THE BOOK
of
SECRETS

OSHO

THE BOOK
of
SECRETS

The Science of Meditation

A CONTEMPORARY APPROACH TO 112 MEDITATIONS
DESCRIBED IN THE VIGYAN BHAIRAV TANTRA

St. Martin's Griffin
New York

Editing by Ma Shivam Suvarna, B. A.
Ma Nirgun, B. A., M. S. W.
Typesetting by Ma Krishna Gopa
Design by Swami Deva Anugito and Ma Krishna Gopa

Sutras from *Zen Flesh, Zen Bones* by Paul Reps
with permission of Charles E. Tuttle Co. Inc.

ISBN 0-312-18058-6

First St. Martin's Griffin Edition: April 1998

Table of Contents

Introduction

What happens when we die?

It is a question that lies at the core of nearly all human spiritual search, and the answer to it often defines the boundary between one religious doctrine and another. Whether one believes in reincarnation or resurrection, heaven or hell, purgatory or paying one's karmic debts, the question of what happens after death occupies an inordinate amount of space in the religious terrain.

In the rich and complex world of Hindu mythology, Shiva represents the face of death and destruction in a "trinity" that also includes creation (Brahma), and sustenance (Vishnu). It is to Shiva that the 5000-year-old sutras of this "Book of Secrets" are attributed. Why? To understand, it will be helpful to know a little more about where he comes from.

He is a complex character, this Shiva, with many aspects. The story goes that once Brahma and Vishnu came to speak to Shiva about some matter of urgency, and found him making love with his wife. Shiva was so absorbed in his lovemaking that he didn't even notice when the two other gods entered his room. Angered by the fact that they had to remain standing there like fools for hours until Shiva finally noticed them, they cursed him and declared that henceforth he would be represented by a phallic symbol. Hence the shivalingam that graces thousands of Shiva temples throughout India. In another of his aspects he is half of the "Shiva-Shakti" duo, the male side of the eternal dance of male and female. And in *The Book of Secrets* he speaks to his consort, Devi, who sits on his lap throughout the entire discourse!

Sex and death, male and female, yin and yang... the paradoxical world not only of Hinduism but all major spiritual traditions of the East.

And meditation—which resolves all paradoxes into mysteries. And springs the trap of the mind so that its owner is finally free to leave the shores of contradiction and enter the river of self-discovery.

Osho says this about it:

Death always occurs in the present. Death, love, meditation—they all occur in the present. So if you are afraid of death, you cannot love. If you are afraid of love, you cannot meditate. If you are afraid of meditation, your life will be useless. Useless not in the sense of any purpose, but useless in the sense that you will never be able to feel any bliss in it. It will be futile.

It may seem strange to connect these three: love, meditation, death. It is not! They are similar experiences. So if you can enter in one, you can enter in the remaining two.

One more thing to understand: Shiva, Brahma and Vishnu all are manifestations of some Ultimate even higher than themselves, some "beyond" which is outside the comprehension even of the gods. Of the three, Shiva is the one who is the most human. Brahma has done his work of creation and is more or less in retirement until some faraway time in the future, after the destruction of this world, when his services might be needed again. Vishnu takes care of the everyday cause-and-effect of things, in a sense the mere household chores, with all the dispassionate accuracy of an accountant. But Shiva, in all his fearsomeness and throbbing life, is the one who longs for a reunion with his original source, who is drunk with some half-remembered vision of his ultimate home. Shiva's sutras are a map that shows the thirsty how to reach the well.

This *Book of Secrets* is a contemporary mystic's commentary on Shiva's 5000-year-old *Vigyan Bhairav Tantra*—literally translated, "techniques for going beyond consciousness." The fact that the word "tantra" means simply "technique" or "method" will be a surprise to many. Tantra in the modern age—predictably, perhaps—is associated almost entirely with sex. In fact, of the 112 meditation techniques described in *The Book of Secrets*, less than a half-dozen are directly concerned with the sexual act. The point of tantra, we discover in the following pages, is not simply to provide people with better sex lives—rather, it is to use countless situations and encounters in the ordinary life of human beings, including sex, as doorways to the experience of meditation. As Osho says, in the first chapter:

These sutras of Shiva are the oldest, most ancient techniques. But you can call them the latest also because nothing can be added to them. They have taken in all the possibilities, all the ways of cleaning the mind, transcending the mind. Not a single method could be added to Shiva's one hundred and twelve methods. It is the most ancient and yet the latest, yet the newest. Old like old hills —the methods seem eternal—and they are new like a dewdrop before the sun, because they are so fresh.

These one hundred and twelve methods of meditation constitute the whole science of transforming mind.

Note Osho's use of the word "science." He emphasizes again and again, not only in *The Book of Secrets* but in nearly all his recorded discourses, that meditation is not a belief system, a doctrine, an "answer" to the question, for example, of what happens when we die. Meditation is an inner state where, in fact, all belief systems, doctrines, and ready made answers have disappeared—leaving only the pure, thought-free awareness that alone is able to perceive reality directly, as it is. But the techniques of meditation are not meditation, either—so don't make that mistake. The techniques are just maps, like scientific formulae. The point is not to study them for their own sake, but to use them, to experiment with them in the laboratory of one's own inner space. Meditation is what can happen as the result of the experiment.

But wait—what does all this have to do with great sex? People who have been able to bring meditation into their lovemaking might tell you to throw away all your "how-to" manuals and learn instead to bring your attention to the here and now. After that, everything will take care of itself.

And what happens when we die? People who have tasted meditation may not be able to give you a precise answer, but they can tell you that they have known and experienced the immortal within themselves, and have come away from the experience knowing that death is just a dream.

Sex, death, and meditation—who better to tie them all together than Shiva, destroyer and lover, the god with the most human of aspirations—to reach higher than himself and unlock the secrets of all that is unknown. And who better to bring the secrets of Shiva's sutras to the present day than Osho, whose insistence is that all of life, from sex to superconsciousness, from spirituality to science, must be reclaimed from all our dark notions of good and evil, of higher and lower, and restored to the luminous wholeness that is our birthright as human beings.

Osho gives quite detailed guidelines in the introductory chapter for using *The Book of Secrets*. A few of them bear emphasizing here, and a few other things about the context in which this book was created will be helpful to the reader in using the book as it was intended.

Each chapter of the book was originally delivered as an extemporaneous talk, addressed to a small gathering of friends and disciples. Osho always speaks without notes or other special preparation, except (in this case, for example) a copy of the sutras he is commenting on, or (elsewhere) a few jokes or anecdotes gathered beforehand that he might use to illustrate a point in the course of his talk.

For those who are accustomed to reading "how-to" and "self-help" books this context might be disconcerting at first. You won't find a lecture here, with points one, two and three to be taken down and repeated back later. There are no footnotes, subtitles, charts, or handy illustrations. To approach the text with those kinds of expectations is to meet frustration in very short order. It will be better to read as you would a story, or poetry, or the lyrics of a song. In an attitude of patience and receptivity, with the assurance that all will be revealed in time.

In the beginning of this *Book of Secrets*, Osho urges his audience to experiment with each of the meditation techniques he talks about, as they go along—"just play with it for three days," he suggests. And he emphasizes the word "play"—not to be serious, not to make "strenuous efforts" or "discipline yourself," but "play." And when you try a technique and find that it really "clicks" with you, a technique that you enjoy and seems to bring something new and fresh into your life, then you can explore it more deeply. In that sense, you as

reader are in a better position than the original audience—you can give as much time as needed to each chapter, to play with each of the techniques given, before moving on to the next.

Of course you can also move straight into the book at any point, should a particular technique really grab your attention and demand that you try it right away.

Do be aware that each of the "sutra chapters" is followed by a chapter containing Osho's responses to questions from his audience. In nearly all cases, the questions relate to the techniques given in the previous chapter. So as you start to experiment, it will be helpful to look into the chapter immediately following the techniques you are playing with. You will very likely find there some extra hint, some greater depth of understanding, some "problem" dissolved.

And finally, remember not to mistake the map for the destination. *The Book of Secrets* is not a series of answers, it's a set of keys. Osho promises at the very beginning that this set of keys is complete, not missing even one pattern for even a single door. The key to your own door is in here somewhere. All you have to do is try the keys, one after the other, until you find one that fits. Then open the door and see for yourself what lies within.

Carol Neiman
Pune, India, 1997

CHAPTER 1

The world of tantra

◆

Devi asks:

O Shiva, what is your reality?
What is this wonder-filled universe?
What constitutes seed?
Who centers the universal wheel?
What is this life beyond form pervading forms?
How may we enter it fully,
above space and time,
names and descriptions?
Let my doubts be cleared!

Some introductory points. First, the world of *Vigyan Bhairav Tantra* is not intellectual, it is not philosophical. Doctrine is meaningless to it. It is concerned with method, with technique—not with principles at all. The word 'tantra' means technique, the method, the path. So it is not philosophical—note this. It is not concerned with intellectual problems and inquiries. It is not concerned with the "why" of things, it is concerned with "how"; not with what is truth, but how the truth can be attained.

Tantra means technique. So this treatise is a scientific one. Science is not concerned with why, science is concerned with how. That is the basic difference between philosophy and science. Philosophy asks, "Why this existence?" Science asks, "How this existence?" The moment you ask the question, How? Method, technique become important. Theories become meaningless; experience becomes the center.

Tantra is science, tantra is not philosophy. To understand philosophy is easy because only your intellect is required. If you can understand language, if you can understand concept, you can understand philosophy. You need not change; you require no transformation. As you are, you can understand philosophy—but not tantra.

You will need a change...rather, a mutation. Unless *you* are different tantra cannot be understood, because tantra is not an intellectual proposition, it is an experience. Unless you are receptive, ready, vulnerable to the experience, it is not going to come to you.

Philosophy is concerned with the mind. Your head is enough; your totality is not required. Tantra needs you in your totality. It is a deeper challenge. You will have to be in it wholly. It is not fragmentary. A different approach, a different attitude, a different mind to receive it is required. Because of this, Devi is asking apparently philosophical questions. Tantra starts with Devi's questions. All the questions can be tackled philosophically.

Really, any question can be tackled in two ways: philosophically or totally, intellectually or existentially. For example, if someone asks, "What is love?" you can tackle it intellectually, you can discuss, you can propose theories, you can argue for a particular hypothesis. You can create a system, a doctrine—and you may not have known love at all.

To create a doctrine, experience is not needed. Really, on the contrary, the less you know the better because then you can propose a system unhesitatingly. Only a blind man can easily define what light is. When you do not know you are bold. Ignorance is always bold; knowledge hesitates. And the more you know, the more you feel that the ground underneath is dissolving. The more you know, the more you feel how ignorant you are. And those who are really wise, they become ignorant. They become as simple as children, or as simple as idiots.

The less you know, the better. To be philosophical, to be dogmatic, to be doctrinaire—this is easy.

To tackle a problem intellectually is very easy. But to tackle a problem existentially—not just to think about it, but to live it through, to go through it, to allow yourself to be transformed through it—is difficult. That is, to know love one will have to be in love. That is dangerous because you will not remain the same. The experience is going to change you. The moment you enter love, you enter a different person. And when you come out you will not be able to recognize your old face; it will not belong to you. A discontinuity will have happened. Now there is a gap, the old man is dead and the new man has come. That is what is known as rebirth—being twice-born.

Tantra is nonphilosophical and existential. So of course Devi asks questions which appear to be philosophical, but Shiva is not going to answer them that way. So it is better to understand it in the beginning; otherwise you will be puzzled, because Shiva is not going to answer a single question. All the questions that Devi is asking, Shiva is not going to answer at all. And still he answers! And really, only *he* has answered them and no one else—but on a different plane.

Devi asks, "What is your reality, my lord?" He is not going to answer it. On the contrary, he will give a technique. And if Devi goes through this technique, she will know. So the answer is roundabout; it is not direct. He is not going to answer "Who am I?" He will give a technique—do it and you will know.

For tantra, doing is knowing, and there is no other knowing. Unless you do something, unless you change, unless you have a different perspective to look at, to look with, unless you move in an altogether different dimension than the intellect, there is no answer. Answers can be given—they are all lies. All philosophies are lies. You ask a question and the philosophy gives you an answer. It satisfies you or doesn't satisfy you. If it satisfies you, you become a convert to the philosophy, but you remain the same. If it doesn't satisfy you, you go on searching for some other philosophy to be converted to. But you remain the same; you are not touched at all, you are not changed.

So whether you are a Hindu or a Mohammedan or a Christian or a Jain, it makes no difference. The real person behind the façade of a Hindu or a Mohammedan or a Christian is the same. Only words differ, or clothes. The man who is going to the church or to the temple or to the mosque is the same man. Only faces differ, and they are faces which are false; they are masks. Behind the masks you will find the same man—the same anger, the same aggression, the same violence, the same greed, the same lust—everything the same. Is Mohammedan sexuality different from Hindu sexuality? Is Christian violence different from Hindu violence? It is the same! The reality remains the same; only clothes differ.

Tantra is not concerned with your clothes, tantra is concerned with you. If you ask a question it shows where you are. It shows also that wherever you are you cannot see; that is why there is the question. A blind man asks, "What is light?" and philosophy will start answering what is light. Tantra will know only this: if a man is asking "What is light?" it shows only that he is blind. Tantra will start operating on the man, changing the man, so that he can see. Tantra will not say what is light. Tantra will tell how to attain insight, how to attain seeing, how to attain vision. When the vision is there, the answer will be there. Tantra will not give you the answer; tantra will give you the technique to attain the answer.

Now, this answer is not going to be intellectual. If you say something about light to a blind man, this is intellectual. If the blind man himself becomes capable of seeing, this is existential. This is what I mean when I say that tantra is existential. So Shiva is not going to answer Devi's questions; still, he will answer—the first thing.

The second thing: this is a different type of language. You must know something about it before we enter into it. All the tantra treatises are dialogues between Shiva and Devi. Devi questions

4

and Shiva answers. All the tantra treatises start that way. Why? Why this method? It is very significant. It is not a dialogue between a teacher and a disciple, it is a dialogue between two lovers. And tantra signifies through it a very meaningful thing: that the deeper teachings cannot be given unless there is love between the two—the disciple and the master. The disciple and master must become deep lovers. Only then can the higher, the beyond, be expressed.

So it is a language of love; the disciple must be in an attitude of love. But not only this, because friends can be lovers. Tantra says a disciple moves as receptivity, so the disciple must be in a feminine receptivity; only then is something possible. You need not be a woman to be a disciple, but you need to be in a feminine attitude of receptivity. When Devi asks, it means the feminine attitude asks. Why this emphasis on the feminine attitude?

Man and woman are not only physically different, they are psychologically different. Sex is not only a difference in the body; it is a difference in psychologies also. A feminine mind means receptivity—total receptivity, surrender, love. A disciple needs a feminine psychology; otherwise he will not be able to learn. You can ask, but if you are not open then you cannot be answered. You can ask a question and still remain closed. Then the answer cannot penetrate you. Your doors are closed; you are dead. You are not open.

A feminine receptivity means a womblike receptivity in the inner depth, so that you can receive. And not only that—much more is implied. A woman is not only receiving something, the moment she receives it, it becomes a part of her body. A child is received. A woman conceives; the moment there is conception, the child has become part of the feminine body. It is not alien, it is not foreign. It has been absorbed. Now the child will live not as something added to the mother, but just as a part, just as the mother. And the child is not only received; the feminine body becomes creative, the child begins to grow.

A disciple needs a womblike receptivity. What-soever is received is not to be gathered as dead knowledge. It must grow in you; it must become blood and bones in you. It must become a part, now. It must grow! This growth will change you, will transform you, the receiver. That is why tantra uses this device. Every treatise starts with Devi asking a question and Shiva replying to it. Devi is Shiva's consort, his feminine part.

One thing more.... Now modern psychology, depth psychology particularly, says that man is both man and woman. No one is just male and no one is just female; everyone is bisexual. Both sexes are there. This is a very recent research in the West, but for tantra this has been one of the most basic concepts for thousands of years. You must have seen some pictures of Shiva as *ardhanarishwar*— half man, half woman. There is no other concept like it in the whole history of man. Shiva is depicted as half man, half woman.

So Devi is not just a consort, she is Shiva's other half. And unless a disciple becomes the other half of the master it is impossible to convey the higher teachings, the esoteric methods. When you become one then there is no doubt. When you are one with the master—so totally one, so deeply one—there is no argument, no logic, no reason. One simply absorbs; one becomes a womb. And then the teaching begins to grow in you and change you.

That is why tantra is written in love language. Something must also be understood about love language. There are two types of language: logical language and love language. There are basic differences between the two.

Logical language is aggressive, argumentative, violent. If I use logical language I become aggressive upon your mind. I try to convince you, to convert you, to make a puppet of you. My argument is "right" and you are "wrong." Logical language is egocentric: "I am right and you are wrong, so I must prove that I am right and you are wrong." I am not concerned with you, I am concerned with my ego. My ego is always "right."

Love language is totally different. I am not concerned with my ego, I am concerned with you. I am not concerned to prove something, to strengthen my ego. I am concerned to help you. It is a compassion to help you to grow, to help you to transform, to help you to be reborn.

Secondly, logic will always be intellectual. Concepts and principles will be significant, arguments will be significant. With love language what is said is not so significant; rather, it is the way it is said. The container, the word, is not important; the content, the message, is more important. It is a heart-to-heart talk, not a mind-to-mind discussion. It is not a debate, it is a communion.

So this is rare: Devi is sitting in the lap of Shiva and asking, and Shiva answers. It is a love dialogue —no conflict, as if Shiva is speaking to himself. Why this emphasis on love, love language? Because if you are in love with your master, then the whole gestalt changes; it becomes different. Then you are not hearing his words, then you are drinking him. Then words are irrelevant. Really, the silence between the words becomes more significant. What he is saying may be meaningful or it may not be meaningful…but it is his eyes, his gestures, his compassion, his love.

That is why tantra has a fixed device, a structure. Every treatise starts with Devi asking and Shiva answering. No argument is going to be there, no wastage of words. There are very simple statements of fact, telegraphic messages with no view to convince, but just to relate.

If you encounter Shiva with a question with a closed mind, he will not answer you in this way. First your closedness has to be broken. Then he will have to be aggressive. Then your prejudices, then your preconceptions have to be destroyed. Unless you are cleared completely of your past, nothing can be given to you. But this is not so with his consort Devi; with Devi there is no past.

Remember, when you are deeply in love your mind ceases to be. There is no past; only the present moment becomes everything. When you are in love the present is the only time, the now is all—

no past, no future. So Devi is just open. There is no defense—nothing to be cleared, nothing to be destroyed. The ground is ready, only a seed has to be dropped. The ground is not only ready, but welcoming, receptive, asking to be impregnated.

So all these sayings that we are going to discuss will be telegraphic. They are just sutras, but each sutra, each telegraphic message given by Shiva, is worth a Veda, worth a Bible, worth a Koran. Each single sentence can become the base of a great scripture. Scriptures are logical—you have to propose, defend, argue. Here there is no argument, just simple statements of love.

Thirdly, the very words *Vigyan Bhairav Tantra* mean the technique of going beyond consciousness. *Vigyan* means consciousness, *bhairav* means the state which is beyond consciousness, and *tantra* means the method: the method of going beyond consciousness. This is the supreme doctrine —without any doctrine.

We are unconscious, so all the religious teachings are concerned with how to go beyond unconsciousness, how to be conscious. For example, Krishnamurti, Zen, they are all concerned with how to create more consciousness, because we are unconscious. So how to be more aware, alert? From unconsciousness, how to move toward consciousness?

But tantra says that this is a duality—unconscious and conscious. If you move from unconsciousness to consciousness, you are moving from one part of the duality to another. Move beyond both! Unless you move beyond both you can never reach the ultimate, so be neither the unconscious nor the conscious; just go beyond, just be. Be neither the conscious nor the unconscious—just be! This is going beyond yoga, going beyond Zen, going beyond all teachings.

'Vigyana' means consciousness, and 'bhairava' is a specific term, a tantra term for one who has gone beyond. That is why Shiva is known as Bhairava and Devi is known as Bhairavi—those who have gone beyond the dualities.

In our experience only love can give a glimpse. That is why love becomes the very basic device to impart tantric wisdom. In our experience we can say that only love is something which goes beyond duality. When two persons are in love, the deeper they move into it, the less and less they are two, the more and more they become one. And a point comes and a peak is reached when only apparently they are two. Inwardly they are one; the duality is transcended.

Only in this sense does Jesus' saying that "God is love" become meaningful; otherwise not. In our experience love is nearest to God. It is not that God is loving, as Christians go on interpreting—that God has a fatherly love for you. Nonsense! "God is love" is a tantric statement. It means love is the only reality in our experience which reaches nearest to God, to the divine. Why? Because in love oneness is felt. Bodies remain two, but something beyond the bodies merges and becomes one.

That is why there is so much hankering after sex. The real hankering is after oneness, but that oneness is not sexual. In sex two bodies have only a deceptive feeling of becoming one, but they are not one, they are only joined together. But for a single moment two bodies forget themselves in each other, and a certain physical oneness is felt. This hankering is not bad, but to stop at it is dangerous. This hankering shows a deeper urge to feel oneness.

In love, on a higher plane, the inner one moves, merges into the other, and there is a feeling of oneness. Duality dissolves. Only in this nondual love can we have a glimpse of what is the state of a bhairava. The state of a bhairava is absolute love with no coming back, from the peak of love there is no falling back. It is remaining on the peak.

We have made Shiva's abode on Kailash. That is simply symbolic: it is the highest peak, the holiest peak. We have made it Shiva's abode. We can go there but we will have to come down, it cannot be our abode. We can go on a pilgrimage. It is a *tirthyatra*—a pilgrimage, a journey. We can touch for a single moment the highest peak; then we will have to come back.

In love this holy pilgrimage happens, but not for all because almost no one moves beyond sex. So we go on living in the valley, the dark valley. Sometimes someone moves to the peak of love, but then he falls back because it is so dizzying. It is so high and you are so low, and it is so difficult to live there. Those who have loved, they know how difficult it is to be constantly in love. One has to come back again and again. It is Shiva's abode. He lives there, it is his home.

A bhairava lives in love; that is his abode. Now he is not even aware of love—because if you live on Kailash you will not be aware that this is Kailash, this is a peak. The peak becomes a plain. Shiva is not aware of love. We are aware of love because we live in nonlove. And because of the contrast we feel love. Shiva is love. The state of bhairava means that one has become love. Not *loving*—one has *become* love, one lives on the peak. The peak has become his abode.

How to make this highest peak possible? Beyond duality, beyond unconsciousness, beyond consciousness, beyond the body and beyond the soul, beyond the world and beyond the so-called moksha, liberation—how to reach this peak? The technique is tantra. But tantra is pure technique, so it is going to be difficult to understand. First let us understand the questions, what Devi is asking.

O Shiva, what is your reality?

Why this question? You can also ask this question, but it will not carry the same meaning. So try to understand why Devi asks, *What is your reality?* Devi is in deep love. When you are in deep love, for the first time you encounter the inner reality. Then Shiva is not the form, then Shiva is not the body. When you are in love, the body of the beloved falls away, disappears. The form is no more and the formless is revealed. You are facing an abyss. That is why we are so afraid of love. We can face a body, we can face a face, we can face a form, but we are afraid of facing an abyss.

If you love someone, if you really love, his body is bound to disappear. In some moments of climax, of peak, the form will dissolve, and through the beloved you will enter the formless. That is why we are afraid—it is falling into a bottomless abyss. So this question is not just a simple curiosity: O Shiva, what is your reality?

Devi must have fallen in love with the form. Things start that way. She must have loved this man as a man, and now when the love has come of age, when the love has flowered, this man has disappeared. He has become formless. Now he is to be found nowhere. O Shiva, what is your reality? It is a question asked in a very intense love moment. And when questions are raised, they become different according to the mind in which they are asked.

So create the situation, the milieu of the question in your mind. Devi must be at a loss—Shiva has disappeared. When love reaches its peak the lover disappears. Why does this happen? This happens because really, everyone is formless. You are not a body. You move as a body, you live as a body, but you are not a body. When we see someone from the outside, he is a body. Love penetrates within, then we are not seeing the person from the outside. Love can see a person as the person can see himself from within. Then the form disappears.

A Zen monk, Rinzai, attained enlightenment, and the first thing he asked was, "Where is my body? Where has my body gone?" He began to search. He called his disciples and said, "Go and find out where my body is. I have lost my body."

He had entered the formless. You are also a formless existence, but you know yourself not directly, but from others' eyes. You know through the mirror. Sometime, while looking in the mirror, close your eyes and then think, meditate: if there was no mirror, how could you have known your face? If there was no mirror, there would have been no face. You do not have a face; mirrors give you

faces. Think of a world where there are no mirrors. You are alone—no mirror at all, not even others' eyes working as mirrors. You are alone on a lonely island; nothing can mirror you. Then will you have any face? Or will you have any body? You cannot have one. You do not have one at all. We know ourselves only through others, and the others can only know the outer form. That is why we become identified with it.

Another Zen mystic, Hyakujo, used to say to his disciples, "When you have lost your head meditating, come immediately to me. When you lose your head, come immediately to me. When you begin to feel there is no head, do not be afraid; come immediately to me. This is the right moment. Now something can be taught to you." With a head, no teaching is possible. The head always comes in between.

Devi asks Shiva, *O Shiva, what is your reality?* —who are you? The form has disappeared; hence the question. In love you enter the other as himself. It is not you answering. You become one, and for the first time you know an abyss—a formless presence.

That is why for centuries together, centuries and centuries, we were not making any sculptures, any pictures of Shiva. We were only making shivalinga —the symbol. The shivalinga is just a formless form. When you love someone, when you enter someone, he becomes just a luminous presence. The shivalinga is just a luminous presence, just an aura of light. That is why Devi asks,

What is your reality?
What is this wonder-filled universe?

We know the universe, but we never know it as wonder-filled. Children know, lovers know. Sometimes poets and madmen know. We do not know that the world is wonder-filled. Everything is just repetitive—no wonder, no poetry, just flat prose. It doesn't create a song in you; it doesn't create a dance; it doesn't give birth to the poetry inside. The whole universe looks mechanical. Children look at it with wonder-filled eyes. When the eyes are wonder-filled, the universe is wonder-filled.

When you are in love, you again become like children. Jesus says, "Only those who are like children will enter my kingdom of God." Why? Because if the universe is not a wonder, you cannot be religious. The universe can be explained—then your approach is scientific. The universe is either known or unknown, but that which is unknown can be known any day; it is not unknowable. The universe becomes unknowable, a mystery, only when your eyes are wonder-filled.

Devi says, *What is this wonder-filled universe?* Suddenly there is the jump from a personal question to a very impersonal one. She was asking, *What is your reality?* and then suddenly, *What is this wonder-filled universe?*

When form disappears, your beloved becomes the universe, the formless, the infinite. Suddenly Devi becomes aware that she is not asking a question about Shiva; she is asking a question about the whole universe. Now Shiva has become the whole universe. Now all the stars are moving in him, and the whole firmament and the whole space is surrounded by him. Now he is the great engulfing factor—"the great encompassing." Karl Jaspers has defined God as "the great encompassing."

When you enter into love, into a deep, intimate world of love, the person disappears, the form disappears, and the lover becomes just a door to the universe. Your curiosity can be a scientific one —then you have to approach through logic. Then you must not think of the formless. Then beware of the formless; then remain content with the form. Science is always concerned with the form. If anything formless is proposed to a scientific mind, he will cut it into form—unless it takes a form it is meaningless. First give it a form, a definite form; only then does the inquiry start.

In love, if there is form then there is no end to it. Dissolve the form! When things become formless, dizzy, without boundaries, every thing entering another, the whole universe becoming a oneness, then only is it a wonder-filled universe.

What constitutes seed?

Then Devi goes on. From the universe she goes on to ask, *What constitutes seed?* This formless, wonder-filled universe, from where does it come? From where does it originate? Or does it not originate? What is the seed?

Who centers the universal wheel?

asks Devi. This wheel goes on moving and moving —this great change, this constant flux. But who centers this wheel? Where is the axis, the center, the unmoving center?

She doesn't stop for any answer. She goes on asking as if she is not asking anyone, as if talking to herself.

What is this life beyond form pervading forms?
How may we enter it fully,
above space and time, names and descriptions?
Let my doubts be cleared!

The emphasis is not on questions but on doubts: *Let my doubts be cleared!* This is very significant. If you are asking an intellectual question, you are asking for a definite answer so that your problem is solved. But Devi says, *Let my doubts be cleared!* She is not really asking about answers. She is asking for a transformation of her mind, because a doubting mind will remain a doubting mind whatsoever answers are given. Note it: a doubting mind will remain a doubting mind. Answers are irrelevant. If I give you one answer and you have a doubting mind, you will doubt it. If I give you another answer, you will doubt that also. You have a doubting mind. A doubting mind means you will put a question mark to anything.

So answers are useless. You ask me, "Who created the world?" and I tell you "A" created the world. Then you are bound to ask, "Who created 'A'?" So the real problem is not how to answer questions. The real problem is how to change the doubting mind, how to create a mind which is not doubting—or, which is trustful. So Devi says, *Let my doubts be cleared!*

Two or three things more…. When you ask a question, you may be asking for many reasons. One may be just this, that you want a confirmation. You already know the answer, you have the answer, you just want it to be confirmed that your answer is right. Then your question is false, pseudo; it is not a question. You may be asking a question not because you are ready to change yourself, but just as a curiosity.

The mind goes on questioning. In the mind questions come as leaves come on a tree. That is the very nature of the mind, to question, so it goes on questioning. It matters not what you are questioning, with anything given to the mind it will create a question. It is a machine to grind out, to create, questions. So give it anything and it will cut it into pieces and create many questions. One question answered, and the mind will create many questions from the answer. This has been the whole history of philosophy.

Bertrand Russell remembers that when he was a child he thought that one day, when he will be mature enough to understand all philosophy, all questions will be answered. Then later, when he was eighty, he said, "Now I can say that my own questions are standing there, as they were standing when I was a child. Now other questions have come up because of these theories of philosophy." So he said, "When I was young I used to say philosophy is an inquiry for ultimate answers. Now I cannot say it. It is an inquiry for endless questions."

So one question creates one answer and many questions. The doubting mind is the problem. Devi says, "Do not be concerned with my questions. I have asked so many things: What is your reality? What is this wonder-filled universe? What constitutes seed? Who centers the universal wheel? What is life beyond form? How can we enter it fully above time and space? But do not be concerned with my questions. Let my doubts be cleared. I ask these

questions because they are in my mind. I ask them just to show you my mind, but do not pay much attention to them. Really, answers will not fulfill my need. My need is…*Let my doubts be cleared!*"

But how can the doubts be cleared? Will any answer do? Is there any answer which will clear your doubts? Mind *is* the doubt. It is not that the mind doubts, *mind* is the doubt! Unless the mind dissolves, doubts cannot be cleared.

Shiva will answer. His answers are techniques—the oldest, most ancient techniques. But you can call them the latest also because nothing can be added to them. They are complete—one hundred and twelve techniques. They have taken in all the possibilities, all the ways of cleaning the mind, transcending the mind. Not a single method could be added to Shiva's one hundred and twelve methods. And this book, *Vigyan Bhairav Tantra*, is five thousand years old. Nothing can be added; there is no possibility to add anything. It is exhaustive, complete. It is the most ancient and yet the latest, yet the newest. Old like old hills—the methods seem eternal—and they are new like a dewdrop before the sun, because they are so fresh.

These one hundred and twelve methods of meditation constitute the whole science of transforming mind. We will enter them one by one. We will try to comprehend first intellectually. But use your intellect only as an instrument, not as a master. Use it as an instrument to understand something, but do not go on creating barriers with it. When we will be talking about these techniques, just put aside your past knowledge, your knowing, whatsoever information you have collected. Put them aside—they are just dust gathered on the road.

Encounter these methods with a fresh mind—with alertness, of course, but not with argumentation. And do not create the fallacy that an argumentative mind is an alert mind. It is not, because the moment you move into arguments you have lost the awareness, you have lost the alertness. Then you are not here.

These methods do not belong to any religion.

Remember, they are not Hindu, just as the theory of relativity is not Jewish because Einstein conceived it. And radio and television are not Christian. No one says, "Why are you using electricity? This is Christian, because a Christian mind conceived it." Science does not belong to races and religions—and tantra is a science. So remember, this is not Hindu at all. These techniques were conceived by Hindus, but these techniques are not Hindu. That is why these techniques will not mention any religious ritual. No temple is needed. You are quite enough of a temple yourself. You are the lab; the whole experiment is to go on within you. No belief is needed.

This is not religion, this is science. No belief is needed. It is not required to believe in the Koran or the Vedas or in Buddha or in Mahavira. No, no belief is needed. Only a daringness to experiment is enough, courage to experiment is enough; that is the beauty. A Mohammedan can practice and he will reach to the deeper meanings of the Koran. A Hindu can practice and he will for the first time know what the Vedas are. And a Jain can practice and a Buddhist can practice; they need not leave their religion. Tantra will fulfill them, wherever they are. Tantra will be helpful, whatsoever their chosen path.

So remember this: tantra is pure science. You may be a Hindu or a Mohammedan or a Parsi or whatsoever—tantra doesn't touch your religion at all. Tantra says that religion is a social affair, so belong to any religion; it is irrelevant. But you can transform yourself, and that transformation needs a scientific methodology. When you are ill, when you have fallen ill or you have caught tuberculosis or anything, then whether you are a Hindu or a Mohammedan makes no difference. The tuberculosis remains indifferent to your Hinduism, to your Mohammedanism, to your beliefs—political, social or religious. Tuberculosis has to be treated scientifically. There is no Hindu tuberculosis, no Mohammedan tuberculosis.

You are ignorant, you are in conflict, you are asleep. This is a disease, a spiritual disease. This disease has to be treated by the tantra. You are irrelevant, your beliefs are irrelevant. It is just a coincidence that you are born somewhere and someone else is born somewhere else. This is just a coincidence. Your religion is a coincidence, so do not cling to it. Use some scientific methods to transform yourself.

Tantra is not very well known. And even if it is known, it is very much misunderstood. There are reasons for it. The higher and purer a science, the less is the possibility that the masses will know of it. We have only heard the name of the theory of relativity. It used to be said that only twelve persons understood it when Einstein was alive. All over the world only one dozen minds could understand it. It was difficult even for Albert Einstein to make it understood to someone, to make it understandable, because it moves so high, it goes above your head. But it can be understood. A technical, mathematical knowledge is needed; a training is needed, and then it can be understood. But tantra is more difficult because no training will help. Only transformation can help.

That is why tantra could never become understood by the masses. And it always happens that when you cannot understand a thing, at least you will misunderstand, because then you can feel, "Okay, I understand." You cannot simply remain in the vacuum.

Secondly, when you cannot understand a thing, you begin to abuse it because it insults you. You cannot understand it! You? *You* cannot understand it? That is impossible. Something must be wrong with the thing itself. One begins to abuse, one begins to talk nonsense, and then he feels, "Now it is okay."

So tantra was not understood; tantra was misunderstood. It was so deep and so high that this was natural. Secondly, because tantra moves beyond duality, the very standpoint is amoral. Please understand these words: 'moral,' 'immoral,' 'amoral.' We understand morality, we understand immorality, but it becomes difficult if something is amoral—beyond both.

Tantra is amoral. Look at it in this way.... A medicine is amoral; it is neither moral nor immoral. If you give it to a thief it will help; if you give it to a saint it will help. It will make no differentiation between a thief and a saint. The medicine cannot say, "This is a thief so I am going to kill him, and this is a saint so I am going to help him." A medicine is a scientific thing. Your being a thief or being a saint is irrelevant.

Tantra is amoral. Tantra says no morality is needed—no particular morality is needed. On the contrary, you are immoral because you have a very disturbed mind. So tantra cannot make a precondition, that first you become moral and then you can practice tantra. Tantra says this is absurd.

Someone is ill, feverish, and the doctor comes and says, "First bring down your fever; first be quite healthy. Only then can I give you the medicine." This is what is happening.

A thief comes to a saint and he says, "I am a thief. Tell me how to meditate." The saint says, "First leave your profession. How can you meditate if you remain a thief?"

An alcoholic comes and he says, "I am an alcoholic. How can I meditate?" The saint says, "The first condition is, leave alcohol, only then can you meditate." The conditions become suicidal. The man is alcoholic or a thief or immoral because he has a disturbed mind, an ill mind. These are the effects, the consequences of the diseased mind, and he is told, "First be well and then you can meditate." But then who needs meditation? Meditation is medicinal. It is a medicine.

Tantra is amoral. It doesn't ask you who you are. Your being a man is enough. Wherever you are, whatsoever you are, you are accepted.

Choose a technique which fits you, put your total energy into it, and you will not be the same again. Real, authentic techniques always will be like that. If I make preconditions, it shows I have a pseudo technique—I say, "First do this and first do

not do that, and then..." And those are impossible conditions because a thief can change his objects, but he cannot become a nonthief.

A greedy man can change the objects of his greed, but he cannot become nongreedy. You can force him or he can force upon himself nongreed, but it is also only because of a certain greed. If heaven is promised he may even try to be nongreedy. But this is greed par excellence. Heaven, *moksha*, liberation, *sat-chit-anand,* existence, consciousness, bliss—they will be the objects of his greed.

Tantra says you cannot change man unless you give him authentic techniques with which to change. Just by preaching nothing is changed. And you can see this all over the world. Whatsoever tantra says is written all over the world. So much preaching, so much moralizing, so many priests, preachers—the whole world is filled with them, yet everything is so ugly and so immoral.

Why is this happening? The same will be the case if you give your hospitals to preachers. They will go there and they will start preaching. And they will make every ill man feel, "You are guilty! You have created this disease; now change this disease." If preachers are given hospitals, what will be the condition of hospitals? The same as the condition of the whole world.

Preachers go on preaching. They go on telling people, "Don't be angry," without giving any technique. And we have heard this teaching for so long that we never even raise the question: "What are you saying? I am angry and you simply say, 'Don't be angry.' How is this possible? When I am angry it means 'I' am anger, and you just tell me, 'Don't be angry.' So I can only suppress myself."

But that will create more anger. That will create guilt—because if I try to change and cannot change myself, that creates inferiority. It gives me a feeling of guilt, that I am incapable, I cannot win over my anger. No one can win! You need certain weapons, you need certain techniques, because your anger is just an indication of a disturbed mind. Change the disturbed mind and the indication will change. Anger is just showing what is within. Change the within and the without will change.

So tantra is not concerned with your so-called morality. Really, to emphasize morality is mean, degrading; it is inhuman. If someone comes to me and I say, "Leave anger first, leave sex first, leave this and that," then I am inhuman. What I am saying is impossible. And that impossibility will make that man feel inwardly mean. He will begin to feel inferior; he will be degraded inside in his own eyes. If he tries the impossible, he is going to be a failure. And when he is a failure he will be convinced that he is a sinner.

The preachers have convinced the whole world that "You are sinners." This is good for them, because unless you are convinced, their profession cannot continue. You must be sinners; only then can churches, temples and mosques continue to prosper. Your being in sin is their success. Your guilt is the base of all the highest churches. The more guilty you are, the more churches will go on rising higher and higher. They are built on your guilt, on your sin, on your inferiority complex. Thus, they have created an inferior humanity.

Tantra is not concerned with your so-called morality, your social formalities, et cetera. That doesn't mean that tantra says to be immoral—no! Tantra is so much unconcerned with your morality that tantra cannot say to be immoral. Tantra gives you scientific techniques for changing the mind, and once the mind is different your character will be different. Once the basis of your structure changes, your whole edifice will be different. Because of this amoral attitude, tantra could not be tolerated by your so-called saints, they all went against it—because if tantra succeeds, then all this nonsense which goes on in the name of religion will have to stop.

See this: Christianity fought very much against scientific progress. Why? Only because if scientific progress is there in the material world, then the time is not very far off when in the psychological

and in the spiritual world also science will penetrate. So Christianity started fighting scientific progress, because once you know that you can change matter through technique, the time is not very far off when you will come to know that you can change mind through techniques—because mind is nothing but subtle matter.

This is tantra's proposition, that mind is nothing but subtle matter; it can be changed. And once you have a different mind you have a different world, because you look through the mind. The world you are seeing, you are seeing because of a particular mind. Change the mind, and when you look there is a different world. And if there is no mind...that is the ultimate for tantra, to bring about a state where there is no mind. Then look at the world without a mediator. When the mediator is not, you are encountering the real, because now no one is between you and the real. Then nothing can be distorted.

So tantra says that when there is no mind, that is the state of a bhairava—a no-mind state. For the first time you look at the world, at that which is. If you have a mind, you go on *creating* a world; you go on imposing, projecting. So first change the mind, then change from mind to no-mind. And these one hundred and twelve methods can help each and everyone. Any particular method may not be of use to you. That is why Shiva goes on relating many methods. Choose any one method which suits you. It is not difficult to know which suits you.

We will try to understand each method and how to choose for yourself one method which can change you and your mind. This understanding, this intellectual understanding will be a basic necessity, but this is not the end. Whatsoever I talk about here, try it.

Really, when you try the right method it clicks immediately. So I will go on talking about methods here every day. You try them. Just play with them —go home and try. The right method, whenever you happen upon it, just clicks. Something explodes in you, and you know that "This is the right method for me." But effort is needed, and you may be surprised that suddenly one day one method has gripped you.

So while I am talking here, parallel to it go on playing with these methods. I say playing because you should not be too serious. Just play! Something may fit you. If it fits you, then be serious, and then go deep into it—intensely, honestly, with all your energy, with all your mind. But before that just play.

I have found that while you are playing your mind is more open. While you are serious your mind is not so open; it is closed. So just play. Do not be too serious, just play. And these methods are simple, you can just play with them.

Take one method and play with it for at least three days. If it gives you a certain feeling of affinity, if it gives you a certain feeling of well-being, if it gives you a certain feeling that this is for you, then be serious about it. Then forget the others, do not play with other methods. Stick to it—at least for three months. Miracles are possible. The only thing is that the technique must be for you. If the technique is not for you, then nothing happens. Then you may go on with it for lives together, but nothing will happen. If the method is for you then even three minutes are enough.

So these one hundred and twelve methods can be a miraculous experience for you, or they may just be a listening—it depends on you. I will go on describing each method from as many angles as possible. If you feel any affinity with it, play with it for three days. If you feel that it fits, that something clicks in you, continue it for three months.

Life is a miracle. If you have not known its mystery, that only shows that you do not know the technique for how to approach it.

Shiva proposes one hundred and twelve methods. These are all the methods possible. If nothing clicks and nothing gives you the feeling that this is for you, then there is no method left for you—remember this. Then forget spirituality and be happy. Then it is not for you.

But these one hundred and twelve methods are for the whole humanity—for all the ages that have passed and for all the ages that have yet to come. In no time has there ever been a single man, and there will never be one, who can say, "These one hundred and twelve methods are all useless for me." Impossible! This is impossible!

Every type of mind has been taken into account. Every possible type of mind has been given a technique in tantra. There are many techniques for which no man exists yet; they are for the future. There are many techniques for which no man exists now; they are for the past. But do not be afraid. There are many methods which are for you.

So we will start this journey from tomorrow.

CHAPTER 2

The path of yoga and the path of tantra

◆

What is the difference between yoga and tantra?

On the path of surrender, how to come to the right technique?

How to know if the technique being practiced will be successful?

There are many questions. The first:

What is the difference between traditional yoga and tantra? Are they the same?

antra and yoga are basically different. They reach to the same goal; however, their paths are not only different, but contrary also. So this has to be understood very clearly. The yoga process is also methodology, yoga is also technique. Yoga is not philosophy. Just like tantra, yoga depends on action, method, technique. Doing leads to being in yoga also, but the process is different.

In yoga one has to fight; it is the path of the warrior. On the path of tantra one does not have to fight at all. Rather, on the contrary, one has to indulge—but with awareness.

Yoga is suppression with awareness; tantra is indulgence with awareness.

Tantra says that whatsoever you are, the ultimate is not opposite to it. It is a growth; you can grow to be the ultimate. There is no opposition between you and the reality. You are part of it, so no struggle, no conflict, no opposition to nature is needed. You have to use nature; you have to use whatsoever you are to go beyond.

In yoga you have to fight with yourself to go beyond. In yoga, the world and *moksha,* liberation —you as you are and you as you can be—are two opposite things. Suppress, fight, dissolve that which

you are so that you can attain that which you can be. Going beyond is a death in yoga. You must die for your real being to be born.

In the eyes of tantra, yoga is a deep suicide. You must kill your natural self—your body, your instincts, your desires, everything. Tantra says accept yourself as you are. It is a deep acceptance. Do not create a gap between you and the real, between the world and *nirvana.* Do not create any gap. There is no gap for tantra; no death is needed. For your rebirth, no death is needed—rather, a transcendence. For this transcendence, use yourself.

For example, sex is there, the basic energy—the basic energy you are born through, born with. The basic cells of your being and of your body are sexual, so the human mind revolves around sex. For yoga you must fight with this energy. Through fight you create a different center in yourself. The more you fight, the more you become integrated in a different center. Then sex is not your center. Fighting with sex—of course, consciously—will create in you a new center of being, a new emphasis, a new crystallization. Then sex will not be your energy. You will create your energy fighting with sex. A different energy will come into being and a different center of existence.

For tantra you have to use the energy of sex. Do not fight with it, transform it. Do not think in terms of enmity, be friendly to it. It is your energy. It is not evil, it is not bad. Every energy is just natural. It can be used for you, it can be used against you. You can make a block of it, a barrier, or you can make it a step. It can be used. Rightly used, it

17

becomes friendly; wrongly used, it becomes your enemy. But it is neither. Energy is just natural. As ordinary man is using sex, it becomes an enemy, it destroys him; he simply dissipates in it.

Yoga takes the opposite view—opposite to the ordinary mind. The ordinary mind is being destroyed by its own desires, so yoga says stop desiring, be desireless. Fight desire and create an integration in you which is desireless.

Tantra says be aware of the desire; do not create any fight. Move into desire with full consciousness, and when you move into desire with full consciousness you transcend it. You are into it and still you are not in it. You pass through it, but you remain an outsider.

Yoga has much appeal because yoga is just the opposite of the ordinary mind, so the ordinary mind can understand the language of yoga. You know how sex is destroying you—how it has destroyed you, how you go on revolving around it like a slave, like a puppet. You know this by your experience. So when yoga says fight it, you immediately understand the language. That is the appeal, the easy appeal of yoga.

Tantra cannot be so easily appealing. It seems difficult: how to move into desire without being overwhelmed by it? How to be in the sex act consciously, with full awareness? The ordinary mind becomes afraid. It seems dangerous. Not that it is dangerous; whatsoever you know about sex creates this danger for you. You know yourself, you know how you can deceive yourself. You know very well that your mind is cunning. You can move in desire, in sex, in everything, and you can deceive yourself that you are moving with full awareness. That is why you feel the danger.

The danger is not in tantra; it is in you. And the appeal of yoga is because of you, because of your ordinary mind, your sex-suppressed, sex-starved, sex-indulging mind. Because the ordinary mind is not healthy about sex, yoga has an appeal. With a better humanity, with a healthy sex—natural, normal—the case would be different. We are not

normal and natural. We are absolutely abnormal, unhealthy, really insane. But because everyone is like us, we never feel it.

Madness is so normal that not to be mad may look abnormal. A Buddha is abnormal, a Jesus is abnormal amidst us. They do not belong to us. This "normalcy" is a disease. This "normal" mind has created the appeal of yoga. If you take sex naturally—with no philosophy around it, with no philosophy for or against—if you take sex as you take your hands, your eyes; if it is totally accepted as a natural thing, then tantra will have an appeal. And only then can tantra be useful for many.

But the days of tantra are coming. Sooner or later tantra will explode for the first time in the masses, because for the first time the time is ripe—ripe to take sex naturally. It is possible that the explosion may come from the West, because Freud, Jung, Reich, they have prepared the background. They did not know anything about tantra, but they have made the basic ground for tantra to evolve. Western psychology has come to a conclusion that the basic human disease is somewhere around sex, the basic insanity of man is sex-oriented.

So unless this sex orientation is dissolved, man cannot be natural, normal. Man has gone wrong only because of his attitudes about sex. No attitude is needed. Only then are you natural. What attitude have you about your eyes? Are they evil or are they divine? Are you for your eyes or against them? There is no attitude! That is why your eyes are normal.

Take some attitude—think that eyes are evil. Then seeing will become difficult. Then seeing will take the same problematic shape that sex has taken. Then you will want to see, you will desire and you will hanker to see. But when you see you will feel guilty. Whenever you see you will feel guilty that you have done something wrong, that you have sinned. You would like to kill your very instrument of seeing; you would like to destroy your eyes. And the more you want to destroy them, the more you will become eye-centered. Then you will start a very absurd activity: you will want to see more and more, and simultaneously you will feel more and more guilty. The same has happened with the sex center.

Tantra says, accept whatsoever you are. This is the basic note—total acceptance. And only through total acceptance can you grow. Then use every energy you have. How can you use them? Accept them, then find out what these energies are —what is sex, what is this phenomenon? We are not acquainted with it. We know many things about sex, taught by others. We may have passed through the sex act, but with a guilty mind, with a suppressive attitude, in haste, in a hurry. Something has to be done in order to become unburdened. The sex act is not a loving act. You are not happy in it, but you cannot leave it. The more you try to leave it, the more attractive it becomes. The more you want to negate it, the more you feel invited.

You cannot negate it, but this attitude to negate, to destroy, destroys the very mind, the very awareness, the very sensitivity which can understand it. So sex goes on with no sensitivity in it. Then you cannot understand it. Only a deep sensitivity can understand anything; only a deep feeling, a deep moving into it, can understand anything. You can understand sex only if you move in it as a poet moves amidst flowers—only then! If you feel guilty about flowers, you may pass through the garden, but you will pass with closed eyes. And you will be in a hurry, in a deep, mad haste. Somehow you have to go out of the garden. Then how can you be aware?

So tantra says, accept whatsoever you are. You are a great mystery of many multidimensional energies. Accept it, and move with every energy with deep sensitivity, with awareness, with love, with understanding. Move with it! Then every desire becomes a vehicle to go beyond it. Then every energy becomes a help. And then this very world is nirvana, this very body is a temple—a holy temple, a holy place.

Yoga is negation; tantra is affirmation. Yoga thinks in terms of duality—that is the reason for the word 'yoga.' It means to put two things together, to "yoke" two things together. But two things are there, the duality is there. Tantra says there is no duality. If there is duality, then you cannot put them together. And howsoever you try they will remain two. Howsoever put together they will remain two, and the fight will continue, the dualism will remain.

If the world and the divine are two, then they cannot be put together. If really they are not two, if they are only appearing as two, only then can they be one. If your body and your soul are two, then they cannot be put together. If you and God are two, then there is no possibility of putting them together. They will remain two.

Tantra says there is no duality; it is only an appearance. So why help appearance to grow stronger? Tantra asks, why help this appearance of duality to grow stronger? Dissolve it this very moment! Be one! Through acceptance you become one, not through fight. Accept the world, accept the body, accept everything that is inherent in it. Do not create a different center in yourself, because for tantra that different center is nothing but the ego. Do not create an ego. Just be aware of what you are. If you fight, then the ego will be there.

So it is difficult to find a yogi who is not an egoist. And yogis may go on talking about egolessness, but they cannot be egoless. The very process they go through creates the ego. The fight is the process. If you fight, you are bound to create an ego. And the more you fight, the more strengthened the ego will be. And if you win your fight, then you will achieve the supreme ego.

Tantra says, no fight! Then there is no possibility of the ego. If we understand tantra there will be many problems, because for us, if there is no fight there is only indulgence. No fight means indulgence for us. Then we become afraid. We have indulged for lives together and we have reached nowhere. But for tantra indulgence is not the indulgence we know. Tantra says indulge, but be aware.

You are angry...tantra will not say do not be angry. Tantra will say be angry wholeheartedly, but be aware. Tantra is not against anger, tantra is only against spiritual sleepiness, spiritual unconsciousness. Be aware *and* be angry. And this is the secret of the method—that if you are aware anger is transformed: it becomes compassion. So tantra says anger is not your enemy; it is compassion in seed form. The same anger, the same energy, will become compassion.

If you fight with it, then there will be no possibility for compassion. So if you succeed in fighting, in suppression, you will be a dead man. There will be no anger because you have suppressed it, but there will be no compassion either because only anger can be transformed into compassion. If you succeed in your suppression—which is impossible —then there will be no sex, but no love either, because with sex dead there is no energy to grow into love. So you will be without sex, but you will also be without love. And then the whole point is missed, because without love there is no divineness, without love there is no liberation, and without love there is no freedom.

Tantra says that these same energies are to be transformed. It can be said in this way: if you are against the world, then there is no nirvana— because this world itself is to be transformed into nirvana. Then you are against the basic energies which are the source.

So tantric alchemy says, do not fight, be friendly with all the energies that are given to you. Welcome them. Feel grateful that you have anger, that you have sex, that you have greed. Feel grateful because these are the hidden sources, and they can be transformed, they can be opened. And when sex is transformed it becomes love. The poison is lost, the ugliness is lost.

The seed is ugly, but when it becomes alive it sprouts and flowers. Then there is beauty. Do not throw away the seed, because then you are also throwing the flowers in it. They are not there yet, not yet manifest so that you can see them. They are unmanifest, but they are there. Use this seed so that you can attain to flowers. So first let there be acceptance, a sensitive understanding and awareness. Then indulgence is allowed.

One thing more which is really very strange, but one of the deepest discoveries of tantra, and that is: whatsoever you take as your enemies—greed, anger, hate, sex, whatsoever—your attitude that they are enemies makes them your enemies. Take them as divine gifts and approach them with a very grateful heart. For example, tantra has developed many techniques for the transformation of sexual energy. Approach the sex act as if you are approaching the temple of the divine. Approach the sex act as if it is prayer, as if it is meditation. Feel the holiness of it.

That is why in Khajuraho, in Puri, in Konarak, every temple has *maithun*, intercourse sculptures. The sex act on the walls of temples seems illogical, particularly for Christianity, for Islam, for Jainism. It seems inconceivable, contradictory. How is the temple connected with maithun pictures? On the outer walls of the Khajuraho temples every conceivable type of sex act is pictured in stone. Why? In a temple it doesn't have any place, in our minds at least. Christianity cannot conceive of a church wall with Khajuraho pictures. Impossible!

Modern Hindus also feel guilty because the minds of modern Hindus are created by Christianity. They are "Hindu-Christians"—and they are worse, because to be a Christian is good, but to be a Hindu-Christian is just weird. They feel guilty. One Hindu leader, Purshottamdas Tandon, even proposed that these temples should be destroyed, that they do not belong to us. Really, it looks like they do not belong to us because tantra has not been in our hearts for a long time, for centuries. It has not been the main current. Yoga has been the main current, and for yoga Khajuraho is inconceivable—it must be destroyed.

Tantra says, approach the sex act as if you are entering a holy temple. That is why they have pictured the sex act on their holy temples. They have said, approach sex as if you are entering a holy temple. Thus, when you enter a holy temple sex must be there in order that the two become conjoined in your mind, associated. Then you can feel that the world and the divine are not two fighting elements, but one. They are not contradictory, they are just polar opposites helping each other. And they can exist only because of this polarity. If this polarity is lost, the whole world is lost. So see the deep oneness running through everything. Do not see only the polar opposites, see the inner running current which makes them one.

For tantra everything is holy. Remember this, for tantra *everything* is holy; nothing is unholy. Look at it this way: for an irreligious person everything is unholy; for so-called religious persons something is holy, something is unholy.

For tantra, everything is holy.

One Christian missionary was with me a few days ago and he said, "God created the world."

So I asked him, "Who created sin?"

He said, "The devil."

Then I asked him, "Who created the devil?"

Then he was at a loss. He said, "Of course, God created the devil."

The devil creates sin and God creates the devil. Then who is the real sinner—the devil or God? But the dualist conception always leads to such absurdities. For tantra God and the devil are not two. Really, for tantra there is nothing that can be called "devil," everything is divine, everything is holy. And this seems to be the right standpoint, the deepest. If anything is unholy in this world, from where does it come and how can it be?

So only two alternatives are there. First, the alternative of the atheist who says everything is unholy. This attitude is okay. He is also a nondualist; he sees no holiness in the world. Then there is the tantric's alternative—he says everything is holy. He is also a nondualist. But between these two are the so-called religious persons, who are not really religious because they are always in a conflict. Their whole

theology is just to make ends meet, and those ends cannot meet.

If a single cell, a single atom in this world is unholy, then the whole world becomes unholy, because how can that single atom exist in a holy world? How can it be? It is supported by everything; to be, it has to be supported by everything. And if the unholy element is supported by all the holy elements, then what is the difference between them? So either the world is holy totally, unconditionally, or it is unholy; there is no middle path.

Tantra says everything is holy, that is why we cannot understand it. It is the deepest nondual standpoint—if we can call it a standpoint. It is not, because any standpoint is bound to be dual. It is not against anything, so it is not any standpoint. It is a felt unity, a lived unity.

These are two paths, yoga and tantra. Tantra could not be so appealing because of our crippled minds. But whenever there is someone who is healthy inside, not a chaos, tantra has a beauty. Only he can understand what tantra is. Yoga has appeal, an easy appeal, because of our disturbed minds.

Remember, it is ultimately your mind which makes anything attractive or unattractive. It is you who is the deciding factor.

These approaches are different. I am not saying that one cannot reach through yoga. One can reach through yoga also, but not through the yoga which is prevalent. The yoga which is prevalent is not really yoga, but the interpretation of your diseased minds. Yoga can be authentically an approach toward the ultimate, but that too is only possible when your mind is healthy, when your mind is not diseased and ill. Then yoga takes a different shape.

For example, Mahavira was on the path of yoga, but he was not really suppressing sex. He had known it, he had lived it, he was deeply acquainted with it. But it became useless to him, so it dropped. Buddha was on the path of yoga, but he had lived through the world, he was deeply acquainted with it. He was not fighting.

Once you know something you become free from it. It simply drops like dead leaves dropping from a tree. It is not renunciation; there is no fight involved at all. Look at Buddha's face—it doesn't look like the face of a fighter. He has not been fighting. He is so relaxed; his face is the very symbol of relaxation...no fight.

Look at your yogis. The fight is apparent on their faces. Deep down much turmoil is there—right now they are sitting on volcanos. You can look in their eyes, in their faces, and you will feel it. Deep down somewhere they have suppressed all their diseases; they have not gone beyond.

In a healthy world, where everyone is living his life authentically, individually, not imitating others but living his own life in his own way, both are possible. He may learn the deep sensitivity which transcends desires; he may come to a point where all desires become futile and drop. Yoga can also lead to this, but to me yoga will lead to it in the same world where tantra can lead to it—remember this. We need a healthy mind, a natural man. In that world where a natural man is, tantra, and yoga also, will lead to transcendence of desires.

In our so-called ill society, neither yoga nor tantra can do this, because if we choose yoga we do not choose it because desires have become useless —no! They are still meaningful; they are not dropping by themselves. We have to force them. If we choose yoga, we choose it as a technique of suppression. If we choose tantra, we choose tantra as a cunningness, as a deep deception—an excuse to indulge.

So with an unhealthy mind neither yoga nor tantra can work. They will both lead to deceptions. A healthy mind, particularly a sexually healthy mind, is needed to start with. Then it is not very difficult to choose your path. You can choose yoga, you can choose tantra.

There are two types of persons basically, male and female. I do not mean biologically, but psychologically. For those who are psychologically basically male—aggressive, violent, extrovert—yoga is their path. For those who are basically feminine, receptive, passive, nonviolent, tantra is their path. So you may note it: for tantra, Mother Kali, Tara, and so many *devis, bhairavis*—female deities—are very significant. In yoga you will never hear mentioned any name of a feminine deity. Tantra has feminine deities; yoga has male gods. Yoga is outgoing energy; tantra is energy moving inward. So you can say in modern psychological terms that yoga is extrovert and tantra is introvert. So it depends on the personality. If you have an introverted personality, then fight is not for you. If you have an extroverted personality, then fight is for you.

But we are just confused, we are just in a mess; that is why nothing helps. On the contrary, everything disturbs. Yoga will disturb you, tantra will disturb you. Every medicine is going to create a new illness for you because the chooser is ill, diseased; so the result of his choice will be illness. So I do not mean that through yoga you cannot reach. I emphasize tantra only because we are going to try to understand what tantra is.

Another question:

On the path of surrender, how does the seeker come to the right technique out of one hundred and twelve methods?

On the path of will there are methods—these one hundred and twelve methods. On the path of surrender, surrender itself is the method, there are no other methods. Remember this. All methods are nonsurrendering, because a method means depending on yourself. You can do something; the technique is there, so you do it. On the path of surrender you are no more, so you cannot do anything. You have done the ultimate, the last: you have surrendered. On the path of surrender, surrender is the only method.

All these one hundred and twelve methods require a certain will; they require something to be done by you. You manipulate your energy, you balance your energy, you create a center in your chaos. You do something. Your effort is significant, basic, required. On the path of surrender only one thing is required—you surrender. We will go deep into these one hundred and twelve methods, so it is good to say something about surrender because it has no method.

In these one hundred and twelve methods there will be nothing about surrender. Why has Shiva not said anything about surrender? Because nothing can be said. Bhairavi herself, Devi herself, has reached Shiva not through any method. She has simply surrendered. So this must be noted. She is asking these questions not for herself, these questions are asked for the whole humanity. She has attained Shiva. She is already in his lap, she is already embraced by him. She has become one with him, but still she is asking.

So remember one thing: she is not asking for herself, there is no need. She is asking for the whole humanity.

But if she has attained, why is she asking Shiva? Can she herself not speak to humanity? She has come through the path of surrender, so she doesn't know anything about method. She herself has come through love; love is enough unto itself, love doesn't need anything more. She has come through love, so she doesn't know anything about any methods, techniques. That is why she is asking.

So Shiva relates one hundred and twelve methods. He also will not talk about surrender because surrender is not a method really. You surrender only when every method has become futile, when you cannot reach by any method. You have tried your best. You have knocked on every door and no door opens, and you have passed through all the routes and no route reaches. You have done whatsoever you can do, and now you feel helpless. In that total helplessness surrender happens. So on the path of surrender there is no method.

But what is surrender and how does it work? And if surrender works, then what is the need of one hundred and twelve methods? Then why go

into them unnecessarily?—the mind will ask. Then okay! If surrender works, it is better to surrender. Why go on hankering after methods? And who knows whether a particular method will suit you or not? And it may take lives to find out. So it is good to surrender, but it is difficult. It is the most difficult thing in the world.

Methods are not difficult. They are easy; you can train yourself. But for surrender you cannot train yourself...no training! You cannot ask how to surrender; the very question is absurd. How can you ask how to surrender? Can you ask how to love?

Either there is love or there is not, but you cannot ask how to love. And if someone tells you and teaches you how to love, remember, then you will never be capable of love. Once a technique is given to you for love, you will cling to the technique. That is why actors cannot love. They know so many techniques, so many methods—and we are all actors. Once you know the trick how to love, then love will not flower because you can create a façade, a deception. And with the deception you are out of it, not involved. You are protected.

Love is being totally open, vulnerable. It is dangerous, you become insecure. We cannot ask how to love, we cannot ask how to surrender. It happens! Love happens, surrender happens. Love and surrender are deeply one. But what is it? And if we cannot know how to surrender, at least we can know how we are maintaining ourselves, how we are preventing ourselves from surrendering. That can be known and that is helpful.

How is it that you have not surrendered yet? What is your technique of nonsurrendering? If you have not fallen in love yet, then the real problem is not how to love. The real problem is to dig deep to find out how you have lived without love, what is your trick, what is your technique, what is your structure—your defense structure, how you have lived without love. That can be understood, and that should be understood.

First thing: we live with the ego, in the ego, centered in the ego. I am, without knowing who I am. I go on announcing, "I am." This "I-am-ness" is false, because I do not know who I am. And unless I know who I am, how can I say "I"? This "I" is a false "I." This false "I" is the ego. This is the defense. This protects you from surrendering.

You cannot surrender, but you can become aware of this defense measure. If you have become aware of it, it dissolves. By and by, you are not strengthening it, and one day you come to feel, "I am not." The moment you come to feel "I am not," surrender happens. So try to find out whether you are. Really, is there any center in you that you can call your "I"? Go deep down within yourself, go on trying to find out where is this "I," where is the abode of this ego.

Rinzai went to his master and he said, "Give me freedom!"

The master said, "Bring yourself. If you are, I will make you free. But if you are not, then how can I make you free? You are already free. And freedom," his master said, "is not your freedom. Really, freedom is freedom from 'you'. So go and find out where this 'I' is, where you are, then come to me. This is the meditation. Go and meditate."

So the disciple Rinzai goes and meditates for weeks, months, and then he comes. Then he says, "I am not the body. Only this much I have found."

So the master says, "This much you have become free. Go again. Try to find out."

Then he tries, meditates, and he finds that "I am not my mind, because I can observe my thoughts. So the observer is different from the observed—I am not my mind." He comes and says, "I am not my mind."

So his master says, "Now you are three-fourths liberated. Now go again and find out who you are."

So he was thinking, "I am not my body. I am not my mind." He had read, studied, he was well informed, so he was thinking, "I am not my body, not my mind, so I must be my soul, my *atma*." But he meditated, and then he found that there is no

atma, no soul, because this atma is nothing but your mental information—just doctrines, words, philosophies.

So he came running one day and he said, "Now I am no more!"

Then his master said, "Am I now to teach you the methods for freedom?"

Rinzai said, "I am free because I am no more. There is no one to be in bondage. I am just a wide emptiness, a nothingness."

Only nothingness can be free. If you are something, you will be in bondage. If you are, you will be in bondage. Only a void, a vacant space, can be free. Then you cannot bind it. Rinzai came running and said, "I am no more. Nowhere am I to be found." This is freedom. And for the first time he touched his master's feet—for the first time! Not actually, because he had touched them many times before also. But the master said, "For the first time you have touched my feet."

Rinzai asked, "Why do you say for the first time? I have touched your feet many times."

The master said, "But you were there, so how could you touch my feet while you were already there? While you are there how can you touch my feet?"

The "I" can never touch anybody's feet. Even though it apparently looks like it touches somebody's feet, it is touching its own feet, just in a roundabout way. "You have touched my feet for the first time," the master said, "because now you are no more. And this is also the last time," the master said. "The first and the last."

Surrender happens when you are not, so *you* cannot surrender. That is why surrender cannot be a technique. You cannot surrender—you are the hindrance. When you are not, surrender is there. So you and surrender cannot cohabit, there is no coexistence between you and surrender. Either you are or surrender is. So find out where you are, who you are. This inquiry creates many, many surprising results.

Raman Maharshi used to say, "Inquire 'Who

am I?'" It was misunderstood. Even his nearest disciples have not understood the meaning of it. They think that this is an inquiry to find out really "Who am I?" It is not! if you go on inquiring "Who am I?" you are bound to come to the conclusion that you are not. This is not really an inquiry to find out "Who am I?" Really, this is an inquiry to dissolve.

I have given many this technique, to inquire within "Who am I?" Then a month or two months later, they will come to me and say, "I have still not found 'Who am I?' The question is still the same; there is no answer."

So I tell them, "Continue. Someday the answer will come." And they hope that the answer will come. There is going to be no answer. It is only that the question will dissolve. There is not going to be an answer, that "You are this." Only the question will dissolve. There will be no one to ask even "Who am I?" And then you know.

When the "I" is not, the real "I" opens. When the ego is not, you are for the first time encountering your being. That being is void. Then you can surrender; then you have surrendered. You *are* surrender now. So there can be no techniques, or only negative techniques like this inquiry into "Who am I?"

How does surrender work? If you surrender, what happens? We will come to understand how methods work. We will go deep into methods, and we will come to know how they work. They have a scientific basis of working.

When you surrender you become a valley; when you are an ego you are like a peak. Ego means you are above everyone else, you are somebody. The others may recognize you, may not recognize you —that is another thing. You recognize that you are above everyone. You are like a peak; nothing can enter you.

When one surrenders, one becomes like a valley. One becomes depth, not height. Then the whole existence begins to pour into him from everywhere. He is just a vacuum, just a depth, an abyss, bottom-

less. The whole existence begins to pour from everywhere. You can say God runs from everywhere to him, enters him from every pore, fills him totally.

This surrender, this becoming a valley, an abyss, can be felt in many ways. There are minor surrenders; there are major surrenders. Even in minor surrenders you feel it. Surrendering to a master is a minor surrender, but you begin to feel it because the master begins to flow into you immediately. If you surrender to a master, suddenly you feel his energy flowing into you. If you cannot feel energy flowing into you, then know well you have not surrendered even in a minor way.

There are so many stories which have become meaningless for us because we do not know how they happened. Mahakashyapa came to Buddha, and Buddha just touched his head with his hand, and the thing happened. And Mahakashyapa began to dance. So Ananda asked Buddha, "What has happened to him? And I have been for forty years with you! Is he mad? Or is he just fooling others? What has happened to him? And I have touched your feet thousands and thousands of times."

Of course, to Ananda, this Mahakashyapa will either look like he is mad or as if he is just deceiving. Ananda was with Buddha for forty years, but there was a problem. He was his elder brother, Buddha's elder brother; that was the problem. When Ananda came to Buddha forty years before, the first thing he said to Buddha was this: "I am your elder brother, and when you initiate me, I will become your disciple. So allow me three things before I become your disciple, because then I cannot demand. One, I will always be with you. Give me this promise, that you will not say to me, 'Go somewhere else.' I will follow you.

"Secondly, I will sleep in the same room where you sleep. You cannot say to me, 'Go out.' I will be with you like your shadow. And thirdly, if I bring anyone at any time, even at midnight, you will have to answer him. You cannot say, 'This is not the time.' And give me these three promises while I am still your elder brother, because once I become your disciple I will have to follow you. You are still younger than me, so give me these promises."

So Buddha promised, and this became the problem. For forty years Ananda was with Buddha, but he could never surrender, because this is not the spirit of surrender.

Ananda asked many, many times, "When am I going to attain?"

Buddha said, "Unless I die, you will not attain."

And Ananda could attain only when Buddha died.

What happened to this Mahakashyapa suddenly? Is Buddha partial—partial to Mahakashyapa? He is not! He is flowing, constantly flowing. But you have to be a valley, a womb, to receive him. If you are above him, how can you receive? That flowing energy cannot come to you, it will miss you. So bow down. Even in a minor surrender with a master, energy begins to flow. Suddenly, immediately, you become a vehicle of a great force.

There are thousands and thousands of stories... just by a touch, just by a look, someone became enlightened. They do not appear rational to us. How is this possible? This is possible! Even a look from the master into your eyes will change your total being, but it can change only if your eyes are just vacant, valleylike. If you can absorb the look of the master, immediately you will be different.

So these are minor surrenders that happen before you surrender totally. And these minor surrenders prepare you for the total surrender. Once you have known that through surrender you receive something unknown, unbelievable, unexpected, never even dreamed of, then you are ready for a major surrender. And that is the work of the master—to help you in minor surrenders so that you can gather courage for a major surrender, for a total surrender.

One last question:

What are the exact indications to know that the particular technique one is practicing will lead to the ultimate?

There are indications. One, you begin to feel a different identity within you. You are no more the same. If the technique fits you, immediately you are a different person. If you are a husband, you are no more the same husband. If you are a shopkeeper, you are never again the same shopkeeper. Whatsoever you are, if the technique fits you, you are a different person; that is the first indication. So if you begin to feel strange about yourself, know that something is happening to you. If you remain the same and do not feel any strangeness, nothing is happening. This is the first indication of whether a technique fits you. If it fits, immediately you are transported, transformed into a different person. Suddenly this happens: you look at the world in a different way. The eyes are the same, but the looker behind them is different.

Secondly, all that creates tensions, conflicts, starts dropping. It is not that when you have practiced the method for years, then your conflicts, anxieties, tensions will drop—no! If the method fits you, immediately they start dropping. You can feel an aliveness coming to you; you are being unburdened. You will begin to feel, if the technique fits you, that gravity has become reversed. Now the earth is not pulling you down. Rather, the sky is pulling you up. How do you feel when an airplane takes off? Everything is disturbed. Suddenly there is a jerk, and gravity becomes meaningless. Now the earth is not pulling you, you are going away from gravity.

The same jerk happens if a meditative technique fits you. Suddenly you take off. Suddenly you feel the earth has become meaningless; there is no gravity. It is not pulling you down, you are being pulled up. In religious terminology this is called "grace." There are two forces—gravity and grace. Grace means you are being pulled upwards; gravity means you are being pulled downwards.

That is why in meditation many people suddenly feel they have no weight. That is why many people feel an inner levitation. So many have reported this to me when the technique fits them:

"This is strange! We close our eyes and we feel that we are a little bit above the earth—one foot, two feet, even four feet above the earth. When we open our eyes we are just on the ground; when we close our eyes we have levitated. So what is this? When we open our eyes we are just on the ground! We never levitated."

The body remains on the ground, but you levitate. This levitation is really a pull from the above. If the technique fits you have been pulled, because the working of the technique is to make you available for the upward pull. This is what the technique means: to make you available for the force which can pull you up. So if it fits, you know—you have become weightless.

Thirdly, whatsoever you will now do, whatsoever, howsoever trivial, will be different. You will walk in a different way, you will sit in a different way, you will eat in a different way. Everything will be different. This difference you will feel everywhere. Sometimes this strange experience of being different creates fear. One wants again to go back and be the same, because one was so attuned with the old. It was a routine world, even boring, but you were efficient in it.

Now everywhere you will feel a gap. You will feel that your efficiency is lost. You will feel that your utility is reduced. You will feel that everywhere you are an outsider. One has to pass through this period. You will become attuned again. You have changed, not the world, so you will not fit. So remember the third thing: When the technique fits you, you will not fit into the world. You will become unfit. Everywhere something is loose, some bolt is missing. Everywhere you will feel that there has been an earthquake. And everything has remained the same; only you, you have become different. But you will be attuned again on a different plane, on a higher plane.

The disturbance is felt just like when a child grows and becomes sexually mature. At the age of fourteen or fifteen every boy feels that he has become strange. A new force has entered—sex. It

was not there before, or it was, but it was hidden. Now for the first time he has become available for a new kind of force. That is why boys are very awkward; girls, boys, when they become sexually mature, they are very awkward. They are nowhere. They are no longer children and they are not yet men, so they are in between, fitting nowhere. If they play with small children they feel awkward—they have become men. If they start making friendships with men they feel awkward—they are still children. They fit with no one.

The same phenomenon happens when a technique fits you. A new energy source becomes available that is greater than sex. You are again in a transitory period. Now you cannot fit in this world of worldly men. You are not a child, and you cannot yet fit in the world of saints; and in between one feels awkward.

If a technique fits you these three things will come up. You may not have expected that I would say these things. You may have expected that I would say you will become more silent, more quiet, and I am saying quite the contrary: you will become more disturbed. When the technique fits you will become more disturbed, not more silent. Silence will come later on. And if silence comes and not disturbance, know well that this is not a technique; this is just getting adjusted to the old pattern.

That is why more people go for prayer than for meditation because prayer gives you a consolation. It fits you, adjusts to you, to your world. Prayer was doing virtually the same thing that psychoanalysts are now doing. If you are disturbed they will make you less disturbed, adjusted to the pattern, to the society, to the family. So by going to a psychoanalyst for one, two or three years you will not get better, but you will be more adjusted. Prayer does the same thing, and priests do the same thing—they make you more adjusted.

Your child has died and you are disturbed, and you go to a priest. He says, "Do not be disturbed. Only those children die early whom God loves more. He calls them up." You feel satisfied. Your child has been "called up." God loves him more. Or the priest says something else: "Do not be worried, the soul never dies. Your child is in heaven."

One woman was here just a few days ago. Her husband had died just during the past month. She was disturbed. She came to me and she said, "Only assure me that he is reborn in a good place and then everything will be okay. Just give me a certainty that he has not gone to hell or he has not become an animal, that he is in heaven or he has become a god or some such thing. If you can just assure me of this, then everything is okay. Then I can bear it; otherwise I am miserable."

The priest would say, "Okay! Your husband is born as a god in the seventh heaven, and he is very happy. And he is waiting for you."

These prayers, they make you adjusted to the pattern...you feel better.

Meditation is a science. It is not going to help you in adjustment, it is going to help you in transformation. That is why I say these three signs will be there as indications. Silence will come, but not as an adjustment. Silence will come as an inner flowering. Then silence will not be an adjustment with the society, with the family, the world, the business—no! Then silence will be a real harmony with the universe.

Then a deep harmony flowers between you and the totality, then there is silence—but that will come later. First you will get disturbed, first you will become mad—because you *are* mad, only unaware.

If a technique fits, it will make you aware of everything that you are. Your anarchy, your mind, your madness, everything will come to light. You are just a dark mess. When a technique fits, it is as if suddenly there is light and the whole mess becomes apparent. For the first time you will encounter yourself as you are. You would like to put the light off and go to sleep again—it is fearful. This is the point where the master becomes helpful. He says, "Do not be afraid. This is just the beginning. And do not escape from it."

At first this light shows you what you are, and if you can go on and on, it transforms you toward what you can be.

Enough for today.

28

CHAPTER 3

Breath –
a bridge
to the universe

◆

Shiva replies:

1 *Radiant one, this experience may dawn between two breaths. After breath comes in (down) and just before turning up (out)—the beneficence.*

2 *As breath turns from down to up, and again as breath curves from up to down—through both these turns, realize.*

3 *Or, whenever in-breath and out-breath fuse, at this instant touch the energy-less, energy-filled center.*

4 *Or, when breath is all out (up) and stopped of itself, or all in (down) and stopped—in such universal pause, one's small self vanishes. This is difficult only for the impure.*

ruth is always here. It is already the case. It is not something to be achieved in the future. *You* are the truth just here and now, so it is not something which is to be created or something which is to be devised or something which is to be sought. Understand this very clearly; then these techniques will be easy to understand and also to do.

Mind is a mechanism of desiring. Mind is always in desire, always seeking something, asking for something. Always the object is in the future; mind is not concerned with the present at all. In this very moment the mind cannot move—there is no space. The mind needs the future in order to move. It can move either in the past or in the future. It cannot move in the present; there is no space. The truth is in the present, and mind is always in the future or in the past, so there is no meeting between mind and truth.

When the mind is seeking worldly objects it is not so difficult, the problem is not absurd; it can be solved. But when the mind starts seeking the truth the very effort becomes nonsense, because the truth is here and now and the mind is always then and there. There is no meeting. So understand the first thing: you cannot seek truth. You can find it, but you cannot seek it. The very seeking is the hindrance.

The moment you start seeking you have moved away from the present, away from yourself, because *you* are always in the present. The seeker is always in the present and the seeking is in the future; you are not going to meet whatsoever you are seeking. Lao Tzu says, "Seek not; otherwise you will miss. Seek not and find. Don't seek and find."

All these techniques of Shiva's are simply turning the mind from the future or the past to the present. That which you are seeking is already there, it is the case already. The mind has to be turned from seeking to nonseeking. It is difficult. If you think about it intellectually it is very difficult. How to turn the mind from seeking to nonseeking?—because then the mind makes nonseeking itself the object! Then the mind says, "Don't seek." Then the mind says, "I should not seek." Then the mind says, "Now nonseeking is my object. Now I desire the state of desirelessness." The seeking has entered again, the desire has come again through the back door. That is why there are people who are seeking worldly objects, and there are people who think they are seeking nonworldly objects. All objects are worldly because "seeking" is the world.

So you cannot seek anything nonworldly. The moment you seek, it becomes the world. If you are seeking God, your God is part of the world. If you are seeking *moksha*—liberation—*nirvana,* your liberation is part of the world, your liberation is not something that transcends the world, because seeking is the world, desiring is the world. So you cannot desire nirvana, you cannot desire nondesire. If you try to understand intellectually, it will become a puzzle.

Shiva says nothing about it, he immediately

proceeds to give techniques. They are nonintellec-tual. He doesn't say to Devi, "The truth is here. Don't seek it and you will find it." He immediately gives techniques. Those techniques are nonintellec-tual. Do them, and the mind turns. The turning is just a consequence, just a by-product—not an object. The turning is just a by-product.

If you do a technique, your mind will turn from its journey into the future or the past. Suddenly you will find yourself in the present. That is why Buddha has given techniques, Lao Tzu has given techniques, Krishna has given techniques. But they always introduce their techniques with intellectual concepts. Only Shiva is different. He immediately gives techniques, and no intellectual understanding, no intellectual introduction, because he knows that the mind is tricky, the most cunning thing possible. It can turn anything into a problem. Nonseeking will become the problem.

There are people who come to me and ask how not to desire. They are desiring nondesire. Some-body has told them, or they have read somewhere, or they have heard spiritual gossip, that if you do not desire you will reach bliss, if you do not desire you will be free, if you do not desire there will be no suffering. Now their minds hanker to attain that state where there is no suffering, so they ask how not to desire. Their minds are playing tricks. They are still desiring, it is only that now the object has changed. They were desiring money, they were de-siring fame, they were desiring prestige, they were desiring power. Now they are desiring nondesire. Only the object has changed, and they remain the same and their desiring remains the same. But now the desire has become more deceptive.

Because of this, Shiva proceeds immediately with no introduction whatsoever. He immediately starts talking about techniques. Those techniques, if followed, suddenly turn your mind: it comes to the present. And when the mind comes to the present it stops, it is no more. You cannot be a mind in the present, that is impossible. Just now, if you are here and now, how can you be a mind? Thoughts cease because they cannot move. The present has no space in which to move; you cannot think. If you are in this very moment, how can you move? Mind stops, you attain to no-mind.

So the real thing is how to be here and now. You can try, but effort may prove futile—because if you make it a point to be in the present, then this point has moved into the future. When you ask how to be in the present, again you are asking about the future. This moment is passing in the inquiry, "How to be present? How to be here and now?" This present moment is passing in the inquiry, and your mind will begin to weave and create dreams in the future: someday you will be in a state of mind where there is no movement, no motive, no seeking, and then there will be bliss—so how to be in the present?

Shiva doesn't say anything about it, he simply gives a technique. You do it, and suddenly you find you are here and now. And your being here and now is the truth, and your being here and now is the freedom, and your being here and now is the nirvana.

The first nine techniques are concerned with breathing. So let us understand something about breathing, and then we will proceed to the tech-niques. We are breathing continuously from the moment of birth to the moment of death. Every-thing changes between these two points. Everything changes, nothing remains the same, only breathing is a constant thing between birth and death.

The child will become a youth; the youth will become old. He will be diseased, his body will become ugly, ill, everything will change. He will be happy, unhappy, in suffering; everything will go on changing. But whatsoever happens between these two points, one must breathe. Whether happy or unhappy, young or old, successful or unsuccessful —whatsoever you are, it is irrelevant—one thing is certain: between these two points of birth and death you must breathe.

Breathing will be a continuous flow; no gap is possible. If even for a single moment you forget to breathe, you will be no more. That is why *you* are not required to breathe, because then it would be difficult. Someone might forget to breathe for a single moment, and then nothing could be done. So, really, *you* are not breathing, because *you* are not needed. You are fast asleep, and breathing goes on; you are unconscious, and breathing goes on; you are in a deep coma, and breathing goes on. *You* are not required; breathing is something which goes on in spite of you.

It is one of the constant factors in your personality—that is the first thing. It is something which is very essential and basic to life—that is the second thing. You cannot be alive without breath. So breath and life have become synonymous. Breathing is the mechanism of life, and life is deeply related with breathing. That is why in India we call it *prana*. We have given one word for both—*prana* means the vitality, the aliveness. Your life is your breath.

Thirdly, your breath is a bridge between you and your body. Constantly, breath is bridging you to your body, connecting you, relating you to your body. Not only is the breath a bridge to your body, it is also a bridge between you and the universe. The body is just the universe which has come to you, which is nearer to you.

Your body is part of the universe. Everything in the body is part of the universe—every particle, every cell. It is the nearest approach to the universe. Breath is the bridge. If the bridge is broken, you are no more in the body. If the bridge is broken, you are no more in the universe. You move into some unknown dimension; then you cannot be found in space and time. So, thirdly, breath is also the bridge between you, and space and time.

Breath, therefore, becomes very significant—the most significant thing. So the first nine techniques are concerned with breath. If you can do something with the breath, you will suddenly turn to the present. If you can do something with breath, you will attain to the source of life. If you can do something with breath, you can transcend

time and space. If you can do something with breath, you will be in the world and also beyond it.

Breath has two points. One is where it touches the body and the universe, and another is where it touches you and that which transcends the universe. We know only one part of the breath. When it moves into the universe, into the body, we know it. But it is always moving from the body to the "no-body," from the "no-body" to the body. We do not know the other point. If you become aware of the other point, the other part of the bridge, the other pole of the bridge, suddenly you will be transformed, transplanted into a different dimension.

But remember, what Shiva is going to say is not yoga, it is tantra. Yoga also works on breath, but the work of yoga and tantra is basically different. Yoga tries to systematize breathing. If you systematize your breathing your health will improve. If you systematize your breathing, if you know the secrets of breathing, your life will become longer; you will be more healthy and you will live longer. You will be more strong, more filled with energy, more vital, alive, young, fresh.

But tantra is not concerned with that. Tantra is concerned not with any systematization of breath, but with using breath just as a technique to turn inward. One has not to practice a particular style of breathing, a particular system of breathing or a particular rhythm of breathing—no! One has to take breathing as it is. One has just to become aware of certain points in the breathing.

There are certain points, but we are not aware of them. We have been breathing and we will go on breathing—we are born breathing and we will die breathing—but we are not aware of certain points. And this is strange. Man is searching, probing deep into space. Man is going to the moon; man is trying to reach farther, from earth into space, and man has not yet learned the nearest part of his life. There are certain points in breathing which you have never observed, and those points are the doors —the nearest doors to you from where you can enter into a different world, into a different being, into a different consciousness. But they are very subtle.

To observe a moon is not very difficult. Even to reach the moon is not very difficult; it is a gross journey. You need mechanization, you need technology, you need accumulated information, and then you can reach it. Breathing is the nearest thing to you, and the nearer a thing is, the more difficult it is to perceive it. The nearer it is, the more difficult; the more obvious it is, the more difficult. It is so near to you that again there is no space between you and your breathing. Or, there is such a small space that you will need a very minute observation, only then will you become aware of certain points. These points are the basis of these techniques.

So now I will take each technique.

1 Watch the gap between two breaths.

Shiva replies: Radiant one, this experience may dawn between two breaths. After breath comes in (down) and just before turning up (out)—the beneficence.

That is the technique: *Radiant one, this experience may dawn between two breaths.*

After breath comes in—that is, down—and just before turning out—that is, going up—*the beneficence.* Be aware between these two points... and the happening. When your breath comes in, observe. For a single moment, or a thousandth part of a moment, there is no breathing—before it turns up, before it turns outward. One breath comes in; then there is a certain point and breathing stops. Then the breathing goes out. When the breath goes out, then again for a single moment, or a part of a moment, breathing stops. Then breathing comes in.

Before the breath is turning in or turning out, there is a moment when you are not breathing. In that moment the happening is possible, because when you are not breathing you are not in the world. Understand this: when you are not breathing you are dead; you *are* still, but dead. But the moment is of such a short duration that you never observe it.

For tantra, each outgoing breath is a death and each new breath is a rebirth. Breath coming in is rebirth; breath going out is death. The outgoing breath is synonymous with death; the incoming breath is synonymous with life. So with each breath you are dying and being reborn. The gap between the two is of a very short duration, but keen, sincere observation and attention will let you feel the gap. If you can feel the gap, Shiva says, *the beneficence.* Then nothing else is needed. You are blessed, you have known; the thing has happened.

You are not to train the breath. Leave it just as it is. Why such a simple technique? It looks so simple. Such a simple technique to know the truth? To know the truth means to know that which is neither born nor dies, to know that eternal element which is always. You can know the breath going out, you can know the breath coming in, but you never know the gap between the two.

Try it. Suddenly you will get the point—and you can get it; it is already there. Nothing is to be added to you or to your structure, it is already there. Everything is already there except a certain awareness. So how to do this? First, become aware of the breath coming in. Watch it. Forget everything, just watch breath coming in—the very passage.

When the breath touches your nostrils, feel it there. Then let the breath move in. Move with the breath fully consciously. When you are going down, down, down with the breath, do not miss the breath. Do not go ahead and do not follow behind, just go with it. Remember this: do not go ahead, do not follow it like a shadow; be simultaneous with it.

Breath and consciousness should become one. The breath goes in—you go in. Only then will it be possible to get the point which is between two

34

breaths. It will not be easy. Move in with the breath, then move out with the breath: in-out, in-out.

Buddha tried particularly to use this method, so this method has become a Buddhist method. In Buddhist terminology it is known as Anapanasati yoga. And Buddha's enlightenment was based on this technique—only this.

All the religions of the world, all the seers of the world, have reached through some technique or other, and all those techniques will be in these one hundred and twelve techniques. This first one is a Buddhist technique. It has become known in the world as a Buddhist technique because Buddha attained his enlightenment through this technique.

Buddha said, "Be aware of your breath as it is coming in, going out—coming in, going out." He never mentions the gap because there is no need. Buddha thought and felt that if you become concerned with the gap, the gap between two breaths, that concern may disturb your awareness. So he simply said, "Be aware. When the breath is going in move with it, and when the breath is going out move with it. Do simply this: going in, going out, with the breath." He never says anything about the latter part of the technique.

The reason is that Buddha was talking with very ordinary men, and even that might create a desire to attain the interval. That desire to attain the interval will become a barrier to awareness, because if you are desiring to get to the interval you will move ahead. Breath will be coming in, and you will move ahead because you are interested in the gap which is going to be in the future. Buddha never mentions it, so Buddha's technique is just half.

But the other half follows automatically. If you go on practicing breath consciousness, breath awareness, suddenly, one day, without knowing, you will come to the interval. Because as your awareness will become keen and deep and intense, as your awareness will become bracketed—the whole world is bracketed out; only your breath coming in or going out is your world, the whole arena for your consciousness—suddenly you are bound to feel the gap in which there is no breath.

When you are moving with breath minutely, when there is no breath how can you remain unaware? You will suddenly become aware that there is no breath, and the moment will come when you will feel that the breath is neither going out nor coming in. The breath has stopped completely. In that stopping, *the beneficence.*

This one technique is enough for millions. The whole of Asia tried and lived with this technique for centuries. Tibet, China, Japan, Burma, Thailand, Sri Lanka—the whole of Asia except India has tried this technique. Only one technique and thousands and thousands have attained enlightenment through it. And this is only the first technique.

But unfortunately, because the technique became associated with Buddha's name, Hindus have been trying to avoid it. Because it became more and more known as a Buddhist method, Hindus have completely forgotten it. And not only that, they have also tried to avoid it for another reason. Because this technique is the first technique mentioned by Shiva, many Buddhists have claimed that this book, *Vigyan Bhairav Tantra*, is a Buddhist book, not a Hindu book.

It is neither Hindu nor Buddhist—a technique is just a technique. Buddha used it, but it was there already to be used. Buddha became a buddha, an enlightened one, because of the technique. The technique preceded Buddha; the technique was already there. Try it. It is one of the most simple techniques—simple compared to other techniques; I am not saying simple for you. Other techniques will be more difficult. That is why it is mentioned as the first technique.

---

2 Watch the turning point between two breaths.

The second technique—all these nine techniques are concerned with breath. *As breath turns from down to up, and again as breath curves from up to down—through both these turns, realize.*

It is the same, but with a slight difference. The emphasis is now not on the gap, but on the turning. The outgoing and ingoing breath make a circle. Remember, these are not two parallel lines. We always think of them as two parallel lines—breath going in and breath going out. Do you think that these are two parallel lines? They are not. Breath going in is half the circle; breath going out is the other half of the circle.

So understand this: first, breathing in and out creates a circle. They are not parallel lines, because parallel lines never meet anywhere. Secondly, the breath coming in and the breath going out are not two breaths, they are one breath. The same breath which comes in, goes out, so it must have a turn inside. It must turn somewhere. There must be a point where the incoming breath becomes outgoing.

Why put such emphasis upon turning? Because, Shiva says, *As breath turns from down to up and again as breath curves from up to down—through both these turns, realize.* Very simple, but he says: realize the turns and you will realize the self.

Why the turn? If you know driving you know about gears. Each time you change the gear, you have to pass through the neutral gear, which is not a gear at all. From the first gear you move to the second or from the second to the third, but always you have to move through the neutral gear. That neutral gear is a turning point. In that turning point the first gear becomes the second and the second becomes the third. When your breath goes in and turns out, it passes through the neutral gear; otherwise it cannot turn out. It passes through the neutral territory.

In that neutral territory you are neither a body nor a soul, neither physical nor mental, because the physical is a gear of your being and the mental is another gear of your being. You go on moving from gear to gear, but you must have a neutral gear where you are neither body nor mind. In that neutral gear you simply are: you are simply an existence—pure, simple, unembodied, with no mind.

That is why there is the emphasis on the turn. Man is a machine—a large, very complicated machine. You have many gears in your body, many gears in your mind. You are not aware of your great mechanism, but you are a great machine. And it is good that you are not aware; otherwise you could go mad. The body is such a great machine that scientists say if we had to create a factory parallel to the human body, it would require four square miles of land, and the noise would be such that one hundred square miles of land would be disturbed by it.

The body is a great mechanical device—the greatest. You have millions and millions of cells and each cell is alive. So you are a big city of roughly sixty trillion cells; there are roughly sixty trillion citizens inside you, and the whole city is running very silently, smoothly. Every moment the mechanism is working. It is very complicated. These techniques will be related at many points with the mechanism of your body and the mechanism of your mind. But always the emphasis will be on those points where suddenly you are not part of the mechanism—remember this. Suddenly you are not part of the mechanism. There are moments when you change gears.

For example, in the night when you drop into sleep you change gears, because during the day you need a different mechanism for a waking consciousness—a different part of the mind functions. Then you drop into sleep, and that part becomes nonfunctioning. Another part of the mind begins to function, and there is a gap, an interval, a turning. A gear is changed. In the morning when you are again getting up, the gear is changed. You are silently sitting, and suddenly someone says something and you get angry—you move into a different gear. That is why everything changes.

If you get angry, your breathing will suddenly change. Your breathing will become irritated, chaotic. A trembling will get into your breathing; you will feel suffocated. Your whole body would like to do something, shatter something, only then can the suffocation disappear. Your breathing will change; your blood will take a different rhythm, a different movement. Different chemicals will have to be released in the body, the whole glandular system will have to change. You become a different man when you are angry.

A car is standing…you start it. Do not put it in any gear, let it be in neutral. It will go on pulling, vibrating, trembling, but it cannot move; it will get hot. That is why, when you are angry and you cannot do something, you will get hot. The mechanism is ready to run and do something and you are not doing—you will get hot. You are a mechanism, but, of course, not only a mechanism. You are more, but the "more" has to be found. When you get into a gear, everything changes inside. When you change the gear, there is a turning.

Shiva says, *As breath turns from down to up, and again as breath curves from up to down— through both these turns, realize.*

Be aware at the turn. But it is a very short turn; very minute observation will be needed. And we are just without any observing capacity; we cannot observe anything. If I say to you, "Observe this flower; observe this flower which I give to you," you cannot observe it. For a single moment you will see it, and then you will begin to think of something else. It may be about the flower, but it will not be *the flower.* You may think about the flower, about how beautiful it is—then you have moved. Now the flower is no more in your observation, your field has changed. You may say that it is red, it is blue, it is white…then you have moved. Observation means remaining with no word, with no verbalization, with no bubbling inside—just remaining *with.* If you can remain with a flower for three minutes, completely, with no movement of the mind, the thing will happen—the beneficence. You will realize.

But we are not at all observers. We are not aware, we are not alert; we cannot pay attention to anything. We just go on jumping. This is part of our heritage, our monkey heritage. Our mind is just

the growth of the monkey mind, so the monkey moves on. He goes on jumping from here to there. The monkey cannot sit still. That is why Buddha insisted so much on just sitting without any movement, because then the monkey mind is not allowed to go on its way.

In Japan they have a particular type of meditation which they call Zazen. The word 'zazen' in Japan means just sitting, doing nothing. No movement is allowed. One is just sitting like a statue— dead, not moving at all. But there is no need to sit like a statue for years together. If you can observe the turn of your breath without any movement of the mind, you will enter. You will enter into yourself or into the beyond within.

Why are these turnings so important? They are important because on turning, the breath leaves you to move in a different direction. It was with you when it was coming in; it will be with you again when it goes out. But at the turning point it is not with you and you are not with it. In that moment the breath is different from you, and you are different from it: if breathing is life, then you are dead; if breathing is your body, then you are no-body; if breathing is your mind, then you are no-mind…in that moment.

I wonder whether you have observed it or not: if you stop your breath, the mind stops suddenly. If you stop your breath just now, your mind will stop suddenly; the mind cannot function. A sudden stoppage of breath and the mind stops. Why? Because they are disjoined. Only a moving breath is joined with the mind, with the body; a nonmoving breath is disjoined. Then you are in the neutral gear. The car is running, the power is on, the car is making a noise—it is ready to go forward—but it is not in gear, so the body of the car and the mechanism of the car are not joined. The car is divided into two. It is ready to move, but the moving mechanism is not joined with it.

The same happens when breath takes a turn. You are not joined with it. In that moment you can easily become aware of who you are. What is this being? What is it to be? Who is inside this house of the body? Who is the master? Am I just the house or is there some master also? Am I just the mechanism or does something else also penetrate this mechanism? In that turning gap, Shiva says, *realize*. He says just be aware of the turning, and you become a realized soul.

---

3 Watch the fusion point of two breaths.

The third breathing technique: *Or, whenever in-breath and out-breath fuse, at this instant touch the energy-less, energy-filled center.*

We are divided into the center and the periphery. The body is the periphery; we know the body, we know the periphery. We know the circumference, but we do not know where the center is. When the out-breath fuses with the in-breath, when they become one, when you cannot say whether it is the out-breath or the in-breath…when it is difficult to demarcate and define whether the breath is going out or coming in, when the breath has penetrated in and starts moving out, there is a moment of fusion. It is neither going out nor moving in. The breath is static. When it is moving out it is dynamic; when it is coming in it is dynamic. When it is neither, when it is silent, nonmoving, you are near to the center. The fusion point of the in and outgoing breath is your center.

Look at it in this way: when the breath goes in, where does it go? It goes to your center, it touches your center. When it goes out, from where does it go out? It moves from your center. Your center has to be touched. That is why Taoist mystics and Zen mystics say that the head is not the center, the navel is your center. The breath goes to the navel, then it moves out. It goes to the center.

As I said, it is a bridge between you and your body. You know the body, but you do not know where your center is. The breath is constantly going to the center and moving out, but we are not taking enough breath. Thus, ordinarily it does not really go to the center—now, at least, it is not going to the center. That is why everyone feels "off center." In the whole modern world, those who can think at all feel they are missing their center.

Look at a child sleeping, observe his breath. The breath goes in; the abdomen comes up. The chest remains unaffected. That is why children have no chests, only abdomens—very dynamic abdomens. The breath goes in and the abdomen comes up; the breath goes out and the abdomen goes down; the abdomen moves. Children are in their center, at their center. That is why they are so happy, so bliss-filled, so energy-filled, never tired—overflowing, and always in the present moment with no past, no future.

A child can be angry. When he is angry, he is totally angry; he becomes the anger. Then his anger is also a beautiful thing. When one is totally angry, anger has a beauty of its own, because totality always has beauty.

You cannot be angry and beautiful, you will become ugly, because partiality is always ugly. And not only with anger. When you love you are ugly because you are again partial, fragmentary; you are not total. Look at your face when you are loving someone, making love. Make love before a mirror and look at your face—it will be ugly, animallike. In love also your face becomes ugly. Why? Love is also a conflict, you are withholding something. You are giving very miserly. Even in your love you are not total; you do not give completely, wholly.

A child even in anger and violence is total. His face becomes radiant and beautiful; he is here and now. His anger is not something concerned with the past or something concerned with the future, he is not calculating, he is just angry. The child is at his center. When you are at your center you are always total. Whatsoever you do will be a total act; good or bad, it will be total. When you are fragmentary, when you are off center, your every act is bound to be a fragment of yourself. Your totality is not responding, just a part, and the part is going against the whole—that creates ugliness.

We all were children. Why is it that as we grow our breathing becomes shallow? It never goes to the abdomen; it never touches the navel. If it could go down more and more it would become less and less shallow, but it just touches the chest and goes out. It never goes to the center. You are afraid of the center, because if you go to the center you will become total. If you want to be fragmentary, this is the mechanism to be fragmentary.

You love—if you breathe from the center, you will flow in it totally. You are afraid. You are afraid to be so vulnerable, so open to someone, to anyone. You may call him your lover, you may call her your beloved, but you are afraid. The other is there. If you are totally vulnerable, open, you do not know what is going to happen. Then *you are* completely, in another sense. You are afraid to be so completely given to someone. You cannot breathe; you cannot take a deep breath. You cannot relax your breathing so that it goes to the center—because the moment breathing goes to the center your act becomes total.

Because you are afraid of being total, you breathe shallowly. You breathe just at the minimum, not at the maximum. That is why life seems so lifeless. If you are breathing at the minimum, life will become lifeless; you are living at the minimum, not at the maximum. You can live at the maximum —then life is an overflowing. But then there will be difficulty. You cannot be a husband, you cannot be a wife, if life is overflowing. Everything will become difficult.

If life is overflowing, love will be overflowing. Then you cannot stick to one. Then you will be flowing all over; all dimensions will be filled by you. And then the mind feels danger, so it is better not to be alive. The more you are dead, the more you are secure. The more you are dead, the more everything is in control. You can control; then you remain the master. You feel that you are the master because you can control. You can control your anger, you can control your love, you can control

everything. But this controlling is possible only at the minimum level of your energy.

Everyone must have felt at some time or other that there are moments when he suddenly changes from the minimum level to the maximum. You go out to a hill station. Suddenly you are out of the city and the prison of it. You feel free. The sky is vast, and the forest is green, and the height touches the clouds. Suddenly you take a deep breath. You may not have observed it.

Now if you go to a hill station, observe. It is not really the hill station that makes the change. It is your breathing. You take a deep breath. You say, "Ah! Ah!" You touch the center, you become total for a moment, and everything is bliss. That bliss is not coming from the hill station, that bliss is coming from your center—you have touched it suddenly.

You were afraid in the city. Everywhere there were others present and you were controlling. You could not scream, you could not laugh. What a misfortune! You could not sing on the street and dance. You were afraid—a policeman was somewhere around the corner, or the priest or the judge or the politician or the moralist. Someone was just around the corner, so you could not just dance in the street.

Bertrand Russell has said somewhere, "I love civilization, but we have achieved civilization at a very great cost." You cannot dance in the streets, but you go to a hill station and suddenly you can dance. You are alone with the sky, and the sky is not an imprisonment. It is just opening, opening and opening—vast, infinite. Suddenly you take a breath deeply, it touches the center and the bliss. But it is not so for long. Within an hour or two, the hill station will disappear. You may be there, but the hill station will disappear.

Your worries will come back. You will begin to think to make a call to the city, to write a letter to your wife, or you will begin to think that since after three days you are going back you should make arrangements. You have just reached and you are making arrangements to leave. You are back.

That breath was not from you really; it suddenly happened. Because of the change of situation the gear changed. You were in a new situation, you could not breathe in the old way, so for a moment a new breath came in. It touched the center, and you felt the bliss.

Shiva says you are every moment touching the center, or if you are not touching you *can* touch it. Take deep, slow breaths. Touch the center; do not breathe from the chest—that is a trick. Civilization, education, morality, they have created shallow breathing. It will be good to go deep into the center, because otherwise you cannot take deep breaths.

Unless humanity becomes nonsuppressive toward sex, man cannot breathe really. If the breath goes deep down to the abdomen, it gives energy to the sex center. It touches the sex center; it massages the sex center from within. The sex center becomes more active, more alive. Civilization is afraid of sex. We do not allow our children to touch their sex centers, their sex organs. We say, "Stop! Don't touch!"

Look at a child when he first touches his sex center, and then say "Stop!" and then observe his breathing. When you say "Stop! Don't touch your sex center!" the breath will become shallow immediately—because it is not only his hand which is touching the sex center, deep down the breath is touching it. And if the breath goes on touching it, it is difficult to stop the hand. If the hand stops, then basically it is necessary, required, that the breath should not touch, should not go deep. It must remain shallow.

We are afraid of sex. The lower part of the body is not only lower physically, it has become lower as a value. It is condemned as "lower." So do not go deep, just remain shallow. It is unfortunate that we can only breathe downwards. If some preachers were allowed, they would change the whole mechanism. They would only allow you to breathe upward into the head. Then you would absolutely not feel sex.

If we are to create a sexless humanity, then we will have to change the breathing system. The breath must go into the head, to the *sahasrar*—the seventh center in the head—then come back to the mouth. This should be the passage: from the mouth to the sahasrar. It must not go deep down because down is dangerous. The deeper you go, the nearer you reach to the deeper layers of biology. You reach to the center, and that center is just near the sex center—just near. It has to be, because sex is life.

Look at it in this way: breath is life from above downwards; sex is life from just the other corner—from down upwards. Sex energy is flowing and breath energy is flowing. The breath passage is in the upper body and the sex passage is in the lower body. When they meet they create life; when they meet they create biology, bioenergy. So if you are afraid of sex, create a distance between the two, do not allow them to meet. So really, civilized man is a castrated man; that is why we do not know about breath, and this sutra will be difficult to understand.

Shiva says, *Whenever in-breath and out-breath fuse, at this instant touch the energy-less, energy-filled center.* He uses very contradictory terms: "energy-less, energy-filled." It is energy-less because your bodies, your minds, cannot give any energy to it. Your body energy is not there, your mind energy is not there, so it is energy-less as far as you know your identity. But it is energy-filled because it has the cosmic source of energy, not because of your body energy.

Your body energy is just fuel energy. It is nothing but petrol. You eat something, you drink something—it creates energy. It is just giving fuel to the body. Stop eating and drinking and your body will fall dead. Not just now, it will take three months at least, because you have reservoirs of petrol. You have accumulated much energy; it can run for at least three months without going to any petrol station. It can run; it has a reservoir. For an emergency, any emergency, you may need it.

This is "fuel" energy. The center is not getting

any fuel energy. That is why Shiva says it is energy-less. It is not dependent on your eating and drinking. It is connected with the cosmic source; it is cosmic energy. That is why he says *energy-less, energy-filled center.* The moment you can feel the center from where breath goes out or comes in, the very point where the breaths fuse—that center—if you become aware of it, then enlightenment.

---

4 Be aware when breathing stops.

The fourth breathing technique: *Or, when breath is all out (up) and stopped of itself, or all in (down) and stopped—in such universal pause, one's small self vanishes. This is difficult only for the impure.*

But then it is difficult for everyone because, he says, *This is difficult only for the impure.*

But who is the pure one? It is difficult for you; you cannot practice it. But you can feel it sometimes suddenly. You are driving a car and suddenly you feel there is going to be an accident. Breathing will stop. If it is out, it will remain out. If it is in, it will remain in. You cannot breathe in such an emergency; you cannot afford it. Everything stops, departs.

Or, when breath is all out (up) and stopped of itself, or all in (down) and stopped—in such universal pause, one's small self vanishes: your small self is only a daily utility. In emergencies you cannot remember it. Who you are—the name, the bank balance, the prestige, everything—just evaporates. Your car is just heading toward another car; another moment and there will be death. In this moment there will be a pause. Even for the impure there will be a pause. Suddenly breathing stops. If you can be aware in that moment, you can reach the goal.

Zen monks have tried this method very much in Japan. That is why their methods seem very weird, absurd, strange. They have done many inconceivable things. A master will throw someone out of

the house. Suddenly the master will begin slapping the disciple without any rhyme or reason, without any cause.

You were sitting with your master and everything was okay. You were just chitchatting, and he will begin to beat you in order to create the pause. If there is any cause the pause cannot be created. If you had abused the master and he starts beating you there is a causality, your mind understands: "I abused him, and he is beating me."

Really, your mind was expecting it already, so there is no gap. But remember, a Zen master will not beat you if you abuse him, he will laugh, because then laughter can create the pause. You were abusing him and you were saying nonsense things to him, and you expected anger. But he starts laughing or dancing. That is sudden; that will create the pause. You cannot understand it. If you cannot understand the mind stops, and when the mind stops, breathing stops. Either way—if breathing stops, mind stops; if mind stops, breathing stops.

You were appreciating the master and you were feeling good, and you were thinking, "Now the master must be pleased." And suddenly he takes his staff and begins to beat you—and mercilessly, because Zen masters are merciless. He begins to beat you; you cannot understand what is happening. The mind stops, there is a pause. If you know the technique, you can attain to your self.

There are many stories that someone attained buddhahood because the teacher suddenly started beating him. You cannot understand it—what nonsense! How can one attain buddhahood by being beaten by someone, or by being thrown out of the window by someone? Even if someone kills you, you cannot attain buddhahood. But if you understand this technique, then it becomes easy to understand.

In the West particularly, in the last thirty or forty years Zen has become very much prevalent—a fashion. But unless they know this technique, they cannot understand Zen. They can imitate it, but imitation is of no use. Rather, it is dangerous. These are not things to be imitated.

The whole Zen technique is based on the fourth technique of Shiva. But this is unfortunate. Now we will have to import Zen from Japan because we have lost the whole tradition; we do not know it. Shiva was the expert par excellence of this method. When he came to marry Devi with his *barat,* his procession, the whole city must have felt the pause...the whole city!

Devi's father was not willing to marry his girl to this "hippie"—Shiva was the original hippie. Devi's father was totally against him. And no father would permit this marriage, so we cannot say anything against Devi's father. No father would permit his daughter's marriage to Shiva. But Devi insisted so he had to agree—unwillingly, unhappily, but he agreed.

Then came the marriage procession. It is said that people began to run, seeing Shiva and his procession. The whole barat must have taken LSD, marijuana. They were "high." And really, LSD and marijuana are just the beginning. Shiva knew and his friends and disciples knew the ultimate psychedelic—*soma rasa.* Aldous Huxley has named the ultimate psychedelic "soma" only because of Shiva. They were high, just dancing, screaming, laughing. The whole city fled. It must have felt the pause.

Any sudden, unexpected, unbelievable thing can create the pause for the impure. But for the pure there is no need of such things. For the pure, the pause is always there. Many times, for pure minds, breathing stops. If your mind is pure—pure means you are not desiring, hankering, seeking anything—silently pure, innocently pure, you can be sitting and suddenly your breath will stop.

Remember this: mind movement needs breath movement. Mind moving fast needs fast movement in breath. That is why when you are in anger, breath will move fast. In the sex act, the breath will move very fast. That is why in Ayurveda—a system of herbal medicine in India—it is said that your life will be shortened if too much sex is allowed. Your life will he shortened, according to Ayurveda, because Ayurveda measures your life in breaths. If your breathing is too fast, your life will be shortened.

Modern medicine says that sex helps blood circulation, sex helps relaxation. And those who suppress their sex may get into trouble—particularly heart trouble. They are right and Ayurveda is also right, but they seem contradictory. But Ayurveda was invented five thousand years before. Every man was doing much labor: life was labor, so there was no need to relax, there was no need to create artificial devices for blood circulation.

But now, for those who are not doing much physical labor, sex is their only labor. That is why modern medicine is also right for modern man. He is not doing any physical exertion, so sex gives the exertion: the heart beats more, the blood circulates faster, the breathing becomes deep and goes to the center. So after the sex act you feel relaxed and you can fall into sleep easily. Freud says that sex is the best tranquilizer, and it is—at least for modern man.

In sex breathing will become fast; in anger breathing will become fast. In sex the mind is filled with desire, lust, impurity. When the mind is pure—no desire in the mind, no seeking, no motivation; you are not going anywhere, but just remaining here and now as an innocent pool...not even a ripple—then breathing stops automatically. There is no need for it.

On this path, the small self vanishes and you attain to the higher self, the supreme self.

I think this will do for today.

CHAPTER 4

Overcoming the deceptions of the mind

◆

How can awareness of the gap in breathing bring enlightenment?

How to work and practice breath awareness simultaneously?

Question:

How is it possible that by simply becoming aware at a particular point in the breathing process one can attain enlightenment? How it is possible to become free from the unconscious by just being aware of such a small and momentary gap in the breathing?

his question is significant, and this question is likely to have occurred to many minds, so many things have to be understood. First, it is thought that spirituality is a difficult attainment. It is neither: that is, it is neither difficult nor an attainment. Whatsoever you are, you are already spiritual. Nothing new is to be added to your being, and nothing is to be discarded from your being; you are as perfect as possible. It is not that you are going to be perfect sometime in the future, it is not that you have to do something arduous to be yourself. It is not a journey to some other point somewhere else; you are not going somewhere else. You are already there. That which is to be attained is already attained. This idea must go deep, only then will you be able to understand why such simple techniques can help.

If spirituality is some attainment, then of course it is going to be difficult—not only difficult, but really impossible. If you are not already spiritual, you cannot be, you never can be, because how can one who is not spiritual be spiritual? If you are not

divine already then there is no possibility, there is no way. And no matter what effort you will make, effort made by one who is not already divine cannot create divinity. If you are not divine, your effort cannot create divinity. Then it is impossible.

But the whole situation is totally opposite: you are already that which you want to attain. The end of longing is already there, present in you. Here and now, this very moment, you are that which is known as divine. The ultimate is here; it is already the case. That is why simple techniques can help. It is not an attainment, but a discovery. It is hidden, and it is hidden in very, very small things.

The persona is just like clothes. Your body is here, hidden in clothes; in the same way your spirituality is here, hidden in certain clothes. These clothes are your personality. You can be naked just here and now, and in the same way you can be naked in your spirituality also. But you do not know what the clothes are. You do not know how you are hidden in them; you do not know how to be naked. You have been in clothes so long—for lives and lives and lives you have been in clothes—and you have been so identified with the clothes, that now you do not think that these are clothes. You think these clothes are you. That is the only barrier.

For example, you have some treasure, but you have forgotten or you have not yet recognized that this is a treasure, and you go on begging in the streets…you are a beggar. If someone says, "Go and look inside your house. You need not be a beggar, you can be an emperor this very moment," the beggar is bound to say, "What nonsense you are talking. How can I be an emperor this very moment? I have been begging for years and still I am a beggar, and even if I go on begging for lives together, I am not going to be an emperor. So how absurd and illogical your statement is, 'You can be an emperor this very moment.'"

It is impossible. The beggar cannot believe it. Why? Because the begging mind is a long habit. But if the treasure is just hidden in the house, then from simple digging, removing the earth a little bit, the treasure will be there. And immediately he will not be a beggar again, he will become an emperor.

It is the same with spirituality: it is a hidden treasure. Nothing is to be achieved somewhere in the future. You have not yet recognized it, but it is there already in you. You are the treasure, but you go on begging.

So simple techniques can help. Digging the earth, removing a little bit, is not a big effort, and you can become an emperor immediately. You have to dig a little bit to remove the earth. And when I say remove the earth, it is not only symbolically that I am saying it. Literally your body is part of the earth, and you have become identified with the body. Remove this earth a little bit, create a hole in it, and you will come to know the treasure.

That is why this question will occur to many. Really, to everyone this question will occur: "So small a technique like this—being aware of your breathing, being aware of the incoming breath and the outgoing breath, and then realizing the interval between the two—is this enough?" Such a simple thing! Is this enough for enlightenment? Is this the only difference between you and Buddha, that you have not realized the gap between two breaths and Buddha has realized it—only this much? It seems illogical. The distance is vast between a Buddha and you. The distance seems infinite. The distance between a beggar and an emperor is infinite, but the beggar can immediately become an emperor if the treasure is already hidden.

Buddha was a beggar like you; he was not a buddha always. At a particular point the beggar died, and he became the master. This is not a gradual process really; it is not that Buddha goes on accumulating and then one day he is not the beggar and he becomes the emperor. No, a beggar can never become an emperor if it is going to be an accumulation, he will remain a beggar. He may become a rich beggar, but he will remain a beggar. And a rich beggar is a bigger beggar than a poor beggar.

Suddenly, one day Buddha realizes the inner treasure. Then he is no more a beggar, he becomes a master. The distance between Gautama Siddhartha and Gautam Buddha is infinite. It is the same distance that is between you and a Buddha. But the treasure is hidden within you as much as it was hidden in Buddha.

Take another example…. One man is born with blind eyes, diseased eyes. For a blind man, the world is a different thing. A small operation may change the whole thing, because only the eyes have to be made all right. The moment the eyes are ready, the seer is hidden behind and he will begin to look from the eyes. The seer is already there, only windows are lacking. You are in a house with no windows. You can break a hole in the wall, and suddenly you will look out.

We are already that which we will be, which we should be, which we are to be. The future is already hidden in the present; the whole possibility is here in the seed. Only a window has to be broken, only a small surgical operation is needed. If you can understand this, that spirituality is already there, already the case, then there is no problem concerning how such a small effort can help.

Really, no big effort is needed. Only small efforts are needed, and the smaller the better. And if you work effortlessly it is still better. That is why it happens, many times it happens, that the more you try, the harder it is to attain. Your very effort, your tension, your occupiedness, your longing, your expectation, becomes the barrier. But with a very small effort, an effortless effort as they call it in Zen—doing as if not doing—it happens easily. The more you are mad after it, the less is the possibility, because where a needle is needed you are using a sword. The sword will not be helpful. It may be bigger, but where a needle is needed a sword will not do.

Go to a butcher—he has very big instruments. And go to a brain surgeon: you will not find such big instruments with the brain surgeon. And if you do find them, then escape immediately! A brain surgeon is not a butcher. He needs very small instruments—the smaller the better.

Spiritual techniques are more subtle; they are not gross. They cannot be, because the surgery is even more subtle. In the brain the surgeon is still doing something with gross matter, but when you are working on spiritual planes the surgery becomes more and more aesthetic. No gross matter is there. It becomes subtle—that is one thing.

Secondly, the questioner asks, "If something is smaller, how can a bigger step be possible through it?" This concept is irrational, unscientific. Now science knows that the smaller the particle, the more atomic, the more explosive—the bigger really. The smaller it is, the bigger the effect. Could you have conceived before 1945, could any imaginative poet or dreamer have conceived that two atomic explosions would wipe out completely two big cities in Japan—Hiroshima and Nagasaki? Two hundred thousand people were simply wiped out of existence within seconds. And what was the explosive force used? An atom! The very smallest particle blew up two big cities. You cannot see the atom. Not only with your eyes can you not see it, you cannot see it by any means. The atom cannot be seen with any instrument; we can only see the effects.

So do not think that the Himalayas are bigger because they have such a big body. The Himalayas are just impotent before an atomic explosion. One small atom can wipe out the whole Himalayas. Size in gross material is not necessarily power. On the contrary, the smaller the unit, the more penetrating. The smaller the unit, the more intensely it is filled with power.

These small techniques are atomic. Those who are doing bigger things do not know atomic science. You will think that a person who is working with atoms is a small person working with small things, and a person who is working with the Himalayas will look very big. Hitler was working with great masses; Mao is working with great masses. And Einstein and Planck, they were working in their laboratories with small units of matter—energy particles. But ultimately, before Einstein's research politicians were just impotent. They were working on a bigger canvas, but they did not know the secret of the small unit.

Moralists always work on big planes, but these are gross. The thing looks very big. They devote their whole lives to moralizing, practicing this and that, to *sanyam*—control. They go on controlling; the whole edifice looks very big.

Tantra is not concerned with this. Tantra is concerned with the atomic secrets in the human being, in the human mind, in human consciousness. And tantra has achieved atomic secrets. These methods are atomic methods. If you can attain them, their result is explosive, cosmic.

Another point is to be noted. If you can say, "How is it that with such a small, simple exercise one can become enlightened?" you are saying this without doing the exercise. If you do it, then you will not say that this is a small, simple exercise. It looks this way because within two or three sentences the whole exercise has been given.

Do you know the atomic formula? Two or three words, and the whole formula is given. And with those two or three words, those who can understand, those who can use those words, can destroy the whole earth. The formula is very small.

These too are formulas, so if you just look at the formula it will look to be a very, very small, simple thing. It is not! Try to do it. When you do it, then you will know that it is not so easy. It looks simple, but it is one of the deepest things. We will analyze the process; then you will understand.

When you take your breath in, you never feel the breath. You have never felt the breath. You will immediately deny this. You will say, "This is not right. We may not be conscious continuously, but we feel the breath." No, you do not feel the breath, you feel the passage.

Look at the sea. Waves are there; you see the waves. But those waves are created by air, wind. You do not see the wind, you see the effect on the water. When you take breath in it touches your nostril. You feel the nostril, but you never know the breath. It goes down—you feel the passage. It comes back—again you feel the passage. You never feel the breath, you just feel the touch and the passage.

This is not what is meant when Shiva says, *Be aware.* First you will become aware of the passage, and when you have become completely aware of the passage, only then will you begin, by and by, to be aware of the breath itself. And when you become aware of the breath, then you will be capable of being aware of the gap, the interval. It is not so easy as it looks.

For tantra, for all seeking, there are layers of awareness. If I embrace you, first you will become aware of my touch upon your body; not of my love, my love is not so gross. And ordinarily we never become aware of love. We are aware only of the body in movement. We know loving movements, we know nonloving movements—but we have never known love itself. If I kiss you, you become aware of the touch, not of my love; that love is a very subtle thing. And unless you become aware of my love the kiss is just dead, it means nothing. If you can become aware of my love, then only can you become aware of me, because that again is a deeper layer.

The breath goes in. You feel the touch, not the breath. But you are not even aware of that touch. If something is wrong, only then do you feel it. If you have some difficulty in breathing, then you feel it; otherwise you are not aware. The first step will be to be aware of the passage where breath is felt to be

touching; then your sensitivity will grow. It will take years to become so sensitive that not the touch, but the movement of breath is known. Then, says tantra, you will have known *prana*—the vitality. And only then is there the gap where breath stops, where breath is not moving—or the center where the breath is touching, or the fusion point, or the turning where the breath, the ingoing breath, becomes outgoing. This will become arduous; then it will not be so simple.

If you do something, if you go into this center, only then will you know how difficult it is. Buddha took six years to come to this center beyond the breath. To come to this turning, he had a long, arduous journey of six years; then it happened. Mahavira was working on it for twelve years; then it happened. But the formula is simple, and theoretically this can happen this very moment—theoretically, remember. There is no barrier theoretically, so why should it not happen this very moment? *You* are the barrier. Except for you this can happen this very moment. The treasure is there; the method is known to you. You can dig, but you will not dig.

Even this question is a trick not to dig, because your mind says, "Such a simple thing? Don't be a fool. How can you become a buddha through such a simple thing? It is not going to be." And then you are not going to do anything, because how can this happen? Mind is tricky. If I say this is very difficult, the mind says, "This is so difficult it is beyond you." If I say this is very simple, the mind says, "This is so simple that only fools can believe in it." And mind goes on rationalizing things, always escaping from doing.

Mind creates barriers. It will become a barrier if you think this is so simple, or this is too difficult—then what are you going to do? You cannot do a simple thing, you cannot do a difficult thing. What are you going to do? Tell me! If you want to do a difficult thing, I will make it difficult. If you are going to do a simple thing, I will make it simple. It is both—it depends on how it is interpreted. But one thing is needed, that you are going to *do*. If you are not going to do then the mind will always give you explanations.

Theoretically, it is possible here and now; there is no actual barrier. But there are barriers. They may not be actual, they may simply be psychological—they may just be your illusions—but they are there. If I say to you, "Do not be afraid—go! The thing that you are thinking is a snake is not a snake, it is just a rope," still the fear will be there. To you it appears to be a snake.

So whatsoever I say is not going to help. You are trembling; you want to escape and run away. I say it is just a rope, but your mind will say, "This man may be in conspiracy with the snake. There must be something wrong. This man is forcing me toward the snake. He may be interested in my death, or something else." If I try to convince you too much that this is a rope, that will only show that I am somehow interested in forcing you toward the snake. If I say to you that theoretically it is possible to see the rope as a rope this very moment, your mind will create many, many problems.

In reality there is no dilemma; in reality there is no problem. There never has been, there never will be. In mind there are problems, and you look at reality through the mind; thus, the reality becomes problematic. Your mind works like a prison. It divides and creates problems. And not only that, it creates solutions which become deeper problems, because in fact there are no problems to be solved. Reality is absolutely unproblematic; there is no problem. But you cannot see anything without problems. Wherever you look, you create problems. Your "look" is problematic. I told you this breath technique; now the mind says, "This is so simple." Why? Why does the mind say this is so simple?

When for the first time the steam engine was invented, no one believed it. It looked so simple—unbelievable. Just the same steam that you know in your kitchen, in your kettle, the steam running an engine, running hundreds and hundreds of passengers and such a load? The same steam that you are so well acquainted with? This is not believable.

Do you know what happened in England? When the first train started, no one was ready to sit in it—no one! Many people were persuaded, bribed, they were given money to sit in the train, but at the last point they escaped. They said, "Firstly, steam cannot do such miracles. Such a simple thing as steam cannot do such miracles. And if the engine starts, that means that the devil is at work somewhere. The devil is running the thing, it is not the steam. And what is the guarantee that once the thing starts you will be capable of stopping it?"

No guarantee could be given because this was the first train. Never had it stopped before, it was only probable. There was no experience, so science could not say, "Yes, it will stop." Theoretically it will stop…but the people were not interested in theories. They were interested if there was any actual experience of stopping a train: "If it never stops then what will happen to us who will be sitting in it?"

So twelve criminals from the jail were brought as passengers. Anyhow they were going to die, anyhow they were sentenced to death, so there was no problem if the train was not going to stop. Then the mad driver who thought that it was going to stop, the scientist who had invented it and these twelve passengers who were anyhow going to be killed, they alone would all be killed. "Such a simple thing as steam," they said at that time. But now no one says this, because now it is working and you know it.

Everything is simple—reality is simple. It seems complex only because of ignorance; otherwise everything is simple. Once you know it, it becomes simple. The knowing is bound to be difficult not because of reality, remember, but because of your mind. This technique is simple, but it is not going to be simple for you. Your mind will create difficulty. So try with it.

Another friend says:

If I try this method of being aware of my breathing, if I pay attention to my breathing, then I cannot do anything else, the whole attention goes to it. And if I am to do anything else then I cannot be aware of my breathing.

This will happen, so in the beginning choose a particular period in the morning, or in the evening, or at any time. For one hour just do the exercise; do not do anything else. Just do the exercise. Once you become attuned to it, then it will not be a problem. You can walk on the street and you can be aware.

Between "awareness" and "attention" there is a difference. When you pay attention to anything it is exclusive; you have to withdraw your attention from everywhere else. So it is a tension really. That is why it is called attention. You pay attention to one thing at the cost of everything else. If you pay attention to your breathing, you cannot pay attention to your walking or to your driving. Do not try it while you are driving because you cannot pay attention to both.

Attention means one thing exclusively. Awareness is a very different thing; it is not exclusive. It is not paying attention, it is being attentive; it is just being conscious. You are conscious when you are inclusively conscious. Your breathing is in your consciousness. You are walking and someone is passing, and you are also conscious of him. Someone is making noise on the road, some train passes by, some airplane flies by—everything is included. Awareness is inclusive, attention exclusive. But in the beginning it will be attention.

So first try in selected periods. For one hour just be attentive to your breathing. By and by you will be able to change your attention into awareness. Then do simple things—for example, walking: walk attentively with full awareness of walking and also of breathing. Do not create any opposition between the two actions of walking and breathing. Be a watcher of both. It is not difficult.

Look! For example, I can pay attention to one face here. If I pay attention to one face, all the faces will not be here for me. If I pay my attention to one face, then all the rest are bracketed out. If I pay attention only to the nose on that face, then the whole face, the remaining face, is bracketed out. I can go on narrowing down my attention to a single point.

The reverse is also possible. I pay attention to the whole face; then eyes and nose and everything are there. Then I have made my focus wider. I look at you not as individuals, but as a group. Then the whole group is in my attention. If I take you as different from the noise that is going on the street, then I am bracketing out the street. But I can look at you and the street as one whole. Then I can be aware of both you and the street. I can be aware of the whole cosmos. It depends on your focus—on its becoming greater and greater. But first start from attention and remember that you have to grow into awareness. So choose a small period. The morning is good because you are fresh, energies are vital, everything is rising; you are more alive in the morning.

Physiologists say that not only are you more alive, but your height is a little more in the morning than in the evening. If you are six feet tall, then in the morning you are six feet and one half inch and in the evening you go back to six feet. Half an inch is lost because your spine settles down when it is tired. So in the morning you are fresh, young, alive with energy.

Do this: do not make meditation the last thing on your schedule. Make it the first. Then when you feel that now it is not an effort, when you can sit for an hour together completely immersed in breathing—aware, attentive—only when you know this, that you have achieved attention of breathing without any effort; when you are relaxed and enjoying it without any forcing, then you have attained it.

Then add something else—for example, walking. Remember both, then go on adding things. After a certain period you will be capable of being aware of your breath continuously, even in sleep. And unless you are aware even in sleep you will not be able to know the depth. But this comes, by and by this comes.

One has to be patient and one has to start rightly. Know this, because the cunning mind will always try to give you a wrong start. Then you can leave it after two or three days and say, "This is hopeless." The mind will give you a wrong start. So always remember to begin rightly, because rightly begun means half done. But we start wrongly.

You know very well that attention is a difficult thing. This is because you are totally asleep. So if you start being attentive to breathing while you are doing something else, you cannot do it. And you are not going to leave the task, you will leave the effort of being attentive to breathing.

So do not create unnecessary problems for yourself. In twenty-four hours you can find a small corner. Forty minutes will do…so do the technique there. But the mind will give many excuses. The mind will say, "Where is the time? There is already too much work to be done. Where is the time?" Or the mind will say, "It is not possible now, so postpone it. Sometime in the future when things are better, then you will do it." Beware of what your mind says to you. Do not be too trusting of the mind. And we are never doubtful. We can doubt everyone but we never doubt our own minds.

Even those who talk so much of skepticism, of doubt, of reason, even they never doubt their own minds. And your mind has brought you to the state you are in. If you are in a hell, your mind has brought you to this hell, and you never doubt this guide. You can doubt any teacher, any master, but you never doubt your mind. With unflinching faith, you move with your mind as the guru. And your mind has brought you to the mess, to the misery that you are. If you are going to doubt anything, doubt first your own mind. And whenever your mind says something, think twice.

Is it true that you do not have any time? Really?

You do not have any time to meditate—to give one hour to meditation? Think twice. Ask again and again to the mind, "Is this the case, that I do not have any time?"

I don't see it. I have not seen a man who does not have more than enough time. I go on seeing people who are playing cards, and they say, "We are killing time." They are going to the movies and they say, "What to do?" They are killing time, gossiping, reading the same newspaper again and again, talking about the same things they have been talking about for their whole lives, and they say, "We don't have any time." For unnecessary things they have enough time. Why?

With an unnecessary thing mind is not in any danger. The moment you think of meditation, mind becomes alert. Now you are moving in a dangerous dimension, because meditation means the death of the mind. If you move into meditation, sooner or later your mind will have to dissolve, retire completely. The mind becomes alert and it begins to say many things to you: "Where is the time? And even if there is time, then more important things are to be done. First postpone it until later. You can meditate at any time. Money is more important. Gather money first, then meditate at your leisure. How can you meditate without money? So pay attention to money, then meditate later on."

Meditation can be postponed easily, you feel, because it is not concerned with your immediate survival. Bread cannot be postponed—you will die. Money cannot be postponed—it is needed for your basic necessities. Meditation can be postponed, you can survive without it. Really, you can survive without it easily.

The moment you go deep in meditation, you will not survive on this earth at least—you will disappear. From the circle of this life, this wheel, you will disappear. Meditation is like death, so the mind becomes afraid. Meditation is like love, so the mind becomes afraid. "Postpone," it says, and you can go on postponing ad infinitum. Your mind is always saying things like this. And do not think I am talking about others. I am talking particularly about *you*.

I have come across many intelligent people who go on saying very unintelligent things about meditation. One man came from Delhi; he is a big government official. He came only for the purpose of learning meditation here. He had come from Delhi, and he stayed seven days here. I told him to go to the morning meditation class on Chowpatty beach in Bombay, but he said, "But that is difficult. I cannot get up so early." And he will never think over what his mind has told him. Is this so difficult? Now you will know: the exercise can be simple, but your mind is not so simple. The mind says, "How can I get up in the morning at six o'clock?"

I was in a big city, and the collector of that city came to meet me at eleven o'clock at night. I was just going to my bed, and he came and said, "No! It is urgent. I am very disturbed. It is a question of life and death," he told me. "So please give me at least half an hour. Teach me meditation; otherwise I might commit suicide. I am very much disturbed, and I am so frustrated that something must happen in my inner world. My outer world is lost completely."

I told him, "Come in the morning at five o'clock."

He said, "That is not possible." It is a question of life and death, but he cannot get up at five o'clock. He said, "That is not possible. I never get up so early."

"Okay," I told him. "Then come at ten."

He said, "That will also be difficult because by ten-thirty I am to be present at my office."

He cannot take one day's leave, and it is a question of life and death. So I told him, "Is it a question of your life and death or my life and death? Whose?" And he was not an unintelligent man, he was intelligent enough. These tricks were very intelligent.

So do not think that your mind is not playing the same tricks. It is very intelligent, and because

you think it is your mind you never doubt it. It is not yours, it is just a social product. It is not yours! It has been given to you, it has been forced upon you. You have been taught and conditioned in a certain way. From the very childhood your mind has been created by others—parents, society, teachers. The past is creating your mind, influencing your mind. The dead past is forcing itself upon the living continuously. The teachers are just the agents—agents of the dead against the living. They go on forcing things upon your mind. But the mind is so intimate with you, the gap is so small, that you become identified with it.

You say, "I am a Hindu." Think again, reconsider it. *You* are not a Hindu. You have been given a Hindu mind. You were born just a simple, innocent being—not a Hindu, not a Mohammedan. But you were given a Mohammedan mind, a Hindu mind. You were forced, encaged, imprisoned in a particular condition, and then life goes on adding to this mind and this mind becomes heavy—heavy on you. You cannot do anything; the mind starts forcing its own way upon you. Your experiences are being added to the mind. Constantly, your past is conditioning your every present moment. If I say something to you, you are not going to think about it in a fresh way, in an open way. Your old mind, your past will come in between, will begin to talk and chatter for or against.

Remember, your mind is not yours, your body is not yours; it comes from your parents. Your mind is also not yours; it also comes from your parents. Who are you?

Either one is identified with the body or with the mind. You think you are young, you think you are old, you think you are a Hindu, you think you are a Jaina, you are a Parsi. You are not! You were born as a pure consciousness. These are all imprisonments. These techniques which look so simple to you will not be so simple, because this mind will create constantly many, many complexities and problems.

Just a few days before, a man came to me and he said, "I am trying your method of meditation, but tell me, in what scripture is it given? If you can convince me that it is given in my religious scripture, then it will be easier for me to do." But why will it be easier for him to do if it is written in a scripture? Because then the mind will not create a problem. The mind will say, "Okay! This belongs to us, so do it." If it is not written in any scripture then the mind will say, "What are you doing?" The mind goes against it.

I said to the man, "You have been doing this method for three months. How are you feeling?"

He said, "Wonderful. I am feeling very wonderful. But tell me...give some authority from the scriptures." His own feeling is not an authority at all. He says, "I am feeling wonderful. I have become more silent, more peaceful, more loving. I am feeling wonderful." But his own experience is not the authority. The mind asks for an authority from the past.

I told him, "It is not written anywhere in your scriptures. Rather, many things which are against this technique are written."

His face became sad. And then he said, "Then it will be difficult for me to do it and to continue it."

Why is his own experience not of any value?

The past—the conditioning, the mind—is constantly molding you and destroying your present. So remember, and be aware. Be skeptical and doubting about your mind. Do not trust it. If you can attain to this maturity of not trusting your mind, only then will these techniques be really simple, helpful, functioning. They will work miracles—they can work miracles.

These techniques, these methods cannot be understood intellectually at all. I am trying the impossible, but then why am I trying? If they cannot be understood intellectually, then why am I talking to you? They cannot be understood intellectually, but there is no other way to make you aware of certain techniques which can change your life totally. You can understand only intellect, and this is a problem. You cannot understand anything else; you can understand only the intellect. And these techniques cannot be understood intellectually, so how to communicate?

Either you should become capable of understanding without intellect being brought in, or some method should be found so that these techniques can be made intellectually understandable. The second is not possible, but the first is possible.

You will have to start intellectually, but do not cling to it. When I say, "Do," try doing. If something begins to happen within you, then you will be capable of throwing your intellect aside and reaching toward me directly without the intellect, without any effort, without the mediator. But start doing something. We can go on talking for years and years, your mind can be stuffed with many things, but that is not going to help. Rather, it may harm you because you will begin to know many things. And if you know many things you will become confused. It is not good to know many things. It is good to know a little and to practice it. A single technique can be helpful; something done is always helpful. What is the difficulty in doing it?

Deep down somewhere there is fear. The fear is that if you do it, it may be that something stops happening—that is the fear. It may look paradoxical, but I have been meeting so many, so many persons who think they want to change. They say they need meditation, they ask for a deep transformation, but deep down they are also afraid. They are dual—double; they have two minds. They go on asking about what to do, never doing it. Why then do they go on asking? Just to deceive themselves that they are really interested in transforming themselves. That is why they are asking.

This gives a façade, an appearance that they are really, sincerely interested in changing themselves. That is why they are asking, going to this guru and that, finding, trying, but they never do anything. Deep down they are afraid.

Erich Fromm has written a book, *Fear of Freedom*. The title seems contradictory. Everyone thinks that they like freedom; everyone thinks that they are endeavoring for freedom—in this world and in "that world" also. "We want *moksha*, liberation, we want to be freed from all limitations, from all slaveries. We want to be totally free," they say. But Erich Fromm says that man is afraid of freedom. We want it, we go on saying that we want it, we go on convincing ourselves that we want it, but deep down we are afraid of freedom. We do not want it! Why? Why this duality?

Freedom creates fear, and meditation is the deepest freedom possible. You are not freed only from outward limitations, you are freed from inner slavery—the very mind, the base of slavery. You are freed from the whole past. The moment you have no mind, the past has disappeared. You have transcended history; now there is no society, no religion, no scripture, no tradition, because they all have their abode in the mind. Now there is no past, no future, because past and future are part of the mind, the memory and the imagination.

Then you are here and now in the present. Now there is not going to be any future. There will be now and now and now—eternal now. Then you are freed completely; you transcend all tradition, all history, body, mind, everything. One becomes free of the fearful. Such freedom—then where will *you* be? In such freedom, can you exist? In such freedom, in such vastness, can you have your small "I" —your ego? Can you say "I am"?

You can say, "I am in bondage," because you can know your boundary. When there is no bondage there is no boundary. You become just a state, nothing more…absolute nothingness, emptiness. That creates fear, so one goes on talking about meditation, about how to do it, and one goes on without doing it.

All the questions arise out of this fear. Feel this fear. If you know it, it will disappear. If you do not know it, it will continue. Are you ready to die in the spiritual sense? Are you ready to be *not*?

Whenever anyone came to Buddha he would say, "This is the basic truth—that you are not. And because you are not you cannot die, you cannot be born; and because you are not you cannot be in suffering, in bondage. Are you ready to accept this?" Buddha would ask, "Are you ready to accept this? If you are not ready to accept this, then do not try meditation now. First try to find out whether you really are or you are not. Meditate on this first: is there any self? Is there any substance within or are you just a combination?"

If you manage to find out, you will find that your body is a combination. Something has come from your mother, something has come from your father, and all else has come from food. This is your body. In this body you are *not*, there is no self. Contemplate on the mind: something has come from here, something from there. Mind has nothing that is original. It is just accumulation.

Find out if there is any self in the mind. If you move deep, you will find that your identity is just like an onion. You peel off one layer and another layer comes up; you peel off another layer and still another layer comes up. You go on peeling layers off, and ultimately you come to a nothingness. With all the layers thrown off, there is nothing inside. Body and mind are like onions. When you have peeled off both body and mind, then you come to encounter a nothingness, an abyss, a bottomless void. Buddha called it *shunya*.

To encounter this shunya, to encounter this void, creates fear. That fear is there. That is why we never do meditation. We talk about it, but we never do anything about it. That fear is there. You know deep down that there is a void, but you cannot escape this fear. Whatsoever you do, the fear will remain unless you encounter it. That is the only way. Once you encounter your nothingness, once you know that within you are just like a space, shunya, then there will be no fear. Then there cannot be any fear, because this shunya, this void, cannot be destroyed. This void is not going to die. That which was going to die is no more; it was nothing but the layers of an onion.

That is why many times in deep meditation, when one comes nearer to this nothingness, one becomes afraid and starts trembling. One feels that one is going to die, one wants to escape from this nothingness back to the world. And many go back; then they never turn within again. As I see it, every one of you have tried in some life or other some meditative technique. You have been near to the nothingness, and then fear gripped you and you escaped. And deep in your past memories, that memory is there; that becomes the hindrance. Whenever you again think of trying meditation, that past memory deep down in your unconscious mind again disturbs you and says, "Go on thinking; do not do it. You have done it once."

It is difficult to find a man—and I have looked into many—who has not tried meditation once or twice in some life. The memory is there, but you are not conscious of it, you are not aware of where the memory is. It is there. Whenever you begin to do something that becomes a barrier, this and that begin to stop you in many ways. So if you are really interested in meditation, find out about your own fear of it. Be sincere about it: are you afraid? If you are afraid, then first something has to be done about your fear, not about meditation.

Buddha used to try many devices. Sometimes someone would say to him, "I am afraid of trying meditation." And this is a must: the master must be told that you are afraid. You cannot deceive the master...and there is no need—it is deceiving yourself. So whenever someone would say, "I am afraid of meditation," Buddha would say, "You are fulfilling the first requirement." If you say yourself that you are afraid of meditation, then something becomes possible. Then something can be done because you have uncovered a deep thing. So what is the fear? Meditate on it. Go and dig out where it comes from, what the source is.

All fear is basically death-oriented. Whatsoever its form, mode, whatsoever its shape, name, all fear is death-oriented. If you move deep, you will find that you are afraid of death.

If someone came to Buddha and said, "I am afraid of death, I have found this out," Buddha would say, "Then go to the burning ghat, go to the cemetery, and meditate on a funeral pyre. People are dying daily—they will be burned. Just remain there at the *marghat*—cemetery—and meditate on the burning pyre. When their family members have gone, you remain there. Just look into the fire, at the burning body. When everything is becoming smoke, you just look at it deeply. Do not think, just meditate on it for three months, six months, nine months.

"When it becomes a certainty to you that death cannot be escaped, when it becomes absolutely certain that death is the way of life, that death is implied in life, that death is going to be, that there is no way out and you are already in it, only then come to me."

After meditating on death, after seeing every day, night and day, dead bodies being burned, dissolved into ashes—just a smoke remains and then disappears—after meditating for months together, a certainty will arise: the certainty that death is inevitable. It is the only certainty really. The only thing certain in life is death. Everything else is uncertain: it may be or it may not be. But you cannot say that it may be or it may not be for death. It is; it is going to be. It has already occurred. The moment you entered life, you entered death. Now nothing can be done about it.

When death is certain there is no fear. Fear is always with things which can be changed. If death is to be, fear disappears. If you can change, if you can do something about death, then fear will remain. If nothing can be done, if you are already in it, then it is absolutely certain that fear will disappear. When fear of death had disappeared, Buddha would allow you to meditate. He would say, "Now you can meditate."

So you also go deep into your mind. And listening to these techniques will be helpful only when your inner barriers are broken, when inner fears disappear and you are certain that death is the reality. So if you die in meditation there is no fear—death is certain. Even if death occurs in meditation, there is no fear. Only then can you move—and then you can move at rocket speed because the barriers are not there.

It is not distance that takes time, but the barriers. You can move this very moment if there is no barrier. You are already there but for the barrier. It is a hurdle race, and you go on putting up more and more hurdles. You feel good when you cross a hurdle; you feel good that now you have crossed the hurdle. And the idiocy of it, the foolishness of it, is that the hurdle was placed there by you in the first place. It was never there. You go on putting up hurdles, then jumping over them, then feeling good; then you go on putting up more hurdles, then jumping. You move in a circle and never, never reach to the center.

Mind creates hurdles because mind is afraid. It will give you many explanations as to why you are not doing meditation. Do not believe it. Go deep, find out the basic cause. Why does a person go on talking about food and yet never eat? What is the problem? The man seems mad!

Another man goes on talking about love and never loves, another man goes on talking about something else and never does anything about it. This talking becomes obsessive; it becomes a compulsion. One goes on, one sees talking as a doing. By talking you feel that you are doing something, so you feel at ease. You are doing something —at least talking, at least reading, at least listening. This is not doing. This is deceptive; do not fall into the deception.

I will be talking here about these one hundred and twelve methods not to feed your mind, not to make you more knowledgeable, not to make you more informed. I am not trying to make you a pundit. I am talking here in order to give you a certain technique which can change your life. So whichever method appeals to you, do not start talking about it—do it! Be silent about it and do it. Your mind will raise many questions. Just inquire deeply first before asking me. Inquire deeply first whether those questions are really significant or if your mind is just deceiving you.

Do, then ask. Then your questions become practical. And I know which question has been asked through doing and which question has been asked just through curiosity, just through intellect. So by and by I will not answer your intellectual questions at all. Do something—then your questions become significant. These questions which say, "This exercise is a very simple one," are not asked after doing. This is *not* so simple. In the end I must repeat again:

You are already the truth.

Only a certain awakening is needed.

You are not to go anywhere else. You are to go into yourself, and the going is possible this very moment. If you can put aside your mind, you enter here and now.

These techniques are for putting your mind aside. These techniques are not really for meditation; they are for putting the mind aside. Once the mind is not there, *you are!*

I think this is enough for today, or even more than enough.

Five techniques of attentiveness

♦

T H E S U T R A S

5 Attention between eyebrows, let mind be before thought. Let form fill with breath essence to the top of the head and there shower as light.

6 When in worldly activity, keep attention between two breaths, and so practicing, in a few days be born anew.

7 With intangible breath in center of forehead, as this reaches heart at the moment of sleep, have direction over dreams and over death itself.

8 With utmost devotion, center on the two junctions of breath and know the knower.

9 Lie down as dead. Enraged in wrath, stay so. Or stare without moving an eyelash. Or suck something and become the sucking.

When one of the great Greek philosophers Pythagoras, reached Egypt to enter a school—a secret esoteric school of mysticism—he was refused. And Pythagoras was one of the best minds ever produced. He could not understand it. He applied again and again, but he was told that unless he goes through a particular training of fasting and breathing he cannot be allowed to enter the school.

Pythagoras is reported to have said, "I have come for knowledge, not for any sort of discipline." But the school authorities said, "We cannot give you knowledge unless you are different. And really, we are not interested in knowledge at all, we are interested in actual experience. No knowledge is knowledge unless it is lived and experienced. So you will have to go on a forty-day fast, continuously breathing in a certain manner, with a certain awareness on certain points."

There was no other way, so Pythagoras had to pass through this training. After forty days of fasting and breathing, aware, attentive, he was allowed to enter the school. It is said that Pythagoras said, "You are not allowing Pythagoras in. I am a different man, I am reborn. You were right and I was wrong, because then my whole standpoint was intellectual. Through this purification, my center of being has changed. From the intellect it has come down to the heart. Now I can feel things. Before this training I could only understand through the intellect, through the head. Now I can feel. Now truth is not a concept to me, but a life. It is not going to be a philosophy, but rather, an experience—existential."

What was that training he went through? This fifth technique was the technique that was given to Pythagoras. It was given in Egypt, but the technique is Indian.

---

5 Focus your attention on the third eye.

The fifth breathing technique: *Attention between eyebrows, let mind be before thought. Let form fill with breath essence to the top of the head and there shower as light.*

This was the technique given to Pythagoras. Pythagoras went with this technique to Greece, and really, he became the fountainhead, the source of all mysticism in the West. He is the father of all mysticism in the West.

This technique is one of the very deep methods. Try to understand this: *Attention between eyebrows....* Modern physiology, scientific research, says that between the two eyebrows is the gland which is the most mysterious part of the body. This gland, called the pineal gland, is the third eye of the Tibetans—*shivanetra:* the eye of Shiva, of tantra. Between the two eyes there exists a third eye, but it is nonfunctioning. It is there, it can function any moment, but it does not function naturally. You have to do something about it to open it. It is not blind; it is simply closed. This technique is to open the third eye.

Attention between eyebrows.... Close your eyes, then focus both of your eyes just in the middle of the two eyebrows. Focus just in the middle, with closed eyes, as if you are looking with your two eyes. Give total attention to it.

This is one of the simplest methods of being attentive. You cannot be attentive to any other part of the body so easily. This gland absorbs attention like anything. If you give attention to it, both your eyes become hypnotized with the third eye. They become fixed; they cannot move. If you are trying to be attentive to any other part of the body it is difficult. This third eye catches attention, forces attention; it is magnetic for attention. So all the methods all over the world have used it. It is the simplest to train you in attention because not only are you trying to be attentive, the gland itself helps you; it is magnetic. Your attention is brought to it forcibly. It is absorbed.

It is said in the old tantra scriptures that for the third eye attention is food. It is hungry; it has been hungry for lives and lives. If you pay attention to it, it becomes alive. It becomes alive! The food is given to it. And once you know that attention is food, once you feel that your attention is magnetically drawn, attracted, pulled by the gland itself, attention is not a difficult thing then. One has only to know the right point. So just close your eyes, let your two eyes move just to the middle, and feel the point. When you are near the point, suddenly your eyes will become fixed. When it becomes difficult to move them, then know you have caught the right point.

Attention between eyebrows, let mind be before thought.... If this attention is there, for the first time you will come to experience a strange phenomenon. For the first time you will see thoughts running before you; you will become the witness. It is just like a film screen: thoughts are running and you are a witness. Once your attention is focused at the third eye center, you become immediately the witness of thoughts.

Ordinarily you are not the witness, you are identified with thoughts. If anger is there, you become anger. If a thought moves, you are not the witness, you become one with the thought, identified, and

you move with it. You become the thought; you take the form of the thought. When sex is there you become sex, when anger is there you become anger, when greed is there you become greed. Any thought moving becomes identified with you. You do not have any gap between you and the thought.

But focused at the third eye, suddenly you become a witness. Through the third eye you become the witness. Through the third eye you can see thoughts running like clouds in the sky or people moving on the street.

You are sitting at your window looking at the sky or at people in the street; you are not identified. You are aloof, a watcher on the hill—different. Now if anger is there you can look at it as an object. Now you do not feel that *you* are angry. You feel that you are surrounded by anger—a cloud of anger has come around you—but you are not the anger. And if you are not the anger, anger becomes impotent, it cannot affect you; you remain untouched. The anger will come and go and you will remain centered in yourself.

This fifth technique is a technique of finding the witness. *Attention between eyebrows, let the mind be before thought.* Now look at your thoughts; now encounter your thoughts. *Let form fill with breath essence to the top of the head and there shower as light.* When attention is focused at the third eye center, between the two eyebrows, two things happen. One is, suddenly you become a witness.

This can happen in two ways. You become a witness and you will be centered at the third eye. Try to be a witness. Whatsoever is happening, try to be a witness. You are ill, the body is aching and painful, you have misery and suffering, whatsoever —be a witness to it. Whatsoever is happening, do not identify yourself with it. Be a witness, an observer. Then if witnessing becomes possible, you will be focused in the third eye.

The vice versa is the case also. If you are focused in the third eye, you will become a witness. These two things are part of one. So the first thing: by being centered in the third eye there will be the arising of the witnessing self. Now you can encounter your thoughts. This will be the first thing. And the second thing will be that now you can feel the subtle, delicate vibration of breathing. Now you can feel the form of breathing, the very essence of breathing.

First try to understand what is meant by "the form," by "the essence of breathing." While you are breathing, you are not only breathing air. Science says you are breathing only air—just oxygen, hydrogen, and other gases in their combined form of air. They say you are breathing air! But tantra says that air is just the vehicle, not the real thing. You are breathing *prana*—vitality. Air is just the medium; prana is the content. You are breathing prana, not only air.

Modern science is still not able to find out whether there is something like prana, but some researchers have felt something mysterious. Breathing is not simply air. It has been felt by many modern researchers also. In particular, one name is to be mentioned: Wilhelm Reich, a German psychologist who called it "orgone energy." It is the same thing as prana. He says that while you are breathing, air is just the container and there is a mysterious content which can be called orgone or prana or *élan vital*. But that is very subtle. Really, it is not material. Air is the material thing—the container is material—but something subtle, nonmaterial, is moving through it.

The effects of it can be felt. When you are with a very vital person, you will feel a certain vitality arising in you. If you are with a very sick person you will feel sucked, as if something has been taken out of you. When you go to the hospital, why do you feel so tired? You are being sucked from everywhere. The whole hospital atmosphere is ill, and everyone there needs more élan vital, more prana. So if you are there, suddenly your prana begins to flow out of you. Why do you feel suffocated sometimes when you are in a crowd? Because your prana is being sucked. While you are alone under the sky in the morning, under the trees, suddenly

you feel a vitality in you—the prana. Each person needs a particular space. If that space is not given, your prana is sucked.

Wilhelm Reich did many experiments, but he was thought to be a madman. Science has its own superstitions, and science is a very orthodox thing. Science cannot feel yet that there is anything more than air, but India has been experimenting with it for centuries.

You may have heard of or you may have even seen someone going into *samadhi,* cosmic consciousness—underground samadhi—for days together, with no air penetrating. One man went into such underground samadhi in Egypt in 1880 for forty years. Those who had buried him all died, because he was to come out of his samadhi in 1920, forty years afterwards. In 1920 no one believed that they would find him alive, but he was found alive. He lived afterwards for ten years more. He had become completely pale, but he was alive. And there had been no possibility of air reaching to him.

He was asked by medical doctors and others, "What is the secret of it?"

He said, "We do not know. We only know this, that prana can enter and flow anywhere." Air cannot penetrate, but prana can penetrate. Once you know that you can suck prana directly, without the container, then you can go into samadhi for centuries even.

By being focused in the third eye, suddenly you can observe the very essence of breath—not breath, but the very essence of breath, prana. And if you can observe the essence of breath, prana, you are at the point from where the jump, the breakthrough happens.

The sutra says, *Let form fill with breath essence to the top of the head....* And when you come to feel the essence of breathing, prana, just imagine that your head is filled with it—just imagine. No need of any effort. I will explain to you how imagination works. When you are focused at the third-eye center, imagine, and the thing happens—then and there.

Now your imagination is just impotent; you go

on imagining and nothing happens. But sometimes, unknowingly, in ordinary life also things happen. You are imagining about your friend and suddenly there is a knock on the door. You say it is a coincidence that the friend has come. Sometimes your imagination works just like coincidence. But whenever this happens, now try and remember and analyze the whole thing. Whenever it happens that you feel your imagination has become actual, go inside and observe. Somewhere your attention must have been near the third eye. Whenever this coincidence happens, it is not a coincidence. It looks that way because you do not know the secret science. Your mind must have moved unknowingly near the third eye center. If your attention is in the third eye, just imagination is enough to create any phenomenon.

This sutra says that when you are focused between the eyebrows and you can feel the very essence of breathing, *let form fill*. Now imagine that this essence is filling your whole head, particularly the top of the head, the *sahasrar*—the highest psychic center. And the moment you imagine, it will be filled. *There*—at the top of the head—*shower as light*. This prana essence is showering from the top of your head as light. And it *will* begin to shower, and under the shower of light you will be refreshed, reborn, completely new. That is what inner rebirth means.

So two things: first, focused at the third eye your imagination becomes potent, powerful. That is why so much insistence has been given on purity. Before doing these practices, be pure. Purity is not a moral concept for tantra, purity is significant—because if you are focused at the third eye and your mind is impure, your imagination can become dangerous: dangerous to you, dangerous to others. If you are thinking to murder someone, if this idea is in the mind, just imagining may kill the man. That is why there is so much insistence on being pure first.

Pythagoras was told to go through fasting, through particular breathing—this breathing— because here one is traveling in a very dangerous land. Because wherever there is power there is

danger, and if the mind is impure, whenever you get power your impure thoughts will take hold of it immediately.

You have imagined many times to kill but the imagination cannot work, fortunately. If it works, if it is actualized immediately, then it will become dangerous—not only to others, but to yourself also, because so many times you have thought to commit suicide. If the mind is focused at the third eye, just thinking of suicide will become suicide. You will not have any time to change, immediately it will happen.

You might have observed someone being hypnotized. When someone is hypnotized, the hypnotist can say anything and immediately the hypnotized person follows. Howsoever absurd the order, howsoever irrational or even impossible, the hypnotized person follows it. What is happening? This fifth technique is at the base of all hypnotism. Whenever someone is being hypnotized he is told to focus his eyes at a particular point—on some light, some dot on the wall or anything, or on the eyes of the hypnotist.

When you focus your eyes at any particular point, within three minutes your inner attention begins to flow toward the third eye. And the moment your inner attention begins to flow toward the third eye, your face begins to change. And the hypnotist knows when your face begins to change. Suddenly your face loses all vitality. It becomes dead, as if deeply asleep. The hypnotist knows immediately when your face has lost the luster, the aliveness. It means that now attention is being sucked by the third eye center. Your face has become dead; the whole energy is running toward the third eye center.

Now the hypnotist immediately knows that anything said will happen. He says, "Now you are falling into a deep sleep"—you will fall immediately. He says, "Now you are becoming unconscious"— you will become unconscious immediately. Now anything can be done. If he says, "Now you have become Napoleon," you will become. You will begin to behave like a Napoleon, you will begin to talk like Napoleon. Your gestures will change. Your unconscious will take the order and will create the actuality. If you are suffering from a disease, now it can be ordered that the disease has disappeared and it will disappear. Or any new disease can be created.

Just putting an ordinary stone from the street in your hand, the hypnotist can say, "This is fire in your hand," and you will feel intense heat; your hand will get burned—not only in the mind, but actually. Actually your skin will get burned. You will have a burning sensation. What is happening? There is no fire, there is just an ordinary stone, cold. How? How does this burning happen? You are focused at the third eye center, your imagination is being given suggestions by the hypnotist, and they are being actualized. If the hypnotist says, "Now you are dead," you will die immediately. Your heart will stop. It *will* stop.

This happens because of the third eye. In the third eye, imagination and actualization are not two things. Imagination is the fact. Imagine, and it is so. There is no gap between dream and reality. There is *no* gap between dream and reality! Dream, and it will become real. That is why Shankara has said that this whole world is nothing but the dream of the divine...the *dream* of the divine! This is because the divine is centered in the third eye— always, eternally—so whatsoever the divine dreams becomes real. If you are also centered in the third eye, whatsoever you dream will become real.

Sariputta came to Buddha. He meditated deeply, then many things, many visions started coming, as it happens with anyone who goes into deep meditation. He began to see heavens, he began to see hells, he began to see angels, gods, demons. And they were actual, so real that he came running to Buddha to tell him that such and such a vision had come to him. But Buddha said, "It is nothing—just dreams. Just dreams!"

But Sariputta said, "They are so real. How can I say that they are dreams? When I see a flower in my vision it is more real than any flower in the world. The fragrance is there; I can touch it. When I see you," he said to Buddha, "I do not see you as

real. That flower is more real than your being here just before me, so how can I differentiate between what is real and what is dream?"

Buddha said, "Now that you are centered in the third eye, dream and reality are one. Whatsoever you are dreaming will be real, and vice versa also."

For one who is centered in the third eye dreams will become real and the whole reality will become just a dream, because when your dream can become real you know there is no basic difference between dream and reality. So when Shankara says that this whole world is just *maya,* a dream of the divine, it is not a theoretical proposition, it is not a philosophical statement. It is, rather, the inner experience of one who is focused in the third eye.

When you are focused in the third eye, just imagine that the essence of prana is showering from the top of the head, just as if you are sitting under a tree and flowers are showering, or you are just under the sky and suddenly a cloud begins to shower, or you are just sitting in the morning and the sun rises and rays begin to shower. Imagine, and immediately there is a shower—a shower of light falling down from the top of your head. This shower re-creates you, gives you a new birth. You are reborn.

6 Focus on the gap during your daily activities.

The sixth breathing technique: *When in worldly activity, keep attention between two breaths, and so practicing, in a few days, be born anew.*

When in worldly activity, keep attention between two breaths.... Forget breaths—keep attentive in between. One breath has come: before it returns, before it is exhaled, there is the gap, the interval. One breath has gone out; before it is taken in again, the gap. *In worldly activity keep attention between two breaths, and so practicing, in a few days, be born anew.* But this has to be done continuously. This sixth technique has to be done continuously. That is why this is mentioned: *When in worldly activity*…. Whatsoever you are doing, keep your attention in the gap between the two breaths. But it must be practiced while in activity.

We have discussed one technique that is just similar. Now there is only this difference, that this has to be practiced while in worldly activity. Do not practice it in isolation. This practice is to be done while you are doing something else. You are eating —go on eating and be attentive of the gap. You are walking—go on walking and be attentive of the gap. You are going to sleep—lie down, let sleep come, but you go on being attentive of the gap. Why in activity? Because activity distracts the mind, activity calls for your attention again and again. Do not be distracted, be fixed at the gap. And do not stop activity, let the activity continue. You will have two layers of existence—doing and being.

We have two layers of existence: the world of doing and the world of being; the circumference and the center. Go on working on the periphery, on the circumference; do not stop it. But go on working attentively on the center also. What will happen? Your activity will become an acting, as if you are playing a part.

You are playing a part—for example, in a drama. You have become Rama or you have become Christ. You go on acting as Christ or as Rama, and still you remain yourself. In the center, you know who you are; on the periphery you go on acting as Rama, Christ or anyone. You know you are not Rama—you are acting. You know who you are. Your attention is centered in you; your activity continues on the circumference.

If this method is practiced, your whole life will become a long drama. You will be an actor playing roles, but constantly centered in the gap. If you forget the gap then you are not playing roles, you have become the role. Then it is not a drama; you have mistaken it as life. That is what we have done. Everyone thinks he is living life. It is not life, it is just a role—a part which has been given to you by the society, by the circumstances, by the culture, by the tradition, the country, the situation. You have

been given a role and you are playing it; you have become identified with it. To break that identification there is this technique.

Krishna has many names. Krishna is one of the greatest actors. He is constantly centered in himself and playing—playing many roles, many games, but absolutely nonserious. Seriousness comes from identification. If you really become Rama in the drama then there are bound to be problems. Those problems will come out of your seriousness. When Sita is stolen you may get a heart attack, and the whole play will have to be stopped. If you really become Rama a heart attack is certain…even heart failure.

But you are just an actor. Sita is stolen, but nothing is stolen. You will go back to your home and you will sleep peacefully. Not even in a dream will you feel that Sita is stolen. When really Sita was stolen, Rama himself was weeping, crying and asking the trees, "Where has my Sita gone? Who has taken her?" But this is the point to understand. If Rama is really weeping and asking the trees, he has become identified. He is no more Rama; he is no more a divine person.

This is the point to remember, that for Rama his real life also was just a part. You have seen other actors playing Rama, but Rama himself was just playing a part—on a greater stage, of course.

India has a very beautiful story about it. I think that the story is unique; nowhere else in any part of the world does such a thing exist. It is said that Valmiki wrote the *Ramayana* before Rama was born, and then Rama had to follow. So really, the first act of Rama was also just a drama. The story was written before Rama was born and then Rama had to follow, so what can he do? When a man like Valmiki writes the story, Rama has to follow. So everything was fixed in a way. Sita was to be stolen and the war had to be fought.

If you can understand this, then you can understand the theory of destiny, *bhagya*—fate. It has a very deep meaning. And the meaning is, if you take it that everything is fixed for you, your life becomes a drama. If you are playing the role of Rama in the drama you cannot change it, everything is fixed, even your dialogue. If you say something to Sita it is just repeating something that is fixed. You cannot change it if life is taken as fixed.

For example, you are going to die on a particular day—it is fixed. When you will be dying you will be weeping, but it is fixed. And such and such persons will be around you—it is fixed. If everything is fixed, everything becomes a drama. If everything is fixed, it means you are just to enact it. You are not asked to live it, you are just asked to enact it.

This technique, the sixth technique, is just to make yourself a psychodrama—just a play. You are focused in the gap between two breaths and life moves on, on the periphery. If your attention is at the center, then your attention is not really on the periphery—that is just "subattention"; it just happens somewhere near your attention. You can feel it, you can know it, but it is not significant. It is as if it is not happening to you. I will repeat this: if you practice this sixth technique, your whole life will be as if it is not happening to you, as if it is happening to someone else.

---

7 A technique to be aware in dreams.

The seventh breathing technique: *With intangible breath in center of forehead, as this reaches heart at the moment of sleep, have direction over dreams and over death itself.*

More and more you are entering deeper layers. *With intangible breath in center of forehead....* If you have known the third eye then you know the intangible breath, the invisible prana in the center of the forehead, and then you know the showering —the energy, the light showers. *As this reaches heart....* When the shower will reach your heart... *at the moment of sleep, have direction over dreams and over death itself.*

Take this technique in three parts. One, you must be able to feel the prana in breath—the intangible

part of it, the invisible part of it, the immaterial part of it. It comes if you are attentive between the two eyebrows; then it comes easily. If you are attentive in the gap, then too it comes, but a little less easily. If you are aware of the center at your navel where breath comes and touches and goes out, it also comes, but with less ease. The easiest way to know the invisible part of breath is to be centered at the third eye. But wherever you are centered, it comes, you begin to feel the prana flowing in.

If you can feel the prana flowing in you, you can know when you are going to die. Six months before the day of your death you begin to know, if you can feel the invisible part of breath. Why do so many saints declare the day of their death? It is easy, because if you can see the content of the breath, the prana flowing into you, the moment the process reverses you can feel it. Before you die, six months before you die, the process reverses: prana begins to flow out of you. Then the breath is not taking it in. Rather, on the contrary, the breath is taking it out—the same breath.

You cannot feel it because you do not know the invisible part—you know only the visible, you know only the vehicle. The vehicle will be the same. Now the breath is carrying prana in, leaving it there; then the vehicle goes back empty. Then again it is filled with the prana and it comes in. So the ingoing breath and the outgoing breath are not the same, remember. The ingoing breath and the outgoing breath are the same as vehicles, but the incoming breath is filled with prana and the outgoing breath is empty. You have taken in the prana and the breath has become empty.

The reverse happens when you are nearing death. The incoming breath comes prana-less, empty, because your body cannot suck prana from the cosmos. You are going to die; there is no need for it. The whole process has reversed. And when the breath goes out, it takes your prana out. One who has been able to see the invisible can know his day of death immediately. Six months before, the process reverses.

This sutra is very, very significant: *With intangible breath in center of forehead, as this reaches heart at the moment of sleep, have direction over dreams and over death itself.* While you are falling into sleep this technique has to be practiced—then only, not at any other time. While you are falling asleep, only then; that is the right moment to practice this technique. You are falling asleep. By and by, by and by, sleep is overtaking you. Within moments, your consciousness will dissolve; you will not be aware. Before that moment comes, become aware—aware of the breath and the invisible part prana, and feel it coming to the heart.

Go on feeling that it is coming to the heart. The prana enters from your heart into the body. Go on feeling that the prana is coming into the heart, and let sleep come while you are continuously feeling it. You go on feeling, and let sleep come and drown you.

If this happens—that you are feeling invisible breath coming into the heart and sleep overtakes you—you will be aware in dreams. You will know that you are dreaming. Ordinarily we do not know that we are dreaming. While you dream you think that this is reality. That too happens because of the third eye. Have you seen anyone asleep? His eyes move upwards and become focused in the third eye. If you have not seen, then see.

Your child is sleeping…just open his eyes and see where his eyes are. His pupils have gone up and they are focused in the third eye. I say look at children, do not look at grown-ups—they are not believable because their sleep is not deep. They will just be thinking that they are asleep. Look at children, their eyes move up. They become focused in the third eye. Because of this focusing in the third eye you take your dreams as real, you cannot feel they are dreams—they are real. You will know when you get up in the morning. Then you will know that "I was dreaming." But this is the later, retrospective realization. You cannot realize in the dream that you are dreaming. If you realize it, then there are two layers: dream is there but you are awake, you are aware. For one who becomes

aware in dreams, this sutra is wonderful. It says, *Have direction over dreams and over death itself.*

If you can become aware of dreams, you can do two things. You can create dreams—one. Ordinarily you cannot create dreams. How impotent man is! You cannot even create dreams. If you want to dream a particular thing you cannot dream it; it is not in your hands. How powerless man is! Even dreams cannot be created. You are just a victim of dreams, not the creator. A dream happens to you; you cannot do anything. Neither can you stop it nor can you create it.

But if you move into sleep remembering the heart being filled with prana, continuously being touched by prana with every breath, you will become a master of your dreams—and this is a rare mastery. Then you can dream whatsoever dreams you like. Just note while you are falling asleep that "I want to dream this dream," and that dream will come to you. Just say, while falling asleep, "I do not want to dream that dream," and that dream cannot enter your mind.

But what is the use of becoming the master of your dreaming? Isn't it useless? No, it is not useless. Once you become master of your dreams you will never dream—it is absurd. When you are master of your dreams, dreaming stops; there is no need for it. And when dreaming stops, your sleep has a different quality altogether, and the quality is the same as of death.

Death is deep sleep. If your sleep can become as deep as death, that means there will be no dreaming. Dreaming creates superficiality in sleep. You move on the surface because of the dreams; because of hanging on to the dreams, you move on the surface. When there is no dreaming you just drop into the sea, its depth is reached.

Death is the same. That is why people in India have always been saying that sleep is a short duration of death, and death is a long sleep—qualitatively they are the same. Sleep is a day-to-day death. Death is a life-to-life phenomenon, a life-to-life sleep. Every day you are tired. You fall into sleep and you regain your vitality, your aliveness in the morning; you are reborn. After a life of seventy or eighty years you are tired completely. Now such short durations of death won't do; you need a great death. After that great death or great sleep, you are reborn with a totally new body.

Once you can know dreamless sleep and can be aware in it, then there will be no fear of death. No one has ever died, no one can die—that is the only impossibility.

Just a day before I was telling you that death is the only certainty, and now I say to you that death is impossible. No one has ever died and no one can die—that is the only impossibility—because the universe is life. You are again and again reborn, but the sleep is so deep that you forget your old identity. Your mind is washed clean of the memories.

Think of it in this way. Today you are going to sleep: it is just as if there were some mechanism—and soon we will have this—like that which can erase on a tape recorder, which can wipe a tape clean so that whatsoever was recorded is no more there. The same is possible with memory, because memory is really just a deep recording. Sooner or later we will have a mechanism which can be put on the head and it will clean your mind completely. In the morning you will no longer be the same person because you won't be able to remember who it was who went to sleep. Then your sleep will look like death. There will be a discontinuity; you won't be able to remember who went to sleep. This is happening naturally. When you die and you are reborn, you cannot remember who died. You start again.

With this technique, first you will become the master of your dreams—that is, dreaming will cease. Or if you want to dream you will be able to dream, but dreaming will become voluntary. It will not be nonvoluntary, it will not be forced upon you; you will not be a victim. Then the quality of your sleep will become just like that of death. Then you will know that death is sleep.

That is why this sutra says: *Have direction over dreams and over death itself.* You will know that death is just a long sleep—and helpful and beautiful because it gives you new life; it gives you everything anew. Death ceases to be...with cessation of dreaming, death ceases to be.

There is another meaning to gaining power over death, direction over death. If you can come to feel that death is just a sleep, you will be able to direct it. If you can direct your dreams, you can direct your death also. You can choose where you are to be born again, to whom, when, in what form; you will become master of your birth also.

Buddha died.... I am not referring to his last life, but to his last-but-one life, before he became Buddha. Before dying he said, "I will be born to such and such parents; such will be my mother, such will be my father. But my mother will die immediately...when I am born my mother will die immediately. Before I am born my mother will have certain dreams." Not only do you gain power from your dreams, you gain power from others' dreams also. So Buddha, as an example, said, "Certain dreams will be there. When I will be in the womb, my mother will have certain dreams. So whenever any woman has these dreams in this sequence, know well I am going to be born to her."

And it happened. Buddha's mother dreamed the same sequence. The sequence was known all over India, because it was no ordinary statement. It was known to everyone, particularly those who were interested in religion and the deeper things of life and the esoteric ways of life. It was known, so the dreams were interpreted. Freud was not the first interpreter—and, of course, not the deepest. Only in the West was he the first.

So Buddha's father immediately called dream interpreters, the Freuds and Jungs of those days, and he asked, "What does this sequence mean? I am afraid. These dreams are rare, and they go on repeating in the same sequence. There are one, two, three, four, five, six dreams continuously being repeated. There are the same dreams, as if one is seeing the same film again and again. What is happening?"

So they told him, "You are going to be the

father of a great soul—one who is going to be a buddha. But then your wife is going to be in danger, because whenever this buddha is born it is difficult for the mother to survive."

The father asked, "Why?" The interpreters said, "We cannot say why, but this soul who is going to be born has made a statement that when he will be born again, the mother will die immediately."

Later on Buddha was asked, "Why did your mother die immediately?" He said, "Giving birth to a buddha is such a big event that everything else becomes futile afterwards. So the mother cannot exist. She will have to be born again to start anew. It is such a climax giving birth to a buddha, it is such a peak, that the mother cannot exist beyond it."

So the mother died. And Buddha had said in his previous life that he would be born while his mother was standing under a palm tree—and it happened. The mother was standing under a palm tree—standing while Buddha was born. And he had said, "I will be born while my mother is standing under a palm tree, and I will take seven steps. Immediately, I will walk. These are the signs I give to you," he said, "so that you will know that a buddha is born." And he carried out everything.

And this is not only so about Buddha. It is so about Jesus, it is so about Mahavira, it is so about many others. Every Jaina *tirthankara* has predicted in his previous life how he is going to be born. And they have given particular dream sequences—that such and such will be the symbols—and they have told how it will happen.

You can direct. Once you can direct your dreams you can direct everything, because dream is the very stuff of this world. This life is made out of the stuff of dreams. Once you can direct your dreams you can direct everything. This sutra says, *over death itself.* Then one can give a certain birth, a certain life to oneself.

We are just victims. We do not know why we are born, why we die. Who directs us—and why? There seems to be no reason. It all seems just a chaos, just accidental. It is because we are not

masters. Once we are masters it is not like this.

8 Watch the turning point with devotion.

The eighth breathing technique: *With utmost devotion, center on the two junctions of breath and know the knower.*

There is a slight difference in the techniques—slight modifications. But though the differences are slight in the techniques, for you they may be great. A single word makes a great difference. *With utmost devotion, center on the two junctions of breath.* The incoming breath has one junction where it turns, the outgoing breath has another junction where it turns. With these two turnings—and we have discussed these turnings—a slight difference is made: that is, slight in the technique, but for the seeker it may be great. Only one condition is added: *With utmost devotion*—and the whole technique becomes different.

In the first form of it there was no question of devotion, just a scientific technique. You do it, and it works. But there are persons who cannot do such dry, scientific techniques. Those who are heart-oriented, those who belong to the world of devotion, for them a slight difference has been made: *With utmost devotion, center on the two junctions of breath and know the knower.*

If you are not of the scientific bent, of the scientific attitude, if you are not a scientific mind, then try this: *With utmost devotion*—with faith, love, trust—*center on the two junctions of breath and know the knower.* How to do this? How? You can have devotion about someone: about Krishna, about Christ you can have devotion. But how can you have devotion about yourself, about this junction of breathing? The phenomenon seems absolutely nondevotional. But that depends....

Tantra says that the body is the temple. Your body is the temple of the divine, the abode of the divine, so do not treat your body as an object. It is sacred, it is holy. And while you are taking a breath in, it is not only you who is taking the breath, it is the divine within you. You are eating, you are moving or walking...look at it in this way: it is not you, but the divine moving in you. Then the whole thing becomes absolutely devotional.

It is said about many saints that they love their bodies. They treat their bodies as if their bodies belong to their beloveds. You can treat your body in this way or you can treat it just like a mechanism —that again is an attitude. You can treat it with guilt, sin; you can treat it as something dirty; you can treat it as something miraculous, as a miracle; you can treat it as the abode of the divine. It depends on you. If you can treat your body as a temple, then this technique will be helpful: *With utmost devotion....*

Try it. While you are eating, try it. Do not think that *you* are eating. Think that it is the divine in you who is eating, and look at the change. You are eating the same thing, you are the same, but immediately everything becomes different. You are giving the food to the divine. You are taking a bath—a very ordinary, trivial thing—but change the attitude: feel that you are giving a bath to the divine in you. Then this technique will be easy: *With utmost devotion, center on the two junctions of breath and know the knower.*

9a **Lie down as dead.**
 b **Stare without blinking.**
 c **Suck something and become the sucking.**

The ninth technique: *Lie down as dead. Enraged in wrath, stay so. Or stare without moving an eyelash. Or suck something and become the sucking.*

Lie down as dead. Try it: suddenly you have gone dead. Leave the body! Do not move it, because you are dead. Just imagine that you are dead. You cannot move the body, you cannot move the eyes, you cannot cry, you cannot scream, you cannot do

anything, you are just dead. And then feel how it feels. But do not deceive. You can deceive, you can slightly move the body. Do not move. If some mosquito is there, then treat the body as if it is dead. It is one of the most used techniques.

Raman Maharshi attained his enlightenment through this technique, but it was not a technique used by him in his life. In his life it suddenly happened, spontaneously. But he must have persisted with this in some past life, because nothing happens spontaneously. Everything has a causal link, a causality. Suddenly one night Raman felt—he was just young, fourteen or fifteen at the time—that he was going to die. And it was so certain in his mind that death had taken over. He couldn't move his body, he felt as if he was paralyzed. Then he felt a sudden choking, and he knew that now the heart was going to stop. He could not even cry and say to another, "I am going to die."

Sometimes it happens in some nightmare—you cannot cry, you cannot move. Even when you become awake for a few moments you cannot do anything. That happened. He had absolute power over his consciousness, but no power over his body. He knew he was there, that he was present, conscious, alert, but he felt he was going to die. And the knowledge became so certain that there was no other possibility, so he just gave up. He closed his eyes and remained there, just waiting to die; he waited there just to die.

By and by the body became stiff. The body died, but then it became a problem. He knew that the body had died, but he was there and he knew it. He knew that he was alive and that the body had died. Then he came back. In the morning the body became okay but the same man never returned—because he had known death. He had known a different realm, a different dimension of consciousness.

He escaped from the house. That death experience changed him completely. He became one of the very few enlightened persons of this age.

This is the technique. This happened spontaneously to Raman, but it is not going to happen spontaneously to you. But try it. In some life it may become spontaneous. It may happen while you are trying it. And if it is not going to happen, the effort is never wasted. It is in you; it remains in you as a seed. Sometime, when the time is ripe and the rains will fall, it will sprout.

Every spontaneity is just like this. The seed was sown some time ago, but the time was not ripe; there were no rains. In another life the time becomes ripe. You are more mature, more experienced, more frustrated with the world—then suddenly, in a certain situation, there are rains and the seed explodes.

Lie down as dead. Enraged in wrath, stay so. Of course, while you are dying it will not be a happy moment. It is not going to be so blissful while you are feeling that you are dead. Fear will take you, anger may come in the mind, or frustration, sadness, sorrow, anguish...anything. It will differ from individual to individual.

The sutra says: *Enraged in wrath, stay so.* If you feel enraged, stay so. If you feel sad, stay so. If you feel anxiety, fear, stay so. You are dead and you cannot do anything, so stay so. Whatsoever is in the mind, the body is dead and you cannot do anything, so stay.

That staying is beautiful. If you can stay for a few minutes, suddenly you will feel that everything has changed. But we start moving. If there is some emotion in the mind, the body begins to move. That is why we call it "emotion"—it creates motion in the body. If you are angry, suddenly your body begins to move. If you are sad, your body begins to move. That is why it is called emotion, because it creates motion in the body. Feel dead and do not allow emotions to move your body. Let them be there, but you *stay so*—fixed, dead. Whatsoever is there...no movement. Stay! No movement.

Or stare without moving an eyelash. This *or stare without moving an eyelash* was the method of Meher Baba. For years together he was staring just at the ceiling of his room. For years together he was just lying dead on the floor, staring at the ceiling without moving an eyelash, without moving his eyes. He would lie down for hours together, just staring, not doing anything. Staring with the eyes is good, because you become fixed again in the third eye. And once you are fixed in the third eye, even if you want to move the eyelids you cannot; they become fixed.

Meher Baba attained through this staring, and you say, "How with these small exercises...?" But for three years he was staring at the ceiling, not doing anything. Three years is a long time. Do it for three minutes and you will feel as if you have been lying there for three years. Three minutes will become very, very long. It will look as if time is not passing and as if the clock has stopped.

Meher Baba stared and stared and stared. By and by thoughts ceased, movement ceased, and he became just a consciousness, he became just a staring. Then he remained silent for his whole life. He became so silent inside by this staring that it became impossible for him to formulate words again.

Meher Baba was in America. There was one man who could read others' thoughts, who could do mind readings, and he was really one of the rarest mind readers. He would close his eyes, sit before you, and within a few minutes he would become attuned with you and he would begin to write what you are thinking. Thousands and thousands of times he was examined, and he was always right, always correct. So someone brought him to Meher Baba. He sat there, and this was the only failure of his life —the only failure. But then again we cannot say it was a failure. He tried and tried, and he began to perspire, but he couldn't catch a single word.

Pen in his hand, he remained there and said, "What type of man is this? I cannot read because there is nothing to read. This man is absolutely vacant. I even forget that someone is sitting there. After closing my eyes, I have to open them again and look to see whether that man is there or whether he has escaped. So it is difficult to concentrate, because the moment I close my eyes I feel I am being deceived—as if that man has escaped and there is no one before me. I have to open my eyes again, and I find that this man is there. And he is not thinking at all." That staring, that constant staring had stopped his mind completely.

Or stare without moving an eyelash. Or suck something and become the sucking. These are slight modifications. Anything will do...you are dead—it is enough.

Enraged in wrath, stay so. Even this part can become one technique. You are in anger: lie down, remain in the anger. Do not move from it, do not do anything, just remain still.

Krishnamurti goes on talking about this. His whole technique depends on this single thing: *Enraged in wrath, stay so.* If you are angry then be angry, and remain angry. Do not move. If you can stay so, anger will go and you will come out a different man. If you are in anxiety, do not do anything. Remain there, stay there. The anxiety will go; you will come out a different man. And once you have looked at anxiety without being moved by it, you will be the master.

Or stare without moving an eyelash. Or suck something and become the sucking. This last one is physical and easy to do, because sucking is the first thing a child has to do. Sucking is the first act of life. When the child is born, he begins to cry. You may not have tried to penetrate into why there is this crying. He is not really crying—it appears to us that he is crying—he is just sucking air. And if the child cannot cry, within a few minutes he will be dead, because crying is the first effort to suck air. The child was not breathing while he was in the womb. He was alive without breathing. He was doing the same which yogis are doing underground. He was just getting prana without breathing—pure prana from the mother.

That is why the love between the child and the mother is an altogether different thing from other loves, because the purest prana—energy—joins both. Now this can never happen again. There was a subtle pranic relationship. The mother was giving her prana to the child, and the child was not breathing at all. When he is born, he is thrown out of the mother into an unknown world. Now the prana, the energy, will not reach him so easily. He has to breathe himself.

The first cry is an effort to suck, and then he will suck the milk from the mother's breast. These are the first basic acts which you have done. Whatsoever *you* have done comes later—these are the first life acts. They can be practiced also. This sutra says: *Or suck something and become the sucking.* Suck something—just suck the air, but forget the air and become the sucking. What does this mean? You are sucking something; you are the sucker, not the sucking. You are standing behind and sucking.

This sutra says, do not stand behind, move in the act and become the sucking. Try anything that will work. You are running—become the running, do not be the runner. Become the running and forget the runner. Feel that there is no runner inside, just the process of running. You are the process, a riverlike process running. Nobody is there inside. It is quiet inside and there is only a process.

Sucking is good, but you will feel that it is very difficult because we have forgotten it completely—but not really completely, however, because we go on substituting for it. The mother's breast is substituted by a cigarette; you go on sucking it. It is nothing but the nipple, the mother's breast and the nipple. And when the warm smoke flows in, it is just like warm milk.

So those who were not really allowed to suck the mother's breast as much as they wanted will smoke later on. This is a substitute, but the substitute will do. While you are smoking a cigarette become the sucking. Forget the cigarette, forget the smoker; become the smoking.

There is the object you are sucking, there is the subject who is sucking, and the process in between of sucking. Become the sucking, become the process. Try it. You will have to try it with many things; then you will find out what is right for you.

You are drinking water, the cold water is going in—become the drinking. Do not drink the water. Forget the water, forget yourself and your thirst, just become the drinking—the very process. Become the coolness, the touch, the entry, and the sucking that has to be given to the process.

Why not? What will happen? If you become the sucking, what will happen? If you can become the sucking, immediately you will become innocent, like a first-day, newly born child—because that is the first process. You will be regressed in a way. But the hankering is there. The very being of man hankers after sucking. He tries many things, but nothing helps because the point is missed. Unless you become the sucking, nothing will help. So try it.

I gave this method to one man. He had tried many things; he had tried many, many methods. Then he came to me, so I asked him, "If I give you only one thing to choose in the whole world, what are you going to choose?" And I told him immediately to close his eyes and tell me, and not think about it. He became afraid, hesitant, so I told him, "Do not be afraid, do not be hesitant. Be frank and tell me."

He said, "This is absurd, but a breast appears before me."

And then he began to feel guilty, so I said, "Do not feel guilty. Nothing is wrong in a breast; it is one of the most beautiful things, so why be guilty?"

But he said, "This has always been an obsession with me." And he said to me, "Please tell me first, then you can proceed with your method and the technique: first tell me why I am so much interested in the breasts of women? Whenever I look at a woman, the first thing I see is the breast. The whole body is secondary."

And it is not so only with him, it is so with everyone—with almost everyone. And it is natural, because the breast of the mother was the first acquaintance with the universe. It is basic. The first contact with the universe was the mother's breast. That is why breasts are so appealing. They look beautiful; they attract, they have a magnetic force. That magnetic force comes from your unconscious. That was the first thing with which you came in contact, and the contact was lovely, it felt beautiful. It gives you food, instant vitality, love, everything. The contact was soft, receptive, inviting. It has remained so in the mind of man.

So I told that man, "Now I will give you the method." And this was the method I gave him, to suck something and become the sucking. I told him, "Just close your eyes. Imagine your mother's breasts or anybody's breasts that you like. Imagine, and start sucking as if there is a real breast. Start sucking." He started sucking. Within three days he was sucking so fast, so madly, he became so much enchanted by it. He told me, "It has become a problem—I want to suck the whole day. And it is so beautiful, and such deep silence is created by it." Within three months the sucking became a very, very silent gesture. The lips stopped, you couldn't even have judged that he was doing something. But inner sucking had started. He was sucking the whole day. It became a mantra, a *japa*—a mantra repetition.

After three months he came to me and said, "Something strange is happening to me. Something sweet is falling from my head onto my tongue continuously. And it is so sweet and so energy filling that I do not need any food, there is no hunger left. Eating has become just a formality. I take something in order not to create any problems in the family. But something is continuously coming to me. It is so sweet, life-giving."

I told him to continue. Three months more, and one day he came just mad, dancing to me, and he said, "Sucking has disappeared, but I am a different man. I am no more the same man who had come to you. Some door has opened within me. Something has broken and there is no desire left. Now I do not want anything—not even God, not even *moksha*, liberation. I do not want anything. Now everything is okay as it is. I accept it and I am blissful."

Try this. Just suck something and become the sucking. It may be helpful to many because it is so basic.

This much for today.

CHAPTER 6

Devices to transcend dreaming

◆

How to be conscious while dreaming?

Why make efforts if we are merely actors on a set stage?

One friend has asked:

Will You please explain to us what are some of the other factors which can make one conscious while dreaming?

his is a significant question for all those who are interested in meditation, because meditation is really a transcending of the process of dreaming. You are constantly dreaming—not only in the night, not only while you are asleep; you are dreaming the whole day. This is the first point to be understood. While you are awake you are still dreaming.

Just close your eyes at any time of the day. Relax the body and you will feel that the dreaming is there. It never disappears, it is only suppressed by our daily activities. It is like the stars in the day. In the night you see the stars. In the day you cannot see them, but they are there always. They are simply suppressed by the sunlight.

If you go into a deep well, then you can see the stars in the sky even in the day. A certain darkness is needed to see the stars. So go into a deep well and look from the bottom, and you will be able to see the stars in the day also. The stars are there. It is not that in the night they are there and in the day they are not, they are always there. In the night you can see them easily. In the day you cannot see them because the sunlight becomes a barrier.

The same is true with dreaming. It is not that

you dream only while you are asleep. In sleep you can feel dreams easily because the activity of the day is no more there; thus that inner activity can be seen and felt. When you get up in the morning, the dreaming continues inside while you start acting on the outside.

This process of activity, of daily activity, simply suppresses the dreaming. The dreaming is there. Close your eyes, relax in an armchair, and suddenly you can feel: the stars are there, they have not gone anywhere. The dreams are there always. There is a continuous activity.

The second point.... If the dreaming continues, you cannot be said to be really awake. In the night you are more asleep, in the day you are less asleep. The difference is relative, because if the dreaming is there you cannot be said to be really awake. Dreaming creates a film over the consciousness. This film becomes like smoke—you are surrounded by it. You cannot be really awake while you are dreaming, whether in the day or in the night. So the second thing: you can only be said to be awake when there is no dreaming at all.

We call Buddha the awakened one. What is this awakening? This awakening is really the cessation of inner dreaming. There is no dream inside. You move there, but there is no dream. It is as if there were no star in the sky; it has become pure space. When there is no dreaming, you become pure space.

This purity, this innocence, this nondreaming consciousness, is what is known as enlightenment —the awakening.

For centuries spirituality all over the world, East or West, has said that man is asleep. Jesus says this, Buddha says this, the Upanishads talk about this: man is asleep. So while you are asleep in the night you are just relatively more asleep; in the day you are less asleep. But spirituality says that man is asleep. This has to be understood.

What is meant by this? Gurdjieff, in this century, emphasized this fact that man is asleep. "In fact," he said, "man *is* a sort of sleep. Everyone is deeply asleep."

What is the reason for saying that? You cannot know, you cannot remember who you are. Do you know who you are? If you meet a person in the street and you ask him who he is and he cannot reply, what will you think? You will think that he is either mad, intoxicated, or just asleep. If he cannot answer who he is, what are you going to think about him? On the spiritual path everyone is like that. You cannot answer who you are.

This is the first meaning when Gurdjieff or Jesus or anyone says that man is asleep: you are not conscious about yourself. You do not know yourself; you have never met yourself. You know many things in the objective world, but you do not know the subject. Your state of mind is as if you had gone to see a film. On the screen the film is running, and you have become so absorbed in it that the only thing you know is the film, the story, whatsoever is appearing on the screen. Then if someone asks you who you are, you cannot say anything.

Dreaming is just the film—*just* the film! It is the mind reflecting the world. In the mirror of the mind the world is reflected; that is what dreaming is. And you are so deeply involved in it, so much identified with it, that you have completely forgotten who you are. This is what being asleep means: the dreamer is lost in the dreaming. You see everything except yourself, you feel everything except yourself, you know everything except yourself. This self-ignorance is the sleep. Unless dreaming ceases completely, you cannot awaken unto yourself.

You might have felt it sometimes while looking at a film for three hours, and suddenly the film stops and you come back to yourself. You remember that three hours have passed, you remember that it was just a film. You feel your tears…you have been weeping because the film was a tragedy to you, or you were laughing, or you were doing something else, and now you laugh about yourself. What nonsense you were doing! It was just a film, just a story. There was nothing on the screen—just a play of light and shadow, just an electrical play. Now you laugh: you have come back to yourself. But where were you for these three hours?

You were not at your center. You had moved completely to the periphery. There, where the film was moving, you had gone. You were not at your center, you were not with yourself. You were somewhere else.

This happens in dreaming; this is what our life is. The film is only for three hours, but this dreaming is running for lives and lives and lives. Even if suddenly the dreaming stops you will not be able to recognize who you are. Suddenly you will feel very faint, even afraid. You will try to move again into the film because that is known. You are acquainted with it, you are well adjusted to it.

For when the stopping of the dreaming happens there is a path, particularly in Zen, which is known as the path of sudden enlightenment. There are techniques in these one hundred and twelve methods, there are many techniques which can give you sudden awakening. But it can be too much, and you may not be capable of bearing it. You may just explode. You may die even, because you have lived with dreaming so long that you have no memory of who you are if there is no dreaming.

If this whole world should suddenly disappear and you alone are left, it would be such a great shock that you would die. The same would happen if suddenly all dreaming disappeared from the consciousness. Your world will disappear, because your world was your dreaming.

We are not really in the world. Rather, "the

world" consists not of things outside us, but of our dreams. So everyone lives in his own dream world.

Remember, it is not one world that we go on talking about. Geographically it is, but psychologically there are as many worlds as there are minds. Each mind is a world of its own. And if your dreaming disappears, your world disappears. Without dreams it is difficult for you to live. That is why sudden methods are not used generally, only gradual methods are used.

It is good to note this: gradual methods are used not because there is any need of gradual processes. You can suddenly jump into realization this very moment. There is no barrier; there has never been any barrier. You are already that realization, you can jump this very moment. But that may prove dangerous, fatal. You may not be capable of bearing it. It is going to be too much for you.

You are attuned only to false dreams. Reality you cannot face, you cannot encounter it. You are a hothouse plant—you live in your dreams. They help you in many ways. They are not just dreams, for you they are the reality.

Gradual methods are used not because realization needs time. Realization needs no time! Realization needs no time at all. Realization is not something to be attained in the future, but with gradual methods you will attain it in the future. So what are the gradual methods doing? They are not really helping you to "realize realization," they are helping you to bear it. They are making you capable, strong, so that when the happening happens you can bear it.

There are seven methods through which immediately you can force your way into enlightenment. But you will not be capable of bearing it. You may go blind—too much of light. Or you may suddenly die—too much of bliss.

This dreaming, this deep sleep we are in, how can it be transcended? This question is meaningful in transcending it: *Will you please explain to us what are some of the other factors which can make one conscious while dreaming?* I will talk about

two methods more. One we discussed yesterday. Today, two more that are even easier.

One is to start acting, behaving as if the whole world is just a dream. Whatsoever you are doing, remember this is a dream. While eating, remember this is a dream. While walking, remember this is a dream. Let your mind continuously remember while you are awake that everything is a dream. This is the reason for calling the world *maya*, illusion, dream.

This is not a philosophical argument. Unfortunately, when Shankara was translated into English, German and French, into Western languages, he was understood to be just a philosopher. That has created much misunderstanding. In the West there are philosophers—for example, Berkeley—who say that the world is just a dream, a projection of the mind. But this is a philosophical theory. Berkeley proposes it as a hypothesis.

When Shankara says that the world is a dream it is not philosophical, not a theory. Shankara proposes it as a help, as a support for a particular meditation. And this is the meditation: if you want to remember while dreaming that this is a dream, you will have to start while you are awake. Normally, while you are dreaming you cannot remember that this is a dream; you think that this is a reality.

Why do you think that this is a reality? Because the whole day you are thinking everything is a reality. That has become the attitude, a fixed attitude. While awake you were taking a bath—it was real. While awake you were eating—it was real. While awake you were talking with a friend—it was real. For the whole day, the whole life, whatsoever you are thinking, your attitude is that this is real. This becomes fixed. This becomes a fixed attitude in the mind.

So while you are dreaming in the night, the same attitude goes on working, that this is real. So let us first analyze. There must be some similarity between dreaming and reality; otherwise this attitude would be somewhat difficult.

I am seeing you. Then I close my eyes and I go

into a dream, and I see you in my dream. In both seeings there is no difference. While I am actually seeing you, what am I doing? Your picture is reflected in my eyes. I am not seeing *you*. Your picture is mirrored in my eyes, and then that picture is transformed through mysterious processes—and science is still not in a position to say how. That picture is transformed chemically and carried somewhere inside the head, but science is still not able to say where—where exactly this thing happens. It is not happening in the eyes; the eyes are just windows. I am not seeing you with the eyes, I am seeing you *through* the eyes.

In the eyes you are reflected. You may be just a picture; you may be a reality, you may be a dream. Remember, dreams are three-dimensional. I can recognize a picture because a picture is two-dimensional. Dreams are three-dimensional, so they look exactly like you. And the eyes cannot say whether whatsoever is seen is real or unreal. There is no way to judge; the eyes are not the judge.

Then the picture is transformed into chemical messages. Those chemical messages are like electrical waves; they go somewhere in the head. It is still unknown where the point is that the eyes come in contact with the surface of seeing. Just waves reach to me and then they are decoded. Then I again decode them, and in this way I know what is happening.

I am always inside, and you are always outside, and there is no meeting. So whether you are real or just a dream is a problem. Even this very moment, there is no way to judge whether I am dreaming or you are really here. Listening to me, how can you say that really you are listening to me, that you are not dreaming? There is no way. That is why the attitude which you maintain the whole day is carried over into the night. And while you are dreaming you take it as real.

Try the opposite; that is what Shankara means. He says that the whole world is an illusion, he says the whole world is a dreaming—remember this. But we are stupid people. If Shankara says, "This is a dream," then we say, "What is the need to do anything? If this is just a dream, then there is no need to eat. Why go on eating and thinking that this is a dream? Don't eat!" But then remember—when you feel hunger, it is a dream. Or eat, and when you feel that you have eaten too much, remember, this is a dream.

Shankara is not telling you to change the dream, remember, because the effort to change the dream is again falsely based on the belief that it is real; otherwise there is no need to change anything. Shankara is just saying that whatever is the case is a dream.

Remember this: do not do anything to change it, just remember it constantly. Try to remember for three weeks continuously that whatsoever you are doing it is just a dream. In the beginning it is very difficult. You will fall again and again into the old pattern of the mind, you will start thinking that this is a reality. You will have to constantly awaken yourself to remind yourself that "This is a dream." If for three weeks continuously you can maintain this attitude, then in the fourth or fifth week, any night while dreaming you will suddenly remember that "This is a dream."

This is one way to penetrate dreams with consciousness, with awareness. If you can remember in the night while dreaming that this is a dream, then in the day you will not need any effort to remember that this is also a dream. You will know it then.

In the beginning, while you are practicing this, it will be just a make-believe. You start just in faith…"This is a dream." But when you can remember in dreaming that this is a dream, it will become a reality. Then in the day, when you get up you will not feel that you are getting up from sleep, you will feel you are simply getting up from one dreaming to another. Then it will become a reality. And if the whole twenty-four hours becomes dreaming, and you can feel and remember it, you will be standing at your center. Then your consciousness will have become double-arrowed.

You are feeling dreams, and if you are feeling

them as dreams you will start to feel the dreamer—the subject. If you take dreams as real, you cannot feel the subject. If the film has become real, you forget yourself. When the film stops and you know that it was unreal, your reality erupts, breaks out; you can feel yourself. This is one way.

This has been one of the oldest Indian methods. That is why we have insisted on the world being unreal. We do not mean it philosophically; we do not say that this house is unreal so you can pass through the walls. We do not mean that! When we say that this house is unreal, it is a device. This is not an argument against the house.

So Berkeley proposed that the whole world is just a dream. One day, in the morning, he was walking with Dr. Johnson. Dr. Johnson was a hardened realist, so Berkeley said, "Have you heard about my theory? I am working on it. I feel that the whole world is unreal, and it cannot be proved that it is real. And the burden of proving it is on those who say that it is real. I say it is unreal—just like dreams."

Johnson was not a philosopher, but he had a very astute logical mind. They are on the street, just walking in the morning on a lonely street. Johnson then takes one stone in his hand and hits Berkeley's leg. Blood oozes out, and Berkeley screams. Johnson says, "Why are you screaming if the stone is just a dream? Whatsoever you say, you believe in the reality of the stone. What you are saying is one thing, and your behavior is something different and contrary. If your house is just a dream, then to where are you returning? Where are you returning after the morning walk? If your wife is just a dream, you will not meet her again."

Realists have always argued this way, but they cannot argue this way with Shankara because his is not a philosophical theory. It is not saying anything about the reality; it is not proposing anything about the universe. Rather, it is a device to change your mind, to change the basic fixed attitude so that you can look at the world in a different, an altogether different way.

This is a problem, continuously a problem for Indian thought—because for Indian thought everything is just a device for meditation. We are not concerned about its being true or untrue. We are concerned about its utility in transforming man.

This is emphatically different from the Western mind. When they propose a theory they are concerned with whether this is true or untrue, whether this can be proved logically or not. When we propose anything we are not concerned about its truth; we are concerned about its utility, we are concerned about its capacity, its capability to transform the human mind. It may be true, it may not be true. Really, it is neither—it is simply a device.

I have seen flowers outside. In the morning the sun rises and everything is just beautiful. You have never been outside, and you have never seen flowers, and you have never seen the morning sun. You have never seen the open sky; you do not know what beauty is. You have lived in a closed prison. I want to lead you out. I want you to come out under the open sky to meet these flowers. How am I to do it?

You do not know flowers. If I talk about flowers, you think, "He has gone mad. There are no flowers." If I talk about the morning sun, you think, "He is a visionary. He sees visions and dreams. He is a poet." If I talk about the open sky, you will laugh. You will start laughing, "Where is the open sky? There are only walls and walls and walls."

So what am I to do? I must devise something which you can understand and which helps you to go out, so I say that the house is on fire and I start running. It becomes infectious: you run after me and go out. Then you will know that what I said was neither true nor false. It was just a device. Then you will know flowers and then you can forgive me.

Buddha was doing that, Mahavira was doing that, Shiva was doing that, Shankara was doing that. We can forgive them later on. We have always forgiven them because once we go out we know what they were doing. And then we understand that it was useless to argue with them because it was not a question of arguing. The fire was nowhere, but we could not understand only that language. Flowers were, but we could not understand the language of the flowers, those symbols were meaningless for us.

So this is one way. Then there is a second method at the other pole. This method makes one pole; the other method makes another pole of the same thing. One method is to start feeling, remembering, that everything is a dream. The other is not to think anything about the world, but just to go on remembering that *you are*.

Gurdjieff used this second method. This second method comes from the Sufi tradition, from Islam. They worked on it very deeply. Remember "I am" —whatsoever you are doing. You are drinking water, you are eating your food—remember, "I am." Go on eating and go on remembering, "I am, I am." Do not forget it! It is difficult because you already think that you know you are, so what is the need to go on remembering this? You never remember it, but it is a very, very potent technique.

When walking remember, "I am." Let the walking be there, go on walking, but be constantly fixed in this self-remembering of "I am, I am, I am." Do not forget this. You are listening to me—just do it here. You are listening to me. Do not be so much merged, involved, identified. Whatsoever I am saying, remember, go on remembering. Listening is there, words are there, someone is talking, you are —"I am, I am, I am." Let this "I am" be a constant factor of awareness.

It is very difficult. You cannot remember continuously even for a single minute. Try it. Put your watch before your eyes and look at the hands moving. One second, two seconds, three seconds... go on looking at it. Do two things: look at the movement of the hand which is showing seconds, and continuously remember "I am, I am." With every second go on remembering "I am." Within five or six seconds you will feel that you have forgotten.

Suddenly you will remember that "Many seconds have passed and I have not remembered 'I am.'"

Even to remember for one complete minute is a miracle. And if you can remember for one minute, the technique is for you. Then do it. Through it you will be capable of going beyond dreams and of knowing that dreams are dreams.

How does it work? If the whole day you can remember "I am," then this will penetrate your sleep also. And when you will be dreaming, continuously you will remember, "I am." If you can remember "I am" in the dream, suddenly the dream becomes just a dream. Then the dream cannot deceive you, then the dream cannot be felt as reality. This is the mechanism: the dream is felt as reality because you are missing the self-remembering; you are missing "I am." If there is no remembering of oneself, then the dream becomes reality. If there is the remembering of oneself, then reality, the so-called reality, becomes just a dream.

This is the difference between dreaming and reality. For a meditative mind, or for the science of meditation, this is the only difference. If you are, then the whole reality is just a dream. If you are not, then the dreaming becomes reality.

Nagarjuna says, "Now I am, for the world is not. While I was not, the world was. Only one can exist." That doesn't mean that the world has disappeared. Nagarjuna is not talking about this world, he is talking about the world of dreaming. Either you can be or the dreams can be—both cannot be.

So the first step will be to continue remembering "I am" constantly; simply "I am." Do not say "Rama," do not say "Shyam." Do not use any name, because you are not that. Simply use "I am."

Try it in any activity and then feel it. The more real you become inside, the more unreal becomes the surrounding world. The reality becomes "I," and the world becomes unreal. The world is real or the "I" is real—both cannot be real. You are feeling that you are just a dream now; then the world is real. Change the emphasis. Become real, and the world will become unreal.

Gurdjieff worked on this method continuously. His chief disciple, P. D. Ouspensky, relates that when Gurdjieff was working on him with this method, and he was practicing for three months continuously this remembering of "I am, I am, I am," after three months everything stopped. Thoughts, dreaming, everything stopped. Only one note remained inside like eternal music: "I am, I am, I am, I am." But then this was not an effort. This was a spontaneous activity going on: "I am." Then Gurdjieff called Ouspensky out of the house. For three months he had been kept in the house and wasn't allowed to move out.

Then Gurdjieff said, "Come with me." They were residing in a Russian town, Tiflis. Gurdjieff called him out and they went into the street. Ouspensky writes in his diary, "For the first time I could understand what Jesus meant when he said that man is asleep. The whole city looked to me as if it was asleep. People were moving in their sleep; shopkeepers were selling in their sleep; customers were buying in their sleep. The whole city was asleep. I looked at Gurdjieff: only he was awake. The whole city was asleep. They were angry, they were fighting, they were loving, buying, selling, doing everything."

Ouspensky says, "Now I could see their faces, their eyes: they were asleep. They were not there. The inner center was missing, it was not there." Ouspensky said to Gurdjieff, "I do not want to go there any more. What has happened to the city? Everyone seems asleep, drugged."

Gurdjieff said, "Nothing has happened to the city, something has happened to you. You have been undrugged; the city is the same. It is the same place you moved around in three months ago, but you couldn't see that other people are asleep because you were also asleep. Now you can see because a certain quality of awareness has come to you. With three months of practicing "I am" continuously, you have become aware in a very small measure. You have become aware! A part of your consciousness has gone beyond dreaming.

That is why you can see that everyone is asleep, dead, moving, drugged, as if hypnotized."

Ouspensky says, "I couldn't bear that phenomenon—everyone asleep! Whatsoever they are doing, they are not responsible for it. They are not! How can they be responsible?" He came back and he asked Gurdjieff, "What is this? Am I deceived somehow? Have you done something to me that the whole city seems asleep? I cannot believe my own eyes."

But this will happen to anyone. If you can remember yourself, then you will know that no one is remembering himself, and in this way each goes on moving. The whole world is asleep. But start while you are awake. Any moment that you remember, start "I am."

I do not mean that you have to repeat the words "I am," rather, have the feeling. Taking a bath, feel "I am." Let there be the touch of the cold shower, and let yourself be there behind, feeling it and remembering "I am." Remember, I am not saying that verbally you have to repeat "I am." You can repeat it, but that repetition will not give you awareness. Repetition may even create more sleep. There are many people who are repeating many things. They go on repeating "Rama, Rama, Rama..." and if they are just repeating without awareness then this "Rama, Rama, Rama..." becomes a drug. They can sleep well through it.

That is why Mahesh Yogi has so much appeal in the West, because he is giving mantras for people to repeat. And in the West sleep has become one of the most serious problems. Sleep is totally disturbed. Natural sleep has disappeared. Only through tranquilizers and drugs can you sleep; otherwise sleep has become impossible. This is the reason for Mahesh Yogi's appeal. It is because if you constantly repeat something, that repetition gives you deep sleep; that is all.

So the so-called transcendental meditation is nothing but a psychological tranquilizer. It is nothing—just a tranquilizer. It helps, but it is good for sleep, not for meditation. You can sleep well, a more calm sleep will be there. It is good, but it is not meditation at all. If you repeat a word constantly it creates a certain boredom, and boredom is good for sleep.

So anything monotonous, repetitive can help sleep. The child in the mother's womb sleeps for nine months continuously, and the reason for this you may not know. The reason is only the "tick-tock, tick-tock" of the heart of the mother. Continuously there is the beat, the heartbeat. It is one of the most monotonous things in the world. With the same beat continuously repeating, the child is drugged. He goes on sleeping.

That is why whenever the child is crying, screaming, creating any problem, the mother puts his head near her heart. Then suddenly he feels good and goes into sleep. Again it is due to the heartbeat. He becomes again a part of the womb. That is why even if you are not a child and your wife, your beloved puts your head on her heart, you will feel sleepy from the monotonous beat.

Psychologists suggest that if you cannot sleep, then concentrate on the clock. Just concentrate on the clock's tick-tock, tick-tock. It repeats the heartbeat, and you can fall asleep. Anything repetitive will help.

So this "I am," the remembering of "I am," is not a verbal mantra. It is not going to be repeated verbally—feel it! Be sensitive to your being. When you touch someone's hand do not only touch his hand, feel your touch also, feel yourself also—that you are here in this touch, present totally. While eating, do not only eat, feel yourself eating as well. This feeling, this sensitivity must penetrate deeper and deeper into your mind.

One day, suddenly, you are awake at your center, functioning for the first time. And then the whole world becomes a dream, then you can know that your dreaming is a dreaming. And when you know that your dreaming is a dreaming, dreaming stops. It can continue only if it is felt as real. It is stopped if it is felt as unreal.

And once dreaming stops in you, you are a different man. The old man is dead; the sleepy man is dead. That human being which you were you are no more. For the first time you become aware; for the first time in the whole world that is asleep, you are awake. You become a buddha, an awakened one.

With this awakening there is no misery, after this awakening there is no death, through this awakening there is no more fear. You become for the first time free of everything. To be free of sleep, to be free of dreaming, is to be free of everything. You attain freedom. Hate, anger, greed disappear. You become just love. Not loving, you become just love!

One question more—and it is relatively the same:

If we are all actors in a play that is already written, how can meditation transform us without the play itself containing a chapter for our transformation at a specific time? And if such a chapter is there already waiting to unfold at its due time, why meditate? Why make any effort at all?

This is the same; it contains the same fallacy. I am not saying that everything is determined. I am not proposing this as a theory to explain the universe. It is a device.

India has always been working with this device of fate. It is not meant by this that everything is predetermined. This is not meant at all! The only reason to propose this is that if you take it that everything is determined, everything becomes a dream. If you take things in this way, if you believe this way—that everything is predetermined; that, for example, you are going to die on a particular day—*everything* becomes a dream. It is not determined, it is not fixed! No one is that much interested in you. The universe is completely unaware of you and when you are going to die. It is so useless a thing. Your death is irrelevant to the universe.

Do not think yourself so important that the whole universe is determining your day of death—the time, the minute, the moment—no! You are *not* the center. It makes no difference to the universe whether you are or you are not. But this fallacy goes on working in the mind. It is created in childhood and it becomes part of the unconscious.

A child is born. He cannot give anything to the world, but he has to take many things. He cannot repay, he cannot give back anything. He is so impotent—just helpless. He will need food, he will need love, he will need shelter, he will need warmth. Everything is to be supplied.

A child is born absolutely helpless—particularly man's child. No animal is so helpless. That is why no animal creates a family—there is no need. But man's child is so helpless, so absolutely helpless, he cannot exist without there being a mother to protect, a father, a family, a society. He cannot exist alone. He would die immediately.

He is so much dependent. He will need love, he will need food, he will need everything, and he will demand everything. And the mother will supply, the father will supply, the family will supply. The child begins to think that he is the center of the whole world. Everything is to be supplied to him; he has but to demand. Just to demand is enough, no other effort is needed.

So the child begins to think of himself as the center, and everything just goes on around him, for him. The whole existence seems to be created for him. The whole existence was waiting for him to come and demand, and everything will be fulfilled. This is a necessity, that his demands should be fulfilled; otherwise he will die. But this necessity becomes very dangerous.

He grows up with this attitude that "I am the center." By and by he will demand more. A child's demands are very simple, they can be supplied. But as he will grow his demands will become more and more complex. Sometimes it will not be possible to supply them, to fulfill them. Sometimes it may be absolutely impossible. He may demand the moon, or anything....

The more he will grow, the more the demands will become complex, impossible. Then frustration sets in, and the child begins to think that now he is being deceived. He has taken it for granted that he was the center of the world. Now problems will be there, and by and by he will be dethroned. When he becomes an adult, he will be completely dethroned. Then he will know that he is not the center. But deep down the unconscious mind goes on thinking in terms of him being the center.

People come and ask me whether their fate is determined. They are asking whether they are so important, so significant for this universe that their fate must be determined beforehand. "What is my purpose?" they ask. "Why was I created?" This childhood nonsense that you are the center creates these questions like, "For what purpose am I created?"

You are not created for any purpose. And it is good that you are not created for any purpose; otherwise you would be a machine. A machine is created for some purpose. Man is not created for some purpose, for something—no! Man is just the outflowing, overflowing creation. Everything simply is. Flowers are there and stars are there and you are there. Everything is just an overflowing, a joy, a celebration of existence without any purpose.

But this theory of fate, of predetermination, is what creates problems, because we take it as a theory. We think that everything is determined, but nothing is determined. However, this technique uses this as a device. When we say everything is determined, this is not said to you as a theory. The purpose is this: that if you take life as a drama, predetermined, then it becomes a dream. For example, if I knew that this day, this night, I was going to talk to you, and it is predetermined what words I should speak on this day, and if it is so fixed that nothing can be changed—that I cannot utter a single new word—then suddenly I am not related at all with this whole process because then I am not the source of action.

If everything is determined and if every word is to be spoken by the universe itself or by the divine or by whatsoever name you choose, then I am no more the source of it. Then I can become an observer—a simple observer.

If you take life as predetermined then you can observe it, then you are not involved. If you are a failure, it was predetermined; if you are a success, it was predetermined. If both are predetermined, both become of equal value—synonymous. Then one is Ravana, one is Rama, and everything is predetermined. Ravana need not feel guilty, Rama need not feel superior. Everything is predetermined, so you are just actors, you are just on a stage playing a role.

To give you the feeling that you are playing a role, to give you the feeling that this is only a predetermined pattern that you are fulfilling, to give you this feeling so that you can transcend it, this is the device. It is very difficult because we are so much accustomed to thinking of fate as a theory—not only as a theory, but as a law. We cannot understand this attitude of taking these laws and theories as devices.

I will explain this to you. One example will be helpful. I was in a city. One man came; he was a Mohammedan, but I didn't know, I was not aware. And he was dressed so that he looked like a Hindu. He not only looked like a Hindu, but he talked as if he was of the Hindu type. He was not a Mohammedan type.

He asked me one question. He said, "Mohammedans and Christians say that there is only one life. Hindus, Buddhists and Jains say there are many lives—a long sequence of lives, so that unless one is liberated one goes on and on being reborn again and again. So what do you say? If Jesus was an enlightened man, he must have known. Or Mohammed, or Moses, they must have known too, if they were enlightened men, that there are many lives and not just one. And if you say that they are right, then what about Mahavira, Krishna, Buddha and Shankara? One thing is certain, that they cannot all be enlightened.

"If Christianity is right then Buddha is wrong, then Krishna is wrong, then Mahavira is wrong. And if Mahavira, Krishna and Buddha are right, then Mohammed, Jesus and Moses are wrong. So tell me. I am very much puzzled; I am in a mess, confused. And both cannot be right. How can both be right? Either there are many lives or there is one. How can both be right?" He was a very intelligent man, and he had studied many things, so he said, "You cannot just escape and say that both are right. Both cannot be right. It is logically so—both cannot be right."

But I said, "This need not be; your approach is absolutely wrong. Both are devices. Neither is right, neither is wrong—both are devices." It became impossible for him to understand what I meant by a device.

Mohammed, Jesus and Moses, they were talking to one type of mind, and Buddha, Mahavira, Krishna, they were talking to a very different type of mind. There are really two source religions—the Hindu and the Jewish. So all the religions born out of India, all the religions born out of Hinduism, believe in rebirth, in many births; and all the religions born out of Jewish thinking—Mohammedanism, Christianity—believe in one life. These are two devices.

Try to understand it. Because our minds are fixed, we take things as theories, not as devices. So many times people come to me and say, "One day you said this is right, and another day you said that is right, and both cannot be right." Of course both cannot be right, but no one is saying that both are right. I am not concerned at all with which is right and which is wrong. I am only concerned with which device works.

In India they use this device of many lives. Why? There are many points. All the religions born in the West, particularly out of Jewish thinking, were religions of poor people. Their prophets were uneducated. Jesus was not educated, Mohammed was not educated, Moses was not. They were all uneducated, unsophisticated, simple, and they were talking with masses who were not sophisticated at all, who were poor, they were not rich.

For a poor man, one life is more than enough, more than enough! He is starving, dying. If you say to him that there are so many lives, that he will go on being reborn and reborn, that he will move in a wheel of a thousand and one lives, the poor man will just feel frustrated about the whole thing. "What are you saying?" a poor man will ask. "One life is too much, so do not talk of a thousand and one lives, of a million lives. Do not speak this. Give us heaven immediately after this life." God becomes a reality only if he can be achieved after this life—immediately.

Buddha, Mahavira and Krishna were talking to a very rich society. Today it has become difficult to understand because the whole wheel has turned. Now the West is rich and the East is poor. Then the West was poor and the East was rich. All the Hindu *avataras,* all the *tirthankaras*—world teachers—of the Jains, all the buddhas—awakened ones—they were all princes. They belonged to royal families. They were cultured, educated, sophisticated, refined in every way. You cannot refine Buddha more. He was absolutely refined, cultured, educated; nothing can be added. Even if Buddha comes today, nothing can be added.

So they were talking to a society which was rich. Remember, for a rich society there are different problems. For a rich society, pleasure is meaningless, heaven is meaningless. For a poor society, heaven is very meaningful. If the society is living in heaven, heaven becomes meaningless, so you cannot propose this. You cannot create an urge to do something for heaven; they are already in it—and bored.

So Buddha, Mahavira and Krishna do not talk about heaven, they talk of freedom. They do not talk of a pleasant world beyond, they talk of a transcendental world where there is neither pain nor pleasure. Jesus' heaven would not have appealed to them—they were already in it.

And secondly, for a rich man the real problem is boredom. For a poor man, promise him pleasure in the future. For a poor man, suffering is the problem. For a rich man, suffering is not the problem; for a rich man, boredom is the problem. He is bored of all pleasures.

Mahavira, Buddha and Krishna, all used this boredom, and they said, "If you do not do anything you are going to be born again and again. This wheel will move. Remember, the same life will be repeated. The same sex, the same richness, the same food, the same palaces again and again: a thousand and one times you will be moving in a wheel."

To a rich man who has known all pleasures this is not a good prospect, this repetition. Repetition is the problem. That is the suffering for him. He wants something new, and Mahavira and Buddha say, "There is nothing new. This world is old. Nothing is new under the heavens, everything is just old. You have tasted all these things before and you will go on tasting them. You are in a wheel, moving. Go beyond it, take a jump out of the wheel."

For a rich man, if you create a device which intensifies his feeling of boredom, only then can he move toward meditation. For a poor man, if you talk about boredom you are saying meaningless things. A poor man is never bored—never! Only a rich man is bored. A poor man is never bored; he is always thinking of the future. Something is going to happen and everything will be okay. The poor man needs a promise, but if the promise is a very long way away it becomes meaningless. It must be immediate.

Jesus is reported to have said that "In my lifetime, in your lifetime, you will see the kingdom of God." That statement has haunted the whole of Christianity for twenty centuries, because Jesus said, "In *your* life, immediately, you are going to see the kingdom of God." And the kingdom of God has not come even yet, so what did he mean? And he said, "The world is going to end soon, so do not waste time! Time is short." Jesus said, "Time is very short. It is foolish to waste it. Immediately the world is going to end and you will have to answer for yourself, so repent."

Jesus created a feeling of immediacy through the concept of one life. He knew, and Buddha and Mahavira also knew. Whatsoever they knew is not told. Whatsoever they devised is known. This was a device to create immediacy, urgency, so that you would begin to act.

India was an old country, rich. There was no question of urgency in promises for the future. There was only one way possible to create urgency, and that was to create more boredom. If a man feels he is going to be born again and again, again and again, infinitely, ad infinitum, he immediately comes and asks, "How to be freed from this wheel? This is too much. Now I cannot continue it anymore because whatsoever can be known I have known. If this is to be repeated it is a nightmare. I do not want to repeat it, I want something new."

So Buddha and Mahavira say, "There is nothing new under the sky. Everything is old and a repetition. And you have repeated for many, many lives, and you will go on repeating for many, many lives. Beware of the repetition, beware of your boredom. Take a jump."

The device is different, but the purpose is the same. Take a jump! Move! Transform yourself! Whatsoever you are, transform yourself from it.

If we take religious statements as devices then there is no contradiction. Then Jesus and Krishna, Mohammed and Mahavira, mean the same thing. They create different routes for different people, different techniques for different minds, different appeals for different attitudes. But those are not principles to be fought and argued about. They are devices to be used, transcended, and thrown.

This much for today.

CHAPTER 7

Techniques to put you at ease

◆

10 *While being caressed, Sweet Princess, enter the caress as everlasting life.*

11 *Stop the doors of the senses when feeling the creeping of an ant. Then.*

12 *When on a bed or a seat, let yourself become weightless, beyond mind.*

M an has a center, but he lives off of it—off the center. That creates an inner tension, a constant turmoil, anguish. You are not where you should be; you are not at your right balance. You are off balance, and this being off balance, off center, is the base of all mental tensions. If it becomes too much, you go mad. A madman is one who has gone out of himself completely. The enlightened man is just the reverse of the madman. He is centered in himself.

You are in between. You have not gone completely out of yourself, and you are not at your center either. You just move in the gap. Sometimes you move very, very far away, so you have moments when you are temporarily mad. In anger, in sex, in anything in which you have moved too far away from yourself, you are temporarily mad. Then there is no difference between you and the madman. The difference is only that he is permanently there and you are temporarily there. You will come back.

When you are in anger it is madness, but it is not permanent. Qualitatively there is no difference; quantitatively there is a difference. The quality is the same, so sometimes you touch madness and sometimes, when you are relaxed, totally at ease, you touch your center also. Those are the blissful moments. They happen. Then you are just like a Buddha or like a Krishna, but only temporarily, momentarily. You will not stay there. Really, the moment you realize that you are blissful you have

moved. It is so momentary that by the time you have recognized the bliss it is finished.

We go on moving between these two, but this movement is dangerous. This movement is dangerous because then you cannot create a self-image, a fixed self-image. You do not know who you are. If you constantly move from madness to being centered in yourself, if this movement is constant, you cannot have a solid image of yourself. You will have a liquid image. Then you do not know who you are. It is very difficult. That is why you even become afraid if you are expecting blissful moments, so you try to fix yourself somewhere in between.

This is what we mean by a normal human being: he never touches his madness in anger and he never touches that total freedom, that ecstasy, either. He never moves from a solid image. The normal man is really a dead man, living between these two points. That is why all those who are exceptional—great artists, painters, poets—they are not normal. They are very liquid. Sometimes they touch the center, sometimes they go mad. They move fast between these two. Of course, their anguish is great, their tension is much. They have to live between two worlds, constantly changing themselves. That is why they feel that they have no identity. They feel, in the words of Colin Wilson, that they are outsiders. In your world of normality, they are outsiders.

It will be helpful to define these four types. First is the normal man who has a fixed, solid identity, who knows who he is—a doctor, an engineer, a professor, a saint—who knows who he is and never moves from there. He constantly clings to the identity, to the image.

Second are those who have liquid images—poets, artists, painters, singers. They do not know who they are. Sometimes they become just normal, sometimes they go mad, sometimes they touch the ecstasy that a buddha touches.

Third are those who are permanently mad. They have gone outside themselves; they never come back into their home. They do not even remember that they have a home.

And fourth are those who have reached their home...Buddha, Christ, Krishna.

This fourth category—those who have reached their home—is totally relaxed. In their consciousness there is no tension, no effort, no desire. In one word, there is no becoming. They do not want to become anything. They are, they have been. No becoming! And they are at ease with their being. Whatsoever they are, they are at ease with it. They do not want to change it, do not want to go anywhere. They have no future. This very moment is eternity for them...no longing, no desire. That does not mean that a buddha will not eat or a buddha will not sleep. He will eat, he will sleep, but these are not desires. A buddha will not project these desires: he will not eat tomorrow, he will eat today.

Remember this. You go on eating in the tomorrow, you go on eating in the future; you go on eating in the past, in the yesterday. It rarely happens that you eat today. While you are eating today, your mind will be moving somewhere else. While you will be trying to go to sleep, you will start eating tomorrow, or else the memory of the past will come.

A buddha eats today. This very moment he lives. He does not project his life into the future; there is no future for him. Whenever future comes, it comes as the present. It is always today, it is always now. So a buddha eats, but he never eats in the mind—remember this. There is no cerebral

eating. You go on eating in the mind. It is absurd because the mind is not meant for eating. All your centers are confused; your entire body-mind arrangement is mixed up, it is mad.

A buddha eats, but he never thinks of eating. And that applies to everything. So a buddha is as ordinary as you while he is eating. Do not think that a buddha is not going to eat, or that when the hot sun is there he is not going to perspire, or when cold winds come he will not feel cold. He will feel it, but he will feel always in the present, never in the future. There is no becoming. If there is no becoming there is no tension. Understand this very clearly. If there is no becoming, how can there be any tension? Tension means you want to be something else which you are not.

You are A and you want to be B; you are poor and you want to be a rich man; you are ugly and you want to be beautiful; or you are stupid and you want to be a wise man. Whatsoever the wanting, whatsoever the desire, the form is always this: A wants to become B. Whatsoever you are, you are not content with it. For contentment something else is needed—that is the constant structure of a mind that is desiring. When you get it, again the mind will say that "This is not enough, something else is needed."

The mind always moves on and on. Whatsoever you get becomes useless. The moment you get it, it is useless. This is desire. Buddha has called it *trishna*: this is becoming.

You move from one life to another, from one world to another, and this goes on. It can continue ad infinitum. There is no end to it, there is no end to desire, desiring. But if there is no becoming, if you accept totally whatsoever you are—ugly or beautiful, wise or stupid, rich or poor—whatsoever you are, if you accept it in its totality, becoming ceases. Then there is no tension; then the tension cannot exist. Then there is no anguish. You are at ease, you are not worried. This nonbecoming mind is a mind that is centered in the self.

On quite the opposite pole is the madman. He

has no being, he is only a becoming. He has forgotten what he is. The A is forgotten completely and he is trying to be B. He no longer knows who he is; he only knows his desired goal. He doesn't live here and now, he lives somewhere else. That is why he looks crazy to us, mad, because you live in this world and he lives in the world of his dreams. He is not part of your world, he is living somewhere else. He has completely forgotten his reality here and now. And with himself he has forgotten the world around him, which is real. He lives in an unreal world—for him, that is the only reality.

A buddha lives this very moment in the being and the madman is just the opposite. He never lives in the here and now, in the being, but always in the becoming—somewhere on the horizon. These are the two polar opposites.

So remember, the madman is not against you, he is against the buddha. And remember also, the buddha is not against you, he is against the madman. You are in between. You are both, mixed; you have madnesses, you have moments of enlightenment, but both are mixed.

Sometimes a glimpse into the center suddenly happens, if you are relaxed. There are moments when you are relaxed. You are in love: for a few moments, for a single moment, your lover, your beloved is with you. It has been a long desire, a long effort, and at last your beloved is with you. For a moment the mind goes off. There has been a long effort to be with the beloved. The mind has been hankering and hankering and hankering, and the mind has always been thinking, thinking about the beloved. Now the beloved is there and suddenly the mind cannot think. The old process cannot be continued. You were asking for the beloved; now the beloved is there, so the mind simply stops.

In that moment when the beloved is there, there is no desire. You are relaxed; suddenly you are thrown back to yourself. Unless a lover can throw you to yourself it is not love. Unless you become yourself in the presence of the beloved, it is not love. Unless mind completely ceases to function in the presence of the lover or the beloved, it is not love.

Sometimes it happens that mind ceases and for a moment there is no desire. Love is desireless. Try to understand this: you may desire love, but love is desireless. When love happens there is no desire; mind is quiet, calm, relaxed. No more becoming, nowhere to go.

But this happens only for a few moments, if it happens at all. If you have really loved someone, then it will happen for a few moments. It is a shock. The mind cannot work because its whole function has become useless, absurd. The one for whom you were longing is there, and the mind cannot think what to do now.

For a few moments the whole mechanism stops. You are relaxed in yourself. You have touched your being, your center, and you feel you are at the source of well-being. A bliss fills you, a fragrance surrounds you. Suddenly you are not the same man you were.

That is why love transforms so much. If you are in love you cannot hide it. That is impossible! If you are in love, it will show. Your eyes, your face, the way you walk, the way you sit, everything will show it, because you are not the same man. The desiring mind is not there. You are like a buddha just for a few moments. This cannot be continued for long because it is just a shock. Immediately the mind will try to find some ways and excuses to think again.

For example, the mind may start thinking you have attained your goal, you have attained your love, so now what? What are you going to do? Then the prophesying starts, the arguments start. You begin thinking, "Today I have reached my beloved, but will it be the same tomorrow also?" The mind has started working. And the moment mind is working you have moved again into becoming.

Sometimes even without love, just through fatigue, tiredness, one stops desiring. Then too one is thrown to oneself. When you are not away from yourself you are bound to be at your self, no matter what may be the cause of it. When one is tired totally, fatigued, when one does not even feel like thinking or desiring, when one is frustrated completely, without any hope, then suddenly one feels at home. Now he cannot go anywhere. All the doors are closed; hope has disappeared—and with it desire, with it becoming.

It will not be for long because your mind has a mechanism. It can go off for a few moments, but suddenly it will come alive again because you cannot exist hopelessly, you will have to find some hope. You cannot exist without desire. Because you do not know how to exist without desire, you will have to create some desire.

In any situation where it happens that suddenly the mind ceases functioning, you are at your center. You are on a holiday, in a forest or at a hill station, or on a beach: suddenly your routine mind will not work. The office is not there, the wife is not there, or the husband is not there. Suddenly there is a very new situation, and the mind will need some time to function in it, to be adjusted to it. The mind feels unadjusted. The situation is so new that you relax, and you are at your center.

In these moments you become a buddha, but these will only be moments. Then they will haunt you, and then you would like to reproduce them again and again and repeat them. But remember, they happened spontaneously, so you cannot repeat them. And the more you try to repeat them, the more it will be impossible for them to come to you.

That is happening to everyone. You loved someone, and in the first meeting your mind ceased for a few moments. Then you got married. Why did you get married? To repeat those beautiful moments again and again. But when they happened you were not married, and they cannot happen in marriage because the whole situation is different. When two people meet for the first time, the whole situation is new. Their minds cannot function in it. They are so overwhelmed by it—so filled by the new experience, by the new life, the new flowering! Then the mind starts functioning and they think, "This is such a beautiful moment! I want to go on repeating it every day, so I should get married."

Mind will destroy everything. Marriage means mind. Love is spontaneous; marriage is calculating. Getting married is a mathematical thing. Then you wait for those moments, but they will never come again. That is why every married man and woman is frustrated—because they are waiting for certain things that happened in the past. Why are they not happening again? They cannot happen because you are missing the whole situation. Now you are not new; now there is no spontaneity; now love is a routine. Now everything is expected and demanded. Now love has become a duty, not a fun. It was fun in the beginning; now it is a duty. And duty cannot give you the same bliss that fun can give. It is impossible! Your mind has created the whole thing. Now you go on expecting, and the more you expect the less is the possibility of its happening.

This happens everywhere, not only in marriage. You go to a master and the experience is new. His presence, his words, his way of life are new. Suddenly your mind stops functioning. Then you think, "This is the man for me, so I must go every day." Then you get married to him. By and by frustration sets in because you have made it a duty, a routine. Now those same experiences will not be coming. Then you think this man has deceived you or that you were fooled somehow. Then you think, "The first experience was hallucinatory. I must have been hypnotized or something. It was not real."

It was real. Your routine mind makes it unreal. And then the mind tries to expect, but the first time it happened you were not expecting. You had come without any expectations, you were just open to receive whatsoever was happening.

Now you come every day with expectations, with a closed mind. It cannot happen. It always happens in an open mind; it always happens in a new situation. That doesn't mean that you have to change your situation daily, it only means: do not allow your mind to create a pattern. Then your wife will be new every day, your husband will be new every day. But do not allow the mind to create a pattern of expectations; do not allow the mind to move in the future. Then your master will be every day new, your friend will be every day new. And everything is new in the world except the mind. Mind is the only thing which is old. It is always old.

The sun is rising anew every day. It is not the old sun. The moon is new; the day, the night, the flowers, the trees…everything is new except your mind. Your mind is always old—remember, always —because mind needs the past, the accumulated experience, the projected experience. Mind needs the past and life needs the present. Life is always blissful—mind never is. Whenever you allow your mind to come in, misery sets in.

These spontaneous moments will not be repeated again, so what to do? How to be in a relaxed state continuously? These three sutras are for this. These are three techniques concerning the feeling of ease, techniques to relax the nerves.

How to remain in the being? How not to move into the becoming? It is difficult, arduous, but these techniques can help. These techniques will throw you upon yourself.

10 Become the caress.

The first relaxation technique: *While being caressed, Sweet Princess, enter the caress as everlasting life.*

Shiva starts with love. The first technique is concerned with love, because love is the nearest thing in your experience in which you are relaxed. If you cannot love, it is impossible for you to relax. If you can relax, your life will become a loving life.

A tense man cannot love. Why? A tense man always lives with purposes. He can earn money, but he cannot love because love is purposeless. Love is not a commodity. You cannot accumulate it; you cannot make a bank balance of it; you cannot

strengthen your ego out of it. Really, love is the most absurd act, with no meaning beyond it, no purpose beyond it. It exists in itself, not for anything else.

You earn money *for* something—it is a means. You build a house for someone to live in—it is a means. Love is not a means. Why do you love? For what do you love? Love is the end in itself. That is why a mind that is calculative, logical, a mind that thinks in terms of purpose, cannot love. And the mind that always thinks in terms of purpose will be tense, because purpose can only be fulfilled in the future, never here and now.

You are building a house—you cannot live in it just now, you will have to build it first. You can live in it in the future, not now. You earn money—the bank balance will be created in the future, not now. Means you will have to use now, and ends will come in the future.

Love is always here; there is no future to it. That is why love is so near to meditation. That is why death is also so near to meditation—because death is also always here and now, it can never happen in the future. Can you die in the future? You can die only in the present. No one has ever died in the future. How can you die in the future? Or how can you die in the past? The past has gone, it is no more, so you cannot die in it. The future has not yet come, so how can you die in it?

Death always occurs in the present. Death, love, meditation—they all occur in the present. So if you are afraid of death, you cannot love. If you are afraid of love, you cannot meditate. If you are afraid of meditation, your life will be useless. Useless not in the sense of any purpose, but useless in the sense that you will never be able to feel any bliss in it. It will be futile.

It may seem strange to connect these three: love, meditation, death. It is not! They are similar experiences. So if you can enter in one, you can enter in the remaining two.

Shiva starts with love. He says, *While being caressed, Sweet Princess, enter the caress as ever-*

lasting life. What does it mean? Many things! One: while you are being loved the past has ceased, the future is not. You move in the dimension of the present. You move in *the now.* Have you ever loved someone? If you have ever loved, then you know that the mind is no longer there.

That is why the so-called wise men say that lovers are blind, mindless, mad. In essence what they say is right. Lovers *are* blind because they have no eyes for the future, to calculate what they are going to do. They are blind; they cannot see the past. What has happened to lovers? They just move here and now without any consideration of past or future, without any consideration of consequences. That is why they are called blind. They are! They are blind for those who are calculating, and they are seers for those who are not calculating. Those who are not calculating will see love as the real eye, the real vision.

So the first thing: in the moment of love, past and future are no more. Then, one delicate point is to be understood. When there is no past and no future, can you call this moment the present? It is the present only between the two—between the past and the future. It is relative. If there is no past and no future, what does it mean to call it the present? It is meaningless. That is why Shiva doesn't use the word "present."He says, *everlasting life.* He means eternity...enter eternity.

We divide time into three parts—past, present, future. That division is false, absolutely false. Time is really past and future. The present is not part of time. The present is part of eternity. That which has passed is time; that which is to come is time. That which is, is not time because it never passes—it is always here. The now is always here. It is *always* here! This now is eternal.

If you move from the past, you never move into the present. From the past you always move into the future; there comes no moment which is present. From the past you always move into the future. From the present you can never move into the future. From the present you go deeper and deeper, into more present and more present. This is everlasting life.

We may say it in this way: from past to future is time. Time means you move on a plane, on a straight line. Or we may call it horizontal. The moment you are in the present the dimension changes: you move vertically—up or down, toward the height or toward the depth. But then you never move horizontally. A Buddha, a Shiva, live in eternity, not in time.

Jesus was asked, "What will happen in your kingdom of God?" The man who asked him was not asking about time. He was asking about what is going to happen to his desires, about how they will be fulfilled. He was asking whether there will be life everlasting or whether there be death; whether there be any misery, whether there will be inferior and superior men. He was asking things of this world when he asked, "What is going to happen in your kingdom of God?"

And Jesus replied—the reply is like that of a Zen monk—"There shall be time no longer."

The man who was replied to in this way may not have understood at all: "There shall be time no longer." Only this one thing Jesus said—"There shall be time no longer," because time is horizontal and the kingdom of God is vertical...it is eternal. It is always here! You have only to move away from time to enter into it.

So love is the first door. Through it, you can move away from time. That is why everyone wants to be loved, everyone wants to love. And no one knows why so much significance is given to love, why there is such a deep longing for love. And unless you know it rightly, you can neither love nor be loved, because love is one of the deepest phenomena upon this earth.

We go on thinking that everyone is capable of love as he is. This is not the case—it is not so. That is why you are frustrated. Love is a different dimension, and if you try to love someone in time you will be defeated in your effort. In time, love is not possible.

I remember one anecdote. Meera was in love

with Krishna. She was a housewife—the wife of a prince. The prince became jealous of Krishna. Krishna was no more; Krishna was not present, Krishna was not a physical body. There was a gap of five thousand years between Krishna's physical existence and Meera's physical existence. So really, how can Meera be in love with Krishna? The time gap was so great.

One day the prince, her husband, asked Meera, "You go on talking about your love, you go on dancing and singing around Krishna, but where is he? With whom are you so much in love? With whom are you talking continuously?" Meera was talking with Krishna, singing, laughing, fighting. She looked mad—she was, in our eyes. The prince said, "Have you gone mad? Where is your Krishna? Whom are you loving? With whom are you conversing? I am here, and you have completely forgotten me."

Meera said, "Krishna is here—you are not here —because Krishna is eternal; you are not. He will always be here, he was always here, he is here. You will not be here; you were not here. You were not here one day, you will not be here another day, so how can I believe that between these two nonexistences you are here? How is an existence possible between two nonexistences?"

The prince is in time, but Krishna is in eternity. So you can be near the prince, but the distance cannot be destroyed. You will be distant. You may be very, very distant in time from Krishna, but you can be near. It is a different dimension, however.

I look in front of me and there is a wall; I move my eyes and there is a sky. When you look in time there is always a wall. When you look beyond time there is the open sky…infinite. Love opens the infinity, the everlastingness of existence.

So really, if you have ever loved, love can be made a technique of meditation. This is the technique: *While being loved, Sweet Princess, enter loving as everlasting life.*

Do not be a lover standing aloof, outside. Become loving and move into eternity. When you are

loving someone, are you there as the lover? If you are there, then you are in time and love is just false, just pseudo. If you are still there and you can say, "I am," then you can be physically near but spiritually you are poles apart.

While in love, *you* must not be—only love, only loving. Become loving. While caressing your lover or beloved become the caress. While kissing, do not be the kisser or the kissed—be the kiss. Forget the ego completely, dissolve it into the act. Move into the act so deeply that the actor is no more. And if you cannot move into love, it is difficult to move into eating or walking—very difficult, because love is the easiest approach for dissolving the ego. That is why those who are egoists cannot love. They may talk about it, they may sing about it, they may write about it, but they cannot love. The ego cannot love!

Shiva says, become loving. When you are in the embrace, become the embrace, become the kiss. Forget yourself so totally that you can say, "I am no more. Only love exists." Then the heart is not beating but love is beating. Then the blood is not circulating, love is circulating. And eyes are not seeing, love is seeing. Then hands are not moving to touch, love is moving to touch.

Become love and enter everlasting life. Love suddenly changes your dimension. You are thrown out of time and you are facing eternity. Love can become a deep meditation—the deepest possible. Lovers have known sometimes what saints have not known. And lovers have touched that center which many yogis have missed. But it will be just a glimpse unless you transform your love into meditation. Tantra means this: the transformation of love into meditation. And now you can understand why tantra talks so much about love and sex. Why? Because love is the easiest natural door from where you can transcend this world, this horizontal dimension.

Look at Shiva with his consort, Devi. Look at them! They don't seem to be two—they are one. The oneness is so deep that it has even gone into symbols. We all have seen the *shivalinga*. It is a phallic symbol—Shiva's sex organ—but it is not alone, it is based in Devi's vagina. The Hindus of the old days were very daring. Now when you see a shivalinga you never remember that it is a phallic symbol. We have forgotten; we have tried to forget it completely.

Jung remembers in his autobiography, in his memoirs, a very beautiful and funny incident. He came to India and went to see Konarak, and in the temple of Konarak there are many, many shivalingas, many phallic symbols. The pundit who was taking him around explained everything to him except the shivalingas. And they were so many, it was difficult to escape this. Jung was well aware, but just to tease the pundit he went on asking, "But what are these?"

So the pundit at last said into his ear, in Jung's ear, "Do not ask me here, I will tell you afterwards. This is a private thing."

Jung must have laughed inside—these are the Hindus of today. Then outside the temple the pundit came near and said, "It was not good of you to ask before others. I will tell you now. It is a secret." And then again in Jung's ear he said, "They are our private parts."

When Jung went back, he met one great scholar—a scholar of oriental thought, mythology, philosophy—Heinrich Zimmer. He related this anecdote to Zimmer. Zimmer was one of the most gifted minds who ever tried to penetrate Indian thought and he was a lover of India and of its ways of thinking—of the oriental nonlogical, mystic approach toward life. When he heard this from Jung, he laughed and said, "This is good for a change. I have always heard about great Indians—Buddha, Krishna, Mahavira. What you relate says something not about any great Indians, but about Indians."

Love for Shiva is the great gate. And for him sex is not something to be condemned. For him sex is the seed and love is the flowering of it, and if you condemn the seed you condemn the flower. Sex can become love. If it never becomes love then it is crip-

pled. Condemn the crippledness, not the sex. Love must flower, sex must become love. If it is not becoming it is not the fault of sex, it is your fault.

Sex must not remain sex; that is the tantra teaching. It must be transformed into love. And love also must not remain love. It must be transformed into light, into meditative experience, into the last, ultimate mystic peak. How to transform love? Be the act and forget the actor. While loving, be love—simply love. Then it is not your love or my love or anybody else's—it is simply *love*. When you are not there, when you are in the hands of the ultimate source, or current, when you are in love, it is not you who is in love. When the love has engulfed you, you have disappeared; you have just become a flowing energy.

D.H. Lawrence, one of the most creative minds of this age, was knowingly or unknowingly a tantra adept. He was condemned in the West completely, his books were banned. There were many cases in the courts only because he had said, "Sex energy is the only energy, and if you condemn it and suppress it you are against the universe. Then you will never be capable of knowing the higher flowering of this energy. And when it is suppressed it becomes ugly—this is the vicious circle."

Priests, moralists, so-called religious people—popes, shankaracharyas and others—they go on condemning sex. They say that this is an ugly thing. And when you suppress it, it becomes ugly. So they say, "Look! What we said is true. It is proved by you. Look! Whatsoever you are doing is ugly and you know it is ugly."

But it is not sex which is ugly, it is these priests who have made it ugly. Once they have made it ugly they are proved right. And when they are proved right you go on making it more and more ugly.

Sex is innocent energy—life flowing in you, existence alive in you. Do not cripple it! Allow it to move toward the heights. That is, sex must become love. What is the difference? When your mind is sexual you are exploiting the other; the other is just an instrument to be used and thrown away. When sex becomes love the other is not an instrument, the other is not to be exploited; the other is not really the other. When you love, it is not self-centered. Rather, the other becomes significant, unique.

It is not that you are exploiting him—no! On the contrary, you both are joined in a deep experience. You are partners of a deep experience, not the exploiter and the exploited. You are helping each other to move into a different world of love. Sex is exploitation. Love is moving together into a different world.

If this moving is not momentary and if this moving becomes meditative—that is, if you can forget yourself completely and the lover and the beloved disappear, and there is only love flowing—then, says Shiva, everlasting life is yours.

---

11 Close your senses, become stonelike.

The second relaxation technique: *Stop the doors of the senses when feeling the creeping of an ant. Then.*

This looks very simple, but it is not so simple. I will read it again: *Stop the doors of the senses when feeling the creeping of an ant. Then.* This is only an example; anything will do. *Stop the doors of the senses when feeling the creeping of an ant,* and then —*then*—the thing will happen. What is Shiva saying?

You have a thorn in your foot—it is painful, you are suffering. Or one ant is there creeping on your leg. You feel the creeping and suddenly you want it to be thrown away. Take any experience! You have a wound—it is painful. You have a headache, or any pain in the body. Anything will do as an object. It is only an example—*the creeping of an ant.* Shiva says: *Stop the doors of the senses when feeling the creeping of an ant.* Whatsoever you are feeling, stop all the doors of the senses.

What is to be done? Close your eyes and think that you are just blind and you cannot see. Close

your ears and think that you cannot hear. With all of the five senses, you just close them. How can you close them? It is easy. Stop breathing for a single moment: all your senses will be closed. When the breath has stopped and all the senses are closed, where is this creeping? Where is the ant? Suddenly you are removed—far away.

One of my friends, an old friend, very aged, fell down the staircase, and doctors said that now he would not be able to move from his bed for three months, he would have to rest for three months. And he was a very restless man; it was difficult for him. I went to see him, so he said, "Pray for me and bless me so that I may die, because these three months are more than death. I cannot remain stonelike. And others are saying, 'Don't move.'"

I told him, "This is a good opportunity. Just close your eyes and think that you are only a stone, you cannot move. How can you move? You are a stone—just a stone, a statue. Close your eyes. Feel that you are now a stone, a statue."

He asked me what will happen. I told him, "Just try. I am sitting here, and nothing can be done. Nothing can be done! You will have to be here for three months anyhow, so try."

He would have never tried, but the situation was so impossible that he said, "Okay! I will try because something may happen. But I don't believe it," he said. "I don't believe that something can happen just by thinking that I am stonelike, dead like a statue, but I will try." So he tried.

I was also not thinking that something was going to happen, because the man was such. But sometimes when you are in an impossible situation, hopeless, things begin to happen. He closed his eyes. I waited, because I was thinking that within two or three minutes he would open them and he would say, "Nothing happened." But he would not open his eyes, and thirty minutes passed. I could feel and see that he had become a statue. All the tension on his forehead disappeared. His face was changed.

I had to leave, but he would not open his eyes.

And he was so silent, as if dead. His breathing calmed down, and because I had to leave, I had to tell him, "I want to go now, so please open your eyes and tell me what has happened."

He opened his eyes a different man. And he said, "This is a miracle. What have you done to me?"

I told him, "I have not done anything at all."

He said, "You must have done something because this is a miracle. When I began to think that I am just like a stone, like a statue, suddenly the feeling came to me that even if I wanted to move my hands it was impossible to do so. I wanted so many times to open my eyes, but they were like stone so I couldn't open them."

He said, "I even became worried about what you will be thinking, as it was so long, but what could I do? I couldn't move myself for these thirty minutes. And when every movement ceased, suddenly the world disappeared and I was alone, deep down in me, myself. Then the pain disappeared."

There was severe pain; he could not sleep in the night without a tranquilizer. But the pain disappeared. I asked him how he felt when the pain was disappearing.

He said, "First I began to feel that it was somewhere distant. The pain was there, but very far away as if happening to someone else. And then by and by, by and by, as if someone is going away and away and you cannot see him, it disappeared. The pain disappeared! For at least ten minutes, the pain was no more. How can a stone body have pain?"

This sutra says, *Stop the doors of the senses.* Become stonelike, closed to the world. When you are closed to the world, really, you are closed to your own body also, because your body is not part of you; it is part of the world. When you are closed completely to the world, you are closed to your own body also. Then, Shiva says, then the thing will happen.

So try it with the body. Anything will do, you will not need some ant creeping on you. Otherwise you will think, "When the ant will creep, I will meditate." And such helpful ants are difficult to find, so

anything will do. You are lying on your bed, you feel the cold sheets—become dead. Suddenly the sheets will go away, away, away, and they will disappear. Your bed will disappear; your bedroom will disappear; the whole world will disappear. You are closed, dead, a stone, like a Leibnitzian monad with no window outside—no window! You cannot move!

And then, when you cannot move, you are thrown back to yourself, you are centered in yourself. Then, for the first time you can look from your center. And once you can look from your center, you can never be the same man again.

12 Let yourself become weightless.

The third relaxation technique: *When on a bed or a seat, let yourself become weightless, beyond mind.*

You are sitting here. Just feel that you have become weightless, there is no weight. You will feel that somewhere or other there is weight, but go on feeling the weightlessness. It comes. A moment comes when you feel that you are weightless, that there is no weight. When there is no weight you are no more a body, because the weight is of the body—not of you. You are weightless.

That is why there were so many experiments done. Someone is dying.... Many scientists all over the world have tried to weigh the person. If there is a slight difference, if when a man is alive the weight is more and when a man is dead the weight is less, then scientists can say that something has moved from the body, that a soul or the self or something that was there is no more—because for science nothing can be weightless, nothing!

Weight is basic to all matter. Even sunrays have weight. It is very, very slight, minute, and they are difficult to weigh, but scientists have weighed them. If you can collect all the sun rays on a five-square-mile plot of ground, their weight will be similar to that of a hair. But sun rays do have weight; they have been weighed. Nothing can be weightless for science. And if something can be weightless then it is immaterial, it cannot be matter. And science has believed for these twenty or twenty-five years that there is nothing except matter.

So when a man dies, if something leaves the body the weight must differ. But it never differs; the weight remains the same. Sometimes it even becomes more—that is the problem. The alive man weighs less; the dead man becomes more weighty. That created new problems, because they were really trying to find out if some weight is lost; then they can say something has left. But it seems that, on the contrary, something has come in. What has happened? Weight is material, but you are not a weight. You are immaterial.

If you try this technique of weightlessness, you just have to conceive of yourself as weightless—and not only conceive, but feel that your body has become weightless. If you go on feeling, feeling, feeling, a moment comes when suddenly you realize that you are weightless. You are already, so you can realize it anytime. You have only to create a situation in which you can feel again that you are weightless.

You have to dehypnotize yourself. This is the hypnosis, the belief that "I am a body and that is why I feel weight." If you can dehypnotize yourself into realizing that you are not a body, you will not feel weight. And when you do not feel weight you are beyond mind, says Shiva: *When on a bed or a seat, let yourself become weightless, beyond mind.* Then the thing can happen. The mind also has weight; everyone's mind has a different weight.

At one time there were some proposals that the weightier the mind, the more intelligent. And generally it is true, but not absolutely, because sometimes very great men had very small minds, and sometimes some stupid idiot's mind weighed very much. But generally it is true, because when you have a bigger mechanism of the mind it weighs more. The mind is also a weight, but your consciousness is weightless. To feel this consciousness, you have to

feel weightlessness. So try it: walking, sitting, sleeping, you can try it.

Some observations…. Why does the dead body become more weighty sometimes? Because the moment the consciousness leaves the body, the body becomes unprotected. Many things can enter it immediately. They were not entering because of you. Many vibrations can enter into a dead body—they cannot enter into you. You are there, the body is alive, resistant to many things. That is why once you are ill, it begins to be a long sequence; one illness, then another, and then another—because once you are ill you become unprotected, vulnerable, nonresistant. Then anything can enter into you. Your presence protects the body. So sometimes a dead body can gain weight. The moment you leave it, anything can enter into the body.

Secondly, when you are happy you always feel weightless; when you are sad you always feel more weight, as if something is pulling you down. The gravitation becomes much more. When you are sad, you are more weighty. When you are happy, you are light. You feel it. Why? Because when you are happy, whenever you feel a blissful moment, you forget the body completely. When you are sad, suffering, you cannot forget the body, you feel the weight of it. It pulls you down—down to the earth, as if you are rooted. Then you cannot move; you have roots in the earth. In happiness you are weightless. In sorrow, sadness, you become weighty.

In deep meditation, when you forget your body completely, you can levitate. Even the body can go up with you. It happens many times. Scientists have been observing one woman in Bolivia. While meditating she goes up four feet, and now it has been observed scientifically; many films have been taken, many photographs. Before thousands and thousands of observers suddenly the woman goes up and gravity becomes nil, nullified. As of yet there is no explanation for what is happening, but that same woman cannot go up while not in meditation. And if her meditation is disturbed, suddenly she falls down.

What happens? Deep in meditation you forget

your body completely, and the identification is broken. The body is a very small thing; you are very big, you have infinite power. The body has nothing in comparison to you.

It is as if an emperor has become identified with his slave, so as the slave goes begging, the emperor goes begging; as the slave weeps, the emperor weeps. When the slave says, "I am no one," the emperor says, "I am no one." Once the emperor recognizes his own being, once he recognizes that he is the emperor and this man is just a slave, everything will change suddenly.

You are infinite power identified with a very finite body. Once you realize your self, then weightlessness becomes more and the weight of the body less. Then you can levitate, the body can go up.

There are many, many stories which cannot yet be proven scientifically, but they will be proven... because if one woman can go up four feet, then there is no barrier. Another can go a thousand feet, another can go completely into the cosmos. Theoretically there is no problem: four feet or four hundred feet or four thousand feet, it makes no difference.

There are stories about Rama and about many others who have disappeared completely with the body. Their bodies were never found dead on this earth. Mohammed disappeared completely—not only with his body; it is said he disappeared with his horse also. These stories look impossible, they look mythological, but they are not necessarily so.

Once you know the weightless force, you have become the master of gravity. You can use it; it depends on you. You can disappear completely with your body.

But to us weightlessness will be a problem. The technique of *siddhasana*, the way Buddha sits, is the best way to be weightless. Sit on the earth—not on any chair or anything, but just on the floor. And it is good if the floor is not of cement or anything artificial. Just sit on the ground so that you are the nearest to nature. It is good if you can sit naked.

Just sit naked on the ground in the Buddha posture, siddhasana—because siddhasana is the best posture in which to be weightless. Why? Because you feel more weight if your body is leaning this way or that way. Then your body has more area to be affected by gravity. If I am sitting on this chair then a greater area of my body is affected by gravity.

While you are standing less area is affected, but you cannot stand for too long. Mahavira always meditated standing—always, because then one covers the least area. Just your feet are touching the ground. When you are standing on your feet, straight, the least amount of gravity works on you —and gravity is weight.

Sitting in a Buddha posture, locked—your legs are locked, your hands are locked—also helps, because then your inner electricity becomes a circuit. Let your spine be straight.

Now you can understand why so much emphasis has been given to a straight spine, because with a straight spine less and less area is covered, so gravity affects you less. With closed eyes, balance yourself completely, center yourself. Lean to the right and feel the gravity; lean to the left and feel the gravity; lean forward and feel the gravity; lean backward and feel the gravity. Then find the center where the least pull of gravity is felt, the least weight is felt, and remain there. Then forget the body and feel that you are not weight—you are weightless. Then go on feeling this weightlessness. Suddenly you become weightless; suddenly you are not the body; suddenly you are in a different world of bodilessness.

Weightlessness is bodilessness. Then you transcend mind also. Mind is also part of the body, part of matter. Matter has weight; you do not have any weight. This is the basis of this technique.

Try any technique, but stick to it for a few days so that you can feel whether it is working or not.

Enough for today.

CHAPTER 8

Total acceptance and nondivision: the meaning of tantric purity

♦

Q U E S T I O N

What does tantra mean by purity?

One of the things being asked about is:

What does tantra mean by purification of the mind, purity of the mind, as a basic condition to further progress?

hatsoever is ordinarily meant by purity is not what is meant by tantra. Ordinarily, we divide everything into bad and good. The division may be for any reason. It may be hygienically, morally or in any other way, but we divide life into two—good and bad. And ordinarily, whenever we say purity we mean goodness —the "bad" qualities should not be allowed and the "good" qualities should be there. But for tantra this division of good and bad is meaningless. Tantra does not look at life through any dichotomy, any duality, any division. Then "What is meant by purity in tantra?" is a very relevant question.

If you ask a saint, he will say that anger is bad, sex is bad, greed is bad. If you ask Gurdjieff, he will say that negativity is bad, that whatsoever emotion is negative is bad and to be positive is good. If you ask Jains, Buddhists, Hindus, Christians or Mohammedans, they may differ in their definition of good and bad—but they have definitions. They call certain things bad and certain things good. So to define purity is not difficult for them. Whatsoever they take as good is pure, whatsoever they take as bad is impure.

But for tantra it is a deep problem. Tantra makes no superficial division between good and bad. Then what is purity? Tantra says that to divide is impure and to live in nondivision is purity. So for tantra purity means innocence—undifferentiated innocence.

A child is there; you call him pure. He gets angry, he has greed, so why do you call him pure? What is pure in childhood? Innocence! There is no division in the mind of a child. The child is unaware of any division into what is good and what is bad. That unawareness is the innocence. Even if he gets angry, he has no mind to be angry, it is a pure and simple act. It happens, and when anger goes, it goes. Nothing is left behind. The child is again the same, as if the anger has never been there. The purity is not touched; the purity is the same. So a child is pure because there is no mind.

The more mind grows, the more the child will become impure. Then anger will be there as a considered thing, not spontaneously. Then sometimes the child will suppress the anger—if the situation does not permit it. And when anger becomes suppressed, then sometimes it will be transferred onto another situation instead. When there is really no need to be angry he will get angry, because the suppressed anger will need some outlet. Then everything will become impure because the mind has come in.

A child can be a thief in our eyes, but a child himself is never a thief because the very concept that things belong to individuals doesn't exist in his mind. If he takes your watch, your money, or anything, it is not a theft for him because the very notion that things belong to someone is nonexistent. His theft is pure while even your nontheft is not pure—the mind is there.

Tantra says that when someone becomes again like a child, he is pure. Of course, he is not a child —only like a child. The difference is there and the similarity is there. The similarity is the innocence regained. Again someone is like a child. A child is standing naked—no one feels the nakedness because a child is still unaware of the body. His nakedness has a quality different from your nakedness. You are aware of the body.

The sage must regain this innocence. Mahavira stands again naked. That nakedness again has the same quality of innocence. He has forgotten his body; he is no longer the body. But one difference is also there, and the difference is great: the child is simply ignorant, hence the innocence. But the sage is wise, that is the reason for his innocence.

The child will one day become aware of his body and will feel the nakedness. He will try to hide, he will become guilty, and he will feel shame. He will come to be aware. So his innocence is an innocence of ignorance. Knowledge will destroy it.

That is the meaning of the biblical story of Adam and Eve being expelled from the Garden of Eden. They were naked like children. They were not aware of the body; they were not aware of anger, greed, lust, sex or anything. They were unaware. They were like children, innocent.

But God had forbidden them to eat the fruit of the tree of knowledge. The tree of knowledge was forbidden but they ate, because anything forbidden becomes inviting. Anything forbidden becomes attractive! They were living in a big garden with an infinite number of trees, but the tree of knowledge became the most important and significant because it was forbidden. Really, this forbidden-ness became the attraction, the invitation. They were as if magnetized, hypnotized by the tree. They couldn't escape it, they had to eat.

But this story is beautiful because the tree is named the tree of knowledge. The moment they ate the fruit of knowledge they became noninnocent. They became aware; they came to realize that they were naked. Immediately, Eve tried to hide her body. With awareness of the body they became aware of everything—anger, lust, greed, everything. They became adult, so they were expelled from the garden.

So in the Bible knowledge is sin. They were thrown out of the garden, they were punished, because of knowledge. Unless they become again like children—innocent, not-knowing—they cannot enter the garden. They can enter the kingdom of God again only if they fulfill this condition of becoming innocent again.

The whole thing is just the story of humanity. Every child is expelled from the garden, not only Adam and Eve. Every child lives his childhood in innocence without knowing anything. He is pure, but the purity is of ignorance. It cannot continue. Unless it becomes a purity of wisdom, you cannot rely on it. It will have to go, sooner or later you will have to eat the fruit of knowledge.

Each child will have to eat the fruit of knowledge. It was easy in the Garden of Eden—just the tree was there. As a substitute for the tree we have schools, colleges and universities. Each child will have to pass, will have to become noninnocent, will have to lose his innocence. The very world needs knowledge, the very existence needs knowledge. You cannot exist in it without knowledge. And the moment knowledge comes, division enters. You begin to divide between what is good and what is bad.

So for tantra the division into good and bad is impurity. Before it you are pure, after it you are pure; in it you are impure. But knowledge is a necessary evil, you cannot escape it. One has to go through it; that is part of life. But one need not remain in it always, one can transcend it. Transcendence makes you again pure and innocent. If divisions lost their meaning, if the knowledge which differentiates between good and evil were no more, you would again look at the world from an innocent attitude.

Jesus says, "Unless you become like children, you cannot enter into my kingdom of God." Unless you become like children...this is the purity of tantra.

Lao Tzu says, "One inch of division, and heaven and hell are set apart." No-division is the mind of the sage—no division at all! A sage doesn't know what is good or what is bad. He is like children but unlike them also, because he has known this division. He has passed through this division and transcended it; he has gone beyond it. He has known darkness and light, but now he has gone beyond it. Now he sees darkness as part of light and light as part of darkness, now there is no division. Light and darkness have both become one—degrees of one phenomenon. Now he sees everything as degrees of one; howsoever polar opposite they are, they are not two. Life and death, love and hate, good and bad, everything is part of one phenomenon, one energy. The difference is only of degrees, and they can never be divided. It cannot be demarked, that "From this point there is division." There is no division.

What is good? What is bad? From where can you define them and demark them as separate? They are always one. They are only different degrees of the same thing. Once this is known and felt, your mind becomes again pure. This is the purity meant by tantra. So I will define tantric purity as innocence, not as goodness.

But innocence can be ignorant—then it is of no use. It has to be lost, you have to be thrown out of it; otherwise you cannot mature. Giving up knowledge and transcendence of knowledge are both part of maturing, part of being really adult. So go through it, but do not remain there. Move! Go on moving! A day comes when you are beyond it.

That is why tantric purity is difficult to understand and can be misunderstood. It is delicate! So to recognize a tantric sage is virtually impossible. Ordinary saints and sages can be recognized because they follow you—your standards, your definitions, your morality. A tantric sage is even difficult to recognize because he transcends all divisions. So really, in the whole history of human growth we know nothing about tantric sages. Nothing is mentioned or recorded about them because it is so difficult to recognize them.

Confucius went to Lao Tzu. Lao Tzu's mind is that of a tantrically awakened sage. He never knew about the word 'tantra'; the word is meaningless for him. He never knew anything about tantra, but whatsoever he has said *is* tantra. Confucius is representative of our mind, he is the archrepresentative. He continually thinks in terms of good and bad, of what should be done and what should not be done. He is a legalist—the greatest legalist ever born. He went to see Lao Tzu, and he asked Lao Tzu, "What is good? What ought one to do? What is bad? Define it clearly."

Lao Tzu said, "Definitions create a mess, because defining means dividing: this is this, and that is that." You divide and say A is A and B is B... you have divided. You say A cannot be B; then you have created a division, a dichotomy, and the existence is one. A is always becoming B, A is always moving into B. Life is always becoming death, life is always moving into death, so how can you define? Childhood is moving into youth and youth is moving into old age; health is moving into disease and disease is moving into health. So where can you demark them as separate?

Life is one movement, and the moment you define you create a mess, because definitions will be dead and life is an alive movement. So definitions are always false. Lao Tzu said, "Defining creates nontruth, so do not define. Do not say what is good and what is bad."

So Confucius said, "What are you saying? Then how can people be led and guided? Then how can they be taught? How can they be made moral and good?"

Lao Tzu said, "When someone tries to make someone else good, that is a sin in my eyes. Who are you to lead? Who are you to guide? And the more guides there are, the more confusion. Leave everyone to himself. Who are you?"

This type of attitude seems dangerous. It is! Society cannot be founded on such attitudes. Confucius goes on asking, and the whole point is that Lao Tzu says, "Nature is enough, no morality is needed. Nature is spontaneous. Nature is enough, no imposed laws and disciplines are needed. Innocence is enough; no morality is needed. Nature is spontaneous, nature is enough. No imposed laws and disciplines are needed. Innocence is enough. Knowledge is not needed."

Confucius came back very much disturbed. He could not sleep for nights. And his disciples asked, "Tell us something about the meeting. What happened?" Confucius answered, "He is not a man, he is a danger, a dragon. He is not a man. Never go to that place where he is. Whenever you hear about Lao Tzu, just escape from that place. He will disturb your mind completely."

And that is right, because the whole of tantra is concerned with how to transcend the mind. It is bound to destroy the mind. Mind lives with definitions, laws and disciplines; mind is an order. But remember, tantra is not disorder, and that is a very subtle point to be understood.

Confucius could not understand Lao Tzu. When Confucius left, Lao Tzu was laughing and laughing and so his disciples asked, "Why are you laughing so much? What has happened?"

Lao Tzu is reported to have said, "The mind is such a barrier to understanding. Even the mind of a Confucius is a barrier. He could not understand me at all, and whatsoever he will say about me will be a misunderstanding. He thinks he is going to create order in the world. You *cannot* create order in the world. Order is inherent in it; it is always there. When you try to create order you create disorder." Lao Tzu said, "He will think that I am creating disorder, and really, he is the one who is creating disorder. I am against all imposed orders because I believe in a spontaneous discipline which comes and grows automatically. You need not impose it."

Tantra looks at things in this way. For tantra, innocence is spontaneity, *sahajata*—to be oneself without any imposition, to be simply oneself, growing like a tree. Not the tree of your garden, but the tree of your forest, growing spontaneously; not guided, because every guidance is a misguidance. For tantra, every guidance is a misguidance. Not guided, not guarded, not directed, not motivated, but simply growing.

The inner law is enough; no other law is needed. And if you need some other law, it only shows that you do not know the inner law, you have lost contact with it. So the real thing is not something imposed. The real thing is again regaining the balance, again moving to the center, again returning to the home so that you gain the real inner law.

But for morality, for religions—so-called religions—order is to be imposed, goodness is to be imposed from above, from without. Religions, moral teachings, priests, popes, they all take you as inherently bad—remember this. They do not believe in the goodness of man; they do not believe in any inner goodness. They believe that you are evil, that unless you are taught to be good you cannot be good; unless goodness is forced from without, there is no possibility of it coming from within.

So for priests, for religious people, for moralists, you are naturally bad. Goodness is going to be a discipline imposed from without. You are a chaos and order has to be brought in by them; they will bring the order. And they have made the whole world a mess, a confusion, a madhouse, because they have been ordering for centuries and centuries, disciplining for centuries and centuries. They have taught so much that the taught ones have gone mad.

Tantra believes in your inner goodness; remember this difference. Tantra says that everyone is born good, that goodness is your nature. It is the case! You are already good! You need a natural growth, you do not need any imposition; that is why nothing is taken as bad. If anger is there, if sex is there, if greed is there, tantra says they are also good. The only thing lacking is that you are not centered in yourself; that is why you cannot use them.

Anger is not bad. Really, the problem is that you are not inside, that is why anger creates havoc. If you are present there inside, anger becomes a healthy energy, anger becomes health. Anger is transformed into energy, it becomes good. Whatsoever is there is good. Tantra believes in the inherent goodness of everything. Everything is holy, nothing is unholy and nothing is evil. For tantra there is no devil, only divine existence.

Religions cannot exist without the devil. They need a God and they need a devil also. So do not be misguided if you see only a God in their temples. Just behind that God, the devil is hiding, because no religion can exist without the devil.

Something has to be condemned, something has to be fought, something has to be destroyed. The total is not accepted, only part. This is very basic. You are not accepted totally by any religion, only partially. They say, "We accept your love, but not your hate. Destroy hate." And this is a very deep problem, because when you destroy hate completely love is also destroyed—because they are not two. They say, "We accept your silence, but we do not accept your anger." Destroy anger and your aliveness is destroyed. Then you will be silent, but not an alive man—only a dead one. That silence is not life, it is just death.

Religions always divide you into two: the evil and the divine. They accept the divine and are against the evil—the evil has to be destroyed. So if someone really follows them, he will come to conclude that the moment you destroy the devil, God is destroyed. But no one really follows them—no one can follow them because the very teaching is absurd. So what is everyone doing? Everyone is just deceiving. That is why there is so much hypocrisy. That hypocrisy has been created by religion. You cannot do whatsoever they are teaching you to do, so you become a hypocrite. If you follow them

you will die; if you do not follow them you feel guilty that you are irreligious. So what to do?

The cunning mind makes a compromise. It goes on paying lip service to them, saying, "I am following you," but it goes on doing whatsoever it wants to do. You continue your anger, you continue your sex, you continue your greed, but you go on saying that greed is bad, anger is bad, sex is bad—that it is a sin. This is hypocrisy. The whole world has become hypocritical, no man is honest. Unless these dividing religions disappear, no man can be honest. This will look contradictory because all the religions are teaching to be honest, but they are the foundation stones of all dishonesty. They make you dishonest; because they teach you to do impossible things, which you cannot do, you become hypocrites.

Tantra accepts you in your totality, in your wholeness, because tantra says, either accept wholly or reject wholly; there is no in between. A man is a whole, an organic whole. You cannot divide it. You cannot say, "We will not accept this," because that which you reject is organically joined to that which you accept.

It is like this.... My body is there. Someone comes and says, "We accept your blood circulation, but we do not accept the noise of your heart. This continuous beating of your heart we do not accept. We accept your blood circulation. It is okay, it is silent." But my blood circulation is through my heart, and the beating is basically related with blood circulation; it happens because of it. So what am I to do? My heart and my blood circulation are an organic unity. They are not two things, they are one.

So either accept me totally or reject me totally, but do not try to divide me because then you will create a dishonesty, a deep dishonesty. If you go on condemning my heartbeat, then I will also start condemning my heartbeat. But the blood won't be able to circulate and I cannot be alive without it. So what to do? Go on as you are, and go on all the time saying something else which you are not, which you cannot be.

It is not difficult to see how heart and blood circulation are related, but it is difficult to see how love and hate are related. They are one. When you love someone, what are you doing? It is one movement, like breath going out. When you love someone, what are you doing? You are going out to meet him, it is a breath going out. When you hate someone, it is a breath coming back in.

When you love, you are attracted to someone. When you hate, you are repelled. Attraction and repulsion are two waves of one movement. Attraction and repulsion are not two things; you cannot divide them. You cannot say, "You can breathe in but you cannot breathe out, or you can breathe out but you cannot breathe in. You are allowed only one thing. Either go on breathing out or go on breathing in, do not do both." How can you breathe in if you are not allowed to breathe out? And if you are not allowed to hate, you cannot love.

Tantra says, "We accept the whole man because man is an organic unity." Man is a deep unity; you cannot discard anything. And this is as it should be —because if man is not an organic unity, then in this universe nothing can be an organic unity. Man is the peak of organic wholeness. The stone lying on the street is a unity. The tree is a unity. The flower and the bird are unities. Everything is a unity, so why not man? And man is the peak—a great unity, a very complex organic whole. Really, you cannot deny anything.

Tantra says, "We accept you as you are. That does not mean there is no need to change; that does not mean that now you have to stop growing. Rather, on the contrary, it means that we accept the basis of growth." Now you can grow, but this growth is not going to be a choice. This growth is going to be a choiceless growth.

Look! For example, when a buddha becomes enlightened we can ask, "Where has his anger gone—where? He had anger, he had sex, so where has his sex gone? Where is it that his anger has gone? Where is his greed?" We cannot recognize any anger in him now. When he is enlightened we cannot recognize any anger in him.

Can you recognize the mud in the lotus? The lotus comes from the mud. If you have never seen a lotus growing from the mud and a lotus flower is brought to you, can you conceive that this beautiful lotus flower has come up from the ordinary mud of a pond? This beautiful lotus coming from ugly mud! Can you recognize the mud anywhere in it? It is there, but transformed. Its fragrance is coming from that same ugly mud. The rosiness of the petals is coming from the same ugly mud. If you hide this lotus flower in mud, within days it will disappear again into its mother. Then again you won't be able to recognize where that lotus has gone. Where? Where is the fragrance? Where are those beautiful petals?

You cannot recognize yourself in Buddha, but you are there—of course, on a greater and higher plane, transformed. The sex is there, the anger is there, the hate is there. Everything which belongs to man is there. Buddha is a man, but he has come to his ultimate growth. He has become a lotus flower; you cannot recognize the mud, but that doesn't mean that the mud is not there. It is there, but not as mud. It is a higher unity. That is why in Buddha you can feel neither hate nor love. That is still more difficult to understand because Buddha appears totally loving—never hating, always silent, never angry. But his silence is different from your silence. It cannot be the same.

What is your silence? Somewhere Einstein has said that our peace is nothing but a preparation for war. Between two wars we have a gap of peace, but that peace is not really peace. It is only the gap between two wars, so it becomes a cold war. Thus, we have two types of war—hot and cold.

After the second world war, Russia and America began a cold war. They are not at peace—just in preparation for another war. They are getting ready. Each war disturbs, destroys. You have to get ready again, so you need a gap, an interval. But if wars really disappear from the world completely, then this type of peace which means cold war will also disappear, because it always happens between two wars. If war disappears completely, this cold war which we call peace cannot continue.

What is your silence? Just a preparation between two angers. When you seem at ease what is it? Are you really relaxed, really at ease, or are you just preparing for another outburst, for another explosion? Anger is a wastage of energy, so you also need time. When you get angry you cannot get angry again immediately. When you move into the sex act, you cannot move again immediately. You will need time, so you will need a period of *brahmacharya*—celibacy—for at least two or three days. It will depend on your age. This celibacy is not really celibacy, you are only preparing again.

Between two sex acts there can be no brahmacharya. You go on calling the period between two meals a fast. That is why in the morning you have "breakfast," but where is the fast? You were just preparing. You cannot go on thrusting food into yourself continuously, you have to have a gap, but that gap is not a fast. Really, it is only a preparation for another meal, not a fast.

So when we are silent, it is always between two angers. When we are at ease, it is always between two peaks of tension. When we are celibate, it is only between two sex acts. When we are loving, it is always between two hatreds—remember this.

So when Buddha is silent, do not think this is your silence. When your anger has disappeared, your silence has disappeared also. They both exist together; they cannot be separated. So when Buddha is a *brahmachari*—a celibate—do not think this is your celibacy. When sex has disappeared, brahmacharya has also disappeared. They both were part of one thing, so they both have disappeared. With a Buddha a very different being is there such as you cannot conceive. You can only conceive of the dichotomy you know. You cannot conceive of what type of man this is, of what has happened to him.

The whole energy has come to a different level,

a different plane of existence. The mud has become a lotus, but it is still there. The mud has not been discarded from the lotus; it has been transformed.

So all of the energies within you are accepted by tantra. Tantra is not for discarding anything whatsoever, but for transformation. And tantra says that the first step is to accept. The first step is very difficult—to accept. You may be getting angry many times every day, but to accept your anger is very difficult. To be angry is very easy; to accept your anger is very difficult. Why? You do not feel so much difficulty in being angry, so why do you feel so much difficulty in accepting it? Getting angry seems not so bad as accepting it. Everyone thinks he is a good man and anger is just momentary, it comes and goes. It doesn't destroy your self-image. You go on remaining good. You say that "It just happened." It is not destructive to your ego.

So those who are cunning will repent immediately. They will get angry and they will repent, they will ask for forgiveness. These are the cunning ones. Why do I call them cunning? Because their anger gives a trembling to their self-image. They begin to feel uneasy. They begin to feel, "I get angry? I am so bad that I get angry?" So the image of a good man trembles. He has to try and make it established again. Immediately he says, "This was bad. I will never do it again. Forgive me." By asking for forgiveness his self-image is established again. He is okay—back to his previous state when there was no anger. He has canceled his anger by asking for forgiveness. He has called himself bad just to remain good.

That is why you can go on for lives together being angry, being sexual, being possessive, being this and that, but never accepting. This is a trick of the mind. Whatsoever you do is just on the periphery. In the center, you remain good. If you accept that "I have anger," in the center you become bad. Then it is not just a question of getting angry, then it is not momentary. Rather, then anger is part of your constitution. Then it is not that someone irritates you into anger. Even if you are alone, the anger is there. When you are not getting angry the anger is still there, because anger is your energy, part of you.

It is not that sometimes it flares up and then goes off—no! It cannot flare up if it is not always present. You can turn off this light, you can turn on this light; but the current must remain continuously there. If the current is not there, you cannot turn it on and off. The current, the anger current, is always there; the sex current is always there, the greed current is always there. You can turn it on, you can turn it off. In situations you change, but inwardly you remain the same.

Accepting means anger is not an act. Rather, *you* are anger. Sex is not just an act; *you* are sex. Greed is not just an act; *you* are greed. Accepting this means throwing away the self-image. And we all have built beautiful self-images. Everyone has built a beautiful self-image—absolutely beautiful. And whatsoever you are doing never touches it, you go on protecting it. The image is protected, so you feel good. That is why you can become angry, you can become sexual, and you are not disturbed. But if you accept and say, "I am sex, I am anger, I am greed," then your self-image falls down immediately.

Tantra says this is the first step, and the most difficult: to accept whatsoever you are. Sometimes we try to accept, but whenever we accept we again do so in a very calculated way. Our cunningness is deep and subtle, and mind has very subtle ways to deceive. Sometimes you accept and say, "Yes, I am angry." But if you accept this, you accept only when you think of how to transcend anger. Then you accept and say, "Okay, I am angry. Now tell me how to go beyond it." You accept sex only to be non-sexual. Whenever you are trying to be something else you are able to accept, because your self-image is again maintained by the future.

You are violent and you are striving to be non-violent, so you accept and say, "Okay, I am violent. Today I am violent, but tomorrow I will be nonviolent, however." How will you become nonviolent? You postpone this self-image into the future. You do not think of yourself in the present. You always think in terms of the ideal—of nonviolence, love and compassion. Then you are in the future. This present is just to become a past, your real self is in the future, so you go on identifying yourself with ideals. Those ideals are also ways of not accepting the reality. You are violent—that is the case. And the present is the only thing that is existential; the future is not. Your ideals are just dreams. They are tricks to postpone the mind, to focus the mind somewhere else.

You are violent; this is the case, so accept it. And do not try to be nonviolent. A violent mind *cannot* become nonviolent. How is this possible? Look deep into it. You are violent, so how can you be nonviolent? Whatsoever you do will be done by the violent mind—whatsoever! Even while striving to be nonviolent, the effort will be done by the violent mind. You are violent, so by trying to be nonviolent you will be violent. In the very effort to be nonviolent, you will try every type of violence.

That is why you go to these strivers for nonviolence. They may not be violent with others, but they are with themselves. They are very violent with themselves—murdering themselves. And the more they get mad against themselves, the more they are celebrated. When they become completely mad, suicidal, then the society says, "These are the sages." But they have only transformed the object of violence, nothing else. They were violent with someone else, now they are violent with themselves—but the violence is there. And when you are violent with someone else the law can protect, the court can help, the society will condemn you. But when you are violent against yourself there is no law. No law can protect you against yourself.

When man is against himself there is no protection, nothing can be done. And no one cares because it is your business. No one else is involved in it: it is your business. So-called monks, so-called saints, they are violent against themselves. No one is interested. They say, "Okay! Go on doing it. It is your business."

If your mind is one of greed, how can you be nongreedy? The greedy mind will remain greedy. Whatsoever is done by it to go beyond greed is not going to help. Of course, we can create new greeds. Ask a greedy mind, "What are you doing just accumulating wealth? You will die and you cannot take your wealth with you." This is the logic of the so-called religious preachers—that you cannot take your wealth with you. But if someone could take it, then the whole logic would fail.

The greedy man feels the logic, of course. He asks, "How can I take wealth with me?" But he really wants to take it. That is why the priest becomes influential. He shows him that it is nonsense to accumulate things which cannot be taken beyond death. He says, "I will teach you how to accumulate things which can be taken. Virtue can be taken, *punya*—good deeds—can be taken, goodness can be taken, but not wealth. So donate the wealth."

But this is an appeal to his greed. This is telling him, "Now we will give you better things which can be carried beyond death." The appeal obtains results. The greedy man feels, "You are right. Death is there and nothing can be done about it, so I must do something which can be carried beyond. I must create some kind of bank balance in the other world also. The world, this bank balance, cannot be with me forever." He goes on talking in these terms.

Go through the scriptures…they appeal to your greed. They say, "What are you doing wasting your time in momentary pleasures?" The emphasis is on "momentary." So find some eternal pleasures; then it is okay. They are not against pleasures, they are just against their being momentary. Look at the greed!

Sometimes it happens that you may find a nongreedy man who is enjoying momentary pleasures, but you cannot find among your saints a man who is not asking for, demanding eternal pleasures. The greed in them is even more. You can find a nongreedy man among ordinary men, but you cannot find a nongreedy man among your so-called saints. They also want pleasures, but they are more greedy than you. You are satisfied with momentary pleasures and they are not. Their greed is bigger. Their greed can only be satisfied with eternal pleasures.

Infinite greed asks for infinite pleasures—remember this. A finite greed is satisfied with finite pleasure. They will ask you, "What are you doing loving a woman? She is nothing but bones and blood. Look deep into the woman you love. What is she?" They are not against the woman, they are against the bones, against the blood, against the body. But if a woman is of gold, then it is okay. They are asking for women of gold.

They are not in this world, so they create another world. They say, "In heaven there are golden damsels—*apsaras*—who are beautiful and who never age." In the Hindu heaven apsaras, the heavenly girls, remain always at sixteen. They never grow older, they are always sixteen—never less, never more. So what are you doing wasting your time on these ordinary women? Think of heaven. They are not against pleasure. Really, they are against momentary pleasure.

If, through some whim, God gives this world eternal pleasure, your whole edifice of religion will fall down immediately; the whole appeal will be lost. If somehow bank balances can be carried beyond death, no one will be interested in creating bank balances in the other world. So death is a great help to the priests.

A greedy man is always attracted by another greed. If you tell him and convince him that his greed is the cause of his misery, and that if he leaves greed he will attain a blissful state, he may try—because now you are not really against his greed. You are giving his greed new pastures. He can move into new dimensions of greed.

So tantra says that a greedy mind cannot become nongreedy, a violent mind cannot become nonviolent. But this seems very hopeless. If this is the case, then nothing can be done. Then what does tantra stand for? If a greedy mind cannot become nongreedy, and a violent mind nonviolent, and a sex-obsessed mind transformed beyond sex, if nothing can be done then what does tantra stand for? Tantra is not saying that nothing can be done. Something can be done, but the dimension is completely different.

A greedy mind has to understand that it is greedy and accept it—not try to be nongreedy. The greedy mind has to go deep within itself to realize the depth of its greed. Not moving away from it, but remaining with it; not moving in ideals—in contradictory ideals, in opposite ideals—but remaining in the present, moving into the greed, knowing the greed, understanding the greed, and not trying to escape from it in any way. If you can remain with your greed, many things will happen. If you can remain with your greed, with your sex, with your anger, your ego will dissolve. This will be the first thing—and what a great miracle it is!

Many people come to me and they go on asking how to be egoless. You cannot be egoless unless you look at the foundations of your ego to find it. You are greedy and you think you are nongreedy—this is the ego. If you are greedy and you know and accept totally that you are greedy, then where can you allow your ego to stand? If you are angry and you say that you are angry—you do not say it to others, but you feel it deep down, you feel the help-lessness—then where can your anger stand? If you are sexual, accept it. Whatsoever is there, accept it.

The nonacceptance of nature creates the ego, the nonacceptance of your suchness—your *tathata,* that which you are. If you accept it, the ego will not be there. If you do not accept it, if you reject it, if you create ideals against it, there will be ego. Ideals are the stuff the ego is made of.

Accept yourself. But then you will look like an animal. You will not look like a man because your concept of man is in your ideals. That is why we go on teaching others not to be like animals, and everyone is an animal. What can you do? You *are* an animal. Accept your animality. And the moment you accept your animality, you have done the first

thing to go beyond animals—because no animal knows that it is an animal, only man can know. That is going beyond. You cannot go beyond by denying.

Accept! When everything is accepted, suddenly you will feel that you have transcended. Who is accepting? Who accepts the whole? That which accepts has gone beyond. If you reject, you remain on the same plane. If you accept, you go beyond. Acceptance is transcendence. And if you accept yourself totally, suddenly you are thrown to your center. Then you cannot move anywhere. You cannot move from your suchness, from your nature, so you are thrown to your center.

All these tantric techniques which we are discussing and trying to understand are different ways of throwing you to your center, of throwing you from the periphery. And you are trying to escape from the center in many ways. Ideals are good escapes. Idealists are the most subtle of egoists.

Many things happen.... You are violent and you create an ideal of nonviolence. Then you need not go into yourself, into your violence; there is no need. Then this is the only need—to go on thinking about nonviolence, reading about nonviolence, and trying to practice nonviolence. You say to yourself, "Do not touch violence," and you are violent. So you can escape from yourself, you can go to the periphery, but then you will never come to the center. That is one thing.

Secondly, when you create the ideal of nonvio-lence, you can condemn others. Now it becomes very easy. You have the ideal to judge everyone with, and you can say to anyone, "You are violent." India has created many ideals; that is why India continuously goes on condemning the whole world. The whole mind of India is condemnatory. It goes on condemning the whole world: everyone else is violent, only India is nonviolent. No one seems to be nonviolent here, but the ideal is good for condemning others. It never changes you, but you can condemn others because you have the ideal, the criterion. And whenever you are violent you can rationalize it—your violence is an altogether different thing.

These past twenty-five years we have been violent many times, but we have never condemned our violence. We have always defended and rationalized it in beautiful terms. If we are violent in Bengal, in Bangladesh, then we say that it is to help the people there to obtain freedom. If we are violent in Kashmir, it is to help Kashmiris. But you know, all those who are warmongering say the same. If America is violent in Vietnam, it is for "those poor people." No one is violent for himself; no one ever has been. We are always violent to help someone. Even if I kill you it is for your own good, it is to help you. And even if you are killed, even if I kill you, just look at my compassion. Even for your own good I can kill you. So go on condemning the whole world.

When India attacked Goa, when India went to war with China, Bertrand Russell criticized Nehru, saying, "Where is your nonviolence now? You are all Gandhians. Where is your nonviolence now?" Nehru replied by banning Bertrand Russell's book in India. The book Russell wrote was banned. This is our nonviolent mind.

This was a good discussion. The book should have been distributed free, because he argued beautifully. He said, "You are a violent people. Your nonviolence was just political. Your Gandhi was not a sage, he was just a diplomatic mind. And you all talk about nonviolence, but when the moment comes you become violent. When others are fighting, you stand on your high altar and you condemn the whole world as violent."

With individuals, with societies, with cultures, with nations, this happens. If you have ideals, you need not transform yourself. You can always hope to be transformed in the future by the ideals themselves, and you can condemn others very easily.

Tantra says to remain with yourself. Whatsoever you are, accept it. Do not condemn yourself, do not condemn others. Condemnation is futile, energies are not changed by it.

The first step is to accept. Remain with the fact —this is very scientific—remain with the fact of anger, greed and sex. And know the fact in its total facticity. Do not just touch it from above, from the surface. Know the fact in its totality, in its total facticity. Move into it to the roots. And remember, whenever you can move to the roots of anything you transcend it. If you can know your sex to the very roots, you become the master of it. If you can know your anger to the very roots, you become the master of it. Then anger becomes just instrumental —you can use it.

I remember many things about Gurdjieff. Gurdjieff taught his disciples to be rightly angry. We have heard about Buddha's words: right meditation, right thinking and right contemplation. We have heard about Mahavira's teaching of right vision and right knowledge. Gurdjieff taught right anger and right greed, and the teaching was influenced by the old tantra tradition. Gurdjieff was condemned very much in the West, because in the West he was a living symbol of tantra.

He would teach right anger; he would teach you how to be angry totally. If you were angry he would tell you, "Go on. Do not suppress it, let it come out in its totality. Move into it. Become anger. Do not withhold, do not stand aside. Take a deep jump into it. Let your whole body become a flare, a fire."

You have never moved this deeply and you have never seen anyone do so, because everyone is more or less cultured. No one is original; everyone is more or less imitating. No one is original! If you can move into anger totally, you will become just a fire, a burning. The fire will be so deep, the flames will be so deep, that the past and future both will cease immediately. You will become just a present flame. And when your every cell is burning, when every part of the body has become fiery and you have become just anger—not angry—then Gurdjieff will say, "Now be aware. Do not suppress. Now be aware. Now suddenly be aware of what you have become, of what anger is."

In this moment of total present-ness one can

become suddenly aware, and you can start laughing at the absurdity of the whole thing, at the foolishness, at the stupidity of the whole thing. But this is not suppression; this is laughter. You can laugh at yourself because you have transcended yourself. Never again will anger be capable of mastering you. You have known anger in its totality, and still you could laugh and still you could go beyond it. You could see from beyond your anger. Once you have seen its totality, you know what anger is. And now you also know that even if the whole energy transforms into anger, still you can be an observer, a witness. So there is no fear. Remember this: that which is not known always creates fear. That which is dark always creates fear. You are afraid of your own anger.

So people go on saying that we suppress anger because it is not good to be angry, it may hurt others. But that is not the real cause. The real cause is that they are afraid of their anger. If they really get angry, they do not know what may happen. They are afraid of themselves. They have never known anger. It is a very fearful thing, hidden inside, so they are afraid of it. That is why they fall in line with the society, with the culture, with the education, and they say, "We must not be angry. Anger is bad. It hurts others."

You are afraid of your anger, you are afraid of your sex. You have never been in sex totally. You have never been in sex so totally that you could have forgotten yourself. You were always there; your mind was always there. And if the mind is there in the sex act, then the act is just pseudo, bogus. The mind must dissolve, you must become just body. There must not be any thinking. If thinking is there, you are divided. Then the sex act is nothing but releasing overflowing energy. It is a release, nothing else. But you are afraid to be totally in sex. That is why you fall in line, why you toe the line with the society and say that sex is bad. You are afraid!

Why are you afraid? Because if you move into

sex totally, you do not know what you can do, you do not know what can happen, you do not know what animal force may come up, you do not know what your unconscious may throw you into. You do not know! Then you will not be the master; you will not be in control. Your self-image may be destroyed. Thus you control the sex act. And the way to control it is to remain in the mind. Let the sex act be there, but local.

Try to understand this "local" and "general." Tantra says a sex act is local when only your sex center is involved. It is local; it is a local release. The sex center keeps on accumulating energy. When it is overflowing you have to release it; otherwise it will create tensions, it will create heaviness. You release it, but it is a local release. Your whole body, your whole self is not involved. Nonlocal, total involvement means that every fiber of the body, every cell of the body, whatsoever you are, is in it. Your whole being has become sexual. Not only your sex center, your whole being has become sexual.

But then you are afraid because then anything is possible. And you do not know what can happen because you have never known the totality. You may do certain things of which you cannot conceive.

Your unconscious will explode. You will become not one animal, but many animals, because you have passed through many lives, through many animal bodies. You may start howling, you may start screaming, you may start roaring like a lion. You do not know.

Anything is possible—that creates fear. You need to be in control so that you never lose yourself in anything. That is why you never know anything. And unless you know, you cannot transcend. Accept, move deep, go to the very roots. This is tantra. Tantra stands for deep experiences. Anything experienced can be transcended; anything suppressed can never be transcended.

This much for today.

CHAPTER 9

Techniques for centering

◆

13 *Or, imagine the five-colored circles of the peacock tail to be your five senses in illimitable
space. Now let their beauty melt within.
Similarly, at any point in space or on a wall—
until the point dissolves. Then your wish for
another comes true.*

14 *Place your whole attention in the nerve, delicate as the lotus thread, in the center of your
spinal column. In such be transformed.*

Man is born with a center, but he remains completely oblivious of it. Man can live without knowing his center, but man cannot be without a center. The center is the link between man and existence; it is the root. You may not know it, knowledge is not essential for the center to be, but if you do not know it you will lead a life that is rootless—as if rootless. You will not feel any ground, you will not feel yourself based; you will not feel at home in the universe. You will be homeless.

Of course, the center is there, but by not knowing it your life will be just a drifting—meaningless, empty, reaching nowhere. You will feel as if you are living without life, drifting, just waiting for death. You can go on postponing from one moment to another, but you know very well that that postponing will lead you nowhere. You are just passing time, and that feeling of deep frustration will follow you like a shadow. Man is born with a center, but not with the knowledge of the center. The knowledge has to be gained.

You have the center. The center is there; you cannot be without it. How can you exist without a center? How can you exist without a bridge between you and existence?...or if you like the word, 'God.' You cannot exist without a deep link. You have roots in the divine. Every moment you live through those roots, but those roots are underground. Just as with any tree, the roots are underground; the tree is unaware of its own roots. You

also have roots. That rootedness is your center. When I say man is born with it, I mean it is a possibility that you can become aware of your rootedness.

If you become aware, your life becomes actual; otherwise your life will be just like a deep sleep, a dream. What Abraham Maslow has called "self-actualization" is really nothing but becoming aware of your inner center from where you are linked with the total universe, becoming aware of your roots: you are not alone, you are not atomic, you are part of this cosmic whole. This universe is not an alien world. You are not a stranger, this universe is your home. But unless you find your roots, your center, this universe remains something alien, something foreign.

Sartre says that man lives as if he has been thrown into the world. Of course, if you do not know your center you will feel a thrown-ness, as if you have been thrown into the world. You are an outsider; you do not belong to this world and this world doesn't belong to you. Then fear, then anxiety, then anguish are bound to result.

A man as an outsider in the universe is bound to feel deep anxiety, dread, fear, anguish. His whole life will be just a fight, a struggle, and a struggle which is destined to be a failure. Man cannot succeed because a part can never succeed against the whole.

You cannot succeed against existence. You can succeed with it, but never against it. And that is the difference between a religious man and a nonreligious man. A nonreligious man is against the universe; a religious man is with the universe. A religious man feels at home. He doesn't feel he has been thrown into the world, he feels he has grown in the world. Remember the difference between being thrown and being grown.

When Sartre says man is thrown into the world, the very word, the very formulation shows that you do not belong. And the word, the choice of the word 'thrown' means that you have been forced without your consent. So this world appears inimical. Then anguish will be the result.

It can be otherwise only if you are not thrown into the world, but you have grown as a part, as an organic part. Really, it would be better to say that you are the universe grown into a particular dimension which we call "human." The universe grows in multidimensions—in trees, in hills, in stars, in planets...in multidimensions. Man is also a dimension of growth. The universe is realizing itself through many, many dimensions. Man is also a dimension along with the height and the peak. No tree can become aware of its roots; no animal can become aware of its roots. That is why there is no anxiety for them.

If you are not aware of your roots, of your center, you can never be aware of your death. Death is only for man. It exists only for man because only man can become aware of his roots, aware of his center, aware of his totality and his rootedness in the universe.

If you live without a center, if you feel you are an outsider, then anguish will result. However, if you feel that you are at home, that you are a growth, a realization of the potentiality of the existence itself—as if existence itself has become aware in you, as if it has gained awareness in you—if you feel that way, if you really realize that way, the result will be bliss.

Bliss is the result of an organic unity with the universe, and anguish the result of an enmity. But unless you know the center you are bound to feel a thrown-ness, as if life has been forced upon you. This center which is there, although man is not aware of it, is the concern of these sutras which we will discuss. Before we enter into *Vigyan Bhairav Tantra* and its techniques concerning the center, two or three things more.

One: when man is born he is rooted in a particular spot, in a particular *chakra*—center—and that is the navel. The Japanese call it *hara;* hence the term *hara-kiri.* Hara-kiri means suicide. Literally, the term means killing the hara—the spine, the center. Hara is the center; destroying the center is the meaning of hara-kiri. But in a way, we have all committed hara-kiri. We have not killed the center, but we have forgotten it, or we have never remembered it. It is there waiting, and we have been drifting away and away from it.

When a child is born he is rooted in the navel, in the hara; he lives through the hara. Look at a child breathing—his navel goes up and down. He breathes with the belly, he lives with the belly—not with the head, not with the heart. But by and by he will have to drift away.

First he will develop another center—that is the heart, the center of emotion. He will learn love, he will be loved, and another center will develop. This center is not the real center; this center is a by-product. That is why psychologists say that if a child is not loved, he will never be able to love.

If a child is brought up in a nonloving situation—a situation which is cold, with no one to love and give warmth—he himself will never be able in his life to love anyone because the very center will not develop. Mother's love, father's love, family, society—they help to develop a center. That center is a by-product; you are not born with it. So if it is not being helped to grow, it will not grow. Many, many persons are without the love center. They go on talking about love, and they go on believing that they love, but they lack the center, so how can they love? It is difficult to get a loving mother, and very difficult and rare to get a loving father. Every father, every mother, thinks that he or she loves. It is not so easy. Love is a difficult growth, very difficult. But if love is not there in the beginning for the child, he himself will never be able to love.

That is why the whole humanity lives without love. You go on producing children, but you do not know how to give them a love center. Rather, on the contrary, the more society becomes civilized, the more it forces into being a third center, which is intellect. The navel is the original center. A child is born with it; it is not a by-product. Without it life is impossible, so it is given. The second center is a by-product. If the child gets love, he responds. In this responding, a center grows in him: that is the heart center. The third center is reason, intellect, head. Education, logic and training create a third center; that too is a by-product.

But we live at the third center. The second is almost absent—or even if it is present, then it is nonfunctioning; or even if it functions sometimes, it functions irregularly. But the third center, the head, becomes the basic force in life because the whole life depends on this third center. It is utilitarian. You need it for reason, logic, thinking. So everyone becomes, sooner or later, head-oriented; you begin to live in the head.

Head, heart, navel—these are the three centers. The navel is the given center, the original one. Heart can be developed, and it is good to develop it for many reasons. Reason is necessary to develop also, but reason must not be developed at the cost of the heart—because if reason is developed at the cost of the heart then you miss the link and you cannot come to the navel again. The development is from reason to existence to being. Let us try to understand it in this way.

The center of the navel is in being; the center of the heart is in feeling; the center of the head is in knowing. Knowing is the farthest from being—feeling is nearer. If you miss the feeling center, then it is very difficult to create a bridge between reason and being—really very difficult. That is why a loving person may realize his at-homeness in the world more easily than a person who lives through intellect.

Western culture has basically emphasized the head center. That is why in the West a deep concern is felt for man. And the deep concern is with his homelessness, his emptiness, his uprootedness. Simone Weil wrote a book, *The Need for Roots*. Western man feels uprooted, as if with no roots. The reason is because only the head has become the center. The heart has not been trained, it is missing.

The beating of the heart is not your heart, it is just a physiological function. So if you feel the beating, do not misunderstand that you have a heart. Heart is something else. Heart means the capacity to feel; head means the capacity to know. Heart means the capacity to feel, and being means the capacity to be one—to be one with something... the capacity to be one with something.

Religion is concerned with the being; poetry is concerned with the heart; philosophy and science are concerned with the head. These two centers, heart and head, are peripheral centers, not real centers, just false centers. The real center is the navel, the hara. How to attain it again? Or how to realize it?

Ordinarily it happens only sometimes—rarely, accidentally it happens—that you come near the hara. That moment will become a very deep, blissful moment. For example, in sex sometimes you come near the hara, because in sex your mind, your consciousness moves downwards again. You have to leave your head and fall down. In a deep sexual orgasm, sometimes it happens that you are near your hara. That is why there is so much fascination about sex. It is not really sex which gives you the blissful experience; really, it is the hara.

In falling down toward sex you pass through the hara, you touch it. But for modern man even that has become impossible, because for modern man even sex is a cerebral affair, a mental affair. Even sex has gone into the head; he thinks about it. That is why there are so many films, so many novels, so much literature, pornography and the like. Man thinks about sex, but that is absurdity. Sex is an experience; you cannot think about it. And if you start thinking about it, it will be more and more difficult to experience it because it is not a concern of the head at all. Reason is not needed.

And the more modern man feels incapable of going deep in sex, the more he thinks about it. It becomes a vicious circle. And the more he thinks about it, the more it becomes cerebral. Then even sex becomes futile. It has become futile in the West, a repetitive thing, boring. Nothing is gained, you just go on repeating an old habit. And ultimately you feel frustrated—as if you have been cheated. Why? Because really, the consciousness is not falling back down to the center.

Only when passing through the hara do you feel bliss. So whatsoever may be the cause, whenever you pass through the hara you feel bliss. A warrior on the field fighting sometimes passes through the hara, but not modern warriors because they are not warriors at all. A person throwing a bomb on a city is asleep. He is not a warrior; he is not a fighter; he is not a *kshatriya*—not Arjuna fighting.

Sometimes when one is on the verge of death one is thrown back to the hara. For a warrior fighting with his sword, any moment death becomes possible, any moment he may be no more. And when fighting with a sword you cannot think. If you think, you will be no more. You have to act without thinking because thinking needs time; if you are fighting with a sword you cannot think. If you think then the other will win, you will be no more. There is no time to think, and the mind needs time. Because there is no time to think and thinking will mean death, consciousness falls down from the head—it goes to the hara, and a warrior has a blissful experience. That is why there is so much fascination about war. Sex and war have been two fascinations, and the reason is this: you pass through the hara. You pass through it in any danger.

Nietzsche says, live dangerously. Why? Because in danger you are thrown back to the hara. You cannot think; you cannot work things out with the mind. You have to act immediately.

A snake passes. Suddenly you see the snake and there is a jump. There is no deliberate thinking about it, that "There is a snake." There is no syllogism; you do not argue within your mind, "Now there is a snake and snakes are dangerous, so I must jump." There is no logical reasoning like this. If you reason like this, then you will not be alive at all. You cannot reason. You have to act spontaneously, immediately. The act comes first and then comes thinking. When you have jumped, then you think.

In ordinary life, when there is no danger you think first, then you act. In danger, the whole process is reversed; you act first and then you think. That action coming first without thinking throws you to your original center—the hara. That is why there is the fascination with danger.

You are driving a car faster and faster and faster, and suddenly a moment comes when every moment is dangerous. Any moment and there will be no life. In that moment of suspense, when death and life are just as near to each other as possible, two points just near and you in between, the mind stops: you are thrown to the hara. That is why there is so much fascination with cars, driving—fast driving, mad driving. Or you are gambling and you have put everything you have at stake—the mind stops, there is danger. The next moment you can become a beggar. The mind cannot function; you are thrown to the hara.

Dangers have their appeal because in danger your day-to-day, ordinary consciousness cannot function. Danger goes deep. Your mind is not needed; you become a no-mind. *You are!* You are conscious, but there is no thinking. That moment becomes meditative. Really, in gambling, gamblers are seeking a meditative state of mind. In danger—in a fight, in a duel, in wars—man has always been seeking meditative states.

A bliss suddenly erupts, explodes in you. It becomes a showering inside. But these are sudden, accidental happenings. One thing is certain: whenever you feel blissful you are nearer the hara. That is certain no matter what the cause; the cause is irrelevant. Whenever you pass near the original center you are filled with bliss.

These sutras are concerned with creating a root-edness in the hara, in the center, scientifically, in a planned way—not accidentally, not momentarily, but permanently. You can remain continuously in the hara, that can become your rootedness. How to make this so and how to create this are the concerns of these sutras.

Now we will take the first sutra which is another of the ways concerning the point, or center.

---

13 Concentrate totally on one object.

First: *Or, imagine the five-colored circles of the peacock tail to be your five senses in illimitable space. Now, let their beauty melt within. Similarly, at any point in space or on a wall—until the point dissolves. Then your wish for another comes true.*

All these sutras are concerned with how to achieve the inner center. The basic mechanism used, the basic technique used is, if you can create a center outside—anywhere: in the mind, in the heart, or even outside on a wall—and if you concentrate totally on it and you bracket out the whole world, you forget the whole world and only one point remains in your consciousness, suddenly you will be thrown to your inner center.

How does it work? First understand this.... Your mind is just a vagabond, a wandering. It is never at one point. It is always going, moving, reaching, but never at any point. It goes from one thought to another, from A to B. But it is never at the A; it is never at the B. It is always on the move. Remember this: mind is always on the move, hoping to reach somewhere but never reaching. It cannot reach! The very structure of the mind is movement. It can only move; that is the inherent nature of the mind. The very process is movement —from A to B, from B to C...it goes on and on.

If you stop at A or B or any point, the mind will fight with you. The mind will say, "Move on," because if you stop the mind dies immediately. It

can be alive only in movement. The mind means a process. If you stop and do not move, mind suddenly becomes dead, it is no more there; only consciousness remains.

Consciousness is your nature; mind is your activity—just like walking. It is difficult because we think mind is something substantial. We think mind is a substance—it is not, mind is just an activity. So it is really better to call it "minding" than mind. It is a process just like walking. Walking is a process; if you stop, there is no walking. You have legs, but no walking. Legs can walk, but if you stop, then legs will be there but there will be no walking.

Consciousness is like legs—your nature. Mind is like walking—just a process. When consciousness moves from one place to another, this process is mind. When consciousness moves from A to B, from B to C, this movement is mind. If you stop the movement, there is no mind. You are conscious, but there is no mind. You have legs, but no walking. Walking is a function, an activity; mind is also a function, an activity.

If you stop at any point, the mind will struggle. The mind will say, "Go on!" The mind will try in every way to push you forward or backward or anywhere—but, "Go on!" Anywhere will do, but do not stay at one point.

If you insist and if you do not obey the mind... it is difficult because you have always obeyed. You have never ordered the mind; you have never been masters. You cannot be because, really, you have never disidentified yourself from the mind. You think you are the mind. This fallacy that you are the mind gives the mind total freedom, because then there is no one to master it, to control it. There is no one! Mind itself becomes the master. It may become the master, but that mastery is just seemingly so. Try once and you can break that mastery—it is false.

Mind is just a slave pretending to be the master, but it has pretended so long, for lives and lives, that even the master believes that the slave is the master.

That is just a belief. Try the contrary and you will know that that belief was totally unfounded.

This first sutra says, *Imagine the five-colored circles of the peacock tail to be your five senses in illimitable space. Now let their beauty melt within.* Think that your five senses are five colors, and those five colors are filling the whole space. Just imagine your five senses are five colors—beautiful colors, alive, extended into infinite space. Then move within with those colors. Move within and feel a center where all these five colors are meeting within you. This is just imagination, but it helps. Just imagine these five colors penetrating within you and meeting at a point.

Of course, these five colors will meet at a point: the whole world will dissolve. In your imagination there are only five colors—just like around the tail of a peacock—spread all over space, going deep within you, meeting at a point. Any point will do, but the hara is the best. Think that they are meeting at your navel—that the whole world has become colors, and those colors are meeting at your navel. See that point, concentrate on that point, and concentrate until the point dissolves. If you concentrate on the point it dissolves, because it is just imagination. Remember, whatsoever we have done is imagination. If you concentrate on it, it will dissolve. And when the point dissolves, you are thrown to your center.

The world has dissolved. There is no world for you. In this meditation there is only color. You have forgotten the whole world; you have forgotten all the objects. You have chosen only five colors. Choose any five colors. This is particularly for those who have a very keen eye, a very deep color sensitivity. This meditation will not be helpful to everyone. Unless you have a painter's eye, a color consciousness, unless you can imagine color, it is difficult.

Have you ever observed that your dreams are colorless? Only one person in a hundred is capable of seeing colored dreams. You see just black and white. Why? The whole world is colored and your dreams are colorless. If one of you remembers that his dreams are colored, this meditation is for him. If someone remembers even sometimes that he sees colors in his dreams, then this meditation will be for him.

If you say to a person who is insensitive to color, "Imagine the whole space filled with colors," he will not be able to imagine. Even if he tries to imagine, if he thinks "red," he will see the word 'red', he will not see the color. He will say "green," and the word 'green' will be there, but there will be no greenness.

So if you have a color sensitivity, then try this method. There are five colors. The whole world is just colors and those five colors are meeting in you. Deep down somewhere in you, those five colors are meeting. Concentrate on that point, and go on concentrating on it. Do not move from it; remain at it. Do not allow the mind. Do not try to think about green and red and yellow and about colors—do not think. Just see them meeting in you. Do not think about them! If you think, the mind has moved. Just be filled with colors meeting in you, and then at the meeting point, concentrate. Do not think! Concentration is not thinking; it is not contemplation.

If you are really filled with colors and you have become just a rainbow, a peacock, and the whole space is filled with colors, it will give you a deep feeling of beauty. But do not think about it; do not say it is beautiful. Do not move in thinking. Concentrate on the point where all these colors are meeting and go on concentrating on it. It will disappear, it will dissolve, because it is just imagination. And if you force concentration, imagination cannot remain there, it will dissolve.

The world has dissolved already; there were only colors. Those colors were your imagination. Those imaginative colors were meeting at a point. That point, of course, was imaginary—and now, with deep concentration, that point will dissolve. Where are you now? Where will you be? You will be thrown to your center.

Objects have dissolved through imagination.

Now imagination will dissolve through concentration. You alone are left as a subjectivity. The objective world has dissolved; the mental world has dissolved. You are there only as pure consciousness.

That is why this sutra says: *At any point in space or on a wall....* This will help. If you cannot imagine colors, then any point on the wall will help. Take anything just as an object of concentration. If it is inner it is better, but again, there are two types of personalities. For those who are introvert, it will be easy to conceive of all the colors meeting within. But there are extroverts who cannot conceive of anything within. They can imagine only the outside. Their minds move only on the outside; they cannot move in. For them there is nothing like innerness.

The English philosopher David Hume has said, "Whenever I go in, I never meet any self. All that I meet are only reflections of the outside world—a thought, some emotion, some feeling. I never meet the innerness, I only meet the outside world reflected in." This is the extrovert mind par excellence, and David Hume is one of the most extroverted minds.

So if you cannot feel anything within, and if the mind asks, "What does this innerness mean? How to go in?" then try any point on the wall instead. There are persons who come to me and ask how to go in. It is a problem, because if you know only outgoing-ness, if you know only outward movements, it is difficult to imagine how to go in.

If you are an extrovert then do not try this point inside, try it outside. The same will be the result. Make a dot on the wall; concentrate on it. Then you will have to concentrate on it with open eyes. If you are creating a center inside, a point within, then you will have to concentrate with closed eyes.

Make a point on a wall and concentrate on it. The real thing happens because of concentration, not because of the point. Whether it is out or in is irrelevant. It depends on you. If you are looking at the outside wall, concentrating on it, then go on concentrating until the point dissolves. That has to

be noted: *until the point dissolves!* Do not blink your eyes, because blinking gives a space for the mind to move again. Do not blink, because then the mind starts thinking. It becomes a gap; in the blinking, the concentration is lost. So no blinking.

You might have heard about Bodhidharma, one of the greatest masters of meditation in the whole history of humankind. A very beautiful story is reported about him.

He was concentrating on something—something outward. His eyes would blink and the concentration would be lost, so he tore off his eyelids. This is a beautiful story: he tore off his eyelids, threw them away, and concentrated. After a few weeks, he saw some plants growing on the spot where he had thrown his eyelids. This anecdote happened on a mountain in China, and the mountain's name is Tah, or Ta. Hence, the name 'tea.' Those plants which were growing became tea, and that is why tea helps you to be awake.

When your eyes are blinking and you are falling down into sleep, take a cup of tea. Those are Bodhidharma's eyelids. That is why Zen monks consider tea to be sacred. Tea is not any ordinary thing, it is sacred—Bodhidharma's eyelids. In Japan they have tea ceremonies, and every house has a tea room, and the tea is served with religious ceremony; it is sacred. Tea has to be taken in a very meditative mood.

Japan has created beautiful ceremonies around tea drinking. They will enter the tea room as if they are entering a temple. Then the tea will be made, and everyone will sit silently listening to the samovar bubbling. There is the steam, the noise, and everyone just listening. It is no ordinary thing ...Bodhidharma's eyelids. And because Bodhidharma was trying to be awake with open eyes, tea helps. Because the story happened on the mountain of Tah, it is called tea. Whether true or untrue, this anecdote is beautiful.

If you are concentrating outwardly, then non-blinking eyes will be needed, as if you no longer have eyelids. That is the meaning of throwing away the eyelids. You have only eyes, without eyelids to close them. Concentrating until the point dissolves. If you persist, if you insist and do not allow the mind to move, the point dissolves. And when the point dissolves, if you were concentrated on the point and there was only this point for you in the world, if the whole world had dissolved already, if only this point remained and now the point also dissolves, then the consciousness cannot move anywhere. There is no object to move to—all the dimensions are closed. The mind is thrown to itself, the consciousness is thrown to itself, and you enter the center.

So whether in or out, within or without, concentrate until the point dissolves. This point will dissolve for two reasons. If it is within, it is imaginary—it will dissolve. If it is outside, it is not imaginary, it is real. You have made a dot on the wall and have concentrated on it. Then why will this dot dissolve? One can understand it dissolving inside—it was not there at all; you just imagined it—but on the wall it is there, so why will it dissolve?

It dissolves for a certain reason. If you concentrate on a point, the point is not really going to dissolve, the mind dissolves. If you are concentrating on an outer point, the mind cannot move. Without movement it cannot live, it dies, it stops. And when the mind stops you cannot be related with anything outward. Suddenly all bridges are broken, because mind is the bridge. When you are concentrating on a point on the wall, constantly your mind is jumping from you to the point, from the point to you, from you to the point. There is a constant jumping; there is a process.

When the mind dissolves you cannot see the point, because really, you never see the point through the eyes; you see the point through the mind *and* through the eyes. If the mind is not there, the eyes cannot function. You may go on staring at the wall, but the point will not be seen. The mind is not there; the bridge is broken. The point is real—it is there. When the mind will come back, you will see it again; it is there. But now you cannot see it. And when you cannot see, you cannot move out.

Suddenly, you are at your center.

This centering will make you aware of your existential roots. You will know from where you are joined to the existence. In you, there is a point which is related with the total existence, which is one with it. Once you know this center, you know you are at home. This world is not alien. You are not an outsider. You are an insider, you belong to the world. There is no need of any struggle, there is no fight. There is no inimical relationship between you and the existence. The existence becomes your mother.

It is the existence that has come into you and that has become aware. It is the existence that has flowered in you. This feeling, this realization, this happening...and there can be no anguish again.

Then bliss is not a phenomenon; it is not something that happens and then goes. Then blissfulness is your very nature. When one is rooted in one's center, blissfulness is natural. One happens to be blissful, and by and by one even becomes unaware that one is blissful, because awareness needs contrast. If you are miserable, then you can feel it when you are blissful. When misery is no more, by and by you forget misery completely. And you forget your bliss also. And only when you can forget your bliss also are you really blissful. Then it is natural. As stars are shining, as rivers are flowing, so are you blissful. Your very being is blissful. It is not something that has happened to you: now it *is you*.

With the second sutra, the mechanism is the same, the scientific basis is the same, the working structure is the same:

---

14 Put your awareness on your spine.

Place your whole attention in the nerve, delicate as the lotus thread, in the center of your spinal column. In such be transformed.

For this sutra, for this technique of meditation, one has to close his eyes and visualize his spinal column, his backbone. It is good to look up in some physiology book the structure of the body, or to go to some medical college or hospital and look at the structure of the body. Then close your eyes and visualize your backbone. Let the backbone be straight, erect. Visualize it, see it, and just in the middle of it visualize a nerve, delicate as the lotus thread, running in the center of your spinal column. *In such be transformed.*

If you can, concentrate on the spinal column, and then on a thread in the middle of it—on a very delicate nerve like a lotus thread running through it. Concentrate on it, and this very concentration throws you to your center. Why?

The spinal column is the base of your whole body structure. Everything is joined to it. Really, your brain is nothing but one pole of your spinal column. Physiologists say it is nothing but a spinal column growth; your brain is really a growth of your spinal column.

Your spine is connected with your whole body —everything is connected to it. That is why it is called the spine, the base. In this spine there is really a threadlike thing, but physiology will not say anything about it because it is not material. In this spine, just in the middle, there is a silver cord—a very delicate nerve. It is not really a nerve in the physiological sense. You cannot operate and find it; it will not be found there.

But in deep meditation it is seen. It is there; it is nonmaterial. It is energy, not matter. And really, that energy cord in your spinal column is your life. Through that you are related to the invisible existence, and through that also you are related to the visible. That is the bridge between the invisible and the visible. Through that thread you are related to the body, and through that thread also you are related to your soul.

First, visualize the spine. At first you will feel very strange, you will be able to visualize it, but as an imagination. And if you go on endeavoring, then it will not be just your imagination. You will become capable of seeing your spinal column.

I was working with a seeker on this technique. I gave him a picture of the body structure to concentrate upon so that he would begin to feel how the spinal column can be visualized inside. Then he started. Within a week he came and said, "This is very strange. I tried to see the picture you gave me, but many times that picture disappeared and I saw a different spine. It is not exactly like the picture you gave to me."

So I told him, "Now you are on the right path. Forget that picture completely, and go on seeing the spine that has become visible to you."

Man can see his own body structure from within. We have not tried it because it is very, very fearful, loathsome; because when you see your bones, blood, veins, you become afraid. So really, we have completely blocked our minds from seeing within. We see the body from without, as if someone else is looking at the body. It is just as if you go outside this room and look at it—then you know the outer walls. Come in and look at the house— then you can look at the inner walls. You see your body from outside as if you are somebody else seeing your body. You have not seen your body from inside. We are capable of it, but because of this fear it has become a strange thing.

Indian yoga books say many things about the body which have been found to be exactly right by new scientific research, and science is unable to explain this. How could they know? Surgery and knowledge of the inside of the human body are very recent developments. How could they know of all the nerves, of all the centers, of all the inner structures? They knew even about the latest findings; they have talked about them, they have worked upon them. Yoga has always been aware about all the basic, significant things in the body. But they were not dissecting bodies, so how could they know?

Really, there is another way of looking at your own body—from within. If you can concentrate within, suddenly you begin to see your body—the inner lining of the body. This is good for those who are deeply body-oriented. If you feel yourself a materialist, if you feel yourself to be nothing but body, this technique will be very helpful for you. If you feel yourself to be a body, if you are a believer in Charvaka or in Marx, if you believe that man is nothing but a body, this technique will be very helpful for you. Then go and see the bone structure of man.

In the old tantra and yoga schools they used many bones. Even now a tantric will always be found with some bones, with a man's skull. Really, that is to help concentration from inside. First he concentrates on that skull, then he closes his eyes and tries to visualize his own skull. He goes on trying to see the outer skull inside, and by and by he begins to feel his own skull. His consciousness begins to be focused. That outer skull, the concentration on it and the visualization, are just helps. Once you are focused inside, you can move from your toes to your head. You can move inside—and it is a great universe. Your small body is a great universe.

This sutra uses the spinal column because within the spinal column there is the thread of life. This is why there is so much insistence on a straight backbone, because if the backbone is not straight you will not be capable of seeing the inner thread. It is very delicate, it is very subtle—it is minute. It is an energy flow. So if the spinal column is straight, absolutely straight, only then can you have glimpses of that thread.

But our spinal columns are not straight. Hindus have tried to make everyone's spinal column straight from the very childhood. Their ways of sitting, their ways of sleeping, their ways of walking were all based, basically, on a straight spinal column. If the spinal column is not straight, then it is very difficult to see the inner core. It is delicate—and really, it is not material. It is immaterial; it is a force. When the spinal column is absolutely straight, that threadlike force is seen easily.

...*In such be transformed.* Once you can feel, concentrate and realize this thread, you will be filled with a new light. The light will be coming from your spinal column. It will spread all over

your body; it may even go beyond your body. When it goes beyond, auras are seen.

Everyone has an aura, but ordinarily your auras are nothing but shadows with no light in them— just dark shadows around you. And those auras reflect your every mood. When you are angry, then your auras become as if blood-filled; they become filled with a red, angry expression. When you are sad, dim, down, then your auras are filled with dark threads, as if you are just near death—everything dead, heavy.

When this spinal column thread is realized, your auras become enlightened. So a Buddha, a Mahavira, a Krishna, a Christ are not painted with auras just as decorations, those auras exist. Your spinal column begins to throw out light. Within, you become enlightened—your whole body becomes a body of light—then it penetrates the outer. So really, for a buddha, for anyone who is enlightened, there is no need to ask anyone what he is. The aura shows everything. And when someone becomes enlightened the master knows it, because the aura reveals everything.

I will tell you one story.... Eno, a Chinese master, was working under his master. When Eno went to his master, the master said, "For what have you come here? There is no need to come to me." He couldn't understand. Eno thought that he was not yet ready to be accepted, but the master was seeing something else. He was seeing his growing aura. He was saying this: "Even if you do not come to me, the thing is bound to happen sooner or later, anywhere. You are already in it, so there is no need to come to me."

But Eno said, "Do not reject me." So the master accepted him and told him to go just behind the monastery, in the kitchen of the monastery. It was a big monastery of five hundred monks. The master said to Eno, "Just go behind the monastery and help in the kitchen, and do not come again to me. Whenever it will be needed, I will come to you."

No meditation was given to Eno, no scriptures to read, study or meditate upon. Nothing was taught to him, he was just thrown into the kitchen. The whole monastery was working. There were pundits, scholars, and there were meditators, and there were yogis, and the whole monastery was agog. Everyone was working and this Eno was just cleaning rice and doing kitchen work.

Twelve years passed. Eno didn't go again to the master because it was not allowed. He waited, he waited, he waited…he simply waited. He was just taken as a servant. Scholars would come, meditators would come, and no one would even pay any attention to him. And there were big scholars in the monastery.

Then the master declared that his death was near, and now he wanted to appoint someone to function in his place, so he said, "Those who think they are enlightened should compose a small poem of four lines. In those four lines you should put all that you have gained. And if I approve any poems and see that the lines show that enlightenment has happened, I will choose someone as my successor."

There was a great scholar in the monastery, and no one attempted the poem because everyone knew that he was going to win. He was a great knower of scriptures, so he composed four lines. Those four lines were just like this…the meaning of it was like this: "Mind is like a mirror, and dust gathers on it. Clean the dust, and you are enlightened."

But even this great scholar was afraid because the master would know. He already knows who is enlightened and who is not. Though all he has written is beautiful, it is the very essence of all the scriptures—mind is like a mirror, and dust gathers on it; remove the dust, and you are enlightened—this was the whole gist of all the Vedas, but he knew that was all that it was. He had not known anything, so he was afraid.

He didn't go directly to the master, but in the night he went to the hut, to his master's hut, and wrote all the four lines on the wall without signing —without any signature. In this way, if the master approved and said, "Okay, this is right," then he would say, "I have written them." If he said, "No!

Who has written these lines?" then he would keep silent, he thought.

But the master approved. In the morning the master said, "Okay!" He laughed and said, "Okay! The man who has written this is an enlightened one."

So the whole monastery began to talk about it. Everyone knew who had written it. They were discussing and appreciating, and the lines were beautiful—really beautiful. Then some monks came to the kitchen. They were drinking tea and they were talking, and Eno was there serving them. He heard what had happened.

The moment he heard those four lines, he laughed. So someone asked, "Why are you laughing, you fool? You do not know anything; for twelve years you have been serving in the kitchen. Why are you laughing?"

No one had even heard him laugh before. He was just taken as an idiot who would not even talk. So he said, "I cannot write, and I am not an enlightened one either, but these lines are wrong. So if someone comes with me, I will compose four lines. If someone comes with me, he can write it on the wall. I cannot write; I do not know writing."

So someone followed him—just as a joke. A crowd came there and Eno said, "Write: There is no mind and there is no mirror, so where can the dust gather? One who knows this is enlightened."

But the master came out and he said, "You are wrong," to Eno. Eno touched his feet and returned to his kitchen.

In the night when everyone was asleep, the master came to Eno and said, "You are right, but I could not say so before those idiots—and they are learned idiots. If I had said that you are appointed as my successor, they would have killed you. So escape from here! You are my successor, but do not tell it to anyone. And I knew this the day you came. Your aura was growing; that was why no meditation was given to you. There was no need. You were already in meditation. And these twelve years' silence—not doing anything, not even meditation

—emptied you completely of your mind, and the aura has become full. You have become a full moon. But escape from here! Otherwise they will kill you.

"You have been here for twelve years, and the light has been constantly spreading from you, but no one observed it. And they have been coming to the kitchen, everyone has been coming to the kitchen every day—thrice, four times. Everyone passes through here; that is why I posted you in the kitchen. But no one has recognized your aura. So you escape from here."

When the spinal column thread is touched, seen, realized, an aura begins to grow around you. *...In such be transformed.* Be filled with that light and be transformed. This is also a centering—a centering in the spinal column. If you are body-oriented, this technique will help you. If you are not body-oriented, it is very difficult, it will be very difficult to visualize from the inside. Then to look at your body from the inside will be difficult.

This sutra will be more helpful for women than for men. They are more body-oriented. They live more in the body; they feel more. They can visualize the body more. Women are more body-oriented than men, but for anyone who can feel the body, who feels the body, who can visualize, who can close his eyes and feel his body from within, this technique will be very helpful for him.

Then visualize your spinal column, and in the middle a silver cord running through it. First it may look like imagination, but by and by you will feel that imagination has disappeared and your mind has become focused on that spinal column. And then you will see your own spine. The moment you see the inner core, suddenly you will feel an explosion of the light within you.

Sometimes this can also happen without any effort. It happens sometimes. Again, in a deep sex act it sometimes happens. Tantra knows: in a deep sex act your whole energy becomes concentrated near the spine. Really, in a deep sex act the spine begins to discharge electricity. And sometimes, even, if you touch the spine you will get a shock. If the intercourse is very deep and very loving and long—really, if the two lovers are just in a deep embrace, silent, nonmoving, just being filled with each other, just remaining in a deep embrace—it happens. It has happened many times that a dark room will suddenly become filled with light, and both bodies will be surrounded with a blue aura.

Many, many such cases have happened. Even in some of your experiences it may have happened, but you may not have noticed that in a dark room, in deep love, suddenly you feel a light around both of your bodies, and that light spreads and fills the whole room. Many times it has happened that suddenly things drop from the table in the room without any visible cause. And now psychologists say that in a deep sex act, electricity is discharged. That electricity can have many effects and impacts. Things may suddenly drop, move or be broken, and even photographs have been taken in which light is visible. But that light is always concentrated around the spinal column.

So sometimes, in a deep sex act also—and tantra knows this well and has worked on it—you may become aware, if you can look within to the thread running in the middle of the spinal column. And tantra has used the sex act for this realization, but then the sex act has to be totally different, the quality has to be different. It is not something to be gotten over with; it is not something to be done for a release; it is not something to be finished hurriedly; it is not a bodily act then. Then it is a deep spiritual communion. Really, through two bodies it is a deep meeting of two innernesses, of two subjectivities, penetrating each other.

So I will suggest to you to try this technique when in a deep sex act—it will be easier. Just forget about sex. When in a deep embrace, remain inside. Forget the other person also, just go inside and visualize your spinal column. It will be easier, because then more energy is flowing near the spinal column, and the thread is more visible because you are silent, because your body is at rest. Love is the deepest relaxation, but we have made love also a great tension. We have made it an anxiety, a burden.

In the warmth of love, filled, relaxed, close your eyes. But men ordinarily do not close their eyes. Ordinarily, women do close their eyes. That is why I said that women are more body-oriented while men are not. In a deep embrace in the act of sex, women will close their eyes. Really, they cannot love with open eyes. With closed eyes, they feel the body more from within.

Close your eyes and feel your body. Relax. Concentrate on the spinal column. And this sutra says very simply: *In such be transformed*. And you will be transformed through it.

Enough for today.

Self-actualization: the basic need

♦

There are many questions. The first:

Is self-actualization a basic need of man?

irst, try to understand what is meant by self-actualization. A.H. Maslow has used this term "self-actualization." Man is born as potentiality. He is not really actual—just potential. Man is born as a possibility, not as an actuality. He may become something; he may attain actualization of his potentiality or he may not attain. The opportunity may be used or it may not be used. And nature is not forcing you to become actual. You are free. You can choose to become actual; you can choose not to do anything about it. Man is born as a seed. Thus, no man is born fulfilled—just with the possibility of fulfillment.

If that is the case—and that *is* the case—then self-actualization becomes a basic need. Because unless you are fulfilled, unless you become what you can be or what you are meant to be, unless your destiny is fulfilled, unless you actually attain, unless your seed becomes a fulfilled tree, you will feel that you are missing something. And everyone is feeling that he is missing something. That feeling of missing is really because of this, that you are not yet actual.

It is not really that you are missing riches or position, prestige or power. Even if you get whatsoever you demand—riches, power, prestige, anything—you will feel this constant sense of something miss-ing within you, because this something missing is not related with anything outward. It is related with your inner growth. Unless you become fulfilled, unless you come to a realization, a flowering, unless you come to an inner satisfaction in which you feel, "Now this is what I was meant to be," this sense of something missing will be felt. And you cannot destroy this feeling of something missing by anything else.

So self-actualization means a person has become what he was to become. He was born as a seed and now he has flowered. He has come to the complete growth, an inner growth, to the inner end. The moment you feel that all your potentialities have become actual, you will feel the peak of life, of love, of existence itself.

Abraham Maslow, who has used this term "self-actualization," has also coined another term: "peak experience." When one attains to oneself, he reaches a peak—a peak of bliss. Then there is no hankering after anything. He is totally content with himself. Now nothing is lacking; there is no desire, no demand, no movement. Whatsoever he is, he is totally content with himself. Self-actualization becomes a peak experience, and only a self-actualized person can attain peak experiences. Then whatsoever he touches, whatsoever he is doing or not doing—even just existing—is a peak experience for him; just to be is blissful. Then bliss is not concerned with anything outside, it is just a by-product of the inner growth.

A buddha is a self-actualized person. That is why we picture Buddha, Mahavira and others—

why we have made sculptures, pictures, depictions of them—sitting on a fully blossomed lotus. That fully blossomed lotus is the peak of flowering inside. Inside they have flowered and have become fully blossomed. That inner flowering gives a radiance, a constant showering of bliss from them. All those who come even within their shadows, all those who come near them feel a silent milieu around them.

There is an interesting story about Mahavira. It is a myth, but myths are beautiful and they say much which cannot be said otherwise. It is reported that when Mahavira would move, all around him, in an area of about twenty-four miles, all the flowers would bloom. Even if it was not the season for the flowers, they would bloom. This is simply a poetic expression, but even if one was not self-actualized, if one were to come in contact with Mahavira his flowering would become infectious, and one would feel an inner flowering in oneself also. Even if it was not the right season for a person, even if he was not ready, he would reflect, he would feel an echo. If Mahavira was near someone, that person would feel an echo within himself, and he would have a glimpse of what he could be.

Self-actualization is the basic need. And when I say basic, I mean that if all your needs are fulfilled, all except self-realization, self-actualization, you will feel unfulfilled. In fact, if self-actualization happens and nothing else is fulfilled, still you will feel a deep, total fulfillment. That is why Buddha was a beggar, but yet an emperor.

Buddha came to Kashi when he became enlightened. The king of Kashi came to see him and he asked, "I do not see that you have anything, you are just a beggar, yet I feel myself a beggar in comparison to you. You do not have anything, but the way you walk, the way you look, the way you laugh makes it seem as if the whole world is your kingdom. And you have nothing visible—nothing! So where is the secret of your power? You look like an emperor." Really, no emperor has ever looked

like that—as if the whole world belongs to him. "You are the king, but where is your power, the source?"

So Buddha said, "It is in me. My power, my source of power, whatsoever you feel around me is really within me. I do not have anything except myself, but it is enough. I am fulfilled; now I do not desire anything. I have become desireless."

Really, a self-actualized person will become desireless. Remember this. Ordinarily we say that if you become desireless, you will know yourself. The contrary is more true: if you know yourself, you will become desireless. And the emphasis of tantra is not on being desireless, but on becoming self-actualized. Then desirelessness follows.

Desire means you are not fulfilled within, you are missing something so you hanker after it. You go on, from one desire to another, in search of fulfillment. That search never ends because one desire creates another desire. Really, one desire creates ten desires. If you go in search of a desireless state of bliss through desires, you will never reach. But if you try something else—methods of self-actualization, methods of realizing your inner potentiality, of making them actual—then the more you will become actual the less and less desires will be felt, because really, they are felt only because you are empty inside. When you are not empty within, desiring ceases.

What to do about self-actualization? Two things have to be understood. One: self-actualization doesn't mean that if you become a great painter or a great musician or a great poet you will be self-actualized. Of course, a part of you will be actualized, and even that gives much contentment. If you have a potentiality of being a good musician, and if you fulfill it and you become a musician, a part of you will be fulfilled—but not the total. The remaining humanity within you will remain unfulfilled. You will be lopsided. One part will have grown, and the remaining will have stayed just like a stone hanging around your neck.

Look at a poet. When he is in his poetic mood

he looks like a buddha. He forgets himself completely—the ordinary man in the poet is as if he is no more there. So when a poet is in his mood, he has a peak—a partial peak. And sometimes poets have glimpses which are only possible with enlightened, buddhalike minds. A poet can speak like a buddha. For example, Kahlil Gibran speaks like a buddha but he is not a buddha. He is a poet—a great poet.

So if you see Kahlil Gibran through his poetry, he looks like Buddha, Christ or Krishna. But if you go and meet the man Kahlil Gibran, he is just ordinary. He talks about love so beautifully—even a buddha may not talk so beautifully. But a buddha knows love with his total being. Kahlil Gibran knows love in his poetic flight. When he is on his poetic flight, he has glimpses of love—beautiful glimpses. He expresses them with rare insight. But if you go and see the real Kahlil Gibran, the man, you will feel a disparity. The poet and the man are far apart. The poet seems to be something which happens to this man sometimes, but this man is not the poet.

That is why poets feel that when they are creating poetry someone else is creating; they are not creating. They feel as if they have become instruments of some other energy, some other force. They are no more. This feeling comes because, really, their totality is not actualized—only a part of it is, a fragment.

You have not touched the sky. Only one of your fingers has touched the sky, and you remain rooted on the earth. Sometimes you jump, and for a moment you are not on the earth; you have deceived gravity. But the next moment you are on the earth again. When a poet is feeling fulfilled, he will have glimpses—partial glimpses. When a musician is feeling fulfilled, he will have partial glimpses.

It is said of Beethoven that when he was on the stage he was a different man, altogether different. Goethe has said that when Beethoven was on stage directing his group, his orchestra, he looked like a god. It could not be said that he was an ordinary

man. He was not a man at all; he was superhuman. The way he looked, the way he raised his hands, was all superhuman. But when he came back from the stage he was just an ordinary man. The man on the stage seemed to be possessed by something else, as if Beethoven was no more there and some other force had entered into him. Back down from the stage he was again Beethoven, the man.

Because of this, poets, musicians, great artists, creative people are more tense—because they have two types of being. Ordinary man is not so tense because he always lives in one: he lives on the earth. But poets, musicians, great artists jump; they go beyond gravity. In certain moments they are not on this earth, they are not part of humanity. They become part of the buddha world—the land of the buddhas. Then again they are back here. They have two points of existence; their personalities are split.

So every creative artist, every great artist is in a certain way insane. The tension is so much! The rift, the gap between these two types of existences is so great—unbridgeably great. Sometimes he is just an ordinary man; sometimes he becomes buddhalike. Between these two points he is divided, but he has glimpses.

When I say self-actualization, I do not mean that you should become a great poet or you should become a great musician. I mean that you should become a total man. I do not say a great man because a great man is always partial. Greatness in anything is always partial. One moves and moves and moves in one direction, and in all other dimensions, all other directions, one remains the same—one becomes lopsided.

When I say become a total man, I do not mean become a great man. I mean create a balance, be centered, be fulfilled as a man—not as a musician, not as a poet, not as an artist, but fulfilled as a man. What does it mean to be fulfilled as a man? A great poet is a great poet because of great poetry. A great musician is great because of great music. A great man is a great man because of certain things he has done—he may be a great hero. A great man in any direction is partial. Greatness is partial, fragmentary. That is why great men have to face more anguish than ordinary men.

What is a total man? What is meant by being a whole man, a total man? It means, firstly, be centered; do not exist without a center. This moment you are something, the next moment something else. People come to me and I generally ask them, "Where do you feel your center—in the heart, in the mind, in the navel, where? In the sex center? Where? Where do you feel your center?"

Generally they say, "Sometimes I feel it in the head, sometimes in the heart, sometimes I do not feel it at all." So I tell them to close their eyes before me and feel it just now. In the majority of cases this happens: they say, "Just now, for a moment, I feel that I am centered in the head." But the next moment they are not there. They say, "I am in the heart." And the next moment the center has slipped, it is somewhere else, at the sex center or somewhere else.

Really, you are not centered; you are only momentarily centered. Each moment has its own center, so you go on shifting. When mind is functioning you feel that the head is the center. When you are in love, you feel it is the heart. When you are not doing anything particularly, you are confused—you cannot find out where the center is, because you can find this out only when you are working, doing something. Then a particular part of the body becomes the center. But *you* are not centered. If you are not doing anything, you cannot find where your center of being is.

A total man is centered. Whatsoever he is doing, he remains in the center. If his mind is functioning, he is thinking; thinking goes on in the head but he remains centered in the navel. The center is never missed. He uses the head, but he never moves to the head. He uses the heart, but he never moves to the heart. All these things become instruments, and he remains centered.

Secondly, he is balanced. Of course, when one is

centered one is balanced. His life is a deep balance. He is never one-sided, he is never at any extreme—he remains in the middle. Buddha has called this the middle path. He remains always in the middle.

A man who is not centered will always move to the extreme. When he eats he will eat much, he will overeat, or he can fast, but right eating is impossible for him. Fasting is easy, overeating is okay. He can be in the world, committed, involved, or he can renounce the world—but he can never be balanced. He can never remain in the middle, because if you are not centered you do not know what middle means.

A person who is centered is always in the middle in everything, never at any extreme. Buddha says his eating is right eating; it is neither overeating, nor fasting. His labor is right labor—never too much, never too little. Whatsoever he is, he is always balanced.

First thing:

A self-actualized person will be centered.

Second thing: he will be balanced.

Thirdly: if these two things happen—centering, balance—many things will follow. He will always be at ease. Whatsoever the situation, the at-easeness will not be lost. I say whatsoever the situation—unconditionally, the at-easeness will not be lost, because one who is at the center is always at ease. Even if death comes, he will be at ease. He will receive death as one receives any other guest. If misery comes, he will receive it. Whatsoever happens, it cannot dislodge him from his center. That at-easeness is also a by-product of being centered.

For such a man, nothing is trivial, nothing is great; everything becomes sacred, beautiful, holy—everything! Whatsoever he is doing, whatsoever, it is of ultimate concern—as if of ultimate concern. Nothing is trivial. He will not say, "This is trivial, this is great." Really, nothing is great, nor is anything small and trivial. The touch of the man is significant. A self-actualized person, a balanced, centered person, changes everything. The very touch makes it great.

If you observe a buddha, you will see that he walks and he loves walking. If you go to Bodhgaya where Buddha attained enlightenment, to the bank of the Niranjana—to the place where he was sitting under the bodhi tree—you will see that the place of his steps has been marked. He would meditate for one hour, then he would walk around. In Buddhist terminology this is called *chakraman*. He would sit under the bodhi tree, then he would walk. But he would walk with a serene attitude, as if in meditation.

Someone asked Buddha, "Why do you do this? Sometimes you sit with closed eyes and meditate, then you walk."

Buddha said, "Sitting in order to be silent is easy, so I walk. But I carry the same silence within. I sit, but inside I am the same—silent. I walk, but inside I am the same—silent."

The inner quality is the same…. When he meets an emperor and when he meets a beggar, a buddha is the same, he has the same inner quality. When meeting a beggar he is not different, when meeting an emperor he is not different; he is the same. The beggar is not a nobody and the emperor is not a somebody. And really, while meeting a buddha, emperors have felt like beggars and beggars have felt like emperors. The touch, the man, the quality remains the same.

When Buddha was alive, every day in the morning he would say to his disciples, "If you have to ask anything, ask." The day he was dying, that morning it was the same. He called his disciples and said, "Now if you want to ask anything, you can ask. And remember, that this is the last morning. Before this day ends, I will be no more." He was the same. That was his daily question in the morning. He was the same! The day was the last, but he was the same. Just as on any other day, he said, "Okay, if you have to ask anything, you can ask—but this is the last day."

There was no change of tone, but the disciples began to weep. They forgot to ask anything.

Buddha said, "Why are you weeping? If you would have wept on another day it would have been okay, but this is the last day. By the evening I will be no more, so do not waste time in weeping. Another day it would have been okay; you could have wasted time. Do not waste your time in weeping. Why are you weeping? Ask if you have anything to ask." He was the same in life and death.

So thirdly, the self-actualized man is at ease. Life and death are the same; bliss and misery are the same. Nothing disturbs him, nothing dislocates him from his home, from his centeredness. To such a man you cannot add anything. You cannot take anything out of him, you cannot add anything to him—he is fulfilled. His every breath is a fulfilled breath, silent, blissful. He has attained. He has attained to existence, to being; he has flowered as a total man.

This is not a partial flowering. Buddha is not a great poet. Of course, whatsoever he says is poetry. He is not a poet at all, but even when he moves, walks, it is poetry. He is not a painter, but whenever he speaks, whatsoever he says becomes a painting. He is not a musician, but his whole being is music par excellence. The man as a totality has attained. So now, whatsoever he is doing or not doing…when he is sitting in silence, not doing anything, even in silence his presence works, creates; it becomes creative.

Tantra is concerned not with any partial growth, it is concerned with you as a total being. So three things are basic: you must be centered, rooted, and balanced; that is, always in the middle —of course, without any effort. If there is effort you are not balanced. And you must be at ease—at ease in the universe, at home in the existence, and then many things follow. This is a basic need, because unless this need is fulfilled you are a man only in name. You are a man as a possibility, you are not actually a man. You can be, you have the potentiality, but the potentiality has to be made actual.

The second question:

Kindly explain contemplation, concentration and meditation.

Contemplation means directed thinking. We all think; that is not contemplation. That thinking is undirected, vague, leading nowhere. Really, our thinking is not contemplation, but what Freudians call association. One thought leads to another without any direction from you. The thought itself leads to another because of association.

You see a dog crossing the street. The moment you see the dog, your mind starts thinking about dogs. The dog has led you to this thought, and then the mind has many associations. When you were a child, you were afraid of a particular dog. That dog comes to the mind and then the childhood comes to the mind. Then dogs are forgotten; then just by association you begin to daydream about your childhood. Then the childhood goes on being connected with other things, and you move in circles.

Whenever you are at ease, try to go backwards from your thinking to where the thoughts came from. Go back, retrace the steps. Then you will see that another thought was there, and that led to this. And they are not logically connected, because how is a dog on the street connected with your childhood?

There is no logical connection—only association in your mind. If I was crossing the street, the same dog would not lead me to my childhood, it would lead to something else. In a third person it would lead to still something else. Everyone has associated chains in the mind. With any one person some happening, some accident will lead to the chain. Then the mind begins to function like a computer. Then one thing leads to another, another leads to another, and you go on, and the whole day you are doing that.

Write down on a sheet of paper whatsoever comes to your mind, honestly. You will be just amazed what is happening in your mind. There is no relation between two thoughts, and you go on doing this type of thinking. You call this thinking?

This is just association of one thought with another, and they lead themselves...you are led.

Thinking becomes contemplation when it moves not through association, but is directed. You are working on a particular problem—then you bracket out all associations. You move on that problem only, you direct your mind. The mind will try to escape to any bypath, to any side route, to some association. You cut off all the side routes; on only one road you direct your mind.

A scientist working on a problem is in contemplation. A logician working on a problem, a mathematician working on a problem is in contemplation. A poet contemplates a flower. Then the whole world is bracketed out, and only that flower and the poet remains, and he moves with the flower. Many things from side routes will attract, but he does not allow his mind to move anywhere. Mind moves in one line, directed. This is contemplation.

Science is based on contemplation. Any logical thinking is contemplation: thought is directed, thinking guided. Ordinary thinking is absurd. Contemplation is logical, rational.

Then there is concentration. Concentration is staying at one point. It is not thinking; it is not contemplation. It is really being at one point, not allowing the mind to move at all. In ordinary thinking mind moves as a madman. In contemplation the madman is led, directed; he cannot escape anywhere. In concentration the mind is not allowed to move. In ordinary thinking, it is allowed to move anywhere; in contemplation, it is allowed to move only somewhere; in concentration, it is not allowed to move, it is only allowed to be at one point. The whole energy, the whole movement stops, sticks to one point.

Yoga is concerned with concentration, ordinary mind with undirected thinking, the scientific mind with directed thinking. The yogic mind has its thinking focused, fixed at one point; no movement is allowed.

And then there is meditation. In ordinary thinking, mind is allowed to move anywhere; in contemplation, it is allowed only in one direction, all other directions are cut off. In concentration, it is not allowed to move even in one direction; it is allowed only to concentrate on one point.

And in meditation, mind is not allowed at all. Meditation is no-mind.

These are four stages: ordinary thinking, contemplation, concentration, meditation.

Meditation means no-mind—not even concentration is allowed. Mind itself is not allowed to be! That is why meditation cannot be grasped by mind. Up to concentration mind has a reach, an approach. Mind can understand concentration, but mind cannot understand meditation. Really, mind is not allowed at all. In concentration, mind is allowed to be at one point. In meditation, even that point is taken away. In ordinary thinking, all directions are open. In contemplation, only one direction is open. In concentration, only one point is open—no direction. In meditation, even that point is not open: mind is not allowed to be.

Ordinary thinking is the ordinary state of mind, and meditation is the highest possibility. The lowest one is ordinary thinking, association, and the highest, the peak, is meditation—no-mind.

And with the second question, it is also asked:

Contemplation and concentration are mental processes. How can mental processes help in achieving a state of no-mind?

The question is significant. Mind asks, how can mind itself go beyond mind? How can any mental process help to achieve something which is not of the mind? It looks contradictory. How can your mind try, make an effort to create a state which is not of mind?

Try to understand. When mind is, what is there? A process of thinking. When there is no-mind, what is there? No process of thinking. If you go on decreasing your process of thinking, if you go on dissolving your thinking, by and by, slowly, you are reaching no-mind. Mind means thinking; no mind means nonthinking. And mind can help. Mind can help in committing suicide. You can commit suicide; you never ask how a man who is alive can help himself to be dead. You can help yourself to be dead —everyone is trying to help. You can help yourself to be dead, and you are alive. Mind can help to be no-mind. How can mind help?

If the process of thinking becomes more and more dense, then you are proceeding from mind to more mind. If the process of thinking becomes less dense, is decreased, is slowed down, you are helping yourself toward no-mind. It depends on you. And mind can be a help, because really, mind is what you are doing with your consciousness this very moment. If you leave your consciousness alone, without doing anything with it, it becomes meditation.

So there are two possibilities: either slowly, gradually you decrease your mind, by and by. If one percent is decreased, then you have ninety-nine percent mind and one percent no-mind within you. It is as if you have removed some furniture from your room—then some space is created there. Then you remove more furniture, and more space is created there. When you have removed all the furniture, the whole room becomes space.

Really, space is not created by removing the furniture, the space was already there. It is only that the space was occupied by the furniture. When you remove the furniture, no space comes in from outside; the space was there, occupied by furniture. You have removed the furniture, and the space is recovered, reclaimed. Deep down mind is space occupied, filled by thoughts. If you remove some thoughts, space is created—or discovered, or reclaimed. If you go on removing your thoughts, by and by you go on regaining your space. This space is meditation.

Slowly it can be done—suddenly also. There is no need to go on for lives together removing the furniture, because there are problems. When you start to remove the furniture, one percent space is created and ninety-nine percent space is occupied.

That ninety-nine percent occupied space will not feel good about the unoccupied space; it will try to fill it. So one goes on slowly decreasing thoughts and then again creating new thoughts.

In the morning you sit for meditation for some time; you slow down your process of thought. Then you go to the market, and again there is a rush of thoughts. The space is filled again. The next day you again do this, and you go on doing this—throwing it out, and inviting it in again.

You can also throw all the furniture out suddenly. It is your decision. It is difficult because you have become accustomed to the furniture. You may feel uncomfortable without the furniture; you will not know what to do with that space. You may become afraid even to move in that space. You have never moved in such freedom.

Mind is a conditioning. We have become accustomed to thoughts. Have you ever observed—or if you have not observed, then observe—that you go on repeating the same thoughts every day. You are like a gramophone record, and then too not a fresh, new one—old. You go on and on repeating the same things. Why? What is the use of it? Only one use, it is just a long habit; you feel you are doing something.

You are lying on your bed just waiting for sleep to come and the same things are repeated every day. Why are you doing this? It helps in a way. Old habits, conditionings, help. A child needs a toy. If the toy is given to him, he will fall into sleep; then you can take away the toy. But if the toy is not there, the child cannot fall into sleep. It is a conditioning. The moment the toy is given to him, it triggers something in his mind. Now he is ready to fall into sleep.

The same is happening with you. The toys may differ. One person cannot fall into sleep unless he starts chanting, "Rama, Rama, Rama..." He cannot fall into sleep! This is a toy. If he chants, "Rama, Rama, Rama..." the toy is given to him; he can fall into sleep.

You feel difficulty in falling asleep in a new room. If you are accustomed to sleeping in particular clothes, then you will need those particular clothes every day. Psychologists say that if you sleep in a nightgown and it is not given to you, you will feel difficulty in falling asleep. Why? If you have never slept naked and you are told to sleep naked, you will not feel at ease. Why? There is no relationship between nakedness and sleep, but for you there is a relationship, an old habit. With old habits one feels at ease, comfortable.

Thinking patterns are also just habits. You feel comfortable—the same thoughts every day, the same routine. You feel everything is okay.

You have investments in your thoughts, that is the problem. Your furniture is not just rubbish to be thrown, you have invested many, many things in it. All the furniture can be thrown immediately, it can be done! There are sudden methods of which we will speak. Immediately, this very moment, you can be freed of your whole mental furniture. But then you will be suddenly vacant, empty, and you will not know who you are. Now you will not know what to do because for the first time your old patterns are no more. The shock may be too sudden. You may even die, or you may go mad.

That is why sudden methods are not used. Unless one is ready, sudden methods are not used. One may go suddenly mad because one may miss all the moorings. The past drops immediately, and when past drops immediately you cannot conceive of the future, because the future was always conceived of in terms of the past.

Only the present remains, and you have never been in the present. Either you were in the past or in the future. So when you are just in the present for the first time, you will feel you have gone berserk, mad. That is why sudden methods are not used unless you are working in a school, unless you are working with a master in a group, unless you are totally devoted, unless you have dedicated your whole life for meditation.

So gradual methods are good. They take a long time, but by and by you become accustomed to space. You begin to feel the space and the beauty of it, and the bliss of it, and then your furniture is removed by and by.

So from ordinary thinking it is good to become contemplative—that is the gradual method. From contemplation it is good to move to concentration—that is the gradual method. And from concentration it is good to take a jump into meditation. Then you are moving slowly, feeling the ground at every step. And when you are really rooted in one step, only then do you begin to go for the next one. It is not a jump, it is a gradual growth. So these four things—ordinary thinking, contemplation, concentration, meditation—are four steps.

The third question:

Is the development of the navel center exclusively free and separate from the growth of the heart and head centers, or does the navel center develop simultaneously with the growth of the heart and the head? And also, please explain in which way the training and techniques for the navel center will differ from the training and techniques for the development of the heart and head centers.

One basic thing to be understood: the heart and head centers are to be developed, not the navel center. The navel center is just to be discovered; it is not to be developed. The navel center is already there. You have to uncover, or discover it. It is there fully developed, you are not to develop it. The heart center and the head center are developments. They are not there to be discovered, they have to be developed. Society, culture, education, conditioning help to develop them.

But you are born with a navel center. Without the navel center you cannot be. You can be without the heart center, you can be without the head center. They are not necessities; it is good to have them, but you can be without them. It will be very inconvenient, but you can be without them. However, without the navel center you cannot be. It is not just a necessity, it is your life.

So there are techniques for how to develop the heart center—how to grow in love, how to grow in sensitivity, how to become a more sensitive mind. There are methods and techniques for how to become more rational, more logical. Reason can be developed, emotion can be developed, but existence cannot be developed. It is already there; it has to be discovered.

Many things are implied in this. One: it may not be possible for you to have a mind, a reasoning faculty, like Einstein. But you can become a buddha. Einstein is a mind center functioning at its perfection. Or someone else...a lover. A Majnu is functioning at his heart center in its perfection. You may not be able to become a Majnu, but you can become a buddha because buddhahood is not to be developed in you, it is already there. It is concerned with the basic center, the original center—the navel. It is already there. You are already a buddha, only unaware.

You are not already an Einstein. You will have to try, and then too there is no guarantee that you will become one. There is no guarantee because really, it seems impossible. Why does it seem impossible? Because to develop the head of Einstein needs the same growth, the same milieu, the same training as was given to him. It cannot be repeated because it is unrepeatable. First you will have to find the same parents, because the training begins in the womb. It is difficult to find the same parents—impossible. How can you find the same parents, the same date of birth, the same home, the same associates, the same friends? You will have to repeat the life of Einstein exactly—ditto! If even one point is missing, you will be a different man.

So that is impossible. Any individual is born only once in this world because the same situation cannot be repeated. The same situation is such a big phenomenon. It means there must be the same world in the same moment! It is not possible—it is impossible. And you are already here, so whatsoever you do, your past will be in it. You cannot become an Einstein. Individuality cannot be repeated.

Buddha is not an individual, Buddha is a phenomenon. No individual factors are meaningful; just your being is enough to be a buddha. The center is already there, functioning; you have to discover it. So the techniques for the heart are techniques for developing something, and the techniques concerning the navel center are concerned with uncovering. You have to uncover. You are already a buddha, you only have to know the fact.

So there are two types of persons—buddhas who know that they are buddhas, and buddhas who do not know that they are buddhas. But all are buddhas. As far as existence is concerned, everyone is the same. Only in existence is there communism; in everything else communism is absurd. No one is equal, inequality is basic in everything else. So it may look like a paradox if I say that only religion leads to communism, but I mean *this* communism: this deep equality of existence, of being. In this you are equal to Buddha, to Christ, to Krishna, but in no other way are two individuals equal. Inequality is basic as far as outer life is concerned; equality is basic as far as inner life is concerned.

So these one hundred and twelve methods are not really for developing the navel center; they are for uncovering it. That is why instantly sometimes one becomes a buddha, because there is no question of creating something. If you can look at yourself, if you can go deep down into yourself, all that you need is already there. It is already the case, so the only question is how to be thrown to that point where you are already a buddha. Meditation doesn't help you to be a buddha, it only helps you to become aware of your buddhahood.

One question more:

Are all enlightened ones navel-centered? For example, is Krishnamurti head- or navel-centered? Was Ramakrishna heart- or navel-centered?

Every enlightened one is navel-centered, but the expression of each enlightened one may flow through other centers. Understand the distinction clearly. Every enlightened one is navel-centered; there is no other possibility. But the expression is a different thing.

Ramakrishna expresses himself from the heart. He uses his heart as the vehicle of his message. Whatsoever he has found at the navel he expresses through his heart. He sings, he dances—that is his way of expressing his bliss. The bliss is found at the navel, nowhere else. He is centered at the navel, but how to say to others that he is centered at the navel? He uses his heart for the expression.

Krishnamurti uses his head for that expression; that is why their expressions are contradictory. If you believe in Ramakrishna you cannot believe in Krishnamurti. If you believe in Krishnamurti you cannot believe in Ramakrishna, because belief is always centered in the expression, not in the experience. Ramakrishna looks childish to a man who thinks with reason: "What is this nonsense—dancing, singing? What is he doing? Buddha never danced, and this Ramakrishna is dancing. He looks childish."

To reason the heart always looks childish, but to the heart reason looks useless, superficial. Whatsoever Krishnamurti says is the same. The experience is the same as it was for Ramakrishna or Chaitanya or Meera. But if the person is head-centered, his explanation, expression is rational. If Ramakrishna sees Krishnamurti he will say, "Come on, let us dance. Why waste your time? Through dance it can be expressed more easily, and it goes deeper." Krishnamurti will say, "Dance? One gets hypnotized through dance. Do not dance. Analyze! Reason! Reason it out, analyze, be aware."

These are different centers being used for expression, but the experience is the same. One can paint the experience—Zen masters have painted their experience. When they became enlightened, they would paint it. They would not say anything, they would just paint it. The *rishis*, sages, of the Upanishads have created beautiful poetry. When they became enlightened they would create poetry. Chaitanya used to dance; Ramakrishna used to sing. Buddha and Mahavira used the head, reason, to explain, to say whatsoever they had experienced. They created great systems of thought to express their experience.

But the experience is neither rational nor emotional: it is beyond both. There have been few persons, very few, who could express through both the centers. You can find many Krishnamurtis, you can find many Ramakrishnas, but only sometimes does it happen that a person can express through both the centers. Then the person becomes confusing. Then you are never at ease with that man because you cannot conceive of any relationship between the two; they appear contradictory.

If I say something, when I say it I must say it through reason. So I attract many people who are rationalistic, head-oriented. Then one day they see that I allow singing and dancing and they become uncomfortable: "What is this? There is no relationship...." But to me there is no contradiction. Dancing is also a way of speaking—and sometimes a deeper way. Reason is also a way of speaking—and sometimes a very clear way. So both are ways of expression.

If you see Buddha dancing, you will be in difficulty. If you see Mahavira playing on a flute, standing naked, then you will not be able to sleep. What happened to Mahavira? Has he gone mad? With Krishna the flute is okay, but with Mahavira it is absolutely unbelievable. A flute in the hand of Mahavira? Inconceivable! You cannot even imagine it. But the reason is not that there is any contradiction between Mahavira and Krishna, Buddha and Chaitanya; it is due to difference of expression. Buddha will attract a particular type of mind—the head-oriented mind—and Chaitanya and Ramakrishna will attract quite the opposite—the heart-oriented mind.

But difficulties arise. A person like me creates difficulties: I attract both, and then no one is at ease. Whenever I am talking, then the head-

oriented person is at ease, but whenever I allow the other type of expression the head-oriented one becomes uneasy. And the same happens to the other—when some emotional method is used the heart-oriented one feels at ease, but when I discuss, when I reason out something, then he is absent, he is not here. He says, "This is not for me."

One lady came just a day before, and she said, "I was at Mount Abu, but then there was a difficulty. The first day when I heard you it was beautiful, it appealed to me; I was just thrilled. But then I saw *kirtan*—devotional chanting and dancing—so I decided to leave immediately; that was not for me. I went to the bus station, but then there was a problem. I wanted to hear you talk, so I came back. I didn't want to miss what you were saying." She must have been in difficulty. She said to me, "It was so contradictory."

It appeared so because these centers are contradictory, but this contradiction is in *you*. Your head is not at ease with your heart; they are in conflict. Because of your inner conflict, Ramakrishna and Krishnamurti appear to be in conflict. Create a bridge between your head and your heart, and then you will know that these are mediums.

Ramakrishna was absolutely uneducated—no development of reason. He was pure heart. Only one center was developed, the heart. Krishnamurti is pure reason. He was in the hands of some of the most vigorous rationalists—Annie Besant, Leadbeater and the theosophists. They were the great system makers of this century. Really, theosophy is one of the greatest systems ever created, absolutely rational. He was brought up by rationalists; he is pure reason. Even if he talks about heart and love, the very expression is rational.

Ramakrishna is different. Even if he talks about reason, he is absurd. Totapuri came to him, and Ramakrishna began to learn Vedanta from him. So Totapuri said, "Leave all this devotional nonsense. Leave this Kali, the mother, absolutely. Unless you leave all this I am not going to teach you, because Vedanta is not devotion, it is knowledge."

So Ramakrishna said, "Okay, but allow me one moment so that I can go and ask the mother if I may leave everything, this whole nonsense. Allow me one moment to ask the mother."

This is a heart-oriented man. Even to leave the mother he will have to ask her. "And," he said, "she is so loving, she will allow me, so you do not bother."

Totapuri could not understand what he had said.

Ramakrishna said, "She is so loving, she has never said no to me at any time. If I say, 'Mother, I am to leave you because now I am learning Vedanta and I cannot do this devotional nonsense, so allow me please,' she will allow. She will give me total freedom to drop it."

Create a bridge between your head and heart, and then you will see that all those who have ever become enlightened speak the same thing, only their languages may differ.

CHAPTER 11

Techniques to penetrate the inner

♦

T H E S U T R A S

15 *Closing the seven openings of the head with your hands, a space between your eyes becomes all inclusive.*

16 *Blessed one, as senses are absorbed in the heart, reach the center of the lotus.*

17 *Unminding mind, keep in the middle—until.*

Man is as if he is a circle without a center. His life is superficial; his life is only on the circumference. You live on the outside, you never live within. You cannot, unless a center is found. You cannot live within, really you have no within. You are without a center, you have only the without. That is why we go on talking about the within, about how to go in, how to know oneself, how to penetrate inwards, but these words do not carry any authentic meaning. You know the meaning of the words, but you cannot feel what they mean because you are never in. You have never been in.

Even when you are alone, in your mind you are in a crowd. When no one is there outside, still you are not within. You go on thinking of others; you go on moving outwards. Even while asleep you are dreaming of others, you are not within. Only in very deep sleep, when there is no dreaming, are you within, but then you become unconscious. Remember this fact: when you are conscious you are never within, and when you are within in deep sleep you become unconscious. So your whole consciousness consists of the without. And whenever we talk about going within, the words are understood but the meaning is not—because the meaning is not carried by the words, the meaning comes through experience.

Words are without meaning. When I say "within,"you understand the word—but only the word, not the meaning. You do not know what within is, because consciously you have never been within. Your mind is constantly outgoing. You do not have any feel of what the inner means or what it is.

That is what I mean when I say that you are a circle without a center—a circumference only. The center is there, but you drop into it only when you are not conscious. Otherwise, when you are conscious you move outwards, and because of this your life is never intense; it cannot be. It is just lukewarm. You are alive as if dead, or both simultaneously. You are deadly alive—living a deadlike life. You are existing at the minimum— not at the maximum peak, but at the minimum. You can say, "I am," that is all. You are not dead; that is what you mean by being alive.

But life can never be known at the circumference. Life can be known only at the center. On the circumference only lukewarm life is possible. So really, you live a very inauthentic life, and then even death becomes inauthentic—because one who has not really lived cannot really die. Only authentic life can become authentic death. Then death is beautiful: anything authentic is beautiful. Even life, if it is inauthentic, is bound to be ugly. And your life is ugly, just rotten. Nothing happens. You simply go on waiting, hoping that something will happen somewhere, someday.

At this very moment there is just emptiness, and every moment has been like that in the past—just empty. You are just waiting for the future, hoping that something will happen someday, just hoping. Then every moment is lost. It has not happened in the past, so it is not going to happen in the future either. It can happen only in this moment, but then you will need an intensity, a penetrating intensity. Then you will need to be rooted in the center, then the periphery will not do. Then you will have to find your moment.

Really, we never think about what we are, and whatsoever we think is just hokum. Once I lived with a professor on a university campus. One day he came and he was very upset, so I asked, "What is the matter?"

He said, "I feel feverish."

I was reading something, so I said to him, "Go to sleep. Take this blanket and rest."

He went to the bed, but after a few minutes he said, "No, I am not feverish. Really, I am angry. Someone has insulted me, and I feel much violence against him."

So I said, "Why did you say that you are feeling feverish?"

He said, "I couldn't acknowledge the fact that I was angry, but really I am angry. There is no fever." He threw off the blanket.

Then I said, "Okay, if you are angry then take this pillow. Beat it and be violent with it. Let your violence be released. And if the pillow is not enough, then I am available. You can beat me, and let this anger be thrown out."

He laughed, but the laughter was false—just painted on his face. It came on his face and then disappeared, it never penetrated in. It never came from within; it was just a painted smile. But the laughter, even false laughter, created a gap. He said, "Not really...I am not really angry. Someone said something before others, and I felt very much embarrassed. Really, this is the thing."

So I said to him, "You have changed your statement about your own feelings three times within half an hour. You said you were feeling feverish, then you said you were angry, and now you say that you are not angry but just embarrassed. Which one is real?"

He said, "Really, I am embarrassed."

I said, "Which? When you said you were fever-ish, you were also certain about that. When you said you were angry, you were also certain about that. And you are also certain about this. Are you one person or many persons? For how long a time is this certainty going to continue?"

So the man said, "Really, I do not know what I am feeling. What it is, I do not know. I am simply disturbed. Whether to call it anger or embarrassment or what, I do not know. And this is not the moment to discuss it with me." He said, "Leave me alone. You have made my situation philosophical. You are discussing what is real, what is authentic, and I am feeling very much disturbed."

This is not only with some other person—X, Y or Z—it is with you. You are never certain, because certainty comes from being centered. You are not even certain about yourself. It is impossible to be certain about others when you are never certain about yourself. There is just a vagueness, a cloudiness; nothing is certain.

Someone was here just a few days ago, and he said to me, "I am in love with someone, and I want to marry her." I looked into his eyes deeply for a few minutes without saying anything. He became restless and he said, "Why are you looking at me? I feel so awkward." I continued looking. He said, "Do you think that my love is false?" I didn't say anything, I just continued looking. He said, "Why do you feel that this marriage is not going to be good?" He said by himself, "I had not really thought it over very much, and that is why I have come to you. Really, I do not know whether I am in love or not."

I had not said a single word. I was just looking into his eyes. But he became restless, and things which were inside began to come up, to bubble up.

You are not certain, you cannot be certain about anything; neither about your love, nor about your hate, nor about your friendships. There is nothing which you can be certain about because you have no center. Without a center there is no certainty. All your feelings of certainty are false and momentary. One moment you will feel that you are certain, but the next moment the certainty will have gone because in each moment you have a different center. You do not have a permanent center, a crystallized center. Each moment is an atomic center, so each moment has its own self.

George Gurdjieff used to say that man is a crowd. Personality is just a deception because you are not a person, you are many persons. So when one person speaks in you, that is a momentary center. The next moment there is another. With every moment, with every atomic situation, you feel certain, and you never become aware that you are just a flux—many waves without any center. Then in the end you will feel that life has been just a wastage. It is bound to be. There is just a wastage, just a wandering—purposeless, meaningless.

Tantra, yoga, religion...their basic concern is how first to discover the center, how first to be an individual. They are concerned with how to find the center which persists in every situation. Then, as life goes on moving without, as the flux of life goes on and on, as waves come and go, the center persists inside. Then you remain one—rooted, centered.

These sutras are techniques to find the center. The center is already there, because there is no possibility of being a circle without a center. The circle can exist only with a center, so the center is only forgotten. It is there, but we are not aware. It is there, but we do not know how to look at it. We do not know how to focus the consciousness on it.

---

15 Close all the openings of your head.

The third technique about centering: *Closing the seven openings of the head with your hands, a space between your eyes becomes all inclusive.*

This is one of the oldest techniques—very much used, and one of the simplest also. Close all the openings of the head—eyes, ears, nose, mouth. When all the openings of the head are closed, your consciousness, which is continuously flowing out, is stopped suddenly; it cannot move out.

You may not have observed, but even if you stop your breathing for a moment, suddenly your mind will stop—because with breathing mind moves on. That is a conditioning with the mind. You must understand what 'conditioning' means, then only will this sutra be easy to understand.

Pavlov, one of the most famous Russian psychologists, has created this term 'conditioning'—or 'conditioned reflex'—a day-to-day word used all over the world. Everyone who is acquainted with psychology even a little knows the word. Two processes of thought—any two processes—can become so associated that if you start with one, the other is also triggered.

This is the famous Pavlovian example. Pavlov worked with a dog. He found that if you put dog food before a dog, its saliva begins to flow. The tongue of the dog comes out and he begins to get ready, prepared for eating. This is natural. When he is seeing the food, or even imagining the food, saliva starts flowing.

But Pavlov conditioned this process with another. Whenever the saliva would start to flow and the food was there, he would do some other things. For example, he would ring a bell, and the dog would listen to the bell ringing. For fifteen days, whenever the food was placed, the bell would ring. Then on the sixteenth day food was not placed before the dog, only the bell was rung. But still the saliva started flowing and the tongue came out, as if the food was there.

But there was no food, only the bell ringing. There is no natural association between the bell ringing and saliva, the natural association is with food. But now the continuous ringing of the bell had become associated with it, and even the ringing of the bell would start the process.

According to Pavlov—and he is right—our whole life is a conditioned process. The mind is a conditioning. Thus, if you stop something in the conditioning, every other associated thing also stops.

For example, you have never thought without breathing. Thinking has always been with breathing. You are not conscious of breathing, but breathing is there continuously, day and night. Every thought, every thinking process is associated with breathing. If you stop your breathing suddenly, thought will also stop. And if all the seven holes—the seven openings of the head—are closed, your consciousness suddenly cannot move out. It remains in, and that remaining in creates a space between your eyes. That space is known as the third eye.

If all the openings of the head are closed you cannot move out, because you have always been moving out from these openings. You remain in, and with your consciousness remaining in it becomes concentrated between these two eyes, between these two ordinary eyes. It remains in between these two eyes, focused. That spot is known as the third eye.

This space *becomes all inclusive*. This sutra says that in this space everything is included, the whole existence is included. If you can feel the space, you have felt all. Once you can feel inside this space between the two eyes, then you have known existence, the totality of it, because this inner space is all inclusive. Nothing is left out of it.

The Upanishads say, "Knowing the one, one knows all." These two eyes can only see the finite. The third eye sees the infinite. These two eyes can only see the material. The third eye sees the immaterial, the spiritual. With these two eyes you can never feel the energy, you can never see the energy; you can see only matter. But with the third eye, energy as such is seen.

This closing of the openings is a way of centering, because once the stream of consciousness cannot flow out, it remains at its source. That source of consciousness is the third eye. If you are centered at the third eye, many things happen. The first is discovering that the whole world is in you.

Swami Ramateertha used to say that "The sun moves in me, the stars move in me, the moon rises in me. The whole universe is in me." When he said this for the first time, his disciples thought he had gone crazy. How can stars be in Ramateertha?

He was talking about the third eye, the inner space. When for the first time the inner space becomes illumined, this is the feeling. When you see that everything is in you, you become the universe.

The third eye is not part of your physical body. The space between our two eyes is not a space which is confined in your body. It is the infinite space which has penetrated in you. Once this space is known, you will never be the same person again. The moment you know this inner space, you have known the deathless. Then there is no death.

When you know this space for the first time, your life will be authentic, intense, for the first time really alive. Now no security is needed, now no fear is possible. Now you cannot be killed. Now nothing can be taken away from you. Now the whole universe belongs to you: you are the universe. Those who have known this inner space, they have cried in ecstasy, "*Aham Brahmasmi!* I am the universe, I am the existence."

The Sufi mystic Mansoor was murdered only because of this experience of the third eye. When for the first time he became aware of this inner space, he started crying, "I am God!" In India he would have been worshipped, because India has known many, many persons who have come to know this inner space of the third eye. But in a Mohammedan country it was difficult. And Mansoor's statement that "I am God—*Ana'l haq!*"—was taken to be something antireligious, because Mohammedanism cannot conceive that man and God can become one. Man is man—the created—and God is the creator, so how can the created become the creator? So this statement of Mansoor's, "I am God," could not be understood; thus, he was murdered. But when he was being murdered, killed, he was laughing. So someone asked, "Why are you laughing, Mansoor?"

Mansoor is reported to have said, "I am laughing because you are not killing me, and you cannot kill me. You are deceived by this body, but I am not this body. I am the creator of this universe, and it was my finger which moved this whole universe in the beginning."

In India he would have been understood easily. The language has been known for centuries and centuries. We have known that a moment comes when the inner space is known. Then one simply goes mad. And this realization is so certain that even if you kill a Mansoor he will not change his statement—because really, you cannot kill him as far as he is concerned. Now he has become the whole. There is no possibility of destroying him.

After Mansoor, Sufis learned that it is good to be silent. So in Sufi tradition, after Mansoor, it has been consistently taught to disciples, "Whenever you come to the third eye, remain silent and do not say anything. Whenever this happens, then keep quiet. Do not say anything, or just go on formally saying things which people believe."

So Islam has now two traditions. One is just the ordinary, the outward, the exoteric; another, the real Islam, is Sufism—the esoteric. But Sufis remain silent, because since Mansoor they have learned that to talk in that language which comes when the third eye opens is to be unnecessarily in difficulty—and it helps no one.

This sutra says: *Closing the seven openings of the head with your hands, a space between your eyes becomes all inclusive.* Your inner space becomes all the space.

---

16 Absorb the senses in your heart.

The fourth centering technique: *Blessed one, as senses are absorbed in the heart, reach the center of the lotus.*

Every technique is useful for a certain type of mind. The technique we have been discussing, the third—closing the openings of the head—can be used by many. It is very simple and not very dangerous. You can use it very easily, and there is also no need to close the openings with your hands. Closing is

needed, so you can use ear plugs and you can use a mask for the eyes. The real thing is to close the openings of your head completely for a few moments—for a few moments or for a few seconds. Try it. Do not practice it—only suddenly is it helpful. When it is sudden it is helpful. When lying in your bed, suddenly close all your openings for a few seconds, and see what is happening within.

When you feel suffocated, go on—unless it becomes absolutely unbearable, because breathing will be closed. Go on, unless it becomes absolutely unbearable. And when it is absolutely unbearable, you will not be able to close the openings any more, so you need not worry. The inner force will throw all the openings open. So as far as you are concerned, continue. When the suffocation comes, that is the moment—because the suffocation will break the old associations. If you can continue for a few moments more, it would be good. It will be difficult and arduous, and you will feel that you are going to die—but do not be afraid, because you cannot die. You cannot die just by closing the openings. But when you feel now you are going to die, that is the moment.

If you can persist in that moment, suddenly everything will be illumined. You will feel the inner space which goes on spreading, and the whole is included in it. Then open your openings. Go on trying it again and again. Whenever you have time, try it. But do not practice it. You can practice stopping the breath for a few moments. But practice will not help, a sudden jerk is needed. In that jerk, the flow into your old channels of consciousness stops, and a new thing becomes possible.

Many practice this even today—many persons all over India. But they practice it, and it is a sudden method. If you practice, then nothing will happen. If I throw you out of this room suddenly, your thoughts will stop. But if we practice it daily, then nothing will happen. It will become a mechanical habit. So do not practice it. Just try it whenever you can. Then suddenly, by and by, you will become aware of an inner space. That inner space comes only to your consciousness when you are on the verge of death. When you are feeling, "Now I cannot continue for a single moment, now death is near," that is the right moment. Persist! Do not be afraid. Death is not so easy. At least up until now not a single person has died using this method.

There are built-in securities, that is why you cannot die. Before death one becomes unconscious. If you are conscious and feeling that you are going to die, do not be afraid. You are still conscious, so you cannot die. And if you become unconscious, then your breath will start. Then you cannot prevent it. So you can use ear plugs, etcetera. Hands are not necessary. Hands were used only because if you are falling into unconsciousness, the hands will become loose and the life process will resume again by itself.

You can use plugs for the ears, a mask for the eyes, but do not use any plugs for the nose or for the mouth, because then it can become fatal. At least the nose should remain open. Close it with your hands. Then when you are actually falling into unconsciousness, the hands will become loose and the breathing will come in. So there is a built-in security. This method can be used by many.

The fourth method is for those who have a very developed heart, who are loving, feeling types, emotional. *Blessed one, as senses are absorbed in the heart, reach the center of the lotus.* This method can be used only by heart-oriented persons. Therefore, understand first what is a heart-oriented person. Then this method can be understood.

With one who is heart-oriented, everything leads to the heart, everything. If you love him, his heart will feel your love, not his head. A head-oriented person, even when loved, feels it cerebrally, in the head. He thinks about it; he plans about it. Even his love is a deliberate effort of the mind.

A feeling type lives without reasoning. Of course, the heart has its own reasons, but it lives without reasoning. If someone asks you, "Why do you love?" if you can answer why, then you are a head-oriented person. And if you say, "I do not

know, I just love," you are a heart-oriented person.

Even if you say that someone is beautiful and that is why you love, it is a reason. For a heart-oriented person, someone is beautiful because they love him. The head-oriented person loves someone because he is beautiful or she is beautiful. The reason comes first, and then comes love. For the heart-oriented, love comes first and then everything else follows. The feeling type is centered in the heart, so whatsoever happens touches his heart.

Just observe yourself. In your life, many things are happening every moment. Where do they touch you? You are passing, and a beggar crosses the street. Where are you touched by the beggar? Do you start thinking about economic conditions? Do you start thinking about how begging should be stopped by law, or about how a socialist society should be created so that there are no beggars? This is a head-oriented man. This beggar becomes just a datum for him. His heart is not touched, only his head is touched. He is not going to do something for this beggar here and now—no! He will do something for communism, he will do something for the future, for some utopia. He may even devote his whole life, but he cannot do anything just now.

The mind is always doing in the future; the heart is always here and now. A heart-oriented person will do something now for this beggar. This beggar is an individual, not a datum. But for a head-oriented man, this beggar is just a mathematical figure. For him, how begging should be stopped is the problem, not that this beggar should be helped—that is irrelevant. So just watch yourself. In many situations, watch how you act. Are you concerned with the heart or are you concerned with the head?

If you feel that you are a heart-oriented person, then this method will be very helpful to you. But know well that everyone is trying to deceive himself that he is heart-oriented. Everyone tries to feel that he is a very loving person, a feeling type—because love is such a basic need that no one can feel at ease if he sees that he has no love, no loving heart. So everyone goes on thinking and believing this, but belief will not do. Observe very impartially, as if you are observing someone else, and then decide—because there is no need to deceive yourself, and it will be of no help. Even if you deceive yourself, you cannot deceive the technique, so when you do this technique you will feel that nothing is happening.

People come to me, and I ask them to what type they belong. They do not know really. They have never thought about it—about what type they are. They have just vague conceptions about themselves, and those conceptions are really just imagination. They have certain ideals and self-images, and they think—or rather, they wish—that they are those images. They are not, and often it happens that they prove to be just the contrary.

There is a reason for it. A person who insists that he is a heart-oriented person may be insisting only because he feels the absence of heart, and he is afraid. He cannot become aware of the fact that he has no heart.

Look at the world! If everyone is right about his heart, then this world cannot be so heartless. This world is our total, so somewhere something is wrong. Heart is not there. Really, it was never trained to be there. Mind is trained, so it is there. There are schools, colleges, universities to train the mind, but there is no place to train the heart. And the training of the mind pays, but the training of the heart is dangerous. If your heart is trained you will become absolutely unfit for this world, because the whole world is run through reason.

If your heart is trained, you will just be absurd in the context of the whole pattern. When the whole world will be moving to the right, you will be moving to the left. Everywhere you will feel difficulty. Really, the more man becomes civilized, the less and less the heart is trained. We have really forgotten about it—that it exists, or that there is any need for its training. That is why such methods, which can work very easily, never work.

Most of the religions are based on heart-oriented techniques—Christianity, Islam, Hinduism and many others. They are based on the heart-oriented person. The older the religion, the more it is based on heart-oriented persons. Really, when the Vedas were written and Hinduism was developing, there were people who were heart-oriented. And to find a mind-oriented person then was really difficult. But now the reverse is a problem. You cannot pray, because prayer is a heart-oriented technique. That is why even in the West, where Christianity—which is a religion of prayer—prevails, prayer has become difficult. Particularly, the Catholic Church is prayer-oriented.

There exists no such thing as meditation for Christianity, but now even in the West people are becoming crazy about meditation. No one is going to church—and even if someone is going, it is just a formal thing, just Sunday religion—because the heart-oriented prayer has become absolutely unknown for man as he is in the West.

Meditation is more mind-oriented, prayer is more heart-oriented. Or we can say that prayer is a technique of meditation for heart-oriented persons.

This technique is also for heart-oriented persons: *Blessed one, as senses are absorbed in the heart, reach the center of the lotus.*

So what is to be done in this technique? *As senses are absorbed in the heart...*Try! Many ways are possible. You touch someone; if you are a heart-oriented person the touch immediately goes to your heart, and you can feel the quality. If you take the hand of a person who is head-oriented, the hand will be cold—not just cold, but the very quality will be cold. A deadness, a certain deadness will be in the hand. If the person is heart-oriented then there is a certain warmth, then his hand will really melt with you. You will feel a certain thing flowing from his hand to you, and there will be a meeting, a communication of warmth.

This warmth comes from the heart. It can never come from the head, because the head is always cool...cold, calculative. The heart is warm, noncalculative. The head always thinks about how to take more; the heart always feels how to give more. That warmth is just a giving—a giving of energy, a giving of inner vibrations, a giving of life. That is why you feel a different quality in it. If the person really embraces you, you will feel a deep melting with him.

Touch! Close your eyes; touch anything. Touch your beloved or your lover, touch your child or your mother or your friend, or touch a tree or a flower, or just touch the earth. Close your eyes and feel a communication from your heart to the earth, or to your beloved. Feel that your hand is just your heart stretched out to touch the earth. Let the feeling of touch be related to the heart.

You are listening to music. Do not listen to it from the head. Just forget your head and feel that you are headless, there is no head at all. It is good to have a picture of yourself without the head in your bedroom. Concentrate on it; you are without the head, do not allow the head to come in. While listening to music, listen to it from the heart. Feel the music coming to your heart, let your heart vibrate with it. Let your senses be joined to the heart, not to the head. Try this with all the senses, and feel more and more that every sense goes into the heart and dissolves into it.

Blessed one, as senses are absorbed in the heart, reach the center of the lotus. The heart is the lotus. Every sense is just the opening of the lotus, the petals of the lotus. Try to relate your senses to the heart first. Secondly, always think that every sense goes deep down into the heart and becomes absorbed in it. When these two things become established, only then will your senses begin to help you. They will lead you to the heart, and your heart will become a lotus.

This lotus of the heart will give you a centering. Once you know the center of the heart, it is very easy to fall down into the navel center, very easy. This sutra does not even mention this—there is no need. If you are really absorbed in the heart totally, and reason has stopped working, then you will fall down. From the heart, the door is opened toward

the navel. Only from the head is it difficult to go toward the navel. Or if you are between the two, between the heart and the head, then too it is difficult to go to the navel. Once you are absorbed in the navel, you have suddenly fallen beyond the heart. You have fallen into the navel center which is the basic one—the original.

That is why prayer helps. That is why Jesus could say, "Love is God." It is not exactly right, but love is the door. If you are deeply in love—with anyone, it doesn't matter who.... Love matters; the object of love doesn't matter. If you are in deep love with anyone, so much in love that there is no relationship from the head, if just the heart is functioning, then this love will become prayer and your beloved or your lover will become divine.

Really, the eye of the heart cannot see anything else, and that is why it happens with ordinary love also. If you fall in love with someone, that someone becomes divine. It may not prove to be very lasting, and it may not prove to be a very deep thing, but in that moment the lover or the beloved becomes divine. The head will destroy the whole thing sooner or later, because the head will come in and try to manage everything. Even love has to be managed. And once the head manages, everything is destroyed.

If you can be in love without the head's management coming in, your love is bound to become prayer and your beloved will become the door. Your love will make you centered in the heart—and once you are centered in the heart, you automatically fall down deep into the navel center.

---

17 Do not choose, keep in the middle.

The fifth centering technique: *Unminding mind, keep in the middle—until.*

Only this much is the sutra. Just like any scientific sutra it is short, but even these few words can transform your life totally. *Unminding mind, keep in the middle—until.*

Keep in the middle.... Buddha developed his whole technique of meditation on this sutra. His path is known as *majjhim nikai*—the middle path. Buddha says, "Remain always in the middle—in everything."

One Prince Shravan took initiation, Buddha initiated him into sannyas. That prince was a rare man, and when he took sannyas, when he was initiated, his whole kingdom was just amazed. The kingdom couldn't believe it, the people couldn't believe that Prince Shravan could become a sannyasin. No one had ever even imagined it, as he was a man of this world—indulging in everything, indulging to the extreme. Wine and women were his whole milieu.

Then suddenly Buddha came to the town, and the prince went to see him for a *darshan*—a spiritual encounter. He fell at Buddha's feet and he said, "Initiate me. I will leave this world."

Those who had come with him were not even aware...this was so sudden. So they asked Buddha, "What is happening? This is a miracle. Shravan is not that type of man, and he has lived very luxuriously. Up to now we couldn't even imagine that Shravan is going to take sannyas, so what has happened? You have done something."

Buddha said, "I have not done anything. Mind can move easily from one extreme to the other. That is the way of the mind—to move from one extreme to another. So Shravan is not doing something new. It is to be expected. Because you do not know the law of the mind, that is why you are so much taken aback."

The mind moves from one extreme to another, that is the way of the mind. So it happens every day: a person who was mad after wealth renounces everything, becomes a naked fakir. We think, "What a miracle!" But it is nothing—just the ordinary law. A person who was not mad after wealth cannot be expected to renounce, because only from one extreme can you move to another—just like a pendulum, from one extreme to the other.

So a person who was after wealth, mad after wealth, will become mad against it, but the mad-

ness will remain—that is the mind. A man who lived just for sex may become a celibate, may move into isolation, but the madness will remain. Before he was living only for sex, now he will be living only against sex—but the attitude, the approach, remains the same.

So a *brahmachari,* a celibate, is not really beyond sex; his whole mind is sex-oriented. He is against, but not beyond. The way of beyond is always in the middle, it is never at the extreme. So Buddha says, "This could have been expected. No miracle has happened. This is how mind works."

Shravan became a beggar, a sannyasin. He became a *bhikkhu,* a monk, and soon other disciples of Buddha observed that he was moving to the other extreme. Buddha never asked anyone to be naked, but Shravan became naked. Buddha was not for nakedness. He said, "That is just another extreme."

There are persons who live for clothes as if that is their life, and there are other persons who become naked—but both believe in the same thing. Buddha never taught nakedness, but Shravan became naked. He was the only disciple of Buddha who was naked. He became very self-torturing. Buddha allowed one meal every day for the sannyasins, but Shravan would take only one meal on alternate days. He became lean and thin. While all the other disciples would sit for meditation under trees, in the shade, he would never sit under any tree. He would always remain in the hot sun. He was a beautiful man and he had a very lovely body, but within six months no one could recognize that he was the same man. He became ugly, dark, black, burned.

Buddha went to Shravan one night and asked him, "Shravan, I have heard that when you were a prince, before initiation, you used to play on a *veena,* a sitar, and you were a great musician. So I have come to ask you one question. If the strings of the veena are very loose, what happens?"

Shravan said, "If the strings are very loose, then no music is possible."

And then Buddha said, "And if the strings are very tight, too tight, then what happens?"

Shravan said, "Then too music cannot be produced. The strings must be in the middle—neither loose nor tight, but just exactly in the middle." Shravan said, "It is easy to play the veena, but only a master can set these strings right, in the middle."

So Buddha said, "This much I have to say to you, after observing you for the last six months—that in life also the music comes only when the strings are neither loose nor tight, but just in the middle. So to renounce is easy, but only a master knows how to be in the middle. So Shravan, be a master, and let these strings of life be just in the middle—in everything. Do not go to this extreme, do not go to that one. Everything has two extremes, but you remain just in the middle."

But the mind is very unmindful. That is why the sutra says, *Unminding mind....* You will hear this, you will understand this, but the mind will not take note. The mind will always go on choosing extremes.

The extreme has a fascination for the mind. Why? Because in the middle, mind dies. Look at a pendulum: if you have any old clock, look at the pendulum. The pendulum can go on moving the whole day if it goes to the extremes. When it goes to the left it is gathering momentum to go to the right. When it goes toward the right, do not think that it is going toward the right—it is accumulating momentum to go toward the left. So the extremes are right-left, right-left.

Let the pendulum stay in the middle, then the whole momentum is lost. Then the pendulum has no energy, because the energy comes from one of the extremes. Then that extreme throws it toward another, then again, and it is a circle...the pendulum goes on moving. Let it be in the middle, and the whole movement will then stop.

Mind is just like a pendulum and every day, if you observe, you will come to know this. You decide one thing on one extreme, and then you move to another. You are angry; then you repent.

You decide, "No, this is enough. Now I will never be angry." But you do not see the extreme.

"Never" is an extreme. How are you so certain that you will never be angry? What are you saying? Think once more—never? Then go to the past and remember how many times you have decided that "I will never be angry." When you say, "I will never be angry," you do not know that by being angry you have accumulated momentum to go to the other extreme.

Now you are feeling repentant, you are feeling bad. Your self-image is disturbed, shaken. Now you cannot say you are a good man, you cannot say that you are a religious man. You have been angry, and how can a religious man be angry? How can a good man be angry? So you repent to regain your goodness again. At least in your own eyes you can feel at ease—that you have repented and you have decided that now there will be no more anger. The shaken image has come back to the old status quo. Now you feel at ease, you have moved to another extreme.

But the mind that says, "Now I will never be angry," will again be angry. And when you are again angry, you will forget completely your repentance, your decision—everything. After anger, again the decision will come and the repentance will come, and you will never feel the deception of it. This has been so always.

Mind moves from anger to repentance, from repentance to anger. Remain in the middle. Do not be angry and do not repent. If you have been angry, then please, at least do this: do not repent. Do not move to the other extreme. Remain in the middle. Say, "I have been angry and I am a bad man, a violent man. I have been angry. This is how I am." But do not repent; do not move to the other extreme. Remain in the middle. If you can remain, you will not gather the momentum, the energy to be angry again.

So this sutra says, *Unminding mind, keep in the middle—until.* And what is meant by *until*? Until you explode! Keep in the middle until the mind dies. Keep in the middle until there is no mind. So, *Unminding mind, keep in the middle—until* there is no mind. If mind is at the extremes, then the middle will be no-mind.

But this is the most difficult thing in the world to do. It looks easy, it looks simple; it may appear as if you can do this. And you will feel good if you think that there is no need for any repentance. Try this, and then you will know that when you have been angry the mind will insist on repenting.

Husbands and wives continue to quarrel, and for centuries and centuries there have been counselors, advisors, great men who have been teaching how to live and love—but they go on quarreling. Freud, for the first time, became aware of the phenomenon that whenever you are in love—so-called love—you are also in hate. In the morning it is love, in the evening it is hate, and the pendulum goes on moving. Every husband, every wife knows this, but Freud has a very uncanny insight. Freud says that if a couple has stopped fighting, know well that love has died.

That love which existed with hate and fight cannot remain, so if you see a couple never fighting, do not think that this is the ideal couple. It means no couple at all. They are living parallel, but not with each other. They are parallel lines never meeting anywhere, not even to fight. They are both alone together—parallel.

Mind has to move to the opposite, so psychology now gives better advice. The advice is better, more deep, more penetrating. It says that if you really want to love—with the mind—then do not be afraid to fight. Really, you must fight authentically so you can move to the other extreme of authentic love. So when you are fighting with your wife, do not avoid it; otherwise the love will also be avoided. When the time for fight is there, fight until the end. Then by evening you will be able to love: the mind will have gathered momentum. The ordinary love cannot exist without fight because there is a movement of the mind. Only a love which is not of the mind can exist without fight, but then it

is a different thing altogether.

A Buddha loving…that is a different thing altogether. But if Buddha comes to love you, you will not feel good because there will be no fault in it. It will be simply sweet and sweet and sweet—and boring, because the spice comes from fight. A Buddha cannot be angry, he can only love. You will not feel his love because you can feel only opposites, you can feel it only in contrast.

When Buddha came back to his home town after twelve years, his wife wouldn't come to receive him. The whole city gathered to receive him except his wife. Buddha laughed, and he said to his chief disciple, Ananda, "Yashodhara has not come. I know her well. It seems she still loves me. She is proud, and she feels hurt. I was thinking that twelve years is a long time and she might not be in love now, but it seems she is still in love—still angry. She has not come to receive me. I will have to go to the house."

So Buddha went. Ananda was with him; it was a condition with Ananda. When Ananda took initiation he made a condition with Buddha, to which Buddha agreed, that he would always remain with him. He was an elder cousin-brother, so Buddha had to concede.

Ananda followed him into the house, into the palace, so Buddha said, "At least for this you remain behind and do not come with me, because she will be furious. I am coming back after twelve years, and I just ran away without even telling her. She is still angry, so do not come with me; otherwise she will feel that I have not even allowed her to say anything. She must be feeling to say many things, so let her be angry, do not come with me."

Buddha went in. Of course, Yashodhara was just a volcano. She erupted, exploded. She started crying and weeping and saying things. Buddha stayed there, waited there, and by and by she cooled down and realized that Buddha had not even uttered a single word.

She wiped her eyes and looked at Buddha, and Buddha said, "I have come to say that I have gained something, I have known something, I have realized something. If you become cool I can give you the message—the truth that I have realized. I have waited so much in order that you could go through a catharsis. Twelve years is a long affair. You must have gathered many wounds, and your anger is understandable; I expected this. That shows that you are still in love with me. But there is a love beyond this love, and only because of that love have I come back to tell you something."

But Yashodhara could not feel that love. It is difficult to feel it because it is so silent. It is so silent, it is as if absent. When mind ceases, then a different love happens. But that love has no opposite to it. When mind ceases, really, whatsoever happens has no opposite to it. With the mind there is always the polar opposite, and mind moves like a pendulum.

This sutra is wonderful, and miracles are possible through it: *Unminding mind, keep in the middle—until.*

So try it. And this sutra is for your whole life. You cannot practice it sometimes, you have to be aware continuously. Doing, walking, eating, in relationship, everywhere—remain in the middle. Try at least, and you will feel a certain calmness developing, a tranquility coming to you, a quiet center growing within you.

Even if you are not successful in being exactly in the middle, try to be in the middle. By and by you will have the feel of what middle means. Whatsoever may be the case—hate or love, anger or repentance—always remember the polar opposites and remain in between. And sooner or later you will stumble upon the exact middle point.

Once you know it you can never forget it again, because that middle point is beyond the mind. That middle point is all that spirituality means.

CHAPTER 12

Beyond mind to the source

♦

Please explain the functions of the navel center, the third-eye center and the spinal cord.

Buddha's asceticism seems the opposite of worldly life and not the middle path. Please explain.

What are some practical ways to develop the heart center?

Should one love in the middle-path way, or be intense in both the love and hate poles?

There are many questions. The first question:

Last night You said that with the dawn of enlightenment, the space between the two eyebrows, the third eye, becomes all inclusive. The other day You said that all enlightened ones are centered in their navel, and on still another day You have explained about the silver cord in the middle of the spine. Thus, we know about three basic things as the roots of man. Please explain the relative significance and relative functions of these three things: the navel center, the third eye and the silver cord.

he basic thing to be understood about these centers is this: whenever you are centered within, the moment you are centered, whatsoever may be the center, you fall down to the navel. If you are centered at the heart, the heart is irrelevant—centering is meaningful. Or if you are centered at the third eye, the third eye is not basic; the basic point is that your consciousness is centered. So whatsoever may be the point of centering, once you are centered—anywhere—you will fall down to the navel.

The basic existential center is the navel, but your functional center may be anywhere. From that center you will fall down automatically. There is no need to think about it. And this is not so only with the heart center or the third-eye center. If you are really centered in reason, in the head, you will also fall down to the navel center.

Centering is the thing, but it is very difficult to be centered in reason, in the head. There are problems. The heart center is based on love, faith, surrender. The head is based on doubt and negation.

To be totally negative is really impossible; to be totally in doubt is impossible. But it has happened sometimes, because the impossible also happens. Sometimes, if your doubt comes to such an intensity that nothing remains which is believed, not even the doubting mind is believed, if the doubt turns upon itself and everything becomes doubt, then you will fall down to the navel center immediately. But this is a very rare phenomenon.

Trust is easier. You can trust totally more easily than you can doubt totally. You can say yes totally more easily than you can say no. So even if you are centered at the head, the *centering* is what is basic: you will fall down to your existential roots. So be centered anywhere. The spine will do; the heart will do; the head will do. Or you can also find other centers in the body.

Buddhists talk about nine *chakras*—nine dynamic centers in the body. Hindus talk about seven chakras—seven dynamic centers in the body. Tibetans talk about thirteen centers in the body. You can find your own also, there is no need to study about these.

Any point in the body can be made an object of centering. For example, tantra uses the sex center for centering. Tantra works with bringing your consciousness to it totally. The sex center will do.

Taoists have used the big toe as the center. Move your consciousness down to the big toe;

remain there, forget the whole body. Let your whole consciousness go to the toe. That will do, because really, on what you are centering is irrelevant. You are centering—that is what is basic. The thing happens because of centering, not because of the center—remember this. The center is not significant, *centering* is significant.

So do not be puzzled, because in so many methods, in one hundred and twelve methods, many centers will be used. Do not become puzzled over which center is more important or which is real, any center will do. You can choose according to your own liking.

If your mind is very sexual, it is good to choose the sex center. Use it, because your consciousness is naturally flowing toward it—then it is better to choose it. But it has become difficult to choose the sex center. That is one of the most natural centers; your consciousness is attracted toward it biologically. Why not use this biological force toward inner transformation? Make it the point of your centering.

But social conditioning, sexually repressive teachings, moralizing—they have done a deep harm. You are disjoined from your sex center. Really, our image of our real selves excludes the sex center. Imagine your body: you will leave your sex organs out of it; that is why many people feel as if their sex organs are something different from them, that they are not part of them. This is why there is so much hiding, so much becoming unconscious.

If someone should come from space, from some other planet, and he should see you, he will not be able to conceive that you have any sex center. If he should listen to your talk, he will not be able to understand that there exists anything like sex. If he moves in your society, in the formal world, he will not know that anything like sex is happening.

We have created a division. A barrier is there, and we have cut off the sex center from ourselves. Really, because of sex we have divided the body into two. The upper means "higher" in our minds and the lower means "lower"—it is condemned.

So "lower" is not just some information about the location of the bottom half, it is an evaluation also. You yourself do not think that the lower body is you.

If someone asks you, "Where are you in your body?" you will point to your head, because that is the highest. That is why brahmins in India will say, "We are the head and the sudras, the untouchables, they are the feet." The feet are lower than the head. Really, you are the head, and the feet and the other parts only belong to you, they are not you. To make this division we have made clothes in two parts—some for the upper body and some for the lower body. This is only to divide the body in two. There is a subtle division.

The lower body is not part of you. It hangs on you—that is another thing. That is why it is difficult to use the sex center for centering. But if you can use it, that is the best, because biologically your energy is flowing toward that center. Concentrate on it. Whenever you feel any sexual urge, close your eyes and feel your energy flowing toward the sex center.

Make it a meditation: feel yourself centered in the sex center. Then suddenly you will feel a change of quality in the energy. Sexuality will disappear, and the sex center will become illumined, full of energy, dynamic. You will feel life at its peak at this center. And if you are centered, sex will really be forgotten completely at that moment. From the sex center you will feel energy flowing all over the body, even transcending the body and going into the cosmos. If you are totally centered at the sex center, suddenly you will be thrown to your basic root, at the navel.

Tantra has used the sex center, and I think tantra has been one of the most scientific approaches toward human transformation, because to use sex is very scientific. When the mind is already flowing toward it, why not use this natural flow as a vehicle?

That is the basic difference between tantra and so-called moralist teachings. Moralist teachers can never use the sex center for transformation—they are afraid. And one who is afraid of sex energy will really find it very, very difficult to transform himself or herself because he is fighting against the current, unnecessarily flowing against the river.

It is easy to flow with the river, just float. And if you can float without any conflict, you can use this center for centering.

Any center will do. You can create your own centers...no need to be traditional. All centers are devices—devices for centering. When you are centered you will come down to your navel automatically. A centered consciousness goes back to the original source.

The second question:

Buddha inspired a large number of persons to become sannyasins—sannyasins who would beg for their meals and live away from society, business and politics. Buddha himself lived an ascetic life. This monastic life seems to be the other extreme of the worldly life. This doesn't seem to be the middle path. Can You explain this?

It will be difficult to understand because you are not aware of what is the other end of worldly life. The other end of life is always death. There have been teachers who said that suicide is the only path. And not only in the past; even now, in the present, there are thinkers who say that life is absurd. If life as such is meaningless, then death becomes meaningful. Life and death are polar opposites, so the opposite to life is death. Try to understand it. And it will be helpful for you to find out the way for yourself.

If death is the polar opposite of life, then mind can move to death very easily—and it happens. When someone commits suicide, have you ever observed that the person who commits suicide was attached too much to life? Only those who are too much attached to life can commit suicide.

For example, you are too attached to your husband or to your wife and you think you cannot live without him or her. Then the husband or the

wife dies, and you commit suicide. The mind has moved to the other end because it was too attached to life. When life frustrates, the mind can move to the other end.

Suicides are of two types—wholesale suicide and gradual suicide. You can commit gradual suicide by withdrawing yourself from life, cutting yourself off, cutting your moorings in life by and by, dying slowly, gradually.

In Buddha's time there were schools which preached suicide. These were the real opposites to life, to worldly life. There were schools which were teaching that to commit suicide is the only way out of this nonsense which we call life, the only way out of this suffering. "If you are alive you will have to suffer," they said, "and there is no way of going beyond misery while you are alive. So commit suicide, destroy yourself." When you hear this it looks like too extremist a view, but try to understand it deeply. It carries some meaning.

Sigmund Freud, after forty years of constant work with the human mind, one of the longest researches one individual can do, came to conclude that man as he is cannot be happy. The very way mind functions creates misery, so at the most less misery or more misery can be the choice. No misery cannot be the choice. If you adjust your mind you will be less miserable, that is all. It looks very hopeless.

The existentialists—Sartre, Camus and others —say that life can never be blissful. The very nature of life is dread, anguish, suffering, so the most one can do is to face it bravely, with no hope. You can only face it bravely, and that is all—with no hope. The situation as such is hopeless. Camus asks, "Well, if this is the situation, then why not commit suicide? If there is no way to go beyond in life, then why not leave this life?"

One of Dostoevsky's characters in one of the greatest novels of the world, *The Brothers Karamazov*, says, "I am trying to find out where your God is just to return to him the entrance ticket— the entrance ticket to life. I don't want to be here.

And if there is any God, he must be very violent and cruel," the character says, "because without asking me he has thrown me into life. It has never been my choice. Why am I alive without my choosing it?"

There were many schools in Buddha's time. Buddha's time was one of the most intellectually dynamic periods in human history. For example, there was Ajit Keshkambal. You may not have heard the name because it is difficult to create a following around those who preach suicide. So no sect exists around Ajit Keshkambal, but he said continuously for five years that suicide alone is the only way.

It is reported that someone asked Ajit, "Then why have you not committed suicide up to now?"

He said, "Just to preach, I have to suffer life. I have a message to give to the world. If I commit suicide, then who will preach? Who will teach this message? Just to give this message, I am here. Otherwise, life is not worth living." It is the opposite extreme of life, of this so-called life which we live.

Buddha's was the middle path. Buddha said, neither death nor life. That is what sannyas means: neither attachment to life nor repulsion, but just being in the middle. So Buddha says that sannyas is to be just in the middle. Sannyas is not negation of life. Rather, sannyas is the negation of both life and death. When you are concerned with neither life nor death, then you become a sannyasin.

If you can see the polar opposites of life and death, then Buddha's initiation into sannyas is just an initiation into the middle path. So a sannyasin is not really against life. If he is, then he is not a sannyasin. Then really, he is a neurotic; he has gone to the other extreme. A sannyasin has a very balanced consciousness—balanced just in the middle.

"If life is misery," the mind says, "then move to the other end." But to Buddhists life is misery because you are at the extreme. That is the Buddhist idea: life is a misery because it is at one extreme, and death will also be a misery because it is another extreme. Bliss is just in the middle, bliss is balance.

A sannyasin is a balanced being—neither lean-ing to the right nor to the left, neither a leftist nor a rightist: just in the middle—silent, unmoving, not choosing this nor that, in a nonchoice, remaining in the center.

So do not choose death. *Choice* is misery. If you choose death you have chosen misery, if you choose life you have chosen misery, because life and death are two extremes. And remember, they are two extremes of one thing. They are not really two, only one thing which has two poles: life and death.

If you choose one, you will have to go against the other pole. That creates misery, because death is implied in life. You cannot choose life without choosing death. How can you? The moment you choose life, you have chosen death. That creates misery because as a result of your having chosen life, death will be there. You have chosen happiness; simultaneously, without your knowing, you have chosen unhappiness, because that is part of it.

If you have chosen love, then you have chosen hate. The other is intrinsic in it, it is hidden there. And one who chooses love will suffer, because then he will hate—and when he comes to hate he will suffer.

Do not choose, be in the middle. In the middle is the truth. At one end is death, at the other end is life. But this energy moving between these two, in the middle, is the truth. Do not choose, because choice means choice of one thing against another thing. To be in the middle means being choiceless. Then you will leave the whole thing. And when you have not chosen, you cannot be made miserable.

Man is made miserable through choice. Do not choose. Just be! It is arduous, it appears impossible —but try it. Whenever you have two opposites, try to be in the middle. By and by you will know the hunch, the feel, and once you know the feel of how to be in the middle—and it is a delicate thing, very delicate, the most delicate thing in life—once you have the feel nothing can disturb you, nothing can make you suffer. Then you exist without suffering.

That is what sannyas means: to exist without

suffering. But to exist without suffering you have to exist without choice, so be in the middle. And Buddha has tried for the first time, so consciously, to create a path of being always in the middle.

The third question:

Enlighten us about a few practical points for the opening and development of the heart center.

The first point: try to be headless. Visualize yourself as headless; move headlessly. It sounds absurd, but it is one of the most important exercises. Try it, and then you will know. Walk, and feel as if you have no head. In the beginning it will be only "as if." It will be very weird. When the feeling will come to you that you have no head, it will be very weird and strange. But by and by you will settle down at the heart.

There is one law.... You may have seen that someone who is blind has more keen ears, more musical ears. Blind men are more musical; their feeling for music is deeper. Why? The energy that ordinarily moves through the eyes now cannot move through them, so it chooses a different path. It moves through the ears.

Blind men have a deeper sensitivity of touch. If a blind man touches you, you will feel the difference, because we ordinarily do much work with touch through our eyes; we are touching each other through our eyes. A blind man cannot touch through the eyes, so the energy moves through his hands. A blind man is more sensitive than anyone who has eyes. Sometimes it may not be so, but generally it is so. Energy starts moving from another center if one center is not there.

So try this exercise I am talking about—the exercise in headlessness—and suddenly you will feel a strange thing: it will be as if for the first time you are at the heart. Walk headlessly. Sit down to meditate, close your eyes, and simply feel that there is no head. Feel, "My head has disappeared." In the beginning it will be just "as if," but by and by you will feel that the head has really disappeared.

And when you feel that your head has disappeared, your center will fall down to the heart—immediately. You will be looking at the world through the heart and not through the head.

When for the first time Westerners reached Japan, they couldn't believe that Japanese had traditionally believed for centuries that they think through the belly. If you ask a Japanese child—if he is not educated in Western ways—"Where is your thinking?" he will point to his belly.

Centuries and centuries have passed, and Japan has been living without the head. It is just a concept. If I ask you, "Where is your thinking going on?" you will point toward the head, but a Japanese will point to the belly, not to the head. And one of the reasons why the Japanese mind is more calm, quiet and collected, is this.

Now this concept has been disturbed because the West has spread over everything. Now there exists no East. Only in some individuals here and there, who are like islands, does the East exist. Otherwise the East has disappeared; now the whole world is Western.

Try headlessness. Meditate standing before your mirror in the bathroom. Look deep into your eyes and feel that you are looking from the heart. By and by the heart center will begin to function. And when the heart functions, it changes your total personality, the total structure, the whole pattern, because the heart has its own way.

So the first thing: try headlessness. Secondly, be more loving, because love cannot function through the head. Be more loving! That is why when someone is in love, he loses his head. People say that he has gone mad. If you are not mad and in love, then you are not in love really. The head must be lost. If the head is there, unaffected, functioning ordinarily, then love is not possible, because for love you need the heart to function—not the head. It is a function of the heart.

It happens that when a very rational person falls in love, he becomes stupid. He himself feels what stupidity he is doing, what silliness. What is he doing? Then he makes two parts of his life. He creates a division. The heart becomes a silent, intimate affair. When he moves out of his house, he moves out of his heart. He lives in the world with the head, and only comes down to the heart when he is loving. But it is very difficult, and ordinarily it never happens.

I was staying in Calcutta at a friend's house, and the friend was a justice of the High Court. His wife told me, "I have only one problem to tell you. Can you help me?"

So I said, "What is the problem?"

She said, "My husband is your friend. He loves you and respects you, so if you say something to him it may be helpful."

So I asked her, "What is to be said? Tell me."

She said, "He remains a High Court judge even in the bed. I have not known a lover, a friend or a husband. He is a High Court judge twenty-four hours a day."

It is difficult, it is difficult to come down from your pedestal. It becomes a fixed attitude. If you are a businessman, you will remain a businessman in the bed also. It is difficult to accommodate two persons within, and it is not easy to change your pattern completely, immediately, anytime you like. It is difficult, but if you are in love you will have to come down from the head.

So for this meditation try to be more and more loving. And when I say be more loving, I mean change the quality of your relationship: let it be based on love. Not only with your wife or with your child or with your friend, but toward life as such become more loving. That is why Mahavira and Buddha have talked about nonviolence. It was just to create a loving attitude toward life.

When Mahavira moves, walks, he remains aware not even to kill an ant. Why? Really, the ant is not his concern. He is coming down from the head to the heart. He is creating a loving attitude toward life as such. The more your relationships are based on love—all relationships—the more your heart center will function. It will start work-ing; you will look at the world through different eyes, because the heart has its own way of looking at the world. The mind can never look in that way —that is impossible for the mind. The mind can only analyze! The heart synthesizes; the mind can only dissect, divide—it is a divider. Only the heart gives unity.

When you can look through the heart, the whole universe looks like one unity. When you approach through the mind, the whole world becomes atomic. There is no unity, only atoms and atoms and atoms. The heart gives a unitary experience, it joins together, and the ultimate synthesis is God. If you can look through the heart, the whole universe looks like one. That oneness is God.

That is why science can never find God. That is impossible, because the method applied can never reach to the ultimate unity. The very method of science is reason, analysis, division. So science comes to molecules, atoms, electrons…. They will go on dividing, but they can never come to the organic unity of the whole. The whole is impossible to look at through the head.

So be more loving. Remember, whatsoever you are doing, the quality of love must be there. This has to be a constant remembering. You are walking on the grass—feel that the grass is alive. Every blade is as much alive as you are.

Mahatma Gandhi was staying with Rabindranath Tagore in Shanti Niketan. And look at their different approaches! Gandhi's nonviolence was a mind affair. He was always reasoning about it, rational about it. He thought about it, he struggled over it, he pondered, contemplated, and then he concluded; he experimented, then he concluded. If you have read his autobiography, you will recall that he has named the book, *Experiments with Truth*. The very word 'experiments' is scientific, of reason—a lab word.

He was staying with Rabindranath, the poet, and they both went for a walk in the gardens. The land was green, alive, so Gandhi said to Rabindranath, "Come out to the lawn."

Rabindranath said, "That is impossible. I cannot walk over the lawn. Every blade is as much alive as I am. I cannot step over so alive a phenomenon."

And Rabindranath was not a preacher of nonviolence—not at all. He never talked about nonviolence, but his approach was through the heart. He feels the grass.

Gandhi pondered over what he said, and then answered, "You are right." This is a mind approach.

Be loving. Even with things, be loving. If you are sitting on a chair, be loving. Feel the chair; have a feeling of gratitude. The chair is giving comfort to you. Feel the touch, love it, have a loving feeling. The chair itself is not important. If you are eating, eat lovingly.

Indians say that food is divine. The meaning is that when you are eating, the food is giving you life, energy, vitality. Be grateful, be loving to it.

Ordinarily we eat food very violently, as if we are killing something, not as if we are absorbing—as if we are killing. Or very indifferently you go on throwing things into your belly, without any feeling. Touch your food lovingly, with gratitude: it is your life. Take it in, taste it, enjoy it. Do not be indifferent and do not be violent.

Our teeth are very violent because of our animal heritage. Animals have no other weapons; nails and teeth are their only weapons of violence. Your teeth are basically a weapon, so people go on killing with their teeth—they kill their food. That is why, the more violent you are, the more you will need food.

But there is a limit to food, so one goes on smoking or one goes on chewing gum. That is violence. You enjoy it because you are killing something with your teeth, grinding something with your teeth, so one goes on chewing gum or *pan*. This is a part of violence. Do whatsoever you are doing, but do it lovingly. Do not be indifferent. Then your heart center will start functioning, and you will come down deep into the heart.

First: try headlessness. Secondly: try love. Thirdly: be more and more aesthetic—sensitive toward beauty, toward music, toward all that touches the heart. If this world can be trained more for music and less for mathematics, we will have a better humanity; if we can train the mind more for poetry and less for philosophy, we will have a better humanity. Because while you are listening to music or playing music the mind is not needed, you drop from the mind.

Be more aesthetic, more poetic, more sensitive. You may not be a great musician or a great poet or a great painter, but you can enjoy, and you can create something in your own right. There is no need to be a Picasso. You can paint your house yourself, you can paint some pictures.

No need to be a maestro, an Alauddin Khan. You can play something in your house; you can play on a flute, no matter how amateurish. But do something which is concerned with the heart. Sing, dance, do something which is concerned with the heart. Be more sensitive to the world of the heart—and not much is needed to be sensitive.

Even a poor man can be sensitive; riches are not needed. You may not have a palace where you can be sensitive. If you are just lying on the beach, it is enough to be sensitive. You can be sensitive to the sand, you can be sensitive to the sun, you can be sensitive to the waves, to the wind, to the trees, to the sky. The whole world is there for you to be sensitive to it. Try to be more sensitive, alive—and *actively* sensitive, because the whole world has become passive.

You go to a cinema hall; someone else is doing something and you just sit there and watch. Someone else is loving on the screen and you are watching. You are just a voyeur—passive, dead, not doing anything. You are not a participant. Unless you are a participant, your heart center will not function. So it is better sometimes to dance.

You are not going to be a great dancer—there is no need. Howsoever awkward, just dance. That will give you the feeling of the heart. While you are dancing your center will be the heart; it can never be at the mind. Jump, play like children. Sometimes forget completely your name, your prestige, your degree. Forget them completely, be childlike. Do not be serious. Sometimes take life as fun, and the heart will develop. The heart gathers energy.

And when you have a heart that is alive, the quality of your mind will also change. Then you can go to the mind, you can function through the mind, but the mind will become just an instrument —you can use it. Then you are not obsessed with it, and you can move away from it any moment you like. Then you are a master. The heart will give you a feeling that you are a master.

And another thing: you will come to know that you are neither the head nor the heart, because you can move from heart to head, from head to heart. Then you know that you are something else—X. If you remain in the head and never move anywhere, you become identified with the head. You do not know that you are different. This movement from heart to head and from head to heart will give you the feeling that you are totally different. Sometimes you are at the heart and sometimes you are at the head, but you are neither heart nor head.

This third point of awareness will lead you to the third center—to the navel. And the navel is not really a center. There, *you are!* That is why it cannot be developed, it can only be discovered.

The fourth question:

You said that Western psychologists now say it is better not to avoid fighting in a love relationship, and that facing it when it comes makes the love more intense. Then You spoke of Buddha's middle path which excludes both extremes. For those who have not yet transcended into the love that is beyond the two poles, which way is preferable for lovers in Your opinion?

Some basic points. Firstly, the love of the mind is bound to be a movement between the two polar opposites of hate and love. With mind, duality is bound to be there. So if you are loving to someone with your mind, you cannot escape the other pole. You can hide it, you can suppress it, you can forget

about it—the so-called cultured are always doing that. But then they become numb, dead.

If you cannot fight with your lover, if you cannot be angry, then the authenticity of the love is lost. If you suppress your anger, that suppressed anger will become a part of you, and that suppressed anger will not allow you total let-go while in love. It is always there. You are withholding it; you have suppressed it.

If I am angry and I have suppressed it, then when I am loving the suppressed anger is there, and that will make my love dead. If I have not been authentic in my anger, I cannot be authentic in my love. If you are authentic, then you are authentic in both. If you are not authentic in one, you cannot be authentic in the other.

All over the world so-called teachings, civilization, culture, they have deadened love completely. And in the name of love this has happened. They say, "If you love someone, then do not be angry; your love is false if you are angry. Then do not fight, then do not hate."

Of course, it looks logical. If you are in love, how can you hate? So we cut off the hate part. But with the hate part cut off, the love becomes impotent. It is as if you have cut off one leg of a man and then you say, "Now you move! Now you can run, you are free to run." But you have cut off a leg, so the man cannot move.

Hate and love are two poles of one phenomenon. If you cut hate, love will be dead and impotent. That is why every family has become impotent. And then you become afraid of letting go. When you are in love you cannot let go completely because you are afraid. If you let go completely the anger, the violence, the hate that is hidden and suppressed may come out. Then you have to force it down continuously. Deep down you have to fight it continuously. And in fighting it you cannot be natural and spontaneous. Then you just pose that you are loving. You pretend, and everyone knows: your wife knows that you are pretending, and you know that your wife is pretending. Everyone is pretending. Then the whole life becomes false.

Two things have to be done in order to go beyond mind. First, go into meditation, and then touch the level of no-mind within you. Then you will have a love that will not have any polar opposite. But then in that love there will be no excitement, no passion. That love will be silent—a deep peace with not even a ripple on it.

A Buddha, a Jesus, they also love. But in that love there is no excitement, no fever. The fever comes from the polar opposite, the excitement comes from the polar opposite. Two polar opposites create tension. But Buddha's love, Jesus' love, is a silent phenomenon, so only those who have reached to the state of no-mind can understand their love.

Jesus was passing, and it was hot, at noon. He was tired, so he just rested under a tree. He didn't know to whom the tree belonged. It belonged to Mary Magdalene. Mary was a prostitute.

She looked from her window and saw this very beautiful man—one of the most beautiful ever born. She felt attracted, and not only attracted, she felt passion. She came out and she asked Jesus, "Come into my house. Why are you resting here? You are welcome."

Jesus saw in her eyes passion, love—so-called love. Jesus said, "Next time, when I am again tired while passing here, I will come to your house. But just now the need is fulfilled. I am ready to move again, so thank you."

Mary felt insulted. This was rare...really, she had never invited anyone before. People would come from far away just to have a look at her. Even kings would come to her, and here was this beggar refusing her. Jesus was just a beggar, a vagabond—just a hippie, and he refused her. So Mary said to Jesus, "Can't you feel my love? This is a love invitation. So come! Do not reject me. Don't you have any love in your heart?"

Jesus said to her in reply, "I also love you—and really, all those who come pretending that they love

you, they do not love you." He said, "Only I can love you."

And he was right. But that love has a different quality. That love does not have the polar opposite, the contrast. Thus the tension is missing, the excitement is missing. He is not excited about love, not feverish. And love is not a relationship for him, it is a state of being.

Go beyond mind; reach to a level of no-mind. Then love flowers, but that love has no opposite to it. Beyond mind there is no opposite to anything. Beyond mind everything is one. Within mind, everything is divided into two. But if you are within mind, it is better to be authentic than to be false.

So be authentic when you feel angry toward your lover or your beloved. Be authentic while you are in anger, and then with no repression, when the moment of love will come, when the mind will move to the other extreme, you will have a spontaneous flow. So with mind, take fighting as part of it. It is the very dynamism of the mind to work in polar opposites. So be authentic in your anger, be authentic in your fight; then you will be authentic in your love also.

So for lovers, I would like to say: be authentic. And if you are really authentic, a unique phenomenon will happen. You will become weary of the whole nonsense of moving in polar opposites. But be authentic; otherwise you will never become weary.

A repressed mind never becomes really aware that he is gripped in polar opposites. He is never really angry, he is never really in love, so he has no real experience of the mind. Thus, I suggest to be authentic. Do not be false. *Be real!* And authenticity has its own beauty. Your lover, your beloved will understand when you are really angry—authentically angry. Only a fake anger or a false nonanger cannot be forgiven. Only a false face cannot be forgiven. Be authentic, and then you will be authentic in love also. That authentic love will compensate, and through this authentic living you will become wearied. You will come to wonder what you are doing—why you are just a pendulum moving from one pole to another. You will be bored, and then only can you decide to move beyond mind and beyond polarity.

Be an authentic man or be an authentic woman. Do not allow any falsity, do not pretend. Be real and suffer reality. Suffering is good. Suffering is really a training, a discipline. Suffer it! Suffer anger and suffer love and suffer hate. Remember only one thing: never be false. If you do not feel love, then say that you do not feel love. Do not pretend; do not try to show that you are loving. If you are angry, then say that you are angry and be angry.

There will be much suffering, but suffer it. Through that suffering a new consciousness is born. You become aware of the whole nonsense of hate and love. You hate the person and you also love the same person, and you go on moving in a circle. That circle will become crystal clear for you, and it becomes crystal clear only through suffering.

Do not escape suffering. You need a *real* suffering. It is like a fire: it will burn you. All that is false will burn and all that is real will be there. This is what existentialists call authenticity. Be authentic, and then you cannot be anymore in the mind. Be nonauthentic, and you will be for lives and lives in the mind.

You will get bored of the duality. But how can one get bored of the duality unless one is really in the duality, not pretending? Then you will know that the so-called love of the mind is nothing but a disease.

Have you observed that a lover cannot sleep? He is not at ease—he is feverish. If you examine him, he will show many symptoms of many diseases. This love, the so-called love of mind and body, is really a disease, but one remains occupied—that is the function of it. Otherwise you will feel unoccupied, as if you are not doing anything in this world. Your whole life will seem vacant, so love is good to fill it.

Mind itself is the disease, so whatsoever belongs to the mind is going to be a disease. Only beyond mind, where you are not divided in duality, where you are one, only there does a different love flower. Jesus calls it love. Buddha calls it compassion. This is just to make a distinction. It makes no difference what you call it.

There is a possibility of a love which has no opposite to it, but that love can come only when you go beyond this love. And to go beyond, I suggest that you be authentic. To be authentic—in hate, in love, in anger, in everything, be authentic: real, not pretending, because only a reality can be transcended. You cannot transcend unreal things.

CHAPTER 13

Inner
Centering

♦

18 *Look lovingly at some object. Do not go to another object. Here in the middle of the object —the blessing.*

19 *Without support for feet or hands, sit only on the buttocks. Suddenly, the centering.*

20 *In a moving vehicle, by rhythmically swaying, experience. Or in a still vehicle, by letting yourself swing in slowing invisible circles.*

21 *Pierce some part of your nectar-filled form with a pin, and gently enter the piercing and attain to the inner purity.*

The human body is a mysterious mechanism. Its working is two-dimensional. In order to go to the outside, your consciousness goes through the senses to meet the world, to meet matter. But this is only one dimension of your body's functions. Your body has another dimension also: it leads you in. If consciousness goes out, then whatsoever you know is matter; if consciousness goes in, then whatsoever you know is nonmatter.

In reality, there is no division: matter and nonmatter are one. But this reality—X—if looked at through the eyes, the senses, appears as matter. This same reality, the X, looked at from within—not through the senses, but through centering—looks like nonmatter. The reality is one, but you can look at it in two ways. One is through the senses; another is not through the senses. All these techniques of centering are really to lead you to a point in yourself where senses are not working, where you go beyond senses.

Three things have to be understood first before we enter the techniques. Firstly, when you see through the eyes, the eyes are not seeing; they are only openings to see. The seer is behind the eyes. That which looks through the eyes is not the eyes. That is why you can close your eyes and still see dreams, visions, images. The seer is behind the senses; he moves through the senses to the world. But if you close your senses, the seer remains within.

If the seer, this consciousness, is centered, suddenly he becomes aware of himself. And when you are aware of yourself you are aware of the total existence, because you and existence are not two. But to become aware of oneself one needs centering. By centering I mean your consciousness not being divided in many directions, your consciousness not moving anywhere, remaining in itself... nonmoving, rooted, without any direction, just remaining there: in.

It looks difficult to remain in, because for our minds even this thinking of how to remain in becomes a going out. We start thinking: the "how" starts thinking. To think about the in, the inner, is also a thought for us—and every thought as such belongs to the outer, never to the inner, because in the innermost center you are simply consciousness.

Thoughts are like clouds. They have come to you, but they do not belong to you. Every thought comes from the outside, from without. You cannot produce a single thought inside, within. Every thought comes from the outside; there is no possibility of creating a thought within. Thoughts are like clouds coming to you. So whenever you are thinking, you are not in—remember. To be thinking is to be out. So even if you are thinking about the inner, the soul, the self, you are not in.

All these thoughts about the self, about the inner, about the within, have come from without; they do not belong to you. To you belongs only simple consciousness, skylike, without the clouds.

So what to do? How to gain this simple consciousness inside? Some devices are used, because directly you cannot do anything. Some devices are needed through which you are thrown in, thrown to it. This center always needs an indirect approach, you cannot approach it directly. Understand this clearly, because this is very basic.

You are playing, and later on you report that it was very blissful, that "I was feeling very happy, I enjoyed it. A subtle happiness has been left behind." Someone listens to you. He is also after happiness—everyone is. He says, "Then I must play, because if through playing happiness is achieved, then I must achieve." He plays also, but he is directly concerned with happiness, with bliss, with enjoyment. Happiness is a by-product. If you are totally in your play, absorbed, happiness results, but if you are constantly hankering for happiness nothing happens. The play is the start.

You are listening to music. Someone says, "I feel very blissful." But if constantly you are directly concerned with bliss, you will not even be able to listen. That concern, that greed for bliss will become a barrier. Bliss is a by-product, you cannot grab it directly. It is so delicate a phenomenon that you have to approach it only indirectly. Do something else and it happens. You cannot do it directly.

Whatsoever is beautiful, whatsoever is eternal is so delicate that if you try to grab it directly it is destroyed. That is what is meant by techniques and devices. These techniques go on telling you to do something. That which you are doing is not significant, that which results is significant. But your mind must be concerned with doing, with technique, not with the result. The result happens—it is bound to happen. But it always happens indirectly, so do not be concerned with the result. Be concerned with the technique. Do it as totally as possible, and forget the result. It happens, but you can become a barrier to it.

If you are concerned only with the result, then it will never happen. And then it becomes very strange. People come to me and say, "You said that if we do meditation this will happen, but we are doing it and this is not happening." And they are

right, but they have forgotten the condition: you have to forget about the result, only then does it happen. You have to be in the act totally. The more you are in the act, the sooner the result happens.

But it is always indirect. You cannot be aggressive about it, you cannot be violent about it. It is such a delicate phenomenon, it cannot be attacked. It only comes to you while you are engaged somewhere else so totally that your inner space is vacant. These techniques are all indirect. There is no direct technique for spiritual happening.

---

18 Look lovingly at an object.

Now the technique—the sixth technique for centering: *Look lovingly at some object. Do not go to another object. Here in the middle of the object —the blessing.*

I should repeat it: *Look lovingly at some object. Do not go to another....* Do not move to another object. *Here in the middle of the object—the blessing.*

Look lovingly at some object.... Lovingly is the key. Have you ever looked lovingly at any object? You may say yes because you do not know what it means to look lovingly at an object. You may have looked lustfully at an object—that is another thing. That is totally different, diametrically opposite. So first, the difference; try to feel the difference.

A beautiful face, a beautiful body—you look at it, and you feel that you are looking at it lovingly. But why are you looking at it? Do you want to get something out of it? Then it is lust, not love. Do you want to exploit it? Then it is lust, not love. Then really, you are thinking of how to use this body, how to possess it, how to make this body an instrument for your happiness.

Lust means how to use something for your happiness; love means your happiness is not at all concerned. Really, lust means how to get something out of it and love means how to give something. They are diametrically opposite.

If you see a beautiful face and you feel love toward the face, the immediate feeling in your consciousness will be how to do something to make this face happy, how to do something to make this man or this woman happy. The concern is not with yourself, the concern is with the other.

In love the other is important; in lust you are important. In lust you are thinking how to make the other your instrument; in love you are thinking how to become an instrument yourself. In lust you are going to sacrifice the other; in love you are going to sacrifice yourself. Love means giving; lust means getting. Love is a surrender; lust is an aggression.

What you say is meaningless: even in lust you talk in terms of love. Your language is not very meaningful, so do not be deceived. Look within, and then you will come to understand that you have not once in your life looked lovingly toward someone or some object.

The second distinction to be made: this sutra says, *Look lovingly at some object.* Really, even if you look lovingly at something material, insentient, the object will become a person. If you look lovingly at it, your love is the key to transform anything into a person. If you look lovingly at a tree, the tree becomes a person.

Just the other day I was talking with Vivek and I told her that when we move to the new ashram we will name every tree, because every tree is a person. Have you ever heard of anyone naming a tree? No one names a tree because no one feels love for it. If the case were otherwise, a tree would become a person. Then it is not just one in a crowd, it becomes unique.

You name dogs and cats. When you name a dog and you call it Tiger or something else, the dog becomes a person. Then it is not just one dog amongst other dogs, it has a personality; you have created a person. Whenever you look lovingly at something, it becomes a person.

And the contrary is also true. Whenever you look with lustful eyes toward a person, the person becomes an object, a thing. That is why lustful eyes are repulsive—because no one likes to become a thing. When you look at your wife with lustful eyes —or at any other woman, or man, with lustful eyes —the other feels hurt. What are you doing, really? You are changing a person, a living person, into a dead instrument. You are thinking of how to "use," and the person is killed.

That is why lustful eyes are repulsive, ugly. When you look at someone with love, the other is raised. He becomes unique. Suddenly he becomes a person. A person cannot be replaced; a thing can be replaced. A 'thing' means that which is replaceable; a 'person' means that which cannot be replaced: there is no possibility of replacing him or her. A person is unique; a thing is not unique.

Love makes anything unique. That is why without love you never feel like a person. Unless someone loves you deeply, you never feel that you have any uniqueness. You are just one in a crowd—just a number, a datum. You can be changed.

For example, if you are a clerk in an office or a teacher in a school or a professor in a university, your professorhood is replaceable. Another professor will replace you; he can replace you at any moment because you are just used there as a professor. You have a functional meaning and significance.

If you are a clerk, someone else is easily able to do the work. The work will not wait for you. If you die this moment, the next moment someone will replace you and the mechanism will continue. You were just a figure—another figure will do. You were just a utility.

But then someone falls in love with this clerk or this professor. Suddenly the clerk is no more a clerk; he has become a unique person. If he dies, then the beloved cannot replace him. He is irreplaceable. Then the whole world may go on in the same way, but the one who was in love cannot be the same. This uniqueness, this being a person, happens through love.

This sutra says, *Look lovingly at some object.* It makes no distinction between an object and a person. There is no need, because when you look lovingly anything will become a person. The very look changes, transforms.

You may or may not have observed what happens when you drive a particular car, say a Fiat. There are thousands and thousands and thousands of Fiats exactly similar, but your car, if you are in love with it, becomes unique—a person. It cannot be replaced; a relationship is created. Now you feel this car as a person. If something goes wrong...a slight sound, and you feel it. And cars are very temperamental. You know the temper of your car —when it feels good and when it feels bad. The car becomes, by and by, a person.

Why? If there is a love relationship, anything becomes a person. If there is a lust relationship, then a person will become a thing. And this is one of the most inhuman acts man can do—to make someone a thing.

Look lovingly at some object.... So what is one to do? When you look lovingly, what are you to do? The first thing: forget yourself. Forget yourself completely! Look at a flower and forget yourself completely. Let the flower be; you become completely absent. Feel the flower, and a deep love will flow from your consciousness toward the flower. And let your consciousness be filled with only one thought—how you can help this flower to flower more, to become more beautiful, to become more blissful. What can you do?

It is not meaningful whether you can do or not; that is not relevant. The feeling of what you can do —this pain, this deep ache over what you can do to make this flower more beautiful, more alive, more flowering—is meaningful. Let this thought reverberate into your whole being. Let every fiber of your body and mind feel it. You will be transfixed in an ecstasy, and the flower will become a person.

Do not go to another object.... You cannot go. If you are in a love relationship, you cannot go. If you love someone in this group, then you forget the whole crowd; only one face remains. Really, you do not see anyone else, you see only one face. All the

others are there, but they are subliminal—just on the periphery of your consciousness. They are *not*. They are just shadows; only one face remains. If you love someone then only that face remains, so you cannot move.

Do not go to another object, remain with one. Remain with a roseflower or remain with a beloved's face. Remain there loving, flowing, with just one heart, with the feeling of, "What can I do to make the loved one happier, blissful?"

Here in the middle of the object—the blessing. And when this is the case you are absent, not concerned with yourself at all, not selfish, not thinking in terms of your pleasure, your gratification. You have forgotten yourself completely, and you are just thinking in terms of the other. The other has become the center of your love; your consciousness is flowing toward the other. With deep compassion, with a deep feeling of love, you are thinking, "What can I do to make the loved one blissful?" In this state, suddenly, *Here in the middle of the object—the blessing.*

Suddenly, as a by-product, the blessing comes to you. Suddenly you become centered.

This looks paradoxical because this sutra says to forget yourself completely, not to be self-centered, to move to the other completely. Buddha is reported to have said continuously that whenever you are praying, pray for others—never for yourself. Otherwise the prayer is just useless.

One man came to Buddha and he said, "I accept your teaching, but only one thing is very difficult to accept. You say that whenever we do prayer we are not to think about ourselves, we are not to ask anything about ourselves. We have to say, 'Whatsoever may be the result of my prayer, let that result be distributed to all. If blessing happens, let it be distributed to all.'" The man said, "This is okay, but can I make only one exception? Not to my immediate neighbor—he is my enemy. Let this blessing be distributed to all except to my immediate neighbor."

The mind is self-centered, so Buddha said,

"Your prayer is useless. Nothing will come out of it unless you are ready to give all, to distribute all, and then all will be yours."

In love you are to forget yourself. It looks paradoxical: then when and how will the centering happen? By being totally concerned with the other, with the other's happiness, when you forget yourself completely and only the other remains there, suddenly you are filled with bliss—the blessing.

Why? Because when you are not concerned with yourself you become vacant, empty; the inner space is created. When your mind is totally concerned with the other, you become mindless within. Then there are no thoughts inside. And then this thought—"How can I be helpful? How can I create more bliss? How can the other be more happy?"—cannot continue anymore, because really, there is nothing you can do. This thought becomes a stop. There is nothing you can do. What can you do? If you think you can do, you are still thinking in terms of yourself—ego.

With the love object one becomes totally helpless—remember this. Whenever you love someone you feel totally helpless. That is the agony of love: one cannot feel what he can do. He wants to do everything, he wants to give the whole universe to the lover or the beloved—but what can he do? If you think that you can do this or that, you are still not in a love relationship. Love is very helpless, absolutely helpless, and that helplessness is the beauty, because in that helplessness you are surrendered.

Love someone and you will feel helpless; hate someone and you can do something. Love someone and you are absolutely helpless—because what can you do? Whatsoever you can do seems insignificant, meaningless; it is never enough. Nothing can be done. And when one feels that nothing can be done, one feels that one is helpless. When one wants to do everything and feels nothing can be done, mind stops. In this helplessness surrender happens. You are empty. That is why love becomes a deep meditation.

Really, if you love someone, no other meditation is needed. But because no one loves, one hundred and twelve methods are needed—and even they may not be enough.

Someone was here the other day. He was telling me, "It gives me much hope. I have heard for the first time from you that there are one hundred and twelve methods. It gives me much hope, but somewhere a depression also comes into the mind: only one hundred and twelve methods? And if these one hundred and twelve methods don't work for me, then is there no one hundred and thirteenth?"

And he is right. He is right! If these one hundred and twelve methods do not work for you, then there is no go. So as he suggests, a depression also follows hope. But really, methods are needed because the basic method is missing. If you can love, no method is needed.

Love itself is the greatest method, but love is difficult—in a way impossible. Love means putting yourself out from your consciousness, and in the same place, where your ego has been in existence, putting someone else. Replacing yourself by someone else means love—as if now you are not and only the other is.

Jean-Paul Sartre says that the other is the hell, and he is right. He is right because the other creates only hell for you. But he is wrong also because if the other can be hell, the other can be heaven. If you live through lust, the other is a hell because then you are trying to kill that person. You are trying to make that person a thing. Then that person will also react and will try to make you a thing, and that creates hell.

So every husband and every wife, they are creating hell for each other because each one is trying to possess the other. Possession is possible only with things, never with persons. You can only be possessed by a person; you can never possess a person. A thing can be possessed, but you try to possess persons. Through that effort persons become things. If I make you into a thing, you will react. Then I am your enemy. Then you will try to make a thing out of me—that creates hell.

You are sitting in your room alone, and then suddenly you become aware that someone is peeping through the keyhole. Observe minutely what happens. Have you felt any change? And why do you feel angry about this Peeping Tom? He is not doing anything to you—just peeping. Why do you feel angry? He has changed you into a thing. He is observing; he has made you into a thing, into an object. That gives you an uneasiness.

And the same will happen to him if you come near the keyhole and look through it. The other will become shattered, shocked. He was a subject just a moment before: he was the observer and you were the observed. Now suddenly he has been caught. He has been observed observing you, and now he has become a thing.

When someone is observing you, suddenly you feel your freedom has been disturbed, destroyed. That is why, unless you are in love with someone, you cannot stare. That stare becomes ugly and violent—unless you are in love. If you are in love then a stare is a beautiful thing, because your stare is not changing the other into a thing. Then you can look directly into the eyes, then you can go deep into the eyes of the other. You are not changing him into a thing. Rather, through your love your look is making him a person. That is why only the stares of lovers are beautiful; otherwise stares are ugly.

Psychologists say there is a time limit. And you all know, observe and you will come to know, what the time limit is for how long you can stare into someone's eyes, if he is a stranger. There is a time limit. One moment more, and the other will become angry. Just a passing look in public can be pardoned because it seems as if you were just seeing, not looking.

A look is a deep thing. If I just see you when passing, no relationship is created. Or I am passing and you look at me, just while passing—no offense is meant so it is okay. But if you suddenly stand and look at me, you become an observer. Then your look will disturb me and I will feel insulted: "What are you doing? I am a person, not a thing. This is not the way to look."

Because of this, clothes have become so meaningful. Only when you love someone can you be easily naked, because the moment you are naked your whole body becomes an object. Someone can look at your whole body, and if he is not in love with you his eyes will turn your whole body, your whole being, into an object. But when you are in love with someone you can be naked without feeling that you are naked. Rather, you would like to be naked, because you would like this transforming love to transform your whole body into a person.

Whenever you are turning someone into a thing, that act is immoral. But if you are filled with love, then in that love-filled moment with any object this phenomenon, this blessing, is possible. It happens.

In the middle of the object—the blessing. Suddenly you have forgotten yourself—the other was there. Then when the right moment comes, when you are no longer present, absolutely absent, the other will also become absent. And between the two the blessing happens. That is what lovers feel. That blessing is also because of an unknown, unconscious meditation.

When two lovers are there, by and by they both become absent. A pure existence remains—without any egos, without any conflict...just a communion. In that communion one feels blissful. It is wrongly inferred that the other has given that bliss to you. That bliss has come because unknowingly you have fallen into a deep meditative technique.

You can do it consciously—and when you do it consciously it goes deeper, because then you are not obsessed with the object. This is happening every day. If you love someone, you feel blissful not because of him or her, but because of love. And why because of love? Because this phenomenon happens—this sutra happens.

But then you become obsessed. Then you think that because of A, because of A's proximity, nearness, because of A's love this blessing happens. Then you think, "I must possess A, because without A being present I may not be able to get this blessing again." You become jealous. If someone else possesses A, then he will be blissful and you will feel miserable, so you want to take away all possibilities of A being possessed by anyone else. A should be possessed only by you, because you have glimpsed a different world through him. Then the moment you try to possess, you will destroy the whole beauty and the whole phenomenon.

When the lover is possessed, love is gone. Then the lover is just a thing. You can use it, but the blessing will never come again, because that blessing was coming when the other was a person. The other was made, created: you created the person in the other, and the other created the person in you. No one was an object. Both were subjectivities meeting—two persons meeting, not one person and one thing.

But the moment you possess, this will become impossible. And mind will try to possess because mind thinks in terms of greed: "One day bliss has happened, so it must happen to me every day. So I must possess." But the bliss happens because there is no possession. And the bliss happens not because of the other, really, but because of you. Remember this, the bliss happens because of you. Because you are so absorbed in the other, the bliss happens.

It can happen with a rose, it can happen with a rock, it can happen with the trees, it can happen with anything. Once you know the situation in which it happens, it can happen anywhere. If you know that you are not, and with a deep love your consciousness has moved to the other—to the trees, to the sky, to the stars, to anyone; when your total consciousness is addressed to the other it leaves you, it moves away from you—in that absence of the self is the blessing.

---

19 Sit on your buttocks only.

The seventh centering technique: *Without support for feet or hands, sit only on the buttocks. Suddenly, the centering.*

This technique has been used by Taoists in China for centuries, and it is a wonderful technique—one of the easiest. Try this: *Without support for feet or hands, sit only on the buttocks. Suddenly, the centering.*

What is to be done? You will need two things. First, a very sensitive body, which you do not have. You have a dead body; it is just a burden to be carried—not sensitive. First you will have to make your body sensitive; otherwise this technique will not work. So first I will tell you something about how to make your body sensitive, and particularly your buttocks, because ordinarily your buttocks are the most insensitive part in your body. They have to be. They have to be because you are sitting the whole day on your buttocks. If they are too sensitive, it will be difficult.

So your buttocks are insensitive—they need to be. Just like the soles of the feet, they are insensitive. Continuously sitting on them, you never feel you are sitting on your buttocks. Have you ever felt it before this? Now you can feel you are sitting on your buttocks, but you have never felt it before—and you have been sitting on your buttocks your whole life, never aware. Their function is such that they cannot be very sensitive.

So first you have to make them sensitive. Try one very easy method.... And this method can be done to any part of the body; then the body will become sensitive. Just sit on a chair, relaxed, and close your eyes. Feel your left hand or your right hand—either one. Feel your left hand. Forget the whole body and just feel the left hand. The more you feel it, the more the left hand will become heavy.

Go on feeling the left hand. Forget the whole body, just go on feeling the left hand as if you are just the left hand. The hand will go on becoming more and more and more heavy. As it goes on becoming heavy, go on feeling it becoming more heavy. Then try to feel what is happening in the hand. Whatever the sensation, note it down: any sensation, any jerk, any slight movement—note down in the mind that this is happening. And go on doing it every day for at least three weeks. At any time during the day, do it for ten minutes, fifteen minutes. Just feel the left hand and forget the whole body.

Within three weeks you will feel you have a new left hand, or a new right hand. It will be so sensitive. And you will become aware of very minute and delicate sensations in the hand.

When you succeed with the hand, then try with the buttocks. Then try: close your eyes and feel that only two buttocks exist; you are no more. Let your whole consciousness go to the buttocks. It is not difficult. If you try, it is wonderful. And the feeling of aliveness that comes in the body is in itself very blissful. Then, when you can feel your buttocks and they can become very sensitive, when you can feel anything happening inside—a slight movement, a slight pain or anything—then you can observe and you can know. Then your consciousness is joined to the buttocks.

First try it with the hand. Because the hand is very sensitive, it is easy. Once you gain the confidence that you can sensitize your hand, this confidence will help you to sensitize your buttocks. Then do this technique. So you will need at least six weeks before you can enter this technique—three weeks with your hand and then three weeks with your buttocks, just making them more and more sensitive.

Lying on the bed, forget the whole body. Just remember that only two buttocks are left. Feel the touch—the bedsheet, the coldness or the slowly coming warmth. Feel it. Lying down in your bathtub, forget the body. Remember only the buttocks—feel. Stand against a wall with your buttocks touching the wall—feel the coldness of the wall. Stand with your beloved, with your wife or husband, buttock to buttock—feel the other through the buttocks. This is just to "create" your buttocks, to bring them to a situation where they start feeling.

Then do this technique: *Without support for feet or hands....* Sit on the ground. *Without*

support for feet or hands, sit only on the buttocks. The Buddha posture will do, *padmasana* will do. Or *siddhasana* will do, or any ordinary asana, but it is good not to use your hands. Just remain on the buttocks, sit only on the buttocks. Then what to do? Just close your eyes. Feel the buttocks touching the ground. And because the buttocks have become sensitive, you will feel that one buttock is touching more. You are leaning on one buttock, and the other is touching less. Then move the leaning to the other. Immediately move to the other; then come to the first. Go on moving from one to the other, and then by and by, balance.

Balancing means that both of your buttocks are feeling the same. Your weight on both of the buttocks is exactly the same. And when your buttocks are sensitive this will not be difficult, you will feel it. Once both your buttocks are balanced, *suddenly, the centering.* With that balance, suddenly you will be thrown to your navel center, and you will be centered inside. You will forget the buttocks, you will forget the body. You will be thrown to the inner center.

That is why I say centers are not meaningful, but centering is—whether it happens at the heart or at the head or at the buttocks, or anywhere. You have seen buddhas sitting. You may not have imagined that they are balancing their buttocks. You go to a temple and see Mahavira sitting, Buddha sitting; you may never have imagined that this sitting is just a balancing on the buttocks. It is—and when there is no imbalance, suddenly that balance gives you the centering.

20 How to meditate in a moving vehicle.

The eighth centering technique: *In a moving vehicle, by rhythmically swaying, experience. Or in a still vehicle, by letting yourself swing in slowing invisible circles.*

It is the same in a different way. *In a moving vehi-*

cle.... You are traveling in a train or in a bullock cart—when this technique was developed there was only the bullock cart. You are moving in a bullock cart on an Indian road—even today the road is the same. But when you are moving, your whole body is moving. Then it is useless.

In a moving vehicle, by rhythmically swaying.... Sway rhythmically. Try to understand; this is very minute. Whenever you are in a bullock cart or in any vehicle, you are resisting. The bullock cart sways to the left, but you resist it. You sway to the right in order to balance; otherwise you will fall down. So you are constantly resisting. Sitting in a bullock cart, you are fighting its movements. It moves to this side, and you have to move to that.

That is why when sitting in a train you become tired. You have not been doing anything. Why do you become so tired? You have been doing much unknowingly. You were fighting the train continuously; there was resistance. Do not resist—this is the first thing. If you want to do this technique, do not resist. Rather, move with the movements, sway with the movements. Become part of the bullock cart, do not resist it. Whatsoever the bullock cart is doing on the road, become part of it. That is why children are never tired of journeying.

Poonam has just come from London with her two children, and she was afraid that they may get ill, that they may get tired because of such a long journey. She became tired, and they came laughing. She became completely tired when she came here. The moment she entered my room she was dead tired, and the two children started playing right then and there. An eighteen-hour-long journey from London to Bombay and they were not a bit tired. Why? Because they do not know how to resist yet.

So a drunkard can sit in a bullock cart for the whole night, and in the morning he will be as fresh as ever, but you will not be. It is because a drunkard cannot resist. He moves with the cart; there is no fight. The fighting is not there, he is one.

In a moving vehicle, by rhythmically sway-

ing.... So do one thing: do not resist. And the second thing, create a rhythm. Create a rhythm in your movements. Make it a beautiful harmony. Forget about the road; do not curse the road and the government—forget them. Do not curse the bullock and the bullock cart, or the driver—forget them. Close your eyes, do not resist. Move rhythmically and create a music in your movement. Make it as if it is a dance. *In a moving vehicle, by rhythmically swaying, experience.* The sutra says the experience will come to you.

Or in a still vehicle.... Do not ask where to get a bullock cart; do not deceive yourself, because the sutra says, *Or in a still vehicle, by letting yourself swing in slowing invisible circles.* Just sitting here, swing in a circle. First take a big circle, then go on slowing it...slowing, slowing, making it smaller and smaller and smaller, until your body is not visibly moving, but inside you feel a subtle movement.

Start with a bigger circle, with closed eyes. Otherwise, when the body stops you will stop. With closed eyes make big circles; just sitting, swing in a circle. Go on swinging, making the circle smaller and smaller and smaller. Visibly you will stop; no one will be able to detect that you are still moving. But inside you will feel a subtle movement. Now the body is not moving, only the mind. Go on making it slower and slower, and experience. That will become a centering. In a vehicle, in a moving vehicle, a nonresisting rhythmical movement will create a centering within you.

Gurdjieff created many dances for such techniques. He was working on this technique. All the dances he was using in his school were, really, swaying in circles. All the dances were in circles—just whirling but remaining aware inside, by and by making the circles smaller and smaller. A time comes when the body stops, but the mind inside goes on moving, moving, moving.

If you have been traveling in a train for twenty hours, after you have come home, after you have left the train, if you close your eyes you will feel that you are still traveling. Still you are traveling.

The body has stopped, but the mind is still feeling the vehicle. So just do this technique.

Gurdjieff created phenomenal dances, very beautiful. In this century he worked miracles—not miracles like Satya Sai Baba. Those are not miracles; any street magician can do them. But Gurdjieff really created miracles. He prepared a group of a hundred people for meditative dancing, and he was showing that dance to an audience in New York for the first time. A hundred dancers were on the stage whirling. Those who were in the audience, even their minds began whirling. There were a hundred white-robed dancers just whirling.

When he indicated with his hand, they would whirl, and the moment he would say, "Stop," there would be dead silence. That was a stop for the audience, but not for the dancers—because the body can stop immediately, but the mind then takes the movement inside; it goes on and on. It was beautiful even to look at, because a hundred persons suddenly became dead statues. It created a sudden shock in the audience also, because a hundred movements—beautiful movements, rhythmical movements—suddenly stopped. You would be looking at them moving, whirling, dancing, and suddenly the dancers stopped. Then your thought would also stop.

Many in New York felt that it was a weird phenomenon: their thoughts stopped immediately. But for the dancers, the dance continued inside, and the inside whirling circles became smaller and smaller until they became centered.

One day it happened that they were coming just to the edge of the stage, dancing. It was expected, supposed, that Gurdjieff would stop them just before they danced down the stage onto the audience. A hundred dancers were just on the edge of the stage. One step more and they would all fall down into the hall. The whole hall was expecting that suddenly Gurdjieff would say stop, but he turned his back to light his cigar. He turned his back to the dancers to light his cigar, and the whole group of a hundred dancers fell down from the

stage upon the floor—on a naked stone floor.

The whole audience stood up. They were screaming, shouting, and they were thinking that many must have broken their bones—it was such a crash. But not a single one was hurt; not even a single bruise was there.

They asked Gurdjieff what had happened. No one had been hurt, and the crash was such that it seemed impossible. The reason was only this: they were really not in their bodies at that moment. They were slowing down their inner circling. And when Gurdjieff saw that now they were completely oblivious of their bodies, he allowed them to fall down.

If you are completely oblivious of your body, there is no resistance. A bone is broken because of resistance. If you are falling down, you resist: you go against the pull of gravity. That going against, that resistance, is the problem—not gravity. If you can fall down with gravity, if you can cooperate with it, then no possibility of being hurt will arise.

This sutra: *In a moving vehicle, by rhythmically swaying, experience. Or in a still vehicle, by letting yourself swing in slowing invisible circles.* You can do it. There is no need of a vehicle, just whirl like children do. When your mind goes crazy, and you feel that now you will fall down, do not stop—go on! Even if you fall down, do not worry about it, close your eyes and whirl. Your mind will get whirled, and you will fall down. When your body has fallen down, inside, feel! The whirling will continue. And it will come nearer and nearer and nearer, and suddenly you will be centered.

Children enjoy this very much because they get a great kick. Parents never allow their children to whirl. It is not good: they should be allowed—rather, encouraged. And if you can make them aware of inner whirling also, you can teach them meditation through their whirling. They enjoy it because they have a bodiless feeling. When they whirl, suddenly children become aware that their body is whirling but they are not. Inside they feel a centering which we cannot feel so easily, because their bodies and souls are still a bit apart; there is a gap.

When you come into your mother's womb, you cannot immediately get totally in the body; it takes time. When a child is born, then too he is not absolutely fixed, his soul is not absolutely fixed to the body; there are gaps. That is why there are many things which he cannot do. His body is ready to do it, but he cannot do it.

If you have observed, you may have noticed that newly born children cannot see with two eyes, they always see with one eye. If you observe, then you will see that when they observe and see anything, they cannot see with two eyes. They always look with one eye—one eye gets bigger. The pupil of one eye will become bigger, and the other pupil will remain small. The consciousness of a newborn child is not yet fixed, it is loose. By and by it will become fixed, and then they will look with two eyes.

They cannot yet feel their own body and others' bodies as different. It is difficult. They are not yet fixed, but fixation will come, by and by.

Meditation is again trying to create a gap. You have become fixed, solidly fixed in your body. That is why you feel, "I am the body." If a gap can be created, then only can you feel that you are not the body but something beyond the body. Swaying and whirling are helpful. They create the gap.

---

21 Concentrate on a pain in your body.

The ninth centering technique: *Pierce some part of your nectar-filled form with a pin, and gently enter the piercing and attain to the inner purity.*

This sutra says, *Pierce some part of your nectar-filled form....* Your body is not just a body, it is filled with you, and that you is the nectar. Pierce your body. When you are piercing your body, you are not pierced—only the body is pierced. But you feel the pierce as if you have been pierced; that is why you feel pain. If you can become aware that only the body is pierced, that you are not pierced, instead of pain you will feel bliss. There is no need to do it with a pin. Many things happen every day; you can use those situations for meditation. Or you can create a situation.

Some pain is there in your body. Do one thing: forget the whole body, just concentrate on the part of the body which is painful. And then a strange thing will be noted. When you concentrate on the part of the body which is painful, you see that part is shrinking. First you feel that the pain, the ache, is in your whole leg. When you concentrate, then you feel it is not in the whole leg. It was exaggerated— it is just at the knee.

Concentrate more, and you will feel it is not on the whole knee but just on a pinpoint. Concentrate more on the pinpoint; forget the whole body. Just close your eyes and go on concentrating in order to find where the pain is. It will go on shrinking; the area will become smaller and smaller. Then a moment will come when it will be just a pinpoint. Go on staring at the pinpoint, and suddenly the pinpoint will disappear and you will be filled with bliss. Instead of pain you will be filled with bliss.

Why does this happen? Because you and your body are two, they are not one. The one who is concentrating is you. The concentration is being done on the body—that is the object. When you concentrate, the gap is broadened, the identification is broken. Just to have concentration you move inside, away from the body. To bring the spot of pain into perspective, you have to move away. That moving away creates the gap. And when you are concentrating on the pain, you forget the identification, you forget that "I am feeling pain."

Now you are the observer and the pain is somewhere else. You are observing the pain, not feeling the pain. This change from feeling to observation creates the gap. And when the gap is bigger, suddenly you forget the body completely; you are aware only of consciousness.

You can try this technique also: *Pierce some part of your nectar-filled body with a pin, and gently enter the piercing*. If there is pain, then first you will have to concentrate on the whole area; then by and by it will come to a pinpoint.

But there is no need to wait. You can use a pin. Use a pin on any part which is sensitive. On the body many spots are blind spots; they will not be useful. You may not have heard about blind spots on the body. Then give a pin to anyone, to your friend, and sit, and tell your friend to pierce your back with the pin at many points. At many points you will feel no pain. You will say, "No, you have not pierced yet. I am not feeling any pain." Those are blind spots. Just on your cheeks there are two blind spots which can be tested.

If you go to Indian villages, many times in religious festivals they will pierce their cheeks with an arrow. It looks like a miracle, but it is not. The cheeks have two blind spots. If you pierce through these blind spots, no blood will come out and there will be no pain. On your back there are thousands of dead spots, where you cannot feel any pain. Your body has two types of spots—sensitive, alive ones, and those that are dead. So find a sensitive spot where you can feel even a slight touch. Then pierce the pin and *enter the piercing*. That is the thing; that is meditation. And *gently* enter the piercing. As the pin moves inside, into your skin, and you feel the pain, you also enter. Do not feel that the pain is entering you; do not feel the pain, do not be identified with it. Enter with the pin. Pierce with the pin.

Close your eyes; observe the pain. As the pain is piercing in, you also pierce you. And with the pin piercing you, your mind will become easily concentrated. Use that point of pain, of intense pain, and observe it. That is what is meant by *gently enter the piercing*.

And attain to the inner purity. If you can enter observing, unidentified, aloof, standing far away, not feeling that the pain is piercing you, but observing that the pin is piercing the body and you are an observer, you will attain to the inner purity; the inner innocence will be revealed to you. For the first time you will become aware that you are not the body. And once you know that you are not the body your life is changed completely, because your whole life is around the body. Once you know you are not the body, you cannot continue this life. The center is being missed.

When you are not the body, then you have to create a different life. That life is the sannyasin's life. It is a different life; the center is different now. Now you exist in the world as a soul, as an *atma*, not as a body. If you exist as a body, then you have created a different world: of material gain, greed, gratification, lust, sex. You have created a world around you; this is the body-oriented world.

Once you know you are not the body, your whole world disappears. You cannot support it anymore. A different world arises which is around the soul—a world of compassion, of love, of beauty, of truth, of goodness, of innocence. The center is shifted, and it is not in the body now. It is in the consciousness.

Enough for today.

CHAPTER 14

Changing the direction of energy

◆

Why is cosmic consciousness—samadhi—called centering?

Explain further how "love alone can be enough" without meditation.

Why is man insensitive?

The first question:

If enlightenment and samadhi mean total consciousness, cosmic consciousness, all-pervading consciousness, then it seems very strange to call this state of cosmic consciousness centering, as the word 'centering' implies one-pointedness. Why is cosmic consciousness, or samadhi, called centering?

entering is the path, not the goal. Centering is the method, not the result. Samadhi is not called centering; centering is the technique to samadhi. Of course, they look contradictory because when one realizes, becomes enlightened, there is no center left.

Jacob Böhme has said that when one comes to the divine it can be described in two ways: either the center is everywhere now, or the center is nowhere; both mean the same thing. So the word 'centering' seems contradictory, but the path is not the goal and the method is not the result. And method can be contradictory. So we have to understand it because these one hundred and twelve methods are methods of centering.

But once you become centered you will explode. Centering is just to gather yourself totally at one point. Once you are gathered at one point, crystallized at one point, that point explodes automatically. Then there is no center—or then the center is everywhere. So centering is a means to explode.

Why does centering become the method? If you are not centered your energy is unfocused, it cannot explode. It is spread out; it cannot explode. Explosion needs great energy. Explosion means that now you are not spread out—you are at one point. You become atomic; you become, really, a spiritual atom. And only when you are centered enough to become an atom can you explode. Then there is an atomic explosion.

That explosion is not talked about because it cannot be, so only the method is given. The result is not talked about. It cannot be talked about. If you do the method the result will follow, and there is no way to express it.

So remember this: basically, religion never talks about the experience itself, it talks only about the method; it shows the how, not the what. The what is left to you. If you do the how, the what will come to you. And there is no way to convey it. One can know it, but he cannot convey it. It is such an infinite experience that language becomes useless. The vastness is such that no word is capable of expressing it. So only the method is given.

Buddha is reported to have said continuously for forty years, "Do not ask me about the truth, about the divine, about nirvana, liberation. Do not ask me anything about such things. Just ask me how to reach there. I can show you the path, but I cannot give you the experience, not even in words." The experience is personal; method is impersonal. Method is scientific, impersonal; experience is always personal and poetic.

What do I mean when I differentiate in this way? Method is scientific. If you can do it, centering will result. That centering is bound to result if the method is done. If the centering is not happening, then you can know that you are missing the point somewhere. Somewhere you have missed the method, you have not followed it. Method is scientific, centering is scientific, but when the explosion comes to you, it is poetic.

By poetic I mean every one of you will experience it in a different way. Then there is no common ground. And everyone will express it in a different way. Buddha says something, Mahavira says something, Krishna says something else, and Jesus, Mohammed, Moses and Lao Tzu, they all differ — not in methods, but in the way they express their experience. Only on one thing do they all agree, that whatsoever they are saying is not expressing that which they have felt. Only on that one point do they agree.

Still, they try. Still, they try to convey somehow, to hint. It seems impossible, but if you have a sympathetic heart something may be conveyed. But that needs a deep sympathy and love and reverence. So really, whenever something is conveyed it doesn't depend on the conveyer, it depends on you. If you can receive it in deep love and reverence, then something reaches you. But if you are critical about it, then nothing reaches. Firstly, it is difficult to express. And even if it is expressed you are critical — then the message becomes impossible; there is no communication.

The communication is very delicate. That is why in all these one hundred and twelve methods it has been left out completely — only hinted at. Shiva says so many times: "Do this, and then the experience," and then he becomes silent. "Do this, and then the blessing," and then he becomes silent.

The blessing, the experience, the explosion: beyond them there is personal experience. With that which cannot be expressed, it is better not to try to express it — because if expression is tried with that which cannot be expressed, it will be misunderstood. So Shiva is silent. He is talking simply of methods, techniques, of how to do it.

But centering is not the end, it is just the path. And why does centering happen, develop, grow into an explosion? Because if much energy is centered at one point, the point will explode. The point is so small and the energy is so great, the point cannot contain it; hence the explosion.

This bulb can contain a particular quantity of electricity. If there is more electricity, the bulb will explode. That is the reason for centering: the more you are centered, the more energy is at your center. The moment there is much energy, the center won't be able to contain it. It will explode.

So it is scientific; it is just a scientific law. And if the center is not exploding, that means you are still not centered. Once you are centered, immediately the explosion follows. There is no time gap. So if you feel that the explosion is not coming, it means that you are still not focused. Still you do not have one center, still you have many centers, still you are divided, still your energy is dissipated, still your energy is moving out.

When the energy moves out you are just being emptied of energy, dissipated. Ultimately you will become impotent. Really, when death comes you have already died; you are just a dead cell. You have been constantly throwing energy outward — so whatsoever may be the quantity of energy, within a period you will become empty. Outgoing energy means death. You are dying every moment; your energy is being emptied; you are throwing your energy, dissipating it.

They say that even the sun which has been there for millions and millions of years, such a great reservoir of energy, is being emptied constantly. And within four billion years it will die. The sun will die simply because there will be no energy to radiate. Every day it is dying because the rays are carrying its energy toward the boundaries of the universe — if there are any boundaries. The energy is going out.

Only man is capable of transforming and changing the direction of energy. Otherwise death is a natural phenomenon — everything dies. Only man is capable of knowing the immortal, the deathless.

So you can reduce this whole thing into a law. If energy is moving out, death will be the result and you will never know what life means. You can only know a slow dying. You can never feel the intensity of being alive. If energy moves out then death is the automatic result—of anything, whatsoever. If you can change the direction of energy—energy not moving out, but moving in—then a mutation, a transformation happens.

Then this energy coming in becomes centered at one point in you. That point is just near the navel—because really, you are born as a navel. You are connected with your mother at the navel. The life energy of the mother is being poured into you through the navel. And once the navel cord is cut, you are separated from the mother, you become an individual. Before that you are not an individual, just part of your mother.

So real birth takes place when the navel cord is cut. Then the child takes its own life, becomes its own center. That center is bound to be just at the navel, because through the navel the energy comes to the child. That was the connecting link. And still, whether you are aware or not, your navel remains the center.

If energy begins to pour in, if you change the direction of the energy so that it comes in, it will hit the navel. It will go on coming in and become centered at the navel. When it is so much that the navel cannot contain it, that the center cannot contain it any longer, the center explodes. In that explosion, again you are no longer an individual. You were not an individual when you were connected with your mother; again you will not be an individual.

A new birth has taken place. You have become one with the cosmos. Now you do not have any center; you cannot say "I." Now there is no ego. A Buddha, a Krishna, goes on talking and using the word 'I.' That is simply formal; they do not have any ego. They are *not*.

Buddha was dying. The day he was to die,

many, many people, disciples, sannyasins, gathered, and they were sad; they were weeping and crying. So Buddha asked, "Why are you weeping?"

Someone said, "Because soon you will be no more."

Buddha laughed and said, "But I have been no more for forty years. I died the day I became enlightened. The center has not been there for forty years. So do not weep, do not be sad. No one is dying now. I am no more! But still the word 'I' has to be used even to denote that I am no more."

Energy moving in is the whole of religion, is what is meant by the religious search. How to move the energy, how to create a total about-turn? These methods help. So remember, centering is not samadhi, centering is not the experience. Centering is the door to the experience, and when there is the experience there is no centering. So centering is just a passage.

You are not centered now. You are multi-centered really—that is why I say you are not centered now. When you become centered, there is only one center. Then the energy that has been moving to multicenters has come back; it is a homecoming. Then you are at your center; then...explosion. Again the center is no more, but then you are not multicentered. Then there is no center at all. You have become one with the cosmos. Then existence and you mean one and the same thing.

For example, an iceberg is floating in the sea. The iceberg has a center of its own. It has a separate individuality; it is separate from the ocean. Deep down it is not separate, because it is nothing but water at a particular degree of temperature. The difference between the ocean water and the iceberg is not in their nature—naturally, they are the same. The difference is only of temperature. And then the sun rises, and the atmosphere becomes hot, and the iceberg begins to melt. Then there is no iceberg: it has melted. Now you cannot find it because there is no individuality, no center in it. It has become one with the ocean.

In you and in Buddha, in those who were crucifying Jesus and in Jesus, in Krishna and in Arjuna, there is no difference in nature. Arjuna is like an iceberg and Krishna is like an ocean. There is no difference in nature. They both are one and the same, but Arjuna has a form, a name—an individual, isolated existence. He feels, "I am."

Through these methods of centering, the temperature will change, the iceberg will melt, and then there will be no difference. That oceanic feeling is samadhi; that being an iceberg is mind. And to feel oceanic is to be a no-mind.

Centering is just the passage, the point of transformation from which the iceberg will be no more. Before it there was no ocean—only an iceberg. After it there will be no iceberg—only ocean. The oceanic feeling is samadhi: it is to feel oneself one with the whole.

But I am not saying to *think* oneself one with the whole. You can think, but thinking is before centering; that is not realization. You do not know —you have only heard; you have read. You wish that someday this may happen to you also, but you have not realized. Before centering you can go on thinking, but that thinking is of no use. After centering there is no thinker. You know! It has happened! You are no more; only the ocean is. Centering is the method. Samadhi is the end.

Nothing has been said about what happens in samadhi because nothing can be said. And Shiva is very scientific. He is not interested at all in telling. He is telegraphic; he will not use a single extra word. So he simply hints: "The experience, the blessing, the happening." Not only this, sometimes he will simply say, "Then." He will say, "Be centered between two breaths and *then.*" And then he will stop. Then sometimes he will simply say, "Be in the middle, just in the middle between two extremes, and *that.*"

These are indications: *that, then,* the experience, the blessing, the happening, the explosion. But then he stops completely. Why? We would like him to say something more.

Two reasons. One: *that* cannot be explained. Why can it not be explained? There are thinkers— for example, modern positivists, language analysts and others in Europe—who say that which can be experienced can be explained. And they have a point to make. They say if you can experience it, then why cannot you tell of it? After all, what is an experience? You have understood it, so why can you not make it understood for others? So they say that if there is any experience, then it can be expressed. And if you cannot express it, it shows simply that there is no experience. Then you are a muddlehead—confused, blurred. And if you cannot even express it, then there is no possibility that you will be able to experience.

Because of this standpoint, they say religion is all hokum. Why can you not express it if you can say you have experienced? Their point appeals to many, but their argument is baseless. Leave aside religious experiences, ordinary experiences also cannot be explained and expressed—very simple experiences.

I have a pain in my head, and if you have never experienced a headache, I cannot explain to you what a headache means. That doesn't mean that I am muddleheaded; that doesn't mean that I am only thinking and I am not experiencing. The headache is there. I experience it in its totality, in its full painfulness. But if you have not experienced a headache, it cannot be explained, it cannot be expressed to you. If you also have experienced it, then of course there is no problem, it can be expressed.

Buddha's difficulty is that he has to talk with nonbuddhas—not non-Buddhists, because non-Buddhists can also be buddhas. Jesus is a non-Buddhist, but he is a buddha. Because Buddha is to communicate with those who have not experienced, there is a difficulty. You do not know what a headache is. There are many who have not known headaches. They have only heard the word; it means nothing to them.

You can talk with a blind man about light, but

nothing is conveyed. He hears the word 'light,' he hears the explanation. He can understand the whole theory of light, but still the word 'light' conveys nothing to him. Unless he can experience, communication is impossible. So note it: communication is possible only if two persons are communicating who have had the same experience.

We are able to communicate in ordinary life because our experiences are similar. But even then, if one is going to split hairs then there will be difficulties. I say the sky is blue and you also say the sky is blue, but how are we to decide that my experience of blue and your experience of blue are the same? There is no possible way to decide.

I may be looking at one shade of blue and you may be looking at a different shade of blue, but what I am looking at inside, what I am experiencing, cannot be conveyed to you. I can simply say "blue." You also say "blue," but blue has a thousand shades —and not only shades: 'blue' has thousands of meanings. In my pattern of mind, blue may mean one thing. To you it may mean something else, because blue is not the meaning. The meaning is always in the pattern of the mind. So even in common experiences it is difficult to communicate.

Moreover, there are experiences which are of the beyond. For example, someone has fallen in love. He experiences something. His whole life is at stake, but he cannot explain what has happened to him, what is happening to him. He can weep, he can sing, he can dance; these are indications that something is happening in him. But what is happening in him? When love happens to someone, what is happening really? And love is not very uncommon. It happens to everyone in some way or other. But still, we have not been able to express yet what happens inside.

There are persons who feel love as a fever, as a sort of disease. Rousseau says that youth is not the peak of human life, because youth is prone to the disease called love. Unless one becomes so old that love loses all meaning, mind remains muddled and puzzled. So wisdom is possible only in very, very old age. Love will not allow you to be wise— that is his feeling.

There are others who may feel differently. Those who are really wise will become silent about love. They will not say anything—because the feeling is so infinite, so deep, that language is bound to betray it. And if it is expressed then one feels guilty, because one can never do justice to the feeling of the infinite. So one remains silent: the deeper the experience, the less the possibility of expression.

Buddha remained silent about God not because there is no God. And those who are very much vocal about God really show they have no experience. Buddha remained silent. Whenever he would go to any town, he would declare, "Please, do not ask anything about God. You can ask anything, but not about God."

Scholars, pundits, who had no experience really but only knowledge, started talking about Buddha and creating rumors, saying, "He is silent because he doesn't know. If he knows then why will he not say?" And Buddha would laugh. That laughter could be understood only by very few.

If love cannot be expressed, then how can God be expressed? Then any expression is harmful— that is one thing. That is why Shiva is silent about the experience. He goes to the point from where a finger can be used as an indication—*then, that,* the experience—and then he becomes silent.

The second reason is: even if it can be expressed in a certain way, even if it can be expressed only partially—even if it cannot be expressed, really, then too some parallels can be created to help. But those too Shiva is not using, and there is a reason. It is because our minds are so greedy that whenever something is said about that experience the mind clings to it. And then the mind forgets the method and remembers only the experience, because method needs effort—a long effort which is sometimes tedious, sometimes dangerous. A long sustained effort is needed.

So we forget about the method. We remember the result and we go on imagining, wishing, desiring the result. And one can fool oneself very easily. One can imagine that the result has been achieved.

Someone was here a few days before. He is a sannyasin—an old man, a very old man. He took sannyas thirty years ago; now he is near seventy. He came to me and he said, "I have come to make some inquiries, to know something."

So I asked him, "What do you want to know?"

Suddenly he changed. He said, "No, not to know really—just to meet you, because whatsoever can be known I have known already."

For thirty years he has been imagining, desiring—desiring bliss, divine experiences—and now, at this late age, he has become weak and death is near. Now he is creating hallucinations that he has experienced. So I told him, "If you have experienced, then keep silent. Be here with me for a few moments because then there is no need to talk."

Then he became restless. He said, "Okay! Then suppose that I have not experienced. Then tell me something."

So I told him, "There is no possibility with me to suppose anything. Either you have known or you have not known." I said, "So be clear about it. If you have known, then keep quiet. Be here for a few moments and then go. If you have not known, then be clear. Then tell me so."

Then he was puzzled. He had come to inquire about some methods. Then he said, "Really, I have not experienced, but I have been thinking so much about *Aham Brahmasmi*—I am the *Brahma*—that sometimes I forget that I have only been thinking. I have repeated it so much, day and night, for thirty years continuously, that sometimes I completely forget that I have not known this. It is just a borrowed saying."

It is difficult to remember what is knowledge and what is experience. They get confused; they get mingled and mixed. And it is very easy to feel that your knowledge has become your experience. The human mind is so deceptive, so cunning, that that is possible. That is another reason why Shiva has remained silent about the experience. He will not say anything about it. He goes on talking about methods, remaining completely silent about the result. You cannot be deceived by him.

That is one of the reasons why this book, one of the most significant of books, has remained altogether unknown. This *Vigyan Bhairav Tantra* is one of the most significant books in the world. No Bible, no Veda, no Gita is so significant, but it has remained completely unknown. The reason? It contains only simple methods without any possibility for your greed to cling to the result.

The mind wants to cling to the result. The mind is not interested in the method; it is interested in the end result. And if you can bypass the method and reach the result, the mind will be extremely happy.

Someone was asking me, "Why so many methods? Kabir has said, '*Sahaj samadhi bhali*—be spontaneous.' Spontaneous ecstasy is good, so there is no need of methods."

I told him, "If you have achieved *sahaj samadhi*—spontaneous ecstasy—then of course no method is useful; there is no need. Why have you come here?"

He said, "I have not achieved yet, but I feel that *sahaj*—the spontaneous—is better."

"But why do you feel that the spontaneous is better?" I said. Because no method is suggested, the mind feels good that you have nothing to do—and without doing, you can have *everything!*

Because of this Zen has become a craze in the West—because Zen says, achieve it effortlessly; there is no need of effort. Zen is right; there is no need for an effort. But remember, to achieve this point of no-effort you will need a long, long effort. To achieve a point where no effort is needed, to achieve a point where you can remain in nondoing, a long effort will be needed. But the superficial conclusion that Zen says no effort is needed has become very appealing in the West. If no effort is needed then the mind says: this is the right thing, because you can do it without doing anything. But no one can do it.

Suzuki, who made Zen known in the West, has

done a service and also a disservice. And the disservice will remain for a longer period. He was a very authentic man, one of the most authentic men of this century, and for his whole life he struggled to carry the message of Zen to the West. And alone, with his own effort, he made it known in the West. And now there is a craze; there are Zen friends all over the West. Nothing appeals like Zen now.

But the point is missed. The appeal has come only because Zen says no method is needed, no effort is needed. You do not have to do anything; spontaneously it flowers.

This is right—but you are not spontaneous, so it will never flower in you. To be spontaneous…. It looks absurd and contradictory, because for you to be spontaneous many methods are needed to purify you, to make you innocent so that you can be spontaneous. Otherwise you cannot be spontaneous in anything.

This *Vigyan Bhairav Tantra* was translated into English by Paul Reps. He has written a very beautiful book, *Zen Flesh, Zen Bones,* and just in the appendix he included this book *Vigyan Bhairav Tantra.* The whole book is concerned with Zen; just in the appendix he added this book also, the one hundred and twelve methods, and he called it a pre-Zen writing. Many Zen followers didn't like this because they said, "Zen says no effort is needed, and this book is concerned only with effort. This book is concerned only with methods, and Zen says no method, no effort is needed. So it is anti-Zen, not pre-Zen." Superficially they are right, but deep down they are not, because to achieve a spontaneous being one has to travel a long way.

One of Gurdjieff's disciples, Ouspensky, used to say, whenever someone would come to him to ask about the path, "We don't know anything about the path. We only teach about some footpaths which lead to the path. The path is not known to us." Do not think that you are already on the path. Even the path is far away. From where you are, from that point, even the path is far away. So first

you have to reach to the path. Ouspensky was a very humble man, and it is very difficult to be religious and to be humble—very, very difficult, because once you begin to feel that you know, the head goes mad. He would always say, "We don't know anything about the path. It is very far away, and there is no need just now to discuss it." Wherever you are, first you have to create a link, a small bridge, a footpath which will lead you to the path.

Spontaneity—*sahaj yoga*—is very far away from you. In the place where you are, you are totally artificial, cultivated and cultured. Nothing is spontaneous—*nothing*, I say, is spontaneous. When nothing is spontaneous in your life, how can religion be spontaneous? When nothing is spontaneous, even love is not spontaneous. Even love is a bargain, even love is a calculation, even love is an effort. Then nothing can be spontaneous. And then to explode spontaneously into the cosmos is impossible.

From the situation you are in, from that situation it is impossible. First you will have to throw away all your artificiality, all your false attitudes, all your cultivated conventions, all your prejudices. Only then will a spontaneous happening be possible. These methods will help you to come to a point from where nothing is needed to be done—just your being is enough. But mind can deceive. And mind easily deceives, because then it can get consolation.

Shiva never talks about any result, just methods. Remember this emphasis. Do something, so that a moment may be possible when nothing is needed, when your central being can just dissolve into the cosmos. But that has to be achieved. Zen's appeal is for the wrong reasons, and the same is true for Krishnamurti, because he says no yoga is needed, no method is needed. Really, he says there is no method of meditation. He is right.

He is right, but Shiva says these one hundred and twelve methods of meditation are there, and Shiva is also right. And as far as *you* are concerned, Shiva is more right. And if you have to choose between Krishnamurti and Shiva, then choose Shiva. Krishnamurti is of no use to you. Even this can be said to help you—that Krishnamurti is absolutely wrong. Remember, I say to help you. And he is harmful. That too I say to help you, because if you get into his argument you will not achieve samadhi. You will achieve only one conclusion—that no method is needed. And that is dangerous. For you method is needed!

There comes a moment when no method is needed, but that moment has not come for you yet. And before that moment, to know about something that is ahead is dangerous. That is why Shiva is silent. He will not say anything of the future, of what will happen. He simply sticks to you, to what you are and what is to be done with you. Krishnamurti goes on talking in terms which cannot be understood by you.

The logic can be felt. The logic is right; it is beautiful. It will be good if you can remember the logic of Krishnamurti. He says that if you are doing some method, then who is doing that method? The mind is doing it. And how can any method done by mind dissolve mind? Rather, on the contrary, it will strengthen it more; it will strengthen your mind more. It will become a conditioning, it will be false.

So meditation is spontaneous; you cannot do anything about it. What can you do about love? Can you practice any method for how to love? If you practice, then your love will be false. It happens, it cannot be practiced. If even love cannot be practiced, how can prayer be practiced? How can meditation be practiced?

The logic is exactly, absolutely right—but not for you, because by listening to this logic continuously you will be conditioned by this logic. And those who have been listening to Krishnamurti for forty years are the most conditioned persons I have come across. They say there is no method, and still they are nowhere.

I say, "You have understood there is no method and you do not practice any method, but has the spontaneity flowered in you?" They say, "No!"

And if I tell them, "Then practice some method," immediately their conditioning comes in. They say, "There is no method."

They have not been practicing any method, and samadhi has not happened. And if you tell them, "Then try some method," they say there is no method. So they are in a dilemma. They have not moved an inch, and the reason is that they have been told something which was not for them.

It is like teaching a small child about sex. You can go on teaching, but you are saying something which is as yet meaningless for the child. And your teaching will be dangerous because you are conditioning his mind. It is not his need; he is not concerned with it. He doesn't know what sex means because his glands are still not functioning, his body is still not sexual. His energy has not yet moved biologically to the sex center, and you are talking to him. Because he has ears, do you think that anything can be taught to him? Because he can nod his head, do you think you can teach him anything?

You can teach, and your teaching can become dangerous and harmful. Sex is not an inquiry for him, it has not become a problem for him. He has not reached that point of maturity where sex becomes significant. Wait! When he begins to inquire, when he matures and when he asks questions, then tell him. And never tell more than he can understand, because that more will become a burden on his head. It is the same with the phenomenon of meditation.

You can be taught only about methods, not about results—that is taking a jump. And without getting a foothold on the method, taking the jump is simply a cerebral affair, a mental affair. And then you will always miss the method.

It is like small children doing arithmetic. They can always go to the back of the book and can know the answer. The answer is there; at the back of the book, the answers are given. They can look at the question, then they can go to the back and know the answer. And once a child knows the answer it is very difficult for him to learn the method, because there seems to be no need. When he already knows the answer, there is no need.

And really, he will do the whole thing in reverse order. Then through any false, pseudo-method he will arrive at the answer. He knows the real thing, he knows the answer, so he can arrive at the answer by just creating a false method. And this happens so much in religion that it seems, as far as religion is concerned, everyone is just doing what children do.

The answer is not good for you. The question is there, the method is there, and the answer must be reached by you. No one else should give you the answer. The real teachers do not help you to know the answer before the process is done, they simply help you to go through the process. In fact, even if you have known somehow, even if you have stolen some answer from somewhere, they will say that this is wrong. It may not be wrong, but they will say, "This is wrong. Throw this—it is not needed." They will debar you from knowing the answer before you *really* come to know it. That is why no answer is given.

Shiva's beloved, Devi, has asked him questions. He is giving simple methods. The question is there, the method is there. The answer is left for you to work out, to live out.

So remember, centering is the method, not the result. The result is cosmic, oceanic experience. There is no center then.

The second question:

You said if one can really love, then love alone is enough and the one hundred and twelve methods of meditation are not needed. As You have explained real love, I feel really that I love, I believe. But the bliss I encounter in meditation feels to be of quite another dimension than the deep contentment I experience from love, and I cannot imagine being without meditation also. So explain more about how love alone without meditation can be enough.

Many things will have to be understood. One, if you are really in love you will not inquire at all about meditation—because love is such a total fulfillment that it is never felt that something is lacking, that some gap is to be filled, that you need something more. If you feel that something more is needed, the gap is there. If you feel that something more is to be done and experienced, then love is just a feeling, not a reality. I do not doubt your belief, you may believe that you are in love. Your belief is authentic; you are not deceiving anyone. You feel that you are in love, but the symptoms show that you are not.

What are the symptoms of being in love? Three things. First, absolute contentment. Nothing else is needed; not even God is needed. Second, no future. This very moment of love is eternity. No next moment, no future, no tomorrow. Love is a happening in the present. And third, you cease to be, you are no more. If you still are, then you have still not entered the temple of love.

If these three things happen…. If you are not, then who is going to meditate? If there is no future, then all methods become useless because methods are for the future, for a result. And if at this very moment you are content, absolutely content, where is the motivation to do anything?

There is a school of psychologists—and this is one of the most significant trends in modern thinking—that started with Wilhelm Reich. He said that every mental disease arises because of the lack of love. Because you cannot feel deep love, because you cannot be in it totally, this unfulfilled being craves for fulfillment in many dimensions.

When I say that "If you can love, nothing is needed," I do not mean that then love is enough. I mean that once you love deeply, love becomes a door—just like any meditation. What is meditation going to do? These three things: it will create contentment; it will allow you to remain in the present, help you to remain in the present; and it will destroy your ego. These three things meditation is going to do—with any method. So you can say it this way: love is the natural method. If the natural method has been missed, then other, artificial methods have to be supplied.

But one can feel that one is in love; then these three things will become criteria for him. He will think that these should be made the touchstones, the measures, and he will observe whether these three things are happening. If they are not happening, then his feeling can be many other things, but not love. And the feeling of love is a great phenomenon, it can be many things. It can be lust; it can be simple sex; it can be just a possessive tendency. It can be just an occupation because you cannot be alone, and you need someone because you are afraid and you need security. The presence of the other helps you to be secure. Or it may be just a sexual relationship.

Energy needs outlets. Energy goes on accumulating—then it becomes a burden. You have to throw it and release it. So your love may be just a release. Love can be many things, and love *is* many things. And ordinarily, love is many things except *love*. To me, love is meditation. So try this: with your lover, be in meditation. Whenever your lover or beloved is present, be in deep meditation. Make this presence of each other a meditative state.

Ordinarily, you are doing the very opposite. Whenever lovers are together they are fighting. When they are separated then they are thinking of each other, and when they are together they are fighting. When they are separated again, then again they are thinking about each other. When they are put together, again the fight starts. This is not love!

So I will suggest some points. Make the presence of your beloved or lover a meditative state. Be silent. Remain close, but be silent. Use each other's presence to drop the mind; do not think. If you are thinking while your lover is with you, then you are not with your lover. How can you be? You are both there, but miles apart. You are thinking your thoughts, your lover is thinking his thoughts. You just appear to be near, but you are not—because when two minds are thinking, they are poles apart.

Real love means cessation of thinking. In the presence of your beloved or lover, cease completely to think; then only are you near. Then suddenly you are one, then bodies cannot separate you. Then deep down within the body, someone has broken the barrier. The silence breaks the barrier—that is one thing.

Make your relationship a sacred phenomenon. When you are really in love, the object of love becomes divine. If it is not, then know well it is not a love relationship; it is impossible. A love relationship is not a profane relationship. But have you ever felt any reverence for your beloved? You may have felt many other things, but never reverence.

It seems inconceivable, but India has tried many, many ways.... That is why India has been insisting that this love relationship between man and woman should be a sacred phenomenon, not a worldly relationship. The lover, the beloved, they become divine. You cannot look at them in any other way.

I wonder, have you ever felt any reverence for your wife? The very thing seems irrelevant—reverence for a wife? There is no question. You can feel condemnation, you can feel everything, but never reverence. The relationship is just worldly; you are using each other. The wife may say that she respects her husband, but I have not seen a single wife who really respects. Traditionally, because it has been a convention to respect the husband, the wife goes on saying she respects, and so she will not even utter his name. Not because of respect, because she can utter anything, but she will not utter his name just traditionally.

Reverence is the second thing. In the presence of your beloved or lover, feel reverence. If you cannot see the divine in your beloved or lover, you cannot see him anywhere else. How can you see him in a tree, where no relationship exists? When no deep intimacy prevails, how can you see him in a rock or a tree? They are unrelated. If you cannot see him in the person you love, if God is not felt there, he cannot be felt anywhere else. And if he can be felt there, sooner or later you will feel him everywhere

—because once the door is thrown open, once you have a glimpse of the divine in any person, then you cannot forget that glimpse. And because of that, then everything becomes a door. That is why I say love itself is a meditation.

So do not think in contrast—whether to love or to meditate. That was not my meaning. Do not try to choose whether to love or to meditate. Love meditatively, or meditate lovingly. Do not create any division. Love is a very natural phenomenon, and it can be used as a vehicle. And tantra has used it as a vehicle—not only love, even sex tantra has used as a vehicle.

Tantra says that in a deep sex act you can meditate more easily than in any other state of mind—because this is a natural, biological ecstasy. But whatsoever is known by the sex act is in a very perverted form. So whenever such things are said you feel uneasy, because whatsoever you have known in the name of sex is not sex. It is just a shadow, because the whole society has cultivated your mind against sex.

Everyone is a suppressed person, so natural sex is impossible. And whenever you are in a sex act, a deep guilt feeling is always present there. That guilt feeling becomes a barrier, and one of the greatest opportunities is lost. You could have used it to go deep down into yourself.

Tantra says, in the sex act be meditative. Feel the whole phenomenon as holy; do not feel guilty. Rather, feel blessed that nature has given you one source through which you can go deep into ecstasy immediately. And then, be totally free in it. Do not repress, do not resist. Let the sexual communion take hold of you. Forget yourself, throw all your inhibitions. Be absolutely natural, and then you will feel a deep music in the body.

When both bodies become one harmony, then you will forget completely that you are—and still, you will be. Then you will forget the "I": there will be no "I," just existence playing with existence, one being with another. And the two will become one. There will be no thinking; future will cease and you

will be in the present this very moment. Without any guilt, without any inhibition, make it a meditation, and then sex is transformed. Then sex itself becomes a door.

If sex becomes a door, by and by sex ceases to be sexual. And a moment comes when sex has gone —only the perfume has remained. That perfume is love. And later on, even that perfume disappears, and then that which remains is samadhi.

Tantra says nothing has to be taken as an enemy. Every energy is friendly; one has just to know how to use it. So do not make any choice. Transform your love into meditation and transform your meditation into love. Then soon you will forget the word and you will know the real thing, which is not the word. The word 'love' is not love, and the word 'meditation' is not meditation, and the word 'God' is not God. These are only words. And if you can penetrate in, then God, meditation, love—they all become one.

One more question:

What are the reasons for man's insensitivities and how to remove them?

When the child is born the child is helpless. The human child, particularly, is totally helpless. He has to depend on others to be alive, to remain alive. This dependence is a bargain. The child has to give many things in this bargain, and sensitivity is one. The child is sensitive; his whole body is sensitive. But he is helpless, he cannot be independent; he has to depend on parents, on family, on society; he will have to be dependent. Because of this dependence and helplessness, the parents, the society, go on forcing things on the child, and he has to yield. Otherwise he cannot remain alive, he will die. So he has to give many things in this bargain.

The first very deep and significant thing is sensitivity: he has to leave it. Why? Because the more the child is sensitive, the more he is in trouble, the more he is vulnerable. A slight sensation, and he begins to cry. The cry has to be stopped by the parents, and they cannot do anything. But if the child goes on feeling every detail of sensation, the child will become a nuisance. And children do become nuisances, so parents have to curtail their sensitivity. The child has to learn resistance, the child has to learn control. And by and by the child has to divide his mind into two. So there are many sensations which he just stops feeling because they are not "good"—he is punished for them.

The child's whole body is erotic. He can enjoy his fingers, he can enjoy his body; the whole body is erotic. He goes on exploring his own body; it is a great phenomenon for him. But the moment comes in his exploration when the child gets to the genitalia. Then it becomes a problem because the father and mother are both repressed. The moment the child, boy or girl, touches the genitalia, the parents become uneasy. This is to be observed deeply. Their behavior suddenly changes, and the child notes it. Something wrong has happened. They start crying, "Don't touch!" Then the child starts feeling that something is wrong with the genitalia, he has to suppress. And the genitals are the most sensitive part of your body—the most sensitive, the most alive part of your body, the most delicate. Once the genitalia are not allowed to be touched and enjoyed, you have killed the very source of sensitivity. Then the child will become insensitive. The more he will grow, the more he will be insensitive.

So first there is a bargain—necessary, but evil. And the moment one begins to understand, this bargain has to be thrown and you have to regain your sensitivity. The second reason for this bargain is because of security.

I was with a friend for many years; I lived in his bungalow. From the very first day I observed that he would not look at his servants. He was a rich man, but he would never look at his servants, he would never look at his children. He would come running into the bungalow, then he would go running from his bungalow to his car. So I asked him, "What is the matter?"

He said, "If you look at your servants they start feeling friendly, and then they start asking about money and this and that. If you talk with your children, then you are not the master, then you cannot control them." So he created a façade of insensitivity around himself. He was afraid that if he talked with a servant, if he should feel that the servant was ill, if he sympathized, then he would have to give some money or some help.

Everyone learns sooner or later that to be sensitive is to be vulnerable to many things. You pull yourself in, you create a barrier around yourself that is a safeguard—a safety measure. Then you can go on through the streets…beggars are begging and there are dirty, ugly slums, but you do not feel anything, you do not really see. In this ugly society one has to create a barrier around himself, a wall—a subtle, transparent wall—behind which he can hide. Otherwise, one is vulnerable, and it will be very difficult to live.

That is why insensitivity sets in. It helps you to be in this ugly world without being disturbed, but there is a cost—and the cost is very much. You are at ease in this world without being disturbed, but then you cannot enter into the divine, into the total, into the whole. You cannot enter the other world. If for this world insensitivity is good and for that world sensitivity is good, that creates the problem.

If you are really interested in entering that world, you will have to create sensitivity, you will have to throw away all these walls, these securities. Of course, you will become vulnerable. You will feel much suffering, but that suffering is nothing in comparison to the bliss you can reach through sensitivity. The more sensitive you become, the more you will feel compassion. But you will suffer because all around you there is hell. You are closed —that is why you cannot feel it. Once you become open, you will be open to both—to the hell of this world and the heaven of that world. You will become open to both.

And it is impossible to remain closed at one point and open at another, because really, either you are closed or you are open. If you are closed, you are closed for both. If you are open, you will be open for both. So remember this: a buddha is filled with bliss, but also filled with suffering.

That suffering is not of his own, it is for others. He is in deep bliss, but he suffers for others. And Mahayana Buddhists say that when Buddha reached to the door of nirvana, the gatekeeper opened the door—this is a myth, and very beautiful—the doorkeeper opened the door, but Buddha refused to enter. The doorkeeper said, "Why are you not coming in? For millennia we have been waiting for you. Every day the news comes that 'Buddha is coming, Buddha is coming!' The whole of heaven is waiting for you. Enter! You are welcome!"

Buddha said, "I cannot enter unless everyone else has entered before me. I will wait! Unless every single human being has entered, heaven is not for me."

Buddha has a suffering for others. As for himself, he is now deep in bliss. See the parallel? You are deep in suffering, and you go on feeling that everyone else is enjoying life. Quite the contrary happens to a Buddha. He is now in deep bliss, and he knows that everyone else is suffering.

These methods are the methods to remove this insensitivity. We will discuss more about *how* to remove it.

Enough.

CHAPTER 15

Seeing the past as a dream

◆

22 *Let attention be at a place where you are seeing some past happening, and even your form, having lost its present characteristics, is transformed.*

23 *Feel an object before you. Feel the absence of all other objects but this one. Then, leaving aside the object-feeling and the absence-feeling, realize.*

24 *When a mood against someone or for someone arises, do not place it on the person in question, but remain centered.*

ne of the great tantrics of this age, George Gurdjieff, says that identification is the only sin. The next sutra, the tenth sutra on centering—which we are going to penetrate tonight—is concerned with identification. So first be crystal clear on what identification means.

You were a child once; now you are not. Someone becomes young, someone becomes old, and childhood becomes a past thing. Youth has gone, but still you are identified with your childhood. You cannot see it as happening to someone else; you cannot be a witness to it. Whenever you see your childhood, you are not aloof from it, you are one with it. Whenever someone remembers his youth, he is one with it.

Really, now it is just a dream. And if you can see your childhood as a dream, as a film passing before you and you are not identified with it, you are just a witness, you will achieve a very subtle insight into yourself. If you see your past as a film, as a dream—you are not part of it, you are just out of it...and really you are—then many things will happen. If you are thinking about your childhood, you are not in it—you cannot be. The childhood is just a memory, just a past memory. You are remaining aloof and looking at it. You are different: you are a witness. If you can feel this witnessing and then see your childhood as a film on a screen, many things will happen.

One: if childhood has become just a dream which you can see, then whatsoever you are just now will become a dream the next day. If you are young, then your youth will become a dream. If you are old, then your old age also will become a dream. One day you were a child; now the childhood has become just a dream and you can observe it.

It is good to start with the past. Observe the past and disidentify yourself from it; become a witness. Then observe the future, whatsoever you imagine about the future, and be a witness to that also. Then you can observe your present very easily, because then you know that whatsoever is present just now was future yesterday, and tomorrow it will become the past. But your witness is never past, never future. Your witnessing consciousness is eternal; it is not part of time. That is why everything that happens in time becomes a dream.

Remember this also: whenever you are dreaming something in the night you become identified with it, and you can never remember in your dream that this is a dream. Only in the morning, when you have awakened from the dream, can you remember that it was a dream and not a reality. Why? Because then you are aloof, not in it. Then there is a gap. Some space is there, and you can see that it was a dream.

But what is your whole past? The gap is there, the space is there. Try to see it as a dream. Now it is a dream; now it is nothing more than a dream, because just as the dream becomes a memory, your past has become just a memory. You cannot prove really that whatsoever you think was your childhood was real or just a dream. It is difficult to prove. It may have been just a dream, it may have been real. The memory cannot say whether it was real or a dream. Psychologists say that old men occasionally get confused between what they have dreamed and what was real.

Children always get confused. In the morning, small children cannot differentiate. Whatsoever they have seen in the dream was not real, but they may weep for a toy destroyed in the dream. And you also, for a few moments after sleep is broken, are still affected by your dream. If someone was murdering you in the dream, even though your sleep is broken and you are wide awake, your heart still beats fast, your blood circulation is fast. You may be still perspiring, and a subtle fear is still there hovering around you. Now you are awake and the dream has passed, but you will take a few minutes to feel that it was simply a dream and nothing else. When you can feel that it was a dream, then you are out of it and there is no fear.

If you can feel that the past was just a dream — you are not to project this and force the idea that the past was just a dream, it is a consequence — if you can observe this; if you can be aware of it without getting involved in it, without being identified with it; if you can stand aloof and look at it, it will become a dream. Anything that you can look at as a witness is a dream.

That is why Shankara and Nagarjuna could say that this world is just a dream. Not that it *is* a dream; they were not fools, not simpletons saying this world actually is a dream. They meant by saying this that they have become witnesses. Even to this world which is so actual, they have become witnesses. And once you become a witness of anything, it becomes a dream. That is the reason why the world is called *maya*, an illusion. It is not that it is unreal, but that one can become a witness to it. And once you become a witness — aware, fully aware — the whole thing drops just like a dream for you, because the space is there and you are not identified with it. But we go on being identified.

Just a few days before I was reading Jean-Jacques Rousseau's *Confessions*. This is a rare book. It is really the first book in world literature in which someone bares himself, totally naked. Whatsoever sins he has committed, whatsoever immorality, he opens himself up, totally naked. But if you read the *Confessions* of Rousseau you are bound to feel that he is enjoying it; he feels very much elated. Talking about his sins, talking about his immoralities, he feels elated. It seems as if he is enjoying it with much relish. In the beginning, in the introduction, Rousseau says, "When the last day of judgment will come, I will say to God, to the Almighty, 'You need not bother about me. Read this book and you will know everything.'"

No one before him has ever confessed so truthfully. And at the end of the book he says, "Almighty God, eternal God, fulfill my only desire. I have confessed everything; now let a big crowd gather to listen to my confessions."

So it is rightly suspected that he may have confessed some sins also which he has not committed. He feels so elated and he is enjoying the whole thing. He has become identified. And there is only one sin which he has not admitted to — the sin of being identified. With whatsoever sin he has committed or not committed he is identified, and that is the only sin for those who know deeply how the human mind functions.

When for the first time he read his *Confessions* amongst a small group of intellectuals, he was thinking that something earthshaking would happen, because he was the first man to confess so truthfully, as he said. The intellectuals listened, and they became more and more bored. Rousseau felt very uneasy because he was thinking something miraculous was going to happen. When he ended, they all felt relieved, but no one said anything. There was complete silence for a few moments. Rousseau's heart was shattered. He was thinking that he had created a very revolutionary thing, earthshaking, historical, and there was simply silence. Everyone was just thinking about how to get away from there.

Who is interested in your sins except yourself? No one is interested in your virtues, no one is interested in your sins. Man is such that he becomes elated, he becomes strengthened in his ego, by his virtues and by his sins also. After writing *Confessions*, Rousseau began to think himself a sage, a saint, because he had confessed. But the basic sin remained. The basic sin is being identified with happenings in time. Whatsoever happens in time is dreamlike, and unless you get unattached from it, not identified with it, you will never know what bliss is.

Identification is misery; nonidentification is bliss. This tenth technique is concerned with identification.

---

22 Look at your past, dis-identified.

The tenth centering technique: *Let attention be at a place where you are seeing some past happening, and even your form, having lost its present characteristics, is transformed.*

You are remembering your past—any happening. Your childhood, your love affairs, the death of your father or mother...anything. Look at it, but do not get involved in it. Remember it as if you are remembering someone else's life. And when this happening is being filmed again, is on the screen again, be attentive, aware, a witness, remaining aloof. Your past form will be there in the film, in the story.

If you are remembering your love affair, your first love affair, you will be there with your beloved; your past form will be there with your beloved. You cannot remember otherwise. Be detached from your past form also. Look at the whole phenomenon as if someone else were loving someone else, as if the whole thing doesn't belong to you. You are just a witness, an observer.

This is a very, very basic technique. It has been used much, particularly by Buddha. There are many forms of this technique; you can find your

own way of approaching this. For example, when you are just falling into sleep at night, just ready to fall into sleep, go backwards through the memories of the whole day. Do not start from the morning. Start right from where you are, just on the bed—the last item—and then go back. Then go back by and by, step by step, just to the first experience in the morning when you first became awake. Go back, and remember continuously that you are not getting involved.

For example, in the afternoon someone insulted you. See yourself, the form of yourself, being insulted by someone, but you remain just an observer. Do not get involved; do not get angry again. If you get angry again, then you are identified. Then you have missed the point of meditation. Do not get angry. He is not insulting you, he is insulting the form that was in the afternoon. That form has gone now.

You are just like a river flowing: the forms are flowing. In your childhood you had one form, and now you do not have that form; that form has gone. Riverlike, you are changing continuously. So when in the night you are meditating backwards on the happenings of the day, just remember that you are a witness—do not get angry. Someone was praising you—do not get elated. Just look at the whole thing as if you are looking indifferently at a film. And backwards it is very helpful, particularly for those who have any trouble with sleep.

If you have any trouble with sleep, insomnia, sleeplessness, if you find it difficult to fall into sleep, this will help deeply. Why? Because this is an unwinding of the mind. When you go back you are unwinding the mind. In the morning you start winding, and the mind becomes tangled in many things, in many places. Unfinished and incomplete, many things will remain on the mind, and there is no time to let them settle at the very moment that they happen.

So in the night go back. This is an unwinding process. And when you will be getting back to the morning when you were just on your bed, to the first thing in the morning, you will again have the same fresh mind that you had in the morning. And then you can fall asleep like a very small child.

You can use this technique of going back for your whole life also. Mahavira used this technique of going back very much. And now there is a movement in America called dianetics. They are using this method and finding it very, very useful. This movement, dianetics, says that all your diseases are just hangovers of the past. And they are right. If you can go backwards and unwind your whole life, with that unwinding many diseases will disappear completely. And this has been proven by so many successful incidents; there are so many successful cases now.

So many persons suffer from a particular disease, and nothing physiological, nothing medical helps; the disease continues. The disease seems to be psychological. What to do about it? To say to someone that his disease is psychological is no help. Rather, it may prove harmful, because no one feels good when you say his disease is psychological. What can he do then? He feels he is helpless.

This going backwards is a miraculous method. If you go back slowly—slowly unwinding the mind to the first moment when this disease happened—if by and by you go back to when for the first time you were attacked by this disease, if you can unwind to that moment, you will come to know that this disease is basically a complex of certain other things, certain psychological things. By going back those things will bubble up.

If you pass through that moment when the disease first attacked you, suddenly you will become aware of what psychological factors contributed to it. And you are not to do anything, you are just to be aware of those psychological factors and go on backwards. Many diseases simply disappear from you because the complex is broken. When you have become aware of the complex, then there is no need of it; you are cleaned of it, purged.

This is a deep catharsis. And if you can do it daily, you will feel a new health, a new freshness coming to you. And if we can teach children to do it daily, they will never be burdened by their past. They will not need ever to go to the past, they will be always here and now. There won't be any hang-up; nothing will be hovering over them from the past.

You can do it daily. It will give you a new insight for going backward through the whole day. The mind would like to start from the morning, but remember, then there is no unwinding. Rather, the whole thing is re-emphasized. If you start from the morning, you are doing a very wrong thing.

There are many so-called teachers in India who suggest to do it—to reflect on the whole day—and they always say to do it again from the morning. That is wrong and harmful, because then you are re-emphasizing the whole thing and the trap will be deepened. Never go from the morning to the evening, always go backward. Only then can you clean the whole thing, purge the whole thing. The mind would like to start from the morning because it is easy: the mind knows it and there is no problem. If you start going backward, suddenly you will feel you have jumped into the morning and you have started going forward again. Do not do that —be aware, go back.

You can train your mind to go back through other things also. Just go back from a hundred— 99, 98, 97…go back. Go from a hundred to one, backwards. You will feel a difficulty because the mind has a habit to go from one to hundred, never from a hundred to one.

In the same way you have to go backward with this technique. What will happen? Going backward, unwinding the mind, you are a witness. You are seeing things that happened to you, but now they are not happening to you. Now you are just an observer and they are happening on the screen of the mind.

While doing this daily, suddenly one day you will become aware during the day, while working in the market, in your office or anywhere, that you can be a witness to events that are happening just now. If you can be a witness later on, and look back at someone who had insulted you without becoming angry about it, why not right now, to what is presently happening?

Someone is insulting you: what is the difficulty? You can pull yourself aside just now and you can see that someone is insulting you, and still you are different from your body, from your mind, from that which is insulted. You can witness it. If you can be a witness to this, you will not get angry; then it is impossible. Anger is possible only when you are identified. If you are not identified, anger is impossible—anger means identification.

This technique says, look at any happening of the past—your form will be there. The sutra says your form, not you. You were never there. Always your form is involved; you are never involved. When you insult me, you do not insult *me*. You cannot insult me, you can insult only the form. The form which I am is there just here and now for you. You can insult that form and I can detach myself from the form. That is why Hindus have always been insisting on being detached from name and form. You are neither your name nor your form. You are the consciousness who knows the form and the name, and the consciousness is different, totally different.

But it is difficult. So start with the past, then it is easy, because now, with the past there is no urgency. Someone insulted you twenty years back, so there is no urgency in it. The man may have died and everything is finished. It is just a dead affair, just dead from the past; it is easy to be aware of it. But once you can become aware there is no difficulty in doing the same with what is happening just here and now.

But to start from here and now is difficult. The problem is so urgent and it is so near that there is no space to move. It is difficult to create space and move away from the incident. That is why the sutra says to start with the past: look at your own form, detached, standing aloof and different, and be transformed through it.

You will be transformed through it because it is a deep cleaning, an unwinding. Then you can know that your body, your mind, your existence in time are not your basic reality. The substantial reality is different. Things come and go upon it without touching it in the least. You remain innocent, untouched; you remain virgin. The whole thing passes, the whole life passes: good and bad, success and failure, praise and blame—everything passes. Disease and health, youth and old age, birth and death—everything passes, and you are untouched by it.

But how to know this untouched reality within you? That is the purpose of this technique. Start with the past. There is a gap when you look at your past; the perspective is possible. Or look at the future. But to look at the future is difficult. Only for a few persons is observing the future not difficult—for poets, for people with imagination who can look into the future as if they are looking at reality. But ordinarily the past is good to use; you can look into the past. For young men it may be good to look into the future. It is easier for them to look into the future because youth is future-oriented.

For old men there is no future except death. They cannot look into the future; they are afraid. That is why old men always start thinking about the past. They always go again and again into their memories, but they commit the same mistake. They start from the past toward their present state of being—that is wrong, they should go backward.

If they can go backward many times, by and by they will feel that their whole past is washed away from them. And then a person can die without the past clinging to him. If you can die without the past clinging to you, you will die consciously, you will die fully aware. Then death will not be a death to you. Rather, it will be a meeting with the deathless.

Clean the whole consciousness of the depth of the past, and your very being will be transformed through it. Try this. This method is not very difficult, only persistent effort is needed; there is no inherent difficulty in the method. It is simple, and you can start with your day. Just tonight on your bed go backward, and you will feel very beautiful, you will feel very blissful. And then the whole day will have passed. But do not be in a hurry, pass it slowly so that nothing is missed. It is a very strange feeling, because many things will come up before your eyes—many things you have really missed while passing through the day because you were too much engaged. But the mind goes on collecting even when you are unaware.

You were passing through a street. Someone was singing, but you might not have paid any attention. You might not have even been aware that you have heard the sound, just passing in the street. But the mind has heard and recorded it. Now that will cling; that will become a burden to you unnecessarily. So go back, but go very slowly, as if a film is being shown to you in very slow motion. Go back and see the details, and then your one day will look very, very long. It is, really, because for the mind there has been so much information, and the mind has recorded everything. Now go back.

By and by you will become capable of knowing everything that has been recorded. And once you can go back, it is just like a tape recorder: it is washed away. By the time you will reach the morning you will fall asleep, and the quality of the sleep will be different—it will be meditative. Then again, in the morning when you feel that you have awakened, do not open your eyes immediately. Go backward into the night.

It will be difficult in the beginning. You may go a little. Some part, some fragment of a dream which you were just dreaming before the sleep was broken may come to your mind. But by and by, with gradual effort, you will be able to penetrate more and more and more, and after a three-month period you will be capable of moving backward to the point when you fell asleep. And if you can go backward deep within your sleep, your quality of sleep and waking will change completely, because then you cannot dream; dreaming will have become futile. If you can go back in the day and in

the night, dreaming is not needed.

Now psychologists say that dreaming is really an unwinding. If you yourself have done it, then there is no need. All that has been hanging in the mind, all that has remained unfulfilled, incomplete, tries to complete itself in the dream.

You were passing and you have seen something —a beautiful house—and a subtle desire arose in you to possess it. But you were going to your office and that was no time for daydreaming, so you just passed by. You did not even notice that the mind had created a desire to possess this house. But now that desire is hanging there, suspended, and if it cannot be removed it will be difficult to sleep.

Difficulties in sleep basically mean only one thing, that your day is still hanging over you and you cannot be relieved of it. You are clinging to it. Then in the night you will see a dream that you have become the owner of this house—now you are living in this house. The moment this dream comes to you, your mind is relieved.

So ordinarily people think that dreams are disturbances to sleep—that is absolutely wrong. Dreams are not disturbances to your sleep. They are not disturbing your sleep, they are really helping; without them you could not sleep at all. As you are you cannot sleep without dreams, because your dreams are helping to complete things which have remained incomplete.

And there are things which cannot be completed. Your mind goes on desiring absurd desires, and they cannot be completed in reality, so what to do? Those incomplete desires go on in you, and they keep you hoping, they keep you thinking. So what to do? You have seen a beautiful woman and you were attracted to her. Now the desire has arisen to possess her. It may not be possible, the woman may not even look at you. So what to do? The dream will help you.

In a dream you can possess the woman, and then the mind is relieved. As far as the mind is concerned, there is no difference between dream and reality. What is the difference? Loving a woman in reality and loving a woman in a dream, what is the difference for the mind? There is no difference. Or this may be the difference, that the dream phenomenon may be more beautiful, because then the woman will not disturb you. It is your dream and you can do anything, and the woman will not create any problems for you. The other is absent completely, you are alone. There is no barrier, so you can do whatsoever you like.

There is no difference for the mind; mind cannot make any distinction between what is dream and what is reality. For example, if you could be put in a coma for one whole year, and you dream on and on, for one year you will not be able to feel in any way that whatsoever you are seeing is a dream. It will be real, and the dream will continue for one year.

Psychologists say that if you can put a man in a coma for a hundred years he will dream for a hundred years, not for a single moment suspecting that whatsoever he is doing is just a dream. And if he dies he will never know that his life was just a dream, that it was never real. For the mind there is no difference: reality and dream are both the same. So mind can unwind itself in dream.

If you do this technique, then there will be no need for dreams. The quality of your sleep will be changed totally, because without dreams you fall to the very bottom of your being, and without dreams you will be aware in your sleep.

That is what Krishna says in the Gita, that while everyone is deeply asleep the yogi is not, the yogi is awake. That doesn't mean that the yogi is not sleeping—he is also sleeping, but the quality of the sleep is different. Your sleep is just like a drugged unconsciousness. A yogi's sleep is a deep relaxation with no unconsciousness. His whole body is relaxed; every fiber and cell of his whole body is relaxed, with no tension left. But he is fully aware of the whole phenomenon.

Try this technique. Start from tonight, try it, and then do it in the morning also. And when you feel that you are attuned to the technique, that you

can do it, after one week try it for your whole past. Just take one day off. Go to some lonely place. It will be good if you fast—fast and be silent. Lie down on some lonely beach or under some tree, and just move toward your past from this point: you are lying on the beach feeling the sand and the sun, and now move backward. Go on penetrating, penetrating, penetrating, and find out the last thing that you can remember.

You will be surprised. Ordinarily you cannot remember much, and you cannot pass the barrier of four or five years of age. Those who have a very good memory may go back to the age barrier of three years, but then suddenly a block comes and everything goes dark. But if you try with this technique, by and by you will break the barrier, and very easily you can come to remember the first day you were born. And that is a revelation.

Back again with your sun and beach, you will be a different man. If you make more effort, you can penetrate to the womb. And you have memories of the womb—nine months of memories with your mother. That nine-month period is also recorded in the mind. When your mother was depressed, you have recorded it because you felt depressed. You were so connected with the mother, so united, so one, that whatsoever happened to your mother was happening to you. When she was angry, you were angry. When she was happy, you were happy. When she was praised, you felt praised. When she was ill, you felt the pain, the suffering, everything.

If you can penetrate to the womb, now you are on the right track. And then, by and by, you can penetrate more and you can remember the first moment when you entered the womb.

Only because of this remembrance, Mahavira and Buddha could say that there are past lives, rebirth. Rebirth is not really a principle, it is just a deep psychological experience. And if you can remember the first moment you entered the womb of your mother, then you can penetrate more and you can remember the death of your past life. Once you touch that point then the method is in your hands; then you can move very easily to all your past lives.

This is an experience, and the result is phenomenal, because then you know that through many, many lives you have lived the same nonsense that you are living now. You have been doing this whole nonsense so many times, repeatedly. The pattern is the same, the format is the same, only the details differ. You loved some other woman, now you love this woman. You gathered money...the coins were of one kind, now the coins are different. But the whole pattern is the same; it is repetitive.

Once you can see that for many, many lives you have lived the same nonsense, how stupid has been this whole vicious circle, suddenly you are awakened and the whole thing becomes a dream. You are thrown away from it, and now you do not want to repeat the same thing in the future.

Desire stops, because desire is nothing but the past being projected into the future. Desire is nothing but your past experience in search of another repetition again. Desire means just an old experience that you want to repeat again—nothing else. And you cannot leave desire unless you become aware of this whole phenomenon. How can you leave it? The past is there as a great barrier, a rocklike barrier. It is upon your head; it is pushing you toward the future. Desires are created by the past and projected into the future. If you can know the past as a dream, all desires become impotent. They fall down, they just wither away—and the future disappears. In that disappearance of past and future, you are transformed.

---

23 Feel an object and become it.

The eleventh centering technique: *Feel an object before you. Feel the absence of all other objects but this one. Then leaving aside the object-feeling and the absence-feeling, realize.*

Feel an object before you—any object. For exam-ple, a rose. Anything will do. *Feel an object before you.* First, feel it. Seeing won't do—feel it. You see a roseflower, but your heart is not stilled, you are not feeling it; otherwise you may start weeping and crying, otherwise you may start laughing and dancing. You are not feeling it, you are just seeing it. And even that seeing may not be complete, because you never see completely. The past, the memory, says that this is a rose, and you pass on. You have not seen it really. The mind says that this is a rose. You know everything about it, as you have known roses before, so what about this one? So you pass on. Just a glimpse is enough to revive the memory of your past experience of roses, and you pass on. Even seeing is not complete.

Remain with the rose. See it, then feel it. What to do to feel it? Smell it, touch it, let it become a deep bodily experience. First close your eyes and let the rose touch your whole face. Feel it. Put it on the eyes, let the eyes touch it; smell it. Put it against the heart, be silent with it; give a feeling to the rose. Forget everything, forget the whole world.

Feel an object before you. Feel the absence of all other objects...because if your mind is still thinking of other things then this feeling will not penetrate deeply. Forget all other roses, forget all other persons, forget everything. Just let this rose remain there. Only the rose, the rose, the rose! Forget everything else, let this rose envelope you completely...you are drowned in the rose.

This will be difficult because we are not so sensitive. But for women it will not be so difficult; they can feel it more easily. For men it may be a little bit more difficult, unless they have a very developed aesthetic sense, like a poet or a painter or a musician—they can feel things. But try. Children can do it very easily.

I was teaching this method to the son of one of my friends. He could feel very easily. When I gave him a roseflower and I told him all that I have told to you, he did it, and he enjoyed it deeply. And then I asked him, "How are you feeling?"

He said, "I have become a roseflower—that is

the feeling. I have become a roseflower." Children can do it very easily, but we never train them; otherwise they could be the best meditators.

Forget all other objects completely. *Feel the absence of all other objects but this one.* This is what happens in love. If you are in love with someone, you forget the whole world. If you are still remembering the world, then know well that this is not love. You have forgotten the whole world; only the beloved or the lover remains. That is why I say love is a meditation. You can use this technique also as a love technique: forget everything else.

Just a few days ago a friend came to me with his wife. His wife was complaining about a certain thing; that is why she had come. The friend said, "I have been meditating for a year and now I am deep in it. And while I meditate I have found it helpful when a peak comes to my meditation to suddenly cry, 'Rajneesh, Rajneesh, Rajneesh!' It helps me, but now a strange thing has happened. When I am making love to my wife, when I come to a sexual peak, I start crying, 'Rajneesh, Rajneesh, Rajneesh!' Because of this my wife is very much disturbed, and she says, 'Are you making love with me, are you meditating, or what are you doing? And why does this "Rajneesh" come in?'"

The man said to me, "It is now very difficult because if I do not cry, 'Rajneesh, Rajneesh!' I cannot achieve a peak. And if I cry, my wife is very much disturbed. She starts crying and weeping and making a scene. So what to do? Thus, I have brought my wife." Of course, his wife's complaint is right, because she does not like for someone else to be present between them. That is why love needs privacy—absolute privacy. The privacy is meaningful, just to forget all else.

In Europe and America, now they are working with group sex. That is nonsense—many couples making love in one room. It is absolute nonsense because then love can never go very deep. It will become just a sex orgy. The presence of others becomes a barrier; then it cannot be meditative.

With any object, if you can forget the whole world you are in a deep love—with a rose or with a stone or with anything. But the condition is to feel the presence of this object and feel the absence of all else. Let this object be the only existential thing in your consciousness. It will be easy if you try with some object you are naturally in love with.

It would be difficult for you to put a stone, a rock, before you and forget the whole world. It would be difficult, but Zen masters have done it. They have rock gardens for meditation. No flowers, no trees, nothing—just rocks and sand. And they meditate on a rock because, they say, if you can have a deep love relationship with a rock, then no man can create a barrier for you. And men are like rocks. If you can love a rock, then you can love a man; then there is no problem. Men are like rocks—even more stony. It is difficult to break them and penetrate them.

But choose some object you naturally love, and then forget the whole world. Relish the presence, taste the presence, feel it, go deep into it and let it go deep into you. *Then, leaving aside the object....* And then comes the most difficult part of this technique. You have left all other objects, and only one object has remained. You have forgotten all, only one has remained.

Now, *leaving aside the object-feeling....* Now leave aside the feeling that you have for this object. *Leaving aside the object-feeling and the absence-feeling*—of other objects. Now there are only two things; everything else is absent. Now leave that absence also. Only this rose, this face, this woman, this man, this rock, is present. Leave this also, and leave the feeling as well. Suddenly you fall into an absolute vacuum and nothing remains. And Shiva says, *Realize.* Realize this vacuum, this nothingness. This is your nature, this is pure being.

It will be difficult to approach nothingness directly—very difficult and arduous. So it is easy to pass through one object as a vehicle. First put one object in the mind, and feel it so totally that you need not remember anything else. Your whole consciousness is filled with this one object. Then leave this also, forget this also.

You fall into an abyss. Now nothing remains, no object. Only your subjectivity is there—pure, uncontaminated, unoccupied. This pure being, this pure consciousness, is your nature. But do it in steps; do not try the whole technique at once. First create an object-feeling. For a few days only do this part, do not do the whole technique.

First, for a few days or for a few weeks, just do one part—the first part. Create an object-feeling; be filled with the object. And use one object, do not go on changing objects, because with every object you will have to make the same effort again. If you have chosen one roseflower, then go on using that roseflower every day. Be filled with it so that one day you can say, "Now I am the flower." Then the first part is fulfilled. When only the flower is there and all else is forgotten, then relish this idea for a few days. It is beautiful in itself—very, very beautiful, vital, powerful in itself.

Just feel it for a few days. And then, when you are attuned to it and it has become easy, then you need not struggle. Then the flower comes there suddenly, the whole world is forgotten and only the flower remains.

Then try the second part: close your eyes and forget the flower also. If you have done the first, the second will not be difficult—remember. But if you try the whole technique in one sitting, the second will be impossible—because if you can do the first, if you can forget the whole world for one flower, you can forget the flower also for nothingness. So the second part will come, but first you have to struggle for it. But the mind is very tricky. The mind will always say to try the whole thing, and then you will not succeed. Then the mind will say, "It is not useful," or, "It is not for me." Try it in parts if you want to succeed. Let the first part be complete, and then do the second. Then the object is not there and only your consciousness remains, just like a light, a flame without anything around it.

You have a lamp and the lamp's light falls on many objects. Visualize it. In your room there are many, many objects. If you bring one lamp into the darkness of the room, all the objects are lighted. The lamp radiates light on every object so that you can see them. Now remain with an object; let there be one object. The lamp is the same, but now only one object is there in its light. Now remove that object also; now light remains without any object.

The same happens with your consciousness. You are a flame, a light; the whole world is your object. You leave the whole world, and you choose one object for your concentration. Your flame remains the same, but now it is not occupied with multiobjects, it is occupied with only one. And then drop that object also. Suddenly there is simply light—consciousness. It is not falling on anything. This Buddha has called *nirvana*; this Mahavira has called *kaivalya*—the total aloneness. The Upanishads have called it the experience of the *Brahma*, or the *atma*. Shiva says that if you can do this single technique, you will realize the supreme.

24 Watch your moods.

The twelfth centering technique: *When a mood against someone or for someone arises, do not place it on the person in question, but remain centered.*

If hate arises for someone or against someone, or love arises for someone, what do we do? We project it on the person. If you feel hate toward me, you forget yourself completely in your hate; only I become your object. If you feel love toward me, you forget yourself completely; only I become the object. You project your love or hate or whatsoever upon me. You forget completely the inner center of your being; the other becomes the center. This sutra says when hate arises or love arises, or any mood for or against anyone, do not project it on the person in question. Remember, you are the source of it.

I love you—the ordinary feeling is that you are the source of my love. That is not really so. I am the source, you are just a screen on which I project my love. You are just a screen; I project my love on you and I say that you are the source of my love. This is not fact, this is fiction. I draw my love energy and project it onto you. In that love energy projected onto you, you become lovely. You may not be lovely to someone else, you may be absolutely repulsive to someone else. Why? If you are the source of love then everyone will feel loving toward you, but you are not the source. I project love, then you become lovely; someone projects hate, then you become repulsive. And someone else doesn't project anything, he is indifferent; he may not even have looked at you. What is happening? We are projecting our own moods upon others.

That is why, if you are on your honeymoon, the moon looks beautiful, miraculous, wonderful. It seems that the whole world is different. And on the same night, just for your neighbor, this miraculous night may not be in existence at all. His child has died—then the same moon is just sad, intolerable. But for you it is enchanting, fascinating; it is maddening. Why? Is the moon the source or is the moon just a screen and you are projecting yourself?

This sutra says, *When a mood against someone or for someone arises, do not place it on the person in question*—or on the object in question. Remain centered. Remember that you are the source, so do not move to the other, move to the source. When you feel hate, do not go to the object. Go to the point from where the hate is coming. Go not to the person to whom it is going, but to the center from where it is coming. Move to the center, go within. Use your hate or love or anger or anything as a journey toward your inner center, to the source. Move to the source and remain centered there.

Try it! This is a very, very scientific, psychological technique. Someone has insulted you—anger suddenly erupts, you are feverish. Anger is flowing toward the person who has insulted you. Now you will project this whole anger onto him. He has not done anything. If he has insulted you, what has he done? He has just pricked you, he has helped your

anger to arise—but the anger is yours. If he goes to Buddha and insults him, he will not be able to create any anger in him. Or if he goes to Jesus, Jesus will give him the other cheek. Or if he goes to Bodhidharma, he will roar with laughter. So it depends.

The other is not the source, the source is always within you. The other is hitting the source, but if there is no anger within you it cannot come out. If you hit a buddha, only compassion will come out because only compassion is there. Anger will not come out because anger is not there. If you throw a bucket into a dry well, nothing comes out. In a water-filled well, you throw a bucket and water comes out, but the water is from the well. The bucket only helps to bring it out. So one who is insulting you is just throwing a bucket in you, and then the bucket will come out filled with the anger, hate, or fire that was within you. You are the source, remember.

For this technique, remember that you are the source of everything that you go on projecting onto others. And whenever there is a mood against or for, immediately move within and go to the source from where this hate is coming. Remain centered there; do not move to the object. Someone has given you a chance to be aware of your own anger—thank him immediately and forget him. Close your eyes, move within, and now look at the source from where this love or anger is coming. From where? Go within, move within. You will find the source there because the anger is coming from your source.

Hate or love or anything is coming from your source. And it is easy to go to the source at the moment you are angry or in love or in hate, because then you are hot. It is easy to move in then. The wire is hot and you can take it in, you can move inward with that hotness. And when you reach a cool point within, you will suddenly realize a different dimension, a different world opening before you. Use anger, use hate, use love to go within.

We use it always to move to the other, and we

213

feel very much frustrated if no one is there to project upon. Then we go on projecting even on inanimate objects. I have seen persons being angry at their shoes, throwing them in anger. What are they doing? I have seen angry persons pushing a door in anger, throwing their anger on the door, abusing the door, using dirty language against the door. What are they doing?

I will end with one Zen insight about this. One of the greatest of Zen masters, Lin Chi, used to say, "While I was young I was very fascinated by boating. I had one small boat, and I would go on the lake alone. For hours together I would remain there.

"Once it happened that with closed eyes I was in my boat meditating on the beautiful night. One empty boat came floating downstream and struck my boat. My eyes were closed, so I thought, 'Some-one is here with his boat, and he has struck my boat.' Anger arose. I opened my eyes and I was just going to say something to that man in anger; then I realized that the boat was empty. Then there was no way to move. To whom could I express the anger? The boat was empty. It was just floating downstream, and it had come and struck my boat. So there was nothing to do. There was no possibility to project the anger on an empty boat."

So Lin Chi said, "I closed my eyes. The anger was there, but finding no way out, I closed my eyes and just floated backward with the anger. And that empty boat became my realization. I came to a point within myself in that silent night. That empty boat was my master. And now if someone comes and insults me, I laugh and I say, 'This boat is also empty.' I close my eyes and I go within."

Use this technique. It may work miracles for you.

CHAPTER 16

Beyond the sin of unconsciousness

♦

How to practice not placing our moods on others without suppressing ourselves?

Why are psychoanalysts in the West not very successful with the "unwinding" technique?

Isn't it true that no method is powerful unless one is initiated into it?

If identification is the only sin, why do many techniques use it and say become one with a thing?

The first question:

The last technique You discussed yesterday said that when a mood against someone or for someone arises, not to place it on the person in question but to remain centered. But when we experiment with this technique on our anger, hatred, etcetera, we feel that we are suppressing our emotion and it becomes a suppressed complex. So please clarify how to be free from these suppressed complexes while practicing the above technique.

xpression and suppression are two aspects of one coin. They are contradictory, but basically they are not different. In expression and in suppression, in both, the other is the center. I am angry—I suppress the anger. I was going to express anger against you; now I suppress the anger against you. But the anger goes on being projected onto you whether expressed or suppressed. This technique is not for suppression. This technique changes the very base of expression and suppression both.

This technique says, do not project it on the other, you are the source. Whether you express it or suppress it, you are the source. The emphasis is neither on expression nor on suppression. The emphasis is on knowing from where this anger arises. You have to move to the center, the source from where anger, hate and love arise. When you suppress you are not moving to the center, you

are struggling with the expression.

Anger has arisen in me. Ordinarily, I can do two things: express it onto someone or repress it. But in both the cases I am concerned with the other and I am concerned with the energy of anger that has come to the surface—not with the source.

This technique is to forget the other completely. Just look at your energy of anger arising and move deep down to find the source within yourself from where it is coming. And the moment you find the source, remain centered in it. Do not do anything with anger—remember. In expression you are doing something with anger; in suppression also you are doing something with anger. Do not do anything with anger; do not touch it, just use it as a path. Just go deep down into it to know from where this has arisen. And the moment you will find the source, it is very easy to be centered there. Anger has to be used, really, as a path to find the source. Any emotion can be used.

When you suppress you are not going to find the source, you are just struggling with energy that has come up and wants to be expressed. You can suppress it, but it will be expressed sooner or later because you cannot struggle forever with the energy that has come up. It has to be expressed. So you may not express it upon A, but then you will express it upon B or C. Whenever you find someone who is weaker than you, you will express the energy. And unless you express it you will feel burdened, tense, heavy and ill at ease.

So it will be expressed. You cannot suppress it continuously. From somewhere it will leak out, because if it is not going to leak out you will be constantly worried by it. So suppression is really nothing but postponing expression. You will simply postpone.

You are angry at your boss and you cannot express it; it is not economical. You will have to push it down, so you just wait until you can express it upon your wife or upon your child or somewhere—upon your servant.... And the moment you reach your home you will express it. You will find causes, of course, because man is a rationalizing animal. He will rationalize; he will find something—something very trivial, but now that will become very meaningful because you have something to express.

Suppression is nothing but postponing. You can postpone for months, for years. And those who know say that you can postpone for lives also, but it will have to be expressed. This technique is not concerned at all with suppression or expression— no! This technique uses your mood, your energy, as a path for you to go deep down within yourself.

Gurdjieff used to create situations in which he would force anger upon you, or hatred, or any other mood, and that was a created phenomenon. You would not be aware of what is going to happen.

Gurdjieff is sitting with his disciples, and as you enter you are not aware of what is going to happen, but they are ready to create anger in you. They will behave in such a way.... Someone will say something, and the whole group will behave so insultingly that you will become furious. Suddenly anger will come up; you are aflame. And when Gurdjieff has seen that now a point has come from where you can either go deep down or you can go out, when the peak has come within you and you are just going to explode, then he will say, "Close your eyes. Now be aware of your anger and go back."

Only then would you realize that the situation was a created one. No one was interested in insulting you—that was just a drama, a psychodrama—but the anger has arisen. And even if you come to know that it was simply a drama, the energy cannot suddenly go down, it will take time. Now you can move down with the falling energy to the source. This energy will just help you to go down to where it has come from; you can connect now with the original source. And this is one of the most successful methods of meditation.

Create any mood...but there is no need because the whole day moods are there. Use any mood to meditate. Then you have forgotten the other completely, and you are not suppressing anything. You are just moving down with some energy which has come up. Every energy comes from the source, so right now the path is warm and you can use that path to go back. And the moment you reach to the original source, the energy will subside into the original source. It is not suppression: the energy has gone back to the original source. And when you become capable of reuniting your energy with your original source, you have become the master of your body, your mind, your energy. You have become the master. Now you will not dissipate your energy.

Once you can know how the energy falls back with you to the center, there is no need of any suppression and there is no need of any expression. Right now you are not angry. I say something— you become angry. From where is this energy coming? A moment before you were not angry, but the energy was in you. If this energy can fall back again to the source, you will again be the same as you were a moment before.

Remember this: energy is neither anger nor love nor hate. Energy is simply energy—neutral. The same energy becomes anger; the same energy becomes sex; the same energy becomes love; the same energy becomes hate. These are all forms of the same energy. You give the form, your mind gives the form, and the energy moves into it.

So remember, if you love deeply you will not have much energy to be angry. If you do not love at all, then you will have much energy to be angry, and you will go on finding situations in which to be angry. If your energy is expressed through sex, you will be less violent. If your energy is not expressed through sex, you will be more violent. That is why militaries will never allow sexual relationships for the soldiers. If it is allowed, the militaries will become absolutely impotent to fight.

That is why, whenever civilization comes to a peak, it cannot fight. So always, more cultured and more civilized societies are overrun and defeated by lesser civilizations—always, because a more developed society cares about its individuals' every need, and sex is included. So when a society is really established, affluent, everybody's sexual need is fulfilled—but when the sexual need is fulfilled you cannot fight. You can fight very easily if the sexual need is not fulfilled. So if you want a world of peace, more freedom for sex will be needed. If you want a world of warring, fighting, then deny sex, suppress sex, create antisex attitudes.

This is a very paradoxical thing: the so-called saints and sages go on talking about peace, and they go on talking against sex also. They go on creating an antisex atmosphere, and at the same time they go on saying that the world needs peace, not war. This is absurd. Hippies are more correct; their slogan is right: "Make Love, Not War." That is right. If you can make love more, really you cannot make war.

That is why the so-called sannyasins who have suppressed sex will always be violent, angry about nothing: just angry, just violent, bubbling, waiting to explode. Their whole energy is unexpressed. Unless the energy falls down to the source, no *brahmacharya*, no real celibacy is possible. You can suppress sex—then it will become violence. If the sex energy moves down to the center, you will be just like a child.

The child has more sex energy than you, but it is still in the source; it has not moved to the body yet. It will move. When the body will be ready and the glands will be ready and the body will be mature, the energy will move. Why does a child look so innocent? The energy is at the source; it has not moved. Again the same thing happens when someone becomes enlightened. The whole energy moves to the source, and the person becomes child-like. That is what Jesus means when he says, "Only those who are like children will be able to enter into my kingdom of God."

What does it mean? Scientifically it means your whole energy has moved back to the source. If you express, it has moved out. And when it is expressed, you are creating a habit for the energy to move out, to leak out. If you suppress, then the energy has not moved to the source and it has not moved out; it is suspended. And a suspended energy is a burden.

That is why, if you really express anger, you feel relief. If you go through sex, you feel relief. If you destroy something, your hate is released and you feel relief. Why is this relief felt? Because suspended energy is burdensome, heavy. Your mind is cloudy with it. You have to throw it out or allow it to move back to the original source; these are the only two things.

If it goes back to the source, it becomes formless. In the source, energy is formless. For example, electricity is formless. When it moves into a fan, it takes one kind of form. When it moves into a bulb, it takes a different form. You can use it in a thousand ways—the energy is the same. The form is given by the mechanism through which it moves.

Anger is a mechanism, sex is a mechanism, love is a mechanism, hate is a mechanism. When energy moves into the channel of hate, it becomes hate. If the same energy moves into love, it becomes love. And when it moves into the source, it is formless energy—pure energy. It is neither hate nor love nor anger nor sex, simply energy. Then it is innocent, because formlessness is absolute innocence. That is why Buddha looks so innocent, childlike. The energy has moved to the source.

Do not express, because you are wasting your energy and helping the other also to waste his. Do not suppress, because then you are creating a suspended phenomenon which will have to be released. Then what to do?

This technique says, do not do anything with the mood itself, just go back to the source from where the mood is coming. And while the mood is hot, the path is clear, visible inside; you can move on it. Use moods for meditation. The result is miraculous, unbelievable. And once you find the key that shows you how to pour the energy back to the source, you will have a different quality of personality. Then you will not be dissipating anything, then it will look stupid.

Buddha has said that whenever you are angry against someone, you are punishing yourself for the misdeed of the other. He has insulted you—that is his deed—and you are punishing yourself by being angry; you are dissipating your energy. This is stupid. But then, listening to Buddha, Mahavira, Jesus, we start repressing; we start suppressing our energy. Then we think that it is not good, that it is stupid to be angry.

So what to do? Suppress the anger, do not be angry, pull yourself in, close yourself. Fight with your anger and suppress it. But then you will be sitting on something which will explode any moment. You are sitting on a Vesuvius—any moment it will explode.

You go on collecting. The whole day's anger is collected; the whole month's anger is collected; the whole year's anger, and the anger of your whole life, and then the anger of many lives, is collected. It is there; it can explode at any moment. Then you become very afraid of being alive even, because any moment anything can go in and you will explode. You become afraid, every moment is an inner struggle.

Psychologists say it is better to express than to suppress, but religion cannot say this. Religion says both are stupid. In expression you are harming the other and also yourself. In suppression you are harming yourself, and you will harm someone else someday. Move to the source so that the energy falls back to the source and becomes formless.

Then you will feel very powerful without being angry. Then you will feel energy—vital energy. You will be alive, you will have an intense life without forms. Anyone will be impressed just by your presence. You need not dominate anyone, just your presence and they will feel that some powerful source has come.

Whenever someone goes to a Buddha or to a Krishna, suddenly his energy feels a change of climate because of such a powerful source. The moment you move near, you are magnetized. No one is magnetizing you, no one is trying anything, there is just the presence. You may feel that someone has hypnotized you, but no one is hypnotizing. The presence of a Buddha—whose energy has become formless, whose energy has gone to the source, who is centered at his source—the very presence is hypnotizing. It becomes charismatic.

Buddha became enlightened. Before his enlightenment he had five disciples. They were ascetics and when Buddha himself was a great ascetic, torturing his body in many, many ways, inventing new and more sadistic techniques to torture himself, those five were his ardent followers. Then Buddha felt that this was wholly, absolutely absurd. Just by torturing one's body one is not going to realize oneself. When he realized this, he left ascetic ways. Those five followers left him immediately. They said, "You have fallen down. You are no more an ascetic." They left him.

When Buddha became enlightened, the first idea that came to his mind was about those five followers. Once they were his followers, so he must go to them. He felt a duty—he must find them and tell them what he has found. So he searched for them, and he traveled in Bihar, from Bodhgaya to Benares, just to find them. They were at Sarnath. Buddha never came back to Benares again, never came back to Sarnath again, because he came only for those five disciples.

He came to Sarnath. It was evening time, the sun was setting, and those five ascetics were sitting on a hillock. They saw Buddha coming, so they said, "That fallen Gautam Buddha, that Gautama Siddhartha who has fallen from the path, is coming. We must not pay any respect to him. We should not pay to him even ordinary respect."

So they closed their eyes. Buddha came nearer and nearer, and those five ascetics began to feel a change—a change of mind. They became uneasy. When Buddha reached just near, suddenly all the five opened their eyes and fell at the feet of Buddha. Buddha said, "But why are you doing this? You decided not to give any respect to me, so why are you doing this?"

They said, "We are not doing it, it is happening. What have you gained? You have become a magnetic force. We are just being pulled. What are you doing to us? Have you hypnotized us?" Buddha said, "No! I have done nothing to you, but something has happened in me. All the energies have fallen to the source, so wherever I move, suddenly a magnetic force is felt."

That is why those who are against Buddha or Mahavira go on saying for centuries, "That man was not good; he was hypnotizing people." No one is hypnotizing. You become hypnotized—that is another thing. When your energy falls back to the original source, you become a magnetic center. This technique is to create this magnetic center in you.

The second question:

Yesterday You said that the meditation technique of unwinding the mind is very significant. But in the West hundreds of Freudian and Jungian psychoanalysts and psychiatrists are practicing this technique, but they are not getting very significant results in trying to transform the being. What are the reasons for their being unsuccessful?

There are many things to be noted. One: Western psychology does not yet believe in the being of man, it believes only in the mind. For Western psychology there is nothing beyond the mind yet. If there is nothing beyond the mind, then whatsoever you do is not going to help man really. At the most

it can help man to be normal—at the most!

And what is normal? What is normalcy? Just the average. If the average man himself is not normal, then being normal means nothing. It simply means you are adjusted to the crowd. So Western psychology is doing only one thing: whenever someone is maladjusted, Western methods make that man again adjusted to the crowd. The crowd is not questioned at all; whether the crowd itself is okay is not the question.

For Eastern psychology, the crowd is not the criterion. Remember this distinction: for Eastern psychology the crowd is not the criterion, society is not the criterion. Society itself is ill. Then what is the criterion? For us a buddha is a criterion. Unless you become buddhalike, you are ill.

For Western psychology society is the criterion, because a buddha cannot be a criterion. They do not believe that there is such a thing as the inner being. If there is no such thing as the inner being, then there cannot be any enlightenment. But when the inner being becomes illuminated, then there is enlightenment.

So Western psychology is really just therapeutic, just a part of medicine. It tries, it helps you to be re-adjusted, but it is not a transcendence. The Eastern effort is for how to transcend the mind, because for us there are no mental diseases, remember. For us there are no mental diseases—rather, the mind is the disease. For Western psychology the mind is not the disease. The mind is you, it is not the disease. The mind can be healthy, and the mind can be ill.

For us the mind is the disease, the mind can never be healthy. Unless you go beyond mind, you can never be healthy. You can be ill and adjusted or you can be ill and maladjusted, but you can never be healthy. So the normal man is not really healthy. He is just within the boundaries, he is ill within the boundaries. The abnormal person is one who has gone beyond the boundaries; and the difference between the two is only of degrees—of quantity, not of quality.

A madman in a madhouse and you—there is

no qualitative difference, only one of degrees. He is a little bit more mad than you; you are within the boundaries. Functionally, you can switch on. He cannot switch on now; he has gone further than you. He has an advanced case, nothing else. You are just on the path and he has reached.

Western psychology tries to bring him back to the fold, to the herd, to the crowd. It makes him normal. It is good; as far as it goes, it is good. But for us, unless a man goes beyond mind he is mad, because for us the mind is madness.

So we are trying to unwind the mind just to know that which is beyond it. They also try unwinding methods just to adjust the mind, but the beyond is not there. And remember this: unless you can go beyond yourself, nothing worthwhile happens. Unless you can reach something which is beyond you, life is meaningless.

Certain other things also.... For Freud and the Freudians, man is really a being that cannot be happy. The very being for them is such that man cannot be happy. If you are not unhappy, that is all. Remember, if you are not unhappy, be satisfied—it is enough. You cannot be happy. Why? Because Freudian psychology says that happiness lies in being instinctual, happiness lies in being like an animal, and that man cannot be. Reason goes on continuously interfering. You can lose your reason and become like an animal; then you can be happy. But then you will not be aware of happiness. This is the paradox for them.

If you fall downward and become like an animal, you will be happy but you will not be aware. If you try to be aware you cannot be happy, because you cannot become like an animal. And reason goes on interfering in everything. Man cannot lose reason and also man cannot live with reason—that is the problem. So you cannot be happy according to Freud. At the most, if you are wise, you can arrange your life in such a way that you will not be unhappy. This is a very negative thing.

For Eastern psychology or metaphysics or religion, a positive goal exists. You can be happy. Not only happy, you can be blissful. And Eastern psychology says that if you can feel that you are unhappy, that shows your potentiality, the possibility that you can be happy; otherwise you would not be able to feel this being unhappy either.

If a man can see darkness he has eyes, and one who can see darkness can see light. Remember, blind men cannot see darkness. You may have been thinking that blind men live in darkness—forget it completely. They cannot see darkness, because even to see darkness eyes are needed. If you can feel unhappiness you have eyes, and if you can feel unhappiness you can feel happiness. Really, if you cannot feel happiness, there is no possibility of feeling unhappiness. These are polar opposites.

You are capable of being totally happy, but then the mind cannot be. Take it in this way: if you fall downward and become just a body, you will be happy. Freud also agreed with this. If you fall downward and forget your reason completely, if you become like an animal, just a body, you will be happy but you will not know it. With the mind you can know it, but then you cannot be happy because the mind goes on disturbing. The body can be happy, but the mind goes on disturbing.

There is another possibility which the East has worked out: go beyond. Freud says that if you fall downward and become an animal, you will be happy but you will not know it; if you are in the mind you can know, but you cannot be happy. Eastern search says that if you go beyond mind you will be happy and also aware. That is a third point —of the beyond.

So these are three points. Man is in the middle; below is the animal existence. Go to a forest and look at the animals. They may not be aware that they are happy, but you will feel that they are happy. Go to the beach in the morning, or go to a garden in the morning and listen to the singing of the birds. They may not know it, but you will feel they are happy. You have never been singing like that. Look deep down into their eyes—they are so unclouded and innocent. They are happy, but you are not happy.

Fall downward and become a body only—then you will be happy. Or go beyond and become the spirit or become the being, and you will be happy. But in the middle you will be always tense, because mind is really not the end. It is just a rope stretched between two realities: body and soul.

So you are just on the rope like a *nata*, a tightrope walker. A tightrope walker cannot be at ease. Either he must go back or he must go forward, but he must not remain on the rope. He must get down from the rope, and there are two possibilities: he can go backward, or he can go forward and beyond. Mind is a rope, and to live with the mind is tightrope walking. You are bound to be unbalanced, uneasy; every moment there is anxiety, anguish. The mind's life is tension. That is why Western psychology succeeds in making you normal, but fails to make you a self-actualized person.

But there are new trends, and people are thinking, and the East is now penetrating the West very deeply. Really, that is the East's way to conquer. The West conquered the East—their way was very gross. The East has its own ways of conquering— very subtle ways, silent ways. Now the East is penetrating the Western mind deeply. Without any violence, without any visible conflict, the East is penetrating the West very deeply. And sooner or later Western psychology will have to evolve concepts about transcending, about how to transcend the mind.

Unwinding can be helpful in both the ways. If you are just trying to create a normal mind, unwinding will be helpful. But then your goal is not transcendence. If your goal is transcendence, then too unwinding can be helpful. All these techniques can be used for ordinary mental peace, and all these techniques can also be used for a real silence which is not of the mind.

There are two types of silence: one of the mind, in which the mind is silent, and another silence when the mind is no more. The silence when the mind is no more, is altogether different from mental peace. In mental peace the mind is there, only not very mad. The madness is slowed down—that is all.

Western psychology must become a metaphysics, only then can man transcend. It must become a philosophy also, and ultimately it must become religion. Only then can man be helped to transcend.

The third question:

You have been explaining many meditation methods to us. However, isn't it true that no method can be all that powerful unless one is initiated into it?

A method becomes qualitatively different when you are initiated into it. I am talking about the methods —you can use them. Once you know the scientific background and the way, the know-how, you can use it, but initiation makes it qualitatively different. If I initiate you into a particular method it will be a different thing, because many things are implied in initiation.

When I talk about a method and I explain it to you, you can use it on your own. The method is explained to you, but whether it will suit you or not, how it will work upon you, what type of person you are, is not discussed. It is not possible.

In initiation, you are more important than the technique. When the master initiates you, he observes you. He finds out what is your type, he finds out how much you have worked through in your past lives, where you are right at this moment, at what center you are functioning right now, and then he decides about the method; he chooses the method. It is an individual approach. The method is not important, you are important; you are being studied and observed and analyzed.

Your past lives, your consciousness, your mind, your body, they are dissected. You are felt deeply in terms of where you are, because the journey begins from that point—the point where you are just now. Just any method will not do.

Then the master chooses a particular method for you, and if he feels that this particular method has to be changed for you, that minute alterations or some additions are needed, he adds, he deletes, he makes the method fit for you. And then he gives the initiation; then he gives the method to you. That is why it is insisted that whenever you are initiated in a method, you are not to talk about it. It has to be secret because it is individual. If you tell it to someone else it may not be helpful, or it may even be harmful.

It has to be kept secret. Unless you achieve and your master says that now you can initiate others, it should not be talked about at all—not uttered, not even to your husband or your wife or your friend. No, it is absolutely secret because it is dangerous, it is very powerful. It has been chosen and made for you. It will work for you, but it is not for any other individual in the world. Really, each individual is so unique that he needs a different method, and with a slight difference a method can become suitable for him.

What I am talking about—these one hundred and twelve methods—they are generalized methods. They are one hundred and twelve generalized methods, all the methods which have been used. This is a general form so that you become acquainted. You can try—if something suits you, you can go on. But this is not initiation into a method. Initiation is a personal, individual affair between the master and the disciple. It is a secret transmission. And many other things are implied in initiation. Then the master chooses a right moment when he will give the method to you, so that it goes deep into the unconscious.

While I am talking, your conscious mind is listening. You will forget. When I have talked about one hundred and twelve methods, you will not even be able to rename them again—the one hundred and twelve. You will forget many completely. You will be able to remember a few, and then you will be mixed up and confused. You will not know what is what.

The master has to choose a right moment when your unconscious is open, and then he gives you the method. Then it goes deep down into the unconscious. So many times initiation is given in sleep, not when you are conscious. Many times initiation is given to you in a deep hypnotic trance, when your conscious mind is completely asleep and your unconscious mind is open.

That is why surrender is so much needed in initiation. Unless you surrender initiation cannot be given, because unless you surrender your conscious mind is always alert and on guard. When you surrender, your conscious mind can then be relieved of its duty and your unconscious mind can come directly in contact with the master.

A right moment has to be chosen, and then you have to be prepared for initiation. It may take months to prepare you. There has to be the right food, the right sleep, and everything has to come to a tranquil point; only then can you be initiated, so initiation is a long process, an individual process. Unless someone is ready to surrender totally, initiation is not possible.

So I am not initiating you into these methods, I am just making you acquainted with these methods. If someone feels that some method suits him deeply and he feels that he should be initiated into that method, I can initiate him into that method. But then it is going to be a long process. Then your individuality has to be completely known. You have to become totally naked so that nothing remains hidden. And then things become very easy —because when a right method is given to a right person at a right moment, it works immediately.

Sometimes it happens that while initiating the disciple, the disciple becomes enlightened, just the initiation becomes the enlightenment. Then the method becomes alive—when it is given by a master privately, individually. Whatsoever I am doing now is not initiating, remember this. This is a scientific approach just to revive the one hundred and twelve methods, to make them known.

If someone is interested, he can be initiated.

And when you are really interested you will seek initiation, because working alone on the method is a very long affair. It may take years, it may take lives, and you may not be able to sustain it for so long a period. Through initiation it becomes very easy, and then the method becomes a transmission. Then through the method the master starts working in you. Initiation is a living relationship with the master, and a long relationship, of course, goes deep. It changes you and transforms you.

The next question:

You quoted George Gurdjieff as saying that identification is the only sin, but in many techniques the process of identification is used. They say, for example, become one with the beloved, become one with the rose, or become one with the master. And, moreover, empathy is supposed to be a meditative and spiritual quality, so the above saying of Gurdjieff's seems to be partially true and useful only for certain techniques.

No! It is not partially true, it is totally true. But you will have to understand. Identification is unconscious, but when you use identification in a meditative technique it is conscious.

For example, your name is Ram. Someone insults "Ram"—immediately *you* feel insulted because you are identified with the name Ram. But this is not a conscious thing for you, it is unconscious. Your mind doesn't work in this way: "I am called Ram. Of course, I am not Ram, this is only my name, and everyone is born nameless. This name is given, and it is arbitrary. This man is only insulting my arbitrary name, so am I to be angry or not?" You would never reason it out in this way. If you reasoned it out in this way, you would not be angry at all. Suddenly someone insults "Ram" and you are insulted, but this is just an arbitrary name. This identification is unconscious, it is not conscious.

When you are identifying with a rose, it is a conscious effort. You are not identified with the rose. You are *trying* to identify yourself with the rose, and you are trying to forget yourself. You are trying to become one with the rose, and you are deeply conscious, aware of the whole process. *You* are doing it. If identification is done consciously, it becomes a meditation. And if you do a certain technique of meditation unconsciously, it is not meditation—remember.

You go on doing your prayer every morning or every night unconsciously, just as a routine affair. While doing it you are not conscious at all of what you are doing. You are not conscious at all of what words you are saying in prayer. You just repeat them like a parrot. This is not meditation. And if you are taking your bath consciously, it is a meditation. So remember this: whatsoever you are doing consciously, with alertness, fully aware, becomes meditation. Even if you kill someone consciously, while fully conscious, it is meditative.

That is what Krishna was saying to Arjuna: "Do not be afraid. Kill, murder, fully consciously, knowing fully that no one is murdered and no one is killed." Arjuna could very easily kill his enemies unconsciously. He could go mad in a rage and kill —that is easy. But Krishna is saying, "Be alert, be fully conscious. Just become the instrument of divine hands, and know well that no one is killed, no one can be killed. The inner being is eternal, immortal. So you are only destroying forms, not that which is behind the forms. So destroy the forms." If Arjuna can be so meditatively aware then there is no violence, no one is killed, no sin is committed.

I will tell you one anecdote in Nagarjuna's life. Nagarjuna was one of the great masters India has produced—of the caliber of Buddha and Mahavira and Krishna. And Nagarjuna was a rare genius. Really, on the intellectual level there is no comparison in the whole world; such a keen and penetrating intellect rarely happens.

He was passing through a city, a capital city, and he always remained naked. The queen of that kingdom was a believer, a follower and a lover of

Nagarjuna, a devotee. So Nagarjuna came to the palace to ask for food. He had one wooden begging bowl.

The queen said, "Give this begging bowl to me. I will cherish it as a gift, and I have another made for you. You can take that."

Nagarjuna said, "Okay!" The other one was golden, and many precious stones were set in it; it was very valuable. Nagarjuna didn't say anything. Ordinarily no sannyasin would take it, he would say, "I cannot touch gold." But Nagarjuna took it. If really gold is just mud, then why make any distinction? He took it.

Even the queen didn't feel it to be good. She felt, "Why? He should have said no. Such a great saint! Why has he taken such a valuable thing while he lives naked, without any clothes, without any possessions? Why should he not reject it?"

If Nagarjuna had rejected it, the queen would have insisted, requested, but then she would have felt better. Nagarjuna took it and went away. One thief saw him passing through the city, and the thief thought, "This man cannot keep this begging bowl, someone is bound to steal it or someone is bound to take it away from him. With the nakedness—how can he protect it?" So he followed...the thief followed Nagarjuna.

Nagarjuna was staying outside the town in an old monastery, alone; the monastery was just in ruins. He went in, he heard the footsteps of the man, but he didn't look behind because he thought, "He must be coming for the begging bowl, not for me, because who would come? No one ever comes following me to these ruins."

He went in. The thief stood behind a wall and waited. Nagarjuna, seeing that he was waiting outside, threw the begging bowl out of the door.

The thief couldn't understand: "What type of man is this? Naked, with such a precious thing, and he has thrown it out." So he asked Nagarjuna, "Can I come in, sir? I have to ask a question."

Nagarjuna said, "I have thrown the bowl out just so that you can come in—to help you to come

in, because I am just going to take my afternoon nap. You would have come for the begging bowl, but then there would have been no meeting with me. So come in."

The thief came in. He said, "Such a precious thing and you have thrown it? And you are such a sage that I cannot lie before you—I am a thief."

Nagarjuna said, "Do not be worried, everyone is a thief. You proceed on, do not waste time about such unnecessary things."

The thief said, "Sometimes, looking at persons like you, my mind also longs to know how this state can be attained. I am a thief; it seems impossible for me. But I hope and I pray that someday I will also be capable of throwing away such a precious thing. Teach me something. I go to many sages, and I am a well-known thief, so everyone knows me. They say, 'First leave your business, your profession, only then can you proceed in meditation.' That is impossible, I cannot leave it, so I cannot proceed in meditation."

Nagarjuna said, "If someone says first leave thieving and then proceed in meditation, then he doesn't know meditation at all—because how is meditation related with theft? There is no relationship. So you go on doing whatsoever you are doing. I will give you a technique; you practice this."

The thief said, "Now it seems we can go on together. So I can go on doing my profession? What is the technique? Tell me immediately!"

Nagarjuna said, "You just remain aware. When you go to steal something, just be fully conscious and aware. When you are breaking into some house, be fully conscious. When you are breaking into a treasury, be fully conscious. When you are taking something out of the treasury, be fully conscious. Do it consciously. Whatsoever you do is no concern of mine. And come after fifteen days, but do not come if you have not practiced. Practice for fifteen days; go on doing whatsoever you are doing, but do it fully consciously."

The third day the thief came back and he said,

"Fifteen days are too long, and you are a very tricky fellow. You have given me such a technique that if I am fully conscious I cannot steal. The last three nights continuously I have been to the palace. I reached the treasury, I opened it, precious things were before me, but then I became fully conscious. And the moment I become fully conscious, I became like a Buddha statue. I could not proceed further; my hand would not move, and the whole treasury seemed useless. So I have been going back there again and again. What am I to do? And you said that leaving my profession was not a condition, but your method seems to have a built-in process."

Nagarjuna said, "Do not come to me again. Now you can choose. If you want to go on stealing, forget meditation. If you want meditation, then forget stealing. You can choose."

The thief said, "You have put me in a dilemma. For these three days I have known that I am alive. And when I came back without taking anything from the palace, for the first time I felt that I was a sovereign, not a thief. These three days have been so blissful that now I cannot leave meditation. You have tricked me; now initiate me and make me your disciple. There is no need to go on trying, three days are enough."

Whatsoever may be the object, if you are conscious it becomes meditation. Try identification consciously—it becomes meditation. Unconsciously, it is a great sin.

You are all identified with many things: "This is mine, that is mine...." You are identified! "This is my country, this is my nation, this is my national flag...." If someone throws your national flag you become furious—what is he doing? You have no nation and all national flags are myths. It is good to play with them like children do; they are toys. But you can murder and be murdered for them, and countries can be created and destroyed for insulting a national flag. And it is just a piece of cloth.

What is happening? You are identified with it. That identification is unconscious. Unconsciousness is sin.

Enough for today.

CHAPTER 17

Several "stop" techniques

◆

T H E   S U T R A S

25 *Just as you have the impulse to do something, stop.*

26 *When some desire comes, consider it. Then, suddenly, quit it.*

27 *Roam about until exhausted and then, dropping to the ground, in this dropping be whole.*

Life has two balances: one is of being and the other of doing. Your being is your nature. It is with you always; you do not have to do anything to get it. It is already the case, you are it. It is not that you possess it, not even that a distance exists between you and it—you are it. You are your being. Doing is an achievement. Whatsoever you do is not already the case. If you do it, it will happen; if you do not do it, it will not happen. All that is not already the case is not your being.

To exist, to survive, you have to do much. And then, by and by, your activity becomes a barrier to knowing your being. Your activity is your circumference—you live on it, you cannot live without it. But it is only the circumference; it is not you, it is not the center. Whatsoever you have is the achievement of your doing; having is the result of doing. But the center is surrounded, engulfed by your doing and your having.

The first thing to note before we proceed into these techniques is that whatsoever you have is not your being, and whatsoever you do or can do is not your being. Your being precedes all doing. Your being precedes all your possessions, all your having. But the mind is constantly involved in doing and having. Beyond mind or below mind exists your being. How to penetrate into that center is what religions have been seeking. This is what has always been the search of all those who are interested in knowing the basic reality of human existence, the ultimate core, the substance of your being. Unless you understand this division between the circumference and the center, you will not be able to understand these sutras which we are going to discuss.

So note the distinction. Whatsoever you have—money, knowledge, prestige, whatsoever you have—it is not you. You have them, they are your possessions; you are different from them. Secondly, whatsoever you do is not your being. You may do it or you may not do it. For example, you laugh, but you may laugh or you may not laugh. You run, but you may run or you may not run. But you are and there is no choice. You cannot choose your being. You are already there.

Action is a choice. You may choose, you may not choose. You may do "this," you may not do "this." You may become a saint or you may become a thief, but your sainthood and your thiefhood are both doings. You can choose, you can change. A saint can become a thief and a thief can become a saint. But that is not your being; your being precedes your sainthood, your thiefhood.

Whenever you have to do something, you have to be there already; otherwise you cannot do it. Who runs? Who laughs? Who steals? Who becomes a saint? The being must precede all activity. The activity can be chosen, but being cannot be chosen. The being is the chooser, not the chosen, and you cannot choose the chooser—he is already there. You cannot do anything about him. Remember this: having, doing, are with you just as a circumference is with the center, but you are the center.

This center is the self, or you may call it the *atma* or whatsoever name you like. This center is your innermost point. How to reach it? And unless one reaches it, knows it, unless one realizes it, one cannot reach to a blissful state which is eternal, one cannot know the deathless, one cannot know the divine.

Unless one realizes this center, one will remain in misery, anguish and suffering. The circumference is the hell. These techniques are the means to enter this center.

25 Stop!

The first stop technique: *Just as you have the impulse to do something, stop.*

All these techniques are concerned with stopping in the middle. George Gurdjieff made these techniques very well-known in the West, but he was not aware of *Vigyan Bhairav Tantra*. He learned these techniques in Tibet from Buddhist lamas. He worked on these techniques in the West, and many, many seekers came to realize the center through these techniques. He called them stop exercises, but the source of these exercises is *Vigyan Bhairav Tantra*.

Buddhists learned from *Vigyan Bhairav*. Sufis also have such exercises; they are also borrowed from *Vigyan Bhairav*. Basically, this is the source book of all techniques which are known all over the world.

Gurdjieff used it in a very simple way. For example, he would tell his students to dance. A group would be dancing—a group of, say, twenty people would be dancing—and suddenly he would say, "Stop!" And the moment Gurdjieff would say stop, they would have to stop totally. Wherever the pause would fall, they would have to stop then and there. No change could be made, no adjustment could be made. If one of your feet was above the earth and you were just standing on one foot, you would have to remain that way. If you fell, that was

another thing, but you were not to cooperate with the fall. If your eyes were opened, they had to remain opened. Now you could not close them. If they closed by themselves, that was another thing. But as far as you were concerned, consciously you had stopped, you had become just like a stone statue.

Miracles happened because in activity, in dance, in movement, when suddenly you stop, a gap happens. This sudden stoppage of all activity divides you into two: your body and you. Your body and you were in movement. Suddenly you stop. The body has the tendency to move. It was in movement, so there is momentum; you were dancing, and there is momentum. The body is not ready for this sudden stop. Suddenly you feel that the body has the impulse to do something, but you have stopped. A gap comes into existence. You feel your body as something distant, far away, with the impulse to move, with momentum for activity. And because you have stopped and you are not cooperating with the body and its activity and its impulse, its momentum, you become separate from it.

But you can deceive yourself. A slight cooperation and the gap will not happen. For example, you feel uncomfortable, but the teacher has said, "Stop!" You have heard the word, but still you make yourself comfortable and then you stop. Then nothing will happen. Then you have deceived yourself, not the teacher, because you missed the point. The whole point of the technique is missed. Suddenly, when you hear the word "Stop!" instantly you have to stop, not doing anything.

Perhaps the posture was inconvenient, you were afraid you might fall down, you might break a bone. But whatsoever happens, now it is not your concern. If you have any concern, you will deceive yourself. This suddenly becoming dead creates a gap. The stopping is at the body and the stopper is the center; the circumference and the center are separate. In that sudden stopping you can feel yourself for the first time; you can feel the center. Gurdjieff used this technique to help many.

This technique has many dimensions, it can be used in many ways. But first try to understand the mechanism. The mechanism is simple. You are in activity, and when you are in activity you forget yourself completely; the activity becomes the center of your attention.

Someone has died, and you are weeping and crying, and tears are falling down. You have forgotten yourself completely. The one who has died has become the center, and around that center this activity is happening—your weeping, your crying, your sadness, your tears. If I suddenly say to you, "Stop!" and you stop yourself completely, you will be totally taken away from your body and the realm of activity. Whenever you are in activity, you are in it, deeply absorbed in it. Sudden stoppage throws you off balance, it throws you out of activity. This being thrown leads you to the center.

Ordinarily, what are we doing? From one activity we move to another. We go on from one activity to another, from A to B and from B to C. In the morning, the moment you are awake activity has started. Now you will be active the whole day. You will change to many activities, but you will not be inactive for a single moment. How to be inactive? It is difficult. And if you try to be inactive, your effort to be inactive will become an activity.

There are many who are trying to be inactive. They sit in a Buddha posture and they try to be inactive. But how can you try to be inactive? The very effort is again an activity. So you can convert inactivity also into activity. You can force yourself to be quiet, still, but that forcing is an activity of the mind. That is why so many try to go into meditation but never reach anywhere—because their meditation is again an activity. They can change.... If you were singing an ordinary song, you can now change to a *bhajan*, to a devotional song. You can sing slow now, but both are activities. You are running, you are walking, you are reading—these are activities. You can pray—that too is an activity. You move from one activity to another.

And with the last thing in the night, when you are falling into sleep, you are still active; the activity has not stopped. That is why dreams happen, because the activity goes on. You have fallen asleep, but the activity continues. In the subconscious you are still active—doing things, possessing things, losing things, moving. Dreaming means you have fallen asleep because of exertion, but the activity is still there continuously.

Only sometimes, for a few moments—and these have become more and more rare for the modern man—only for a few moments dreaming stops and you are totally asleep. But then that inactivity is unconscious. You are not conscious, you are fast asleep. The activity has ceased; now there is no circumference, now you are at the center—but totally exhausted, totally dead, unconscious.

That is why Hindus have always been saying that *sushupti*, dreamless sleep, and *samadhi*, the ultimate ecstasy, are similar—the same, with only one difference. But the difference is great: the difference is of awareness. In sushupti, in dreamless sleep, you are at the center of your being—but unaware. In samadhi, in the ultimate ecstasy, in the ultimate state of meditation, also you are at the center—but aware. That is the difference, but it is a great difference, because if you are unaware, even if you are at the center it is meaningless. It refreshes you, it makes you more alive again, it gives you vitality—in the morning you feel fresh and blissful—but if you are unaware, even if you are at the center your life remains the same.

In samadhi you enter yourself fully conscious, fully alert. And once you are at the center fully alert, you will never be the same again. Now you will know who you are. Now you will know that your possessions, your actions are just on the periphery; they are just the ripples, not your nature.

The mechanism of these techniques of stopping is to throw you suddenly into inactivity. The point must come suddenly, because if you try to be inactive you will turn it into activity. So do not try, and suddenly be inactive. That is the meaning of "Stop!" You are running and I say, "Stop!" Do not try, just stop! If you try, you will miss the point. For example, you are sitting here. If I say stop, then stop immediately then and there; not a single moment is to be missed. If you try and adjust, and you settle down and then say, "Okay, now I will stop," you have missed the point. *Suddenly* is the base, so do not make any effort to stop—just stop!

You can try it anywhere. You are taking your bath—suddenly order yourself to "Stop!" and stop. Even if it is only for a single moment, you will feel a different phenomenon happening within you. You are thrown to the center and suddenly everything stops—not only the body. When the body stops totally, your mind stops also. When you say, "Stop!" do not breathe then. Let everything stop… no breathing, no body movement. For a single moment remain in this stop, and you will feel you have penetrated suddenly, at rocket speed, to the center. And even a glimpse is miraculous, revolutionary. It changes you, and by and by you can have more clear glimpses of the center. That is why inactivity is not to be practiced. Use it suddenly, when you are unaware.

So a master can be helpful. This is a group method. Gurdjieff used it as a group method because if you say "Stop!" you can deceive yourself easily. First you make yourself comfortable and then you say "Stop!" Or even if consciously you have not made any preparation for it, unconsciously you may be prepared. Then you may say, "Now I can stop." If it is done by the mind, if there is a planning behind it, it is useless; then the technique will not be of any help. So in a group it is good. A master is working with you, and he says, "Stop!" He will find moments when you are in a very inconvenient posture, and then a flash happens, a sudden lightning.

Activity can be practiced; inactivity cannot be practiced—and if you practice it, it becomes just another activity. You can be inactive only suddenly. Sometimes it happens that you are driving a car, and suddenly you feel there is going to be an accident, that another car has reached near yours and in just a moment there will be a crash. Suddenly your mind stops, breathing stops, everything stops. So many times in such accidents one is thrown to the center. But you may miss the point even in an accident.

I was in a car and there was an accident, and one of the most beautiful accidents possible. Three persons were with me, but they missed the whole thing completely. It could have been a revolution in their lives, but they missed. The car went down into a river bed, into a dry river bed, from a bridge. The car was totally upside down, and the three persons with me began crying, they began weeping.

One woman was there and she was crying. She was just beside me and she was crying, "I am dead! I am dead!"

I told her, "If you were dead, then no one would be here to say this."

But she was trembling, and she said, "I am dead! What will happen to my children?" Even after we carried her out of the car she was trembling and saying the same thing: "What will happen to my children? I am dead!" It took at least half an hour for her to calm down.

She missed the point. It was such a beautiful thing: suddenly she could have stopped everything. And one couldn't do anything. The car was falling from the bridge, so her activity was not needed at all. One couldn't do anything. But still the mind can create activity. She started thinking about her children, and then she began crying, "I am dead!" A subtle moment was missed. In dangerous situations the mind stops automatically. Why? Because mind is a mechanism and it can work with only routine things—that which it has been trained to do.

You cannot train your mind for accidents, otherwise they would not be called accidents. If you are ready, if you have passed through rehearsals, then they are not accidents. 'Accident' means that the mind is not ready to do anything. The thing is so sudden, it leaps from the unknown—mind cannot do anything. It is not ready, it is not trained for it. It is bound to stop unless you start something else, unless you start something for which you are trained.

This woman who was crying about her children was not at all attentive to what was happening. She was not even aware that she was alive. The present moment was not in her focus of consciousness. She had moved away from the situation to her children, to death and to other things. She had escaped. As far as her attention was concerned, she had escaped from the situation completely.

But as far as the situation was concerned, nothing could be done; one could only be aware. Whatsoever was happening was happening. One could only be aware. As far as the present moment is concerned, in an accident what can you do? It is already beyond you, and the mind is not prepared for it. The mind cannot function, so the mind stops.

That is why dangers have a secret appeal, an intrinsic appeal: they are meditative moments. If you race a car and it goes beyond ninety miles per hour, and then beyond one hundred and then beyond one hundred and ten and beyond one hundred and twenty, then a situation comes in which anything can happen and you will not be able to do anything. Now really, the car is beyond control, going beyond control. Suddenly the mind cannot function; it is not ready for it. That is the thrill of speed—because a silence creeps in, you are thrown to the center.

These techniques help you to move to the center without any accidents, without any danger. But remember, you cannot practice them. When I say you cannot practice them, what do I mean? In a way you can practice them: suddenly you can stop. But the stopping must be sudden, you must not be prepared for it. You should not think about it and plan it and say that "At twelve o'clock I will stop." Let the unknown happen to you when you are unprepared. Move in the unknown, the uncharted, without any knowledge. This is one technique: *Just as you have the impulse to do something, stop.* This is one dimension.

For example, you have the impulse to sneeze. You are feeling that the impulse is coming, you are feeling the sneeze coming. Now a moment comes when you cannot do anything—it will happen. But in the very beginning of the feeling, when you feel the sensation of a sneeze coming to you, the moment you become aware, stop! What can you do? Can you stop the sneeze? If you try to stop the sneeze, the sneeze will come sooner, because stopping will make your mind more conscious about it and you will feel the sensation more. You will become more sensitive, your total attention will be there, and that attention will help the sneeze to come out sooner. It will become unbearable. You cannot stop the sneeze directly, but you can stop yourself.

What can you do? You feel the sensation that the sneeze is coming: stop! Do not try to stop the sneeze, just you yourself stop. Do not do anything. Remain completely unmoving, with not even your breath going in or coming out. For a moment, stop, and you will feel that the impulse has gone back, that it has dropped. And in this dropping of the impulse a subtle energy is released which is used in going toward the center, because in a sneeze you are throwing some energy out—in any impulse.

'Impulse' means you are burdened with some energy which you cannot use and cannot absorb. It wants to move out, it wants to be thrown out; you want a relief. That is why after you sneeze you will feel good, a subtle well-being. Nothing has happened, you have simply released some energy which was superfluous, a burden. Now it is no more there, you are relieved of it. Then you feel a subtle relaxation inside.

That is why physiologists, Pavlov, B. F. Skinner and others, say sex is also like sneezing. They say physiologically there is no difference, sex is just like sneezing. You are overburdened with energy, you want to throw it out. Once it is thrown out your mechanism relaxes, you become unburdened. Then you feel good. That good feeling is just a release, according to physiologists, and as far as physiology goes they are right. Whenever you have some impulse, *just as you have the impulse to do something, stop!* Not only with a physiological impulse, any impulse can be used.

For example, you were going to drink a glass of water. You have touched the water, the glass—suddenly stop. Let the hand be there, let the desire to drink, the thirst be there inside, but you stop completely. The glass is outside, the thirst is inside; the hand is on the glass, the eyes are on the glass—stop suddenly. No breathing, no movement, as if you have become dead. The very impulse, the thirst, will release energy, and that energy is used for going to the center. You will be thrown to the center. Why? Because any impulse is a movement outward. Remember, 'impulse' means energy moving outward.

Remember another thing: energy is always in movement—either going out or coming in. Energy can never be static. These are the laws. If you understand the laws, then the mechanism of the technique will be easy. Energy is always in movement. Either it is moving out or moving in; energy can never be static. If it is static it is not energy, and there is nothing which is not energy, so everything is moving somewhere.

When an impulse, any impulse, comes to you, it means energy is moving out. That is why your hand goes to the glass—you have moved out. A desire has come to do something. All activities are movements toward that which is without from that which is within—movements from within to without.

When you stop suddenly, the energy cannot be static in you. You have become static, but the energy cannot be static in you, and the mechanism through which it was moving out is not dead, it has stopped. So what can the energy do? The energy cannot do anything other than move inward. Energy cannot be static. It was going out. You have stopped, the mechanism has stopped, but the mechanism which can lead it toward the center is there. This energy will move inward.

You are converting your energy and changing its dimension every moment without knowing it.

You are angry, and you feel the urge to beat someone or to destroy something or to do something violent—try this. Take someone—your friend, your wife, your child, anyone—and hug, kiss or embrace him or her. You were angry, you were going to destroy something; you wanted to do some violent thing. Your mind was destructive, the energy was moving toward violence. Love someone immediately.

In the beginning you may feel that this is just like acting. You will wonder, "How can I love? How can I love in this moment? I am angry!" You do not know the mechanism. In this moment you can love deeply because the energy has been aroused, it has arisen. It has come to a point where it wants to be expressed, and energy needs movement. If you just start loving someone, the same energy will move into love and you will feel a rush of energy that you may not have ever felt.

There are persons who cannot go into love unless they are angry, unless they are violent. There are people who can only go into deep love when their energy is moving violently. You may not have observed, but it happens daily: couples will fight before they make love. Wives and husbands fight, become angry, become violent, and then they make love, and they may not have understood what was happening. Then it becomes a mechanical habit—whenever they fight they will love. And the day they do not fight they will not be able to love.

Particularly in Indian villages, where wives are still beaten, if a certain husband stops beating his wife it is known that now he has stopped loving her. And even wives understand that if the husband has become totally nonviolent toward them, it means the love has stopped. He is not fighting, so it means he is not loving.

Why? Why is fight so associated with love? It is associated because the same energy can move in different dimensions. You may call it "love" or "hate." They look opposite, but they are not so opposite, because the same energy is moving. So a person who becomes incapable of hate becomes incapable of love, according to your definitions of love. A person who cannot be violently angry becomes incapable of the love which you know. He may be capable of a different quality of love, but that is not your love. A Buddha loves, but that love is totally different. That is why Buddha calls it compassion; he never calls it love. It is more like compassion, less like your love, because your love implies hate, anger, violence.

Energy can move, can change directions. It can become hate, it can become love—the same energy. And the same energy can move inward also, so whenever you have the impulse to do something, stop! This is not suppression. You are not suppressing anything, you are just playing with energy—just playing with energy and knowing the workings of it, how it works inwardly. But remember, the impulse must be real and authentic; otherwise nothing will happen.

For example, when there is no thirst you move to a glass of water and then suddenly you stop. Nothing will happen because there is nothing to happen—the energy was not moving. You were feeling love toward your wife, your husband, your friend. You wanted to hug, to kiss—stop! But the impulse must be there authentically. If the impulse is not there and you were just going to console someone, to kiss because the kiss is expected, and then you stop, then nothing will happen because nothing was moving inside.

So first remember the impulse must be authentic, real. Only with a real impulse does energy move, and when a real impulse is suddenly stopped the energy becomes suspended. With no dimension from where to move out, it turns in. It has to move, it cannot remain there.

But we are so false that nothing seems real. You eat your meal because of the clock, because of the time, not because of hunger. So if you stop, nothing will happen because there was really no hunger behind it, no impulse. No energy was moving there. That is why if you take your meal at one o'clock, at one o'clock you will feel the hunger. But the hunger

is false; it is just a mechanical habit, just a dead habit. Your body is not hungry. If you do not eat you will feel something is missing, but if you can remain for one hour without eating you will forget it, the hunger will have subsided.

A real hunger will grow more; it is bound to grow. If your hunger was real, then at two you will feel more hungry. If the hunger was false, then at two you will have completely forgotten. Really, there will be no hunger at two. Even if you want to eat, now you will not feel hungry. The hunger was just a false, mechanical feeling. No energy was moving, it was just the mind saying to you that now this is the time to eat, so eat.

If you are feeling sleepy, stop! But the feeling must be real; that is the problem. And that is the problem for us now, it was not so in Shiva's time. When the *Vigyan Bhairav Tantra* was preached for the first time, it was not so. Man was authentic, humanity was real, pure, nothing was false about it. With us everything is false. You pretend that you love; you pretend that you are angry. You go on pretending and then you forget yourself whether you are pretending or whether anything real is left. You never say what is in you, you never express it. You go on expressing what is not there. Watch yourself and you will come to know it.

You say something, but you feel something else. Really, you wanted to say quite the opposite, but if you say the real thing you will become totally unfit —because the whole society is false, and in a false society you can exist only as a false person. The more adjusted, the more false, because if you want to be real you will feel a maladjustment.

That is why renunciation came into existence, because of a false society. Buddha had to leave not because it had any positive meaning, but only a negative meaning—because with a false society you cannot be real. Or at every moment you are in a constant struggle, unnecessarily dissipating energy. So leave the unreal, leave the false, so that you can be real. That was the basic reason for all renunciation.

But watch yourself, how unreal you are. Watch the double mind. You are saying something, but you are feeling quite the contrary. Simultaneously, you are saying one thing in your mind and something else without. Thus, if you stop anything which is not real, the technique will not help. So find something authentic about yourself and try to stop that. Not everything has become false, many things are still real. Fortunately, everyone is real sometimes; in some moment everyone is real. Then stop it.

You are feeling angry, and you feel it is real. You are going to destroy something, beat your child, or do something: stop! But do not stop with a consideration. Do not say, "Anger is bad, so I should stop"—no! Do not say, "This is not going to help the child, so I should stop." No mental consideration is needed, because if you consider, then the energy has moved into consideration. This is an inner mechanism.

If you say, "I should not beat my child because it is not going to do any good to him, and this is not good for me also. This is useless and this never helps," the same energy which was going to become anger has become consideration. Now you have considered the whole thing, and the energy has subsided. It has moved into consideration, into thinking. Then you stop, but then there is no energy to move in. When you feel angry, do not consider it, do not think about it being good or bad; do not think at all. Suddenly remember the technique and stop!

Anger is pure energy...nothing bad, nothing good. It may become good, it may become bad—that will depend on the result, not on the energy. It can become bad if it goes out and destroys something, if it becomes destructive. It may become a beautiful ecstasy if it moves within and throws you to the center; it may become a flower. Energy is simply energy—pure, innocent, neutral. Do not consider it. You were going to do something—do not think, simply stop and then remain stopped. In that remaining you will have a glimpse of the inner center. You will forget the periphery and the center will come into your vision.

Just as you have the impulse to do something, stop! Try it. Remember three things…. One, try it only when a real impulse is there. Secondly, do not think about stopping, just stop. And thirdly, wait! When you have stopped, no breathing, no movement—wait and see what happens. Do not try. When I say to wait, I mean do not try now to think about the inner center. Then you will again miss. Do not think of the self, of the atma. Do not think that now the glimpse is there, now the glimpse is coming. Do not think, just wait. Let the impulse, the energy move by itself. If you start thinking about the Brahma and the atma and the center, the energy will have moved into this thinking.

You can waste this inner energy very simply. Just a thought will be enough to give it a direction; then you will go on thinking. When I say stop, it means stop totally, fully. Nothing is moving, as if the whole time has stopped. There is no movement—simply you are! In that simple existence, suddenly the center explodes.

---

26 Face any desire.

The second stop technique: *When some desire comes, consider it. Then, suddenly, quit it.*

This is a different dimension of the same technique. *When some desire comes, consider it. Then, suddenly, quit it.* You feel a desire—a desire for sex, a desire for love, a desire for food, anything. You feel a desire: consider it. When the sutra says consider it, it means do not think for or against it, just consider the desire, what it is.

A sexual desire comes to the mind. You say, "This is bad." This is not consideration. You have been taught that this is bad, so you are not considering this desire, you are consulting the scriptures, you are consulting the past—the past teachers, the *rishis*—sages. You are not considering the desire itself, you are considering something else. You are considering many things—your conditioning, your upbringing, your education, your culture, your civilization, your religion—but not the desire.

This simple desire has come. Do not bring in the mind, the past, the education, the conditioning; do not bring in values. Just consider this desire—what it is. If your mind could be washed completely of all that has been given to you by the society, of all that your parents have given to you—the education, the culture—if your total mind could be washed out, the desire for sex will arise. It will arise, because that desire is not given to you by the society. That desire is biologically built in; it is in you.

For example, if a child is born and no language is taught, the child will not learn any language. He will remain without language. A language is a social phenomenon; it has to be taught. But when the right moment comes, the child will feel sexual desire. That is not a social phenomenon, it is biologically built in. The desire will come at the right mature moment. It is not social, it is biological —deeper. It is built into your cells.

Because you were born out of sex, every cell of your body is a sex cell; you consist of sex cells. Unless your biology can be washed off completely, the desire will be there. It will come—it is already there. When a child is born the desire is already there, because the child is a by-product of a sexual meeting. He comes through sex; his whole body is built with sex cells. The desire is there, only a time is needed before his body becomes mature enough to feel that desire, to enact that desire. The desire will be there whether you are taught that sex is bad or good, whether you are not taught that sex is hell or heaven, whether you are taught this way or that way, for or against—because both are teachings.

The old traditions, the old religions, Christianity particularly, go on preaching against sex. The new cults of hippies and yippies and others have started the opposite movement. They say sex is good, sex is ecstatic, sex is the only real thing in the world.

Both are teachings. Do not consider your desire according to some teaching. Just consider the desire in its purity, as it is—a fact. Do not interpret it.

'Consideration' here means not interpreting, but just looking at the fact as it is. The desire is there: look at it directly, immediately. Do not bring in your thoughts or ideas, because no thought is yours and no idea is yours. Everything has been given to you, every idea is a borrowed thing. No thought is original—no thought can be original. Do not bring in thinking, just look at the desire, at what it is, as if you do not know anything about it. Face it! Encounter it! That is what is meant by *consider it*.

When some desire comes, consider it. Just look at the fact—at what it is. Unfortunately, it is one of the most difficult things to do. Compared to this, reaching to the moon is not so difficult or reaching to the peak of Everest is not so difficult. It is highly complicated—reaching to the moon is highly complicated, infinitely complicated, a very complex phenomenon. But compared to living with a fact of the inner mind it is nothing, because the mind is so subtly involved in everything you do. It is always there. Look at the word.... If I say "sex," the moment I say it you have decided for or against. The moment I say "sex," you have interpreted: "This is not good. This is bad." Or, "This is good." You have interpreted even the word.

Many persons came to me when the book *From Sex to Superconsciousness* was published. They came and they said, "Please change the title." The very word 'sex' makes them disturbed—they have not read the book. And those who have already read the book also say to change the title.

Why? The very word gives you a certain interpretation. Mind is so interpretive that if I say 'lemon juice,' your saliva starts flowing. You have interpreted the words. In the words 'lemon juice' there is nothing like lemon, but your saliva starts flowing. If I wait for a few moments, you will become uneasy because you will have to swallow. The mind has interpreted; it has come in. Even with words you cannot remain aloof, without interpreting. It will be very difficult, when a desire arises, to remain aloof, to remain just a dispassionate observer, calm and quiet, looking at the fact, not interpreting it.

I say, "This man is a Mohammedan." The moment I say, "This man is a Mohammedan," the Hindu has thought that this man is bad. If I say, "This man is a Jew," the Christian has decided that this man is not good. The very word 'Jew,' and in the Christian mind comes the interpretation; the traditional, conventional idea flares up. This Jew is not to be considered, the old interpretation will have to be imposed on this Jew.

Every Jew is a different Jew. Every Hindu is a different, unique individual. You cannot interpret him because you know other Hindus. You may have come to conclude that all the Hindus you have known are bad, but this Hindu is not in your experience. You are interpreting this Hindu according to your past experience. Do not interpret, interpretation is not consideration. Consideration means consider *this* fact—absolutely this fact. Remain with this fact.

Rishis have said that sex is bad. It may have been bad for them; you do not know. You have the desire, a fresh desire, with you. Consider it, look at it, be attentive to it. *Then, suddenly, quit it.*

There are two parts to this technique. First, remain with the fact—aware, attentive of what is happening. When you feel a sexual desire, what is happening in you? See how you become feverish, how your body begins to tremble, how you feel a sudden madness creeping in, how you feel as if you are possessed by something else. Feel it, consider it. Do not exercise any judgment, just move into this fact—the fact of sexual desire. Do not say it is bad!

If you have said that, the consideration has stopped, you have closed the door. Now your face is not toward the desire—your back is. You have moved away from it. You have missed a moment in which you could have gone deep down into your biological layer of being. You are clinging to the social layer, which is the uppermost.

Sex is deeper than your *shastras*—scriptures—because it is biological. If all the shastras can be destroyed—and they can be destroyed, many times they have been—your interpretation will be lost. But sex will remain; it is deeper. Do not bring superficial things in. Just consider the fact and move within, and feel what is happening to you. What happened to particular rishis, to Mohammed and Mahavira, is irrelevant. What is happening to you this very moment? This alive moment, what is happening to you?

Consider it, observe it. And then the second part...this is really beautiful. Shiva says, *Then, suddenly, quit it.*

Suddenly—remember. Do not say, "This is bad, so I am going to leave it. I am not going to move with this idea, this desire. This is bad, this is sin, so I will stop it, I will suppress it." Then a suppression will happen, but not a meditative state of mind. And suppression is really creating by your own hands a deceived being and mind.

Suppression is psychological. You are disturbing the whole mechanism and suppressing energies which are going to burst out any day. The energy is there, you have simply suppressed it. It has not moved out, it has not moved in, you have simply suppressed it. It has simply moved sideways. It will wait and it will become perverted, and perverted energy is the basic problem with man.

Psychological diseases are by-products of perverted energy. Then it will take such shapes, such forms, which are not even imaginable, and in those forms it will try again to be expressed. And when it is expressed in a perverted form, it leads you into a very, very deep anguish, because there is no satisfaction in any perverted form. And you cannot remain perverted, you have to express it. Suppression creates perversion. This sutra is not concerned with suppression. This sutra is not saying to control, this sutra is not saying to suppress. The sutra says, *Suddenly, quit it.*

What to do? The desire is there; you have considered. If you have considered it, it will not be difficult; the second part will be easy. If you have not considered it, look at your mind. Your mind will be thinking, "This is good. If we can quit sexual desire suddenly, this is beautiful." You would like to do it, but your liking is not the question. Your liking may not be your liking, but just the society's. Your liking may not be your own consideration, but just tradition. First consider, do not create any liking or disliking. Just consider, and then the second part becomes easy—you can quit the desire.

How to quit it? When you have considered a thing totally, it is very easy; it is as easy as dropping this paper from my hand. *Quit it....* What will happen? A desire is there. You have not suppressed it and it is moving out, it is coming up; it has stirred your whole being. Really, when you consider a desire without interpretation your whole being will become a desire.

When sex is there and if you are not against it or for it, if you have no mind about it, then just by looking at the desire your whole being will be involved in it. A single sex desire will become a flame. Your whole being will be concentrated in the flame, as if you have totally become sexual. It will not only be at the sex center, it will spread all over the body. Every fiber of your body will be trembling. The passion will have become a flame. Now, quit it. Don't fight with it, simply say, "I quit it."

What will happen? The moment you can simply say, "I quit," a separation happens. Your body—your passionate body, your body filled with sex desire—and *you* become two. Suddenly, in a moment, they are two poles apart. The body is writhing with passion and sex, and the center is silent, observing. No fight is there, just a separation—remember this. In fight you are not separate. When you are fighting you are one with the object. When you have just quit it, you are separate. Now you can look at it as if someone else is there, not you.

One of my friends was with me for many years. He was a constant chain smoker, and he tried and

tried, as smokers do, not to smoke. One day, suddenly in the morning, he would decide, "Now I am not going to smoke," and by the evening he would be smoking again. And he would feel guilty and he would defend it, and then for a few days he would not gather courage again to decide not to smoke. Then he would forget what happened. Then one day, again he would say, "Now I am not going to smoke," and I would just laugh because this had happened so many times. Then he himself became fed up with the whole thing—with this smoking and then deciding not to smoke, and this constant vicious circle.

He wondered what to do. He asked me what to do, so I told him, "Do not be against smoking—that is the first thing to do. Smoke, and be with it. For seven days do not be against it; do this thing."

He said, "What are you telling me? I have been against it and even then I could not leave it, and you are saying not to be against it. Then there is no possibility of leaving it."

So I told him, "You have tried with the inimical attitude and you have been a failure. Now try the other—the friendly attitude. Do not be against it for seven days."

Immediately he said, "Then will I be able to leave it?"

So I told him, "Then again...you are still inimical toward it. Do not think about leaving it at all. How can one think about leaving a friend? For seven days just forget it. Remain with it, cooperate with it, smoke as deeply as possible, as lovingly as possible. When you are smoking, just forget everything; become the smoking. Be totally at ease with it, in deep communion with it. For seven days, smoke as much as you like and forget about leaving it."

These seven days became a consideration. He could look at the fact of smoking. He was not against it, so now he could face it. When you are against something, or someone, you cannot face it. The very being against becomes a barrier. You cannot consider...How can you consider an enemy? You cannot look at him, you cannot look into his eyes; it is difficult to face him. You can look deeply only into the eyes of one you love; then you penetrate deep. Otherwise eyes can never meet.

So he looked into the fact deeply. For seven days he considered it. He was not against, so the energy was there, the mind was there, and it became a meditation. He had to cooperate with it; he had to become the smoker. After seven days he forgot to tell me. I was waiting for him to say, "Now the seven days have ended, so now how can I leave it?" He forgot completely about the seven days. Three weeks passed and then I asked him, "Have you forgotten completely?"

He said, "The experience has been so beautiful, I do not want to think about anything else now. It is beautiful, and for the first time I am not struggling with the fact. I am just feeling what is happening to me."

Then I told him, "Whenever you feel the urge to smoke, simply quit." He didn't ask me how to quit it, he had simply considered the whole thing and the whole thing became so childish, and there was no struggle. So I said, "When you feel again the urge to smoke, consider it, look at it, and leave it. Take the cigarette in your hand, stop for a moment, then leave the cigarette. Let it drop, and as the cigarette drops let the urge also drop inside."

He didn't ask me how to do it, because consideration makes one capable—you can do it. And if you cannot do it, remember, you have not considered the fact. Then you were against it, all the time thinking how to leave it. Then you cannot quit it. When suddenly the urge is there and you quit it, the whole energy takes a jump inward. The technique is the same, only the dimensions differ: *When some desire comes, consider it. Then, suddenly, quit it.*

---

27 Exhaust yourself and drop to the ground.

Third: *Roam about until exhausted and then, dropping to the ground, in this dropping be whole.*

The same! This stop technique is the same. *Roam about until exhausted.* Just run in a circle. Jump, dance, and run again until you are exhausted—until you feel that now not a single step more can be taken. But you will have to understand that your mind will say that now you are completely exhausted. Do not pay any attention to the mind. Go on running, dancing, jumping. Go on! Do not pay any attention. The mind will say that now you are exhausted, now you cannot go on anymore. Continue until you feel—not think, until you feel—that the whole body is tired, that "A single step more has become impossible, and if I move I will fall down."

When you feel that you are falling down and now you cannot move, that the body has become heavy and tired and completely exhausted, *then, dropping to the ground, in this dropping be whole.* Then drop! Remember, be so exhausted that dropping happens of itself. If you continue, you will drop. The point has come—you are just on the verge of dropping. Then, the sutra says, drop, and *in this dropping be whole.*

That is the central point in the technique: when you are dropping, be whole. What is meant? Do not drop just according to the mind—that is one thing. Do not plan it; do not try to sit, do not try to lie down. Drop as a whole, as if the whole body is one and it has dropped. And you are not dropping it, because if you are dropping it then you have two parts: you who is dropping it and the body which has been dropped. Then you are not whole. Then you are fragmentary, divided. Drop it as a whole; drop yourself totally. And remember, drop! Do not arrange it. Fall down dead. *In this dropping be whole.* If you can drop in this way, you will feel for the first time your whole being, your wholeness. You will feel for the first time your center—not divided, but one, unitary.

How can it happen? The body has three layers of energy. One is for day-to-day affairs, which is very easily exhausted. It is just for routine work. The second is for emergency affairs; it is a deeper layer. When you are in an emergency, only then is it used. And the third is the cosmic energy, which is infinite. The first can be easily exhausted. If I say to you to run, you will take three or four rounds and you will say, "I am feeling tired." Really, you are not feeling tired—the first layer is exhausted. In the morning it will not be so easily exhausted; in the evening it will be exhausted very easily because the whole day you have been using it. Now it needs repair; you will need a deep sleep. From the cosmic reservoir it can again get energy enough to work. This is the first layer.

If I tell you to run just now, you will say, "I am feeling sleepy, I cannot run." And then someone comes and says, "Your house is on fire." Suddenly the sleepiness has gone. There is no tiredness, you feel fresh; you start running. What has happened so suddenly? You were tired, and the emergency has made you connected with the second layer of energy, so you are fresh again. This is the second layer. In this technique, the second layer has to be exhausted. The first layer is exhausted very easily. Continue. You will feel tired, but continue. And within a few moments a new surge of energy will come, and you will feel again renewed and there will be no tiredness.

So many people come to me and they say, "When we are in a meditation camp, it seems miraculous that we can do this much. In the morning, for one hour meditating actively, chaotically, going completely mad. And then in the afternoon we do an hour, and then in the night also. Three times a day we can go on meditating chaotically." Many have said that they feel that this is impossible, that they cannot continue and they will be dead tired, and the next day it will be impossible to move any limb of the body. But no one gets tired. Three sessions every day, doing such exertions, and no one is tired. Why? Because they are in contact with the second layer of energy.

But if you are doing it alone—go to a hill and do it alone—you will become tired. When the first layer is finished you will feel, "Now I am tired." But in a big group of five hundred people doing meditation, you feel, "No one is tired, so I should continue a little more." And everyone is thinking the same: "No one is tired, so I should continue a little more. If everyone is fresh and doing, why should I feel tired?"

That group feeling gives you an impetus, and soon you reach the second layer. And the second layer is very big—an emergency layer. When the emergency layer is also tired, finished, only then are you in contact with the cosmic, the source, the infinite.

That is why much exertion is needed—so much that you feel, "Now it is going beyond me." The first moment you feel it is going beyond you, it is not going beyond you—it is just going beyond the first layer. And when the first layer is finished, you will feel tired. When the second layer is finished, you will feel, "If I do anything now, I will be dead." So many come to me, and they say that whenever they reach deep in meditation, a moment comes when they become afraid and scared and they say, "Now I am afraid. It seems as if I am going to die. Now I cannot penetrate any further. A fear grips me, as if I am going to die, now I will not be able to come out of meditation."

That is the right moment—the moment when you need courage. A little courage, and you will penetrate the third, the deepest, infinite layer.

This technique helps you very easily to fall into that cosmic ocean of energy: *Roam about until exhausted and then, dropping to the ground, in this dropping be whole.* And when you drop to the ground totally, for the first time you will be whole, unitary, one. There will be no fragments, no divisions. The mind with its divisions will disappear, and the being that is undivided, indivisible, will appear for the first time.

CHAPTER 18

Remaining with the facts

◆

Is permissiveness in expression a growth toward authenticity?

Why does one sometimes feel uneasy when stopping anger, sex, etcetera?

If there is unawareness during an authentic impulse, how to stop?

Isn't initiation and the grace of the master more important than techniques, and how to become capable of receiving?

The first question:

You said last night that modern man has become inauthentic in expressing anger, violence, sex, etcetera. You say that in India students and the younger generation are less violent in their emotional expressions than are Western youth. Does this mean that Western youth are becoming more authentic in their expressions? Is permissiveness in the expression of sex and anger a growth toward being authentic in emotional expressions?

any things have to be considered. One, to be authentic means to be totally factual. Ideologies, theories, isms, distort you and they give you a false persona. You cultivate faces, then whatsoever you show, you are not. The reality is missed and you are suddenly acting and acting. Your life becomes less alive and more a game in which you are enacting something —not your real soul, but the culture, the education, the society, the civilization. Man can be cultivated —and the more you are cultivated, the less real you are.

The reality is your uncultivated self, untouched by society. But that is dangerous. A child, if left to himself, will be just an animal. He will be authentic, but he will be an animal; he will not become a man. So that is not possible, that alternative is closed. We cannot leave a child to himself. We have to do something, and whatsoever we do will disturb the real self. It will give clothing, it will give faces and masks to the child. He will become a man, but then he will become an actor; he will not be real. If you leave him to himself he will be like an animal—authentic, real, but not a man. So it is a necessary evil that we have to teach him, we have to cultivate and condition him. Then he becomes a man, but unreal.

The third possibility opens with these techniques of meditation. All techniques of meditation are really unconditionings. Whatsoever society has given to you can be taken away again, and then you will not be an animal. Then you will be something more than man. You will be a superman— real, but not an animal.

How does it happen? A child has to be given culture, education. There is no possibility of leaving him to himself. If you leave him to himself, he will never become a man; he will remain an animal. He will be real, but he will miss the world, the dimension of consciousness which opens with man. So we have to make him a man, and he becomes unreal.

Why does he become unreal? Because this man is just imposed from without. Inside he remains the animal. From outside we impose humanity on him. He is divided; he is split in two. Now the animal goes on living within, and the man without. That is why whatsoever you do and say is a double bind. You have to maintain a face which has been given to you, and you continuously have to satisfy your animal also. That creates problems, and everyone becomes dishonest. The more you are idealistic, the

247

more you will have to be dishonest, because the ideal will say, "Do this," and the animal will be quite the contrary. He would like to do something else that is quite the opposite.

Then what can one do? One can deceive others and oneself; one can maintain a face, a false face, and go on living the life of the animal. That is what is happening. You live a life of sex, but you never talk about it. You talk about bramacharya, celibacy. Your sex life is just pushed into the dark—not only from society, not only from your family, but even from your own conscious mind. You push it into the dark as if it is not a part of your being. You go on doing things which you are against because your biology cannot change just by education.

Remember, your inheritance—your biological cells, your structure—cannot be changed just by ideological education. No school, no ideology can change your inner animal. Only a scientific technique can change the inner being. Just moral teachings will not help unless you have a scientific technique to change your total inner consciousness. Only then will you not be double, you will become single.

The animal is single, unitary; the saint, too, is single and unitary. Man is double because man is just between the two, the animal and the saint—or, you can say, between God and dog. Man is just in-between. Inside he remains the dog; outside he pretends to be God. That creates a tension, anguish, and everything becomes false. You could fall down and become an animal; then you would be more authentic than man. But then you would miss much—you would miss the possibility to become God.

The animal cannot become God because the animal has no problems to transcend. Remember, the animal cannot become God because there is nothing to be transformed. The animal is at ease with himself; there is no problem, no struggle, no need for transcendence. The animal is not even conscious, he is simply unconsciously authentic. But the animal *is* authentic, although the authentic-ity is unconscious. No animal can lie; that is impossible. But it is not because animals maintain a morality, they cannot lie because they are not aware of the possibility that one can be false.

They are bound to be true, but that truth is not their choice, it is their slavery. An animal is bound to be true, not because he has chosen to be true, but because he cannot choose the other alternative. There is no alternative for him; he can only be himself. There is no possibility to be false because he is unconscious of possibilities.

Man is conscious of possibilities. Only man can be untrue. That is a growth, that is evolution. Man can be untrue and that is why he can be true. Man can choose. Animals are bound to be true; that is their slavery, not their freedom. If you are true, that is an achievement because you could always be untrue. The possibility is open, but you have not chosen it, you have chosen the other. It is a conscious choice.

Of course, then man is always in difficulties. Choosing is always difficult, and the mind wants to choose something which is easy to do. The mind wants to have the thing with the least resistance. To lie is easy; to be false is easy. To appear loving is easy; to *be* loving is very difficult. To create a façade is easy; to create a being is difficult. So man chooses the simple, the easy, which can be done without any effort and without any sacrifice.

With man, freedom comes into existence. Animals are just slaves. With man, freedom comes into existence, choice comes into existence—then difficulties and anxieties. With man, the untrue, the false, enters. You can deceive. Up to this point it is a necessary evil.

Man cannot be simple and pure in the same way as animals, but he can be more simple and pure, and he can be more impure and more complex. He can be more simple and more pure and more innocent, but he cannot be simple and pure and innocent just like animals. That innocence is unconscious, and man has become conscious. Now he can do two things: he may go on with his falseness, and constantly remain a divided being in conflict with himself. Or he may become conscious of the whole phenomenon of what has happened and what is happening to him, and he may decide not to be false. He may leave all that is false. He may sacrifice, he may choose to sacrifice, whatsoever can be gained by being false. Then he becomes again authentic.

But this authenticity is different, qualitatively different from the authenticity of an animal. The animal is unconscious. He cannot do anything—he is forced by nature to be authentic. When a man decides to be authentic, no one is forcing him; on the contrary, everything is forcing him to be inauthentic—the society, the culture, all that exists around him is forcing him to be inauthentic. He *decides* to be authentic. This decision makes you a self, and this decision gives you a freedom which no animal can attain and no false man can attain.

Remember, whenever you lie, deceive, are dishonest, you are forced to do that. That is not your choice, not a real choice. Why do you lie? Because of the consequences, because of the society: you will suffer if you say the truth. You lie and you escape suffering.

Really, the society has forced you to lie; it was not your choice. If you say the truth, it is your choice, no one is forcing you to say the truth. Everything is forcing you to say a lie, to be dishonest. That is more convenient, safe, secure. Now you are entering danger, insecurity, but this is your choice. With this choice, for the first time you attain a self.

So animal authenticity is one thing, and man's authenticity is qualitatively different—it is a conscious choice. So a buddha is one again. He is like an animal, with only one difference: he is simple, pure, innocent like an animal, but unlike an animal because he is conscious. Now everything is a conscious choice. He is alert, aware.

The question is: *Does this mean that Western youth is becoming more authentic?* In a sense, yes. It is becoming more authentic because it is falling

toward the animal. It is not a choice. Rather, again, it is the easiest course—to fall down. Western youth is more authentic than Eastern youth in the sense that they are now falling deeper down toward the animal. Eastern youth is false. Their behavior looks like a façade—not real, but phony. But these two are not really the only alternatives.

Eastern youth is false, cultured, cultivated, forced to be something which is not real. Western youth has revolted against this, revolted toward the authenticity of the animal. That is why sex and violence have taken more and more of a grip on the Western youth. In a way they are more authentic, but in a way the greater possibility is lost.

A buddha is in revolt and a hippie is also in revolt, but the revolts are different; the quality differs. A buddha is also revolting against the conditioning, but he is going beyond it—toward a unity which is higher than man and higher than the animal. You can revolt and go down toward the animal. Then you are also going toward a unity, but that is going down, below man.

But in a way, revolt is good—because once revolt comes into the mind, the day is not far off when you will come to understand that this revolt is just going backwards. A revolt is needed which must go forward. So Western youth may come to understand sooner or later that their revolt is good, but the direction is wrong. Then it will become possible in the West for a new humanity to be born.

In this sense, the Eastern phoniness is not worth anything. It is better to be authentic, to be revolting, because a revolting mind will not take much time to see that the direction is wrong. But a phony youth may continue for millennia, may not be even aware that there is a possibility to revolt and to go beyond. But between the two, neither is worth choosing; the third alternative is the way.

Man must revolt against conditioning and go beyond. If you fall below, then you may have the pleasure of revolting, but the revolt has become destructive—it is not creative. Religion is the deepest revolt, but you may not have thought about it in that way. We take religion as the most orthodox thing—the traditional, the conventional. It is not. Religion is the most revolutionary thing in human consciousness, because it can lead you toward the unity which is higher than animal, higher than man. These techniques are concerned with that revolution.

So when Shiva says be authentic, he means do not be phony, do not continue to be phony. Be aware about your false persona, about your clothing, dresses, masks—and then be authentic. Whatsoever you are, realize it.

The real problem is that one becomes deceived by one's own deceptions. You talk about compassion.... In India we talk so much about compassion, nonviolence, everyone thinks that he is nonviolent, but if you look at a person's acts, at his relationships, at his gestures, he is violent. But he is not aware that he is violent. He may be violent even in his nonviolence. If he is trying to force others to be nonviolent, that is violence. If he is forcing himself to be nonviolent, that is violence. To be authentic means he must understand and realize what is his real state of mind—not ideas, not principles, but the state of mind. What is his state of mind? Is he violent? Is he angry?

This is what is meant by Shiva when he says be authentic. Know what is the real, your fact, because only a fact can be changed. If you want to transform yourself, you must know your facticity. You cannot change a fiction. You are violent and you think that you are nonviolent—then there is no possibility of any transformation. That nonviolence is nowhere, so you cannot change. And the violence is there, but you are not aware of it, so how can you change it?

First know the facts as they are. How to know the facts? Encounter them without your interpretations. That is what yesterday's sutra said: *consider.* Your servant has come—consider how you look at your servant. Your boss has come into the room—consider how you look at your boss. Is the look the same when you look at your servant as when you

look at your boss? Are your eyes the same, or is there any difference? If there is any difference, you are a violent man.

You do not look personally at the man, at the human being, your look is an interpretation. If he is rich you look in a certain way; if he is poor you look in a different way. Your look becomes economical. You are not looking at the man right before you, you are looking at some bank balance. And if the man is poor, your look has a subtle violence in it, a degrading, insulting look. If the man is rich you have a subtle appreciation, a welcome. A deep concern is there always, whatsoever you are doing.

Look at your concern. You are angry at your son or at your daughter, and you say you are angry for his or her sake, for his or her good. Go deep down; consider whether it is true. Your son has been disobedient and you are angry. You say you want to change him because it is for his own good. Look within and consider the fact. Is the fact that you are thinking about his good, or do you simply feel insulted because he has disobeyed you? You feel hurt because he has disobeyed you. Your ego is hurt because he has disobeyed you.

If your ego is hurt, this is the fact, and you go on pretending that that is not the thing—that you are just thinking about his good, and that is why you are angry. You are angry just for him; you are not really angry. How can you be angry? You are a loving father, so you are not angry at all. How can you be angry? You love him so much, but because he is going on a wrong path, because of your love, you want to change him, and that is why you are angry. You are just pretending to be angry to help him.

But is this the fact? Are you just pretending, or do you feel hurt because he has disobeyed you? And are you so sure that whatsoever you say is right for him? Go deep down within yourself, look at the fact, consider it—and be authentic. If you are really offended by his disobedience, then know it well that you are offended and you feel hurt, and that is why you are angry. This is being authentic.

Then you can do much for a change in you because facts can be changed; fictions cannot be changed. With everything that you are doing or you are thinking, go deep down. Dig out the facts, and do not allow interpretations and words to color it.

If this consideration is there, by and by you will become authentic. And this authenticity will not be like that of an animal. This authenticity will be like that of a saint, because the more you know how ugly you are, the more you know how violent you are, the more you penetrate inside your facts and become aware of the nonsense that you are doing, the more this awareness will help you. And by and by your ugliness will drop away, will wither away, because if you are aware of your ugliness it cannot continue.

If you want it to continue, do not be aware of it and create a façade of beauty around it. Then you will see the beauty, and the ugliness will remain behind, never to be seen directly. Everyone else will see it—that is the problem. The son will see that the father is not angry for his good. He will see that the father is angry because he has been disobeyed and he feels hurt; the son will know it. You cannot hide your ugliness from others. You can hide it only from yourself. Your look will reveal to everyone that there is violence. You can only deceive yourself that there was compassion.

That is why everyone thinks of himself as a very superior being, and no one else agrees with him. Your wife doesn't agree with you that you are a superior being. Your children are not in agreement with you that you are a superior being. Your friends do not agree, no one agrees with you that you are a superior being.

They have a popular saying in Russia that if everyone says their mind totally, exactly as it is, there will not be four friends in the whole world. Impossible! Whatsoever your friend thinks about you, he never says to you. That is why friendship continues. But he is always saying things behind you, and you are saying what you think about your friend behind him. No one says honestly what he thinks because then there will be no possibility of any friendship. Why? No one agrees with you, and the reason is only this: you can only deceive yourself, you cannot deceive anyone else. Only self-deception is possible.

And when you think you are deceiving others you are simply deceiving yourself. It may be that others pretend to you that they have been deceived by you, because there are moments when it is convenient to play the role of being deceived. It may be beneficial for the person. You talk to someone about your greatness.... Everyone is talking directly or indirectly about his greatness, his superiority. Someone may agree with you. If it is beneficial to him, he will pretend to you that he is being deceived by you, but he knows inside who you are.

You cannot deceive anyone unless someone is ready to be deceived; that is another thing. By authenticity I mean: remember your facticity. Always sort it out from your interpretations. Throw away your interpretations and look at the fact of what you are. And do not be afraid—much ugliness is there. If you are afraid, then you will never be able to change it. If it is there, accept that it is there; consider it.

This is what consideration means: consider it, look at it in its total nakedness. Move around it, go to its roots, analyze it. See why it is there, how you help it to be there, how you feed it, how you protect it, how it has grown to be such a big tree. See your ugliness, your violence, your hatred, your anger, how you have protected it, how you have helped it to grow up to now. Look at the roots; look at the whole phenomenon.

And Shiva says that if you consider it totally you can drop it immediately, this very moment, because it is you who have been protecting it. It is you who have been helping it to become rooted in you. It is your creation. You can drop it immediately—just now. You can leave it, and then there is no need to look again toward it. But before you can do this, you will have to know it—what it is, the whole mechanism, the whole complexity of it, how you help it every moment.

If someone says something insulting to you, how do you react? Have you ever thought about it —that he may be right? Then look! He may be right. There is every possibility of him being more right than you are about yourself, because he is aloof, far away; he can observe.

So do not react. Wait! Tell him, "I will consider what you have said. You have insulted me, and I will consider the fact. You may be right. If you are right, then I will give you my thanks. Let me consider it. And if I find that you are wrong I will inform you." But do not react. Reaction is different.

If you insult me, I say to you, instead of reacting, "Wait. Come back after seven days. I will consider whatsoever you have said—you may be right. I will put myself in your place and will observe myself; I will create a distance. You may be right, so let me look at the fact. It is very kind of you to have pointed it out, so I will look at it. If I feel that you are right, I will thank you; if I feel that you are wrong, I will inform you that you are wrong." But what is the need of reaction?

You insult me—then what do I do? I insult you immediately then and there. I escape consideration, I have reacted. You insulted me, so I have insulted you.

And remember, reaction can never be right. It can *never* be right! If you insult me, you create the possibility of my being angry. And when I am angry, I am not conscious. I will say something which I have never thought about you. This very moment, because of your insults, I react in a violent way. A moment later I may repent.

Do not react—consider the facts. And if your consideration is total, you can drop anything. It is in your hands. Because you are clinging to it, it is there. But you can drop it immediately, and there will be no suppression—remember. When you have considered a fact, there will never be any suppression. Either you like it and you continue it, or you do not like it and you drop it.

The second question:

According to last night's technique, when anger, violence, sex, etcetera, arises, one should consider it and then suddenly quit it. But when one does it, one sometimes feels sick and uneasy. What are the reasons for these negative feelings?

Only one reason: your consideration is not total. Everyone wants to quit anger without understanding it; everyone wants to quit sex without understanding it. And there is no revolution without understanding. You will create more problems and you will create more misery for yourself. Do not think of renouncing anything, just think of how to understand it; understanding, not renunciation. There is no need of thinking to quit anything. The only need is to understand it in its totality. If you have understood it in its totality, the transformation will follow. If it is good for you, if it is good for your being, it will grow. If it is bad for you, it will drop. So the real thing is not quitting, it is understanding.

Why do you think about renouncing anger? Why? Because you have been taught that anger is bad. But have *you* understood it as bad? Have *you* come to a personal conclusion, through your own deepening insight, that anger is bad? If you have come to this conclusion through your own inner search, there will be no need to quit it—it will have already disappeared. The very fact of knowing that this is poisonous is enough. Then you are a different man.

But you go on thinking of leaving, quitting, renouncing. Why? Because people say that anger is bad, and you are simply influenced by whatsoever they say. Then you go on thinking that anger is bad, and when the moment comes you go on being angry.

This is how a double mind is created. You remain with anger, and yet you always think anger is bad. This is inauthenticity. If you think that anger is good, then do it and do not say that anger is bad. Or if you say anger is bad, then try to understand whether this is your realization or whether someone else has said it to you.

Everyone is creating misery around himself because of others. Someone says this is bad and someone says that it is good, and they go on forcing these ideas in your mind. The parents are doing this, the society is doing this, and then one day you are just following others' ideas. And the difference between your nature and others' ideas causes a split; you become schizophrenic. You will do something and you will believe in the very contrary. That will create guilt. Everyone feels guilty. Not that everyone *is* guilty, everyone feels guilty because of this mechanism.

They say anger is bad. Everyone has said to you that anger is bad, but no one has told you how to know what anger is. Everyone says sex is bad. They have been teaching, teaching, that sex is bad, and no one says what sex is and how to know it. Ask your father, and he will become uneasy. He will say, "Do not talk about such bad things!" But these bad things are facts. Even your father could not escape it; otherwise you would not have been born. You are a naked fact. And no matter what your father says about sex, he couldn't escape it. But he will feel uneasy if you ask him because no one has told him; his parents never told him why sex is bad.

Why? And how to know it? And how to go deep into it? No one will tell this to you, they will just go on labeling things: this is bad and that is good. That labeling creates misery and hell.

So one thing to remember—for any seeker, a real seeker, this is a basic thing to be understood: remain with your facts, try to know them. Do not allow the society to force its ideology on you. Do not look at yourself through others' eyes. You have eyes; you are not blind. And you have the facts of your inner life. Use your eyes! That is what consideration means. And if *you* consider, then this will not be a problem.

But when one does it, one sometimes feels sick and uneasy. You will feel this if you have not understood the facts; you will feel uneasy, because it is subtle repression. You know already that anger is bad. If I say to consider it, you consider it only so that it can be renounced. That renouncing is there, always present in your mind.

Someone was here, a very old man, sixty years of age. He is a very religious man—and not only a religious man, but a type of religious leader. He has been teaching many people and he has written many books. He is a moralizer, and now, at the age of sixty, he comes to me and he says, "You are the only person to whom I can tell my real problems. How can I get rid of sex?"

And I have heard him speak about the misery of sex. He has written books, and he has tortured his sons and daughters. If you want to torture someone, morality is the best trick—the easiest. Immediately you create guilt in the other person. That is the subtlest torture. Talk about brahmacharya and you will create guilt, because it is so difficult to be a brahmachari, to be a pure celibate. It is so difficult, and when you talk about brahmacharya and the other cannot be, he feels guilty.

You have created guilt; now you can torture. You have made the other man degraded, inferior. Now he will never be at ease. He will have to live in sex and he will feel guilty. He will always think about brahmacharya, and he won't know what to do. His mind will think of brahmacharya, and his body will live with sex. Then he will go against his body. Then he will think, "I am not my body. This body is an evil thing." And once you create guilt in someone, you have destroyed a mind, poisoned it.

The old man came and asked how to get rid of sex, so I told him first to be aware of the fact—and he had missed much opportunity. Now the sex will be weak, and the awareness will need more effort. When sex is violent and the energy is there and sex is young, you can be aware of it very easily. It is so forceful, it is not difficult to see and know and feel it. This man, at the age of sixty, now feeble, weak, ill, will have difficulty in being aware of sex.

When he was young he was thinking about brahmacharya. He couldn't have lived that; he has five children. Then he was thinking about brahmacharya and missing the opportunity. And now he is thinking of what to do about sex. So I told him to be aware of it—to forget his teachings and burn his books, and not to say anything about sex to anyone without knowing it himself. I told him to be aware of it.

So he said, "If I try to be aware, in how many days will I get rid of it?" This is how the mind works. He is ready even to be aware, but just to get rid of it.

So I told him, "If you are not aware of it, who is deciding to get rid of it? How do you conclude that sex is bad? Is this taken for granted? Is there no need to discover it within yourself?"

Do not think of renouncing anything. Renunciation means you are just being forced by others. Be individual. Do not allow society too much domination over you, do not be a slave. You have eyes, you have consciousness, you can see your sex, anger and other desires. Use your consciousness, use your eyes. Be aware.

Think of yourself as if you are alone. No one is there to teach you. What will you do? Start from the very beginning, from ABC, and go inside. Be totally aware. Do not decide, do not be in haste, do not conclude so soon. If you can reach a conclusion through your own awareness, that very conclusion will become a transformation. Then you will not feel any unease, there will be no repression. Only then can you quit anything. I am not saying, be aware to quit. Remember, I am saying: if you are aware, you can quit anything.

Do not make awareness a technique to quit. Quitting is just a consequence. If you are aware you can quit anything, but you may not decide to quit; there is no necessity. You may never decide to quit. Sex is there—if you become fully aware of it, you may not decide to quit it. If with full awareness you decide not to quit it, then sex has its own beauty. If

with full awareness you decide to quit it, then your renunciation is also beautiful.

Try to understand me. Whatsoever comes, whatsoever happens through awareness is beautiful, and whatsoever happens without awareness is ugly. That is why your so-called brahmacharis, celibate monks, are basically ugly. Their whole way of life is ugly. That celibacy has not come as a consequence, it is not their own search.

Now look at a person like D.H. Lawrence. His sex is beautiful, more beautiful than the renunciation of your celibate monks, because his sex is with full awareness. Through inner search he has come to conclude that he is going to live with sex. He has accepted the fact; now there is no hitch, no guilt. Rather, sex has become glorious. So a D.H. Lawrence, fully aware of his sex, accepting it, living it, has a beauty of his own.

A Mahavira, fully aware of the fact and then coming to leave it, to quit it, has a beauty of his own. They both are beautiful—D.H. Lawrence and Mahavira. They *both* are beautiful! But the beauty is not of sex and not of quitting sex, the beauty is of awareness.

This must also be constantly remembered—that you may not come to the same conclusion as Buddha; there is no necessity. You may not come to the same conclusion as Mahavira; there is no inevitability. If there is any inevitability, there is only one, and that is of awareness. When you are fully aware, whatsoever happens to you is beautiful, is divine.

Look at the sages of the past: Shiva sitting with Parvati. Parvati is sitting in his lap in a deep love gesture. You cannot conceive of Mahavira in such a pose—impossible! You cannot conceive of Buddha in such a pose. Just because Rama is pictured with Sita, Jains cannot accept him as an *avatara,* as a divine incarnation, because he is still with women. It is impossible for Jains to conceive of him as an incarnation of God, so they say he is a great man— a *mahamanava,* but not an avatara. He is a great man, but still a man because the woman is there.

When the woman is there, you cannot go beyond man; the counterpart is there, so you are still a man. Of course, Rama was a great man, but not beyond man, Jains say.

If you ask Hindus, they have not talked about Mahavira at all—not even talked about him, not even mentioned him in their books—because for the Hindu mind, man alone without a woman is half, a fragment, not the whole. Rama alone is not the whole, so Hindus say "Sitaram." They put the woman first. They will never say "Ramsita," they will say "Sitaram." They will say "Radhakrishna." They will put woman first for a basic reason—because man is born out of woman and man alone is half. With woman he becomes whole.

So no Hindu god is alone. The other part, the other half, is there. Sitaram is really the whole; Radhakrishna is the whole. Krishna alone is half. There is no need for Rama to quit Sita and there is no need for Krishna to quit Radha. Why? They are fully aware.

You cannot find a more aware man, a more conscious man than Shiva, but he is sitting with Parvati in his lap. It creates problems. Then who is right? Is a Buddha right or is a Shiva right? Problems are created because we do not know that everyone flowers individually. Buddha and Shiva both are fully conscious, but it happens to Buddha that he leaves something in this full consciousness—that is his choice. It happens to Shiva in his full consciousness that he accepts everything. They are both at the same point of realization, of awareness, but their expression is different.

So do not fall into any pattern. No one knows what will happen when you become aware. Do not decide before becoming aware that you are going to quit this and that. Do not decide—no one knows. Wait! Be aware, and let your being flower. No one knows what will happen. With everyone there is an unknown possibility of flowering. And you need not follow anyone—because every following is dangerous, destructive; every imitation is suicide. Wait!

These techniques are only to make you aware. And when you are aware, you can quit anything or you can accept anything. When you are not aware, remember what is happening: neither can you accept, nor can you quit. You have sex—neither can you accept it totally and forget about it, nor can you quit it. I say either accept it and forget, or quit it and forget.

But you cannot do either of the two; you will always be doing both. You will accept and then you will think of quitting, and this is a vicious circle. When you have had sex, then for a few hours or a few days you will think of quitting it. Really, you are doing nothing else but regaining energy. When you have regained energy, you will again think of having it. And this will go on for your whole life. It has been so for so many lives. When you become fully aware, you can decide. Either you accept it—then that acceptance gives a beauty—or you quit it—then that quitting is also beautiful.

One thing is certain: when you are aware you can forget it—either way. It is not a problem then. Your decision is total and the problem drops. But if you feel any uneasiness, it means you have not considered, you have not been aware.

So be more aware. Consider the fact more—more deeply, more individually, without the conclusions of others.

The third question:

When an impulse is authentic, I am unaware. How can I exercise "Stop"?

This is a very significant question. It is easy to stop anything when you are false, and it is difficult to stop anything when you are authentic. When the anger is real, you will forget about the technique of "Stop!" When the anger is false you will remember, you can do it. But when the anger is false there is no meaning, there is no energy. You can stop it, but it is useless. When the anger is real, only then is the energy there, and if you stop it the energy will take an inner turn.

So what to do? Try to be aware not of anger directly, but of easier things. You are walking—be aware of it. Do not start with anger, start with easier things. You are walking—be aware of it, there is no problem. Then suddenly stop your walk. Start with easy things, and then go on to a deeper, more complex thing. Do not start with complex things, do not jump to sex immediately. It is more subtle, and you will need a deeper awareness for it.

So first create awareness with easier things. You are walking, you are taking a bath, you feel thirsty, you feel hungry—start with these things, all very ordinary things. You were just going to speak something to someone: Stop! even in the middle of a sentence. You were going to relate a story you have related a thousand times, and you have bored everyone with it. You were again starting, "Once there was a king...." Stop! Start with easy things, more easy things.

There is a fly on your head and you were just going to send it away with your hand: Stop! Let the fly be there, let your hand remain stopped. Do it with easy things so that you have the feeling, the feel of stopping with awareness. Then move to complex things.

Anger is a very complex thing; take a mechanical thing. Every day in the morning you step out of your bed. Have you observed? You step out every day in the same way. If your right foot comes first, it comes first always. Tomorrow morning when the right foot is coming out, stop and let the left foot come.

Do it with easier things; then there is nothing to sacrifice but a habit. Always you start walking with the right foot first: Stop! Anything...anything can be used. Find something—the easier, the better. And when you become a master of easier things and you can stop suddenly, and you can have the feel of awareness, a sudden calmness comes to you. For a second, an inner silence explodes.

Gurdjieff used to train his disciples in very easy things. For example, you say something and you nod your head. Then he would say to you, "Say the same thing, but do not nod your head." It is a mechanical habit. I am saying something; I make a gesture with my hand. Gurdjieff would say, "Do not make this gesture when you say this thing—remember this. Make any other gesture, but remember only this: when you are saying this, do not make this gesture. Be aware of it."

Use anything—anything! You always start your conversation with a particular sentence—do not start with it. Someone says something and you have a mechanical response—do not respond that way, say something else. Or if you have started saying the old thing, stop in the middle. Stop with a jerk, suddenly. Try this, and only when you feel a mastery, move to complex things.

This is one of the basic tricks of the mind, that it will always tell you to jump to a complex thing. Then you are a failure, then you will never try again; you know that it cannot be done. This is a trick of the mind. The mind will say, "Okay, now you know that the exercise of stopping will be a failure when you are angry, hot and angry." Then you will not try again.

Try with cold things; do not move to the hot. And when you can do it with cold things, then move to the hot. With gradual steps feel the path, and do not be hasty; otherwise nothing will be accomplished.

The last question:

After hearing about so many meditation techniques in *Vigyan Bhairav Tantra*, I am beginning to feel that the inner door cannot really open by techniques, but that it really depends on things like initiation, the grace of the master, etcetera. Is that not really the case? And when and how can one become capable of receiving initiation?

Really, the grace of the master is again a technique. Just by changing the words, nothing changes. It means surrender. You can receive the grace of the master only when you surrender, and surrender is a technique. If you do not know how to surrender, you will not receive any grace. So really, grace is not given, it is received. No one can give grace—you can receive it. With an enlightened person the grace is flowing always. It is there; it is just his nature.

Just as a lamp is burning and the light is radiating, the enlightened person is always radiating grace. It is not any effort. It is flowing effortlessly, it is there. If you can receive, you can receive. If you cannot receive, you cannot receive.

So it may look paradoxical if I say this, but it is the truth: the grace is not given by the master, it is received by the disciple. But how to be a disciple? Again, it is a technique. How to surrender? How to become receptive? Surrendering is the most difficult of things. You cannot surrender your anger, you cannot surrender your sadness, so how can you surrender your total being? You cannot surrender nonsensical things, you cannot surrender your diseases, so how can you surrender yourself?

Surrendering means surrendering totally. You leave everything totally to your teacher, to your master. You say, "Now I am no more. Now you are —do whatsoever you like." And when you wait, and when you do not again go and ask him when he is going to do this or that, you have surrendered, you are finished. There is nothing to be asked anymore. In the right moment the thing will happen. But how to do it?

This also will need a very great awareness. Ordinarily, stupid people think that surrender is very easy. That is stupidity. They think that if you go and touch the feet of a master you have surrendered. Just touching the feet can be a surrender, but do not think that because you have touched the feet you have surrendered. Surrendering is an inner attitude. It is putting yourself off, forgetting yourself completely. Only the master remains; you are no more. Only the master is.

This can be done only with a very deep awareness. What is that awareness? That awareness will come if you go on doing these techniques and you feel continuously that you are helpless. But do not decide on your helplessness before doing them—it will be false. First do them, and do them authentically. If the techniques happen to help you, there will be no need of surrender; you will be transformed. If you do them authentically, really, fully, if you are not deceiving yourself and still nothing happens, then you will feel a helplessness. You will feel, "I cannot do anything." If this goes deep in you, this feeling of helplessness, only then will you be capable of surrendering—not before.

Do you feel helpless? No one feels helpless. *No one* feels helpless! Everyone knows, "I can do. If I want, I can do. It is because I do not want to that I am not doing." Everyone thinks that if they wish, if they will, they will do. They think, "The moment I will it, I will do it. The only reason I am not doing it is because I am not willing it just now."

But no one feels helpless. If someone says that through the grace of the master it can happen, you think you are ready just this very moment. If it is a question of doing something, you say you can do it whenever you want, but if it is a question of grace you say, "Okay! If it can be received from someone, I can receive it this very moment."

You are not helpless, you are just lazy, and there is a great difference. In laziness no grace can be received—only in helplessness. And helplessness is not part of laziness. Helplessness comes only to those who first make every effort to reach, to penetrate, to do. When you have done everything and nothing happens, you feel helpless. Only then can you surrender to someone. Then your surrendering will become a technique.

That is the last of techniques, but people try it first. That is the last, the ultimate. When nothing happens by doing, if there is only helplessness and helplessness and helplessness, if you lose all hope and your ego is shattered, then you know that nothing can be done alone. Then your hand reaches to the feet of a master. It is a different type of reach: you are helplessly searching for him, your whole being moves to his feet. You become just a womb to receive.

Then the grace is available. It has never been unavailable; it is always available. In every age, in every period, there are enlightened persons. But unless you are ready to lose yourself, you will not be in contact with him. You may be just sitting behind him or just sitting by the side of him, but there will be no contact.

There are three types of distances. One distance is of space. You are sitting there, I am sitting here, and there is space between the two points. This is a distance in space. You can come near and the distance will be less. You can just touch me and the distance is lost—but only in space.

There is a second type of distance—in time. Your beloved has died, your friend has died. In space, one point has disappeared completely, there is infinite distance. But in time, you will feel your friend just nearby. You close your eyes, and the friend is there. In time it may be that the person who is sitting by your side is more distant than your beloved who is no more in the world. The beloved is dead—then by and by, there will be a greater distance of time. People say time heals. When that time is very, very, very distant, the memory becomes more and more faint, and it disappears.

A third distance exists, a third dimension, which is love. If you are in love with someone, then he may be on another star, but in your love he is just near you. He may have died, there may be centuries of distance between you and him, but in love there is no distance.

Someone can be near Buddha just now. Twenty-five centuries means nothing because the distance is of love. In space there is no Buddha now; the body has disappeared. In time there is a distance of twenty-five centuries, but in love there is no distance. If someone is in love with Buddha, time and space distances disappear. He is just here, and you can receive his grace.

You may be just sitting by the side of a Buddha. There is no gap as far as space is concerned; there is

no distance as far as time is concerned. But if there is no love, then there is infinite distance. So someone may have lived with Buddha without being in contact, and someone may be just here now who is in contact with Buddha.

Grace happens in the dimension of love. For love everything is always eternally present. So if you are in love, grace can happen. But love is surrendering; love means now the other has become more important than yourself. Now for the other's life, you are ready to die. For the other to live, you will sacrifice yourself. The other has become the center; you are just the periphery. By and by you disappear completely, and the other remains. In that right moment, grace is received.

So do not think of a master as one who can give you grace. Think of becoming a helpless disciple—totally surrendered, in love. The master will come to you. When the disciple is ready, the master always comes. It is not a question of physical presence; when you are ready, from an unknown dimension of love, grace happens. But do not think about grace as an escape.

Because I am talking about so many techniques, I know there are two possibilities: you may try some, or you may just become confused, and the latter is more possible. With one hundred and twelve techniques, listening to one and then another and then another continually, you will become confused. You will think it is beyond you—so many techniques, so what to do and what not to do?

It may come to your mind that it is better to receive grace, *gurukripa*, than to go into this jungle-like world of techniques—this is very complex, so it is easier to receive grace. But that will not happen to you if this is your way of thinking. Try these techniques, and try honestly. If you are a failure, then that very failure will become your surrender. That is the ultimate technique.

Okay?

CHAPTER 19

A technique for the intellectual and a technique for the feeling type

◆

28 *Suppose you are gradually being deprived of strength or of knowledge. At the instant of deprivation, transcend.*

29 *Devotion frees.*

For tantra, man himself is the disease. It is not that your mind is disturbed—rather, your mind is the disturbance. It is not that you are tense within, but rather, you are the tension. Understand the distinction clearly. If the mind is ill then the illness can be treated, but if the mind itself is the illness, then this illness cannot be treated. It can be transcended, but it cannot be treated. That makes the basic difference between Western psychology and Eastern tantric and yogic psychology; that is the difference between Eastern tantra and yoga, and Western psychology.

Western psychology thinks that the mind can be healthy, the mind as it is can be treated and helped —because for Western thinking there is no transcendence, as there is nothing beyond mind. Transcendence is possible only if there is something beyond, so that you can live in your present state and move further. But if there is no beyond and the mind is the end, then transcendence is impossible.

If you think you are just a body, then you cannot transcend your body—because who will transcend and to where will you transcend? If you are simply the body, then you cannot go beyond the body. If you can go beyond the body, that means you are not simply the body, but something plus. That "plus" becomes the dimension to move into.

Similarly, if you are just the mind and nothing else, then no transcendence is possible. Then we can treat individual diseases.... Someone is men-tally ill—we can treat the illness. We will not touch the mind, but we will treat the illness and make the mind normal. And no one will think about whether the normal mind itself is healthy or not.

The normal mind is just a skeptical mind. Freud says that as everyone is, we can only bring a diseased mind to normality. But whether everyone is healthy or not, that question cannot be raised. We take it for granted that the average mind is okay. So whenever someone goes beyond that average mind, moves somewhere else, he has to be brought back and readjusted. Thus, the whole of Western psychology has been an effort toward readjustment—readjustment to the ordinary mind, the average mind.

In this sense, there are thinkers, particularly one very intelligent thinker, Geoffrey, who says that genius is a disease because genius is abnormal. If normality is health, then genius is disease. A genius is not normal; he is in a certain way mad. His madness may be useful, so we allow him to live.

An Einstein or a Van Gogh or an Ezra Pound— poets, painters, scientists, mystics—they are mad, but their madness is allowed for two reasons: either their madness is harmless or their madness is utilitarian. Through their madness they contribute something which normal minds cannot contribute. Because they are mad they have moved to one extreme, and they can see certain things that the normal mind cannot see. So we can allow these madmen—and we even make them Nobel laureates. But they are ill.

If normality is the criterion and the standard of

health, then everyone who is not normal is ill. Geoffrey says that a day will come when we will treat scientists and poets in the same way we treat madmen: we will make them readjust to the average mind. This attitude is because of a particular hypothesis that mind is the end and there is no beyond.

Just opposite to this attitude is the Eastern approach. We say here that mind itself is the disease. So whether normal or abnormal, we will make only the distinction of "normally ill" and "abnormally ill." A normal man is normally ill. He is not so much ill that you can detect it, he is just average. Because everyone else is like him, his illness cannot be detected. Even the person, the psychoanalyst who treats him, is himself a normally ill person. Mind itself is the disease for us.

Why? Why call mind itself the disease? We will have to approach it from a different dimension, then it will be easy. For us, the body is death; for the Eastern approach, the body is death. So you cannot create a perfectly healthy body; otherwise it will not die. You can create a certain balance, but the body as such, because it is going to die, is prone to be ill. So health can only be a relative thing. The body cannot be perfectly healthy—it cannot be.

That is why medical science has no standard and no definition of what health is. They can define diseases, they can define a particular disease, but they cannot define what health is. Or at the most they can only define negatively that when a person is not ill, not particularly ill, he is healthy. But to define health in a negative way looks absurd, because then disease becomes the primary thing by which you define health. But health cannot be defined, because really, the body can never be really healthy. Every moment the body is only in a relative balance, because death is progressing with life; you are dying also. You are not simply alive, you are dying simultaneously.

Death and life are not two ends far away from each other. They are like two legs simultaneously walking—and they both belong to you. This very moment you are alive and dying, both. Something is dying within you every moment. Within a span of seventy years, death will reach the goal. Every moment you will go on dying and dying and dying, and then you will die.

The day you were born you started dying. The birthday is also the death-day. If you are dying continuously—and death is not something which will come from without, but something which will grow within—then the body can never be really healthy. How can it be? When it is dying every moment, how can it be really healthy? It can only be relatively healthy. So if you are normally healthy, it is enough.

It is the same with the mind. The mind cannot be really healthy, whole, because the very existence of the mind is such that it is bound to remain diseased, ill at ease, tense, anxious, in anxiety. The very nature of the mind is such, so we will have to understand what is this nature.

Three things.... One, mind is a link between the body and the no-body which is within you. It is a link between the material and the nonmaterial within you. It is one of the most mysterious bridges. It bridges two quite contradictory things—matter and spirit.

If you can, conceive the paradox. Usually you make a bridge over a river where both the banks are material. In this case, mind is the bridge between one bank which is material and the other which is nonmaterial...between the visible and the invisible, between the dying and the nondying, between life and death, between body and spirit—or whatsoever you name these two banks. Because mind bridges such contradictory things, it is bound to remain tense; it cannot be at ease.

It is always moving from the visible to the invisible, from the invisible to the visible. Every moment the mind is in deep tension. It has to bridge two things which cannot be bridged. That is the tension, that is the anxiety. You are every moment in anxiety.

I am not talking about your financial anxiety or other such anxieties—they are boundary anxieties, frame anxieties. The real anxiety is not that, the real anxiety is that of the buddha. You are also in that anxiety, but you are so much burdened by your day-to-day anxieties, you cannot discover your basic anxiety. Once you find your basic anxiety, you will become religious.

Religion is a concern for the basic anxiety. Buddha became anxious in a different way. He was not worried about finance, he was not worried about a beautiful wife, he was not worried about anything. There was no worry; ordinary worries were not there. He was secure, safe, the son of a great king, the husband of a very beautiful wife, and everything was available. The moment he desired anything he would get it. All that was possible was possible for him.

But suddenly he became anxiety-ridden—and that anxiety was a basic anxiety, a primary anxiety. He saw a dead man being carried away, and he asked his chariot driver what had happened to this man.

The driver said, "This man is dead now. He has died."

This was Buddha's first encounter with death, so he asked immediately, "Is everyone prone to death? Am I also going to die?"

Look at the question. You may not have asked it. You may have asked who has died, why he has died, or you might have said that he looks too young and this is not the age to die. Those anxieties are not basic; they are not concerned with you. You may have felt sympathetic, you may have felt sad, but still that is just on the circumference—and you will have forgotten within a few moments.

Buddha turned the whole question toward himself and he asked, "Am I going to die?"

The chariot driver said, "I cannot lie to you. Everyone is prone to death, everyone is going to die."

Buddha said, "Then turn back the chariot. If I am going to die, then what is the use of life? You have created a deep anxiety in me. Unless this anxiety is resolved, I cannot be at ease."

What is this anxiety? It is a basic anxiety. So if you become aware of the very basic situation of life —of body, of mind—a subtle anxiety will creep in, and then that anxiety will continue to tremble within you. Whatsoever you are doing or not doing, the anxiety will be there—a deep anguish. The mind is bridging an abyss, an impossible abyss. The body is going to die, and you have something —X—within you which is deathless.

These are two contradictions. It is as if you are standing in two boats which are moving in opposite directions. Then you will be in a deep conflict. That conflict is the conflict of the mind. The mind is between two opposites—that is one thing.

Secondly, mind is a process, not a thing. The word 'mind' is a false notion. When we say "mind," it appears as if there is something like a mind within you. There is nothing! Mind is not a thing, mind is a process. So it is better to call it "minding," not mind. We have a word in Sanskrit, *chitta*, which means minding. Not mind, but minding—a process.

A process can never be silent. A process will always be tense; a process means a turmoil. And mind is always moving from the past to the future. The past goes on being a burden on it, so it has to move into the future. This constant movement creates another tension within you. If you become too much conscious about it, you may go mad.

So that is why we are always engaged in something or other; we do not want to be unoccupied. If you are unoccupied, then you will become conscious of the inner process, of the minding, and that will give you very strange and peculiar tensions. So everyone wants to be occupied in some way or other. If there is nothing else to do, one goes on reading the same newspaper again and again. Why? Can you not sit silently? It is difficult, because if you sit silently you become aware of the totally tense process within.

So everyone is in search of escapes. Alcohol can give that—you become unconscious. Sex can give that—for a moment you forget yourself completely. Television can give that, music can give that...anything where you can forget yourself and become occupied so much that for the time being you are as if you are not. This constant escaping from oneself is really because of this process of minding. If you are unoccupied—and unoccupiedness means meditation—if you are totally unoccupied, you will become aware of your inner processes. And mind is the basic process within.

That is why so many people come to me and say they have come to meditate, but when they start meditating they become more tense. They say, "We were not so tense before and we were not so worried before. Ordinarily the whole day we are not so much worried, but when we sit down quietly and start meditating, thoughts rush upon us; they crowd in." That is something new, so they think it is because of meditation that thoughts are crowding them.

It is not because of meditation. Thoughts are crowding you every moment of your existence, but you are so occupied outwardly, you cannot be conscious of it. Whenever you sit down you become conscious, you become conscious of something you have been escaping constantly. Mind, minding, is a process, and a process is an effort. Energy is wasted in it, dissipated in it. It is necessary; it is needed for life, it is part of the struggle for survival. It is a weapon—and one of the most violent weapons.

That is why man could survive over other animals. The animals are more strong physically, but they lack a subtle weapon—minding. They have dangerous teeth, dangerous nails; they are more powerful than man; they can instantly kill a man completely. But they lack one weapon—minding. Because of that weapon, man could kill, survive.

So the mind is a survival measure. It is needed; it is necessary, and it is violent. The mind is violent, it is part of the long violence man has had to pass through. It has been built through violence. So whenever you sit down, you will feel inner violence —thoughts rushing, violent thoughts, a turmoil, as

if you are going to explode. That is why no one wants to sit silently.

Everyone comes and says, "Give me some support, some inner support. I cannot just sit silently. Give me a name that I can repeat like 'Rama, Rama, Rama....' Give me a name that I can repeat; then I can be silent."

Really, what are you doing? You are creating a new occupation. Then you can be silent because the mind is still occupied. Now you are focused on "Rama, Rama, Rama," on chanting; the mind is still not unoccupied. The mind as a process is bound to be always ill; it cannot be so balanced as silence needs.

Thirdly, mind is created from without. When you are born you have just the capacity for mind, but no mind—just a possibility, a potentiality. So if a child is brought up without society, without a society, the child will grow, he will have a body, but not a mind. He will not be able to speak any language; he will not be able to think in concepts. He will be like any animal.

Society trains your capacity into an actuality, it gives you a mind. That is why a Hindu has a certain mind and a Mohammedan has a different mind. Both are men, but their minds are different. A Christian has a different mind.... These minds are different because different societies have cultivated them with different purposes, different goals.

A child, a boy, is born, or a girl is born—they do not have minds, they have only the possibility that the mind can sprout. It can be there, but it is not there; it is just a seed. Then you train them. Then a boy becomes one mind and a girl becomes a different mind, because you teach them differently. Then a Hindu becomes different and a Mohammedan becomes different. Then a theist is different and an atheist is different. These minds are brought up in you. They are conditioned, forced upon you.

Because of this, mind as such is always old and orthodox. There can be no progressive mind. This statement may look strange: there can be no progressive mind. Mind is orthodox because it is a conditioning. So these so-called progressives are as much orthodox about their progressiveness as any orthodox person. Look at a communist. He thinks he is very progressive, but Marx's *Das Kapital* is just as authoritative upon him as the Koran on any Mohammedan, or the Gita on any Hindu. And if you start criticizing Marx, the communist feels as much hurt as any Jain will feel if you start criticizing Mahavira. Mind is orthodox because it is conditioned by the past, by the society, by others, for certain purposes.

Why am I making you aware of this fact? Because life changes every moment and mind belongs to the past. Mind is always old and life is always new. There is bound to be tension and conflict.

A new situation arises…. You fall in love with a woman, and you have a Hindu mind and the woman is Mohammedan. Now there will be conflict. Now there is going to be much anguish unnecessarily. The woman is Mohammedan, and life has brought you to a situation where you fell in love with her. Now life gives you a new phenomenon, and mind does not know how to deal with it. There is no know-how, so there will be conflict.

That is why, in a very changing world, people become uprooted; their lives become anxious. This was not so in past ages. Man was more silent—not so really, but he appeared more silent because the state of affairs around him was so static and the mind was not in much conflict. Now everything is changing so fast, and the mind cannot change so fast. Mind clings to the past, and everything changes every moment.

That is why there is so much anxiety in the West. In the East there is less anxiety. This is strange because the East has to face more basic problems. Food is not there, clothes are not there, houses are not there; everyone is just starved. But they are in less anxiety, and the West is in more anxiety. The West is affluent, scientifically and technologically developed, with a higher state of living, so why so much anxiety? Because technology gives life such a rapid change that the mind cannot cope

with it. Before you are adjusted to a new thing, the new has become old and has changed.

Again the gap! Life is bringing about new situations, and the mind always tries to react with the old conditioning. That gap goes on growing. The more the gap will be there, the more will be the anxiety. Mind is orthodox and life is not orthodox.

These are the reasons why mind itself is the disease. So what to do? If you are going to treat the mind, there are easy ways. Psychoanalysis is easy. It may take a long time, it may not succeed, but still it is not difficult. But this transcendence of the mind is difficult, arduous, because you have to leave the mind completely. You have to take wing and go beyond, and leave the mind as it is—do not touch it.

For example, I am here and the room is hot. I can do two things. I can air-condition the room and continue to live in the room. I can go on making arrangements so that the room is not hot, but then every arrangement has to be looked after and then every arrangement creates its own anxieties and problems. There is another possibility: I can leave the room and go out.

This is the difference. The West goes on living in the same room of the mind, trying to adjust, to make arrangements, so that living in the mind becomes at least normal. It may not be very blissful, but it becomes less and less unhappy. It may not reach a point, a peak of happiness, but one is saved from much suffering; there is less and less suffering.

Freud has said that there is no possibility for man to be happy. At the most, if you can arrange your mind in such a way that you are normal, you will be less unhappy than others, that is all. This is very hopeless. But Freud is a very genuine, authentic thinker, and his insight is right in a way because he cannot see beyond the mind.

That is why the East has not really developed any psychology comparable to Freud, Jung or Adler. And that is strange because the East has been talking about the mind for at least five thousand years.

With five thousand years of talking about mind, meditation, going beyond, why couldn't the East create psychology? Psychology is a very recent development in the West. Why couldn't the East create a psychology? Buddha was here who talked about the deepest layers of the mind. He talked about the conscious, he talked about the subconscious, he talked about the unconscious. He must have known. But why couldn't he develop psychologies about the conscious, subconscious and unconscious?

The reason is this: the East has not been interested in the room. It talks about the room a little in order to go beyond, to go out. We have been interested in the room just to find the door; that is all. We are not interested in details about the room; we are not going to live in it. So the only interest has been in knowing where the door is and how to go out. We have talked about the room only so that the door can be located—so that we can know how to open it and go out.

This has been our whole interest. That is why psychology could not be developed in India. If you are not interested in the room, you will not make maps of the room; you will not measure every wall and every inch of space. You are not bothered about these things. You are only interested in where the door is, where the window is, so that you can jump out. And the moment you are out you will forget the room completely, because then you are under the great infinite sky. You will not even remember that there was a room and you lived in a cave, while all the time the infinite sky was beyond—and you could have moved out at any moment. You will forget the room completely. If you can go beyond the mind, what happens? The mind remains the same, you do not make any change in the mind, but you go beyond it and everything changes.

Then you can come back to the room again if you need to, but you will be a different person. This going out and coming in will have made you qualitatively different. A man who has been living in a room, and who has not known what it is like on the outside, is not really a man; he lives like a beetle, he lives like an insect. When he moves out to the sky—the open sky—and to the sun and the clouds and the infinite expanse, he becomes different immediately. This impact of the infinite makes him for the first time a man, a consciousness.

Now he can move into the room again, but he will be a different man. Now the room can only be something which is used. It is not now a prison; he can move out any moment. Then the room becomes just something to be used, something utilitarian. Previously he was imprisoned in it; now he is not imprisoned. He is now a master, and he knows the sky is outside and the infinite is awaiting him. And even this room is part of that infinite now, even this small, limited sky and space within the room is the space, the same space which is outside. The man comes in again and lives in the room, uses the room, but now he is not imprisoned in it. This is a qualitative change.

The East is concerned with how to go beyond the mind and then use it. Do not be identified with the mind—that is the message. And all the techniques of meditation are concerned only about how to find the door, how to use the key, how to unlock the door and go out.

We will discuss two methods today. The first is concerned with stopping in the middle of an activity. We discussed three stop methods before; now this one remains.

28 Imagine yourself losing all energy.

The fourth stop method: *Suppose you are gradually being deprived of strength or of knowledge. At the instant of deprivation, transcend.*

You can do it in an actual situation or you can imagine a situation. For example: lie down, relax, and feel as if your body is going to die. Close your eyes; start feeling that you are dying. Soon you will feel that your body is becoming heavy. Imagine: "I am dying, I am dying, I am dying." If the feeling is authentic, the body will start becoming heavy; you will feel as if your body has become like lead. You want to move your hand, but you cannot move; it has become so heavy and dead. Go on feeling that you are dying, dying, dying, dying, dying, and when you feel that now the moment has come—just a jump and you will be dead—then suddenly forget your body and transcend.

Suppose you are gradually being deprived of strength or of knowledge. At the instant of deprivation, transcend. When you feel that the body is dead, what is meant now by transcending? Look at the body. Up to now you were feeling that you are dying; now the body has become a dead weight. Look at the body. Forget that you are dying and now be the observer. The body is lying dead and you are looking at it. There will be a transcendence. You will be out of your mind, because a dead body needs no mind. A dead body relaxes so much that the very process of the mind stops. You are there and the body is there, but the mind is absent. Remember, mind is needed for life, not for death.

If suddenly you come to know that within an hour you will die, what will you do in that hour? One hour left, and it is certain that you are going to die after one hour—exactly after one hour. What will you do? Your thinking will drop completely because the whole of thinking is concerned with either the past or the future.

You were planning to purchase a house or to purchase a car, or you were planning to marry someone or divorce someone. You were thinking many things, and they were constantly on your mind. Now, with only one hour more, there is no meaning in marriage and no meaning in divorce. Now you can leave all the planning to others, who are going to live. With death planning ceases, with death worrying ceases, because every worry is life-oriented.

You have to live tomorrow; that is why there is worry. So all those who have been teaching meditation to the world have always been saying: do not think of tomorrow. Jesus says to his disciples, "Do not think of the tomorrow," because if you think of

the tomorrow you cannot go into meditation. Then you move into worries. But we are so fond of worries that not only do we think of the tomorrow, we think of the other life. So we plan not only for this life, we plan for the other life, beyond death, also.

One day I was passing through a street and someone gave me a pamphlet. A very beautiful house was painted on the cover and a very beautiful garden. It was lovely—divinely lovely. And in very big capital letters was the question: "Do you want such a beautiful house and such a beautiful garden? And without any price, without any cost—for free?" I turned it over. The house was not of this earth. It was a Christian pamphlet, and it read, "If you want such a beautiful house and such a beautiful garden, believe in Jesus. Those who believe in him will get such houses free of cost in the kingdom of God."

The mind goes on not only thinking of tomorrow, but thinking of beyond death, arranging and making reservations for the afterlife. Such a mind cannot be a religious mind. A religious mind cannot think of tomorrow. So those who think of the afterlife are constantly worried about whether God will behave rightly with them or not.

Churchill was dying and someone asked him, "Are you ready to meet the father there in heaven?"

Churchill said, "That is not my worry. I am constantly worried whether the divine father is ready to meet me."

But either way one goes on worrying about the future. Buddha said, "There is no heaven and no afterlife." And he said, "There is no soul, and your death will be total and complete; nothing will survive." People thought he was an atheist. He was not, he was just trying to create a situation in which you can forget the tomorrow and can remain in this very moment, here and now. Then meditation follows very easily.

So if you are thinking of death—not the death which will come, or is to come later—fall down on the ground and lie dead. Relax and feel, "I am dying, I am dying, I am dying." And not only think it, feel it in every limb of the body, in every fiber of the body. Let death creep in. It is one of the most beautiful meditations. When you feel that the body is a dead weight and you cannot move your hand, you cannot move your head and everything has become dead, suddenly look at your own body.

Mind will not be there. You can look! You will be there, consciousness will be there. Look at your body—it will not look like yours, it will be just a body. The gap between you and the body will be clear, crystal clear. There will be no bridge. The body is lying dead and you are there standing as a witness, not in it—*not* in it!

Remember, the feeling that you are in the body is because of the mind. If the mind is not there, if it is absent, you will not say you are in the body or out of the body. You will simply be there, no in or out. "In" and "out" are both relative terms associated with the mind. Simply, you will be there witnessing. This is transcendence. You can do it in many ways.

Sometimes it is possible in actual situations.... You are ill and you are feeling that there is no hope, you are going to die. This is a very useful situation. Use it for meditation. You can try it in other ways also. Suppose you are gradually being deprived of strength. Lie down and feel as if the whole existence is sucking your strength out. You are being sucked from everywhere—your strength is being sucked. Soon you will be impotent, completely devoid of strength. Your energy is flowing out, being taken out. Soon nothing will be left inside. That is how life is: you are being sucked out, everything that is around you is sucking you out. One day you will be just a dead cell; everything will have been sucked out. The life will have flown out of you, and only the dead body will remain there.

Even this very moment you can do it. Imagine this: lie down and feel that the energy is being sucked out. Within a few days you will have the knack of how energy goes out. And when you feel that everything has moved out, nothing is now left within you, transcend: *At the instant of deprivation, transcend.* When the last quantum of energy is leaving you, transcend. Be an onlooker; just become a witness. Then this universe and this body, both, are not you. You are looking at the phenomenon.

This transcendence will bring you out of the mind. This is the key. And you can do it in many ways, whatsoever is your liking. For example, we were talking about a run around. Exhaust yourself; go on running and running and running. Do not stop by yourself, let the body fall. When every fiber is exhausted, you will fall down. When you are falling down, become aware. Just look and see that the body is falling down. Sometimes a very miraculous happening happens. You remain standing and the body has fallen down, and you can look at it. You can look, as only the body has fallen down and you are still standing. Do not fall with the body. Roam around, run, dance, exhaust the body —but remember, you are not to lie down. Then the inner consciousness also moves with the body and lies down.

You are not to lie down, you just go on doing it until the body falls by itself. Then it falls like a dead weight. Immediately, you feel the body is falling and you cannot do anything. Open your eyes, be alert, do not miss the point. Be alert and see what is happening. You may be still standing, and the body has fallen down. And once you know it, you can never forget that you are different from the body.

This 'standing out' is the real meaning of the English word 'ecstasy.' Ecstasy means to stand out. And once you can feel you are out of the body, there is no mind in that moment, because mind is the bridge that gives you the feeling that you are in the body. If you are out of the body for a single moment, there will be no mind in that moment. This is transcendence. Then you can move in the body, then you can move in the mind, but now you cannot forget the experience. That experience has become part and parcel of your being; it will be there always. Go on doing it every day, and many things happen through such a simple process.

The West is always worried about how to tackle mind, and it tries to find many ways. But still, nothing works or seems to work. Everything becomes a fashion and then dies. Now psychoanalysis is a dead movement. New movements are there— encounter groups, group psychology, action psychology and many other things—but just like a fashion they come and go. Why? Because within mind, at the most you can only make arrangements. They will be disturbed again and again. Making arrangements with the mind is making a house on sand, or making a house of playing cards. It is always wavering, and the fear is always there that now it is going. At any moment it may not be there.

Going beyond the mind is the only way to be inwardly happy and healthy, to be whole. Then you can move in the mind and use the mind, but the mind becomes the instrument and you are not identified with it. So two things: either you are identified with the mind—this is illness for tantra—or you are not identified with the mind. Then you use it as an instrument, and then you are healthy and whole.

---

29 Devote yourself.

The fifth stop technique is very simple in one sense and the most difficult in another, and it is only of two words. The fifth technique says, *Devotion frees.*

Just two words: *Devotion frees.* It is simply one word really, because "frees" is the consequence of devotion. What is meant by devotion? In *Vigyan Bhairav Tantra* there are two types of techniques. One is for those who are intellectually oriented, scientifically oriented, and another is for those who are heart-oriented, emotion-oriented, poetically oriented. And there are only two types of minds, the scientific mind and the poetic mind— and these are poles apart. They meet nowhere, and

they cannot meet. Sometimes they run parallel, but still, there is no meeting.

Sometimes it happens in a single individual that he is a poet and a scientist. Rarely, but sometimes it happens that he is both a poet and a scientist. Then he has a split personality. He is really two persons, not one. When he is a poet, he forgets the scientist completely; otherwise the scientist will be disturbing. And when he is a scientist, he has to forget the poet completely and move into another world, with another arrangement of concepts—ideas, logic, reason, mathematics.

When he moves to the world of poetry, the mathematics is no more there—music is there. Concepts are no more there, words are there—but liquid, not solid. One word flows into another, and one word can mean many things or it may not mean anything. The grammar is lost; only the rhythm remains. It is a different world.

Thinking and feeling—these are the two basic types. The first technique I taught was for a scientific mind. The second technique, *devotion frees,* is for a feeling type. Remember to find out your type. And no type is higher or lower. Do not think that the intellectual type is higher or the feeling type is higher—no! They are simply types. No one is higher or lower. So just think factually what is your type.

This second technique is for the feeling type. Why? Because devotion is toward something else and devotion is a blind thing. In devotion the other becomes more important than you. It is a trust. The intellectual cannot trust anybody; he can only criticize. He cannot trust. He can doubt, but he cannot trust. And if sometimes some intellectual comes to trust, it is never authentic. First he tries to convince himself about his trust; it is never authentic. He finds proofs, arguments, and when he is satisfied that the arguments help, the proofs help, then he trusts. But he has missed the point, because trust is not argumentative and trust is not based on proofs. If proofs are there, then there is no need of trust.

You do not believe in the sun, you do not

believe in the sky—you know. How can you believe in the sun rising? If someone asks what is your belief about the sun rising, you do not have to say, "I believe in it. I am a great believer." You say, "The sun is rising and I know it." No question of belief or disbelief. Is there someone who disbelieves in the sun? There is no one. Trust means a jump into the unknown without any proofs.

It is difficult for the intellectual type, because the whole thing becomes absurd, foolish. First proofs must be there. If you say, "There is a God. Surrender yourself to God," first God has to be proven. But then God becomes a theorem—of course proven, but useless. God must remain unproven; otherwise he is of no use, because then trust is meaningless. If you believe in a proven God, then your God is just a theorem of geometry. No one believes in the theorems of Euclid—there is no need, they can be proven. That which can be proven cannot be made a basis of trust.

One of the most mysterious Christian saints, Tertullian, said, "I believe in God because he is absurd." That is right. That is the attitude of the feeling type. He says, "Because he cannot be proven, that is why I believe in him." This statement is illogical, irrational, because a logical statement must be like this: "These are the proofs of God; therefore I believe in him." And he says, "Because there are no proofs, and no argument can prove that God is, therefore I believe in him." And he is right in a way, because trust means a jump into the unknown without any reasons. Only a feeling type can do that.

Forget devotion, first understand love; then you will be able to understand devotion. You fall in love. Why do we say "falling in love"? Nothing falls—just your head. What falls in love but your head? You fall down from the head. That is why we say "falling in love"—because the language is created by intellectual types. For them love is a lunacy, love is madness; one has *fallen* in love. It means, now you can expect anything from him... now he is mad, now no reasoning will help, you

cannot reason with him. Can you reason with someone who is in love? People try. People try, but nothing can be proven.

You have fallen in love with someone. Everyone says, "That person is not worthwhile," or "You are entering a dangerous terrain," or "You are proving yourself foolish; you can find a better partner." But nothing will help, no reasoning will help. You are in love—now reason is useless. Love has its own reasoning. We say "falling in love." It means now your behavior will be irrational.

Look at two lovers, at their behavior, their communication. It becomes irrational. They start using baby talk. Why? Even a great scientist, when he falls in love, will use baby language. Why not use a highly developed, technological language? Why use this baby talk? Because highly technological language is of no use.

One of my friends married a girl. The girl was Czechoslovakian. She did know a little English, however, and this man knew a little Czechoslovakian; they got married. He was a highly educated man, a professor in a university, and the girl was also a professor. But the man said to me—I was staying with him—"It is very difficult because I know only technological Czech, technological terminology, and she also only knows technological English, so we cannot have baby talk. So it is strange. Our love is just that somewhere on the surface we feel; it cannot move deep. The language becomes the barrier. I can talk as a professor—as far as my subject is concerned I can talk about it—and she can talk about her subject. But love has been the subject of neither of us."

So why do you fall into baby talk? Because that was your first love experience, with your mother. Those words that you uttered first were love words. They were not head-oriented, they came from the heart; they belonged to feeling. They had a different quality.

So even when you have a very developed language, when you love you again fall back—you fall back into baby talk. Those words are different.

They do not belong to this category of the mind; they belong to the heart. They may not be so expressive, so meaningful. Still, they are more expressive and more meaningful—but their meaning is of a different dimension altogether. Only if you are very deeply in love will you fall silent. Then you cannot talk with your beloved, or you can talk just by the way, but really, there is no talk.

If the love goes deep, words become useless; you remain silent. If you cannot remain silent with your beloved, know well there is no love—because it is very difficult to live in silence with someone you are not in love with. With a stranger you immediately start talking. When you are riding in a train or in a bus you immediately start talking, because to sit by the side of a stranger silently is very difficult, awkward. There is no other bridge, so unless you create a language bridge there is no bridge.

No inner bridge is possible with that stranger. You are closed in yourself and he is closed in himself, and two enclosures are just side by side. There is every fear of colliding and of danger, so you create a bridge. You start talking about the weather or about anything, any nonsense that gives a feeling that you are bridged and you are communicating. Two lovers will fall silent, and when two lovers start talking again you can know well that the love has disappeared; they have become strangers.

So go and look…. Wives and husbands, whenever they are alone, they will talk about anything. And they both know, they both are aware that there is no need to talk, but it is so difficult to remain silent. So anything, any trivia will do, but talk so that you can have the feeling that communication is there. But two lovers will fall silent. Language will disappear because language belongs to reason. First it will become a baby talk, and then this will disappear. Then they will be silently in communication. What is their communication? It is irrational. They feel attuned to a different dimension of existence, and they feel happy in that attunement. And if you ask them to prove what is their happiness, they cannot prove it.

No lover has been able to prove up to now why he is happy in love. Why? Because love implies much suffering. Still, lovers are happy. Love has a deep suffering, because when you become one with someone it is always difficult. Two minds become one…it is not only two bodies becoming one. That is the difference between sex and love. If only two bodies become one, it is not very difficult and there is no suffering. It is one of the easiest things; any animal can do it. It is easy. But when two people are in love it is very difficult, because two minds have to dissolve, two minds have to be absent. Only then is the space created, and love can flower.

No one reasons about love; no one can prove that love gives happiness. No one can even prove that love exists. And there are scientists, behaviorists, followers of Watson and Skinner, who say love is just an illusion. There is no love; you are just in an illusion. You feel that you are in love, but there is no love, you are just dreaming. And no one can prove they are wrong. They say that love is just a hallucination, a psychedelic experience. Nothing real, just body chemistry influencing you, just hormones, chemicals, influencing your behavior and giving a false well-being to you. No one can prove them wrong.

But the miracle is this, that even a Watson will fall in love. Even a Watson will fall in love, knowing well that this is just a chemical affair. And even a Watson will be happy. But love cannot be proven, it is so inner and subjective. What happens in love? The other becomes important—more important than you. You become the periphery and he becomes the center.

Logic always remains self-centered, mind always remains ego-centered: I am the center and everything just encircles around me—for me, but I am the center. This is how reason works. If you move with reason too much, you will come to the conclusion to which Berkeley came. He said, "Only I exist, everything else is just an idea in the mind. How can I prove that you are there, sitting there just before me? How can I prove reasonably, rationally, that you are really there? You may be just a dream. I may be just dreaming and talking; you may not be there at all. How can I prove to myself that really you are there? I can, of course, touch you, but I can touch you even in a dream. And even in a dream I feel it when I touch someone. I can hit you and you will scream, but even in a dream, if I hit someone the dream figure screams. So how can I make a distinction that my audience here, just now, is not a dream but a reality? It may be just a fiction."

Go to a madhouse, and you will find people sitting alone talking. To whom are they talking? I may be talking to no one. How can I prove rationally that you are really here? So if reason goes to the extreme, to the very logical extreme, then only I remain and everything else becomes a dream. This is how reason works.

Quite the contrary is the path of the heart. I become the mystery and you—thou, the other, the beloved—become the real. If you move to the very extreme, then it becomes devotion. If your love comes to such an extreme point that you forget completely that you are, you have no notion of yourself and only the other remains, that is devotion.

Love can become devotion. Love is the first step; only then can devotion flower. But for us even love is a faraway reality, sex is the only real thing. Love has two possibilities: either it falls into sex and becomes a bodily thing, or it rises into devotion and becomes a thing of the spirit. Love is just in-between. Just below it is the abyss of sex, and beyond it is the open sky—the infinite sky of devotion.

If your love grows deeper, the other becomes more and more significant—so significant that you begin to call the other your god. That is why Meera goes on calling Krishna, God. No one can see Krishna, and Meera cannot prove that Krishna is there, but she is not interested in proving it at all. She has made that point, Krishna, her love object. And remember, whether you make a real person your love object or whether it is just your imagination, it makes no difference, because the whole transformation comes through devotion, not through the

beloved—remember this. Krishna may not be there at all; it is irrelevant. For the lover, it is irrelevant.

For Radha, Krishna was there in reality. For Meera, Krishna was not there in reality. That is why Meera is a greater devotee than Radha. And even Radha would become jealous of Meera, because for Radha the real person was there. It is not so difficult to feel Krishna's reality when he is present. But when Krishna is no more there, Meera alone is living in a room and talking to Krishna, and living for him who is nowhere. For her, he is everything and all. She cannot prove it; it is irrational. But she took a jump and she became transformed. Devotion freed her.

I want to emphasize the fact that it is not a question of whether Krishna is there or not. It is not! This feeling that Krishna is there, this total feeling of love, this total surrender, this losing oneself into one who may be or may not be, this *losing* itself is the transformation. Suddenly one is purified—totally purified—because when the ego is not there you cannot be impure in any way. Because ego is the seed of all impurity.

The feeling of ego is the root of all madness. For the feeling world, for the world of the devotee, ego is the disease. Ego dissolves, and it dissolves in only one way; there is no other way. There is only one way: the other becomes so important, so significant, that by and by you fade out and disappear. One day you are no more; just a consciousness of the other remains.

And when you are no more, the other is also not the other, because he is the other only when you are there. When the "I" disappears, the "thou" also disappears. In love you take the first step—the other becomes important. You remain, but for certain moments there may be a peak when you are not. Those are rare peaks of love, but ordinarily you remain and the lover is there. When the lover becomes more important than you, you can die for him or her. If you can die for someone, there is love. The other has become the meaning of your life.

Only if you can die for someone can you live for

someone. If you cannot die for someone, you cannot live for someone. Life acquires a meaning only through death. In love, the other has become important, but you are still there. In some higher peaks of communication you may disappear, but you will come back; this will be only for moments. So lovers have glimpses of devotion. That is why in India the beloved used to call her lover her god. Only in peaks does the other become divine, and the other becomes divine only when you are not. This can grow. And if you make it a *sadhana*—a spiritual practice—if you make it an inner search, if you are not just enjoying love but transforming yourself through love, then it becomes devotion.

In devotion you surrender yourself completely. And this surrender can be to a god who may not be in the sky or who may be, or to a master who may not be awakened or who may be, or to a beloved who may not be worthwhile or who may be—that is irrelevant. If you can allow yourself to dissolve for the other, you will be transformed.

Devotion frees. That is why we have glimpses of freedom only in love. When you are in love, you have a subtle freedom. This is paradoxical because everyone else will see that you have become a slave. If you are in love with someone, those around you will think that you both have become slaves to each other. But you will have glimpses of freedom.

Love is freedom. Why? Because ego is the bondage; there is no other bondage. You may be in a prison and you cannot escape. If your beloved comes into the prison, the prison disappears that very moment. The walls are there still, but they do not imprison you. Now you can forget them completely. You can dissolve into each other and you can become for each other a sky in which to fly. The prison has disappeared; it is no more there. And you may be under the open sky without love, totally free, untethered, but you are in a prison because you have nowhere to fly. This sky will not do.

Birds fly in that sky, but you cannot. You need a different sky—the sky of consciousness. Only the other can give you that sky, the first taste of it.

When the other opens for you and you move into the other, you can fly.

Love is freedom, but not total. If love becomes devotion, then it becomes total freedom. It means surrendering yourself completely. So those who are of the feeling type, this sutra is for them: *Devotion frees.* Take Ramakrishna.... If you look at Ramakrishna you will think that he is just a slave to the goddess Kali, to Mother Kali. He cannot do anything without her permission; he is just like a slave. But no one was more free than him. When he was appointed for the first time as priest in Dakshineshwar, at the temple, he started behaving strangely. The committee, the trustees gathered, and they said, "Throw this man out. He is behaving undevotionally." This happened because first he would smell a flower and then the flower would be put at the feet of the goddess. That is against the ritual. A smelled flower cannot be offered to the divine—it has become impure.

First he would taste the food which was made for the offering, and then he would offer it. And he was the priest so the trustees asked him, "What are you doing? This cannot be allowed."

He said, "Then I will leave this post. I will move out of the temple, but I cannot offer food to my Mother without tasting it. My mother used to taste...whenever she would prepare something, she would taste it first and then only would she give it to me. And I cannot offer a flower without smelling it first. So I can go out, and you cannot stop me, you cannot prevent me. I will go on offering it anywhere, because my Mother is everywhere; she is not confined in your temple. So wherever I will be, I will be doing the same thing."

It happened that someone, some Mohammedan, told him, "If your Mother is everywhere, then why not come to the mosque?" He said, "Okay, I am coming." He remained there for six months. He forgot Dakshineshwar completely; he was in a mosque.

Then his friend said, "Now you can go back." He said, "She is everywhere." So one may think that Ramakrishna is a slave, but his devotion is such that now the beloved is everywhere. If you are nowhere, the beloved will be everywhere. If you are somewhere, then the beloved will be nowhere.

CHAPTER 20

Ordinary love and the love of a Buddha

◆

Q U E S T I O N S

Should love be continuous, and when does it become devotion?

Why does tantra give the body so much importance?

Tell us something about attachment and freedom.

The first question:

It seems very difficult to love someone for twenty-four hours a day. Why does it happen so? Should love be a continuous process? And at which stage does love become devotion?

ove is not an act; it is not something that you do. If you do it, it is not love. No doing is involved in love; it is a state of being, not an act. No one can do anything continuously for twenty-four hours. If you are doing love, then of course you cannot do it for twenty-four hours. With any act you will get tired; with any act you get bored. And then, after any act, you have to relax. So if you are doing love, you will have to relax into hate, because you can relax only into the opposite.

That is why our love is always mixed with hatred. You love this moment, and the next moment you hate the same person. The same person becomes the object of both love and hate; that is the conflict of lovers. Because your love is an act, that is why there is this misery.

So the first thing to be understood is that love is not an act; you cannot do it. You can be in love, but you cannot "do" love. Doing is absurd. But other things are also implied. It is not an effort because if it were an effort you would get tired. It is a state of mind.

And do not think in terms of relationship, think in terms of states of mind. If you are in love, this is a state of mind. This state of mind may be focused on one person or it may be unfocused—on the whole. When it is focused on one person, it is known as love. When it becomes unfocused, it becomes prayer. Then you are just in love—not with someone, but just in love, as you are breathing.

If breathing were an effort you would get tired of it, and you would have to relax and then you would die. If it were an effort, then at some time you might forget to do it and then you would die. Love is just like breathing, it is a higher plane of breathing. If you do not breathe, your body will die. If you are not in love, your spirit cannot be born.

So take love as a breathing of the soul. When you are in love your soul becomes vital, alive, just like it is breathing. But think in this way. If I say to you, "Only breathe when you are near me and do not breathe anywhere else," then you will die. And the next time you will be near me you will be just dead and you will not even be able to breathe near me.

That has happened with love. We possess—the love object is possessed and the lover says, "Don't love anybody else. Only love me." Then the love is atrophied and then the lover cannot love, it becomes impossible. It doesn't mean that you have to love everyone, but you have to be in a loving state of mind. It is just like breathing: even if your enemy is there you will breathe.

That is the meaning of Jesus' saying, "Love your enemy." It has been a problem for Christianity, how to understand this saying, "Love your enemy." It seems contradictory. But if loving is not an act, if it is just a state of mind, then there is no question of enemy or friend. You are in love.

Look at it from the other side. There are persons who are continuously in hate, and whenever they try to show love they have to make much effort. Their love is an effort because their continuous state of mind is hate.

That is why effort is needed. There are persons who are continuously sad; then their laughter is an effort. They have to fight against themselves. Then their laughter becomes a painted laughter—just false, imposed, put together, not coming from deep within but just arranged, no spontaneity in it but just artificial.

There are persons who are continuously in anger—not angry at something or someone, just angry. Then love becomes an effort. On the other hand, if love is your state of mind, anger will be an effort. You can do it, but you cannot be angry. Then you will have to create it artificially; it will be false.

If a Buddha tries to be angry, much effort will be needed, and then too it will be false. And only those who do not know him can be deceived. Those who know him, they know that that anger is false, just painted, created. It is not coming from within; that is impossible. A Buddha, a Jesus, cannot hate. Then effort is needed. If they want to show hatred, then they will have to "do" it.

But you do not need any effort to be hateful; you need effort to be loving. Change the state of mind. How to change the state of mind? How to be loving? And it is not a question of time, of how to be loving twenty-four hours a day. This is absurd—this question is absurd.

It is not a question of time. If you can be loving in a single moment that is enough, because you never have two moments together. Only one moment is given. When one is lost, a second is given. You have only one moment always with you. If you know how to be loving in one single

moment, you know the secret. You need not think about twenty-four hours, or of the whole life.

Only a single moment of love and you know how to fill a moment with love. Then the second moment will be given to you, and you can fill that second moment also with love. So remember, it is not a question of time. There is a question only of a single moment, and a single moment is not part of time. A single moment is not a process; a single moment is just now.

Once you know how to enter a single moment with love, you have entered eternity: time is no more. A buddha lives in the now; you live in time. Time means thinking of the past, thinking of the future. And while you are thinking of the past and of the future, the present is lost.

You are engaged with the future and the past, and the present is being lost—and the present is the only existence. The past is no more and the future has yet to be; they both are not, they are nonexistential. This very moment, this single atomic moment, is the only existence—here and now. If you know to be loving, you know the secret. And you will never be given two moments together, so you need not bother about time.

A single moment is always—and it is always in the shape of now. Remember, there are not really two types of "nows." This single moment is the same; it doesn't differ in any way from the moment that has gone before it, and it doesn't differ in any way from the moment that is going to follow it.

This atomic now is always the same. That is why Eckhart says, "It is not that time passes. Time remains the same. Rather, we go on passing." Pure time remains the same; we go on passing. So do not think about twenty-four hours, and then you need not think of the present moment.

One thing more. Thinking needs time; living doesn't need time. You cannot think in this very moment. In this very moment, if you want to be, you will have to cease thinking, because thinking is basically concerned with either the past or the future. Of what can you think in the present? The moment you think, it has become the past.

A flower is there—you say this is a beautiful flower. This saying is now no more in the present; it has become the past. When you come to grasp something in thinking, it has become the past. In the present you can be, but you cannot think. You can be with the flower, but you cannot think about it. Thinking needs time.

So in another way, thinking is time. If you do not think, there is no time. That is why in meditation you feel a timelessness. That is why in love you feel a timelessness. Love is not thinking, it is a cessation of thought. You are! When you are with your beloved, you are not thinking about love, you are not thinking about the beloved. You are not thinking at all. And if you are thinking, then you are not with your beloved, you are somewhere else. Thinking means absence from the now...you are not there.

That is why those who are too much obsessed with thinking cannot love, because even when they are there, even if they reach to the original divine source, even if they meet God, they will go on thinking about him and they will miss him completely. You can go on thinking about and about and about, but it is never the fact.

A moment of love is a timeless moment. Then there is no question of thinking how to love twenty-four hours. You never think about how to live twenty-four hours, how to be alive twenty-four hours. Either you are alive or you are not. So the basic thing to be understood is not time, but now —how to be here and now in a state of love.

Why is there hate? When you feel hatred, go to the cause of it. Only then can love flower. When do you feel hatred? When you feel that your existence, your life, is in danger, when you feel that your existence can be annihilated, suddenly hate surges in you. When you feel that you can be destroyed, you start destroying others. That is a safety measure. It is just a part of you that is struggling for survival. Whenever you feel that your existence is in danger, you are filled with hatred.

So unless you come to feel that your existence cannot be in danger, that it is impossible to annihilate you, you cannot be filled with love. A Jesus can be in love because he knows something which is deathless. You cannot be in love because you know only that which belongs to death. And every moment death is there; every moment you are afraid. How can you love when you are afraid? Love cannot exist with fear. And fear is there, so you can only create a make-believe that you love.

And again, your love is really nothing but a safety measure. You love so that you will not fear. Whenever you believe that you are in love, you are less afraid. For the moment you can forget death. An illusion is created in which you can feel that you are accepted by the existence; you are not denied, rejected. That is why there is so much need of love and of being loved.

Whenever you are being loved by someone, you create around you an illusion that you are needed by the existence—at least by someone. You are needed by someone, so you are not just futile. You are not just accidental—you are needed somewhere. Without you the existence will miss something. That gives you a feeling of well-being. You feel a purpose, a destiny, a meaning, a worthiness.

When you are not loved by anyone you feel rejected, you feel denied, you feel meaningless. Then you feel there is no purpose, no destiny. If no one loves you and you die, there will be no feeling of your absence, it will not be felt that you are no more. No one will feel that you were, and now you are no more.

Love gives you the feeling of being needed. That is why in love one becomes or feels less afraid. Whenever love is not there you become more fearful, and in fear, as a protection, you become hateful. Hate is a protection. You are afraid of being destroyed; you become destructive.

In love, you feel that you are accepted, welcome —not an uninvited guest, but rather that you are invited, welcome, waited for, received, that the existence is happy that you are. The one who loves you becomes the representative of the whole existence.

But this love is basically fear-based. You are protecting against fear, against death, against the inhuman indifference of existence.

Really, existence is indifferent—at least on the surface. The sun, the sea, the stars, the earth, they are totally indifferent to you; no one is worried about you. And it is apparently clear that you are not needed. Without you everything will be as good as it is with you; nothing will be lost. Look at the existence superficially: no one, nothing, cares about you. They may not even be aware of you. The stars are not aware of you; even the earth which you call "Mother" is not aware of you. And when you die, the earth will not be sad. Nothing will have changed; things will be as they are and as they always have been. With you or without you, there is no difference.

You feel you are just an accident. You were not needed; uninvited you have come...just a chance product. This creates fear. This is what Kierkegaard calls "anguish." There is a subtle continuous fear—you are not needed.

When someone loves you, you feel that a different dimension has come into existence. Now at least one person will be there who will weep, who will feel sorry, who will be sad. There will be tears; you will be needed. At least there will be one person who will always feel your absence if you are not. At least for one you have gained a destiny, a purpose.

That is why there is so much need of love. And if you are not loved, you are uprooted. But this love is not the love I am talking about. This is a relationship and a mutual creation of illusion—a mutual illusion: "I need you, you need me. I give you this illusion that without you my purpose, my meaning, my life will be lost; you give me this illusion that without me everything will be lost. So we both are helping each other to be in an illusion. We are creating one separate, private existence in which we become meaningful, in which the whole indifference of this vast space is forgotten."

Two lovers live in each other; they have created

a private world. That is why love needs so much privacy. If you are not in privacy, the world goes on impinging upon you. It goes on telling you that whatsoever you are doing is just a dream, and this is a mutual illusion. Love needs privacy because then the whole world is forgotten. Only two lovers exist, and the indifference, the total indifference of existence, is forgotten. You feel loved, welcomed. Without you nothing will be the same. At least in this private world nothing will be the same without you. Life is meaningful.

I am not talking about this love. This is really illusory. It is a cultivated illusion, and man is so weak that he cannot live without this illusion. Those who can, live without this illusion. A buddha can live without this illusion, and then he will not create it.

When it becomes possible to live illusionlessly—to live without illusion—a second, a different dimension of love comes into being. It is not that one person needs you. It is coming to understand, to realize, that you are not different from this existence which looks so indifferent. You are part of it, organically one with it. And if a tree is flowering, it is not separate from you. You have flowered in the tree and the tree has become conscious in you.

The sea and the sand and the stars, they are one with you. You are not an island, you are organically one with this universe. The whole universe is within you and the whole of you is in this universe. Unless you come to know it and feel it and realize it, you will not get that love which is a state of mind.

If you come to realize this, you will not need to create a private illusion that someone loves you. Then there is meaning, and if no one loves you, no meaning is lost. Then you are not afraid at all because even death will not annihilate you. It may annihilate the form, it may annihilate the body, but it cannot annihilate *you* because you are the existence.

This is what happens in meditation. This is for what meditation is meant. In it you become a part, an opening. You come to feel, "Existence and I are one." Then you are welcomed, and there is no fear and there is no death. Then love flows from you. Then love is not an effort—you cannot do anything except love. Then it is like breathing. Deep inside you breathe love; in and out you breathe love.

This love grows into devotion. Then ultimately you will even forget it just as you forget your breathing. When do you remember your breathing? Have you observed? You remember only when something is wrong. When you feel any difficulty, then you know that you have been breathing; otherwise there is no need even to be aware of it. And if you are aware of your breathing, that shows that something is wrong with your breathing process. There is no need of being aware of the breathing process. Silently it goes on.

So when you are aware of your love, the love that is a state of mind, it means that something is still wrong. By and by even that awareness is lost. You simply breathe love in and out. You have forgotten everything, even that you love. Then it has become devotion. That is the ultimate peak, the ultimate possibility—you may call it anything.

Love can become devotion only when this awareness is lost, forgotten. It doesn't mean that you have become unconscious, it only means that the process has become so silent that there is no noise around it. You are not unconscious of it, but you are not conscious of it either. It has become so natural. It is there, but it does not create any disturbance inside; it has become so harmonious.

So remember, when I am talking about love, I am not talking about your love. But if you try to understand your love, it will become a step toward growing into a different kind of love. So I am not against your love. I am simply stating the fact that if your love is fear-based, it is just ordinary, animal love. And no derogation, no condemnation is implied; it is simply a fact.

Man is afraid. He needs someone who gives him the feeling that he is welcomed, that he need not be afraid. At least with one person you need

not be filled with fear. This is good as far as it goes, but this is not what Buddha or Jesus called love. They called love a state of mind, not a relationship. So go beyond relationship, and by and by just be loving. First you will not be capable of it unless you move into meditation. Unless you come to know the deathless within, unless you come to know a deep unity between the inner and the outer, unless you feel that you are existence, it will be difficult.

So these techniques of meditation are just to help you grow from relationship into a state of mind. And do not think of time at all; time is irrelevant for love.

The second question:

Most of the techniques which You have discussed have used the body as an instrument. What are the reasons for the body to be given so much importance by tantra?

Many basic points are to be understood. One, you are your body. Right now you are just your body and nothing else. You may have notions about the soul, the *atma*, etcetera—those are simply notions, just ideas. As you are right now you are just a body. And do not go on deceiving yourself that you are the deathless soul, the immortal atma. Do not go on deceiving yourself. That is just an idea, and that idea too is fear-based.

You do not know whether the soul exists or not; you have never penetrated to the innermost core where one realizes the deathless. You have only heard about it, and you cling to the idea because you are afraid of death. You know death is real, so you go on wishing and believing that something in you must be there which is deathless. This is a wish fulfillment.

I am not saying that there is no soul, I am not saying that there is nothing which is deathless. No, I am not saying that. But as far as you are concerned, you are just the body with an idea that there is a soul which is deathless. This is just in the mind, and this too you have collected because of the fear. That is why the weaker you will become, the older, the more you will become a believer in the immortal soul and God. Then you will go to the church or the temple or the mosque. If you go to the mosque or the church or the temple, you will find that old men, just on the verge of death, are gathered there.

Youth is basically atheistic; always this has been so. The younger you are, the less theistic. The younger you are, the more you are an unbeliever. Why? Because you are still strong and you feel less fear, and you are still ignorant of death. Death is far away somewhere, it happens only to others. It happens only to others, not to you. But the older you grow, you will by and by begin to feel that now it is going to happen to you also.

Death comes near, and one begins to believe. So all beliefs are fear-based. And one who believes because of fear is really deceiving himself. You are the body right now—this is a fact. You do not know anything about the deathless, you know only about the "deathful." But the deathless is there; you can know it. Believing won't do, only knowing can help. You can realize it, but just ideas are of no use unless they become a concrete experience.

So do not be deceived by ideas and do not take ideas and beliefs for experiences. That is why tantra always starts with the body—because that is a fact. You have to start from the body because you are in the body. And that too is not right. When I say you are in the body, that too is not right. As far as you are concerned you *are* the body, not *in* the body. You do not know anything about what is in the body, you know only the body. That experience of something beyond body is still far away.

If you go to metaphysicians, to theologians, they are going to start with the soul. But tantra is absolutely scientific. It starts from where you are, not from where you can be. Starting from where you can be is absurd—you cannot start from where you can be, you can start only from where you are.

Tantra has no condemnation against the body.

Tantra is a total acceptance of things as they are. Christian theologians, and those of other religions also, are condemnatory, against the body. They create a dualism, a dichotomy, that you are two. And the body is the enemy, the evil for them, so fight with it. This duality is basically wrong, and this duality will divide your mind into two and will create a split personality.

Religions have helped the human mind to be schizophrenic. Any division will divide you deeply, and you will become two, or you will become many. And everyone is a crowd of many divisions, with no organic unity and with no center. You are not an individual as far as the meaning of the word is concerned. The word means indivisible, 'individual' means indivisible. But you are just divided into many things.

Not only are your mind and your body divided, your soul and your body are divided also. The nonsense has gone so deep that even the body is divided: the lower body is evil and the upper body is good. It is stupid, but it is there. Even you yourself cannot feel at ease with your lower body. Some uneasiness creeps in. There is division and division and division....

Tantra accepts everything. Whatsoever is, is accepted wholeheartedly. That is why tantra could accept sex totally. For five thousand years tantra has been the only tradition which has accepted sex totally, the only one all over the world. Why? Because sex is the point where you are, and any movement is going to be from the point where you are.

You are at the sex center; your energy is at the sex center. And from that point it has to move up, far beyond. If you reject the center itself, then you can go on deceiving yourself that you are moving, but you cannot move. Then you are rejecting the only point from where movement is possible. So tantra accepts the body, accepts sex, accepts everything. And tantra says, wisdom accepts everything and transforms it; only ignorance rejects. Only ignorance rejects—wisdom accepts everything.

Even a poison can become a medicine, but only through wisdom.

The body can become a vehicle to that which is beyond body, and sex energy can become a spiritual force. And remember, when you ask, "What are the reasons that the body is given so much importance in tantra?" why do you ask? Why?

You are born as a body, you live as a body, you become ill as a body; you are treated, given medicine, helped, made whole and healthy as a body. You become young as a body, you will become old as a body, you will die as a body. Your whole life is body-centered, centered around the body. You will love someone, you will make love to someone and you will create other bodies, you will reproduce other bodies.

What are you doing the whole life? Preserving yourself. What are you preserving with food, with water, with shelter? The body is preserved. What are you doing by reproducing? The body is being reproduced. The whole life, 99.9 percent, is body-oriented. You can go beyond, but that journey has to be through the body, by the body, and you have to use the body. But why do you ask?—because the body is just the outer thing. Deep down the body is a symbol of sex.

So those traditions which are against sex will be against the body. Those traditions which are not against sex can only be friendly toward the body. Tantra is absolutely friendly, and tantra says that the body is sacred, holy. For tantra, to condemn the body is a sacrilege. To say that the body is impure or to say that the body is sin is nonsense for tantra —a very poisonous teaching. Tantra accepts the body—not only accepts it, but says that the body is holy, pure, innocent. You can use it and you can make it a vehicle, a medium, to go beyond! It helps even in going beyond.

But if you start fighting with the body, you are lost. If you start fighting with it, you will become more and more diseased. And if you go on fighting with it, you will miss an opportunity. Fighting is negative; tantra is a positive transformation. Do

not fight with it—there is no need.

It is as if you are sitting in a car and you start fighting with the car. Then you cannot move because you are fighting with the vehicle—which has to be used, not fought against. And you will destroy the vehicle by your fighting, and then it will be more and more difficult to move.

The body is a beautiful vehicle—very mysterious, very complex. Use it, do not fight with it. Help it. The moment you go against it you are going against yourself. It is as if a man wants to reach somewhere, but he fights with his own legs and cuts them. Tantra says, know the body and know the secrets of it. Know the energies of it and know how those energies can be transformed—how they can be moved and turned into different dimensions.

For example, take sex, which is the basic energy in the body. Ordinarily, sex energy is just used for reproduction. One body creates another body and it goes on. The biological utility of sex energy is only in reproduction. But that is only one of the uses, and the lowest. No condemnation is implied, but it is the lowest. The same energy can do other creative acts also. Reproduction is a basic creative act—you create something. That is why a woman feels a subtle well-being when she becomes a mother: she has created something.

Psychologists say that because man cannot reproduce like woman, because man cannot become a mother, he feels a certain unease, and to destroy that unease or to overcome it he goes on creating other things. He will paint, he will do something in which he becomes a creator, in which he becomes a mother. That is one of the reasons why women are less creative and men are more creative—because women have a natural dimension in which to be creative. They can become mothers and they can have a fulfillment, an easy fulfillment. A deep biological creativity is felt.

But man lacks that and feels somewhere an imbalance. He wants to create, so he will substitute something. He will paint, he will sing, he will dance. He will do something in which he also becomes a mother. Sex energy, psychologists say now—and tantra has always been saying that—is always the source of all creation. So it happens that if a painter is really deep in his creation, he may forget sex completely. When a poet is very involved with his poetry, he will forget sex completely. He need not force any brahmacharya, any celibacy, upon himself.

Only monks, noncreative monks living in a monastery, need to force brahmacharya—because if you are creative, the same energy which moves through sex moves into creation. You can forget it completely, and there is no need to make any effort to forget it because that is impossible. You cannot make any effort to forget anything, because the very effort will make you remember it again and again. That is futile—in fact, suicidal. You cannot try to forget anything.

That is why those who force themselves to be brahmacharis, celibates, become simply cerebral sex perverts. Then sex revolves in the mind: the whole thing goes on in the mind—not in the body, but in the mind. And that is worse, because then the mind becomes totally mad. Any creativity will help sex to disappear.

Tantra says, if you move into meditation sex will disappear completely; it can disappear completely. The whole energy is being absorbed at higher centers—and your body has many centers. Sex is the lowest center, and man exists at the lowest center. The more energy moves higher, the more the higher centers begin to flower. When the same energy comes to the heart, then it becomes love. When the same energy comes higher still, new dimensions and new experiences begin to flower. And when the same energy is at the highest, at the last peak in your body, it has reached that which tantra calls *sahasrar*—the last chakra in the head.

Sex is the lowest chakra and sahasrar is the highest, and between these two the sex energy moves. It can be released from the sex center. When it is released from the sex center you become a cause to reproduce someone else. When the same energy is released from the sahasrar, from the head into the cosmos, you give a new birth to yourself. It is also reproduction, but not biologically. Then it is spiritually a reproduction; then you are reborn. In India we used to call such a person "twice-born"—*dwij*. Now he has given himself a new birth. The same energy has moved.

Tantra has no condemnations, only secret techniques for how to transform. That is why tantra talks so much about the body—it is needed. The body has to be understood, and you can start only from where you are.

The third question:

You said that love can make you free. But ordinarily we see that love becomes attachment, and instead of freeing us it makes us more bound. So tell us something about attachment and freedom.

Love becomes attachment because there is no love. You were just playing, deceiving yourself. The attachment is the reality; the love was just a foreplay. So whenever you fall in love, sooner or later you discover you have become an instrument—and then the whole misery begins. What is the mechanism? Why does it happen?

Just a few days ago a man came to me and he was feeling very guilty. He said, "I loved a woman, I loved her very much. The day she died I was weeping and crying, but suddenly I became aware of a certain freedom within me, as if some burden had left me. I felt a deep breath, as if I had become free."

That moment he became aware of a second layer of his feeling. Outwardly he was weeping and crying and saying, "I cannot live without her. Now it will be impossible, or the life will be just like death. But deep down," he said, "I became aware that I am feeling very good, that now I am free."

A third layer began to feel guilt. It said to him, "What are you doing?" And the dead body was lying there just before him, he said to me, and he began to feel a great deal of guilt. He said to me,

"Help me. What has happened to my mind? Have I betrayed her so soon?"

Nothing has happened; no one has betrayed. When love becomes attachment, it becomes a burden, a bondage. But why does love become an attachment? The first thing to be understood is that if love becomes an attachment, you were just in an illusion that it was love. You were just playing with yourself and thinking that this was love. Really, you were in need of attachment. And if you go still deeper, you will find that you were also in need of becoming a slave.

There is a subtle fear of freedom, and everyone wants to be a slave. Everyone, of course, talks about freedom, but no one has the courage to be really free, because when you are really free you are alone. If you have the courage to be alone, then only can you be free.

But no one is courageous enough to be alone. You need someone. Why do you need someone? You are afraid of your own loneliness. You become bored with yourself. And really, when you are lonely, nothing seems meaningful. With someone you are occupied, and you create artificial meanings around you.

You cannot live for yourself, so you start to live for someone else. And the same is the case with the someone else also: he, or she, cannot live alone, so he is in search to find someone. Two persons who are afraid of their own loneliness come together and they start a play—a play of love. But deep down they are searching for attachment, commitment, bondage.

So sooner or later, whatsoever you desire happens. This is one of the most unfortunate things in this world. Whatsoever you desire comes to happen. You will get it sooner or later and the foreplay will disappear. When its function is done, it will disappear. When you have become a wife and husband, slaves to each other, when marriage has happened, love will disappear because love was just an illusion in which two persons could become slaves to each other.

Directly you cannot ask for slavery; it is too humiliating. And directly you cannot say to someone, "Become my slave." He will revolt. Nor can you say, "I want to become a slave to you," so you say, "I cannot live without you." But the meaning is there; it is the same. And when this—the real desire—is fulfilled, love disappears. Then you feel bondage, slavery, and then you start struggling to become free.

Remember this. It is one of the paradoxes of the mind: whatsoever you get you will get bored with, and whatsoever you do not get you will long for. When you are alone, you will long for some slavery, some bondage. When you are in bondage, you will begin to long for freedom. Really, only slaves long for freedom, and free people try again to be slaves. The mind goes on like a pendulum, moving from one extreme to the other.

Love doesn't become attachment. Attachment was the need; love was just a bait. You were in search of a fish named attachment, love was just a bait to catch the fish. When the fish is caught, the bait is thrown. Remember this, and whenever you are doing something, go deep within yourself to find out the basic cause.

If there is real love, it will never become attachment. What is the mechanism for love to become attachment? The moment you say to your lover or beloved, "Love only me," you have started possessing. And the moment you possess someone you have insulted him deeply, because you have made him into a thing.

When I possess you, you are not a person then, but just one more item amongst my furniture—a thing. Then I use you, and you are my thing, my possession, so I won't allow anyone else to use you. It is a bargain in which I am possessed by you, and you make me a thing. It is the bargain that now no one else can use you. Both partners feel bound and enslaved. I make a slave of you, then you in return make a slave of me.

Then the struggle starts. I want to be a free person, and still I want you to be possessed by me;

you want to retain your freedom and still possess me—this is the struggle. If I possess you, I will be possessed by you. If I do not want to be possessed by you, I should not possess you.

Possession should not come in between. We must remain individuals and we must move as independent, free consciousnesses. We can come together, we can merge into each other, but no one possesses. Then there is no bondage and then there is no attachment.

Attachment is one of the ugliest things. And when I say ugliest, I do not mean only religiously, I mean aesthetically also. When you are attached, you have lost your loneliness, your aloneness: you have lost everything. Just to feel good that someone needs you and someone is with you, you have lost everything, you have lost yourself.

But the trick is that you try to be independent and you make the other the possession—and the other is doing the same. So do not possess if you do not want to be possessed.

Jesus said somewhere, "Judge ye not so that ye should not be judged." It is the same: "Possess not so that ye should not be possessed." Do not make anyone a slave; otherwise you will become a slave.

So-called masters are always slaves of their own slaves. You cannot become a master of someone without becoming a slave—that is impossible.

You can only be a master when no one is a slave to you. This seems paradoxical, because when I say you can only be a master when no one is a slave to you, you will say, "Then what is the mastery? How am I a master when no one is a slave to me?" But I say only then are you a master. Then no one is a slave to you and no one will try to make a slave out of you.

To love freedom, to try to be free, means basically that you have come to a deep understanding of yourself. Now you know that you are enough unto yourself. You can share with someone, but you are not dependent. I can share myself with someone. I can share my love, I can share my happiness, I can share my bliss, my silence, with someone. But that is

a sharing, not a dependence. If no one is there, I will be just as happy, just as blissful. If someone is there, that is also good and I can share.

When you realize your inner consciousness, your center, only then will love not become an attachment. If you do not know your inner center, love will become an attachment. If you know your inner center, love will become devotion. But you must first be there to love, and you are not.

Buddha was passing through a village. One young man came to him and said, "Teach me something: how can I serve others?"

Buddha laughed at him and said, "First be. Forget others. First be yourself and then everything will follow."

Right now you are not. When you say, "When I love someone it becomes an attachment," you are saying you are not, so whatsoever you do goes wrong because the doer is absent. The inner point of awareness is not there, so whatsoever you do goes wrong. First *be,* and then you can share your being. And that sharing will be love. Before that, whatsoever you do will become an attachment.

And lastly: if you are struggling against attachment, you have taken a wrong turn. You can struggle. So many monks, recluses, sannyasins are doing that. They feel that they are attached to their house, to their property, to their wives, to their children, and they feel caged, imprisoned. They escape, they leave their homes, they leave their wives, they leave their children and possessions, and they become beggars and escape to a forest, to a loneliness. But go and observe them. They will become attached to their new surroundings.

I was visiting a friend who was a recluse living under a tree in a deep forest, but there were other ascetics also. One day it happened that I was staying with this recluse under his tree, and a new seeker came while my friend was absent. He had gone to the river to take a bath. Under his tree the new sannyasin started meditating.

The man came back from the river, and he pushed that new man away from the tree and said,

"This is my tree. You go and find another, some-where else. No one can sit under my tree." And this man had left his house, his wife, his children. Now the tree had become a possession—you cannot meditate under his tree.

You cannot escape so easily from attachment. It will take new forms, new shapes. You will be deceived, but this will be there. So do not fight with attachment, just try to understand why it is there. And then know the deep cause: because you are not, this attachment is there.

Inside you, your own self is so much absent that you try to cling to anything in order to feel safe. You are not rooted, so you try to make anything your roots. When you are rooted in your self, when you know who you are, what this being is which is in you and what this consciousness is which is in you, then you will not cling to anyone.

That doesn't mean you will not love. Really, only then can you love because then sharing is possible—and with no conditions, with no expec-tations. You simply share because you have an abundance, because you have so much it is over-flowing.

This overflowing of yourself is love. And when this overflowing becomes a flood, when by your own overflowing the whole universe is filled and your love touches the stars, in your love the earth feels good and in your love the whole universe is bathed, then it is devotion.

CHAPTER 21

Three looking techniques

♦

30 *Eyes closed, see your inner being in detail. Thus see your true nature.*

31 *Look upon a bowl without seeing the sides or the material. In a few moments become aware.*

32 *See as if for the first time a beauteous person or an ordinary object.*

Tonight's techniques are concerned with the practice of looking. Before we enter these techniques, something has to be understood about the eyes, because all these seven techniques depend on them. The first thing: eyes are the most nonbodily part in the human body, the least bodily. If matter can become nonmatter, then such also is the case with eyes. Eyes are material, but simultaneously they are also nonmaterial. Eyes are a meeting point of you and your body. Nowhere else in the body is the meeting so deep.

The human body and you are much separated, a great distance is there. But at the point of the eyes you are nearest to your body and the body is nearest to you. That is why eyes can be used for the inner journey. A single jump from the eyes can lead you to the source. That is not possible from the hand, not possible from the heart, not possible from anywhere else in the body. From elsewhere you will have to travel long; the distance is great. But from the eyes a single step is enough to enter into yourself. That is why eyes have been used continuously in religious yogic and tantric practices.

The first reason is because you are *nearest* from there. That is why, if you know how to look into someone's eyes, you can look into his depths. He is there. He is not so present anywhere else in the body, but if you can look into his eyes you will find him there. It is a difficult art to look into someone else's eyes, and it comes to you only when you have taken a jump from your own eyes within; otherwise you cannot look. If you have not looked within beyond your own eyes, you cannot have a look into someone else's eyes. But if you know how to look into the eyes, you can touch the depth of the person.

That is why only in love can you look straight and stare into another's eyes. Otherwise, if you stare into someone's eyes he will feel offended. You are trespassing; this is a trespass. You can look at the body—there is no trespass. But the moment you stare into somebody's eyes, you are trespassing his individuality, you are trespassing his individual freedom, you are entering him without any invitation. That is why there is a limit, and now the limit can be measured. At the most you can be allowed to look for three seconds. You can be allowed just a casual look and then you have to move your eyes; otherwise the other will feel offended. Looking is violent, because you can have a glimpse of his inner secrets, and that cannot be allowed.

Only in deep love can you look into another's eyes, because love means that now you do not want to maintain any secrets. You are now open to the other and the other is always welcome and invited to enter you. And when lovers look into each other's eyes, there is a meeting which is not of the body. So the second thing to be remembered: your mind, your consciousness, your soul, whatsoever is within you, can be glimpsed through the eyes.

That is why a blind man has a dead face. It is

291

not only that the eyes are lacking, but that the face is dead—not alive. Eyes are the light of the face; they enlighten your face, they give it an inner aliveness. When the eyes are not there, your face lacks aliveness. And a blind man is really closed. You cannot enter him so easily. That is why blind men are very secretive and you can rely upon a blind man. If you give him a secret, you can rely upon him. He will maintain it, and it will be difficult to judge whether he has a secret. But with a man who has alive eyes, it can be judged immediately that he has a secret.

For example, you are traveling without a ticket on a railway train. Your eyes will go on betraying that you are without a ticket. It is a secret; no one knows, only you know. But your eyes will have a different look, and you will look at anyone who enters the train with a different quality. If the other could understand the quality, he would know immediately that you are without a ticket. The look will be different when you have a ticket.

So if you are hiding a secret, your eyes will reveal it. And to control the eyes is very difficult. The most difficult thing in the body to control is the eyes. So everyone cannot become a great detective because the basic training of the detective is the training of the eyes. His eyes should not reveal anything, or they should reveal the opposite. When he is traveling without a ticket, his eyes should reveal that he has a ticket. It is very difficult because eyes are not voluntary, they are nonvoluntary.

Now many experiments are being done on the eyes. Someone is a *brahmachari,* a celibate, and he says he has no attraction toward women, but his eyes will reveal everything. He may be hiding his attraction. If a beautiful woman enters the room, he may not look at her, but even his not looking at her will be revealing. There will be an effort, a subtle suppression, and the eyes will show it. Not only that, the surface of the eyes will expand. When a beautiful woman enters, the pupils of the eyes will expand immediately to allow the beautiful woman more space to go in. And you cannot do

anything about it because those pupils and their expansion is nonvoluntary. It is absolutely impossible to control them.

So the second thing to remember is that your eyes are the doors to your secrets. If anyone wants to enter into your secret world, your privacy, your eyes are the doors. If you know how to unlock them, you will become vulnerable, open. And if you want to enter into your own secret life, your inner life, then again you will have to use the same locking and unlocking system. You will have to work on your eyes, only then can you enter.

Thirdly, eyes are very liquid, moving. They are in constant movement, and that movement has its own rhythm, its own system, its own mechanism. Your eyes are not moving at random, anarchically. They have a rhythm of their own and that rhythm shows many things. If you have a sexual thought in the mind, your eyes move differently—with a different rhythm. Just by looking at your eyes and the movement, one can say what type of thought is moving inside. When you feel hungry and a thought of food is inside, eyes have a different movement.

So now even your dreams can be penetrated. Your eye movements can be recorded while you are asleep. And remember, even in dreams your eyes behave similarly. If you are seeing a naked woman in your dream, this can be judged from your eye movements. Now there are mechanical devices to record the movements of the eyes.

These eye movements are called REM—rapid eye movements. They can be recorded on a graph, just like an electrocardiogram. Your eye movements from a whole night's sleep can be continuously recorded. And then the graph can show when you were dreaming and when you were not, because when you are not dreaming the eyes stop and become static. When you are dreaming they move, and the movement is like when you are seeing something on a screen. If you are seeing a film, the eyes have to move. In the same way, in your dream your eyes move: they are seeing something. They follow the movements of the film. For your eyes there is no difference between an actual film being shown on the screen or just a dream film.

So these REM recorders tell how much you dreamt in the night and for how many moments you were not dreaming, because the eyes stop their movement when you are not dreaming. There are many persons who say they never dream. They just have a very absent minded memory—nothing else. They cannot remember, that is the only thing. They are actually dreaming, for the whole night they are dreaming, but they cannot remember. Their memory is not good, that is all. So in the morning when they say there was no dream, do not believe them.

Why do the eyes move when there is a dream, and why do the eyes stop when there is no dream? Each eye movement is joined to the thought process. If thinking is there, the eyes will move. If there is no thinking, the eyes will not move—there is no need.

So remember this third point also, that eye movements and thinking are joined together. That is why if you stop your eyes and their movements, your thought process will stop immediately. Or if your thought process stops your eyes will stop automatically.

And one point more, the fourth. The eyes move continuously from one object to another. From A to B, from B to C, they go on moving. Movement is their nature. It is just like a river flowing, movement is its nature. And because of that movement, they are so alive! Movement is also life.

You can try to stop your eyes at a particular point, at a particular object, and not allow them to move, but movement is their nature. You cannot stop movement, but you can stop your eyes: understand the distinction. You can stop your eyes at a particular fixed point—on a dot on the wall. You can stare at the dot; you can stop your eyes. But movement is their nature. So they may not move from object A to object B because you have forced them to remain at A, but then a very strange phenomenon happens.

Movement is bound to be there. If you do not allow them movement from A to B, they will move from outwards to inwards. Either they can move from A to B, or if you do not allow this outward movement they will move inwards. Movement is their nature, they need movement. If you suddenly stop and do not allow them to move outwards, they will start moving inwards.

So there are two possibilities of movement. One is from object A to object B—this is an outward movement. This is how it is happening naturally. But there is another possibility which is of tantra and yoga—not allowing movement from one outside object to another and stopping this movement. Then the eyes jump from an outside object to the inner consciousness, they begin to move inwards. Remember these four points; then it will be easy to understand the techniques.

---

30 Close the eyes and stop their movement.

The first looking technique: *Eyes closed, see your inner being in detail. Thus see your true nature.*

Eyes closed.... Close your eyes. But just closing is not enough. Total closing means to close your eyes and stop their movements; otherwise the eyes will continue to see something which is of the outside. Even with closed eyes you will see things—images of things. Actual things are not there, but images, ideas, collected memories—they will start flowing. They are also from outside, so your eyes are still not totally closed. Totally closed eyes means nothing to see.

Understand the difference. You can close your eyes; that is easy, everyone closes them every moment. In the night you close your eyes, but that will not reveal the inner nature to you. Close your eyes so that nothing remains to be seen—no outside object, no inside image of any outside object, just a blank darkness as if you have suddenly gone blind. Not blind only to reality, but to the dream reality also.

One has to practice it. A long period will be needed, it cannot be done suddenly. You will need a long training. Close your eyes. Anytime you feel that it is easy and you have time, close your eyes and then inwardly stop all movements of the eyes. Feel! Do not allow any movement, stop all movements of the eyes. Feel as if they have become stones, and then remain in that "stony" state of the eyes. Do not do anything; just remain there. Suddenly, someday, you will become aware that you are looking inside yourself.

You can go just outside this building, move around the building and have a look, but that is looking at the building from the outside. Then you can enter into the room and you can stand in this room and have a look. That is looking at the building from the inside. When you are taking a round outside, you see the walls, but only one side, the outside of the walls. When you come in, the walls are the same, but now you will see the inside of the walls.

You have seen your body only from the outside. You have seen your body in a mirror or you have seen your hands from the outside. You do not know what the inside of your body is. You have never entered into your own self; you have never been at the center of your body and being, to look around at what is there from the inside.

This technique is very helpful for having a look from the inside, and that transforms your total consciousness, your total existence—because if you can have a look from the inside, you immediately become different from the world. This false identity that "I am the body" is only because we have been looking at our bodies from the outside. If you can have a look from the inside, the looker becomes different. And then you can move your consciousness in your body, from your toe to your head; you can now have a round inside the body. And once you become capable of having a look from the inside and moving there, then it is not difficult to go outside at all.

Once you know how to move, once you know

that you are separate from the body, you are freed from a great bondage. Now you have no gravitational pull; now you have no limitation. Now you are absolute freedom. You can go out of the body; you can go and come. And then your body becomes just an abode.

Close your eyes, see your inner being in detail and move from limb to limb inside. Just go to your toe. Forget the whole body, move to the toe. Stay there and have a look. Then move through the legs, come on upwards, go to every limb. Then many things happen.

Then your body becomes such a sensitive vehicle, you cannot even imagine it. Then if you touch someone, you can move into your hand totally and that touch will become transforming. That is what is meant by a master's touch: he can move to any limb totally, and then he is concentrated there. If you can move to any part of your body totally, that part becomes alive—so much alive that you cannot imagine what happens to that part. Then you can move to the eyes totally. If you can move to your eyes totally and then look into someone's eyes, you will penetrate him; you will go to his very depths.

Now psychoanalysts are trying to go to the depths through psychoanalysis. Then they take one year, two years, three years…. This is a sheer wastage of time. And life is so short that if three years are taken to analyze a person's mind, it is nonsense. And then too you cannot rely on whether the analysis is complete or not. You are groping in the dark. The Eastern approach has been through the eyes. No need of analyzing the person for such a long time. The work can be done by just entering through his eyes totally, touching his depths, knowing many things about him of which even he is not aware.

The master has many things to do. One of the basic things is this: to analyze you, to go deep into you, to move into your darker realms which are unknown to you. And if he says to you that something is hidden in you, you will not believe it. How can you believe it? You are not aware of it. You know only one part of the mind—a very small fragment which is just the upper part, just the first layer. Behind it there are hidden nine layers which are not known to you, but through your eyes a penetration is possible.

Close your eyes; *see your inner being in detail.* The first, outer part of the technique is to look at your body inwardly—from your inner center. Stand there and have a look. You will be separated from the body because the looker is never the looked at. The observer is different from the object.

If you can see your body totally from the inside, then you can never fall into the illusion that you are the body. Then you will remain different—totally different: inside it but not it, in the body but not the body. This is the first part. Then you can move; then you are free to move. Once freed from the body, freed from the identity, you are free to move. Now you can move into your mind—deep down. Those nine layers which are within and unconscious can now be entered into.

This is the inner cave of the mind. If you enter this cave of the mind, you will become separate from the mind also. Then you will see that the mind is also an object which you can look at, and that which is entering the mind is, again, separate and different. This entering into the mind is what is meant by: *see your inner being in detail.* Body and mind both should be entered and looked at from within. Then you are simply a witness, and this witness cannot be penetrated.

That is why it is your innermost core: that is you. That which can be penetrated, that which can be seen, is not you. When you have come to that which cannot be penetrated, that in which you cannot move, which cannot be observed, then only have you come to the real self. You cannot witness the witnessing source, remember—that is absurd.

If someone says that "I have witnessed my witness," that is absurd. Why is it absurd? Because if you have witnessed your witnessing self, then the witnessing self is not the witnessing self. That which has witnessed it is the witness. That which

you can see, you are not; that which you can observe, you are not; that which you can become aware of, you are not.

But a point comes, beyond the mind, where simply you are. Now you cannot divide your single existence into two: object and subject. Simple subjectivity is there, just witnessing. This is very, very difficult to comprehend through intellect because all the categories of the intellect are broken there.

Because of this logical difficulty, Charvaka—the expounder of one of the most logical philosophical systems in the world—says that you cannot know the self; there is no self-knowledge. And because there is no self-knowledge, how can you say that there is a self? Whatsoever you know is not the self. The knower is the self, not the known, so you cannot say logically that "I have known my self." That is absurd, illogical. How can you know your self? Then who will be the knower and who will be the known? Knowledge means a dichotomy, a division between object and subject, the knower and the known.

So Charvaka says that all those who say they have known the self are talking nonsense. Self-knowledge is impossible because the self is irreducibly the knower. It cannot be converted into the known.

Then Charvaka says that if you cannot know the self, how can you say that there is self? Those like Charvaka, who do not believe in the presence of a self, are called *anatmavadin.* They say no self is; they say there is no self—that which cannot be known is not. And they are right logically. If logic is all, they are right. But this is the mystery of life, that logic is only the beginning—not the end. A moment comes when logic ends, but you do not end. A moment comes when logic is finished, but you are still there. Life is illogical. That is why it is difficult to comprehend, to conceive of what is meant when it is said that only the witness remains.

For example, if there is a lamp in this room, you see many objects around you. When the lamp is turned off, there is darkness and nothing can be seen. When the lamp is put on, there is light and you can see everything in the room. But have you ever observed what is happening? If there are no objects, will you be able to see the lamp and its light? You will not be able to see its light, because to be seen the light must reflect something. It must strike an object. The rays must go to an object and then be reflected, then they will reach to your eyes. So first you see objects, then you infer that light is there. When you burn a lamp or a candle, you never see the light first. First you see the objects, and because of the objects you come to know about the light.

Scientists say that if there are no objects then light cannot be seen. Look at the sky: it looks blue but it is not blue, it is filled with cosmic rays. It looks blue because there are no objects. Those rays cannot reflect and come to your eyes. If you go into space and there are no objects, then there will be darkness. Of course, rays will be passing just by your side, but there will be darkness. To know the light some objects have to be there.

Charvaka says that if you enter within and come to the point where only the witness has remained and there is nothing to be witnessed, how can you know about it? Some object must be there to be witnessed; only then can you know the witnessing. Logically, scientifically, it is right. But existentially it is not right.

Those who really move inside come to a point where there is no object left but just the consciousness of being. You are, but nothing is there to be seen—only the seer. There is simple subjectivity without any object around it. The moment you come to this point, you have entered your ultimate goal of being. You can call it the alpha, the beginning, or you can call it the omega, the end. It is both, alpha and omega. This is called "self-knowledge."

Linguistically the word is wrong because linguistically nothing can be said about it. Language becomes meaningless when you enter the world of the one. Language is meaningful only when you are in the world of two. In the world of duality language is meaningful because language is created in, is part of, the dualistic world. It becomes meaningless when you enter the one, the nondual. That is why those who know have remained silent—or even if they say something they hurriedly add that whatsoever they are saying is just symbolic, and whatsoever they are saying is not exactly true, it is false.

Lao Tzu said that that which can be said cannot be true, and that which is true cannot be said. He remained silent; for most of his life he would not write anything. He said, "If I say something it will be untrue, because nothing can be said about the realm where only the one remains."

Eyes closed, see your inner being in detail— body and mind both. *Thus see your true nature.* See your body and mind, your structure. And remember, body and mind are not two things. Rather, you are both: body-mind—psychosomatic. Mind is the finer part of the body and body is the grosser part of the mind.

So if you can become aware of the structure of body-mind, if you can become conscious of the structure, you are freed from the structure, you are freed from the vehicle, you have become different. And this knowing that you are separate from the structure is your true nature. That is what you really are. This body will die, but that true nature never dies. This mind will die and change, and die again and again, but that true nature never dies. That true nature is eternal. That is why that true nature is neither your name nor your form. It is beyond both.

So how to do this technique? Total closing of the eyes is needed. If you try it, close your eyes and then stop the movements. Let your eyes become just like stones. No movements allowed. Suddenly, any day while practicing this, it will happen that you will be able to look within. The eyes which were always looking outside will turn in and you will have a glimpse inside.

Then there is no difficulty. Once you have a glimpse inside, you know what to do and how to move. Only the first glimpse is difficult; after that you have the knack. Then it becomes just like a trick. Any moment you can close your eyes, make your eyes static, you can enter the realm.

Buddha was dying. It was the last day of his life, and he asked his disciples if they wanted to ask any questions. They were weeping, crying, and they said, "You have told us so much. Now nothing is left to ask."

Buddha had a habit of asking thrice. He would never stop after asking once. He would ask again, and then he would ask still again whether you had any question to ask. Many times Buddha was asked, "Why do you ask a single thing three times?" He said, "Because man is so unaware, so unconscious, he may not have heard the first time and he may have missed the second time."

Thrice he asked, and thrice his *bhikkhus*, monks, his disciples said, "Now we do not want to ask anything. You have said so much."

Then he closed his eyes and said, "If you do not have anything to ask, before death occurs to the body I will move from it. Before death enters the body I will move from it."

He closed his eyes. His eyes became static and he started moving. It is said that there were four parts to his movement inwards. First he closed his eyes; secondly, his eyes became static, there were no movements. If you had then the instrument for recording REM, the graph would not have come. The eyes became static—that was the second thing. Thirdly, he looked at his body; then fourthly, he looked at his mind.

This was the whole journey. Before death occurred he was back at his center, in his original source. That is why this death is not called death: we call it *nirvana*, and this is the difference. We call it nirvana—cessation—not death. Ordinarily, we die because death occurs to us. It never occurred to Buddha. Before death came, he had already returned to the source.

Death occurred only to the dead body—he was not there to be found. So in Buddhist tradition it is said that he never died. Death could not catch him. It followed him as it follows everyone, but he could not be trapped; he tricked death out of it. He must have been laughing—standing beyond, and death was there only with a dead body.

This technique is the same. Make four parts of it and move. And when you know one glimpse, the whole thing will become very easy and simple. Then any moment you can move in and come out, and go in and come out, just like coming out of your house and going in…coming out and going in.

---

31 Look at an object as a whole.

The second looking technique: *Look upon a bowl without seeing the sides or the material. In a few moments become aware.*

Look at anything. A bowl or any object will do, but look with a different quality. *Look upon a bowl without seeing the sides or the material.* Look upon any object, but with these two conditions…. Do not look at the sides, look at the object as a whole. Ordinarily, we look at parts. It may not be done so consciously, but we look at parts. If I look at you, first I see your face, then your torso, and then your whole body. Look at an object as a whole, do not divide it in parts. Why? Because when you divide something in parts, the eyes have an opportunity to move from one part to another. Look at a thing as a whole. You can do it.

I can look at all of you in two ways. I can look from this side and then move. I can look at A, then at B, then I look at C and go on moving. When I look at A, B and C, I am not present—or just present on the fringe, but not focused. When I look at B, I am leaving A. When I look at C, A has been completely lost; he has gone out of my focus. I can look at this group in this manner, but I can look at the whole group without dividing it into individuals, into units, taking it as a whole.

Try it. First look at a thing moving from one

fragment to another. Then suddenly look at this thing as a whole; do not divide it. When you look at a thing as a whole, the eyes have no need to move. In order not to give any opportunity for movement, this has been made a condition: look at an object totally, taken as a whole. And secondly, look without seeing the material. If the bowl is of wood, do not see the wood; just see the bowl, the form. Do not see the substance.

It may be of gold, it may be of silver—observe it. Do not look at the material of which it is made, just look at the form. The first thing is to look at it as a whole. Secondly, look at it as a form, not as a substance. Why? Because substance is the material part, form is the spiritual part, and you are to move from the material to the nonmaterial. It will be helpful.

Try it. You can try it with anyone. Some man or some woman is standing: look, and take the man or woman wholly into your look, totally into it. It will be a weird feeling in the beginning because you are not habituated this way, but it is very beautiful in the end. And then, do not think about whether the body is beautiful or not, white or black, man or woman. Do not think, just look at the form. Forget the substance and just look at the form.

In a few moments become aware. Go on looking at the form as a whole. Do not allow the eyes any movement. Do not start thinking about the material. What will happen? You will suddenly become aware of your self. Looking at something, you will become aware of your self. Why? Because for the eyes there is no possibility to move outwards. The form has been taken as a whole, so you cannot move to the parts. The material has been dropped; pure form has been taken. Now you cannot think about gold, wood, silver, etcetera.

A form is pure form. No thinking about it is possible. A form is just a form; you cannot think about it. If it is of gold, you can think many things. You would like, you may like to steal it, or to do something with it, or to sell it, or you can think about the price—many things are possible. But of

pure form, no thinking is possible. Pure form stops thinking. And there is no possibility of changing from one part to another; you have taken it as a whole.

Remain with the whole and the form. Suddenly you will become aware of yourself, because now the eyes cannot move. And they need movement, that is their nature. So your look will move toward you. It will come back, it will return home, and suddenly you will become aware of your self. This becoming aware of one's self is one of the most ecstatic moments possible. When for the first time you become aware of your self, it has such beauty and such bliss that you cannot compare it with anything else you have known.

Really, for the first time you become your self; for the first time you know you are. Your being is revealed in a flash.

But why does it happen? You might have seen, in children's books particularly, a picture—or in some psychological treatises, but I hope everyone has seen it somewhere or other—a picture of an old woman, and in the same lines a beautiful young woman is also hidden. There is one picture, the same lines, but two figures are in it: one old woman, one young woman.

Look at the picture; you cannot become aware of both simultaneously. You will become aware either of one or the other. If you have become aware of the old woman, you cannot see where the young woman is hiding. But if you try to find her, it will be difficult, and the very effort will become a barrier. Because you have become aware of the old woman, she will have become a fixed thing in your eyes. With this fixed thing, you are trying to find the young woman. It is impossible, you will not be able to find her. You have to do a technique.

Just stare at the old woman, forget the young woman completely. Stare at the old woman, at the old woman figure. Stare! Go on staring. Suddenly the old woman will disappear, and you will become aware of the young woman hiding there. Why? If you try to find her you will miss. This type of picture is given to children like a puzzle, and it is said to them, "Find the other." Then they start trying to find her, and because of that they miss.

The trick is not to try to find her, just stare at the figure and you will become aware. Forget the other, no need to think about it. Your eyes cannot remain at one point, so if you stare at the old woman figure the eyes will become tired. Then suddenly they will move from the figure, and in that movement you will become aware of the other figure which is hidden just by the old woman's side, in the same lines. But the miracle is that when you become aware of the young woman, you cannot see the old woman. But you know that both are there now.

In the beginning you may not have believed that the young woman is hiding, but now you know because you have seen the old woman first. Now you know that the old woman is there, but while looking at the young one you cannot simultaneously become aware of the old one. And if you become aware of the old one, you will miss the young one again. Both cannot be seen simultaneously; you can see only one at a time.

The same happens with the outside and the inside look. You cannot have both looks simultaneously. When you are looking at a bowl or at any object, you are looking out: the consciousness is moving out, the river is flowing out. You are focused on the bowl. Go on staring at it. That very staring will create the opportunity to move in. Your eyes will become tired, they would like to move. Finding nothing to move outward, suddenly the river will turn back—that remains the only possibility. You will have forced your consciousness to fall back. And when you become aware of *you*, you will miss the bowl; it will not be there.

That is why a Shankara or a Nagarjuna says the whole world is illusory; they have known it so. When we come to know ourselves, the world is not. Really, the world is not illusory; it is there. But you cannot see both worlds simultaneously—that is the problem. So when a Shankara enters into himself, when he comes to know his self, when he

becomes a witness, the world is not there. So he is right. He says it is *maya*—illusion. It simply appears to be; it is not there.

Be aware of the fact. When you know the world, you are not. You *are* there, but hidden, and you cannot believe that you are hidden there; the world is too much present for you. And if you start to look for yourself directly, it will be difficult, the very effort may become a barrier. So tantra says, fix your stare somewhere in the world, on any object, and do not move from there, remain there. This very effort to remain there will create the possibility for the consciousness to begin to flow upwards—backwards. Then you will become aware of your self.

But when you become aware of your self, the bowl will not be there. It is there, but *for you* it will not be there. So Shankara says the world is illusory because when you come to know your self the world is not there. It disappears like a dream.

But Charvaka and Epicurus and Marx, they are also right. They say the world is true, and your self is just false; it is nowhere to be found. They say science is real. Science says only matter is, only objects are; there is no subject. They are right, because the eyes are focused on the object.

A scientist is constantly focusing on objects. He forgets the self completely. Both Shankara and Marx are right in one sense and wrong in another. If you are fixed upon the world, if your look is fixed on the world, the self will look illusory—like it is just a dream. If you are looking inwards, the world will become a dream. Both are real, but you cannot be aware of both simultaneously—that is the problem. And nothing can be done. You will meet the old woman or you will meet the young woman, and one will become maya, illusory. But this technique can be used easily. It will take a little time, but it is not difficult.

Once you know the turning of consciousness, you can do it anywhere. Just riding in a bus or sitting in a train you can do it—anywhere. No need of a bowl or any particular object, you can do it with anything. With anything, stare, stare, stare ...and suddenly turn inwards, and the train disappears. Of course, when you come back from your inner journey you will have traveled, but the train will have disappeared. From one station you will reach to another, and in between there will have been no train—just a gap. Of course, the train was there; otherwise how can you come to the other station? But it was not there for you; for you it was not.

Those who can practice this technique can live in the world very easily. Any moment they can make anything disappear—remember this. You are bothered with your wife or with your husband— you can have her or him disappear. The wife is there sitting just by your side and she is not there. She is maya, she has disappeared. Just by staring and then turning your consciousness inwards, she has ceased to be there. And it has happened many times.

I remember Socrates. His wife Xanthippe was very much worried about him, and any wife would have been in the same dilemma. To have a Socrates as a husband is one of the most difficult things to tolerate. Socrates is good as a teacher, but not as a husband.

One day it happened...and because of it his wife has been condemned for two thousand years continuously, but that is not just; I do not think she has done anything wrong. Socrates was sitting there, and he must have been doing something like this technique—it is not recorded, I am just assuming. His wife came with a tray, a teapot, to give him tea. She must have found that he was not there, so it is reported that she poured the tea upon Socrates, over his face. Then suddenly he came back.

His face remained burned for his whole life. And because of this his wife has been condemned, but no one knows what Socrates was doing there —because no wife would do this suddenly, there is no need. He must have done something; something must have been happening there. That is why Xanthippe had to throw tea over him. He must have been in an inner trance, and the burning sensation of the tea must have brought him back, the consciousness must have returned.

I assume that this was the case because there are many other cases reported about Socrates which are similar. For forty-eight hours he was not found. He was sought all over, the whole of Athens went in search of Socrates, but he was not to be found anywhere. Then he was found outside the city, miles away, standing under a tree. Half of his body was just under snow. Snow was falling, and he was just frozen, standing there with open eyes. But he was not looking at anyone.

When the crowd gathered around, they looked into his eyes and they thought that he was dead. His eyes were just like stones—looking, but not looking at anyone; just static, unmoving. They felt his heart, it was beating slowly; he was alive. They had to give him shocks, only then did he come back to look at them. Immediately he asked, "What is the time now?" He had missed forty-eight hours completely, they never existed for him. He was not in this world of time and space.

So they asked, "What were you doing? We thought you were dead already...forty-eight hours!"

He said, "I was staring at the stars, and just suddenly it happened that the stars disappeared. And then, I don't know...then the whole world disappeared. But I remained in such a cool, calm, blissful state that if it is death it is worth thousands of lives. If it is death, then I would like to enter it again and again."

It may have happened without his knowledge, because Socrates was not a yogi, not a tantric. He was not in any way concerned consciously with any spiritual practice. But he was a great thinker, and it may have happened as an accident that he was staring at the stars in the night, and suddenly his look turned back, inwards. You can do it. And stars are really good objects.

Lie down on the ground, look at the black sky, and then fix yourself on one star. Concentrate on it, stare at it. Narrow down your consciousness to one

300

star; forget other stars. Concentrate, narrow down your gaze. Other stars will be there just on the fringe, on the boundary. But by and by they will disappear, and only one star will remain. Then go on staring. A moment will come when that star will disappear. And when that star disappears, you will appear to yourself.

---

32 Look at an object as if for the first time.

The third looking technique: *See as if for the first time a beauteous person or an ordinary object.*

Some basic things first; then you can do this technique. We look at things always with old eyes. You come to your home; you look at it without looking at it. You know it—there is no need to look at it. You have entered it again and again for years together. You go to the door, you enter the door, you may unlock the door. But there is no need to look.

This whole process goes on robotlike, mechanically, unconsciously. If something goes wrong…only if your key is not fitting into the lock, then you look at the lock. If the key fits, you never look at the lock. Because of mechanical habits, repeatedly doing the same thing again and again, you lose the capacity to look; you lose the freshness to look. Really, you lose the function of your eyes—remember this. You become basically blind, because eyes are not needed.

Remember the last time you looked at your wife. The last time you looked at your wife or at your husband may have been years ago. For how many years have you not looked? You just pass, giving a casual glimpse, but not a look. Go again and look at your wife or at your husband as if you were looking for the first time. Why? Because if you are looking for the first time, your eyes will be filled with a freshness. They will become alive.

You are passing through a street, and a beautiful woman passes. Your eyes become alive—lighted. A sudden flame comes to them. This woman may be a wife to someone. He will not look at her; he may be as blind as you have become seeing your wife. Why? For the first time eyes are needed, the second time not so much, and the third time they are not needed. After a few repetitions you become blind.

We live blindly. Be aware: when you meet your children, are you looking at them? You are not looking at them. This habit kills the eyes; the eyes become bored—repeatedly there is the old again and again. And nothing is old really, it is just that your habit makes you feel that it is so. Your wife is not the same as she was yesterday, she cannot be; otherwise she is a miracle. Nothing can be the same the next moment. Life is flux, everything is flowing, nothing is the same.

The same sunrise will not happen again. In a sense also, the sun is not the same. Every day it is new; basic changes have occurred. And the sky will not be the same again, this morning is not going to come again. Every morning has its own individuality, and the sky and the colors will not gather in the same pattern again. But you go on moving as if everything is just the same.

They say nothing is new under the sky. Really, nothing is old under the sky. Only the eyes become old, accustomed to things; then nothing is new. For children everything is new, that is why everything gives them excitement. Just a colored stone on a beach, and they become so excited. You will not be excited even seeing God himself coming to your house. You will say, "I know him, I have read about him." Children are so excited because their eyes are new and fresh, and everything is a new world, a new dimension.

Look at children's eyes—at the freshness, the radiant aliveness, the vitality. They look mirrorlike, silent but penetrating. Only such eyes can reach within.

So this technique says, *See as if for the first time a beauteous person or an ordinary object.* Anything will do. Look at your shoes. You have been using them for years, but look as if for the first time and see the difference; the quality of your consciousness suddenly changes.

I wonder whether you have seen Van Gogh's painting of his shoe. It is one of the rarest things. There is just an old shoe—tired, sad, as if just on the verge of death. It is just an old shoe, but look at it, feel it, and you will feel what a long, boring life this shoe must have passed through. It is so sad, just praying to be taken away from life, tired completely, every nerve broken, just an old man, an old shoe. It is one of the most original paintings. But how could Van Gogh see it?

You have even older shoes with you—more tired, more dead, more sad, depressed—but you have never looked at them, at what you have done to them, how you have behaved with them. They tell a life story about you because they are your shoes. They can say everything about you. If they could write, they would write a most authentic biography of the person they had to live with— every mood, every face. When their owner was in love he behaved differently with the shoes, when he was angry he behaved differently. The shoes were not concerned at all, but everything has left a mark.

Look at Van Gogh's painting, and then you will see what he could see in the shoes. Everything is there—a whole biography of the person who was using them. But how could he see? To be a painter, one has to regain the child's look, the freshness. He can look at everything—at most ordinary things even. He can look!

Cézanne has painted a chair, just an ordinary chair, and you may even wonder...why paint a chair? There is no need. But he worked on that painting for months at a time. You may not have stopped for a single moment to look at it, and he worked for months on it because he could look at a chair. A chair has its own spirit, its own story, its own miseries and happinesses. It has lived, it has passed through life. It has its own experiences, memories. They are all revealed in Cézanne's painting. But do you look at your chair? No one looks at it, no one feels it.

Any object will do. This technique is just to make your eyes fresh—so fresh, alive, radiantly vital, that they can move within and you can have a look at your inner self. *See as if for the first time.* Make it a point to see everything as if for the first time, and sometime, suddenly, you will be surprised at what a beautiful world you have been missing. Suddenly become aware and look at your wife as if for the first time. And it will be no wonder if you feel again the same love you felt the first time, the same surge of energy, the same attraction in its fullest. But look as if for the first time at *a beauteous person or an ordinary object.* What will happen? You will regain your eyesight. You are blind. Just now, as you are, you are blind. And this blindness is more fatal than physical blindness, because you have eyes and still you cannot look.

Jesus says many times, "Those who have eyes, let them see. Those who have ears, let them hear." It seems that he was talking to blind men or to deaf men. But he goes on repeating it. What was he—a superintendent in some institute for the blind? He goes on repeating, "If you have eyes, look." He must be talking with ordinary men who have eyes. But why this insistence on, "If you have eyes, look"? He is talking about the eyes which this technique can give you.

Look at everything you pass as if for the first time. Make it a continuous attitude. Touch everything as if for the first time. What will happen? If you can do this, you will be freed from your past. The burden, the depth, the dirtiness, the accumulated experiences—you will be freed from them.

Every moment, move from the past. Do not allow it to enter within you; do not allow it to be carried—leave it. Look at everything as if for the first time. This is a great technique to help you to be freed from the past. Then you are constantly in the present, and by and by you will have an affinity with the present. Then everything will be new. Then you will be able to understand Heraclitus' saying that you cannot step twice in the same river. You cannot see a person twice—the same person—because nothing is static. Everything is river-like, flowing and flowing and flowing. If you are freed from the past and you have a look which can see the present, you will enter the existence. And this entry will be double: you will enter into everything, into its spirit, and you will enter into yourself also because the present is the door. All meditations in one way or the other try to get you to live in the present. So this technique is one of the most beautiful techniques—and easy. You can try it, and without any danger.

If you are looking afresh even when passing through the same street again, it is a new street. Meeting the same friend as if he is a stranger, looking at your wife as you looked for the first time when she was a stranger, can you really say that he or she is not still a stranger? You may have lived for twenty years or thirty years or forty years with your wife, but can you say that you are acquainted with her? She is still a stranger, you are two strangers living together. You know the outer habits of each other, the outer reactions, but the inner core of the being is unknown, untouched.

Look freshly again, as if for the first time, and you will see the same stranger. Nothing, *nothing*, has become old; everything is new. This will give a freshness to your look, your eyes will become innocent. Those innocent eyes can see. Those innocent eyes can enter into the inner world.

CHAPTER 22

Unblocking the third eye

♦

How do the looking techniques affect the third eye?

Why do persons involved in psychic sciences have tense and fearful eyes?

Why does the stopping of eye movement create psychic tensions?

The first question:

Explain the relationship of the two eyes with the third eye. In which way do the techniques concerned with looking affect the third eye?

irstly, two points are to be understood. One, the energy of the third eye is really the same as that which moves in the two ordinary eyes—the same energy. It begins to move in a new center. The third eye is already there, but nonfunctioning, and it cannot see unless these ordinary eyes become unseeing.

The same energy has to move in it. When the energy is not moving in the two eyes it can move in the third, and when it moves in the third the two eyes will become unseeing. They will be there, but you won't be able to see through them. That energy that looks through them will be absent; it will move through a new center. That center is between these two eyes. It is already there, complete; any moment it can function. But it needs energy to function, and that same energy has to be diverted.

Secondly, when you are seeing through the two eyes, you are seeing through the physical body. The third eye is not really a part of the physical body. It is part of the second body which is hidden—the subtle body, the *sukshma sharir*. It has a corresponding spot in the physical body, but it is not part of it. That is why physiology cannot believe that there exists a third eye or anything like it,

because your skull can be analyzed, penetrated, x-rayed, and there is no point, no physical entity which can be said to be the third eye. The third eye is part of the subtle body, the *sukshma sharir*.

When you die your physical body dies, but your *sukshma sharir*, your subtle body, moves with you; it takes another birth. Unless the subtle body dies, you can never be freed from the circle of birth–death, rebirth–redeath. The circle moves on.

The third eye belongs to the subtle body. When the energy is moving through the physical body, you are looking through the physical eyes. That is why through the physical eyes you cannot look at anything other than the physical, than the material. The two eyes are physical. Through these eyes you cannot look at anything, cannot see anything which is not physical.

Only with the third eye functioning can you enter a different dimension. Now you can see things which are invisible to the physical eyes, but are visible to the subtle eyes. Then, with the third eye functioning, if you look at a person you look at his soul, at his spirit, not at his body—just like you look at the physical body through the physical eyes, but you cannot see the soul. The same happens when you look through the third eye: you look and the body is not there, just the one who resides in the body.

Remember these two points. Firstly, the same energy has to move. It has to be taken away from the ordinary physical eyes and allowed to move through the third eye. Secondly, the third eye is not part of the physical body. It is part of the subtle body, the second body that is within. Because it is part of the subtle body, the moment you can look through it you look at the subtle world. You are sitting here. If a ghost is sitting here you cannot see it, but if your third eye is functioning you will see the ghost, because subtle existence can be seen only through the subtle eye.

How is the third eye related with this technique of looking? It is deeply related. Really, this technique is to open the third eye. If your two eyes stop completely, if they become nonmoving, static, like stones, with no movement in these eyes, the energy stops flowing through them. If you stop them, the energy stops flowing through them. The energy flows; that is why they move. The vibration, the movement, is because of the energy. If the energy is not moving, your eyes will become just like a dead man's eyes—stony, dead.

Looking at a spot, staring at it without allowing your eyes to move anywhere else, will give a staticness. Suddenly the energy which was moving through the two eyes will not be moving through these eyes. And energy has to move; energy cannot be static. Eyes can be static, but energy cannot be static. When these eyes are closed to the energy, if suddenly the doors are closed and the energy cannot move through these eyes, it tries to find a new path. And the third eye is just near, just between the two eyebrows, half an inch deep. It is just near—the nearest point.

If your energy is released from these eyes, the first thing that can happen is that it will move through the third eye. It is just as if water is flowing and you close one hole: it will find another—the nearest which can be found with the least resistance. It will find it automatically; you do not have to do anything specifically. With these physical eyes, you just have to stop energy from moving through them, and then energy will find its own path and it will move through the third eye.

This movement through the third eye transforms you into a different world. You start seeing things you have never seen, you start feeling things you have never felt, you start smelling things you have never smelled. A new world, a subtle world, starts functioning. It is already there. The eye is there; the world, the subtle world, is already there. Both are there, but not revealed.

Once you function in that dimension, many things become apparent to you. For example, if a person is going to die, if your third eye is functioning you will become immediately aware that he is going to die. No physical analysis, no physical diagnosis can say that certainly he is going to die. At the most, we can talk about probabilities. We can say perhaps he will die, and this statement will be conditional: "If such and such remains the case, he may die; if something can be done he may not die."

Medical diagnosis cannot yet be certain about death. Why? So much development and yet so much uncertainty about death! Really, medical science is trying to deduce death, to infer death, through physical symptoms, and death is a subtle phenomenon, not physical. It is an invisible phenomenon of a different dimension. But with the third eye functioning, you suddenly feel that a man is going to die. How do you feel it? Death has an impact. If the man is going to die, then death has already cast its shadow there, and that shadow can be felt with the third eye at any time.

When a child is born, those who have had much deep practice using the third eye can see the time of his death that very moment. But then the shadow is very subtle. When a person is going to die in six months, then anyone whose third eye functions a little can see the death six months before it comes. The shadow darkens. Really, around you a dark shadow settles down and that can be felt, but not with these two eyes.

With the third eye, you begin to see auras. A person comes to you; he cannot deceive you, because whatever he says is meaningless unless it corresponds to his aura. He may say he is a person who never gets angry, but the red aura will show that he is filled with anger. He cannot deceive as far as his aura is concerned, because he is completely unaware of the aura. Whatsoever he says can be judged through his aura, whether it is right or wrong. With the third eye you start seeing radiations, auras.

In the old days, that was how someone was initiated. Unless the aura was right, the master would wait, because your wish fulfillment was not the question. You may have wanted to be initiated, but that was not enough unless your aura said that you were ready. So for years the disciple had to wait until the aura was ready; it had nothing to do with his desire to be initiated—that is futile. Sometimes even for lives, one had to wait.

For example, Buddha resisted the temptation to initiate women for many years. So much pressure was put upon him; still he would reject this. Ultimately he agreed to initiate women, but then he said, "Now my religion will not be alive after five hundred years; I have compromised. But because you are forcing me, I will initiate women."

What was the reason why he would not initiate women? One basic reason was this: with man, sexual energy can be regulated very easily. A man can become a celibate very easily. With a woman's body it is difficult because menses is a regular phenomenon—unconscious, uncontrollable, nonvoluntary. Semen ejaculation can be controlled, but menses cannot be controlled. Or, if one tries to control it, then it will have very bad effects on the body.

The moment a woman enters her period of menses, her aura changes completely: it becomes sexual, aggressive, depressed, all that is negative surrounds the woman, and this happens every month. Only because of this Buddha was not ready to initiate women. He said that it was difficult because every month the menses moves in a circle, periodically, and nothing can be done voluntarily. Something can be done, but it was difficult to do that in Buddha's time. Now it can be done.

Mahavira completely denied any possibility of a woman being liberated from a woman's body. He said that a woman has to be born again as a man,

and only then can she be liberated. So for a woman all the effort should be channeled to enter a new birth as a man. Why? It was a problem of the aura.

If you initiate a woman, every month she will fall down and the whole effort will be lost. There was no discrimination, no evaluation about whether or not woman and man are equal; that was not the question. But for Mahavira the question was this: how to help? So he found an easier way: to help a woman to be reborn as a man. That was easier. It meant that a woman had to wait for another life, and the whole effort had to be directed toward the goal that she should be born in a male body.

This appeared easier to Mahavira than to initiate a woman, because every month she comes back down to the original state and all effort is lost. But these two thousand years have done much. Particularly, tantra has done much.

Tantra has found different doors, and tantra is the only system in the world which makes no differentiation between man and woman. Rather, on the contrary, it says that a woman can become easily liberated, and the reason is the same, only looked at from a different angle. Tantra says that because a woman's body is periodically regulated, she can detach herself from her body more easily than man. Because man's mind is more involved in the body, that is why he can regulate it. Man's mind is more involved in the body; that is why he can control his sex.

Woman's mind is not so involved in the body. The body functions as an automaton—different, on a different layer, and the woman cannot do anything about it. It is like an automatic mechanism; it goes on. Tantra says that because of this woman can detach herself from her body very easily. And if this becomes possible—this detachment, this gap—then there is no problem.

So it is a very paradoxical thing: if a woman decides to be celibate and to detach herself from her body, she can maintain her purity more easily than a man. Once the detachment is there, then she can forget the body completely. Man can detach himself very easily, can control very easily, but his mind is more involved in the body. That is why he can control, but then he will have to control every day, continuously. And because feminine sex is passive, it is very easy for a woman to be relaxed about sex. Man's sex is active. It is easy for him to control it, but difficult for him to relax about it.

So tantra has been trying to find many, many ways, and tantra is the only system which says there is no difference, that even a feminine structure can be used. So tantra is the only path which gives women equal status. Otherwise, every religion, whatsoever it may say, deep down feels that women are inferior. It may be Christianity, it may be Islam, it may be Jainism, it may be Buddhism, but deep down it feels this, and the reason is the diagnosis through the third eye, the aura—the forming of the aura every month at the time of menses.

With the third eye you become capable of seeing things which are there, but which cannot be seen with ordinary eyes. All the methods about looking affect the third eye, because looking means a certain energy moving outward from you toward the world. If blocked, if suddenly blocked, the energy will find another path, and the third eye is just near.

In Tibet there were even surgical operations for the third eye. Sometimes it happens that your third eye is blocked because you have not used it for millennia. If the third eye is blocked and you stop your eyes, you will feel a certain uneasiness because the energy is there and there is no path where to move. In Tibet they devised certain operations to have the passage cleared. This can be done. And if it is not done, then many things can happen.

Just two or three days before, one sannyasin—she is here—came to me. She said, "There is a very hot sensation at the third eye." And not only was there the sensation, the skin had become burned as if really someone had burned it from the outside. The sensation, the burning, was inside, but the skin was affected. It became completely burned. She was afraid—what had happened? The feeling was pleasant, the warmth was very pleasant as if something were melting. Something was happening, but even the physical body had become affected, as if actual fire had touched it.

The reason? The third eye had started functioning, the energy began to move in it. It had been cold for lives together; energy never moved through it. When for the first time energy moves there is the warmth. When for the first time energy moves there is the burning sensation. And because the passage has to be created and forced, it may become like fire. It is concentrated energy hammering on the third eye.

In India we have been using sandalwood powder and other things, ghee and other things, just on the third-eye spot. We call this mark a *tilak*. It is put just on the third-eye spot in order to give a certain coolness from the outside, so if warmth comes within and fire moves within it should not affect the skin outside. Not only can the skin be burned by it, sometimes even holes have appeared on the skull.

I was reading one of the most penetrating books about one of the very deep mysteries of human existence on the earth. There have always been proposals that man came from some other planet, because there seems to be no possibility that man suddenly evolved on earth. There seems to be no possibility really that man could have evolved from a baboon or a chimpanzee. And there has been no link, because if man evolved from the chimpanzee to be man, there must be links—something that is between man and chimpanzee—but there is no such thing. With all the available data and discoveries, we have not yet found a single body structure, a skull or anything, which we can say is a link between the chimpanzee and man.

Evolution means steps. A chimpanzee cannot suddenly become a man—stages must have been followed. But there is no proof, so Darwin's theory remains a hypothesis. There are no in-between links.

So there have always been fantastic proposals

that man must have appeared on the earth suddenly. A man's skull dating very far back, a hundred thousand years back, has been found. But in comparison with other skulls there is nothing lacking in it. It is the same type of skull, with the same brain, with the same structure. We have not evolved really as far as brain structure is concerned.

So it seems man suddenly appeared on earth. He must have come from some other planet. For example, now we are traveling into space, and if we find some planet worth living upon we will populate it; then suddenly man will appear there. I was reading a book about such a proposal, and the author has been finding many things to help his hypothesis.

There is one thing that I wanted to tell you about in connection with this matter of looking. He has found one skull in Mexico and one in Tibet. Both of these skulls have holes at the third-eye spot, and the holes are such that they could only have been made by a gun bullet. The skulls are at least one-half million to one million years old. If the holes were made by an arrow, they could not be round. They are so round that they could not have been made by an arrow; only a bullet could make such holes. So that author tries to prove by this that bullets existed one million years before. Otherwise how were these two men killed?

But really, that doesn't prove anything about bullets. Whenever the third eye is blocked completely and the energy moves suddenly, this hole can appear. The energy is just like a bullet coming from within—just like a bullet. It is concentrated fire; it will create a hole. Those two skulls with holes show not that those men were killed by bullets, but simply that there was a third eye phenomenon. The third eye was blocked completely; energy became concentrated. The eyes were stopped completely; energy could not move, and it became fire. Then it exploded. Just so that there would not be such an accident, in Tibet they discovered and devised methods to make a hole so that the energy could move easily.

So whenever you are trying this looking, remember this: if you feel a burning sensation, do not be afraid. But if you feel that the energy has become a great fire as if a live bullet is there and wants to penetrate the skull—stop the method and come immediately to me. Do not do it further. If you feel as if a bullet is there and it wants to penetrate the skull, stop. Open your eyes and move them as much as you can. Immediately the sensation will drop, the energy will have moved through the eyes. And unless I say something to you do not proceed, because sometimes it has happened that the skull is broken.

Nothing is wrong even if it happens. Even if one dies in it nothing is wrong, because one has achieved something which is beyond death. But just to be safe, stop whenever you feel that something wrong can happen—with any method, not only with this. With any method, if you feel something wrong is possible, stop.

In India now, many methods are being taught and many, many seekers suffer unnecessarily, because those who teach are not even aware of the dangers. And those who follow, they follow in a blind way. They do not know where they are moving or what they are doing.

I am talking about these one hundred and twelve methods specifically because of this—so that you become aware of all the methods, all the possibilities, the dangers, and so that you can then find out which will suit you best. Then if you proceed in any method, you will be fully aware of what can happen, what you have to be aware of, and when something happens how you have to tackle it.

The second question:

It is observed that the practitioners of psychic sciences possess tense and fearful eyes. Explain what this indicates and how to overcome this phenomenon.

Those who practice hypnotism, mesmerism, magnetism, or things like this, will have very tense eyes —obviously, because they are trying to move their energy through the eyes forcibly. They are bringing their total energy near the eyes just to influence, impress or dominate someone. Their eyes will become tense because then their eyes are flooded with energy, more than they can tolerate. Their eyes will be red, tense, and if you look at them you will feel a sudden shivering: they are using their eyes in a very political way. If they look at you, they are sending their energy to dominate you. And through eyes, domination is very easy.

This was the case with Rasputin, who dominated Russia, before Lenin, just through his eyes. He was an ordinary peasant, uneducated, but with very magnetic eyes, and he came to know how to use this. The moment he would look at you, you would forget yourself, and in that moment he could send any suggestion to you telepathically and you would follow it. That is how he dominated the czar and the czarina, the royal family, and through them, the whole of Russia. Nothing could be done without his will.

You can have those eyes also; it is not difficult. You have just to learn how to bring your total body energy to the eyes. They become flooded, and then, whenever you look at someone your energy starts flowing toward him. It envelopes the person, penetrates his mind, and in this flooded shock his thinking stops. And this is not a very rare thing that happens just with man, it happens all over the animal kingdom. There are many animals who will just look at their prey, and if the prey looks at them he is done for. Then the prey's eyes become fixed; he cannot move, he cannot escape.

Hunters know this well, and hunters develop very powerful eyes because they are always in search in the darkness for animals. Their eyes become powerful. Thieves and hunters by and by gather more energy in their eyes automatically, because of their work.

Suddenly a lion comes before a hunter, and he is without weapons and he cannot do anything. Then this is what has been done always: the hunter can stare into the eyes of the lion, and now it will depend on whether he has more magnetic eyes or the lion. If the lion is less magnetic and the hunter can bring his total energy to his eyes…. And it is easy, he can do this, because when death is there one can do anything. When death is there the hunter can put his total energy at stake. If the hunter can look directly into the eyes of the lion and forget everything and just look, if he can just become the look, then the whole energy will move from his eyes and the lion will escape. He will be trembling with fear.

Through the eyes you can cause your whole energy to flood out, but when you do that your eyes will be tense: you will not be able to sleep, you will not be able to relax. So all those who are trying to dominate others will be restless. If you look at their faces their eyes will be alive, but their faces will be dead. Look at any hypnotist: his eyes will be very much alive, but his face will be dead, because his eyes are sucking the whole energy and nothing is left anywhere else.

Do not do this because it is useless to dominate anyone. The only useful thing is to dominate yourself. It is useless, a wastage of your energy. Nothing is achieved through it—just an egoistic feeling that you can dominate. So this is evil, a black art. That is the difference between black magic and white magic. Black magic means using your energy, wasting it, in dominating others. White magic means using the same methods, but using your energy in dominating your own life, becoming a master of yourself.

And remember, sometimes similarities happen…. If a buddha moves amongst you, you will be dominated by him, although he is not dominating you. He is not trying to dominate you, but you will be dominated because he is the master of himself. And he is such a master that all around him whosoever moves will become a slave. But there is no conscious effort on his part. Rather, on the contrary, he will continually insist, "Be your own master—

remember this." And this insistence is because of this knowledge.

Buddha knows that whosoever comes around him will become a slave. He is not doing anything; he is not trying to dominate anyone, but he knows this will happen. His last dying words were, "Be a lamp unto yourself."

He was dying, and Ananda asked him, just a day before his actual death, "When you will be no more, what shall we do?"

He said, "It is good that I shall be no more. Then you can be your own master. Be a lamp unto yourself; forget me. It is good, because when I am no more you will be freed from my domination."

Those who try to dominate others will try in every way to make a slave of you. That is evil, satanic. Those who become their own masters will help you to become masters, and they will try in every way to cut their influence. That can be done in many ways.

For example, I will tell a more recent incident. Ouspensky, the chief disciple of Gurdjieff, was working under Gurdjieff for ten years. It was very difficult to work under Gurdjieff. He was a man of infinite magnetism. Whosoever would come around him would be pulled.

With such people, either you are pulled or you become afraid and go against them, but you cannot remain indifferent. You are either for or against; you cannot be indifferent to such people. And that going against is just a safety measure. If you come around a person who is magnetic, either you will become a slave to him or, just to protect yourself, you will become an enemy, because that is a protection.

Ouspensky came to him, stayed with him, worked with him, and there was no theoretical knowledge to be imparted. Gurdjieff was a man of action. He would give techniques, and one had to work. Then Ouspensky achieved a certain crystallization. He became an integrated man; he was transformed. He was not fully enlightened yet, but he was not fast asleep as we are. He was in between, just on the verge.

When you feel that the morning is near, when you start listening to the noises which indicate morning is near, you are asleep, but not totally asleep. The sleep is just on the verge of going. You are not yet awake, you may again fall into a sleep. You are just on the surface, just near awakening.

And when Ouspensky was just near awakening, he was thinking that now Gurdjieff will help him more because this was the moment. But suddenly Gurdjieff started behaving in such a strange way that Ouspensky had to leave. He started up in such strange ways with him, did such absurd things, contradictory, nonsensical—on the surface—that Ouspensky had to leave him on his own account.

Gurdjieff never told him to leave. On his own account he left him, went against him, said that he had gone mad. He started teaching, and he always said, "I am teaching according to Gurdjieff, my teacher, but now he is mad." He would say, "According to the early Gurdjieff...." He would not talk about the later Gurdjieff.

But the basic reason why Gurdjieff did this is deep compassion. That was the moment when Ouspensky had to be left alone; otherwise he would have become a constant dependent. The moment came when he had to be thrown out, and in such a way that he would never become aware that he had been thrown out consciously.

Persons like Buddha or Gurdjieff will affect you without their conscious effort and you will be pulled toward them. But they will try in every way to ensure that you are not pulled in that way, that you are not attracted hypnotically, that you are not dominated by them. And they will help to make you masters, standing on your own feet.

Those who are trying to dominate others, their eyes will be tense, evilish. You will not feel any innocence in their eyes, you will not feel purity in their eyes. You will feel attraction, but the attraction will be like alcohol. You will feel a magnetic pull, but the pull will not be to free you but to enslave you.

Remember, never use any energy to dominate anyone. Because of this, Buddha, Mahavira, Jesus, they made it a point, and they went on hammering, that the moment you enter the spiritual search, be filled with love for everyone, even for your enemy —because if you are filled with love you will not be attracted to the inner violence which wants to dominate.

Only love can become an antidote. Otherwise when the energy comes to you and you are over-filled with it, you will start dominating. This happens every day. I have come across many, many people.... I start helping them, they will grow a little, and the moment they feel that a certain energy is coming to them they will start dominating others, they will try now to use it.

Remember, never use spiritual energy to dominate. You are wasting your efforts. Sooner or later you will be empty again, and you will fall down suddenly. And this is pure wastage, but it is very difficult to control it because you become aware that now you can do certain things. If you touch someone who was ill and he becomes okay, how can you resist touching others now? How can you resist?

If you cannot resist, you will waste your energy. Something has happened to you, but soon you will throw it away unnecessarily. And really, the mind is so cunning that you may be thinking that you are helping others by healing them. That may be just a cunning trick of the mind, because if you have no love, how can you be so concerned with others' diseases, their illnesses, their health? You are not concerned. Really, now this is a power. If you can heal, you can dominate them.

You may say, "I am just helping them," but even in your help you are simply trying to dominate them. Your ego will be fulfilled. This will become a food for your ego. So all the old treatises say beware. They say beware because when the energy comes to you, you are at a dangerous point. You can waste it, you can throw it away. When you feel any energy, make it a secret; do not allow

anyone to know about it.

Jesus said, "If your right hand is doing something, do not allow the left hand to know about it." In the Sufi mystic tradition, they say when energy starts coming, do not even pray before others, do not go to a mosque with others. Why? When the energy comes and someone is praying, and there are many persons present, they will feel immediately that something is happening. So the Sufis say that then you should do your prayers deep in the night—at midnight—when everyone is asleep and no one can be aware of what is happening to you. Do not tell anyone what is happening to you.

But the mind is just a chattering box. If something happens, immediately you will go and spread the good news that something has happened to you. Then you have wasted it. And if people are impressed, then all you have gained is their good opinion and nothing else. This is not a good bargain. Wait! A moment will come when your energy becomes accumulated; it reaches a point where it becomes integrated, transformed. Then things will happen around you without your doing anything. And only then can you help others to be their own masters—when you are your own master.

I remember one Sufi mystic, Junnaid. One day a man came to him and he said, "Junnaid, master, great master, I have come to know your inner secret. People say you have a golden secret and that you have not told it to anyone until now. I will do anything you say, but tell me the secret."

Junnaid said, "I have been keeping it, hiding it, for thirty years, so how much time can you wait? You will have to go through a preparation. It is a thirty-year secret but I will tell it to you. But for how much time will you keep patient?"

The man became afraid, scared. He said, "How long do you suggest?"

Junnaid said, "At least thirty years. It is not too much, I am not asking too much."

The man said, "Thirty years? I will think it over."

Junnaid said, "Then if you come back again, I will not be ready to give it to you in thirty years. Remember, if you decide just now, then okay. Otherwise I will also have to think." So the man agreed.

It is said that he remained for thirty years with Junnaid. Then the last day came, and he went to Junnaid and said to him, "Now communicate your secret."

Junnaid said, "I will give it to you on one condition: that you will keep it a secret. You are not to tell it to anyone. This secret must die with you, unknown."

The man said, "Why have you wasted my whole life? Thirty years I was waiting for the secret just to tell others, and now there is a condition! Then what is the use of knowing it if I cannot tell it to others? If you make this condition, then please do not tell it to me; otherwise it will haunt me, I will know something which I cannot tell to others. So be kind enough and do not tell it to me. You have wasted my thirty years. A little life is left, so let me live it relaxedly. This will be too much, knowing something without telling it to others."

Whatsoever you gain through any spiritual method, let it remain secret. Do not go on spreading it, do not try to use it in any way. Let it remain unused, pure. Only then will it be used for inner transformation. If you use it outwardly, it is a wastage.

The third question:

You mentioned that rapid eye movements indicate mental processes and that if eye movements are stopped the mental processes will also stop. But this physiological control of the mental processes, this stopping of eye movements, seems to create psychic tensions such as happens when we keep our eyes closed under a blindfold for a long time.

Firstly, your mind and your body are not two things as far as tantra is concerned. Remember that always. Do not say, "physiological process" and "mental process." They are not two—just two parts of one whole. Whatsoever you do physiologically affects the mind. Whatsoever you do psychologically affects the body. They are not two, they are one.

You can say that the body is a solid state of the same energy and the mind is a liquid state of the same energy. So no matter what you are doing physiologically, do not think that this is just physiological. Do not wonder how it is going to help any transformation in the mind. If you take alcohol, what happens to your mind? Alcohol is taken in the body, not in the mind, but what happens to the mind? If you take LSD, it goes into the body, not into the mind, but what happens to the mind?

Or if you go on a fast, fasting is done by the body, but what happens to the mind? Or from the other end: if you think sexual thoughts, what happens to your body? The body is affected immediately. You think in the mind of a sex object and your body starts getting ready.

There was a theory by William James. In the first part of this century it apparently looked very absurd, but in a sense it is right. He and another scientist named Lange proposed this theory which is known as the James-Lange theory. Ordinarily, we say you are afraid and that is why you escape and run away, or you are angry and that is why your eyes get red and you start beating your enemy.

But James and Lange proposed quite the contrary. They said that because you run away, that is why you feel fear; and because your eyes get red and you start beating your enemy, you feel anger. It is just the opposite. They said that if this is not so, then we want to see even one instance of anger when the eyes are not red and the body is not affected and one is simply angry. Do not allow your body to be affected and try to be angry—then you will know that you cannot be angry.

In Japan parents teach their children a very simple method of controlling anger. They say whenever you feel angry, do not do anything with the anger, just start taking deep breaths. Try it, and you will not be able to get angry. Why? Just because you take deep breaths, why can you not get angry? It becomes impossible to get angry. Two reasons.... You start taking deep breaths—but anger needs a particular rhythm of breathing. Without that rhythm anger is not possible. A particular rhythm in breathing or chaotic breathing is needed for anger to be.

If you start taking deep breaths it is impossible for the anger to come out. If you are consciously taking deep breaths, then the anger cannot express itself. It needs a different breathing which should be allowed. You need not do it; the anger will do it itself. With deep breathing you cannot be angry.

And secondly, your mind shifts. When you feel angry and you start to take deep breaths, your mind is shifted from anger to breathing. The body is not in a state to be angry, and the mind has shifted its concentration toward something else. Then it is difficult to be angry. That is why the Japanese are the most controlled people on earth. It is just a training from childhood.

It is difficult anywhere else to find such an incident, but in Japan it happens even today. It is happening less and less because Japan is becoming less Japanese. It is becoming more and more westernized, and the traditional methods and ways are becoming lost. But it was happening, and it still happens today.

One of my friends was there in Kyoto, and he wrote me a letter saying, "I have seen such a beautiful phenomenon today that I want to write about it to you. And when I come back, I will want to understand how it is possible. One man was struck by a car. He fell down, stood up, thanked the driver, and went away—he thanked the driver!"

In Japan it is not difficult. He must have taken a few deep breaths, and then it was possible. You are transformed into a different attitude, and you can thank even a person who was just going to kill you, or who has already tried to kill you.

Physiological processes and psychological processes are not two things, they are one, and you can start from either pole to affect and change the other. And any science will do that. For example, tantra believes deeply in the body. Only philosophy is vague, airy, verbal; it may start from something else. Otherwise, any scientific approach is bound to start from the body because that is within your reach. If I talk of something which is beyond your reach, you may listen to it, you may gather it in your memory, you may talk about it, but nothing happens. You remain the same. Your information is increased, but not your being. Your knowledge goes on increasing, but your being remains the same poor mediocrity; nothing happens to it.

Remember, the body is what is within your reach; just now you can do something with it and change your mind through the body. By and by you will become a master of the body, and then you will become a master of the mind. And when you become a master of the mind, you will change the mind by and by, and you will be moving beyond it. If the body changes, you move beyond body. If the mind changes, you move beyond mind. And always do something which you *can* do.

For example, you may not be capable of becoming a master of anger, like a buddha, just now. How can you? But you can change your breathing and then you can feel the subtle effect, the change. Do it. If you feel filled with passion, sexual passion, take a few deep breaths and feel the effect: the passion will have dispersed.

Aldous Huxley's wife, Laura Huxley, has written a beautiful book—just simple devices for doing certain things. If you feel angry, Laura Huxley says, just tighten up your face. You can tighten in such a way—for example, in your closet—so that no one will be able to see.

A person is sitting just in front of you and you feel angry—so just tighten up your face. Go on tightening it as much as you can, and then suddenly relax and feel the difference. The anger will have gone. Or if it has not gone, do it again. Go on doing it—twice, thrice.... What happens? If you tighten your face muscles and you go on tightening and tensing them, the energy that was going to become anger moves into the face.

And it is very easy for it to move into the face. When you are angry, how do you feel? You feel you want to beat someone with your fists. The energy is there, so use it. If you can use it, it is dispersed. Your face will become relaxed, and the other person will not even be able to know that you were angry. It will appear as if nothing has happened to you. And once you know these things, you become more and more aware that energy can be transformed, diverted, checked, released, or prevented from being released, or used in a different way. If you can use your energy you become the master. Then one day you may not use it at all; you may preserve it.

This exercise is not good for a buddha—to clench the fists. This is not good for a buddha because this is wasting energy. But this is good for you. At least the other is saved from you, and a vicious circle is saved. If you get angry he will get angry, and there is no end to it. It may disturb your whole night, and it may continue as a hangover for a week. And then, because of this hangover, you may do many things you never intended to do. Do not say that this is just physiological. You are physiological, so what can be done? You are a physique; you cannot deny that fact. Use your energy. There is no need of denying it.

If you close your eyes, sometimes you may feel a certain tension gathering there, or an uneasiness. Then there are certain things you can do. One, when you close your eyes do not become tense about it, let them be relaxed. You can close your eyes forcibly—then you will get tense. Then your eyes will get tired and inside you will feel uneasiness. Relax the face, relax the eyes, and let them be closed. I say, let them be closed; do not close them. Relax! Feel relaxed. Drop the eyelids and let the eyes be closed. Do not force them! If you force them, that is not good.

If you cannot feel the difference, then do this: first force them to close. Let your whole face become tense, strained, and then close your eyes

forcibly. For a few moments remain strained, then relax. Then again close your eyes relaxedly. Then you will feel the difference. Do not strain to do anything—that will tire you.

Two, when the eyes are closed and your face is relaxed, look as if everything has become dark. A deep darkness is around you. Imagine you are amidst darkness, in a deep, velvety darkness, surrounded by it, in a deep, dark night. Go on feeling this darkness. That will help your eyes to stop their movements. With nothing to be seen, the eyes will stop. Be in darkness.

You can do it in a dark room. Open your eyes, look at the darkness, then close them and feel the darkness. Again open your eyes, feel the darkness; close your eyes, feel it inside. Darkness is deeply relaxing. Darkness is outside and inside you; everything is dead—dark and dead. Both are related. That is why we paint death as black, dark. All over the world death is painted as black, and people fear darkness.

While doing this method, feel darkness, love darkness, and feel inside that you are going to die. Darkness is all around, and you are dying. The eyes will stop. You will feel that they cannot move, they will have stopped. In that stopping, suddenly the energy will go up and start hammering the third eye. When it starts hammering, you will hear it, you will feel it. A warmth will come, a fire will flow —a liquid fire trying to find a new path.

Do not be afraid. Help it, cooperate with it, let it move, become it. And when the third eye opens for the first time, the darkness will disappear and there will be light—light without a source. You have seen light, but always with a source. Either it comes from the sun or from the stars or from the moon or from the lamp, but some source is there.

When your energy moves through the third eye, you will come to know a light without source. It is not coming from any source, it is simply there, not coming from anywhere. That is why the Upanishads say that God is not like the sun or like a flame. He is sourceless light. There is no source anywhere, simply light is there, just as if it is morning.

The sun has not arisen, but the night has disappeared. In between there is the dawn—the pre-dawn. Or in the evening, the sun has set and the night has not yet come. Just in between there is the margin. That is why Hindus have chosen *sandhya* as a proper time for meditation. *Sandhya* is the in-between time—neither night nor day, just the line that divides. Why? Just as a symbol. The light is there, but without a source. The same will happen inside, light will be there without a source. Wait for it; do not imagine it.

The last thing to be remembered: you can imagine anything, so it is dangerous to tell you many things. You can imagine them. You will close the eyes and you will feel and imagine that now the third eye has opened or is opening, and you can imagine light also. Do not imagine; resist imagination. Close your eyes. Wait! Whatsoever comes, feel it, cooperate with it, but wait. Do not jump ahead; otherwise nothing will happen. You will be having a dream—a beautiful, spiritual dream, but nothing else.

People go on coming to me and they say, "We have seen this and we have seen that." But they have imagined it—because if really they had seen, they would be transformed. But they are not transformed. They are the same persons, only now a spiritual pride is added. They have some dreams—beautiful, spiritual dreams: someone is seeing Krishna playing on his flute, someone is seeing light, someone is seeing kundalini rising. They go on seeing things, and they remain the same—mediocre, stupid, dull. Nothing has happened to them; they go on relating that this is happening, that is happening, but they remain the same—angry, sad, childish, stupid. Nothing has changed.

If you really see the light which is there waiting for you, to be seen through the third eye, you will be a different person. And then you need not tell anyone. People will come to know you are a different person. You cannot even hide it; it will be felt. Wherever you will move, others will feel that "Something has happened to this man."

So do not imagine; wait, and let things take their own course. You do the technique, and then wait. Do not jump ahead.

CHAPTER 23

Several more looking methods

◆

33 *Simply by looking into the blue sky beyond clouds, the serenity.*

34 *Listen while the ultimate mystical teaching is imparted. Eyes still, without blinking, at once become absolutely free.*

35 *At the edge of a deep well look steadily into its depths until—the wondrousness.*

36 *Look upon some object, then slowly withdraw your sight from it, then slowly withdraw your thought from it. Then.*

We live on the surface of ourselves —just at the fringe, the boundary. The senses are just on the boundary and your consciousness is way deep down at the center. We live in the senses; that is natural. But that is not the ultimate flowering, it is just the beginning. And when we are living in the senses, we are basically concerned with objects, because senses are irrelevant unless there is concern with some object of enjoyment. For example, eyes are useless unless there is something to be seen, ears are useless unless there is something to be heard, and hands are useless unless there is something to be touched.

We live in the senses, therefore we have to live in objects. The senses are just on the boundary of the being, in the body, and objects are not even on the boundary, they are beyond the boundary. So three points have to be understood before we enter the techniques.

First, the consciousness is at the center. Second, the senses through which the consciousness moves out are at the boundary. And third, the objects in the world to which the consciousness moves through the senses are beyond the boundary. These three things have to be remembered: consciousness at the center, senses at the boundary and objects beyond the boundary. Try to understand it clearly, because then the techniques will be very simple.

Look at it from many directions. One: senses are just in-between, just in the middle. At one side is consciousness, at another side is the world of objects. Senses are just in the middle—between the two. From the senses you can move either way: either you can go to the objects or you can go to the center. Either way the distance is the same. From the senses, doors open both ways—move to the objects or move to the center.

You are at the senses. That is why one of the most famous Zen masters, Bokuju, has said that *nirvana* and the world are the same distance away. So do not think that nirvana is very far away. The world and nirvana, this world and that other world, are both at the same distance.

This saying has created much confusion because we feel that nirvana is very, very far away—that *moksha*, liberation, the kingdom of God, is very, very far away. We feel that the world is just near, just here. But Bokuju says, and he says rightly, that both are at the same distance.

The world is here, and nirvana is also here. The world is near, and nirvana is also near. For nirvana you have to move inwards, for the objects you have to move outwards; the distance is the same. From my eyes, my center is just as near as you are near me. I can see you if I move outward, I can see myself if I move inward. We are at the doors of the senses, but naturally the bodily needs are such that consciousness moves outwards. You need food, you need water to drink, you need a house to live in. These are your bodily needs and these can only be found in the world, so quite naturally, consciousness moves through the senses toward the world. Unless you create a need which can only be fulfilled when you move inward, you will never move inward.

For example, if a child were born self-sufficient, if he didn't need any food, he would not look at his mother at all. The mother would become irrelevant, meaningless, because for the child the mother is not the meaning, food is the meaning. The mother is his first food, and because the mother gives him food and satisfies a basic need, without which he will die, he starts loving the mother. That love comes secondly, as a shadow, because the mother is fulfilling a basic need.

So those mothers who are feeding their children through bottles should not expect much love because for the child food is the need, not the mother. The mother will come into his being, enter into his being only through food. That is why food and love are deeply related—very, very deeply related. If your love need is fulfilled, you will need less food. If your love need is not fulfilled, you will need more food. So those who love and who are loved will not gather much fat. There are other reasons also, but this is one of the most basic—they will not eat much. If love is not fulfilled, then food becomes a substitute. Then they will eat much.

For the child, food is the basic need. But if a child should be born who can be self-sufficient, who does not need any food, who does not need any outward help to be alive, he will not move in the world at all. Do you think he will move? There would be no need. And unless a need is there, the energy will never move. We move outwardly not because we are sinners. We move outwardly because we have needs which can be fulfilled only through objects—objects which can be gained if we move in the world of objects.

Why do you not move inward? Because you have not yet created the need to move inward. Once the need is there, it is as easy to move inward as to move outward. What is that need? That need is concerned with religion. You cannot be religious unless that need is there. How is that need created? By what process does one become aware of a deep need which helps you move inward?

Three things are to be remembered. Firstly, death. Remember, all life-needs force you to move outward. If you want to move inward, death must become a basic concern; otherwise you cannot move inward. That is why it happened that persons like Buddha, who became deeply conscious of death, started moving inward. Only when you become aware of death will you create the need to look back.

Life looks outward. Unless you become aware of death, religion is meaningless for you. That is why animals have no religion. They are alive, they are as much alive as man, or even more, but they cannot be conscious of death, they cannot conceive of death, they cannot see death in the future. They see that others are dying, but it never occurs to the animal mind that this death is an indication of his death also.

For the animal mind death always occurs to others. And if for you also death is just something which happens to others, you still live in the animal mind. If you are not aware of death, you have not yet become man. That is the basic difference between animal and man—an animal cannot be aware of death, only man can be. If you are not aware of death you are not a man yet, and only man creates the need to move inward.

To me, 'man' means awareness of death. I am not saying become afraid of death; that is not awareness. Just be aware of the fact that death is coming nearer and nearer and you have to be prepared for it.

Life has its own needs, death creates its own needs. That is why younger societies are irreligious—because younger societies are not yet aware of the phenomenon of death; it has not become a central concern for them. An older society—for example, India, one of the oldest societies in existence—is so much aware of death. Because of that awareness, deep down India is religious. So the first thing: become aware of death. Think about it, look at it, contemplate it. Do not be afraid, do not escape the fact. It is there and you cannot escape it.

It has come into existence with you.

Your death is born with you; now you cannot escape it. You have hidden it in yourself—become aware of it. The moment you become aware that you are going to die, that death is certain, your total mind will start looking in a different dimension. Then food is a basic need for the body, but not for the being, because even if you get food death will occur. Food cannot protect you from death, food can only help you to postpone. If you get a good shelter, a good house, it will not protect you from death; it will only help you to die conveniently, comfortably. And death, whether it happens comfortably or uncomfortably, is the same.

In life you may be poor or rich, but death is the great equalizer. The greatest communism is in death. Howsoever you live, it makes no difference; death happens equally. In life, equality is impossible; in death, inequality is impossible. Become aware of it, contemplate it. And it is not only that death is certain somewhere in the future; with the idea that it is very far away, you will again not be able to contemplate it. The mind has a very small range; the focus of the mind is very small. You cannot think beyond thirty years. After thirty years there will be death…it is as if you are not going to die. Thirty years is so long, the distance is so much, it is as if death is not going to occur.

If you want to contemplate death, know another fact about it: it can occur the next moment, it is possible the very next moment. You may not be able to hear my whole sentence, I may not be able to complete it. My mother's father used to tell me that when I was born he consulted one astrologer, one of the best-known astrologers of those days. The astrologer was to make my *kundali*—birth chart. But the astrologer studied it and he said, "If this child survives after seven years, only then will I make the chart. It seems impossible that he can survive for more than seven years, so it is useless. If the child is going to die in seven years it is useless to make the kundali; it will be of no use. And it has been my habit," the astrologer said, "that unless I

am certain that the kundali will be useful I never make it." So he didn't make it.

Fortunately, or unfortunately, I survived. Then my mother's father went to the astrologer, but he was dead, so he never could make my kundali. He was dead, and I have been constantly wondering about this. He was aware of the fact that this child may die, but he was not aware of the fact that he may die. It seems that he was absolutely unconcerned—and he was no ordinary man. But no one is concerned with his own death. Knowingly, cunningly, we are not concerned with it because it creates a fear. So I have always suspected that that astrologer might have never looked at his own kundali, otherwise he would have become aware.

Death is possible the very next moment, but the mind will not believe it. I say it and your mind will say, "No! How is it possible the next moment? It is far away." But that is a trick. If you postpone, you cannot contemplate. It must be so near that you can focus on it. And when I say that the next moment it is possible, I mean it. It can happen, and whenever it will happen will be the next moment. Just before it, you could not have conceived that it was going to happen.

A person is dying; just a moment before he could never have thought that death is so near. It always happens in the next moment—remember. It has always happened that way, and this will be the way always. It always happens in the next moment. Bring it near so that you can focus on it, and that very focusing will help you to enter in; a new need will be created.

Secondly, you go on living. You go on creating artificial meanings and purposes for this very moment. You never think of your life as a whole, whether it has any meaning or not. You go on creating new meanings, and you push yourself on with those meanings. That is why a poor man lives a more meaningful life than a rich man—because a poor man has many things to get, and that gives a meaning to his life. If you are really rich, it means you have everything that is possible and this world cannot offer anything to you. Then your life becomes meaningless. Now you cannot create any meaning for this moment, for this day, to help you live. That is why the richer a society, the more affluent a culture, the more meaninglessness is felt. Poorer societies never feel meaninglessness.

A poor man is concerned with having a house. For years together he will work for it. His life has a meaning; something has to be achieved. And when he gets the house he will be happy for a few days at least, but then bigger houses are there…. So he will go on moving, doing this and that, never thinking about his life as a whole, whether it has any meaning or not. He never takes life as a whole.

Just imagine that you have everything—the house, the car that you long for, and all your dreams are fulfilled. So now what? Just imagine that whatsoever you need is there, you have it. Now what? Suddenly meaning disappears. You are standing on an abyss; nothing can be done, you become meaningless. You are already meaningless, just not aware. Even if you get the whole world, then what? What is fulfilled?

Alexander was coming to India, and he met a great saint, Diogenes. Diogenes was one of the most penetrating minds ever born. He lived naked like Mahavira; he is the Mahavira of Greek civilization and culture. He left everything, renounced everything, not because through renouncing things he was going to get anything—that is not real renouncing, not authentic renunciation. If you renounce something to get something, that is a bargain. If you think that you are going to have some reservation in heaven and that is why you renounce, it is not renunciation. If you renounce the bodily pleasures to have spiritual pleasures, this is not renunciation.

Diogenes renounced everything, not because out of it he was going to get something. He renounced just to see if, when he has nothing, there is any meaning or not. He thought that if one possesses nothing, if even then one has a meaning, a purpose, a destiny, then death cannot annihilate anything, because death can annihilate only possessions—and the body is also a possession. He left everything. He had only one thing, a wooden bowl out of which to drink water. He thought, "This is not much of a possession." Then one day he saw a child drinking water with his hands. He immediately threw away the bowl. He said, "If a child can drink water with his hands, am I more weak than a child?"

When Alexander was coming to India to conquer, to make a world empire, somebody informed him that just on the way, where he would be stopping, there lived a great sage who was just the opposite of him. He was told, "You are going to make a world empire, and he has even thrown away his bowl because he says that as he is happy without it, why carry this burden? And you say that unless the whole world becomes your empire, you cannot be happy. So he is just at the opposite pole, and it would be good if you meet him."

Alexander was fascinated. The opposite always fascinates, it has a deep sexual attraction. Just as man is attracted to woman or woman is attracted to man, there is the same attraction with the opposite. Alexander could not bypass Diogenes, but it was not good for him to go to Diogenes, and it was impossible that Diogenes would come to him—there was no solution.

Diogenes was informed. Many, many messengers came to inform him that "The great Alexander is passing this way. It would be good if you meet him." He said, "The great Alexander? Who has said this to you? I think he himself has. So tell your great Alexander that he has nothing to give to me, and there is no need for him to meet me—and I am a very small man." He used to say, "Really, I am a dog, not a man at all—just a dog, so there is no need. It is below his dignity to meet this dog."

Then Alexander had to come. Diogenes is reported to have said, "I hear you are going to win the whole world, so I thought, I closed my eyes and thought, 'Okay! If I have won the whole world, then what?' This has been my problem constantly:

if I have won the whole world, then what?" It is reported that Alexander, after hearing this, became very sad. "Then what?" he said to Diogenes. "Do not talk such things. You make me very sad."

Diogenes said, "But you will become very sad when you win the whole world. What can I do? I am just imagining, and I have come to conclude that this is useless. You are making a suicidal effort. You yourself are trying to win the whole world—so then what? If you succeed, then what?"

Alexander returned from Diogenes very disturbed, upset, sad. He said to his companions, "This man is very dangerous. He has shattered my dreams." And he could never forget, could never forgive Diogenes. The day he died, he remembered him again, and he said, "It may be that that fellow was right: then what?"

So the next thing is that whatsoever you are doing, whatsoever you are achieving, remember to ask, "If I succeed, then what?" Is there any meaning in it all, or is there just some artificial meaning given by you only to divide, to create an illusion around you so that you feel you are doing something worthwhile—and all the time you are really wasting life and energy, not doing anything worthwhile? There is only one thing worthwhile: if you can become happy without anything, without any dependence, if you can be blissful alone, totally alone. If nothing is needed for your bliss, only then can you be blissful; otherwise you will be in misery, always in misery.

Dependence is misery, and those who depend on possessions, those who depend on accumulated knowledge, those who depend on this or that, they are helping their own misery to become accumulated more and more. So the next point to remember is to ask whether you have any meaning, or whether you are just floating along without any meaning. Are you just making believe that this or that is the meaning of your existence?

One man used to come to me. He used to say that if his son gets into college, that would be all he would need and he would be very happy. He was a poor man, a very ordinary clerk, and that was the only dream, that his son would get into college. Then the son got into college. Now the son has become a forest official. A few months back the son was here and he told me, "I am getting only six hundred rupees per month. I have two children and this is my only dream, that they can get a good education; that is all. I am working hard. If they can be well educated and if I can send one of my children to some foreign country to study, that is all I ask."

His father is no more; he has died. This was his meaning in life, his purpose—to make his boy educated and well placed. Now the boy is well placed, and now the boy has the same purpose, to help his children become educated and well placed. And he will die, and those children will go on doing the same nonsense.

What is the meaning of all this? What are you doing? Just passing time? Just destroying life? Or have you got some authentic meaning which you can say makes you happy, blissful? This is the second consideration which will turn you inward.

And thirdly, man goes on forgetting. You go on forgetting things. You were angry yesterday, and you repented it. Now you have forgotten, and if the same stimulus is given again, you will be angry again. This has been so for your whole life, you go on repeating the same things.

It is said that it is very extraordinary to find a man who learns through life—very rare. Really, no one learns. If you learn, then you cannot commit the same mistake twice. But you go on committing the same mistake again and again. Rather, the more you commit it, the more you become prone to commit it. You are angry again and again, and again and again you repent it, and you have not learned anything. Given the stimulus, you will be angry, and you will do the same madness, and then you will repent again—that is also part of it. And then you will again be ready to be stimulated and to be angry.

The third thing: if you want to turn in, learn!

Whatsoever you are doing, learn through it. Take the essential out of it. Look back at what you have been doing with your life and your energy and your time—the same mistakes, the same foolishnesses, the same stupidities, again and again.

So you move in a wheel. However, it is not good to say that you move the wheel; rather, the wheel moves you. Mechanically, you go on and on and on. That is why in India we have called the world *sansara*. *Sansara* means the wheel which goes on, and you are just clinging to some spoke on it and you go on moving.

Unless you learn something about this wheel, this vicious circle, this sansara, unless you learn something about it, you will not leave the spoke and jump out of it. So three words, three key words:

Death: make it a constant contemplation.

Meaning: go on searching for it in your life.

And learn: learn through your life, because there is no other learning. Scriptures won't give you anything.

If your own life cannot give you something, nothing can give it to you. Learn through your own life, conclude through it. What have you been doing with yourself? If you are in a wheel, jump out of it. But to know that you are in a wheel, you will have to go deep into understanding and learning. These three things will help you to turn in.

Now the techniques:

---

33 Look into the limitless sky.

Simply by looking into the blue sky beyond clouds, the serenity.

Now you see why I have said so many things—because the techniques are very easy, and you can do them and nothing will result. Then you will say, "What type of techniques are these? We can do them, they are so simple."

You can look at the blue sky beyond the clouds and nothing will happen. Then you will say, "Shiva is not talking rationally, reasonably. He is saying anything, whatsoever comes to his mind. What kind of technique is this? *Simply by looking into the blue sky beyond clouds, the serenity,* one will become serene."

But if you remember: death, meaning, learning, this technique will help you immediately to turn in. *Looking into the blue sky beyond clouds....* Just looking, not thinking. The sky is infinite, it ends nowhere. Just look into it. There is no object, that is why the sky is chosen. The sky is not an object. Linguistically it is, existentially the sky is not an object because an object begins and ends. You can go around an object, you cannot go around the sky. You are in the sky, but you cannot go around it. So you may be the object for the sky, but the sky cannot be your object. You can look into it, but you cannot look at it, and that looking into it goes on and on…it never ends.

So look into the blue sky and go on looking. The object is infinite, there is no boundary to it. Do not think about it, do not say it is beautiful. Do not say, "How lovely!" Do not appreciate the color, do not start thinking. If you start thinking, you have stopped. Now your eyes are not moving into the blue, the infinite blue. Just move, just look—do not think. Do not create words; they will become barriers. Not even "blue sky" should be said. Do not verbalize.

There should be just a pure, innocent look into the blue sky. It never ends. You will go on and on and on and on, and suddenly, because there is no object, just a vacuum, suddenly you will become aware of yourself. Why? Because if there is any vacuum your senses become useless. Senses are only useful if there is an object.

If you are looking at a flower, then you are looking at something—the flower is there. The sky is not there. What do we mean by a sky? That which is not there. 'Sky' means space. All objects are in the sky, but the sky is not an object. It is just the vacuum, the space in which objects can exist. The sky itself is just pure emptiness. Look at this pure emptiness. That is why the sutra says: *beyond the clouds*. Because clouds are not the sky, they are objects floating in the sky. You can look at the clouds, but that will not help. Look into the blue sky—not at the stars, not at the moon, not at the clouds, but at objectlessness, emptiness. Look into it.

What will happen? In emptiness there is no object to be grasped by the senses. Because there is no object to be grasped, clung to, senses become futile. And if you are looking into the blue sky without thinking, suddenly you will feel that everything has disappeared, there is nothing. In that disappearance you will become aware of yourself. Looking into this emptiness, you will become empty. Why? Because your eyes are like a mirror. Whatsoever is before them is reflected. I see you and you are sad—then a sudden sadness enters into me. If a sad person enters into your room, you become sad. What has happened? You have looked at sadness. You are like a mirror, the sadness is reflected in you.

Someone laughs heartily—suddenly you feel a laughter coming to you also. It has become infectious. What has happened? You are like a mirror, you are reflecting things. You look at a beautiful object—it is reflected in you. You look at an ugly object—it is reflected in you. Whatsoever you are seeing penetrates deep into you. It becomes part of your consciousness.

If you are looking into the emptiness, there is nothing to be reflected—or only the blue infinite sky. If it is reflected, if you feel the blue infinite sky within, you will become serene, you will find serenity. And if really you can conceive of emptiness—where sky, blue, everything disappears: just an emptiness—inside also emptiness will be reflected. And in emptiness, how can you be worried, how can you be tense?

In emptiness, how can the mind function? It stops, it disappears. In the disappearance of the mind—the mind that is tense, worried, filled with thoughts that are relevant, irrelevant—in that disappearance of the mind, *the serenity*.

One thing more. Emptiness, if reflected in, becomes desirelessness. Desire is tension. You desire and you become worried. You look at a beautiful woman—a sudden desire arises. You look at a beautiful house—you want to possess it. You look at a beautiful car just passing by your side—you want to be in it, you want to drive it. A desire has come in, and with the desire mind becomes worried: "How to get it? What to do to get it?" The mind becomes frustrated or hopeless—or hopeful, but it is all dreaming. Many things can happen.

When desire is there, you are disturbed. The mind is shattered into fragments, and many plans, dreams, projections start; you become mad. Desire is the seed of madness.

But emptiness is not an object; it is just emptiness. When you look at emptiness, no desire arises; it cannot arise. You do not want to possess emptiness, you do not want to love emptiness, you do not want to make a house out of it. Emptiness? You cannot do anything with it! All movement of the mind stops, no desire arises, and with the nonarising of desire, *the serenity*. You become silent, serene. A sudden peace explodes in you. You have become like the sky.

Another thing. Whatsoever you contemplate, you become like it, you become that, because mind can take infinite forms. Whatsoever you desire, your mind takes its form, you become it. That is why a person who is just after riches, gold, after money, his mind becomes just a treasure—nothing else. Shake him, and you will hear the sound of rupees inside, nothing else. Whatsoever you desire, you become that. So be conscious of what you are desiring because you are becoming that.

The sky is the most empty thing. It is just near you and it costs nothing, and you do not have to go somewhere—to the Himalayas or to Tibet—to find the sky. Technology has destroyed everything, but the sky is still there; you can use it. Use it before they destroy it—any day they will destroy it. Look, penetrate into it. And the look must be a nonthinking one, remember this. Then you will feel the same sky within, the same dimension within, the same space and blueness and emptiness. That is why Shiva says, *Simply by looking into the blue sky beyond clouds, the serenity.*

34 A secret method.

The next looking technique: *Listen while the ultimate mystical teaching is imparted. Eyes still, without blinking, at once become absolutely free.*

Listen while the ultimate mystical teaching is imparted. This is a secret method. In this esoteric tantra, the master gives you the teaching secretly, the doctrine secretly, or the mantra secretly. When the disciple is ready then the mantra, or the supreme secret, will be imparted, communicated to him, privately. Just in his ear it will be whispered. This technique is concerned with that whispering. *Listen while the ultimate mystical teaching is imparted.*

When the master has decided that now you are ready and the secret of his own experience can be communicated, when the moment has come when he can say to you that which is unsayable, then this technique has to be used. *Eyes still, without blinking, at once become absolutely free.* When the master is imparting his secret to you in your ear, whispering it, let your eyes be totally still, no movement of the eyes. That means the mind should be quiet, thoughtless.

No blinking, not even a slight movement, because that will show a disturbance within. Just become an empty ear with no movement within. The consciousness is just waiting to be impregnated, just open, receptive, passive, no activity on its own part. And when this will happen, this moment when you are totally empty, not thinking anything but just waiting...not waiting for something, because then it will become thinking, not waiting for something but just waiting; when this static moment, this nondynamic moment will

happen; when everything has stopped, time is not flowing and mind is totally vacant—it becomes no-mind. Only into a no-mind can a master impart.

And he is not going to give a very long discourse, he will give just one or two or three words. In that silence those one, two or three words will penetrate to your very core, to the very center, and they will become a seed there. In this passive awareness, in this silence, *at once become absolutely free.*

One can become free only by becoming free of the mind, there is no other freedom. Freedom from the mind is the only freedom. Mind is the bondage, the slavery, the servitude. So a disciple has to wait with his master for the right moment when he will call him and impart. He is not to ask, because asking means desire. He is not to expect, because expectation means conditions, desire, mind. He is just to wait. And when he is ready, when his waiting becomes total, the master can do anything.

Sometimes the master can do very trivial things, and the thing will happen. And ordinarily, even if a Shiva goes on talking about one hundred and twelve methods, nothing will happen because the preparation is not there. You can throw seeds on stones, but nothing will happen. The fault is not of the seeds. You can throw a seed out of season, but nothing will happen. The fault is not of the seed. The right season is needed, the right moment is needed, the right soil is needed. Only then will the seed become alive and transform.

So sometimes very trivial things work. For example, Lin Chi became enlightened while he was just sitting on his master's verandah and the master came out and just laughed. He looked at Lin Chi—into his eyes—and laughed uproariously. Lin Chi started laughing, bowed down, and left. But he had been waiting there for six years, that verandah was his abode for six years.

The master would come day after day, month after month, and he would not even look at him. And Lin Chi was waiting there. Then after two years, for the first time he looked at him. Then two more years passed, and for the first time he patted him. Then Lin Chi waited and waited, and after six years, one day suddenly the master came out, stared into Lin Chi's eyes, and Lin Chi must have done this technique: *Listen while the ultimate mystical teaching is imparted. Eyes still, without blinking, at once become absolutely free.*

The master looked and used laughter as a medium. He was a great master. Really, words were not needed, just laughter. Suddenly there was that laughter, and something happened in Lin Chi. He bowed down, laughed, left, and told everyone that now he was no more, that he was liberated, free. He was no more, that is what liberation means. *You* are not liberated, you are liberated from yourself.

Lin Chi used to tell how it happened. For six years he was waiting. It was a long waiting, a patient waiting. He was just waiting on the verandah, and every day the master would come. And he would wait for the right moment—when he would become ready, then the master would do something. Just by waiting for six years, you will fall into meditation. What can you do? He might have thought for a few days about old things, but if you do not give new food every day to the mind, by and by it stops. How long can you chew again and again on the same thing?

He might have been thinking about past things, and by and by, because no new stimulus was given, thinking stopped. He was not allowed to read, he was not allowed to talk, he was not allowed to move and meet anyone. He was just allowed to fulfill the basic bodily needs and wait on the verandah.

Silently he waited, day after day—day in, day out, day and night. Summer would come and pass away, and winter would come and pass away, and there would be rain and it would pass away, he must have forgotten time. He must have forgotten for how many days he had been there. And then one day suddenly the master appeared, and he looked deeply into his eyes. Lin Chi's eyes must have suddenly become static, nondynamic. This was the moment; six years were wasted for this.

There was no movement of the eyes, because a single movement and he may miss. Everything must have become silent—and then suddenly, the uproarious laughter, the master began laughing madly. That laughter must have been heard deep down at the very core, it must have reached.

So when Lin Chi was asked, "What happened to you?" he said, "When my master laughed, suddenly I recognized that the whole world is just a joke. In his laughter, this was the message: the whole world is just a joke, just a drama. All seriousness disappeared. And if the whole world is just a joke, who is in bondage? And who needs to be free?" So Lin Chi said, "There was no bondage at all. I was thinking that I was bound, and that is why I was trying to be free, and then suddenly the master laughed and the bondage fell away."

Sometimes it has happened with such things; you can never conceive of how it was possible. There are many Zen stories.... One Zen master became aware when the gong was beaten. Just while he was hearing the gong being beaten, the sound, something shattered in him. One Zen nun became aware, enlightened, while she was carrying two pails of water. Suddenly the bamboo broke, and the earthen pots fell down. The sound, the breaking of the pots and the water flowing out of them, and she became enlightened.

What happened? You can break many pots but nothing will happen. A right moment had come. She was coming back. Her master had said, "This night I am going to give you the secret, so go and take a bath, and bring two pails of water for me. I will take a bath and impart to you the secret for which you have been waiting." She must have felt ecstatic—the moment had come. She took a bath, filled the pots, and carried them back.

It was a full-moon night, and just when she was passing on the footpath from the river to the ashram, suddenly the bamboo broke.

When she reached, the master was waiting, and he looked at her and he said, "Now there is no need, it has happened. Now I have nothing to convey. You have already received."

That old nun used to say, "With that bamboo breaking, something broke in me also. Those pails falling down, those broken earthen pots, and I saw my body broken. I looked at the moon. Everything was silent, serene, and I became silent and serene. From that moment, I have not been, I am no more." This is what liberation, freedom means.

---

35 Look into a deep well.

The next looking technique: *At the edge of a deep well look steadily into its depths until—the wondrousness.*

The techniques are similar, with a slight difference. *At the edge of a deep well look steadily into its depths until—the wondrousness.* Look into a deep well. The well will be reflected in you. Forget thinking completely, stop thinking completely, just go on looking into the depth. Now they say mind has its own depth, like a well. Now in the West, they are developing depth psychology. They say mind is not just a surface, the surface is just a beginning; there are depths—many depths, hidden depths.

Look into a well without thinking. The depth will be reflected in you, the well will become just an outer symbol of the inner depth. And go on looking *until —the wondrousness,* until you feel wonder-filled.

Do not stop before this moment. Go on looking, go on looking, go on looking, day after day, month after month. Just go to a well, look deep, with no thoughts moving in the mind. Just meditate on depth, become one with it. Go on meditating; one day your thoughts will not be there. Any moment it can happen. Suddenly you will feel you have the same well within you, the same depth. And then a very strange feeling will come to you, you will feel wonder-filled.

Chuang Tzu was passing over a bridge with his master, Lao Tzu. Lao Tzu is reported to have said to Chuang Tzu, "Remain here. Go on looking down from this bridge to the river until the river stops and the bridge starts flowing. Then come to me." The river is flowing, the bridge never flows. But Chuang Tzu was given this meditation—to wait on this bridge. It is said he made a hut on the bridge and remained there. Months passed...he would just sit on the bridge, looking down for the moment when the river would stop and the bridge would flow. Then he would go to the master.

One day it happened: the river stopped and the bridge started flowing. How can it happen? If thought stops completely, then anything is possible, because it is fixedness of thought which says that the river is flowing and the bridge is static. This is just relative.

Einstein says, and physics says, that everything is relative. You are traveling in a train, a fast train. What happens? The trees flow by, they run by. And if the train is really smooth and you do not feel that the train is running, you are just looking through the windows, the trees are moving, not the train.

Einstein has said that if in space two trains are running, or two spaceships are running side by side with the same speed, you will not be able to feel that they are moving. You can feel a moving train because you see the static things by the side. If there is nothing—for example, if the trees are also moving in the same direction with the same speed —you will feel static. Or when a train passes in the opposite direction, your speed is doubled. You feel your train has become faster.

It has not become faster. It is the same train with the same speed, but a train going in the opposite direction gives you the feeling of double speed. If speed is relative, then it is just a fixedness of the mind to think that the river is flowing and the bridge is static.

Continuously meditating, meditating, meditating, Chuang Tzu came to realize that everything is relative. The river is flowing because you take the bridge as static. The bridge is also flowing, deep down nothing is static in this world. Atoms are moving, electrons are moving; the bridge is a constant movement within. Everything is flowing; the bridge is also flowing. Chuang Tzu must have had a glimpse of the atomic structure of the bridge.

Now they say this wall which looks static is not static. Movement is there, every electron is running, but the movement is so fast you cannot see it. That is why you feel it as static.

If this fan goes on with a faster movement, faster and faster, you will not be able to see its wings or the spaces between them. You will not be able to see this. And if it moves faster still, you will see simply one circular disc that is static. Nothing will be moving in it because eyes cannot catch that fast movement.

So Chuang Tzu must have had a glimpse of the atomic structure of the bridge. He waited and waited, and the fixed mind dissolved. Then he saw that the bridge was flowing—and the movement was so fast that the river was just static in comparison to it. He came running to Lao Tzu and Lao Tzu said, "Okay! Now do not ask me. The thing has happened to you." What had happened? No-mind had happened.

In this technique, *At the edge of a deep well look steadily into its depth until—the wondrousness.* When you feel wonder-filled, when the mystery descends upon you, when mind is no more but simply mystery—a milieu of mystery—then you will be capable of knowing yourself.

---

36 Withdraw yourself completely.

Another looking technique: *Look upon some object, then slowly withdraw your sight from it, then slowly withdraw your thought from it. Then.*

Look upon some object. Look at a flower, but remember what that *look* means. Look! Do not think. I need not repeat it. Always remember that look means: look, do not think. If you think, it is not a look; then you have contaminated everything. It must be a pure look, a simple look.

Look upon some object. Look at a flower, a rose. *Then slowly withdraw your sight from it—* very slowly. The flower is there, first look at it. Drop thinking, go on looking. When you feel that now there is no thought, simply the flower is there in your mind, nothing else, now slightly move your eyes away. By and by the flower recedes, goes out of focus, but the image will remain with you. The object will have gone out of focus; you will have turned your look away. The image, the outer flower is no more there, but it is reflected— reflected in your mirror of consciousness. It will be there! *Then slowly withdraw your sight from it, then slowly withdraw your thought from it.*

So first, withdraw from the outer object. Then only the inner image remains, the thought of the roseflower. Now withdraw that thought also. This is very difficult, the second part, but if the first part is done exactly as it is said, it will not be so difficult. First withdraw your sight from the object. Then close your eyes, and just as you have removed your eyesight from the object, remove yourself from the image. Withdraw yourself; become indifferent. Do not look at it inside, just feel that you have gone away from it. Soon the image will also disappear.

First the object disappears, then the image disappears. And when the image disappears, Shiva says, *Then.* Then you are left alone. In that aloneness one realizes oneself, one comes to the center, one is thrown to the original source.

This is a very good meditation—you can do it. Take any object, but let the object remain the same every day so that the same image is created inside and you remove yourself from the same image. Images in the temples were used for this technique. Now images are there, but the technique is lost. You go to a temple—this is the technique to do. Look at the statue of Mahavira or Buddha or Rama or Krishna or any other. Look at the statue, concentrate on it; focus the whole mind so that the statue becomes an image inside. Then close your eyes. Remove your eyes from the statue, then close them. And then remove the image, wipe it out completely.

Then you are there in your total aloneness, in your total purity, in your total innocence. Realizing that is freedom, realizing that is truth.

CHAPTER 24

Doubt or faith, life or death: the bases of different paths

♦

Should a mixed type do two different kinds of techniques?

As tantra is life-affirmative, how can death orientation be used?

How can the mind be transformed only by bringing the body to a deathlike state?

The first question:

I feel that neither am I the feeling type altogether, nor am I the intellectual type. I am a mixed type. Should I do two different kinds of techniques alternatively? Please guide.

his is a significant question. Many things will have to be understood. One: whenever you feel that you are neither the intellectual type nor the emotional type, know well that you belong to the intellectual type, because confusion is part of it. The emotional type is never confused. One who belongs to the emotional type will not feel such confusion. Emotion is always total and whole, intellect is always fragmented, divided, confused. That is the very nature of intellect. Why? Because intellect depends on doubt and emotion depends on faith. Wherever doubt is, division will be, and doubt can never be total. How can it be? The very nature of doubt is doubting. You cannot doubt a thing totally. If you doubt a thing totally, it becomes faith.

Doubt is always confusion, and basically, when you doubt, you also doubt your doubt. You cannot be certain about it. A doubting mind cannot be even certain about doubt. So layers of confusion will be there, and each layer will be based on another layer of doubt and confusion.

The intellectual type always feels this way. The feeling will always be there that "I am nowhere, I do not belong anywhere," or "Sometimes I am here and sometimes there, sometimes this and sometimes that." But the emotional type is at ease with himself. Because trust is the base, emotion is not divided; it is whole, individual. So if you have any doubt, if you cannot feel certain to what type you belong, know well you belong to the intellectual type. Then practice techniques which are meant for the intellectual type. If you do not feel any confusion, then only do you belong to the emotional type, the feeling type.

For example, a Ramakrishna: he is a feeling type. You cannot create doubt in him; that is impossible, because a doubt can be created only when basically the doubt exists already. No one can create doubt in you if it is not already hidden there. Others can only help it to come out, they cannot create it. Neither can faith be created. That too others can help to manifest, to come out.

Your basic type cannot be changed, so it is very essential to know your basic type—because if you are doing something which doesn't suit you, fit with you, you are wasting time and energy. And you will get more and more confused because of your wrong efforts. Neither can doubt be created in you, nor faith. You already have the seed of either this or that. If you have doubt, then it is better not to think of faith at all, because that will be a deception and hypocrisy. If you have doubt, do not be afraid—even doubt can lead to the divine. You have to use it.

I will repeat: even doubt can lead to the divine —because if your doubt can destroy the divine,

335

then it is stronger, more powerful than the divine. Even doubt can be used, it can be made a technique. But do not deceive. There are persons who go on teaching that if you have doubts, you can never reach to the divine. So what to do? Then you have to force it underneath, suppress it, hide it, create a false belief. But that will be only on the surface, it will never touch your soul. Deep down you will remain in doubt, and just on the surface a façade of belief will be created.

That is the difference between faith and belief. Belief is always false. Faith is a quality; belief is a concept. Faith is the quality of your mind; belief is just acquired. So those who have doubt and are afraid of it, they cling to beliefs; they say, "I believe," but they have no faith. Deep down they know their doubt. They are always afraid of it. If you touch, criticize their belief, they will immediately get angry. Why? Why the anger, this irritation? They are not irritated by you, they are irritated by their own doubt which you are helping to come up. If a man of faith is there you can criticize him and he is not going to get angry, because you cannot destroy faith.

A Ramakrishna is the type, or a Chaitanya or a Meera—they are feeling types. One of the most beautiful minds of Bengal, Keshav Chandra, went to meet Ramakrishna. He went not just to meet him, but to defeat him, because Ramakrishna was just an illiterate, not a scholar at all. And Keshav Chandra was one of the greatest minds ever born on Indian soil, one of the most keen, logical intellects. It was certain that Ramakrishna would be defeated. When Keshav Chandra came, all the intellectuals of Calcutta gathered at Dakshineshwar just to see Ramakrishna defeated. Keshav Chandra started arguing, but he must have felt very awkward because Ramakrishna enjoyed his arguments very much—in fact, too much. When he would propose some argument against God, Ramakrishna would start jumping, dancing.

He felt very awkward, so he said, "What are you doing? You have to answer my arguments."

Ramakrishna is reported to have said, "By my seeing you, my faith is strengthened. Such an intellect is impossible without God." That is how a feeling type looks at things. "And I predict," said Ramakrishna, "that sooner or later you will be a greater devotee than me because you have a greater mind. With such a mind, how can you fight the divine? With such a keen mind? Even a fool, an idiot like me, has reached. How can you remain without reaching?"

He was not angry, not arguing, but he defeated Keshav Chandra. Keshav Chandra touched his feet and he said, "You are the first theist I have met with whom argument is futile. Looking at your eyes, looking at you and the way you have behaved with me, this is the first glimpse for me that the divine is possible. You are the proof without giving any proof." Ramakrishna became the proof.

The intellectual type has to proceed through doubt. Do not force any belief upon yourself; that will be deceiving yourself. You cannot deceive anyone else, you can only deceive yourself. Do not force, be authentic. If doubt is your nature, then proceed through doubt. Doubt as much as possible, and do not choose any technique which is based on faith—that is not for you. Choose some technique which is scientifically experimental. No need to believe.

There are two types of methods. One is experimental. You are not told to believe, you are told to do it, and the consequence will be the belief, the faith. A scientist cannot believe. He can take a hypothesis to work on, to experiment with, and if the experiment comes out right, if the experiment proves that the hypothesis is right, then he reaches to a conclusion. Faith is achieved through experiment. So there are techniques in these one hundred and twelve techniques which do not require any faith on your part.

That is why Mahavira, Buddha.... They are intellectual types, just as Ramakrishna and Chaitanya are feeling types. Because of this Buddha says that there is no need to believe in God; there is no God.

He says, "Do what I say, do not believe in me. Experiment with what I say, and if your experience proves it right then you can believe it."

Buddha says, "Do not believe in me, do not believe what I say. Do not believe something because I have said it. Experiment with it, go through it, and until you achieve your own conclusion remain in doubt. Your own experience will become your faith."

Mahavira said, "No need to believe in anyone—not even in the master. Just do the technique."

Science never says to believe. It says, do the experiment, go to the lab. This is for the intellectual type. Do not try faith before you do the experiment. You cannot try it—you will falsify everything. Be real unto yourself. Remain real and authentic.

Sometimes it has happened that even atheists have reached the divine because of finding their truth about themselves. Mahavira is an atheist; he doesn't believe in God. Buddha is an atheist; he doesn't believe in any God. So a miracle happened with Buddha. It is said about him that he was the most godless man and the most godlike. Both—godless and godlike. He was absolutely intellectual, but he reached because he never deceived himself, he went on doing experiments. For six years continuously he was doing this experiment and that, and he did not believe. Unless something were proven true by experience, he would not believe it. So he would do something, and if nothing happened he would leave it.

One day he reached. Just by doubting and doubting and doubting, experimenting, a point came...a point came when nothing remained to be doubted. Without any object, the doubt fell. There was no object to doubt now. He had doubted everything, and even doubt became futile. Doubt dropped, and in that dropping he realized. Then he realized that the doubt was not the real thing: rather, the doubter was, and you cannot doubt the doubter. The doubter is there to say, "No, this is not right."

It may not be right, it may be right, but who is it who is saying that this is not right or this is right? That source of saying is right, is true. You can say there is no God, but you cannot say, "I am not," because the moment you say "I am not," you have accepted yourself. Who is making this statement? You cannot deny yourself without at the same time recognizing yourself. That is impossible.

Even to deny you have to be there. You cannot say to someone, some guest who is knocking on the door, "I am not in the house." How can you say this? This is absurd, because your saying that "I am not in the house," proves that you are there.

Buddha doubted everything, but he could not doubt himself. When everything was doubted and became useless, ultimately he was thrown to himself. And there, doubt was impossible, so doubt fell. Suddenly he was awakened to his own reality, to his own source of consciousness, the very ground of consciousness. So he was godless, but he became godlike. Really, on this earth a more godlike person has never walked, but his instinct was intellectual.

Both types of techniques are there. If you feel you are intellectual, confused, doubting, do not try faith techniques, they are not for you. Every technique is not for everyone. If you have faith, there is no need to try any other method, no need. If you have faith, then try those methods which require faith as a presupposition. But be authentic; that is basic. That is a very essential thing to remember continuously.

It is very easy to deceive, because we imitate. You may start imitating Ramakrishna without knowing that you are not of that type. If you imitate, you will be an imitation; nothing real will happen to you. You can imitate Buddha. This is happening every day because we are born into religions. Because of that, much nonsense continues. You cannot be born into a religion, you have to choose. Religion has nothing to do with blood, bones, birth—nothing!

Someone is born a Buddhist. He may be a feeling type, but he will follow Buddha. Then his whole life will be wasted. Someone is born an intellectual type.

He may be born a Mohammedan or he may be born into a devotional cult. His life will be wasted and he will become false. The whole world is irreligious because religion is foolishly associated with birth. There is no relationship at all. You have to choose consciously, because first you have to understand your type and then you have to choose. The world will be deeply religious the day we allow everyone to choose his religion, method, technique, path.

But religion has become organizational, politically organizational. That is why the moment a child is born we force religion upon him, we condition him into a religion. The parents are afraid that he may move into another organization. Before he becomes conscious he must be destroyed, crippled, forced. Before he becomes conscious and can think about things, his mind must be conditioned so that he cannot think freely. You cannot think freely because whatsoever you think has been preconditioned.

I was reading Bertrand Russell. He says, "Intellectually, I conceive of Buddha as being greater than Jesus. But deep down in my heart, that is impossible: Jesus is greater than Buddha. At the most, if I force myself, then I will put them parallel, equal. Intellectually, I feel Buddha is a giant. Jesus is nothing before him."

Why this feeling? Because Bertrand Russell is himself the intellectual type, so Buddha has an appeal for him; Jesus has no appeal. But the mind has been conditioned into Christianity. This is not truth because these comparisons are meaningless, they simply show something about Bertrand Russell— neither about Buddha nor about Jesus, because no comparison is possible. For someone who is of the feeling type, Jesus will look greater than Buddha. But if he is a Buddhist, if he is born a Buddhist it will be difficult. His own mind will feel uneasy if he thinks that someone is greater than Buddha. It is difficult, impossible in a way, because whatsoever you think has been fed into you—it has already been fed in.

Your mind is something like a computer. The information has been fed in, evaluation has been

fed in. You are already based on some nonsensical concepts, traditions. You cannot throw them away easily; that is why religion is just a word. Very few people can become religious, because very few people can rebel against their own conditioning. Only a revolutionary mind can become religious— a mind which can see a thing, the facts of it, and then decide what to do.

But feel your type, try to feel your type. It is not difficult. The first thing: if you feel confused, you are the intellectual type. If you feel certain, trusting, then proceed with the different techniques which require trust as a basic thing. And secondly, remember, never do both the techniques. That will create more confusion in you. Nothing is wrong, both are right; Ramakrishna is right, Buddha is right. Remember one thing: in this world, many things can lead you to truth—many paths. There is no monopoly. Even contradictory paths, absolutely contradictory paths, can lead you to the same point.

There is no "one" path. On the contrary, if you go deep and realize, you will come to know that there are as many paths as there are travelers, because each individual has to proceed from the point where he is standing already. He cannot use a ready-made path. Basically, you create your path by your movement. There is no ready-made path already there, there are no highways that are ready-made. But every religion tries to force on you this idea that the path is ready and you have just to travel over it. That is wrong. This inner search is more like the sky than the earth.

A bird is flying, he will leave no footprints in the sky. The sky will remain a vacuum. The bird has flown—he has not left any footprints, no bird can follow in his footprints. The sky is always empty. Another bird, any bird who has to fly, will create his own path.

Consciousness is like a sky, not like the earth. A Mahavira moves, a Buddha moves, a Meera moves, a Mohammed moves.... You can see their movement, you can see their achievement, but the moment they move, the path disappears. You cannot follow, deadlike, you cannot imitate. You have to find your own path.

First think about your type and then choose methods. In these one hundred and twelve methods, many are for the intellectual type, many are for the emotional type. But do not think that because you are a mixed type you have to follow both. That will create more confusion, and you will be divided so deeply that you may even go mad, schizophrenic; you may become split. Do not do that.

The second question:

To know death is certain, You said yesterday. This seems to be the approach of Buddha, who was life-negative. But tantra's approach is life-affirmative, not negative, so how can this death orientation be used in tantra?

Buddha is not really life-negative. He appears so, he appears to be life-negative because he focuses on death. To us he appears to be in love with death, but he is not. On the contrary, he is in love with eternal life. To find that life which is deathless, he focuses on death. Death is not his love, he has to focus on death just to find something which is beyond death. And Buddha says that if there is nothing beyond death then life is futile—but only then is life futile. He never says life is futile, he says that if nothing is beyond death, then life is futile. And your life is futile, he says, because your life is not beyond death. Whatsoever you think is your life is just a part of death. You are fooled by that. You think it is life and it is nothing but death on its way.

A man is born—he is on his way to die. Whatsoever he becomes, whatsoever he achieves, possesses, nothing will help: he is moving toward death. This so-called life is moving toward death. How can we call it life? That is Buddha's question. A life which moves toward death, how to call it life? Life which implies death inevitably is just

hidden death, not life; it is gradual death. By and by you are dying, and you go on thinking that you are living.

Right now you feel you are living, but you are dying. Every moment you are losing life and gaining death. A tree is known by its fruits, Buddha says, so your tree of life cannot be called life because death is the fruit. A tree is known by its fruit, and if on your tree of life only fruits of death come, then you were deceived by the tree. And another thing: if a tree gives a particular fruit, it shows that that particular fruit was the seed of the tree; otherwise that particular fruit could not come out of the tree. So if life gives the fruit of death, death must have been the seed.

Let us understand this. You are born, and you think that birth is the beginning—it is not. Before this birth, you died in another life. That death was the seed of this birth, and then again, death will become the fruit. And that fruit will become the seed for another birth.

Birth leads to death, death precedes birth. So if you want to see life as it really is, it is surrounded on both the sides by death. Death is the beginning and death is again the end, and life is just the illusion in between. You feel alive between two deaths; the passage joining one death to another you call life. Buddha says this is not life. This life is *dukkha*—misery. This life is death. That is why he appears to us who are deeply life-hypnotized, obsessed about being alive in any way, as life-negating. To us, just to be alive seems to be the end. We are so much afraid of death that Buddha appears in love with death, and that looks abnormal. He seems to be suicidal. This is what many have criticized Buddha for.

Albert Schweitzer has criticized Buddha because he feels that Buddha is obsessed with death. He is not obsessed with death, we are obsessed with life. He is simply analyzing things, finding out what are the facts. And the deeper you go, the more you will find he is right. Your life is just false, fake, overtaken by death, just a clothing—inside there is death. Buddha focuses on death because he says, "If I can find out what death is, only then can I find out what life is. And if I can know what both death and life are, then there is a possibility that I may transcend both and know something which is beyond birth and death, beyond both." He is not negative, not life-denying, but he appears so.

Tantra appears life-affirmative, but that again is our interpretation. Neither is Buddha life-denying, nor is tantra life-affirmative; the source is the same. Buddha focuses on death, tantra focuses on life. And both are one, so wherever you want to start, start. But go so deeply that you come to know the other also.

Buddha focuses on the end—death. Tantra focuses on the beginning—life. That is why Buddha seems to be too much in love with death and tantra seems to be too much in love with sex, love, body, life. In the end there is death and in the beginning there is sex. Because tantra focuses itself on the beginning, sex becomes very important. So how to go deep and know what sex is, how to reveal the mystery of love, how to penetrate into the beginning, into the seed, so that you can go beyond—that is tantra's approach.

Buddha focuses on death, and he says to meditate deeply on death: move into it and know the whole reality of it. Both are two ends of the same thing. Sex is death, and death is very sexual. It will be difficult to understand.

There are many insects which die with their first intercourse. The first sex act, and death occurs. There is a species of spider in Africa in which the male dies in copulation. He cannot come down from the copulation; he is just on the female, and he dies there. The first copulation becomes death, and it is very horrible. At the moment of ejaculation he dies. Actually, he is not even really dead: he is still in the pangs of death. The moment the spider, the male spider, ejaculates, death starts and the female starts eating him. He never dismounts. The female starts eating him, and by the time the sexual act is finished, he is half eaten.

Sex and death are so interconnected. Because of this, man became afraid of sex. Those who want to live more, who are fascinated with long life, they will be always afraid of sex, and for those who think that they can become immortal, brahmacharya, celibacy, will be their cult. No one has yet been immortal and no one can be, because you are born out of sex. If you were born out of brahmacharya, then it could be possible. If your father and mother were celibates, then only could you be immortal.

Sex has already entered with your birth. Whether you go into sex or not makes no difference, you cannot escape death. Your very being starts with sex, and sex is the beginning of death. Because of this Christians say Jesus was born from a virgin mother. Just to say that he is no mortal, no ordinary mortal, they say he was born to a virgin mother. "He is no ordinary mortal"—just to say this, just to say that death has no power over him, they had to create this myth.

This is a part of a long myth. If he was born out of sex, then death would have its power over him. Then he could not escape death, because with sex, death enters. So they say that he was born without any sex act; he was not a by-product of sex. They say that because he was the son of a virgin mother, he could revive again—resurrect. They crucified him, but they could not kill him. He remained alive because he was not a by-product of sex. They could not kill him. If really Jesus was born out of a virgin mother, it is impossible to kill him. Death is impossible. When the beginning is not, how can the end be? If he was not born out of a virgin mother, then death will be the certain, inevitable end.

So the whole myth has to be maintained. If you say that he was not born out of a virgin mother, then the second part of the myth, resurrection, becomes false. If you say he resurrected, that he denied death, escaped death, that death could not kill him, that he could not be crucified really, that those who were crucifying him were deceived, that he was alive and he remained alive, then you have to maintain the first part of the myth.

I am not saying anything for or against, I am simply saying that the whole myth has to be maintained, one part only cannot be maintained. If sex is there before birth, then death will be there. Because of this deep association, many times many societies have become afraid of sex. That fear is of death. Even if you accept sex, a certain fear remains there. Even if you move into sex, a certain fear remains there. No one allows himself a total let-go in it. The fear is there, you are on guard. You cannot go into it totally; you cannot let yourself go completely because that let-go is just like death.

Neither is tantra for your idea of life, nor is Buddha against the real life. Tantra starts from one part—the beginning; Buddha starts with the end. And tantra is more scientific than Buddha, because it is always good to begin at the beginning. You are already born; death is far away. Birth has occurred—you can work on it more deeply—death has to occur. It is still in the imagination; it is not a reality to you. And when you see someone die, you never see death. You see someone dying, never the death—the process which happens to him inside. You cannot see it; it is invisible, it is individual. And the individual himself cannot say anything because the moment he goes through the process he is no more. He cannot come back, he cannot step back and tell what has happened.

So whatsoever is known about death is just inference. No one knows anything about death actually. Unless you can remember your past lives, you cannot actually know anything about death. You have died many times; that is why Buddha had to revive many techniques about remembering past lives. Because your death of this life is in the future, how can you concentrate on it? How can you meditate on it? It has not happened yet. It is very vague, dark, unknown. What can you do? You can only think about it, but that thinking will also be borrowed. You will be repeating what others have said. Someone has said something about death, and you will be repeating it. How can you meditate on death? You can see others dying, but that is not a

real entry into it. You are just an outsider.

It is just as if someone is eating a sweet.... You look at him, but how can you feel what is happening to him, what taste, what sweetness, what fragrance is happening to him? What is going on in him you cannot know. You can just look at his mouth, his behavior, or you can see the expression on his face—but this is all inference, not actual experience.

You cannot know what is happening to him unless he says something, but whatsoever he says will be words to you, and again not an experience. Buddha talked about his past deaths, but no one believed him. If I tell you something about my past deaths, deep down you will not believe it. How can you believe it? You do not have any access to the reality of it. You are just closed at this birth, and the death of this life has not come yet. It always happens to others; it has not happened to you yet.

It is difficult to meditate on death. As a base, you will have to move into past lives, you will have to go digging into past memories. Buddha and Mahavira both used the technique of *jati smaran*—the technique of going into past lives. Only then can you meditate on death.

Tantra is more scientific. It starts with life, with birth, with sex, which is a fact to you. Death is still a fiction. But remember, the end of both is the same. They both are in search of eternal life—life which is deathless. Either transcend the beginning or transcend the end, either jump from one pole or from another. And remember, you can jump out of it only from a pole, you cannot jump from the middle.

If I want to jump out of this room, either I have to move to this side to the extreme, or to that side to the extreme. I cannot jump out from the middle of the room, because jumping is possible only from the extreme pole. And there are two extreme poles in life—birth and death. Tantra starts from birth. It is more scientific, more real. You are already in it, so you can meditate upon it. Sex is a fact, so you can meditate upon it, you can move deep within it.

Death is not a fact. A very rare mind is needed to conceive of death; a very keen intellect is needed to penetrate into the future. Rarely it happens that a buddha will conceive of death so deeply that the future becomes the present. But it is always for rare individuals.

Tantra can be used by anyone who has any interest, who has any desire to search in order to know what real life is. But tantra also uses death just to help you move inwards—not for you to meditate on it, not for you to jump out of it, but to help you move inwards.

Buddha also talked about birth just to make it a part of the meditation on death. The other part can be used as a help, but is not the center. Tantra says, if you can think about death, your life will take a different meaning, shape and significance. Your mind will start thinking in new dimensions which without death would be difficult or even impossible. The moment you begin to feel that this life is going to end in death, death becomes a certainty and you cannot cling to this life, mind starts moving beyond. That is what I was saying yesterday.

If you think about just this life, your mind will go outwards: it will go out and out and out to the objects. If you begin to look and see that death is hidden everywhere, then you cannot cling to objects. Your mind will start moving inwards.

Just the other day a young girl came to me. She is an Indian girl who fell in love with an American boy. But after she fell in love and they were just thinking and planning to get married, the boy fell ill and it was discovered, diagnosed, that he had a certain type of cancer that is incurable. Death was certain. He could be alive two or three or four years at the most. The boy tried to persuade the girl not to marry him now. He said, "Death is so certain, why waste your life with me?"

But the more he insisted—this is how the mind functions—the more the girl became adamant about wanting to marry him. This is how mind works—in paradoxes. If I would have been in the place of that boy, I would have insisted on marry-

ing; then the girl would have escaped. Then there was no possibility of marriage. Then I would not have seen that girl again. But the boy insisted—out of his love, but out of a foolish mind, without knowing how mind functions—that she should not marry him. Anyone would have done the same. And because he was insisting, the girl felt it to be a matter of conscience: she insisted on marrying him.

Then they got married. Now, after marriage, the girl is surrounded constantly by death. She is sad; she cannot love the boy. It is easy to die for anyone, it is very difficult to live. It is very easy to die…to be a martyr is such an easy thing. It is such an easy thing to be a martyr because it is a momentary thing, you can do it in a single moment.

If you love me and I say, "Jump out of this building," you can jump because you feel you love me. But if I say, "Okay, now live with me for thirty years," it is very difficult.

You can become a martyr in a single moment. To die for someone, for something, is the easiest thing in the world; to live for something is the most arduous and difficult thing. She became a martyr, but now she has to live enclosed in death's presence. She cannot love. She cannot see the face of her husband, because the moment she sees it the cancer is there, death is there just by the corner. Any moment it can happen, so she is in constant agony.

What has happened? Death has become a certainty. Now life has no interest for her, everything has dropped and has become death. She came from America just to meet me. She wants to meditate because life seems futile. Life has become equivalent to cancer, so now she has come here to ask me, "Teach me meditation. How can I move beyond life?" Unless life becomes futile you never think about moving beyond it.

I told her that apparently her marriage looks very unfortunate, but it may prove very fortunate. Everyone's husband is going to die, but when is not certain. Everybody's wife is going to die, but when is not certain. Death is certain, only the date is not certain. And who knows, even the date may be certain—you do not know. That is why ignorance is very blissful. She could have loved that boy if still they were ignorant; apparently nothing would be wrong. But now love has become impossible, life has become impossible. Death is always there, constantly present between the two of them.

So I asked her, "Why are you not loving him more because he is going to die? Love him more."

She said, "How can I love? We are always three; the privacy is lost. I am there and my husband is there, and between us two, death. There is no privacy left."

Death is too much; it is impossible to live with. It can become a turning. If you can become aware of death, says tantra, use it as a turning inwards. No need to go into details about death, no need to go on contemplating about it. Do not make it an obsession. Just the awareness that death is there will help you to move inwards, to be meditative.

The third question:

How can the mind be transcended and transformed only by bringing the body to a deathlike state?

The mind is constantly active. While you are active meditation is impossible, because meditation means a deep inactivity. You can know yourself only when everything has become still, silent and quiet. Only then, in that silence, do you happen to encounter yourself. Otherwise, in activity you are so much occupied with something or other, you cannot feel your own presence. You go on forgetting yourself. Continuously, with this or that object, you go on forgetting yourself.

Activity means being related with something outside. You are active because you are related with something outside, doing something outside. Inactivity means you have returned home; you are not doing anything. In the Greek language, leisure is called *schole*. The English word 'school' comes from this Greek word; school means leisure. You can learn something only when you are at leisure;

learning happens in leisure. If you are active, doing this and that, you cannot learn.

Schools were for the leisure class—those who could afford leisure. Their children were sent to schools, to places of leisure. They were not to do anything but learn; they were allowed total inactivity as far as the world was concerned. They were freed from all worldly activity, and then they could learn.

The phenomenon is similar if you want to learn about your own presence: you will have to be completely inactive, just being, not doing anything. All the ripples must cease, all activity must evaporate. You are, simply you are. In that moment, for the first time you become aware of your own presence. Why? Because the presence is so subtle. Occupied with a gross object, engaged with gross activity, you cannot become aware of such a subtle presence. It is a very silent music, your presence. And you are so much filled with noise, and every type of noise is occupying you, that you cannot hear that still, small voice within.

Cease being engaged in outward noises and activities. Then that still, small voice for the first time is heard; that soundless sound, that soundless music is felt. You enter the subtle and leave the gross. Activity is gross; inactivity is subtle. And your presence is the most subtle thing in the world. To feel that, you will have to cease; you will have to be absent from everywhere so that your total presence comes in and you can encounter yourself. That is why in many techniques it is suggested to make your body as if it is dead. It means simply being inactive like a dead man.

While you are meditating, let your body enter death. It will be imagination, but even that will help. Do not ask how imagination can help. Imagination has its own function. For example, now scientific experiments are done…. You sit down, there is a doctor, and he is observing your pulse rate. Inside, you just start being angry; you imagine that you are fighting, angry—your pulse rate will go higher.

Inside, just imagine you are dying, that you are just going to die. Become silent and feel death descending. Your pulse rate will come down. The pulse rate is a physical thing, and you were just imagining. Imagination is not unreal; it is also real. If you can really imagine, even real death can occur. If you can really imagine, you can affect physical things.

You might have observed some display of hypnosis. Or if not, you can do this easily at home; it is not difficult, it is very easy. Use your child as the medium. If the child is a girl, it is better than using a boy, because a boy is more doubting than a girl, and a boy is always in a fighting mood instead of a cooperative mood. A boy means that—a fighting mood.

Cooperation is needed. Just tell the child to relax, and go on suggesting, "You are going into a deep trance, going into a deep trance, going into a deep trance, falling asleep. Your eyelids are becoming heavy, heavy, heavier...." And use a monotonous voice: "Heavier, heavier, heavier...." Let your voice be monotonous, as if you are also becoming sleepy.

Within five minutes the child will be fast asleep. This is not ordinary sleep, this is a hypnotic trance. It is basically, qualitatively different from sleep, because now the child can hear only your voice. There is nothing else that he or she can hear. If someone else talks, the child is deaf. If you talk— the person who has hypnotized him—he can still hear. He will follow your orders.

Try to do some experiments. Say to the child, "This is a burning hot coal that I am putting in your hand. You will be burned." Put any ordinary thing in the child's hand—a piece of stone that is cold, with nothing hot about it. The child will throw it immediately because the mind has the suggestion that it is a burning coal, hot, and that his or her hand is going to be burned. He will throw it, he will scream as if he has touched something hot.

But a miracle happens. You will come to know that his hand is really burned. What is happening?

There was no possibility of being burned by a cold stone, but the child is burned exactly as if there was a burning coal put in his hand. It was just imagination. That is why those who have penetrated the human mind say that imagination is as real a fact as anything. Imagination is not just imagination, because it results in actual fact.

Do this experiment.... Fall down on the ground, lie still and feel you are going to die. The body is becoming dead. By and by you will feel a heaviness coming over the body. The whole body will become a dead weight, a lead weight. Tell yourself that "Even if I want to remove my hand from the position where it is, I cannot move it." Then try to remove it, and you will not be able to do so. Now the imagination is working.

In this state where you feel the body has become a dead weight, you can cut yourself off from the world of activity easily. That is why this is suggested. You can now become inactive because you are dead. Now you can feel that everything has died and the bridge from you to the world is broken. The body is the bridge. If the body is dead, you cannot do anything. Can you do anything without the body? You cannot do anything without the body.

Any activity is through the body. Mind can think about it but cannot do it. You have become impotent; you cannot do anything. You are inside, the world is outside; the vehicle is dead and the bridge is broken. In this state of the body being dead and the bridge being broken, your energy will start moving inwards, because there is no way to move out. The outer way is closed and blocked, so now you move inwards. See yourself standing at the heart center; look within at the details of the body. You will feel very strange when for the first time you can look from within your own body.

Tantra, yoga, ayurveda, all the old physiologies, all the old physiological doctrines, their work was revealed and made known through such inner meditative techniques. Modern physiology is known through dissection, but ancient physiology was known through meditation, not dissection. And now there is a school, a school of very avant-garde medical thinkers who say that when you dissect a body and come to know something, you come to know something which is dead—and whatsoever is inferred from a dead part is irrelevant to a live body.

They may be right. If you take my blood out and then examine it, you are examining dead blood. It is not the same blood which was in me. Outwardly it is the same, but in me it was a live process, a live current, alive, part of a mechanism, of an organic whole. Now it is dead. It is as if you pull my eyes out and then examine them. When they were with me I was behind them and in them. Now they are dead stones, and whatsoever you come to know about those eyes is not about my eyes, because the basic, essential part is missing: I am not there.

Those eyes were part of a big whole. Their whole quality consisted in being part of a big whole. Now they are independent, not part of anything. The pattern is lost, the live contact is lost. All the traditions of yoga and tantra say that unless you can come to know the living body, your knowledge is false. But how to come to know the living body? There is only one way: you enter into yourself, and move within to see the details of the body. A different world was revealed through these techniques, an alive world.

So the first thing: be centered at the heart, and look around at your body, move. Two things will happen. One: you will not feel now that you are the body—you cannot feel it. You are the observer, one who is aware, alert, looking at, not being looked at. For the first time the body will become just a clothing; you will be different from it. And the second thing: immediately you will feel, "I cannot die."

This will seem strange—using a method, an imaginary method of death, and then coming to the deathless point. You will come to know suddenly, "I cannot die." You have seen others who have

died. What happened to them? Their bodies became dead; that is why you inferred that they were dead. Now you can see that the whole body is lying dead, and you are alive.

So bodily death is not your death. The body dies, and you move on. And if you persist in this technique, the time is not very far away when you can come out of your body and look at your body from without, at your body lying dead just before you. It is not very difficult. Once you experience this, you will never be the same person again. You will be reborn; you will become *dwij*—twice born. Now a new life starts.

I was telling you yesterday about an astrologer who had promised to work on my life's birth chart. He died before he had done it, so his son had to prepare the chart, but he was also puzzled. He said, "It is almost certain that this child is going to die at the age of twenty-one. Every seven years he will have to face death." So my parents, my family, were always worried about my death. Whenever I would come to the end of a seven-year cycle, they would become afraid. And he was right. At the age of seven I survived, but I had a deep experience of death—not of my own, but of the death of my maternal grandfather. And I was so much attached to him that his death appeared to be my own death.

In my own childish way I imitated his death. I would not eat for three days continuously, would not drink water, because I felt that if I did so it would be a betrayal. I loved him so much, he loved me so much, that when he was alive I was never allowed to go to my parents. I was with my maternal grandfather. He said, "When I die, only then can you go." He lived in a very small village, so I couldn't go to any school because there was no school. He would never leave me, but then the time came when he died. He was part and parcel of me. I had grown with his presence, his love.

When he died I felt that it would be a betrayal to eat. Now I didn't want to live. It was childish, but through it something very deep happened. For three days I remained lying down; I would not come out of the bed. I said, "Now that he is dead, I do not want to live." I survived, but those three days became a death experience. I died in a way, and I came to realize—now I can tell about it, though at that time it was just a vague experience —I came to feel that death is impossible. This was a feeling.

Then at the age of fourteen, my family again became disturbed that I would die. I survived, but then I again tried it consciously. I said to them, "If death is going to occur as the astrologer has said, then it is better to be prepared. And why not give a chance to death? Why should I not go and meet it halfway? If I am going to die, then it is better to die consciously."

So I took leave from my school for seven days. I went to my principal and I told him, "I am going to die."

He said, "What nonsense you are talking! Are you committing suicide? What do you mean you are going to die?"

I told him about the astrologer's prediction that the possibility of death would confront me every seven years. I told him, "I am going into retreat for seven days to wait for death. If death comes, it is good to meet it consciously so that it becomes an experience."

I went to a temple just outside of my village. I arranged with the priest that he should not disturb me. It was a very lonely, unvisited temple—old, in ruins. No one ever came to it. So I told him, "I will remain in the temple. You just give me once a day something to eat and something to drink, and the whole day I will be lying there waiting for death."

For seven days I waited. Those seven days became a beautiful experience. Death never came, but on my part I tried in every way to be dead. Strange, weird feelings happened. Many things happened, but the basic note was this—that if you are feeling you are going to die, you become calm and silent. Nothing creates any worry then because all worries are concerned with life. Life is the basis of all worries. When you are going to die anyway one day, why worry?

I was lying there. On the third or fourth day a snake entered the temple. It was in view, I was seeing the snake, but there was no fear. Suddenly I felt very strange. The snake was coming nearer and nearer, and I felt very strange. There was no fear, so I thought, "When death is coming, it may be coming through this snake, so why be afraid? Wait!"

The snake crossed over me and went away. Fear had disappeared. If you accept death, there is no fear. If you cling to life, then every fear is there.

Many times flies came around me. They would fly around, they would creep over me, on my face. Sometimes I felt irritated and would have liked to throw them off, but then I thought, "What is the use? Sooner or later I am going to die, and then no one will be here to protect the body. So let them have their way."

The moment I decided to let them have their way, the irritation disappeared. They were still on the body, but it was as if I was not concerned. They were as if moving, as if creeping on someone else's body. There was a distance immediately. If you accept death, a distance is created. Life moves far away with all its worries, irritations, everything. I died in a way, but I came to know that something deathless is there. Once you accept death totally, you become aware of it.

Then again at the age of twenty-one, my family was waiting. So I told them, "Why do you go on waiting? Do not wait. Now I am not going to die."

Physically, someday I will die, of course. However, this prediction of the astrologer helped me very much because he made me aware very early on about death. Continuously, I could meditate and could accept that it was coming.

Death can be used for deep meditation because then you become inactive. Energy is released from the world; it can move inwards. That is why a deathlike posture is suggested. Use life, use death, for discovering that which is beyond both.

CHAPTER 25

From words to pure sounds to being

◆

37 *Devi, imagine the Sanskrit letters in these honey-
filled foci of awareness, first as letters, then more
subtly as sounds, then as most subtle feeling. Then,
leaving them aside, be free.*

38 *Bathe in the center of sound, as in the continuous
sound of a waterfall. Or, by putting the fingers in
the ears, hear the sound of sounds.*

Jean-Paul Sartre wrote an autobiography. He has called it *Words*. The name is very meaningful. It is the autobiography of every man—words and words and words. You are filled with words, and this process of words continues the whole day, even in the mind. When you are sleeping, you are still filled with words, thoughts.

The mind is just an accumulation of words, and everyone is too much obsessed with the mind. That is why self-knowledge becomes more and more impossible. The self is beyond the words, or behind the words, or below the words, or above the words, but never in the words. You exist not in the mind, but just below the mind, behind the mind, above the mind—never in the mind. You are focused in the mind, but you are not there. Standing out, you are focused in the mind. Because of this constant focusing, you have become identified with the mind. You think you are the mind, this is the only problem, the basic problem, and unless you are aware that you are not the mind, nothing meaningful can happen to you. You will live in misery.

This identification is the misery. It is as if one is identified with a shadow. Then the whole life becomes false. Your whole life is false, and the basic error is that you are identified with the mind. You think you are the mind: this is the ignorance. You can develop your mind, but in that way ignorance will not be dissolved. You can become very

intelligent, you can become very talented, you may even become a genius. But if the identification with the mind is there, you remain basically mediocre because you remain identified with a false shadow. How does it happen? Unless you understand the mechanism of how it happens you cannot go beyond it, and all the techniques of meditation are nothing but processes to go beyond, to go beyond the mind.

Meditation techniques are not against the world, they are against the mind—and not really against the mind, but against identification. How are you identified with the mind? What is the mechanism that is working? Mind is a need—a great need, particularly for humanity. And that is the basic difference between man and the animals. Man thinks, and he has used thinking as a weapon for his struggle to survive. He could survive because he could think; otherwise he is more helpless than any animal, more weak than any animal. Physically, it was impossible for him to survive. He could survive because he could think. Because of thinking, he has become the master of the earth.

If thinking has been so deeply helpful, then it becomes easy to understand why man has become identified with the mind. You are not so much identified with the body. Of course, religions go on saying, "Do not be identified with the body," but no one is really identified with the body—no one! You are identified with the mind, not with the body, and this identification with the body is not so fatal as the identification with the mind—because the body is more real. The body exists, it is related to existence very deeply. Mind is just a shadow.

Identification with the mind is more subtle than identification with the body, but we are identified with the mind because mind has been such a great help to survive—not only against animals, against nature, but against other human beings also. If you have a keen, intelligent mind, you will win against other human beings as well. You will succeed, you will become more rich, because you will be more calculating and more cunning. Against other human beings also, mind is the weapon. That is why we are so much identified—remember this.

Against death, against disease, against nature, against animals, against other human beings, mind has been your protection, your security. And mind has done much, so obviously we think of ourselves as mind. If someone says that your body is ill you do not feel offended, but if someone says that your mind seems ill you do feel offended. If your body is ill, you do not feel offended. Why? You are not identified with the body. But if your mind is ill and someone says you are psychologically ill, mentally ill, insane, you feel offended. Now this is something about you, not about your body.

You behave with the body as if it is a vehicle, something you possess, but not so with the mind. With the mind, you are the mind; with the body, you are the master. The body is a slave—you possess it.

This mind has created a division in your being also, and that is the second basic cause of why we are identified with it. You think not only about external things, you think about internal things also. For example, the body has many instincts. You think about your instincts also. Not only do you think, you fight against your instincts, so there is a constant internal fight. There is sex: the mind fights it, or tries to mold it in its own way. It suppresses it, perverts it, tries to control it.

The mind is fighting inside also. That fight creates a division between you and your body. And really, you start thinking that the body is something inimical, not a friend, because the body goes on doing things which the mind is against. The body is

not going to listen to the mind, so the mind feels offended, defeated. It attacks the body, and then a division is created. And you are always identified with the mind, never with the body.

The mind is your ego. That is your "I." If the body feels sexuality, you can divide. You can say, "This is the body, not me. I am against it. I have taken a vow of celibacy, I am against it. This is the body; this is not me." Then who are you? The mind which has taken a vow? This mind is your ego, and you go against the body because the body is very ego-destroying. Whatsoever you decide, it never listens.

All the ascetic nonsense was born because of this: the body will not listen. The body is nature, the body is a part of the cosmic whole, the body has its own laws. Those laws are unconscious; it functions according to them. The mind tries to create its own laws over and above the body. Then a conflict is created. Then the mind starts fighting the body. Then the mind will starve the body; it will try in every way to kill it.

That is what has happened in the past: so-called religious people have been really mad against their bodies. And whatsoever they were doing was less for God and more against the body. Really, to be in search of God became synonymous with being against the body. Religious persons took the attitude, "Kill the body, destroy the body. The body is the enemy." And really, this is not a religious attitude, but one of the most irreligious attitudes, because it is the most egoistical. This is the ego; the ego feels offended.

You decide not to be angry again, and then anger comes: your ego feels defeated. Your decision is thrown overboard, and the anger comes. And when the anger comes you feel this is coming from the body. You decide against sex and sex comes: you feel offended, so you try to punish the body. Asceticism is nothing but punishment—punishing your own body in order to force it to behave according to the ego.

This mind, this process of thinking, this ego, is

just a fragment of your whole total being, and this fragment is trying to be the sovereign. This is not possible, the fragment cannot be the sovereign. It is going to fail; that is why there is so much frustration in life. You can never succeed—you are trying the impossible. The fragment cannot be the sovereign. The whole is bigger and the whole is more powerful.

It is just as if a branch of a tree tries to control the whole tree, even the roots. How can a branch control the whole tree, and how can it force the roots to follow it? That is impossible. Whatsoever it thinks, it is mad; the branch has gone mad. It may go on thinking and dreaming, conceiving of some future where the tree will be following it, but it is not possible; it will have to follow the tree. It is alive only because of the tree and the roots. And the roots were there before it was. The roots are the source of it also.

Your mind is just a fragment of your body; it cannot control it. The very effort to control the body will create frustration and failure. And the whole humanity has been a failure because of this. Everyone is suffering, in conflict, in anguish, in anxiety, trembling, because the impossible is being tried. But the ego always likes to try the impossible. The possible has no challenge for it; the impossible is a challenge. And if the impossible can be done, then the ego will feel very good—because this cannot be done. You can try to do it, but you will waste your life trying that which cannot be done.

Because of this inner effort to become the master, you are identified with the mind. Who would like to be identified with a slave? Who would like to be identified with the unconscious? It is useless. The unconscious is negated because it cannot be grasped. And with the unconscious there is no ego; you cannot feel "I."

Try to understand it in this way: when sex overpowers you, really you cannot say "I." It is as if something greater than you has taken possession—as if you are in a strong current. You are no more; something else is driving you. That is why these words are meaningful...that is why those who are against sex will say, "Sex possessed me."

Anger possesses you, hunger possesses you. They are something greater than you, and you are just taken by the current. It is fearful. It is very fearful because then you are no more. It is a sort of death. That is why you are so much against sex—it is a sort of death. Those who are against sex will always be afraid of death, and those who are not against sex and can flow in it easily, spontaneously, will never be afraid of death. See the association: those who are against sex will always be afraid of death, and those who are afraid of death will be always against sex.

Those who are afraid of death will always create theories of immortality; they will always think about life beyond death. Those who think about immortality will always be against sex—these are alternatives. Sex gives you a fear. What is the fear? You are no more in it, something greater than you possesses you. You are thrown overboard; you are no more in it.

So even those who are not against sex, they too never move really deep into sex. They never move; they are always holding back, trying to remain there, not allowing themselves, not ready for a let-go. That is why orgasm, such a natural thing, has become so impossible for man and woman. A deep orgasm means you have been in something which was greater than you. You have been in something where you were not, the ego was not.

The ego is struggling to control everything, and mind helps you. In the effort you become identified with the mind, and this identification is the misery, it is a false shadow. Mind is a very utilitarian instrument. You have to use it, but do not become identified with it. It is a good instrument—necessary. Use it! But do not feel that *you* are the mind, because once you start feeling you are the mind, you cannot use it. The mind starts using you. Then you are simply drifting with the mind.

All the meditation techniques are an effort to give you a glimpse of that which is not mind. So how to go beyond it? How to leave it and look at it even for a single moment?

37 Beyond words and sounds.

The first sound technique: *Devi, imagine the Sanskrit letters in these honey-filled foci of awareness, first as letters, then more subtly as sounds, then as most subtle feeling. Then, leaving them aside, be free.*

Words are sounds. Thoughts are words in sequence, in logical sequence, in a particular pattern. Sound is basic. With sound words are created, and then with words thoughts are created, and then with thoughts religion and philosophy, everything. Deep down is the sound.

This technique uses a reverse process. Shiva says: *Devi, imagine the Sanskrit letters in these honey-filled foci of awareness, first as letters, then more subtly as sounds, then as most subtle feeling. Then, leaving them aside, be free.*

We live in philosophy. One is a Hindu, one is a Mohammedan, one is a Christian, or something else. We live in philosophies, systems of thought, and they have become so important that we can die for them. Man can die for words, for mere words. Someone calls his conception of the absolute a lie, or someone calls Rama or someone calls Christ or something else a lie—then man can fight, for a mere word he can kill the other. The word has become so important. This is nonsense, but this is history and this is how we are still behaving.

A single word can create such a disturbance in you that you are ready to kill or to die for it. We live in philosophies, systems of thought. What are philosophies? Thoughts arranged logically, systematically, in a pattern. And what are thoughts? Words arranged in a system, meaningfully. And what are words? Sounds, upon which it is agreed that they mean either this or that. So sounds are basic; they are the basic structure of the mind.

Philosophies are the peak, but the bricks by which the whole structure is raised are sounds.

What is wrong? A sound is just a sound, and the meaning is given by us, agreed upon by us; otherwise it has no meaning. The meaning is invested by us, projected by us; otherwise 'Rama' is just a sound—it is meaningless. We give it a meaning, and then we create a system of thought around it. Then this word becomes very significant, then we make a philosophy around it. Then you can do something, anything, for it. You can die or you can live for it. If someone insults this sound 'Rama,' you can become infuriated. And what is this? Just an agreement, a legal agreement that "This word means this." No word means anything in itself, it is simply a sound.

This sutra says to go in the reverse order—go backwards. Come to the sounds; then, more basic than sounds, a feeling is somewhere hidden. This has to be understood. Man uses words. Words mean sounds with meanings that are agreed upon. But animals, birds use sounds without any linguistic meaning. They do not have any language, but they use sounds with feeling. A bird is singing: it has a "feeling" meaning in it, it is indicating something. It may be a call for the partner, for the beloved, or it may be a call for the mother, or the child may be feeling hungry and just showing his distress. It is indicating a feeling.

Above sounds there are words, thoughts, philosophies; below sounds are feelings. And unless you can get below feelings, you cannot get below mind. The whole world is filled with sounds, only the human world is filled with words. And even a child who cannot use language uses sounds. Really, the whole language developed because of particular sounds that every child is using all over the world.

For example, in any language the word 'mother' is somehow related with 'ma.' It may be 'mater,' it may be 'Mutter,' it may be 'mata,' it may be 'ma,' —anything—but somewhere it is related with the sound 'ma' in all the languages, more or less. The child can utter 'ma' most easily. The first sound which the child can utter is ma. Then the whole structure is based on this 'ma.' A child utters 'ma' because it is the first sound which is easy for the child to utter. This is the case anywhere, in any part of the world, in any time. Just because of the structure of the throat and the body, 'ma' is the easiest sound to utter.

And the mother is the nearest and the first person who is meaningful. So the first sound becomes associated with the first person who is meaningful, and from this mother, mater, mata, ma, all the other words are derived. But when the child for the first time utters 'ma,' he has no linguistic meaning for it, but a feeling is there. And because of that feeling the word becomes associated with the mother. That feeling is more basic than the sound.

So this sutra says first to imagine the Sanskrit letters. Any language will do. Because Shiva was talking to Parvati, that is why he said Sanskrit. You can use English or Latin or Arabic, any language will do. Sanskrit has no significance except in that Shiva was talking to Parvati in Sanskrit. It is not that Sanskrit is something superior to any other language, any language will do. First feel inside, in your consciousness, *the honey-filled foci of awareness* filled with letters: A, B, C, D...any letters of any language. This can be done, and it is a very beautiful exercise. If you want to do it, close your eyes and just see your consciousness inside being filled with words.

Think of consciousness as a blackboard, then: A, B, C.... Visualize all the words, all the letters. Visualize these first as letters. A: look at it as A as you write it. Write it with consciousness and look at it. Then by and by, forget the letter A and just remember the sound of A—just the sound. Start with visualization—because eyes are predominant for us. Ears are not so predominant. We are eye-oriented, eye-centered. Again, the reason is the same. Because eyes help us to survive more than anything else, our consciousness is ninety percent in the eyes. Conceive of yourself without eyes, and your whole

life goes dead—then a very minor part remains.

So first visualize. Use your eyes inwards and see the letters. Letters are more related to ears than eyes because they are sounds, but for us, because we are reading, reading, reading, they have become associated with eyes. Basically, they are associated with ears—they are sounds. Start with the eyes, then forget the eyes by and by. Then move away from the eyes to the ears. First imagine them as letters, then see them, hear them *more subtly as sounds, then as most subtle feelings.* And this is a very beautiful exercise.

When you say A, what is the feeling? You may not have been aware of it. What is the feeling inside you? Whenever you use any sound, what type of feeling comes into existence? We are so feeling-less that we have simply forgotten. When you see a sound, what happens inside? You go on using it and the sound is even forgotten. You go on seeing it. If I say A, you will see it first. In your mind, A will become visible; you will visualize it. When I say A, do not visualize it. Just hear the sound A, and then go and find out what happens in your feeling center. Does nothing happen?

Shiva says, move from letters to sounds, uncover sounds through the letters. Uncover sounds, and then, through the sounds also, uncover feelings. Be aware of how you feel. They say that man has now become very insensitive; he is the most insensitive animal on earth.

I was reading about one poet, a German poet, and he relates one incident of his childhood. His father was a lover of horses, so he had many horses at the house, a big stable, but he would not allow this child to go to the stable. He was afraid, as the child was very small. But when the father was not there the child would sometimes steal into the stable where he had a friend—a horse. Whenever the child would go in, the horse would make some sounds.

And the poet has written, "Then I also started making sounds with the horse, because there was no possibility of language. Then, in communication with that horse, for the first time I became aware of sounds—their beauty, their feeling."

You cannot be aware with a man because he is dead. A horse is more alive, and he has no language. He has pure sound. He is filled with his heart, not with his mind. So that poet remembers, "For the first time, I became aware of the beauty of sounds and their meaning. This was not the meaning of words and thoughts, but a meaning filled with feeling." If someone else was there, the horse would not make those sounds, so the child could understand that the horse meant, "Do not come in. Someone is here and your father will be angry."

When there was no one, the horse would make the sounds meaning, "Come in. There is no one." So the poet remembers that "It was a conspiracy, and he helped me very much, that horse helped me very much. And when I would go and love that horse, he would move his head in a particular way when he liked it. When he did not like it, he would not move his head in that way. When he liked it, then it was a certain thing, he would express it. When he was not in the mood, then he would not move in a certain way."

And this poet says, "This continued for years. I would go and love that horse, and that love was so deep, I never felt any affinity with anyone else so deeply. Then one day when I was stroking his neck and he was moving and enjoying it ecstatically, suddenly for the first time I became aware of my hand, that I was stroking, and the horse stopped. Now he would not move his neck." And that poet says, "Then for years I tried and tried, but there was no response, the horse would not reply. Only later on did I become aware that because I became aware of my hand and myself, the ego came in and the communication broke. I couldn't recapture again that communication with the horse."

What happened? That was a feeling communication. The moment ego comes, words come, language comes, thought comes, then the layer is changed completely. Now you are above sounds; then you were below sounds. Those sounds are

feelings, and the horse could understand feelings. Now he couldn't understand, so the communication broke. The poet tried and tried—but no effort is successful because even your effort is the effort of your ego.

He tried to forget his hand, but he couldn't forget. How can you forget? It is impossible. And the more you try to forget it, the more you remember. So you cannot forget anything with effort. Effort will simply emphasize the memory more. The poet says, "I became fixed with my hand; I couldn't move that horse. I would go up to my hand, and then there was no movement. The energy would not move into that horse and he became aware of this."

How did the horse become aware? If I suddenly start speaking some other language, then the communication is broken, then you will not be able to understand me. And if this language were not known to you, you would suddenly stop because now the language is unknown to you. Thus, the horse stopped.

Every child lives with feeling. First come sounds, then those sounds are filled with feeling. Then come words, then thoughts, then systems, religions, philosophies. Then one goes farther and farther away from the center of feeling.

This sutra says, come back, come down—down to the state of feeling. Feeling is not your mind: that is why you are afraid of feeling. You are not afraid of reasoning. You are always afraid of feeling because feeling can lead you into chaos. You will not be able to control. With reason, the control is with you; with the head, you are the head. Below the head you lose the head, you cannot control, you cannot manipulate. Feelings are just below the mind—a link between you and the mind.

Then Shiva says, *Then, leaving them aside, be free.* Then leave the feelings. And remember, only when you come to the deepest layer of feelings can you leave them. You cannot leave them just now. You are not at the deepest layer of feelings, so how can you leave them? First you have to leave philosophies—Hinduism, Christianity, Moham-medanism—then you have to leave thoughts, then you have to leave words, then you have to leave letters, then you have to leave sounds, then you have to leave feelings—because you can leave only that which is there. You can leave that step upon which you are standing; you cannot leave a step upon which you are not standing.

You are standing at the step of philosophy, the one farthest away. That is why I insist so much that unless you leave religion you cannot be religious.

This sutra, this technique, can be done very easily. The problem is not with feelings, the problem is with words. You can leave a feeling, just as you can undress—as you can get out of your clothes. You can throw off your clothes; you can leave feelings simply in that way. But right now you cannot do it, and if you try to do it, it will be impossible. So go step by step.

Imagine letters—A, B, C, D—then change your emphasis from the written letter to the heart sound. You are moving deep, the surface is left behind. You are sinking deep—then feel what feeling comes through a particular sound.

Because of such techniques, India could discover many things. It could discover which sounds are related to particular feelings. Because of that science, the *mantra* was developed. A particular sound is related to a particular feeling, and it is never otherwise. So if you create that sound within you, that feeling will be created. You can use any sound, and then the related feeling will be created around you. That sound creates the space to be filled by a particular feeling.

So do not use just any mantra, that is not good; it may be dangerous for you. Unless you know, or unless a person who gives you the mantra knows, what particular sound creates what particular feeling, and whether that feeling is needed by you or not, do not use any mantra. There are mantras which are known as death mantras. If you repeat them, you will die within a particular time. Within a particular period you will die, because they create

in you a longing for death.

Freud says that man has two basic instincts: libido—eros—the will to live, the will to be, the will to continue, the will to exist. And thanatos—the will to die. There are particular sounds through which, if you repeat them, the will to die will come to you. Then you would like just to drop into death. There are sounds which give you eros—which give you more libido, which give you more lust to live, to be. If you create those sounds within you, that particular feeling will overwhelm you. There are sounds which give you a feeling of peace and silence, there are sounds which create anger. So do not use any sound, any mantra, unless it is given to you by a master who knows what is going to happen through it.

When you come down from sounds, you will be aware. Each sound has its counterpart in feeling. Each sound has a corresponding feeling that goes with it, just hidden behind it. Then move to the feeling; forget the sound and move to the feeling. It is difficult to explain, but you can do it. And there were techniques for this. Particularly in Zen, there were techniques. A particular mantra would be given to a seeker. If he was doing it rightly inside, the master could know from the face. The master could know from the face whether he was doing it rightly or not because a particular feeling would come. If the sound is created, then the feeling is bound to come, and it will be on the face. You cannot deceive a master. He knows by your face what is happening inside.

Dogo was a great master, but he himself was very much disturbed, when he was a disciple, about how his master came to know what he was experiencing. And the Zen master moved with his staff and he would hit you immediately. If something goes wrong with your sound inside, he will hit you immediately. So Dogo asked, "But how do you know? And you hit me exactly in the right moment. How do you know?"

The face expresses the feeling, not the sound. The sound cannot be expressed by the face, but the face is bound to express the feeling. And the deeper you move, the more your face becomes flexible to express, more liquid. It immediately shows what is happening inside. This face which you have right now will drop because this is a mask—this is not a face. When you move in, masks fall down because they are not needed. Masks are needed for others.

Because of this, the old masters insisted on moving away from the world. This was so that you could move away from the mask easily; otherwise others will be there, and because of them you have to carry masks. You do not love your wife or your husband, but you have to carry a mask—a loving face, a false loving face. The moment you enter the house, you arrange the face: you come in and you start laughing. This is not your face.

Zen masters insisted that first one should attain the original face, because with the original face everything becomes easy. Then the master can simply know what is happening. So enlightenment was never reported. If some seeker attained enlightenment, he was not to report to the master that he had attained because the master would simply know. He would tell the disciple. No disciple was allowed to tell the master, "I have attained." There was no need. The face will show, the eyes will show, the very movement, the walking, will show. Whatsoever he does, every gesture will show that he has attained.

When you move from sounds to feelings, you move into a very, very ecstatic world, an existential world. You move away from the mind. Feelings are existential; that is what the word means—you feel them. You cannot see them, you cannot hear them, you simply feel them. When you come to this point, you can take the jump. This is the last step. Now you are standing near an abyss; you can jump.

And if you jump from the feelings, you jump into yourself. That abyss is you—not as your mind, but as your being; not as the accumulated past, but as the present, here and now.

You move from the mind to the being, and the bridge, the link, is the feelings. But to come to the feelings you will have to leave many things—words, sounds, the whole deception of the mind. *Then, leaving them aside, be free.*

You *are* free. This saying, *be free,* doesn't mean that you have to do something to be free. *Then, leaving them aside, be free* means you are free! Being is freedom; mind is bondage. That is why it is said that mind is the *sansara,* the world.

Do not leave the world…you cannot leave it. If the mind is there, you will create another world; the seed is there. You can move to a mountain, to a retreat, but you will move with the mind; you cannot leave it here. The world moves with you, you will create another world. Even in your retreat you will start creating it again, because the seed is there. You will create relationships again. It may be with the trees, it may be with birds, but you will create relationships again, you will create expectations again, and you will go on spreading the net because the seed is there. You will again be in a world.

Mind is the world, and you cannot leave mind anywhere. You can leave it only if you move within. So the only Himalaya is this; no other Himalaya will do. If you move within from words to feelings, and from feelings to being, you are moving away from the world. And once you know this inner abyss of being, then you can be anywhere, even in hell. Then it makes no difference. It makes no difference then! If you are without mind, hell cannot enter you, and with mind *only* hell enters. The mind is the door to hell.

Leaving them aside, be free. But do not try directly with feelings, you will not succeed. Try first with words. But with words also you will not succeed if you do not leave philosophies, if you do not leave thoughts. Words are just units—and if you give significance to words you cannot leave them.

Know well that language is a human creation. It is utilitarian, necessary, and the meanings we have given to sounds are our own creation. If you can understand this well, then you can move easily. If someone is saying something against the Koran, or against the Vedas, how do you feel? Can you laugh about it or does something clench within you? Can you laugh about it? Someone is insulting the Gita or someone is saying some derogatory thing against Krishna or Rama or Christ—can you laugh? Can you see through the words, that these are mere words? No, you will be hurt. Then it is difficult to lose words.

See that words are just words—noises with agreed-upon meanings and nothing else. Be convinced of it. And it is so! First become detached from words. If there is detachment from words, then you can understand that these are just noises.

It is just like in the military where they use numbers. One soldier is number 101: he can become identified with '101.' And if someone says something derogatory against the number 101, he will feel insulted, he will start fighting. And '101' is just a number, but he has become identified with it. Your name is just a number, just an index number. Things will be difficult otherwise, so we have labeled you. That is just a label; any other label can do the same work. But it is not just a label for you, it has gone deep; your name has become the center of your ego.

So they say, the so-called wise ones, they say, "Live for your name. See that your name remains pure. Respectability of your name must be there, and even if you die your name will live." It was never there, it is just a code number. You will die and the name will live.... When you yourself cannot live, how is the label going to live?

Look at words—at their futility, their meaninglessness, and do not become attached to any word. Only then can you do this technique.

38 Feel yourself in the center of sounds.

The second sound technique: *Bathe in the center of sound, as in the continuous sound of a waterfall. Or, by putting the fingers in the ears, hear the sound of sounds.*

This technique can be done in many ways. One way is to begin by just sitting anywhere. Sounds are always present. It may be in a market or it may be at a Himalayan retreat: sounds are there. Sit silently, and with sound there is something very special. Whenever there are sounds, you are the center. All the sounds come to you from everywhere, from all directions.

With sight, with eyes, this is not so. Sight is linear. I see you—then there is a line toward you. Sound is circular, it is not linear. So all sounds come in circles and you are the center. Wherever you are, you are always the center of sound. For sounds, you are always God, the center of the whole universe. Every sound is coming to you, moving toward you, in circles.

This technique says, *Bathe in the center of sound.* Wherever you are, if you are doing this technique, just close your eyes and feel the whole universe filled with sound. Feel as if every sound is moving toward you and you are the center. Even this feeling that you are the center will give you a very deep peace. The whole universe becomes the circumference and you are the center, and everything is moving toward you, falling toward you.

...As in the continuous sound of a waterfall. If you are sitting by the side of a waterfall, close your eyes and feel the sound all around you, falling on you from every side, creating a center in you from every side. Why this emphasis on feeling that you are in the center? Because in the center there is no sound. The center is without sound, that is why you can hear sounds; otherwise you could not hear them. A sound cannot hear another sound. Because you are soundless at your center, you can hear sounds. The center is absolute silence. That is why you can hear sounds entering you, coming to you, penetrating you, encircling you.

If you can find out where is the center, where is the field in you to where every sound is coming, suddenly sounds will disappear and you will enter into soundlessness. If you can feel a center where every sound is being heard, there is a sudden transference

357

of consciousness. One moment you will be hearing the whole world filled with sounds, and another moment your awareness will suddenly turn in and you will hear the soundlessness, the center of life.

Once you have heard that, then no sound can disturb you. It comes to you, but it never reaches you. It is always coming to you, but it never reaches you. There is a point where no sound enters. That point is *you*. Do it in a market, there is no other place like a market. It is so much filled with sounds, mad sounds. But do not start thinking about sounds—that this is good and that is bad, and this is disturbing and that is very beautiful and harmonious. You are not supposed to think about sounds, you are simply supposed to think of the center. You are not supposed to think about every sound moving toward you—whether it is good, bad, beautiful. You are just to remember that you are the center and all the sounds are moving toward you—every sound, whatsoever the sort.

In the beginning you will get dizzy because you have not been hearing whatsoever is happening all around. Your hearing is selective, your seeing is selective. And now scientific research says that ninety-eight percent is not heard, only two percent of whatsoever is happening all around you is heard. Otherwise, if you heard one hundred percent of what is happening all around you, you will simply go mad. Previously, it was thought that the senses are the doors, the openings, the windows for the outside to enter inside. Now they say they are not doors, and they are not so open as it was thought. Rather, they are like a watchman, a censor, who is every moment watching what is to be allowed in or not.

Only two percent of happenings are allowed in —and you are already mad with two percent. With one hundred percent, with a total opening, with everything opened, every sense opened, functioning, and everything being allowed in, you will go mad. So when you try this method, in the first step you will feel a dizziness coming to you. Do not be afraid, go on feeling the center—and allow every-thing, whatsoever is happening. Allow everything to move in.

Relax yourself, relax your watch towers, your senses; relax everything, let everything enter you. You have become more liquid, open; everything is coming to you, all sounds are moving toward you. Then move with the sounds, and come to the center where you hear them.

Sounds are not heard in the ears, the ears cannot hear them. The ears only do a transmission work, and in the transmission they cut out much which is useless for you. They choose, they select, and then those sounds enter you. Now find out within where is your center. The ears are not the center, you are hearing from somewhere deep down. The ears are simply sending you selected sounds. Where are you? Where is your center?

If you are working with sounds, then sooner or later you will be surprised—because the center is not in the head. It appears to be in the head because you have never heard sounds, you have heard only words. With words the head is the center, with sounds it is not the center. That is why in Japan they say that man thinks not through the head, but through the belly—because they have been working with sounds for a long time.

You have seen in every temple a gong. That is placed there to create sounds around a seeker. Someone is meditating, and the gong is sounded or a bell is rung. A disturbance seems to have been created by the very sound of the bell; someone is meditating, and this bell or gong seems disturbing. In a temple, every visitor who comes will hit the gong or ring the bell. With someone meditating there, this would seem to be a constant disturbance. It is not, because the person is waiting for this sound.

So every visitor is helping. Again and again the bell is hit, and the sound is created and the medita-tor again enters himself. He looks at the center, where this sound goes deep. There is one hit on the bell—the visitor has done that. Now the second hit will be inside the meditator, somewhere inside.

Where is it? The sound always hits at the belly, at the navel, never in the head. If it hits in the head, you can understand well that it is not sound, it is words. Then you have started thinking about the sound. Then the purity is lost.

Now there is much research about children who are in the womb. They are also hit by sounds and they react to sounds. They cannot react to language. They have no head yet, they have no reasoning, and they do not yet know language and the agreed-upon customs of the society. They do not know about language, but they hear the sounds. And every sound affects the child more than it affects the mother, because the mother cannot hear the sounds—she hears the words. And we are creating mad sounds, chaotic, and those sounds are hitting the unborn children. They will be born mad; you have already disturbed them too much.

Even plants are affected by sound. They grow more if some musical sounds are created around them; they grow less if some chaotic sounds are created around them. You can help them to grow. You can help them in many ways through sounds.

Now they say that because of traffic noises—which are not harmonious and cannot be—man is going mentally insane, and it seems that the limit has come. If it grows more, then there is no hope for man. These sounds are hitting you continuously, but if you think about them they will hit your head, and that is not the center; the navel is the center. So do not think about them.

All the mantras are meaningless sounds. And if some master says that "This is the meaning of this mantra," then it is not a mantra at all. A mantra needs to be, of necessity, without meaning. It has some work, but no meaning. It has to do something within you, but it has no meaning because it has just to be a pure sound within you. That is why we evolved the mantra *aum*. It is meaningless, it is just a pure sound. If this pure sound is created within you, if you can create it within, then too the same technique can be used.

Bathe in the center of sound, as in the continu- *ous sound of a waterfall. Or, by putting the fingers in the ears, hear the sound of sounds.* You can create the sound just by using your finger, or anything which closes your ears forcibly. Then a certain sound is heard. What is that sound, and why do you hear it when the ears are closed, when the ears are plugged?

It happened in America that a train passed through a certain neighborhood in the middle of the night, somewhere about 2:00 a.m. A new line was inaugurated and the train stopped moving on the old route. But a very strange phenomenon happened. The people who were living in that neighborhood where the train had stopped moving complained to the police that at about 2:00 a.m. something mysterious was heard. There were so many reports, it had to be investigated—what was the matter? Strange sounds were heard at about two. They were never heard when the train was passing; the people had become accustomed to the train.

Now suddenly the train stopped. They were waiting to hear it in their sleep; they had become accustomed to it, conditioned. They were waiting, and the sound was not there. Absence was heard, and this absence was something new. They felt uneasy about it, they couldn't sleep. So for the first time it was understood that if you are constantly hearing something and it stops, you will hear the absence of it. So do not think that you will simply not hear it. You will hear the absence, the negative part of it will be heard.

If I look at you, and then if I close my eyes, I see your negative. If you look at the window and then close your eyes you will see the negative of the window, and the negative can be so forceful that if you suddenly look at the wall the negative will be projected on the wall. You will be seeing the negative.

Just as there are negatives of photographs, there are negative sounds. Not only can the eyes see the negative, the ears can even hear the negative. So when you close your ears, you hear the negative world of sounds. All the sounds have stopped. Suddenly a new sound is heard. This sound is the absence of sound. A gap has come in. You are missing something, and then you hear this absence.

Or, by putting the fingers in the ears, hear the sound of sounds. That negative sound is known as the sound of sounds—because it is not really a sound, but its absence. Or, it is a natural sound, because it is not created by anything.

All sounds are created. The sound you hear when you close your ears is not a created sound. If the whole world becomes absolutely silent, then you will hear the silence also. Pascal is reported to have said, "The moment I think about the infinite cosmos, the silence of the infinite cosmos makes me very much afraid." The silence makes him afraid because sounds are only on the earth. Sounds need atmosphere. The moment you go beyond the earth's atmosphere there are no sounds—only absolute silence. That silence you can create even on the earth, if you close both of your ears completely. Then you are on the earth, but you have moved; you have dropped below sounds.

Astronauts are being trained for many things, and one thing is to be in the silence. They have to be trained in silent chambers so that they become accustomed to soundlessness; otherwise they will go mad. Many problems face them, and this is one of the deepest problems: how to be away from the human world of sounds. Then you become isolated.

If you are lost in the forest and you hear a certain word, you may not know the source but you are less afraid. Someone is there! You are not alone! In soundlessness, you are alone. In a crowd, if you close both of your ears totally and move in, you are alone. The crowd has disappeared, because it was through sounds that you could know others were there.

Putting the fingers in the ears, hear the sound of sounds. This absence of sound is a very subtle experience. What will it give to you? The moment there are no sounds, you fall back upon yourself. With sounds we move away, with sounds we move to the

other. Try to understand this: with sounds we are related to the other, we communicate with the other.

So even a blind man is not in so much difficulty as a man who cannot speak, who is dumb. Observe a person who is dumb: he looks inhuman. A blind man never looks inhuman, but a dumb person looks inhuman; the face gives a feeling of something which is not human. And a dumb person is in more difficulty than a blind man. With the blind man the problem is that he cannot see, but he can communicate. He can become a part of a greater humanity, he can become a part of a society, of a family; he can love, he can speak. A dumb man is suddenly out of society. He cannot speak, he cannot communicate, he cannot express.

Try to imagine yourself in an air-conditioned glass room, a soundproof room. No sound can enter to you, and you cannot scream, you cannot do anything to express yourself, the sound will not go out. In a glass room you can see the whole world moving around you, but neither can you speak to them nor can they speak to you. You will feel hopelessly frustrated, and the whole thing will become a nightmare.

A dumb man is in a nightmare continuously. Without communicating he is not part of humanity. Without expression he cannot flower. He cannot reach anyone and no one can reach him. He is with you and far away, and the gap is unbridgeable.

If sound is the vehicle to move to the other, then soundlessness becomes the vehicle to move to oneself. With sound you communicate with the other; with soundlessness you fall down into your own abyss, into yourself. That is why so many techniques use soundlessness to move within.

Become absolutely dumb and deaf—even if only for a few moments—and you cannot go anywhere else than to yourself. Suddenly you will find that you are standing within; no movement will be possible. That is why silence was practiced so much. In it, all the bridges for moving to the other are broken.

Gurdjieff used to give long silent periods to his

disciples, and then he would insist that not only was language not to be used, but there was to be no communication, no gesture at all—neither with the eyes nor the hands. No communication was to be used. Silence means *no* communication. So he would force the group to live in a house—twenty, thirty or forty people in one bungalow, in one house—and than he would say, "Remain here in this house as if you are alone. You cannot go out." Forty persons would be there, and he would say, "Move in the house, live in the house as if you are alone. No communication! Do not recognize that the other is, not even by the eyes. Move completely as if you are the only person residing in the house." With three months of living in this way, absolutely dumb and deaf, with no possibility of communicating, there would be no possibility to move out.

I do not know whether you have observed or not, but in society those who can talk much become prominent; those who can communicate their thoughts easily become leaders—religious, political, literary, any type. Those who can communicate their thoughts, those who can talk efficiently, they become leaders. Why? They can reach more people, they can reach to greater masses.

Have you ever heard of any dumb person becoming a leader? You can find a blind man becoming a leader; there is no problem. And sometimes he may become a great leader, because all that his eyes are not doing, all those energies will be transferred to his ears. But a dumb man cannot become a leader in any walk of life. He cannot communicate, he cannot become social.

Society is a language. Language is basic to social existence—to relationship. If you leave language, you are alone. The world may be filled with millions, but if you lose language you are alone.

Meher Baba stayed continuously for forty years in silence. What was he doing in silence? Really, you cannot do anything in silence because every act is somehow related with others. Even in imagination, if you do something you will have to imagine others; you cannot do it alone. If you are absolutely alone, action becomes impossible. Even the imagination to act becomes impossible. Acting is related to others. If you drop language inside, all doing drops. You are, but you are not doing anything.

Meher Baba would tell his disciples, by writing a note, "On this particular date I am going to break my silence," and then he would not break it. This continued for forty years, and then he died in silence. What was the problem? Why should he say, "Now, this year, on this day, on this date, I am going to speak?" And why should he postpone it again? What was happening inside? Why would he not keep his promise?

Once you know silence for such a long time, you cannot fall back to sounds again; it becomes impossible. There is a rule, and he didn't follow the rule so he could not come back. There is a rule that one should not remain silent for more than three years. Once you cross the limit, you cannot come back to the world of sounds. You may try, but it is impossible. It is easy to move from sounds to silence, but it is very difficult to move from silence to sounds. Beyond three years many things simply become impossible. The mechanism cannot function the same way again. It has to be used continuously; at the most, one can remain silent for three years. Beyond that, if you remain silent the mechanism which can produce sounds and words cannot be used again, it becomes dead.

Secondly, the person becomes so silent remaining with himself alone that it will now be a misery to communicate. Then to say something to someone will be like talking to a wall, because the person who has remained silent for such a long time knows that you cannot understand whatsoever he is saying. Regardless of what he is saying, he knows he is not saying that which he wants to say. The whole thing has gone. After such a deep silence, he cannot move again to the world of sounds.

So Meher Baba tried and tried, but he couldn't bring himself to speak again. He wanted to say something, and he had something worth saying, but the mechanism and the movements necessary to come back to a lower realm were impossible. Thus, he died without saying what he wanted to say.

It will be helpful to understand this: whatsoever you are doing, always go on doing the opposite with it. Go on changing to the opposite always. Remain silent for a few hours, then talk. Do not become fixed in anything—you will be more alive and more moving. Do meditation for a few days, and then stop suddenly and do everything that can create tension in you. Then move again to meditation.

Go on moving between the opposites, you will be more alive and dynamic. Do not get fixed. Once you get fixed, you will not be able to move to the other extreme, and the ability to move to the other extreme means life. If you are not able to move, you are already dead. This movement is very good.

Gurdjieff advised his disciples to have sudden changes. He would insist on fasting and then he would say, "Now eat as much as you can." Then suddenly he would say, "Go on a fast." Then again he would say, "Start eating." He would say, "Be awake for a few days and nights continuously, then

fall asleep for a few nights." This movement between the polar opposites gives you a dynamism, an aliveness.

Or, by putting the fingers in the ears, hear the sound of sounds. In one technique, two opposites have been shown. *Bathe in the center of sound, as in the continuous sound of a waterfall*—this is one extreme. *Or, by putting the fingers in the ears, hear the sound of sounds*—this is another extreme.

One part is to hear the sounds coming to your center; another part is to stop all sounds and feel the soundless center. Both these have been given in one technique for a special purpose—so that you can move from one to the other.

The *or* is not a choice to do this or that. Do both! That is why both have been given in one technique. First do one for a few months, then do the other for a few months. You will be more alive, and you will know two extremes. And if you can move to the two extremes easily, you can remain young forever. Those who get fixed at any extreme become old and die.

CHAPTER 26

Acceptance of the peaks and the valleys

◆

Q U E S T I O N S

Should we consciously channel and regulate instincts?

How to turn horrible noises into positive sound?

The first question:

Last night You discussed the censorship and suppression by the conscious mind of the unconscious instincts, and You said that the unconscious instincts belong to the animal heritage in man's evolution. Then is it not good to channel and regulate them according to the intelligence, discrimination and art of living which belong to the conscious mind?

Man is an animal, but not only an animal: he is more also. But that "more" cannot deny the animal, it has to absorb it. Man is more than an animal, but the animal cannot be denied. It has to be absorbed creatively. You cannot leave it aside, it is in your very roots; you have to use it creatively. So the first thing to remember is not to be negative about your animal heritage. Once you start thinking in negative terms you will become destructive to yourself, because you are ninety-nine percent animal.

If you create a division, you are fighting a losing battle; you cannot win. The result of your fight will be quite the opposite, because ninety-nine percent is animal. Only one percent of the mind is conscious, and this one percent cannot win against the ninety-nine percent. It is going to be defeated. That is why there is so much frustration, because everyone is defeated by his own animal. You can never succeed. Of necessity you are going to be a failure, because that one percent cannot succeed against the ninety-nine percent. It cannot even be divided from the ninety-nine percent.

It is just like a flower: it cannot go against the roots, it cannot go against the whole tree. And while you are against your animal heritage, you are being fed by it. You are alive because of it. If your animal dies this moment, you will die immediately. Your mind exists as a flower; your animal heritage is the whole tree. Do not be negative—that is suicidal. And if you are divided against yourself, you can never attain anything which is blissful.

You are creating a hell, and the hell is nowhere else but in a divided personality. In the split personality is the hell. And hell is not something geographical, hell is psychological—and heaven also. The personality which is a whole, one unit, with no inner division and conflict, is heaven.

So the first thing I would like to say is, do not be negative. Do not divide yourself, do not go against yourself, do not become two. The animal that is there is not something bad. The animal in you is a great potential. That is your past and also your future, because much is hidden in it. Uncover it, develop it, allow it to grow and go beyond it, but do not fight with it. That is one of the basic teachings of tantra.

Other traditions are divisive. They divide you, they create a fight within you. Tantra is not divisive, it doesn't believe in fight. Tantra is absolutely positive; it doesn't believe in saying no. Tantra believes in saying yes—yes to the whole of life. And through "yes" the transformation happens, and through "no" there is only disturbance—no transformation is possible. Against whom are you fighting? Against yourself? How can you win? And the major part of you is from the animal, so the major part will win. So those who fight, they are creating their own defeats. If you want to be defeated, fight. If you want to win, do not fight.

Victory needs knowledge, not fight. Fight is a subtle violence. And this is strange, but this has happened: those who talk about nonviolence to others are very violent against themselves. There are teachings and traditions which say, "Do not be violent to anyone," but those same teachings are very violent as far as you are inwardly concerned. They teach you to be violent with yourself, but not to be violent with others.

All types of asceticism, renunciation, negative attitudes, life-denying philosophies, are based on maintaining a violent attitude toward yourself. They tell you to be violent with yourself.

Tantra is absolutely nonviolent. It says, if you cannot be nonviolent with yourself, you cannot be nonviolent with anyone else—that is impossible. A person who is violent to himself will be violent to everyone; in his nonviolence also he will be just hiding his violence. Aggression can be turned against yourself, but that aggressive attitude is destructive.

But that doesn't mean to remain the animal which you are. The moment you accept your heritage, the moment you accept your past, the future becomes an opening. Through acceptance is the opening. The animal is the past; it need not be the future. There is no need to go against the past —and you cannot go. Use it creatively.

What can be done to use it creatively? The first thing is to be profoundly aware of its existence. Those who fight are not aware of it. Because they are afraid, they push the animal behind, they push the animal into the unconscious. Really, there need not be any unconscious, but because of suppression the unconscious is created. You feel many things within which you condemn without understanding

them. A man who understands condemns nothing; there is no need. He can even use poison as a medicine because he knows. Everything can be used creatively. Because you do not know, in ignorance poison is poison. With wisdom it can become the elixir.

The person who is fighting against his sex, anger, greed, against the animal, what will he do? He will suppress. Fighting is suppression. He will push down anger, sex, greed, hatred, jealousy. He will push everything down somewhere underground, and he will create a false structure above ground. The structure will be false because the energies have not been transformed which can make it real. The structure is phony; underground, the real energies have been repressed. Those real energies will always remain there working, any moment they can explode. You are just sitting on a volcano, and every moment that volcano is trying to erupt. If it does, your structure will be shaken.

Whatsoever you have built in the name of religion, morality, culture, is a phony structure that is above ground—just a false façade. Underground the real man is hiding. So your animal is not very far away; your façade is just skin-deep. Someone insults you, and the gentleman disappears and the animal comes out. The gentleman is just skin-deep; the volcano is just near. Any moment it can be brought out, and when it comes out, your intelligence, your morality, your religion, your so-called being above animal things, simply disappear. When the real asserts itself, the false disappears. Only when the real goes back underground does the false come again.

When you are angry, where is your mind, where is your consciousness, where is your morality? Where are your vows that you have taken so many times—that "Now I am not going to be angry again"? When anger comes they all simply disappear. When anger has moved again to its cave, its underground cave, you start repenting. Those phony fellows have gathered again. They start talking, condemning, and planning for the future, and again in the future the same will happen: when anger will come the shadows will disappear.

Your consciousness right now is just a shadow. It is not a real thing; it has no substance in it. You can take a vow of *brahmacharya,* of celibacy—it makes no difference to your sex instinct. The sex instinct simply goes underground, and when it comes up, your vows of brahmacharya, of celibacy, will prove to be made of just very dreamlike stuff. They cannot face the real thing.

So these are the two attitudes. You can either suppress sex—then you will never go beyond it—or you can use your sex energy in a creative way. Not saying no to it, but giving it a deep yes; not forcing it to go underground, but creating a structure above ground with it. Then you will be a real man. It will be difficult, obviously; that is why we choose the easier path. It is easier to have a false structure, because nothing is needed. Only one thing is needed: to deceive yourself, that is all. If you can deceive yourself, you can create a false structure very easily. Nothing will change really, but you will go on thinking that everything has changed.

This is easy, to create an illusion. To create a reality is a difficult task, it is arduous. But it is worthwhile, because once you have created something with real energies, your structure cannot be shattered. If sex is above ground, then you can create something out of it—for example, love. If sex is transformed, it becomes love; if it is suppressed, it becomes hatred.

You become afraid of love if you suppress sex. A person who has suppressed sex will always be afraid of love, because the moment love comes sex will follow. Love is of the soul and sex is of the body, so love cannot be allowed to happen because then sex will follow. It will be just somewhere near, by the corner. So a person who has suppressed sex cannot be loving. He may show it, he may pretend that he is very loving, but he cannot be because he is so afraid. He cannot touch you with a loving hand because the fear is there. The loving hand can any moment turn out to be a sexual touch, so he will be afraid; he will not allow you to touch him.

He may create many justifications for it but the real thing is fear—fear of the instinct which he has repressed. And he will be filled with hatred, because any energy that is repressed reverses itself and goes to its original nature.

Sex moves easily toward love; that is a natural flow. If you prevent it, if you create hindrances to its path, it will become hatred. So your so-called saints and so-called moral teachers, if you look deep into them you will find them filled with hatred. And that is bound to be, it is natural. Sex is hidden there, any moment it can erupt. They are sitting on a dangerous volcano. If you push down energies, you are just postponing a task, and the more it is postponed, the more difficult it will be.

Tantra says, create your life with real energies—and real energies are all animal energies. But when I say animal, there is no condemnation in it. The word 'animal' for me is not condemnatory, as it is for you. The animal is beautiful in itself, the animal in itself is nothing to be condemned. The animal within you is pure energy, moving according to natural laws.

It has been asked, "What should we do consciously? Should we not channel? Should we not control?" No! Your consciousness is not to control, your consciousness is not to channel. Your consciousness can do only one thing: your consciousness is to understand, and understanding in itself becomes the transformation.

Tantra will say, understand sex, do not try to channel it. If you do not understand it, every effort is bound to be a failure, and harmful. So do not do anything. First understand it, and through understanding the path will be revealed. You are not to force your energies on that path. Through understanding you come to know the law, just like in science. What are you doing in science? You come to understand a law; a natural mystery is revealed. Once the natural mystery is revealed, you can use the energy creatively.

Without your knowing the inherent law, all efforts are doomed. So tantra says, understand the animal, because in the animal is hidden the potential for your future. Really, it can be said that in the animal God is hidden. The animal is your past, God is your future—but the future is hidden in your past, in seed form. Understand whatsoever your natural forces are. Accept them, understand them. Your mind is not to be there mastering; it is not there to control them and fight with them, it is there to understand them.

Really, if you understand them, you are using your mind rightly. Understand sex, understand anger, understand greed. Be alert; try to find out their ways—how they work, what are their functions. And be constantly aware of the very movement of these animal instincts within. If you can be conscious of these animal instincts, there will be no division, you will not have an unconscious mind. If you can move with these instincts deep within, you will have only a conscious mind; there will be no unconscious.

The unconscious is there because of repression. You have closed the major part of your being to consciousness because you are afraid. You cannot look at your own reality. You are so afraid that you have already moved out of the house—you just live on the verandah. You never go in because the fear is there: if you come face to face with yourself, all your imagination, all your illusions about yourself will fall down.

You think yourself to be a saint, you think yourself to be a religious person, you think yourself to be this and that. If you face your reality, all these illusions will evaporate. And everyone has created an image of himself. That image is false, but we cling to the image and this clinging becomes the barrier toward moving within.

So the first thing is to accept the animal. It is there, and nothing is wrong about it. It is your past, and you cannot deny your past, you can only use it. If you are wise, you will use it and create a better future out of it. If you are foolish you will fight with it, and through fight the future will be destroyed. Fight with a seed, and you will destroy it. Use it, give it soil, help it, protect it so that the seed becomes a tree, an alive tree, and the future blossoms through it.

The animal is your seed. Do not fight with it. Tantra has no condemnation against it, simply love for it, because the whole future is hidden in it. Know it well, and then you can use it and you can thank it.

I have heard that when Saint Francis died, when he was just on his deathbed, suddenly he opened his eyes and thanked his body before going to his death. Before moving to the other world, he thanked his body. He said, "Much was hidden in you, and you helped me so much. And I was so ignorant, and there were times when I even fought with you. There were times I even thought about you in inimical terms. But you were always a friend, and it is because of you I could move to such a state of consciousness."

This thanksgiving to the body is beautiful. But Saint Francis could understand it only in the end. Tantra says, try to understand in the beginning. If you only thank your body when you are dying, it will be of no use.

Your body is a treasury of hidden forces, of mysterious possibilities. Tantra says that in your body is the whole cosmos in miniature, it is just a miniature of the whole cosmos. Do not fight with it. What is your sex if the body is a miniature? If really this is so, that your body is the whole cosmos in miniature, what is sex? That which is creation in the cosmos is sex in you. Throughout the whole cosmos, creation is going on every moment—that is sex in you. And if there is so much force in it, it is because you are needed to be a creator.

If sex is so powerful, it only means for tantra that you cannot be allowed to be noncreative; you must create. If you cannot create something greater, then at least create life. If you cannot create anything better than you, then at least create someone who will replace you when you die. Sex is so forceful because the cosmos cannot allow you to be noncreative, and you are fighting with it. Use it.

There is no need to use sex only in reproduction. In every creation sex is used. That is why a great poet, a great painter, may not feel so much of an urge for sex. But the reason is not that he is a saint. The reason is simply that he is creating something greater and the need is fulfilled.

A great musician is creating music. No father can feel so much fulfilled as a musician feels when great music is created, and no son can give so much happiness to any parent as a great piece of music can give to the musician, or great poetry can give to the poet. Because he is creating on higher realms, nature relieves him of lower creation; the energy has moved higher. Tantra says, do not fight with the energy, allow the energy to move higher. And there are many realms of higher movement and many dimensions.

Buddha is neither a painter nor a musician nor a poet, but he has gone beyond sex. What has happened to him? The highest creation is the creation of oneself. The highest creation is the creation of total consciousness within, creation of a whole within, oneness. That is the peak, the Himalayan peak. Buddha is at that peak, he has created himself. When you move in sex, you create your body; the replica is created. When you move higher, you create spirit, you create soul. Or if you will allow me the expression, you create God.

You have heard that God created the world, but I say to you that you have the potentiality to create God—and unless you create him you will never be fulfilled. So do not think that God is in the beginning. Rather, it will be better to think that God is in the end. God is not the cause of the world, but the teleology, the very end, the very peak. If you flower in your totality, you will become a god. That is why we call Buddha a god—and he never believed in God. This is very paradoxical. He never believed in God; he is one of the deepest atheistic minds ever born. He says there is no God, but we called Buddha himself divine.

H.G. Wells has written that Gautam Buddha was the most godless man and the most godlike. What happened to this Gautam? He created, he gave birth to the highest peak, the highest possibility. The ultimate had happened in him; then he was no longer creating anything—there was no need. It would have been futile for Buddha to write poetry, it would have been futile for him to paint. It would have been childish. He created the ultimate; he gave himself a new birth. The old was used completely to give birth to the new. And because it is an ultimate phenomenon, the whole past had been used. The past disappeared, the animal was no more, because when the tree is born the seed disappears. The seed cannot be there.

Jesus says, unless a seed of corn falls to the ground and dies, nothing can happen. Once the seed falls to the ground and dies, the new life bubbles up through it. The death is only a death of the seed, of the past. But there can be no death without giving birth to the new; something new will come out of it.

Tantra says, do not try to control. Who are you to control, and how will you be able to control? Your control will be just illusory. Try to understand. Try to understand the inner nature, the phenomenon, the dynamics of the energies, and that understanding will automatically change you. Change is not an effort. If change is an effort, then it cannot create bliss.

Bliss never happens through effort. Effort is always tension-creating; it gives anguish. Effort is always ugly because you are forcing something. Understanding is not an effort; it is beautiful, it is a spontaneous happening. Do not control. If you try, you will be a failure, and you will destroy yourself. Understand! Let understanding be the only law, the only *sadhana*—spiritual practice. Leave everything to understanding. If understanding cannot do anything then it cannot be done, so forget it. All that can be done can be done through understanding.

So tantra says, accept things because acceptance will be needed to understand. You cannot understand anything if you deny. If I hate you, I cannot look into your eyes, I cannot see your face. I will turn about, I will escape from you, I will not look at you directly. When I love you, only then can I look into your eyes. When I love you deeply, only then can I see your face.

Only love sees a face; otherwise you never see faces. You move, you look, but that look is just casual, not deep. It touches, but it never penetrates. But when you love, then your whole energy becomes your eyes. Then the energy moves, touches deep, goes deep down into the other person, meets at his center of being. Then only can you see and know.

That is why in the old biblical language they have used the word 'know' for sex, for love—for deep love. It is not coincidental. In the Bible it is reported that "Adam knew his wife Eve, and then Cain was born." This use of 'know' for deep love, for sex, is strange but very meaningful, because when you know someone it means you have loved someone. There is no other way to know someone.

And it is not only with persons, it is so with energies also. If you want to know your inner being and the multidimensional phenomenon of energies, love! Do not hate the animal, love it. And you are not unrelated to it, you are part of it. The animal has pushed you to this point where you have become man—be grateful to it.

It is sheer ungratefulness when people go on condemning the animal in man. This is sheer ingratitude. The animal has pushed you to this point where you have become man, and the animal can push you to the point where you can become God. It is the animal that is pushing you. Understand it —its ways, how it works—and that understanding will become transformation.

So no control, no effort to become the boss— no! Why are you so afraid of your animal? Because your mind is really impotent; that is why you are so afraid. Why do you want to control it? If you are really the master, the animal will follow you. But you know well that the animal is the master and

you have to follow him. That is why there is this whole effort to become the master.

You know very well that anything real that happens, happens through the animal, and anything bogus that happens, happens through the mind. This awareness creates fear. That is why you want to try to become the master, but a master is never born out of effort. Only slaves try to become masters. A master is simply a master.

I will tell you one story.... It happened in the house of a great warrior. One night he suddenly became aware of a mouse. He was a great warrior, a great swordsman. He became very angry because the mouse was sitting just in front of him and looking into his eyes. No one had ever dared so much as the mouse was daring. So he pulled out his sword, but the mouse would not run. Then he attacked the mouse, but suddenly the mouse jumped and the sword was broken in pieces; it fell on the floor.

Of course, the warrior became just mad. He tried and tried, and the more he tried, the more he was defeated. It is difficult to fight with a mouse, and once you have started fighting you have accepted defeat. The mouse became bold. With every failure of the warrior, the mouse became more bold. He simply jumped on the warrior's bed. The warrior went out and asked his friends what to do. "This has never happened in my life," he said. "No one can dare so much as an ordinary mouse! But it seems miraculous—I am totally defeated."

So the friends said, "It is nonsense to fight with a mouse. It is better to bring in a cat."

But the rumor went out that the warrior had been defeated—and even the cats heard it, so no cat was ready to come. All the cats gathered. They elected a leader and said, "You go, because it is not an ordinary mouse—the warrior has been defeated. We are ordinary cats, and this is a great warrior. If he is defeated, where are we? So we will wait outside and let you go in."

The leader became afraid—leaders are always afraid. They are leaders because cowards are there, and those cowards choose them. They are leaders of the cowards. If there were no cowards, there would not be any leaders. Basically, they are chosen by cowards, so they are leaders of cowards.

The cat had to go, as every leader has to go—because the followers were pushing him. Now that the leader was chosen, nothing could be done, the cat had to go. She entered, afraid, trembling, nervous. The mouse was sitting on the bed. The cat had never seen such a mouse: he was just sitting on the bed. She started thinking what to do, what method to apply, and while she was thinking what to do, what method to apply, what technique—about old experiences and memories, about what to do with this situation—while she was thinking, the mouse suddenly attacked. The cat ran away, because this had never happened in the past! There is no mention in history of a mouse attacking a cat.

She came out and fell dead, so the warrior was advised by the neighborhood that "Now ordinary cats won't do. You go to the palace, bring the king's cat. Only a royal cat can do something. This is not an ordinary case." So the warrior had to go to the king and ask for the cat.

The cat from the palace came. The warrior was very afraid when the cat was coming with him because that cat looked just very ordinary. He was afraid that this was again going to be a failure, because the cat who had died was bigger, greater, a great leader, and this ordinary cat…? It seemed that the king was just joking—this cat won't do. But the warrior couldn't say anything to the king.

He came with that ordinary cat. The cat entered, killed the mouse and came out. All the cats were waiting. They gathered around and they said, "What is the trick? Our leader has died, the warrior has been defeated by the mouse, and you simply killed him. You came out with the dead mouse."

The cat said, "I am a cat and he is a mouse. There is no other technique. I am a cat—that is enough. What is the use of any technique? Being a cat is enough. When I entered, it was enough that a cat should enter. I am a cat."

Really, this is a Zen story. If your mind were the master, there would be no need for effort. Every effort is just to deceive yourself: you are not the cat, and you are fighting with the mouse. Become a master! But how to become a master? Tantra says, understanding will make you a master, nothing else. Understanding is the secret of all mastery. If you know it well, you are the master. If you do not know, you will go on fighting. Then you will remain the slave, and the more you fight, the more you will be defeated. You are fighting with a mouse.

The second question:

Are there no horrible noises if we listen from the center of the body? What about the screeching city noises that have been a source of irritation to us all of our lives—can we turn these into positive sound?

This always remains a basic question: how to change something, how to change negative sounds into positive ones. You cannot! If you are positive, then nothing is negative for you. If you are negative, then everything will be negative for you. You are the source of all that exists around you; you are the creator of your own world. And we are not living in one world, remember. There are as many worlds as there are minds. Each mind is living in its own world; it creates the world.

So if everything looks negative and everything looks destructive and everything looks inimical, against you, it is because you do not have the positive center in you. So do not think about how to change negative noises. If you feel negativity all around you, it simply shows you are negative within. The world is just a mirror, and you are reflected in it.

I was staying in a village rest house. It was a very poor village, but it was filled with many dogs. They all gathered in the night around the rest house; it must have been their usual habit. The rest house was a good place—big trees, shadows, and they must have been resting there every night. So I was staying there, and one minister of a particular state was staying there. The minister became very disturbed because the dogs were barking, creating much nuisance. Half the night passed and the minister couldn't sleep, so he came to me.

He said, "Are you asleep?" I was fast asleep, so he came near to me, made me wake up and asked me, "Please tell me how you could fall into sleep amid such noises all around. At least twenty to thirty dogs are there, and they are fighting and barking and doing everything that dogs ordinarily do. So what to do? I cannot sleep, and I am so tired after the whole day's journey. If I cannot sleep, it will be difficult for me. Tomorrow I have to go again on a tour, and I will leave early in the morning. Sleep doesn't seem to come, and I have tried all the methods I have learned and heard about—chanting a mantra, praying to God, etcetera. I have done everything, but nothing happens, so what to do now?"

So I told him, "Those dogs are not gathered here for you or to disturb you. They are not even aware that a minister is staying here; they do not read newspapers. They are completely ignorant. They are not here purposefully, they are not concerned with you. They are doing their work. Why are you getting disturbed?"

So he said, "Why should I not? How not to? With so much barking, how can I go into sleep?"

So I told him, "Do not fight with the barking. You are fighting—that is the problem, not the noise. The noise is not disturbing you, you are disturbing yourself because of the noise. You are against the noise, so you have a condition. You are saying, 'If the dogs stop barking, then I will sleep.' The dogs won't listen to you. You have a condition. You feel that if the condition is fulfilled, then you can sleep. This condition is disturbing you. Accept dogs! Do not make a condition that 'If they stop barking, then I will sleep.' Just accept.

"Dogs are there and they are barking; do not resist, do not fight, do not try to forget those noises. Accept them and listen to them, they are beautiful. The night is so silent, and they are barking so vitally—just listen. This will be the mantra, the right mantra: just listen to them."

So he said, "Okay! I do not believe that this will help, but as there is nothing else to do, I will try." He fell asleep, and the dogs were still barking. In the morning he said, "This is miraculous. I accepted them; I withdrew my condition. I listened. Those dogs became very musical, and their barking, their noise, was not disturbing. Rather, it became a sort of lullaby, and I fell into deep sleep because of it."

It depends on your mind. If you are positive, then everything becomes positive. If you are negative, then everything turns negative, everything turns sour. So please remember this—not only about noises, but about everything in life. If you feel that something negative exists around you, go and find the cause within. It is you. You must be expecting something, you must be desiring something, you must be making some conditions.

Existence cannot be forced to go according to you; it flows in its own way. If you can flow with it, you will be positive. If you fight with it, you will become negative and the whole cosmos around you will turn negative.

It is just like a person who is trying to float upstream: then the stream is negative. If you are trying to float upstream in a river, then the river will seem negative and you will feel that the river is fighting you, that the river is pushing you downwards. The river is trying to move you downstream, not upstream, so it will seem as if the river is fighting you. The river is completely unaware of you, blissfully unaware. And it is good; otherwise the river will have to go into a madhouse. The river is not fighting with you, you are fighting with the river. You are trying to float upstream.

I will tell you one anecdote.... A great crowd gathered around Mulla Nasruddin's house, and they said, "What are you doing? Your wife has fallen into the stream and the river is in a flood. Go immediately; otherwise the stream will take your wife to the sea." The sea was just near.

So Mulla came running to the bank, jumped into the stream, and started swimming upstream to find where his wife was.

The crowd screamed, "What are you doing, Nasruddin? Your wife couldn't have gone up-stream. She has gone downstream."

Mulla said, "Do not disturb me. I know my wife very well. If anyone else had fallen into the stream, he would have gone downstream. Not my wife, however. She must have gone upstream. I know my wife well, I have lived with her for forty years."

The mind is always trying to go upstream, to move upstream. Fighting with everything, you create a negative world around you. Obviously, this has to happen. The world is not against you, but because you are not with the world, you feel it is against you. Float downstream, and then the river will help you to float. Then your energy will not be needed. The river will become a boat, it will take you. You will not lose any energy by floating downstream, because once you float downstream you have accepted the river, the current, the flow, the direction—everything. Then you have become positive towards it. When you are positive, the river is positive to you.

You can make everything positive only by making yourself positive toward life. But we are not positive toward life. Why? Why are we not positive toward life? Why are we negative? Why this constant struggle? Why can we not have a total let-go with life? What is the fear?

You may not have observed: you are afraid of life—very much afraid of life. It may sound odd to say that you are afraid of life, because ordinarily you feel that you are afraid of death, not of life. This is the usual observation, that everyone is afraid of death. But I tell you, you are afraid of death only because you are afraid of life. One who is not afraid of life will not be afraid of death.

Why are we afraid of life? Three reasons. Firstly, your ego can exist only if it goes upstream.

Floating downstream, your ego cannot exist. Your ego can exist only when it fights, when it says no! If it says yes, always yes, it cannot exist. The ego is the basic cause of saying no to everything.

Look at your ways, at how you behave and react. Look at how the no comes immediately to the mind, and how yes is very, very difficult—because with no you exist as an ego. With yes your identity is lost, you become a drop in the ocean. Yes has no ego in it; that is why it is so difficult to say yes—very difficult.

You understand me? If you are going upstream, you feel *you* are. If you just let go and you start floating with the stream wheresoever it leads, you do not feel that you are. Then you have become part of the stream. This ego, this thinking yourself to be isolated as an "I," creates the negativity around you. This ego creates the ripples of negativity.

Secondly, life is unknown, unpredictable, and your mind is very narrow: it wants to live in the known, in the predictable. Mind is always afraid of the unknown. There is a reason: it is because mind consists of the known. Whatsoever you have known, experienced, learned, mind consists of that. The unknown is not part of the mind. The mind is always afraid of the unknown, the unknown will disturb the mind, so the mind is closed for the unknown. It lives in its routine, it lives in a pattern. It moves in particular grooves, known grooves. It goes on moving, moving, just like a gramophone record. It is afraid to move into the unknown.

Life is always moving into the unknown, and you are afraid. You want life to go according to your mind, according to the known, but life cannot follow you. It always moves into the unknown. That is why we are afraid of life, and whenever we get any chance we try to kill life, we try to fix it. Life is a flux. We try to fix it because with the fixed, prediction is possible.

If I love someone, immediately my mind will start working on how to marry that person, because marriage fixes things. Love is a flux, love cannot be predicted. No one knows where it will lead, or whether it will lead anywhere. No one knows! It is floating with the stream, and you do not know where the stream is going. It may not be there the next day, the next moment.

You cannot be certain of the next moment. But the mind wants certainty, and life is insecurity. Because the mind wants certainty, the mind is against love. The mind is for marriage because marriage is a fixed thing. Now you have fixed things, so now the flux is broken. Now the water is not flowing—it has become ice. Now you have something dead; you can predict. Only dead things are predictable. The more something is alive, the more it is unpredictable. No one knows where life will move.

So we do not want life, we want dead things. That is why we go on possessing things. It is difficult to live with a person; it is easy to live with things. So we go on possessing things and things and things. It is difficult to live with a person. And if we have to live with a person, we will try to make a thing out of that person, we cannot allow the person.

A wife is a thing, a husband is a thing. They are not persons, they are fixed things. When the husband comes to the house, he knows that the wife will be there, waiting. He knows, he can predict. If he feels like loving, he can love—the wife will be available. The wife has become a thing. The wife cannot say, "No, today I am not in the mood to love." Wives are not supposed to say such things. Not in the mood? They are not supposed to have moods. They are fixed institutions—institutes. You can rely on the institute; you cannot rely on life. Thus, we turn persons into things.

Look at any relationship. In the beginning it is a relationship of 'I' and 'thou,' but sooner or later it becomes a relationship of 'I' and 'it.' The 'thou' disappears, and then we go on expecting things. We say, "Do this. This is the duty of a wife and that is the duty of a husband. Do this!" You will have to do it. It is a duty; it has to be done mechanically. You cannot say, "I cannot do it."

This fixedness is a fear of life. Life is a flux; nothing can be said about life. I love you this moment, but the next moment the love may disappear. The moment before it was not there; this moment it is there. And it is not because of me that it is there, it just happened. I couldn't have forced it to be here. It just happened, and that which has happened can unhappen at any moment, you cannot do anything. The next moment it may disappear; there is no certainty for the next moment.

But the mind wants certainty, so it turns love into marriage. The living thing becomes dead. Then you can possess it, then you can rely on it. The next day also there will be love. This is the absurdity of the whole thing: you have killed the thing in order to possess it, and then you can never enjoy it because it is no more, it is dead.

In order that you could possess the wife, she has been killed. The beloved has become a wife, and now you expect that the wife should behave like the beloved. That is absurd, the wife cannot behave like the beloved. The beloved was alive, the wife is dead. The beloved was a happening, the wife is an institution. And when the wife is not behaving like the beloved, then you go on saying, "Don't you love me? You loved me before." But this is not the same person. This is not even a person, this is a thing. First you killed her to possess her, and now you want aliveness out of her. Then the whole misery is created.

We are afraid of life because life is a flux. The mind wants certainty. If you really want to be alive, be ready to be insecure. There is no security and there is no way to create security! There is only one way: do not live, then you will be secure. So those who are dead are absolutely secure. An alive person is insecure. Insecurity is the very central core of life, but the mind wants security.

Thirdly, in life, in existence, there is a basic duality. Existence exists as duality, and the mind wants to choose one part and deny the other. For example, you want to be happy, you want pleasure; you do not want pain. But the pain is part of pleasure, the other aspect of it. The coin is one. On one side is pleasure, on another side is pain. You want pleasure, but you do not know that the more you want pleasure, the more pain will follow; and the more you become sensitive to pleasure, the more you become sensitive to pain also.

So a person who wants pleasure should be ready to accept pain. This is just like valleys and hills. You want peaks, hills, but you do not want valleys—so where will the valleys go? And without the valleys, how can there be peaks? Without valleys there can be no peaks. If you love peaks, love valleys also. They become part of the destiny.

The mind wants one thing and it denies the other, and the other is part of it. The mind says, "Life is good, death is bad." But death is one part, —the valley part—and life is the peak part. Life cannot exist without death. Life exists *because* of death. If death disappeared, life would disappear, but the mind says, "I want only life, I do not want death." Then the mind moves in a dream world which exists nowhere, and it starts fighting with everything, because in life everything is related to the opposite. If you do not want the opposite, a fight starts.

A person who understands this—that life is duality—accepts both. He accepts death, not as against life, but as part of it, as the valley part. He accepts night as the valley part of the day. One moment you feel blissful; the next moment you are sad. You do not want to accept the next moment— that is the valley part. And the higher the peak of bliss, the deeper will be the valley, because deeper valleys are only created by higher peaks. So the higher you move, the lower you will be falling. And this is just like waves rising high: then there is a valley part.

Understanding means being aware of this fact —not only being aware, but having a deep acceptance of the fact, because you cannot move away from the fact. You can create a fiction…and we have been creating fictions for centuries. We have put hell somewhere deep down and heaven high up somewhere. We have created an absolute division between them, which is nonsense, because hell is the valley part of heaven. It exists with heaven; it cannot exist apart.

This understanding will help you to be positive; then you will be able to accept everything. By positive I mean that you accept everything because you know that you cannot divide existence.

I take a breath in, and immediately I have to throw it out. I inhale and then exhale. If I were only to inhale and not to exhale, I would die; or if I were only to exhale and not to inhale, then too I would die, because inhaling and exhaling are part of one process, a circle. I can inhale only because I exhale. Both are together and they cannot be divided.

This is what a liberated man is—undivided. It happens if this understanding comes to him. I call a man liberated, enlightened, who accepts the very duality of existence.

Then he is positive.

Then whatsoever happens is accepted.

Then he has no expectations.

Then he makes no demands on existence.

Then he can float downstream.

CHAPTER 27

Soundlessness, soundfulness and total awareness

◆

39 *Intone a sound, as AUM, slowly. As sound enters soundfulness, so do you.*

40 *In the beginning and gradual refinement of the sound of any letter, awake.*

41 *While listening to stringed instruments, hear their composite central sound; thus omnipresence.*

**I** wonder whether or not you have heard about the concept of antimatter. A new concept has entered recently in the world of physics—the concept of anti-matter. It has been felt always that nothing can exist in the universe without its opposite. It is impossible to conceive of anything which exists alone without its opposite. The diametrically opposite must be there whether known or not. The shadow cannot exist without light, life cannot exist without death, morning cannot exist without night, man cannot exist without woman—or the same with anything you can think of.

The diametrically opposite pole is inevitably needed. This was always proposed in philosophy, but now this is a proposition of physics. And very absurd notions have developed because of this concept. Time moves from the past to the future, but now physicists say that if time moves from the past to the future, there must be somewhere the opposite time process, which moves from the future to the past; otherwise this time process cannot be—but it is. The opposite, the diametrically opposite must be there somewhere—antitime. Moving from the future to the past? It looks very absurd. How can something move from the future to the past?

They also say that matter exists, so antimatter must be existing somewhere. What will be the anti-matter? Matter is density. Suppose a stone is here in my hand. What is that stone? Around it is space and in the space there is a density of matter. That density is matter. What will be the antimatter? They say antimatter will be just a hole in space. Density is matter, and there is also a hole in space with nothing in it. A space will be around it, but it will be just a hole of nothingness. They say antimatter must exist to balance matter. Why am I talking on this? Because these sutras which are to follow are based on this "anti" phenomenon.

Sound exists, but tantra says sound can exist only because of silence; otherwise sound will be impossible. Silence is antisound. So wherever there is sound, just behind it there is silence. It cannot exist without silence; it is the other aspect of the same coin. So I utter a word; for example, aum. The more I utter it, just side by side, just behind it is the antiphe-nomenon, soundlessness. So if you can use sounds as a technique to enter soundlessness, you will enter meditation. If you can use a word to go beyond words, you will move into meditation. Look at it in this way: mind is the word; meditation is no-mind. Mind is filled with sound and words and thought. Just by the corner is the other extreme—no-mind.

Zen masters have called meditation the state of no-mind. What is mind? If you analyze it, it is a process of thought. Or if you analyze it in terms of physics, then it is a process of sounds. This sound process is mind; then just near it the no-mind exists. And you cannot move into the no-mind without using the mind as the jumping board, because you cannot even conceive of what no-mind is without understanding what mind is. Mind has to be used as a jumping board, and from that jumping board you can have a plunge into the no-mind.

There have been two opposing schools. One school is there—it is known as Sankhya. Sankhya says mind has not to be used, because if you use mind you cannot go beyond it. The same is the teaching of J. Krishnamurti; he is a Sankhyaite. You cannot use mind. If you use mind you cannot go beyond it, because the very use of the mind will strengthen it, will make it more powerful. When you use it, you will be in its clutches. Using it, you cannot go beyond it. So don't use mind. That is why Krishnamurti is against all techniques of meditation: because any technique is bound to use mind as a base. Mind has to be used if you are going to use a technique. Any technique is bound to be a sort of conditioning—or a reconditioning, or an unconditioning, or whatsoever name you give to it, but it is going to be with the mind.

Sankhya philosophy says that mind cannot be used; just understand this and take a jump. But yoga says this is impossible. Even this understanding is to be done by mind. Even with this understanding—that you cannot use mind, that no technique will be of help, that every technique will become a hindrance and whatsoever you do will create a new conditioning—you will still be using mind, you will move within mind. This too has to be understood by mind.

So yoga says there is no way in which mind is not used; mind will have to be used. It should not be used positively, it should be used negatively. It should not be used in such a way that it is strengthened, it should be used in such a way that it is weakened. And techniques are the ways to use the mind in such a way that you use it to jump beyond it. You use it just to go beyond it—as a jumping board.

If mind can be used as a jumping board—and yoga and tantra believe that it can—then something which belongs to mind has to be trained. Sound is one of the basic things; you can use sound to go into soundlessness.

39 Intone a sound and become it.

The third sound technique: *Intone a sound, as AUM, slowly. As sound enters soundfulness, so do you.*

Intone a sound, as AUM, slowly. For example, take aum. This is one of the basic sounds. A-U-M: these three sounds are combined in it. A-U-M are three basic sounds. All sounds are made of them or derived from them; all sounds are combinations of these three sounds. So these three are basic. They are as basic as in physics the electron, neutron and proton are basic. This has to be deeply understood.

Gurdjieff speaks of "The Law of the Three." He says existence in the absolute sense is one. In the absolute sense, in the ultimate sense, there is only one. But that is absolute, and whatsoever we see is relative. Whatsoever we see is never absolute; the absolute is always hidden. It cannot be seen, because the moment we see something, it is divided. It is divided in three: the seer, the seen, and the relationship. I am seeing you; I am here, you are there, and between the two there is the relationship of knowledge, of seeing, of vision, of cognition. The process is divided into three. The absolute is divided into three; the moment it is known it becomes three. Unknown, it remains one. Known, it becomes three. The known is relative; the unknown is absolute.

So even our talk about the absolute is not absolute, because the moment we say "the absolute," it has become known. Whatsoever we know, even the word 'absolute' is relative. That is why Lao Tzu insists so much that truth cannot be said. The moment you say it, it has become untrue because it has become relative. So whatsoever word we use —the truth, the absolute, *para-brahma*, Tao— whatsoever word we use, the moment we use it, it has become relative and it has become untrue. The one has become divided into three.

So Gurdjieff says that the law of the three is basic for the universe that we know. And if we go deep we will find, we are bound to find, that everything will be reduced to three. This is the law of the three. Christians have called it the trinity—God the father, Jesus the son, and the Holy Ghost. Indians have called it *Trimurti:* the three faces of Brahma, Vishnu, and Mahesh or Shiva. Now physics says that if we move, if we go on moving through analysis to the very base, then matter will be reduced to three: the electron, neutron and proton.

Poets have said that if we go deep in search for human aesthetic feeling, emotion, then there is *satyam, shivam, sundaram*—the true, the good and the beautiful. Human feeling is based on these three. Mystics have said that if we analyze ecstasy, *samadhi,* then there is *sat-chit-anand*—existence, consciousness and bliss.

The whole human consciousness, in whatsoever dimension it works, comes to the law of the three. 'Aum' is a symbol of the law of the three. A-U-M: these three are basic sounds. The atomic sounds, you can call them. These three sounds have been combined in aum, so aum is just near the absolute, just behind it is the absolute, the unknown. And aum is the last station as far as sounds are concerned. If you move beyond aum, you move beyond sound; then there is no sound. A-U-M: these three are the last, they are the boundary of existence. Beyond these three you move into the unknown, into the absolute.

Physicists say that now we have come to the electron, it seems we have come to the limit, to the very limit, because the electron cannot be said to be matter. Electrons are not visible; they have no material property. And they cannot be called nonmatter either because all matter consists of them, is constituted of them. If they are neither matter nor nonmatter, what to call them? No one has seen electrons, they are just inferred; it is mathematically assumed that they are there. Their effects are known, but they have not been seen. Now we cannot move beyond them. The law of the three is the limit, and if you move beyond the law of the three you move into the unknown. Nothing can be

said then. Even about electrons very little can be said.

Aum is the limit as far as sound is concerned, you cannot move beyond. That is why aum has been used so much, in India, and all over the world. The Christian-Mohammedan 'amen' is nothing but aum in a different form; the same basic notes are there. The English words 'omnipresent,' 'omnipotent,' 'omniscient' contain it: the prefix 'omni' is a derivation of aum. So 'omnipresent' refers to that which is present in the whole of the aum, in the whole of existence. 'Omnipotent' means that which is absolutely potent. 'Omniscient' means that which has seen the aum, the whole, the law of the three. The whole universe comes under it.

Christians, Mohammedans, have been using after their prayers 'amen.' But Hindus have made a complete science out of it—the science of sound and the science of how to transcend sound. And if mind is sound, then no-mind must be soundlessness, or—and both mean the same—soundfulness.

This has to be understood. The absolute can be described in either of two ways—negative or positive. The relative has to be described in both the ways—negative and positive: it is a duality. When you try to express the absolute, you can use either positive terms or negative terms, because human languages have two types of terms—negative and positive. When you are going to describe the absolute, the indescribable, you have to use some terms symbolically. So it depends on the mind.

For example, Buddha liked to use negative terms. He would say soundlessness; he would never say soundfulness. 'Soundfulness' is a positive term. Buddha would say soundlessness, but tantra uses positive terms. The whole thinking of tantra is positive. That is why the term used here is 'soundfulness': *enter soundfulness*. Buddha describes his absolute in negative terms: *shunya,* nothingness. The Upanishads describe the same absolute as *Brahma*—absoluteness. Buddha will use nothingness and the Upanishads will use absoluteness, but both mean the same thing.

When words lose meaning you can use either the negative or the positive, because all words are either negative or positive; you just have to choose one. You can say for a liberated soul that he has become the whole. This is a positive way of saying it. Or you can say he is no more—he has become nothingness. This is a negative way of saying it.

For example, if a small drop of water meets the ocean, you can say that the drop has become nothingness, the drop has lost its individuality, the drop is no more. This is a Buddhist way of saying things. It is good, it is right as far as it goes, because no word goes very far. So as far as it goes, it is good. "The drop is no more"—that is what is meant by *nirvana*. The drop has become nonbeing, it is not. Or you can use Upanishadic terms. The Upanishads will say that the drop has become the ocean. They are also right, because when the boundaries are broken, the drop has become the ocean.

So these are simply attitudes. Buddha likes negative terms, because the moment you say anything positive it becomes limited, it looks limited. When you say that the drop has become the ocean, Buddha will say that the ocean is also finite. The drop remains the drop; it has become a little bigger, that is all. Howsoever bigger makes no difference. Buddha will say that it has become a little bigger, but it remains. The finite has not become infinite. The finite remains finite, so what is the difference? A small drop and a big drop...for Buddha, that is the only difference between 'ocean' and 'drop'— and it is right, mathematically it is so.

So Buddha says that if the drop has become the ocean, then nothing has happened. If you have become a god, then nothing has happened, you have only become a bigger man. If you have become Brahma nothing has happened, you are still finite. So Buddha says that you have to become nothing, you have to become shunya—empty of all boundaries and attributes, empty of everything that you can conceive of, just emptiness. But Upanishadic thinkers will say that even if you are empty *you are*. If you have become emptiness *you* are still there, because

emptiness exists, emptiness is. Nothingness is also a way of being, a way of existence. So they say, why belabor the point and why unnecessarily use negative terms? It is good to be positive.

It is your choice, but tantra almost always uses positive terms. The very philosophy of tantra is positive. It says, do not allow no, do not allow the negation. Tantrics are the greatest of yea-sayers. They have said yes to everything, so they use positive terms. The sutra says, *Intone a sound, as AUM, slowly. As sound enters soundfulness, so do you....*

Intone a sound, as AUM, slowly. The intoning of a sound is a very subtle science. First you have to intone it loudly, outwardly; then others can hear it. And it is good to start loudly. Why? Because you can also hear it clearly when you intone it loudly; because whatsoever you say it is to others, and this has become a habit. Whenever you are talking you are talking to others, and you hear yourself talk only when you are talking to others. So start from the natural habit.

Intone the sound aum, then by and by, feel attunement with the sound. When you intone the sound aum, be filled with it, forget everything else. Become the aum, become the sound. And it is very easy to become the sound, because sound can vibrate through your body, through your mind, through your whole nervous system. Feel the reverberation of aum. Intone it, and feel it as if your whole body is being filled with it, every cell is vibrating with it.

Intoning is also in-tuning. Tune yourself with the sound, become the sound. And then, as you feel a deep harmony between you and the sound, and you develop a deep affection for it—and the sound is so beautiful and so musical: aum—then the more you intone it, the more you will feel yourself filled with a subtle sweetness. There are sounds which are bitter, there are sounds which are very hard. Aum is a very sweet sound, the purest. Intone it and be filled with it.

And when you begin to feel harmonious with it,

you can drop intoning loudly. Then close your lips and intone it inwardly, but inwardly also first try it loudly. Intone inwardly, but loudly, so that the sound spreads all over your body, touches every part, every cell of your body. You will feel vitalized by it, you will feel rejuvenated, you will feel a new life entering you—because your body is a musical instrument. It needs harmony, and when the harmony is disturbed you are disturbed.

That is why when you hear music you feel good. Why do you feel good? What is music but just some harmonious sounds? Why do you feel such a well-being when there is music around you? And when there is chaos, noise, why do you feel so disturbed? You yourself are deeply musical. You are an instrument, and that instrument re-echoes things.

Intone aum inside, and you will feel that your whole body dances with it. You will feel that your whole body is undergoing a cleansing bath; every pore is being cleansed. But as you feel it more intensely, and as it penetrates you more, go on becoming more and more slow, because the slower the sound, the deeper it can go. It is just like homeopathy. The smaller the dose, the deeper it penetrates – because if you want to go deeper, you have to go more subtly, more subtly, more subtly....

Crude, coarse sounds cannot enter your heart. They can enter your ears, but they cannot enter your heart. The passage is very narrow, and the heart is so delicate that only very slow, very rhythmic, very atomic sounds are allowed to enter it. And unless a sound enters your heart, the mantra is not complete. The mantra is complete only when the sound enters your heart—the deepest, most central core of your being. Then go on being more slow, more slow, more slow.

And there are also other reasons for making these sounds slower and more subtle: the more subtle a sound is, the more intense an awareness you will need to feel it inside. The more coarse the sound, the less need there is of any awareness. A coarse sound will hit you, you will become aware

of it; but then it is violent.

If a sound is musical, harmonious, subtle, then you will have to listen to it inside and you will have to be very alert to listen to it. If you are not alert, you will go to sleep and miss the whole point. That is the problem with a mantra, with any chanting, with any use of sound: it can create sleep. It is a subtle tranquilizer. If you continuously repeat any sound without being alert about it, you will fall asleep, because then the repetition becomes mechanical. "Aum, aum, aum…" becomes mechanical, and then repetition creates boredom.

Boredom is a basic necessity for sleep. You cannot get to sleep unless you are bored. If you are excited, you cannot get to sleep. That is why the modern man is becoming incapable of going to sleep. What is the reason? There is so much excitement. It was never like this before.

In the old, past world, life was a deep boredom, a repetitious boredom. If you go to a village hidden somewhere in the hills, there life is a boredom. It may not look to you like a boredom because you have not lived there, and on a holiday you may feel very excited. But that excitement is because of Bombay, not because of those hills. Those hills are completely boring. Those who are living there are bored and asleep. There is only the same thing, the same routine with no excitement, with no change, and nothing ever happens. There is no news. Things go on as they have always, they go on repeating in a circular way. As seasons repeat, as nature repeats, as day and night move in a circle, everything moves in a village, in an old village, in a circle. That is why villagers can fall to sleep so easily: everything is just boring.

Modern life has become so exciting—nothing repeats. Everything goes on becoming new, changing. Life has become unpredictable, and you are so excited you cannot fall asleep. Every day you can see a new film, every day you can hear a new speech, every day you can read a new book, every day something new is possible.

This constant excitement continues. When you

go to your bed, the excitement is there. The mind wants to be awake; it seems futile to fall asleep. There are thinkers who are saying that this is pure wastage—if you live for sixty years, twenty years are wasted in sleep. Sheer wastage! Life is so much excitement, why waste any of it? But in the old world, in the old days, life was not an excitement. It was a circular movement of the same repetition. If anything excites you, it means it is new.

If you repeat a particular sound, it creates a circle within you. It creates boredom; it creates sleep. That is why Mahesh Yogi's transcendental meditation is known in the West as a nonmedical tranquilizer. It is because it is a simple repetition of a mantra. But if your mantra becomes just a repetition without an alert *you* inside, an alert *you* constantly listening to you, listening to the sound, it may help sleep, but it cannot help anything else. As far as it goes, it is good. If you are suffering from insomnia, transcendental meditation is good.

Otherwise, it helps—but not unless you use the mantra with an alert inner ear. Then you have to do two things: go on reducing the pitch of the mantra, reducing the sound, making it more slow and more subtle, and at the same time, simultaneously, go on becoming more alert, more alert. As the sound becomes subtle, become more alert; otherwise you will miss the whole point.

So two things have to be done: sound has to be slowed down, and you have to become more alert. The more sound becomes subtle, the more alert you are. To make you more alert the sound has to be made more subtle, and a point comes when sound enters soundlessness, or soundfulness, and you enter total awareness. When the sound enters soundlessness or soundfulness, by that time your alertness must have touched the peak. When the sound reaches the valley, when it goes to the downmost, deepest center in the valley, your alertness has gone to the very peak, to the Everest. And there, sound dissolves into soundfulness or soundlessness, and you dissolve into total awareness.

This is the method: *Intone a sound, as AUM,*

slowly. As sound enters soundfulness, so do you. And wait for the moment when the sound has become so subtle, so atomic, that now, any moment, it will take a jump from the world of the laws, the world of the three, and it will enter the world of the one, the absolute. Wait! This is one of the most beautiful experiences possible to man— when sound dissolves. Then suddenly you cannot find where the sound has gone.

You were hearing it subtly, deep down: "Aum, aum, aum…" and then it is no more there. You have entered the world of the one. The world of the three is no more. This, tantra says, is soundfulness; Buddha says soundlessness.

This is a way—one of the most used, one of the most helpful. Mantras became so important because of this. Because sound is already there and your mind is so filled with it, you can use it as a jumping board. But there are difficulties, and the first difficulty is sleep. Whosoever uses a mantra must be aware of this difficulty. That is the hindrance— sleep. You are bound to fall into sleep because it is so repetitious, it is so harmonious, it is so boring—you will fall victim. And do not think that your sleep is your meditation. Sleep is not meditation.

Sleep is good in itself, but beware. If you are using the mantra for sleep, then it is okay. But if you are using the mantra for spiritual awakening, then beware of sleep. For those who use a mantra, sleep is the enemy—and it so easily happens. And it is so beautiful, because it is a different type of sleep; remember that too. When it comes from a mantra, this is not ordinary sleep. This is a different kind of sleep.

The Greeks have called it *hypnos,* and from hypnos the word 'hypnotism' has been derived. In yoga they call it *yoga tandra*—a particular sleep which happens to the yogi and not to the ordinary man. It is hypnos—an induced sleep, not an ordinary sleep. And the difference is very basic, so try to understand it—because if you try a mantra, any sound, this is going to be your problem. The greatest problem to face is sleep.

Hypnosis uses the same technique—creating boredom. The hypnotist goes on repeating a certain word or certain sentences. He is continuously repeating, and you become bored. Or he gives you a light to concentrate on. Seeing a light continuously, you get bored.

In many temples, churches, people are fast asleep. Listening to scriptures, they fall asleep. They have heard those scriptures so many times, it has become a boredom. There is no excitement, they already know the story.

If you go on seeing the same film again and again, you will be fast asleep: no excitement for the mind, no challenge, and there is nothing to see. You have heard the *Ramayana* so many times, you can be asleep and without any difficulty you can go on hearing in your sleep. And you will never feel that you were asleep because you will never miss anything in the story: you know it already.

Preachers' voices are very deeply sleep-inducing, monotonous. You can talk monotonously, in the same pitch, then sleep happens. Many psychologists advise their patients with insomnia to go and hear a religious talk, that gives sleep easily. Whenever you are bored, you will fall asleep, but that sleep is hypnosis, that sleep is yoga tandra. And what is the difference? That is not natural. It is unnatural, and with particular attributes.

One, when you fall asleep through a mantra or through hypnosis, you can create any illusion easily and the illusion will be as real as possible. In ordinary sleep you can create dreams, but the moment you are awake you will know that they were dreams. In hypnosis, in yoga tandra, you can create visions, and when you will be out of it you will not be able to say that they were dreams. You will say that they were more real than the life around you. That is one of the basic differences.

You can create any illusion. So if a Christian falls into hypnosis, he will see Christ. If a Hindu falls, he will see Krishna playing on his flute. It is beautiful! And the quality of hypnosis is that you will believe that this is real. That is the danger, and

no one can convince you that this is unreal. The feeling is such that you *know* this is real. You can say that the whole life is unreal, *maya*, illusion, but you cannot say that whatsoever you have seen in hypnosis, in yoga tandra, is unreal. It is so alive, so colorful, so attractive and magnetizing.

That is why if someone says something to you while you are hypnotized, you will believe him absolutely. There can be no doubt; you cannot doubt him. You may have seen some hypnotic sessions. Whatsoever the hypnotist says, the hypnotized person believes and starts acting out. If he says to a man, "You are a woman. Now walk on the stage," the man will walk like a woman. He cannot walk like a man because hypnosis is deep trust; it is faith. There is no conscious mind to think, no reasoning mind to argue. You are simply the heart, you simply believe. There is no way not to believe, you cannot question. The questioning mind is asleep—that is the difference.

In your ordinary sleep, the questioning mind is present, it is not asleep. In hypnosis your questioning mind is asleep, and you are not asleep. That is why you can hear the hypnotist say anything to you and you will follow his instructions. In ordinary sleep you cannot hear, but your reasoning is not asleep. So if something happens which can be fatal to you, your sleep will be broken by your reason.

A mother is sleeping with her child. She may not hear anything else, but if the child gives even a very small sound, a small signal, she will be awake. If a child feels a little uneasy, she will be awake. The reasoning mind is alert. You are asleep, but your reasoning mind is alert. So even sometimes in dreams, you can feel that they are dreams. Of course, the moment you feel this your dream will be broken. You can feel that it is absurd, but the moment you feel it the dream will be broken. Your mind is alert, a part is constantly watching.

But in hypnosis, or in yoga tandra, the watcher is asleep. That is the problem with all those who want to use sound to go into soundlessness or soundfulness, to go beyond. They must be aware that the mantra should not become an auto-hypnotic technique. It must not create auto-hypnosis.

So what can you do? You can do only one thing: while you are using your mantra, while you are intoning your mantra, do not simply intone it. At the same time be alert and listen to it also. Intone it and listen to it both. Otherwise, if you are not listening consciously, it will become your lullaby and you will fall into deep sleep. That sleep will be very good—you will feel refreshed after it, alive; you will feel a certain well-being—but this is not the point.

40 Listen to a fading sound.

The fourth technique on sound: *In the beginning and gradual refinement of the sound of any letter, awake.*

Sometimes teachers have used this technique very much. They have their ingenious ways. For example, if you enter a Zen master's hut, he may suddenly give a scream. You will become startled, but if you know why he is doing this you know he is doing it just to make you awake. Any sudden thing makes you awake. Any sudden sound can make you awake.

Suddenness breaks your sleep, and ordinarily we are asleep. Unless something goes wrong, we are not out of sleep, we go on doing things sleepily. That is why we never feel the sleep. You go to your office, you drive the car, you come back to your home, you love your children, you talk to your wife, so you think you are not sleepy at all. How can you do all of these things in a sleep? You think that isn't possible, but do you know anything about sleepwalkers—about those who walk in their sleep? Their eyes are open, and they are asleep, and they can do many things. But they will not remember in the morning that they have done them.

They may go to the police station and report

that something is wrong, that someone came into their house at night and was creating mischief, and they themselves have been found to be responsible. But in the night, in their sleep, they walk and do certain things, then they come back into their beds and continue their sleep, and in the morning they cannot remember what has happened. They can open doors, they can use keys, they can do many things. Their eyes are open, and they are asleep.

In a deeper sense, we are all sleepwalkers. You can go to your office, you can come to your home, you can do certain things; you will repeat the same things you have always repeated. You will tell your wife, "I love you," and you will not mean anything by it. The words will be just mechanical. You are not even aware that you are telling your wife, "I love you." You are simply doing things as if you are fast asleep. This whole world is a world of sleepwalkers for a person who has become awakened. A Buddha feels that way, a Gurdjieff feels that way—that everyone is fast asleep and still doing things.

Gurdjieff used to say that whatsoever is happening in this world is absolutely what can be expected —wars, fights, riots, murder, suicide. Someone asked Gurdjieff, "Can something be done to stop wars?" He said, "Nothing can be done—because those who are fighting, they are fast asleep, and those who are pacifists, they are fast asleep. And everyone is going on in a sleep. These happenings are natural, inevitable. Unless man is awake, nothing can be changed, because these are all just by-products of his sleep. He will fight; he cannot be stopped from fighting. Only the causes can be changed."

Once he was fighting for Christianity, for Islam, for this and that. Now he is not fighting for Christianity, now he is fighting for communism, for democracy. Causes will change, excuses will change, and the fight will continue, because man is asleep and you cannot expect anything else.

This sleepiness can be broken. You have to use certain techniques. This technique says, *In the begin-*

ning and gradual refinement of the sound of any letter, awake. Try with any sound, with any letter— aum, for example. In the beginning, when you have not yet created the sound, *awake.* Or when the sound moves into soundlessness, then awake.

How can you do it? Go to a temple. A bell is there or a gong. Take the bell in your hand and wait. First become totally alert. The sound is going to be there and you are not to miss the beginning. First become totally alert, as if your life depends on this, as if someone is going to kill you this very moment, and you will be awake. Be alert—as if this is going to be your death. And if there is thought, wait, because thought is sleepiness. With thought you cannot be alert. When you are alert, there is no thought. So wait. When you feel that now the mind is without thought, that there is no cloud and you are alert, then move with the sound.

Look when the sound is not there, then close your eyes. Then look when the sound is created, struck; then move with the sound. The sound will become slower and slower, subtler and subtler and subtler, and then it will not be there. Then go on with the sound. Be aware, alert. Move with the sound to the very end. See both the poles of the sound, both the beginning and the end.

Try it with some outer sound like a gong or a bell or anything, then close your eyes. Utter any sound inside—aum or anything—and then do the same experiment with it. It is difficult; that is why we do it outwardly first. When you can do it outwardly, then you will be able to do it inwardly. Then do it. Wait for the moment when the mind is vacant, then create the sound inside. Feel it, move with it, go with it, until it disappears completely.

Until you can do this…it will take time. A few months will be needed, at least three months. In these three months, you will become more and more alert. The presound state and the after-sound state have to be watched. Nothing is to be missed. Once you become so alert that you can watch the beginning and the end of a sound, through this process you will have become a totally different person.

Sometimes this looks very absurd. Such simple techniques, how can they change you? Everyone is so disturbed, in anguish, and these methods seem so simple. They seem like tricks. If you go to Krishnamurti and tell him that this is the method, he will say, "This is a mental trick. Do not be tricked by it. Forget it, throw it!"

It looks so. Obviously, it looks like a trick. How can you be transformed through such simple things? But you do not know—they are not simple. When you do them, then you know that they are very arduous. If you just hear me telling about them, they are simple. If I tell you, "This is poison and if you take one drop of it you will die," if you do not know anything about poison you will say, "What are you talking about? Just a drop of this liquid, and a person like me who is healthy, strong, will die?" If you do not know anything about poison, then only can you say this. If you know something about it, you cannot say this.

This seems to be very simple: intoning a sound and then becoming aware in the beginning and in the end. But awareness is very difficult, and when you try it then you will know that it is not child's play. You are not aware—and when you try it, for the first time you will know that you have been asleep your whole life. Right now you think you are already aware. Try this. With any small thing, try this.

Tell yourself that "I will be awake, alert, for ten breaths," and then count the breaths. "For ten breaths only," tell yourself, "I will remain alert. And I will count from one to ten, the incoming breath, the outgoing, the incoming, the outgoing. I will remain alert."

You will miss. Two or three, and you will have moved somewhere else. Then suddenly you will become aware that "I have missed. I am not counting the breaths." Or you can count, but when you have counted to ten you will become aware that "I was counting in my sleep. I was not alert."

Alertness is one of the most difficult things. Do not think that the methods are simple. Whatsoever the technique, alertness is the thing to be attained. All else is just a help.

And you can devise your own methods. But remember only one thing: alertness must be there. You can do anything in sleep; then there is no problem. The problem arises only when it is a condition to do it alertly.

---

41 Listen to a stringed instrument.

The fifth sound technique: *While listening to stringed instruments, hear their composite central sound; thus omnipresence.*

The same! You are hearing an instrument—a sitar, or anything. Many notes are there. Be alert and listen to the central core, the backbone of it around which all the notes are flowing, the deepest current which holds all the notes together—that which is central, just like your backbone. The whole body is held by the backbone. Listening to the music, be alert, penetrate the music, and find the backbone of it—the central thing which goes on flowing, holding everything together. Notes come and go and disappear, but the central core flows on. Become aware of it.

Basically, originally, music was used for meditation; particularly Indian music developed as a method of meditation, Indian dancing developed as a method of meditation. For the doer it was a deep meditation, and for the audience also it was a deep meditation. A dancer or a musician can be a technician. If there is no meditation in it, he is a technician. He can be a great technician, but then the soul is not there, only the body. The soul comes only when the musician is a deep meditator.

And music is just the outward thing. While playing on his sitar, one is not only playing on his sitar, he is also playing on his alertness inside. The sitar goes on outwardly and his intense awareness moves inside. The music flows outwardly, but he is alert, constantly aware of the innermost core of it.

And that gives samadhi. That becomes ecstasy. That becomes the highest peak.

It is said that when the musician has really become the musician, he will break his instrument —because it is of no use. If he still needs his instrument, he is not a real musician yet. He is just learning. If you can play with music, with meditation, sooner or later the inner music will become more important, and the outer will become not only less important: ultimately it will become a disturbance. If your consciousness moves inside and can find the inner music, then the outer music will be a disturbance. You will throw the sitar, you will throw the instrument away from you, because now you have found the inner instrument. But it cannot be found without the outer; with the outer you can become alert more easily. Once you have become alert, leave the outer and move inwards. And for the listener also, the same!

But what are you doing when you listen to music? You are not meditating. On the contrary, you are using music as something like alcohol. You are using it to be relaxed, you are using it for self-forgetfulness. This is the misfortune, the misery: the techniques which were developed for awareness are being used for sleep. And this is how man goes on doing mischief with himself.

If something is given to you which can make you awake, you will use it to make yourself more sleepy. That is why for millennia teachings were kept secret—because it was thought to be useless to give techniques to a sleepy man. He will use them for sleep; he cannot do otherwise. So techniques were given only to particular disciples who were ready to shake their sleep, who were ready to be shattered out of their sleepiness.

Ouspensky dedicates one book to George Gurdjieff as "the man who disturbed my sleep." Such people *are* disturbers. Persons like Gurdjieff or Buddha or Jesus, they are disturbers. That is why we take revenge upon them. Whosoever disturbs our sleep, we will crucify him. He doesn't look good to us. We may have been dreaming beautiful dreams and he comes and disturbs our sleep. We want to kill him. The dream was so beautiful.

The dream may be beautiful and it may not be beautiful, but one thing is certain: it is a dream, and futile, useless! And if it is beautiful, then it is more dangerous because it can attract you more, it can become a drug.

We have been using music as a drug, dancing as a drug. And if you want to use music and dancing as drugs, then they will become not only drugs for your sleep, they will become drugs for sexuality also. So remember this point: sexuality and sleep go together. The more sleepy the person, the more sexual; the more awake, the less sexual. Sex is basically rooted in sleep. When you awake you will be more loving, the whole energy of sex will have been transformed to love.

This sutra says: *While listening to stringed instruments, hear their composite central sound—their complete central sound—thus omnipresence.* And then you will know what is to be known, or what is worth knowing. You will become omnipresent. With the music, finding the composite central core, you will become awake, and with that awakening you will be everywhere.

Right now, you are somewhere—a point which we call the ego. If you can become awake, this point will disappear. You will not be anywhere then, you will be *everywhere*—as if you have become the all. You will have become the ocean, you will have become the infinite.

The finiteness is with the mind.

The infiniteness enters with meditation.

CHAPTER 28

Meditation: an unburdening of repressions

◆

As repression works automatically in us, how to tell apart the false and real in ourselves?

Would You explain the process of mantra initiation and the reasons for secrecy of the mantra?

Can You compare the chaotic music used in Your Dynamic Meditation, and rock music in the West?

The first question:

Repression has become an automatic reaction in our bodies and minds which we do not even recognize or want to change anymore. How can we learn to tell between a false image and a real one in ourselves?

Many things have to be understood. One: all your faces are false; you do not have any real face. That is why the question arises over which is false and which is real. If you have the real, you know. Then the question never arises. All the faces are unreal, false, so you do not have any comparisons to make. You do not know the real—that is the difficulty. You have not seen the real, and the real is not seen naturally; much effort is needed to find it.

In Zen they say that the real is the original face —the face you had before your birth and the face you will have after your death. That means that all the faces in life, so-called life, are false. How to find out what is the real face? You will have to go back to before your birth. That is the only way to find the real face, because the moment you are born you have started being false. You have started being false because it pays to be false.

The child is born, and he has started to be a politician. The moment he is related to the world, to the parents, to the family, he is in politics. Now he has to take care about his faces. He will smile as a bribery. He will try to find out in what ways he should behave so that he is accepted more, loved more, appreciated more. And sooner or later the child will find out what is condemned by the parents, by the family, and he will start repressing it. Then the false has entered.

So all the faces you have are false. Do not try to find out the real one among your present faces. They are all false, similarly false. They are useful— that is why they have been adopted—utilitarian, but not true. And the deepest deception is that whenever you become aware that your faces are false, you will create another face which you will think is the real.

For example, a person who lives an ordinary life, in an ordinary world, with a business, a family, comes to realize the whole of his falseness, the whole inauthenticity of his life, so he renounces it. He becomes a sannyasin and leaves the world, and he may be thinking that now the face is real. It is again a false face. It has been adopted as a reaction to other faces, and with a reaction you can never get to the real. By reacting to a false face you will create another false face. So what is to be done?

The real is not something which has to be achieved. The false is your achievement. The real is not something to be achieved, it is not something to be cultivated. It is something to be discovered! It is already there. You need not try to attain it, because any effort will only lead to some other false face. For a false face effort is needed; it has to be cultivated. For the real face you have not to do anything, it is already there. If you simply leave your clinging to the false faces, the false will drop and that which is real will remain. When you have nothing to drop, and only that which cannot be dropped is there, you will come to realize what is real.

Meditation is the way to drop the false faces. That is why there is so much insistence on being thoughtless—because without thought you cannot create a false face. In a thoughtless state of awareness, you will be real—because it is basically thought which creates false faces and masks. When there is no thought there can be no face. You will be faceless, or with the real face—and both mean the same.

So be aware of your thought process. Do not fight with it, do not repress it. Simply have awareness: the thoughts are there just like clouds in the sky, and you are looking at them without any prejudice, either for or against. If you are against, you will be fighting—and that very fight will create a new thought process. If you are for them, you will forget yourself and you will float in the current of the thought process. You will not be there as a conscious witness. If you are for, you will be in the process. If you are against, you will create another process in reaction.

So do not be for and do not be against. Allow the thoughts to move, let them go wherever they are going, be in a deep let-go, and simply witness. Whatsoever is passing, witness. Do not judge; do not say, "This is good, this is bad." If the thought of a divine being comes, do not say, "Beautiful!" The moment you say this you are identified with it, and you are cooperating with the thought process. You are helping it, you are giving energy to it, you are feeding it. And if you are feeding it, it can never drop.

Or if there is a thought, a sexual thought, do not say, "This is bad, this is sin." Because when you say, "This is sin," you have created another series of thoughts. Sex is a thought, sin is a thought, God is a thought. Be neither for nor against. Simply look with unprejudiced eyes, just watching indifferently.

This will take time. Because your mind is so occupied with notions, it is very difficult. The moment we see something we have judged it. We do not wait; there is not even a single moment's gap. You see a flower, and you have already said, "It is beautiful." In the very seeing the interpretation comes in.

You will have to be constantly aware to drop this mechanical habit of judging. You see a face and you have already judged—ugly, good, bad, or anything else. This judgment has become so deep-rooted that we cannot see anything simply. The mind enters immediately. It becomes an interpretation; it is not a simple vision. Do not interpret. Simply *see*.

Sit down in a relaxed posture or lie down. Close your eyes and allow your thoughts to move. If you say, "Bad!" if you condemn, then you start repressing them. Then you are not allowing them to move independently. That is why there is so much need for dreams, because whatsoever you are repressing during the day you will have to release in the night. That which is repressed goes on forcing its expression, it needs expression. So whatsoever you repress you dream. Dreams are cathartic.

Now modern sleep research says that you can be deprived of sleep and not much harm will result, but you cannot be deprived of your dreams. The old idea that sleep is very necessary has been found to be false. Instead of sleep, dreams are very necessary, and sleep is necessary only because you cannot dream without sleep.

Researchers have developed techniques with which it can now be judged from the outside whether you are dreaming or whether you are simply asleep. If you are simply asleep, they will disturb the sleep—the whole night long. When you are dreaming they will allow it, when you are not dreaming they will disturb the sleep, and no bad result comes out of it.

But if they should disturb you when you are dreaming and allow you to sleep when you are not dreaming, within three days you will begin to feel dizzy, and within seven days you will feel a deep uneasiness. Your body and mind both will feel ill. Within three weeks you will feel a certain type of insanity. What happens? It is because dreams are cathartic. If you go on repressing during the day and if the repressions are not allowed to be expressed, they will accumulate in you, and that accumulation of repression is insanity.

In meditation you are not to repress any thought. But it is difficult because your whole mind consists of judgments, theories, isms, doctrines, beliefs. So one who is very deeply obsessed with any idea, a philosophy or a religion, cannot really enter into meditation. It is difficult because his obsession will become the barrier. So if you are a Christian or a Hindu or a Jain, it will be difficult for you to enter meditation because your philosophy gives you judgments: this is good and that is not good, this has to be repressed, this is not to be allowed.

All philosophies are repressive and all religions, all ideologies, are repressive, because they give you interpretations. They do not allow you to see life as it is. They force interpretations on it.

One who wants to go deep into meditation has to be aware of this nonsense of ideology. Just be a simple man without any philosophy, with no attitude toward life. Just be a seeker—one who is in an inquiry, in a deep inquiry to know what life is. Do not force any ideology over and above it. Then it will be very easy to move into meditation.

Because of this, the greatest meditator the world has ever known, Gautam Buddha, insisted that no ideology is needed, no philosophy is needed, no concepts about life are needed. Whether God is or is not is meaningless, irrelevant. Whether *moksha*, liberation, exists or not is meaningless. Whether your soul is immortal or not is meaningless.

Buddha was so much antiphilosophy not because *he* was antiphilosophy, but because antiphilosophy can become the basic ground for a meditator to jump into the unknown. Philosophy means knowing something about the unknown without knowing it. It is just preconceptions, hypotheses, man-constructed ideologies.

This is to be remembered as a very foundational fact: do not judge, let the mind flow easily. As the river flows, let the mind flow easily; just sit on the bank watching. And this watching should be pure —without any interpretations. Sooner or later, when the water has flown, when the repressed ideas have moved, you will find gaps coming. A thought will go, and another thought will not be coming, and there will be a gap—an interval. In that interval, nothingness happens. In that interval you will have the first glimpse of your real face, of the original face.

When there is no thought there is no society. When there is no thought there is no other. When there is no other, no society, you need not have any face. Thoughtlessness is facelessness. In that interval, when one thought has gone and another has not appeared, in that interval, for the first time you will know in reality what is your face—the face you had when you were not born and the face you will have when you die.

All the faces in life are false. And once you know the real face, once you feel this inner nature which Buddhists call *buddha swabhava*—the nature of the inner buddha—when you come to feel this inner nature even once, even with a single glimpse, you will be a different person, because now you will constantly know what is false and what is real. Then you will have the criterion. Then you can compare, and there will be no need to ask what is real and what is unreal. The question comes only because you do not know what is real, and whatsoever you know is all unreal.

Only through meditation will you be able to learn what is a false image and what is a real, authentic face. Of course, the mind is automatic, and whatsoever you have done has become mechanical. It is hard to break this mechanicalness.

The first thing to be understood: mechanicalness is a necessity of life—and your body has an inner mechanism. Colin Wilson has called it the inner robot; you have a robot within you. Once trained, once you are trained in anything, that training is passed to the robot. You can call it memory, you can call it mind,—anything—but the word robot is good because it is absolutely mechanical, automatic. It functions in its own way.

You are learning to drive. While you are learning, you will have to be aware, alert. A danger is there. You do not know how to drive and anything can happen, so you will have to be alert. That is why learning is so painful, one has to be alert constantly. When you have learned driving, the driving has been given to the robot part of your mind. Now you can go on smoking, singing, listening to the radio or talking to a friend, or even loving your girlfriend. You can go on doing anything and the robot part of your being will drive.

You will not be needed; you are relieved of the burden. The robot will do everything. You will not even have to remember where to turn; you need not. The robot will know where to turn, where to stop, where not to stop, what to do and what not to do. You are not needed; you are relieved of the job. The robot does everything.

If something very sudden happens, some accident or something that the robot cannot tackle because it is not trained in it, only then will you be needed. Suddenly there will be a jerk in your body. The robot will be replaced and you will come in its place. You can feel that jerk. When suddenly you feel that an accident is going to happen, there is a jerk inside. The robot moves away; it gives place to you. Now *you* are driving. But when the accident is avoided, again the robot will take over. You will relax and the robot will drive.

And this is necessary for life because there are so many things to do—so many things! And if there is no robot to do them, you will not be capable of doing them at all. So a robot is needed, it is a necessity.

I am not against the robot. Go and give unto the robot whatsoever you learn, but remain the master. Do not allow the robot to become the master. This is the problem: the robot will try to be the master, because the robot is more efficient than

you. Sooner or later the robot will say to you, "Be completely retired. You are not needed. I can do things more efficiently."

Remain the master. What can be done in order for you to remain the master of the robot? Only one thing is possible, and that is: sometimes, without any danger, take the reins into your hands. Tell the robot to relax, come into the seat, and drive the car—without any danger, because in danger it is again automatic, the jerk, the replacement of the robot by you is automatic.

You are driving; suddenly, without any necessity, tell the robot to relax. You come into the seat and drive the car. You are walking; suddenly remember and tell the body that "Now I will walk consciously. The robot is not allowed. I am the master and I will move the body consciously." You are hearing me: it is the robot part which is hearing me. Suddenly give a jerk to it; do not allow the mind to come in. Hear me directly, consciously.

What do I mean when I say hear consciously? When you are hearing unconsciously, you are just focused on me and you have forgotten yourself completely. I exist, the speaker exists, but the listener is unconscious. You are not aware of yourself as the listener. When I say take the reins in your hands, I mean be aware of the two points: the speaker and the listener. And if you are aware of the two points, the speaker and the listener, you have become the third—the witness.

This witnessing will help you to remain the master. And if you are the master, your robot cannot disturb your life. It *is* disturbing your life. Your total life has become a mess because of this robot. It helps, it is efficient, but it goes on taking everything from you—even those things which should not be given to it.

You have fallen in love; it is beautiful in the beginning because it has not been given to the robot yet. You are learning. You are alive, aware, alert, and love has a beauty. But sooner or later the robot will take it over. You will become a husband or a wife, and you will have given the charge to the robot.

Then you will say to your wife, "I love you," but *you* will not be saying it. The robot will be saying it, the gramophone record. Then it is a recorded thing. You just play it again and again, and your wife will understand it—because whenever your robot says, "I love you," it means nothing. And when your wife says, "I love you," you too will know it is nothing, because a sentence given by a gramophone record only creates noise. It makes no sense; there is no sense in it.

Then you will want to do everything, yet *you* are not doing it. Then love becomes a burden and one even wants to escape from love. All your feelings, all your relationships are now directed by the robot. That is why sometimes you insist on not doing a certain thing, but the robot insists that you do it because the robot is trained to do it. And you are always a failure and the robot always succeeds.

You say, "I am not going to be angry again," but your saying it is meaningless because the robot is trained. And the training has been long, so just a sentence in the mind that "I am not going to be angry again," will not have any effect. This robot has been long trained. So next time when someone insults you, your decision not to be angry will be of no help. The robot will take charge immediately and the robot will do whatsoever it is trained to do. And then in the end, when the robot has done it, you will repent.

But the difficulty, the deep difficulty is this, that even this repentance is done by the robot, because you have always done that—after the anger you have repented. The robot has learned that trick also; it will repent, and again you will do the same thing.

That is why many times you feel that you have done something, said something, behaved in a certain way, in spite of yourself. What does this expression, "in spite of yourself" mean? It means that there is another self within you which can act, which can do something in spite of you. Who is that self? The robot!

What to do? Do not take vows that "I will not

be angry again." They are self-defeating; they will not lead you anywhere. Rather, on the contrary, whatsoever you are doing, do it consciously. Take charge from the robot—with any ordinary thing. When eating, eat consciously. Do not do it mechanically, as you have done every day. When smoking, smoke consciously. Do not allow your hand to move to the packet unconsciously, do not bring the cigarette out unconsciously. Be conscious, alert— and there is a difference.

I can raise my hand mechanically, just without any awareness; I can raise my hand with full awareness flowing in my hand. Try it! You will feel the difference. When you are aware, your hand will be raised very slowly, very silently, and you will feel that the hand is filled with the awareness. And when the hand is filled with the awareness, your mind will be thoughtless, because your whole awareness will have moved to the hand. Now no energy is left to think.

When you raise your hand automatically, mechanically, you go on thinking and your hand goes on moving. Who is moving that hand? Your robot. Move it yourself! Do it in the day at any time, any moment, while doing anything. Take charge from the robot. Soon you will be able to have a mastery over the robot. But do not try it with difficult situations—that is suicidal. We always try with difficult situations, but because of the difficulty you never win. Start with simple situations, where even if you are not so efficient no harm is going to result.

We always try with difficult situations. For example, one man thinks, "I am not going to be angry." Anger is a very difficult situation and the robot will not leave it to you. And it is better that the robot should do it because he knows more than you. You decide about sex—not to do something or to do something—but you cannot follow it through. The robot will take over. The situation is very complex, and more efficient handling is needed than you can give it right now.

Unless you become so perfectly aware that you

can tackle any complex situation without the help of the robot, the robot will not allow you to do it. And this is a very necessary defense mechanism. If it were otherwise, you would make a great mess of your life—if you were to go on taking things away from the robot in difficult situations.

Try! Start with simple things such as walking. Try with this; there is no harm. You can say to the robot that "There is not going to be any harm. I am just walking, taking a walk, and I am not going anywhere—just walking. So there is no need of you; I can be nonefficient."

And then be aware and walk slowly. Be filled with awareness throughout your whole body. When one foot moves, move with it. When one foot leaves the ground, leave the ground with it. When the other foot touches the ground, touch the ground with it. Be perfectly aware. Do not do anything else with the mind; just turn the whole mind into awareness.

It will be difficult because the robot will interfere continuously. Every moment the robot will try and will say, "What are you doing? I can do it better than you." And he *can* do it better. So try it with nonserious things, with noncomplex things, simple things.

Buddha has told his disciples to walk, eat and sleep with awareness. If you can do these simple things, then you will also know how to enter into difficult things with awareness. Then you can try.

But we always try with difficult things; then we are defeated. Then the defeated feeling gives you a deep pessimism about yourself. You start thinking that you cannot do anything. That is very helpful for the robot. The robot will always help you to do something when you are in difficulty because then you are defeated. Then the robot can say to you, "Leave it to me. I can always do it better than you can do it."

Start with simple things. Zen Buddhists, Zen monks, have been so many times reported to have been doing this. When Basho was asked, "What is your meditation? What is your *sadhana*, spiritual practice?" he said, "When I feel hungry I eat and when I feel sleepy I go to sleep. This is all."

The man who was asking said, "But this we all do. What is special about it?"

Basho repeated it again. He said, "When I am hungry 'I' eat and when I feel sleepy 'I' sleep." And that is the difference. When you feel hungry your robot eats, when you feel sleepy your robot sleeps. Basho said "I," and that is the difference.

If you become more aware in your day-to-day work, in your ordinary life, the awareness will grow. And with that awareness you will not be just a mechanical thing. For the first time you become a person—now you are not one. And a person has a face and a mechanical thing has many masks—no face.

If you are a person—alive, alert, aware—you can have an authentic existence. If you are just a mechanical device, you cannot have any authentic existence. Each moment will change you; each situation will change you. You will be just a floating thing with no inner core, with no inner being. Awareness gives you the inner presence. Without it you feel that you are, but you are not.

Someone asked Buddha, "I want to serve humanity. Tell me how I can serve."

Buddha looked at the man very deeply, penetratingly, with deep compassion, and then he said, "But where are *you*? *Who* will serve humanity? You are not yet. First be, and when you are, you need not ask me. When you are, you will do something which just happens to you which is worth doing."

Gurdjieff noted that everyone comes with the notion that he is, that he already is. Someone came to Gurdjieff and asked, "I am very insane inside. My mind goes on in conflicts, in contradictions, so tell me what I can do to dissolve this mind, to have mental peace, inner calm."

Gurdjieff said, "Do not think about the mind, you cannot do anything about it. The first thing is to be present. First *you* have to be; then you can do something. *You* are not."

What is meant by this "You are not"? It means that you are a robot, a mechanical thing, working according to mechanical laws. Start being alert. Join awareness with anything you are doing—and start with simple things.

The second question:

Explain the meaning, preparation and process of mantra deeksha—mantra initiation. And what are the reasons why individuals must keep the mantra secret?

First try to understand what initiation is, what is *deeksha*. It is a deep communion, a deep transfer of energy from the master to the disciple. Energy always flows downwards. Every energy flows downwards, just like water flows downwards. The master—one who has attained, one who has known, one who has become—is the highest peak of energy possible, of purest energy…the Everest of energy. This energy can flow downwards to anyone who is receptive, humble, surrendered. This surrendered attitude—the receptive attitude, a deep humbleness—will be needed to receive. Otherwise you yourself are a peak; you are not a valley. Then the energy cannot flow downwards to you.

You are a different sort of peak, the peak of ego—not of energy, not of being, not of bliss, not of consciousness. You are a density of ego, of 'I-ness.' You are a peak, and with this peak no initiation is possible. Ego is the barrier because ego closes you and you cannot surrender.

To be a disciple, to be initiated, one has to surrender himself totally. And there is no partial surrender. Surrender means total. You cannot say, "I partially surrender"—it makes no sense. Then you are still there with your ego. Ego has to be surrendered, and when you surrender the ego you become receptive, open. You become like a valley, and then the peak can flow downwards to you. And I am not talking symbolically, it is so actually.

Have you ever been in love? Then you can feel that love actually flows between two bodies, it is an actual flow. Energy is being transmitted, transferred, received, given. But love is on the same level. You both can remain peaks of ego, and still love can be.

But with a master you are not on the same level. And if you try to be on the same level, initiation becomes impossible. Love is possible, but initiation becomes impossible. Initiation is possible only when you are on a lower level—just humble, surrendered, open to receive—when the disciple is feminine, just womblike, passive, able to receive. The master is the male factor in initiation.

This secret of initiation is now completely lost because the more we are educated, the more civilized, the more cultured, then the more egoistic we become. And now, to surrender has become very, very impossible. It has always been difficult, but now it is impossible.

Initiation is a transfer of inner energy, actual energy, and the master can enter in you and can transform you if you are ready and receptive. But then deep trust is needed—more trust than is needed in love—because you do not know what is going to happen. You are completely in the dark.

Only the master knows what is going to happen and what he is doing. He knows; you cannot know. And there are things that cannot be said about what is going to happen because with the human mind there are many problems. One problem is this: that if something is said before it happens, it will change the happening. It cannot be said.

So there are many things which the master cannot say to you. He can do them to you, but he cannot say them to you. That doing is initiation. He actually moves in you—in your body, in your mind. He cleanses you, changes you. The only thing required is your total trust, because without it there is no opening and he cannot enter you: your doors are closed.

You are always defending yourself. Life is a struggle—a struggle for survival, to survive. This struggle gives you a closing. You are closed, afraid; you are afraid to be vulnerable. Someone may enter, someone may do something within you. So you shrink yourself, you remain closed—just hiding behind, constantly defending. In initiation you have to lose this defense; this armor of defense has to be thrown away. You become vulnerable, and then the master can enter you.

For example, it is just like a deep love act. You can rape a woman, but you cannot rape a disciple. You can rape a woman because it is a bodily rape, and the body can be raped and entered without any consent. Without the will of the woman you can rape. It is a forced thing. The body is material; things can be forced on it.

Something just like this happens in initiation. The master enters your spirit, not your body. Unless you are ready and receiving, the entrance is not possible. A disciple cannot be raped because it is not a bodily question. It is a question of spirit, and you cannot force entry into a spirit. No violence is possible with it.

So when the disciple is ready and open, just like a loving woman, inviting and receptive, ready, in a deep let-go, only then can the master enter and work. And centuries of work can be done in moments. You may not be able to do in many lives certain things which can be done in a moment. But then you have to be vulnerable, totally trusting. You do not know what is going to happen and what he will do inside you.

A woman is afraid because the sexual act is a journey into the unknown for her. Unless she loves the man, unless she is ready to suffer, to carry the burden of a child, to carry the child for nine months and then make a life commitment to it, unless she is deeply in love, she will not allow the man to enter her body—because it is not simply her body, it is her whole life. When she is in deep love, then she is ready to suffer, to sacrifice. And to sacrifice and suffer in deep love is blissful.

But the problem with the disciple is deeper. It is not a question only of a physical birth, of a new child, it is *his* rebirth. He himself is going to be reborn. He will die in a certain sense and he will be

born in a certain different sense. And this is possible if the master enters him, but the master cannot force it. No force is possible, the disciple can only invite it.

And that is the problem—a very great problem in spiritual discipleship, because the disciple goes on defending himself or herself, goes on creating more and more armor around him. He behaves with his master in the same way he would behave with anyone in the world; the same defense mechanisms go on working. And then time is wasted unnecessarily, energy is wasted, and the moment is delayed which can happen right now. But this is natural, and sometimes even with great masters disciples have missed the chance.

Ananda, one of the great disciples of Buddha and the nearest, couldn't attain liberation while Buddha was alive. Buddha was with Ananda for forty years, and Ananda couldn't attain. But many who came after Ananda attained, and then it became a problem. And Ananda was one of the nearest—the closest. He was sleeping in the same room with Buddha, he was moving with Buddha for forty years continuously. He was like a shadow to Buddha; as much as he knew about Buddha even Buddha might not have known.

But he couldn't attain; he remained the same. And a very ordinary thing was the only barrier: he was an elder cousin-brother of Buddha. This created the ego.

Buddha died...a great council met to write down whatsoever Buddha had said. It had to be written then. Soon those who lived with Buddha would be no more, so everything had to be recorded. But the council would not allow Ananda, and only he knew the greater experiences, the statements of Buddha, his life, his biography. This was all known to Ananda; no one knew so much.

But the council decided that Ananda could not be allowed because he was still unenlightened. He could not record Buddha's sayings because an ignorant man cannot be believed. He would not deceive, but with an ignorant man nothing is reliable. He may think that something happened, and he may relate it authentically as far as he knows, but he is a man who is not yet awakened. Whatsoever he has seen and heard in sleep could not be believed, so only those would record who had become awakened—they decided.

Ananda was weeping just outside the door. The door was closed, and he remained just by the door for twenty-four hours, weeping, crying and screaming. But they would not allow him. For these twenty-four hours he was weeping, weeping, and then suddenly he became aware what had been the barrier—why he hadn't been able to attain while Buddha was alive, what had been the barrier.

Then he went back into his memories. A forty-year-long life with Buddha! He remembered the first day when he came to him for initiation. But he had one condition, and that was why he missed the whole initiation. He could not be initiated because he made a condition.

He came to Buddha and he said, "I have come to be a disciple of yours. Once I become your disciple, you will be the master and I will have to follow whatsoever you say, I will have to obey. But right now I am your elder brother, and I can order you and you will have to obey. You are not the master, I am not the disciple. Once I am initiated, you will be the master and I will be the disciple. Then I will not be able to say anything, so before I become a disciple these are my three conditions. Say yes to these three conditions; then initiate me."

The conditions were not very big, but a condition is a condition and then your surrender is not total. They were very small conditions, very loving conditions. He said, "One, I will always be with you. You cannot tell me to move anywhere else. While I am alive I will be your shadow; you cannot order me away. Give me the promise—because later on I will be just a disciple, and if you order me away I will have to follow. This will be a promise given to an elder brother—that I will be with you. You cannot tell me to move anywhere else. I will just be your shadow; I will sleep in the room where you sleep.

"Secondly, whenever I will say, 'Meet this man,' you will have to meet him. Whatsoever your reason for not meeting, you will have to agree. If I want that someone should be given your *darshan*—spiritual presence—you will have to give it.

"And thirdly, if I say that someone has to be initiated, you cannot refuse. Grant me these three conditions. Promise me and then initiate me. I will not ask anything again because then I shall be just a disciple."

When he remembered this, while he was weeping, crying before the door of the council, after he went back into his memories, he suddenly became aware that the initiation was not there because he had not been receptive. Buddha had agreed. He said, "Okay!" and he followed the three conditions his whole life. But Ananda missed, the nearest one missed.

And the moment he realized this he became enlightened. That which couldn't happen with Buddha happened when he was no more: he surrendered.

If there is surrender, even an absent master can help you. If there is no surrender, even an alive master who is present cannot help you. So in initiation, in any initiation, surrender is needed.

Mantra initiation means that when you have surrendered, the master will enter you—your body, your mind, your spirit. He will move in you to find a sound for you, so that whenever you chant that sound you will be a different man in a different dimension.

A mantra cannot be given unless you have surrendered totally, because mantra giving means the master has entered you and felt the deep harmony, the inner music of your being. And then he gives a symbolic sound which is in harmony with your inner music. The moment you chant that sound you enter the world of your inner music, the inner harmony is entered.

That sound is just a key, and a key cannot be given unless the lock is known. So I cannot give you a key unless I know your lock, because a key is meaningful only when it can unlock. Any key will not do, and everyone is a particular lock—you need a particular key. That is why mantras are to be kept secret.

If you give your mantra to someone he may experiment with it, but that key will not suit that lock. And sometimes, when you force a wrong key into a lock you can destroy the lock, you can disturb the lock. You can so much disturb it that even when a right key is found it may not work. That is why mantras are to be kept absolutely secret. They are not told to anyone; that is a promise you make. The master gives you a key, it is a key only for you. You cannot go on distributing it —for many that would be harmful.

You will be allowed to give keys only when your lock is totally opened. But then you will not give *this* key to anyone. Then you will have become capable of entering into the other. Then you will be able to feel the lock and devise a key for it.

The key is always devised by the master. If there is a heap of keys, one who doesn't know may think all keys are the same. There may be only very small differences, minute differences, and even the same word can be used differently. For example, aum. This has three sounds—'A-U-M.' If emphasis is given on the 'U,' the mid-sound, it is one key. If emphasis is given on the 'A,' it is a different key. If the emphasis is given on the 'M,' it is still a different key; it will open different locks. That is why there is so much emphasis on the exact use of the mantra as it is given by the master.

So the master gives the mantra in your ear; he chants it exactly as it should be used. He chants it in your ear, and you have to become so alert that your whole consciousness comes to the ear. He chants it, and then it enters into you. You have to remember it now—the exact use of it. That is why individuals must keep their mantras secret; they should not be made public. They are dangerous, and if you are initiated you know it. If a master has really given you a key, you know it. You treasure it like anything; you cannot go on distributing it. It can be harmful for others and it can be harmful for

you also—for many reasons.

Firstly, you are breaking a promise, and the moment the promise is broken your contact with the master is broken. You will not be in contact with him again. If the promise is kept, there is a constant contact.

Secondly, if you give the mantra to anyone and talk about it, it comes to the surface of the mind. The deeper roots are broken, it becomes a gossip.

Thirdly, if you can keep anything secret, the more you keep it secret, the deeper it goes. It is bound to go deeper.

It is said of Marpa that when he was given the secret mantra by his master, the promise was there that the mantra would be kept absolutely secret. "You are not to talk about it," he was told.

Then Marpa's master appeared in his dream and he said, "What is your mantra?" Even in the dream Marpa kept his promise, he refused to tell it. And it is said that because of the fear that someday in a dream the master may come or send someone, and he may be so asleep that he would break the secret and the promise would be broken, he stopped sleeping altogether. He would not sleep!

He had not been sleeping for seven or eight days, and his master asked Marpa, "Why are you not sleeping? I see you do not go to sleep at all, so what is the matter?"

Marpa said, "You are playing tricks with me. You came in a dream and you were asking for the mantra. I cannot tell even you. Once the promise is there, it will not come out of my mouth even in a dream. But then I became fearful. In sleep, who knows! Someday I may forget."

If you are so aware of keeping the promise that even in a dream you remember it, then it is going deep. It is going deep, it is entering inner realms. And the deeper it moves, the more it will be a key to you —because the lock is at the deepest layer. Try with anything. If you can keep it a secret, it will move deep. If you cannot keep it a secret, it will move out.

Why do you want to say something to someone? Why do you chatter? Really, anything that you chatter about you are relieved of. Once you tell it you are relieved of it; it has moved out.

The whole psychoanalysis is nothing but this. The psychoanalyst is just listening and the patient goes on talking. It helps the patient—because the more he talks about his problems, inner conflicts and associated ideas, the more he is relieved of them. The reverse happens when you can keep a secret. At no moment are you allowed to talk about it. It will enter deep, deep, and one day it will hit the exact lock.

One question more:

In reference to the meditation techniques based on sounds, please explain the difference between the chaotic music played in Your Dynamic Meditation and the shake or rock music of the West.

Your mind is in chaos. That chaos has to be brought out, acted out. Chaotic music can be helpful, so if you are meditating and chaotic music is played or chaotic dancing is there around you, it will help to bring out your chaos. You will flow in it, you will become unafraid of expression. And this chaotic music will hit your chaotic mind within and will bring it out. It helps.

Rock, jazz, or other music which is chaotic in a way also helps something to come out, and that something is repressed sexuality. I am concerned with all your repressions. Modern music is more concerned just with your repressed sex, but there is a similarity. However, I am not concerned only with your repressed sex, I am concerned with all your repressions—sexual or not sexual.

Rock music, or other music like that, is so influential in the West because of Christianity. Christianity has been repressing sex for twenty centuries. They have forced sex to go so deep down inside that every man has become a pervert deep down. So the West has to relieve itself of the sin that Christianity has done with man, with his mind, through music, through dance, through chaotic painting, chaotic poetry—in every dimension.

In the West mind has to be completely freed somehow from the whole centuries-long past of repression. In every way they are doing it. All that is influential today is chaotic. But sex is not the only thing, there are many other things also. Sex is the basic thing, it is very important, but there are other things also. Your anger is repressed, your sadness is repressed, even your happiness is repressed.

Man as he is is a repressed being. He is not allowed to do anything, he has just to follow rules. He is not a free agent but just a kept slave, and the whole society is a big prison. The walls are very subtle: they are glass walls, transparent. You cannot see them, but they are, and everywhere. Your morality, your culture, your religion, they are all walls. They are transparent, you cannot see them, but whenever you want to cross them you are thrown back.

This state of mind is neurotic. The whole society is ill. That is why I so much insist on chaotic meditation. Relieve yourself, act out whatsoever society has forced on you, whatsoever situations have forced on you. Act them out, relieve yourself of them, go through a catharsis. The music helps.

Once you can throw out everything that has been repressed in you, you will become natural again, you will be a child again. And with that child many possibilities open. With you everything is closed. When you become again a child, then only can your energies be transformed. Then you are pure, innocent, and with that innocence and purity transformation is possible.

Perverted energies cannot be transformed. Natural, spontaneous energy is needed. That is why I insist so much on acting out things: so that you can throw the society out. The society has entered you very deeply. It has not left *you* anywhere; it has entered from everywhere. You are a citadel, and the society has entered from everywhere. Its police, its priests, they have done much to make you a slave. You are not free, and man can attain to bliss only when he becomes a total freedom.

For you to be made a total freedom the whole society has to be thrown out of you, but that doesn't mean that you are going to become anti-social. Once you throw the society out, once you become aware of your pure freedom inside, you can live with the society; there is no need to be opposed. But then the society cannot enter into you. You can move in it, you can act in it, but then the whole thing becomes just a psychodrama—you are acting. Now the society cannot kill you, cannot make a slave of you; you are acting knowingly.

Those who become antisocial simply show that they are still bound to the same society. All the antisocial movements in the West are reactionary, not revolutionary. You are reacting to the same society, you are related to the same society in a reverse manner. You are standing on your head, that is all. You are doing *shirshasana*—the headstand posture —but you are the same person. Whatsoever the society is insisting upon, you are doing quite the contrary—but you are still following the society. This will not help.

If you are opposed you will never be beyond the society, you will always be part of it. If the society dies, you will die. Think of what in the West they now call the establishment—the society that is established—and the alternate societies of hippies, yippies, or others. They exist as a part of this establishment. If the establishment is dissolved, they will be nowhere. They cannot exist by themselves; they are just a reaction.

You cannot create a society of hippies by itself. Hippies can exist only as an alternate society *with* an establishment—just as a reaction. They cannot exist independently. So howsoever much they may think they are independent, they are not independent. The establishment is their source, their life. Once the establishment is not there, they will be at a loss where to move and what to do. Whatsoever they are doing is dictated by the establishment. They go against it, but the directions, the instructions are given by the establishment.

If the establishment says short hair, you can be long-haired. But if there is no establishment, then what to do? If the establishment says cleanliness,

you can be dirty. But if there is no establishment and no fuss about cleanliness, you are nowhere. If the establishment says this, you can do that—quite the reverse—but you follow the establishment.

So antisocials are not revolutionaries. They are reactionaries, a part and a product of the same society—those who have moved against it in bitterness.

A meditator, a sannyasin, is not antisociety, he is beyond society. He is not against the establishment, neither is he for it—but he takes it nonseriously. He knows it is just a play; he moves in it like an actor. And if you can move in the society like an actor on the stage, it never touches you; you remain beyond it. So do not be for it, do not be against it.

But how can you do it? You can do it only when you have thrown the society out of you. If it is there, then there are two paths open to you: follow it or go against it. But you are bound to it; you are in bondage. First one has to clean oneself of society, then for the first time you become an individual. Right now you are not, you are just a social unit.

When the society is thrown out, when its entire presence is thrown out, you are again back to your childhood: you have become innocent. And this innocence is deeper than that which any child can have, because you know the fall as well and now you have risen. It is a resurrection. You have experienced, you have known the whole nonsense. Now you are again pure. This purity becomes the temple for the divine.

Once you can throw the society out of you, without any bitterness, without going against it or being involved in any reaction…if you can simply throw society out of you, the divine can enter into you.

With society in, the divine will remain out; with society out, the divine can enter—because the divine means existence. Society is a human, local phenomenon. Existence is greater, infinite. It is not concerned with man, morals, traditions, it is concerned with the very roots of being. One has to be beyond society, not against it, remember. And this chaotic method helps you. It is a catharsis.

CHAPTER 29

Methods for the dropping of mind

◆

42 *Intone a sound audibly, then less and less audibly as feeling deepens into this silent harmony.*

43 *With mouth slightly open, keep mind in the middle of the tongue. Or, as breath comes silently in, feel the sound 'HH.'*

44 *Center on the sound 'AUM' without any 'A' or 'M.'*

antra divides life into two dimensions: one is the *sansara*—that which is, the world; and the other is *moksha*—that which can be, the ultimate, the hidden which can become manifest. But there is no contradiction between these two. The hidden is just here and now, in the world—of course, unknown to you, but not nonexistent. It is there. The ultimate and the immediate are not two things, but just two dimensions of one existence.

So for tantra there is no contradiction, there is no duality. The one appears as two because of our limitations; because we cannot see the whole. The moment we can see the whole, one appears as one. The division is not in reality, but in our limited knowledge. That which we know is sansara—the world; and that which is unknown but which can be known is moksha—the transcendental, the ultimate, the absolute.

For other traditions, there is a conflict between the two; for tantra there is no conflict. This has to be understood very deeply in the mind and in the heart. Unless this is understood deeply, you will never be able to understand the viewpoint of tantra. And whatsoever is your belief, that belief is of duality. Whether you are a Christian or a Mohammedan or a Hindu or a Jain, your belief is of duality, of conflict. The world appears to be something which is against the divine, and you have to fight the world to reach the divine. This is the common belief of all so-called religions, particularly organized religions.

Mind can understand duality very easily. Rather, it can understand only duality because the very function of the mind is to divide. The very function of the mind is to cut the whole into fragments.

The mind works like a prism, and when a ray of light enters the prism it is divided into seven colors. Mind is a prism and reality is divided through it. That is why mind revels in analysis. It goes on dividing things into fragments, and it cannot prevent itself unless there is nothing to be divided anymore. So mind has a tendency to reach to the atomic, the lowest division. It goes on dividing, dividing, until a moment comes when no division is possible. If division is still possible, it will divide still further.

Mind goes to the fragment, to the minutest fragment, and reality is a whole, not the fragment. So a completely reverse process is needed to know the real: a process which is of synthesis, not of analysis; a process which crystallizes, not one which divides. A no-mind process is needed.

Tantra denies divisions and tantra says that the whole is whole. The part that we know is the world, the part that is hidden is the divine, or God, or whatsoever you name it—but the hidden is just here and now. You are not aware of it, but it is here and now. It is already. For you it will be in the future, but in the existence it is here and now. You may have to travel to it; you may have to attain a no-mind attitude of looking at things—then it will be revealed. You are just standing and the morning sun is rising, but you are standing with closed eyes.

The morning is here and now, but for you it is not here and now. When you will open your eyes, only then will it become a fact for you.

In the existence the morning exists, but not for you. You are closed to it, it is hidden for you. For you there is only darkness and the light is hidden. But if you open your eyes, any moment the morning will become a fact to you. It was already a fact, only you were blind.

Tantra says that the world is already the divine, but you are blind. So whatsoever you know in your blindness is to be called the world, and whatsoever is hidden because of your blindness is the divine. This is one of the basic tenets—that this sansara is the moksha, this very world is divine, this very world is the ultimate. The immediate and the ultimate are not two, but one. The here and there are not two, but one. Because of this insistence, many things become possible for tantra. One: tantra can accept everything, and the deep acceptance relaxes you completely. Nothing else can relax you.

If there is no division between this world and that, if the transcendental is imminent here and now, if matter is just the body of the divine, then nothing is denied, nothing is condemned and you need not be tense. Even if it may take ages for you to come to realize the divine, there is no hurry for tantra. It is already there, and time is not lacking. It is eternally here; whenever you will open your eyes you will find it. And whatsoever you are already getting is the hidden divine.

So the Christian attitude of condemnation, of sin, or other such religious attitudes, is totally a lie to tantra—and absurd, because if you condemn something you also become divided inwardly. You cannot divide things only outwardly. If you divide, you also will be divided in parallel. If you say that this world is wrong, then your body will become wrong because your body is part of this world.

If you say that this world is something which is a hindrance to reaching the ultimate, then your whole life will be condemned and you will feel guilty. Then you cannot enjoy, then you cannot live,

then you cannot laugh. Then seriousness will become your face. You can be only serious; you cannot be nonserious, you cannot be playful.

That has happened to all the minds all over the world. They become dead, serious. Through seriousness they become dead because they cannot accept life as it is. They deny it, and they feel that unless they deny they cannot reach the other world.

So the other world becomes the ideal, the future, the desire, the vision, and this world becomes a sin. Then one feels guilty with it. And any religion that makes you guilty, makes you neurotic. It drives you crazy! In this sense, tantra is the only healthy religion. And whenever any religion becomes healthy, it becomes tantra—it becomes tantric. So every religion has two aspects. One is the outer aspect: the church, the organization, the publicized, the public face, the exoteric. This aspect is always life-denying. The other aspect is the inner core. Every religion has that too: the esoteric. It is always tantric—totally accepting.

Unless you accept the world totally, you cannot be at ease within. Nonacceptance creates a tension. Once you accept everything as it is, you are at home in the world. Tantra says this is a basic thing: you must be at home. Only then does something more become possible. If you are tense, divided, in conflict, in anguish, in guilt, how can you transcend? You are so mad inside, you cannot travel further. You are so engaged here, so much possessed by the here, you cannot go beyond.

This seems paradoxical. Those who are too much against the world are too much in it; they have to be. You cannot go away from your enemy, you are possessed by the enemy. If the world is your enemy, no matter what you do or pretend to do you will remain worldly. You may even renounce it, but your very approach will be worldly.

I have seen one saint, a very renowned one.... He will not touch money, and if you put some coins before him, he will close his eyes. This is neurotic, this man is ill! What is he doing? But people worship him because of this. They think he is so otherworldly. He is not, he is too much in the world. Even you are not so much in the world. What is he doing? He has just reversed the process; now he is standing on his head. He is the same man —the same man who was greedy for money. Constantly he must have been thinking of money, accumulating possessions. Now he has become quite the opposite, but he remains the same within. Now he is against money, now he cannot touch it.

Why this fear? Why this hatred? Remember, whenever there is hatred it is love in reverse. You can hate a thing only if you have been in love with it. Hate is always possible only through love. You can be against something only if you have been so much for it, but the basic attitude remains the same: this man is greedy.

I asked this man, "Why are you so afraid?"

He said, "Money is the hindrance. Unless I use will against my greed toward money, I cannot reach the divine."

So now it is only a new sort of greed. He is in a bargain: if he touches money he loses the divine. And he wants to get the divine, he wants to possess the divine, so he is against the money.

Tantra says, do not be for the world, do not be against the world, just accept it as it is. Do not create any problem out of it. How is this going to help you? If you do not create any problem out of it, if you do not grow neurotic over it—this way or that—if you remain simply in it and accept it as it is, your whole energy is relieved from it and can move to the hidden realm, to the hidden dimension.

Acceptance in this world becomes transcendence for that. Total acceptance here will lead you, will transform you to the other dimension, the hidden dimension, because all your energy is relieved; it is not engaged here. Tantra believes deeply in the concept of *niyati*—fate. Tantra says, take this world as your fate and do not be worried about it. Once you take it as your niyati, as your fate, you accept it, whatsoever it is. You are not worried about changing it, about making it differ-

ent, about making it according to your desire. Once you accept it as it is and you are not bothered by it, your total energy is relieved, and then this energy can penetrate inwards.

These techniques can be helpful only if you take this attitude; otherwise they will not be helpful. And they look so simple. If you start them directly as you are, they will seem simple, but you will not succeed in them. The basic framework is lacking. Acceptance is the basic framework. Once the acceptance is there in the background, these very simple methods will work wonders.

---

42 Use sound as a passage toward feeling.

The sixth method concerning sound: *Intone a sound audibly, then less and less audibly as feeling deepens into this silent harmony.*

Any sound will do, but if you love a certain sound it will be better, because if you love a certain sound then the sound is not just sound. When you intone the sound, then you are also intoning a hidden feeling with it, and by and by the sound will be dropped and only feeling will remain.

The sound has to be used as a passage toward feeling. Sound is mind and feeling is heart. Mind has to use a passage toward the heart. It is difficult to enter the heart directly. Because we have been missing it so much and for so many lives, we do not know from where to move to the heart. How to enter it? The door seems closed.

We go on talking about the heart, but that talk also is just in the mind. We say that we love through the heart, but this too is cerebral; in the head. Even the talk of the heart is in the head. And we do not know where the heart is. I do not mean the physical part of it, we know about that. But then physicians will say, medical science will say, that there is no possibility of love in it. It is just a pumping system. Nothing else is in it, and all else is just myth and poetry and dreaming.

But tantra knows a deep center hidden behind your physical heart. That deep center can only be reached through the mind because we are standing in the mind. We are there in the head, and any travel inwards has to begin from there. Mind is sound. If all sound stops, you won't have any mind. In silence there is no mind—that is why there is so much insistence on silence. Silence is a no-mind state.

Ordinarily we say, "My mind is silent." This is absurd, meaningless, because mind means absence of silence. So you cannot say that the mind is silent. If mind is, there cannot be any silence, and when silence is, there is no mind. So there is no such thing as a silent mind; there cannot be. It is just like saying that someone is alive-dead. It makes no sense. If he is dead, then he is not alive. If he is alive, then he is not dead. You cannot be alive-dead.

So there is nothing like a silent mind. When silence comes, mind is not there. Really, mind goes out and silence comes in; silence comes in and mind goes out. Both cannot be there. Mind is sound. If the sound is systematic you are sane, if the sound has gone chaotic you are insane; but in both the cases sound is there, and we exist at the point of the mind.

So how to drop from that point to the inner point of the heart? Use sound, intone sound. One sound will be helpful. If there are many sounds in the mind, it is difficult to leave them. If there is only one sound, it can be left easily. So first many sounds are to be sacrificed for one sound. That is the use of concentration.

Intone one sound. Go on intoning it, first audibly so that you can hear it, and then by and by, slowly, inaudibly. No one else can hear it then, but you can hear it inside. Make it more quiet, make it less and less audible, and then suddenly drop it. There will be silence, an explosion of silence—but feeling will be there. Now there will be no thought, but feeling will be there.

That is why it is good to use a sound, a name, a mantra, for which you have some feeling. If a Hindu uses "Rama," he has some feeling for it. It is not simply a word for him, it is not only in his head. The vibrations reach to his heart also. He may not be aware, but it is deep-rooted in his bones, in his very blood. There has been a long tradition, a long conditioning, for many lives. If you have been attached to one sound continuously, it is very deep-rooted. Use it. It can be used.

A Christian can use "Rama," but it will remain in the mind, it will not go deep. It is better that he uses "Jesus" or "Maria" or something else. It is very easy to be influenced by a new idea, but it is difficult to use it. You do not have any feeling for it. Even if you are convinced in the mind that this will be better, this conviction is on the surface.

One of my friends was living in Germany. He was there for thirty years and he completely forgot his mother tongue—he was a Maharashtrian and his mother tongue was Marathi. But he had forgotten it, for thirty years he was using German. German became just like his mother tongue. I say just like because no other tongue can become your mother tongue. There is no possibility because the mother tongue remains deep down inside of you. He consciously forgot it, and he was not able to speak or understand it.

Then he fell ill, and he was so ill that his whole family had to go there to see him. He was unconscious, but sometimes consciousness would come. Whenever he would become conscious he would speak German and whenever he would become unconscious he would mutter in Marathi. Consciously he couldn't understand anything of Marathi; unconsciously he couldn't understand anything of German.

Deep in the unconscious Marathi remained; it was the mother tongue. And you cannot replace the mother tongue. You can put other things over and above it, you can overimpose other things, but you cannot replace it. Deep down, it will remain.

So if you have a feeling for a certain sound, it is better to use it. Do not use an intellectual sound, it will be of no help because the sound has to be used to make a passage from the mind to the heart. So use some sound for which you have a deep love, a certain feeling.

If a Mohammedan uses "Rama," it is very difficult, the word means nothing to him. That is why the two oldest religions never believe in conversion —Hinduism and Judaism. They are the two oldest religions, the two original religions; all other religions are just offshoots of these two. Christianity and Islam are offshoots of the Jewish tradition; Buddhism, Jainism, Sikhism are offshoots of Hinduism. These two original religions never believed in conversion, and the reason was this: that you can convert a man intellectually, but you cannot convert a man from his heart. You can convert a Hindu into a Christian, you can convert a Christian into a Hindu, but the conversion will remain of the mind.

Deep down a converted Hindu remains a Hindu. He may go to a church and he may pray to Mary or to Jesus, but his prayer remains of the head. You cannot change the unconscious. And if you hypnotize him, you will find he is a Hindu. If you hypnotize him and let him reveal his unconscious, you will find he is a Hindu.

Hindus and Jews never believed in conversion because of this basic fact. You cannot change a man's religion because you cannot change his heart and unconscious feelings. And if you try, then you disturb him, because you give him something which will remain on the surface and you divide him. Then he becomes a split personality. Deep down he is a Hindu; on the surface he is a Christian. He will use Christian sounds, mantras, which will not go deep, and he cannot use Hindu sounds which can go deep. You have disturbed his life.

So find a certain sound for which you have some feeling. Even your own name may be helpful. If you do not have any feeling for anything else, then your own name will be helpful. There are many cases on record…. One very famous mystic,

Bukkh, used his own name, because he said, "I do not believe in any God. I do not know about him, I do not know what his name is. There are names I have heard, but there is no proof that they are his name. And I am in search of myself, so why not use my own name?" So he would use his own name, and just by using his own name he would drop down into silence.

If you do not have any love for anything else, use your own name. But it is very difficult because you are so condemning toward yourself that you do not have any feeling, you do not have any respect toward yourself. Others may be respectful toward you, but you are not respectful toward yourself.

So the first thing is to find any sound that will be helpful: for example, your lover's name, your beloved's name. If you love a flower, then "rose" will do, anything—any sound that you feel good using, uttering, listening to, from which you feel a certain well-being coming to you. If you cannot find one, then there are some suggestions from traditional sources. "Aum" can be used, "amen" can be used, "Maria" can be used, "Rama" can be used, or Buddha's name, or Mahavira's name, or any name that you have a love for. But a feeling must be there. That is why the master's name can be helpful, if you have the feeling. But feeling is essential!

Intone a sound audibly, then less and less audibly as feeling deepens into this silent harmony. And go on reducing the sound. Intone it more slowly, more inaudibly so that even you have to make an effort to hear it inside. Go on dropping, go on dropping, and you will feel the change. The more sound will drop, the more you will be filled with feeling. When sound disappears, only feeling remains. This feeling cannot be named. It is a love, a deep love, but not toward anyone—this is the difference.

When you use a sound or a word, the love is attached to a label. You say, "Rama, Rama, Rama…." You have a deep feeling for this word, but the feeling is addressed to "Rama," narrowed down to "Rama." When you go on reducing the "Rama," a moment will come when "Rama" disappears, the sound disappears. Now only the feeling remains, the feeling of love—not toward Rama, it is now not addressed. There is simply a feeling of love—not toward anyone, not even toward; there is simply a feeling of love, as if you are in an ocean of love.

When it is not addressed, then it is of the heart. When it is addressed, it is of the head. Love toward someone is through the head; simple love is of the heart. And when love is simple, unaddressed, it becomes prayer. If it is addressed, it is not yet prayer; you are just on the way. That is why I say if you are a Christian you cannot start as a Hindu, you should start as a Christian. If you are a Mohammedan you cannot start as a Christian, you should start as a Mohammedan. But the deeper you go, the less you will be a Mohammedan or a Christian or a Hindu.

Only the start will be Hindu, Mohammedan or Christian. The more you will proceed toward the heart, as the sound will be less and less and feeling more and more, you will be less a Hindu, less a Mohammedan. When the sound disappears, you will simply be a human being—not Hindu, not Mohammedan, not Christian.

It is like the difference between 'sects' and 'religion.' Religion is one, sects are many. Sects help you to begin. If you think that they are the end, then you are finished. They are just the beginning. You have to leave them and go beyond, because the beginning is not the end. In the end there is religion; in the beginning there is just a sect. Use the sect to go toward religion; use the limited to go toward the unlimited; use the finite to go toward the infinite.

Any sound will do. Find your own sound. And when you intone it, you will feel whether you have a loving relationship with it, because the heart will start vibrating. Your whole body will begin to be more sensitive. You will feel as if you are falling into something warm, just like your beloved's lap; something warm begins enveloping you. And this is

a physical feeling also, not simply a mental feeling. If you intone a sound which you love, you will feel a certain warmth around you, inside you. Then the world is not a cold world, it is warm.

If you have gone to a Hindu temple, then you must have heard of the *garbhagriha*—the womb house. The innermost center of the temple is known as *garbha*—the womb. You might not have observed why it is called the womb. If you intone the sound of the temple—and every temple has its own sound, its own mantra, its own *ishta devata*, its own deity, and the related mantra of the deity—if you intone that sound, the same warmth as there is in the womb of the mother is created. That is why the garbha, the womb of the temple, is made just similar to the womb of the mother: round-shaped, almost closed, with only one opening.

When Christians came for the first time to India and discovered Hindu temples, they felt that these temples were really unhygienic—not ventilated at all, with only one little door. But the womb is with only one door and not ventilated at all. That is why the temple was made only with one door, just like a womb, and if you intone that sound, that womb becomes alive. And also it is called the garbha because you can get a new birth there, you can become a new man.

If you intone a sound that you love, that you have feeling for, you will create a sound-womb around you. So it is good not to practice this method under the open sky. You are very weak, you cannot fill the whole sky with your sound. It is better to choose a small room, and if the room is such that it vibrates your sound it is good, it will help you. And if you can choose the same place every day, it will be very good. It becomes charged. If the same sound is repeated every day, every atom, the very space becomes a milieu.

That is why followers of other religions are not allowed in the temples. In Mecca no one can enter if he is not a Mohammedan, and this is good. Nothing is wrong in it, it is because Mecca belongs to a particular science. One who is not a Mohammedan goes there with a sound which will be disturbing to the whole milieu. If a Mohammedan is not allowed into a Hindu temple, there is no insult in it. And all those social reformers who do not know anything about temples, religion and esoteric science, they go on giving slogans, nonsense slogans, and they are disturbing everything.

A Hindu temple is for Hindus because a Hindu temple is a particular place—a created place. For millennia they have been working on it to make it alive, and anyone can disturb it. That disturbance is very dangerous. A temple is not a public place. It is for a particular purpose and for particular people; it is not for visitors. That is why visitors were not allowed in the old days. Now they are allowed because we do not know what we are doing. A visitor should not be allowed. It is not a place to see, to go to for sightseeing. It is a created space filled with particular vibrations.

If it is a Rama temple and you were born in a family where Rama's name has been sacred, loved, then when you enter an alive space which is always filled with Rama's name, even if you do not want to chant, even if you are not using the Rama mantra, you will start chanting. The space all around will press you. Those vibrations all around will hit you, and you will start chanting from deep down. So use a place—a temple is good.

These methods are temple methods. A temple is good, or a mosque or a church. Your own house is not good for these methods, because with so many sounds you have a chaotic space around you and you are not so strong that just by your sound you can change the space. So it is better to go to a certain place which belongs to a certain sound, and then use it. And it is good to go to the same place every day.

By and by you will become powerful. By and by you will drop down from the mind to the heart. Then you can do this method anywhere and the whole cosmos becomes your temple. Then there is no problem. But in the beginning it is good to choose the place, and if you can even choose the

time, exactly the same time every day, it is good because then the temple waits for you. Right at that exact time, the temple waits for you. It is more receptive; it is happy that you have come. And I mean physically; this is not a symbolic thing, but a physical one.

It is just as if you take your meals every day at a particular time. At that particular time your whole body feels the hunger. The body has its own inner clock, it feels the hunger exactly at that time. If you go to sleep every day at a particular time, your whole body gets ready at that particular period. If you change every day your sleeping time and your food time, you are disturbing your body.

Now they say your age will be affected by it. If you go on daily changing your body routine, then if you were going to be alive for eighty years you will be alive only for seventy years. Ten years will be lost. And if you go regularly with the body clock, then if you were going to live for eighty years you will live for ninety very easily. Ten years can be added.

Exactly like this, everything all around you has its own clock, and the world moves in cosmic time. If you enter the temple at exactly the same time every day, the temple is ready for you and you are ready for the temple. These two readinesses meet, and the results are magnified a thousandfold.

Or you can create a small corner in your house. But then do not use that corner for any other purpose, because every purpose has its own vibrations. If you use that corner for a business purpose or you play cards there, that space becomes confused. And now these confusions can even be recorded on mechanical devices; it can be known if the space is confused.

If you can create a corner in your house, a small temple, it is very good. If you can afford a small temple, that is the first thing to be tried. But do not use it for any other purpose. Let it be absolutely private for you, and results will come very soon then.

43 Focus your mind on the tongue.

The seventh sound technique: *With mouth slightly open, keep mind in the middle of the tongue. Or, as breath comes silently in, feel the sound 'HH.'*

Mind can be focused anywhere in the body. Ordinarily, we have focused it in the head, but it can be focused anywhere. And with a change of the focus, your qualities change. For example, in many Eastern countries—Japan, China, Korea—traditionally it has been taught that mind is in the belly, not in the head. And because of this, those who thought that mind is in the belly had different qualities of mind. You cannot have those qualities because you think mind is in the head.

Really, the mind is nowhere. The brain is in the head; the mind is not there. 'Mind' means your focusing. You can focus it anywhere, and once focused it is very difficult to remove it from that point. For example, now psychologists and workers who are doing in-depth human research say that when you are making love your mind must move from the head to the genital area; otherwise your sex will be a frustration. If it remains in the head, you cannot go deep into sex. No orgasm will result, the experience will not be orgasmic. It will not give you a peak. You may produce children, but you will not have known what is the highest peak of love.

You have not known that about which tantra talks or Khajuraho depicts, you cannot. Have you seen Khajuraho? Or if you have not seen Khajuraho, you might have seen pictures of the Khajuraho temple. Then look at the faces, at couples making love. Look at the faces, the faces look divine. They are in the act of sex, but the faces are as ecstatic as any buddha's face. What is happening to them? This sex is not cerebral. They are not making love through the head; they are not thinking about it. They have dropped down from the head. Their focusing has changed.

Because of this dropping from the head, the consciousness has moved to the genital area. The mind is no more. The mind has become no-mind. Their faces have the same ecstasy as a buddha has. This sex has become a meditation. Why? Because the focus has changed. If once you can change the focus of your mind, if you can remove it from the head, the head is relaxed, the face is relaxed. Then all tensions have dissolved. You are not there, the ego is not there.

That is why the more mind becomes intellectual, rational, the less capable it becomes of love, because love needs a different focusing. In love you need a focusing near the heart; in sex you need a focusing near the genital center. If you are doing mathematics, the head is okay. But love is not mathematics and sex is absolutely not. And if the mathematics continues in the head and you are making love, you are simply wasting energy. Then this whole effort will be disgusting.

But mind can be changed. Tantra says there are seven centers, and mind can be changed to any center. Each center has a different functioning. If you concentrate on a particular center, you become a different man.

In Japan there has been a military group, which is just like the *kshatriyas* in India, known as the *samurai*. They are trained to be soldiers, and their first training is to bring the mind down to just two inches below the navel. In Japan this center is called the *hara*. The samurai are trained to bring the mind to the hara. Unless a soldier can bring his mind's focusing to the hara, he is not allowed to go to fight, and this is right. The samurai are the greatest fighters the world has ever known, the greatest warriors; in the world there is no comparison with a samurai. He is a different man, a different being, because his focusing is different.

They say that when you are fighting there is no time. Mind needs time to function; it calculates. If you are attacked and your mind thinks about how to protect, you have missed the point already, you have lost. There is no time. You must function

414

timelessly and mind cannot function timelessly, mind needs time. Howsoever short, mind needs time.

Below the navel there is a center, the hara, which functions timelessly. If the focusing is at the hara and the fighter is fighting, then this fight is intuitive, not intellectual. Before you attack him, he knows. It is a subtle feeling in the hara, not in the head. It is not an inference, it is a psychic telepathy. Before you attack him, before you think of attacking him, the thought has reached him. His hara is hit and he is ready to protect himself. Even before you have attacked, he is in defense, he has protected himself.

Sometimes, if two persons are fighting and both are samurai, defeating the other is a problem. Neither can defeat the other; it is a problem. No one can be declared the winner. In a way it is impossible because you cannot attack the man— before you attack, he knows.

There was one Indian mathematician…. The whole world was wonderstruck because he would not calculate. Ramanujam was his name. You would give him the problem and he would give you the answer immediately. One of England's best mathematicians, Hardy, visited Ramanujam. Hardy was one of the best mathematicians ever born, and he had to work with a particular problem for six hours. But Ramanujam was given the same problem and he answered immediately. There was no possibility for the mind to function in this way, as the mind needs time.

Ramanujam was asked again and again, "How do you do it?" He would say, "I don't know. You give me the problem, and the answer comes to me. It comes from somewhere below. It is not from my head." It was coming from the hara. He was not aware, he was not trained, but this is my feeling: he must have been a Japanese in his previous birth because in India we have not worked much upon the hara.

Tantra says, focus your mind on different centers and the results will be different. This technique is concerned with focusing on the tongue, in the middle of the tongue. *With mouth slightly open* —as if you are going to speak. Not closed, but slightly open as if you are going to speak; not like when you are speaking, but like when you are just going to speak.

Then keep the mind in the middle of the tongue. You will have a very strange feeling, because the tongue has a center just in the middle which controls your thoughts. If you suddenly become aware and you focus on that, your thoughts will stop. Focus as if your whole mind has come to the tongue—just in the middle. Let the mouth be slightly open as if you were going to speak, and then focus the mind as if it is not in the head. Feel it as if it is in the tongue, just in the middle.

The tongue has the center of speech, and thought is speech. What are you doing when you are thinking? Talking within. Can you think anything without talking within? You are alone; you are not talking to anyone, you are thinking. What are you doing while you are thinking? Talking within, talking to yourself. Your tongue is involved. Next time, while you are thinking, be aware: feel your tongue. It is vibrating as if you are talking to someone else. Then feel it again, and you can feel that the vibrations are centered in the middle. They arise from the middle and then they spread all over the tongue.

Thinking is talking within. If you can bring your total consciousness, your mind, to the center of the tongue, thinking stops. So those who have been practicing silence, they are simply practicing not talking. If you stop talking outwardly, then you will become very deeply aware of talking inside. And if you remain completely silent for one month or two months or one year, not talking, you will feel your tongue vibrating violently. You are not feeling it because you go on talking and the vibrations are released. But even now, if you stop and become conscious while thinking, you will feel your tongue vibrating a little. Stop your tongue completely and then try to think—you cannot think. Stop your tongue completely as if it is frozen; do not allow it to move. You cannot think then.

The center is just in the middle, so bring your mind there. *With mouth slightly open, keep mind in the middle of the tongue. Or, as breath comes silently in, feel the sound 'HH.'*

This is the second technique. It is just similar: *Or, as breath comes silently in, feel the sound 'HH.'*

With the first technique your thinking will stop, you will feel a solidity within—as if you have become solid. When thoughts are not there you become immovable; thoughts are the inner movement. And when thoughts are not there and you have become immovable, you have become part of the eternal, which only appears to move but which is immovable, which remains unmoved.

In thoughtlessness you become part of the eternal, the unmoved. With thought you are part of the movement, because nature is movement. The world is movement, that is why we have called it the sansara, the wheel—it is moving and moving and moving. The world is movement and the hidden, the ultimate, is unmoved, unmoving, immovable.

It is just like a wheel that is moving, but a wheel is moving on something which never moves. A wheel can move only because in the center there is something which never moves, which remains unmoved. The world moves and the transcendental remains unmoved. If your thoughts stop, suddenly you drop from this world to the other. With the movement stopped inside, you become part of the eternal—that which never changes.

Or, as breath comes silently in, feel the sound 'HH.' Open your mouth slightly, as if you are going to speak. Then inhale, and be aware of the sound which is created by inhaling. It is just 'HH'—whether you are exhaling or inhaling. You are not to make the sound, you are just to feel the incoming breath on your tongue. It is very silent. You will feel 'HH.' It will be very silent, very slightly audible. You have to be very alert to be aware of it. But do not try to create it. If you create it, you have

missed the point. Your created sound will be of no help, it is the natural sound that happens when you inhale or exhale.

But the technique says while inhaling, not exhaling—because while exhaling you will go out, and with the sound *you* will go out, while the effort is to go in. So while inhaling, hear the sound 'HH.' Go on inhaling and go on feeling the sound 'HH.' Sooner or later you will feel that the sound is not being created only at the tongue, it is being created in the throat also. But then it is very, very inaudible. With very deep alertness you can become aware of it.

Start from the tongue, then by and by be alert; go on feeling it. You will hear it in the throat, then you will start hearing it in the heart. And when it reaches the heart, you have gone beyond mind. All these techniques are just to give you a bridge from where you can move from thought to no-thought, from mind to no-mind, from the surface to the center.

---

44 A method for those with a sensitive ear.

The eighth sound technique: *Center on the sound 'AUM' without any 'A' or 'M.'*

Center on the sound 'AUM'—A-U-M, AUM—*without any 'A' or 'M.'* Just the 'U' remains. This is a difficult technique, but for some it may be suitable, particularly for those who work with sound: musicians, poets, those who have a very sensitive ear, for them this technique can be helpful. For others, those who have no sensitive ear, this is very difficult because it is very delicate.

You have to intone aum, and you have to feel in this aum three sounds separately: A-U-M. Intone aum, and in the sound you have to feel three sounds—A-U-M. They are there, infused together. A very delicate ear can be aware, can hear A-U-M separately while intoning. They are separate—very close, but separate. If you cannot hear them separately, then this technique cannot be done. Your ears will have to be trained for it.

In Japan, particularly in Zen, they train the ears first. They have a method of training the ears. The wind is blowing outside—it has a sound. The master will say, "Concentrate on it. Feel all the nuances, the changes: when the sound is angry, when the sound is furious, when the sound is compassionate, when the sound is loving, when the sound is strong, when the sound is delicate. Feel the nuances of the sound. The wind is blowing through the trees—feel it. The river is running—feel the nuances."

For months together the seeker, the meditator, will be sitting by the side of the river, listening to it. It has different sounds. Everything is changing. In the rain it will be flooded; it will be very much alive, overflowing. The sounds will be different. In the summer it will be reduced to nothingness, sounds will cease. But there will be inaudible sounds if one is listening, if you listen. All the year round the river will be changing, and one has to be aware.

In Hermann Hesse's book *Siddhartha*, Siddhartha lives with a boatman. And there is no one, just the river, the boatman and Siddhartha. And the boatman is a very silent man. He has lived all his life with the river. He has become silent, he rarely speaks. Whenever Siddhartha feels lonely, the boatman tells him to go to the river, to listen to the river. It is better than listening to human words.

And then by and by, Siddhartha is attuned to the river. Then he begins to feel its moods—the river changes moods. Sometimes it is friendly and sometimes it is not, and sometimes it is singing and sometimes it is weeping and crying, and sometimes there is laughter and sometimes there is sadness. And then he begins to feel the slight, delicate differences. His ear becomes attuned.

So in the beginning you may feel it to be difficult, but try. Intone aum, go on intoning it, feeling A-U-M. Three sounds are combined together in it: aum is a synthesis of three sounds. Once you start

feeling them differently, then drop 'A' and 'M.' Then you cannot say aum: 'A' will be dropped, 'M' will be dropped. Then 'U' will remain. Why? What will happen? The real thing is not the mantra. It is not A-U-M or the dropping. The real thing is your sensitivity.

First you become sensitive of three sounds, which is very difficult. And when you become so sensitive that you can drop the 'A' and 'M' and only the middle sound remains, in this effort you will lose your mind. You will be so much engrossed in it, so deeply attentive to it, so sensitive to it, that you will forget to think. And if you think, you cannot do this.

This is just an indirect way to bring you out of your head. So many ways have been tried, and they look very simple. You wonder, "What can happen? Nothing will happen by such simple methods." But miracles happen, because it is just indirect. Your mind is being focused on something very subtle. If you focus, you cannot go on thinking; mind will drop. Suddenly one day you will become aware, and you will wonder what has happened.

In Zen they use koans. One of the famous koans they tell to the beginner is, "Go and try to hear the sound of one hand. You can create a sound with two hands. If one hand can create a sound, hear it."

One small boy was serving a Zen master. He would see many people coming. They would come to the master, put their head at his feet, and then they would ask the master to tell them something to meditate on. He would give them a koan. The boy was just doing some work for the master, he was serving him. He was just nine or ten years of age.

Seeing every day many people coming and going, one day he also came very seriously, put his head at the master's feet, and then asked him, "Give me some koan, some object for meditation."

The master laughed, but the boy was very serious, so the master said, "Okay! Try to hear the sound of one hand. And when you have heard it, then come to me and tell me."

The boy tried and tried. He couldn't sleep the

whole night. In the morning he came and he said, "I have heard. It is the sound of the wind blowing through the trees."

The master said, "But where is the hand involved in it? Go again and try." So he would come every day. He would find some sound and then he would come, and the master would say, "This is also not it. Go on trying, go on trying!"

Then one day the boy didn't come. The master waited and waited, and then he told his other disciples to go and find out what had happened—it seemed the boy had heard. So they went around.

He was sitting under a tree, absorbed—just a newborn buddha. They came back and they said, "But we are afraid to disturb the boy. He is looking just like a newborn buddha. It seems he has heard the sound."

So the master came, put his head at the boy's feet and asked him, "Have you heard? It seems you have heard."

The boy said, "Yes, but it is soundlessness."

How did this boy develop? His sensitivity developed. He tried every sound, he listened attentively. Attention developed. He would not sleep. The whole night he would listen for what is the sound of one hand. He was not so intellectual as you are, so he never thought that there cannot be any sound of one hand. If the koan is given to you, you are not going to try. You will say, "What nonsense! There cannot be any sound with one hand."

But the boy tried. The master had said there must be something in it, so he tried. He was a simple boy, so whenever he would hear something, whenever he would feel this was something new, he would come again. But by this process his sensitivity developed. He became attentive, alert, aware. He became one-pointed. He was in search, and the mind dropped because the master said, "If you go on thinking you may miss. Sometimes there is the sound which is of one hand. Be so alert that you do not miss it."

He tried and tried. There is no sound of one hand, but that was just an indirect method to create sensitivity, awareness. And one day, suddenly, everything disappeared. He was so attentive that only attention was there, so sensitive that only sensitivity was there, so aware—not aware of something, but simply aware! And then he said, "I have heard it, but it is soundlessness. It is soundlessness!" But you have to be trained to be attentive, to be alert.

This is just a method to make you very delicately aware of the subtle nuances of sound. Just doing this, you will forget aum. Not only will 'A' drop, not only will 'M' drop, but one day suddenly you will also drop, and there will be soundlessness, and you will be a newborn buddha sitting under a tree.

CHAPTER 30

Surrendering in sex and surrendering to a master

◆

If tantra teaches to be in the middle, how can one understand the difference between indulgence and repression?

Is there any connection between opening up to a master and opening up in sex?

The first question:

Last night You discussed the attitude of total acceptance as the basic ground for all tantric *sadhana*, or spiritual practice. If I remember correctly, on another day You said that the science of tantra teaches to be in the middle in everything, being free from the extremes in life. In this reference, explain how one can come to understand the difference between indulgence and repression in one's sex life.

Accepting the total life means the middle path. If you deny, you move to the opposite extreme. Denial is extreme. If you deny anything, you deny it for something; then you move to one extreme. If one denies sex, he will move to *brahmacharya*, celibacy—to the other extreme. If you deny brahmacharya, you will move to indulgence—to the other extreme. The moment you deny, you have accepted the extreme path.

Acceptance of totality is to be automatically in the middle. You are neither for something nor against something. You have not chosen, you are just floating in the stream. You are not moving toward a goal—you have no choice. You are in a let-go.

Tantra believes in a deep let-go. When you choose, your ego comes in. When you choose, your will comes in. When you choose, you are moving against the whole universe—you have your own choice. When you choose, you are not choosing the universal flow: you are standing aloof, isolated; you are like an island. You are trying to be yourself against the whole flux of life.

Nonchoosing means you are not to decide where life goes. You allow life to move, to take you with it, and you have no fixed goal. If you have a fixed goal, you are bound to choose. Life's goal is your goal. You are not moving against life; you have no ideas of your own against life. You leave yourself, you surrender yourself to the life force itself. This is what tantra means by total acceptance.

And once you accept life in its totality things start happening, because this total acceptance frees you from your ego point. Your ego point is the problem, because of it you create problems. There are no problems in life itself; existence is problemless. You are the problem and you are the creator of the problem, and you create problems out of everything. Even if you meet God, you will create problems out of him. Even if you reach paradise, you will create problems out of paradise—because you are the original source of the problems. You are not going to surrender. This nonsurrendering ego is the source of all problems.

Tantra says that it is not a question of achieving something, it is not a question of achieving brahmacharya. If you achieve brahmacharya against sex, your brahmacharya will remain basically sexual. Two extremes, howsoever opposite, are parts of one whole—two aspects of one thing. If you choose one, you have chosen the other also. The other will be hidden now, repressed. What does repression mean? Choosing one extreme against the other, which is a basic part of it.

You choose brahmacharya against sex, but what is brahmacharya? It is just the reversal of sex energy. You have chosen brahmacharya, but you have also chosen sex with it. Now brahmacharya will be on the surface, and deep down there will be sex. You will be disturbed because your choice will create the disturbance. You can choose only one pole, but the other pole follows automatically. And you are against the other pole, so now you will be disturbed.

Tantra says, do not choose: be choiceless. Once you understand this, the question will never arise of what is indulgence and what is repression. Then there is no repression and no indulgence. The question arises only because you are still choosing. There are people who come to me and they say, "We will accept life, but if we accept life when will brahmacharya happen?" They are ready to be in total acceptance, but the readiness is false, just superficial. Deep down they are still clinging to the extremes.

They want brahmacharya—celibacy. They have not achieved it by fighting with sex, so when they hear me they think, "As we have not been able to achieve it through fighting, now we should achieve it through acceptance." But the achieving mind, the motivated mind, the greedy mind, is there—and the goal is there, the choice is there.

If you have something to achieve, you cannot accept the totality; the acceptance is not total. Then you are also trying acceptance as a technique to achieve something. Acceptance means: now you leave that achieving mind, that motivated mind that is always for something, hankering for something—you leave it! You allow life to flow freely, just as the wind is flowing through the trees. You allow life to be free, to move freely through you; you have no resistance. Wherever it leads, you are ready to move. You have no goal. If you have any goal then you will have to resist life, then you will have to fight it.

If a tree has some goal, some leaning, some idea, then it cannot allow the wind to move freely through it. If it wants to go south, then the wind which is forcing it north will be the enemy.

If you have some goal, you cannot accept life as a friend. Your goal creates the enmity. If you expect something out of life, you are forcing yourself on life, you are not allowing life to happen to you. Tantra says, things happen when you do not expect them, things happen when you do not force them, things happen when you are not hankering after them.

But this is a consequence, not a result. And be clearly aware of the difference between 'consequence' and 'result.' A result is consciously desired; a consequence is a by-product. For example, if I say to you that if you are playing happiness will be the consequence, you will try it for a result. You go and you play, and you are waiting for the result of happiness. But I told you it will be the consequence, not the result.

Consequence means that if you are really in the play, happiness will happen. If you constantly think about happiness, then it has to be a result; it will never happen. A result is from a conscious effort; a consequence is just a by-product. If you are deep in play, you will be happy. But the very expectation, the conscious longing for happiness, will not allow you to be deep in play. The longing for the result will become the barrier and you will not be happy.

Happiness is not a result, it is a consequence. If I tell you that if you love you will be happy, happiness will be a consequence, not a result. If you think that because you want to be happy you must love, nothing will come out of it. The whole thing will be bogus because one cannot love for any result. Love happens! There is no motivation behind it.

If there is motivation, it is not love. It may be anything else. If I am motivated and I think that because I long for happiness I will love you, this love will be false. And because it will be false, happiness will not result out of it. It will not come; that is impossible. But if I love you without any motivation, happiness follows like a shadow.

Tantra says, acceptance will be followed by transformation, but do not make acceptance a technique for transformation. It is not. Do not long for transformation—only then does transformation happen. If you desire it, your very desire is the hindrance. Then there is no question of what indulgence is and what repression is.

This question comes to the mind only because you are not ready to accept the whole. Accept it, let it be indulgence and accept it. If you accept it, you will be thrown to the middle. Or let it be repression and accept it. If there is acceptance, you will be thrown to the middle. Through acceptance you cannot remain with the extreme. 'Extreme' means denial of something—accepting something and denying something. 'Extreme' means being for something and against something. The moment you accept whatsoever is the case you will be thrown to the middle, you will not remain with the extreme.

So forget any intellectual understanding of what repression is and what indulgence is. It is nonsense and it will not lead you anywhere. Just accept, wherever you are. If you are in indulgence, accept it. Why be afraid of it?

But there is a problem. If you are in indulgence, you can remain in indulgence only if you are simultaneously trying to transcend it. That gives a good feeling to the ego: you can feel good and you can postpone. You know this is not going to be forever. You feel, "Today I am indulgent, but tomorrow I will be beyond it." The tomorrow helps you to be in indulgence today. You know that "Today I am drinking alcohol or smoking, but this is not going to be for all my life. I know this is bad, and tomorrow I am going to leave it."

That hope for tomorrow helps you to indulge today, and that is a good trick. Those who want to indulge, they must have great ideals. Those ideals give you opportunity. Then you need not feel very guilty about whatsoever you are doing because in the future everything is going to be okay; this is just for the moment. This is a trick of the mind. So those who indulge, they always talk of nonindulgence. Those who indulge, they go to the masters who are against it. And you can see a deep relationship....

If you are after riches, money, power, you will always worship someone who is against riches—the ascetic. One who has renounced will be your ideal. A rich society can worship and respect only one who has renounced riches. Look around and you will see. If you are indulging in sex, you must respect a person who has gone beyond it, who has become a brahmachari. You will worship him. He is the ideal; he is your future. You are thinking that someday you are going to be like this man. You worship him.

And if one day some rumor comes to you that he is indulging in sex, the respect is gone, because you cannot respect yourself. You are so self-condemning of whatsoever you are that if you find that your master is just like you, the respect is gone. He must be just the opposite. Then he gives you hope. Then he can lead you to the opposite end. Then you can follow him.

So there is always a very deep relationship between the followers and the master. You will always see them on opposite poles: the follower will be just on the opposite pole, and he is a follower only because of this. If you are obsessed with food, then you can respect only a person who goes for long fasting. He is "the miracle." You hope someday to attain the same. He is your future. You can worship him and respect him. He is the image, but this image helps you to be whatsoever you are; it is not going to change you. The very effort to change, the very idea to change, is the hindrance. This is the insight of tantra.

Tantra says, whatsoever you are, accept it. Do not create any ideals. They are dreams—and false. Accept whatsoever is. Do not call it good or bad, do not try to justify it or rationalize it. Live in the moment and see that this is the case. Remain with the fact and accept it. This is difficult—very difficult, arduous. Why is it so difficult? Because then your ego is shattered. Then you know that you are a sexual animal. Then the high ideal of brahmacharya cannot help your ego at all. Then you know that you are ninety-nine percent an animal… and that one percent I leave you just not to shock you too much.

With the ideals of Mahavira, Buddha, Krishna, Christ, you feel you are ninety-nine percent divine and only one percent is lacking. So sooner or later, by the grace of God, you will attain it. You feel happy as you are. That will not help. That will not help at all. That can help only to postpone the real problem, the real crisis, and unless you face that crisis you will never be transformed. One has to pass through it; one has to suffer it. But only the facticity of life leads you toward the truth. Fictions will not help.

So remain with the fact. Whatsoever you are—animal or whatever—is okay. Sex is there, anger is there, greed is there: okay, so it is there. It is so, such is the case. The universe happens to you in this way; you have found yourself in this way. It is how life has made you; it is how life is forcing you, leading you to somewhere.

Relax and allow life to lead you. What is the difficulty in relaxing? The difficulty is that if you relax, you cannot maintain the ego. Ego can be maintained only in resistance. When you say no, ego is strengthened. When you say yes, ego simply disappears.

That is why it is so difficult to say yes to anything. Even in ordinary things it is so difficult to say yes. We want to say no. The ego, the "I," feels good only when it is fighting. If you are fighting with someone else, it is good, the ego feels good. If you are fighting with yourself the ego feels even better, because to fight with someone else creates more problems around you. When you are fighting with yourself, there is no problem around you. When you are fighting with someone else, the society will create problems for you. When you are fighting with yourself, the whole society will worship you. It is good because you are not harming anyone.

And really, if you are someone who is harming yourself, if you are not allowed to harm yourself you will harm others. Otherwise where will that energy move? So society is always happy with those idiots who are harming themselves. The society feels good because their violence is directed back, they will not do any harm.

That is why we call them *sadhus*—the good ones. They are good ones because they can do much harm—they are doing it—but they are doing it to themselves. They are suicidal. A killer, a murderer, can become suicidal if he turns against himself, so the society feels good, unburdened of a murderer if he becomes suicidal. The society pays respect, appreciates him. But the person remains the same—he remains violent. Now he is violent with himself, or he remains greedy but he talks of nongreed.

But look! Try to understand the talk of nongreed. The base is always greed. They say that if you are nongreedy, only then will you achieve paradise. And what is to be gained in paradise? Everything that greed would like.

So be nongreedy to achieve paradise. If you are not a celibate, you will not go to heaven. And what are you going to achieve in heaven? All that you condemn here on earth. Then beautiful women are allowed, and there is no comparison—because anyone who is beautiful on earth will become ugly. This is what the *shastras,* scriptures, say. And the women that are in heaven never become old, they remain fixed at the age of sixteen. So be celibate here so that you can indulge there.

But what type of logic is this? The motivation remains the same. The motivation remains exactly the same, only the objects change, the time sequence changes. You are postponing your desires for the future. This is a bargain.

Tantra says, try to understand this whole working of the mind, and then it is good not to fight, then it is good to flow as you are and accept it. We are afraid because if we accept, then how will we change? Tantra says, acceptance is transcendence.

You have tried fighting and you have not changed. Look at your whole life, analyze it, and if you are honest you will find that you have not changed a single bit, not an inch. Move back toward your childhood. Analyze your whole life, and no matter what you may be talking and thinking, the exact, actual life has remained the same. And you have been fighting continuously. Nothing happens out of it.

So now try tantra. Tantra says, do not fight; no one ever changes with fight. Accept! Then there is no question of what is indulgence and what is repression, and what is brahmacharya and what is this and that. Whatsoever is, you accept it and flow with it. You dissolve your ego resistance, you relax into the existence and go wherever it leads. If the destiny of the existence is that you are meant to be an animal, then, says tantra, be an animal.

What will happen out of it and how does it happen? Tantra says, total transformation happens —because once you accept, the inner division dissolves, you become one. Then there are not two in you—the saint and the animal, the saint repressing the animal and the animal throwing the saint aside every moment. Then there is no two in you, you become one.

And this oneness gives energy. All your energy is wasted in inner fight and conflict. This acceptance makes you one. Now there is no animal who is to be condemned and no saint who is to be appreciated. You are whatsoever you are. You have accepted it, you have relaxed with it, so your energy becomes one. Then you are a whole and not divided against yourself.

This wholeness is an alchemical transformation. With this wholeness you have energy. Now you are not wasting your life. There is no inner conflict; you are at ease within. This energy which you gain through nonconflict becomes your awareness.

Energy can move in two dimensions. If it moves in fight, you are wasting it every day. If it accumulates and there is no fight, a moment comes just like when you go on heating water to a hundred degrees: then the water becomes something else, it evaporates. Then it is no more liquid, it becomes a gas. It will not become transformed at ninety-nine degrees. It will become transformed only at a hundred degrees.

The same happens inwards. You are wasting your energy every day, and the evaporating point never comes. It cannot come because energy is not accumulated at all. Once the inner fight is not there, energy goes on accumulating and you feel more and more strong.

But not the ego, the ego feels strong only when fighting. When there is no fight, the ego becomes impotent. You feel strong, and that "you" is a totally different thing. You cannot know about it unless you are whole. Ego exists with fragments, division. This "you"—the self, or what we call the *atma*—exists only when there is no division, no inner fight. 'Atma' means the whole; 'self' means the undivided energy.

Once this energy is undivided, it goes on accumulating. You are producing it every day, life energy is produced in you, but you are wasting it in fight. This same energy comes to a point where it becomes awareness—this is automatic, tantra says this is automatic. Once you know how to be whole, you will become more and more aware, and the day will come when your total energy will be transformed into awareness.

When the energy is transformed into awareness many things happen, because then the energy cannot move to sex. When it can move to a higher dimension, it will not move to a lower dimension. Your energy goes on moving to the lower dimension because there is no higher for you. You do not have the level of energy where it can move into the higher, so it moves into sex. It moves into sex and you become afraid of it, so you create the ideal of brahmacharya and you become divided. Then you become less and less energetic. You are wasting energy.

This is a very potent experience—that when you are weak you feel more sexual. It looks absolutely absurd in biological terms, because biology will say that when you are more potent you will feel more sexual. But this is not the case.

When you are weak, ill, you will feel more sexual. When you are healthy and a subtle well-being is there, you will not feel so sexual.

And the quality of sex will also be different. When you are weak, the sexuality will be a sort of disease and a vicious circle will be created. Through sex you will become more weak, and the more weak you become the more sexual you will feel. And the sex will become cerebral, it will move into your head.

When you are healthy, when a well-being is there, when you feel blissful, relaxed, you are not so sexual. Then even if sex happens, it is not a disease. Rather, it is an overflowing. A totally different quality is there. When sex is an overflowing, it is just love expressing itself through bioenergy. It is creating a deep sharing, a deep contact through bioenergy. It is a part of love.

When you are weak and sex is not overflowing it is a violence against yourself, and when it is a violence against yourself it is never love. A weak person can have sex, but his sex is never love. It is more or less rape, and rape to both the parties; to himself also it is a rape. But then a vicious circle is created: the more weak he feels, the more sexual he feels.

But why does this happen? Biology has no explanation for it, but tantra has an explanation. Tantra says that sex is an antidote against death. Sex means life for society. You may die, but life will continue. So whenever you feel weak, feel that death is near, then sex will become very important because you may die at any moment. Your energy layer has gone down. You may die at any moment, so indulge in sex so someone can live. Life should go on.

For tantra, old men are more sexual than young men. And this is a very deep insight. Young men are more sexually potent, but not so sexual; old men are less sexually potent, but more sexual. So if

we can enter an old man's mind, then we can know what is happening.

As far as sex energy is concerned, it is less in old men, more in young men. But as far as sexuality is concerned—sexuality means thinking about sex—it is more in old men than in young men. Death is coming near and sex is the antidote to death, so now the weakening energy would like to produce someone. Life must continue. Life is not concerned with you, life is concerned with itself. This is a vicious circle.

And the same happens in the reverse order also. If you are overflowing with energy, sex becomes less and less important and love becomes more and more important. And then sex can happen just as a part of love, as a deep sharing. The deepest sharing can be of bioenergy because that is the life force. To whomsoever you love you want to give something. Giving is part of love, in love you give things. The greatest gift can be of your life energy. In love, sex becomes a deep gift of bioenergy, of life. You are giving a part of yourself.

Really, in every act of sex you are giving yourself totally. Then a different circle is created; the more you feel love, the more you become strong. The more you feel love, the more you share love, then the more strong you become because in love the ego is dissolved. In love you have to flow with life.

You need not flow with life in politics. Rather, you will be a fool if you flow with life in politics, because there you have to force yourself against life; only then can you rise in politics. If you are doing business you will be a fool if you flow with life. You will be nowhere, because you have to fight, you have to compete, you have to be violent. The more violent and the more mad, the more you will succeed there. It is a struggle.

Only in love is there no competition, no fight, no violence. You succeed in love only when you surrender. So love is the only antiworldly thing in the world, the only nonworldly thing in the world. And if you are in love you will become more a whole, undivided; more energy will be accumulated. The more the energy, the less will be the sexuality. And a moment comes when the energy comes to a point where transformation happens, and energy becomes awareness. Sex disappears, and only a loving kindness, a compassion, remains.

Buddha has a glow of loving compassion; this is sex energy transformed. But you cannot achieve it through fight, because fight creates division and division makes you more sexual. This is the insight of tantra—absolutely different from whatsoever you may have been thinking about sex and brahmacharya. Only through tantra does a real brahmacharya, a real purity and innocence, happen. But then it is not a result, it is a consequence. It follows total acceptance.

The second question:

My mind thinks that it is anxious to receive Your message, yet toward the end I find myself resisting and getting tired. I suspect that if I were open sexually I would allow myself to receive without any closing. Is there any connection between opening to a master and opening up in sex? My background gives a negative and passive meaning to surrender. I know I will not go deeper unless I am able to overcome this negativity that seems to be engraved in my psyche. Is surrender possible when the opposite is planted so deeply?

Yes, there is a connection between surrender and sex, because sex is the first surrender, a biological surrender, which you can experience easily. What does surrender mean? It means to be open, unafraid, vulnerable. It means allowing the other to enter you. Biologically, naturally, sex is the basic experience where without any effort you allow someone to enter you, or someone to be so deeply close to you that you are not armored against him. You are not resisting, not holding yourself back, but you are flowing...relaxed, not afraid, not thinking of the future, of the result, of the consequences, but just being in the moment. Even if

death occurs you will accept it.

In deep love, lovers have always felt that this is the right moment to die. And if death occurs, then even death can be welcomed in this moment. They are open—even for death they are open. If you are open for life, you will be open for death. If you are closed for life, you will be closed for death.

Those who are afraid of death are basically afraid of life. They have not lived, that is why they are so afraid of death. And the fear is natural. If you have not lived at all you are bound to be afraid of death, because death will deprive you of the opportunity to live and you have not lived yet. So if death comes, then when will you live?

One who has lived deeply is not afraid of death. He is fulfilled, and if death comes he can welcome it, accept it. Now whatsoever life can give, life has given. Whatsoever can be known in life, he has known it. Now he can move into death easily. He would like to move into death so that he can know something unknown, something new. In sex, in love, you are fearless. You are not fighting for something in the future; this very moment is paradise, this very moment is eternal.

But when I say this, I do not necessarily mean that you have experienced it through sex. If you are afraid, resisting, then in sex you can have a biological release, a sexual release, but you will not attain to the ecstasy tantra talks about.

Wilhelm Reich says you have not known sex at all unless in sex you can attain a deep orgasm. It is not only a release of sex energy, your whole body must become relaxed. Then the sex experience is not localized at the sex center, but it spreads all over the body. Your every cell is bathed in it, and you have a peak—a peak in which you are not a body. If you cannot attain a peak in sex, a peak in which you are not a body, you have not known sex at all. That is why Wilhelm Reich says a very paradoxical thing: he says sex is spiritual.

This is what tantra says, and the meaning is that in deep sex you will not be a body at all; you will become just a spirit that is hovering. Your body will be left far behind; you will have forgotten it completely. It will be no more. You will not be part of the material world, you will have become immaterial. Only then is there orgasm. That is what tantra says about *sambhog*—intercourse.

There comes a total relaxation, a feeling that now you are fulfilled, a feeling that there is no need to desire anything. Unless this feeling happens to you in sex—this feeling of desirelessness—you have not known sex at all. You may have produced children, but that is easy—and a different thing.

Only man can achieve this spirituality in sex; otherwise sex is just an animal instinct. But when teachers or monks condemn sex, you nod your head that they are right. When tantra says something it is difficult to believe in it because it is not your experience. That is why tantra couldn't become a universal message yet. But the future is good—because the more man will become wise and understanding, the more tantra will be felt and understood.

Only within these hundred years has psychology laid foundations for a world which will be tantric. But you nod your head with someone who is condemning sex because you also have the same experience. You know that nothing happens in it, and after sex you feel depressed. That is why there is so much condemnation. Every time you move into it you feel depressed, later on you repent.

Tantra, Wilhelm Reich, Freud and others who know, agree absolutely that if you achieve an orgasm in sex the glow will last for hours afterwards. You will feel absolutely different...without any worries, without any tensions. Euphoria will result, they say; ecstasy will be there. And that ecstasy happens only when there is really a let-go—when you are not holding yourself back, you are not fighting; you are just moving with the life energy.

Life energy has two layers, and it will be good to understand this. I was talking about breath, and I told you that breath was something like a link between your voluntary system and your non-voluntary system. In your body the major part is nonvoluntary. The blood circulates, and you are not asked to do anything. You cannot do anything, it just goes on circulating. Only during these last three hundred years could man know that blood circulates. Before that it was thought that blood just filled the body—not that it was circulating, because you cannot feel its circulation. It goes on working without you, without your knowledge. It is nonvoluntary.

You eat food, then the body starts working. Beyond your mouth you are not needed. The moment food goes beyond your mouth the body takes it, the nonvoluntary system goes on working on it. And it is good that it works this way. If it were left to you, you would create a mess. It is such a great work that if you had to do it you would not be able to do anything else. If you had taken a cup of tea, it would be enough to keep you engaged the whole day—to work it out, to transform it into blood. And the work is so much.

The body works nonvoluntarily, but there are a few things you can do voluntarily. I can move my hand, but I cannot move the blood that moves in the hand. I cannot do anything directly with the bone that moves in the hand. I cannot do anything with the system that works, but I can move my hand. I can move my body, but I cannot do whatsoever goes on within it, I cannot interfere. I can jump, I can run, I can sit, I can lie down, but inside I cannot do anything. Just on the surface I am allowed freedom.

Sex is a very mysterious phenomenon. You start it, but a moment comes when you are no more. Sex is started as a voluntary thing, then there is a limit. If you cross that limit you cannot come back; if you do not cross that limit you can come back. So sex is both voluntary and nonvoluntary. There is a limit up to which your mind will be needed. But if you do not lose your mind, your head, your reason, your consciousness, your religion, your philosophy, your way of life, if you do not lose your mind, then the boundary will not be crossed and you will be experiencing sex in the voluntary realm.

This is what is happening. Then after sex you will feel depressed, against it—and you will be thinking of renouncing life and taking a vow against sex. Of course, these vows will not go on for long. Within twenty-four hours you will be okay and ready to move again into sex. But it becomes a repetition and the whole thing seems futile. You accumulate energy, then you throw it—and nothing results out of it. And this is a long boredom, a drab thing. That is why monks and teachers who are against sex appeal to you: they are talking about something you can understand.

But you have not known the nonvoluntary sex, the deepest biological dimension. You have not touched it, and you always come back from the limit because that limit creates fear. Beyond that limit your ego will not be, beyond that limit you will not be. The sex energy will take hold of you, it will possess you. Then you will be doing something which you cannot control.

Unless you can move to this uncontrolled phenomenon, you cannot achieve orgasm. And once you know this uncontrolled life energy, you are no more in it. You have become just a wave in a great ocean, and things are just happening. You are not forcing them to happen.

Really, you are not active—you have become passive. In the beginning you are active, and then a moment comes when you become passive. And when you become passive, only then does orgasm happen. If you have known it then you can understand many things. Then you can understand religious surrender also. Then you can understand the surrender of a disciple to a master. Then you can understand the surrender of someone to the existence itself. But if you do not know any surrender it is difficult even to conceive of what it means.

So it is right: sex is deeply related with surrender. If you have known deep sex you will be more capable of surrendering, because you have known a deep pleasure that follows surrender, you have known a bliss that comes as a shadow of surrender.

Then you can trust.

Sex is biological surrender. *Samadhi*—cosmic consciousness—is existential surrender. Through sex you touch life. Through samadhi, ecstasy, you touch existence, you move even deeper than life; the basic existence is touched. Through sex you move from yourself to another person; in samadhi you move from yourself to the whole, to the cosmos.

Tantra is, if you will allow me, "cosmic sex"! It is a falling in love with the whole cosmos, it is a surrender toward the whole cosmos. And you have to be passive. To a limit you have to be active, but beyond that limit you are not needed; you are a hindrance then. Then leave it to the life force, leave it to existence.

The second thing: if you go on thinking about surrender as negative and passive, nothing is wrong in it. It is passive and negative, but the negativity and the passivity is nothing condemnable. In our minds, the moment we hear the word 'negative' some condemnation enters, the moment we hear 'passive' some condemnation enters—because for the ego both of these are deaths.

Nothing is wrong in being passive. Passivity is a way to be in deep contact with the universe. And you cannot be active with it—that is the difference between religion and science. Science is active with the universe, religion is passive with the universe. Science is just like the male mind—active, violent, forcing; religion is a feminine mind—open, passive, receptive. Receptivity is always passive. And truth is not to be created, it is to be received.

You are not going to create the truth. The truth is already there. You have to receive it. You have to become the host and then the truth will become your guest. And a host has to be passive. You have to be like a womb to receive it, but your mind is trained for activity—to be active, to do something—and this is the realm where whatsoever you do will become a hindrance. Do not do—just be! This is what passivity means: do not do anything. Just be, and allow that which is already there to happen to you. You are not needed creatively, actively, to do something. You are needed just to receive. Be passive; do not interfere. Nothing is wrong with passivity.

Poetry happens when you are passive. Even the greatest discoveries of science have happened in passivity. But the attitude of science is active. Even the greatest things in science happen only when the scientist is passive, just waiting, not doing anything. And religion is basically passive.

What is Buddha doing when he is meditating? Our language, our terms, give a false impression. When we say Buddha is meditating, it appears, because of the terms used, that he is doing something. But meditation means not doing. If you are doing something, nothing will happen.

But all doing is just like sex: in the beginning you have to be active, then a moment comes when activity ceases and you have to be passive. When I say "Buddha is meditating," I mean Buddha is no more. He is not doing anything, he is just passive— a host waiting, just waiting. And when you are waiting for the unknown, you cannot even expect anything. You do not really know what is going to happen, because if you know then the waiting becomes impure and the desire enters. You do not know anything.

All that you had known has ceased, all the known has dropped. The mind is not functioning, it is just simply awaiting, and then everything happens to you. The whole universe falls into you, the whole universe enters from all sides into you. All the barriers are withdrawn. You are not withholding yourself.

Nothing is wrong with passivity. Rather, your activity is the problem. But we are trained for activity because we are trained for violence, struggle, conflict. And it is good as far as it goes, because in the world you cannot be passive. In the world you have to be active, fighting, forcing your way. But that which is so helpful in the world is not helpful when you move toward a deeper existence. Then you have to reverse your steps. Be active if you are

moving in politics, in society, for riches or for power. Be inactive if you are moving into God, into religion, into meditation. Passivity is the way there.

And nothing is wrong about the negative either. 'Negative' only means that something has to be dropped. For example, if I want to create space in this room, what am I going to do? What is the process to create space? Can I bring space from outside and fill this room? I cannot bring space from outside. The space is already here—that is why it is a room—but it is filled with people or furniture or things, so I take the things and people out of it. Then the space is discovered, not brought. It was already here, but filled. So I do a negative process, I empty it.

Negativity means emptying yourself, not doing something positive, because that which you are trying to discover is already there. Just throw out the furniture. Thoughts are the furniture in the mind. Just throw them out and the mind becomes a space, and when the mind is a space it becomes your soul, your atma. When it is filled with thoughts, desires, it is mind; vacant, empty, it is not mind. Negation is a process of elimination.

So do not be afraid of the words 'negative' and 'passive.' If you are afraid, you can never surrender. Surrender *is* passive and negative. It is not something you are doing; rather, you are leaving your doings, you are leaving the very notion that you can do. You cannot do—this is the basic feeling. Only then is there surrender. It is negative because you are moving into the unknown, the known is left.

When you surrender to a master it is one of the miracles, because you do not know what is going to happen and what this man is going to do to you. And you can never be certain whether he is real or not. You cannot know to whom you are surrendering and where he is going to lead you. You will try to make certain, but the very effort means that you are not ready for surrender.

If you are absolutely certain before you surrender that this man is going to lead you somewhere

—to a paradise—and then you surrender, it is not a surrender at all. You have not surrendered. Surrender is always to the unknown. When everything is known, there is no surrender. When you have already checked that this is going to happen, and that two and two are going to make four, then there is no surrender. You cannot say "I surrender" because the four is already made certain.

In uncertainty, in insecurity, is the surrender. So it is easy to surrender to God because, really, there is no one to whom you are surrendering and you remain the master. It is difficult to surrender to a living master because then you are no longer the master. With God you can go on deceiving, because no one is going to ask you....

I was reading a Jewish anecdote. One old man was praying to God, and he said, "My neighbor 'A' is very poor, and last year I prayed to you but you have not done anything for him. My other neighbor 'B' is crippled, and I prayed last year also, but you have not done anything." And so on and so forth, he continued. He talked about all the neighbors, and then in the end he said, "Now I will pray again this year. If you forgive me, I can also forgive you."

But he was talking alone. Every talk with the divine is a monologue, the other is not there. So it is up to you, what you are doing is up to you, and you remain the master. That is why there is so much insistence in tantra to surrender to a living master, because then your ego is shattered. And that shattering is the base. That shattering is the base, and only then something can arise out of it.

But do not ask me what you can do to surrender. You cannot do anything. Or, you can do only one thing: be aware of what you can do by doing, what you have gained by doing—be aware! You have gained much: you have gained many miseries, anguishes, nightmares. That is what you have gained through your own effort, this is what ego can gain. Be aware of the misery that you have created—positively, actively, without surrendering. Whatsoever you have done to your life, be aware of

it. That very awareness will help you one day to throw it all and to surrender. And remember that you will be transformed not by surrender to a particular master, but by surrender itself.

So the master is irrelevant, he is not the point. People go on coming to me and they say, "I want to surrender, but to whom?" That is not the point, you are missing the point. It is not a question of to whom. Just the surrendering helps, not the person to whom you have surrendered. He may not be there or he may not be authentic or he may not be an enlightened one. He may just be a rogue, that is not the point. It is irrelevant. You have surrendered—that helps because now you are vulnerable, open. You have become feminine. The male ego is lost, and you have become a feminine womb.

The person you have surrendered to may be bogus or he may not be. That is not the point. You have surrendered, now something can happen to you. And many times it has happened that even with a false master disciples have become enlightened. You may be surprised, even with a false master disciples have become enlightened.

It is reported of Milarepa that he went to a master and he surrendered. Milarepa was a very faithful man, very trusting, so when the master said, "You will have to surrender to me, only then can I help," he said, "Okay, I surrender."

But many persons were jealous. The old followers of that master were jealous of Milarepa because Milarepa was such a different type of man. He was a very magnetic force. They became afraid that if this man remained there he would become the chief disciple, the next master. So they said to their master, "This man seems to be false, so first check whether his surrender is real."

The master said, "How should we examine him?"

They said, "Tell him to jump from this hill"—they were sitting on a hill.

So the master said, "Milarepa, if you have really surrendered, jump from this hill."

So he did not wait even to say yes, he jumped.

The disciples thought he would be dead; then they went down. It took hours for them to go to the valley. He was just sitting under a tree meditating, and he was happy—as happy as he had never been.

So they gathered, and the disciples thought that it must be a coincidence. The master was also surprised, how could this happen? So he asked Milarepa privately, "What did you do? How did it happen?"

He said, "When I surrendered, there was no question of *my* doing. You have done something."

The master knew well that he had not done anything, so he tried again. One house was on fire, so he told Milarepa to go in and sit there and only to come out when the whole house had become ashes. Milarepa went in. He stayed there for hours, then the house was just ashes. When they reached there he was just buried in the ashes—but as alive and as blissful as ever. Milarepa touched his master's feet and said, "You are doing miracles."

So the master said, "It is difficult to think that it is again a coincidence."

But the followers said, "This is nothing but a coincidence. Try again. At least three trials are needed."

They were passing through a village and the master said, "Milarepa, the boat has not yet come and the ferryman has not kept his promise, so you go. Walk on the water, go to the other bank and tell the ferryman to come."

Milarepa walked, and then the master really thought it was a miracle. He walked and went to the other bank and brought the ferry. The master said, "Milarepa, how are you doing it?"

He said, "I just take your name and go on. It is your name, master, that helps me."

So the master thought, "If my name helps so much…." He tried to walk on the water also, but he drowned, and no one has ever heard about him again.

How did it happen? Surrender is the thing—not the master, not the thing to which you surrender. The statue, the temple, the tree, the stone—anything will do. If you surrender, you become vulnerable to existence. Then the whole existence takes you into its arms.

This story may be just a parable, but the meaning is that when you surrender, the whole existence is for you. The fire, the hill, the river, the valley—nothing is against you because you are not against anything. The enmity is lost.

If you fall from a hill and your bones are broken, it is the bones of your ego. You were resisting, you didn't allow the valley to help you. You were helping yourself. You were thinking yourself more wise than existence. Surrender means you come to realize that whatsoever you do will be stupid, foolish. And you have done many stupid things for many lives.

Leave it to existence itself. You cannot do anything.

You have to realize that you are helpless. This realization that "I am helpless" helps the surrender to happen.

CHAPTER 31

From sound to inner silence

◆

T H E   S U T R A S

45 *Silently intone a word ending in 'AH.' Then in the 'HH,' effortlessly, the spontaneity.*

46 *Stopping ears by pressing and the rectum by contracting, enter the sound.*

47 *Enter the sound of your name and, through this sound, all sounds.*

Tantra is not a philosophy. Rather, it is a science with one difference: science is objective, tantra is subjective. But still, it is a science and not a philosophy. Philosophy thinks about the truth, the unknown, the ultimate; science tries to discover what is. Science enters the immediate, philosophy thinks of the ultimate. Philosophy is always looking toward the sky, science is more down to earth.

Tantra is not concerned with the ultimate. It is concerned with the immediate, the here and now. Tantra says, the ultimate is hidden in the immediate, so you need not worry about the ultimate. By worrying about the ultimate you will miss the immediate, and the ultimate is hidden in the immediate. So by thinking about the ultimate you will miss both. If the immediate should be missed, because of it you will miss the ultimate also. So philosophy is just smoke. The approach of tantra is scientific, but the object is different from that of so-called science.

Science tries to understand the object, the objective world, the reality that is before your eyes. Tantra is the science of the reality that is behind your eyes, the subjectivity, but the approach is scientific. Tantra doesn't believe in thinking, it believes in experimenting, in experiencing. And unless you can experience, everything is just a wastage of energy.

I am reminded of one incident. Mulla Nasruddin was crossing a street. Just in front of a church he was knocked down by a hit-and-run driver. He was an old man, and a crowd gathered. Someone was saying, "That man cannot survive."

The priest of the church ran out. He came near and he found out that the old man was just going to die, so he prepared to administer the last rites. He came near and asked the dying Mulla, "Do you believe in God the Father? Do you believe in God the Son? Do you believe in God the Holy Ghost?"

Mulla opened his eyes and said, "My God! I am dying and he is asking me puzzles!"

All philosophy is like this: it is asking puzzles while you are dying. Every moment you are dying, every moment everyone is on his deathbed—because death can occur at any moment. But philosophy goes on asking and answering puzzles. Tantra says it is good for children to philosophize, but those who are wise will not waste their time in philosophy. They should try to know—not to think, because through thinking there is no knowledge. Through thinking you go on webbing words, creating patterns of words. It leads nowhere, you remain the same—no transformation, no new insights. The old man just goes on gathering dust.

Knowing is a different phenomenon. It does not mean thinking about, it means going deep into the existence itself in order to know, moving into the existence. Remember this, that tantra is not a philosophy. It is science—a subjective science. The approach is scientific and nonphilosophic. It is very down to earth, concerned with the immediate. The immediate is to be used as a door to the ultimate, the ultimate happens if you enter the immediate. It is there, and there is no other way to reach to it.

Philosophy is not a way in the eyes of tantra, it is a false way. It only appears that this is a way. It is a door which is not; it simply appears to be a door, it is a false door. The moment you try to enter it you come to know that you cannot enter, it is just a painted door, there is no door in reality. Philosophy is a painted door. If you sit by its side and go on thinking and thinking, it is good. If you try to enter it, it is a wall.

So every philosophy is good for philosophizing. For experiencing, every philosophy is impotent. That is why there is so much insistence on technique in tantra, because a science can do nothing but give technology, whether of the outside world or of the inside. The very word 'tantra' means technique. That is why, in this small and yet one of the greatest and deepest books, only techniques are given, no philosophy, just one hundred and twelve techniques to reach the ultimate through the immediate.

---

45 Intone a word ending in 'AH.'

The ninth technique concerning sound: *Silently intone a word ending in 'AH.' Then in the 'HH,' effortlessly, the spontaneity.*

Silently intone a word ending in 'AH.' Any word that ends in AH—intone it silently. Emphasis should be given to the ending AH. Why? Because the moment this sound AH is intoned, your breath goes out. You may not have observed it, but now you can observe: whenever your breath goes out you are more silent, and whenever your breath comes in you are more tense—because the outgoing breath is death and the incoming breath is life. Tension is part of life, not of death. Relaxation is part of death; death means total relaxation. Life cannot be totally relaxed, it is impossible.

Life means tension, effort. Only death is relaxed. So whenever a person becomes absolutely relaxed, he is both—alive outwardly and dead within. You can see in the face of a buddha both life and death simultaneously. That is why there is so much silence and calm, they are part of death. Life is not relaxation. You relax in the night when you are asleep. That is why the old traditions say that death and sleep are similar. Sleep is a temporary death and death is permanent sleep. That is why night relaxes you, it is the outgoing breath. The morning is the incoming breath.

The day makes you tense and the night relaxes you. Light makes you tense, darkness relaxes you. That is why you cannot sleep when there is light, it is difficult to relax because light is similar to life, it is antideath. Darkness is similar to death, it is pro-death.

So darkness has deep relaxation in it, and those who are afraid of darkness cannot relax. It is impossible, because every relaxation is dark. And darkness surrounds your life on both the sides. Before you are born you are in darkness; when life ceases you are again in darkness. Darkness is infinite, and this light and this life are just a moment in it, just a wave arising and then falling back. If you can remember the darkness that surrounds both the ends, you will be relaxed here and now.

Life, death—they are two sides of existence. The incoming breath is life, the outgoing breath is death. So it is not that you die someday, you are dying with every breath. That is why the Hindus have been counting life in breaths, they do not count life in years. Tantra, yoga, all the old Indian systems, they count life in breaths: how many breaths you are going to live. So they say if you breathe very fast, with too much breathing in a short time, you will die very soon. If you breathe very slowly and your breaths are less in an interval, you will live very long.

And this is so. If you go and observe animals, those animals whose breathing is very slow live long. Take the elephant: the elephant lives long, the breath is very slow. Then there is the dog: the dog dies soon, the breath is very fast. Whenever you find an animal in which the breath is fast, any animal, that animal will not have a long life. A long life is always with slow breath.

Tantra and yoga and other Indian systems count your life in breaths. Really, with every breath you are born and with every breath you are dying. This mantra, this technique, uses the outgoing breath as the method, the medium, the vehicle, to go deep into silence. It is a death method. *Silently intone a word ending in 'AH.'* The breath has gone —that is the reason for a word ending in AH.

This AH is meaningful because when you say AH it completely empties you. The whole breath has moved out; nothing remains within. You are totally empty—empty and dead. For a single moment, for a very small interval, life has moved out of you. You are dead—empty. This emptiness, if realized, if you can become aware of it, will change you completely. You will be a different man.

Then you will know well that this life is not your life and this death is also not your death. Then you will know something which is beyond the incoming and outgoing breath—the witnessing soul. And this witnessing can happen easily when you are empty of breath, because life has subsided and with it all tensions have subsided. So try it, it is a very beautiful method. But the ordinary process, the ordinary habit, is to emphasize the incoming breath, never the outgoing breath.

We always take the breath in, but we never throw it out. We take it in and the body throws it out. Observe your breathing and you will know. We take it in. We never exhale, we only inhale. The exhaling is done by the body because we are afraid of death, that is the reason. If it was in our power we would not exhale at all, we would inhale and then control it within. No one emphasizes exhaling —inhaling is emphasized. Because we have to do exhaling after inhaling, that is why we go on suffering it. We tolerate it because we cannot inhale without exhaling.

So exhaling is accepted as a necessary evil, but basically we are not interested in exhaling. And this is not only about breath, this is our whole attitude toward life. We cling to everything that comes to us; we will not leave it. This is the miserliness of the mind. And remember, there are many implications in it. If you are suffering from constipation, this will be the basic cause: you always inhale and never exhale. The mind which never exhales but just inhales will suffer from constipation. The constipation is the other end of the same thing. He cannot exhale anything, he goes on accumulating, he is afraid. The fear is there. He can only accumulate, but anything that is accumulated becomes poisonous.

If you only inhale and do not exhale, your very breath becomes poison to you; you will die because of it. You can turn a life-giving force into poison if you behave in a miserly way, because the exhaling is absolutely necessary. It throws all the poisons out of you.

So really, death is a purifying process and life is a poisoning process. This will look paradoxical. Life is a poisoning process because to live you have to use many things—and the moment you have used them they turn into poison, they are converted into poisons. You take a breath in, you use oxygen, and then what remains becomes poison. It was life only because of the oxygen, but you have used it. So life goes on changing everything into a poison.

Now there is a great movement in the West— ecology. Man has been using everything and turning it into poison, and the very earth is just on the verge of dying. Any day it can die because we have turned everything into poison. Death is a purifying process. When your whole body has become poisonous, death will relieve you of the body. It will renew you, it will give you a new birth; a new body will be given to you. Through death all the accumulated poisons are dissolved back into nature. You are given a new mechanism.

And this happens with every breath. The outgoing breath is similar to death—it takes poisons out. And when it is going out, everything ebbs within. If you can throw the whole breath out, completely out so that no breath remains within, you touch a point of silence that can never be touched while the breath is in.

It is just like the ebb and tide: with every breath a tide of life comes to you, with every exhalation everything ebbs—the tide has gone. You are just a vacant, empty shore. This is the use of this technique. *Silently intone a word ending in 'AH.'* Emphasize the exhaling breath. And you can use it for many changes in the mind. If you are suffering from constipation, forget intaking. Just exhale and do not inhale. Let the body do the work of inhaling; you just do the work of exhaling. You force the breath out and do not inhale. The body will inhale by itself; you need not worry about it, you are not going to die. The body will take breath in, you just throw it out and let the body take it in. Your constipation will go.

If you are suffering from heart disease, just exhale, do not inhale. Then you will not suffer from heart disease. If while just going upwards on a staircase, or anywhere, you feel tired—very much tired, suffocated, breathless—simply do this: just exhale, do not inhale. Then you can climb up any amount of steps and you will not be tired. What happens? When you go with an emphasis on exhaling, you are ready to let go, you are ready to die. You are not afraid of death; that makes you open. Otherwise you are closed—fear closes you.

When you exhale, the whole system changes and accepts death. There is no fear, you are ready to die. And one who is ready to die can live. Really, only one who is ready to die can live. He alone becomes capable of life—because he is not afraid.

One who accepts death, welcomes it, receives it as a guest, lives with it, goes deep into life. Exhale, do not inhale, and that will change your total mind. Because of its simple techniques tantra never appeals, because we think, "My mind is such a complex thing." It is not complex—just foolish. And fools are very complex. A wise man is simple. Nothing is complex in your mind, it is a very simple mechanism. If you understand, you can change it very easily.

If you have not seen anybody dying, if you have been protected from seeing death as Buddha was protected, you cannot understand anything about it. Buddha's father was afraid because some astrologer said, "This boy is going to be a great sannyasin. He will renounce the world."

The father asked, "What is to be done to protect him from doing such a thing?"

So those astrologers thought and thought, and then they concluded and they said, "Do not allow him to see death, because if he is not aware of death he will never think of renouncing life."

This is beautiful—very meaningful. That means all religion, all philosophy, all tantra and yoga, is basically death-oriented. If you are aware of death, only then does religion become meaningful. That is why no animal except man is religious, because no animal is aware of death. They die, but they are not aware. They cannot conceive or imagine that there is going to be death.

When one dog dies, other dogs never imagine that death is going to happen to them also. Always someone else dies, so how can a dog imagine that "I am going to die"? He has never seen himself dying. Someone else, some other dog dies, so how can he connect that "I am going to die"? No animal is aware of death; that is why no animal renounces. No animal can become a sannyasin. Only a very high quality of consciousness can lead you to renounce—when you become aware of death. And if even by being a man you are not aware of death, you belong to the animal kingdom; you are not yet a man. You become a man only when you encounter death. Otherwise there is no difference between you and the animal.

Everything is similar; only death makes the difference. With death encountered, you are no more animal, something has happened to you which never happens to an animal. Now you will be a different consciousness.

So Buddha's father protected him from seeing any type of death—not only man's death, but the death of animals and even of flowers. So the gardeners were instructed not to allow the child to see a dead flower, a pale flower dying on the branch, a pale leaf, a dry leaf. No, nowhere should he come to realize that something dies—he may infer from it that "I am going to die." And you do not infer it even seeing your wife dying, your mother, your father, your child. You weep for them, but you never conceive that this is a sign that "I am going to die."

But the astrologers said, "The boy is very, very sensitive, so protect him from any type of death." And the father was overconscientious. He would not allow even an old man or an old woman to be seen, because oldness is just death heard from a distance; death is there from a distance, just coming. So Buddha's father would not allow any old man or old woman to be seen by the child. If Buddha suddenly became aware that just by stopping the breath a man could die, it would be very difficult for him. "Just because no breath is coming in, how can a man die?" he would wonder. "Life is such a big, complex process."

If you have not seen anyone dying, even you cannot conceive that just by stopping the breath a man will die. Just by stopping the breath? Such a simple thing, and how can such a complex life die?

It is the same with these methods. They look simple, but they touch the basic reality.

When the breath is going out, when you are completely emptied of life, you touch death, you are just near it, and everything becomes calm and silent within you.

Use it as a mantra. Whenever you feel tired, whenever you feel tense, use any word which ends in AH. "Allah" will do—any word that brings your total breath out so that you exhale completely and you are emptied of breath. The moment you are emptied of breath you are emptied of life also. And all your problems belong to life, no problem belongs to death. Your anxiety, your anguish, your anger, your sadness, they all belong to life.

Death is nonproblematic. Death never gives any problem to anyone. And even if you think that "I am afraid of death and death creates a problem," it is not death that creates the problem but your clinging to life. Only life creates problems; death dissolves all problems. So when the breath has moved completely out...AHHH...you are emptied of life. Look within at that moment when the breath is completely out. Before taking another breath in, go deep down in that interval and become aware of the inside calm, the silence. In that moment you are a buddha.

If you can catch that moment, you have known a taste of what Buddha might have known. And once known, you can detach this taste from the incoming-outgoing breath. Then the breath can go on coming in, going out, and you can remain in that quality of consciousness that you have come to know. It is always there; one has just to discover it. And it is easier to discover when life is emptied out.

Silently intone a word ending in 'AH.' Then in the 'HH,' effortlessly, the spontaneity. And when the breath goes out...HHH...everything is emptied. *Effortlessly:* in this moment, there is no need to make any effort. *The spontaneity:* just be aware, be spontaneous, be sensitive, and realize this moment of death.

In this moment you are just near the door, very, very near to the ultimate. The immediate has moved out, the superfluous has moved out. In this moment you are not the wave, you are the ocean—just near, just near! If you can become aware you will forget that you are a wave. Again the wave will come, but now you can never be identified with it, you will remain the ocean. Once you have known that you are the ocean, you can never again be the wave.

Life is waves...death is the ocean. That is why Buddha so much insists that his *nirvana* is death-like. He never says you will attain life immortal, he says you will simply die totally. Jesus says, "Come to me and I will give you life, and life abundant." Buddha says, "Come to me to realize your death. I will give you death totally." Both mean the same thing, but Buddha's terminology is more basic. But you will become afraid of it. That is why

Buddha had no appeal in India; he was uprooted completely. We go on saying that this land is a religious land, but the most religious person couldn't get roots here.

What type of religious land is this? We have not produced another Buddha; he is incomparable. And whenever the world thinks India to be religious, the world remembers Buddha—no one else. Because of Buddha, India is thought to be religious. What type of religious land is this? Buddha has no roots here, he was totally uprooted. He used the language of death—that is the cause, and brahmins were using the language of life. They say the *Brahma* and he says *nirvana*. 'Brahma' means life, infinite life; and 'nirvana' means just cessation, death—total death.

Buddha says, "Your ordinary death is not total; you will be born again. I will give you a total death, and you will never be born again." A total death means now no birth is possible. So this so-called death, Buddha says, is not death. It is just a rest period, you will become alive again. It is just a breath gone out. You will take the breath in again, you will be reborn. Buddha says, "I will give you the way so that the breath will go out and will never come in again—total death, nirvana, cessation."

We become afraid because we cling to life. But this is the paradox: the more you cling to life, the more you will die, and the more you are ready to die, then the more you become deathless. If you are ready to die, then there is no possibility of death. No one can give you death if you accept it, because through that acceptance you become aware of something within you which is deathless.

This incoming breath and outgoing breath are the life and death of the body, not of "me." But "I" do not know anything other than the body; "I" am identified with the body. Then it will be difficult to be aware when the breath comes in, easy to be aware when the breath goes out. When the breath is going out, for that moment you have become old, dying, emptied completely of the breath; you are dead for a moment.

In the 'HH,' effortlessly, the spontaneity. Try it! Any moment you can try it. Just riding in a bus or traveling in a train or moving to the office, whenever you have time intone a sound like 'Allah'—any sound ending with AH. This 'Allah' helped so much in Islam—not because of any Allah there in the sky, but because of this AH. This word is beautiful. And then the more one goes on using this word 'Allah, Allah....' It becomes reduced. Then what remains is 'Lah, Lah....' Then it is reduced further; then it remains as 'Ah, Ah....' It is good, but you can use any word that ends in AH—or just AH will do.

Have you observed that whenever you are tense you will sigh...AHHH...and you will feel relaxed. Or whenever you are in joy, overjoyed, you say AHHH...and the whole breath is thrown out and you feel within a tranquility that you have never felt. Try this: when you are feeling very good, take the breath in and then see what you feel. You cannot feel that well-being that comes with AHHH.... It is coming because of the breath going out.

So languages differ, but these two things never differ. All over the world, whenever someone feels tired he will say AHHH.... Really, he is calling for death to come and relax him. Whenever one feels overjoyed, blissful, he says AHHH.... He is so overfilled with joy that he is not afraid of death now. He can relieve himself completely, relax completely.

And what will happen if you go on trying it? You will become fully aware of something within you—the spontaneousness of your being, of *sahaj*, of being spontaneous. That you are already, but you are too much engaged with life, too much occupied with life. You cannot become aware of the being which is behind.

When you are not occupied with life, with the incoming breath, the being behind is revealed; there is a glimpse. But the glimpse will become, by and by, a realization. And once it is known you cannot forget it—and this is not something which you are creating. That is why it is spontaneous, it is not something you are creating. It is there, you have simply forgotten. It is a remembrance, it is a re-discovery.

Try to see children, very small children, taking their breaths. They take them in a different way. Look at a child sleeping. His belly comes up and down, not the chest. If you are sleeping and you are being observed, your chest comes up and down; your breath never goes down to the belly. The breath can go down to the belly only if you exhale and do not inhale. If you inhale and do not exhale, the breath cannot go down to the belly. The reason why breath goes to the belly is that when one exhales, the whole breath is thrown out and then the body takes it in. And the body takes only that amount which is needed—never more, never less.

The body has its own wisdom, and it is more wise than you. Do not disturb it. You can take more—then it will be disturbed. You can take less—then it will be disturbed. The body has its own wisdom, it only takes that amount which is needed. When more is needed, it creates the situation. When less is needed, it creates the situation. It never goes to the extreme, it is always balanced. But if *you* inhale it is never balanced, because you do not know what you are doing, you do not know what is the need of the body. And the need changes every moment.

Allow the body! You just exhale, you just throw it out, and then the body will take breath in—and it will take it deeply and slowly, and the breath will go down to the belly. It will hit the navel point exactly and your belly will go up and down.

If you inhale, then you never exhale totally. Then the breath is in and you go on inhaling, so the breath which is already in will not allow your breath to go down to the very bottom. Then just shallow breathing happens. You go on taking breath in, and the poisonous breath is there, filling you up.

They say that you have six thousand sacs in your lungs and only two thousand are touched by your breath. The four thousand are always filled with poisonous gases which need to be exhaled, and that two-thirds portion of your chest creates much anxiety, much anguish and misery in the mind, in the body. A child exhales, he never inhales. Inhaling is done by the body itself.

When the child is born, the first thing he is going to do is cry. With that cry his throat opens, with that cry comes the first AHHH.... The oxygen and air that had been given by the mother is exhaled. This is his first effort with breathing. That is why if a child is not crying, then the doctor will become uneasy, because he has not shown the sign of life. He still feels dependent on the mother. He must cry! That cry shows that now he is becoming an individual; the mother is not needed, he will take his own breath. And the first thing is that he is going to cry in order to exhale that which was given by the mother, and then his body will start functioning, inhaling.

A child is always exhaling, and when the child starts inhaling, when the emphasis moves to inhaling, be aware. He has already become old; he has learned things from you. He has become tense. Whenever you are tense, you cannot take a deep breath. Why? Your stomach becomes rigid. Whenever you are tense your stomach becomes rigid, it won't allow breath to go down. Then you have to take shallow breaths.

Try with AH. It has a beautiful feeling around it. Whenever you feel tired, AHHH...throw the breath. And make it a point to emphasize exhaling. You will be a different man, and a different mind will evolve. With the emphasis on breathing in, you have developed a miser mind and a miser body. With exhaling, that miserliness will disappear and with it many problems. Possessiveness will disappear.

So tantra will not say leave possessiveness. Tantra says change your system of breathing, you cannot possess then. Observe your own breathing and your moods, and you will become aware. Whatsoever is wrong is always associated with the emphasis that is given to the incoming breath and whatsoever is good, virtuous, beautiful, true, is always associated with exhaling. Whenever you are speaking a lie, you will hold your breath in. Whenever you speak truth, you never hold the breath. You fear to lie, so you hold the breath. You are afraid something may go out with the out-moving breath, that your hidden truth may be revealed.

Go on trying this AH more and more. You will be more healthy in body, more healthy in mind, and a different quality of calm, at-easeness, tranquility will develop.

---

46 Closing ears and contracting rectum.

The tenth sound method: *Stopping ears by pressing and the rectum by contracting, enter the sound.*

We are not aware of the body or how the body functions and what is its Tao, what is its way. But if you observe, then you can very easily become aware. If you stop your ears and pull your rectum up, contract your rectum, everything will stop for you. It will be as if the whole world has become nonmoving—as if everything has become static, stopped. Not only movements, you will feel as if time has stopped.

What happens when you pull the rectum up, contract it? When both ears are closed simultaneously, with closed ears you will hear a sound within. But if the rectum is not pulled up, that sound is released by the rectum. That sound is very subtle. If the rectum is pulled up, contracted, and the ears are closed, you will see within you a pillar of sound—and that sound is of silence. It is a negative sound. When all sounds have ceased, then you feel the sound of silence or the sound of soundlessness. But it will be released from the rectum.

So close the ears and pull the rectum up. Then you are closed from both the sides, and your body becomes closed and just filled with sound. This feeling of being filled with sound gives a deep fulfillment. So we will have to understand many things around it, only then will it become possible for you to have the feeling of what happens.

We are not aware of the body—that is one of the basic problems for a seeker. And the society is against becoming aware of the body because society is afraid of the body. So we train every child not to be aware of the body, we make every child insensitive. We create a distance between the child's mind and body, so he is not very much aware of the body, because body awareness will create problems for the society.

Many things are implied. If the child is aware of the body, he will become aware of sex sooner or later. And if he is too much aware of the body, he will feel too sexual, sensuous. So we have to kill the very root. He should be made dull about his body, insensitive, so he never feels it. You do not feel your body. You feel it only when something wrong happens, when something goes wrong.

You have a headache, then you feel your head. Some thorn is there, then you feel your feet. When your body aches, you feel that you have a body. You feel it only when something goes wrong, and then too not right away. You are never aware of your diseases immediately. You become aware only when a period has passed and when the disease goes on knocking at your consciousness: "I am here." Only then do you become aware. So no one really goes to the doctor in time. Everyone reaches there late, when the disease has entered deep and has done much wrong.

If a child has grown up with sensitivity he will become aware of the disease even before the disease happens. And now, in Russia particularly, they are working on the theory that a disease can be known even six months before its happening if someone is very deeply sensitive about his body, because subtle changes start long in advance. They prepare the body for the disease. The impact is felt even six months before.

But never mind disease, we never become aware even of death. If you are going to die tomorrow, you are not aware even today. A thing like death which may happen the next moment, and you are not aware this moment. You are totally dead to your body, insensitive. This whole society, the whole culture up to now, creates this dullness, this deadness, because it has been against the body. You are not allowed to feel it. Only in accidents can you be pardoned, forgiven for being aware of it; otherwise, do not be aware of the body.

This creates many problems, particularly for tantra, because tantra believes in deep sensitivity and knowledge of the body. You go on moving and your body goes on doing many things and you are unaware. Now much work is being done on body language. The body has its own language, and psychiatrists and psychologists and psychoanalysts in particular are being trained for body language, because they say you cannot believe the modern man. Whatsoever he says cannot be believed. Rather, one must observe his body, that will give a more true clue.

A man enters a psychiatrist's office. The old psychiatry, Freudian psychoanalysis, will talk and talk with the man to bring out whatsoever is hidden in his mind. Modern psychiatry will observe his body because that gives clues. If a man is an egoist, if ego is his problem, he stands in a different way than a humble man. His neck has a different angle than a humble man's, his spine is not flexible but dead, fixed. He looks wooden, not alive. If you touch his body it has a wooden feeling, not the warmth of a living body. He is like a soldier just moving to the front.

Look at the soldier moving to the front. He has a wooden shape, a wooden feeling, and that is needed by a soldier because he is going to die or to kill. He must not be much aware of the body, so his whole training is to create a wooden body. Soldiers marching look like toys, like dead toys marching.

If you are humble you have a different body; you sit differently, you stand differently. If you feel inferior you stand differently; if you feel superior you stand differently. If you are always in fear, you stand in such a way as if you are protecting yourself from some unknown force. That is always

there. If you are not afraid, you are just like a child playing with his mother; there is no fear. Wherever you go you are unafraid, at home with the universe around you. The man who is afraid is armored. And when I say armored it is not only symbolically, physiologically he is armored.

Wilhelm Reich was working very much on body structure, and he came to see some deep associations between mind and body. If a man is afraid, his stomach is not flexible. You touch his stomach and it is like a stone. If he becomes fearless, his stomach relaxes immediately. Or if you relax the stomach, then the fear disappears. Massage the stomach to relax, and you will feel more fearless, less afraid.

A person who is loving has a different quality of body and warmth—he is warm bodily. A person who is not loving is cold, physiologically he is cold. Cold and other things have moved into your body and they have become barriers, they do not allow you to know about your body. But the body goes on working in its own way and you go on working in your own way—a rift is created. That rift has to be broken.

I have seen that if someone is suppressive, if he has suppressed his anger, then his fingers, his hands, have the sensation of a suppressed anger. And a person who knows how to feel it can feel just by touching your hand that you have suppressed anger. And why in the hand? Because anger has to be released by the hands. If you have suppressed anger then in your teeth, in your gums, it is suppressed—and it can be felt by touching. It gives a vibration that "I am suppressed here."

If you have suppressed sex, then in your erotic zones it is there. If a person has suppressed sex, then if you touch his erotic zones you can feel it. With any erotic zone touched, sex is there if it has been suppressed. The zone will become afraid and will withdraw from your touch, it will not be open. Because the person inside is withdrawing, the part of the body will withdraw. It will not allow you to bring about an opening.

Now they say that fifty percent of women are frigid, and the reason is that we teach girls to be more suppressive than boys. So they have suppressed, and when a girl suppresses her sexual feelings up to the age of twenty, it has become a long habit—twenty years of suppression. Then when she will love, she will talk about love, but her body will not be open; the body will be closed. And then an opposite, a diametrically opposite phenomenon happens: two currents oppose each other. She wants to love but her body is repressive, the body withdraws; it is not ready to come closer.

If you see a woman sitting with a man, if the woman loves the man she will be inclining toward him, the body will be inclining. If they are sitting on a sofa, both of their bodies will be inclining toward each other. They are not aware, but you can see it. If the woman is afraid of the man, her body will be inclining to the opposite direction. If a woman loves a man she will never cross her legs when sitting near him. If she is afraid of the man she will cross her legs. She is not aware, this is not done consciously. It is body armor. The body protects itself and works in its own ways.

Tantra became aware of this phenomenon; the first awareness of such deep body feeling, sensitivity, was with tantra. And tantra says that if you can use your body consciously, the body becomes the vehicle to move to the spirit. Tantra says it is foolish, absolutely idiotic, to be against the body. Use it! It is a vehicle. And use its energy in such a way that you can go beyond it.

Now, *Stopping ears by pressing and the rectum by contracting, enter the sound.*

Many times you have been contracting the rectum and sometimes the rectum is released even without your consciousness. If you suddenly become afraid, the rectum is released. You may defecate in fear, you may urinate in fear. Then you cannot control it. If a sudden fear grips you, your bladder will relax, your rectum will relax. What happens? In fear, what happens? Fear is a mental thing, so why do you urinate in fear? Why is the control lost?

There must be some deep connecting root.

Fear happens in the head, in the mind. When you are unafraid this never happens. The child really has no mental control over his body. No animal controls his urine, bladder or anything. Whenever the bladder is full it is released. No animal controls it, but man has to control it of necessity. So we force a child to control when he should go to the bathroom and when not. We tell him he has to control, we give timings. So the mind takes over the control of a function which is nonvoluntary. That is why it is so difficult to train the child for the toilet. And now psychologists say that if we stop toilet training, humanity will very much improve.

Toilet training is the first repression of the child and its natural spontaneity, but it seems difficult to listen to these psychologists. We cannot listen to them because then the children will create many problems. We have to train them of necessity. Only a very, very rich, affluent society will be able not to bother. Poor societies have to manage, we cannot afford it. If the child urinates anywhere, if he urinates on the sofa, we cannot afford it, so we have to train. This training is mental. The body really has no built-in program for it.

Man is an animal as far as body is concerned, and the body knows no culture, no society. That is why when you are in deep fear, the control mechanism that you have imposed on the body is relaxed. You are not in control; you are thrown off control. You can control only in normal conditions. In emergencies you cannot control because for emergencies you have never been trained. You have only been trained for the normal, day-to-day, routine world. In an emergency the control is lost, your body starts functioning in its own animal way. But one relationship can be understood, that with a fearless man this will never happen. So this has become a sign of a coward.

If in fear you urinate or defecate, this shows you are a coward. A fearless man will not behave in this way, because a fearless man is taking deep breaths.

His body and his breathing system are related, there is no gap. With a man who is a coward there is a gap, and because of that gap he is always over-burdened with urine and defecation. So whenever an emergency comes, that overburdenedness has to be thrown, he has to be unburdened. And it has a reason in nature. A coward who is unburdened can escape more easily with his stomach relaxed, can run more easily. A burdened stomach will become a hindrance, so it is helpful for a coward to be relaxed.

Why am I talking about this? I am just saying that you have to be aware of your mental processes and your stomach processes; they are deeply related. Psychologists say that fifty to ninety percent of your dreams are because of your stomach processes. If you have taken a very heavy meal you are bound to see nightmares. They are not related with the mind, it is just that the heavy stomach creates them.

Many dreams can be created by outside tricks. If you are sleeping, your hands can be crossed on your chest and immediately you will start dreaming some nightmare. A pillow can be put on your chest and you will dream that some demon is sitting on your chest just going to kill you. And this has been one of the problems. Why is there such a burden from the small weight of a pillow? If you are awake, there is no weight; you do not feel anything heavy. But why is it that a small pillow placed on you in the night when you are sleeping is felt as being so heavy that it is as if you have been burdened with a big stone or a rock? Why is so much weight felt?

The reason is this: when you are aware, when you are awake, your mind and body are not corre-lated; the gap is there. You cannot feel the body and its sensitivity. While asleep, the control, the culture, the conditioning, dissolves; you have again become a child and your body has become sensi-tive. Because of that sensitivity, a small pillow is felt as a rock. It is magnified because of sensitivity—the sensitivity magnifies it. So body-mind processes

are deeply related, and if you know what happens you can use this.

Rectum closed, pulled upwards, contracted, creates a situation in the body in which sound can be felt if present. You will feel a pillar of sound in silence within the closed space in your body. Close the ears and pull up the rectum, and then just remain with what is happening inside you. Just remain in that vacant state which is created by these two things. Your life energy is moving within and it has no way to go out. Sound goes out either from your ears or from your rectum. Those are the two doors from where the sound can move out. If is not moving out, you can feel it more easily.

And what will happen when you feel this inner sound? With the very phenomenon of hearing the inner sound, your thoughts dissolve. Just try it anytime during the day, just pull up the rectum and put your fingers in the ears. Press the ears and pull up the rectum. You will feel that your mind has stopped. It will not be functioning; thoughts will have stopped. That constant flow of thoughts is not there. It is good! And if one goes on doing it when-ever there is time, in the day if you can do it for five or six times, within three or four months you will become an expert in it. And then such a well-being flows out of it!

And the inner sound, once heard, remains with you. Then you can hear it the whole day. The market is noisy, the road is noisy, the traffic is noisy, but if even in that noise you have heard the inner sound, you will feel the still small voice that goes on inside. And then nothing will disturb you. If you can feel your inner sound, then nothing from the outside can disturb you. You remain silent; whatsoever happens around you makes no difference.

---

47 Use your name as a mantra.

The last sound technique: *Enter the sound of your name and, through this sound, all sounds.*

Your own name can be used as a mantra very easily, and it is very helpful because your name has gone very deep into your unconscious. Nothing else has gone so deep. If we are all sitting here, and we all fall asleep and someone comes and calls "Rama," no one will listen except the person whose name is Rama. He will listen to it; he will be disturbed in his sleep. No one else will listen to the sound 'Rama,' but why does this man listen? It has gone down deep; it is not conscious now, it has become unconscious.

Your name has gone very deep within you, but there is a very beautiful phenomenon about your name: you never call it, others call it. Others use it; you never use it.

I have heard that in the First World War, for the first time in America rationing was created. Thomas Edison was a very great scientist, but he was very poor so he had to stand in the queue for his ration card. And he was such a great man that no one ever used his name before him. There was no need to use his name for himself, and no one else would use his name because he was so much respected. Everyone would call him "Professor," so he had forgotten what his name was.

He was standing in the queue, and when his name was called, when it was asked who Thomas Alva Edison was, he just stared blankly. Again the name was called, then someone who was a neighbor to Edison said to him, "Why are you standing? Your name is being called. It is your name, Professor."

Then he became aware and he said, "But how can I recognize it? No one calls me Edison. It has been so long...they just call me Professor."

You never use your own name. Only others use it—you have heard it used by others. But it has gone deep, very deep. It has penetrated like an arrow into your unconscious. If you yourself use it, then it becomes a mantra. And for two reasons it helps: one, when you use your own name, if your name is "Rama" and you use "Rama, Rama, Rama..." suddenly you feel as if you are using

someone else's name—as if it is not yours. Or if you feel that it is yours, you feel that there is a separate entity within you which is using it. It may belong to the body, it may belong to the mind, but he who is calling "Rama, Rama..." becomes a witness.

You have always called others' names. When you call your own name it looks as if it belongs to someone else, not to you, and it is a very revealing phenomenon. You can become a witness to your own name, and with the name your whole life is involved. Separated from the name, you are separated from your whole life. And this name has penetrated deep within you because everyone has called you this from your very birth, you have always heard this. So use this sound, and with this sound you can go to the very depths to which the name has gone.

In the old days we gave everyone a name of God—everyone. Someone was Rama, someone was Narayana, someone was Krishna, someone was Vishnu, or something like that. They say all the Mohammedan names are the names of God. And all over the world that was the practice, to give a name which is really a name of God.

This was for good reasons. One reason was this technique—because if your name can be used as a mantra it will serve you a double purpose. It will be your name—and you have heard it so much, so many times, and all your life it has penetrated deep. Then also, it is the name of God. So go on repeating it inside, and suddenly you will become aware that "This name is different from me." Then by and by this name will have a sanctity of its own. You will remember any day that "Narayana" or "Rama" is God's name. Your name has turned into a mantra.

Use it! This is very good! You can try many things with your name. If you want to be awakened at five o'clock in the morning, no alarm is so exact as your own name. Just repeat thrice inside, "Rama, you have to be awake by five o'clock sharp."

Repeat it three times, and then just fall asleep. You will be awakened at five o'clock because "Rama," your name, is very deep in the unconscious.

Call your name and tell yourself, "At five o'clock in the morning, let me be awakened." Someone will awaken you. And if you continue this practice, one day you will suddenly realize that at five o'clock someone calls you and says, "Rama, be awake." That is your unconscious calling you.

This technique says, *Enter the sound of your name and, through this sound, all sounds.* Your name becomes just a door for all names. But enter the sound. First, when you repeat "Rama, Rama, Rama..." it is just a word. But it means something when you go on repeating "Rama, Rama, Rama...."

You must have heard the story of Valmiki. He was given this mantra "Rama," but he was an ignorant man—uneducated, simple, innocent, childlike. He started repeating "Rama, Rama, Rama..." but he was repeating so much that he forgot completely and reversed the whole thing. Instead he was chanting "Mara, Mara...." He was chanting "Rama, Rama, Rama..." so fast that it became "Mara, Mara, Mara...." And he achieved the goal through "Mara, Mara, Mara...."

If you go on repeating the name fast inside, soon it will not be a word: it will become a sound, just meaningless. And then there is no difference between Rama and Mara—no difference! Whether you call Rama or Mara, it makes no sense, they are not words. It is just the sound, just the sound that matters. Enter the sound of your name. Forget the meaning of it, just enter the sound. Meaning is with the mind, sound is with the body. Meaning is in the head, sound spreads all over the body. So forget the meaning. Just repeat it as a meaningless sound, and

through this sound you will enter all sounds. This sound will become the door to all sounds. And 'all sounds' means all that exists.

This is one of the basic tenets of Indian inner search, that the basic unit of the existence is sound and not electricity. Modern science says that the basic unit of the existence is electricity, not sound, but they also say that sound is a form of electricity. Indians, however, have always been saying that electricity is nothing but a form of sound.

You may have heard that through a particular *raga*, a particular sound, fire can be created. It can be created because—this is the Indian idea—that sound is the basis of all electricity. So if you hit sound in a particular frequency, electricity will be created.

On long bridges, if a military group is passing, they are not allowed to march because many times it has happened that because of their march the bridge falls. It is because of sound, not because of their weight. If they cross marching, then the particular sound of their feet breaks the bridge.

In old Hebrew history, the city of Jericho was very protected by great walls and it was impossible to break those walls by guns. But through a particular sound the walls were broken, and that sound was the secret of the breaking of those walls. If that sound is created before walls, the walls will give way.

You have heard the story of Ali Baba: a particular sound and the rock moves. These are allegories. Whether they are right or not, one thing is certain: if you can create a particular sound so continuously that meaning is lost, mind is lost, the rock at your heart will be removed.

CHAPTER 32

"No-fight" is the central teaching

◆

Q U E S T I O N S

Do these techniques belong to yoga or actually to the central subject matter of tantra?

How to make sex meditative, and should any special sexual positions be practiced.

Is 'anahat nad' a sound or soundlessness?

The first question:

Beloved Master, please explain whether the techniques You have discussed so far from Vigyan Bhairav Tantra *belong to the science of yoga instead of to the actual and central subject matter of tantra. What is the central subject matter of tantra?*

This question arises to many. The techniques that we have discussed also belong to yoga. They are the same techniques, but with a difference; you can use the same techniques with a very different philosophy behind them. The framework, the pattern differs, not the technique. You may have a different attitude toward life, just the contrary to tantra.

Yoga believes in struggle; yoga is basically the path of will. Tantra does not believe in a struggle; tantra is not the path of will. Rather, on the contrary, tantra is the path of total surrender. Your will is not needed. For tantra your will is the problem, the source of all anguish. For yoga your surrender, your will-lessness is the problem.

Your will is weak, that is why you are in anguish, suffering—for yoga. For tantra, because you have a will, because you have an ego, an individuality, that is why you are suffering. Yoga says, bring your will to absolute perfection and you will be liberated. Tantra says, dissolve your will completely, become totally emptied of it, and that will

be your liberation. And both are right; this creates the problem. For me, both are right.

But the path of yoga is a very difficult one. It is just nearly impossible that you can attain to the perfection of the ego. It means you become the center of the whole universe. The path is very long, arduous, and really, it never reaches to the end. So what happens to the followers of yoga? Somewhere on the path, in some life, they turn to tantra.

Intellectually yoga is conceivable, existentially it is impossible. It is possible you will reach by yoga also, but it almost never happens. It happens very rarely, such as to a Mahavira. Sometimes centuries and centuries pass and then a man like Mahavira appears who has achieved through yoga. But he is rare, an exception, and he breaks the rule.

But yoga is more attractive than tantra. Tantra is easy, natural, and you can attain through tantra very easily, very naturally, effortlessly. And because of this, tantra never appeals to you as much. Why? Anything that appeals to you appeals to your ego. Whatsoever you feel is going to fulfill your ego will appeal to you more. You are gripped in the ego, thus yoga appeals to you very much.

Really, the more egoistic you are, the more yoga will appeal to you, because it is pure ego effort. The more impossible, the more it is appealing to the ego. That is why Mount Everest has so much appeal. There is so much attraction to reach to the top of a Himalayan peak because it is so difficult. And when Hillary and Tensing reached Mount Everest, they felt a very ecstatic moment. What was that? It was because the ego was fulfilled—they were the first to reach the top of Everest.

When the first man landed on the moon, can you imagine how he felt? He was the first in all history. And now he cannot be replaced; he will remain the first in all the history to come. Now there is no way to change his status. The ego is fulfilled deeply. There is no competitor now, and there cannot be. Many will land on the moon but they will not be the first. Many can land on the moon and many can go to Everest—but yoga gives you a higher peak. And the more unreachable the end, the more there is the perfection of the ego— pure, perfect, absolute ego.

Yoga would have appealed to Nietzsche very much because he felt that the energy which is working behind life is the energy of will—the will to power. Yoga gives you that feeling. You are more powerful through it.

The more you can control yourself, the more you can control your instincts, the more you can control your body and the more you can control your mind, then the more you feel powerful. You become a master inside. But this is through conflict; this is through struggle and violence. And it always happens more or less that a person who has been practicing yoga for many lives comes to a point where the whole journey becomes drab, dreary, futile, because the more ego is fulfilled, the more you will feel it is useless. Then the follower of the path of yoga turns to tantra.

But yoga appeals because everyone is an egoist. Tantra never appeals in the beginning. Tantra can appeal only to those who have worked on them- selves, who have really been struggling through yoga for many lives. Then tantra appeals to them because they can understand. Ordinarily you will not be attracted by tantra, and if you are attracted you will be attracted by the wrong reasons, so try to understand them also.

You will not be attracted by tantra in the first place because it asks you to surrender, not to fight. It asks you to float, not to swim. It asks you to move with the current, not to go upstream. It tells

you nature is good; trust nature, do not fight it. Even sex is good. Trust it, follow it, flow into it; do not fight it. "No-fight" is the central teaching of tantra. Flow. Let go! This cannot appeal, there is no fulfillment of your ego through it. In the first step it asks for your ego to be dissolved, in the very begin- ning it asks you to dissolve it.

Yoga also asks you, but at the end. First it will ask you to purify it. And if it is purified completely it dissolves, it cannot remain. But that is the last in yoga, and in tantra that is the first.

So tantra will not appeal generally. And if it does appeal, it will appeal for wrong reasons. For example, if you want to indulge in sex then you can rationalize your indulgence through tantra. That can become the appeal. If you want to indulge in wine, in women, in other things, you can feel attracted toward tantra. But really, you are not attracted to tantra. Tantra is a façade—a trick. You are attracted to something else which you think tantra allows you. So tantra always appeals for wrong reasons.

Tantra is not to help your indulgence, it is to transform it. So do not deceive yourself. Through tantra you can deceive yourself very easily, and because of this possibility of deception Mahavira would not describe tantra. This possibility is always there. And man is so deceptive that he can show one thing when he really means another, he can rationalize.

For example, in China, in old China, there was something like tantra—a secret science. It is known as Tao. Tao has similar trends to tantra. For exam- ple, Tao says that it is good, if you want to be freed of sex, that you should not stick to one person—to one woman or one man. You should not stick to one person if you want to be freed. Tao says that it is better to go on changing partners.

This is absolutely right, but you can rationalize it; you can deceive yourself. You may just be a sex maniac and you can think, "I am doing tantra practice, so I cannot stick to one woman. I have to change partners." And many emperors in China practiced it. They had big harems only for this.

But Tao is meaningful if you look deep down into human psychology. If you know only one woman, sooner or later your attraction for that woman will wither away, but your attraction for women will remain. You will be attracted by the other sex. This woman, your wife, will really not be of the opposite sex. She will not attract you, she will not be a magnet for you. You will have become accustomed to her.

Tao says that if a man moves amidst women, many women, he will not only go beyond one, he will go beyond the opposite sex. The very knowledge of many women will help him to transcend. And this is right—but dangerous, because you would like it not because it is right but because it gives you license. That is the problem with tantra.

So in China also that knowledge was suppressed, it had to be suppressed. In India tantra was also suppressed because it said many dangerous things—dangerous only because you are deceptive. Otherwise they are wonderful. Nothing has happened to the human mind that is more wonderful and mysterious than tantra; no knowledge is so deep.

But knowledge always has its dangers. For example, now science has become a danger because it has come to know many deep secrets. Now it knows how to create atomic energy. Einstein is reported to have said that if he is again given a life, rather than being a scientist he would like to be a plumber, because as he looks back his whole life has been futile—not only futile, but dangerous to humanity. And he has given one of the deepest secrets, but to a mankind which is self-deceptive.

I wonder...the day may come soon when we will have to suppress scientific knowledge. There are rumors that there are secret discussions amid scientists about whether to disclose more or not—whether they should stop the search or whether they should go further, because now it is dangerous ground.

Every knowledge is dangerous; only ignorance is not dangerous, you cannot do much with it.

Superstitions are always good—never dangerous. They are homeopathic. If the medicine is given to you, it is not going to harm you. Whether it is going to help you or not depends on your own innocence, but one thing is certain: it is not going to harm you. Homeopathy is harmless; it is a deep superstition. If it works, it can only help. Remember, if something can only help then it is deep superstition. If it can do both, help and harm, then only is it knowledge. A real thing can do both, help and harm. Only an unreal thing can just help. But then the help never comes from the thing, it is always a projection of your own mind. So, in a way, only illusory things are good; they never harm you.

Tantra is science, and it is deeper than atomic knowledge because atomic science is concerned with matter and tantra is concerned with you, and you are always more dangerous than any atomic energy. Tantra is concerned with the biological atom, with you, the living cell, with life consciousness itself and how its inner mechanism works.

That is why tantra became so much interested in sex. One who is interested in life and consciousness will automatically become interested in sex because sex is the source of life, of love, of all that is happening in the world of consciousness. So if a seeker is not interested in sex, he is not a seeker at all. He may be a philosopher, but he is not a seeker. And philosophy is, more or less, nonsense—thinking about things which are of no use.

I have heard that Mulla Nasruddin was interested in girls, but he had very bad luck with girls, no one would like him. He was going to meet a certain girl for the first time, so he asked a friend, "What is your secret? You are wonderful with women, you simply hypnotize them, and I am always a failure, so give me some clue. I am going on a date for the first time with a girl, so give me some secrets."

The friend said, "Remember three things: always talk about food, family and philosophy."

"Why about food?" Mulla asked.

The friend said, "I talk about food because then the girl feels good—because every woman is interested in food. She is food for the child, for the whole humanity she is food, so she is basically interested in food."

Mulla said, "Okay. And why family?"

So the man said, "Talk about her family so your intentions look honorable."

Then Mulla said, "And why about philosophy?"

The man said, "Talk about philosophy, that makes the woman feel that she is intelligent."

So Mulla rushed to his date. Immediately when he saw the girl he said, "Hello, do you like noodles?"

The girl was startled and said, "No!"

Then the Mulla asked the second question: "Have you got two brothers?"

The girl was even more startled and wondered, "What type of date is this?" She said, "No!"

So for a moment Mulla was at a loss. He wondered, "How to start talking about philosophy?" Just for a moment he was at a loss, and then he asked, "Now, if you had a brother, would he like noodles?"

Philosophy is more or less nonsense. Tantra is not interested in philosophy, tantra is interested in actual existential life. So tantra never asks whether there is a God or whether there is *moksha*, liberation, or whether there is hell or heaven. Tantra asks basic questions about life. That is why there is so much interest in sex and love. They are basic. *You are* through them; you are part of them.

You are a play of sex energy and nothing less, and unless you understand this energy and transcend it you will never be anything more. You are, right now, nothing but sex energy. You can be more, but if you do not understand this and you do not transcend it you never will be more. The possibility is just there as a seed. That is why tantra is interested in sex, in love, in natural life.

But the way to know it is not through conflict. Tantra says you cannot know anything if you are in a fighting mood because then you are not receptive. Then because you are fighting the secrets will be hidden from you—you are not open to receive.

And whenever you are fighting you are always outside. If you are fighting sex you are always outside; if you surrender to sex you reach the very inner core of it, you are an insider. If you surrender then many things become known.

You have been in sex, but always with a fighting attitude behind it. That is why you have not known many secrets. For example, you have not known the life-giving forces of sex. You have not known them because you cannot know—that needs for you to be an insider.

If you are really flowing with sex energy, totally surrendered, sooner or later you will arrive at the point where you will know that sex cannot only give birth to a new life, sex can give you more life. To lovers sex can become a life-giving force, but for that you need a surrender. And once you are surrendered, many dimensions change.

For example, tantra has known, Tao has known, that if you ejaculate in the act, then it cannot be life-giving to you. There is no need to ejaculate; ejaculation can be totally forgotten. Tantra and Tao both say ejaculation is because you are fighting, otherwise there is no need of it.

The lover and the beloved can be in a deep sexual embrace, just relaxing into each other with no hurry to ejaculate, with no hurry to end the affair. They can just relax into each other. And if this relaxation is total, they both will feel more life. They both will enrich each other.

Tao says a man can live for one thousand years if he is not in any hurry with sex, if he is deeply relaxed. If a woman and man are deeply relaxed with each other, simply melting into each other, absorbed into each other, not in any hurry, not in any tension, many things happen—alchemical things happen—because the life juices of both, the electricity of both, the bioenergy of both, meet. And just by this meeting, because they are anti— one is negative, one is positive; they are antipoles —just by meeting with each other deeply, they invigorate each other, make each other vital, more alive.

They can live for a long time, and they can live never becoming old. But this can only be known if you are not in a fighting mood. And this seems paradoxical. Those who are fighting sex, they will ejaculate sooner because the tense mind is in a hurry to be relieved of the tension.

New research says many surprising things, many surprising facts. Masters and Johnson have worked scientifically for the first time with what happens in deep intercourse. They have come to realize that seventy-five percent of men are premature ejaculators—seventy-five percent! Before there is a deep meeting they have ejaculated and the act is finished. And ninety percent of women never have any orgasm; they never reach to a peak, to a deep, fulfilling peak—ninety percent of women!

That is why women are so angry and irritated, and they will remain so. No meditation can help them to be peaceful and no philosophy, no religion, no ethics will make them at ease with the men with whom they are living. They are in frustration, in anger, because modern science and old tantra both say that unless a woman is deeply fulfilled orgasmically she will be a problem in the family. That which she is lacking will create irritations and she will be always in a fighting mood.

So if your wife is always in a fighting mood, think again about the whole thing. It is not simply the wife—you may be the cause. And because women are not achieving orgasm, they become anti-sex. They are not willing to go into sex easily. They have to be bribed; they are not ready to go into sex. Why should they be ready if they never achieve any deep bliss through it? Rather, they feel after it that the man has been using them. They feel like a thing which has been used and then discarded.

The man is satisfied because be has ejaculated. Then he moves and goes to sleep, and the wife goes on weeping. She has been just used, and the experience has not been in any way fulfilling to her. It may have relieved her husband or lover or friend, but it has not been in any way fulfilling to her.

Ninety percent of women do not even know what orgasm is. They have never known it; they have never reached a peak of such a blissful convulsion of the body that every fiber vibrates and every cell becomes alive. They have not reached it, and this is because of an antisexual attitude in the society. The fighting mind is there, and the woman is so repressed that she has become frigid.

The man goes on doing the act as if it is a sin. He feels it as guilt, it is not to be done. And while he is making love to his wife or beloved, he is thinking of some *mahatma*—some so-called saint—of how to go to the mahatma and how to transcend this sex, this guilt, this sin.

It is very difficult to get rid of the mahatmas, they are even there while you are making love. You are not two; one mahatma must be there. If there is no mahatma, then God is watching you doing this sin. The concept of God in people's minds is just that of a Peeping Tom—he is always watching you. This attitude creates anxiety, and when anxiety is there ejaculation comes soon.

When there is no anxiety, ejaculation can be postponed for hours—even for days. And there is no need of it. If the love is deep, both parties can invigorate each other. Then ejaculation completely ceases, and for years two lovers can meet with each other without any ejaculation, without any wastage of energy. They can just relax with each other. Their bodies meet and relax; they enter sex and relax. And sooner or later, sex will not be an excitement. It is an excitement right now. Then it is not an excitement, it is a relaxation, a deep let-go.

But that can happen only if you have first surrendered inside to the life energy—the life force. Only then can you surrender to your lover or beloved. Tantra says this happens, and it says how it can happen.

Tantra says, never make love while you are excited. This seems very absurd because you want to make love when you are excited. And normally, both partners excite each other in order that they can make love. But tantra says that in excitement you are wasting energy. Make love while you are calm, serene, meditative. First meditate, then make love, and when making love do not go beyond the limit. What do I mean by "do not go beyond the limit"? Do not become excited and violent, in order that your energy will not be dispersed.

If you see two persons making love you will feel that they are fighting. If small children sometimes see their father and mother making love, they think the father is going to kill the mother. It looks violent, it looks like a fight. It is not beautiful, it looks ugly.

It must be more musical, harmonious. The two partners must be as if they are dancing, not fighting —as if singing one harmonious melody, just creating an atmosphere in which both may dissolve and become one. And then they relax. This is what tantra means. Tantra is not sexual at all, tantra is the least sexual thing and yet it has so much concern with sex. And if through this relaxation and let-go nature reveals to you its secrets, it is no wonder. Then you begin to be aware of what is happening. And in that awareness of what is happening many secrets come to your mind.

Firstly, sex becomes life-giving. As it is now it is death-giving, you simply dying through it, wasting yourself, deteriorating. Secondly, it becomes the deepest natural meditation. Your thoughts cease completely. When you are totally relaxed with your lover, your thoughts cease. The mind is not there, only your heart beats. It becomes a natural meditation. And if love cannot help you into meditation, nothing will help, because everything else is just superfluous, superficial. If love cannot help, nothing will help.

Love has its own meditation. But you do not know love; you know only sex and you know the misery of wasting energy. Then you get depressed after it. Then you decide to take a vow of *brahmacharya*, celibacy. And this vow is taken in depression, this vow is taken in anger, this vow is taken in frustration. It is not going to help.

A vow can be helpful if taken in a very relaxed, deeply meditative mood. Otherwise you are simply showing your anger, your frustration and nothing else, and you will forget the vow within twenty-four hours. The energy will have come again, and just as an old routine you will have to release it.

Tantra says, sex is very deep because it is life. But you can be interested in tantra for the wrong reasons. Do not be interested in tantra for wrong reasons, and then you will not feel that tantra is dangerous. Then tantra is life-transforming.

Some tantric methods have been used by yoga also, but with a conflict, a fighting attitude. Tantra uses the same methods, but with a very loving attitude—and that makes a great difference. The very quality of the technique changes. The technique becomes different because the whole background is different.

It has been asked, *What is the central subject matter of tantra?* The answer is *you!* You are the central subject matter of tantra: what you are right now and what is hidden in you that can grow, what you are and what you can be. Right now you are a sex unit, and unless this unit is understood deeply you cannot become a spirit, you cannot become a spiritual unit. Sexuality and spirituality are two ends of one energy.

Tantra starts with you as you are; yoga starts with what your possibility is. Yoga starts with the end; tantra starts with the beginning. And it is good to start with the beginning. It is always good to begin with the beginning, because if the end is made the beginning, then you are creating unnecessary misery for yourself. You are not the end—not the ideal. You have to become a god, the ideal, and you are just an animal. And this animal goes berserk because of the ideal of the god; it goes mad, it goes crazy.

Tantra says, forget the god. If you are the animal, understand this animal in its totality. In that understanding itself, the god will grow. And if it cannot grow through that understanding then forget it, it can never be. Ideals cannot bring your possibilities out; only the knowledge of the real will help. So you are the central subject matter of tantra, as you are and as you can become, your actuality and your possibility—they are the subject matter.

Sometimes people get worried. If you go to understand tantra, God is not discussed, *moksha*—liberation—is not discussed, nirvana is not discussed. What type of religion is tantra? Tantra discusses things which make you feel disgusted, which you do not want to discuss. Who wants to discuss sex? Everyone thinks he knows about it. Because you can reproduce, you think you know.

No one wants to discuss sex and sex is everyone's problem. No one wants to discuss love because everyone feels he is a great lover already. And look at your life! It is just hatred and nothing else. And whatsoever you call love is nothing but a relaxation, a little relaxation, of the hatred. Look around you, and then you will know what you know about love.

Baal Shem, a fakir, went to his tailor every day for his robe, and the tailor took six months to make a simple robe for the fakir. The poor fakir! When the robe was ready and the tailor gave it to him, Baal Shem said, "Tell me, even God had only six days to create the world. Within six days God created the whole world and you took six months to make this poor man's robe?"

Baal Shem remembered the tailor in his memoirs. The tailor said, "Yes, God created the world in six days, but look at the world, at what type of world it is. Yes, he created the world in six days, but look at the world!"

Look around you; look at the world you have created. Then you will come to know that you do not know anything, you are just groping in the dark. And because everyone else is also groping in the dark, it cannot be that you are living in light. If everyone else is groping in the dark you feel good, because then you feel there is no comparison.

But you are also in the dark, and tantra starts with you as you are. Tantra wants to enlighten you about basic things which you cannot deny. If you try to deny them, it is at your own cost.

The second question:

How can one convert the sex act into a meditative experience? Should one practice any special positions in sex?

Positions are irrelevant; positions are not very meaningful. The real thing is the attitude—not the position of the body, but the position of the mind. But if you change your mind you may want to change your positions, because they are related. But they are not basic.

For example, the man is always on the woman—on top of the woman. This is an egoist posture because the man always thinks he is better, superior, higher—how can he be below the woman? But all over the world in primitive societies the woman is above the man. So in Africa this posture is known as the missionary posture, because when Christian missionaries went to Africa, the primitives just could not understand what they were doing. They thought it would kill the woman.

The man-on-top posture is known in Africa as the missionary posture. African primitives say this is violent that man should be on top of the woman. She is weaker, delicate, so she must be on top of the man. But it is difficult for man to think of himself as lower than woman, under her.

If your mind changes, many things will change. It is better that the woman should be on top, for many reasons. If the woman is on top she will be passive, so she is not going to do much violence; she will simply relax. And the man under her cannot do much, he will have to relax. This is good. If he is on top he is going to be violent, he will do much. And nothing is needed to be done on her part. For tantra you have to relax, so it is good that the woman should be on top. She can relax better than any man. The feminine psychology is more passive, so relaxation comes easy.

Positions will change, but do not be bothered about positions much. Just change your mind. Surrender to the life force, float in it. Sometimes, if you are really surrendered, your bodies will take the right position that is needed in that moment. If both partners are deeply surrendered, their bodies will take the right posture that is needed.

Every day situations change, so there is no need to fix postures beforehand. That is a problem, that you try to fix it beforehand. Whenever you try to fix it, this is a fixing by the mind; then you are not surrendering.

If you surrender then you let things take their own shape, and that is a wonderful harmony—when both partners have surrendered. They will take many postures or they will not take them and will just relax. That depends on the life force, not on your cerebral decision beforehand. You need not decide anything beforehand. Decision is the problem. Even to make love, you decide. Even to make love, you go and consult books.

There are books on how to make love. This shows what type of human mind we have produced. You even consult books on how to make love. Then it becomes cerebral; you think everything. Really, you create a rehearsal in the mind and then you enact it. Your action is a copy, it is never real then. You are enacting a rehearsal. It becomes acting, it is not authentic.

Just surrender and move with the force. What is the fear? Why be afraid? If you cannot be unafraid with your lover, then where will you be unafraid? And once you have the feeling that the life force helps by itself and takes the right path that is needed, it will give you a very basic insight into your whole life. Then you can leave your whole life to the divine that is your beloved.

Then you leave your whole life to the divine. Then you do not think and you do not plan; you do not force the future according to you. You just allow yourself to move into the future according to the divine, according to the total.

But how to make the sex act a meditation? Just by surrendering it becomes so. Do not think about it, let it happen. And be relaxed, do not move ahead. This is one of the basic problems with the mind: it always moves ahead. It is always seeking the result, and the result is in the future. You are never in the act, you are always in the future seeking a result. That seeking of a result is disturbing everything, it damages everything.

Just be in the act. What is the future? It is to come, you need not worry about it. And you are not going to bring it with your worries. It is already coming; it has already come. So you forget about it, you just be here and now.

Sex can become a deep insight into being here and now. That is, I think, the only act now left in which you can be here and now. You cannot be here and now while in your office, you cannot be here and now while you are studying in your college, you cannot be here and now anywhere in this modern world. Only in love can you be here and now.

But even then you are not. You are thinking of the result. And now many modern books have created many new problems. You read a book on how to make love, and then you are afraid about whether you are making it rightly or wrongly. You read a book on how a posture is to be taken, or what type of posture is to be used, and then you are afraid about whether you are taking the right posture or not.

Psychologists have created new worries in the mind. Now they say the husband must remember whether his wife is achieving orgasm or not, so he is worried over it. And this worry is not going to help in any way, it is going to become a hindrance.

The wife is worried whether she is helping the husband to relax totally or not. She must show that she is feeling very blissful. Then everything becomes false. Both are worried about the result, and because of this worry the result will never come.

Forget everything. Flow in the moment and allow your bodies their expression. Your bodies know well; they have their own wisdom. Your bodies are constituted of sex cells. They have a built-in program; you are not asked at all. Just leave it to the body and the body will move. This leaving it to nature together, both together, this let-go, will create meditation automatically.

And if you can feel it in sex, then you know one thing: that whenever you surrender you will feel the same. Then you can surrender to a master. It is a love relationship. You can surrender to a master, and then while you are putting your head at his feet, your head will become empty. You will be in meditation.

Then there is even no need of a master. Then go out and surrender to the sky. You know how to surrender—that is all. Then you can go and surrender to a tree. But it looks foolish because we do not know how to surrender. We see a person—a villager, a primitive man—going to the river, surrendering himself to the river, calling the river the mother, the divine mother, or surrendering himself to the rising sun, calling the rising sun a great god, or going to a tree and putting his head at the roots and surrendering.

For us it looks superstitious. You say, "What nonsense he is doing! What will the tree do? What will the river do? They are not goddesses. What is the sun? The sun is not a god." Anything becomes a god if you can surrender. So your surrender creates divinity. There is nothing divine, there is only a surrendering mind which creates divinity.

Surrender to a wife and she becomes divine. Surrender to a husband and he becomes divine. The divinity is revealed through surrender. Surrender to a stone and there is no stone now: that stone has become a statue, a person—alive.

So just know how to surrender. And when I say how to surrender, I do not mean to know a technique; I mean you have a natural possibility of surrendering in love. Surrender in love and feel it there. And then let it spread all over your life.

The third question:

Please explain whether the _anahat nad_—soundless sound—is a type of sound or whether it is total soundlessness. And also explain how the state of total soundfulness can be equal to total soundlessness.

Anahat nad is not a type of sound, it is soundlessness, but this soundlessness is heard. To express it is difficult because then the logical question arises of how soundlessness can be heard.

Let me explain it…. I am sitting on this chair. If I go away from this chair, will you not see my absence in the chair? It cannot be seen by one who has not seen me sitting here, he will simply see the chair. But a moment before I was here and you have seen me sitting here. If I move away and you look at the chair, you will see two things: the chair and my absence. But that absence will be seen only if you have seen me and you have not forgotten me, that I was there.

We are hearing sounds; we only know sounds. So when that soundlessness comes, anahat nad, we feel that every sound has disappeared and absence is felt. That is why it is called anahat nad. It is also called nad; 'nad' means sound. But 'anahat' changes the quality of the sound. 'Anahat' means uncreated, so it is uncreated sound.

Every sound is a created sound. Whatsoever sounds you have heard, they are all created. That which is created will die. I can clap my hands—a sound is created. It was not there before and now it is no more; it was created and it has died. A created sound is known as _ahat nad_. Uncreated sound is known as anahat nad—the sound that is always. Which is that sound that is always? It is not really a sound. You call it a sound because the absence is heard.

If you live by a railway station and one day the railway union goes on strike, you will hear something no one can hear. You will hear the absence of the trains coming and going and moving.

I was traveling in the past for at least three weeks every month. In the beginning it was very difficult to sleep in the train, and then it became difficult to sleep at home. When I was no longer sleeping only in trains, the sound of the train was missed. Whenever I would reach home it would be difficult, because I would miss and I would feel the absence of the railway sounds.

We are accustomed to sounds. Every moment is filled with sound. Our heads are constantly filled by sounds and sounds and sounds. When your mind goes away, moves up or down, goes beyond or below, when you are not in the world of sounds, you can hear the absence. That absence is sound-lessness.

But we have called it anahat nad. Because it is heard we call it nad—sound; and because it is not really a sound we call it anahat—uncreated. "Un-created sound" is contradictory. Sound *is* created—"uncreated" contradicts. So all deep experiences of life have to be expressed in contradictory terms.

If you go and ask a master like Eckhart or Jacob Böhme, or Zen masters like Hyakujo or Obaku or Bodhidharma or Nagarjuna, or Vedanta and the Upanishads, everywhere you will find two contra-dictory terms whenever a deeper experience is talked about.

The Vedas say, "He is and he is not"—about God. You cannot find a more atheistic expression: "He is and he is not." He is far away and he is near. He is far away and he is also near. Why contradic-tory statements? The Upanishads say, "You cannot see him, but unless you see him you have not seen anything." What type of language is this?

Lao Tzu says that "Truth cannot be said"—and he is saying it! This too is a saying. He says that "Truth cannot be said; if it is said it cannot be true," and then he writes a book and says some-thing about the truth. It is contradictory.

One student came to a great old sage. The student said, "If you can forgive me, master, I want to relate to you something about myself. I have become an atheist; now I do not believe in God."

So the old sage asked, "For how many days have you been studying scriptures? For how many days?"

So the seeker, the student said, "Nearabout twenty years I have been studying the Vedas, the scriptures."

So the old man sighed and said, "Just twenty years and you have the nerve to say that you have

become an atheist?"

The student was puzzled. What was this old man saying? So he said, "I am puzzled. What are you saying? You make me more confused than when I came here."

The old man said, "Go on studying the Vedas. In the beginning one says God is. Only in the end does one say God is not. To become an atheist you will have to travel much into theism. God is at the beginning; God is not at the end. Do not be in a hurry." The student was even more puzzled.

"God is and God is not" has been uttered by those who know. "God is" is uttered by those who do not know and "God is not" is also uttered by those who do not know. Those who know, they utter both simultaneously: God is and God is not.

'Anahat nad' is a contradictory term, but used with much consideration, with deep consideration, it is meaningful. It says that the phenomenon is felt as a sound and it is not a sound. It is felt as a sound because you have only felt sounds, you do not know any other language. You know only the language of sounds; that is why it is felt as sound. But it is silence, not sound.

And the question further says: *Explain how the state of soundfulness can be equal to total sound-lessness.* It is always so. The zero and the absolute both mean the same!

For example, if I have a jar which is completely empty and I have another jar which is completely filled, both are complete. One is completely empty, another is completely filled. But both are complete, both are perfect. If the jar is half-filled, it is half-filled and half-empty. You can call it half-empty, you can call it half-filled. But if it is completely empty or completely filled, one thing is common to both: completeness.

Soundlessness is complete. You cannot do any-thing more to make it more soundless. Understand this: it is complete, nothing can be done. You have come to a point beyond which there is no move-ment possible. And if a sound is total you cannot add anything to it. You have come to another limit;

you cannot go beyond it. This is common and this is what is meant.

One can say it is soundlessness because no sound is heard, everything has become absent. You cannot take anything further from it; it is complete. Or you can say it is a complete sound, a full sound, absolute sound; nothing can be added to it. But in both the cases the indication is for perfection, absoluteness, wholeness.

It depends on the mind. There are two types of minds and two types of expressions. For example, if you ask Buddha, "What will happen in deep meditation? When one achieves *samadhi* what will happen?" he will say, "There will be no *dukkha*—there will be no pain." He will never say there will be bliss, he will simply say there will be no pain—

just painlessness. If you ask Shankara, he will never talk about pain. He will simply say, "There will be bliss—absolute bliss."

And both are expressing the same experience. Buddha saying "no pain" refers to the world. He says, "All the pains I have known are not there. And whatsoever is there, I cannot relate it in your language."

Shankara says, "There is bliss, absolute bliss." He never talks about the world and its pain. He is not referring to your world, he is referring to the experience itself. He is positive, Buddha is negative. But their indications are toward the same moon.

Their fingers are different, but what their fingers indicate is the same.

CHAPTER 33

The spirituality of the of the tantric sex act

◆

48 *At the start of sexual union keep attentive on the fire in the beginning, and so continuing, avoid the embers in the end.*

49 *When in such embrace your senses are shaken as leaves, enter this shaking.*

50 *Even remembering union, without the embrace, transformation.*

51 *On joyously seeing a long-absent friend, permeate this joy.*

52 *When eating or drinking, become the taste of food or drink, and be filled.*

Sigmund Freud has said somewhere that man is born neurotic. This is a half-truth. Man is not born neurotic, but he is born in a neurotic humanity and the society around drives everyone neurotic sooner or later. Man is born natural, real, normal, but the moment the newborn becomes part of the society neurosis starts working. As we are, we are neurotic, and the neurosis consists of a split—a deep split. You are not one: you are two or even many. This has to be understood deeply; only then can we proceed in tantra.

Your feeling and thinking have become two different things: this is the basic neurosis. Your thinking part and your feeling part have become two, and you are identified with the thinking part, not with the feeling part. And feeling is more real than thinking; feeling is more natural than thinking. You have come with a feeling heart, but thinking is cultivated; it is given by society. And your feeling has become a suppressed thing. Even when you say that you feel, you only think that you feel. The feeling has become dead, and this has happened for certain reasons.

When a child is born, he is a feeling being: he feels things. He is not a thinking being yet. He is natural, just like anything natural in nature—just like a tree or like an animal. But we start molding him, cultivating. He has to suppress his feelings because without suppressing his feelings he is always in trouble. When he wants to cry he cannot cry because his parents will not approve of it. He

will be condemned. He will not be appreciated, he will not be loved. He is not accepted as he is. He must behave: he must behave according to a particular ideology, ideals. Only then will he be loved.

Love is not for him as he is. He can be loved only if he follows certain rules. Those rules are imposed; they are not natural. The natural being begins to become suppressed, and the unnatural, the unreal, is imposed over it. This unreal is your mind, and a moment comes when the split is so great that you cannot bridge it. You go on forgetting completely what your real nature was—or is. You are a false face; the original face is lost. And you are also afraid to feel the original, because the moment you feel it the whole society will be against you. So you yourself are against your real nature.

This creates a very neurotic state. You do not know what you want; you do not know what are your real, authentic needs. And then you go on after nonauthentic needs because only the feeling heart can give you the sense, the direction, of what are your real needs. When they are suppressed you create symbolic needs. For example, you may go on eating more and more, stuffing yourself with food, and you may never feel that you are filled. The need is for love; it is not for food. But food and love are deeply related, so when the need for love is not felt, or is suppressed, a false need for food is created and you can go on eating. Because the need is false, it can never be fulfilled, and we live in false needs. That is why there is no fulfillment.

You want to be loved; that is a basic need—natural. But it can be diverted into a false dimen-

465

sion. For example, the love need, the need to be loved, can be felt as a false need if you try to divert the attention of others to yourself. You want that others should pay attention to you, so you may become a political leader. Great crowds may pay attention to you, but the real basic need is to be loved. And even if the whole world is paying attention to you, that basic need cannot be fulfilled. That basic need can be fulfilled even by a single person loving you, paying attention to you because of love.

When you love someone, you pay attention to him. Attention and love are deeply related. If you suppress the need for love, then it becomes a symbolic need; then you need the attention of others. You may get it, but then too there will be no fulfillment. The need is false, disconnected from the natural, basic need. This division in the personality is neurosis.

Tantra is a very revolutionary concept—the oldest and yet the newest. Tantra is one of the oldest traditions and yet nontraditional, even anti-traditional, because tantra says unless you are whole and one you are missing life altogether. You should not remain in a split state: you must become one. What to do to become one? You can go on thinking, but that is not going to help because thinking is the technique to divide. Thinking is analytical. It divides; it splits things. Feeling unites, synthesizes, makes things one. So you can go on thinking, reading, studying, contemplating. It is not going to help unless you fall back to the feeling center. But it is very difficult, because even when we think about the feeling center, we *think!*

When you say to someone, "I love you," be aware of whether it is just a thought or whether it is a feeling. If it is just a thought, then you are missing something. A feeling is of the whole: your whole body, mind, everything you are, is involved. In thinking, only your head is involved, and that too not totally, but just a fragment of it. There is only a passing thought; it may not be there the next moment. Only a fragment is involved, and that creates much misery in life—because with a frag-

mentary thought, you give promises which you cannot fulfill. You can say, "I love you and I will love you forever." However, the second part is a promise which you cannot fulfill because it is given by a fragmentary thought. Your whole being is not involved in it. And what will you do tomorrow when the fragment has gone and the thought is no more there? Now the promise will become a bondage.

Sartre said somewhere that every promise is going to be false. You cannot promise because you are not whole. Just a part of you promises, and when the part is no more there on the throne and another part has taken over, what are you going to do? Who will fulfill the promise? Hypocrisy is born because when you go on trying to fulfill, pretending that you are fulfilling, then everything becomes false. Tantra says fall down deep within to the feeling center. What to do and how to fall back? Now I will enter the sutras. These sutras, each sutra, is an effort to make you whole.

---

48 In the sex act, do not seek the release.

The first sutra: *At the start of sexual union keep attentive on the fire in the beginning, and so continuing, avoid the embers in the end.*

Sex can be a very deep fulfillment, and sex can throw you back to your wholeness, to your natural, real being, for many reasons. Those reasons have to be understood. One, sex is a total act. You are thrown off your mind, off balance. That is why there is so much fear of sex. You are identified with the mind, and sex is a no-mind act. You become headless; you do not have any head in the act. There is no reasoning, no mental process. And if there is any mental process, there is no real, authentic sex act. Then there is no orgasm, no fulfillment. Then the sex act itself becomes a local thing, something cerebral, and it has become so.

All over the world, so much hankering, so much lust for sex, is not because the world has become more sexual. It is because you cannot even enjoy sex as a total act. The world was more sexual before. That is why there was no such hankering for sex. This hankering shows that the real is missing and there is only the false. The whole modern mind has become sexual because the sex act itself is no more there. Even the sex act is transferred to the mind. It has become mental; you think about it.

Many people come to me...they say they go on thinking about sex; they enjoy thinking about it, reading, seeing pictures, pornography. They enjoy this, but when the actual moment for sex comes they suddenly feel they are not interested. They even feel they have become impotent. They feel vital energy when they are thinking. When they want to move into the actual act, they feel there is no energy, even no desire. They feel that the body has become dead.

What is happening to them? Even the sex act has become mental. They can only think about it; they cannot do it because doing will involve their whole being. And whenever there is any involvement of the whole, the head becomes uneasy because then it can no more be the master; it can no more be in control.

Tantra uses the sex act to make you whole, but then you have to move in it very meditatively. Then you have to move in it forgetting all that you have heard about sex, studied about sex, all that the society has told you: the church, your religion, the teachers. Forget everything and get involved in it in your totality. Forget to control! Control is the barrier. Rather, be possessed by it; do not control it. Move in it as if you have become mad. The "no-mind" state looks like madness. Become the body, become the animal, because the animal is whole. And as modern man is, only sex seems to be the easiest possibility to make you whole because sex is the deepest, the biological center within you. You are born out of it. Your every cell is a sex cell; your whole body is a sex-energy phenomenon.

This first sutra says, *At the start of sexual union keep attentive on the fire in the beginning, and so continuing, avoid the embers in the end.* And this makes the whole difference. For you, the sex act is a release. So when you move in it you are in a hurry. You just want a release. Overflowing energy will be released; you will feel at ease. This at-easeness is just a sort of weakness. Overflowing energy creates tensions, excitement. You feel something has to be done. When the energy is released, you feel weak. You may take this weakness as relaxation. Because the excitement is no more, the overflowing energy is no more, you can relax. But this relaxation is a negative relaxation. If you can relax just by throwing energy, it is at a very great cost. And this relaxation can only be physical. It cannot go deeper and cannot become spiritual.

This first sutra says don't be in a hurry and do not hanker for the end: remain with the beginning. There are two parts to the sex act—the beginning and the end. Remain with the beginning. The beginning part is more relaxed, warm. But do not be in a hurry to move to the end. Forget the end completely.

At the start of sexual union, keep attentive on the fire in the beginning. While you are overflowing, do not think in terms of release; remain with this overflowing energy. Do not seek ejaculation; forget it completely. Be whole in this warm beginning. Remain with your beloved or your lover as if you have become one. Create a circle.

There are three possibilities. Two lovers meeting can create three figures—geometrical figures. You may have even read about it or even seen an old alchemical picture in which a man and woman are standing naked within three geometrical figures. One figure is a square, another figure is a triangle and the third figure is a circle.

This is one of the old alchemical and tantric analyses of the sex act. Ordinarily, when you are in the sex act, there are four persons, not two, and this is a square: four angles are there because you yourself are divided in two—into the thinking part and the feeling part. Your partner is also divided in two; you are four persons. Two persons are not meeting there, four persons are meeting. It is a crowd, and there can be no deep meeting really. There are four corners, and the meeting is just false. It looks like a meeting, but it is not. There can be no communion because your deeper part is hidden and your beloved's deeper part is also hidden. Only two heads are meeting, only two thinking processes are meeting —not two feeling processes. They are hidden.

The second type of meeting can be like a triangle. You are two—two angles of the base. For a sudden moment you become one, like the third angle of the triangle. For a sudden moment your two-ness is lost and you become one. This is better than a square meeting because at least for a single moment there is oneness. That oneness gives you health, vitality. You feel alive and young again.

But the third is the best and the third is the tantric meeting: you become a circle. There are no angles, and the meeting is not for a single moment. The meeting is really nontemporal; there is no time in it. And this can happen only if you are not seeking ejaculation. If you are seeking ejaculation, then it will become a triangle meeting—because the moment there is ejaculation the contact point is lost.

Remain with the beginning; do not move to the end. How to remain in the beginning? Many things are to be remembered. First, don't take the sex act as a way of going anywhere. Don't take it as a means, it is the end in itself. There is no end to it; it is not a means. Secondly, do not think of the future, remain with the present. And if you cannot remain in the present in the beginning part of the sex act, then you can never remain in the present—because the very nature of the act is such that you are thrown into the present.

Remain in the present. Enjoy the meeting of two bodies, two souls, and merge into each other, melt into each other. Forget that you are going anywhere. Remain in the moment going nowhere, and melt. Warmth, love, should be made a situation for two persons to melt into each other. That is why, if there is no love, the sex act is a hurried act. You are using the other; the other is just a means. And the

other is using you. You are exploiting each other, not merging into each other. With love you can merge. This merging in the beginning will give many new insights.

If you are not in a hurry to finish the act, the act, by and by, becomes less and less sexual and more and more spiritual. Sex organs also melt into each other. A deep, silent communion happens between two body energies, and then you can remain for hours together. This togetherness moves deeper and deeper as time passes. But don't think. Remain with the moment deeply merged. It becomes an ecstasy, a samadhi, cosmic consciousness. And if you can know this, if you can feel and realize this, your sexual mind will become nonsexual. A very deep *brahmacharya,* celibacy, can be attained. Celibacy can be attained through it!

This looks paradoxical because we have been always thinking in terms that if a person has to remain celibate he must not look at the other sex, he must not meet the other sex. He must avoid, escape. A very false celibacy happens then: the mind goes on thinking about the other sex. And the more you escape from the other, the more you have to think, because this is a basic, deep need.

Tantra says do not try to escape; there is no escape possible. Rather, use nature itself to transcend. Don't fight; accept nature in order to transcend it. If this communion with your beloved or your lover is prolonged with no end in mind, then you can just remain in the beginning. Excitement is energy. You can lose it; you can come to a peak. Then the energy is lost and a depression will follow, a weakness will follow. You may take it as relaxation, but it is negative.

Tantra gives you a dimension of a higher relaxation which is positive. Both partners melting with each other give vital energy to each other. They become a circle, and their energy begins to move in a circle. They are giving life to each other, renewing life. No energy is lost. Rather, more energy is gained because through the contact with the opposite sex your every cell is challenged, excited. And if you can merge into that excitement without leading it to a peak, if you can remain in the beginning without becoming hot, just remaining warm, then those two "warmths" will meet and you can prolong the act for a very long time. With no ejaculation, with no throwing energy out, it becomes a meditation, and through it you become whole. Through it your split personality is no more split; it is bridged.

All neurosis is a "splitness." If you are bridged again, you become again a child—innocent. And once you know this innocence you can go on behaving in your society as it requires. But now this behavior is just a drama, an acting. You are not involved in it. It is a requirement, so you do it. But you are not in it; you are just acting.

You will have to use unreal faces because you live in an unreal world; otherwise the world will crush you and kill you. We have killed many real faces. We crucified Jesus because he started behaving like a real man. The unreal society will not tolerate it. We poisoned Socrates because he started behaving like a real man. Behave as the society requires; do not create unnecessary troubles for yourself and others. But once you know your real being and the wholeness, the unreal society cannot drive you neurotic; it cannot make you mad.

At the start of sexual union keep attentive on the fire in the beginning, and so continuing, avoid the embers in the end. If ejaculation is there, energy is dissipated. Then there is no more fire. You are simply relieved of your energy without gaining anything.

---

49 Shaking in sex.

The second sutra: *When in such embrace your senses are shaken as leaves, enter this shaking.*

When in such embrace, in such deep communion with the beloved or the lover, *your senses are shaken as leaves, enter this shaking.* We have even become afraid: while making love you do not allow your bodies to move much, because if your bodies are allowed much movement the sex act spreads all over your body. You can control it when it is localized at the sex center. The mind can remain in control. When it spreads all over your body, you cannot control it. You may start shaking, you may start screaming, and you will not be able to control your body once the body takes over.

We suppress movements. Particularly, all over the world, we suppress all movements, all shaking for women. They remain just like dead bodies. You are doing something to them; they are not doing anything to you. They are just passive partners. Why is this happening? Why all over the world do men suppress women in such a way? There is fear—because once a woman's body becomes possessed, it is very difficult for a man to satisfy her: because a woman can have chain orgasms; a man cannot have. A man can have only one orgasm; a woman can have chain orgasms. There are cases of multiple orgasms reported. Any woman can have at least three orgasms in a chain, but man can have only one. And with man's orgasm, the woman is aroused and is ready for further orgasms. Then it is difficult. Then how to manage it?

She needs another man immediately, and group sex is a taboo. All over the world we have created monogamous societies. We seem to feel that it is better to suppress the woman. So, really, eighty to ninety percent of women never know what orgasm is. They can give birth to children; that is another thing. They can satisfy the man; that is also another thing. But they themselves are never satisfied. So if you see such bitterness in women all over the world—sadness, bitterness, frustration—it is natural. Their basic need is not fulfilled.

Shaking is just wonderful because when you shake in your sex act the energy starts flowing all over the body, the energy vibrates all over the body. Every cell of the body is involved then. Every cell becomes alive because every cell is a sex cell.

When you were born, two sex cells met and your body was created; those two sex cells are everywhere in your body. They have multiplied and multiplied and multiplied, but your basic unit remains the sex cell. When you shake all over your body, it is not only a meeting of you with your beloved. Within your body also, each cell is meeting with the opposite cell. This shaking shows it. It will look animallike, but man *is* an animal and there is nothing wrong in it.

This second sutra says, *When in such embrace your senses are shaken as leaves....* A great wind is blowing and a tree is shaking. Even the roots are shaking, every leaf is shaking. Just be like a tree. A great wind is blowing, and sex *is* a great wind—a great energy blowing through you. Shake! Vibrate! Allow every cell of your body to dance, and this should be for both. The beloved is also dancing, every cell vibrating. Only then can you both meet, and then that meeting is not mental. It is a meeting of your bioenergies.

Enter this shaking, and while shaking don't remain aloof. Don't be a spectator, because mind is the spectator. Don't stand aloof! Be the shaking, become the shaking. Forget everything and become the shaking. It is not that your body is shaking: it is *you,* your whole being. You become the shaking itself. Then there are not two bodies, two minds. In the beginning, there are two shaking energies, and in the end just a circle—not two.

What will happen in this circle? One, you will be part of an existential force—not a societal mind, but an existential force. You will be part of the whole cosmos. In that shaking you will be part of the whole cosmos. That moment is of great creation. You are dissolved as solid bodies. You have become liquid—flowing into each other. The mind is lost, the division is lost. You have a oneness.

This is *advaita,* this is nonduality. And if you cannot feel this nonduality, then all the philosophies of nonduality are useless. They are just words. Once you know this nondual existential moment, then only can you understand the Upanishads. Then only you can understand the mystics—what they are talking about when they talk of a cosmic oneness, a wholeness. Then you are not separate from the world, not alien to it. Then the existence becomes your home. And with that feeling that "Now I am at home in the existence," all worries are lost. Then there is no anguish, no struggle, no conflict. This is what Lao Tzu calls Tao, what Shankara calls advaita. You can choose your own word for it, but through a deep love embrace it is easy to feel it. But be alive, shaking, and become the shaking itself.

---

50 Make love without the partner.

The third sutra: *Even remembering union, without the embrace, transformation.*

Once you know this, even the partner is not needed. You can simply remember the act and enter into it. But first you must have the feeling. If you know the feeling, you can enter into the act without the partner. This is a little difficult, but it happens. And unless it happens, you go on being dependent, a dependency is created. For so many reasons it happens. If you have had the feeling, if you have known the moment when you were not there but only a vibrating energy had become one and there was a circle with the partner, in that moment there was no partner. In that moment only you are, and for the partner you are not: only he or she is. That oneness is centered within you; the partner is no more there. And it is easier for women to have this feeling because they are always making love with closed eyes.

During this technique, it is good if you have your eyes closed. Then only an inner feeling of a circle, only an inner feeling of oneness, is there. Then just remember it. Close your eyes; lie down as if you are with your partner. Just remember and start feeling it. Your body will begin to shake and vibrate. Allow it! Forget completely that the other is not there. Move as if the other is present. Only in the beginning is it 'as if.' Once you know, then it is not 'as if,' then the other is there.

Move as if you are actually going into the love act. Do whatsoever you would have done with your partner. Scream, move, shake. Soon the circle will be there, and this circle is miraculous. Soon you will feel that the circle is created, but now this circle is not created with a man and woman. If you are man, then the whole universe has become woman; if you are woman, then the whole universe has become man. Now you are in a deep communion with the existence itself, and the door, the other, is no more there.

The other is simply a door. While making love to a woman, you are really making love to existence itself. The woman is just a door, the man is just a door. The other is just a door for the whole, but you are in such a hurry you never feel it. If you remain in communion, in deep embrace for hours together, you will forget the other and the other will just become an extension of the whole. Once this technique is known you can use it alone, and when you can use it alone it gives you a new freedom—freedom from the other.

It really happens that the whole existence becomes the other—your beloved, your lover—and then this technique can be used continuously, and one can remain in constant communion with the existence. And then you can do it in other dimensions also. Walking in the morning, you can do it. Then you are in communion with the air, with the rising sun and the stars and the trees. Staring at the stars in the night, you can do it. Looking at the moon, you can do it. You can be in the sex act with the whole universe once you know how it happens.

But it is good to start with human beings because they are nearest to you—the nearest part of the universe. But they are dispensable. You can take a jump and forget the door completely—*Even remembering union...transformation*—and you *will* be transformed, you will become new.

Tantra uses sex as a vehicle. It is energy; it can be used as a vehicle. It can transform you, and it can give you transcendental states. But as we are using sex, it looks difficult for us—because we are using it in a very wrong way, and the wrong way is not natural. Even animals are better than us: they are using it in a natural way. Our ways are perverted. Constant hammering on the human mind that sex is sin has created a deep barrier within you. You never allow yourself a total let-go. Something is always standing aloof condemning, even for the new generation. They may say they are not burdened, obsessed, that sex is not a taboo for them, but you cannot unburden your unconscious so easily. It has been built over centuries and centuries; the whole human past is there. So while you may not be condemning it as sin consciously, the unconscious is there constantly condemning it. You are never totally in it. Something is always left out. That left-out part creates the split.

Tantra says move in it totally. Just forget yourself, your civilization, your religion, your culture, your ideology. Forget everything. Just move in the sex act: move in it totally; do not leave anything out. Become absolutely nonthinking. Only then does the awareness happen that you have become one with someone. And this feeling of oneness can then be detached from the partner and it can be used with the whole universe. You can be in a sex act with a tree, with the moon, with anything. Once you know how to create this circle, it can be created with anything—even without anything.

You can create this circle within yourself because man is both man and woman, and woman is both woman and man. You are both because you were created by two. You were created by man and woman both, so half of you remains the other. You can forget everything completely, and the circle can be created within you. Once the circle is created within you—your man is meeting your woman, the inner woman is meeting the inner man—you are in an embrace within yourself.

And only when this circle is created is real celibacy attained. Otherwise all celibacies are just perversions, and then they create their own problems. When this circle is created inside, you are freed.

This is what tantra says: Sex is the deepest bondage, yet it can be used as a vehicle for the highest freedom. Tantra says poison can be used as medicine, but wisdom is needed. So do not condemn anything. Rather, use it. And do not be against anything. Find out ways how it can be used and transformed. Tantra is a deep, total acceptance of life. It is the only approach of its kind. All over the world, in all the centuries that have gone by, tantra is unique. It says don't throw anything and don't be against anything and don't create any conflict, because with any conflict you will be destructive with yourself.

All the religions are against sex, afraid of it, because it is such a great energy. Once you are in it you are no more, and then the current will take you anywhere; that is why the fear. So create a barrier in which you and the current become two, and do not allow this vital energy to have any possession over you: be the master of it.

Only tantra says that this mastery is going to be false, diseased, pathological, because you cannot really be divided with this current. You are it! So all divisions will be false, arbitrary—and basically no division is possible because you *are* the current, a part and parcel of it, just a wave in it. You can become frozen and you can separate yourself from the current, but that frozenness will be deadness. And humanity has become dead. No one is really alive; you are just dead weights floating in the stream. Melt!

Tantra says try to melt. Do not become like icebergs: melt and become one with the river. Becoming one with the river, feeling one with the river, merging in the river, be aware and there will be transformation. There *is* transformation. Transformation is not through conflict, it is through awareness. These three techniques are very, very scientific, but then sex becomes something other than what you know. Then it is not a temporary

relief, then it is not throwing energy out. Then there is no end to it. It becomes a meditative circle.

---

51 When joy arises, become it.

A few more related techniques: *On joyously seeing a long-absent friend, permeate this joy.*

Enter this joy and become one with it—any joy, any happiness. This is just an example: *On joyously seeing a long-absent friend....* Suddenly you see a friend you have not seen for many, many days or many, many years. A sudden joy grips you. But your attention will be on the friend, not on your joy. Then you are missing something, and this joy will be momentary. Your attention is focused on the friend: you will start talking, remembering things, and you will miss this joy and this joy will go.

When you see a friend and suddenly feel a joy arising in your heart, concentrate on this joy. Feel it and become it, and meet the friend while being aware and filled with your joy. Let the friend be just on the periphery, and you remain centered in your feeling of happiness.

This can be done in many other situations. The sun is rising, and suddenly you feel something rising within you. Then forget the sun; let it remain on the periphery. You be centered in your own feeling of rising energy. The moment you look at it, it will spread. It will become your whole body, your whole being. And do not just be an observer of it; merge into it. There are very few moments when you feel joy, happiness, bliss, but you go on missing them because you become object-centered.

Whenever there is joy, you feel that it is coming from without. You have met a friend; of course, it appears that the joy is coming from your friend, from seeing him. That is not the actual case. The joy is always within you. The friend has just become a situation. The friend has helped it to come out, has helped you to see that it is there. And this is not only with joy, but with everything: with anger, with sadness, with misery, with happiness, with everything it is so. Others are only situations in which things that are hidden in you are expressed. They are not causes; they are not causing something in you. Whatsoever is happening, is happening *to you*. It has always been there; it is only that meeting with this friend has become a situation in which whatsoever was hidden has come out in the open—has come out. From the hidden sources it has become apparent, manifest. Whenever this happens remain centered in the inner feeling, and then you will have a different attitude about everything in life.

Even with negative emotions, do this. When you are angry, do not be centered on the person who has aroused it. Let him be on the periphery. You just become anger. Feel anger in its totality; allow it to happen within. Don't rationalize; don't say that this man has created it. Do not condemn the man. He has just become the situation. And feel grateful towards him that he has helped something which was hidden to come into the open. He has hit you somewhere, and a wound was there hidden. Now you know it, so become the wound.

With negative or positive, with any emotion, use this, and there will be a great change in you. If the emotion is negative, you will be freed of it by being aware that it is within you. If the emotion is positive, you will become the emotion itself. If it is joy, you will become joy. If it is anger, the anger will dissolve.

And this is the difference between negative and positive emotions: if you become aware of a certain emotion, and by your becoming aware the emotion dissolves, it is negative. If by your becoming aware of a certain emotion you then become the emotion, if the emotion then spreads and becomes your being, it is positive. Awareness works differently in both cases. If it is a poisonous emotion, you are relieved of it through awareness. If it is good, blissful, ecstatic, you become one with it. Awareness deepens it.

So to me this is the criterion: if something is deepened by your awareness, it is something good.

If something is dissolved through awareness, it is something bad. That which cannot remain in awareness is sin and that which grows in awareness is virtue. Virtue and sin are not social concepts, they are inner realizations.

Use your awareness. It is just as if there is darkness and you bring in light: the darkness will be no more there. Just by bringing light in, the darkness is no more there, because, really, it was not. It was negative, just an absence of light. But many things will become manifest which are there. Just by bringing in light, these shelves, these books, these walls, will not disappear. In darkness they were not; you could not see them. If you bring light in, darkness will be no more there, but that which is real will be revealed. Through awareness all that is negative like darkness will dissolve—hatred, anger, sadness, violence. Then love, joy, ecstasy, will for the first time become revealed to you. So, *On joyously seeing a long-absent friend, permeate this joy.*

52 Eat and drink consciously.

The fifth tantra technique: *When eating or drinking, become the taste of food or drink, and be filled.*

We go on eating things; we cannot live without them. But we eat them very unconsciously, automatically, robotlike. If the taste is not lived, you are just stuffing. Go slow, and be aware of the taste. And only when you go slow can you be aware. Do not just go on swallowing things. Taste them unhurriedly and become the taste. When you feel sweetness, become that sweetness. And then it can be felt all over the body—not just in the mouth, not just on the tongue, it can be felt all over the body! A certain sweetness—or anything else—is spreading in ripples. Whatsoever you are eating, feel the taste and become the taste.

This is how tantra appears to be quite the contrary from other traditions. Jains say no taste—*ashwad*. Mahatma Gandhi had it as a rule in his ashram—ashwad: do not taste anything. Eat, but do not taste; forget the taste. Eating is a necessity, but do it in a mechanical way. Taste is desire, so do not taste. Tantra says taste it as much as possible; be more sensitive, alive. And not only be sensitive —become the taste.

With ashwad, with no taste, your senses will be deadened. They will become less and less sensitive. And with less sensitivity, you will not be able to feel your body, you will not be able to feel your feelings. Then you will just remain centered in the head. This centeredness in the head is the split. Tantra says do not create any division within yourself. It is beautiful to taste; it is beautiful to be sensitive. And if you are more sensitive you will be more alive, and if you are more alive, then more life will enter your inner being. You will be more open.

You can eat things without tasting; it is not difficult. You can touch someone without touching; it is not difficult. We are already doing it. You shake hands with someone without touching him because to touch, you have to come to the hand, you have to move to the hand. You have to become your fingers and your palm as if you, your soul, have come to the hand. Only then can you touch. You can take someone's hand in your hand and withdraw. You can withdraw; then the dead hand is there. It appears to be touching, but it is not touching.

We are not touching! We are afraid to touch somebody because symbolically touch has become sexual. You may be standing in a crowd, in a tram, in a railway compartment, touching many persons, but you are not touching them and they are not touching you. Only bodies are there in contact, but you are withdrawn. And you can feel the difference: if you really touch someone in the crowd, he will feel offended. Your body can touch, but you must not move in that body. You must remain aloof—as if not in the body, as if there is only a dead body touching.

This insensitivity is bad. It is bad because you are defending yourself against life. You are so much afraid of death, and you are already dead. You need not really be afraid because no one is going to die; you are already dead. And that is why you are afraid—because you have not lived. You have been missing life and death is coming.

A person who is alive will not be afraid of death because he is living. When you are really living there is no fear of death. You can even live death. When death comes, you will be so sensitive to it that you will enjoy it. It is going to be a great experience. If you are alive you can even live death, and then death is no more there. If you can even live death, if you can even be sensitive to your dying body as you are withdrawing to the center and dissolving, if you can live even this, then you have become deathless.

*When eating or drinking, become the taste of the food or drink, and be filled...*by the taste. When drinking water, feel the coolness. Close your eyes, drink it slowly, taste it. Feel the coolness and feel that you have become that coolness, because the coolness is being transferred to you from the water; it is becoming a part of your body. Your mouth is touching, your tongue is touching, and the coolness is transferred. Allow it to happen to the whole of your body. Allow its ripples to spread, and you will feel a coolness all over your body. In this way your sensitivity can grow, and you can become more alive and more filled.

We are frustrated, feeling vacant, empty, and we go on talking that life is empty. But we are the reasons why it is empty. We are not filling it and we are not allowing anything to fill it. We have an armor around us—a defense armor. We are afraid to be vulnerable, so we go on defending against everything. And then we become tombs—dead things.

Tantra says be alive, more alive, because life is God. There is no other God than life. Be more alive, and you will be more divine. Be totally alive, and there is no death for you.

CHAPTER 34

Cosmic orgasm through tantra

◆

Q U E S T I O N S

Are You teaching us indulgence?

How often should one indulge in sex in order to help and not hinder the meditation process?

Doesn't orgasm deplete one's meditative energies?

You said the sex act should be slow, but total and uncontrolled. Please explain these two things.

efore I take your questions some other points have to be clarified, because those points will help you understand more what tantra means. Tantra is not a moral concept. It is neither moral nor immoral. It is amoral. It is a science, and science is neither. Your moralities and concepts concerning moral behavior are irrelevant for tantra. Tantra is not concerned with how one should behave; it is not concerned with ideals. It is concerned basically with what is, with what you are. This distinction has to be understood deeply.

Morality is concerned with ideals—how you should be, what you should be. Therefore, morality is basically condemning. You are never the ideal so you are condemned. Every morality is guilt-creating. You can never become the ideal; you are always lagging behind. The gap will always be there because the ideal is the impossible, and through morality it becomes more impossible. The ideal is there in the future, and you are here as you are, and you go on comparing. You are never the perfect man; something is always lacking. Then you feel guilt; you feel a self-condemnation.

One thing, tantra is against self-condemnation because condemnation can never transform you. Condemnation can only create hypocrisy. Then you try to pretend, to show, that you are what you are not. Hypocrisy means you are the real man, not the ideal man, but you pretend, you try to show, that you are the ideal man. Then you have a split within you; you have a false face. The unreal man is born,

and tantra is basically a search for the real man, not for the unreal man.

Of necessity, every morality creates hypocrisy. It will do so inevitably. Hypocrisy will remain with morality. It is part of it—the shadow. This will look paradoxical because moralists are the men who condemn hypocrisy the most, and they are the creators of it. And hypocrisy cannot disappear from the earth unless morality disappears. They both will exist together; they are two aspects of the same coin. Morality gives you the ideal and you are not the ideal; that is why the ideal is given to you. Then you start feeling that you are wrong, and that this wrongness is natural, it is given to you; you are born with it, and you cannot immediately do anything about it. You cannot transform it, it is not so easy. You can only suppress it, that is easy.

But there are two things you can do. You can create a false face; you can pretend to be something you are not. That saves you. Then you can move more easily in the society—more conveniently. And inwardly you have to suppress the real because the unreal can be imposed only if the real is suppressed. So your reality goes on moving downward into the unconscious and your unreality becomes your conscious. Your unreal part becomes more dominant and the real recedes back. You are divided, and the more you try to pretend, the greater will be the gap.

The child is born as one, whole. That is why every child is so beautiful. The beauty is because of wholeness. The child has no gap, no split, no divisions, no fragments. The child is one. The real and unreal are not there. The child is simply real, authentic. You cannot say that the child is moral. The child is neither moral nor immoral. He is just unaware that there is anything moral or immoral. The moment he becomes aware, a split starts. Then the child begins behaving in unreal ways because to be real becomes more and more difficult.

This happens of necessity, remember, because the family has to regulate, the parents have to regulate. The child has to be civilized, educated, given manners, cultivated; otherwise it will be impossible for the child to move in the society. He has to be told, "Do this, don't do that." And when we say, "Do this," the child's reality may not be ready to do it. It may not be real; there may not be any real desire within the child to do it. And when we say, "Don't do this or don't do that," the child's nature may like to do it.

We condemn the real and we enforce the unreal, because the unreal is going to be helpful in an unreal society and the unreal is going to be convenient. Where everyone is false, the real is not going to be convenient. A real child will be in a basic difficulty with the society because the whole society is unreal. This is a vicious circle. We are born in a society, and hitherto not a single society has existed on the earth which is real. And this is vicious! A child is born in a society, and a society is already there with its fixed rules, regulations, behaviors and moralities which the child has to learn.

When he will grow he will become false. Then children will be born to him, and he will help make them false, and this goes on and on. What to do? We cannot change the society. Or if we try to change the society, we will not be there when the society will be changed. It will take an eternity of time. What to do?

The individual can become aware of this basic split within: that the real has been suppressed and the unreal has been imposed. This is pain, this is suffering, this is hell. You cannot get any satisfaction through the unreal because through the unreal only unreal satisfactions are possible, and this is

natural. Only through the real can real satisfactions happen. Through the real you can reach reality; through the real you can reach the truth. Through the unreal you can only reach more and more hallucinations, illusions, dreams, and through dreams you can deceive yourself, but you can never be satisfied.

For example, in a dream, if you feel thirsty, you may dream you are drinking water. This will be helpful and convenient for the sleep to continue. If this dream where you dream you are drinking water is not there, your sleep will be broken. A real thirst is there. It will break the sleep; the sleep will be disturbed. Dream is a help; it gives you the feeling that you are drinking water. But the water is false. Your thirst is simply deceived; it is not removed. You may continue to sleep, but the thirst is there suppressed.

This is happening not only in sleep: in your whole life this is happening. You are searching for things through the unreal personality which is not there, which is just a façade. If you do not get them, you will be in misery; if you get them, then too you will be in misery. If you do not get them the misery will be less—remember. If you get them, the misery will be deeper and more.

Psychologists say that because of this unreal personality we basically never want to reach the goal—never *want* to reach—because if you reach the goal you will be totally frustrated. You live in hope; in hope you can continue. Hope is a dream. You never reach the goal, so you never come to realize that the goal is false.

A poor man struggling for riches is more happy in the struggle because in the struggle there is hope. And with the unreal personality only hope is happiness. If the poor man gets riches, he will become hopeless. Now frustration will be the natural consequence. Riches will be there, but no satisfaction. He will have achieved the goal, but nothing will have happened. His hopes are shattered. That is why the moment a society becomes affluent it becomes disturbed.

If America is so much disturbed today, it is because hopes are achieved, goals are achieved, and now you cannot deceive yourself any more. So if in America the younger generation is revolting against all the goals of the older generation, it is because of this: that they all proved nonsense.

In India we cannot conceive of this. We cannot conceive of young people voluntarily going poor—going hippie. Voluntarily going poor? We cannot conceive of it. We still have hope. We are hoping for the future: that someday the country will become rich and then there will be heaven. Heaven is always in the hoping.

Because of this unreal personality, whatsoever you try, whatsoever you do, whatsoever you see, becomes unreal. Tantra says truth can happen to you only if you are again grounded in the real. But to be grounded in the real you have to be very courageous with yourself because the unreal is convenient and the unreal is so much cultivated and your mind is so much conditioned, that you will become afraid of the real.

Someone has asked:

You said yesterday to be in the love act totally—to enjoy, to feel the bliss of it, to remain in it, and when the body starts shaking, to be the shaking. Then what are You teaching us—indulgence?

This is perversion! This is the unreal personality speaking to you. The unreal personality is always against enjoying anything. It is always against you: you must not enjoy. It is always for sacrificing things, for your sacrificing yourself for others. It looks beautiful because you have been brought up in it. Sacrifice yourself for others—this is altruism. If you are trying to enjoy yourself this is selfish. And the moment someone says, "This is selfish," it becomes a sin.

But I tell you, tantra is a basically different approach. Tantra says that unless you can enjoy yourself you cannot help anyone to enjoy. Unless you are really contented with yourself, you cannot serve others; you cannot help others toward their contentment. Unless you are overflowing with your own bliss you are a danger to society, because a person who sacrifices always becomes a sadist.

If your mother goes on talking to you and says that "I have sacrificed myself for you," she will torture you. If the husband goes on saying to the wife that "I am sacrificing," he will be a sadistic torturer. He will torture because sacrifice is just a trick to torture the other.

So those who are always sacrificing are very dangerous—potentially dangerous. Be aware of them, and do not sacrifice. The very word is ugly. Enjoy yourself; be bliss-filled. And when you are overflowing with your own bliss, that bliss will reach to others also. But that is not a sacrifice. No one is obliged to you; no one needs to thank you. Rather, you will feel grateful to others because they have been participating in your bliss. Words like 'sacrifice,' 'duty,' 'service,' are ugly; they are violent.

Tantra says that unless you are filled with light, how can you help others to be enlightened? Be selfish; only then can you be altruistic. Otherwise the whole concept of altruism is nonsense. Be happy; only then can you help others to be happy. If you are sad, unhappy, bitter, you are going to be violent with others and you will create misery for others.

You may become a *mahatma*, a so-called great saint; that is not very difficult. But look at your mahatmas. They are trying in every way to torture everyone who comes to them, but their torturing is very deceptive. They torture you for your own sake; they torture you for your own good. And because they are torturing themselves you cannot say to them, "You are preaching something to us which you are not practicing." They are already practicing it. They are torturing themselves; now they can torture you. And when a torture is for your own good, that is the most dangerous torture: you cannot escape it.

And what is wrong with enjoying yourself? What is wrong in being happy? If there is anything wrong it is always in your unhappiness, because an unhappy person creates ripples of unhappiness all around him. Be happy! And the sex act, the act of love, can be one of the deepest means through which bliss can be attained.

Tantra is not teaching sexuality. It is simply saying that sex can be a source of bliss. And once you know that bliss, you can go further because now you are grounded in reality. One is not to remain with sex forever, but you can use sex as a jumping point. That is what tantra means: you can use sex as a jumping point. And once you have known the ecstasy of sex, you can understand what mystics have been talking about—a greater orgasm, a cosmic orgasm.

Meera is dancing. You cannot understand her; you cannot even understand her songs. They are sexual; their symbology is sexual. This is bound to be because in human life the sex act is the only act in which you come to feel a nonduality, in which you come to feel a deep oneness, in which the past disappears and the future disappears and only the present moment—the only real moment—remains. So all those mystics who have really known oneness with the divine, oneness with existence itself, they have always used sexual terms and symbols for their experience to express it. There is no other symbology, there is no other symbology which comes near to it.

Sex is just the beginning, not the end. But if you miss the beginning, you will miss the end also, and you cannot escape the beginning to reach the end.

Tantra says take life naturally; do not be unreal. Sex is there as a deep possibility, a great potentiality. Use it! And what is wrong in being happy in it? Really, all moralities are against happiness. Someone is happy, and you feel something has gone wrong. When someone is sad, everything is okay. We live in a neurotic society where everyone is sad. When you are sad, everyone is happy because everyone can sympathize with you. When you are happy, everyone is at a loss. What to do with you? When someone sympathizes with you, look at his face. The face gleams; a subtle shining comes to the

face. He is happy sympathizing. If you are happy, then there is no possibility for this. Your happiness creates sadness in others; your unhappiness creates happiness. This is neurosis! The very foundation seems to be mad.

Tantra says be real, be authentic to yourself. Your happiness is not bad, it is good. It is not sin! Only sadness is sin, only to be miserable is sin. To be happy is virtue because a happy person will not create unhappiness for others. Only a happy person can be a ground for others' happiness.

Secondly, when I say that tantra is neither moral nor immoral I mean that tantra is basically a science. It looks at you, at what you are. It means that tantra is not trying to transform you, but it actually does transform you through reality. The difference between magic and science is the same as between morality and tantra. Magic also tries to transform things simply through words, without knowing the reality. The magician can say that now the rains will stop; he cannot really stop them. Or he can say that rains will come—but he cannot start them, he can just go on using words.

Sometimes coincidences will be there, and then he will feel powerful. And if the thing is not going to happen according to his magic prophecy he can always say, "What has gone wrong?" That possibility is always hidden in his profession. With magic everything starts with "if." He can say, "If everyone is good, virtuous, then the rains will come on a particular day." If the rains come it is okay; if the rains are not coming then "everyone is not virtuous, there is someone who is a sinner."

Even in this century, the twentieth century, a person like Mahatma Gandhi could say, when there was famine in Bihar, "It is because of the sin of the people living in Bihar that the famine has come"— as if the whole world is not sinning, only Bihar! Magic starts with "if," and that "if" is great and big.

Science never starts with if because science first tries to know what is real—what reality is, what the real is. Once the real is known it can be transformed. Once you know what electricity is, it can be changed, transformed, used. A magician does not know what electricity is. Without knowing electricity, he is going to transform, he is thinking to transform! Those kind of prophecies are just false—illusions.

Morality is just like magic. It goes on talking about the perfect man, and without knowing what man is—the real man. The perfect man remains as a dream. It is used just to condemn the real man. Man never reaches it.

Tantra is science. Tantra says first know what the reality is, what man is, and don't create values and don't create ideals right now; first know what is. Do not think of the "ought," just think of the "is." And once the "is" is known, then you change it. Then you have the secret.

For example, tantra says do not try to go against sex, because if you go against sex and try to create a state of *brahmacharya*, celibacy, purity, it is impossible. It is just magical. Without knowing what sex energy is, without knowing of what sex is constituted, without going deep into the reality of it, the secrets of it, you can create an ideal of brahmacharya. Then what will you do? You will simply suppress. And a person who is suppressing sex is more sexual than a person who is indulging in it because through indulgence the energy is released. Through suppression it is there, moving in your system continuously.

A person who suppresses sex starts seeing sex everywhere. Everything becomes sexual. Not that everything is sexual, but now he projects. Now he projects! His own hidden energy is now projected. Everywhere he will look he will see sex, and because he is condemning himself he will start condemning everyone. You cannot find a moralist who is not violently condemning. He is condemning everyone; to him everyone is wrong. Then he feels good, his ego is fulfilled. Why is everyone wrong? Because he sees everywhere the same thing he is suppressing. His own mind will become more and more sexual, and more and more he will be afraid. This brahmacharya is perversion, it is unnatural.

A different quality, a different type of brahmacharya, happens to the follower of tantra, but the very process is totally, diametrically opposite. Tantra first teaches how to move in sex, how to know it, how to feel it, how to come to the deepest possibility hidden in it, to the climax, how to find the essential beauty, the essential happiness and bliss that is hidden there.

Once you know that secret you can transcend it because, really, in a deep sexual orgasm it is not sex which gives you bliss, it is something else. Sex is just a situation. Something else is giving you the euphoria, the ecstasy. That something else can be divided into three elements. But when I speak about those elements, do not think that you can understand them just from my words. They must become part of your experience. As concepts they are useless.

Because of three basic elements in sex you come to a blissful moment. Those three are, firstly, time-lessness: you transcend time completely. There is no time. You forget time completely; time ceases for you. Not that time ceases, it ceases for *you;* you are not in it. There is no past, no future. In this very moment, here and now, the whole existence is concentrated. This moment becomes the only real moment. If you can make this moment the only real moment without sex, then there is no need of sex. Through meditation it happens.

Secondly, in sex for the first time you lose your ego, you become egoless. So all those who are very egoistic, they are always against sex, because in sex they have to lose their egos. You are not, nor is there the other. You and your beloved are both lost into something else. A new reality evolves, a new unit comes into existence in which the old two are lost—completely lost. The ego is afraid. You are no more there. If without sex you can come to a moment when you are not, then there is no need of it.

And thirdly, in sex you are natural for the first time. The unreal is lost, the faces, the façades are lost; the society, the culture, the civilization, is lost.

You are a part of nature. As trees are, as animals are, as stars are, you are a part of nature. You are in a greater something—the cosmos, the Tao. You are floating in it. You cannot even swim in it; *you* are not. You are just floating—being taken by the current.

These three things give you the ecstasy. Sex is just a situation in which it happens naturally. Once you know and once you can feel these elements, you can create these elements independently of sex. All meditation is essentially the experience of sex without sex, but you have to go through it. It must become part of your experience, not just be there as concepts, ideas, thoughts.

Tantra is not for sex, tantra is to transcend. But you can transcend only through experience—existential experience—not through ideology. Only through tantra does brahmacharya happen. This looks paradoxical, but it is not. Only through knowledge does transcendence happen. Ignorance cannot help you towards transcendence; it can only help you towards hypocrisy.

Now I will take more questions.

Someone has asked:

How often should one indulge in sex in order to help and not to hinder the meditation process?

The question arises because we go on misunderstanding. Your sex act and the tantric sex act are basically different. Your sex act is to relieve; it is just like sneezing out a good sneeze. The energy is thrown out and you are unburdened. It is destructive, it is not creative. It is good—therapeutic. It helps you to be relaxed, but nothing more.

The tantric sex act is basically, diametrically opposite and different. It is not to relieve, it is not to throw energy out. It is to remain in the act without ejaculation, without throwing energy out; to remain in the act merged—just at the beginning part of the act, not the end part. This changes the quality; the complete quality is different then.

Try to understand two things. There are two types of climaxes, two types of orgasm. One type of orgasm is known. You reach to a peak of excitement, then you cannot go further: the end has come. The excitement reaches to a point where it becomes nonvoluntary. The energy jumps into you and goes out. You are relieved of it, unburdened. The load is thrown; you can relax and sleep.

You are using it like a tranquilizer. It is a natural tranquilizer: a good sleep will follow—if your mind is not burdened by religion. Otherwise even the tranquilizer is destroyed. If your mind is not burdened by religion, only then can sex be a tranquilizing thing. If you feel guilt, even your sleep will be disturbed. You will feel depression, you will start condemning yourself and you will begin to take oaths that now you won't indulge anymore. Then your sleep will become a nightmare afterwards. If you are a natural being not too much burdened by religion and morality, only then can sex be used as a tranquilizer.

This is one type of orgasm—coming to the peak of excitement. Tantra is centered on another type of orgasm. If we call the first kind a peak orgasm, you can call the tantric orgasm a valley orgasm. In it you are not coming to the peak of excitement, but to the very deepest valley of relaxation. Excitement has to be used for both in the beginning. That is why I say that in the beginning both are the same, but the ends are totally different.

Excitement has to be used for both: either you are going toward the peak of excitement or to the valley of relaxation. For the first, excitement has to be intense—more and more intense. You have to grow in it; you have to help it to grow towards the peak. In the second, excitement is just a beginning. And once the man has entered, both lover and beloved can relax.

No movement is needed. They can relax in a loving embrace. When the man feels or the woman feels that the erection is going to be lost, only then is a little movement and excitement required. But then again relax. You can prolong this deep embrace for hours with no ejaculation, and then both can fall into deep sleep together. This—*this*—is a valley orgasm. Both are relaxed, and they meet as two relaxed beings.

In the ordinary sexual orgasm you meet as two excited beings—tense, full of excitement, trying to unburden yourselves. The ordinary sexual orgasm looks like madness; the tantric orgasm is a deep, relaxing meditation. Then there is no question of how often one should indulge. You can indulge as much as you like because no energy is lost. Rather, energy is gained.

You may not be aware of it, but this is a fact of biology, of bioenergy, that man and woman are opposite forces. Negative–positive, yin–yang, or whatsoever you call them, they are challenging to each other. And when they both meet in a deep relaxation, they revitalize each other. They both revitalize each other, they both become generators, they both feel livelier, they both become radiant with new energy, and nothing is lost. Just by meeting with the opposite pole energy is renewed.

The tantric love act can be done as much as you like. The ordinary sex act cannot be done as much as you like because you are losing energy in it, and your body will have to wait to regain it. And when you regain it, you will only lose it again. This looks absurd. The whole life is spent in gaining and losing, regaining and losing: it is just like an obsession.

The second thing to be remembered: you may or may not have observed that when you look at animals you can never see them enjoying sex. In intercourse, they are not enjoying themselves. Look at baboons, monkeys, dogs or any kind of animals. In their sex act you cannot see that they are feeling blissful or enjoying it—you cannot! It seems to be just a mechanical act, a natural force pushing them towards it. If you have seen monkeys in intercourse, after the intercourse they will separate. Look at their faces: there is no ecstasy in them, it is as if nothing has happened. When the energy forces itself, when the energy is too much, they throw it.

The ordinary sex act is just like this, but moralists have been saying quite the contrary. They say,

"Do not indulge, do not 'enjoy.'" They say, "This is as animals do." This is wrong! Animals never enjoy; only man can enjoy. And the deeper you can enjoy, the higher is the kind of humanity that is born. And if your sex act can become meditative, ecstatic, the highest is touched. But remember tantra: it is a valley orgasm, it is not a peak experience. It is a valley experience!

In the West, Abraham Maslow has made this term 'peak experience' very famous. You go into excitement towards the peak, and then you fall. That is why, after every sex act, you feel a fall. And it is natural: you are falling from a peak. You will never feel that after a tantric sex experience. Then you are not falling. You cannot fall any further because you have been in the valley. Rather, you are rising.

When you come back after a tantric sex act, you have risen, not fallen. You feel filled with energy, more vital, more alive, radiant. And that ecstasy will last for hours, even for days. It depends on how deeply you were in it. If you move into it, sooner or later you will realize that ejaculation is wastage of energy. No need of it—unless you need children. And with a tantric sex experience, you will feel a deep relaxation the whole day. One tantric sex experience, and even for days you will feel relaxed—at ease, at home, nonviolent, nonangry, nondepressed. And this type of person is never a danger to others. If he can, he will help others to be happy. If he cannot, at least he will not make anyone unhappy.

Only tantra can create a new man, and this man who can know timelessness, egolessness and deep nonduality with existence will grow. A dimension has opened. It is not far away, the day is not very far away, when sex will simply disappear. When sex disappears without your knowledge, when suddenly one day, you realize that sex has disappeared completely and there is no lust, then brahmacharya is born. But this is arduous. It looks arduous because of too much false teaching, and you feel afraid of it also because of your mind's conditioning.

Of two things we are very much afraid: sex and death—and both are basic. A really religious seeker will enter both. He will experience sex to know what it is because to know sex is to know life. And he would also like to know what death is because unless death is known you cannot know what eternal life is. If you can enter sex to its very center you will know what life is, and if you can enter into death voluntarily, to its very center, then the moment you touch the center of death you become eternal. Then you are immortal because death is something that happens just on the periphery.

Sex and death both are basic for a real seeker, but for ordinary humanity both are taboo. No one talks about them, and both are basic and both are deeply related. They are so deeply related that even upon entering sex you enter a certain death—because you are dying. The ego is disappearing; time is disappearing; your individuality is disappearing. You are dying! Sex is also a subtle death. And if you can know that sex is a subtle death, death can become a great sexual orgasm.

A Socrates entering death is not afraid. Rather, he is very much enthusiastic, thrilled, excited to know what death is. There is a deep welcome in his heart. Why? Because if you have known the small death of sex and you have known the bliss that follows it, you would like to know the greater death, the greater bliss that is hidden behind it. But for us both are taboo. For tantra, both are basic dimensions for search. One has to go through them.

Someone has asked:

If one experiences kundalini—the rising of energy up the spinal passage—does not it deplete one's meditative energies to have orgasm?

All the questions are basically without understanding of what the tantric sex act is. Ordinarily, it is so. If your energy, your kundalini, goes up, rises and rushes up towards the head, you cannot have an ordinary orgasm. And if you try to have it, you will

be in a deep conflict within, because energy is moving up and you are forcing it down. But the tantric orgasm is not a difficulty. It will be a help. Energy moving up is not contradictory to tantric orgasm. You can relax, and that relaxation with your beloved will help the energy move higher.

In the ordinary sex act it is a difficulty. That is why all those techniques which are not tantric are against sex—because they do not know that a valley orgasm is possible. They know only one kind —the ordinary orgasm, and then it is a problem for them. For yoga it is a problem because yoga is trying to force your sex energy upwards. Your sex energy moving upwards is what is called kundalini.

In the sex act it moves downwards. Yoga will say to be a celibate, because if you are doing both —yoga and indulging in sex—you are creating chaos in your system. On the one hand you are trying to pull energy up, and on the other hand you are throwing energy out—down. You are creating chaos.

That is why yoga techniques are against sex, but tantra is not against sex because tantra has a different type of orgasm, a valley orgasm, which can help. And no chaos, no conflict, is created; rather, it will be helpful. If you are escaping, if you are a man and you are escaping from woman or if you are a woman escaping from man, then whatsoever you do the other remains in your mind and goes on pulling you down. This is paradoxical, but this is a truth.

While in a deep embrace with your beloved you can forget the other. Only then do you forget the other. A man forgets that woman exists; a woman forgets that man exists. Only in a deep embrace the other is no more, and when the other is no more your energy can flow easily. Otherwise the other goes on pulling it down.

So yoga and ordinary techniques try to get you to escape from the other—the opposite sex. You have to escape. You have to be aware—continuously struggling and controlling. But if you are against the other sex, that very "againstness" is a constant strain and goes on pulling you down.

Tantra says no strain is needed; be relaxed with the other. In that relaxed moment the other disappears and your energy can flow up, but it flows up only when you are in a valley. It flows down when you are at a peak.

One more question:

Last night You said that the full act should be slow and unhurried, but You also said that one should not have any control over the sexual act and that one should become total. This confuses me. Please explain these two things.

It is not control. Control is a different thing and relaxation is totally different. In sex, you are relaxing in it, not controlling it. If you are controlling it, there will be no relaxation. If you are controlling it, sooner or later you will be hurried to finish it because control is a strain. And every strain creates tension, and tension creates a necessity, a need, to release. It is not a control; you are not resisting something. You are simply not in a hurry because sex is not happening in order to move somewhere. You are not going somewhere. It is just a play; there is no goal. Nothing is to be reached, so why hurry?

But a man who is always, in every act, present totally…. If you are hurried in everything, you will be hurried in your sex act also, because *you* will be there. A person who is very much time-conscious will be hurried in his sex act also—as if time is being wasted. So we ask for instant coffee and for instant sex. With coffee it is good, but with sex it is simply nonsense. There can be no instant sex. It is not work and it is not something which you can hurry. Through hurry you will destroy it; you will miss the very point. Enjoy it because through it a timelessness is to be felt. If you are in a hurry, then timelessness cannot be felt.

Tantra says go unhurriedly, slowly enjoying it just as if you are going for a walk in the morning— not as if you are going to the office. That is a differ-

ent thing. When you are going to the office you are in a hurry to reach somewhere, and when you are on a walk in the morning you are not in a hurry because you are not going anywhere. You are simply going, there is no hurry, there is no goal. You can return from any point.

This unhurriedness is basic to create the valley; otherwise the peak will be created. And when this is said, it does not mean that you have to control. You are not to control your excitement, because that is contradictory. You *cannot* control excitement. If you control it, you are creating a double excitement. Just relax! Take it as a play; do not make any end. The beginning is enough.

In the act, close your eyes. Feel the other's body, feel the other's energy flowing towards you and be merged in it, melt in it. It will come. The old habit may persist for a few days; then it will go. But do not force it to go. Just go on relaxing, relaxing, relaxing, and if there is no ejaculation do not feel that something has gone wrong. A man feels that something has gone wrong if there is no ejaculation; he tends to feel that something has gone wrong. Nothing has gone wrong! And do not feel that you have missed something: you have not missed. In the beginning it will be felt as if you are missing something, because the excitement and the peak will not be there. Before the valley comes you will feel that you are missing something, but this is just an old habit. Within a period, within a month or three weeks, the valley will start appearing, and when the valley appears you will forget your peaks. No peak is worth this. But you have to wait, and do not force it and do not control it. Just relax.

Relaxation is a problem—because when we say, "Relax," in the mind it is translated as if some effort is to be made. Our language gives this appearance. I was reading one book. The book is entitled, *You Must Relax*. You *must!* The very "must" will not allow you to relax, because when it becomes a goal, you must, and if you are not able you will feel frustrated. The very must gives you a feeling of hard effort—of an arduous journey. You cannot relax if you are thinking in terms of must.

Language is a problem. There are certain things which language always expresses wrongly. For example, relaxation: if I say to relax, then too it becomes an effort and you will ask, "How to relax?" With how you miss the point. You cannot ask "How?" Then you are asking for a technique, and technique will create effort, effort will create tension. So if you ask me how to relax, I will say do not do anything, just relax. Just lie down and wait, do not do anything! All that you can do will be the barrier; it will create the hindrance.

If you start counting from one to a hundred and back from a hundred to one, you will remain awake the whole night. And if sometimes you have fallen asleep because of counting, it is not because of counting. It is because you counted and counted, and then you became bored—because of that boredom. It is not because of counting—only because of boredom. And then you forgot counting and then sleep came. But sleep comes, relaxation comes, only when you are not doing anything: this is the problem.

When I say "sex act" it looks like you need an effort. You do not! Just start playing with your beloved or your lover; just go on playing. Feel each other, be sensitive to each other, just like small children playing or just like dogs playing—animals playing. Just go on playing, and do not think about the sex act at all. It may happen, it may not happen.

If it happens through just playing, it will lead you to the valley more easily. If you think about it, then you are already ahead of yourself; you are playing with your beloved, but you are *thinking* of the sex act. Then the playing is false. You are not here and the mind is in the future, and this mind will always move in the future.

When you are in the sex act, the mind is thinking about how to finish it. It is always ahead of you. Do not allow it! Just play, and forget about any sex act. It will happen. Then allow it to happen. Then it will be easy to relax, and when it happens just relax. Be together. Be in each other's presence and feel happy.

Negatively, something can be done. For example, when you get excited you breathe fast because excitement needs fast breathing. For relaxation it is good, helpful, if you breathe deeply, not fast but slow, breathing very easily—being at ease. Then the sex act can be prolonged.

Don't talk, don't say anything, because that creates disturbance. Don't use mind, use bodies. Use mind only to feel what is happening. Don't think, just feel what is happening—the warmth that is flowing, the love that is flowing, the energy that is encountered. Just feel it.

Be aware, and that too should not be made a strain. Float effortlessly. Then only will the valley appear, and once the valley appears *you* are transcended.

Once you feel and realize the valley, the relaxed orgasm, it is already a transcendence. Then sex is not there. It has become a meditation—a *samadhi*.

CHAPTER 35

Turning inward toward the real

◆

THE SUTRAS

53 O lotus-eyed one, sweet of touch, when singing, seeing, tasting, be aware you are and discover the ever-living.

54 Wherever satisfaction is found, in whatever act, actualize this.

55 At the point of sleep, when the sleep has not yet come and the external wakefulness vanishes, at this point Being is revealed.

56 Illusions deceive, colors circumscribe, even divisibles are indivisible.

Civilization is a training in how to become unreal. Tantra is the reverse process—how to prevent yourself from becoming unreal, and if you have already become unreal, how to touch the reality which is hidden within you, how to contact it again, how to be again real. The first thing to be understood is how we go on becoming unreal, and once this process is understood many things change immediately. The very understanding becomes mutation.

Man is born undivided. He is neither a body nor a mind. He is born undivided, as one individual. He is both body and mind. Even to say that he is both is wrong. He is body-mind. Body and mind are two aspects of his being, not two divisions—two polarities of something which we may call life, energy or anything—XYZ—but body and mind are not two things.

The very process of civilization, education, culture, conditioning, starts with the division. Everyone is taught that he is two, not one, and then, of course, one begins to be identified with the mind and not with the body. The very thinking process becomes your center and the thinking process is just a periphery. It is not the center because you can exist without thinking. Once you existed without thinking: thinking is not a necessity to exist. If you go deep in meditation *you* will be, and there will be no thinking. If you become unconscious *you* will be, but there will be no thinking. Moving into deep sleep *you* will be, but there will be no thinking.

Thinking is just on the periphery; your being is somewhere else—deeper than thinking. But you are being taught continuously that you are two, body and mind, and that, really, you are the mind and you possess the body. The mind becomes the master and body becomes the slave, and you go on struggling against the body. This creates a rift, a gap, and that gap is the problem. All neurosis is born out of that gap; all anxiety is born out of that gap.

Your being is rooted in your body, and your body is not just something separate from existence. It is part of it. Your body is the whole universe. It is not something limited, finite. You may not have observed it, but try to observe where your body really ends—where! Do you think that your body ends where your skin ends?

If the sun which is so far away just goes dead, instantly you will be dead here. If the sun rays stop coming, you will be no more here. Your body cannot exist without the sun being there so far away. The sun and you are somehow deeply related. The sun must be included in your body; otherwise you cannot exist. You are part of its rays.

In the morning you see flowers open; their opening is really the rising of the sun. In the night they will close; their closing is the setting of the sun. They are just rays that are spread out. You exist here because there, so far away, the sun exists. Your skin is not really your skin. Your skin goes on spreading; even the sun is included. You are breathing; you can breathe because the air is there, the atmosphere is there. Each moment you exhale and inhale the atmosphere in and out.

If for a single moment there were no air, you would be dead. Your breath is your life. If your breath is your life, then the whole atmosphere is part of you. You cannot exist without it. So where does your body really end? Where is the limit? There is no limit! If you observe, if you go deep, you will find there is no limit. Or, the limit of the universe is your body limit. The whole universe is involved in you, so your body is not just your body; it is your universe and you are grounded in it. Your mind too cannot exist without the body. It is part of it, a process of it.

Division is destructive, and with the division you are bound to become identified with the mind. You think, and without thinking there is no division. You think, and you become identified with your thinking. Then you feel as if you possess the body. This is a complete reversal of the truth. You do not possess the body; neither is the body possessing you. They are not two things. Your existence is one, a deep harmony of opposite poles. But opposite poles are not divided, they are joined together. Only then can they become opposite poles. And the opposition is good. It gives challenge, it gives stamina, it creates energy. It is dialectical.

If you were really one, without opposite poles within, you would be dull and dead. These two opposite poles, body and mind, give you life. They are opposite and at the same time complementary—and basically and ultimately one. One current of energy runs in both. But once we get identified with the thinking process, we think that we are centered in the head. If your legs are cut, you will not feel that *you* are cut. You will say, "My legs are cut." But if your head is cut, *you* are cut. You are murdered.

If you close your eyes to feel where you are, immediately you will feel you are in your head. You are not there—because when for the first moment you entered life in your mother's womb, when the male and female cells met, there was no head. But life was started. You were there, and there was no

head. In that first meeting of two alive cells, you were created. The head came later on, but your being was there. Where is that being? It is not in your head. Really, it is nowhere—or everywhere in your body. It is nowhere; you cannot pinpoint where it is. And the moment you pinpoint it you miss the whole thing. It is everywhere. Your life is everywhere, it is spread out all over you. And not only all over you; if you follow it, you will have to go to the very ends of the universe. It is everywhere!

With the identification that "I am my mind," everything becomes false. You become unreal because this identity is false. This has to be broken. Tantra techniques are to break down this identity. The effort of tantra is to make you headless, uncentered, everywhere or nowhere. And why does humanity, why do human beings become false and unreal with the mind? Because mind is an epiphenomenon—a process which is necessary, useful, but secondary; a process which consists of words, not of realities. The word 'love' is not love, the word 'god' is not God. But mind consists of words, of a verbal process, and then love itself becomes less significant than the word 'love.' For the mind, the word is more significant. God becomes less significant than the word 'god.' For the mind it is so. Words become more meaningful, significant. They become primary, and we start living in words. And the more you live in words the more shallow you become, and you will go on missing the reality which is not words. Reality is existence.

Living in the mind is as if someone is living in a mirror. In the night, if you go to a lake and the lake is silent and there are no ripples, the lake becomes a mirror. You can look at the moon in the lake, but that moon is false—just a reflection. The reflection comes from the real, but the reflection is not real. Mind is just a reflecting phenomenon. The reality is reflected in it, but reflections are not real. And if you get caught in reflections, you will miss reality completely. That is why, with the mind, with mind reflections, everything wavers. A slight wave, a slight wind, will disturb your mind. Reality is not disturbed, but the mind is disturbed by anything. Mind is a reflecting phenomenon, and we are living in mind.

Tantra says come down. Descend from your thrones, come down from your heads. Forget the reflections and move towards the reality. All the techniques which we are discussing are concerned with this: how to be away from the mind so that you can move into reality.

Now we will discuss the techniques.

53 Self-remembering.

The first self-remembering technique: *O lotus-eyed one, sweet of touch, when singing, seeing, tasting, be aware you are and discover the ever-living.*

We are living, but we are not aware that we are or that we are living. There is no self-remembering. You are eating or you are taking a bath or you are taking a walk: you are not aware that you are while walking. Everything is, only you are not. The trees, the houses, the traffic, everything is. You are aware of everything around you, but you are not aware of your own being—that you are. You may be aware of the whole world, but if you are not aware of yourself that awareness is false. Why? Because your mind can reflect everything, but your mind cannot reflect you. If you are aware of yourself, then you have transcended the mind.

Your self-remembering cannot be reflected in your mind because you are behind the mind. It can reflect only things which are in front of it. You can just see others, but you cannot see yourself. Your eyes can see everyone, but your eyes cannot see themselves. If you want to see yourself you will need a mirror. Only in the mirror can you see yourself, but then you will have to stand in front of the mirror. If your mind is a mirror, it can reflect the whole world. It cannot reflect you because you cannot stand before it. You are always behind, hidden behind the mirror.

This technique says, while doing anything—singing, seeing, tasting—be aware that you are and discover the ever-living, and discover within yourself the current, the energy, the life, the ever-living. But we are not aware of ourselves.

Gurdjieff used self-remembering as a basic technique in the West. The self-remembering is derived from this sutra. The whole Gurdjieffian system is based on this one sutra. Remember yourself, whatsoever you are doing. It is very difficult. It looks very easy, but you will go on forgetting. Even for three or four seconds you cannot remember yourself. You will have a feeling that you are remembering, and suddenly you will have moved to some other thought. Even with this thought that "Okay, I am remembering myself," you will have missed, because this thought is not self-remembering. In self-remembering there will be no thought; you will be completely empty. And self-remembering is not a mental process. It is not that you say, "Yes, I am." Saying "Yes, I am," you have missed. This is a mind thing, this is a mental process: "I am."

Feel *I am*, not the words 'I am.' Don't verbalize, just feel that you are. Don't think, *feel!* Try it. It is difficult, but if you go on insisting it happens. While walking, remember you are, and have the feeling of your being, not of any thought, not of any idea. Just feel. I touch your hand or I put my hand on your head: don't verbalize. Just feel the touch, and in that feeling feel not only the touch, but feel also the touched one. Then your consciousness becomes double-arrowed.

You are walking under trees; the trees are there, the breeze is there, the sun is rising. This is the world all around you; you are aware of it. Stand for a moment and suddenly remember that you are, but don't verbalize. Just feel that you are. This nonverbal feeling, even if for only a single moment, will give you a glimpse—a glimpse which no LSD can give you, a glimpse which is of the real. For a single moment you are thrown back to the center of your being. You are behind the mirror; you have transcended the world of reflections; you are existential. And you can do it at any time. It doesn't need any special place or any special time. And you cannot say, "I have no time." When eating you can do it, when taking a bath you can do it, when moving or sitting you can do it—anytime. No matter what you are doing, you can suddenly remember yourself, and then try to continue that glimpse of your being.

It will be difficult. One moment you will feel it is there, the next moment you will have moved away. Some thought will have entered, some reflection will have come to you, and you will have become involved in the reflection. But don't be sad and don't be disappointed. This is so because for lives together we have been concerned with the reflections. This has become a robotlike mechanism. Instantly, automatically, we are thrown to the reflection. But if even for a single moment you have the glimpse, it is enough for the beginning. And why is it enough? Because you will never get two moments together. Only one moment is with you always. And if you can have the glimpse for a single moment, you can remain in it. Only effort is needed—a continuous effort is needed.

A single moment is given to you. You cannot have two moments together, so don't worry about two moments. You will always get only one moment. And if you can be aware in one moment, you can be aware for your whole life. Now only effort is needed, and this can be done the whole day. Whenever you remember, remember yourself.

O lotus-eyed one, sweet of touch, when singing, seeing, tasting, be aware you are, and discover the ever-living. When the sutra says *be aware you are,* what will you do? Will you remember that "My name is Rama" or "Jesus" or something else? Will you remember that you belong to such and such a family, to such and such a religion and tradition? To such and such a country and caste and creed? Will you remember that you are a communist or a Hindu or a Christian? What will you remember?

The sutra says be aware you are; it simply says, "You are." No name is needed, no country is

needed. Let there be simple existence: you are! So don't say to yourself who you are. Don't answer that "I am this and that." Let there be simple existence, that you are.

But it becomes difficult because we never remember simple existence. We always remember something which is just a label, not existence itself. Whenever you think about yourself, you think about your name, religion, country, many things, but never the simple existence that you are.

You can practice this: relaxing in a chair or just sitting under a tree, forget everything and feel this "you-areness." No Christian, no Hindu, no Buddhist, no Indian, no Englishman, no German—simply, you are. Have the feeling of it, and then it will be easy for you to remember what this sutra says: *Be aware you are, and discover the ever-living.* And the moment you are aware that you are, you are thrown into the current of the ever-living. The false is going to die; only the real will remain.

That is why we are so much afraid of death: because the unreal is going to die. The unreal cannot be forever, and we are attached to the unreal, identified with the unreal. You as a Hindu will have to die; you as Rama or Krishna will have to die; you as a communist, as an atheist, as a theist, will have to die; you as a name and form will have to die. And if you are attached to name and form, obviously the fear of death will come to you, but the real, the existential, the basic in you, is deathless. Once the forms and names are forgotten, once you have a look within to the nameless and the formless, you have moved into the eternal.

Be aware you are, and discover the ever-living. This technique is one of the most helpful, and it has been used for millennia by many teachers, masters. Buddha used it, Mahavira used it, Jesus used it, and in modern times Gurdjieff used it. Among all the techniques, this is one of the most potential. Try it. It will take time; months will pass.

When Ouspensky was learning with Gurdjieff, for three months he had to make much effort, arduous effort, in order to have a glimpse of what self-remembering is. So continuously, for three months, Ouspensky lived in a secluded house just doing only one thing: self-remembering. Thirty persons started that experiment, and by the end of the first week twenty-seven had escaped; only three remained. The whole day they were trying to remember—not doing anything else, just remembering that "I am." Twenty-seven felt they were going crazy. They felt that now madness was just near, so they escaped. They never turned back; they never met Gurdjieff again.

Why? As we are, really, we are mad. Not remembering who we are, what we are, we are mad, but this madness is taken as sanity. Once you try to go back, once you try to contact the real, it will look like craziness, it will look like madness. Compared to what we are, it is just the reverse, the opposite. If you feel that this is sanity, that will look like madness.

But three persisted. One of the three was P. D. Ouspensky. For three months they persisted. Only after the first month did they start having glimpses of simply being, of "I am." After the second month, even the 'I' dropped, and they started having the glimpses of "am-ness"—of just being, not even of 'I,' because 'I' is also a label. The pure being is not 'I' and 'thou'; it just is.

And by the third month even the feeling of am-ness dissolved because that feeling of am-ness is still a word. Even that word dissolves. Then you are, and then you know what you are. Before that point comes you cannot ask, "Who am I?" Or you can go on asking continuously, "Who am I?"—just continuously inquiring, "Who am I? Who am I?" and all the answers that will be provided by the mind will be found false, irrelevant. You go on asking, "Who am I? Who am I? Who am I?" and a point comes where you can no more ask the question. All the answers fall down, and then the question itself falls down and disappears. And when even the question, "Who am I?" disappears, you know who you are.

Gurdjieff tried from one corner: just try to remember you are. Raman Maharshi tried from another corner. He made it a meditation to ask, to inquire, "Who am I?" And don't believe in any answers that the mind can supply. The mind will say, "What nonsense are you asking? You are this, you are that, you are a man, you are a woman, you are educated or uneducated, rich or poor." The mind will supply answers, but go on asking. Don't accept any answer because all the answers given by the mind are false. They are from the unreal part of you. They are coming from words, they are coming from scriptures, they are coming from conditioning, they are coming from society, they are coming from others. Go on asking. Let this arrow of "Who am I?" penetrate deeper and deeper. A moment will come when no answer will come.

That is the right moment. Now you are nearing the answer. When no answer comes, you are near the answer because mind is becoming silent—or you have gone far away from the mind. When there will be no answer and a vacuum will be created all around you, your questioning will look absurd. Whom are you questioning? There is no one to answer you. Suddenly, even your questioning will stop. With the questioning, the last part of the mind has dissolved because this question was also of the mind. Those answers were of the mind and this question was also of the mind. Both have dissolved, so now *you are*.

Try this. There is every possibility, if you persist, that this technique can give you a glimpse of the real—and the real is ever-living.

54 Feel the satisfaction.

The second self-remembering technique: *Wherever satisfaction is found, in whatever act, actualize this.*

You feel thirsty, so you drink water. A subtle satisfaction is attained. Forget the water, forget the thirst. Remain with the subtle satisfaction that you are feeling. Be filled with it; simply feel satisfied.

But the human mind is mischievous. It only feels dissatisfactions, discontent. It never feels satisfaction; it never feels content. If you are dissatisfied, you will feel it and you will be filled by it. When you are thirsty, you feel it: you are filled with thirst, you feel it in the throat. If it grows you feel it all over your body, and a moment will come when it is not that *you* are thirsty, you will feel that you have become the thirst. If you are in a desert and there is no hope of getting water, you will not feel that *you* are thirsty; you will feel that you have become the thirst.

Dissatisfactions are felt, miseries are felt, pains are felt. Whenever you suffer, you become the suffering. That is why the whole life becomes a hell. You have never felt the positive; you have always felt the negative. Life is not such a misery as we have made it; misery is just our interpretation. A Buddha is happy here and now, in this very life. A Krishna is dancing and playing on a flute. In this very life here and now, where we are in misery, Krishna is dancing. Life is neither misery, nor is life bliss. Bliss and misery are our interpretations, our attitudes, our approaches, how we look at it. It is your mind—how it takes it.

Remember, and analyze your own life. Have you ever taken account of happy moments, of contents, of satisfactions, of blissful glimpses? You have not taken any account, but you have taken every account of your pain, suffering, misery, and you go on accumulating. You are an accumulated hell, and this is your own choice. No one else is forcing you into this hell; this is your own choice. The mind takes the negative, accumulates it and becomes negative itself. And then this is a self-perpetuating misery. The more negatives you have within the mind, the more negative you become, the more negatives are accumulated. The similar attracts the similar, and this has been for lives and lives. You miss everything because of your negative approach.

This technique gives you a positive approach, a total reversal to the ordinary mind and its process. *Wherever satisfaction is found, in whatever act, actualize this*—feel it, become one with it. Don't take it just as a passing phase. The satisfaction can become a glimpse of a greater positive existence.

Everything is just a window. If you become identified with a pain, you are looking from a window, and the window of pain, of suffering, opens only towards hell. If you are one with a satisfactory moment, a blissful moment, an ecstatic moment, you are opening another window. The existence is the same, but your windows are different.

Wherever satisfaction is found, in whatever act, actualize it—wherever! No conditions: wherever! You see a friend and you feel happy; you meet your lover or beloved and you feel happy: *actualize this*. Be happiness in that moment, and make that happiness a door. Then you are changing the mind, and you will start accumulating happiness. Your mind will turn positive, and the same world will look different.

One Zen monk, Bokuju, is reported to have said, "The world is the same, but nothing is the same because the mind changes. Everything remains the same, but nothing is the same because I am not the same."

You go on trying to change the world, and no matter what you do the world will remain the same because you remain the same. You can get a bigger house, you can get a bigger car, you can get a more beautiful wife or a husband, but nothing will change. The bigger house will not be bigger. The beautiful wife or husband will not be more beautiful. The bigger car will remain the smaller one because you are the same. Your mind, your approach, your ways of seeing are the same. You go on changing things without changing yourself. So a miserable person leaves a hut and moves to a palace, but the miserable person remains the same. He was miserable in a hut; now he will be miserable in a palace. This misery may be palatial, but he will be miserable.

You go on carrying your misery with you, and

wherever you move you will be with yourself. So no outer change is basically a change; it is just an appearance. You simply feel that there has been a change, but there is no change. Only one change, only one revolution, only one mutation can be there, and that is if your mind changes from negative to the positive. If your outlook is focused on misery, you live in hell; if your outlook is focused on happiness, the very hell becomes the heaven. Try this! This will change your very quality of life.

But you are interested in quantity. You are interested in how to get more rich—in quantity, not in quality. You can have two houses and two cars, a bigger bank account, many things. Quantity changes: it becomes more and more. But your quality remains the same, and richness is not of things. Richness is of the quality of your mind, of your life. Even a poor man can be a rich man as far as quality is concerned, and even a rich man can be a poor man. Almost always this is the case, because a person concerned with things and quantity is totally unaware that a different dimension is there within him—the dimension of quality. And that dimension changes only when your mind is positive.

From tomorrow morning, for the whole day, remember this: whenever you feel something beautiful, satisfactory, something blissful—and there are many moments in a twenty-four-hour day—be aware of it. There are many moments when heaven is just near you, but you are so attached and involved with the hell that you go on missing it. The sun rises, the flowers open, the birds sing and the breeze blows through the trees. It is happening! A small child looks at you with innocent eyes, and a subtle feeling of bliss enters into you; or someone smiles and you feel blissful.

Look all around, and try to find the blissful; be filled with it. In that moment forget everything. Be filled with it, taste it, and allow it to happen to your whole being. Be one with it. The fragrance of it will follow you. It will go on resounding within you the whole day, and the resounding, the echoing feeling, will help you to be more positive.

This is accumulative. If you start in the morning, in the evening you will be more open to the stars, to the moon, to the night, to the darkness. Do it for twenty-four hours experimentally, just to have a feeling of what it is. Once you can feel that the positive leads you to a different world because you become different, you are not going to leave it. The whole emphasis will have changed from negative to positive. Then you look at the world in a different, a new way.

I am reminded of one anecdote. One of Buddha's disciples was taking leave from his master. The disciple's name was Purnakashyapa. He asked Buddha, "Where am I to go? Where am I to go to preach your message?"

Buddha said, "You yourself can choose where."

So he said, "I will go to a far corner of Bihar" —it was known as Sooka—"I will move to Sooka province."

Buddha said, "It is better if you change your choice because the people of that province are very cruel, violent, mischievous, and no one has yet dared to go there to teach them nonviolence, love, compassion. So please change your choice."

But Purnakashyapa said, "Allow me to go there *because* no one has gone there, and someone has to be there."

Buddha said, "Then I will ask you three questions before I allow you to go. If the people of that province insult you, humiliate you, how will you feel it?"

Purnakashyapa said, "I will feel they are very good if they simply insult me. Then they are not beating me. They are good people; they could have beaten me."

Buddha said, "Then the second question: if they start beating you, how will you feel?"

Purnakashyapa said, "I will feel they are very good people. They could have killed me, but they are simply beating me."

Then Buddha said, "Now the third question: if they really kill you and murder you, then at the moment when you are dying how will you feel?"

Purnakashyapa said, "I will thank you and them. If they kill me, they will have freed me of a life where many errors were possible. They will have freed me so I will feel thankful."

So Buddha said, "Now you can go anywhere. The whole world is heaven for you. Now there is no problem. The world is a heaven, so you can go anywhere."

With this mind, nothing is wrong with the world. With your mind, nothing can be right. With a negative mind, everything is wrong—not that it is wrong; it is wrong because a negative mind can see only what is wrong.

Wherever satisfaction is found, in whatever act, actualize this. This is a very delicate process, but very sweet also, and the more you proceed in it, the sweeter it becomes. You will be filled with a new sweetness and fragrance. Just look for the beautiful; forget the ugly. Then a moment comes when the ugly also becomes the beautiful. Just look to the happy moment, and a moment comes when there is nothing which you can call unhappy. There is no unhappy moment then. Be concerned with the blissful, and sooner or later there will be no misery. Everything is beautified by a positive mind.

---

55 Be aware of the gap between waking and sleep.

The third self-remembering technique: *At the point of sleep, when the sleep has not yet come and external wakefulness vanishes, at this point Being is revealed.*

There are some turning points in your consciousness. At these turning points you are nearer to your center than at other times. You change gears, and whenever you change a gear you pass through the neutral gear. That neutral gear is nearer. In the morning, when sleep is going, vanishing, and you are feeling awake but not yet awake, just at the midpoint, you are in a neutral gear. There is a point when you are not asleep and not awake, just in the middle. There you are in a neutral gear. From sleep to waking, your consciousness changes the whole mechanism. It jumps from one mechanism to another. Between the two mechanisms, there is no mechanism; there is a gap. Through that gap you can have a glimpse of your being. The same happens in the night when you are again jumping from your waking mechanism to your sleeping mechanism, from your consciousness to the unconscious. For a single moment there is no mechanism, no grip of the mechanism on you, because you have to take a jump from one to another. Between the two if you can be awake, between the two if you can become aware, between the two if you can remember yourself, you will have a glimpse of your real being.

How to do it? While going to sleep, relax. Close your eyes, make the room dark. Just close your eyes and start waiting. The sleep is coming; just wait, don't do anything, just wait! Your body is relaxing, the body is becoming heavy: feel it. Have the feeling of it. Sleep has its own mechanism, it starts working. Your waking consciousness is vanishing. Remember, because the moment will be very subtle and the moment will be atomic. If you miss, you miss. It is not a very long period—a single moment, a very small gap, and you will change from waking to sleep. Just wait, fully aware. Go on waiting. This will take time. It takes at least three months. Only then can you have the glimpse one day of the moment which is just in the middle. So don't be in a hurry. You cannot do it just now; you cannot do it tonight. But you have to start and you may have to wait for months.

Ordinarily, within three months, one day it happens. It is happening every day, but your awareness and the meeting of the gap cannot be planned. It is a happening. You just go on waiting, and someday it happens. Someday, suddenly you become aware that you are neither awake nor asleep—a very weird phenomenon. You may even become afraid because you have known only the two: you know when you are asleep, you know when you are awake. But you don't know a third point in your being when you are neither. At the first impact of it you may become afraid and scared. Don't get scared and don't be afraid. Anything which is so new, unknown previously, is bound to give a certain fear because this moment, when you will have experienced it again and again, will give you another feeling also: that you are neither alive nor dead, neither this nor that. This is an abyss.

These two mechanisms are like two hills; you jump from one peak to another. If you remain in the middle you fall into an abyss, and the abyss is bottomless: you go on falling, you go on falling. Sufis have used this technique, and before they give this technique to a seeker, they give another practice also, just to safeguard. Whenever this technique is given in Sufi systems, before it another practice is given, and that is to imagine with closed eyes that you are falling into a deep well—dark, deep and bottomless. Just imagine falling into a deep well—falling and falling and falling, eternally falling. There is no bottom, you cannot reach to the bottom. Now this fall cannot stop anywhere. You can stop; you can open your eyes and say no more, but this fall in itself cannot stop. If you continue, the well is bottomless, and it gets more and more dark.

In Sufi systems, this well exercise—this bottomless, dark well exercise—is to be practiced first. It is good, helpful. If you have practiced it and you have realized the beauty of it, the silence, then the deeper you go into the well, the more silent you become. The world is left far away, and you feel that you have gone far away, far away, far away. Silence grows with darkness, and deep down there is no bottom. Fear comes to your mind, but you know that this is just imagination so you can continue.

Through this exercise you become capable of this technique, and then, when you fall into the well between waking and sleeping, it is not imagination; it is a real fact. And it is bottomless, the abyss is bottomless. That is why Buddha has called this nothingness emptiness—*shunya*. There is no end to it. Once you know it, you also have become endless. It is difficult to have this glimpse while awake. Then it is impossible, of course, while you are asleep because then the mechanism is functioning, and it is difficult to detach yourself from the mechanism. But there is a moment in the night and in the morning another moment—in twenty-four hours there are these two moments—when it is very easy, but one has to wait.

At the point of sleep, when sleep has not yet come and external wakefulness vanishes, at this point Being is revealed: then you know who you are, what is your real being, what is your authentic existence. We are false while we are awake, and you know it well. You are false while you are awake. You smile when tears would have been more real. Your tears are also not believable. They may be just a façade, ceremonial, a duty. Your smile is false, and those who study faces can say that your smile is just a painted smile. There are no roots within; the smile is just on your face, just on your lips. It is nowhere else in your being. There are no roots, there are no limbs. It is imposed. The smile is not coming from within to without; the smile has been forced from without.

Whatsoever you say and whatsoever you act is false, and it is not necessarily the case that you are doing this false business of life knowingly—not necessarily! You may be totally unaware—and you are! Otherwise it will be very difficult to carry such false nonsense continuously. It is automatic. This falseness continues while you are awake, and it continues even while you are asleep—in a different way, of course. Your dreams are symbolic, not real. It is surprising that even in your dreams you are not real, even in your dreams you are afraid, and you create symbols.

Now psychoanalysis goes on doing this business of analyzing your dreams. They have a big business because you cannot analyze your own dreams. They are symbolic, they are not real. They say something only in metaphors. If you want to kill your mother and get rid of her, you are not going to kill her even in your dream. You will kill someone else who looks like your mother. You will kill your aunt or someone else, but not your mother. Even in dreams you cannot be real. Then psychoanalysis is needed; a professional is needed to interpret—but you may describe the whole thing in such a way that even psychoanalysis is deceived.

Your dreams are also totally false. If you are real while you are awake, your dreams will be real. They will not be symbolic. If you want to kill your mother you will see a dream in which you kill your mother, and no interpreter will be needed to show you what your dream means. But we are so false. In dream you are alone, but still afraid of the world and the society.

To kill a mother is the greatest sin, and I wonder whether you have ever thought about why to kill a mother is the greatest sin. It is the greatest sin because everyone feels a deep enmity toward his mother. It is the greatest sin, and it is taught, your mind is conditioned, that even to think of harming your mother is a sin. She has given birth to you. All over the world, in all societies, the same is taught. There is not a single society on the earth which will not agree to this, that to kill a mother is the greatest sin. She has given you birth and you are killing her?

But why this teaching? Deep down there is the possibility that everyone goes against his mother of necessity—because the mother has not only given birth to you, she has been the instrument of falsifying you; she has been the instrument of forcing you to be unreal. She has made you whatsoever you are. If you are a hell, she has a part in it, the greatest part. If you are miserable, your mother is there somewhere, hidden in you because the mother has given you birth, she has brought you up—or, really, she has brought you down from your reality. She has falsified you. The first untruth happened between you and your mother; the first lie happened between you and your mother—the first lie!

Even when there is no language and the child cannot speak, he can lie. The child sooner or later becomes aware that many of his feelings are not approved by his mother. Her face, her eyes, her behavior, her mood, everything shows that something in him is not accepted, appreciated. Then he starts suppressing. Something is wrong. There is no language yet; his mind is not functioning. But his whole body starts suppressing. Then he begins to feel that sometimes something is appreciated by the mother. He depends on the mother, his life depends on the mother. If the mother leaves him, he will be no more. His whole existence is centered on the mother.

Everything the mother shows, does, speaks, behaves, is significant. If the child smiles, and the mother loves him and gives him warmth and milk and hugs him, he is learning politics. He will smile while there is no smile in him because now he knows he can persuade the mother. He will smile a false smile. Then the liar is born, the politician has come into existence. Now he knows how to falsify, and this he learns in his relationship with his mother. This is the first relationship with the world. When he will become aware of his misery, of his hell, of his confusions, he will find that his mother is hidden somewhere.

There is every possibility that you may feel inimical towards your mother. That is why every culture insists that it is the greatest sin to kill your mother. Even in thought, even in dream, you cannot kill your mother. I am not saying that you *should* kill her, I am simply saying that your dreams are also false—symbolic, not real. You are so false that you cannot even dream a real dream.

These are our two false faces: one is there while you are awake, one is there while you are asleep. Between these two false faces there is a very small door, an interval. In that interval you can have a glimpse of your original face when you were not related to your mother, and through the mother to the society; when you were alone with yourself; when *you were*—not this and that, there was no division. Only the real was; there was no unreal. You can have a glimpse of that face, that innocent face between these two mechanisms.

Ordinarily we are not concerned with dreams, we are concerned with our waking hours. But psychoanalysis is more concerned with your dreams, not with your waking hours, because it feels that in waking hours you are a greater liar. In dreams something can be caught. You are less aware when you are asleep, and you are not forcing things, you are not manipulating. Then something real can be caught. You may be a celibate, a monk in your waking hours, but you have suppressed the sex urge. Then it will force itself into your dreams; your dreams are going to be sexual. It is very difficult to find a monk who is without sexual dreams—rather, impossible. You can find a criminal without sexual dreams, but you cannot find a religious man without sexual dreams. A debauchee may be without sexual dreams, but not so-called saints, because whatsoever you force down while you are awake will erupt in your dreams and will color your dreams.

Psychoanalysts are not concerned with your waking life because they know it is totally false. If something of the real can be glimpsed, it can be glimpsed only through your dreams. But tantra says that even dreams are not so real. They are more real—and this will look paradoxical because we think that dreams are unreal—they are more real than your waking hours because then you are less on guard. The censor is asleep and things can come up, the suppressed can express itself—of course symbolically, but symbols can be analyzed.

And all over the world human symbols are the same. You may speak a different language while awake, but while dreaming you speak the same language. All over the world the dream language is one. If sex is repressed, then the same symbols will come up. If the urge for food, the urge to eat, hunger, is repressed, then the same symbols will come—or similar ones. The dream language is one, but in dreams there are still problems because they are symbolic. And a Freud may interpret them in a different way, a Jung in a different way and an Adler still in a different way. And if you are analyzed by a hundred psychoanalysts, there will be a hundred interpretations. You will be still more confused than you were before, more confused with a hundred interpretations of one thing.

Tantra says in neither waking nor sleeping are you real. You are real only in-between. So don't be concerned with the waking, and don't be concerned with dreaming and sleep. Be concerned with the gap; be aware of the gap. While passing from one state to another have a glimpse. And once you know when the gap comes, you become the master of it. You have the key; you can open that gap anytime and enter into it. A different dimension of being, the real dimension, opens.

---

56 Think of the world as an illusion.

The fourth self-remembering technique, and the last: *Illusions deceive, colors circumscribe, even divisibles are indivisible.*

This is a rare technique, one not much used, but one of the greatest teachers in India, Shankara, has used it, and Shankara has based his whole philosophy on this technique. You know his philosophy of *maya*—illusion. Shankara says everything is illusory. Whatsoever you are seeing, hearing, feeling, all is illusion. It is not real because the real cannot be contacted by senses. You are hearing me and I am seeing you hearing me: it may be just a dream, and there is no way how to judge whether it is a dream or not. I may be just dreaming that you are here listening to me. How am I to know that this is real and not a dream? There is no way.

Chuang Tzu is reported to have said that one night he dreamt that he had become a butterfly. In the morning he was very sad—and he was not a man to have sadness, he was never known to be sad. His disciples gathered and said, "Chuang Tzu, Master, why are you so sad?"

Chuang Tzu said, "Because of a dream."

The disciples laughed and said, "Because of a dream you are sad—you who have been always teaching us not to be sad even if the whole world causes you sadness? And just a dream has caused you sadness? What are you talking about?"

Chuang Tzu said, "It is such a dream that it causes me very, very deep confusion, sadness, misery. I dreamt in my dream that I had become a butterfly."

The disciples said, "What is so puzzling in it?"

Chuang Tzu said, "Now this is the puzzle: if Chuang Tzu can dream that he can become a butterfly, why not the reverse? The butterfly may dream that it has become a Chuang Tzu. So now I am disturbed. What is right and what is wrong? What is real and what is unreal? Was it Chuang Tzu who was dreaming of becoming a butterfly or has the butterfly now gone to sleep and dreamt that it has become a Chuang Tzu? If one is possible, then the other is possible." And it is said that Chuang Tzu never could get over this puzzle. This remained for his whole life.

How to decide that I am not in a dream talking to you? How to decide that you are not dreaming I am talking? With senses no decision is possible, because while dreaming, dreams look real—as real as anything. When you dream, you always feel it is real. When dreams can be felt as real, why can reality not be felt as dream?

Shankara says with senses there is no possibility to know whether the thing confronting you is real or unreal. And if there is no possibility to know whether it is real or unreal, Shankara calls it maya: it is illusion. Illusion doesn't mean unreal. Illusion means an impossibility to decide whether it is real or unreal—remember this.

In Western languages 'maya' has been translated very wrongly, and it gives the feeling in Western terms that 'illusion' means 'unreal.' It does not! 'Illusion' means the inability to decide whether the thing is real or unreal. This confusion is maya.

This whole world is maya, a confusion. You cannot decide; you cannot be decisive about it. It is always escaping you, always changing, turning into something else. It is fantasy, a dreamlike thing. This technique is concerned with this philosophy. *Illusions deceive*—or, that which deceives is illusion—*colors circumscribe, even divisibles are indivisible*. In this world of illusion nothing is certain. This whole world is like rainbows. They appear to be, but they are not. If you are far away they are, but if you come nearer they dissolve. The nearer you come, the more they are not. If you reach to a point where you were seeing a rainbow, it is no more there.

The whole world is like rainbow colors, and it is so. When you are far away everything is hopeful; when you come nearer the hope disappears. And when you reach the goal, only ashes are there—just a dead rainbow. The colors have disappeared, and things as they appeared are not. As you feel them to be, they are not.

Even divisibles are indivisible. Your whole mathematics, your whole calculating system, all your concepts, all your philosophy, just become futile. If you try to understand this illusion, your very effort confuses you more. Nothing is certain there; everything is uncertain—a flux, a flux of change, with no possibility for you to decide whether this or that is true or false. What will happen? If you take this attitude, what will happen? If you really go deep in this attitude that everything which cannot be decided is illusory, you will automatically, spontaneously turn to yourself. Then the only point where you can have a center is in your own being. That is certain.

Try to understand this: I may dream in the night that I have become a butterfly, and I cannot decide in that dream whether this is real or unreal. In the morning I may be puzzled like Chuang Tzu whether instead the butterfly may have been dreaming. These are two dreams, and there is no way to compare which is real and which is unreal.

But Chuang Tzu is missing one thing—the dreamer. He is thinking only of dreams, comparing dreams and missing the dreamer—the one who dreams that Chuang Tzu has become a butterfly, the one who is thinking that it may be quite the reverse: that the butterfly is dreaming that she has become Chuang Tzu. Who is this observer? Who was asleep and is now awake? You may be unreal, you may be a dream to me, but I cannot be a dream to myself, because even for a dream to exist a real dreamer is needed. Even for a false dream a real dreamer is needed. Even a dream cannot exist without a real dreamer. So forget dream. This technique says forget dream. The whole world is illusion, you are not. So don't go after the world, there is no possibility to gain certainty there. And now this appears to be proven even by scientific research.

For the last three centuries science was certain, and Shankara looked to be just a philosophical mind, poetic.... For three centuries science was certain, but now, during these two last decades, science has become uncertain. Now the greatest scientists say nothing is certain, and with matter we will never be certain. Everything has again become uncertain. Everything looks like a flux, changing. Only appearance looks certain. The deeper you go, the more everything becomes uncertain, indefinite. Shankara says, and tantra has always been saying, that the world is illusory. Even before Shankara

was born, tantra was preaching one technique—that the whole world is illusory, so think of it as a dream. If you can think of it as a dream—and if you think at all, you will come to realize it as a dream—then your whole focus of consciousness will turn inwards, because there is a deep urge to find the truth, the real.

If the whole world is unreal, then there is no shelter in it. Then you are moving after, following shadows, and wasting time and life and energy. Then move inwards. One thing is certain: "I am." Even if the whole world is illusory, one thing is certain: there is someone who knows this is illusory. The knowledge may be illusory, the known may be illusory, but the knower cannot be. This is the only certainty, the only rock on which you can stand.

This technique says look at the world: it is a dream, illusory, and nothing is as it appears. It is just a rainbow. Go deep in this feeling. You will be thrown to yourself. With that coming to one's own self, you come to a certain truth, to something which is indubitable, which is absolute.

Science can never be absolute. It is going to be relative. Only religion can be absolute because it searches not the dream, it searches for the dreamer; not for the observed, but for the observer, the seer, the one who is aware.

CHAPTER 36

From maya (illusion) to reality

◆

How can self-remembering transform the human mind?

If one should emphasize the positive, isn't this a choice that is against accepting the total reality?

What is the guru's role and significance in this world of maya?

The first question:

In which way can the practice of self-remembering transform the human mind?

an is not centered in himself. He is born centered, but the society, the family, the education, the culture, they push him off center, and they put him off center in a very cunning way, knowingly or unknowingly. So everyone becomes, in a sense, eccentric—off the center. There are reasons, survival reasons for it. When a child is born he has to be forced into a certain discipline. He cannot be allowed freedom. If he is allowed total freedom, he will remain with the center—spontaneous, living with himself, living himself.

He will be original as he is. He will be authentic, and then there will be no need to practice any self-remembering. There will be no need to practice any meditation because he will never go off the center. He will remain with himself—centered, rooted, grounded in his own being. But this has not yet been possible. Meditation is, therefore, medicinal. The society creates the disease, and then the disease has to be treated.

Religion is medicinal. If really a human society based in freedom can be evolved, there would be no need of religion. Because we are ill medicine is needed, and because we are off center methods of centering are needed. If someday it becomes possible on earth to create a healthy society, healthy in the inner sense, there will be no religion. But it seems difficult to create such a society.

The child has to be disciplined. What are you doing when you are disciplining a child? You are forcing something which is not natural to him. You are asking and demanding something which he will never do spontaneously. You will punish him, you will appreciate, you will bribe him, you will do everything to make him social—to take him away from his natural being. You will create a new center in his mind which was never there, and this center will grow and the natural center will go into oblivion, into the unconscious.

Your natural center has moved into the unconscious, into the dark, and your unnatural center has become your conscious. There is really no division between unconscious and conscious; the division is created. You are one consciousness. This division comes because your own center has been forced to some dark corner. Even you are not in contact with it; you are not allowed to be in contact with it. You yourself have become unconscious that you have a center. You live what the society, the culture, the family have taught you to live: you live a false life.

For this false life a false center is needed. That center is your ego, your conscious mind. That is why, no matter what you do, you will never be blissful—because only the real center can happen, only the real center can explode, can come to the climax, the optimum, of the possibility of bliss. The false center is a shadow game. You can play with it, you can hope with it, but ultimately nothing but frustration comes out of it. With a false anxiety that is bound to be so.

In a way everything is forcing you not to be yourself, and this cannot be changed just by saying that this is wrong, because society has its own needs. A child, when born, is just like an animal—spontaneous, centered, grounded, but so independent. He cannot become part of an organization. He is disturbing. He has to be forced, cultivated and changed. In this cultivation he has to be pushed off center.

We live on the periphery and we live only to the extent that the society allows us. Our freedom is false because the rules of the game, of the social game, are so deeply fixed that you may feel that you are choosing this and that, but you are not choosing. The choice comes from your cultivated mind, and this goes on in a mechanical way.

I am reminded of a man who married eight women in his life. He married one woman, then divorced her, then married another—very cautiously, very carefully, *very* carefully, in order not to fall into the old trap again. In every way he calculated, and he was thinking that this new woman was going to be totally different than the first one. But within a few days, with the honeymoon not yet even over, the new woman started to prove herself to be just the same as the old one, the first one. Within six months the marriage was shattered again. He married a third woman and now he was still more cautious, but again the same thing happened.

He married eight women, and every time the woman turned out to be the same as the old one. What was happening? And he was choosing very cautiously now, very carefully. What was happening? The chooser was unconscious. He couldn't change the chooser, and the chooser was always the same so the choice was going to be the same. And the chooser works unconsciously.

You go on doing this and that, and you go on changing outward things, but you remain the same. You remain off center. Whatsoever you do, howso-ever it is apparently different, it ultimately proves to be the same. The results are always the same; the outcome is always the same; the consequence is always the same.

Whenever you feel you are choosing and you are free, then too you are not free and you are not choosing. The choice is also a mechanical thing. Scientists say, biologists particularly, that the mind becomes imprinted, and that happens very early. The first two or three years are the years for imprinting, and things become fixed in the mind. Then you go on doing the same; you go on repeating in a mechanical way. You are moving in a vicious circle.

The child is forced to be off center. He has to be disciplined; he has to learn obedience. That is why we give so much value to obedience. And obedience destroys everyone, because obedience means now you are not the center: the other is the center, you are just to follow him.

Education is a necessity in order to survive, but we make this necessity to survive an excuse for submitting. We force everyone to be obedient. What does it mean? Obedient to whom? Always someone else—the father, the mother, someone else is there, and you have to be obedient to him. Why so much insistence for obedience? Because your father was forced to be obedient when he was a child; your mother was forced to be obedient when she was a child. They were forced off their centers; now they are doing the same. They are doing the same with their children, and these children will do the same again. This is how the vicious circle moves on.

Freedom is killed, and with freedom you lose your center. Not that the center is destroyed; it cannot be destroyed while you are alive. It would be good if it was destroyed; you would be more at ease with yourself. If you were totally false and there was no real center hidden within you, you would be at ease. There would be no conflict, no anxiety, no struggle.

The conflict comes into existence because the real remains there. It remains in the center, and just on the periphery an unreal center is created. Between these two centers a constant struggle, a constant anxiety, tension, is created. This must be transformed, and there is only one way: the false must disappear and the real must be given its place. You must be regrounded into your center, into your being; otherwise you will be in anguish.

The false can disappear. The real cannot disappear unless you die. While you are alive the real will be there. The society can do only one thing: it can push it deep down and it can create a barrier so that even you become unconscious of it. Can you remember any moment in your life when you were spontaneous, when you just lived in the moment—when you were living yourself and you were not following someone else?

I was reading one memoir of a poet. His father had died, and the dead body was put in a coffin. The poet, the son, was weeping, crying, and then suddenly he kissed the forehead of his father's dead body and said, "There, now that you are dead, I can do this. I always wanted to kiss you on your forehead, but while you were alive it was impossible. I was so afraid of you."

You can kiss only a dead father—and even if the alive father allows you to kiss, the kiss is going to be false; it cannot be spontaneous. A young boy cannot even kiss his mother spontaneously because always the fear of sex is there; the bodies must not come too closely in contact, even with the mother. Everything becomes false. There is fear and falsity —no freedom, no spontaneousness, and the real center can function only when you are spontaneous and free.

Now you will be able to understand what is my attitude towards this question: *In which way can the practice of self-remembering transform the human mind?* It will reground you; it will give you again roots into your own center. By self-remembering, you are forgetting everything other than yourself: the society, the mad world around you, the family, the relationships, everything, you are forgetting. You are simply remembering that you are.

This remembrance is not given by the society to you. This self-remembrance will detach you from all that is peripheral. And if you can remember, you will fall back to your own being, to your own center. The ego will be there just on the periphery, but you will be able to see it now. Like any other object, you will be able to observe it. And once you become capable of observing your ego, your false center, you will never be false again.

You may need your false center because you have to live in a society which is false. You will be able to use it now, but you will never be identified with it. It will be instrumental now. You will live in your center. You will be able to use the false as a social convenience, a convention, but you will not be identified with it. Now you know you can be spontaneous, free. Self-remembering transforms you because it gives you the opportunity to be yourself again—and to be oneself is the ultimate and to be oneself is the absolute.

The peak of all the possibilities, of all the potentialities, is the divine—or whatsoever you want to call it. God is not somewhere in the past; he is your future. You have heard it said again and again that God is the father. More significantly, he is going to be your son, not the father, because he is going to evolve out of you. So I say God the son because the father is in the past and the son is in the future.

You can become divine, God can be born out of you; if you are authentically yourself, you have taken the basic step. You are going towards divinity, towards total freedom. As a slave you cannot move to that. As a slave, as a false person, there is no path leading towards the divine, to the ultimate possibility, the ultimate flowering of your being. First you must be centered in yourself. Self-remembering helps and only self-remembering helps; nothing else can transform you. With the false center there is no growth, only accumulation—and remember the distinction between accumulation and growth. With the false center you can accumulate: you can accumulate wealth, you can accumulate knowledge, you can accumulate anything, without any growth.

Growth happens only to the real center. Growth is not an accumulation; you are not burdened by growth. Accumulation is a burden.

You can know many things without knowing anything. You can know much about love without knowing love. Then it is an accumulation. If you know love, then it is growth. You can know much about love with the false center; you can love only with the real center. Real centers can mature. The false can only get bigger and bigger without any growth, without any maturity. The false is just a cancerous growth, an accumulation, burdening you like a disease.

But you can do one thing: you can change your focus totally. From the false, you can move your eyes to the real. This is what is meant by self-remembering: whatsoever you are doing, remember yourself—that you are. Don't forget it. The very remembering will give an authentic reality to whatsoever you are doing. If you are loving, first remember that you are; otherwise you will be loving from the false center. And from the false center you can only pretend; you cannot love. If you are praying, first remember that you are; otherwise the prayer is going to be just nonsense, just a deception. And you are not deceiving anyone else, you are deceiving yourself.

First remember that you are, and this remembering that "I am" must become so basic that it follows you like a shadow. Then even while asleep it will enter, and you will remember. If you can remember the whole day, by and by it enters even in your dreams, even in your sleep, and you will know that "I am."

The day you can know even in your sleep that you are, you are grounded in your center. Now the false is no more; it is not a burden to you. You can use it now, it is instrumental. You are not a slave to it, you have become the master.

Krishna says in the Gita that while everyone is asleep, the yogi is not: he is awake. It is not meant that the yogi lives without sleep, because sleep is a biological, bodily necessity. What is meant is that

he remembers even in his sleep that he is—that "I am." Sleep is just on the periphery. In the center the remembrance is there.

The yogi remembers even while he is asleep, and you are not remembering yourself while you are even awake. You are walking on the street, but you are not remembering that you are. Try, and you will feel a change of quality. Try to remember that you are. Suddenly a new lightness comes to you, the heaviness disappears; you become weightless. You are thrown off the false center to the real one again, but it is difficult and arduous because we are so much grounded in the false. It will take time, but no transformation is possible without self-remembering becoming effortless for you. You simply start remembering yourself; otherwise no transformation is possible.

The second question:

Last night You said that one should always see life in its positive dimensions and one should not give emphasis to the negative. Is this not a choice? And is this not against encountering the total reality—that which is?

It is a choice, but one who is negative cannot take a jump towards choicelessness. If he can take it, it is good, but it is impossible. From the negative, it is impossible to take a jump towards choicelessness because the negative mind means that you can see only the ugly, you can see only death, you can see only misery. You cannot see any positive elements in life. And, remember, it is difficult to lose misery.

It may look very strange when I say this, but it is difficult to take a jump from misery; it is easier to take a jump from happiness. It is easier to take a jump when you are happy because with happiness courage comes, with happiness the possibility of a higher bliss opens, with happiness the whole world looks like a home. With misery the world is like a hell, and there is no hope; everything is just hopeless. Then you cannot take any jump. In misery one becomes a coward, and one clings to misery because at least this misery is known.

You cannot be adventurous when you are unhappy. Adventure needs a subtle happiness in you. Then you can leave the known. You are so happy that you are not afraid of the unknown. And the happiness has become such a deep phenomenon to you that you know that wherever you will be you will be happy. With the positive mind you know there is no hell, and wherever you are the heaven will be. You can move into the unknown because now you know that heaven moves with you.

You have heard that you enter heaven or hell. This is nonsense. No one enters heaven, no one enters hell. You carry your own hell and heaven with you, and wherever you enter, you enter with your hell or heaven. Heaven and hell are not doors. They are burdens; you carry them with you.

Only with a dancing heart—happy, blissful, positive—can you take a jump into the uncharted. That is why I say that from the negative you cannot be choiceless. You cling to your misery. It is known. You are acquainted with it, you are related to it, and it is better to remain with the known misery than with the unknown. At least you have become accustomed to it, and you know its ways. You have created certain defense mechanisms, an armor around you to be safe from this misery. An unknown misery will create new defense mechanisms. It is always better to be with the known misery than with an unknown misery.

With happiness, quite the reverse is the case. With happiness, one wants to move into the unknown happiness because the known gets boring. You never get bored with the known misery; you enjoy it. Look at people talking about their misery: they enjoy it, they magnify their misery; they have a subtle happiness.

With happiness you get bored. You can move into the unknown. The unknown is alluring, and the choiceless is the door for the unknown. This is how one has to move: from the negative to the positive and from the positive to the choiceless.

First make your mind positive. From hell move to heaven, and from heaven you can move to *moksha*—to the ultimate which is neither. From misery move to bliss, and only then you can move to the beyond which is beyond both. That is why the sutra said first to transform your mind from negative to positive, and this change is just a change of focusing.

Life is both or neither. It *is* both or neither; it depends on you, on how you see it. You can look at it with a negative mind, and then it looks like hell. It is not hell; this is only your interpretation.

You change your outlook: look positively. And this is what is meant by the attitude of the atheist. I don't call a man an atheist or theist because he believes in God or not. I call a man a theist if he has a positive attitude and an atheist if he has a negative attitude. It is not a question of saying no to God; it is a question of saying no to life. The theist is one who says yes and looks always from a yea-saying mind. Then everything changes totally.

If a negative mind comes to a rose, to a garden, many roses may be there, but he will count only the thorns. The first thing for the negative mind is the thorns; that is significant. Flowers are just illusory; only thorns are real. He will count, and, of course, for each flower a thousand thorns exist. And once he has counted a thousand thorns he cannot believe in one flower. He will say this one flower is just illusory. How can such a beautiful flower exist with such ugly thorns, violent thorns? It is impossible, it is unbelievable. And even if it exists, it means nothing now. One thousand thorns have been counted, and the flower disappears.

A positive mind will start with the rose, with the flower. And once you are in a communion with the rose, once you know the beauty, the life, the unearthly flowering, thorns disappear. And one who has known the rose in its beauty, in its highest possibility, one who has looked deep into it, for him now even thorns will not look like thorns. The eyes filled with the rose are different now. Now the thorns will look just like a protection for this flower. They will not be enemies; they will look just like part of the happening of flowers.

Now this mind will know that this flower happens and these thorns are needed, they protect. Because of these thorns this flower could happen. This positive mind will feel grateful even to thorns. And if this approach deepens, a moment comes when thorns become flowers. With the first approach the flower disappears—or the flower even becomes a thorn. Only with a positive mind can you get the state of a nontense mind. With a negative mind you will remain tense, with so many miseries all around. Such a negative, inventive mind goes on revealing miseries and miseries and hells and hells.

In Buddha's time, there was one really famous teacher. His name was Sanjay Belattiputta. He was an absolutely negative thinker. Buddha thought of seven hells, so someone came to Sanjay Belattiputta and told him that Buddha said there are seven hells. Sanjay Belattiputta said, "Go and tell your Buddha he doesn't know anything. There are seven hundred hells. He doesn't know anything! Only seven? There are seven hundred hells, and I have counted all of them."

If you have a negative mind, even seven hundred are not much. You will find more; there is no end to it. The positive mind can be non-tense. Really, if you are positive how can you be tense and if you are negative how you can be non-tense? With a negative mind there can be no association with meditation. The negative mind is antimeditative; it cannot meditate. A single mosquito is enough to destroy all meditation. With a negative mind, the door is closed for tranquility, for stillness, for silence. The negative mind is self-perpetuating for misery. How can it take a jump toward choicelessness?

Krishnamurti goes on talking about choicelessness, and the audience is negative. They listen, but they never understand. And when they are not understanding, Krishnamurti gets disturbed because they are not understanding him. Only a positive mind can understand what he is saying, but a posi-tive mind need not go anywhere—neither to any Krishnamurti nor to any Rajneesh, nowhere. Only a negative mind is in search of a teacher, of a master.

To talk to the negative mind about choicelessness, about going beyond duality, about living both negative and positive, is meaningless. Not that this is untrue—it is true, but meaningless. The one who is listening must be taken into account. He is more important than the one who is talking. As I see it, you are negative. First you need a transformation towards positivity. From your no-saying you must become a yea-sayer. You must look at life with a yes attitude, and with a yes attitude this very earth is totally transformed. Only then, when you have attained a positive attitude, can you take a jump towards choicelessness—and that will be easy, very easy!

Misery cannot be renounced. It is difficult; you cling to it. Only happiness can be renounced because then you know that when you renounce the negative you gain the positive and a positive happiness. You renounce the negative and you gain happiness: just by renouncing the negative you attain to happiness. If you now renounce this happiness, this positive mind also, you open the doors for the infinite. But you must first have a feel of the positive. Only then, *only* then, can you take a jump.

The third question:

In the last technique yesterday, You explained that in this world of maya, the inner consciousness of the seeker is the only real center for him. In this reference, please explain the significance and role of the guru in this world of maya.

This world of maya is not a world of maya for you; it is very real, and the role of the guru is to show you that it is not real. It is real for you, so how can you think that it is unreal? You can think about unreality only if you have a glimpse of the real; only then can you compare. This world is not maya, illusory, for you. You have heard, you have read that this world is maya, and you may have memorized it just like a parrot, so you also call this world illusory.

Every day someone comes to me who calls this world illusory and then he says, "My mind is very much bothered. I am very tense, so tell me how to attain peace?" And this world is illusory! If this world is illusory, how can your mind be tense? If you have known that this world is illusory, the world will have disappeared, and with the world all its misery. But the mind still is. You don't know that this world is illusory.

In the morning when the sleep has disappeared, and with it the dream, are you worried about the dream? Are you worried that in the dream you felt ill or that you were even dead? While the dream was there, you were worried, you were ill, you were asking for a doctor, for some medicine. But in the morning, the moment you are not asleep and the dream has disappeared, you are not worried. Now you know it was a dream, and you are not ill.

If someone comes to me and says, "I know that it was a dream that I was ill, but now tell me something: where am I to get the medicine to get over that illness?" what will it show? It will show he is still asleep; it will show that he is still dreaming. The dream is still there.

In India, this parrotlike speech that "the whole world is illusory" has gone deep into the mind, but in the false center. It is not a growth. We have heard, the Upanishads, the Vedas and the *rishis* have been saying for centuries, that the world is illusory. They have propagated the idea so strongly that those who are asleep and dreaming, they think they are awake. The whole world is asleep, but their misery shows that the world is real, their anguish shows that the world is real.

The role of the guru is to give you a glimpse of the real—not a teaching, but an awakening. The guru is not a teacher, the guru is an awakener. He has not to give you doctrines. If he gives you doctrines, he is a philosopher. If he talks about the world as illusory and argues and proves that the world is illusory, if he discusses, debates, if he intellectually gives you a doctrine, he is not a guru, he is not a master. He may be a teacher, a teacher of a particular doctrine, but he is not a master, not a guru.

A guru is not a giver of doctrines. He is a giver of methods—of methods which can help you to come out of your sleep. That is why a guru is always a disturber of your dreams, and it is difficult to live with a guru. It is very easy to live with a teacher because he never disturbs you. Rather, he goes on increasing your accumulation of knowledge. He helps you to be more egoist; he makes you more knowledgeable. Your ego is more fulfilled. Now you know more, you can argue more. You can teach yourself, but a guru is always a disturber. He will disturb your dream and your sleep, and you may have been dreaming a very beautiful dream. You may have been on a trip, a beautiful trip. He will disturb it, and you will get angry.

A guru is always in danger from his disciples. Any moment they can kill him because he is going to disturb; that is what his work is. He cannot help you to be yourself as you are because you are false. He has to destroy your false identity. It is painful. That is why, unless there is a very deep love, the work is impossible. A very deep intimacy is needed; otherwise hate will be there. So a guru cannot allow you to be near him unless you have surrendered; otherwise you are going to be an enemy. Only with your total surrender can a guru work, because it is a spiritual surgery.

Of necessity, much suffering will be there for the disciple, and if he is not in deep intimacy with the guru it is impossible. He will not be ready to suffer so much. He has come in search of bliss and the guru gives him suffering. He has come to feel euphoria, and the guru creates a hell for him. In the beginning hell will be there because your image will be shattered, your expectations will be shattered. Whatsoever you have known, you will have to throw it. Whatsoever you are, he will undo it. Really, you are passing through a death.

In India, in the old days, we said *Acharya mrityuh*. It means that the master, the guru, is a death. He is! And unless you trust him so totally, this surgical operation is impossible because in the beginning there will be suffering. Your anguish will come up; all your suppressed hells will be revealed. And only if you believe, if you have deep faith and trust in him, can you remain with him; otherwise you will escape, because this man is disturbing you completely.

So, remember, the guru's work is, his role is, to make you aware of your falsity, and because of your false center your world is false. The world is not really illusory, it is not maya. It is maya because your eyes are illusory. They are dream-filled. You project your dreams all around, and the reality is falsified. The same world will become real when your eyes are real. When the false center is broken and you are again rooted in your real center, in your being, this world will become the *nirvana*.

Zen masters have been continuously saying that this world is nirvana, this very world is moksha, liberation. It is only a question of eyes. With false eyes everything is falsified; with real eyes everything is real. Your false entity creates a false world around you. And don't think that you all live in one world. You cannot! Each one lives in his own world, and there are as many worlds as there are minds because each mind creates its own world, its own milieu. Even if you are living in a family, the husband lives in his own world and the wife in her own world, and there are collisions every day between these two worlds. They never meet; they collide. Meeting is impossible.

With mind there can be no meeting—only collision, conflict. When mind is not, there can be a meeting. The wife lives in her own world, in her own expectations. The husband for her is not the real husband that is there in the world, he is just her own image. The husband lives in his own world, and the real wife is not his wife. He has an image of a wife, and whenever this wife falls short of his image there is struggle, conflict, anger, hatred. He loves his own image of a wife and the wife loves her own image of a husband, and these both are illusory; they exist nowhere. This real wife is there and this real husband is there, but they cannot meet because between these two real things are the unreal wife and the unreal husband. They are always there; they won't allow a meeting of the real ones.

Everyone is living in his own world, in his own dreams, expectations, projections. There are as many worlds as there are minds. Those worlds are illusory, maya. When your false center disappears, the whole world changes. Then it is a real world. Then for the first time you see things as they are. Then there is no misery because with illusion expectation disappears, and with reality there can be no misery. Then one comes to feel, "It is so! Fact is fact!" Only with fictions are there problems, and fictions never allow you to know fact. These fictions of the mind are maya.

The role of the guru is to shatter the fictions so that the fact becomes available to you and you become available to the fact. That "facticity" is truth. Once you know that facticity, even the guru will be different. If you come to a guru now, you come with your own image of him. Someone comes to me: he comes with his own image of me. And then, if I am not following his image, he is in difficulty. But how am I to follow his image? And if I try to follow everyone's image, I will be in a mess. And every disciple thinks I should be like this or that; he has his own concept of a guru. If I am not fulfilling his concepts he becomes frustrated, but this is how it is going to be. A disciple comes with a mind, and this is the problem. I have to change his mind, to destroy it. He comes with a mind and he looks at me also with his mind.

I was staying in a home with a family. The family was Jain, so they wouldn't eat in the night. The old man of the family, the grandfather, he was a lover of my books. He had never seen me, and it is easy to love a book: a book is a dead thing. He came to meet me. He was very old, and even to come from his room was difficult for him. He was ninety-two, and he came to meet me. I told him I would come to his room, but he said, "No! I respect you so much, I will come." So he came, and he was praising me very much.

He said, "You are just like a *tirthankara*, like the highest in Jain mythology, Mahavira." The greatest teachers are known as tirthankaras, so he said, "You are just like a tirthankara." He was praising and praising me, and then evening came and darkness descended.

Someone from the house came and said, "Now it is getting late. You come for your evening meal."

So I said, "Wait a little because of this old man. Let him say whatsoever he wants to say; then I will come."

The old man said, "What are you saying? Are you going to eat in the night?"

I said, "It is okay with me."

So he said, "I take my words back. You are no tirthankara. A person who doesn't even know that to eat in the night is the greatest sin, what else can he know?"

Now this man cannot have any meeting with me. Impossible! If I was not eating in the night, I was a tirthankara, a great master. I had not eaten yet. I had just said that I would eat in the night, and suddenly I am no more a tirthankara. The old man said to me, "I have come to learn something from you, but now that is impossible. Now I feel I must teach you something."

When this world becomes an illusion, your guru will also be part of it and will disappear. That is why, when the disciple awakens, there is no guru. This will seem very paradoxical: when the disciple *really* awakens, there is no guru.

There are beautiful songs of Saraha, a Buddhist mystic. With every song the last ending line is "and Saraha disappeared." He teaches something; he gives some teachings. He says, "Neither the world is nor the nirvana is, neither the good nor the bad. Go beyond, and Saraha disappears." It has been a puzzle. Why does Saraha go on saying "and Saraha disappears"? If you really attain to the song, to

whatsoever he has said—"There is neither good nor bad, nor the world nor the nirvana"—if the disciple really awakens to this, Saraha will disappear. Where will be the guru? The guru was part of the disciple's world. Now there will be no entities like the guru and the disciple; they will have become one. When the disciple awakens, he becomes the guru, and Saraha disappears. Then the guru is no more there. Even the guru is part of your dream, of your illusioned world. But because of this many problems arise.

Krishnamurti goes on saying there is no teacher —and he is right. This is the ultimate truth. When you have awakened, you are the teacher and there is no other teacher. But this is the ultimate truth, and before this happens the teacher is because the disciple is. The disciple creates the teacher; it is the disciple's need.

So remember this: if you meet a wrong teacher, you deserve a wrong teacher; that is why you meet a wrong teacher. A wrong disciple cannot meet a right teacher. You create your teacher, your master. A small teacher or a great teacher depends on you; you will meet the person you deserve. If you meet a wrong person it is because of you. You are responsible for it, not the wrong person. The guru also is part of your mind, it is part of the dreamworld. But unless you become awakened, you will need someone to disturb you, someone to help. This someone is a guru if he gives you methods. He is simply a teacher if he gives you only doctrines, principles, teachings, but you may need him right now.

Think of it in this way: even in a dream there is something which can help you to come out of it. Even in a dream something can help you to come out of it. You can try it just while falling asleep. Go on repeating in the mind, "Whenever there is a dream, my eyes will open." For three weeks go on continuously repeating it just when you are falling asleep: "Whenever there is a dream, my eyes will open; suddenly I will be awakened." And you will be awakened. Even from a dream you can be awakened by a certain method. Just when falling asleep, say to yourself—if your name is Ram, say —"Ram, awaken me at five o'clock in the morning." Repeat it twice, and then silently fall asleep. Sooner or later you will get the trick. Exactly at five o'clock someone will awaken you. Even in dream, even in sleep, methods can be used which will awaken you. The same is the case for the spiritual sleep you are in.

A master can give you methods which will be helpful for this. Then whenever you are falling into a dream, the methods will not allow you to fall, or whenever you have fallen into a dream suddenly you will be awakened. When this awakening becomes natural to you there is no need for the guru. When you have awakened the guru disappears, but you will still feel gratitude for the guru because he helped you.

Sariputta was one of the greatest disciples of Buddha. He became enlightened in his own right; he became a buddha himself. Then Buddha said to Sariputta, "Now you can go and move; now my presence is not needed for you. You yourself have become a master in your own right, so you can go and help others to come out of their sleep."

Sariputta, when leaving Buddha, touched his feet. Someone asked Sariputta, "You yourself have become enlightened, so why are you touching Buddha's feet?"

Sariputta said, "Now there is no need to touch his feet, but this situation could happen only because of him. Now there is no need, but this could happen only because of him."

Sariputta moved away, but wherever he was, in the morning he would prostrate himself in the direction where Buddha was; in the evening he would prostrate himself and everyone would ask, "What are you doing? To whom you are prostrating yourself?" because Buddha was far away, miles away.

He would say, "To my teacher who has disappeared. I am myself now the guru, but it was not possible before him. It became possible only because of him."

So even when the teacher disappears, when the guru disappears, the disciple will feel a deep gratitude, the greatest gratitude that is possible.

There is a need while you are asleep for someone to disturb you. And if you allow someone, that is what surrender means. If you say, "Okay, I allow you to disturb me," that is what surrender means —a trust. Trust means that now even if this man leads you towards misery, you will be ready to move. You will not question him anymore. Wherever he leads you, you trust in him. He is not going to harm you.

If you don't trust, then no progress is possible because you feel he is going to harm you. You feel, in your terms, that he is going to harm you in many ways, and if you think, "I am to protect myself," then no further work is possible. If you mistrust your surgeon, you will not allow him to make you unconscious. You don't know what he is going to do, and you will say, "Do the operation, but allow me to be conscious so I can go on seeing what you are doing. I cannot trust you."

You trust your surgeon. He makes you unconscious because things are such that in your conscious state surgery would be impossible to do; your consciousness would interfere. That is why trust is blind. It means you are ready even to become unconscious, even to become blind. You are ready to follow him wherever he leads. Only then does a deeper, inner surgery become possible. And it is not only a physical, physiological surgery; it is psychological. Much pain will be felt, much anguish, because catharsis is needed and you have to be thrown back to your own center which you have forgotten completely, pulled back to your roots again which you have left behind miles away.

This is going to be arduous and difficult; it even takes years. But if the disciple is ready to surrender, it can even happen in seconds. It depends on the intensity of surrender. Unnecessary time is wasted because the guru has to go slowly—slowly so that you are prepared to trust more, and he has to do many things unnecessarily just to create trust. Just to do the surgery he has to create many things unnecessarily which can be discarded. No need to waste time and energy on them, but they are needed just to create trust.

I quoted Saraha; Saraha is one of the eighty-four *siddhas*—one of the eighty-four Buddhist mystics—who attained. Saraha says to those disciples who have become masters, "Behave in such a way that others can trust you. I know now that you need no morality; I know now that you need no rules. You have gone beyond, and you can do whatsoever you like and you can be whatsoever you like. Now no system, no morality exists for you. But behave in such a way so that disciples can trust you." So great masters have behaved in such a way that the society approves. It is not because they need to behave in that way; it is only an unnecessary thing to create trust. So if Mahavira behaves in the pattern that Jains have set, it is not because there is any inner necessity. He behaves that way only so that Jains can follow and become disciples, so that they can trust.

That is why many problems arise whenever a teacher starts behaving in a new way. Jesus behaved in a new way which was not known to the Jewish community. There was nothing wrong in it, but this became the problem. Jews couldn't trust him. Their masters of old had behaved differently and this man was behaving differently. He was not following the rules of the game, so they couldn't trust him. Thus, they had to crucify him.

And why did Jesus behave in such a way? India was behind it. He was here for many years before he appeared in Jerusalem. He was taught here in a Buddhist monastery, and he tried to follow Buddhist rules there where no Buddhist society existed. In a Jewish community he was behaving as if he was living in a Buddhist community, and that created the whole problem. He was killed, misunderstood, murdered, and the reason was only this —that Jews couldn't trust him.

A teacher, a guru, has unnecessarily to create many things around him, to do many things, just to create trust. But even then, problems arise because everyone comes with his own expectations: "The guru must be like this or like that."

Surrender means you leave your expectations, you allow the guru to be as he is and you allow him to do whatsoever he wants to do. Even if pain results, you are ready for it. Even if he leads you towards death you are ready for it, because ultimately he will lead you to a deep death. Only after it is rebirth possible. Resurrection is possible only when your old identity has been crucified.

CHAPTER 37

Techniques to witness the fluxlike film of life

◆

57 *In moods of extreme desire, be undisturbed.*

58 *This so-called universe appears as a juggling, a picture show. To be happy, look upon it so.*

59 *O Beloved, put attention neither on pleasure nor on pain, but between these.*

60 *Objects and desires exist in me as in others. So accepting, let them be transformed.*

he original mind is like a mirror: it is pure, and it remains pure, but dust can gather upon it. The purity is not lost, the dust cannot destroy the purity, but the purity can be covered up. This is the condition of the ordinary mind—covered with dust. Hidden behind the dust, the original mind remains pure. It cannot become impure, that is impossible. And if it was possible for it to become impure, then there would be no way to regain the purity again. In itself it remains pure, just covered by dust.

Our mind is the original mind plus dust, the buddha-mind plus dust, the divine mind plus dust. Once you know how to uncover it, how to reclaim it from the dust, you have known all that is worth knowing and you have attained all that is worth attaining. All these techniques are concerned with how to free your mind from the day-to-day dust that is bound to gather upon it. Dust is but natural. Just like with a traveler passing from many, many roads, dust is gathered—and for many, many lives you have been a traveler. You have traveled long distances, and much dust has gathered.

Many points have to be understood before we enter the techniques. One, the East is basically different from the West in its attitude towards inner transformation. Christianity thinks that something has happened to man's being itself—the sin. The East thinks that nothing has happened to the being itself; nothing can happen. The being remains in its absolute purity; there has been no sin. So man is not condemned in the East, he is not something degraded. On the contrary, he remains the divine that he is, that he has always been, and it is natural that dust will gather. Dust is bound to gather.

So there is no sin, just a false identification.

We become identified with the mind, with the dust. Our experience, our knowledge, our memories, all are dust. Whatsoever you have known, whatsoever you have experienced, whatsoever has been your past, is all dust. Regaining the original mind means regaining the purity—without experiences, without knowledge, without memories, without the past.

The whole past is dust, but we are identified with the past and not with the consciousness that is always present. Think of it in this way: whatsoever you know is always of the past, and you are here and now in the present. All your knowledge is dust. "Knowing" is your purity, knowledge is dust. The capacity to know, the energy to know, knowing, is your original nature. Through that knowing you gather knowledge. That knowledge is dustlike. Here and now, this very moment, you are absolutely pure, but you are not identified with this purity, you are identified with the past, the accumulated past. So all meditative techniques are basically methods to remove yourself from the past and to allow you to plunge into the here and now.

Buddha was searching for how to regain this purity of consciousness, how to be free from the past, because unless you are free from the past you will remain in bondage, you will be a slave. The past is heavy on you, and because of the past the present is never known. The past is known; the present is a very minute atomic moment. You go on missing it because of the past, and because of the past you go on projecting into the future. The past is projected into the future, and both are false. The past is no more, the future is yet to be. Both are not, and that which is, is hidden between these two which are not.

Buddha was in search; he went from one teacher to another. He searched, and he went to many teachers, all of the known teachers. He consulted them, he allowed them to work upon him, he cooperated. He disciplined himself in many ways, but he was not fulfilled, and the difficulty was this: the teachers were interested in the future, in some liberated state somewhere beyond death, after the life is over. They were interested in some God, some *nirvana*, some *moksha*—some liberated state—somewhere in the future, and Buddha was interested in the here and now, so there was really no meeting. He said to every teacher, "I am interested in the here and now, in how to be total, complete and pure here and now." And they would say, "Apply this method, do this, and if you do it rightly, someday in the future, in some future life, in some future state, you will attain."

Sooner or later he left every teacher, and then he tried by himself alone. What did he do? He did a very simple thing. Once you know it, it is very simple and obvious, but when you don't know it, it is so arduous and so difficult, it seems impossible. He did only one thing: he remained with the present moment. He forgot his past and he forgot his future. He said, "I will be here and now. I will simply exist." If you can exist even for a single moment, you have known the taste—the taste of your pure consciousness. And once it is tasted you can never forget it. Then the taste, the flavor, remains with you, and that flavor becomes a transformation.

Many are the ways how to uncover yourself from your past, how to throw the dust and have a look into the mirror of your own mind. All these techniques are different ways, but with every technique a deep understanding is needed: remember that. These techniques are not mechanical because they are to uncover consciousness. They are not mechanical things. You can use these techniques mechanically, and if you use them as mechanical techniques you may gain a certain stillness of mind, but that won't be the original purity. You may gain a certain silence, but that silence will be cultivated. That too belongs to the dust part of the mind, not to the original layer. Don't use them mechanically. A deep understanding is needed, and with understanding they can be helpful to uncover your being.

57 Be undisturbed by desires.

The first witnessing technique: *In moods of extreme desire, be undisturbed.*

In moods of extreme desire, be undisturbed: When desire grips you, you are disturbed. Of course, that is natural. Desire grips you, then your mind starts wavering and many ripples go on, on the surface. The desire pulls you somewhere into the future; the past pushes you somewhere into the future. You are disturbed, you are not at ease. Desire is, therefore, a dis-ease.

This sutra says, *In moods of extreme desire, be undisturbed.* But how to be undisturbed? Desire means disturbance, so how to be undisturbed— and in extreme moments of desire? You will have to do certain experiments; only then will you understand what it means. You are in anger, anger grips you, you are temporarily mad, possessed, you are no more in your senses. Suddenly remember to be undisturbed—as if you are undressing. Inside, become naked, naked from the anger, undressed. Anger will be there, but now you have a point within you which is not disturbed.

You will know that anger is there on the periphery. Like fever, it is there. The periphery is wavering; the periphery is disturbed. But you can look at it. If you can look at it, you will be undisturbed. Become a witness to it, and you will be undisturbed. This undisturbed point is your original mind. The original mind cannot be disturbed; it is never disturbed—but you have never looked at it. When anger is there, you become identified with the anger. You forget that anger is something other than you. You become one with it, and you start acting through it, you start doing something through it.

Two things can be done. In anger you will be violent to someone, to the object of your anger. Then you have moved to the other. Anger is just in-between you and the other. Here I am, then there is anger, and there you are—the object of my anger. From anger I can travel in two dimensions: either I can travel to you; then you become my center of consciousness, the object of my anger. Then my mind becomes focused on you, the one who has insulted me. This is one way how you can travel from anger. There is another way: you can travel to yourself. You don't move to the person whom you feel has caused the anger. You move to the person who feels to be angry; you move to the subject and not to the object.

Ordinarily, we go on moving to the object. If you move to the object, the dust part of your mind is disturbed, and you will feel, "'I' am disturbed." If you move within to the center of your own being, you will be able to witness the dust part; you will be able to see that the dust part of the mind is disturbed, but "I am not disturbed." And you can experiment upon this with any desire, any disturbance.

A sexual desire comes to your mind; your whole body is taken by it. You can move to the sexual object, the object of your desire. The object may be there, it may not be there. You can move to the object in imagination also. But then you will get more and more disturbed. The further you go away from your center, the more you will be disturbed. Really, the distance and disturbance are always in proportion. The more distant you are from your

center, the more you are disturbed; the nearer you are to the center, the less you are disturbed. If you are just at the center, there is no disturbance.

In a cyclone, there is a center which is undisturbed—in the cyclone of anger, the cyclone of sex, the cyclone of any desire. Just in the center there is no cyclone, and a cyclone cannot exist without a silent center. The anger also cannot exist without something within you which is beyond anger.

Remember this: nothing can exist without its opposite. The opposite is needed there.

Without it, there is no possibility of it existing. If there were no center within you which remains unmoved, no movement would be possible there. If there were no center within you which remains undisturbed, no disturbance could happen to you. Analyze this and observe this. If there were no center of absolute undisturbance in you, how could you feel that you are disturbed? You need a comparison. You need two points to compare.

Suppose a person is ill: he feels illness because somewhere within him, a point, a center of absolute health exists. That is why he can compare. You say that your head is aching. How is it that you know about this ache, this headache? If you were the headache, you could not know it. You must be someone else, something else—the observer, the witness, who can say, "My head is aching."

This ache can be felt only by something which is not the ache. If you are ill, you are feverish, you can feel it because you are not the fever. The fever cannot feel that there is fever; someone is needed who is beyond it. A polarity is needed. When you are in anger, and if you feel you are in anger, it means that a point exists within you which is still undisturbed and which can be a witness. You may not look at that point, that is another thing. You may not see yourself at that point, that is another thing. But it is there always in its pristine purity; it is there.

This sutra says, *In moods of extreme desire, be undisturbed.* What can you do? This technique is not for suppression. This technique is not saying that when there is anger suppress it and remain undisturbed—no! If you suppress, you will create more disturbance. If the anger is there and an effort to suppress is there, it will double the disturbance. When anger is there, close your doors, meditate on the anger, allow the anger to be. You remain undisturbed, and don't suppress it.

It is easy to suppress; it is easy to express. We do both. We express if the situation allows, and if it is convenient and not dangerous for you. If you can harm the other and the other cannot harm you, you will express the anger. If it is dangerous, if the other can harm you more, if your boss or whoever you are angry at is more strong, you will suppress it.

Expression and suppression are easy, witnessing is difficult. Witnessing is neither; it is not suppressing, it is not expressing. It is not expressing because you are not expressing it to the object of anger. It is not being suppressed either. You are allowing it to be expressed—expressed in a vacuum. You are meditating on it.

Stand before a mirror and express your anger—and be a witness to it. You are alone, so you can meditate on it. Do whatsoever you want to do, but in a vacuum. If you want to beat someone, beat the empty sky. If you want to be angry, be angry; if you want to scream, scream. But do it alone, and remember yourself as a point which is seeing all this, this drama. Then it becomes a psychodrama, and you can laugh at it and it will be a deep catharsis for you. Afterwards you will feel relieved of it—and not only relieved of it, you will have gained something through it. You will have matured; a growth will have come to you. And now you will know that even while you were in anger there was a center within you which was undisturbed. Now try to uncover this center more and more, and it is easy to uncover it in desire.

That is why tantra is not against desire. It says be in desire, but remember the center which is undisturbed. So tantra says that even sex can be used. Move in sex, but remain undisturbed. Be a witness. Go on being a deep observer. Whatsoever

is happening, is happening on the periphery; you are just an onlooker, a spectator.

This technique can be very useful, and much benefit can happen to you through it. But it will be difficult because when you become disturbed, you forget everything. You may forget that you have to meditate. Then try it in this way: don't wait for the moment when anger happens to you. Don't wait for the moment! Just close your room, and think of some past experience of anger when you went mad. Remember it, and re-enact it. That will be easy for you. Re-enact it, do it again, relive it. Do not just remember it, relive it. Remember that someone had insulted you and what was said and how you reacted to him. React again, replay it.

You may not know that mind is just a tape-recording device. And now scientists say, now it is a scientific fact, that if your memory centers are touched with electrodes, they start replaying. For example, you were once angry: the incident is recorded, in the same sequence as it happened, just as if on a tape-recording in your brain. If it is touched by an electrode, it will start replaying. You will have the same feeling again. Your eyes will go red, your body will start trembling and will become feverish, the whole thing will be re-enacted. The moment the electrode is put away, it stops. If you give it energy again, it starts from the very beginning again.

Now they say that mind is a recording machine, and you can re-enact anything. But don't just remember: relive. Start feeling the experience again, and the mind will get the idea. The incident will come to you; you will relive it. In reliving it, remain undisturbed. Start from the past. This is easy because now it is a play, the actual situation is not there. And if you become capable of doing this, then you will be able to do it when the situation for anger is really there, when a real situation is there. And this can be done with every desire, and it is to be done with every desire.

This re-enacting something from the past will do much. Everyone has scars in his mind; unhealed wounds are there. If you re-enact them, you will be unburdened. If you can go to your past and do something which has remained incomplete, you will be unburdened from your past. Your mind will become fresher; the dust will be thrown away. Remember in your past something which you feel has remained suspended. You wanted to kill someone, you wanted to love someone, you wanted this and that, and that has remained incomplete.

That incomplete thing goes on hovering on the mind like a cloud. It influences everything that you are and that you are doing. That cloud has to be dispersed. Move back on the time track and bring back desires which have remained incomplete, and relive the wounds which are still green. They will be healed. You will become more whole, and through this you will have the knack of how to remain undisturbed in a situation which is disturbed.

In moods of extreme desire, be undisturbed. Gurdjieff used this technique very much. He created situations, but to create situations a school is needed. You cannot do that alone. Gurdjieff had a small school in Fontainebleau, and he was a taskmaster. He knew how to create situations. You would enter the room, and a group would be sitting there. You would enter the room where a group was sitting, and something would be done so that you would get angry. And it would be done so naturally that you could never imagine that some situation was being created for you. But it was a device. Someone would insult you by saying something, and you would get disturbed. Then everyone would help the disturbance and you would become mad. And when you were right at the point where you could explode, Gurdjieff would shout, "Remember! Remain undisturbed!"

A situation can be created, but only in a school where many persons are working on themselves. And when Gurdjieff would shout, "Remember! Remain undisturbed," now you would know that this was a created situation. The disturbance cannot disappear so suddenly, so immediately, because it

has physical roots. Your glands had thrown poison in the blood; your body had become affected.

Anger cannot disappear so immediately. Even now that you had come to know that you had been deceived, that no one was insulting you and no one meant anything by it, it would be difficult to do anything. The anger is there, your body is filled with it—but suddenly your temperature cools down. Only on the body, on the periphery, does the anger remain. At the center you suddenly cool down, and you know that a point exists within you which is undisturbed. You start laughing. Your eyes are red with anger; your face is violent, animallike, but you start laughing. You know two things now —a point which is undisturbed and a periphery which is disturbed.

You can help. Your family can become a school; you can help each other. Friends can become a school and they can help each other. You can decide with your family...the whole family can decide that now a situation has to be created for the father or for the mother, and then the whole family works to create the situation. When the father or mother goes completely mad, then everyone starts laughing and says, "Remain completely undisturbed." You can help each other, and the experience is simply wonderful. Once you know a cool center within you in a hot situation, you cannot forget it, and then in any hot situation you can remember it, reclaim it, regain it.

In the West now one technique, a therapeutic technique, is used; it is called psychodrama. It helps, and it is also based on techniques like this. In psychodrama you just enact, you just play a game. In the beginning it is a game, but sooner or later you become possessed. And when you become possessed your mind starts functioning, because your mind and your body function automatically. They function automatically!

So if you see an actor acting in a psychodrama who, in a situation of anger, really becomes angry, you may think that he is simply acting, but it is not so. He might have really become angry; it may not be acting at all now. He is possessed by the desire, by the disturbance, by the feeling, by the mood, and if he is really possessed, only then does his acting look real.

Your body cannot know whether you are playing or whether you are doing it for real. You may have observed yourself at some time in your life that you were just playing at being angry, and you didn't know when the anger became real, or you were just playing and you were not feeling sexual. You were playing with your wife or with your girlfriend, or with your husband, and then suddenly it became real. The body takes it, and the body can be deceived. The body cannot know whether it is real or unreal, particularly with sex. If you imagine it your body thinks it is real.

Sex is one of the most imaginary centers in the body, so just by imagining, you can have a sexual orgasm. You can deceive the body. In dream, you can have a sexual release; even in dream, the body is deceived. You are not making love to anyone; just in dream, in fantasy, in imagination, you are making love. But the body can release sexual energy, and even a deep orgasm can be felt. What is happening? How is the body deceived? The body cannot know what is real and what is unreal. Once you start doing something, the body thinks it is real and it starts behaving in a real way.

Psychodrama is a technique based on such methods. You are not angry, you are simply acting angry—and then you get into it. But psychodrama is beautiful because you know that you are simply acting, and then on the periphery anger becomes real, and just behind it you are hidden and looking at it. Now you know that you are not disturbed, but the anger is there, the disturbance is there. The disturbance is there, and yet the disturbance is not.

This feeling of two forces working simultaneously gives you a transcendence, and then in real anger also you can feel it. Once you know how to feel it, you can feel it in real situations also. Use this technique; this will change your total life. Once you know how to remain undisturbed, the world is not

misery for you. Then nothing can create any confusion in you; really, nothing can hurt you. Now there is no suffering for you, and once you know it you can do another thing.

Gurdjieff used to do it. He was able to change his face at any moment. He would be laughing, he would be smiling, he would be looking happy with you, and suddenly he would become angry without any cause. And it is reported about him that he became so proficient at this art that if two persons were sitting near him, one on each side, he could be angry with half of his face and he could be smiling with the other half of his face. Then one person would report, "What a beautiful man Gurdjieff is," and the other would say, "What an ugly man!" He would look at one person from one side smiling, and he would look at the other side angrily.

Once you can detach your center from the periphery, you can do it. Once the center is detached completely, if you can remain undisturbed in anger, in desire, you can play with desires, with anger, with disturbances.

This technique is to create a feeling of two extremes within you. They are there, two polar opposites are there. Once you become aware of this polarity, you become for the first time a master of yourself. Otherwise others are your masters; you are just a slave. Your wife knows, your son knows, your father knows, your friends know, that you can be pushed and pulled. You can be disturbed, you can be made happy and unhappy. If someone else can make you happy and unhappy, you are not a master, you are just a slave. The other has a hold. Just by a single gesture he can make you unhappy; just by a small smile he can make you happy.

So you are just at the mercy of someone else; the other can do anything to you. And if this is the situation, then all your reactions are simply reactions, not actions. You simply react. If someone insults you and you become angry, your anger is not an action, it is a reaction. If someone appreciates you and you start smiling and feeling good, great, this is a reaction, not an action.

Buddha was passing by a village, and some persons gathered there. They were against him, and they insulted him. Buddha listened, and then he said, "I am to reach to the other village in time, so can I go now? If you have said whatsoever you have come to say, if it is finished, then I can move. Or, if you have to say something more to me, while returning I will wait here. You can come and tell me."

Those persons were just surprised. They couldn't understand. They had been insulting him, using bad words, abusing him, so they said, "But we are not saying something to you, we are abusing and insulting you."

Buddha said, "You can do that, but if you want any reaction from me you have come late. Ten years before, if you had come with such words, I would have reacted. But now I have learned how to act, I am a master of myself now; you cannot force me to do anything. So you will have to go back. You cannot disturb me; nothing can disturb me now because I have known my own center."

This knowledge of the center or this grounding in the center makes you a master. Otherwise you are a slave, and a slave of so many—not only of one master, but of many. Everything is a master, and you are a slave to the whole universe. Obviously, you will be in trouble. With so many masters pulling you in so many directions and dimensions, you are never together, you are not in a unity, and pulled in so many dimensions, you are in anguish. Only a master of oneself can transcend anguish.

---

58 See the world as a drama.

The second witnessing technique: *This so-called universe appears as a juggling, a picture show. To be happy, look upon it so.*

This whole world is just like a drama, so don't be too serious about it. Seriousness will force you into trouble, you will get into trouble. Don't be serious about it. Nothing is serious; this whole world is just a drama.

If you can look to the whole world as a drama you will regain your original consciousness. The dust gathers because you are so serious. That seriousness creates problems, and we are so serious that even while seeing a drama we gather dust. Go to a picture house and look at the spectators. Don't look at the screen, forget the picture; don't look at the screen, just look at the spectators in the hall. Someone will be weeping and tears will be rolling down, someone will be laughing, someone will become sexually excited. Just look at people. What are they doing? What is happening to them? And there is nothing on the screen, just pictures— pictures of light and shadow. The screen is vacant.

But how are they getting excited? They are weeping, crying, laughing. The picture is not just a picture, the film is not just a film. They have forgotten that it is just a story, they have taken it seriously. It has become "alive"! It is "real"! And this is happening everywhere, not only in a picture house. Look at the life that is all around you. What is it?

Many people have lived on this earth. Where you are sitting, at least ten dead bodies are buried in that place, and they too were serious like you. Now they are no more. Where have their lives gone? Where have their problems gone? They were fighting—fighting for a single inch of earth, and the earth is there and they are no more.

And I am not saying that their problems were not problems. They were—as your problems are problems. They were serious—problems of life and death. But where are their problems? And if the whole humanity should disappear any day, the earth will be there, the trees will grow, the rivers will flow and the sun will rise, and the earth will not feel any absence or wonder where humanity is.

Look at the expanse: look backwards, look forwards, look to all dimensions at what you are, what your life is. It looks like a long dream, and everything that you take so seriously this moment becomes useless the next moment. You may not even remember it.

Remember your first love, how serious it was. Life depended on it. Now you don't remember it at all, it is forgotten. And whatsoever you are thinking that your life depends on today will be forgotten. Life is a flux, nothing remains. It is like a moving film, everything changing into everything else. But in the moment you feel it is very serious, and you get disturbed. This technique says, *This so-called universe appears as a juggling, a picture show. To be happy, look upon it so.*

In India we have called this world not a creation of God, but a play, a game, a *leela*. This concept of leela is beautiful, because creation seems serious. The Christian, the Jewish God is very serious. Even for a single disobedience, Adam was thrown out of the Garden of Eden—and not only was *he* thrown out, because of him, the whole humanity. He was our father, and we are suffering because of him. God seems to be so serious. He should not be disobeyed. And if he is disobeyed, he is going to take revenge, and the revenge has been so long.

The sin doesn't seem to be so serious. Really, Adam committed it because of God's own foolishness. God the Father said to Adam, "Don't go near the tree, the Tree of Knowledge, and don't eat its fruit." This prohibition becomes an invitation, and this is psychological. In that big garden, only that Tree of Knowledge became attractive. It was prohibited.

Any psychologist can say, God committed an error. If the fruit of that tree was not to be eaten, it was good not to talk about it at all. There was no possibility of Adam reaching to that tree, and the whole humanity would have been in the garden. But this saying, this order, "Don't eat," created the trouble; this "don't" created the whole trouble.

Because Adam disobeyed he was thrown out of heaven, and the revenge seems so long. And Christians say Jesus was crucified just to redeem us—to redeem us from that sin that Adam committed. So the whole Christian concept of history hangs on two persons, Adam and Jesus. Adam committed the sin, and Jesus suffered to redeem us from it and allowed himself to be crucified. He suffered so that Adam's sin may be forgiven. But it doesn't seem that God has forgiven yet. Jesus was crucified, but humanity goes on suffering in the same way.

The very concept of God as a father is ugly, serious. The Indian concept is not of a creator. God is just a player; he is not serious. This is just a game. Rules are there, but rules of a game. You need not be serious about them. Nothing is sin—only error, and you suffer because of error, not because God punishes you. You suffer because of the rules you don't follow. God is not punishing you. The whole concept of leela gives life a dramatic color; it becomes a long drama. And this technique is based on this concept: *This so-called universe appears as a juggling, a picture show. To be happy, look upon it so.*

If you are unhappy, you have taken it too seriously. And don't try to find any way how to be happy. Just change your attitude. You cannot be happy with a serious mind. With a festive mind, you can be happy. Take this whole life as a myth, as a story. It is one, but once you take it this way you will not be unhappy. Unhappiness comes out of too much seriousness. Try for seven days; for seven days remember only one thing, that the whole world is just a drama—and you will not be the same again. Just for seven days! You are not going to lose much because you don't have anything to lose.

You can try it. For seven days take everything as a drama, just as a show. These seven days will give you many glimpses of your buddha-nature, of your inner purity. And once you have the glimpse you cannot be the same again. You will be happy, and you cannot conceive of what type of happiness can happen to you because you have not known any happiness. You have known only degrees of unhappiness: sometimes you were more unhappy, sometimes less unhappy, and when you were less unhappy you called it happiness. You don't know what happiness is because you cannot know. When you have a concept of the world in which you are taking it very seriously, you cannot know what happiness is. Happiness happens only when you are grounded in this attitude, that the world is just a play.

So try this, and do everything in a very festive way, celebrating, doing an act—not a real thing. If you are a husband, play, be a play husband; if you are a wife, be a play wife. Make it just a game. And there are rules, of course; any game to be played needs rules. Marriage is a rule and divorce is a rule, but don't be serious about them. They are rules, and one rule begets another. Divorce is bad because marriage is bad: one rule begets another! But don't take them seriously, and then look how the quality of your life immediately changes.

Go to your home this night, and behave with your wife or husband or your children as if you are doing a part in a drama, and see the beauty of it. If you are playing a part you will try to be efficient, but you will not get disturbed. There is no need. You will do the part and go to sleep. But remember, it is a part, and for seven days continuously follow this attitude. Then happiness can happen to you, and once you know what happiness is you need not move into unhappiness, because it is your choice.

You are unhappy because you have chosen a wrong attitude towards life. You can be happy if you choose a right attitude. Buddha pays so much attention to right attitude. He makes it a base, a foundation—right attitude. What is right attitude? What is the criterion? To me this is the criterion: the attitude that makes you happy is the right attitude, and there is no objective criterion. The attitude that makes you unhappy and miserable is the wrong attitude. The criterion is subjective; your happiness is the criterion.

59 Stay in the middle between two polarities.

The third witnessing technique: *O Beloved, put attention neither on pleasure nor on pain, but between these.*

Everything is polar, and mind moves from one polarity to another, never staying in-between. Have you known any moment when you were neither happy nor unhappy? Have you known any moment when you were neither healthy nor sick? Have you known any moment when you were neither this nor that, when you were just in-between, just in the middle, right in the middle? Mind moves from one pole to another immediately. If you are happy, sooner or later you will move to unhappiness, and you will move immediately: the happiness will disappear and you will be unhappy.

If you are feeling good, sooner or later you will feel bad, and there is no point where you stay in-between. You move immediately from this to that. Just like the pendulum of an old clock, you move from left to right, from right to left, and the pendulum goes on moving. There is a secret law: when the pendulum is going to the left, it appears to be going to the left, but it is gathering momentum to go right. When it is going to the left, it is gathering energy, momentum, to go right; when it is going right, it is gathering momentum to go left. So what appears is not the whole. When you are becoming happy, you are gathering momentum to be unhappy. So whenever I see you laughing, the moment is not far away when you will be weeping.

In Indian villages the mothers know this, so when a child starts laughing too much they say, "Stop him; otherwise he will weep." It is bound to be so. If a child is so happy, the next step can be nothing but unhappiness. Thus, they stop him. Otherwise he will be unhappy. But the same applies to the reverse, and that is not known. When a child is weeping and you try to stop him, you are not only stopping his weeping; you are stopping his next step. He cannot be happy now. When a child is weeping, allow him. Help him to weep more so that when weeping is finished he has gathered momentum. Now he can move to the right, he can be happy.

Now psychoanalysts say that when a child is weeping and screaming, don't stop him, don't try to persuade him, don't distract him. Don't try to focus his mind somewhere else; don't bribe him to stop. Don't do anything. Just remain silent near him, and allow him to weep and cry and scream so that he can move easily to happiness. Otherwise, neither will he be able to weep nor will he be able to be happy. That is how we all have become. We cannot do anything. The smile is halfhearted, the tear is also halfhearted; everything is confusion.

But this is the natural law of mind. It moves from one pole to another. This technique is to change this natural law: *O Beloved, put attention neither on pleasure nor on pain, but between these.* Any of the polarities can be chosen, and try to be just in-between. What can you do to be in-between? How will you be in-between? One thing: when pain is there, what can you do? When pain is there, you want to escape from it. You don't want it; you try to go away from it. Your effort is to go to the opposite—to be happy, to be joyful.

When there is happiness, what do you do? Your effort is to cling to it so that the other pole may not enter—to *cling* to it! When happiness is there you cling; when pain is there you escape. This is the natural attitude. If you want to change this natural law and transcend it, when pain is there don't try to escape. Remain with it. You will disturb the whole natural mechanism. You have a headache: remain with it. Close your eyes, meditate on the headache; remain with it. Don't do anything. Just be a witness; don't try to escape.

When happiness is there and you are feeling especially blissful in any particular moment, don't cling to it. Close your eyes and remain a witness to it all. Clinging or escaping are natural for the dust-covered mind. If you remain a witness, sooner or later you will fall in-between because the natural law is to move to the polarity, to the polar opposite. If you remain a witness, you are in-between.

Buddha has called his whole philosophy *majjhim nikai*—the middle way, because of this technique. He says remain in the middle always; no matter what the polarity, remain always in the middle. By witnessing one remains in the middle. The moment you lose your witnessing you either become attached or repulsed. If you are repulsed you will go to the other extreme; if you are attached you will try to remain at this extreme, but you will never be in-between. Just be a witness. Don't be attracted, don't be repulsed. The headache is there; accept it. It is there as a fact. As a tree is there, as the house is there, as the night is there, the headache is there. Accept it and close your eyes. Don't try to escape from it.

You are happy; accept the fact. Don't cling to it, and don't try not to become unhappy; don't try anything. If unhappiness comes, allow it. If happiness comes, allow it. Just remain a watcher on the hill, just seeing things. The morning comes, and then evening comes, and then the sun rises, and then the sun sets and there are stars and darkness, and again the sun rises—and you are just a watcher on the hill. You cannot do anything. You simply see. The morning has come; you note the fact, and you know that now the evening will come because the evening follows the morning. And when the evening comes you note the fact, and you know that now the morning will be coming because the morning follows the evening.

When pain is there, you are just a watcher. You know that pain has come, and sooner or later it will go, and the polar opposite will come. And when happiness has come, you know that it is not going to remain always. Unhappiness will be just hidden somewhere, it will be coming. You remain a watcher. If you can watch without attraction and without repulsion you will fall in the middle, and once the pendulum stops in the middle you can look for the first time at what the world is.

While you are moving, you cannot know what the world is; your movement confuses everything. Once you are not moving, you can look at the world. For the first time you know what reality is. A nonmoving mind knows what reality is; a moving mind cannot know what reality is. Your mind is just like a camera: you go on moving and taking shots, but whatsoever comes is just a confusion because the camera must not move. If the camera is moving, the pictures are going to be just a confusion.

Your consciousness is moving from one polarity to another, and whatsoever you know of reality is just a confusion, a nightmare. You don't know what is what; everything is confused, missed. If you remain in the middle and the pendulum has stopped, if your consciousness is focused now, centered, then you know what reality is. Only a mind that is unmoving can know what the truth is. *O Beloved, put attention neither on pleasure nor on pain, but between these.*

---

60 Acceptance.

The fourth witnessing technique: *Objects and desires exist in me as in others. So accepting, let them be transformed.*

This technique can be very helpful. When you are angry, you always justify your anger, but when someone else gets angry you always criticize. Your madness is natural, but others' madness is just perversion. Whatsoever you do is good—or even if it was not good, it was necessary to do. You always find some rationalization for it.

The same is done by others, but then the same rationalization is not given. If you are angry, you say it was necessary to help the other. If you were not angry, the other would have been destroyed, he would have got a wrong habit, so it was good to give him punishment. It was just for his good. But when someone gets angry at you, the same ratio-

nalization is not applicable. Then he is mad, he is evil.

We have double standards—one standard for one oneself and another standard for everyone else. This double-standard mind is going to be in deep misery always. This mind is not just, and unless your mind is just you cannot have a glimpse of the truth. Only a just mind can leave this double standard.

Jesus says, "Don't do to others what you would not like done to you." This means a similar standard is needed. This technique is based on the idea of a single standard: *Objects and desires exist in me as in others.* ... You are not exceptional, although everyone thinks he is exceptional. If you think you are exceptional, know well this is how every ordinary mind thinks. To know that one is ordinary is the most extraordinary thing in this world.

Someone asked Suzuki about his teacher: "What was exceptional in your teacher, Suzuki?" Suzuki was a Zen master, so he said, "The only thing I will never forget is this, that I have never seen a man who thought himself so ordinary. He was just ordinary, and that is the most extraordinary thing, because every ordinary mind thinks he is exceptional, extraordinary."

But no one is extraordinary, and if you know this you become extraordinary. Everyone is just like everyone else. The same desires that hover around you hover around everyone else. But you call your sex love; others' love you call sex. Whatsoever you do, you protect it. You say it is good. That is why you are doing it, and the same thing done by others is not the same. And this happens not only to persons; it happens to races, nations. This is why the whole world has become a mess, because of this.

If India goes on strengthening its army it is for defense, and if China goes on strengthening its army it is for attack. Every government in the world calls its military organization defense. Then who attacks? If everyone is defending, who is the aggressor? If you move into history, you cannot find anyone who is an aggressor. Of course, the defeated ones prove to be aggressors. The defeated ones always prove to be aggressors because they cannot write history. The victorious ones write history.

If Hitler could have won, then the history would have been different. Then he would have been the savior of the world, not the aggressor. Then Churchill and Roosevelt and the other allies would have been the aggressors, and it would have been good if they were destroyed. But because Hitler couldn't win he was the aggressor, and Churchill and Roosevelt and Stalin and the other allies saved humanity. Not only with persons, but with everything we do—as nations, as races—the same logic moves. We are something different and the other is different.

No one is different! A religious mind knows that everyone is the same, so if you give rationalizations for yourself, please give the same rationalizations to others also. If you criticize others, then apply that same criticism to yourself. Don't create two standards. One standard will transform your being totally because with one standard you become just, and for the first time you can look straight into reality, as it is. *Objects and desires exist in me as in others. So accepting, let them be transformed.*

Accept them and they will be transformed. What are we doing? We accept that they exist in others. Whatsoever is wrong exists in others; whatsoever is right exists in you. Then how can you be transformed? You are already transformed. You think that you are already good and everyone else is bad; the world needs a transformation, not you. That is why there are always leaders, movements, prophets. They go on crying from the rooftops to change the world, to create a revolution, and we have been making revolutions and revolutions and nothing changes.

Man remains the same and the earth remains in the same misery. Only faces and labels change, but misery continues. It is not a question of how to change the world. The world is not wrong; you are wrong. The question is how to change yourself.

"How to change myself?" is the religious quest; "How to change everyone else?" is political. But the politician thinks he is okay; really, he is the model of how the whole world should be. He is the model, he is the ideal, and it is up to him to change the whole. Whatsoever the religious man sees in everyone else he sees in himself also. If there is violence, he immediately wonders whether the violence exists in him or not. If there is greed, if he sees greed somewhere, his first reflection is over whether the same greed is in him or not. And the more he searches the more he finds that he is the source of all evil. Then it is not a question of how to change the world; it is a question of how to change oneself. And the change starts the moment you accept one standard. Then you are already changing.

Don't condemn others. I don't mean condemn yourself—no! Just don't condemn others. And if you are not condemning others, you will have a deep compassion for them, because the same problems are there. If someone commits a sin, a sin in the eyes of the society, you start condemning him, never thinking that you also have the seed to commit that sin within you. If someone commits a murder you condemn him, but have you not always been thinking to kill someone, to murder? Is not the potential seed there always? The man who has committed murder was not a murderer a moment before, but the seed was there. And the seed is with you also. A moment later, who knows? You may be a murderer.

So don't condemn him. Rather, accept. Then you will feel a deep compassion for him because whatsoever he has done any man is capable of doing; you are capable of doing it.

A noncondemning mind will have compassion; a noncondemning mind will have a deep acceptance. He knows that this is how humanity is and that "this is how I am." Then the whole world will become just a reflection of your own self. It will become a mirror. Then every face becomes a mirror for you; you look at yourself in every face.

Objects and desires exist in me as in others. So accepting, let them be transformed. Acceptance becomes transformation. This is difficult to understand because we always reject, and then too we cannot transform anything. You have greed, but you reject it. No one wants to think of himself as greedy. You are sexual, but you reject it. No one wants to feel oneself as sexual. You are angry, you have anger, but you reject it. You create a façade, and you try to justify it. You never feel that you are angry or that you are anger.

But rejection never transforms anything. It simply suppresses, and that which is suppressed becomes more powerful. It moves to your roots, to your unconscious deep down within you, and it begins functioning from there. And from that darkness of the unconscious it becomes more powerful. You cannot accept it now because you are not even conscious of it. Acceptance brings everything up. There is no need to suppress.

You know you are greedy, you know you have anger, you know you are sexual, and you accept them as natural facts without any condemnation. There is no need to suppress them. They come to the surface of the mind, and from the surface of the mind they can be thrown very easily. From the deep center they cannot be thrown. And when they are on the surface you are always aware of them, but when they are in the unconscious you become unaware. And a disease of which you are aware can be cured; a disease of which you are unaware cannot be cured.

Bring everything up to the surface. Accept your humanity, your animality. Whatsoever is there, accept it without any condemnation. It is there, and be aware of it. Greed is there; don't try to make it nongreed. You cannot. And if you try to make it nongreed, you will simply suppress it. Your nongreed will simply be another form of greed and nothing else. Don't try to change it into the other; you cannot change it. If you want to try to change greed, what will you do? And a greedy mind can be

attracted only towards the ideal of nongreed if some further greed is possible through it. If someone says that "If you leave all your riches you will be allowed in my kingdom of God," then you can even renounce. A further greed becomes possible. This is a bargain.

Greed has not to become nongreed; greed is to be transcended. You cannot change it.

How can a violent mind become nonviolent? If you force yourself to be nonviolent, this will be a violence to yourself. You cannot change one into another, you can simply be aware and accepting. Accept greed as it is. By acceptance is not meant that there is no need to transform it. By acceptance is meant only that you accept the fact, the natural fact, as it is. Then move in life knowing well that greed is there. Do whatsoever you are doing, remembering well that greed is there. This awareness will transform you. It transforms because knowingly you cannot be greedy, knowingly you cannot be angry.

For anger, for greed, for violence, unawareness is a basic requirement, just as you cannot knowingly take poison, just as knowingly you cannot put your hand into a flame. Unknowingly you can put it. If you don't know what a flame is, what fire is, you can put your hand in it. But if you know that fire burns, you cannot put your hand in it.

The more your knowingness grows, the more greed becomes a fire and anger becomes poison. They simply become impossible. Without any suppression, they disappear. And when greed disappears without any ideal of nongreed, it has a beauty of its own. When violence disappears without making you nonviolent, it has a beauty of its own.

Otherwise a nonviolent man is deeply violent. That violence is there hidden, and you can have a glimpse of it from his nonviolence also. He will force his nonviolence upon himself and upon others in a very violent way. That violence has become subtle. This sutra says that acceptance is transformation, because through acceptance awareness becomes possible.

CHAPTER 38

Toward
the authentic being

♦

How does the modern mind become identified with the dust of past experience?

If one feels life as a psychodrama, then also one feels lonely. Then what is the right attitude towards life?

How to grow in stillness and playfulness simultaneously.

You said acceptance transforms, but why then does acceptance of senses and desires make me feel animallike instead?

The first question:

In which way does the modernized original mind become identified with the dust of the past knowledge and experience?

ind is pure, and no impurity can enter it. That is impossible. The mind is just the buddha-nature, the ultimate. And when I say mind, I don't mean your mind, I simply mean the mind where no I and you exist. You are the impurity. Just behind you is the original mind. You are the dust. So first try to analyze what you are, and then you will be able to understand how the original mind becomes identified with the past, with memories, with dust.

What are you? Right now, if I ask you what you are, you can answer in two ways. One will be a verbal answer, and in that verbal answer you will relate your past. You will say, "My name is this. I belong to this family or that, to this religion or that, to this country or that. I am educated or uneducated, rich or poor." These are all past experiences, they are not you. You have been through them, you have passed through them, they have been the passage, but your past goes on accumulating.

This will be the verbal answer, but this is not the real answer. This is your mind arguing, the false ego. Right now, if you leave all of your past—if you forget your father, your parents, your family, your religion, your country, all which is accidental

—if you forget all that is accidental and just remain with yourself here and now, then who are you? No name will come to your consciousness, no form—just a simple awareness that you are. You won't be able to say who you are. You will simply say, "I am." The moment you answer the who, you move into the past.

You are a simple consciousness, a pure mind, an innocent mirror. Right now, this very moment, you are. Who are you? Just a simple awareness that "I am." Even the I is not needed. The deeper you move, the more you will feel just am-ness, existence. This existence is the pure mind, but this existence has no form; this is formless—*nirakar.* This existence has no name; it is nameless—*anam.*

It will be difficult for you to be introduced by this which you really are. In the society, relating with others, you will need some name, some form. Your past supplies you name and form. That name and form are useful. Without them it will be difficult to survive. They are needed, but they are not you; they are just labels. Because of this utilitarian need, the original mind becomes identified with name and form.

A child is born. He is a simple consciousness, but you have to call him, you have to give him a name. In the beginning, the child will use his own name. He will not say, "I am feeling hungry"; he will say, "Ram is feeling hungry"—Ram is his name. He will say, "Ram is feeling very angry." Only later on will he learn that this cannot be used in this way; he cannot call himself Ram. Ram is the name that he is to be called by others. Then he will learn the use of "I."

First he will become identified with "Ram," the name that others call him; then he will become identified with "I." This is utilitarian. You need it. Without it survival will be difficult. Because of this utilitarian necessity, one becomes identified. You can go beyond this identification, and the moment you start going beyond and reclaiming your original consciousness, you have started meditation, and you can start meditation only when you become frustrated with your name and form and the world that belongs to it.

Religion starts when you become frustrated, totally frustrated, with the world of name and form and when the whole thing looks meaningless. It is! Ultimately it *is* meaningless. This feeling of meaninglessness of the world that is created around name and form makes you uneasy. That uneasiness is the beginning of a religious search. You become uneasy because with this label you cannot become totally identified. The label remains a label; you remain what you are. This label covers you a little, but it cannot become your totality. And sooner or later you become fed up with this label. You want to know who you really are. And the moment you ask sincerely, "Who am I?" you are on a different journey; you are transcending.

This identification is natural. There is another reason why it is so easy to become identified. This is a room; if I say to you, "Look at the room," where will you look? You will look at the walls. The walls are not the room: the room is just roominess; it is not the walls, the walls are just the boundaries of the space that we call room. But if I tell you to look at the room, you will look at the walls because the roominess cannot be looked at.

You are just inner space; your name and form are the walls. They give you a boundary, they give you a definition, they give you a definite place. You can be identified with that definiteness; otherwise you are just a zero, *shunya*—a nothingness. That nothingness is there, that inner space is there.

Look at it in this way. You breathe in, you breathe out. If you breathe in and breathe out silently and there is no thinking in the mind, if you are simply sitting under a tree breathing in and breathing out, what will you feel? You will feel that there is outer space, there is inner space. The breath comes into the inner space, the breath moves out to the outer space, but where are you? There are simply two spaces. Your throat is just a door, a swinging door. When the breath comes in, the breath forces the door and moves in. When the breath goes out, it again forces the door and goes out. Your throat is just a swinging door, and there are two spaces—the outer and the inner. And if this door is broken, then there are not even two spaces—just one space.

You will become afraid if you feel a nothingness within. You want to be something definable, definite. There is no one who is definite inside; the outer space is infinite and the inner space is also infinite. That is why Buddha insisted that there is no soul, no *atma*. You are just a vacant space— infinite.

It is difficult to feel oneself as this infinite space unless you make an arduous effort. One becomes identified with the boundaries. It is easier to feel oneself that way—with the boundaries. Your name is just a boundary, your body is just a boundary, your thoughts are just a boundary.

For outer utility, for your own convenience also, you become identified. Then, once you become identified, accumulation goes on and on and on, and with accumulation you feel a fulfillment of the ego. You are identified with your riches, then you go on accumulating. You have a feeling you are growing greater, bigger. You have a big house, then a bigger house, then a still bigger house, so you feel that you are getting bigger and bigger, and that is how greed is born.

Greed is nothing but an expansion, an effort to expand the ego. But howsoever great you become in your ego, you can never become infinite, and you *are* infinite within. If you can look into the nothingness you are infinite within. That is why ego is never satisfied. Ultimately it is frustrating. It cannot become infinite; it will remain finite.

This is how one always has a spiritual discontent. You are infinite. Nothing less will be helpful for you and nothing less will ever satisfy you. But every boundary is going to be finite. It is needed, it is necessary in a way, useful, but it is not true, it is not the truth. This inner mirror, this inner mind, is pure consciousness—just consciousness.

Just look at the light. You say the room is filled with light, but how do you see the light? You have never seen light itself, you cannot see it; you always see something lighted. Light falls on the walls, light falls on the books, light falls on other persons. It is reflected on those objects. Because you can see objects, you say light is there. When you cannot see objects, you say there is darkness. You have never seen light pure in itself. It is always seen reflected on some object.

Consciousness is even purer than light. It is the purest possibility in existence. If you become totally silent, all boundaries disappear and you will not be able to say who you are. You simply are, because there is no object you can feel yourself to be in contrast with. You cannot say that you are a subject, soul, or even a consciousness. Because of this purity of consciousness, you always know yourself through something else; you cannot know yourself directly. So when you create boundaries, you feel that you know yourself. With a name you feel you know yourself; with your riches you feel you know yourself. Something around you becomes the boundary and the pure consciousness is reflected back.

When Buddha attained enlightenment he said, "I am no more." When you attain to that state you will also say, "I am no more," because without a boundary how can you be? When Shankara attained, he said, "I am all." Both mean the same. If you are the all, you are no more. All or nothing —only two possibilities are there, but in both the possibilities you are not. If you are all, the *Brahma*, then you are not. If you are not, totally a

nothingness, then too you are not. Because of this, it is a necessary part of life to become identified. And it is good, because unless you become identified you cannot become unidentified. Unless you become identified, you cannot become unidentified! At least once, one has to become identified.

It is like this: if you are born healthy and have never been ill, you will never be aware of your health. You cannot be, because awareness of health needs a background of disease and illness. You will have to fall ill to know that you were healthy or what health is. The other pole will be needed. Eastern esoteric science says this is why the world is, so that you can experience that you are divine. The world gives a contrast.

Go into a school, and you will see that the teacher is writing on a blackboard with white chalk. He can write on a white board too, but then it will be meaningless because it will be invisible, it won't be seen. Only on a blackboard can one write with white chalk so that it is seen. The blackboard is a necessity for the white writing to become visible.

The world is just a blackboard, and you become visible because of it. This is an inherent polarity, and it is good. That is why in the East we have never said that the world is bad; we take it just as a school, a training. It is good because only in contrast will you be able to know your purity. When you come into the world you become identified. With identification you enter; the world starts. So you will have to fall ill to know your inner health.

This has been a basic question all over the world: Why is this world there? Why is it at all? Many answers have been given, but those answers are just superfluous. Only this attitude seems to be very deep and meaningful—that the world is just a background; without it you cannot become aware of your inner consciousness.

I will tell you one story. One man—very rich, the richest in his country—became disturbed, became frustrated. He felt that life was meaningless. He had everything that could be purchased, but all that could be purchased proved meaningless. Only something that could not be purchased could have real meaning. He had everything he could purchase—he could have purchased the whole world—but what to do now? He was frustrated and deep discontent was within.

So he gathered all his valuables, ornaments, gold, jewels, everything, into a big bag, and he started on a journey just to find a man who could give him something valuable, a glimpse of happiness. Then be would present his whole life's earnings to him. He went from one teacher to another, traveled and traveled, but no one was able to give him even a glimpse. And he was ready to give everything—his whole kingdom.

Then he reached a village and asked for Mulla Nasruddin, who was a fakir living there. A village man told him, "Mulla Nasruddin is just sitting outside the town, meditating under a tree. You go there, and if he cannot give you a glimpse of happiness then forget it. Then you can go to all the corners of the world, but you will never get it. If this man cannot give you a glimpse, then there is no possibility."

So the man was very excited. He came to Nasruddin, who was sitting under a tree. The sun was setting. The man said, "I have come for this purpose. My whole life's earnings are here in this bag, and I will give them to you if you can give me a glimpse of happiness."

Mulla Nasruddin listened. The evening was descending, it was becoming dark. Without answering him, Mulla Nasruddin snatched the bag from the rich man and ran away. Of course, the rich man followed him crying, weeping and screaming. The village streets were known to Mulla Nasruddin; they were not known to the rich man as he was a stranger, so he couldn't find him. From all over the village people from the whole village started following them. Nasruddin was just running round and round. The man was mad. He was crying, "I have been robbed of all my life's riches. I am a poor man! I have become a beggar!" He was weeping—weeping like anything.

Then Nasruddin reached the same tree, and he just put the bag before the tree and went behind the tree to hide there. The man came there, he fell on the bag, and started weeping in happiness. Nasruddin looked from behind the tree and said, "Are you happy, man? Have you had a little glimpse?"

The man said, "I am as happy as anyone can be on this earth."

What happened? To have a peak, a valley is needed. To feel happiness, unhappiness is needed. To know the divine, the world is needed. The world is just a valley. The man was the same, the bag was the same. Nothing new had happened, but now he said that he was happy—as happy as anyone can be on this earth—and just a few minutes before he was miserable. Nothing had changed. The man was the same, the bag was the same, the tree was the same. Nothing had changed, but the man was now happy, dancing.

The contrast had happened. Consciousness becomes identified because through identification the world is, and through the world you can regain yourself.

When Buddha attained he was asked, "What have you achieved?" He said, "Nothing. On the contrary, I have lost much. I have not attained anything because now I know that whatsoever I have attained was always there; it was my nature. It was never taken away from me, so I have not achieved anything. I have achieved that which was already there, which was already achieved. I have lost only my ignorance."

Identification is ignorance. It is part of this great play—this cosmic *leela*, this cosmic play—that you will have to lose yourself to find yourself again. This losing yourself is just a way, and the only way, to regain yourself. If you have lost too much already, you can regain. If you have not yet lost yourself enough, you will have to lose more. And nothing can be done before that; no help is possible before that. Unless you are lost completely in the valley, in the darkness, in the *sansara*, in the world, nothing can be done. Lose so that you can gain. This looks paradoxical, but this is how the world is, how the very process is.

The second question:

If one begins to feel that life is a psychodrama, then one also feels detached and lonely. Thus, the intensity, sincerity, the depth of living is lost. Please suggest what to do in this situation. What then is the right attitude toward life?

If one begins to feel that life is a psychodrama, then one also feels detached and lonely.... Then feel it! Why create a problem? If you feel detached and lonely, then feel it! But we go on creating problems. Whatsoever happens, we will create a problem out of it. Feel lonely and detached—and if you can be at ease with your loneliness, it will disappear. If you start doing something with it to transcend it, it will never disappear; it will remain there. Now a modern trend in psychology and psychoanalysis says that anything can disappear if you remain with it without creating any problems, and this has been one of the oldest teachings of tantra.

For the last ten or twelve years, in Japan, a small psychotherapeutic technique has been in use. Western psychoanalysts and psychiatrists have been studying it. It is a Zen therapy, and it is wonderful. If someone goes neurotic or psychotic, that man or woman is simply put into a lonely room and he or she is told, "Remain with yourself, whatsoever you are. Neurotic? Okay! Then be neurotic and live with it." And the doctors do not interfere. Food is provided, needs will be fulfilled, attention will be given, but there is no interference. The patient has to live with himself, and within ten days he starts changing. Western psychoanalysis works for years, and basically nothing changes.

What happens to this Zen patient? There is no interference from outside. There is just acceptance of the fact that "Okay, you are neurotic. Nothing can be done." Zen says that one tree is small and

another tree is very big, so okay: one is small, another is big, and nothing can be done. Once you accept a thing, you are already transcending it.

One of the most original psychiatrists of England, R.D. Laing, has now proposed that if we can leave a madman to himself, just paying loving attention to him, fulfilling his needs and not interfering with him, he will get over his madness within three or four weeks. His proposal is that no madness can last for more than ten days if it is not interfered with. If you interfere, then you prolong the process.

What happens when you are not interfering in anything? You feel lonely, so feel lonely: it is how you are. But when you feel lonely you start doing something, and then you are divided. Then one part of you feels lonely and another part tries to change it. This is absurd. It is just pulling yourself up by your legs or the strings of your shoes—pulling yourself up to the sky. Absurd! You are lonely, so what can you do? There is no one else to do anything. You are alone, so be lonely. This is your fate; this is how you are. What will happen if you accept it? If you accept it, your fragmentariness will disappear, you will become one, you will be whole—not divided.

If you are depressed, so be depressed; don't do anything. And what can you do? Whatsoever you do will be done out of depression, so it will create more confusion. You can pray to God, but you will pray so depressingly that you will even make God depressed through your prayers. Don't do that violence. Your prayer is going to be a depressed prayer.

You can meditate, but what will you do? The depression will be there. Because you are depressed, whatsoever you do the depression will follow. More confusion will be created, more frustration, because you cannot succeed. And when you cannot succeed you will feel more depressed, and this can go on ad infinitum. It is better to remain with the first depression than to create a second circle and then a third circle. Remain with the first; the original is beautiful. The second will be false, and the third will be a far-off echo. Don't create these. The first is beautiful. You are depressed, so this is how existence is happening to you at this moment.

You are depressed, so remain with it. Wait and watch. You cannot be depressed for long because in this world nothing is permanent. This world is a flux. This world cannot change its basic law for you so that you remain depressed forever. Nothing is here forever; everything is moving and changing. Existence is a river; it cannot stop for you, just for you, so that you remain depressed forever. It is moving, it has already moved. If you look at your depression, you will feel that even your depression is not the same the next moment; it is different, it is changing. Just watch, remain with it and don't do anything. This is how transformation happens through nondoing. This is what is meant by "effortless effort."

Feel depression, taste it deeply, live it. It is your fate. Then suddenly you will feel it has disappeared because the man who can accept even depression cannot be depressed. A man, a mind, who can accept even depression cannot remain depressed! Depression needs a nonaccepting mind. "This is not good, that is not good; this should not be, that should not be; this must not be like this." Everything is denied, rejected—not accepted. No is basic. Even happiness will be rejected by such a mind. Such a mind will find something to reject in happiness also.

One man came to me just the other day and he said, "Meditation is going deep and I am feeling very happy, but I am suspicious. This happiness must be illusory because I have never felt any happiness before. I must be in a delusion; so much doubt has come to me. Now, please clarify my doubt." Even if happiness happens to a mind who has been always rejecting, he will feel a doubt about it. He will feel that something has gone wrong. He is happy, so he will feel something has gone wrong. Just by meditating for a few days this is not possible.

A nonaccepting mind will nonaccept anything, but if you can accept your loneliness, your depres-sion, your sadness, you are transcending already. Acceptance is transcendence. You have taken the very ground away, and then the depression cannot stand there.

Try this: whatsoever your state of mind, accept it and wait for when the state changes itself. You are not changing it; you can feel the beauty that comes when states change by themselves. You can know that it is just like the sun rising in the morning and then setting in the evening. Then again it will rise and again it will set, and it will go on. You need not do anything about it. If you can feel your states of mind changing by themselves, you can remain indifferent, you can remain away, miles away, as if the mind is going somewhere else. The sun is rising, setting; the depression is coming, the happiness is coming, going—but you are not in it. It goes and comes by itself; the states come and move.

If one begins to feel that life is a psychodrama, then one also feels depressed and lonely. So feel it! *Thus, the intensity, sincerity, the depth of living is lost.* Let it be lost, because the sincerity and depth that can be lost was not real. It was pseudo, false, and it is better that the false thing is lost. How can a real depth be lost? The very definition of a "real depth" is that it cannot be lost, no matter what you do. If you can disturb a buddha, then he is not a buddha. Whatsoever you do, he remains undisturbed. That unconditional undisturbance is the buddha-nature. The real cannot be lost. The real is always unconditional.

If I love you and I say, "Don't be angry, otherwise my love will be lost," then the sooner such a love is lost, the better. If the love is real, whatsoever you do makes no difference; the love will remain. And only then does it have any worth.

So if just by looking at the world as a psychodrama, as a drama, your intensity, your depth of living is lost, then it is not worth preserving. It was false. Why is it lost? Because it was really an act in a drama, and you were thinking that it was real so you felt it was deeper. Now you know it was just a drama. If it was just a drama and the sincerity is lost, the sincerity was false. You were thinking it was real, and it was not real. Just by looking at life as a drama, it disappeared.

It is just as if a rope was there lying in a dark room and you felt that it was a snake, but there was no snake. Now you come with a lamp, and with the lamp the snake is lost and only the rope remains. If with the lamp the snake is lost, then it was never there.

If you look at life as a drama, that which is false will be lost and that which is real will, for the first time, appear in you. Wait! Let the false be lost, and wait! There will be a gap, an interval, before the false disappears and the real comes. There will be a gap. When false shadows will have disappeared completely and your eyes will not be filled by them, and your eyes will have become detached from the false shadows, you will be able to look at the real that was always there. But one has to wait.

Please suggest what to do in this situation. Nothing! Please don't do anything. You have created a mess because of too much of your doing. You are such a good doer, you have confused everything around you—not only for yourself, but for others also. Be a nondoer; that will be compassion towards yourself. Be compassionate. Don't do anything, because with a false mind, a confused mind, everything becomes more confused. With a confused mind, it is better to wait and not to do anything so that the confusion disappears. It will disappear; nothing is permanent in this world. You need only a deep patience. Don't be in a hurry.

I will tell you one story. Buddha was traveling through a forest. The day was hot—it was just midday—he felt thirsty, so he said to his disciple Ananda, "Go back. We crossed a little stream. You go back and bring, fetch, some water for me."

Ananda went back, but the stream was very small and some carts were passing through it. The water was disturbed and had become dirty. All the dirt that had settled in it had come up, and the water was not drinkable now. So Ananda thought,

"I shall have to go back." He came back and he said to Buddha, "That water has become absolutely dirty and it is not drinkable. Allow me to go ahead. I know there is a river just a few miles away from here. I will go and fetch water from there."

Buddha said, "No! You go back to the same stream." As Buddha had said this Ananda had to follow it, but he followed it with half a heart as he knew that the water could not be brought. And time was being unnecessarily wasted and he was feeling thirsty, but when Buddha said it he had to go.

Again he came back and he said, "Why did you insist? That water is not drinkable."

Buddha said, "You go again." And as Buddha said it, Ananda had to follow.

The third time he reached the stream, the water was as clear as it had ever been. The dust had flowed away, the dead leaves had gone, and the water was pure again. Then Ananda laughed. He brought the water and he came dancing. He fell at Buddha's feet and he said, "Your ways of teaching are miraculous. You have taught me a great lesson—that just patience is needed and nothing is permanent."

And this is Buddha's basic teaching: nothing is permanent, everything is fleeting—so why be so worried? Go back to the same stream. By now everything should have changed. Nothing remains the same. Just be patient: go again and again and again. Just a few moments, and the leaves will have gone and the dirt will have settled again and the water will be pure again.

Ananda also asked Buddha, when he was going back for the second time, "You insist that I go, but can I do something to make that water pure?"

Buddha said, "Please don't do anything; otherwise you will make it more impure. And don't enter the stream. Just be outside, wait on the bank. Your entering the stream will create a mess. The stream flows by itself, so allow it to flow."

Nothing is permanent; life is flux. Heraclitus has said that you cannot step twice in the same river. It is impossible to step twice in the same river because the river has flowed on; everything has changed. And not only has the river flowed on, you have also flowed on. You are also different; you are also a river flowing.

See this impermanency of everything. Don't be in a hurry; don't try to do anything. Just wait! Wait in a total nondoing. And if you can wait, the transformation will be there. This very waiting is a transformation.

The third question:

The practice of witnessing makes me quiet, still, and silent, but then the friends around me say that I have become serious. There seems to be some substance in what they say. Please explain how one can grow simultaneously in stillness and playfulness.

If you have really become silent, you will not pay attention to what others are saying. If others' opinions are still important, you are not silent. Really, you are waiting for them to say something or for them to approve and appreciate that you have become silent. Your silence needs their approval? You need them to certify it? Then you are not confident that you have become silent.

Others' opinions are meaningful only because you don't know anything. Opinion is never knowledge. You go on gathering others' opinions because you don't know what you are, who you are, what is happening to you. You have to ask others, "What is happening to me?" You have to ask others? If you are really silent, quiet, still, then there are no friends and no opinion is meaningful. Then you can laugh. Let them say whatsoever they say.

But you become affected. Whatsoever they say goes deep in you; you become disturbed. Your silence is false, forced, cultivated. It is not a spontaneous flowering within you. You may have forced yourself to be silent, but you were boiling within. Then the silence is just on the surface. If someone says you are not silent, or if someone says this is not good, or if someone says this is false, then you are disturbed and the silence is gone. The silence is gone, that is why you are asking me this. *There*

seems to be some substance in what they say. You have become serious. So what is wrong in being serious? If you are born serious, to be serious, you will be serious. You cannot force playfulness; otherwise your playfulness will be serious, and you will destroy the whole play. There are serious players. They get so serious in their games and plays that it becomes even more anxiety-creating.

I was reading the memoirs of someone who was a great industrialist, much worried with day-to-day problems. Someone suggested golf: "Play golf. That will be anxiety-reducing." He started playing golf, but he was the same man. He became so excited about his golf that he couldn't sleep, he was playing the whole night. The industry was a burden, and now golf became a second burden—and a stronger one. He played golf, but with a serious mind, the same mind.

If you are serious, you are serious. Nothing can be done about it. Be serious and remain serious. Then you have already started being playful; then you are playful about your seriousness, not serious about it. You take it as a play, so you say, "Okay, God has given me this role, so I will be a serious man and I will play my seriousness." Then it will have disappeared deep down. Do you understand me?

You can create seriousness out of your playfulness or you can create playfulness out of your seriousness. If you are a sad one, a serious one, tell everyone, "I am born serious and I am going to remain so"—and don't get serious about it. Be! Simply be, and then you can laugh about it and it will disappear. And you will not even become aware of when it has disappeared.

And don't pay attention to what others say. This is a disease. They will drive you crazy—the others. Who are these others and why are you so much interested in them? They drive you crazy and you drive them crazy because you are the other to them. Why pay so much importance to others' opinions? Pay attention to your own experiences and remain true to your own experiences. If you feel good in being serious, it is okay! If you feel you have become quiet and silent and still through your practice of witnessing, why be interested and why be disturbed by what others say?

But we are not confident, so we must gather others' opinions. We must go on a signature campaign: "You think I have become a buddha, so please sign." When everyone signs it and you have gathered many signatures, at least the majority, you think you are a buddha. This is not the way to be an enlightened one.

And *please explain how one can grow simultaneously in stillness and playfulness.* One grows! There has never been any case that is otherwise. One grows simultaneously in stillness and playfulness, but if your stillness is false then the problem arises. All those who have known silence have always been playful, nonserious. They could laugh, and they could laugh not only at others, they could laugh at themselves.

Bodhidharma entered China fourteen hundred years ago, from India. He put one of his shoes on his head; one was on one of his feet and one was on his head. The Emperor of China, Wu, had come to welcome him. He became disturbed. There were many, many rumors, of course, that this man was strange, but he was an enlightened one and the emperor wanted to welcome him to his kingdom. He became disturbed. His courtiers, they also became disturbed. What type of man was this? And he was laughing.

It was not good to say anything before others, so when everyone had gone and Bodhidharma and the emperor retired into Bodhidharma's room, the emperor asked, "Please tell me, why are you making such a fool of yourself? Why are you carrying one shoe on your head?"

Bodhidharma laughed and said, "Because I can laugh at myself, and it is good to show you my reality. I am such a man, and I don't pay more importance to my head than I pay to my feet; both are the same to me. Higher and lower have disappeared. And, moreover, I want to tell you that I don't pay any significance to what others say about me. This is good. The first moment that I entered, I wanted you to know what type of man I am."

This Bodhidharma was a rare jewel; very few have existed who can be compared to him. What was he showing? He is simply showing that on this path of spirituality you are to go alone, as an individual. Society becomes irrelevant.

Someone had come to do an interview with George Gurdjieff. The man who came was a big journalist. Gurdjieff's disciples were very much excited because now the story was going to be in a big newspaper, and their master's photo and their master's news were going to be published. They cared very much; they payed much attention to the journalist. They virtually forgot their master, and they hung around the journalist. Then the interview began, but really, it never began. When the journalist asked some questions to Gurdjieff, Gurdjieff said, "Wait a minute."

Just by his side was sitting a lady. Gurdjieff asked, "What day is today?"

The lady said, "Sunday."

Gurdjieff said, "How is that possible? Just the day before it was Saturday, so how can it be Sunday today? Just the other day you said it is Saturday, and now it is Sunday. How, after Saturday, can Sunday come?"

The journalist stood up. He said, "I am going. This man seems to be mad." All the disciples just couldn't understand what had happened. When the journalist had left, Gurdjieff was laughing.

What others say is not relevant. Be authentic to what you feel, but be authentic! If real silence happens to you, you will be able to laugh.

It is said about Dogen, one Zen master, that when he attained enlightenment many people asked, "What did you do after that?"

He said, "I ordered a cup of tea." What is there to do next? Everything is finished. And Dogen was serious about his playfulness, playful about his seriousness. Really, what remains?

Don't pay much attention to what others say

and remember only one thing: don't force and cultivate stillness. A cultivated stillness will be serious, ill, tense. But how can a real silence come to you? Try to understand this. You are tense, you are unhappy, you are depressed, angry, greedy, violent. A thousand diseases are there. Still, you can practice silence. These diseases will be within you, and you can create a layer of silence. You can do transcendental meditation; you can use a mantra. The mantra is not going to change your violence, neither is it going to change your greed. It is not going to change anything deep. The mantra can just give a tranquilizing effect. Just on the periphery, you will feel more silent. This is just a tranquilizer, a sound tranquilizer, and tranquilizing is possible through many ways—many ways. When you repeat a mantra continuously, you become sleepy. Any continuous repetition of a sound creates boredom and sleep. You feel relaxed, but this relaxation is just on the surface. Within, you remain the same.

Go on practicing a mantra every day, and you will feel a certain stillness—but not really, because your diseases have not changed, your personality structure remains the same. It is just whitewashed. Stop the mantra, stop the practice, and all your diseases will come up again.

This is happening everywhere. Seekers move from one teacher to another. They go on moving, practicing, and when they stop their practice they find they are the same; nothing has happened. Nothing will happen in this way. These are cultivated silences. You have to go on cultivating them. Of course, if you go on cultivating them, they remain with you just like a habit, but if you break the habit they disappear. A real silence comes not by just using some superficial technique, but by being aware of all that you are—not only being aware, but remaining with the fact of what you are.

Remain with the fact. This is very difficult because the mind wants change. How to change violence, how to change depression, how to change unhappiness? The mind seeks change to create somehow a better image in the future. Because of this, one goes on seeking this and that method.

Remain with the fact, and don't try to change it. Do this for one year. Fix a date, and say that "From this date, for one year, I will not think in terms of change. I will remain with whatsoever I am; I will just be alert and aware." I am not saying that you are not to do anything, but that alertness is the only effort. You have to be alert, not thinking in terms of change; remaining whatsoever you are—good, bad or whatsoever. One year, with no attitude of change, just being alert, suddenly one day you will find you are no more the same. Alertness will have changed everything.

In Zen, they call it zazen—just sitting and doing nothing. Whatsoever happens, happens; you are just sitting. Zazen means just sitting, doing nothing. In Zen monasteries, monks will sit for years, the whole day. You will think they are meditating. They are not! They are just sitting silently. And by silence it is not that they are using some mantra to create any silence; they are simply sitting. If a leg goes dead, they feel it. They are alert. If the body feels tired, they are alert: the body feels tired. This is how the body has to feel. If thoughts are moving, they know it. They are not trying to stop them; they are not trying to push them away. They are not doing anything. Thoughts are just there like clouds in the sky, but they know the clouds cannot destroy the sky, they come and go.

So thoughts are moving in the sky of consciousness; they come and go. They don't force them, they don't stop them, they don't do anything. They are just alert that the thoughts are moving. Sometimes depression comes, a cloud; everything becomes shadowy. Sometimes happiness comes, a sunshine; everything starts dancing, as if flowers have opened all over the consciousness. But they are not disturbed by either this or that, by cloudy weather or by sunshine. They just wait and see that things are moving. They are just sitting on the bank of a river, and everything goes on moving. They don't try to change anything.

If a bad thought comes, they don't say, "This is

bad," because the moment you say, "This is bad," you have a greed to change it. The moment you say, "This is bad," you have pushed it away; you have condemned it, and you would like to change it into something good. They simply say this is this, that is that—no condemnation, no evaluation, no justification. Simply watching, witnessing.

Sometimes they forget witnessing. Then too they are not disturbed. They know that "Of course it is so," that "I forgot to witness; now I remember and I will witness again." They don't create any problem. They live what is. Years come and go, and they go on sitting and seeing what is.

Then one day everything disappears. Just like a dream, everything disappears and you are awakened. This awakening is not a practiced thing; this awakening is not cultivated. This awakening is your nature, your basic nature. It has erupted because you could wait patiently and watch, and you didn't create any problems. Remember this as a very basic thing: don't create problems. Don't create problems!

One lady was here just two or three days ago. She said, "My mind is sexual, so what can I do?" Someone else came and said, "I feel very inferior; an inferiority complex is there. What can I do?" So I told that man, "You feel inferior, so feel inferior; know that you feel like that. What to do? There is nothing to do. One feels sexual, so feel sexual. Know that you are sexual." But the moment I say such things to someone, he feels shocked. He had come for a technique to change himself.

No one accepts himself; you are such enemies to yourself. You have never had any love for yourself; you have never been at ease with yourself. And this is surprising: you expect everyone to love you, and you yourself cannot even love yourself. You are so against yourself, you would like to shatter yourself in every way and create another. If you were allowed you would create another man. And you would not be satisfied with that either because you would still remain behind it.

Love yourself, accept yourself, and don't create unnecessary problems. And all problems are unnecessary; there are no necessary problems. I have not come across any. Remain with your facticity, and transformation will happen. But it is not a result, you cannot force it to happen. It is a consequence, not a result. If you accept yourself and remain alert, it comes. You cannot force it, you cannot say that "I will force it to come." And if you force, a false thing will happen to you, and then that false thing can be disturbed by anyone—*by anyone.*

The last question:

You said that acceptance transforms, but why is it that when I accept my senses and desires I feel that I have become animallike instead of transformed?

This is your transformation; this is your reality. And what is wrong in being an animal? I have not seen a single man who can be compared to any animal.

Suzuki used to say, "I love a frog, even a frog, more than a man. Look at a frog sitting near a pond: how meditatively a frog sits! Look at him, how meditative he is—not disturbed by the whole world going on, just sitting and sitting and meditating, one with existence."

Suzuki said, "When I was unenlightened I was a man, and when I became enlightened I became just like a cat."

Look at a cat: she knows the secret of how to relax and she has not read any books about relaxation. How to relax? Look at a cat. No man can be a better teacher than a cat. The cat is relaxed and alert. If you relax, you go to sleep. The cat is alert even in her sleep, and the body is so flexible, so relaxed in every moment.

What is wrong in being an animal? Man, through his ego, has created comparisons. He says, "We are not animals."

But no animal would like to be a human being. They are at ease, at home in existence. They are not worried, they are not tense. Of course, they don't create any religion because they don't need to. They don't have any psychoanalysts—not because they are undeveloped, but because they don't need any.

What is wrong with animals? Why this condemnation? This condemnation is part of the human ego. Man thinks in terms of being the superior one, the highest in the hierarchy. No animal has consented to this hierarchy. Darwin said that man has evolved out of monkeys, but if you ask monkeys I am afraid they will not say that man is an evolution; they will say he is a degradation. Man thinks himself as the center. There is no need for this. This is only egoistic nonsense.

If you feel like being an animal, nothing is wrong in it. Be one, and be one totally—and be one with full alertness. That alertness will first uncover your animal because that is your reality. Your humanity is just false, skin-deep. Someone insults you, and the animal comes out—not the human being. Someone condemns you, and the animal comes out—not the human being. It is

there, and your humanity is just skin-deep. If you accept everything, this skin-deep humanity will disappear. This is a false thing, and you can become aware of your real animal. And it is good to become aware of reality. If you go on being alert, within this animal you will find the divine. And it is always better to be a real animal than to be an unreal man. Reality is the point.

So I am not against animals, I am only against falsities. Don't be a false human being. Be a real animal, and with that reality you will have become authentic, substantial. Now go on being alert, and by and by you will come to a deeper layer which is more real than the animal—and that is the divine.

The divine is not only in you, remember; it is in all animals. It is not only that it is in animals—it is in all the trees, it is in the rocks. The divine is the basic center in everything. You can lose it only by being false, and you can gain it again by being real.

CHAPTER 39

From the wave to the cosmic ocean

◆

61 *As waves come with water and flames with fire, so the Universal waves with us.*

62 *Wherever your mind is wandering, internally or externally, at this very place, this.*

63 *When vividly aware through some particular sense, keep in the awareness.*

Sri Aurobindo says somewhere that the whole life is yoga—and it is so. Everything can become a meditation. And unless everything becomes a meditation, meditation has not happened to you. Meditation cannot be a part, a fragment. Either it is—and when it is you are wholly in it—or it is not. You cannot make a part of your life meditative. That is impossible, and that is what is being tried everywhere.

You can become meditative, not a part of you; that is impossible because meditation is a quality of your being. It is just like breathing: you go on breathing whatsoever you are doing. Irrelevant of what you are doing, you go on breathing. Walking, sitting, lying, sleeping, you continue breathing. You cannot arrange it in such a way that sometimes you breathe and sometimes you don't breathe. It is a continuum.

Meditation is an inner breathing, and when I say an inner breathing, I mean it literally; it is not a metaphor. Just as you are breathing air you can breathe consciousness, and once you start breathing consciousness in and out you are no more just a physical body. And with that start, beginning with a higher breathing—a breathing of consciousness, of life itself, as it were—you enter a different realm, a different dimension. That dimension is metaphysics.

Your breathing is physical; meditation is metaphysical. So you cannot make a part of your life meditative. You cannot meditate in the morning and then forget it. You cannot go to a temple or to a church and meditate there and come out of your meditation as you come out of the temple. That is not possible, and if you try it you will be trying a false thing. You can enter a church and you come out of it, but you cannot enter meditation and come out of it. When you enter, you have entered. Wherever you go now meditation will be you. This is one of the basic, primary, elemental facts to be remembered always.

Secondly, you can enter meditation from anywhere because the whole life is in a deep meditation. The hills are meditating, the stars are meditating, the flowers, the trees, the elements are meditating, the very earth is meditating. The whole life is meditating, and you can enter it from anywhere; anything can become an entrance. This has been used. That is why there are so many techniques; that is why there are so many religions; that is why one religion cannot understand another—because their entrances are different. And sometimes there are religions which are not known even by the name of religion. You will not recognize certain persons as religious because their entrance is so different.

For example, a poet. A poet can enter meditation without going to any teacher, without going to any temple, without in any way being religious, so-called religious. His poetry, his creativity, can become an entrance; he can enter through it. Or a potter who is just creating earthen pots can enter meditation just by creating earthen pots. The very craft can become an entry. Or an archer can become meditative through his archery, or a gardener, or anyone can enter from anywhere. Whatsoever you can do can become a door. If the quality of awareness changes while you are doing something, it becomes a technique. So there can be as many techniques as you can imagine. Any act can become a door. So the act, the technique, the way, the method, is not primary, but the quality of consciousness that you bring to the act is the basic thing.

Kabir, one of India's greatest mystics, was a weaver, and he remained a weaver even when he attained. He had thousands and thousands of disciples, and they would come and they would tell him, "Now stop your weaving. You don't need it. We are here and we will serve you in every way."

Kabir would laugh and he would say, "This weaving is not just weaving. I am making clothes—that is the outer act—but something goes on within me simultaneously that you cannot see. This is my meditation." How can a weaver be a meditator through weaving? If the quality of the mind that you bring to weaving is meditative, then the act is not relevant, it is irrelevant.

Another mystic was a potter; his name was Gora. He worked on earthen pots, and he would dance and he would sing while he was making his pots. While he was making a pot on the wheel, as the pot would center on the wheel he would also center within himself. One would see only one thing: the wheel was moving, the earthen pot was emerging and he was centering the earthen pot. You were seeing only one centering. Another centering was happening simultaneously: he was also being centered. While centering the pot, while helping the pot to emerge, he was also emerging in the unseen world of inner consciousness. When the pot was created, that was not the real thing he was working on; he was also creating himself.

Any act can become meditative, and once you know how an act becomes meditative you can transform all your acts into meditation. Then the whole life becomes yoga. Walking on the street or working in the office or just sitting and not doing anything—just idling, or anything—can become

meditation. So remember, meditation doesn't belong to the act; it belongs to the quality you bring to the act.

Now we will enter the techniques.

61 Experience existence as wave-ing.

First: *As waves come with water and flames with fire, so the Universal waves with us.*

First try to understand what a wave is, and then you can feel how this consciousness of waves can help you to enter into meditation. You see waves in the ocean. They appear; they are in a sense, and still in a deeper sense they are not. This is the first thing to be understood about a wave. The wave appears; it is there in a sense, but still it is not there in a deeper sense. In a deeper sense only the ocean is. You cannot have a wave without the ocean, and even while the wave is there, only the ocean is. The wave is just a form, not a substance. The ocean is substantial; the wave is just a form.

Because of language many problems are created. Because we say wave, it looks as if a wave is some thing. It would be better if we use not wave, but waving. There is no wave, just waving—just an activity, not a thing; just a movement, not a substance; just a process, not matter. The matter is the ocean; the wave is just a form. The ocean can be silent. The waves will disappear, but the ocean will be there.

The ocean can be silent or in movement or in much activity or in no activity, but you cannot find a silent wave. A wave is activity, not a substance. When the activity is there, the wave is there: it is a waving, a movement—a simple form of movement. But when the silence comes, when inactivity comes, the wave is no more and the ocean is there. In both the cases the ocean is the reality. The wave is just a play-form. The wave happens and disappears, the ocean remains.

Secondly, waves appear as individuals. Each

wave has its own personality—unique, different from any other. No two waves are similar. Some waves are big, some waves are small. They have their own peculiar characteristics. Each wave has its own character, and, of course, each wave is different from the other. One wave may rise, another may die. While one is rising, another is dying. Both cannot be the same because one is rising, another is dying. Still, the reality behind both is the same. They look different, they look separate, they look individual, but the look is fallacious. Deep down only one ocean is, and no matter how they look unrelated they are related. And while one wave is rising and another is dying, you may not see any relationship; the relationship may not appear, because how can a rising wave be related to a dying wave?

An old man is dying and a child is born: how are they related? If they are related, they will die both together or they will be born together. The child is born and the old man has died; one wave is dying, another is arising. But the rising wave may be gathering energy from the dying wave. The dying wave may be helping it, by its death, to rise. The dispersing wave may be the cause of the wave that is rising.

Deep down they are related to one ocean. They are not different; they are not unrelated, they are not separate. Their individuality is false and illusory. They are nonindividual. Their duality appears to be, but it is not so: their nonduality is the truth.

Now I will read the sutra again: *As waves come with water and flames with fire, so the Universal waves with us.* We are just waves in a cosmic ocean. Meditate on it, allow this feeling to go deep down within you. Start feeling your breathing as just the rising of a wave. You breathe in, you breathe out, and the breath that is entering you was someone else's breath just a moment before and the breath that is leaving you will become someone else's breath the next moment. Breathing is just waving in the ocean of life. You are not separate— just waves. You are one deep down. We have a

togetherness; individuality is false and illusory. Hence, the ego is the only barrier. Individuality is false. It appears to be, but it is not real. The real is the nonindividual, the oceanic, the togetherness.

That is why every religion is against the egoistic attitude. The person who says there is no God may not be irreligious, but the person who says "I am" is irreligious.

Gautam Buddha was an atheist; he didn't believe in any God. Mahavira Vardhaman was an atheist; he didn't believe in any God. But they achieved, they arrived, they realized the totality, the wholeness. If you don't believe in any God you may not be irreligious, because God is not basic to religion. Nonego is basic to religion. And even if you believe in God, with an egoist mind you are irreligious. With a nonegoistic mind there is no need to believe in a God. You fall into the divine automatically. With no ego you cannot cling to the wave; you have to fall into the ocean. With the ego, you go on clinging to the wave. Look at life as an ocean, and feel yourself just as a wave, and allow this feeling to enter in you.

You can use this technique in many ways. While breathing, feel that the ocean is breathing in you. The ocean comes to you, goes out, comes in, goes out. With every breath feel a wave rising, with every exhalation feel a wave dying. And between the two, who are you? Just a nothingness, *shunya* —a void. With that feeling of the void you will be transformed. With that feeling of nothingness all your misery will disappear, because misery needs a center—and a false center at that. The void is your real center. With it there is no misery; you are in a deep ease. Because you are not, who can be tense? You are bliss-filled. It is not that you are bliss-filled, but because you are not, only bliss is. Without you, can you create misery?

That is why Buddha never says that in that state, the ultimate state, there will be *ananda*— bliss. He never says it. He says that there will be no misery, that is all. To talk about bliss may mislead you, so Buddha says don't ask about bliss; simply try to know how you can be without misery. And that means how you can be without yourself.

What is our problem? The problem is that the wave thinks itself separate from the ocean; then there are problems. If a wave thinks itself separate from the ocean, the fear of death will immediately come. The wave has to die and the wave can see all around dying waves. And you cannot deceive yourself for long. The wave is seeing that other waves are dying, and the wave knows that even in its rising, death is hidden somewhere, because those other waves a moment before were rising and now they are falling down, dispersing.

So you are to die. If the wave thinks itself separate from the ocean the fear of death is bound to appear sooner or later. But if the wave knows that it is not and only the ocean is, there is no fear of death. Only a wave can die, not the ocean. I can die, but not life. You can die, you will die—but not the cosmos, not the existence. The existence goes on waving. It has waved in you, it will wave in others. And while your wave may be disappearing, just by your dispersal other waves will arise and the ocean continues.

Once you detach yourself from the wave form, and you become one and feel one and realize oneness with the ocean, the formless, there is no death for you. Otherwise the fear of death will create misery. In every pain, in every anguish, in every anxiety, the basic fear is of death. You are afraid, trembling. You may not be conscious of it, but if you penetrate within you will find that every moment there is a trembling because you are going to die.

You may create many securities, you may create a citadel around you, but nothing is going to help. Nothing is going to help! Dust unto dust! You are going to fall back down. Have you ever observed or have you ever meditated on the fact that when you are just walking on the road dust clings to your shoe? The dust may have been the body of a Napoleon, of an Alexander. Somewhere, Alexander is just dust now, and the dust clinging to your shoe

may have once been the body of Alexander.

The same is going to be the case with you. Now you are here, and the next moment you will not be; the same is going to be the case with you! Sooner or later the dust will go unto dust, the wave will disappear. Fear grips. Just imagine yourself as dust clinging to somebody's shoe or imagine some potter making an earthen pot of you, of your body, or of your beloved's body, or imagine yourself moving into a worm or becoming a tree. But this is happening. Everything is a form and form has to die. Only the formless is eternal. If you cling to the form, if you identify yourself with the form, if you feel yourself as a wave form, you are getting into trouble by yourself. You are the ocean, not the wave.

This meditation can help; it can bring a metamorphosis for you, it can become a mutation. But allow it to spread all through your life. While breathing, think; while eating, think; while walking, think. Think two things—that the form is always the wave and the formless is always the ocean. The formless is deathless; the form is mortal. And it is not that you will die someday, you are dying every day. Childhood dies and youth-hood is born; then youth-hood dies and the old age is born; then the old age dies and the form disappears.

Every moment you are dying into something else; something else is born. Your first day of birth is not the first day of your only birth; that is simply part of many more births to come. And your death of this life is not the first death; it is only the death of this life. You have been dying before. Every moment something is dying and something else is born. A part of you dies; another part is born.

Physiologists say that within seven years nothing old remains in your body; everything changes —every cell. If you are going to live for seventy years, ten times over your body is renewed again and again. Every seven years you have a new body. Not suddenly, but every moment something is changing.

You are a wave, and that too not substantial; every moment you are changing. And a wave cannot be static; a wave has to be changing, a wave has to be constantly in movement. There can be no phenomenon like a nonmoving wave. How can there be? A nonmoving wave makes no sense. There is movement, process; you are a process, a movement. If you become identified with this movement and process and think yourself confined between birth and death, you will be in misery. Then you are taking appearance as reality. This is what Shankara calls *maya*—illusion. The ocean is the *Brahma*, the ocean is the truth.

So think yourself as a wave, or as a continuum of waves rising and falling, and just be a witness to this. You cannot do anything. These waves will disappear. That which has appeared will have to disappear; nothing can be done about it. Every effort is absolutely useless. Only one thing can be done, and that is to be a witness of this wave form. Once you become a witness, suddenly you will become aware of something which is beyond the wave, which transcends the wave, which is in the wave also and out of the wave also, which forms the wave and still goes beyond, which is the ocean.

As waves come with water and flames with fire, so the Universal waves with us. The universal waves with us. You are not, the universal is—and he is waving through you. Feel it, contemplate over it, meditate on it. Allow it to happen to you in many, many ways.

I told you about breathing. A sex desire arises in you: feel it—not as your desire, but just as the ocean waving in you, just as life pulsating, just as life having a wave in you. You meet in a love act: don't think of it as two waves meeting, don't think of it as two individuals meeting. Rather, think of it as two individuals merging. There are no more two individuals. Waves have disappeared; only the ocean has remained. Then the sex act becomes a meditation. Whatsoever happens to you, feel it not as if it is happening to you, but as if it is happening to the cosmos. You are just a part of it—just a wave on the surface. Leave everything to the universe.

Dogen, a Zen master, used to say, when he felt hungry he would say, "It seems the universal feels hungry through me." When he would feel thirsty he would say, "The existence is thirsty within me." This is what this meditation will lead you to. Then everything disperses from your ego and becomes part of the universe. Then whatsoever happens, happens to existence itself; you are no more here. Then there is no sin, then there is no responsibility.

I don't mean that you will become irresponsible; I don't mean that you will become a sinner. Sin will be impossible because sin can happen only around an ego. There will be no responsibility because sin can happen only around an ego. There will be no responsibility because now you cannot be irresponsible. Only you are, so to whom can you be responsible? And now if you see someone dying, you will feel you are dying with him, within him. The universe is dying and you are part of it. And if you will see some flower flowering, you will flower with it. The whole universe will become you now. To be in such a deep affinity and harmony is to be in *samadhi*.

Meditation is the way, and this harmony of oneness, this feeling of oneness with all, is the end, is the goal. Try it! Remember the ocean and forget the wave. And whenever you remember the wave and start behaving as the wave, remember, you are doing something wrong and you will create misery because of it.

There is no God who is punishing you. Whenever you fall a prey to some illusion, you punish yourself. The law, *dharma*, the Tao is there. If you move in harmony with it, you feel blissful. If you move against it, you feel yourself to be in misery. There is no one sitting there in the skies to punish you. There is no record of your sins; there is no need for this. It is just like gravity. If you walk rightly, the gravity is a help. You cannot walk without it. If you walk wrongly, you will fall down, you may get a fracture. But no one is punishing you; it is just the law, the gravity—the impersonal gravity.

If you walk wrongly and you fall down, you will

have a fracture. If you walk rightly, you use gravity. The energy can be used wrongly or rightly. When you feel yourself as a wave, you are against the universal law, you are against the reality. Then you will create misery for yourself. This is what the law of *karma* means. There is no law-giver; God is not a judge. To be a judge is ugly, and if God were a judge, he would be completely bored, or else he would have gone mad by now. He is not a judge, he is not a controller, he is not a law-giver. The universe has its own laws, and the basic law is that to be real is to be in bliss, to be unreal is to be in misery.

62 Use mind as the door to meditation.

The second technique: *Wherever your mind is wandering, internally or externally, at this very place, this.*

This mind is the door—this very mind. Wherever it is wandering, whatsoever it is thinking, contemplating, dreaming, this very mind, this very moment, is the door. This is a very revolutionary method because we never think that the ordinary mind is the door. We think that some supermind—a Buddha, a Jesus—can enter, that they have some superhuman mind. This very mind that you have—this mind which goes on dreaming and imagining relevant or irrelevant thoughts, which is crowded with ugly desires, passions, anger, greed, all that is condemned, which is there beyond your control, pulling you here and there, pushing you from here and there, constantly a madhouse—this very mind, says this sutra, is the door. *Wherever your mind is wandering*—wherever, remember; the object is not relevant—wherever your mind is wandering, *internally or externally, at this very place, this.*

Many things have to be understood. One, the ordinary mind is not so ordinary as we think. The ordinary mind is not unrelated to the universal mind: it is part of it. Its roots go down to the very center of existence; otherwise you cannot be. Even

a sinner is grounded into the divine; otherwise he cannot be. Even if the devil is there, he cannot be without divine support.

Existence itself is possible only because of the groundedness into the being. Your mind is dreaming, imagining, wandering, tense, in anguish, in misery. Howsoever it moves and wheresoever it moves, it remains grounded in the totality. Otherwise is not possible. You cannot go away from existence; that is impossible. This very moment you are grounded in it.

So what is to be done? If this very moment we are grounded in it, then it will appear to the egoist mind that nothing is to be done. We are already the divine, so why so much fuss? You are grounded in the divine, but you are unaware of the fact. When mind is wandering, there are two things—the mind and the wandering, the objects in the mind and the mind itself, clouds wandering in the sky and the sky. There are two things—the clouds and the sky.

Sometimes it may happen, it happens, that there are so many clouds that the sky disappears, you cannot see it. But even if you cannot see it, it has not disappeared; it cannot disappear. There is no way to help the sky to disappear. It is there; hidden or unhidden, visible or invisible, it is there.

But clouds are also there. If you pay attention to the clouds, the sky has disappeared. If you pay attention to the sky, the clouds are just accidental, they come and they go. You need not be too much worried about them. They come and they go. They have been coming, they have been going. They have not been destroying the sky even an inch, they have not made the sky dirty; they have not even touched it. The sky remains virgin.

When your mind is wandering, there are two things: one is the clouds, the thoughts, the objects, images, and the other is the consciousness, the mind itself. If you pay too much attention to the clouds, to objects, thoughts, images, you have forgotten the sky. You have forgotten the host; you have become too much interested in the guest. Those thoughts, images, wandering, are just guests.

If you focus yourself on the guests, you forget your own being. Change the focus from the guests to the host, from the clouds to the sky. Do it practically.

A sex desire arises: this is a cloud. Or a greed arises to have a bigger house: this is a cloud. You can become so obsessed with it that you forget completely to whom it has arisen, to whom it has happened. Who is behind it? In what sky is this cloud moving? Remember that sky, and suddenly the cloud disappears. You need just a change of focus from the object to the subject, from the outer to the inner, from the cloud to the sky, from the guest to the host—just a change of focus.

Lin Chi, one Zen master, was speaking. Someone said from the crowd, "Answer me only one question: Who am I?"

Lin Chi stopped speaking. Everyone was alert. What answer was he going to give? But he didn't answer. He came down from his chair, walked, came near to the man. The whole crowd became attentive, alert. They were not even breathing. What was he going to do? He should have answered from the chair; there was no need. The man became afraid, and Lin Chi came near him with his piercing eyes. He took the man's collar in his hand, gave him a shake and asked him, "Close your eyes! And remember who is asking this question, 'Who am I?'" The man closed his eyes—afraid, of course. He went within to seek who had asked this question, and he would not come back.

The crowd waited and waited and waited. His face became silent, calm, still. Then Lin Chi had to shock him again. "Now come out and tell everybody, 'Who am I?'"

The man started laughing and he said, "What a miraculous way of answering a thing! But if someone asks me this now, I am going to do the same. I cannot answer."

It was just a change of focus. You ask the question "Who am I?" and your mind is focused on the question and the answer is hidden just behind the question in the questioner. Change the focus; return to yourself.

This sutra says, *Wherever your mind is wandering, internally or externally, at this very place, this.* Move from the objects to the mind itself, and you are no more an ordinary mind. You are ordinary because of the objects. Suddenly you become a buddha yourself. You are already a buddha, you are just burdened with many clouds. And not only are you burdened; you are clinging to your clouds, you won't allow them to move. You think that clouds are your property. You think that the more you have, the better: you are richer. And your whole sky, your inner space, is just hidden. In a way, it has disappeared amidst the clouds and clouds have become your life. The life of the clouds is *sansara*—the world.

This can happen in a single moment even, this change of focus—and it always happens suddenly. I don't mean that you need not do anything and it will happen suddenly; you will have to do much. But it will never happen gradually. You will have to do and do and do, and one day, suddenly, a moment comes when you are at the right temperature to evaporate. Suddenly there is no water; it has evaporated. Suddenly you are not in the object. Your eyes are not focused to the clouds; suddenly they have turned inward to the inner space.

It never happens gradually that one part of your eyes has turned inward and one part is with the outward clouds—nor does it happen in percentages, that now you have become ten percent inner and ninety percent outer, now twenty percent inner and eighty percent outer—no! When it happens it happens a hundred percent, because you cannot divide your focusing. Either you see the objects or you see yourself—either the world or the Brahma. You can come back to the world, you can change your focus again; you are the master. Really, only now are you the master—when you can change your focus as you like.

I remember Marpa, one Tibetan mystic. When he realized—when he became a buddha, when he turned inward, when he came to encounter the inner space, the infinity—someone asked him,

"Marpa, how are you now?"

Marpa's answer is exceptional, unexpected. No buddha has answered that way. Marpa said, "As miserable as before."

The man was bewildered. He said, "As miserable as before?"

But Marpa laughed. He said, "Yes, but with a difference, and the difference is that now the misery is voluntary. Sometimes, just for a taste of the world, I move outwards, but now I am the master. Any moment I can go inwards. And it is good to move in the polarities. Then one remains alive. I can move!" Marpa said, "I can move now. Sometimes I move in the miseries, but now the miseries are not something which happen to me. I happen to them and I remain untouched." Of course, when you move voluntarily, you remain untouched.

Once you know how to change your focus inwards, you can come back to the world. Every buddha has come back to the world. Again he focuses, but now the inner man has a different quality. He knows that this is his focusing. These clouds are allowed to move. These clouds are not masters; they cannot dominate you. You allow them, and it is beautiful. Sometimes, when the sky is filled with clouds, it is beautiful; the movement of the clouds is beautiful. If the sky remains itself, the clouds can be allowed to move. The problem arises only when the sky forgets itself and only clouds are there. Then everything becomes ugly because the freedom is lost.

This sutra is beautiful. *Wherever your mind is wandering, internally or externally, at this very place, this.* This sutra has been used deeply in Zen tradition. Zen says your ordinary mind is the buddha-mind. Eating, you are a buddha; sleeping, you are a buddha; carrying water from the well, you are a buddha. You are! Carrying water from the well, eating your food, lying down on your bed, you are a buddha. Inconceivable! It looks puzzling, but it is the truth.

If when carrying water you simply carry the water, if you don't make any problem out of it and you simply carry water, if your mind is unclouded and the sky vacant, if you are just carrying water, then you are a buddha. Eating, just eat without doing anything else. When we are eating we are doing thousands and thousands of things. The mind may not be here at all. Your body may be eating just like a robot; your mind may be somewhere else.

One university student was here some days before. His examination is coming near, so he came to ask me, "I am very much confused and the problem is this: I have fallen in love with a girl. While I am with the girl, I think of my examination, and while I read I think only of my girl. So what to do? While reading, studying, I am not there, I am with my girl in my imagination. And with my girl, I am never with her; I am thinking about my problems, about my examination which is drawing near. So everything has become a mess."

This is how everyone has become a mess, not only that boy. While in the office you think of the house; while in the house you are in the office. And you cannot do such a magical thing. While in the house you can be only in the house, you cannot be in the office. And if you are in the office, you are not sane, you are insane. Then everything gets into everything else. Then nothing is clear. And this mind is a problem.

While drawing water from a well, carrying water from a well, if you are simply doing this simple act, you are a buddha. So many times, if you go to Zen masters and ask them, "What do *you* do? What is your *sadhana*? What is your meditation?" they will say, "While feeling sleepy, we sleep. While feeling hungry, we eat. And that is all, there is no other sadhana." But this is very arduous. It looks simple: if while eating you can just eat, if while sitting you can just sit, not doing anything else; if you can remain with the moment and not move away from it, if you can be merged with the moment with no future, no past, if this moment now is the only existence—then you are a buddha, this very mind becomes a buddha-mind.

When your mind wanders, don't try to stop it. Rather, become aware of the sky. When mind wanders, don't try to stop it, don't try to bring it to some point, to some concentration—no! Allow it to wander, but don't pay much attention to the wandering—because for or against, you remain concerned with the wandering.

Remember the sky, allow the wandering, and just say, "Okay, it is just a traffic on the road. Many people are moving this way and that. The same traffic is going on in the mind. I am just the sky, not the cloud." Feel it, remember it, and remain in it. Sooner or later you will feel that the clouds are slowing down and there are bigger gaps between the clouds. They are not so dark, not so dense. The speed has slowed down, and intervals can be seen, and the sky can be looked at. Go on feeling yourself as the sky and not the clouds. Sooner or later, someday, in some right moment when your focus has really gone inwards, clouds will have disappeared and you are the sky, the ever-pure sky, the ever-virgin sky.

Once you know this virginity, you can come back to the clouds, to the world of the clouds. Then that world has its own beauty. You can move in it, but now you are a master. The world is not bad; the world as the master is the problem. With you as the master, you can move in it. Then the world has a beauty of its own. It is beautiful, it is lovely, but you need to know that beauty and that loveliness as a master within.

---

63 Be aware who is sensing.

The third technique: *When vividly aware through some particular sense, keep in the awareness.*

You see through your eyes. Remember, you see *through* your eyes. Eyes cannot see; you see through them. The seer is hidden behind, the eyes are just the opening, just the windows. But we go on thinking that we see by the eyes; we go on thinking we hear by the ears. No one has ever heard by the ears. You hear *through* the ears, not *by* the ears. The hearer is hidden behind. The ears are just receptive organs.

I touch you, I give you a loving touch, a hand-clasp. The hand is not touching you, I am touching you, through the hand. The hand is just instrumental, so there can be two types of touch—when I really touch you and when I just avoid touch. I can touch your hand and avoid touch. I may not be there in my hand, I may have withdrawn. Try this, and you will have a different, a distant feeling. Put your hand on someone and withdraw yourself. A dead hand is there, not you. And if the other is sensitive, he will feel a dead hand. He will feel insulted. You are deceiving; you are just showing that you are touching, and you are not touching.

Women are very sensitive about it; you cannot deceive them. They have a greater sensitivity of touch, of body touch, so they know. The husband may be talking beautiful things. He may have brought flowers and he may be saying, "I love you," but his touch will show that he is not there. And women have an instinctive feeling when you are with them and when you are not with them. It is difficult to deceive them unless you are a master. Unless you are a master of your own self, you cannot deceive them. But a master would not like to become a husband, that is the difficulty.

Whatsoever you say will be false; your touch will show it. Children are very sensitive, you cannot deceive them. You may pat them, but they know that this is a dead pat. If your hand is not a flowing energy, a loving energy, they know. Then it is just as if a dead thing is being used. When you are present in your hand in your totality, when *you* have moved, when your center of being has come to the hand, when your soul is there, then the touch has a different quality.

This sutra says that the senses are just doors, receiving stations, mediums, instruments, receptors. You are hidden behind. *When vividly aware through some particular sense, keep in the awareness.* While hearing music, don't forget yourself in the ear, don't lose yourself into the ear. Remember the awareness that is hidden behind. Be alert! While seeing someone... Try this. You can try it right now, looking at me. What is happening? You can look at me by the eyes, and when I say by the eyes, it means you are not aware that you are hidden behind the eyes. You can look at me through the eyes, and when I say through the eyes, then the eyes are just in between you and me. You are standing there behind the eyes, looking through the eyes, just as if someone looks through a window or specs.

Have you seen some clerk in a bank looking from above his specs? The specs have slipped down on his nose, and he looks. Just look that way at me, towards me, as if you are looking from above your eyes, as if the eyes have slipped down a little on your nose and you are standing behind looking at me. Suddenly you will feel a change in the quality. Your focus changes; eyes become just doors. This becomes a meditation.

When hearing, just hear through the ears and remain aware of your inner center. When touching, just touch through the hand and remember the inner one who is hidden behind. From any sense you can have a feeling of the inner center, and every sense goes to the inner center. It has to report. That is why, when you are seeing me and you are hearing me, when you see me through the eyes and you hear me through the ears, deep down you know that you are seeing the same man whom you are also hearing. If I have some body odor your nose will smell it.

Then three different senses report to one center. That is why you can coordinate. Otherwise it will be difficult: if your eyes see and your ears hear, it will be difficult to know whether you are hearing the same man whom you are seeing or two different ones, because these two senses are different and they never meet. Your eyes have never known about your ears and your ears have not heard about your eyes. They don't know each other,

they have never met; they have not even been introduced.

So how does everything become synthesized? Ears hear, eyes see, hands touch, the nose smells, and suddenly somewhere inside you know that this is the same man that you are hearing and seeing and touching and smelling. This knower is different from the senses. Every sense reports to this knower, and in this knower, in the center, everything falls, fits and becomes one. This is miraculous.

I am one, outside you. I am one! My body and body's presence, my body odor, my speaking, are one. Your senses will divide me. Your ears will report if I say something, your nose will report if there is some odor, your eyes will report if I can be seen and am visible. They will divide me into parts. But again, somewhere within you, I will become one. Where I become one within you is your center of being. That is your awareness, and you have forgotten it completely. This forgetfulness is the ignorance, and the awareness will open the doors for self-knowledge. And you cannot know yourself in any other way.

When vividly aware through some particular sense, keep in the awareness. Remain with the awareness; keep in the awareness; remain alert. It is difficult in the beginning. We go on falling asleep, and it seems arduous to look through the eyes. It is easy to look by the eyes. In the beginning you will feel a certain strain—if you try to look through the eyes. Not only will you feel a strain; the person you look at will also feel a strain.

If you look at someone through the eyes, he will feel as if you are trespassing upon him, as if you are doing something unmannerly. If you look through the eyes, the other will become aware suddenly that you are not behaving properly, because your look will become piercing, your look will go deeper. If it comes from your depth, it will penetrate to the other's depth. That is why society has a built-in security: don't look too deeply into anyone unless you are in love. If you are in love, you can look deeply into the other; you can penetrate to the very depth because the other is not afraid. The other can be naked, totally naked, the other can be vulnerable, the other can be open to you. But ordinarily, if you are not in love, you are not allowed to see directly, to see penetratingly.

In India, a person who looks in such a way, penetratingly at someone, is called a *luchcha*. A luchcha means a seer. The word 'luchcha' comes from *lochan*; lochan means eyes, and luchcha means one who has become eyes towards you. So don't try it on someone you don't know; he will think you are a luchcha.

First try with objects—a flower, a tree, the stars in the night. They will not feel trespassed upon and they will not object. Rather, they will like it and will feel very good and appreciated. First try with them, then with loving persons—your wife, your child. Sometimes take your child into your lap and look at him through the eyes, and the child will understand.

He will understand more than anyone else because he is still uncrippled by the society, still unperverted, still natural. He will feel deep love if you look through the eyes; he will feel your presence.

Look at your lover or beloved, and then only, by and by, as you get the feel of it and as you become more artful about it, you will be able to look at anyone—because then no one will be able to know that someone has looked so deeply. And once you have this art of standing always alert behind your senses, the senses cannot deceive you. Otherwise the senses deceive you.

In a world which is just an appearance, they have deceived you to feel it as real. If you can look through the senses and remain alert, the world will by and by appear to you as illusory, dreamlike, and you will be able to penetrate to the substance—to the very substance of it.

That substance is the Brahma.

CHAPTER 40

Sudden enlightenment and its obstacles

◆

If authentic experience is sudden, what is the gradual growth and clarity that we feel?

What happens to polar opposites when one is in the witnessing consciousness?

When is the buddha-mind revealed in the state of thoughtless awareness?

What are the reasons that one doesn't have an explosive catharsis while doing Your meditations?

The first question:

You said that either one sees the world or the *Brahma* and that no gradually increasing perception of the Brahma is possible. But in experience we feel that as we become aware and more silent and still, the feeling of the divine presence becomes gradually clearer and clearer. What is this gradual growth and clarity if the authentic experience is never gradual, but sudden?

his has been a very ancient problem: Is enlightenment sudden or gradual? Many things have to be understood. There has been a tradition which says that enlightenment is gradual and that everything can be divided into degrees, everything can be divided into steps—that like anything else, knowledge can also be divided; you can become more and more wise, you can become more and more enlightened. This has been widely accepted because the human mind cannot conceive of anything sudden. Mind wants to divide, analyze. Mind is a divider. Degrees can be understood by the mind, but suddenness is non-mental—beyond mind.

If I say to you that you are ignorant and that gradually you will become wise, this is comprehensible, you can comprehend it. If I say to you, "No, there is no gradual growth. Either you are ignorant or you become enlightened, there is a sudden jump," then the question arises of *how* to become

enlightened. If there were no gradualness, there could be no progress. If there were no degree of growth, no degrees, then you could not make progress, you could not proceed. From where to begin? In a sudden explosion, the beginning and the end are both the same. There is no gap between the beginning and the end, so from where to begin? The beginning is the end.

It becomes a puzzle for the mind, it becomes a *koan*. But sudden enlightenment seems to be impossible. It is not that it is impossible, but that the mind cannot conceive of it. And, remember, how can the mind conceive of enlightenment? It cannot. It has been widely accepted that this inner explosion is also gradual growth. Even many enlightened persons have conceded that to your minds, and they have said, "Yes, there is a gradual growth."

It is not that there is. They have said it and accepted your attitude, your way of perception. They have been in a deep compassion for you. They know that if you start thinking that it is gradual, the start will be good, but there will be no gradual growth. But if you start, if you go on seeking it, someday the sudden thing will happen to you. And if it is said that enlightenment is only sudden and no gradual growth is possible, you are not even going to start and it will never happen. Many enlightened persons have said that enlightenment is a gradual thing just to help you, just to persuade you to start.

Something is possible through gradual process, but not enlightenment—not enlightenment, something else. And that something else becomes helpful. For example, if you are making water to evaporate it, heating it, evaporation will come suddenly. At a certain point, at a hundred degrees, evaporation will happen—suddenly! There will be no gradual growth between water and vapor. You cannot divide; you cannot say that this water is a little vapor and a little water. Either it is water or it is all vapor. Suddenly the water jumps into the state of vapor. There is a jump—not gradual growth. But by heating you are gradually giving heat to the water. You are helping it to reach the hundred-degree point, the evaporating point. This is a natural growth. Up to the evaporating point, the water will grow in the sense of being more and more hot. Then evaporation will happen suddenly.

So there have been masters who were wise, compassionate, who used the language of the human mind which you can understand, telling you, "Yes, there is a gradual growth." It gives you courage and confidence and hope, and a possibility that it can happen to you also: you cannot attain in a sudden explosion, but by and by, step by step, with your limitations, with your weaknesses, you can grow to it. It may take many lives, but still there is hope. You will just get heated by all your efforts.

The second thing to remember: even hot water is still water. So even if you become more clear in your mind, more pure in your perceptions, more moral, more centered, you are still man, not a buddha, not enlightened. You become more silent, more still, calmer. You feel a deep bliss, but still you are a man, and your feelings are really negative, not positive.

You feel calm because you are now less tense. You feel blissful because now you are clinging less to your miseries; you are not creating them. You feel collected. It is not that you have come to realize the one, but only because now you are less divided. Remember this: your growth is negative. You are just hot water. The possibility is there that at any moment you will come to the point where evaporation happens. When it happens, you will not feel

calmness, you will not even feel blissful, you will not feel silent, because these attributes are relative to their opposites. When you are tense, you can feel silence. When you feel noise, you can feel stillness. When you are divided, fragmentary, you can feel oneness. When you are in suffering, anguish, you can feel bliss.

That is why Buddha was silent—because language cannot now express that which is beyond polarities. He cannot say, "Now I am filled with bliss," because even this feeling that "Now I am filled with bliss" is possible only with a background of suffering and anguish. You can feel health only with a background of illness and disease; you can feel life only with a background of death. Buddha cannot say, "Now I am deathless," because death has disappeared so completely that deathlessness cannot be felt.

If the misery has disappeared so completely, how can you feel blissful? If the noise and the anguish are so absolutely nonexistent, how can you feel silence? All these experiences, feelings, are related to their opposites. Without their opposites they cannot be felt. If darkness disappears completely, how can you feel light? It is impossible.

Buddha cannot say, "I have become light!" He cannot say, "Now I am filled with light." If he says such things, we will say he is not yet a buddha. He cannot utter such things. Darkness must be there if you want to feel light; death must be there if you want to feel deathlessness. You cannot avoid the opposite. It is a basic necessity for any experience to exist. So what is Buddha's experience? Whatsoever we know, it is not that. It is neither negative nor positive, neither this nor that. And whatsoever can be expressed, it is not that.

That is why Lao Tzu insists so much that truth cannot be said, and the moment you say it you have falsified it. Already it is untrue.

Truth cannot be said because of this: it cannot be divided into polar opposites, and language is meaningful only with polar opposites. Language becomes meaningless otherwise. Without the contrary, language loses meaning.

So there is a tradition which says that enlightenment is gradual, but that tradition is not really the truth. It is just a half-truth uttered in compassion for human minds. Enlightenment is sudden, and it cannot be otherwise. It is a jump! It is a discontinuity from your past! Try to understand: if something is gradual, the past goes on remaining in it. If something is gradual, then there is a continuity. There is no gap. If from ignorance to knowledge there is gradual growth, the ignorance cannot completely disappear. It will remain, it will continue, because there has been no discontinuity, there has been no gap. So the ignorance may become more polished, the ignorance may become more knowledgeable. The ignorance may appear wise, but it is there. The more polished it is, then, of course, the more dangerous. The more knowledgeable it is, then the more cunning one is and the more capable of deceiving oneself.

Enlightenment and ignorance are absolutely separate, discontinuous. A jump is needed—a jump in which the past dissolves completely. The old is gone; it is no more, and the new has appeared which was never there before.

Buddha is reported to have said, "I am not that one who was seeking. The one who has appeared now never was before." This looks absurd, illogical, but it *is* so. It is so! Buddha says, "I am not he who was seeking; I am not he who was desiring enlightenment; I am not he who was ignorant. The old man is dead completely. I am a new one. I never existed in that old man. There has been a gap. The old has died and the new is born."

For the mind to conceive of this is difficult. How can you conceive of it? How can you conceive of a gap? Something must continue. How can something disappear completely and something new appear? It was absurd for logical minds, it was absurd for scientific minds, just two decades before. But now, for science, it is not absurd. Now they say that deep down in the atom electrons appear and disappear, and they take jumps. From one point the

electron takes a jump to another; in between the two it is not. It appears at point A, then disappears and reappears at point B, and within the gap it is no more. It is not there. It becomes absolutely nonexistent.

If this is so, it means that nonexistence is also a sort of existence. It is difficult to conceive of, but it is so: nonexistence is also a sort of existence. It is as if something moves from the visible to the invisible, as if something moves from form to formlessness.

When Gautama Siddhartha, the old man who died in Gautam Buddha, was seeking, he was a visible form. When the enlightenment happened, that form completely dissolved into the formless. For a moment there was a gap; there was no one. Then from that formlessness a new form arose. This was Gautam Buddha. Because the body continues in the same way, we think that there is a continuity, but the inner reality changes completely. Because the body continues in the same way, that is why we say "Gautam Buddha"—that "Gautama Siddhartha has now become Gautam the awakened; he has become a buddha." But Buddha himself says, "I am not he who was seeking. I am a totally different one."

It is difficult for the mind to conceive of this—and for the mind many things are difficult, but they cannot be denied just because they are difficult for the mind. The mind has to yield to those impossibilities which are incomprehensible to it. Sex cannot yield to the mind; the mind has to yield to sex. This is one of the most basic inner facts—that enlightenment is a discontinuous phenomenon. The old simply disappears and the new is born.

There has been another tradition, a later tradition, of those who have been insisting all through history that enlightenment is sudden—that it is not gradual. But those who belong to it are very few. They stick to the truth, but they are bound to be very few because no following can be created if sudden enlightenment is the case. You simply cannot understand it, so how can you follow it? It is shocking to the logical structure and it seems absurd, impossible. But remember one thing: then you move into deeper realms. Whether of matter or of mind, you will have to encounter many things of which a superficial mind cannot conceive.

Tertullian, one of the greatest Christian mystics, has said, "I believe in God because God is the greatest absurdity. I believe in God because mind cannot believe in God." It is impossible to believe in God; no proof, no argument, no logic can help the belief in God. Everything goes against him, against his existence, but Tertullian says, "That is why I believe—because only by believing in an absurdity can I move away from my mind."

This is beautiful. If you want to move away from your mind, you will need something of which your mind cannot conceive. If your mind can conceive of it, it will absorb it into its own system, and then you cannot transcend your mind. That is why every religion has insisted on some point which is absurd. No religion can exist without some absurdity just as a foundation in it. From that absurdity you either turn back and say, "I cannot believe so I will go away." Then you remain yourself—or you take a jump, you turn away from your mind. And unless your mind is killed the enlightenment cannot happen.

Your mind is the problem, your logic is the problem, your arguments are the problem. They are on the surface. They look true, but they deceive. They are not true. For example, look how the mind's structure functions. The mind divides everything in two, and nothing is divisible. Existence is indivisible; you cannot divide it—but mind goes on dividing it. It says that "this" is life and "this" is death. What is the actual fact? The actual fact is that both are the same. You are both alive and dying this very moment; you are doing both. Rather, you *are* both—death and life.

Mind divides. It says, "this" is death and "this" is life. Not only does it divide; it says that both are opposites, enemies, and that death is trying to destroy life. And it looks okay: death is trying to destroy life. But if you penetrate deeper, deeper

than the mind, death is not trying to destroy life! You cannot exist without death. Death is helping you to exist. It is every moment helping you to exist. If for a single moment death stops working, you will die.

Death is every moment throwing away many parts in you which have become nonfunctional. Many cells die; they are removed by death. When they are removed, new ones are born. You are growing: something is dying and something is being born continuously. Every moment there is death and life, and both are functioning. In language I have to call them two. They are not two; they are two aspects of one phenomenon. Life and death are one; "life-death" is a process. But mind divides. That division looks okay for us, but that division is false.

You say "this" is light and "that" is dark; you divide. But where does darkness start and where does light end? Can you demarcate them? You cannot demark them. Actually, whiteness and blackness are two poles of a long greyness, and that greyness is life. On one pole blackness appears and on another pole whiteness appears, but the reality is grey, and that grey contains both in itself.

Mind divides and then everything looks clear-cut. Life is very confusing; that is why life is a mystery. And because of this, mind cannot understand life. It is helpful to create clear-cut concepts. You can think easily, conveniently, but you miss the very reality of life. Life is a mystery, and mind demystifies everything. Then you have dead fragments, not the whole.

With the mind you will not be able to conceive of how enlightenment is sudden, how you will disappear and something new will be there which you had never known before. But don't try to understand through mind. Rather, practice something which will make you more and more hot. Rather, try to attain some fire which will make you more and more hot. And then one day suddenly you will know that the old has disappeared; the water is no more, this is a new phenomenon. You have evaporated, and everything has changed totally.

Water was always flowing downwards, and after evaporation the new phenomenon is rising upwards. The whole law has changed. You have heard about one law, Newton's law of gravity, which says that the earth attracts everything downwards. But the law of gravity is only one law. There is another law. You may not have heard about it because science has yet to uncover it, but yoga and tantra have known it for centuries. They call it levitation. Gravity is the pull downwards and levitation is the pull upwards.

The story of how the law of gravity was discovered is well-known. Newton was sitting under a tree, under an apple tree, and then one apple fell down. Because of this he started thinking, and he felt that something is pulling the apple downwards. Tantra and yoga ask, "How did the apple reach upwards in the first place? How?" That must be explained first—how the apple reached the upward position, how the tree is growing upwards. The apple was not there; it was hidden in a seed, and then the apple traveled the whole journey. It reached the upward position and only then did it fall down. So gravity is a secondary law. Levitation was there first. Something was pulling the apple upwards. What is that?

In life we easily know gravity because we are all pulled downwards. The water flows downwards; it is under the law of gravity. When it evaporates, suddenly the law also evaporates. Now it is under levitation, it rises upwards.

Ignorance is under the law of gravity; you always move downwards, and whatsoever you do makes no difference. You have to move downwards. In every way you will have to move downwards, and struggle alone will not be of much help unless you enter a different law—the law of levitation. That is what *samadhi* is—the door for levitation. Once you evaporate, once you are no more water, everything changes.

It is not that now you can control; there is no need to control, now you simply cannot flow downwards. As it was impossible before to rise upwards, now it is impossible to flow downwards.

It is not that a buddha tries to be nonviolent; he cannot do otherwise. It is not that he tries to be loving; he cannot do otherwise. He has to be loving. That is not a choice, not an effort, not any cultivated virtue, it is simply that now this is the law: he rises upwards. Hate is under the law of gravity; love is under levitation.

This sudden transformation doesn't mean that you are not to do anything and that you are simply to wait for the sudden transformation. Then it will never come. This is the puzzle. When I say—or someone else says—that enlightenment is sudden, we think that if it is sudden nothing can be done, that we must simply wait. When it will happen, it will happen, so what can one do? If it is gradual you can do something.

But I say to you that it is not gradual, and yet you can do something. And you have to do something, but that something will not bring you enlightenment. That something will bring you near the phenomenon of enlightenment. That something will make you open for the phenomenon of enlightenment to happen. So enlightenment cannot be an outcome of your efforts; it is not. Through your efforts you simply become available for the higher law of levitation. Your availability will come through your effort, not enlightenment. You will become open, you will become nonresistant, you will become cooperative for the higher law to work. And once you are cooperative and nonresistant, the higher law starts functioning. Your efforts will yield you, your efforts will make you more receptive.

It is just like this: you are sitting in your room with closed doors. The sun is outside, but you are in darkness. You cannot do anything to bring the sun in, but if you simply open the doors your room becomes available. You cannot bring the sun in, but you can block it out. If you open your doors, the sun will enter, the waves will come; the light will come into the room. You are not really bringing the light, you are simply removing the hindrance. The light comes by itself.

Understand it deeply: you cannot do anything to reach enlightenment, but you are doing many things to hinder it—to hinder it from reaching to you. You are creating many barriers, so you can only do something negatively: you can throw the barriers, you can open the doors. The moment the doors are open, the rays will enter, the light will touch you and transform you.

All effort in this sense is to destroy the barriers, not to attain enlightenment. All effort is negative. It is just like medicine. The medicine cannot give you health; it can only destroy your diseases. Once the diseases are not there, health happens; you become available. If diseases are there, health cannot happen.

That is why medical science, Eastern or Western, has not yet been able to define what health is. They can define each disease exactly—they know thousands and thousands of diseases and they have defined them all—but they cannot define what health is. At the most they can say that when there is no disease you are healthy. But what is health? Something which goes beyond mind. It is something which is there: you can have it, you can feel it, but you cannot define it.

You have known health, but can you define it, what it is? The moment you try to define it you will have to bring disease in. You will have to talk something about disease, and you will have to say, "No-disease is health." This is ridiculous. To define health you need disease? And disease has definite qualities. Health also has its own qualities, but they are not so definite because they are infinite. You can feel them; when health is there you know it is there. But what is it? Diseases can be treated, destroyed. Barriers are broken and the light enters. Similar is the phenomenon of enlightenment. It is a spiritual health. Mind is a spiritual disease, and meditation is nothing but medicine.

Buddha is said to have said, "I am a medicine man, a *vaidya*—a physician. I am not a teacher and I have not come to give you doctrines. I know a certain medicine which can cure your diseases. And don't ask about health. Take the medicine, destroy the disease, and you will know what health is. Don't ask about it." Buddha says, "I am not a metaphysician, I am not a philosopher. I am not interested in what God is, in what soul is, in what *kaivalya*, aloneness, *moksha*, liberation, and *nirvana* is. I am not interested! I am simply interested in what disease is and in how it can be cured. I am a medicine man." His approach is absolutely scientific. He has diagnosed human dilemma and disease. His approach is absolutely right.

Destroy the barriers. What are the barriers? Thinking is the basic barrier. When you think, a barrier of thoughts is created. Between you and the reality a wall of thoughts is created, and thoughts are more dense than any stone wall can be. And then there are many layers of thought. You cannot penetrate through them and see what the real is. You go on thinking about what the real is and you go on imagining what the real is, and the real is here and now waiting for you. If you become available to it, it will happen to you. You go on thinking about what the real is, but how can you think if you don't know?

You cannot think about something which you don't know; you can only think about something which you already know. Thinking is repetitious, tautological; it never reaches to anything new and unknown. Through thinking you never touch the unknown; you only touch the known, and it is meaningless because you already know it. You can go on feeling it again and again; you may enjoy the feeling, but nothing new comes out of it.

Stop thinking. Dissolve thinking, and the barrier is broken. Then your doors are open and the light can enter. And once the light enters, you know that the old is no more.

You know now that that which you are is absolutely the new. It never was before, you had never known it; but you may even say that this is the ancientmost—it was there always, not known to you.

You can use both expressions, they mean the same. You can call it the ancientmost—the Brahma who has always been there, and you can say that you were missing it continuously. Or you can say that this is the most new—that which has happened only now and never was before. That too is right because for you this is the new. If you want to speak about the truth, you will have to use paradoxical expressions. The Upanishads say, "This is the new and this is the old. This is the most ancient and this is the most new. It is the far and the near both." But then language becomes paradoxical, contradictory.

And you ask me, *What is this gradual growth and clarity if the authentic experience is never gradual, but sudden?* This clarity is of the mind; this clarity is of a lessening of disease; this clarity is of the falling of barriers. If one barrier falls you are less burdened, your eyes are less clouded. If another barrier falls you are still more unburdened, your eyes become still more clear. But this clarity is not of enlightenment; this clarity is only of a lessening disease, not of health. When all barriers disappear, with those barriers your mind also disappears. Then you cannot say, "Now my mind is clear, it is no more." Then you simply say, "Now there is no mind."

When there is no mind, then the clarity is of enlightenment. Then the clarity is of enlightenment! —that is absolutely different. Then another dimension has opened. But you will have to pass through clarities of mind. Remember always that no matter how clear your mind becomes, it is still a barrier. No matter how transparent your mind becomes, even if it becomes a transparent glass and you can look to the other side, still it is a barrier and you will have to break it completely. So sometimes it happens that when one is meditating one becomes more and more clear, more sane, more still; silence is felt. Then one clings to meditation and thinks that everything is achieved. Great masters have always been emphasizing that a day comes when you have to throw your meditation also.

I will tell you one story—one Zen story. Bokuju was meditating—meditating very deeply, meditating with his whole heart. His master would come every day, and he would just laugh and go back. Bokuju became annoyed. The master would not say anything, he would just come and look at him, laugh and go away. And Bokuju was feeling very good in meditation. His meditation was deepening, and he needed someone to appreciate him. He was waiting for the master to pat him and say, "Good, Bokuju. You did well." But the master just laughed. The laughter felt insulting—as if Bokuju was not progressing, and he was progressing. As he progressed more, the laughter grew more and more insulting. It was impossible to tolerate it now.

One day the master came, and Bokuju was feeling absolutely silent as far as mind can go; there was no noise within, no thought. The mind was absolutely transparent; no barrier was felt. He was filled with a subtle deep happiness, joy was bubbling all over, he was in ecstasy. Thus he thought, "Now my master will not laugh. Now the moment has come, and he is going to tell me, 'Now, Bokuju, you have become enlightened.'"

That day the master came; the master came with a brick in his hand, and he started rubbing that brick on the rock on which Bokuju was sitting. He was so silent, and the rubbing of the brick created noise. He became annoyed. At last he couldn't tolerate it, so he opened his eyes and asked his master, "What are you doing?"

The master said, "I am trying to make this brick a mirror, and by continuously rubbing it I hope that someday this brick will become a mirror."

Bokuju said, "You are behaving stupidly. This stone, this brick, is not going to become a mirror. No matter how much you rub it, it is not going to become a mirror."

The master laughed and said, "Then what are you doing? This mind can never become enlightened, and you go on rubbing and rubbing it. You are polishing it, and you are feeling so good that when I laugh you feel annoyed." And suddenly, as the master threw his brick, Bokuju became aware. When the master threw his brick, suddenly he felt that the master was right, and the mind broke. Then from that day on there was no mind and no meditation. He became enlightened.

The master said to him, "Now you can move anywhere. Go, and teach others also. First teach them meditation; then teach them nonmeditation. First teach them how to make the mind clear, because only a very clear mind can understand that now even this clear mind is a barrier. Only a deeply meditative mind can understand that now even meditation has to be thrown."

You cannot understand it right now. Krishnamurti goes on saying that there is no need of any meditation, and he is right. But he is talking to wrong persons. He is right, there is no need for any meditation, but he is wrong because of to whom he is saying this. Those who cannot even understand what meditation is, how can they understand that there is no need for any meditation? This is going to be harmful for them because they will cling to this idea. They will feel that this idea is very good, there is no need of meditation, so "We are already enlightened."

Listening to Krishnamurti, many feel that now there is no need of meditation and that those who are meditating are foolish. They may waste their whole life because of this thought, and this thought is right. There comes a point when meditation has to be thrown; there comes a point when meditation becomes a barrier. But wait for this point to come. You cannot throw something which you don't have. Krishnamurti says, "No need of meditation; don't meditate." But you have never meditated, so how can you say, "Don't meditate"?

A rich man can renounce his riches, not a poor man. To renounce you need something to renounce in the first place. If you meditate, you can renounce it one day—and that is the last renunciation, and that is the greatest. Wealth can be renounced, it is easy. Family can be renounced, it is not difficult. The whole world can be renounced because everything is outer and outer and outer. The last thing is meditation, the innermost wealth. And when you renounce it, you have renounced yourself. Then no self remains—not even the meditating self, the great meditator. Even that image is broken. You have fallen into nothingness. Only in this nothingness, the discontinuity. The old has disappeared and the new has happened. You become available through meditation.

Whatsoever is felt through meditation, don't think that it is enlightenment. These are just glimpses of a lessening disease, of a dispersing disease. You feel good. The disease is less, so you feel relatively healthy. Real health is not yet there, but you are more healthy than before and it is good to be more healthy than before.

The second question:

You said that life exists in polar opposites like love and hate, attraction and repulsion, virtue and vice, etcetera. But what happens to these polar opposites when one is in the witnessing consciousness?

Don't ask, wait for the happening, for what happens. You can ask and some answer can be given, but that answer cannot become an authentic answer for you. And never jump ahead. Don't ask what happens when one dies. What happens? Whatsoever is said will be meaningless because you are still alive. What happens when someone is dead? You will have to pass through it. Unless you are dead you cannot know it. Whatsoever is said can be believed on trust, but this is meaningless.

Rather, ask how to be dead so that you can know what happens. No one else can die for you; no one else's experience can be an experience for you. You will have to die. Death cannot be another's experience for you, it has to be your own. Similar is the case here. What happens when polarities disappear? In a way nothing happens. Happening dissolves because all happening is polar. When love and hate both dissolve—and they *do* dissolve —what happens? When you love, you hate also— and you hate the same person you love. Hate is just hidden, and when hate comes up love goes down.

Jesus says, "Love your enemies," and I say that you cannot do otherwise. You *do* love your enemies. You hate them so much, and without love that is impossible. Love is just the other aspect of the coin. And where is the demarcation where love ends and hate begins? There is just a grey extension. When do you hate someone and when do you love? Can you demark it? You love and hate the same person; any moment hate can become love and love can become hate. This is the polarity of mind, this is how mind functions. Don't become worried about it. If you know, you will never become worried. If you love someone, you know hate will be there. If someone loves you, you will expect both—love and hate.

But what happens in a buddhalike consciousness when love and hate both disappear? What happens? It is difficult to express what happens, but whatsoever has been felt around Buddha is more like love without hate. It has been felt around Buddha; it is not that Buddha feels it so. Buddha cannot feel love now because he cannot feel hate. He cannot feel love, but around him everyone has felt a deep love flowing. We can describe it as love without hate, but then the quality is different.

With our love, hate is inevitably present. It colors it, it changes the quality of it. Hate gives a passion to love, a force, an intensity, a focused quality, a concentration, while Buddha's love becomes a dispersed phenomenon. Intensity is not there. It cannot burn you, it can only warm you. It is not a fire, it is just a glow. It is not a flame, it is just like the morning light when the sun has not yet risen and the night has disappeared. It is just the moment of interval—light without any fire, without any flame. We have felt it as love, and as the purest, because there is no hate. Even to feel this type of love, you have to be a very deeply meditative mind. You need a mind which can meditate; otherwise

such a delicate and diffuse phenomenon will not be felt. You have to be very deeply sensitive.

You can only feel gross love, and that grossness is given by hate. If someone simply loves you without any hate, it will be difficult for you to feel his love. You will have to grow to become more transparent, delicate, sensitive. You will have to become like a very sensitive musical instrument; only then will the breeze sometimes come to you. And the breeze is so nonviolent now that it will not hit you, it will be just a delicate touch. If you are very, very aware, you will feel it; otherwise you will miss it.

But this is our feeling around a buddha, not Buddha's feeling. Buddha cannot feel love or hate. Really, the polar opposites disappear, and simple presence remains. Buddha is a presence, not a mood. You are moods, not a presence. Sometimes you are hate, one mood, sometimes you are love— another mood; sometimes you are anger, another mood, sometimes you are greed—another mood. You are moods, you are never a pure presence, and your consciousness goes on being modified by your moods. Each mood becomes the master. It modifies the consciousness, cripples it, changes it, colors it, deforms it.

A buddha is without moods. Now hate has gone, love has gone, anger has gone, greed has gone—and nongreed also, nonanger also. They have disappeared! They both have disappeared! He is a simple presence. If you are sensitive, you will feel love flowing from him, you will feel compassion. If you are not sensitive, if you are gross, if your meditation has not developed, you will not feel him at all. A buddha will move amidst you, and you will not even become aware that some phenomenon is passing—something rare, something which passes only once in centuries. You will not become aware!

Or, if you are very gross, antimeditative, you will even become angered by his presence. Because his presence is subtle, you may even become violent because of his presence. His presence may be disturbing to you. If you are very gross, antimeditative, you will become an enemy of a buddha and he will not have done anything. If you are open, sensitive, you will become a lover, and he will not have done anything. Remember this: when you become an enemy, it is you; when you become a friend, it is you. A buddha is a simple presence, he is available. If you become an enemy, you turn your back. You will simply miss something for which you may have to wait for lives to come again.

Ananda was weeping the day Gautaum Buddha was passing away, and Buddha said in the morning, "Now this is my last day. Now the body is going to be finished." Ananda was near. He was the first to whom Buddha said, "This is my last day, so go and tell everyone that if they have to ask something they can ask."

Ananda started weeping and crying, so Buddha said, "Why are you weeping? For this body? I have been teaching and teaching and teaching that this body is false, it is already dead—or are you weeping for my death? Don't weep, because I have died forty years ago. I died the day I became enlightened, so this body is only disappearing now. Don't weep."

Ananda said a beautiful thing. He said, "I am not weeping for your body or for you, I am weeping for myself. I am yet unenlightened, and now how many lives will pass before again a buddha will be available? And I may not be again able to recognize you."

Unless you become enlightened, your clarity of mind can be clouded at any moment. Before you become enlightened, you can fall back again and again. Nothing is certain. So Ananda said, "I am weeping for myself. I am yet unenlightened, I have not yet reached the goal, and you are entering nothingness."

Many, even Buddha's own father, couldn't recognize that his son was no more his son—that something had happened into this body which rarely happens. The darkness had disappeared and the eternal light was burning there, but he couldn't recognize it.

Many were against him; many tried to kill him. But it is all up to you: whether you become a friend, a lover or an enemy depends on you, on your sensitivity, on your mind—how your mind feels.

But a buddha is not doing anything, he is simply a presence. Just by his presence much happens around him. Those who can feel love, they will feel he is in deep love with them. And the deeper you can feel, the more you will grow in the feeling that his love is deepening towards you. If you can become a real lover, you will feel that a buddha is a lover to you. If you become an enemy, and you feel hate, you will feel that a buddha is an enemy and you will feel that he has to be killed, destroyed. It depends on you. A buddha is a nondoer; he is simply being, he is there. So what happens is difficult to say because whatsoever we say will be a mood. If we say he becomes a lover, that he has a great love, it will be false. That will be our feeling.

Jesus' followers felt that he was simply love and Jesus' enemies thought he had to be crucified—so it depends on you. It depends on you how you take it, how you are capable of taking it, how much open you are. But from the side of an enlightened one, nothing can he said. He can simply say that now he is: without doing anything he is—just a presence, a being.

The third question:

You said that when a person is totally in the present moment without any thought in the mind, then he is a buddha-mind. But even when there is no thought in me and I am in the moment, absorbed, with no past or future, I do not feel the buddha-nature. Please explain when in this thoughtless awareness the buddha-mind is revealed.

The first thing: if you are aware that there is no thought in your mind, there is thought. Even this is a thought, that now there is no thought in you. This thought is the last thought. Allow it also to disappear. And why are you waiting for when the buddha-nature is going to happen to you? That again is a thought. It will not happen in that way—never!

I will tell you one story. One king came to Gautam Buddha. He was a devotee, a great devotee, and he had come for the first time for his darshan—for his audience. In one of his hands, in his left hand, he had one beautiful golden ornament, priceless, with many jewels in it. It was the most precious that he had—a rare piece of art. He had come to present it to Buddha just to show his devotion. He came near. In his left hand was that priceless jeweled ornament; he was going to present it. Buddha said, "Drop it!" He was disturbed. He never expected this. He was shocked. But because Buddha was saying "Drop it!" he dropped it.

In his other hand, in his right hand, he had brought a beautiful rose. He thought that Buddha might not like stones; he might just think that this was a childish thing that he had brought. But it was good to have an alternative, so he brought a beautiful rose. A rose is not so gross, not so material. It has a spirituality, something of the unknown is there. And Buddha might like it because he says life is flux, and the flower is in the morning and in the evening it is no more. It is the most fluxlike thing in the world. So he put his other hand in front of Buddha and he wanted to present the flower. Buddha again said, "Drop it!" Then he felt very disturbed. Now he had nothing to present. But when Buddha again said to drop it, he dropped it.

Then suddenly he became aware of the "I." He thought, "Why am I presenting things when I can present myself?" When he became aware, with both his hands empty, he presented himself. But Buddha again said, "Drop it!" Now he had nothing to drop—just empty hands—and Buddha said, "Drop it!"

Mahakashyapa, Sariputta, Ananda and his other disciples were there, and they started laughing. The man became aware that even to say that "I present myself to you" is egoistic. Even to say, "Now I am here and I surrender to you," is not surrender. So

he himself fell down. Buddha smiled and said, "You understand well."

Unless you drop even this idea of surrendering, unless you drop even this idea of empty hands, it is not surrender. One has to drop even emptiness in the hand. It is easy to understand the dropping of things...but then the hands were empty and Buddha said, "Drop it! Don't even cling to this emptiness!" When you do meditation, you have to drop thoughts. When thoughts are dropped, a thought remains and the thought is, "Now I have become thoughtless." There is a subtle feeling, a thought that "Now I have achieved and now there is no thought. Now the mind is vacant. Now I am empty."

But this emptiness is filled with this thought. And whether thoughts are there or a thought is there makes no difference. Drop the thought also. And why are you waiting for the buddha-nature? *You* cannot wait because you will not be there. You will never meet Buddha; when Buddha happens you will not be there, so your hopes are futile. You are wasting time, you will not be there.

Kabir has said, "When I was, you were not. Now you are, and where has Kabir gone? When I was seeking and seeking and desiring and hungering for you, you were not. I was there. Now you are there, and please tell me, where has Kabir gone? Where is that seeker who was seeking and seeking and hungering and weeping and crying for you? Where has that Kabir gone?"

You will not be there when Buddha happens. So don't wait, don't desire, because your desire of "When will Buddha happen to me?" and "When will I become a buddha-nature? When will I become enlightened?"—this very desire will create a barrier, the last barrier. For the achieving of total freedom, the desire for freedom is the last barrier. To be enlightened, even this desire for enlightenment has to be thrown, has to be cast away.

One of the great Zen masters, Lin Chi, used to say, "If you meet Buddha anywhere, kill him immediately! If you meet Buddha anywhere in your meditation, kill him immediately!" He means it. This desire to be a buddha, to be enlightened, if you meet it anywhere, kill it immediately. Only then does it happen. Total desirelessness is needed, and when I say total desirelessness, I mean that even the desire for total desirelessness must be dropped. You are, without any desire. You are, without any thought, not even aware that there is no thought, that there is no desire. Then it happens.

The last question:

What are the possible reasons for not having an explosive catharsis? I constantly, even with today's shaktipat meditation, have only a very mild catharsis. Does it necessarily mean that I am not open or not open enough, or are there other possible reasons? My concern over this then becomes a distraction to me during the meditation and after.

The first thing to be noted, to be remembered: catharsis will happen deeply if you just help it to happen, if you just cooperate with it. Mind is so suppressed, and you have so much pushed things down, that to reach them your cooperation is needed. So whenever you feel even a light catharsis, help it to become stronger. Don't just wait. If you feel that your hand is trembling, don't just wait, help it to tremble more. Don't feel, think that it has to be spontaneous so you have to wait. If it has to be spontaneous then you will have to wait for years, because for years you have been suppressing and the suppression was not spontaneous. You have done it on purpose.

You will have to do quite the opposite now. Only then can the suppressions be brought to the surface. You feel like weeping; you weep mildly. Help it along! Make it a deep scream! You don't know that from the very beginning you have been suppressing your crying, you have not cried really. From the very beginning the child wants to cry, to laugh. The crying is a deep necessity in him. Through crying, every day he goes through catharsis.

The child has many frustrations. This is bound

to be; it is of necessity. The child wants something, but he cannot say what, he cannot express it. The child wants something, but the parents may not be in a position to fulfill it. The mother may not be available there. She may be engaged in some other work, and he may not be cared for. At that moment no attention is paid to him, so he starts crying. The mother wants to persuade him, to console him, because she is disturbed, the father is disturbed, the whole family is disturbed. No one wants him to cry, crying is a disturbance; everyone tries to distract him so that he may not cry. We can bribe him. The mother can give him a toy, the mother can give him milk—anything to create a distraction or to console him—but he should not cry.

But crying is a deep necessity. If he can cry and is allowed to cry, he will become fresh again; the frustration is thrown through crying. Otherwise, with a stopped crying, the frustration is stopped. Now he will go on piling it up, and you are a piled-up cry. Now psychologists say that you need a primal scream. Now a therapy is developing in the West just to help you to scream so totally that every cell of your body is involved in it. If you can scream so madly that your whole body screams in it, you will be relieved of much pain, much suffering that is accumulated. You will become just like a child— fresh and innocent again.

But that primal scream is not going to come suddenly. You will have to help it. It is so deep down, and there are so many layers of repression, that don't just wait—help it. When you want to cry, cry wholeheartedly! Give total energy to it and enjoy it. Help it. And the second thing—enjoy it, because if you are not enjoying what you are doing it cannot go deep. It will be superficial. If you are screaming, then enjoy it. Enjoy the very thing, feel good. If you are feeling somewhere that "What I am doing is not good; what will others say? What a childish thing I am doing," even a slight feeling like this will become repression. Enjoy it and be playful about it. Enjoy and be playful. Just inquire more and more whether it can become deeper, whether you can help it along more—in what ways you can help it along more.

If you are sitting and crying, then maybe…if you start jumping the cry will become deeper. Or if you lie down on the floor and start thrashing about, maybe it will become deeper. Try, help it along, and enjoy it—and you will feel there are many ways in which you can help it along. Enjoy trying to deepen it, and once it takes over then you will not be needed. Once it comes to the right source where energy is hidden, once you touch the right source and the energy is released, then you are not needed. You can flow automatically, spontaneously. And when it starts flowing spontaneously,

you will be cleansed completely.

It is just like flowers being cleansed after a rain. Then they become new. Every bit of dust, whatsoever has gathered upon one, is no more there; they are themselves. In life we gather dust. This catharsis is just a cleansing. Help it along, enjoy it, and one day the primal scream will come. Just go on doing it. It cannot be predicted when it will come. When the primal scream will come cannot be said because man is very complex. It can come this very moment; it may take years. One thing is certain: if you help it, enjoy it and play with it, it is going to come.

CHAPTER 41

Tantric methods for awareness and nonjudgment

◆

64 *At the start of sneezing, during fright, in anxiety, above a chasm, flying in battle, in extreme curiosity, at the beginning of hunger, at the end of hunger, be uninterruptedly aware.*

65 *The purity of other teachings is an impurity to us. In reality, know nothing as pure or impure.*

ife is a paradox. To reach near you have to travel far, and that which is already achieved you have to achieve again. Nothing is lost. Man remains natural, man remains pure, man remains innocent; it is only that he forgets it. The purity is not disturbed, the innocence is not destroyed. Only a deep forgetfulness is there.

That which is to be achieved you are already. In essence, nothing new is to be achieved. You have only to discover, uncover, unfold that which is already the case; hence both the difficulty of spiritual endeavor and the simplicity. I say "both".... It is very simple if you can understand, but it is very difficult because you have to understand that which you have completely forgotten, that which is so obvious that you never become aware of it, that which is just like your breathing. It goes on continuously, uninterruptedly, but because it goes on continuously, uninterruptedly, you need not be aware of it. Your awareness is not needed; it is not a basic requirement. You can forget it or you can remember it; it is a choice.

Sansara and *nirvana*, the world and the liberated state of consciousness, are not two things, just two attitudes, just two choices. You can choose either. You can be in the world because of a certain attitude, and the same world becomes nirvana, the same world becomes absolute bliss, just by changing the attitude. You remain the same, everything remains the same; just a change of focus, a change of emphasis, a change of choice, is required. It is easy. Once absolute bliss is achieved, you will laugh about it. Once it is known, you will not be able to understand why you were missing it, how you could miss it. It was there always just waiting to be looked at, and it was yours.

A buddha laughs. Anyone who achieves it laughs because the whole thing seems to be ridiculous. You were searching for something which was never lost. The whole effort was absurd. But this happens only when you have achieved it, so those who have achieved it say it is very simple. But those who have not achieved it, they say it is the most arduous thing, the most difficult—really, not simply difficult, but the most impossible thing.

These methods which we will be discussing are told by someone who has achieved—remember this. They will look too simple, and they are. To our minds things so simple cannot be appealing—because if techniques are so simple and the abode is so near, if you are already in it, if techniques are so simple and the home is so near, you will look ridiculous to yourself. Then why are you missing it? Rather than feel the ridiculousness of your own ego, you will think that such simple methods cannot help.

That is a deception. Your mind will tell you that these simple methods cannot be of any help—that they are so simple they cannot achieve anything. To achieve divine existence, to achieve the absolute and the ultimate, how can such simple methods be used? How can they be of any help? Your ego will say that they cannot be of any help.

Remember another thing: ego is always interested in something which is difficult, because when something is difficult there is a challenge, and if you can overcome the difficulty your ego will feel fulfilled. The ego is never attracted towards anything which is simple—never! If you want to give your ego a challenge, then you have to have something difficult devised. If something is simple there is no appeal, because even if you can conquer it there will be no fulfillment of the ego. In the first place, there was nothing to be conquered, the thing was so simple. Ego asks for difficulties—some hurdles to be crossed, some peaks to be conquered. And the more difficult the peak, the more at ease your ego will feel.

Because these techniques are so simple, they will not have any appeal to your mind. Remember, that which appeals to the ego cannot help your spiritual growth. Only that which has no appeal to your ego can be a help towards transformation. But this is what happens: if some teacher says that this or that is very difficult, very arduous, that only after lives and lives and lives will you have any possibility for any glimpse, your ego will feel good.

These techniques are so simple that right now, here and now, the thing is possible. But then there is no contact with your ego. If I say that right now, here, this very moment you can achieve all that is possible to man, that you can become a Buddha or a Christ or a Krishna in this very moment here and now without losing a single instant, then there will be no contact with your ego. You will say, "This is not possible. I must go somewhere else to search for it." And these techniques are so simple that you can achieve all that is possible to human consciousness at any moment that you decide to achieve it.

When I say that these techniques are simple, I mean many things. First, spiritual explosion is not caused by anything; it is not a causal phenomenon. If it were caused by something, then time would be needed, because time is necessary for the cause to take place. And if time is needed, then it cannot be the case, it cannot happen this very moment. Then you will have to wait for tomorrow or for another life. The next moment will be needed. If anything is

causal, then the cause has to take place, and then after the cause the effect will follow, and you cannot produce the effect right now without the cause; time will be needed. But a spiritual happening is not a causal phenomenon. You are already in that state; just a remembering is needed. It is not a causal phenomenon.

It is just like this: in the morning somebody has suddenly awakened you, and you cannot recognize where you are. For a moment you may not even recognize who you are. In a sudden awakening from deep sleep, you may not be able to recognize the place, the time, but within a moment you will recognize. The more alert you will become, the more you will recognize who you are, where you are and what has happened. This is not a causal thing—just a question of alertness. With a growing alertness, you will recognize.

All these techniques are for a growing alertness. You are already the person you long to be, you are already where you want to reach. You have reached your home already. You have never left it really. You have always been there, but dreaming, asleep. You can fall asleep here and then you can dream, and in your dream you can move anywhere; you can go to hell or to heaven or anywhere.

Have you ever observed that whenever you are in your dream, one thing is certain?—that you are never in the room in which you are asleep. Have you observed that fact? You can be anywhere, but you will never be in the same room, on the same cot where you are. Because you are already there, there is no need to dream about it. Dream means you have to trek away.

You may be sleeping in this room, but you will never dream of this room. There is no need, you are already there. The mind desires something which is not, so the mind moves. It may go to London, to New York, to Calcutta, to the Himalayas, to Tibet, to anywhere. It may go anywhere, but it will never be here. It can be anywhere, but never here—and you are here.

This is the case. You are dreaming. Your divine

existence is here; you are *that*. But you have been trekking long.... And each dream creates a new sequence of dreaming. Each dream creates new dreams, and you go on dreaming and dreaming and dreaming.

All these techniques are just to make you alert so that you can come out of your dreams back to the place where you have always been, to the state which you have never missed. And you cannot miss it, it is your nature—it is *swabhav*. It is your very being, so how can you miss it? These techniques are just to help your alertness to grow more, to help it become more intense. With the intensity of awareness, everything changes. The more intense the awareness, the less the possibility for dreaming; you become more and more alert about the real. The less intense the awareness, the more you drift into dreaming. So the whole phenomenon is that a nonalert state of mind is the world, and an alert state of mind is nirvana. Nonalert, you are what you appear to be. Alert, you are what you are.

So the whole question is one of how to change your nonalert state of mind into an alert state of mind, how to become more aware, how to get out of sleep and dreaming. That is why techniques can be of help. Even an alarm clock can be of help—just an artificial device, just an alarm clock. If the alarm goes on, it can help to bring you out of your dreaming. But you can deceive it also; you can even dream about it, and then the whole thing is falsified. When the alarm goes, you can dream, you can make a dream around the alarm also. You can dream that you have entered a temple and the bells are going on. Now you have deceived the alarm. It could have broken your sleep, but you can change it into dream itself; you can make it part of your dreaming.

If you can make it part of your dreaming, if it can be absorbed into a dreaming process, then it cannot help you. You can dream anything, and then it will not look like an alarm. It will have become something else. You have entered a temple and the bells are.... Now there is no need to wake up. You have changed the alarm, the real thing,

into a dream, and a dream cannot be disturbed by another dream, it can only be helped.

These techniques are all artificial in a way. They are just devices to help bring you out of your dreaming state, but you can make them also part of your dream. Then you miss the point. Then you *miss* the point! Try to understand this because this is very basic. And once understood, it will be helpful; otherwise you can go on deceiving yourself.

For example, I say, "Take a jump into sannyas." That is just a device. Your old identity is broken; your old name becomes as if it belongs to someone else. You can look at your past more detachedly. You can be a witness. You are aloof, a distance is created. I give you a new name and a new robe just to create the distance. But you can make it part of your dreaming; then you will miss the whole point. You can still think in terms of the old—that the old man, A, has taken sannyas. You feel, "*I* have taken sannyas." "I" remain the old. "I" have changed my robe, my name, but "I" remain the old, and the old continues. Now this sannyas is just something added to the old. It is not discontinuous, it is continuous. If it is continuous, if *you* have taken sannyas, you the old one, if *you* have changed your robe and name, you have missed the point.

You must be dead, you must not be the old now. You must feel that the old has died, that this is a new entity which you never knew, that this is not a growth out of the old. This is discontinuous with the old. Then the device will have helped. Then the alarm will have worked and the technique is useful. You are not missing the point. All these techniques are such that you can miss or you can use them; it depends. But remember well, the techniques are just techniques. If you understand the spirit, you may become alert even without any technique.

For example, the alarm clock may not be needed. Go deeply into it. Why do you need an alarm clock? If you want to get up early in the morning at three, why do you need an alarm clock? Deep down you know that you can deceive yourself, and deep down you know that if you really want to get up at three, you will get up at three and no clock is needed. But with the clock, the responsibility is put off. Now you will not be responsible. Now if something goes wrong, the clock is responsible. You can sleep with ease now. Now the clock is there; you can sleep without any disturbance.

But if you really want to get up early at three, you will get up early at three. No clock is needed. This very intensity to get up will bring the happening. This will to get up at three may be so intense, you may not be able to sleep at all, and there will be no need to get up; you will already be awake the whole night. But to sleep well the clock is needed. Then you can go to sleep. But you can deceive. When the alarm goes off, you can deceive; you can dream about it.

These techniques are helpful only because your intensity is low. If you are really intense, there is no need of any technique; you can be alert. But your intensity is not such. Even with the technique you may start dreaming, and many possibilities are there. The first possibility is that you will not believe that such simple techniques can be of any help. This is the first thing. Then there is no contact. Secondly, you may think that a very, very long process is needed, that it will come gradually. But there are certain things that only happen suddenly, they never come gradually.

I am reminded that Mulla Nasruddin was asked to give his blessings to one of his neighbor's sons on his birthday. So he said, "Son, I hope you live one hundred and twenty years plus three months." Everyone was wondering at this "plus three months."

The son asked, "But why? It is okay—one hundred and twenty years. Why plus three months?"

So Mulla Nasruddin said, "I would not like you to die so suddenly. Just one hundred and twenty years, and suddenly you die? I would not like you to die so suddenly; that is why plus three months."

But even with "plus three months" you will die suddenly anyway. Whenever you are going to die, you will die suddenly. Every death is a sudden death. No death is gradual because either you are alive or dead. There is no gradual process. One moment you are alive and the next moment you are dead. There is no time process; death is sudden.

Samadhi is also sudden. Spiritual explosion is also sudden. It is like death. It is more like death than it is like life; it is sudden. It can happen at any moment. If you are ready, these techniques can be of help. They will not bring it gradually; really, they will gradually bring you to be ready for the sudden happening. Remember this distinction: they are preparing you so that the sudden samadhi happens.

These techniques are not techniques for samadhi; they are techniques to prepare you, and then samadhi happens. So how you use these techniques depends on you. But don't think that a very long process is needed, because that may be just a trick. The mind says a very long process is needed so that you can postpone. You can say, "Tomorrow I will do it or the day after tomorrow," and you can go on postponing forever. A postponing mind goes on always postponing. It is not a question of whether you are going to do it tomorrow; there is only a question because you are not going to do it today, that is all. Tomorrow will again be a today, and the same mind will say, "Okay, I am going to do it tomorrow."

And, remember, you never postpone for years. You postpone for one day because if you postpone for years you cannot deceive yourself. You say, "It is only a question of one day. Just today I am not doing it; tomorrow I will do it." And the gap is so small that you never feel you are postponing it forever.

Tomorrow never comes, it is always today. And this mind which thinks in terms of tomorrow will *always* think in terms of tomorrow. And it never comes, it has never been, it will never be. All that you have is this very moment, so don't go on postponing.

Now we will enter the techniques.

64 At the beginning of a strong sensation, be aware.

The first technique: *At the start of sneezing, during fright, in anxiety, above a chasm, flying in battle, in extreme curiosity, at the beginning of hunger, at the end of hunger, be uninterruptedly aware.*

It looks so simple: at the start of sneezing, during fright, in anxiety or before hunger or after hunger, *be uninterruptedly aware.* Many things have to be understood. Very simple acts like sneezing can be used as devices, because howsoever simple they look, they are very complex, and the inner mechanism is a very delicate thing. Whenever you feel that a sneeze is coming become alert, and the sneeze may not come at all. It may simply disappear, because a sneeze is a nonvoluntary thing—unconscious, nonvoluntary.

You cannot sneeze voluntarily; you cannot will it. How can you? How helpless man is! You cannot will a single sneeze. Howsoever you may try, you cannot bring it out. A single sneeze—such a small thing, but you cannot will it. It is nonvoluntary; volition is not needed. It does not happen because of your mind; it is because of your total organism, your total body.

And the second thing: when you become alert, when the sneeze is coming—you cannot bring it, but when it is coming—if you become alert, it may not come, because you are bringing something new to the process: the alertness. It may disappear, but when the sneeze disappears and you are alert, there is a third thing. First, a sneeze is nonvoluntary. You bring in a new thing—alertness. When the alertness comes, the sneeze may not come. If really you are alert, it will not; it may not happen at all. Then a third thing happens. The energy that was going to be released through a sneeze, where does it move? It moves to your alertness. Suddenly there is a flash, a lightning. You become more alert. The energy that was going to be thrown by the sneeze moves into alertness. Suddenly you become more alert.

In that flash, in that lightning, even enlightenment is possible. That is why I say that these matters are so simple, they look absurd. Their promise seems to be too much. Just through sneezing, how can one become enlightened? But sneezing is not just sneezing; you are totally involved in it. Whatsoever you do or whatsoever happens to you is a total involvement. Observe again: whenever a sneeze happens, you are totally in it with the whole body, the whole mind. It is not just your nose in which the sneeze is happening; every fiber, every cell of your body is involved in it. A subtle trembling, a subtle wavering goes all over the body, and with it the whole body becomes concentrated. And when the sneeze has happened, the whole body relaxes. But it is difficult to bring alertness to it. If you bring alertness to it, it will not happen, and if it happens you can know that the alertness was not there. That is why you should be alert.

*At the start of sneezing...*because if it has started, nothing can be done. The arrow has gone; you cannot change it now. The mechanism has started. The energy is on its way to being released, it cannot be stopped. Can you stop a sneeze in the middle? How can you stop it in the middle? By the time you are ready, it has already happened. You cannot stop it in the middle.

Just at the beginning, become alert. The moment you feel the sensation that it is coming, become alert. Close your eyes and be meditative. Bring your total consciousness to the focus just where you are feeling the sensation of an oncoming sneeze. Just at the beginning, remain alert. The sneeze will disappear, and the energy will be transformed into more alertness. And because in the sneeze the whole body is involved, the whole mechanism is involved—it is a release mechanism and you are alert at this moment—there will be no mind, there will be no thought, no meditation.

In a sneeze, thinking stops. That is why so many people like snuff. It unburdens them, their minds feel more relaxed because for a moment thinking stops. Snuff gives them a glimpse of no-thinking.

Through snuff, when the sneeze comes, they are not minds, they become bodies. The head disappears for a single moment, but it feels good.

If you become habituated to snuff, it is very difficult to leave it. It is more penetrating a habit than smoking; smoking is nothing before it. It penetrates more deeply, because smoking is conscious and sneezing is unconscious. To leave snuff is more difficult than to leave smoking. And smoking can be changed, substitutes can be found—but there is no substitute for snuff, because, really, sneezing is a very unique phenomenon in the body.

The only other thing that can be compared and which has been compared is the sex act. Those who think in terms of physiology, they say that the sex act is just sneezing through the sex organ—and the similarity is there. It is not one hundred percent right because much more is involved in sex, greater things are involved in it. But in the beginning, just in the beginning, the similarity is there.

Something is thrown out from the nose and you feel relieved, and something is thrown out from the sex organ and you feel relieved. And both are nonvoluntary. You cannot move into sex with will. If you try, you will be a failure—particularly men, because man's sex organ has to do something. It is active. You cannot will its act, and if you try, then the more you try, the more it will be impossible. It can happen, but you cannot make it happen. Because of this, in the West sex has become a problem. This half century in the West sex knowledge has developed, and everyone has become so conscious about it that the sex act is becoming more and more impossible.

If you are alert, sex will be impossible. If a man is alert while making love, the more he is alert, the more it will be difficult. He will not be able to get an erection. It cannot be willed, and if you will it you will lose it. The same method, the same technique, can be used in sex. Just in the beginning, when you feel the sensation of an erection just coming to you but it has not yet come, you just feel the vibration, become alert. The vibration will be lost, and the same energy will move into alertness.

Tantra has used this. It has tried in many ways. A beautiful naked woman will be there just as an object for meditation, and the seeker, the meditator, will sit before the nude woman meditating on her body, her form, her proportions, just waiting for the first sensation in his sex center. The moment the sensation is there, he will close his eyes. He will forget the woman. He will close his eyes, and he will become alert of the sensation. Then sex energy is being transformed into alertness.

He is allowed to meditate on the nude woman only up to the point when the sensation is felt. Then he has to close his eyes and move to his own sensation and become alert there, the same as is done in sneezing. And why does this flash happen? Because mind is not there. The basic thing is that if the mind is not there and you are alert, you will have satori, you will have the first glimpse of samadhi.

Thought is the barrier. So if thought disappears in any way, the thing will happen. But thought must disappear; only then is alertness there. Thought can disappear even in sleep; thought can disappear when you go unconscious; thought can disappear when you take some drug. Thought disappears, but then there is no alertness to be aware of the phenomenon that is hidden behind thought. So I define meditation as thoughtless consciousness. You can become thoughtless and unconscious; then there is no meaning. You can be conscious with thought; you are already that.

Bring these two things together—consciousness and thoughtlessness. When they meet, meditation happens, meditation is born. And you can try with very small things because nothing is really small. Even a sneeze is a cosmic phenomenon. In existence, nothing is great and nothing is small. Even a minute atom can destroy the whole world, and even a sneeze, a very atomic phenomenon, can transform you.

So don't see things as small or big. There is nothing small and nothing big. If you have the penetrating eye, then very small things are vital. Between atoms universes are hidden, and between the universe and an atom you cannot say which is great and which is small. Even a single atom is a universe in itself, and the greatest universe is nothing but atoms.

So don't think in terms of great and small. Just try. Don't say, "What can happen in a sneeze? I have been sneezing my whole life, and nothing has happened."

Bring in this technique: Just *at the start of sneezing, during fright...*when you feel afraid and fear enters, just when you feel the fear enter, become aware and fear will disappear. With alertness, there can be no fear. How can you be afraid when you are alert? You can be afraid only when you lose alertness. Really, a coward is not a person who is afraid; a coward is a person who is asleep, and a brave man is a person who can bring his alertness to the moments of fear. So fear disappears.

In Japan, they train their warriors for alertness. The basic training is for alertness, and everything else is secondary: swordsmanship, archery, everything is secondary. It is known, it is said about the great Zen master Rinzai that he never succeeded—never succeeded in his archery—to get to the right point, to the right aim. His arrow always missed; it never reached to the right point. And he is known as one of the greatest archers, so it is asked, "How is Rinzai known as the greatest archer when he never succeeded in any aim and the point was always missed? His arrow never reached to the right point, so how is he known as one of the greatest archers?"

The followers of Rinzai say, "It is not the end, it is the beginning. We are not concerned with the arrow reaching to the end, we are concerned with when the arrow starts its journey. We are concerned with Rinzai. When the arrow leaves the bow, he is alert; that is all. It is not the result, that is irrelevant."

One man was a disciple to Rinzai. He was a great archer himself, he never missed his aim, and then he came to Rinzai to learn, so someone said,

"To whom are you going to learn? He is not a master; he is not even a disciple. He is a failure, and you are a great master and you are going to Rinzai to learn?"

So that archer said, "Yes, because I have succeeded technically. But as far as my consciousness is concerned, I am a failure. He is technically a failure, but as far as his consciousness is concerned he is the archer and the master—because when the arrow leaves he is alert, and that is the point."

This archer who was a master technically had to learn for years under Rinzai, and every day he was one hundred percent accurate in his aiming. Rinzai would say, "No, you are a failure. Technically the arrow leaves rightly—but you are not there, you are not alert. You loose it in your sleep."

In Japan they have been training their warriors to be alert first, and everything else is secondary. A warrior is a brave man if he can be alert. And it was felt in the Second World War that you cannot match Japan's warriors; their bravery is incomparable. From where does it come? Physically they are not so strong, but in consciousness, in alertness, fear cannot enter. They are not afraid, and whenever fear comes they will try Zen methods.

This sutra says, *During fright, in anxiety....* When you feel anxious, much anxiety-ridden, try it. What is one to do? What do you ordinarily do when anxiety is there? What do you do? You try to solve it. You try alternatives, and you get more and more into it. You will create a bigger mess because anxiety cannot be solved through thinking. It cannot be dissolved through thinking because thinking itself is a sort of anxiety. So you help it to grow more. Through thinking, you cannot come out of it; you will go deeper into it. This technique says don't do anything with anxiety. Just be alert. Just be alert!

I will tell you one old anecdote about Bokuju, another Zen master. He lived alone in a cave, all alone, but during the day, or even in the night, he would sometimes say loudly, "Bokuju"—his own name—and then he would say, "Yes, I am here." And no one else was there.

Then his disciples used to ask him, "Why are you calling 'Bokuju,' your own name, and then saying, 'Yes sir, I am here'?"

He said, "Whenever I get into thinking, I have to remember to be alert, and so I call my own name, 'Bokuju.' The moment I call 'Bokuju' and I say, 'Yes sir, I am here,' the thinking, the anxiety disappears."

Then, in his last days, for two or three years, he never called Bokuju, his name, and never had to reply, "Yes sir, I am here."

The disciples asked, "Master, now you never do this."

So he said, "But now Bokuju is always there. He is *always* there, and there is no need. Before I used to miss him. Sometimes the anxiety would take me, cloud me all over, and Bokuju was not there. So I had to remember 'Bokuju,' and the anxiety would disappear...."

Try this. This is a beautiful thing. Try your name. When you feel deep anxiety, just call your name—not Bokuju or any name, but your name—and then reply to it, "Yes sir, I am here," and feel the difference. Anxiety will not be there. At least for a single moment you will have a glimpse beyond the clouds, and that glimpse can be deepened. Once you know that if you become alert anxiety is not there, it disappears, you have come to a deep knowing of your own self and the mechanism of inner working.

...Above a chasm, flying in battle, in extreme curiosity, at the beginning of hunger, at the end of hunger, be uninterruptedly aware.

You can use anything. Hunger is there, become alert. What to do when you feel hunger is there? What has happened? When you feel hunger you never see it as something happening to you. You become the hunger. You feel, "I am hungry." The real feeling is that "I am hunger," but you are *not* hunger; you are only conscious of it. It is something happening on the boundary. You are the center, you have become aware of it. It is an object. You remain the subject, you are a witness. You are not

hunger; hunger is happening to you. You were there when hunger was not and you will be there when hunger will have gone. So hunger is an accident; it happens to you.

Become alert, then you will not be identified with it. If you feel hunger, become alert that hunger is there. Look at it, encounter it, face it. What will happen? The more you become alert, the farther away will the hunger be felt; the less alert, the nearer. If you are not alert, exactly at the center you will feel, "I am hunger." If you become alert, hunger is thrown away. Hunger is there, you are here. Hunger is an object, you are a witness.

Fasting has been used only because of this, for this technique. Fasting in itself is of no use. If you are not doing this technique with the hunger, fasting is foolish—just foolish, of no use. Mahavira used fasting with this technique, and Jainas have been simply using fasting without this technique. Then it is foolish. You are just destructive, and it cannot be of any help. You can be hungry for months and identified with hunger, feeling that "I am hungry." It is useless, harmful. There is no need to go on a fast. Every day you can feel it, but there are problems. That is why fasting may be helpful.

Ordinarily, we stuff ourselves with food before we feel hunger. In the modern world there is no need to feel hunger. You have a time fixed for your meals, and you take them. You never ask whether the body is feeling hungry or not; at a fixed hour you take your meals. Hunger is not felt. You may say, "No, when it is one o'clock I feel hungry." That may be a false hunger; you feel it because it is one o'clock, your time. Someday you can play a trick. Tell your wife or your husband to change the clock. It is twelve, and the clock will show that it is one. You will feel hunger. Or it is already one hour fast: it is two exactly, and the clock shows one; then you will feel hunger. You look at the clock and you feel hunger. This is artificial, false, it is not real.

So fasting may be helpful. If you fast, then for two or three days you will feel a false hunger. Only after the third or fourth day will real hunger be felt;

your body will demand, not the mind. When mind demands, it is false. When the body demands, it is real. And when it is real and you become alert, you become totally different from your body. Hunger is a body phenomenon. Once you can feel that hunger is different from you and you are a witness to it, you have transcended the body.

But you can use anything, these are just examples. This technique can be used in many ways; you can devise your own way. But insist on one thing: if you are trying with hunger, then go on at least for three months with hunger. Then only will you be disidentified with your body someday. Don't change the device every day because a deepening is needed with any technique.

So choose anything for three months. Stick to it, apply the technique, go on working with it, and always remember to be aware in the beginning. In the middle it will be very difficult, because once the identity is felt that *you* are hungry, you cannot change it. You can get changed mentally. You can say, "No, I am not hunger, I am a witness." That is false. This is the mind talking, this is not a feeling experience. Just try to be aware in the beginning, and, remember, you are not to say that "I am not hunger." This is how mind can deceive. You can say, "The hunger is there, but I am not hunger. I am not body, I am the *Brahma.*" You are not to say anything. Whatsoever you say will be false because you are false.

This chanting that "I am not the body" will not help. You go on saying "I am not the body" because you "know" that you *are* body. If you really know that you are not the body, what is the use of saying "I am not the body"? There is no use, it will look stupid. Be aware, and then the feeling that "I am not the body" will be there. This will not be a thought, this will be a feeling. This will not be felt in the head, this will be felt all over your being. You will feel the distance—that the body is far away, that "I am absolutely different." And there is not even a possibility of mixing both. You cannot. The body is the body; it is matter, and you

are consciousness. They can live together, but they never mix. They cannot become mixed.

---

65 Do not judge.

The second technique: *The purity of other teachings is an impurity to us. In reality, know nothing as pure or impure.*

This is one of the basic messages of tantra. It is very difficult to conceive of it because it is absolutely nonethical, nonmoral. I will not say immoral because tantra is not concerned with morality or immorality. Tantra says it is irrelevant. This message is to help you to grow beyond purity and impurity, beyond division really, beyond dichotomy, duality. Tantra says existence is nondual, it is one, and all distinctions are man-created—all distinctions, remember. Distinctions as such are man-created. Good-bad, pure-impure, moral-immoral, virtue-sin: all these concepts are man-created. They are attitudes of man; they are not real. What is impure and what is pure? It depends on your interpretation. What is immoral and what is moral? It depends on your interpretation.

Nietzsche has said somewhere that all morality is interpretation. So something can be moral in this country and immoral in the neighboring country, something can be moral to a Mohammedan and immoral to a Hindu, moral to a Christian and immoral to a Jaina. Or something can even be moral to the older generation and immoral to the younger generation. It depends; it is an attitude. Basically, it is a fiction. The fact is simply the fact. The naked fact is simply the fact; it is neither moral nor immoral, pure nor impure.

Think of the earth without human beings. Then what will be pure and what will be impure? Everything will be—simply be. Nothing will be pure and nothing will be impure; nothing will be good and nothing will be bad. With man, mind comes in. Mind divides. It says "this" is good and "that" is bad. This division not only creates a division in the world; this division creates a division in the divider also. If you divide, you are also divided in that division, and you cannot transcend your inner division unless you forget outer divisions. Whatsoever you do to the world, you have done to yourself also.

Naropa, one of the greatest masters of siddha yoga, says, "An inch division, and hell and heaven are set apart"—an inch division! But we go on dividing; we go on labeling, condemning, justifying. Look at the bare fact of existence and don't label it. Only then can tantra's teachings be understood. Don't say good or bad; don't bring your mind to the fact. The moment you bring your mind to the fact, you have created a fiction. Now it is not a fact, it is not a reality: it is your projection. This sutra says, *The purity of other teachings is an impurity to us. In reality, know nothing as pure or impure.*

The purity of other teachings is an impurity to us—tantra says, "What is very pure for other teachings, a virtue, is a sin for us, because their concept of purity divides. For them something becomes impure."

If you call a man a saint, you have created the sinner. Now you will have to condemn someone somewhere because the saint cannot exist without the sinner. And look now at the absurdity of our efforts: we go on trying to destroy sinners, and we conceive of and hope for a world where there will be no sinners—only saints. This is nonsense because saints cannot exist without sinners. They are the other aspect of the same coin. You cannot destroy one aspect of the coin, they both will exist. Sinners and saints are both part and parcel of one thing. If you destroy the sinners, saints will disappear from the world. But don't be afraid; let them disappear because they have not proved to be of any worth.

Sinners and saints are both part of one interpretation, of one attitude towards the world, in which one says, "This is good and that is bad." And you cannot say that "This is good" unless you say that "That is bad." The bad is needed to define the good. So the good depends on the bad, your virtue depends on sin, and your saints are impossible; they cannot exist without the sinners. So they must be grateful to the sinners; they cannot exist without them. In relation to them, in comparison to them, howsoever much they condemn the sinners, they are part and parcel of the same phenomenon. Sinners can disappear from the world only when saints disappear—not before that; and sin will not be there when there is no concept of virtue.

Tantra says that the fact is real and the interpretation is unreal. Don't interpret. *In reality, know nothing as pure or impure.* Why? Because purity and impurity are *our* attitudes imposed on reality. Try this. This technique is arduous, not simple— because we are so much oriented towards dual thinking, based, rooted in dual thinking, that we are not even aware of our condemnations and justifications. If someone starts smoking here, you may not have consciously felt anything, but you have condemned. Deep down within you, you have condemned. Your look may have condemned or no look may have condemned. You may not have looked at the person, and you have condemned.

This is going to be difficult because the habit has become so deep-rooted. You go on—just by your gestures, your sitting, your standing—you go on condemning, justifying, not even aware of what you are doing. When you smile at a person or when you don't smile at a person, when you look at someone or you don't look, you just ignore someone, what are you doing? You are imposing your attitudes. You say something is beautiful; then you will have to condemn something as ugly. And this dual attitude is simultaneously dividing you, so within you there will be two persons.

If you say that someone is angry and anger is bad, what will you do when you will feel angry? You will say that this is bad, then there will be problems because you say that "This is bad; this anger in me is bad." Then you have started to divide yourself into two persons—a bad person, an evil person within, and a good person, a saint. Of course, you are bound to be identified with the saint within, so the devil, Satan, the evil within you is to be condemned. You are divided in two. Now there will be a constant fight, a conflict. Now you cannot be an individual; you will be a crowd, a house divided against itself. Now there will be no peace, no silence. You will feel only tensions and anguish. This is what you are feeling, but you don't know why.

A divided person cannot be at peace. How can he be? Where to put your devil? You have to destroy it, and it is *you*; you cannot destroy it. You are not two. The reality is one, but because of your divisive attitude you have divided the outer reality. Now the inner is also divided accordingly—so everyone is fighting with himself. It is as if you are fighting against one hand—fighting the right hand with the left hand—and the energy is one. In my right hand and left hand, I am; I am flowing in both. But I can oppose one against the other, my right hand against my left hand, and I can create a conflict, a bogus fight. Sometimes I can deceive myself that the right hand has won, and now the left is down. But this is a deception, because I know that it is me in both and any moment I can put the left up and the right down. I am in both; both the hands are mine.

So howsoever much you think you have put your saint above and crushed the devil down, know that at any moment you can change the positions, and the saint will be down and the devil will be up. That creates fear, insecurity, because you know that nothing is certain. You know you are so loving this moment and you have crushed your hatred down, but you are afraid because at any moment the hatred can come up and the love will be just crushed down. And it can happen at any moment because within you are both.

Tantra says don't divide, be undivided; only then will you be victorious. How to be undivided? You don't condemn, don't say "this" is good and "that" is bad. Just withdraw all conceptions of purity and impurity. Look at the world, but don't say what it is. Be ignorant, don't be too much wise. Don't label, remain silent, noncondemnatory, nonjustifying. If you can remain silent about the world, by and by this silence will penetrate within. And if the division is not there outwardly, the division will disappear from the inner consciousness, because both *can* exist together.

But this is dangerous for society. That is why tantra was suppressed. This is dangerous! Nothing is immoral, nothing is moral; nothing is pure, nothing is impure. Things are as they are. A real tantric will not say that a thief is bad; he will say that he is a thief, that is all. And by using the word "thief" there is no condemnation in his mind. This "thief" is just a fact, not a condemnation. If someone says that "Here is a man who is a great saint," he will say, "Okay! He is a saint." But there is no evaluation in it. He will not say, "He is good," he will say, "Okay! He is a saint and that man is a thief," just like this is a rose and that is not a rose, this tree is high and that tree is low, night is dark and day is light—but without comparison.

But this is dangerous. Society cannot exist without condemning one thing and without appreciating the other—society cannot exist! Society exists on duality. That is why tantra was suppressed. It was thought to be antisocial, but it is not. It is not! But that very attitude of nonduality is transcendental. It is not antisociety, it is transcendental; it is beyond society.

Try this. Just move in the world without any values, just with natural facts: someone is this, someone is that. And then, by and by, you will feel a nondivision within yourself. Your polarities will be coming together, your "bad" and your "good" will be coming together. They will merge into one, and you will become one unity. There will be nothing as pure, nothing as impure. Know the reality.

The purity of other teachings is an impurity to us: tantra says that "What is basic for others is poisonous for us." For example, there are teachings which are based on nonviolence. They say violence is bad, nonviolence is good. Tantra says that nonviolence is nonviolence, violence is violence; nothing is good and nothing is bad.

There are teachings which are based on celibacy —*brahmacharya*. They say that brahmacharya is good, sex is bad. Tantra says sex is sex, brahmacharya is brahmacharya. One is a brahmachari and one is not. But these are simple facts, no values are attached to them. And tantra will never say that the brahmachari is good, the celibate is good, and that the one who is in sex is bad. Tantra will not say that. Tantra accepts things as they are. And why? Just to create a unity within you.

This is a technique to create a unity within you, to have a total existence within, undivided, nonconflicting, not opposed. Only then is silence possible. One who is trying to move to some place against something can never be at peace. How can he be? And one who is divided within himself, fighting with himself, how can he win? It is impossible. You are both, so who is going to win? No one is going to win, and you will be at loss because you will dissipate your energy in fighting unnecessarily. This is a technique to create a unity in yourself. Allow valleys to disappear; don't judge.

Jesus says somewhere, "Judge ye not so that ye may not be judged." But this was impossible for the Jews to understand, because the whole Jewish conception is morality-oriented: "This is good and that is not good." Jesus in his teaching, "Judge ye not," is talking in terms of tantra. If he was murdered, crucified, it is because of this. He had a tantra attitude— "Judge ye not."

So don't say that a prostitute is bad—who knows? And don't say that a puritan is good—who knows? And ultimately they both are part of one game. They are based on each other, on a mutual existence. So Jesus says, "Judge ye not," and this is what this sutra means: "Judge ye not so that ye may not be judged."

If you are nonjudging, not taking any moral standpoint, simply observing facts as they are, not interpreting them according to yourself, then you cannot be judged. You are transformed completely. Now there is no need for *you* to be judged by any divine power—there is no need! You have become divine yourself; you have become God yourself. Be a witness, not a judge.

CHAPTER 42

Alertness through tantra

♦

Doesn't an immoral life create hindrances in meditation?

Does a tantric object if one follows certain laws of life, calling them moral?

If nothing is impure, then how can the teaching of others be impure?

Does an unexpressed emotional desire return to the source and make a person energetic?

Isn't it suppression to make an effort to avoid suppression or indulgence?

The first question:

Is it not true that an immoral life creates hindrances in meditation?

hat is meditation? It is not your character, it is not what you do. It is what you are. It is not the character; it is the consciousness that you bring to whatsoever you do. The doing is irrelevant. Whether you are doing it consciously or not is the question, whether moral or immoral. Are you alert? If you are alert, meditation happens. If you are not alert, you live in sleep.

You can be moral while fully asleep, there is no problem. Rather, it is better to be moral if you want to be fully asleep because then society will not disturb you. Then no one will be against you. You can sleep conveniently. The society will help you.

You can be moral without being meditative, but the immorality will always be just behind you. Just like a shadow it will follow, and your morality will be just skin deep because your morality can only be imposed from without when you are asleep. It can only be pseudo, false, a façade, it cannot become your being. You will become moral outwardly, but inwardly you will remain immoral. And the more moral you become outwardly, the more immoral you will be within—in the same proportion, because your morality is bound to be nothing but a deep suppression. You cannot do anything else while asleep; you can only suppress.

And through this morality you will also become false. You will not be a person, but simply a "persona"—just a pseudo entity. Misery will follow, and you will consequently be on the verge of explosion—explosion of all that you have suppressed. It is there waiting for you. And if you are really honest in being moral while asleep, you will go mad. Only a dishonest person can remain moral without being mad. That is what hypocrisy means. Hypocrites just show that they are moral, but they are not, and they find ways and means to be immoral, constantly remaining moral on the surface or pretending to be moral. Then only can you remain sane; otherwise you will go insane.

This so-called morality leaves only two alternatives. If honest, you will become insane; if dishonest, you will become a hypocrite. So those who are clever, cunning, they are hypocrites. Those who are simple, innocent, who become victims of such teachings, go mad.

While asleep, real morality cannot happen to you. And what do you mean by "real morality"? Something which is a spontaneous flowering out of your being, not imposed from without. And real morality is not in opposition to immorality; a real morality is just an absence of immorality, it is not in opposition. For example, you can be taught to love your neighbors, to love everyone, to be loving. It can become a moral attitude, but the hate remains within. You force yourself to be loving, and a forced love cannot be real, cannot be authentic. It is not going to fulfill either you or the other person whom you love. No one can be fulfilled by this false love.

It is just like false water. No one's thirst can be quenched by it. The hatred is there, and the hatred is trying to assert. And a false love cannot be a real hindrance to it. Rather, the hatred will penetrate the false love and will even poison it, and your loving will become just a sort of hatred. It is very tricky and cunning.

A real morality happens to a person who has gone deep within himself—and the deeper you move, the more loving you become. It is not something forced against hatred; it is not something antagonistic to hatred. The deeper you move, the more love flows out of you. It has nothing to do with hatred at all; it is not concerned with hatred at all. The moment you reach to your center, you are loving without any moral imposition. You may not even be aware that you are loving. How can you be aware? This love will just be so natural that it will be just like breathing, just like your shadow following you. You will simply be loving.

Tantra teaches the inner journey. Morality will happen, but that will be a consequence, not a prerequisite. Be clear about this distinction. Tantra says don't be entangled with moral and immoral concepts. They are outer. Rather, move within. So the techniques are there for how to move within. And don't be concerned with moral and immoral, pure and impure; don't be concerned with distinctions. Just move within. Forget the outer—the outer world, the society and whatsoever the society has taught you. All that society teaches is bound to be dualistic, it is bound to be suppressive, it is bound to be a conflict within you. And if the conflict is there, you cannot move within.

So forget the conflict and forget all that creates conflict. Simply move within. The deeper you go, the more moral you will become, but that morality will not be the morality of the society. You will be moral without being moral—without being conscious that you are moral, because there is nothing opposed to it within you. You are simply loving because you feel blissful when you are loving. It is a bliss in itself. There is no end to it; no result is needed. It is not that you will get into the kingdom of God if you love. It is not a bargain. The morality that society preaches and so-called religions preach is a bargain: "Do this and you will get that. If you don't do this you will not get that. You will even be punished." It is a bargain.

Tantric morality is not a bargain, it is a happening. The deeper you move, the more you start living in the moment. You feel that to love is bliss. It is not a step, a condition, a bargain towards something else; it is enough unto itself. You love because you feel blissful in loving. You are not doing anything for your neighbor; you are not obliging anyone else. It is a pleasure to be loving. It is good for you right here and now. There is no future heaven or hell. Just now it creates the heaven, and the kingdom of God enters you. And this happens with all the virtues; they flower spontaneously.

Now look at the question: *Is is not true that an immoral life creates hindrances in meditation?* Really, the contrary is the truth. A meditative life creates hindrances in immoral life. Immoral life cannot create any hindrances. Immoral life means that you are nonmeditative—nothing else; you are fast asleep. That is why you are doing harm to yourself.

For tantra, the basic thing is meditation, alertness, awareness. Nothing else is more basic than that. When someone is immoral, it shows that he is not alert. It is just a symptom. The immoral life is just a symptom that he is not alert. What is ordinary teaching doing? Ordinary teachers will tell to this sleeping man who is immoral to be moral. He may change from immorality to morality, but the sleep continues.

So the whole effort is wasted because the real disease was not immorality; immorality was just a symptom. The disease was nonalertness, nonmeditativeness. That is why he was immoral. You can convert him to morality. You can create fear, and you can make afraid only that person who is asleep; otherwise you cannot create fear. You can create a fear about hell and you can create a profit motive for heaven. Both of these things are possible only while you are asleep. If you are not asleep, you cannot be threatened and you cannot be motivated because of profit. Those two things are meaningful only to the mind that is asleep.

So create the fear of punishment, and a person will move from immorality to morality—but he will move because of fear. Create a profit motive, and then he can move from immorality to morality —but he will move because of lust, greed, profit motivation. Greed and fear are part of the sleeping mind. He remains asleep, nothing basic is changed.

He is good for the society; that is okay. For the society the immoral person is a problem, but the moral person is not a problem. So society has solved its problems, but the man remains asleep. For himself, nothing is solved; he is now more convenient for the society. Previously, he was inconvenient. Try to observe the fact: an immoral person is inconvenient to the society, but he is convenient for himself. A moral person becomes convenient to the society, but he becomes inconvenient to himself.

So it is only that the coin is put upside down. That is why immoral persons look more happy and gay, and a moral person is serious, sad, burdened. The immoral person is fighting with the society and the moral person is fighting with himself. The immoral person feels worried only because there is always a fear of being caught. He is afraid of being caught, but he is enjoying. If no one catches him, if there is no fear of being caught, he is okay.

The moral person is caught in a struggle with himself. Nothing is okay with him; he is only okay with the society. Morality is a lubricant, it helps you to move easily with others. But then you become uneasy with yourself. Uneasiness remains either with the society or with yourself. Only when you become awakened does uneasiness leave you.

Tantra is concerned with the basic disease, not with the symptoms. Morality is removing symptoms. So tantra says don't be concerned with moral or immoral concepts. It does not mean that tantra says become immoral. How can tantra tell you to become immoral when tantra cannot even tell you to become moral? Tantra says the whole thing is irrelevant: don't talk about morality and immorality; come to the root. You can be moral or immoral, but that is only the symptom. Come to the root! The root is that you are asleep—fast asleep.

How to break this sleeping pattern? How to be aware and how not to fall again and again into sleep? That is what tantra is concerned with—and once you become alert your character will change. But that is a consequence. Tantra says you need not worry about it; that is a consequence. Inevitably it happens, so you need not worry about it. You are not to bring it, it will happen. You simply become more and more alert, and you will be less and less immoral. But this morality that will happen to you is not forced; it is not something done by you on your part. You are just trying to be alert, and it happens.

How can an alert man be violent? How can an alert man feel hatred and anger? It may look paradoxical, but it is so. One who is asleep cannot be without hatred. It is impossible. He can only pretend that there is no anger, no hatred. He can only pretend that there is love, compassion, kindness, sympathy. Those are all pretensions. Quite the contrary happens to the one who has awakened. If anger is needed, he can only pretend. He cannot be angry; he can only pretend! If anger is needed— and sometimes it is needed—he can only pretend. He cannot be sad, but if it is needed he can pretend that he is sad. Now these are impossible.

Love is natural now, as hatred was before. Love was a pretension before. Now hatred can only be a pretension—if it is needed. Jesus fighting with the moneychangers in the great temple was pretending. He cannot be angry, but he has chosen to pretend. He cannot be really angry. He cannot be angry, but he can use anger—as you use love and cannot be loving.

You use love for certain purposes. Your love is just to get something else; it is never simply love. You may be trying to get money, you may be trying to get sex, you may be trying to get something—ego fulfillment, a victory, a feeling that you are very powerful. You may be trying to get anything else, but it is never love.

A buddha can be angry if he thinks that it is going to help. Because of his love sometimes he may be angry, but that is only a pretension and only fools are befooled by it. Those who know, they will simply laugh. As meditation deepens, says tantra, you start changing. And it is beautiful when change happens to you. If you "do" it, it can never be something very deep because doing is just on the surface. So tantra says, allow it to happen from the being, from the very center. Let it flow from the center towards the periphery; don't force it from the periphery to the center. That is impossible.

Tantra will not say moral or immoral. The only thing is if you are asleep, try to change it. Allow yourself to become more and more alert, wherever you are. "If you are immoral," tantra says, "it is okay. We are not concerned with your immorality, we are concerned with your sleep and with how to transform it into alertness. Don't fight with the immorality. Just try to transform your sleep."

If you are moral it is okay. Tantra is not going to tell you first to become immoral and then to try. Neither does the immoral one have any need to transform himself into a moral person, nor does the moral person have to transform himself into an immoral one in order to get into meditation. All that they need is to change their quality of consciousness. So wherever you are, a sinner or a saint, for tantra there is no distinction. If you are asleep, then try the techniques for alertness. And don't try to change symptoms. The sinner is ill and the so-called saint is also ill because both are asleep.

The illness is the sleep, not your character. Your character is just a by-product. And whatsoever you do while remaining asleep will not make any basic change. Only one thing can change you and create a mutation and that is alertness. The question is one of how to become more and more alert. So whatsoever you do, make it an object of alertness.

If you do some immoral act, do it meditatively. It will not be long before the act will dissolve by itself and disappear. Then you will not be able to do it—not because you have created an armor against it, but because now you are more alert. And how can you do a thing which needs sleep as a requisite? You cannot do it.

Understand well this basic distinction between tantra and what others teach. Tantra is more scientific. It goes to the very root of the problem, transforms you from the very being—not from your outer sheath of character, of morality and immorality, of acts and doings. Whatsoever you do is just on the periphery; whatsoever you are is never on the periphery. The quality of the act, not the act itself, is meaningful for tantra.

For example, one butcher came to Nan Yin. He was a butcher and Nan Yin was a Buddhist monk who believed in nonviolence. His whole profession was of violence. The whole day he was killing animals. But when the butcher came to Nan Yin, he asked him, "What am I to do? My profession is one of violence. So am I to leave my profession first and is it that only then I can be a new man, or is there some other way?"

Nan Yin said, "We are not concerned with what you do. We are concerned with what you are. So you go on doing whatsoever you are doing, but be more alert. While killing, remain alert, meditative, and go on doing whatsoever you are doing. We are not concerned."

Nan Yin's followers became disturbed—because here was a person who was a follower of Buddha, a believer in nonviolence, allowing a butcher to continue. One disciple said, "This is not good. And we never expected that a person like you would allow a butcher to remain a butcher. And when he was asking, you should have told him to drop this. He himself was ready."

Nan Yin is reported to have said, "You can change the butcher's profession easily; he was himself ready. But in that way you cannot change his quality of consciousness. He will remain a butcher."

He may become a saint, but the quality of the mind will remain that of a butcher. That will be a deception for others and for himself also. Go and look at your so-called saints. Many of them remain butchers. The quality, the attitude, the violence, their very look towards you, is condemning, violent. You are a sinner and they are saints. When they see you, the very look is such that you are condemned, you are thrown into hell.

Nan Yin said, "So it is not good to change his outer life; it is better to bring a new quality to his mind. And it is good to let him remain a butcher, because he is disturbed by his butchery and violence. If he becomes a saint he will remain a butcher, but then he will not be disturbed. His ego will be strengthened. So this is good. He is disturbed that violence is there, and he has become at least this much aware—that this is not good. He is ready to change, but just readiness to change will not help. A new quality of the mind has to be developed. Let him meditate."

After one year had passed, the man came. He had become a different man. He was still a killer, but the man had changed although the doing remained the same. He came to Nan Yin again and he said, "Now I am a different man. I meditated and meditated and meditated, and my whole life has become a meditation because you told me to meditate in whatsoever I am doing. I am butchering animals, but the whole day I am meditating. Now what do you tell me to do?"

So Nan Yin said, "Now do not come to me. Allow your awareness to make a path for you. You need not come to me."

So the butcher said, "Now, only if you say remain in the profession will I pretend to be there. But as far as I am concerned, I am no more there. So if you allow me, I am not going back. But if you say to go, then it is okay. I will go and pretend, and I will continue."

This is how, when your quality changes—the quality of your consciousness changes—you become a different person altogether. And tantra is concerned with you, not with what you do.

The second question:

If one follows certain laws of life and calls this moral, then is there any objection from a tantric?

Tantra has no objections, but this having no objection is not the problem. Tantra has no objection whatsoever; tantra is not in any way condemning. It is not concerned to tell you, "Do this," or "Don't do that." If you feel good, if you feel happy following certain principles, then follow them. But following certain principles can never lead you to happiness because you are not going to change through principles and through following them. You will remain the same.

Principles are always borrowed, ideals are always borrowed. Someone else has given them to you. They are not your own; they have not grown out of your own experience. They are without roots. The society, the religion to which you are born, the teachers you happened to be near, they have given them to you. You can follow them and you can force yourself accordingly, but then you will be a dead person—not alive. You may create a certain peace around yourself, but that will be the peace of the cemetery—dead. You may be less vulnerable to disturbances, more closed in because of the principles, but then you will become less sensitive and less alive. So so-called principled men are always dead.

Look at them: they look silent, still, peaceful, at ease, but a certain deadness is always around them. The aura of death is always there. You cannot feel the feast of life around them, the festivity of being alive, the celebration of being alive. You can never feel that around them. They have created an armor around them—a safety armor. Nothing can penetrate them. The walls of their principles and character stop everything, but then they are behind the walls, imprisoned, and they are their own prisoners. If you choose this, tantra has no objection. You are free to choose a life which is not a life at all.

Once Mulla Nasruddin visited a cemetery, and he saw a very beautiful marble mausoleum. Inscribed on it was the name "Rothschild." Mulla is reported to have said, "Aha! Ahhh! This is what I call life. This is what I call living—a beautiful marble mausoleum." But howsoever beautiful it is, it is not life. It is marble—beautiful, rich—but not life. You can create a mausoleum out of your life through principles, ideals, impositions, but then you will be dead, although less vulnerable because death is not vulnerable.

Death is a security; life is always insecure. Anything can happen to a live person; nothing can happen to a dead person. He is secure. There is no future, no possibility for change. The last thing has happened to him—death. Now nothing can happen.

Principled personalities are dead personalities. Tantra is not interested in them. Tantra has no objection—if you feel good being dead, it is your choice. You can commit suicide, and this is a suicide. But tantra is for those who want to be more alive, and the truth, the ultimate, is not death, it is life. Remember that: the ultimate is not death. It is life—more life. Jesus has said, "Abundant life, infinite life."

So by being dead you can never reach to the ultimate. If it is life, and "abundant life," then by being dead you will never be in contact with it. Just by being more alive, more vulnerable, more sensitive, less principled and more alert, you will reach it. Why do you seek principles? You may not have observed why. It is because with principles you need not be alert. You need not be alert! If you live through principles you need not be alert.

Suppose I make a principle out of nonviolence and then I stick to it, or I make it a principle to be truthful and I stick to it; then it becomes a habit. I create a habit of being truthful, of always speaking the truth. It becomes a mechanical habit; now there is no need to be alert. I cannot speak lies because a principle, a habit, will always create a barrier. The society depends on principles, on inculcating and educating the children with principles. Then they become incapable, really, of being otherwise. If a person becomes incapable, he is dead.

Your truth can be alive only if it comes through alertness, not through principle. Each moment you have to be alert in order to be true. Truth is not a principle; it is something born out of your alertness. Nonviolence is not a principle; if you are alert you cannot be violent. But that is difficult and arduous. You will have to transform yourself totally. It is easy to create a life according to principles, rules and regulations. Then you need not worry. You need not worry about being more alert and aware; you can follow the principles.

Then you are just like a railway train running on the tracks. Those tracks are your principles. You are not afraid because you cannot miss the path. Really, you don't have any path; you have just mechanical rails on which your train is running. You will reach the destination, you need not be afraid. You will be asleep and the train will reach. It is running on dead paths; they are not alive.

But tantra says that life is not like that, it is more like a river. It is not running on iron rails, on tracks; really, it is like a river. The path has not even been charted before. As the river flows, the path is created. As the river moves, the path is created. The river will reach to the sea, and this is how life should be if you understand the tantra way.

Life is like a river. There is no precharted way; there are no maps to be given to you which are to be followed. Just be alive and alert, and then wheresoever life leads you go with full confidence in it. Tantra is a trust—a trust in the life force. Allow it to lead you, don't force it. Surrender to it and allow it to lead you towards the sea. Just be alert, that is all. While life leads you towards the sea just be alert so that you don't miss anything.

It is very important to remember that tantra is not simply concerned with the end; it is also concerned with the means. It is also concerned with the path, not only the destination. If you are alert, even this life will be a bliss. The very movement of the river is a bliss in itself. Passing through the valleys, through the rocks, falling down from the hills, moving into the unknown is itself a bliss.

Be alert here also, because the ocean, the ultimate, cannot just be a happening in the end. It cannot be. It is a growth. The river is "growing" to be the sea. It is not simply going to meet the sea, it is "growing" to be the sea, and this is possible only through rich experience, alert experiences, moving, trusting. This is how tantra looks at the search—at the human search. Of course, it is dangerous. If rivers can be run through predetermined paths, there would be less danger, fewer errors. But the whole beauty of aliveness would be lost.

So don't be a follower of principles. Just be a creator of more and more consciousness. Those principles will happen to you, but you will never feel imprisoned in them.

The third question:

The second sutra discussed yesterday says, "The purity of other teachings is an impurity to us. In reality, know nothing as pure or impure." If nothing is impure, then how can the teachings of others be impure?

Really, nothing is impure, but the teaching that something is pure and something is impure has to be discarded. Only in that sense does the sutra mean, "The purity of other teachings is an impurity to us." Nothing is pure and nothing is impure, but if someone teaches that something is pure and something is impure, tantra says that this has to be discarded. Only in this sense does the sutra say that "The purity of other teachings is an impurity to us." This is just a discarding. It is just saying don't make any distinctions, remain innocent.

But look at the complexity of life. If I say remain innocent, and if you then try innocence, that innocence will not be innocent. How can it be? If you have "tried" it, it has become a calculated thing. Then it cannot be innocent. If you try it, it cannot be! So what is to be done? Just discard

those things which create cunningness. Don't try to create any innocence; you cannot. Just discard those things which create cunningness in your mind. This is negative. When you have discarded the root causes of cunningness, innocence will have happened to you.

Nothing is pure or impure. But what is to be done then? Your mind is filled with distinctions: "This is pure and that is impure." So tantra says, "For us this is the only impurity. This mind filled with concepts of purity and impurity is the only impurity. If you can discard it, you have become pure."

This sutra is meaningful in another sense also. There are teachings with very fixed rules. For example, Catholic Christian teachings or Jaina teachings in India are against sex; they say that sex is impure, ugly, sin. Tantra says that nothing is ugly, nothing is impure, nothing is sin. Even sex can become a path—even sex can become a path towards salvation. It depends on you. It is not sex, it is you who determines the quality of it.

Even prayer can become a sin—and sex can become a virtue. It depends on you. The value is not in the object, the value is brought to it by you. Look at it—at this phenomenon—in a different way. Tantra says that even sex can become salvation, but then come to sex without any notions of purity and impurity, good or bad, morality and immorality. Come to sex as pure energy, just energy. Move in that energy as if you are moving into the unknown. Don't fall asleep, be alert! When sex brings you to the very root of your being, be alert. Don't fall asleep on the path. Be alert and experience everything, whatsoever is happening—the relaxation that comes, the tension that happens, the peak that comes, and the valley in which you are thrown back.

Your ego dissolves for a moment; you become one with your beloved or with your partner. For a moment, the two are not there. The bodies are two, but deep down there is a communion and they have become one. Be alert! Don't miss this moment in sleep. Be alert, see what is happening. This oneness is what was hidden in the sex act. The sex was just the outer core. Now this is the meaning— the central point. This is what you were longing for, this is what the hankering was for. This was for what there was the search—this unity, this dissolving of the ego, this feeling of oneness, this ecstasy of nontension, this ecstasy of relaxation. This was the meaning, the goal, and this is what you were searching for through this woman and that, through this man and that. You were searching and searching, but no woman can fulfill it, no man can give it.

Only through a deep tantric awareness does the sex act completely disappear, and a deep ecstasy is revealed. So tantra says it is you: if you can bring meditation to your love, to your sex, the sex is transformed. So tantra doesn't say that this is pure or that is impure—and if you want to use the old terminology of purity and impurity, then I will say that for tantra sleep is impure, alertness is pure, and all else is just meaningless.

The fourth question:

If an emotional desire or mood becomes exhilarating for us, and if we do not express it outwardly, does this energy necessarily go back to the source and make the person fresh and energetic?

Not necessarily! But if you are aware, then it is so, necessarily. Any energy, *any* energy, needs roots to move, and no energy can be destroyed. Energy is indestructible. It can only change into different forms; it can never become nothing. So when you try to suppress any energy, you are doing absolute nonsense with yourself. Energy cannot be suppressed; it can only be transformed. A suppressed energy will become a cancer. If you feel anger, two ordinary routes are available: either express it or suppress it. If you express it, then it becomes a chain, because then you create anger in the other person and he will express it—and there is no end to it. Then you will express it, and it can continue

for years. It continues! That is how everyone is living. It goes on and on.

Those who know deeply, they say that for lives also, for lives together, it goes on and on. You have been angry with a person in your past life, and still in this life you are repeating the same pattern with the same person. You are not aware, you are blissfully unaware. So it is good if you think something new is happening. Ninety-nine percent of the time nothing new is happening; old patterns are just being repeated again and again.

Sometimes you suddenly see a stranger, and you become angry. He has not done anything—you have not even met him before—but you feel depressed or angry or violent, or you want just to escape from this person. You feel bad. Why? It is some old pattern. Energy never dies, it remains, so if you express it, you are falling into an eternal chain. Someday you will have to come out of it. And the whole thing is useless, it is just wastage. Don't start the chain.

Then the other ordinary alternative is to suppress it, and when you suppress it you are creating a wound within yourself. That will be a suffering. That will create problems. And the anger will go on being suppressed, and you will become a volcano of anger.

So it may be that you are not now expressing your anger, but now your whole personality will become angry. There will be no eruptions, no one will see you beating someone and being violent, but now your whole personality will become angry because so much anger within poisons you. Now whatsoever you do the angry part is there. Even while you are loving someone, the angry part is there—in everything. If you are eating your food, the angry part will be there. You will be violent with your food, you will not be loving. If you are opening a door, the angry part will be there. You will be violent with the door.

One day in the morning, Mulla Nasruddin was passing down a street shouting oaths and saying very angrily, "The devil will take possession of your spirit and beets will grow in your belly"—and so it went on and on.

One man looked at him and said, "Mulla, whom are you cursing so much so early in the morning?"

Mulla said, "Who? I don't know. But don't worry, someone will turn up sooner or later."

If you are filled with anger, this happens: you are just waiting, and sooner or later someone will turn up. Inside you are bubbling with fire, just waiting for some objects, some medium, someone who should help you to unburden yourself. Then your whole personality becomes angry or violent or sexual. You can suppress sex, and then the suppressed sex becomes your whole personality. Then wherever you look you will see sex, in whatsoever you touch you will see sex, whatsoever you do will be a sexual act. You can suppress sex very easily; it is not difficult. But then sex will spread all over you. Your every fiber, every cell will become sexual.

Look at the celibates. Their minds become totally sexual; they dream about sex, they fight with sex, constantly they fantasize about sex. They are obsessed. That which could have been natural has become perverted. If you express it you create a chain, if you suppress you create a wound, and both are not good. So tantra says that whatsoever you do—for example, if you are angry, when you feel that anger is coming—be uninterruptedly aware. Don't suppress it and don't express it. Do a third thing, take the third alternative: be suddenly aware that anger is coming. This awareness changes the energy that is moving as anger into a different energy. The very energy that is known as anger becomes compassion. Through alertness there is the transmutation.

The same energy which is known as sex becomes *brahmacharya*, spirituality, through awareness. Alertness is the alchemy. Through it everything changes. Try it, and you will come to know. When you bring alertness, awareness, to any mood, any feeling, any energy, it changes its nature and quality. It is never the same again, and a new route opens. It is not going back again to the same place where

it was, from where it came; it is not moving outwards. The horizontal movement has stopped. With alertness it becomes vertical, it moves upwards. That is a different dimension. A bullock cart moves horizontally; an airplane moves vertically—upwards.

I would like to tell you one parable. One fakir, a Sufi, used to say that someone was presented an airplane, a very small aircraft, by a friend, who was a great king. But the man was poor. He had heard about airplanes, but he had never seen one. He knew only bullock carts, so he thought that this was a new device—a new type of bullock cart. He used his two bullocks to bring the airplane home, and then he used the airplane as a bullock cart. He was very happy. Of course, the small aircraft worked as a bullock cart. But then, by and by, just from being curious he started studying it. Then he came to understand that bullocks were not needed. It had a motor and it was able to go by itself, so he fueled it and used it as a motor car.

But then by and by, he became aware of the wings, and he thought, "Why are they there?" And it seemed to him that the man who had devised this machine must have been very intelligent, a genius; thus, he could not have added something unnecessarily. The wings showed that the machine could fly also. So he tried. Then the airplane came to its own; it became vertical.

You are using the mind that you have as a bullock cart. The same mind can become a motor car; then bullocks will not be needed. It has an inbuilt mechanism, but then too it will be moving horizontally. However, the same mind has wings. You have not observed, that is why you don't know that it has wings. It can fly! It can move upwards! And once it moves upwards, once your energies start moving upwards, the whole world is different. Your old questions simply fall down and your old problems are no more there, because you are now moving vertically.

All those problems were there because you were moving horizontally. The problems of a bullock cart are not problems for an airplane. The road was not good, so there was a problem. The road was blocked, so there was a problem. Now this is not a problem because the road is not used at all. Whether blocked or not, whether good or not, it is irrelevant.

Moral teachings are bullock-cart teachings; tantra's teaching is vertical. That's why all those problems are irrelevant for tantra. The energy that you know as anger, sex, greed or whatsoever, is moving horizontally. Once you bring your alertness to it, you have brought a new dimension. Just by being alert, you move upwards.

Why? Observe the fact: when you are alert, you are always above the fact. Become alert about anything, and you are always above the fact. The fact is somewhere below, down, and you are looking from above, from a peak. Whenever you have witnessed something you have moved upwards, and the thing has remained below. If this attention is really authentic and you can be uninterruptedly aware, then the energy that was moving horizontally as anger, as sex, will move into this new dimension. It will come near to you, to the witness. Then you have started flying. And for lives and lives you have been using the device which is meant for flying as a bullock cart, unnecessarily creating problems because you were just not knowing what is possible for you.

The fifth question:

You said that one should neither suppress nor indulge in anger, but that one should remain passively alert and meditative. Obviously, it will need a sort of inner effort to avoid suppression or indulgence, but then is this not also a sort of suppression?

No! It is an effort, but not "a sort of suppression." Every effort is not suppression. There are three types of effort. One is the effort which is expression. When you express your anger, it is an effort. Then the second type of effort is when you suppress it. When you express what you are doing, you are forcing your energy outwards to the person, to the object; you are throwing out your energy, the other is the target. Energy moves to the other; it is an effort. When you suppress, you return the energy to the original source, to your own heart. You force it back. It is an effort, but the direction is different. In expression it moves away from you; in suppression it again moves near you.

The third thing, alertness, passive alertness, is also an effort, but the dimension is different. The energy moves upwards. In the beginning it is an effort. When I say be passively alert, in the beginning even passivity is bound to be an effort. Only by and by, as you become more acquainted with it, will it not be an effort. And when it is not an effort, it becomes more passive—and the more passive, the more magnetic. It pulls the energy upwards.

But in the beginning everything is going to be an effort, so don't become a victim of words. It creates problems. Mystics have always been talking about effortlessness; they say don't make any effort. But in the beginning even this is going to be an effort. When we say be effortless we only mean don't force the effort. Allow it to come through awareness. If you force it, you will become tense. If you become tense, anger cannot move upwards. Tension is horizontal; only a nontense mind can be above, hovering like a cloud.

Look at the clouds floating with no effort. Just bring your witnessing in like a floating cloud. In the beginning it is going to be an effort, but remember only that it is going to become effortless. You will be forcing it and allowing it more and more.

This is difficult because language creates the difficulty. If I tell you to relax, what will you do? You will make a sort of effort. But then I tell you don't make any effort, because if you make any effort that will create tension and you will not be able to relax. I tell you to simply relax. Then you are at a loss, and you are bound to ask, "Then what do you mean? If I am not going to make any effort then what am I supposed to do?"

You are not supposed to do anything, but in the beginning that nondoing will look like a doing. So I will say, "Okay! Make a little effort, but remember that the effort is to be left behind. Use it as a starter just in the beginning. You cannot understand nondoing; you can only understand doing. So use the language of doing and action. Start, but use effort only as a starter. And remember, the sooner you leave it behind, the better."

I have heard that when Mulla Nasruddin became very old, he became a victim of insomnia, he couldn't sleep. Everything was tried—hot baths, pills, tranquilizers, syrups—but nothing was of any help. Everything was of no avail. And the children were disturbed because Mulla would not sleep himself, and he would not allow anyone in the house to sleep. So the whole night had become a nightmare for the whole family.

They searched desperately for any method, any medicine that would help Mulla to sleep, because the whole family was going crazy. So finally they brought a hypnotist. The children came very happily, and they told old Mulla, "Now you need not be worried, papa. This is a miracle man. He creates sleep within minutes. He knows the very magic of it, so don't be worried. Now there is no fear, and you will sleep."

The hypnotist showed a watch with a chain to Nasruddin and said, "Only very little faith will do the miracle. You need a little trust towards me. Just trust me, and you will fall like a small babe into deep sleep. Look at this watch."

He started moving that watch left and right. Nasruddin looked at it, and the hypnotist said, "Left-right, left-right. Your eyes are becoming tired, tired, tired. You are falling asleep, asleep, asleep, asleep."

Everyone was in joy—happy. Mulla's eyes closed, his head moved down, and he felt like a small babe going into deep sleep. A very rhythmic breathing came. The hypnotist took his fee, and he put his finger on his lips, just to indicate to the children he was not to be disturbed now. Then he sneaked out. The moment he was out, Mulla opened one eye and said, "That nut! Has he gone yet?"

He was making an effort to relax, so he relaxed "like a babe." He had started breathing rhythmically and closed his eyes, but it was all an effort. He was helping the hypnotist. He thought that he was helping the hypnotist—but it was effort on his part, so nothing happened. Nothing could happen. He was awake. If he could have just been passive, if he could have heard what was being said, looked at what was being shown, the sleep would have happened. No effort on his part was necessary; only passive acceptance was necessary. But even for you to bring your mind to that passive acceptance, in the beginning you will need effort.

So don't be afraid of effort. Start with effort, and just remember that effort has to be left behind and you have to move beyond effort. Only when you have moved beyond will you be passive, and that passive awareness brings the miracle.

With passive awareness, mind is no more there. For the first time your inner center of being is revealed, and there is a reason. Effort is needed for anything that is to be done in the world. If you want to do something in the world, anything, effort is needed. But if you want to do something in the inner, no effort is needed. Just relaxation is needed. Nondoing is the art there just as doing is the art in the outward, the outside world.

This passive alertness is the key. But don't become disturbed by language. Start with effort. Just keep in mind that you have to leave it, and go on leaving it. Even leaving will be an effort—but a moment comes when everything has gone. Then you are there, simply there not doing anything—just there, being. That "beingness" is *samadhi,* and all that is worth knowing, worth having, worth being, happens to you in that state.

CHAPTER 43

Finding the changeless through the changing

◆

66 *Be the unsame same to friend as to stranger, in honor and dishonor.*

67 *Here is the sphere of change, change, change. Through change consume change.*

orthrope says somewhere that the Western mind has been continuously searching for the theoretical component of existence—the causal link for how things happen, what is the cause, how the effect can be controlled, how man can manipulate nature. And the Eastern mind, says Northrope, has been on a different adventure. The search has been to find the aesthetic component of reality—not the theoretical, but the aesthetic.

The Eastern mind has not been much involved with the search to know how to manipulate nature, but it has been interested in how to be one with nature—not in how to conquer it, but in how to be in a deep friendship, a deep participation with it. The Western mind has been in a conflict, a struggle; the Eastern mind has been in a mystique, a love relationship. I don't know whether Northrope will agree with me or not, but my feeling is that science is a hatred, a relationship of hatred with nature; hence, struggle, fight, conquering, the language of victory.

Religion is a love relationship; hence, no conflict, no struggle. In another way, science is a male attitude and religion a female attitude. Science is aggressive, religion is receptive. The Eastern mind is religious. Or, if you allow me, I will say that wherever a religious mind is, it is Eastern. The scientific mind is Western. It makes no difference whether a man is born in the East or the West. I am using East and West as two attitudes, two approaches, not as two geographical denominations. You can be born in the West, but you may not belong there; you may be Eastern through and through. You may be born in the East, but you may not belong; you may be scientific, the approach may be mathematical, intellectual.

Tantra is absolutely Eastern. It is a way of participating with reality—a way how to be one with it, how to dissolve boundaries, how to move in an undifferentiated realm. Mind differentiates, creates boundaries, definitions, because mind cannot work without definitions, without boundaries. The more clear-cut the boundaries, the better the possibility for the mind to work. So mind cuts, divides, chops everything.

Religion is a dissolving of boundaries in order to move to the undifferentiated where there is no definition, where there is no limit to anything, where everything moves into everything else, where everything is everything else. You cannot cut, you cannot chop existence. The consequences are bound to be very different in each approach. By the scientific approach, by dividing, chopping, you can come only to dead particles, atoms, because life is something which cannot be cut into divisions. And the moment you cut it, it is no more there. It is as if someone goes to study a symphony by studying each single note. Each single note is part of the symphony, but it is not the symphony. The symphony is created by many notes dissolving into each other. You cannot study a symphony by studying notes.

I cannot study you by studying your parts, you

are not just a total of parts, you are more than that. When you divide and cut and analyze, life disappears; only dead parts are left. That is why science will never be capable of knowing what life is, and whatsoever is known through science will be about death—matter—it will never be about life. Science may become capable of manipulating life, of knowing the parts, the dead parts. It may be capable of manipulating life, but still *life* is not known, not even touched. Life remains unknowable for science. By the very method of its technology, its methodology, by the very approach, life cannot be known through it.

That is why science goes on denying—denying anything else other than matter. The very approach debars any contact with that which is life. And the vice versa happens also: if you move deeply into religion, you will start denying matter. Shankara says that matter is illusion, it is not there; it simply appears to be. The whole Eastern approach has been to deny the world, matter, anything material. Why? Science goes on denying life, the divine, consciousness. Deeper religious experiences go on denying matter—all that is material. Why? Because of the very approach. If you look at life without differentiation, matter disappears. Matter is life divided, differentiated. Matter means life defined, analyzed into parts.

So, of course, if you look at life undifferentiatedly and become part of it, in a deep participation, if you become one with existence as two lovers become one, matter disappears. That is why Shankara says that matter is illusion. If you participate in existence, it is. But Marx says that consciousness is just a by-product, it is not substantial; it is just a function of matter. If you divide life, then consciousness disappears, becomes illusory. Then only matter is.

What I am intending to say to you is this: Existence is one. If you approach it through analysis, it appears material, dead. If you approach it through participation, it appears as life, as divine, as consciousness. If you approach it through

science there is no possibility of any deep bliss happening to you, because with dead matter bliss is impossible. At the most it can only be illusory. Only with a deep participation is bliss possible.

Tantra is a love technique. The effort is to make you one with existence. So you will have to lose many things before you can enter. You will have to lose your habitual pattern of analyzing things; you will have to lose the deep-rooted attitude of fighting, of thinking in terms of conquering.

When Hillary reached to the highest peak of the Himalayas, Mount Everest, all of the Western world reported it as a conquering—a conquering of Everest. Only in a Zen monastery in Japan, on a wall newspaper, it was written, "Everest has been befriended"—not conquered! This is the difference: "Everest has been befriended"; now humanity has become friendly with it. Everest has allowed Hillary to come to it. It was not a conquering. The very word 'conquer' is vulgar, violent. To think in terms of conquering shows aggressiveness. Everest has received Hillary, welcomed him, and now humanity has become friendly; now the chasm is bridged. Now we are not unacquainted. One of us has been received by Everest. Now Everest has become part of human consciousness. This is a bridging.

Then the whole thing becomes totally different. It depends on how you look at it. Remember this before we enter the techniques. Remember this: tantra is a love effort towards existence. That is why so much of sex has been used by tantra: because it is a love technique. It is not only love between man and woman; it is love between you and existence, and for the first time existence becomes meaningful to you through a woman. If you are a woman, then existence becomes for the first time meaningful to you through a man.

That is why sex has been so much discussed and used by tantra. Think of yourself as absolutely asexual—as if all sex were removed from you the day you were born. Just think: all sex was completely removed from you the day you were born.

You will be unable to love; you will be unable to feel any affinity with anyone. It will be difficult to get out of yourself. You will remain enclosed, you will not be able to approach, to go out to meet someone. There in existence, you will be a dead thing, closed from everywhere.

Sex is your effort to reach out. You move from yourself; someone else becomes the center. You leave your ego behind, you go away from it to meet someone. If you really want to meet you will have to surrender, and if the other also wants to meet you he will also have to move out. Look at the miracle in love—at what happens. You move to the other and the other moves to you. He comes into you and you go into him or into her. You have changed places. Now he becomes your soul and you become her soul or his soul. This is a participation. Now you are meeting. Now you have become a circle. This is the first meeting where you are not enclosed in the ego. This meeting can become just a stepping-stone toward a greater meeting with the universe, with existence, with reality.

Tantra is based not on intellect, but on heart. It is not an intellectual effort, it is a feeling effort. Remember this, because that will help you to understand the techniques. Now we will enter the techniques.

---

66 Be aware of that which never changes in you.

The first technique: *Be the unsame same to friend as to stranger, in honor and dishonor.*

Be the unsame same—this is the base. What is happening in you? Two things are happening. Something in you remains continuously the same, it never changes. You may not have observed it, you may not have encountered it yet, but if you observe you will come to know that something in you remains constantly the same. Because of that sameness, you can have an identity. Because of that sameness, you feel yourself centered; otherwise you

will be a chaos. You say, "My childhood." Now what has remained of it? *Who* says, "My childhood"? Who is this "my," "me," "I"?

Nothing has remained of your childhood. If your pictures of your childhood are shown to you for the first time, you will not be able to recognize them. Everything has changed. Your body is no more the same; not a single cell has remained the same. Physiologists says that the body is a flux, it is riverlike. Every moment many cells are dying and many new ones are born. Within seven years your body will have changed completely. So if you are going to live seventy years, ten times over your body has renewed itself completely.

Every moment your body is changing, and your mind. You cannot recognize a photograph of your childhood, and if it were possible to give you a photograph of your mind, of your childhood mind, it would be impossible to recognize it. Your mind is even more of a flux than your body. Every moment everything changes. Even for a single moment nothing remains the same. In the morning you were different as far as your mind is concerned. In the evening you are totally a different person.

When someone would come to meet Buddha, before the person would depart, take leave of him, Buddha would say, "Remember, the man who has come to meet me is not the man who is going back. You are totally different now. Your mind has changed." Meeting with a Buddha is, of course, bound to change your mind for better or worse, but you cannot be the same.

You came here with a different mind; you will go with a different mind. Something has changed. Something new has been added, something has been deleted. And even if you are not meeting anyone, if you are just remaining by yourself, then too you cannot remain the same. Every moment the river is moving.

Heraclitus has said, "You cannot step twice in the same river." The same can be said about man: you cannot meet the same man again—impossible! And because of this fact, and because of our ignorance of it, life becomes a misery—because you go on expecting the other to be the same. You marry a girl and you expect her to be the same. She cannot be! Unmarried, she was different; married, she is completely different. A lover is something else, a husband is something totally different. You cannot expect your lover to meet you through your husband. That is impossible. A lover is a lover; a husband is a husband. The moment a lover becomes a husband, everything has changed. But you go on expecting. That creates misery—unnecessary misery. If we can recognize this fact that mind goes on moving and changing continuously, we will escape many, many miseries without any cost. All you need is simple awareness that mind changes.

Someone loves you and then you go on expecting love. But the next moment he hates you; then you are disturbed—not because of his hate, but only because of your expectation. He has changed. He is alive, so he is bound to change. But if you can see the reality as it is you will not be disturbed. The one who was in love a moment before can be in hate a moment later, but wait! One moment later he will be in love again. So don't be in a hurry, just be patient. And if the other can also see this changing pattern, then he will not be fighting for changing patterns. They change; that is natural.

So if you look at your body, it changes. If you try to understand your mind, it changes. It is never the same. Even for two consecutive moments, nothing is the same. Your personality goes on like a flux. If this is all and there is nothing which remains the same continuously, eternally, timelessly, then who will remember that this was "my childhood"? Childhood has changed, the body has changed, the mind has changed. Then who remembers? Then who knows about childhood and about youth and about old age? Who knows?

This knower must remain the same; this witness must remain the same. Only then can the witness have a perspective. The witness can say, "This was my childhood, this was my young age, this was my old age. This moment I was in love,

and this moment the love changed into hatred." This witnessing consciousness, this knower, is always the same.

So you have two realms or two dimensions existing together in you. You are both—the changing which is always changing and the nonchanging which is always remaining nonchanging. If you become aware of these two realms, then this technique will be helpful: *Be the unsame same.* Remember this: *Be the unsame same.* You are bound to be "unsame" on the periphery, but at the center remain the same.

Remember that which is the same. Just remembering will be enough; you need not do anything else.

It is nonchanging. You cannot change it, but you can forget it. You can be so engrossed, obsessed with the changing world around you—with your body, with your mind—that you may completely forget the center. The center is so much clouded by the changing flux—and, of course, there are problems: that which is constantly the same is difficult to remember because change creates problems.

For example, if a constant noise goes on around you, you will not be aware of it. If a clock on the wall goes on, tick-tock, tick-tock the whole day, you are never aware of it. But if suddenly it stops, you will immediately become aware. If something is constantly the same, there is no need to take any notice. When something changes, the mind has to take notice. It creates a gap, and the pattern vibrates. You were hearing it continuously, so there was no need to hear it. It was there, it became part of the background. But if now suddenly the clock stops, you will become aware. Your consciousness will suddenly come to the gap.

It is just as if one of your teeth falls out; then your tongue goes continuously to the place. When the tooth was there the tongue never tried to touch it. Now the tooth is not there—just a gap is there—then the whole day, howsoever you try, you cannot help it: the tongue goes to the gap. Why?

Because something is missing and the background has changed. Something new has entered.

Whenever something new enters, you become conscious—for many reasons. It is a safety measure. It is needed for your life—to survive. When something changes you have to become aware. It may be dangerous. You have to take notice, and you have to adjust again to the new situation that has come into being. But if everything is as it was, there is no need. You need not be aware. And this same element in you, what Hindus have called *atma*, the soul, has been there always from the very beginning, if there was any beginning. And it is going to the very end, if there is going to be any end. It has been eternally the same, so how can you be aware of it?

Because it is so permanently the same, eternally the same, you are missing it. You take notice of the body, you take notice of the mind because they are changing. And because you take notice of them, you start thinking that you are them. You know only them; you become identified.

The whole spiritual effort is to find the same amidst the unsame—to find the eternal in the changing, to find that which is always the same. That is your center, and if you can remember that center, only then will this technique be easy—or if you can do this technique, remembering will become easy. From both the ends you can travel.

Try this technique. The technique is to *be the unsame same to friend as to stranger.* To the friend and to the enemy, or to the stranger, be the "unsame same." What does it mean? It seems contradictory. In a way you will have to change, because if your friend comes to meet you, you will have to meet him differently, and if a stranger comes you will have to meet him differently. How can you meet a stranger as if you know him already? You cannot. The difference will be there, but still, deep down remain the same. The attitude must remain the same, but the behavior will be "unsame." You cannot meet an unknown person as if you know him already. How can you? You

can pretend at the most, but pretensions will not do. The difference will be there.

There is no need to pretend with a friend that he is a friend. With a stranger, even if you try to act as if he is a friend, it will be pretension—something new. You cannot be the same; unsameness will be necessary. As far as behavior is concerned you will be different, but as far as your consciousness is concerned you can be the same. You can look at the friend as at the stranger.

It is difficult. You may have heard, "Look at the stranger as if he is a friend," but that is not possible if what I am saying is not possible. First look at your friend as the stranger; only then you can look at the stranger as at the friend. They are correlated.

Have you ever looked at your friends as if they are strangers? If you have not, then you have not looked at all. Look at your wife: do you really know her? You may have lived with her for twenty years or even more, and the more you live with her, the more is the possibility that you will go on forgetting that she is a stranger—and she remains a stranger. Howsoever you love her, it will not make any difference.

Really, if you love her more, the more strange she will look—because the more you love, the deeper you penetrate and the more you know how riverlike she is, moving, changing, alive, every moment different. If you don't look deeply, if you just stick to the level that she is your wife, that this is her name or that, then you have chosen a particular fragment, and you go on thinking of that particular fragment as your wife. And whenever she has to change, she has to hide her changes. She may not be in a loving mood, but she has to pretend because you expect love from your wife.

Then everything becomes false. She is not allowed to change; she is not allowed to be herself. Then something is being forced. Then the whole relationship goes dead. The more you love, the more you will feel the changing pattern. Then each moment you are a stranger. You cannot predict; you cannot say how your husband is going to behave tomorrow morning. You can predict only if you have a dead husband; then you can predict. Predictions are possible only about things, never about persons. If some person is predictable, know well he is dead; he has died. His living is just false, so you can predict. Nothing is predictable about persons because of the change.

Look at your friend as at a stranger; he *is* one! Don't be afraid. We are afraid of strangers, so we go on forgetting that even a friend is a stranger. If you can look at the stranger in your friend also, you will never get frustrated because you cannot expect anything from a stranger. You take your friends for granted; hence, expectations and then frustrations—because no one can fulfill your expectations, no one is here to fulfill your expectations. Everyone is here to fulfill his own expectations, no one is here to fulfill you. Everyone is here to fulfill himself or herself, but you expect others to fulfill you and others expect you to fulfill them. Then there is conflict, violence, struggle and misery.

Go on always remembering the stranger. Don't forget, even your closest friend is a stranger—as far removed from you as possible. If this feeling happens to you, this knowing, then you can look at the stranger and you can find a friend there also. If a friend can be a stranger, then a stranger can be a friend. Look at a stranger: he doesn't know your language, he doesn't belong to your country, he doesn't belong to your religion, he doesn't belong to your color. You are white and he is black or you are black and he is white. You cannot communicate through language; you don't belong to the same church. So there is no common ground in nation, religion, race or color—no common ground! He is totally a stranger. But look into his eyes, and the same humanity is there, that is the common ground; and the same life, that is the common ground; and the same existence, that is the root of your being friends.

You may not understand his language, but you can understand him. Even silence can be communicative. Just by your looking deep down into his eyes, the friend will be revealed. And if you know how to look, then even an enemy cannot deceive you. You can look at the friend in him. He cannot prove that he is not your friend. Howsoever far removed, he is near you because you belong to the same existential current, to the same river to which he belongs. You belong to the same earth of being.

If this happens, then even a tree is not far away from you, then even a stone is not far away from you. A stone is very strange. There is no meeting ground, no possibility of any communication—but the same existence is there. The stone also exists, the stone also participates in being. He is there—I call it "he"—he also takes up space, he also exists in time. The sun also rises for him, as it rises for you. One day he was not, as you were not, and one day you will die and he will also die. The stone will disappear. In existence we meet. The meeting is the friendship. In personality we differ, in manifestation we differ; in essence we are one.

In manifestations we are strangers, so howsoever close we come we remain far away. You can sit close, you can embrace each other, but there is no possibility to come more close. As far as your changing personality is concerned, you are never the same. You are never similar; you are always strangers. You cannot meet there because before you can meet you have changed. There is no possibility of meeting. As far as bodies are concerned and minds are concerned there can be no meeting, because before you can meet you are no more the same.

Have you ever observed? You feel love for someone—a very deep upsurge. You are filled with it, and the moment you go and say, "I love you," it has disappeared. Have you observed? It may not be there now, it may be just a memory. It was there, but it is not there now. The very fact that you asserted it, made it manifest, has made it enter into the realm of change. When you felt it, it may have been deep in the essence, but when you bring it out you are bringing it into the pattern of time and change, it is entering into the river. When you say, "I love you," by then it may have disappeared completely. It is so difficult, but if you observe, it will become a fact. Then you can look. In the friend there is the stranger and in the stranger the friend. Then you can remain *the unsame same.* You change peripherally; you remain the same in the essence, in the center.

In honor and dishonor.... Who is honored and who is dishonored? You? Never! Only that which is changing, and that you are not. Someone honors you; if you take it that he is honoring *you,* you will be in difficulty. He honors a particular manifestation in you, not you. How can he know you? You don't even know yourself. He honors a particular manifestation; he honors something which has come into your changing personality. You are kind, loving; he honors it. But this kindness and this love are just on the periphery. The next moment you will not be loving, you may be filled with hate. There may be no flowers, only thorns. You may not be so happy. You may be just sad, depressed. You may be cruel, angry. Then he will dishonor you. Then again the loving manifestation. Others come in contact not with you, but with your manifestations.

Remember this, they are not honoring and dishonoring *you.* They cannot do either because they don't know you; they cannot know you. If even you are not aware of yourself, how can they be? They have their own formulas, they have their theories, they have their measurements and criteria. They have their touchstones and they say, "If a man is such and such we will honor him, and if a man is such and such we will dishonor him." So they act according to their criteria, and you are never near their touchstones—only your manifestations.

They can call you a sinner one day and a saint another. They can call you a saint today, and the next day they may go against you, stone you to death. What is happening? They come in contact with your periphery, they never come in contact with you. Remember this, that whatsoever they are saying, it is not about you. You remain beyond; you remain outside. Their condemnations, their

appreciations, whatsoever they do is not really concerned with you, just with your manifestations in time.

I will tell you one Zen anecdote. One young monk lived near Kyoto. He was beautiful, young, and the whole town was pleased. They honored him. They believed him to be a great saint. Then one day everything turned upside down. One girl became pregnant, and she told her parents that this monk was responsible. So the whole town turned against him. They came, and they burned his cottage. It was morning, and a very cold morning, a winter morning, and they threw the child onto the monk.

The father of the girl told him, "This is your child, so take the responsibility."

The monk simply said, "Is it so?" And then the child started weeping, so he forgot about the crowd and began caring for the child.

The crowd went and destroyed the whole cottage, burned it down. Then the child was hungry and the monk was without any money, so he had to go to beg in the city for the child. Who will give him anything now? Just a few moments before he was a great saint, and now he is a great sinner. Who will give him anything now? Wherever he tried, they closed their doors in his face. They condemned him completely.

Then he reached to the same house—to the house of the girl. The girl was very much distressed, and then she heard the child weeping and screaming, and the monk standing there just saying, "Don't give anything to me, I am a sinner. But the child is not a sinner; you can give milk to this child." Then the girl confessed that just to hide the real father of the child, she had taken the name of the monk. He was absolutely innocent.

So the whole town turned around again. They fell at his feet, started asking his forgiveness. And the father of the girl came, took the child back with weeping eyes, tears rolling down, and he said, "But why did you not say so before? Why did you not refuse in the morning? The child does not belong to you."

The monk is reported to have said again, "Is it so?" In the morning he had said, "Is it so? This child belongs to me?" And in the afternoon he said, "Is it so? This child doesn't belong to me?"

This is how this sutra has to be applied in life. In honor and dishonor, you must remain *the unsame same*. The innermost center must remain the same, whatsoever happens to the periphery. The periphery is bound to change, but you must not change. And because you are two, the periphery and the center, that is why opposite, contradictory terms have been used: *Be the unsame same....* And you can apply this technique to all opposites: in love and hate, poverty and richness, comfort and uncomfort, or in anything, remain *the unsame same*.

Just know that the change is happening only to your periphery; it cannot happen to you, it is impossible. So you can remain detached, and this detachment is not forced. You simply know it is so. This is not a forced detachment; this is not any effort on your part to remain detached. If you *try* to remain detached, you are still on the periphery; you have not known the center. The center is detached; it has always been so. It is transcendental. It is always the beyond. Whatsoever happens below never happens to it.

Try this in polar situations. Go on feeling something in you which is the same. When someone is insulting you, focus yourself to the point where you are just listening to him—not doing anything, not reacting—just listening; he is insulting you. And then someone is praising you. Just listen. Insult-praise, honor-dishonor: just listen. Your periphery will get disturbed. Look at it also; don't change it. Look at it; remain deep in your center, looking from there. You will have a detachment which is not forced, which is spontaneous, which is natural.

And once you have the feeling of the natural detachment, nothing can disturb you. You will remain silent. Whatsoever happens in the world, you will remain unmoved. Even if someone is killing you, only the body will be touched—not you. You will remain beyond. This "beyondness"

leads you into existence, into that which is bliss, eternal, into that which is true, which is always, into that which is deathless, into life itself. You may call it God or you can choose your term. You can call it *nirvana*, whatsoever you like, but unless you move from the periphery to the center and unless you become aware of the eternal in you, religion has not happened to you, neither has life happened to you. You are missing, simply missing all. That is possible—to miss the ecstasy of living.

Shankara says that "I call the man a *sannyasin* who knows what is changing and what is non-changing, who knows what is moving and what is nonmoving." This, in Indian philosophy, is known as discrimination—*vivek*. To discriminate between these two, the realm of the change and the realm of the unchanging—this is called *vivek*, discrimination, awareness.

This sutra can be used very, very deeply and very easily with whatsoever you are doing. You feel hunger? Remember the two realms. Hunger can only be felt by the periphery because the periphery needs food, needs fuel. You don't need food, you don't need any fuel, but the body needs them. Remember, when hunger happens it is happening to the periphery; you are just the knower of it. If you were not there, it would not be known. If the body were not there, it would not happen. By your absence only knowledge will not be there because the body cannot know. The body can have it, but it cannot know it. You know it; you cannot have it.

So never say that "I am hungry." Always say within, "I know that my body is hungry." Give emphasis to your knowing. Then the discrimination is there. You are becoming old; never say, "I am becoming old." Just say, "My body is becoming old." Then in the moment of death also you will know, "I am not dying; my body is dying. I am changing bodies, just changing the house." If this discrimination deepens, one day, suddenly, there will be enlightenment.

67 Remember that everything changes.

The second sutra: *Here is the sphere of change, change, change. Through change consume change.*
The first thing to understand is that everything you know about is change; except for you, the knower, everything is change. Have you seen anything which is not change? This whole world is a phenomenon of change. Even the Himalayas are changing. They say—the scientists who work on it—that they are growing; these Himalayas are the youngest mountains in the world, still a child, really, still growing. They have not yet become mature; they have not reached to the point from where something begins to decline. They are still rising.

If you compare them with Vindhyachal, another mountain, they are just children. Vindhyachal is one of the oldest—and some say the oldest mountain in the world. It is so old, it is decreasing, coming down. For centuries it has been coming down—just dying, in its old age. So even a Himalaya which looks so stable, unchanging, unmoving, is changing. It is just a river of stones. Stones make no difference; they are also riverlike, floating. Comparatively everything is changing. Something looks more changing, something looks less changing, but that is only relative.

Nothing is unchanging that you can know. Remember my point: nothing that you can know is unchanging. Nothing is unchanging except the knower. But that is always behind. It always "knows"; it is really never known. It can never become the object; it is always the subject. Whatsoever you do or know, it is always behind. You cannot know it. When I say this, don't get disturbed. When I say that you cannot know it, I mean you cannot know it as an object. I can look at you, but how can I look at myself in the same way? It is impossible because to be in a relationship of knowledge two things are needed—the knower and the known.

So when I look at you, you are the known and I am the knower, and the knowledge can exist as a bridge. But where to make the bridge when I look at myself, when I am trying to know myself? There only I am, alone—totally alone. The other bank is missing, so where to create the bridge? How to know myself?

So self-knowledge is a negative process. You cannot know yourself directly; you can simply go on eliminating objects of knowledge. Go on eliminating the objects of knowledge. When there is no object of knowledge, when you cannot know anything, when there is nothing but the vacuum, the emptiness—and this is what meditation is: just eliminating all objects of knowledge—then a moment comes when consciousness is, but there is nothing to be conscious of; knowing is, but there is nothing to know. The simple, pure energy of knowing remains and nothing is left to be known. There is no object.

In that state when there is nothing to be known, it is said that you know yourself in a certain sense. But that *knowledge* is totally different from all other knowledge. It is misleading to use the same word for both. There have been mystics who have said that self-knowledge is contradictory, the very term is contradictory. Knowledge is always of the other; self-knowledge is not possible. But when the other is not, something happens. You may call it self-knowledge, but the word is misleading.

So whatsoever you know is change. Everywhere, even these walls, are constantly changing. Now physics supports this. Even the wall which looks so stationary, nonchanging, is changing every moment. A great flux is on. Every atom is moving, every electron is moving. Everything is moving fast, and the movement is so fast that you cannot detect it. That is why the wall looks so permanent. In the morning it was like this, in the afternoon it was like that, in the evening it was like this, yesterday it was like this and tomorrow it will be like this. You look at it as if it is the same, but it is not. Your eyes are not capable of detecting such great movement.

The fan is there. If the fan is moving very fast, you will not be able to see the space, it will look like just one circle. Space cannot be seen because the movement is fast, and if the movement is so fast you will not see that the fan is moving at all. You will not be able to detect the movement. The fan will look stationary; you will even be able to touch it. It will be stationary, and your hand will not even be able to enter into the gaps, because your hand cannot move so fast as to go into the gaps. Before you move, another blade will have come. Before you move, still another blade will have come. You will always touch the blade, and the movement will be so fast that the fan will look like it is non-moving. So things that are nonmoving are very fast moving: that is why there is the appearance that they are stationary.

This sutra says that everything is change: *Here is the sphere of change....* On this sutra Buddha's whole philosophy stands. Buddha says that everything is a flux, changing, nonpermanent, and that one should know this. Buddha's emphasis is so much on this point, his whole standpoint is based on it. He says, "Change, change, change: remember this continuously." Why? If you can remember change, detachment will happen. How can you be attached when everything is changing?

You look at a face; it is very beautiful. When you look at a face that is very beautiful, there is a feeling that this is going to remain. Understand it deeply. Never expect that this is going to remain. But if you know that this is changing fast, that this is beautiful this moment and it may be ugly the next, how can you feel any attachment? It is impossible. Look at a body: it is alive; the next moment it will be dead. All is futile, if you feel the change.

Buddha left his palace, his family—his beautiful wife, his child—and when someone asked him why, he said, "Where there is nothing permanent, what is the use? The child will die." And the night Buddha left, the child was born. He was just a few hours old. Buddha went into his wife's room to have a last look. The wife's back was towards the door. She was holding the child in her arms in sleep. Buddha wanted to say goodbye, but then he resisted. He said, "What is the use?"

A moment came in his mind when a thought flashed that "The child is just one day old, a few hours old, and I must have a look." But then he said, "What is the use? Everything is changing. This day the child is born, and the next day the child will die. And one day before he was not here. Now he is here, and one day again he will not be here. So what is the use? Everything is changing." He left—turned back and left.

When someone asked, "Why have you left all that?" he said, "I am in search of that which never changes, because if I stick to that which changes there is going to be frustration. If I cling to that which is changing, I am stupid, because it will change, it will not remain the same. Then I will be frustrated. So I am in search of that which never changes. If there is anything which never changes, only then does life have any worth and meaning. Otherwise everything is futile." He based his whole teaching on change.

This sutra is beautiful. This sutra says, *Through change consume change.* Buddha would never say the second part. The second part is basically tantric. Buddha will say that everything is change; feel it, and then you will not cling to it. And when you don't cling to it, by and by, by leaving everything that changes, you will fall into yourself to the center where there is no change. Just go on eliminating change, and you will come to the unmoving, to the center—the center of the wheel. That is why Buddha has chosen the wheel as the symbol of his religion: because the wheel moves, but the center on which it moves remains unmoving. So the *sansara*—the world—moves like a wheel. Your personality moves like a wheel, and your innermost essence remains the center on which the wheel moves. It remains unmoving.

Buddha will say life is change. He will agree with the first part. The next—the second part—is typically tantric: *Through change consume change.*

Tantra says don't leave that which is changing; move into it. Don't cling, but move. Why be afraid? Move into it, live it out. Allow it to happen, and you move into it. Consume it through itself. Don't be afraid, don't escape. Where will you escape? How can you escape? Everywhere there is change. Tantra says everywhere is change. Where will you escape? Where can you go?

Wherever you go the change will be there. All escape is futile, so don't try to escape. Then what to do? Don't cling. Live the change, be the change. Don't create any struggle with it. Move with it. The river is flowing; you flow with it. Don't even swim; allow the river to take you. Don't fight with it, don't waste your energy by fighting with it; just relax. Be in a let-go and move with the river.

What will happen? If you can move with a river without any conflict, without any direction of your own, if the river's direction is your direction, suddenly you will become aware that you are not the river. You will become aware that you are not the river! Feel it. Someday try it in a river. Go there, relax, and allow the river to take you. Don't fight; become the river. Suddenly you will feel that the river is all around, but you are not the river.

In fighting you may forget this. That is why tantra says, *Through change consume change.* Don't fight. There is no need because in you the change cannot enter. So don't be afraid. Live in the world. Don't be afraid because in you the world cannot enter. Live it. Don't choose this way or that.

There are two types of people: one that will cling to the world of change and one that will escape. But tantra says it is change, so to cling is futile and to escape also. What is the use? Buddha says, "What is the use of remaining in the world of change?" Tantra says, "What is the use of escaping from it?"

Both are futile. Rather, allow it to happen. You are not concerned with it; it is happening, you are not even needed for it. You were not and the world was changing, and you will not be and the world will go on changing—so why create any fuss about it?

Consume change through change. This is a very deep message. Consume anger through anger, consume sex through sex, consume greed through greed, consume the *sansara* through the sansara. Don't fight with it, be relaxed, because fight creates tensions and fight creates anxiety, anguish, and you will be unnecessarily disturbed. Allow the world to be as it is.

There are two types of persons. One type is those persons who cannot allow the world to be as it is. They are called revolutionaries. They will change it, they will struggle to change it. They will destroy their whole life in changing it, and it is already changing. They are not needed, they will only consume themselves. They will burn out in changing the world, and it is already changing. No revolution is really needed. The world is a revolution; it is changing.

You may wonder why India has not created great revolutionaries. It is because of this insight that everything is already changing. Why are you disturbed to change it? You can neither change it nor stop the change. It *is* changing. Why waste yourself?

One type of personality always tries to change the world. In religion's eyes he is neurotic. Really, he is afraid of coming to himself, so he goes on and becomes obsessed with the world. The state has to be changed, the government has to be changed, the society, the structure, the economics, everything has to be changed, and he will die, and he will never have a moment of ecstasy in which he could know what he was, and the world will continue and the wheel will go on moving. It has seen many revolutionaries, and it goes on moving. Neither can you stop it nor can you accelerate the change.

This is a mystic's attitude: mystics say there is no need to change the world. But mystics are also of two types. One will say there is no need to change the world, but there is a need to change oneself. He also believes in changing—not in changing the world, but himself.

But tantra says there is no need to change anyone—neither the world nor yourself. That is the deepest core of mysticism. You need not change the world and you need not change yourself. You are just to know that everything is changing, and to float in the change and relax in the change.

And the moment there is no effort to create any change, you can relax totally—because if the effort is there you cannot relax. Then tension will be there because in the future something of value is going to happen: the world is going to change. The world is going to become communistic, or the earthly paradise is to come, or some utopia in the future, or you are going to enter into the kingdom of God, or into *moksha*. Somewhere in paradise the angels are waiting to welcome you—but "somewhere" is the future. With this attitude you are going to be tense.

Tantra says forget it. The world is already changing and you are also already changing. Change is existence, so don't become worried about it. It is already happening without you; you are not needed. You just float in it with no anxiety for the future, and suddenly amidst change you will become aware of a center within you which never changes, which has remained always as it is—the same.

Why does it happen? Because if you are relaxed, then the changing background gives you the contrast, and through it you can feel the non-changing. If you are in any effort to change the world or yourself, you cannot look at the small unmoving center within you. You are so much obsessed with change, you are not able to have a look at what is the case.

The change is all around. The change becomes the background, the contrast, and you are relaxed. So there is no future in your mind—no future thoughts. You are here now; this moment is all. Everything is changing, and suddenly you become aware of a point within you which has never changed. *Through change consume change.* This is what is meant by *Through change consume change.*

Don't fight. Through death become deathless; through death allow death to die. Don't fight with it. The tantra attitude is difficult to conceive of, because our minds want to do something and this is a nondoing. It is just relaxing, not doing, but this is one of the most hidden secrets. If you can feel this, you need not bother about anything else. This one technique can give you all.

Then you need not do anything because you have come to know the secret that through change, change can be consumed, and through death, death can be consumed, and through sex, sex can be consumed, and through anger, anger can be consumed. Now you have come to know the secret that through poison, poison can be consumed.

CHAPTER 44

Secrets of love and liberation

♦

Why has modern man become incapable of love?

To realize the center, must the peripheral movements cease?

Isn't it difficult to dissolve change through change without anxiety and disappointment?

What is tantra's attitude toward handling the modern city life of tensions and exertions?

The first question:

In reference to Your statement that tantra is a love technique, please explain why modern man and woman have become incapable of love.

ove is spontaneous. It cannot be con-trolled. You cannot "make" love; you cannot do anything about it. And the more you do, the more you will miss it. You have to allow it to happen. You are not needed for it. Your presence is the hindrance. The more you are absent, the better. When you are not, love happens. Because of their inability to be absent, modern man and woman have become incapable of love. They are only capable of doing things. The whole modern mind is based on doing. Whatsoever can be done, modern man can do more efficiently than any man that has ever existed. Whatsoever can be done, we can do more efficiently. We are the most efficient century; we have turned everything into technology—into a problem of how to "do" it. We have developed one dimension and that is the dimension of doing, but in developing this dimension we have lost much.

At the loss of being we have learned how to do things, so that which can be done we do better than anyone—better than any society that ever existed on earth. But when the question of love comes, a problem arises because love cannot be done. And not only is this so with love; we have become incapable of all that cannot be done.

For example, meditation: we have become incapable of it, it cannot be done. Or play: we have become incapable of it, it cannot be done. Or joy, happiness: we have become incapable of them because they cannot be done. They are not acts; you cannot manipulate them. On the contrary, you have to let yourself go. Then joy happens to you, then happiness comes to you, then love enters you, then love takes possession. And because of this possession we have become afraid.

Modern man, the modern mind, wants to possess everything and not be possessed by anything. Modern man wants to be the master of everything, and you can only be the master of things—not of happenings. You can be the master of a house, you can be the master of a mechanical device; you cannot be the master of anything which is alive. Life cannot be mastered; you cannot possess it. On the contrary, you have to be possessed by it. Only then is there contact with it.

Love is life, and it is greater than you. You cannot possess it. I would like to repeat it: love is greater than you; you cannot possess it. You can only allow yourself to be possessed by it; it cannot be controlled. The modern ego wants to control everything, and you become scared of whatsoever you cannot control. You become afraid, you close the door. You close that dimension completely because fear enters. You will not be in control. With love you cannot be in control, and the whole trend which has led to this century was one of how to control. All over the world, and particularly in the West, the trend is for how to control nature,

621

how to control everything, how to control energies.

Man must become the master, and you have become the master—of course, only of those things which are possible to possess, and side by side you have been developing an incapacity for those things which cannot be possessed. You can possess money; you cannot possess love. And because of this we have been turning everything into a thing. You even go on turning persons into things because then you can possess them. If you love a person, you are not the master; no one is the master. Two persons love each other, and no one is the master—neither the lover nor the beloved. Rather, love is the master and both are possessed by a greater force than themselves, encircled by a greater force—a whirlwind. If they try to possess each other, they will miss. Then they can possess each other. Then the lover will become the husband and the beloved will become the wife. Then they can possess, but a husband is a thing and a wife is a thing. They are not persons. You can possess them. They are dead entities, legal labels—not alive.

We go on turning persons into things just to possess them, and then we feel frustrated—because we wanted to possess the person and the person cannot be possessed. When you possess a person, he is no more a person; he is a dead thing, and you cannot be fulfilled by a dead thing. Look at this contradiction: you can be fulfilled only by persons, never by things, but your mind desires possessions —so you turn them into things. Then you cannot be fulfilled. Then frustration sets in.

Possessiveness, the attitude to possess, has killed the capacity to love. Don't think in terms of possession. Rather, think in terms of being possessed. That is what surrender means—being possessed: you allow yourself to be possessed by something greater than you. Then you will not be in control. Then a greater force will take you. Then the direction will not be yours. Then you cannot choose the goal. Then the future is unknown; you cannot be secure now. Moving with a greater force than yourself, you are insecure, afraid.

If you are afraid and insecure, it is better not to move with great forces. Just work with lower forces than you; then you can be the master, and you can decide the goal beforehand. Then you will achieve the goal, but you will not get anything out of it. You will have just wasted your life.

The secret of love and the secret of prayer and the secret of anything that can make you fulfilled is surrender—the capacity to be possessed. The problem with love exists because this capacity is not there. There are other reasons also, but this is the base. The first reason is too much emphasis on intellect, reason. So man is lopsided. Your head has grown and your heart has remained absolutely neglected. And love is not a capacity of the intellect. It has a different center; it has a different focus, source. It is in your heart, it is your feeling; it is not reasoning. But the whole modern education consists of reasoning, logic, intellect, mind. The heart is not even talked about. It is denied, really; it is just a poetic fiction.

It is not! It is a reality! Just look at it in this way: if from the very beginning a child is brought up without any training of the mind or the reasoning, without any intellectual training, will he have an intellect? He cannot!

There have been such cases. Sometimes it has happened that wolves have brought up a human child. Just ten years before, one child was caught in a forest. The wolves had brought him up. He was fourteen years of age. He couldn't even stand on two legs; he would run on all fours. He couldn't speak a single word; he would roar like a wolf. He was in every way a wolf, and fourteen years of age. Those who caught him named him Ram. The child took six months to learn the name. Within a year the child died, and the psychologists who worked on him suspected that he died because of too much strain on the intellect. This forcing, this training to get him to stand on two feet, this memory training to get him to remember the name, the effort to make him a human being, killed him.

He was robust in health when he was caught—

more healthy than any human being ever is. He was just like an animal. But this training killed him. Every effort was made so that if you could have asked him, "What is your name?" he would be able to say, "Ram." This was his whole intellect. After six months of constant training, punishment, creating a profit motive in him, the only proof that the child could give of his intellect was this much: he would be able to say "Ram." What happened? If someone from Mars could get hold of this child, he would think that humanity has no mind, no intellect, no reason.

The same has happened to the heart. Without training it is as if it is not. It has been completely neglected, so your whole life energy has been forced towards the head, not towards the heart, and love is a functioning of the heart center. This is why modern man has become incapable of love: modern man has become incapable of the heart. He calculates, and love is not a calculation. He knows arithmetic and love is not arithmetic. He thinks in terms of logic and love is illogical. He always tries to rationalize everything. Whatsoever he is doing reason must support it, and love is not supported by reason.

Really, when you fall in love you throw your reason completely. That is why we say man "falls" in love. Falls from where? Falls from the head down into the heart. We use this term of condemnation, "falling in love," because the head, the reason, cannot look at it without condemning it. It is a fall.

Is love really a fall or a rising? Do you become more with it or do you become less? Do you expand or do you shrink? With love you become more! Your consciousness is more, your feeling is more, your ecstatic sensation is more, your sensitivity is more. You are more alive, but one thing is less: reasoning is less. You cannot reason it out; it is blind. As far as reason is concerned it is blind. The heart has its own reason—that is another thing—and the heart has its own eyes, but that is another thing. The eyes of reason are not there, so reason says it is a fall; you have fallen.

Unless the heart center starts functioning again man will not be capable of love, and the whole misery of modern life is because unless he loves he cannot feel any meaning in his life. Life looks meaningless. Love gives it meaning; love is the only meaning. Unless you are capable of love you will be meaningless, and you will feel that you are existing without any meaning, futilely, and suicide will become attractive. Then you will like to kill yourself, to finish with yourself, to end, because what is the use of existing?

Mere existing cannot be tolerated. Existence must have a meaning; otherwise, what is the use? Why go on prolonging yourself unnecessarily? Why go on repeating the same pattern every day? Getting out of the bed and doing the same thing, and again falling asleep and the next day the same pattern: why?

You have done it so far, and what has happened? And you will do it unless death comes and relieves you of your body. So what is the use? Love gives meaning. It is not that through love any result comes into being or any goal—no! Through love every moment becomes of value in itself. Then you never ask this. If someone asks what is the meaning of life, know well that love is lacking. Whenever someone asks what is the meaning of life, he is asking because he has not been able to flower in a love experience. Whenever someone is in love, he never asks what is the meaning of life. He knows the meaning; there is no need to ask. He knows the meaning! The meaning is there: love is the meaning in life.

And through love prayer is possible because prayer is again a love relationship—not between two individuals, but between one individual and existence itself. Then the whole existence becomes your beloved or lover. But it is possible only through love experience that you can grow into prayer or into meditation, and the ultimate ecstasy is just like love. That is why Jesus says that "God is love," not that "God is loving."

Christians have been interpreting it in this way —that God is kind, loving. That is not the meaning. Jesus says that God is love. He simply equates God and love. You can say "love" or you can say "God"; they both mean the same. God is not loving; God is love itself. If you can love, you have entered the divine. And when your love grows to such an infinity that it is not concerned with anyone in particular—rather, it has become a diffused phenomenon; when there is no lover for you; rather, the whole existence, all that is, has become the lover or beloved—then it has become prayer.

And tantra is a love method. So the first thing is how to love, and then the second thing is how to grow in love so that love becomes prayer. But one must start from love. And don't be afraid of love because that fear shows you are afraid of the heart. The head is cunning; the heart is innocent. With the head you feel protected; with the heart you become vulnerable, open. Anything can happen.

That is why we have become closed. The fear is there: if you are vulnerable, anything can happen to you; someone can deceive you. With the mind no one can deceive you; you can deceive others. But I tell you be ready to be deceived, but don't close the heart. Be ready to be deceived, but don't close the heart! That vulnerability to be deceived is of worth because you will not lose anything by it. And if you are ready to be deceived infinitely, only then can you believe in the heart. If you are calculative, cunning, clever, much too clever, then you will miss the heart. And modern man is so educated, so sophisticated, so clever; that is why he has become incapable of love.

Women were not like this, but they are following modern man fast, they are copying modern man fast. Sooner or later they will become just like man, or they may even overtake him. Now they are also becoming incapable because the same head orientation, the same effort to be cunning and clever, is there now. They may form a "Women's Liberation Movement" or anything like it, but it is not heart-oriented. It is just a copy of the same stupidity that man has been doing with himself. You may go to the other extreme, but if you react, even in your reaction you are following.

A great crisis is there. It is difficult now to prevent women all over the world from copying man and his nonsense because man seems to be so successful. He is successful in a way; he has become the master of things. Now he possesses the whole world. Now he feels he has conquered nature, and "success succeeds; nothing succeeds like success."

Now women feel that man has succeeded and has become the master, so they must copy him. But look also at the thing in which man has failed completely. He has lost his heart; he cannot love. Reason alone is not enough, and reason in control is dangerous. The heart must be higher than reason because reason is just an instrument and the heart is you. The heart must be allowed to use reason— not vice versa. But you have been doing that. The head is allowed to dominate; in its domination, the head has killed the heart.

And thirdly, one thing more has to be remembered as to why modern man has become incapable of love. Love is basically a sort of madness, a sort of deep participation with nature, a sort of dissolving of the ego. It is primal. You are born out of love; your every cell of the body is a love cell. Your very energy, your life energy, is a love energy. You exist in it, but there is no ego in that energy. You cannot feel "I." That energy is unconscious, and when you move in love *you* become unconscious. Only a fragment of your mind is conscious, and in that fragment of the mind exists the ego.

The mind has three layers. First is the unconscious: when you are deeply asleep with no dreams, you are in it. The child in the mother's womb is absolutely unconscious, he is just part of the mother. The child is not aware that "I am separate"; he is just part of the mother. There is no separation, no defined existence. He is undifferentiated from the mother and from existence itself. There is no fear because fear comes only when you become aware of yourself. The child is totally at ease; he is unconscious.

And the second layer is of consciousness. It is a very small fragment. One tenth part of the unconscious has become conscious in you through training, education, society, family. It was needed for survival, so a part of you has become conscious. But that part also gets tired very soon; that is why you need sleep. In sleep you become again a child in the womb. You have fallen back, the conscious is no more there. It has become part of the unconscious. That is why sleep is so refreshing. In the morning you feel alive again, fresh, because you have fallen back into the mother's womb.

You may not have observed this.... Observe someone who is deeply asleep. More or less, he will be in the same posture in which he was in his mother's womb. And if you can be in the right posture, sleep will follow more easily. If you feel any difficulty in falling asleep, just feel your mother's womb, as if you are in it. Imagine it, and take the posture in which you would have been in your mother's womb. In that posture you will fall deeply asleep. You need the same warmth; otherwise the sleep will be disturbed. You need the same warmth as there was in your mother's womb.

That is why hot milk is good. If you sip hot milk before you go to sleep it will be good, because that again makes you a child. Milk is child's food, and if it is hot you are again at your mother's breast. Hot milk is good for sleep only because of this reason: you fall back into childhood, you are reduced into a child. Sleep refreshes you. Why? Because the conscious mind gets tired. It is just a part, and the whole is unconscious. It has to fall back to the whole to become revived. It is again resurrected. That is why in the morning you feel good and morning looks beautiful—not only because morning is beautiful, but because again you have a child's eyes. The afternoon is not so beautiful. The world is the same, but you have lost those innocent eyes again. And the evening becomes ugly because you are tired.

You have lived too much in the conscious. This conscious has ego as the center. These are two ordinary states which we know. The third state, that with which tantra and yoga are concerned, is the superconscious. 'Superconscious' means that your whole unconscious has become conscious. In the unconscious there is no ego; you are total. In the superconscious, again there is no ego; you are total. But in between the two the conscious mind has a center—the ego.

This ego is the problem, this ego creates problems. You cannot fall in love because then you will have to become unconscious, just as unconscious as you become in sleep. Or, if you want to rise to prayer, you have to become totally conscious like a Buddha or like a Meera. So love becomes impossible, prayer becomes impossible.

The ego creates the barrier. You cannot lose yourself, and love is losing, dispersing, dissolving, melting. If you melt into the unconscious, it is love; if you melt into the superconscious it is prayer—but both are a melting. So what is to be done? Remember this: you cannot do anything about it. Let it be deeply noted: you cannot do anything about love, about prayer. Your conscious mind is impotent; it cannot do anything. It has to be lost, it has to be put aside. And then remember surrender: whenever you want to move beyond yourself, surrender is the way—either in love or in prayer.

Whenever you long to move beyond, somewhere else where you are not, then surrender, let-go is the path. Allow something to happen to you; don't manipulate. And once you know how to allow, many things will start happening. You may not be even aware of what is possible for you, of what a great, tremendous energy you have closed within yourself which can explode and then become an ecstasy. Your whole life will be filled with consciousness, light and bliss, but you don't know it. It is just as if every atom is an atom bomb: if one atom explodes, tremendous energy is released. And every heart is also an atom bomb. If it explodes in love or prayer, tremendous energy is released.

But you have to explode and lose yourself. The

seed has to lose itself; only then is the tree born. And if the seed resists and says, "No, I must survive," then the seed can survive, but the tree will never be born. And unless the tree is born the seed will feel frustrated, because the tree is the meaning. The seed will feel frustrated! The seed can feel fulfilled only when the tree is there flowering. But then the seed has to lose itself, die.

Modern man has become incapable of love because he has become incapable of death. He cannot die to anything. He clings to life; he cannot die to anything.

In old English, three or four hundred years ago, this was a usual expression. The lover would say to the beloved, "I want to die in you." This was a love expression. It is beautiful! "I want to die in you." Love is a death—a death of the ego. Only then is your real self born, and modern man is very, very afraid of death. In every way, surrender is death, love is death, and life also is a continuous death. If you are afraid, you will miss life itself.

Be ready to die every moment. Die to the past, die to the future, and die in the present moment. Don't cling and don't resist. Don't make any effort for life, and you will have abundant life. Life will happen to you if you are ready to die. This looks paradoxical, but this is the law. Jesus says that one who is ready to lose will gain, and one who clings will lose everything.

The second question:

You said last night that the periphery is always changing, whereas the innermost center is eternally unmoving. To realize the center is it necessary that the peripheral movement must cease? Can that be? How and when?

You have missed the whole point. The whole point was not to make any effort to change the periphery. Allow the periphery to be as it is. And you cannot change it. It is the nature of the periphery to move and change. You cannot make it static. Nature is a flux. It is so; you cannot make it static. And don't

waste your time and opportunity of life trying to make it static. Just know it as change. Be the witness of it, and you will come to feel the innermost center which is not change. The world is change, your personality is change, your body-mind is change, but you are not; you are not the change. What is the use of struggling with change? No need!

Tantra says please be reestablished in your center, be aware of the center which is unmoving, and allow the whole existence to move. It is not a disturbance at all. It becomes a disturbance only if you cling to it or if you try to make it unmoving. Then you are falling into absurdities, foolish efforts. They will not succeed; you will be a failure. Know well that life is a change, but somewhere within this change there is an unmoving center also. Just become aware of it. That very awareness is enough to liberate you. That very feeling that "I am unmoving" liberates. That is the truth. You know it, and you are different.

Don't fight with shadows! And the whole life is a shadow because change is nothing but a shadow. The unchanging is the real; the changing is the unreal. So don't ask whether the peripheral change and movement has to be forced to cease in order to realize the center. There is no need, and you cannot force it. It cannot cease! The world goes on; only it will not go on in you. You can remain in the world, and there is no need for the world to be in you. The world is not the disturbance. When you get involved in it, when you become the change, when you feel that you have become the change, then it creates problems.

Problems are created not by the changing periphery. They are created by the identification that "I am this change." You have fallen ill; illness is not really the disturbance. When you feel that "*I have fallen ill*," it is a disturbance. If you can be a witness to that illness, if you can feel that illness is a happening somewhere on the periphery—that it is not happening to you, it is happening to someone else and you are just the witness—then death also can happen and you will be just a witness.

Alexander was returning from India. Some friends had requested him to bring back a sannyasin from India. They said, "When you come with conquered possessions, don't forget: bring a sannyasin also. We want to see what a sannyasin is —what type of a man renounces the world. We want to know what has happened to one who has renounced all desires, what type of bliss comes to one who leaves all hankering, thirst or hunger for the future, for possessions and things."

Just at the last moment Alexander remembered. In the last town from where he was to leave India to go back to his country, he told his soldiers to go and find a sannyasin. They went to the town, and they asked an old man of the town. He said, "Yes there is a sannyasin, a great sannyasin, but it will be difficult. It will be very difficult to persuade him to go with Alexander to Athens."

But the soldiers were soldiers, so they said, "Don't you be worried about it. We can force anyone. Just tell us where he is. We know how to force him, so there is no need to persuade. If Alexander tells even the whole town to follow him, you will have to follow, so what of a single sannyasin?"

But the old man laughed, and the soldiers couldn't understand because they had never encountered a sannyasin. They reached the sannyasin. He was standing naked on the bank of the river, and they told him, "Alexander orders that you have to come with us. Every care will be taken, there will be no inconvenience for you; you will be the royal guest. But you have to come with us to Athens."

The sannyasin laughed and he said, "It will be very difficult for your Alexander to take me with him. No force in this world can force me to follow. You will not be able to understand, but it is better that you bring your Alexander."

Alexander was disturbed. He felt insulted, but he wanted to see this man. He came with a naked sword and he said, "If you say no, then immediately you lose your life. I will cut your head." The name of the sannyasin was—as it is reported in Alexander's records—Dandamesh.

The sannyasin laughed and said, "You came a little late. You cannot kill me now because I have killed myself already. You are a little late. You can cut my head, but you cannot cut me because I have become a witness. So when this head will fall down on the earth, you will see it falling down and I will also see it falling down. But you cannot cut me; you cannot even touch me. So don't waste time, you can cut! Raise your sword and cut my head."

Alexander couldn't kill that man. It was impossible because it was useless. The man was so beyond death, it was impossible to kill him. You can only be killed if you cling to life. That clinging to the changing pattern makes you a mortal. If you don't cling, you are as you have always been— immortal. Immortality is your birthright; it has always been there. You become a mortal only if you cling. So there is no question, there is no need to force the changing periphery to be static. There is no need, and you *cannot* make it static. It will go on, the wheel will go on. All that you can do is to know that you are not the wheel. You are the axis, not the wheel.

The third question:

Man being as he is, is it not difficult for him to dissolve change through change, sex through sex, et cetera, without attachments and with their consequent anxiety and disappointment?

Man as he is *can* do this, and this is suggested *only* for man as he is. Tantra is a medicine for *you*—for those who are ill. So don't think that it is not for you. It is for you and you can do it, but you will have to understand what is meant when you say that there is the possibility of falling into attachments, and then the consequences will be there and frustration. You have not understood. "Consume change through change" means that even if there is attachment don't fight with it. Be attached, but be a witness also.

Let the attachment be there; don't fight with it.

Tantra is a nonfighting process. Don't fight! Frustration will come, of course, so be frustrated. But be a witness also. You were attached, and you were a witness. Now the frustration has come, and you know well that it had to come. Now be frustrated, but be a witness. Then through attachment, attachment is consumed, and through frustration, frustration is consumed.

Try this when you feel miserable. Be miserable; don't fight with it. Try this, it is wonderful. When there is misery and you feel miserable, close your doors and be miserable. Now what can you do? You are miserable, so you are miserable. Now be totally miserable. Suddenly you will become aware of the misery. And if you try to change it you will never become aware, because your effort, your energy, your consciousness is directed towards change, towards how to change this misery. Then you start thinking about how it came, and what to do now to change it. Then you are missing a very beautiful experience—the misery itself.

Now you are thinking about the causes and you are thinking about the consequences and you are thinking about the method for how to forget it, how to go beyond it, and you are missing misery itself, and misery is there and that can be liberating. Just don't do anything. Don't analyze how the misery is created; don't think about what consequences are going to follow. They will follow, so you can see later on. There is no haste. Be miserable, simply miserable, and don't try to change it.

Try this: see for how many minutes you can remain miserable. You will start laughing about the whole thing; the whole thing will look stupid, because if you are totally miserable, suddenly your center is beyond misery. That center can never be miserable, it is impossible! If you remain with the misery, the misery becomes the background, and your center which can never be miserable suddenly rises above, and then you are miserable and you are not miserable: the "same unsame." Now you are consuming misery through misery. This is what is meant. You are not doing anything; you are simply consuming misery through misery. Misery will disappear as clouds disappear, and the sky will be open and you will be laughing, and you have not done anything. And you cannot do anything; all that you can do will create more confusion and more misery.

Who has created this misery? You, and now you are trying to change it. It will get worse. You are the creator of the misery. You have created it, you are the source, and now the source itself is trying. What can you do? Now the patient is treating himself, and he has created the whole thing. Now he is thinking of surgery. It is suicidal. Don't do anything. The inside is very deep. You have tried so many times to stop misery, to stop depression, to stop this and that, and nothing has happened. Now try this: don't do anything; allow the misery to be there in its totality. Allow it to happen in its full intensity, and remain nondoing. Just be with it and see what happens.

Life is change. Even the Himalayas are changing, so your misery cannot be unchanging. It will change by itself, and you will see that it is changing—that it is disappearing and it is going away, and you feel unburdened and you have not done anything.

Once you know the secret you can consume anything through itself, but the secret is to be silently without doing anything. Anger is there, so be, just *be*. Don't do anything. If you can do this much, this nondoing, if you can just be there—present, witnessing, but making no effort to change anything, allowing things to have their own way—you will consume anything. You *can* consume anything.

The last question:

Tantra says do not struggle or swim, but let go and float in the river of life. But experience shows that the modern city life of speed and heavy technology creates constant tensions and exertions physically and mentally. What will be tantra's attitude about it? Is it not good to avoid unnecessary exertions?

Life has always been so, modern or primitive. Tensions are there, anxieties are there. Objects change, but man remains the same. Two thousand years back you were driving a bullock cart; now you are driving a car—but the driver remains the same. The bullock cart has changed—things are different now, you are driving a car—but the driver remains the same. He was anxious about his cart, tense about his cart; now you are tense and anxious about your car. Objects change, but the mind remains the same.

So don't think that because of the modern life you are so much in anxiety. It is because of you, not because of modern life, and you will be in anxiety anywhere, in any type of civilization. Go to a village for a few days—two or three days—and you will feel good for a while because even diseases need readjustment. But within three days you will be adjusted to the village, and then anxieties will start coming, disturbances will be felt again. Now the causes will not be the same, but you are the same.

Sometimes it happens that you may be disturbed because of city traffic and noise, and you may be saying that you cannot sleep at night because there is so much traffic and noise. Then go to a village, and you will not be able to sleep because there is no traffic and no noise. You will have to come back because the village looks dead, dull—because there is no life.

People go on reporting such feelings to me. I told one friend to go to Kashmir, to Pahalgam. He came back and said that life is dull there, that there is no life. You can enjoy for one or two days valleys and hills, and then one gets bored. He had been telling me here that city life was getting on his nerves, and now he said that those hills were getting boring and he began longing to come back home.

You are the problem; Kashmir will not be of any help. It is not Bombay that disturbs you or London or New York; it is *you!* And it is not that London has created you: you have created London.

It is not the traffic and the noise and the mad rush: you have created this—you and others like you. Look! The cause is within you. It is not that you are tense because of noise. The noise is there because you are tense, and you cannot live without it. That is why it is there. You need it, you cannot live without it. And in villages people are suffering. They want to come to Bombay or to New York or to London, and the moment they get the opportunity they run. And I have been listening to people who go on talking about the beautiful village life, but they never go to live there. They *never* go to live there, they simply talk about it.

Who prevents you? Why not go? Go to the forest—who prevents you? You will not like it, you cannot like it. Right now you will like it for a few days because it is a change, and then? Then you will get bored. You will find it dull, and you will like to escape from there.

This city life is created by your mad mind. You are not becoming mad because of these cities; these cities are built because of your mad mind. They are built for you and by you, and they exist for you. And unless this mad mind changes, these cities cannot disappear, they will have to remain. They are your by-product.

Remember one thing: whenever you feel that something is wrong, first find out the cause in yourself. Don't go anywhere. Out of a hundred times, ninety-nine times you will find the cause within yourself. And if you find the cause within you, ninety-nine times out of a hundred, the hundredth cause will disappear by itself.

You are the cause of whatsoever is happening to you. *You* are the cause, and the world is just a mirror. But it is consolatory always to find the cause somewhere else. Then you never feel guilt, you never feel self-condemned. You can always point out that here is the cause, and unless this cause changes, "How can I change?" You can escape into it; this is a trick. So your mind always goes on projecting causes somewhere else. The wife is disturbed because of the husband; the mother is disturbed because of the children, and the children are disturbed because of the father. Everyone is disturbed because of someone else, and everyone always thinks that the cause exists outside.

Mulla Nasruddin was passing down a street. It was evening, and the darkness was descending. Suddenly he became aware that the street was empty with no traffic, and he became afraid. A group of people were coming toward him, and he had been reading about *dacoits,* robbers, murderers. So he created fear, he started trembling. He thought, he projected, that now these murderers and dacoits were coming, and they were bound to kill him, so how to escape them? He looked all around.

There was a cemetery, so he jumped over the wall of the cemetery. There was a ready-made grave for someone, so he thought that it would be good to be dead in this grave. They will feel that he is dead, so there won't be any need to murder him.

So Mulla lay down. The group was just a marriage procession, but they saw this man trembling and jumping. Then they became afraid and wondered what was the matter and who this man was. They thought, "He seems to be up to some mischief. He is hiding there." So the whole procession stopped, and they jumped over the wall. Mulla became more afraid. Now they came near and they asked, "What are you doing here? Why are you here in this grave?"

So Mulla said, "You are asking a very difficult question. I am here because of you and you are here because of me."

And this is happening everywhere. You are disturbed because of someone else; he is disturbed because of you. And you are just creating everything around you, projecting, and then becoming afraid, scared, and making efforts to defend. And then there is misery and frustration and conflict and depression and fighting.

The whole thing is stupid, and it will remain unless you change your attitude. And always try first to find the cause within you. How can the traffic noise disturb you? How? If you are against it, it will disturb. If you have the attitude that it disturbs, it will disturb. But if you accept it, if you allow it to happen without any reaction, then you may even start enjoying it. It has its own melody, its own music. You have not heard it, but that doesn't mean that it doesn't have its own music. Someday forget yourself and listen to the traffic noise. Just listen, and don't bring in your attitudes that this is disturbing, that this is not good. Don't bring in your attitudes, just listen to the melody! In the beginning it will look chaotic. That too is because of the mind. If you relax totally, sooner or later everything will fit into a harmonious whole and even the traffic noise will become music. You can enjoy it and you can dance to its tune. It depends on you.

Nothing disturbs unless you think that it disturbs. For example I will tell you that many things have disturbed humanity because there was a certain concept that they disturb. When the concept changes the things remain the same, but they don't disturb. For example, masturbation disturbed the whole world. Just half a century before, the whole world was disturbed by masturbation. Every teacher, every father, every mother was disturbed, and every child was disturbed. And still in the larger, ignorant world, the disturbance remains. And then physiologists and psychologists discovered that masturbation cannot disturb anyone; it is natural, and nothing is wrong with it. There is absolutely nothing wrong with it, but the old teaching was that if you become mad, it was because of masturbation.

Everything was forced down, reduced to masturbation. And more or less every child was doing it, every boy was doing it, so every boy was afraid. He was doing it, and he was afraid that now he was going to be mad, inferior, crazy, eccentric, ill, and his life would be wasted. But he couldn't resist. He had to do it, and these ideas entered into the mind and had effects. They affected him, and many went mad, many remained inferior, many remained stupid because of it, and it has no relationship at all.

Modern science, modern research says that rather it is healthy. Medical science says that it is good because a boy at the age of thirteen or fourteen or a girl at the age of twelve or thirteen becomes sexually mature. If nature were allowed they would have to get married immediately. They are ready to reproduce, but civilization of necessity forces that they will have to remain unmarried for ten years at least or even more. But medicine says that fourteen to twenty, these six years, are the most sexually potent. A boy is never so potent again as he is then. The energy is bubbling up; the whole body is ready to burst into sex. But the society says no, the energy should not be allowed to move. However, the energy is moving and the child cannot do anything, and whatsoever he is going to do will have effects because of the philosophy around him. He will feel he is doing something wrong, he will feel guilt, and that guilt will follow like a shadow. And many diseases will happen because of the idea, not because of the act.

Medicine says that it is healthy because he is relieved of unnecessary energy. That unnecessary energy would create problems otherwise, so it is healthy. Now, particularly in America and England and other Western developed countries who know much more about physiology, masturbation is being propagated. Now there are films on how to masturbate to show to the children, and every teacher will be teaching sooner or later how to masturbate rightly. They say it is healthy, and now those who think it is healthy feel very healthy about it.

I don't think it is either—it is neither healthy nor unhealthy. The idea is the thing. If it is healthy and the concept is stretched, then it will become healthy. Now in the West they say not only that masturbation never affected anyone's intelligence adversely, but that the better the intelligence, the more masturbation will be there. So a boy who is masturbating more will be of higher IQ than the boy who is not masturbating. And they have reasons for saying this, because even for a boy to discover masturbation is a sign of intelligence: he is finding out a way.

The society has closed the door for marriage, and the nature is forcing the energy. The intelligent one will find a way and the nonintelligent one will just be blocked, he will not be able to find the way. Now studies show that those boys who masturbate are more intelligent. If this idea is spread, and it is bound to be, sooner or later the whole world will be having this idea. Then masturbation will be healthy, and you will feel a well-being from it.

Now every parent is afraid because the parent knows what he did when he was young. When his boy comes to the same age, he becomes afraid and he starts looking around at what the boy is doing. He is afraid, and if he catches the boy he will punish him. But the new knowledge says don't punish the boy—no! Rather, teach him. If he is not masturbating, then go to the doctor and find out what is wrong. If this knowledge becomes well spread, then this will happen.

But both are positions. *Both* are positions! And when some boy masturbates, he is very suggestive in that moment—because when sexual energy is being released, he becomes vulnerable, open, flexible, and his mind is silent. Any idea put in at that moment will have its effects—so if you tell him, "You are going to be ill because of it," he will feel ill. If you tell him, "You are going to be healthy because of it," he will become healthy. If you say to him, "You will be stupid for your whole life if you do this," he will remain a dunce. If you say, "Now this is a good sign of intelligence," he may develop a higher IQ. You are simply suggesting something to him in a very vulnerable moment. Whatsoever you think starts happening.

Buddha is reported to have said that every thought will become actual, so be aware. If you think that the traffic noise disturbs you, it will disturb you: you are ready for disturbance. If you think that a family life is a bondage, it will be a bondage for you: you are ready for this. If you think that poverty will help to make you liberated, it will help. Ultimately it is you who is creating a world around you, and whatsoever you think becomes the noosphere, the milieu, and you exist in it.

Tantra says remember this causality, it is always within you. And if you know this, then you will not cause anything. If you know this, you will not cause anything for yourself. And when someone is not causing anything, he is liberated. Then he is not in misery and not in bliss. Bliss is your creation and misery is also your creation. You can change your misery into bliss because it is your creation.

The liberated one, the enlightened one, is really in neither because he has ceased to cause anything around him. He simply is! That is why Buddha never says that the enlightened one is blissful. Whenever someone asked him, "Tell us something about someone who has gone beyond—whether he is in perfect bliss," Buddha laughed and said, "Don't ask. I can say only this much, that he is not in misery. I cannot say anything more. He is not in misery; that is all I can say."

Why so much insistence on the negative? Because Buddha knows. When you have come to know that you were the cause of your misery, then you know well that the bliss also was caused by you. Then one ceases to cause anything. That is what *nirvana* is: a cessation of causing anything around you. Then you are, simply—no misery, no bliss. If you can understand, only this is bliss. There is no misery and no bliss, because if there is bliss then misery is there; you are still causing something. And if you can cause bliss, then you can cause misery, and you will become bored of the bliss also.

How much can you stand it—how much? Have you ever thought about it? Twenty-four hours in bliss: will you be able to stand it? You will become bored, and you will go on seeking teachers who can teach you how to become miserable again. If the world becomes blissful, I cannot conceive that there won't be any teachers. There will be teachers, because then people will need misery. Someone will be needed to tell them how to become miserable again, just for a change. Then you can go back to your bliss, and you will feel it more—because only then can you feel it more, when you have missed it.

Teachers will be there! Now they are teaching how to become blissful; then they will teach how to become miserable, how to have a taste of hell. A little change will be helpful, healthy.

But you are the cause, and you will become enlightened the moment you have known that the world you are living in was caused by you. When you will not cause it, it will have disappeared. The traffic will go on, the noise will be there, and everything will be there as it is, but you will not be there because you will have disappeared with the cause.

CHAPTER 45

Remaining with the real

◆

68 *As a hen mothers her chicks, mother particular knowings, particular doings, in reality.*

69 *Since, in truth, bondage and freedom are relative, these words are only for those terrified with the universe. This universe is a reflection of minds. As you see many suns in water from one sun, so see bondage and liberation.*

Eno had asked a person, "What is the problem? What are the roots so that man can be solved and man can make some efforts to know who he is?" Why shouldn't he know without any effort? Why should there be any problem at all? You are, you know you are—so why can't you know who you are? Where do you miss? You are conscious. You are conscious that you are conscious. A life is there; you are alive. Why are you not aware who you are? What becomes the barrier? What prevents you from this basic self-knowledge? If you can understand the barrier, the barrier can be dissolved very easily.

So the real question is not how to know oneself. The real question is to know how you are not knowing yourself, how you are missing such an obvious reality, such a basic truth which is so near to you, how you go on not seeing. You must have created a device; otherwise it is difficult to escape from oneself. You must have created walls; you must, in some sense, be deceiving yourself.

So what is that trick of escaping from oneself, of not knowing oneself? If you don't understand that trick, whatsoever you do will not be of any help—because the trick remains, and you go on asking how to know oneself, how to know the truth, how to know the reality, and consequently you go on helping the barrier. You go on creating it also, so whatsoever you do will be of no use.

Really, nothing positive is needed to know oneself, only something negative. In a way, you have only to destroy the barrier that you yourself have constructed, and the moment that barrier is not there you will know. Knowing happens when the barrier is not; you cannot make any positive effort for it. You have just to be aware of how you are missing it.

So a few things have to be understood as to how you are missing it. One: you live in your dreams, and then dreams become barriers. Reality is not a dream. It is there, you are surrounded by it everywhere. Inside and outside, it is there—you cannot miss it—but you are dreaming. Then you move in a different dimension which is not a reality. Then you go on moving in a dreamworld. Then dreams become like clouds around you, and they create the barrier. Unless mind ceases dreaming, the truth cannot be known. And when you see through dreams the reality is distorted, and your eyes are filled with dreams, and your ears are filled with dreams, and your hands are filled with dreams.

So whatsoever you touch is touched through the dreams, and whatsoever you see is seen through dreams, and whatsoever you hear is heard through the dreams, and you distort everything. Whatsoever reaches you, reaches through dreams, and they change everything, they color everything. Because of the dreaming mind you are missing the reality outside and the reality inside. You can go on finding ways and means how to come to reality, but you will be trying that too through your dreaming mind.

So you can dream religious dreams—you can dream dreams about reality, about truth, about

God, about Christ and Buddha—but that too will be dreaming. Dreaming must cease; dreaming cannot be used to know reality.

What do I mean when I say "dreaming"? You are hearing right now, but a dream is there, and that dream is constantly interpreting what is being said. You are not hearing me; you are hearing yourself, because simultaneously you are interpreting—are you not? You are thinking about what is being said. What is the need to think? Just hear, don't think, because if you think you cannot hear, and if you go on thinking and hearing, then whatsoever you hear is your own noise. Then it is not what is being said. Stop thinking; let the passage of hearing be clear of thoughts. Then that which is said will be heard.

When looking at the flower, stop dreaming. Don't allow your eyes to be filled with thoughts and dreams about the past and future, with what you know about flowers. Don't even say that "This flower is beautiful," because then you are missing the reality. These words will become a barrier. You say, "This flower is beautiful," and words have come in: the reality is interpreted through the words. Don't allow words to gather around you. Look directly, hear directly and touch directly.

When you touch someone, just touch; don't say that the skin is beautiful, smooth. Then you are missing, you have moved in dream. Whatsoever the skin is, it is here now. Touch it and allow the skin itself to be revealed to you. You look at a beautiful face. Look at it, and allow the face to enter itself. Don't interpret it, don't say anything. Don't bring your past mind in.

The first thing: dreams are created by your past mind. It is the past mind continuously moving around you. Don't allow the past to come in and then don't allow the future. The moment you see a beautiful face, a beautiful body, immediately desire arises. You want to possess. You see a beautiful flower and you want to pluck it. Then you have moved. The flower is there, but you have moved into desire, into the future. Now you are not here.

So either you are in the past which is not, or you are in the future which has not come yet, and you are missing that which is there right now.

So the first thing to remember: words should not be allowed to exist between you and reality. With less words there are less barriers; with no words there are no barriers. And then you face reality directly; immediately you are face to face. Words destroy everything because they change the very meaning.

I was reading someone's biography. She was describing one day after just coming out of her bed. The woman writes that "One day, in the morning, I opened my eyes." Then immediately, she says, "But it is not right to say that I opened my eyes. 'I' didn't do anything. The eyes opened by themselves." She changes the sentence and she writes, "No, it is not good to say that I opened my eyes. I did not do anything. There was no effort on my part; it was not an action at all." Then she writes, "The eyes opened by themselves." But then she feels this is too absurd because the eyes belong to her, so how can they open themselves? So what to do?

Language never says what is. If you say, "I opened my eyes," it is a lie. If you say, "The eyes opened by themselves," it is a lie again, because eyes are just fragments. They cannot open themselves. The whole organism is involved. And whatsoever we say is like that. If you go to aboriginal societies in India—and there are many aboriginal tribes—they have a different language structure. Their language structure is more basic and more real, but they cannot create much poetry. Their language structure cannot be helpful for dreaming.

If it is raining, we say, "It is raining." They ask, "What do you mean by 'it'? What do you mean by 'it'?" They have simply the word rain. What do you mean by "it"? What is raining? They just say "rain." Rain is the reality, but we go on adding things—and the more words are added, the more we are lost, far away, thrown far away from reality.

Buddha used to say, "When you say, 'A man is walking,' what do you mean? Where is the man?

Only the walking is. What do you mean by 'the man'?" When we say, "A man is walking," it appears that there is something like a man and something like walking—two things added together. Buddha says there is walking.

When you say, "The river is flowing," what do you mean? There is just flowing, and that flowing is the river. The walking is the man, the seeing is the man, standing and sitting is the man. If you eliminate all these—walking, sitting, standing, thinking, dreaming—will there be a man left behind? There will be no man behind. But language creates a different world, and by constantly moving into words we go on moving away.

So the first thing to remember is how not to allow words unnecessarily. When there is a need, you can use them, but when there is no need remain empty, remain nonverbal, *mouna*, remain silent. There is no need to be constantly verbalizing things.

Secondly, don't project. Don't verbalize, don't project. Look at what is there. Don't add things and then look. You see a face. When you say, "It is beautiful," you are putting something into it, or if you say, "It is ugly," you are again putting something into it. A face is a face. Beauty and ugliness are your interpretations. They are not there, because the same face may be beautiful to someone and ugly to someone else, and to a third it may be neither. He may be indifferent; he may not even look at it—at the same face. The face is simply a face. Don't put things into it; don't project. Your projections are your dreams, and if you project then you miss. And this is happening every day.

You see that a face is beautiful; then desire is created. The desire is not for that face or that body; it is for your own interpretation, your own projection. The person that is there, the real person, has been used as a screen, and you have projected yourself. And then disillusion is bound to be there because the real face cannot be forced into unreality by your projection. Sooner or later the projection will have to be dropped, and the real face will

come out, and then you will feel that you have been cheated. You will say, "What has happened to this face? This face was so beautiful and this person was so beautiful, and now everything has gone ugly." Again you are interpreting. The person remains whatsoever he is, but your interpretations and projections go on, and you are never allowing energy to assert itself. You go on suppressing it. You are suppressing inwardly and outwardly also. You never allow the reality to assert itself.

I am reminded that one day a neighbor asked Mulla Nasruddin whether he could have his horse for a few hours. The Mulla said, "I would gladly give my horse to you, but my wife has gone with the horse and they will be out for the whole day." Just at this moment the neigh of the horse was heard from the stable, so the man looked at Mulla Nasruddin. Nasruddin said, "Okay, whom do you believe—me or the horse? And the horse is a notorious liar to boot. Whom do you believe?"

We create an untrue world around us because of our projections, but if the reality asserts and the horse neighs from the stable, we ask, "Whom do you believe?" We always believe ourselves, not the reality that goes on asserting. It is asserting every moment, but we go on forcing our illusions. That is why every man feels disillusioned in the end. It is not because of reality. Every man and woman feels disillusioned in the end, as if the whole life has been a waste. But now you cannot do anything, you cannot undo it. Time is no more with you. Time has flown and death is near and you are disillusioned, and now the opportunity is lost.

Why does everyone feel disillusioned? Not only those who are unsuccessful in life, but those who are successful in life, they also feel the same. It is okay if unsuccessfuls feel disillusioned, but even those who succeed feel this way. Napoleons and Hitlers and Alexanders, they also feel disillusioned. The whole life has been a waste. Why? Is the cause really in reality, or is the cause in the dreams which you were projecting? And then you could not project them and the reality asserted itself, and ultimately reality wins and you are defeated. You can win only if you are not projecting.

So remember the second thing: look directly at things as they are. Don't project, don't interpret, don't force your mind upon things. Allow the reality to assert itself, whatsoever it is. This is always good, and howsoever beautiful your dreams they are bad, because you are bound on a journey of disillusion. And the sooner you are disillusioned, the better. But once one illusion is gone, immediately you start creating another to replace it.

Allow a gap. Between two illusions, allow a gap. Allow an interval so the reality can be seen. This is very arduous—to look at the reality as it is. It may not be according to your desires. There is no need for it to be according to your desires. But then you have to live with reality, to live in it—and you *are* in it! It is better to come to terms with reality than to go on deceiving yourself, and you are not aware how you go on projecting. Someone says something, and you understand something else. And you base things on your understanding, and then you make a house of cards out of it, you create a palace of cards. It was never said! Something else was meant!

Always see what is there. Don't be in a haste. It is better not to understand something than to misunderstand. It is better to remain ignorant consciously than to think that you know. Look into your relationships—at the husband, the wife, the friend, the teacher, the master, the servant—look! Everyone is thinking in his own ways, interpreting the other, and there is no meeting, no communication. Then they are fighting, in constant conflict. The conflict is not between two persons, the conflict is between false images. Be alert so that you don't have any false image of anyone else. Remain with the real, howsoever hard, howsoever arduous and difficult, even if sometimes it seems impossible. But once you know the beauty of remaining with the real, you will never be a victim of dreaming.

And thirdly, why do you dream? It is a substitute. Dreaming is a substitute. If you cannot get whatsoever you desire in reality, then you start dreaming. For example, if you have fasted the whole day, in the night you will dream. You will dream about food, of being invited by a great emperor, or some such thing. You will be eating and eating and eating in your dreaming. The whole day you were fasting, and now in the night you are eating. If you are sexually suppressive, then your dreams will become sexual. Through your dreams it can be known what you are suppressing in the day. Your daytime fast will be shown by your dream. Dreams are substitutes, and psychologists say that it will be difficult for man as he is to live without dreams. And they are right in a way. As man is it will be difficult to live without dreams, but if you want a transformation, then you have to live without dreams. Why are dreams created? Because of desires. Unfulfilled desires become dreams.

Study your desiring; be aware and observe it. The more you observe it, the more it will disappear. And then you will not create webs in the mind, and you will not move in a private world of your own. Dreams cannot be shared; even two intimate friends cannot share their dreams. You cannot invite anyone into your dreams. Why? You and your lover cannot both be in the same dream. Your dream is yours; another's dream is another's. They are private. Reality is not so private, only madness is private. Reality is universal, you can share it; you cannot share dreams. They are your private madness—fictions. So what is to be done?

One can, in the day, live so totally that nothing is left suspended. If you are eating, eat totally. Enjoy it so totally that you don't need any dream in the night. If you are loving someone, love so totally that no love enters into your dreams. Whatsoever you do in the day, do it so totally that nothing is suspended on the mind, nothing is incomplete which has to be completed in dreams. Try this, and within a few months you will have a different quality of sleep. Dreams will go on becoming less and less, and deep sleep will deepen. And when in the night dreams are less, in the day projections will be less because, really, your sleep continues and your dream continues. With closed eyes in the night and with opened eyes in the day, they continue. Inside a current goes on.

Any moment, close your eyes and wait, and you will see that the film has come back; the dream is running. It is always there, just waiting for you. It is just like the stars in the day. They have not disappeared, but only because of the sunlight you cannot see them. They are there waiting, and when the sun will set they will start appearing.

Your dreams are just that way—moving within you even while you are awake. They are just waiting. Close your eyes, and they start functioning. When dreams are less in the night, in the day you will have a different quality of waking. If your night changes, your day changes; if your sleep changes, your waking changes. You will be more alert. With less dreams running within, you will be less asleep. You will look more directly.

So don't leave anything suspended, that is one thing. And whatsoever you are doing, remain with the act. Don't move anywhere else. If you are taking a shower, be there. Forget the whole world. Now this shower is the whole universe. Everything has ceased; the world has disappeared. There is only you and the shower. Remain there. Move with each act so totally that you are neither lagging behind nor jumping ahead; you are with the act. Then dreams will disappear, and with less dreaming you will be more able to penetrate the reality.

---

68 Be hope-less.

Now the technique. The technique is concerned with this. *As a hen mothers her chicks, mother particular knowings, particular doings, in reality.*

The key term is *in reality.* You are also mothering many things, but in dreams—not in reality. You are also doing many things, but in dream—not in reality. Don't mother dreams, don't help dreaming

to grow more in you; don't give your energy to dreaming. Withdraw yourself from all dreams. It will be difficult because you have invested so much in your dreaming. If you suddenly withdraw yourself totally from dreaming, you will feel as if you are sinking and dying, because you have always lived in a postponed dream. You have never been here and now, you are always somewhere else. You have been hoping.

Have you heard the Greek parable of Pandora's box? To revenge a certain deed on the part of a man, Pandora was sent a box, and the box had all the diseases that are now rampant in humanity. They were not there before, and when the box was opened the diseases were released. Pandora, being afraid after seeing the diseases, closed the box. Only one disease remained there and that was hope; otherwise man would have dissipated—all these diseases would have killed him, but because of hope he continued.

Why are you living? Have you ever asked? There is nothing to live for here and now. There is just hope. You are carrying a Pandora's box. Why are you living right now? Why do you get up every morning? Why do you start the whole day again—again and again? Why this repetition? What is the reason? You cannot find any reason right now for why you are living, and if you find something it will be something in the future—a hope that something is going to happen: someday "something" is going to happen. You don't know when that day will come; you even don't know what it is that is going to happen—but someday "something is going to happen," and so you go on prolonging yourself, you go on carrying yourself.

Man lives just in hope, and this is not life because hope means dream. Unless you live here and now, you are not alive. You are a dead weight, and that tomorrow which will fulfill all your hopes is never to come. When death will come, then only will you realize that now there is no tomorrow, and now you cannot postpone. Then you will feel disillusioned, cheated—but no one has cheated you;

you are the master of the whole mess.

Try to live in the moment, in the present, and don't cherish hopes, whatsoever their nature. They may be worldly, they may be otherworldly; it makes no difference. They may be religious—somewhere in the future, in the other world, in heaven, in the *nirvana*, after death—but it makes no difference. Don't hope. Even if you feel a subtle hopelessness here, remain here. Don't move from the moment here and now. Don't move! Suffer it, but don't allow the hope to enter in.

Through hope dreaming enters. Be hopeless. If life is hopeless, be hopeless. Accept it, but don't cling to any future event. Then suddenly there will be a change. Once you remain in the present moment, dreams stop—because then they cannot arise. The source has been withdrawn. You cooperate with them, you mother them; that is why they arise. Don't cooperate with them, don't mother them.

This sutra says . . . *mother particular knowings.* Why particular knowings? You also mother, but you mother particular theories, not knowings; particular scriptures, not knowings; particular hypotheses, systems, philosophies, world views—but never particular knowings. This sutra says throw them away. Scriptures, theories, they are of no use. Have your own experience which is real, your own knowings, and mother them. Howsoever trivial, a real knowing is something. You can base your life upon it. Whatsoever they are, always think of real, particular knowings that *you* have known.

Have you known anything? You know many things, but everything is borrowed. Someone has said them, someone has given them to you. Teachers, parents, society, they have conditioned your mind. You "know" about God, you "know" about love, you "know" about meditation. You don't know anything really! You have not tasted anything, this all is borrowed. Someone else has tasted, the taste is not your own. Someone else has seen, but you have your eyes and you have not used

them. Someone else has experienced—a Buddha has experienced, a Jesus has experienced—and you just go on borrowing their knowings. They are false! For you, they are of no use. They are more dangerous than ignorance, because ignorance is yours and the knowledge is borrowed.

It is better to be ignorant; at least the ignorance is yours. It is authentic, it is real, sincere and honest! Don't go on with borrowed knowledge. Otherwise you will forget that you are ignorant, and you will remain ignorant.

This sutra says ...*mother particular knowings.* Always try to know something in a way that is fresh, direct, immediate. Don't believe in anyone. Your belief will lead you astray. Trust yourself—and if you cannot trust yourself, how can you trust anybody else?

Sariputta came to Buddha and said, "I have come to believe in you. I have come! Help me to build faith in you."

Buddha is reported to have said, "If you don't believe in yourself, how can you believe in me? So forget me. First have trust in yourself, believe in yourself. Only then can you have trust in someone else."

So remember this: you cannot trust anybody if you cannot even trust yourself. The first trust is always within. Only then can it flow, only then can it overflow; it can reach to others. But how can you trust if you don't know anything? How can you trust in yourself if you don't have any experience? Try to trust in yourself. Don't think that this experience of looking through others' eyes is only with the absolute. It is with ordinary experiences also. But let them be your own. They will help you to grow, they will make you mature, they will make you ripened.

This is really strange: you look with others' eyes, you live with others' lives. You call a rose beautiful. Really, is it your feeling or just a teaching that is spread around you that a rose is beautiful? Is this your knowing? Have you known it? You say that moonlight is good, beautiful. Is it your knowing, or is it just that poets have been singing about it and you are repeating it? If you are like a parrot, you cannot live your life authentically. Whenever you assert anything and whenever you say anything, first check within whether it is your knowledge and your experience.

Throw out all that is not yours—it is of no use—and cherish and mother all that is yours, because only through that will you grow. *Mother particular knowings, particular doings, in reality.* Always remember "in reality." Do something. Have you done anything ever, or have you been just following others, just following orders? "Love your wife": have you really loved her? Or are you just doing a duty because it has been said, because it has been taught: Love your wife, or love your mother, love your father, love your brother—so you are loving and you are following! Have *you* really loved any time when you were there? Was it ever the case that no teaching was working and no other was being followed? Were you ever authentically in love? You can deceive yourself; you can say, "Yes!" But find out before you say anything. If you have loved, you would be transformed; the particular act of love would have changed you. But it has not changed you because your love is false. And the whole life has become false. You go on doing things that are not your own. Do your own thing and mother it.

Buddha is good, but you cannot follow him. Jesus is good, beautiful, but you cannot follow him. And if you follow, you will become ugly. You will be a carbon copy. You will be false, and you will not be accepted by the existence. Nothing false is accepted. Love a Buddha, love a Jesus, but don't be their carbon copies. Don't imitate. Always allow your own self to move in its own way. You will become Buddha-like one day, but the path will be basically your own. One day you will become a Jesus, but you will have traveled along a different route, you will have experienced different things. One thing is certain: whatsoever may be the route and whatsoever may be the experience, it must be authentic, real, and your own. Then you will reach one day. Through falsity you cannot reach the truth; falsity will lead to more falsity.

Do something, remembering well that it is you who are doing it without following anybody. Then even a very small act, just a smile, may become a source of *satori,* a source of *samadhi,* cosmic consciousness. You come back to your home and smile at your children. That smile is false; you are pretending. You are smiling because a smile is expected. It is a painted smile. Nothing else is smiling in you but the lips. They are manipulated; the smile is mechanical. And you can become so habituated in this that you may completely forget how to smile. You may laugh, but the laughter may not be coming from your center.

Always remember, no matter what you are doing, observe whether your center is involved in it or not, because if it is not involved it is better not to do a thing. Don't do it! No one is forcing you to do anything. Don't do it! Preserve your energy for the moment when something real happens to you; then do it. Don't smile, preserve the energy. The smile will come, and then it will change you completely. Then it will be total. Then every cell of your body will smile. Then it will be an explosion—nothing painted.

And children know, you cannot deceive them. The moment you can deceive them, they are no more children. They know when your smile is false, they can detect it; anyone who is real will detect it. Your tears are false, your smile is false. These are small acts, but you are made up of small acts. So don't think to do something big—that then you will do this. If you are false in small things you will always be false.

It is easy to be false in big things. If you are false in small things, it is very easy to be false in big things, because big things are always on exhibition. They are for others to see, so you can very easily be false.

You can be a saint if saintliness is respected. Then you are on exhibition—just an exhibition piece. You can be a saint because it is respected and ego-fulfilling, but everything will be false. Just think, if a society changes its attitudes as they have been changed in Soviet Russia or in China, immediately saints disappear—because there is no respect for them.

I remember one of my friends, a Buddhist *bhikkhu* who went to Soviet Russia in Stalin's days. He told me that whenever somebody would shake hands with him, suddenly the man would shrink and would say, "You have the hands of a bourgeois." He had very beautiful hands. As a bhikkhu he had never done anything; he was a beggar, a royal beggar, so there had been no labor. His hands were very smooth, beautiful, feminine. In India, whenever someone touched his hands he would say, "So beautiful!" In Russia, whenever someone would touch his hands, he would shrink away, and the condemnation would come into his eyes and he would say, "So you have bourgeois hands, the hands of an exploiter." He came back and told me, "I felt so condemned there that I longed to be a laborer."

Saints disappeared from Russia because now there is no respect. All that saintliness which was there was only on exhibition; it was a showpiece, painted. Only real saints can exist now in Russia. For unreal ones there is no possibility because you will have to struggle there to be a saint, and the whole society will be against you. In India, the easiest way to survive and exist is to be a saint. Everyone respects you. You can be false, and falsity pays.

Remember this: from the very morning, when you open your eyes, try to be real and authentic. Don't do anything which is false. Only for seven days, go on remembering. Don't do anything which is false. Whatsoever is lost, let it be lost. Whatsoever you lose, lose it. But remain real, and within seven days a new life will be felt within you. The dead layers will be broken and a new living current will come to you. You will feel alive again for the first time—a resurrection.

Mother doings…mother knowings…in reality—

not in dream. Do whatsoever you like to do, but think—really, are you doing it, or is your mother doing it through you or your father doing it through you? Because dead men, dead parents, societies, old generations gone long ago are still functioning within you. They have created such conditionings that you go on fulfilling *them*—and they were fulfilling their dead fathers and mothers, and you are fulfilling your dead fathers and mothers, and no one is fulfilled. How can you fulfill someone who is dead? But the dead are living through you.

Always observe when you do something, whether your father is doing it through you or you are doing it. When you get angry, is it your anger or is it the way your father used to be angry? You are just imitating. I have seen patterns going on, being repeated. If you marry, your marriage is going to be just approximately the same as your father's and your mother's. You will act like your father, your wife will act like her mother, and you will create the same mess again. When you get angry, observe: are you there or someone else? When you love, remember, are you there or someone else? When you speak something, remember, are you speaking or your teacher? When you make a gesture, remember, is it yours or is someone else present in your hand? It will be difficult, but this is *sadhana*. This is what spiritual effort means.

And leave all falsities. You may feel a certain dullness for a time being, because all your falsities will drop and the real will take time to come and assert itself. There will be a period of a gap. Allow that period, and don't be afraid and don't become scared. Sooner or later your false selves will drop, masks will drop, and your real face will come into being. Only through that real face can you encounter God. That is why this sutra says, *As a hen mothers her chicks, mother particular knowings, particular doings, in reality.*

69 Go beyond bondage and freedom.

The second sutra: *Since, in truth, bondage and freedom are relative, these words are only for those terrified with the universe. This universe is a reflection of minds. As you see many suns in water from one sun, so see bondage and liberation.*

This is a very deep technique, one of the deepest, and only very rare minds have tried it. Zen is based on this technique. This technique is saying a very difficult thing—difficult to comprehend, not difficult to experience. But first comprehension is needed.

This sutra says that the world and nirvana are not two things, they are one; that heaven and hell are not two things, they are one; and that bondage and liberation are not two things, they are one. It is difficult because we can only conceive of something easily if it is in terms of polar opposites.

We say that this world is bondage, so how to get out of this world and be liberated? Then liberation is something which is opposite, which is not bondage. But this sutra says that both are the same—liberation and bondage—and unless you are freed from both you are not freed. Bondage binds, and liberation also. Bondage is a slavery, and liberation is also.

Try to understand this. Look at a person who is trying to go beyond bondage. What is he doing? He leaves his home, he leaves his family, he leaves the riches, he leaves the things of the world, he leaves society just to get out of bondage, out of the fetters of the world. Then he creates new fetters for himself. Those fetters are negative.

I have seen one saint who cannot touch money. He is respected—he is bound to be respected by those who are mad after money. He has moved to the other pole. If you put money in his hand, he will throw it as if there were some poison or as if you have put some scorpion in his hand. He will throw it and he will become scared. A subtle trembling comes to his body.

What is happening? He has been fighting with money. He must have been a greedy man—too much greed. Only then can he move to this extreme. He may have been too much obsessed with money. He is still obsessed, but now in the reverse direction. However, the obsession is still there.

I have seen one sannyasin who cannot look at any female face. He becomes afraid. He will always look down, he will never look up if some woman is there. What is the problem? He must have been too much sexual, obsessed with sex. He is still obsessed, but then he was running after this woman or that and now he is running from women—from this one and that. But he is still obsessed with women. Whether he is running after or running from, his obsession remains. He thinks that now he is liberated from women, but this is a new bondage. You cannot become liberated by reaction. The thing you go against will bind you negatively; you cannot escape it. If someone is against the world and for liberation, he cannot be liberated; he will remain in the world. The attitude of being against is a bondage.

This sutra is very deep. It says: *Since, in truth, bondage and freedom are relative....* They are not opposite, they are relative. What is freedom? You say, "Not bondage." And what is bondage? You say, "Not freedom." You can define them by each other. They are just like hot and cold, not opposite. What is hot and what is cold? They are just degrees of the same phenomenon—degrees of temperature—but the phenomenon is the same, and they are relative. If there is in one bucket cold water and in another there is hot water and you put in both your hands—one hand in the hot and one in the cold—what will you feel? A difference of degrees.

And if at first you cool down both your hands on ice and then you put both your hands into the hot and the cold water, what will happen? Now again you will feel a difference. Your cold hand will now feel more hot in the hot water than it felt before. And if your other hand has become cold, much colder than the cold water, then that water will now look hot; you will not feel it as cool. It is relative. There are only degrees of difference, but the phenomenon is the same.

Tantra says that bondage and liberation, *sansara* and *moksha,* are not two things, but a relative phenomenon—of the same thing. So tantra is unique. Tantra says that you have to be liberated not only from bondage; you have to be liberated from moksha also. Unless you are liberated from both, you are not liberated.

So the first thing: don't try to go against anything because you will move to something which belongs to it. It looks opposite, but it is not. Don't move from sex to *brahmacharya.* If you are trying to move from sex to brahmacharya, your brahmacharya will be nothing but sexuality. Don't move from greed to no-greed because that no-greed will again be a subtle greed. That is why if a tradition teaches to be nongreedy, it gives you some profit motive in it.

I was staying with a saint, and he told his followers, "If you leave greed you will get much in the other world. If you leave greed, you will gain much in the other world!" Those who are greedy, greedy for the other world, will be influenced by this. They may be motivated, and they will be ready to leave many things to gain. But the motive to gain remains; otherwise how can a greedy man move toward nongreed? Some motive must be there which fulfills his greed deeply.

So don't create opposite poles. All opposites are related; they are degrees of the same phenomenon. If you become aware of this, you will say that both poles are the same. If you can feel this, that both poles are the same, and if this feeling deepens, you will be liberated from both. Then you are neither for sansara nor for moksha. Really, then you are not asking for anything; you have stopped asking. In that stopping, you are liberated. In that feeling that everything is the same, the future will have dropped. Where can you move now? Sex and brahmacharya both are the same, so where is one to move? And if greed and nongreed are the same

and violence and nonviolence are the same, where has one to move?

There is nowhere to move. Then movement ceases; there is no future. You cannot desire anything because all desires will be the same; the difference will be just of degrees. What can you desire? Sometimes I ask people—when they come to me, I ask them—"What do you really desire?" Their desire is based in them as they are. If they are greedy, they desire nongreed; if they are sexual, obsessed with sex, they desire brahmacharya, how to be beyond sex, because they are miserable in their sex.

But this desire for brahmacharya is based, rooted, in their sexuality. They ask, "How to get out of this world?" The world is too much on them, they are too much burdened and they are clinging too much—because the world cannot burden you unless you cling to it. The burden is in your head—not because of the burden, but because of you, you are carrying it. And they are carrying the whole world; then they get burdened. And in this experience of misery there arises a new desire for the opposite, so then they start hankering for the opposite.

They were running after money, so now they run after meditation. They were running after something in this world; now they are running after something in that world. But the running remains, and the running is the problem. The object is irrelevant. Desire is the problem. What you desire is meaningless. You desire, that is the problem, and you go on changing objects. Today you desire A, tomorrow you desire B, and you think you are changing. Then the day after tomorrow you desire C, and you think you are transformed. But *you* are the same. You desired A, you desired B, you desired C, and A-B-C are not you. You desire—that is you, and that remains the same. You desire bondage, then you get frustrated, fed up; then you desire liberation. You desire, and desire is the bondage.

So you cannot desire liberation. Desire is bondage, so you cannot desire liberation. When desire ceases, liberation is. That is why this sutra says, *In truth, bondage and freedom are relative.* So don't become obsessed with the opposite.

These words are only for those terrified with the universe. These words of bondage and freedom are for those who are terrified with the universe.

This universe is a reflection of minds. Whatsoever you see in this universe is a reflection. If it looks like bondage, it means it is your reflection. If it looks like liberation, again it is your reflection.

As you see many suns in water from one sun, so see bondage and liberation. The sun rises, and there are many ponds—dirty and pure, big and small, beautiful and ugly—and one sun reflects in many ponds. One who goes on counting the reflections will think that there are many, many suns. One who looks not into the reflections but to the reality will see one. The world, as you look at it, reflects you. If you are sexual, the whole world seems sexual. If you are a thief, the whole world seems to be in the same profession.

Once Mulla Nasruddin and his wife were fishing, and the place was restricted; only license holders could fish there. Suddenly a policeman appeared, so Mulla's wife said, "Mulla, you have the license so you run away. Meanwhile, I will escape."

So Mulla started running. He ran and ran and ran, and the policeman followed. Of course, Mulla left the wife there, and the policeman followed him. Mulla ran and ran until he felt that now his heart would explode. But by that time the policeman caught hold of him. The policeman was also perspiring, and he said, "Where is your license?" So Mulla produced his papers. The policeman looked at them and they were okay. So he said, "Why are you running, Nasruddin? Why did you run away?"

Nasruddin said, "I am going to a doctor, and he says after every meal to run for half a mile."

The policeman said, "Okay, but you saw me running after you, chasing you, yelling, so why didn't you stop?"

Nasruddin said, "I thought that maybe you go to the same doctor."

It is logical; it is what is happening. Whatsoever you see all around you is more a reflection of you than of any real thing there. You look at yourself mirrored everywhere. The moment you change, the reflection changes. The moment you become totally silent, the whole world becomes silent. The world is not a bondage; bondage is a reflection. And the world is not liberation; liberation is again a reflection.

A Buddha finds the whole world in nirvana. A Krishna finds the whole world celebrating in ecstasy, in bliss; there is no misery. But tantra says that whatsoever you see is a reflection unless all seeing disappears and only the mirror is seen with nothing reflected in it. That is the truth.

If something is seen, it is just a reflection. Truth is one; many can only be reflections. Once this is understood—not theoretically, but existentially, through experience—you are liberated, liberated from both bondage and liberation. Naropa, when he became enlightened, was asked by someone, "Have you achieved liberation now?" Naropa said, "Yes and no both. Yes, I am not in bondage, and no because that liberation was also a reflection of bondage. I thought about it because of bondage."

Look at it in this way: you are ill, then you long for health. That longing for health is part of your illness. If you are really healthy, you will not long for health. How will you? If you are really healthy, where is the longing? What is the need? If you are really healthy, you never feel that you are healthy. Only ill, diseased persons feel that they are healthy. What is the need? How can you feel that you are healthy? If you are born healthy and you have never been ill, will you be able to feel your health? Health is there, but it cannot be felt. It can be felt only through contrast, through the opposite. Only through the opposite are things felt. If you are ill, you can feel health—and if you are feeling health, remember, you are still ill.

So Naropa says, "Yes and no both. 'Yes' because there is no bondage now, but with the bondage liberation has also disappeared; that is why 'no.' It was part of it. Now I am beyond both —neither in bondage nor in liberation."

Don't make religion a search, a desire. Don't make moksha, liberation, nirvana, an object of desiring. It happens when there is no desiring.

CHAPTER 46

The tantric way to freedom from desires

◆

Is the motive towards liberation a desire or an intrinsic human thirst?

How can one be transformed by being total in actions that are of anger and violence?

Can You tell us something about the quality of an enlightened one's sleep?

The first question:

You said yesterday that the motivation towards liberation or samadhi is also a tension and a barrier, but is it not correct that it is not a desire but an aspiration—the intrinsic thirst of the human being?

ou must understand what desire means, and religions have confused you much about it. If you desire something of the world, they call it desire. If you desire something of the other world, they call it by a different name. This is absurd. Desire is desire! It makes no difference what the object of desire is. The object may be anything—of this world, material, or of another world, spiritual—but desiring remains the same.

Every desire is a bondage. Even if you desire God, it is a bondage; even if you desire liberation it is a bondage. And liberation cannot happen unless this desiring goes away totally. So remember, you cannot desire liberation, that is impossible; that is contradictory. You can become desireless, and then liberation happens. But that is not a result of your desire. Rather, it is a consequence of no-desire.

So try to understand what desire is. Desire means that right now you are not okay, you are not at ease. This very moment you are not at ease with yourself, and something else in the future, if fulfilled, will bring you peace. The fulfillment is always in the future; it is never here and now. This tension of the mind for the future is desire. Desire means you are not in the present moment, and all that is there is only the present moment. You are somewhere in the future, and the future is not. It never has been, it will never be. All that is, is always the present—this moment.

This projection of your fulfillment somewhere in the future is desire. So what that future fulfillment is, is irrelevant. It may be the kingdom of God, heaven, *nirvana*, it may be anything, but if it is in the future, it is desire. And you cannot desire in the present, remember; that is not possible. In the present you can only be, you cannot desire. How can you desire in the present?

Desire leads into the future, into fantasy, dreaming. That is why so much insistence by Buddha for no-desire, because only in no-desire do you move into reality. With desire you move into dreams. The future is a dream, and when you project into the future you are going to be frustrated. You are destroying reality right now for future dreams, and this habit of the mind will remain with you. It is being strengthened every day. So when your future comes it will come in the form of the present, and your mind will again move to some other future. Even if you could reach God, you will not be satisfied. The way you are, it is impossible. Even in the presence of the divine, you will have moved away into the future.

Your mind is always moving into the future. This movement of the mind in the future is desire. Desire is not concerned with any object, with whether you desire sex or you desire meditation—it makes no difference. Desiring is the thing—that you desire. It means you are not here. It means you are not in the real moment, and the present moment is the only door into existence. The past and future are not doors, they are walls.

So I cannot call any desire spiritual. Desire as such is worldly. Desire is the world. There is no spiritual desire; there cannot be. That is a trick of the mind, a deception. You don't want to leave desiring, so you change the objects. First you were desiring wealth, prestige, power. Now you say you don't desire and that these are worldly things. You condemn them, and those who desire them are condemned in your eyes. Now you desire God, the kingdom of God, nirvana, moksha, the eternal, *sat-chit-anand,* the *Brahma.* Now you desire these, and you feel very good. You think you are transformed, but you have not done anything. You remain the same.

You are just playing tricks with yourself, and now you are in a greater mess because you think that this is not desiring. You remain the same. The mind remains the same; the functioning of the mind remains the same. You are not yet here. The objects of desire have changed, but the running, the dreaming, remains, and the dreaming is the desire—not the object.

So try to understand me. I say that every desire is worldly because desire is the world. So it is not a question of changing the desire, it is not a question of changing objects. It is a question of a mutation, of a revolution from desire to no-desire; from desire to no-desire, not from old desires to new desires, from worldly desires to otherworldly desires, from material desires to spiritual desires—no! From desire to no-desire is the revolution!

But how to move from desire to no-desire? You can move only if there is some desire. If some profit motive, some greed, some gain is there, only then can you move from desire to no-desire. But then you are not moving at all. I say that with no-desire you will attain eternal bliss. This is right—that with no-desire eternal bliss happens—but if I say to you that with no-desire you will gain eternal

happiness, you will make it an object of desire and then you will have missed the point completely.

It is not a result, it is a consequence of deep understanding. So try to understand that with desire there is misery, and don't think that you know it already. You don't know; otherwise how can you move into desire? You have not yet become aware that desire is misery, desire is hell. Be aware! When you desire something be aware. Then move with the desire in full alertness, and then you will reach hell.

Every desire leads to misery, whether fulfilled or not. If fulfilled, it leads sooner; unfulfilled it takes time—but every desire leads to misery. Be alert of the whole process, and move with it. There is no hurry because nothing can be done in a hurry, and spiritual growth is not possible in a hurry. Move slowly, patiently. Watch every desire and then watch how every desire becomes a door to hell. If you are watchful, sooner or later you will realize that desiring is hell. The moment that realization happens, there will be no desire. Suddenly desires will disappear, and you will be in a state of no-desire. I don't say desirelessness, I simply say "no-desire."

You cannot practice it, remember; only desires can be practiced. How can you practice no-desire? You cannot practice it, you can only practice desires. But if you are alert, you will become aware that they lead to misery. And when each desire leads to misery, when this becomes a realization to you—not mere opinion and knowledge, but a realized fact—desiring disappears, it becomes impossible. How can you lead yourself into misery? You are always leading yourself to happiness—thinking that you are—and always moving into misery. This has been happening for lives and lives. You always think this or that is the door of heaven, and when you have entered you always realize that this is hell. And this has been without any exception; it is always the case.

Move with mindfulness in every desire, and allow every desire to lead you to misery. Then, suddenly, one day the maturity will happen to you, this ripeness will happen to you: you will realize that every desire is misery.

The moment you realize it, desiring disappears. There is no need to do anything now; desiring simply falls away, withers away, and you are in a state of no-desire. In that no-desire nirvana is, the perfect, the absolute bliss is. You may call it God, the kingdom of God or whatsoever you choose to call it, but remember well that it is not a result of your desiring. It is a consequence of nondesiring, and nondesiring cannot be practiced.

Those who "practice" nondesiring, they are deluding themselves. There are many all over the world—*bhikkhus,* sannyasins—who are practicing nondesiring. You cannot practice nondesiring; no negative thing can be practiced. Underneath they are desiring, they are hankering after God, the peace that will happen, the bliss that is waiting for them somewhere in the future beyond death. They are desiring; they only call their desiring "spiritual desire."

You can deceive yourself very easily. Words are very deceptive and you can rationalize. You call a poison "ambrosia," and when you call it ambrosia it appears as ambrosia. Words hypnotize; that is one thing. But this feeling, this realization that desire is misery, must be yours.

Mary Stevens has written somewhere that she was visiting a friend's home, and her friend's daughter was blind. Mary Stevens was very puzzled because the girl would say, "He is ugly, I don't like him"; and "The color of this dress is beautiful."

As she was blind, Mary Stevens asked, "How do you feel that someone is ugly and that a color is beautiful?"

The girl said, "My sisters say this to me." This is knowledge.

Buddha has said that desire is misery and you go on repeating. This is knowledge. You are desiring, and you have never seen that desire is misery. You have simply heard Buddha. This will not do. You are simply wasting your life and opportunity.

Your own experience can change you; nothing else changes. Knowledge cannot be borrowed. If borrowed, it is just a fake. It looks like knowledge, but it is not. But why do we follow a Buddha or a Jesus —why? Because of our greed. We look at Buddha's eyes, and they are so peaceful that greed arises, desire arises for how to attain this. Buddha is so blissful—every moment in ecstasy. A desire arises for how to be Buddha-like. We also desire such states.

Then we go on asking how Buddha achieved this, how it happens. The "how" creates many problems because then Buddha will say that in "no-desire" it happens. And he is right, it *has* happened in no-desire. But when we hear that in no-desire it happens, we start practicing no-desire, we start leaving desires, and the whole effort is a desire to be Buddha-like.

Buddha was not trying to be like someone else; he was not asking to be a buddha. He was simply trying to understand his own misery—and the more understanding dawned upon him, the more misery disappeared. Then one day he came to understand that desire is poison. If you have desire you have fallen a victim; now there is no possibility of your ever being happy. You can only hope— have hope and frustration, then more hope and more frustration: this will be your circle. And when you become more frustrated you hope more, because that is the only consolation. You go on moving in the future because in the present you always have frustration, and the frustration is coming because of your past.

In the past this present was the future, and you hoped for it. Now it is a frustration. Then you hope again for the future, and when it will become the present you will again become frustrated. Then you will hope again. Then more frustration, more hope, and with more hope, still more frustration. This is a vicious circle. This is what the wheel of *sansara* is.

But no buddha can give you his own eyes. And it is good that he cannot give them to you; otherwise you will remain a fake always, eternally. Then you will never become authentic. It is good to suffer because only through suffering will you become authentic and real. So the first thing: move with your desires so that you can understand what they really are. Experience whatever suffering is hidden there. Let it be revealed to you. Only that is austerity—only that is *tapascharya*.

Naropa has said that if you can be alert every desire leads you to nirvana, and this is the meaning, because if you are alert, you know that every desire is misery. And when you have searched every nook and corner of desiring, suddenly you stop. In that stopping is the happening, and it is always there. That happening is always waiting for you, just waiting to meet you in the present. But you are never in the present, you are always dreaming. Reality sustains you; because of the real you are alive, because of the real you exist. But you go on moving in the unreal. The unreal is very hypnotizing.

I have heard one Jewish joke. Two old friends met after many, many years. Then one friend said to the other, "I have not seen you in twenty-five years. How is your son, your boy Harry?"

The other said, "There is a son; he is a great poet. All over the land his voice is heard, his songs are sung, and those who know poetry say that sooner or later he is going to become a Nobel laureate."

The other friend said, "Marvelous! And tell me about your second son, Benny. How is he?"

The friend said, "I am so happy about my second son. He is a leader, a great political leader. Thousands and thousands follow him, and I am sure that sooner or later he is going to be the prime minister of this land."

Then the friend said, "My! So fortunate you are! And what about your third son Izzie?"

The father became very sad and said, "Izzie? He is still Izzie. He is a tailor. But I tell you that if it was not for Izzie we would all be starving."

But the father was sad because Izzie is just a tailor. And the poet and the great politician, the great leader—they are dreams. Izzie is the reality—

the tailor. "But if not for Izzie, we would all be starving," he said.

You could not exist were it not for this moment. *That* is real. But you are never happy about it. You are happy in your dreams for the future about Nobel laureates, prime ministers. Right now, "Izzie is just a tailor." Your reality is where you are grounded; your dreams are not your ground. They are false. Come to terms with your reality in the present moment. Encounter it, face it whatsoever it is, and don't allow the mind to move into the future. The future is desire. If you can be here and now, you are a buddha. If you cannot be here and now, then everything is just dream stuff.

And you will have to come back because dreams cannot lead you anywhere. They can only lead you to hope and frustration, but nothing real happens through them. But remember my point that you cannot imitate. You will have to pass through suffering. Suffering is the path. It purifies you, it makes you alert, it makes you aware. The more you are aware, the less you are desire-filled. If you are perfectly aware, no desire happens, and meditation means nothing else but perfect awareness.

The second question:

Please explain how it is possible that one can be spiritually transformed by being total in actions that are of anger, hatred and violence.

Yes, you can be totally transformed through anger, through hatred, through violence. And there is no other way—because you exist in violence, in anger, in greed, in passion. From where you exist, *only* from there, does the way start. I will not tell you to create nongreed against your greed; I will tell you to be greedy totally, but with a fully alert mind—to be violent, to be angry, but be total so that you suffer totally, so that you can feel the whole poison of it. You must pass through this fire. No one else can pass for you; no proxy is possible. You will have to pass through it, and you always think that someone else will do it.

Christians go on thinking that through Jesus there is salvation. It has not happened yet. The world remains the same. Two thousand years have passed since Jesus was crucified, but we go on hoping that someone else will suffer and we will reach to bliss. No! Everyone has to carry his own cross. Jesus was crucified; he reached the goal. You cannot reach. You will have to pass through that crucifixion yourself. And this is the crucifixion—that anger is there, passion is there, violence is there, greed is there, jealousy is there.

What are you doing with them? The society teaches to create the antipole. Greed is there, so suppress it and create a nongreedy mind. Anger is there, so suppress it. Don't be angry. Push the energy back and smile. What happens? Anger goes on being accumulated within, and you go on becoming more and more angry, because more and more energy is accumulated within as anger—suppressed. It becomes your unconscious reservoir, and against this anger you go on smiling. That smile becomes false, because while anger is knocking within how can you smile? You can smile, but then it will be just a false thing.

So you are divided into two—a false smile and a real anger. The false smile becomes your personality and the real anger remains your soul. You are divided against yourself, and a constant fight will be there. And you cannot be happy with the false smile. No one else is deceived. You cannot be happy with a real anger hidden behind always trying to come out. A false smile and a real anger—this is the situation. All that is good is false and all that is bad is real. The real you carry within and the false you show outside. This is schizophrenic, and every man has become schizophrenic, divided—not only divided, but constantly fighting with himself. The whole life and energy is wasted and dissipated in this fight. And the fight is stupid, but this is happening.

What I am suggesting is, don't create any falsity around you. The false will never lead you to the real; the false will lead you to more that is false.

Don't do the false, and allow the real total expression. When I say this you may become scared, because violence is there and you may want to kill someone. So do I mean to go and kill? No! Meditate on it. Close your room and allow your violence. You can express it on a pillow, on a picture, on anything. There is no need to go and kill someone, because that is not going to help. That will create more problems and a chain.

On the pillow, write the name of your enemy or your friend—and remember, we are more angry at our friends than at our enemies. Just put a picture of your wife or husband on a pillow, and bring your violence out. Beat the pillow, kill the pillow, and do whatsoever you feel. And don't feel that you are doing a stupid thing. This is what you want to do with the real object, and that will be more stupid. Don't think that this is silly. This is how you are: you are silly, and you cannot change by just repressing it. Look at this silliness, see that this is how you are. Allow yourself full expression; act it out. And if you can be real, you will realize for the first time what anger, what violence is hidden within you. You are a volcano, and this can erupt from you at any moment.

In any situation, the volcano may erupt. It is erupting every day. Someone kills someone, and just a day before he was as normal as you. No one ever suspected that he was going to be a murderer. No one suspects about you, and you have so many thoughts in your mind to murder. You have thought, you have planned it many times. The idea to murder someone else or yourself has come to you. It has happened to you if you are not absolutely idiotic. Psychologists say that an intelligent man is bound to think of suicide at least ten times in his life—at least ten times!—and ten thousand times you think to murder someone. You never do it, that is another thing. But you can do it; the possibility is always there.

Make your anger a total act in meditation, and then see what happens. You will feel it coming from your whole body. If you allow it, then every cell of your body will be in it. Every pore, every fiber of the body will become violent. Your whole body will be in a mad situation. It will go mad, but allow it, and don't withhold. Move with the river, and after the cyclone is over, you will feel for the first time a deep center within you. A subtle calmness will happen. When the anger has gone, there will be no repentance because you have not done it to anyone. There will be no guilt. You will be unburdened. When this anger is thrown out and silence comes, that silence is real—not forced.

You can sit down like a buddha in *padmasana*, in a yogic posture. You can force yourself, but the monkey within you goes on jumping. Now only the body is static. The mind is more mad than it ever was before. Whenever you sit for meditation, you feel what is happening. You are never so noisy within when you are not meditating, so why does so much noise happen whenever you meditate? Why does the mind go so vagrant? Why do so many thoughts come in a cloud? It is because your body is static, and through this staticness of your body you can feel the monkeyness of the mind more. The contrast is there.

But forced silence is of no use. Either you will not succeed in it or if you will succeed you will move into sleep. A forced silence, if successful, becomes sleep. It is good as far as sleep is concerned; otherwise it is useless. A real silence always happens only when some pent-up energy is released totally. The disturbance was because of that pent-up energy. That forced energy was trying to erupt, that was the problem, that was the disturbance within. When it is released, you are unburdened.

Then every fiber in your being is relaxed. In that relaxedness you can say that you are in a state of no-anger. It is not against anger; it is simply absence of anger. Remember, the real is always the absence, not the opposite—*not* the opposite! It is always the absence—an absence of greed, an absence of sex, an absence of jealousy—but in that absence, your reality flowers because the diseases have gone. Now your inner health can flower. And once it

starts flowering you will not accumulate anger. You accumulate anger only because you are missing yourself.

Really, you are not angry at anyone else, you are angry within yourself. But you go on projecting that anger onto others; otherwise you will go mad, so you go on finding excuses. Really, you are angry because you are missing yourself, you are missing your destiny. That which is possible for you is not happening, and that is why you are angry. Nothing is happening to you, and time goes on flowing. Death is coming nearer, and you remain as unfulfilled as ever, and there seems to be no possibility to be fulfilled. Because of this, because you are not realizing your potentialities, because you have not become that which you can become, you are angry, violent. And then you go on finding excuses.

You throw your anger on this, on that. Really, it is not a question of anger, and if you make it a question of anger, your diagnosis is wrong. It is a question of self-realization. Why is one violent? Why is one destructive? Because he is angry against himself, against his very being; because he is. And then he feels to be against the whole world.

A buddha is silent, nonviolent, not because he has practiced it, but because now he has realized himself. Now the flower has come to its total flowering, so nothing is there to release. He is fulfilled. Simple gratefulness to the existence remains. Now there is no complaint; nothing is wrong. When you really flower, everything is okay; all is good. Because of this Buddha couldn't see problems. All is good! That is why Buddha is not a revolutionary. To be a revolutionary, you must be able to see misery, you must be able to feel the whole mess around, the hell. To be a revolutionary, you must have a feeling that everything is wrong. Only then are you a revolutionary. Buddha was here in this land, Mahavira was here in this land, but they were not revolutionaries. Why? This question arises: why?

When one is at ease with oneself, all is good. He cannot be destructive, he can only be creative. His revolution can only be a creative one, and you cannot see anything creative. When someone destroys something, only then does it become news; only then can you see it.

A Lenin is seen as a revolutionary, not as a buddha. All over the world now there are revolutionaries, and they go on growing. And the reason? It is because fewer and fewer persons are realizing their potentiality. They are violent and they want to destroy—because if there is no meaning in their lives how can they feel that there can be meaning in others' lives? A Mahavira is even aware not to kill an insect, not even to kill a mosquito, because he has realized himself. Now he knows what is possible even for a mosquito. A mosquito is not just a mosquito; this is a possibility. An infinite possibility is there: this mosquito can become divine. He cannot destroy it, it is impossible. He can only help. He is only concerned with how to help so that the potential becomes the actual.

You are just seeds. A great destiny is hidden, but nothing is being realized. The potential is wasted; the seed remains the seed. You feel anger. The modern generation is much angrier than older generations because there is more awareness of the possibility and less fulfillment. Now the new generation knows what is possible much more than the older generation. This generation is alive to the fact that much is possible. But nothing is happening and nothing is becoming actual, so there is more frustration. If you cannot be creative, at least you can be destructive; you feel your power in being destructive. Anger, violence, are destructive forces. They are there because creativity is not there.

Don't go against them. Rather, help them to be released. Don't suppress them; allow them to evaporate from you. Then that which you think is opposite is present. When they have evaporated, you will suddenly realize that silence is there, that love is there, compassion is there. They are not to be cultivated. They are just like a stream hidden in rocks. You remove the rocks and the stream starts flowing. The stream is not against the rocks, not the opposite of the rocks. Just the absence of the rocks, and an opening happens and the stream starts flowing.

Love is in you like a stream, anger is in you like a rock. Remove it. But you go on forcing it inside, more inside. Then you are forcing the stream as well to go more inside. Throw this rock. There is no need to hit someone with it. You want to hit someone because you don't know how to throw it without hitting anyone. That is what I am teaching: to throw it without hitting anyone. There is no need to hit anyone. And if you can throw this rock without hitting anyone, everyone will profit out of it. You may not be throwing it on others' heads, but it was always there and others feel it.

When you are angry, howsoever you suppress it your anger is felt. You vibrate it; around you a subtle sadness happens. Everyone becomes alert that some disease has entered. Everyone wants to leave you; you become repulsive. Your very attitude gives a bad odor to you.

You may not be aware, but biochemists say that when someone is in love or in anger or in sex, different odors are released from the body—actually, not metaphorically. When you are in anger, a bad odor is released from your body. When you are in love, the quality is different. In sexual passion, a different odor is released.

Animals are attracted by odor—because when the female is ready, a subtle odor is released from her sex glands and the male is attracted. Without that odor the female is not ready. That is why you see dogs smelling: they can smell sex. If you are sexual, you are also releasing a subtle odor. If you are angry, then too—because different chemicals are released in the blood system. Consciously no one may notice, but unconsciously everyone notices it. You are a burden—repulsive, destructive. Throw this poison out of your system.

So remember this: it is good to release in the vacuum. And the sky is big enough, it will not return it back to you. It will simply absorb it, and you will be released. So do anything meditatively and totally, even anger, even violence, even sex. It is easy to conceive of how to be angry alone, but you can also create a sexual orgy alone meditatively. And you will have a different quality after that.

While all alone, just close your room and move as if in the sex act. Allow your whole body to move. Jump and scream; do whatsoever you feel like doing. Do it totally. Forget everything—societal inhibitions, et cetera. Move in the sex act alone meditatively, but bring your total sexuality to it.

With the other, the society is always present because the other is present. And it is so difficult to be in such a deep love that you can feel as if the other is not present. Only in a very deep love, in a very deep intimacy, is it possible to be with your lover or beloved as if he is not or she is not.

This is what intimacy means: if you are as if alone with your lover or beloved or your spouse in the room with no fear of the other, then you can move in the sex act totally; otherwise the other is always an inhibiting presence. The other is looking at you: "What will she think? What will he think? What are you doing? Behaving like an animal?"

One lady was here just a few days before. She came to complain against her husband. She said, "I cannot tolerate it. Whenever he loves me, he starts behaving like an animal."

When the other is present, the other is looking at you: "What are you doing?" And you have been taught that there are some things which you can do and some things which you are not to do. It inhibits; you cannot move totally.

If love is really there, then you can move as if you are alone. And when two bodies become one, they have a single rhythm. Then the two-ness is lost, and sex can be released totally. And it is not like in anger; anger is always ugly, but sex is not always ugly. Sometimes it is the most beautiful thing possible—but only sometimes. When the meeting is perfect, when the two become one rhythm, when their breaths have become one and their *prana*, energy, flows in a circle, when the two have disappeared completely and the two bodies have become one whole, when the negative and positive, the male and female, are no more there, then sex is the most beautiful thing possible. But that is not always the case.

If it is not possible, you can bring your sex act to a climax of frenzy and madness while alone, in a meditative mood. Close the room, meditate in it, and allow your body to move as if you are not controlling it. Lose all control!

Spouses can be very helpful, and particularly in tantra: your wife, your husband or your friend can be very helpful if you both are experimenting deeply. Then allow each total uncontrol. Forget civilization as if it never existed; move back into the Garden of Eden. Throw that apple—the fruit of the tree of knowledge. Be Adam and Eve in the Garden of Eden before they were expelled. Move back! Just be like innocent animals, and act out your sexuality in its totality. You will never be the same again.

Two things will happen. Sexuality will disappear. Sex may remain, but sexuality will disappear completely. And when there is no sexuality, sex is divine. When the cerebral hankering is not there, when you are not thinking about it, when it has become a simple involvement—a total act, a movement of your whole being, not only of the mind—it is divine. Sexuality will disappear first, and then sex may also disappear, because once you know the deeper core of it, you can achieve that core without sex.

But you have not known that deeper core, so how can you achieve it? The first glimpse comes through total sex. Once known, the path can be traveled in other ways also. Just looking at a flower, you can be in the same ecstasy in which you are when you meet with your spouse in a climax. Just watching the stars, you can move in it.

Once you know the path, you know it is within you. The spouse only helps you to know it, and you help your spouse to know it. It is within you! The other was just a provocation. The other was just a challenge to help you know something which was always within you.

And this is what is happening between a master and a disciple. The master can become only a challenge to you to show that which has always been hidden in you. The master is not giving you anything. He *cannot* give; there is nothing to give. And all that can be given is worthless because it will only be a thing.

That which cannot be given but which can only be provoked is worthwhile. A master is just provoking you. He challenges you to help you to come to a point where you can realize something which is already there. Once you know it, there is no need of a master.

Sex may disappear, but first sexuality disappears. Then sex becomes a pure, innocent act; then sex also disappears. Then there is *brahmacharya*, celibacy. It is not opposite to sex; it is just its absence. And remember this difference. This is not in your awareness.

Old religions go on condemning anger and sex as if both are the same or as if both belong to the same category. They do not! Anger is destructive; sex is creative. All old religions go on condemning them in a similar way, as if anger and sex, greed and sex, jealousy and sex are similar. They are not! Jealousy is destructive—*always!* It is never creative; nothing can come out of it. Anger is always destructive, but not so with sex! Sex is the source of creativity. The divine has used it for creation. Sexuality is just like jealousy, anger and greed: it is always destructive. Sex is not—but we don't know pure sex, we know only sexuality.

A person who is looking at a pornographic picture or one who is going to see a film, a movie of sexual orgies, is not seeking sex; he is seeking sexuality. There are persons I know who cannot make love to their wives unless they first go through some dirty magazines or books or pictures. When they see these pictures, then they are excited. The real wife is nothing to them. A picture, a nude picture, is more exciting to them. That excitement is not in the gut; that excitement is in the mind, in the head.

Sex transferred to the head is sexuality; thinking about it is sexuality. Living it is a different thing, and if you can live it you can go beyond it. Anything lived totally leads you beyond. So don't be afraid of anything. *Live it!* If you think it is destructive to others, move in it alone, do not do it with others. If you think it is creative, then find a partner, find a friend. Become a couple, a tantric couple, and move in it totally. If you still feel that the other's presence is inhibiting, then you can do it alone.

The last question:

Does an enlightened person ever dream? Can You tell us something about the quality and nature of an enlightened person's sleep?

No, an enlightened person cannot dream. And if you like dreams very much, never become enlightened. Beware! Dreaming is part of sleep. The first thing is that for dreaming to happen you have to move into sleep. For ordinary dreams you have to move into sleep. In sleep you become unconscious. When you are unconscious, dreams can happen. They happen only in your unconsciousness.

An enlightened person is conscious even while asleep. He cannot become unconscious. Even if you give him an anaesthetic—chloroform or something like that—only his periphery goes to sleep. He remains conscious; his consciousness cannot be disturbed.

Krishna says in the Gita that while everyone is asleep the yogi is awake. It is not that yogis are not going to sleep in the night; they also sleep, but their sleep has a different quality. Only their bodies sleep, and then their sleep is beautiful. It is a rest.

Your sleep is not a rest. It may even be an exertion, and in the morning you may feel more exhausted than you ever felt in the evening. A whole night's sleep, and in the morning you feel more exhausted—what is happening? You are a miracle!

The whole night was an inner turmoil. Your

body was not at rest because the mind was so active. And the activity of the mind is bound to be an exertion for the body, because without the body the mind cannot act. The activity of the mind means parallel activity of the body, so the whole night your body is moving and is active. That is why in the morning you feel more exhausted.

What does it mean for someone to become enlightened? It means one thing: now he is perfectly conscious. Whatsoever goes on in his mind, he is aware. And the moment you are aware, certain things completely stop. Just through awareness they stop. It is just like this room is dark and you bring a candle: the darkness will disappear. Everything will not disappear; these bookcases will be here, and if we are sitting here we will be here. By bringing the candle only darkness disappears.

When someone becomes enlightened, now he has an inner light. That inner light is awareness. Through that awareness sleep disappears—nothing else. But because sleep disappears, the quality of everything changes. Now whatsoever he is going to do will be in his perfect alertness, and that which needs unconsciousness as a prerequisite now becomes impossible.

He cannot be angry—not because it is a decision not to be angry; he *cannot* be angry. Anger can exist only when you are unconscious. Now unconsciousness is not there, so the base is not there and anger is not possible. He cannot hate; hate exists only when you are unconscious. He becomes love —not because of any decision on his part. When light is there, when consciousness is there, love flows; it is natural. Dreaming becomes impossible because dream needs, first of all, unconsciousness, and he is not unconscious.

Buddha's disciple, Ananda, said to him, after sleeping and living in the same room, in the same place with Buddha, "This is a miracle; this is very strange. You never move in your sleep." Buddha always remained in one posture the whole night. The way he would sleep in the beginning, that would be the way he would come out of it, and his

hand would remain in the exact place where it was put.

You might have seen Buddha's picture showing him sleeping. His posture is called "the lying posture." He would remain in this same posture the whole night. Ananda watched him for years. Whenever he would look at Buddha sleeping, he would be the same the whole night. So Ananda asked, "Tell me, what are you doing the whole night? You remain in one posture."

Buddha is reported to have said, "Only once did I move in my sleep, but then I was not a buddha. Just before, just a few days before the enlightenment happened, I moved in my sleep. But then suddenly I became aware and I wondered, 'Why am I moving?' I moved unconsciously without any knowing on my part. But after enlightenment there is no need. If I want I can move, but there is no need. And the body is so relaxed...."

Consciousness penetrates even in sleep. But you can have a fixed posture the whole night and you will not be enlightened. You can practice it; it is not difficult. You can force yourself; then within a few days you will be able to do this. But that is not the point. If you look at a Jesus moving, do not think, "Why is he moving?" It depends. If Jesus moves in his sleep, he is conscious. If he wants to move, he moves.

For me, it happens quite the reverse. Before coming to awareness I slept always in one posture the whole night. I do not remember ever moving. But since then I have been moving the whole night. Even five minutes are enough for me in one posture. I have to move again and again. I am so aware that it is not a sleep at all really. So it depends. But you can never deduce anything from the outside. Always, this is only possible from the inside.

For an enlightened one, awareness will remain there even in his sleep, and then dreams are not possible. They require unconsciousness—that is one thing, and they require suspended experiences —that is the second thing. And for an enlightened one there is no suspended experience, no incomplete experience. Everything is complete. He has eaten his food; now he is not thinking about eating again. When he feels hungry he will eat again, but meanwhile there is no thought of eating.

He has taken his bath; now he is not thinking of the bath tomorrow. When the time comes, if he is alive, he will take it. If the situation permits it will happen, but there is no thinking. Acts are there, but not any thinking about them.

What are you doing? You are constantly rehearsing—constantly rehearsing for tomorrow as if you are an actor and you are to show someone. Why are you rehearsing? When the time comes, you will be there.

The enlightened person lives in the moment, in the act, and he lives so totally that it is not incomplete. If something is incomplete, then it will be completed in a dream. Dream is a completion. It happens because the mind cannot allow anything to be incomplete. If something is incomplete, there is an inner uneasiness. It wonders how to complete it. Then in a dream you complete it, and you are at ease. Even if it is completed in a dream, for the mind it is a relaxation.

What are you dreaming? You are just completing your incomplete acts which you could not complete in the day. In the day you may have wanted to kiss a woman, and you could not kiss. Now you will kiss her in your dream, and your mind will feel relaxed; a tension is released.

Your dreaming is nothing but your incompleteness, and an enlightened person is complete. Whatsoever he is doing, he is doing it so wholly, so totally, that nothing remains suspended. There is no need for any dreaming. Dreaming in the night will cease and thinking in the day will cease.

It is not that he will become unable to think. He can think if he needs. If you ask him a question he will think immediately, but no rehearsal is needed. First you think and then you reply, but his reply is his thinking. He thinks and replies. That is also not good to say, because actually there is no gap. It is simultaneous. He thinks out loud, but there is no rehearsal, no thinking, no dreaming. He lives life. With thinking and dreaming you miss life.

CHAPTER 47

Tantric meditation using light

◆

70 *Consider your essence as light rays from center to center up the vertebrae, and so rises "livingness" in you.*

71 *Or in the spaces between, feel this as lightning.*

72 *Feel the cosmos as a translucent ever-living presence.*

Man can be considered in three ways: in terms of the normal, the abnormal and the supernormal. Western psychology is basically concerned with the abnormal, the pathological, with the man who has fallen down from the normal, who has fallen down from the norm. Eastern psychology, tantra and yoga, consider man from the standpoint of the supernormal—of the one who has gone beyond the norm. Both are abnormal. One who is pathological is abnormal because he is not healthy, and one who is supernormal is abnormal because he is *more* healthy than any normal human being. The difference is of negative and positive.

Western psychology developed as part of psychotherapy. Freud, Jung, Adler and other psychologists were treating the abnormal man, the man who is mentally ill. Because of this the whole Western attitude towards man has become erroneous. Freud was studying pathological cases. Of course, no healthy man would go to him—only those who were mentally ill. They were studied by him, and because of that study he thought that now he understood man. Pathological men are not really men; they are ill, and anything based on a study of them is bound to be deeply erroneous and harmful. This has proved harmful because man is looked at from a pathological standpoint. If a particular state of mind is chosen and that state is ill, pathological, then the whole image of man becomes disease-based. Because of this attitude, the whole Western

society has fallen down—because the ill man is the base, the perverted has become the foundation.

And if you study only the abnormal, you cannot conceive of any possibility of supernormal beings. A buddha is impossible for Freud, not conceivable. He must be fictitious, mythological. A buddha cannot be a reality. Freud has only come in contact with ill men who are not even normal, and whatsoever he says about normal man is based on the study of abnormal man. It is just like a physician who is doing a study. No healthy man will go to him, there is no need. Only unhealthy people will go. By studying so many unhealthy people, he creates a picture in his mind of man, but that picture cannot be of man. It cannot be because man is not only illnesses. And if you base your concept of man on illnesses, the whole society will suffer.

Eastern psychology, particularly tantra and yoga, also has a concept of man, but that concept is based on the study of the supernormal—Buddha, Patanjali, Shankara, Nagarjuna, Kabir, Nanak— on persons who have reached to the peak of human potentiality and possibility. The lowest has not been considered, only the highest. If you consider the highest your mind becomes an opening; you can grow because now you know higher reaches are possible. If you consider the lowest, no growth is possible. There is no challenge. If you are normal you feel happy. It is enough that you are not perverted, that you are not in a mental asylum. You can feel good, but there is no challenge.

But if you seek the supernormal, the highest possibility that you can become, if someone has become that possibility, if that possibility has become actual in someone, then a possibility for growth opens. You can grow. A challenge comes to you, and you need not be satisfied with yourself. Higher reaches are possible and they are calling you. This must be understood deeply. Only then will the psychology of tantra be conceivable. Whatsoever you are is not the end. You are just in the middle. You can fall down, you can rise up. Your growth has not finished. You are not the end product; you are just a passage. Something is constantly growing in you.

Tantra conceives of and bases its whole technique on this possibility of growth. And remember, unless you become that which you can become, you will not be fulfilled. You *must* become that which you can become—it is a must! Otherwise you will be frustrated, you will feel meaningless, you will feel that there is no purpose in life. You can carry on, but there can be no joy in it. And you may succeed in many other things, but you will fail with yourself. And this is happening. Someone becomes very rich and everyone thinks that now he has succeeded. Everyone except himself thinks that he has succeeded. He knows his failure. Wealth is there, but he has failed. You are a great man, a leader, a politician. Everyone thinks that they have succeeded, but they have failed. This world is strange: you succeed in everyone's eyes except your own.

People come to me daily. They say they have everything, but now what? They are failures, but where have they failed? As far as outward things are concerned they have not failed, so why do they feel this failure? Their inner potentiality has remained potent. They have not flowered. They have not achieved what Maslow calls "self-actualization." They are failures—inner failures, and ultimately, what others say is meaningless. What you feel is meaningful. If you feel that you are a failure, others may think that you are a Napoleon or an Alexander the Great, but it makes no difference. Rather, it depresses you more. Everyone thinks that you are

a success, and now you cannot say that you are not —but you know you are not. You cannot deceive yourself. As far as self-actualization is concerned you cannot deceive. Sooner or later you will have to call upon yourself and look deeply into yourself at what has happened. The life is wasted. You have given up an opportunity and gathered things which mean nothing.

Self-actualization refers to the highest peak of your growth, where you can feel a deep content, where you can say, "This is my destiny, this is for what I was meant, this is why I am here on earth." Tantra is concerned with that self-actualization— with how to help you grow more. And remember, tantra is concerned with you, not with ideals. Tantra is not concerned with ideals; it is concerned with you as you are and as you can become. The difference is great. All teachings are concerned with ideals. They say become like Buddha, become like Jesus, become like this or that. They have ideals, and you have to become like those ideals. Tantra has no ideal for you. Your unknown ideal is hidden within you; it cannot be given to you. You are not to become Buddha, there is no need. One Buddha is enough, and no repetition is of any value. Existence is always unique, it never repeats; repetition is boredom. Existence is always new, eternally new, so even a Buddha is not repeated—such a beautiful phenomenon, left unrepeated.

Why? Because even if a Buddha is repeated it will create boredom. What is the use? Only the unique is meaningful; copies are not meaningful. Only if you are firsthand is your destiny fulfilled. If you are secondhand, you have missed.

So tantra never says be like this or that; there is no ideal. Tantra never talks about ideals; hence, the name "tantra." Tantra talks about techniques— never about ideals. It talks of *how* you can become; it never says what. It exists because of that how. Tantra means technique; the very word "tantra" means technique. It is concerned with "how" you can become, it is not concerned with "what." That "what" will be supplied by your growth. Just use the technique, and by and by your inner potentiality will become actual. The uncharted possibility will become opened, and as it opens you will realize what it is. And no one can say what it is. Unless you become it, no one can predict what you can become.

So tantra gives you only techniques—never ideals. This is how it is different from all moral teachings. Moral teachings always give ideals. Even if they talk about techniques, those techniques are always for particular ideals. Tantra gives no ideal to you; you *are* the ideal, and your future is unknown. No ideal from the past can be of any help because nothing can be repeated, and if it is repeated it is meaningless.

Zen monks say to remember and be alert. If you meet Buddha in your meditation, kill him immediately; don't allow him to stand there. Zen monks are Buddha's followers, and yet they say kill Buddha immediately if you meet him in your meditation, because the personality, the ideal of Buddha may become so hypnotizing that you may forget yourself, and if you forget yourself you have missed the path. Buddha is not the ideal; you are the ideal, your unknown future. That has to be discovered.

Tantra gives you techniques of discovery. The treasure is within you. So remember this second thing: it is very difficult to believe that you are the ideal—difficult for you to believe because everyone is condemning you. No one accepts you, not even you yourself. You go on condemning yourself. You always think in terms of being like someone else, and that is false, dangerous. If you go on thinking like that you will become a fake and everything will be phony. Do you know from where the word 'phony' comes? It comes from telephone. In the early days of the telephone, the transmission was so false, so unreal, that a real voice and a phony voice were heard from the telephone—a phony voice that was mechanical. The real voice was lost—just in those beginning days. From there comes the word 'phony.' If you are imitating someone else, you will become phony, you will not be real. A mechanical device will be there all around you, and your reality, your real voice, will be lost. So don't be phony, be real.

Tantra believes in you. That is why there are so few believers in tantra—because no one believes in himself. Tantra believes in you and says that you are the ideal, so don't imitate anyone. Imitation will create a pseudo personality around you. You can go on moving with that pseudo personality thinking it is yourself, but it is not. So the second thing to remember is that there is no fixed ideal. You cannot think in terms of the future; you can only think in terms of the present—just the immediate future in which you can grow.

No fixed future is there, and it is good that there is no fixed future; otherwise there would be no freedom. If there were a fixed future, man would be a robot. You have no fixed future. You have multipossibilities; you can grow in many ways. But the only thing that will give you ultimate contentment is that you grow—that you grow in such a way that every growth produces further growth. Techniques are helpful because they are scientific. You are saved from unnecessary wandering, unnecessary groping. If you don't know any techniques, you will take many lives. You will reach the goal because the life energy within you will move unless it comes to the point where no movement is possible. It will go on moving to the highest peak, and that is the reason why one goes on being born again and again. Left to yourself you will reach—but you will have to travel very, very long, and the journey will be very tedious and boring.

With a master, with scientific techniques, you can save much time, opportunity and energy. And sometimes within seconds you can grow so much that within lives even you will not be able to grow that much. If a right technique is used growth explodes, and these techniques have been used in thousands of years of experiments. They were not devised by one man; they were devised by many, many seekers, and only the essence is given here. In these one hundred and twelve techniques, all techniques from all over the world have been covered.

Nowhere does there exist any technique which has not been covered in this one hundred and twelve; they are the whole spiritual search in essence. But all the techniques are not for everyone, so you will have to try them out. Only certain techniques will be helpful to you, and you will have to find them out. There are two ways: either by your own trial and error, until you stumble upon something which starts working and you start growing, and then you move in it; or you surrender to some teacher and he finds out what will suit you. These are the two ways. You can choose.

Now the techniques.

---

70 Visualize light rays rising up your spine.

The first light technique: *Consider your essence as light rays rising from center to center up the vertebrae, and so rises "livingness" in you.*

Many yoga methods are based on this. First understand what it is; then the application. The vertebrae, the spine, is the base of both your body and mind. Your mind, your head, is the end part of your spine. The whole body is rooted in the spine. If the spine is young, you are young. If the spine is old, you are old. If you can keep your spine young, it is difficult to become old. Everything depends on your spine. If your spine is alive, you will have a very brilliant mind. If the spine is dull and dead, you will have a very dull mind. The whole yoga tries in many ways to make your spine alive, brilliant, filled with light, young and fresh.

The spine has two ends: the beginning is the sex center and the end is *sahasrar*, the seventh center at the top of the head. The beginning of the spine is attached to the earth, and sex is the most earthly thing in you. From the beginning center in your spine you are in contact with nature, with what Sankhya has called *prakriti*—the earth, the material. From the last center, or the second pole, sahasrar, in the head, you are in contact with the divine.

These are the two poles of your existence. First is sex and second is the sahasrar. There is no word for sahasrar in English. These are the two poles. Either your life will be sex-oriented or sahasrar-oriented. Either your energy will be flowing down from the sex center back to the earth, or your energy will be released from the sahasrar into the cosmos. From the sahasrar you flow into the *Brahma*, into the absolute Existence. From sex you flow down into the relative existence. These are the two flows, the two possibilities. Unless you start flowing upwards, your misery will never end. You may have glimpses of happiness, but only glimpses—and very illusory ones.

When the energy starts moving upwards you will have more and more real glimpses. And once it reaches the sahasrar and is released from there, you will have the absolute bliss with you. That is *nirvana*. Then there is no glimpse; you become the bliss itself. So the whole thing for yoga and tantra is how to move energy upwards through the vertebrae, through the spinal column, how to help it move against gravity. Sex is very easy because it follows gravitation. The earth is pulling everything down, back; your sex energy is pulled by the earth. You may not have heard it, but astronauts have felt this—that the moment they move beyond the earth's gravity they don't feel much sexuality. As the body loses weight, sexuality dissolves, disappears.

The earth is pulling your life energy down and this is natural, because the life energy comes from the earth. You eat food and you are creating life energy within you; it comes from the earth, and the earth is pulling it back. Everything goes to its source. And if it continues to move in this way, life energy going back again and again, and you are moving in a circle, you will go on moving for lives and lives. You can go on moving this way infinitely unless you take a jump just like the astronauts. Like the astronauts, you have to take a jump and move beyond the circle. Then the pattern of earth's gravitation is broken. It can be broken!

The techniques for how it can be broken are

here—for how the energy can move vertically and rise up within you, reaching new centers; for how new energies can be revealed within you, making you a new person with every move. And the moment the energy is released from your sahasrar, the opposite pole of sex, you are no more man. Then you don't belong to this earth; you have become divine. That is what is meant when we say Krishna is God or Buddha is God. Their bodies are just like yours—their bodies will have to fall ill and they will have to die—everything happens in their bodies as it happens to you. Only one thing is not happening in their bodies which is happening to you: the energy has broken the gravitation pattern.

But that you cannot see, it is not visible to your eyes. But sometimes when you are sitting by the side of a buddha, you can feel this. Suddenly you feel an upsurge of energy within you, and your energy starts moving upwards. Only then do you know that something has happened. Just by being in contact with a buddha your energy begins to move upwards towards the sahasrar. A buddha is so powerful that even the earth is less powerful; it cannot pull your energy downwards. Those who have felt this around a Jesus, a Buddha, a Krishna, have called them God. They have a different source of energy which is stronger than the earth.

How can the pattern be broken? This technique is very useful for breaking the pattern. First understand something basic. One, if you have observed at all you must have observed that your sex energy moves with imagination. Just through imagination your sex center starts functioning. Really, without imagination it cannot function. That is why if you are in love with someone it functions better—because with love imagination enters. If you are not in love it is very difficult. It will not function.

This is the reason why male prostitutes were not found in the old days, only women prostitutes. It is difficult for a male prostitute if he has no love, and how can he have love just because of money? You can pay a man to have intercourse with you, but if he has no imagination for you he cannot function.

Women can function because their sex is passive. Really, their functioning is not needed. They can be totally detached; they may not be feeling anything at all. Their bodies can just be there like corpses. With a prostitute you are not making love with a real body—only with a dead corpse. But women can easily be prostitutes because their sex is passive.

The sex center functions through imagination. That is why even in dreams you can get erections and ejaculations. They are actual. Dreams are just imagination. It has been observed that every man, if physically fit, will have at least ten erections in the night. With every movement of the mind, with only a slight thought of sex, the erection will come.

Your mind has many energies, many faculties, and one is will. But you cannot will sex. For sex will is impotent. If you try to love someone, you will feel you have gone impotent. So never try. Will never functions with sex; only imagination will function. Imagine, and the center will start to function. Why am I emphasizing this fact? Because if imagination helps the energy to move, then you can move it upwards or downwards just by imagination. You cannot move your blood by imagination; you cannot do anything else in the body by imagination. But sex energy can be moved by imagination. You can change its direction.

This sutra says, *Consider your essence as light rays*—think of yourself, your being, as light rays—*from center to center up the vertebrae*—up your spine—*and so rises "livingness" in you.* Yoga has divided your spine into seven centers. The first is the sex center and the last is sahasrar, and between these two there are five centers. Some systems divide into nine, some into three, some into four. Division is not very meaningful, you can make your own division. Just five centers are enough to work with; the first is the sex center, the second is just behind the navel, the third is just behind the heart, the fourth is behind your two eyebrows, just in-between, in the middle of the forehead. And the fifth, sahasrar, is just on the top of your head. These five will do.

This sutra says, *Consider yourself...*which means imagine yourself—close your eyes and imagine yourself just as if you are light. This is not just imagination. In the beginning it is, but it is reality also because everything consists of light. Now science says that everything consists of electricity, and tantra has always said that everything consists of light particles—and you also. That is why the Koran says that God is light. *You* are light! Imagine first that you are just light rays; then move your imagination to the sex center. Concentrate your attention there and feel that light rays are rising upwards from the sex center, as if the sex center has become a source of light and light rays are moving in an upsurge—upwards towards the navel center. Division is needed because it will be difficult for you to connect your sex center with the sahasrar. So smaller divisions will be of help. If you can connect, no divisions are needed. You can just drop all divisions from your sex center onwards, and the energy, the life force will rise up as light towards the sahasrar. But divisions will be more helpful because your mind can conceive of smaller fragments more easily.

So just feel that the energy—just the light rays—is rising up from your sex center to your navel like a river of light. Immediately you will feel a warmth rising in you. Soon your navel will become hot. You can feel the hotness; even others can feel that hotness. Through your imagination the sex energy will have started to rise. When you feel that now the second center at the navel has become a source of light, that the rays are coming and being collected there, then start to move to the heart center. As the light reaches the heart center, as the rays are coming, your heartbeat will be changed. Your breathing will become deeper, and a warmth will come to your heart. Go on upwards.

Consider your essence as light rays from center to center up the vertebrae, and so rises "livingness" in you. And as you will feel warmth, just side by side you will feel a "livingness," a new life coming to you, an inward light rising up. Sex energy has

two parts: one is physical and one is psychic. In your body everything has two parts. Just like your body and mind, everything within you has two parts—one material and the other spiritual. Sex energy has two parts. The material part is semen; it cannot rise upwards, there is no passage for it. Because of this, many physiologists of the West say that tantra and yoga methods are nonsense and they deny them completely. How can sex energy rise up? There is no passage and sex energy cannot rise. They are right and still wrong. Semen, the material part, cannot rise—but that is not the whole of it. Really, it is only the body of sex energy, it is not the sex energy. The sex energy is the psychic part of it, and the psychic part can rise. And for that psychic part, the spinal passage is used—the spinal passage and its centers. But that has to be felt and your feelings have gone dead.

I remember that a certain psychotherapist wrote somewhere about a patient, a woman. He was telling her to feel something, but the psychotherapist felt that whatever she did she was not feeling, but thinking about feeling—and that is a different thing. So the therapist put his hand on the woman's hand and pressed it, telling her to close her eyes and relate what she felt. She said immediately, "I feel your hand."

But the therapist said, "No, this is not your feeling. This is just your thinking, your inference. I have put my hand in your hand; you say you are feeling my hand. But you are not. This is inference. What do you feel?"

So she said, "I feel your fingers."

The therapist again said, "No, this is not feeling. Don't infer anything. Just close your eyes and move to the place where my hand is; then tell me what you feel."

Then she said, "Oh! I was missing the whole thing. I feel pressure and warmth."

When a hand touches you, a hand is not felt. Pressure and warmth are felt. The hand is just inference, it is intellect, not feeling. Warmth and pressure, that is feeling. Now she was feeling. We have lost feeling completely. You will have to develop feeling; only then can you do such techniques. Otherwise, they will not function. You will just intellectualize, you will just think that you are feeling, and nothing will happen. That is why people come to me and say, "You tell us this technique is so significant, but nothing happens." They have tried, but they are missing a dimension—the feeling dimension. So first you will have to develop that, and there are some methods which you can try.

You can do one thing. If you have a small child in your house, follow the child around for one hour every day. It will be better and more fulfilling than following a buddha. Allow the child to move on all fours, and you also move on all fours. Just follow the child moving on all fours, and you will feel for the first time a new life energy coming to you. You will again become a child. Look at the child and just follow. He will go to every corner; he will touch everything—not only touch, he will taste everything, he will smell everything. Just follow, and do whatsoever he is doing.

You were also a child once; you have done this. The child is feeling. He is not intellectualizing, he is not thinking. He feels a smell, so he moves to that corner from where it is coming. He sees an apple, so he tastes it. Just taste like a child. Watch when he is eating the apple, look at him: he is totally absorbed in it. The whole world has dropped, the world is no more there—only the apple. Even the apple is not and the child is not—only the eating. Just follow a small child for one hour. That hour will be so enriching, you will become again a child.

Your defense mechanisms will drop, your armor will drop, and you will start looking at the world as a child looks—from the feeling dimension. When you feel that now you can feel, not think, you will enjoy the texture of the carpet on which you are moving like a child, the pressure, the warmth—and just by innocently following a child. Man can learn much from children, and sooner or later your real innocence will erupt. You were once a child

and you know what it means to be one. You have simply forgotten.

The feeling center must start functioning; only then will these techniques be of any help. Otherwise you will go on thinking that energy is rising, but there will be no feeling. And if there is no feeling, imagination is impotent, futile. Only a feeling imagination will give you a result. You can do many other things and there is no need to make a specific effort to do them. When you go to sleep just feel your bed, feel the pillow—the coldness. Just turn on to it, play with the pillow.

Close your eyes and listen to the noise of the air conditioner, or of the traffic or of the clock or anything. Just listen. Don't label, don't say anything. Don't use the mind. Just live in the sensation. In the morning, in the first moment of waking, when you feel that now sleep has gone, don't start thinking. For a few moments you can again be a child—innocent, fresh. Don't start thinking. Don't think about what you are going to do and when you are starting for the office and what train you are going to catch. Don't start thinking. You will have enough time for all that nonsense. Just wait. For a few moments just listen to the noise. A bird is singing or the wind is passing through the trees or a child is crying or the milkman has come and is making sounds or the milk is being poured. With anything that happens, feel it. Be sensitive to it, open to it. Allow it to happen to you, and your sensitivity will grow.

When taking a shower, feel it all over the body —every drop of water touching you. Feel the touch, the coldness, the warmth! Try this the whole day whenever you have the chance, and everywhere there is a chance—everywhere! When just breathing, feel the breath—its movement within and its going out—just feel it! Just feel your own body. You have not felt it.

We are so afraid of our own bodies. No one touches his own body in a loving way. Have you ever given any love to your own body? The whole civilization is afraid of anyone touching himself because from childhood touching has been denied. It appears to be masturbatory to touch oneself in a loving way. But if you cannot touch yourself in a loving way your body will go dull and dead. It has gone so. Touch your eyes with your palms. Feel the touch, and your eyes will feel fresh and alive immediately. Feel your body all over. Feel your lover's body, your friend's body. Massage is good. Two friends can massage each other and feel each other's bodies. You will become more sensitive.

Create sensitivity and feeling. Then it will be easy for you to do these techniques, and then you will feel "livingness" arising in you. Don't leave this energy anywhere. Allow it to come to the sahasrar. Remember this: whenever you do this experiment, don't leave it in the middle. You have to complete it. Take care that no one disturbs you. If you leave this energy somewhere in the middle, it can be harmful. It has to be released. So bring it to the head and feel as if your head has become an opening.

In India we have pictured sahasrar as a lotus— as a thousand-petalled lotus. 'Sahasrar' means thousand-petalled—an opening of a thousand petals. Just conceive of the lotus with a thousand petals, opened, and from every petal this light energy is moving into the cosmos. Again, this is a love act—not with nature now, but with the ultimate. Again, it is an orgasm.

There are two types of orgasms: one is sexual and the other spiritual. The sexual comes from the lowest center and the spiritual from the highest center. From the highest you meet the highest and from the lowest you meet the lowest. Even while actually in the sex act, you can do this exercise; both the partners can do this. Move the energy upwards, and then the sex act becomes *tantra sadhana*; it becomes meditation.

But don't leave the energy somewhere in the body at some center. Someone may come and you will have some business, or some phone call will come and you will have to stop. So do it at such a time that no one will disturb you, and don't leave the energy in any center. Otherwise that center

where you leave the energy will become a wound, and you may create many mental illnesses. So be aware; otherwise don't do this. This method needs absolute privacy and no disturbance, and it must be done completely. The energy must come to the head, and it should be released from there.

You will have various experiences. When you will feel that the rays are starting to come up from the sex center, there will be erections or sensations at the sex center. Many, many people come to me very afraid and scared. They say that whenever they start meditation, when they start to move deep, there is an erection. They wonder, "What is this?" They are afraid because they think that in meditation sex should not be there. But you don't know life's functioning. It is a good sign. It shows that energy is now there alive. Now it needs movement. So don't become scared and don't think that something is wrong. It is a good sign. When you start meditation the sex center will become more sensitive, alive, excited, and in the beginning the excitement will be just the same as any sexual excitement—but only in the beginning. As your meditation becomes deeper, you will feel energy flowing up. As the energy flows, the sex center becomes silent, less excited.

When the energy will really move to the sahasrar, there will be no sensation at the sex center. It will be totally still and silent. It will have become completely cool, and the warmth will have come to the head. And this is physical. When the sex center is excited, it becomes hot; you can feel that hotness, it is physical. When the energy will move, the sex center will become cooler and cooler and cooler, and the hotness will come to the head.

You will feel dizzy. When the energy comes to the head, you will feel dizzy. Sometimes you may even feel nausea because for the first time energy has come to the head and your head is not acquainted with it. It has to become tuned. So don't become afraid. Sometimes you may immediately become unconscious, but don't be afraid. This happens. If so much energy moves suddenly and explodes in the head, you may become unconscious. But that unconsciousness cannot remain for more than one hour. Within one hour the energy automatically falls back or is released. You cannot remain that way for more than one hour. I say one hour, but in fact it is exactly forty-eight minutes. It cannot be more than that. It never has been in thousands of years of experiments, so don't be afraid. If you do become unconscious, it is okay. After that unconsciousness you will feel so fresh that it is as if you have been in sleep for the first time, in the deepest sleep.

Yoga calls it by a special name—*yoga tandra:* yogic sleep. It is very deep; you move to your deepest center. But don't be afraid. And if your head becomes hot, it is a good sign. Release the energy. Feel as if your head is opening like a lotus flower— as if energy is being released into the cosmos. As the energy is released, you will feel a coldness coming to you. You have never felt the coldness that comes after this hotness. But do the technique completely; never do it incompletely.

71 Visualize a spark of light jumping from one chakra to the next.

The second light technique: *Or in the spaces between, feel this as lightning.*

This is a very similar method with a slight difference: *Or in the spaces between, feel this as lightning.* Between one center and another, as rays are coming, you can feel it like lightning—just a jump of light. For some people the second will be more suitable and for others the first. This is why there is a modification. There are people who cannot imagine things gradually and there are people who cannot imagine in jumps. If you can think and imagine gradually, then the first method is good. But if you try the first method and you suddenly feel that from one center the rays jump directly to the second, then don't do the first method. The

second is better for you. *Feel this as lightning*—like a spark of light jumping from one center to the next. And the second is more real because, really, light jumps. There is no gradual, step-by-step growth. Light is a jump.

Look at the electric light. You think it is constant, but that is illusory. There are gaps, but the gaps are so small that you cannot detect them. Electricity comes in jumps. One jump, and then there is a gap of darkness. Another jump, and then there is a gap of darkness. But you never feel the gap because the jump is so fast. Otherwise, every moment there is darkness. Again there is a jump, light comes, then again darkness. Light jumps, it never travels. For those who can conceive of jumps, the second modification is best. *Or in the spaces between, feel this as lightning.* Just try it. If you feel good with the rays coming gradually, it is okay. If you don't feel good and rays are jumping, then forget about rays. Think of this as lightning in the sky, in the clouds, just jumping from one place to another.

For women the first technique will be easier and for men the second. The feminine mind can conceive of gradualness more easily and the male jumps more easily. The male mind is "jumpy"; it jumps from one thing to another. There is a subtle uneasiness in the male mind. The female mind has a gradual process, it is not jumpy. That is why female and male logic are very different. A man goes on jumping from one thing to another, and for women this is inconceivable. For them there must be growth—gradual growth. But choose. Try these, and choose whichever you feel is good for you.

Two or three things more about this method. With lightning you may feel such hotness that it may seem unbearable. If you feel that, don't try it. Lightning can give you much heat. If you feel this, that it is unbearable, then don't try this. Then with the first method, if you are at ease, then it is good. Otherwise with uneasiness don't try it. Sometimes the explosion can be so great that you may become afraid of it, and once afraid you will never be able to do it again. Then fear enters.

So one has to be aware always not to become afraid of anything. If you feel that fear will come and it is too much for you, don't try it. Then the first method with light rays is best. If you feel that even with light rays too much hotness is coming to you—and it depends because people differ—then conceive of the rays as cool, imagine them as cool. Then instead of feeling warmth you will feel a coldness with everything. That too will be effective. So you can decide; try and decide. Remember, with this technique, and with others also, if you feel very uneasy or anything unbearable, don't do it. There are other methods, and this one may not be for you. With unnecessary disturbance inside, you will create more problems than you will solve.

In India, because of this, we have developed a particular yoga which we call *sahaj yoga*. Sahaj means spontaneous, easy, natural. Always remember sahaj. If you feel any technique spontaneously coming to you, if you feel more affinity with it, if you feel better with it—more healthy, more alive, more at home—then that is the method for you. Move with it; you can trust it. Don't create unnecessary problems. And the inner mechanism is very complex. If you do something which is too much for you, you may destroy many things. So it is better to move with something which feels harmonious to you.

72 Feel the presence of the ever-living existence.

The third light technique: *Feel the cosmos as a translucent ever-living presence.*

This again is concerned with light: *Feel the cosmos as a translucent ever-living presence.* If you have taken any drugs such as LSD or some such thing, the whole world around you becomes a light phenomenon of colors that are translucent, alive. This is not because of LSD. The world is such, but your

eyes have become dull. The LSD is not creating a colorful world around you; the world is already colorful, nothing is wrong with the world. It is a rainbow of colors—a mystery of colors and translucent light. But your eyes have become dull. That is why you can never feel it in such colorfulness.

LSD is just clearing your eyes. It is not making the world colorful; it is just helping your dullness to go chemically, and then the whole world erupts before you. It is a new thing. Even an ordinary chair becomes a marvelous phenomenon. Just a shoe on the floor takes on new colors, a new youth. Ordinary traffic noise becomes musical. Trees you have always seen but never looked at are born anew though you have always passed them by and you know you have seen them. Every leaf of a tree is a miracle.

And this is how reality is. It is not LSD which is creating this reality. LSD is just destroying your dullness, your insensitivity, and you look at the world as one should really look. But LSD can give you only a glimpse, and if you depend on it, sooner or later even LSD will not be able to remove your dullness. Then you will need greater doses, and then you will become immune to greater doses. And, really, if you then leave LSD or other drugs, the world will be duller than it has ever been. Then you will become even more insensitive.

Just a few days ago a girl came to see me. She said she could not feel any orgasm in the love act. She has tried many men, but she cannot feel any orgasm. The peak never comes, and she has become frustrated. So I asked her to tell me her whole love and sex life—the whole story. Then I discovered that she had been using an electric vibrator. Now in the West they are using these. Once you use an electric vibrator as a male penis, then no male can satisfy you because an electric vibrator is, after all, an electric vibrator. Then your vagina and clitoris will go dead, dull, and then orgasm will become impossible. Then there won't be any possibility of any orgasm. You will now need a more powerful electric vibrator, and this can go to such an extreme that your total sexual mechanism will become stony. And this is happening to our every sense. If you use any outer device, you will become dull.

LSD will make you dull ultimately because with it you are not growing. If *you* grow, then it is a different process. Then you become more sensitive, and as you become more sensitive the world becomes different. Now you can sense many things you never sensed before because you were not sensitive.

This technique is based on inner sensitivity. First grow in sensitivity. Just close your doors, make the room dark and light a small candle. Sit near the candle with a very loving attitude—rather, with a prayerful attitude. Just pray to the candle, "Reveal yourself to me." Take a bath, throw cold water on your eyes, then sit in a very prayerful mood before the candle. Look at it and forget everything else. Just look at the small candle—the flame and the candle. Go on looking at it. After five minutes you will feel that many things are changing in the candle. They are not changing in the candle, remember; your eyes are changing.

With a loving attitude, with the whole world closed out, with total concentration, with a feeling heart, just go on looking at the candle and the flame. Then you will discover new colors around the flame, new shades which you were never aware were there. They are there; the whole rainbow is there. Wherever light is, the rainbow is there because light is all colors. You need a subtle sensitivity. Just feel it and go on looking at it. Even if tears start flowing, go on looking at it. Those tears will help your eyes to be more fresh.

Sometimes you may feel that the flame, the candle, has become mysterious. It is not the ordinary candle you brought with you; it has taken on a new glamour, a subtle divineness has come into it. Go on doing this. You can also do this with many other things.

One of my friends was telling me that a group of five or six persons had been experimenting with rocks. I had told them how to experiment, and then they reported to me. They were experimenting with rocks on the bank of a lonely river. They were trying to feel them with their hands, with their faces, touching the rocks with their tongues, smelling the rocks. In every way possible they were feeling the rocks—just ordinary rocks which they found on the bank.

They tried this for a whole hour, everyone with a rock. And then, my friend reported, there was a miracle. Everyone said, "Could I keep this rock? I have fallen in love with it!" An ordinary rock! If you have a sympathetic relationship with it, you will fall in love. And if you don't have that sensitivity, then even with a very beautiful person you are with a rock; you cannot fall in love.

Sensitivity must grow. Your every sense must become more alive. Then you can experiment with this technique. *Feel the cosmos as a translucent ever-living presence.* Everywhere light is—in many, many shapes, forms, light is happening everywhere. Look at it! And everywhere light is because the whole phenomenon is based on the foundation of light. Look at a leaf or a flower or a rock, and sooner or later you will feel rays coming out of it. Just wait patiently. Don't be in a hurry because nothing is revealed when you are in a hurry. In a hurry you are dull. Wait silently with anything, and you will discover a new phenomenon which was always there, but of which you were not alert—not aware of it.

Feel the cosmos as a translucent ever-living presence, and your mind will become completely silent as you feel the presence of the ever-living existence. You will be just a part in it, just a note in the great symphony. No burden, no tension...the drop has fallen into the ocean. But great imagination will be needed in the beginning, and if you are also trying with other sensitivity training it will be helpful.

You can try many ways. Just take someone's hand into your hand. Close your eyes and feel the life in the other. Feel it, and allow it to move towards you. Feel your own life and allow it to move towards the other. Sit near a tree and touch the bark of the tree. Close your eyes and feel the life arising in the tree, and you change immediately.

I have heard about one experiment. A doctor was experimenting with people to see whether their feelings changed their biochemistry. Now he has reported that feeling changes biochemistry immediately. He experimented with a group of twelve persons. He collected their urine before the experiment, and the urine was ordinary, normal.

Each person was put under a different stress. One was shown a film of horror, anger, violence, cruelty—it was just a film. For thirty minutes he was shown a film of horror. Of course, with the film his emotions changed. He felt stress. To another a very joyful film was shown. He felt happy. And so on went the experiment for twelve persons. Then their urine was taken again and the urine analysis showed that everyone's urine was different now. The chemicals had changed in the body. The person who felt horror was ill now; the person who felt hope, happiness, joy, was healthy now. His urine was different, the chemicals of the body were different.

You are not aware of what you are doing with yourself. When you go to see a murder film, you don't know what you are doing. You are changing your body chemistry. If you are reading a detective novel, you don't know what you are doing. You are killing yourself. You will become excited, you will become afraid, a tension will come to you. That is how you enjoy the detective novel. The more tense you become, the more you enjoy it. The more the suspense over what is going to happen, the more you get excited—and you are changing your body chemistry.

All these techniques also change your body chemistry. If you feel the whole world as filled with life, light, then you are changing your body chemistry. And this is a chain reaction. When your body chemistry changes, you can look at the world and it will look more alive. And if it looks more alive, your body chemistry will change again, and then it becomes a chain.

If this method is done for three months, you will be living in a different world because you will be different now.

CHAPTER 48

The potentiality of the seed

◆

What is the difference between an inspiration and an ideal, and is being inspired by someone wrong for a seeker?

What is normal, and why is there so much pathology nowadays?

How can one "feel" awareness unless one achieves it, and how to imagine that which has not yet happened?

The first question:

Last night You said that a Krishna, a Christ, a Buddha, is the climax of human possibility and growth, and then You said that yogic and tantric psychology put no ideal before man and that to have an ideal is a mistake according to tantra. In this reference please explain what is the difference between an inspiration and an ideal. What is the significance of inspiration in a seeker's life? Please tell whether even being inspired by a great man is a mistake on the path of a meditator.

Buddha, a Krishna or a Christ, is not an ideal for you; you are not to follow them. If you follow them you will miss them, and your own buddhahood will never be achieved. Buddhahood is the ideal, not Buddha. Christhood is the ideal, not Jesus. Buddhahood is different from Gautam Buddha; Christhood is different from Jesus. Jesus is only one of the Christs. You can become a Christ, but you can never become a Jesus. You can become a Buddha, but you can never become Gautam. Gautam became a buddha and *you* can become a buddha. Buddhahood is a quality, it is an experience! Of course, when Gautam became a buddha, Gautam had his own individuality. You have your own individuality. When you will become a buddha, these two buddhas will not be the same. The innermost experience will be the same, but the expression will be different—abso-

lutely different. No comparison is possible. Only at the innermost core will you be the same.

Why? Because at the innermost core there is no individuality. The individual is on the periphery. The deeper you move, the more the individual dissolves. At the innermost core you are as if no one. At the innermost core you are just a deep void, a nothingness—a *shunya,* a zero. And because of this nothingness there is no difference, because two nothings cannot be different. But two somethings are bound to be different. Two "somethings" can never be the same and two "nothings" can never be different. When one becomes just absolutely nothing, a zero point, that is similar in a Jesus, in a Krishna, in a Buddha. When you will reach to the ultimate, you will reach to this shunya—this nothingness.

But your personality, your expression of that ecstasy, is bound to be different. A Meera will dance; a Buddha can never dance. It is impossible to conceive of Buddha dancing, it looks absurd. But Meera sitting under a bodhi tree like a Buddha also looks absurd. She will lose everything, she will not be a Meera at all; she will be imitation. The real Meera can only be conceived of as dancing in ecstasy in her own love madness. That is her expression. The innermost core is the same. With Buddha sitting under the bodhi tree and Meera dancing in mad ecstasy, the innermost core is the same. In the dancing Meera and in the silently sitting Buddha who is just like a statue, the innermost core is the same but the periphery is different. The dancing and the silent sitting are just on the periphery. If you move within Meera, as you go deeper the dance will cease, the Meera will cease. If you go deep into Buddha, the sitting will cease, the Buddha will cease as an individual.

You can become a buddha, but you can never become a Gautam Buddha: that is what is meant. Don't make them your ideals; otherwise you will start imitating them. And what can you do if you imitate? You can force something from without, but that will be a fake phenomenon. You will become pseudo—just painted. You will look Buddha-like—more than Buddha. You can look, but that will be just a look, an appearance; deep down you will remain the same—and this will create a duality, a conflict, an inner anguish, and you will be in suffering.

You can be in bliss only where you are authentically yourself. You can never feel any happiness when you are acting as someone else. So remember tantra's message: *you* are the ideal. You are not to imitate anyone; you are to discover yourself. Looking at a buddha, there is no need to imitate him. When you are looking at a buddha, the possibility hits deep in you that something of the beyond can happen. 'Buddha' is just a symbol that something has happened to this man—and if it can happen to this man, it can happen to *every* man. Then the whole possibility of humanity is revealed.

In a Jesus, in a Meera, in Chaitanya, just a possibility is revealed, the future is revealed. You need not be whatsoever you are. Something more is possible. So a buddha is just a symbol of the future. Don't imitate him; rather, let his life, his being, the phenomenon that is happening, become a new thirst in you, that is all. You must not be content with yourself as you are right now. Let a buddha become a discontent in you, a thirst to transcend, to go beyond, to move into the unknown. When you reach to the peak of your own being, you will know what happened to Buddha under the bodhi tree or what happened to Jesus on the cross or what happened to Meera when she was dancing in the streets. You will know, but your expression will be your own. You are not going to be a Meera or a Buddha or a Jesus. You are going to be yourself, and you have never been before. You are unique.

So nothing can be said; you are not predictable. No one can say what will happen, how you will manifest it. Whether you will sing, dance, paint or remain silent no one can say. And it is good that nothing can be said, nothing can be predicted. That is the beauty. If it is predictable that you will be like this or that, then you will become a mechanical thing.

Predictions are possible only about mechanical devices. Human consciousness is unpredictable; that is its freedom. So when tantra says don't follow ideals, it doesn't mean to deny Buddha. No, it is not a denial. Really, it is how you can find your own buddhahood. Following another, you will miss it. Following your own path, you can gain it, you can achieve it.

Someone came to a Zen master, Bokuju. Bokuju's master was very famous, well known, a very great man, so someone asked, "Are you really following your master?"

Bokuju said, "Yes, I am following him."

But the man who asked the question was disturbed because it was well known all over the country that Bokuju was not following his master at all. So the man said, "Are you trying to deceive me? Everyone knows and you are also aware that you are not following your master at all, and still you say that you are following. What do you mean?"

Bokuju said, "I am following my master—because my master never followed his master. This is what I have learned from him. He was himself!"

This is how a Buddha, a Jesus is to be followed. This is how! They are unique! If you are really following them, *you* must be unique.

Buddha never followed anyone, and he achieved enlightenment only in that moment when he had completely stopped following. When he became himself, when he left all paths, all teachings, all doctrines, then he could achieve. If you follow him, you are not following him. It is not paradoxical, it only looks so. If you follow him as a dead routine, if you imitate him, you are not following him. He never followed anyone, and only then could he become the peak. Understand him, don't follow him; and then a subtle following will happen. But that is inner—not an imitation.

In Nietzsche's great work *Thus Spake Zarathustra*, the last message of Zarathustra to his disciple is: "Beware of me. Now I have told everything that was to be told to you. Now beware of me. Don't follow me; just forget me. Leave me and go away."

This is the last message of all the great masters. No great master would like to make you a puppet because then he is killing you. He is a murderer then. He will help you to be yourself. And if you cannot be yourself in the intimacy and communication with your master, then where will you be yourself?

The master means an opportunity for you to be yourself. Only small minds, narrow minds who pretend to be masters and who are not masters, will try to impose themselves on you. Great masters will help you to grow on your own path, and great masters will create every barrier so that you don't become a victim of following. They will create every barrier! They will not allow it because your tendency will be to follow. It is easy, imitation is easy; to be authentic is arduous. And when you imitate you don't feel responsible for it, the master is responsible. No great master has ever allowed anyone to imitate. He will create every hindrance so that you cannot imitate him. He will throw you by every means to yourself.

I am reminded of one Chinese saint who was celebrating his master's enlightenment day. Many followers had come. They said, "But we never heard that this man was your master. We never knew that you belonged to this man." That old man was dead.

They said, "Only today did we come to hear and know that you are celebrating your master's enlightenment day. This man was your master? But how? We never saw you with him!"

The saint replied, "I had been with him, but he had refused. He had refused to become my master, and because of his refusal I could become myself. Now, whatsoever I am is because of his refusal. I am his disciple. He could have accepted me; then I would have thrown all responsibility on his shoulders. But he refused, and he was the last man. There was no comparison. When he refused, I could not go to anyone else because he was the only shelter. If he had refused, then there was no meaning, no purpose in going anywhere. I left going to anyone. He was the last. If he would have accepted me, I would have forgotten myself. But he refused, and he refused very rudely. The refusal became a shock and a challenge, and I decided that now I would not go to anyone. If this man had refused, then there was no one worth going to. Then I started working on my own, and only then did I realize by and by why he had refused. He had thrown me to myself, and only then did I know that he had accepted me. Otherwise why should he refuse?"

This looks contradictory, but this is how the deeper dynamism of consciousness works. Masters are mysterious. You cannot judge them; you cannot be sure what they are doing unless the whole thing happens. Then only retrospectively will you be able to know what they were doing. Now it is impossible. On the middle path you cannot judge what is happening, what is being done. But one thing is certain: imitation cannot be allowed.

Inspiration is a different thing. Through inspiration you start on the journey, not on any effort of copying. You move on your own path. Inspiration is just a challenge. A thirst arises, and then you move.

Tantra says be inspired, but don't become imitators. Always remember that you are your own goal. No one else can be, and unless you achieve that point from where you can say, "I have achieved my destiny and now I am fulfilled," don't stop. Go on transcending, go on being in discontent, go on moving. And if you don't make any ideal, then you can be enriched by everyone.

The moment you become obsessed with an ideal, you are closed. If you become obsessed with Buddha, then Jesus is not for you, then how can Mohammed be for you? Then you are obsessed with an ideal; then you are trying to copy it. Then all the contrary ones, all the different ones are inimical in your mind. How can a follower of Mahavira conceive of being open to Mohammed? It is impossible. He is totally different. Not only different, they are contraries. They look like polar opposites. If you put both in your mind you will be in deep conflict, so you cannot put both.

That is why followers are always enemies of others' followers. They create enmity in the world. A Hindu cannot conceive that Mohammed can be enlightened; a Mohammedan cannot conceive that Mahavira can be enlightened; a follower of Krishna cannot conceive that Mahavira can be enlightened, that Jesus can be enlightened. Jesus looks so sad and Krishna looks so blissful. Krishna's bliss and Jesus' sadness are total opposite poles. Jesus' followers cannot conceive of Krishna being enlightened. So much misery in the world and he is playing on his flute? It looks to be too selfish. The whole world is suffering, and he goes on dancing with his *gopis*?

The followers of Jesus will think this to be profane—but I say "followers." A Jesus and a Buddha and a Krishna can exist together without any problem, without any conflict. Rather, they will enjoy each other very much—but not the followers. Why? Why is this so? This will be so because there is a deep psychological reason. The follower is not concerned with Mohammed or Mahavira; he is concerned with himself. If he thinks both are good, he will be in difficulty. Then whom to follow and what to do? Mohammed is with his sword in his hand and Mahavira says that even to kill an insect means that for lives you will suffer. Mohammed is with his sword, so what to do? Mohammed goes to war, and Mahavira escapes from life completely. He escapes so much that he is afraid even to breathe, because while you breathe, many lives—many, many lives—are killed through it. He is afraid to breathe and Mohammed goes to war.

How can a follower of either make accommodations for the opposite? Then his heart will be divided and he will be in constant conflict. To avoid this, he says that everyone else is wrong and only this is right. But this is his problem. This is created because he is trying to imitate. There is no need. If you are not an imitator, then you can taste the water of many rivers and many wells, and there is no problem if the taste differs. Rather, it is beautiful. You are enriched by this. Then you are open to Mohammed and Mahavira and Christ and Zarathustra and everyone. They all inspire you towards yourself. They are not ideals; they all help you to be yourself. They are not pointing towards themselves, they are pointing towards you in different ways, in different methods. They are pointing to one goal, and that is *you*.

Laura Huxley has written a book. The name of the book is *You Are Not the Target*. But I tell you, you *are* the target of all these—of Buddha, of Mahavira, of Krishna, of Christ. They all indicate towards you. You are the target, you are the goal. Through you life is trying, striving, to achieve a unique peak. Be happy about it! Be grateful about it! Life is trying to achieve a unique goal through you, and that goal can be achieved only through you. No one else can achieve it. You are meant for it, you are destined for it. So don't waste time following others. But that doesn't mean not to get inspired. Really, if you are not following anyone you can become inspired easily. If you are following, you have become dead. You will not get inspired. Inspiration is an openness; following is being closed.

The second question:

You spoke of Western psychology being rooted in Freudian concepts of pathology and of Eastern psychology using the supernormal as the base from which to evaluate a man. But as I look around me in the modern world, I see that most people fit Freud's categories of pathology. One in a million fits the category of supernormal and a small number actually fit the societal ideal of normal. Why is there so much pathology nowadays and what would You consider to be the definition of normal?

Many things will have to be understood. It is not so —it is not that very few are there who achieve their peaks. Many are there, but you don't have the eyes to see them. Whenever you look around you, you see that which you can see. How can you see that which you cannot see? Your capacity to see determines many things. You hear that which you can hear, not that which is there. If a buddha passes, you may not be able to recognize. And you really were there when Buddha passed, but you missed him. You were there! You were there when Jesus was alive, but you crucified him. It is difficult to see because you see in your own ways. You have concepts, you have categories, you have attitudes. Through them you look at a Buddha and a Jesus.

Jesus looked like a criminal to you. When Jesus was crucified he was crucified with two criminals; on each side there was a thief. Three persons were crucified together, and Jesus was just between two thieves. Why? He was considered to be an immoral criminal somehow, and you were there to judge. Even if Jesus comes right now, you will judge again in the same way because your judgment, your criteria, have not changed.

Jesus lived and stayed with anyone and everyone. He stayed in a prostitute's house, and the whole village went against him. But his values were different. The prostitute came, washed his feet with her tears and said, "I am guilty. I am a sinner and you are my only hope. If you come to my home, I will be relieved of my guilt. I will become alive again. If Jesus could come to my house, then I am accepted."

So Jesus went. He stayed there, but the whole town went against him. What type of man is he, staying with a prostitute? But for Jesus love is the value, and no one has given such a loving invitation ever. He couldn't say no. And if Jesus had said no, he could not have been an enlightened man. Then he would have just been seeking after social respectability. He was *not* seeking after respectability.

In another village, the whole town came to Jesus with a woman who had sinned. In the Old Testament it is written that if someone sins she should be stoned to death. It is not that *he* should be, it is that *she* should be stoned to death, because only women sin; man never sins—because all these scriptures are written by men. And this was a great problem, so they asked Jesus about it. They were playing a trick, because if Jesus would have said, "No, don't kill this woman, don't be the judges," then they could say, "You are against the scriptures." And if Jesus would have said, "Yes, kill this woman, stone her to death," then they would say, "Where has gone your message 'Love your enemy' and where has gone your message 'Judge ye not that ye should be not judged'?"

So they were playing a trick. They were creating a dilemma—a logical dilemma. Whatsoever Jesus would have said, he would be trapped. But you cannot trap an enlightened man, it is impossible. It is impossible, and the more you try to trap him... you will get trapped with him. So Jesus said, "The scripture is absolutely correct. But come forward only those who have never sinned. Take these stones in your hands and murder this woman, but only those who have never sinned." The crowd started disappearing. Those who were standing in front went back—because who will stone this woman?

But they became enemies of Jesus. And when I say "they," I mean you. You have always been here. You cannot recognize, you cannot see. You are blind! That is why you always feel that the world is bad and there is no enlightenment—that everyone is pathological. It is not so, but you can only see pathology because you are pathological. You can understand illness because you are ill. You cannot understand health because you have never been healthy. The language of health simply escapes you.

I have heard about one Jewish mystic, Baal Shem. Someone came and asked Baal Shem, "Which is more significant, which is more valuable —wealth or wisdom?"

The man was asking the question for a reason, so Baal Shem laughed and said, "Of course, wisdom is more significant, more valuable."

Then the man said, "Then, Baal Shem, the second question: I always see you, the wise man, waiting on the wealthy. You always go to rich people's houses. I have never seen any wealthy man waiting on you, the wise one, and you say that wisdom is more valuable than wealth. Then explain this phenomenon to me."

Baal Shem laughed and said, "Yes, wise men go to the wealthy ones because they are wise and they know the value of wealth, and the wealthy ones are just wealthy—simply wealthy and nothing else— and they cannot understand the value of wisdom. Of course, I go—because I understand the value of wealth. And those poor idiots? They are just wealthy—nothing else. They cannot understand the value of wisdom, so they never come to me."

If you see a saint going to a palace, you will say, "Okay! This man is not a saint." It is finished because you look through your own eyes. Wealth has meaning for you. You can only follow a saint who renounces wealth because you are wealth-obsessed. You look through you, and whatsoever you say is more about you than about anyone else. It is always about you; you are the reference. When you say that Buddha is not enlightened, you don't mean that. You simply mean, "For me he does not look enlightened."

But who are you? And does his enlightenment depend in any way on your attitude, your approach, your standpoint? You have fixed categories of thought and you go on using them. To you pathology is recognizable, but enlightenment is not. And you cannot understand that which is higher than you—remember. You can only understand that which is lower than you or at the most on the same level. You cannot understand the higher, that is impossible. To understand the higher you will have to move higher. You can understand the lower.

Look at it in this way: a madman cannot understand you. It is impossible for a madman to understand you; he looks through his madness. But you can understand a madman. He is lower than you. The normal human being can understand abnormals who have gone below, pathological, but he cannot understand higher ones. Even a Freud is afraid.

Jung has written in his memoirs that once it happened to him that he wanted to analyze Freud's dreams. He was one of Freud's greatest disciples. They were traveling to the United States on a ship, so for many days they were together. One day Jung gathered courage. He was the most intimate disciple in those days, and he asked Freud, "I would like to analyze your dreams, so just tell me any dream. For many, many days we will be together, so I will analyze it."

What did Freud say? Freud said, "What do you mean? If you analyze my dreams I will lose my authority. I cannot tell you my dreams." He was so afraid because in his dreams the same pathology, the same illnesses will be revealed as he is revealing in others' dreams. He said, "I cannot lose my authority. I cannot tell you about my dreams."

Freud, the greatest psychologist of this age, is prone to all the illnesses that anyone else is. When Jung said that "I am going to leave you," he fell from his chair and became unconscious. He swooned. For hours he was unconscious because he was so shocked just by the idea of a disciple leaving him, just by a disciple saying, "I am going to leave you."

If you say to a buddha, "I am going to leave you," can you conceive of him falling down and becoming unconscious? Even with all of the ten thousand disciples leaving him, he will be happy—so happy that he will feel it will be good if you go. Why? Your psychologists are also like you. They are not from above. They have the same problems, so one psychologist goes to another psychologist to be analyzed. It is not like one doctor going to another doctor to be treated. For doctors it is okay; they can be forgiven. But for psychologists it seems absurd. One psychologist going to another to be analyzed? What does it mean? He is an ordinary man. Psychology is just a profession.

Buddha is not in any profession, he is not an ordinary man. He has awakened to a new reality; he has reached to a new state of being. Now he can look from a peak. He can understand you, but you cannot understand him. And howsoever he tries, it is really impossible to make you understand him. You will go on misunderstanding him unless you are caught not by his words, but by his personality—unless you are caught by his magnetism, not by his words. Unless you become just like an iron piece and you are caught by his magnetism, you will not be able to understand him; you will misunderstand. That is why you cannot see. But the world always has its enlightened persons. Pathology is recognized because we are pathological, so we can see and understand it.

Secondly, even if there is only one—only a single human being who has ever achieved enlightenment throughout human history, even if there is only one buddha, he is enough to show you the possibility. If it can happen to one human being, why can it not happen to you? If one seed can become a flower, then every seed has the potentiality to become a flower. You may be just a seed, but now you know your future. Now you are aware that much more is possible.

But with the human mind the reverse is happening. It has been happening always. You see a cocoon and then it breaks, and then the butterfly moves. With man it seems to be quite the reverse. Man is born as the butterfly, and then he enters the cocoon. Every child is more buddhalike than he will ever be again. Look at a child, look at the eyes. They are more buddhalike than any adult's eyes. The way he sits, the way he moves—the grace, the beauty, the living in the moment, even his anger is beautiful. It is so total, and whenever anything is total it is beautiful.

Look at a child in anger jumping and screaming. Just look! Don't be concerned with yourself, that he is disturbing you. Just look at the phenomenon. The anger is beautiful—because the child is so totally in it that nothing is left behind. He *is* the anger, and he is so authentic that nothing is being suppressed. He is not withholding, he has moved and become anger. Look at the child when he loves, when he welcomes you, when he comes near to you: he is like a buddha. But soon you will help him, the society will help him to enter the cocoon, and then he will die in it.

From the cradle we enter into the grave immediately. That is why so much pathology is there—because no one is allowed to be natural. The pathology is forced. You are caged, imprisoned in a dead pattern, and then your spontaneous being suffers and you cannot come out of it. That is why so much pathology is there. This pathology is man-created—and the more man becomes civilized, the more pathological he becomes. So now this is a criterion: if in your country there are less madmen, know well that you are less civilized. If in your country the madmen are growing, and everyone is going insane and everyone is going to the psychoanalyst, know well you are the most civilized country in the world.

When any country achieves the optimum, everyone will have become mad. Civilization drives you mad because it is not allowing you to be your natural self. Everything is suppressed, and with suppression everything is disturbed. You cannot even breathe naturally; anything else is out of the question. Even your breath is unnatural. You cannot breathe deeply because the society does not allow you deep breathing.

Breathe deeply, because if you take deep breaths you cannot suppress your instincts. If you want to suppress anything, you can observe the changes in breathing in yourself. If you are angry and you want to suppress it, what will you do? Immediately you will stop breathing. With anger breathing goes deep, because anger will need a hot flow of blood in you, anger will need more oxygen. Anger will need some chemical changes within you, and through breathing those changes happen. So whenever you feel angry and you want to repress it, you will not be able to breathe naturally. You will take shallow breaths.

Look at a child and tell him not to do something. Immediately his breathing will be shallow. Then he will not be able to breathe deeply, because if he takes deep breaths he cannot follow your commands. Then he will do whatsoever he likes to do. So no one is even taking deep breaths. If you take deep breaths, your sex center is massaged from within and the society is against this. Take slow breaths, shallow breaths. Don't go deep, then the sex center is not hit!

Really, civilized man has become incapable of deep sexual orgasm because he cannot take deep breaths. In the love act your breathing must be so deep that your whole body becomes involved. Otherwise you will not achieve orgasm, and then you will feel frustrated. So many people come to me and they say, "There is no pleasure in sex. We go on doing it like a mechanical act, and energy is only lost. After it we feel frustrated, depressed." The reason is not sex, the reason is only that they are not getting into it totally. It becomes local, so only semen is released. Then they feel weak, and nothing is gained through it.

If the whole body is involved like an animal, if every cell of the body is excited and starts shaking, if the whole body becomes like an electric force and feeling moves, if you become egoless, headless, and thinking is not there, if you are the body moving in a rhythm, vibrating in a rhythm, then you will have a deep pleasure out of it. You will feel relaxed—in a certain sense, fulfilled.

But this cannot happen because you cannot take deep breaths. You are so afraid.... Look at the body. The body has two poles. One pole is for intake—your head is for intake. The upper pole is for intake of food, air, impressions, thoughts, anything. You take in from the upper part; this is one pole. The lower body is for release. It is not for intake, you cannot take anything in from the lower. The lower body is to release, to relax. You take from the upper, and from the lower you release it.

But the civilized man only takes in—never releases. That creates pathology. You go mad. It is just like eating food and then continuing to store it, never defecating. You will go mad. The other pole has to be used. If someone is a miser, automatically he becomes constipated. Look at any miser: he will be suffering from constipation. Miserliness is a sort of spiritual constipation. So go on hoarding, don't leave anything.

Those who are against sex without knowing what they are doing are misers. They go on taking in food, but they will not release the sex energy. Then they will go mad. There is no need to release it only from the sex center. There is another possibility —to release it from *sahasrar*, the highest center at the top of the head. That is what tantra teaches. But it must be released, you cannot hoard it. Nothing can be hoarded in the world. The world is a movement, it is a river. Take in and give out. If you take in and never give out, you will become mad.

That is what is happening: everyone is taking and no one is giving. You become afraid when a moment of giving comes. You want just to take— even with love. You want that someone should love you. The basic need is that you should love someone, then you will be released. If someone loves you that will not help, because then you are taking in again. Both of these poles must be balanced; then health happens. And that is what I call a normal being. A normal being is one whose taking in and giving out is parallel, balanced. He is normal.

I call that man abnormal whose taking in is too much and whose giving out is unbalanced. He is not giving out at all. Even if he gives sometimes, it has to be forced. It is not his own. You can snatch something from him, you can force him to give, but he will not give. His giving out is just like an enema, it is not natural. You can force, so he will defecate. But *he* is not defecating, he is not ready. It is abnormal to just go on hoarding everything. Then he will go mad, because the whole system is disturbed. This is abnormal, and supernormal is the one who gives and never takes in.

These are three things—the abnormal one who takes in and never gives out, the normal one whose give and take are balanced, and the supernormal who never takes in and only gives. A buddha is a giver; a madman is a taker. He is at the opposite pole of a buddha. If both poles are balanced, you are a normal man. At least be normal, because if you cannot be normal you will fall down and you will become abnormal.

That is why *dana*—giving—is so much emphasized in all religions. Give! Whatsoever it is, give, and don't think in terms of taking. Then you will become supernormal. But that is a very far-off thing. First be normal, be balanced. Whatsoever you take in, give it back to the world. You just be the passage. Don't hoard. Then you will never become mad, you will never be neurotic, schizophrenic, psychotic or whatsoever you may call it.

My definition of a normal man is one who is balanced—absolutely balanced. Nothing is retained. He takes the breath in and then he allows it to move out. The incoming breath and the outgoing breath are just the same—balanced. Try to be balanced, and always remember that you must give back that which you have received. You will be alive, healthy, silent, peaceful, happy. A deep rhythm will happen to you, and this rhythm happens through a balance of give and take.

But we go on thinking in terms of taking in more and more. Whatsoever you take in without

giving it out again will create disturbance, tension, suffering. You will become a hell. Before you take something in, always think to let something out. Have you observed that you always emphasize the breath that goes in? You never emphasize the breath that goes out. You take the breath in, and then the body throws the breath out. Reverse it: you will be more normal. Emphasize the outgoing breath. Throw the breath out as much as you can, and let the body take in.

When you take in and you have not released, your lungs become filled with carbon dioxide. Then you go on taking in, and you never release the entire lungs. You go on forcing the carbon dioxide inwards. Then your breathing becomes shallow, and the entire lungs are filled with carbon dioxide. First throw it out, and forget about taking in. The body will take care of that itself. The body has its own wisdom, and it is more wise than you. Throw the breath out and forget taking in. Don't be afraid, you are not going to die. The body will take in, and it will take in as much as is needed. As much as you have thrown out it will take in, and the balance will be there. If you take in, then you will disturb the balance because the hoarding mind is there.

I have stayed in many, many houses and I see that people have collected so many things that they cannot live, there is no space to live—and they go on hoarding. They go on hoarding, and they think that someday the things will be needed. Whatsoever is not needed, don't hoard it. And if something is needed more by someone else than you, it is better to give it. Be a giver, and you will never be pathological. All the old civilizations were based on dana—on giving, and this modern civilization is based on hoarding. That is why more people are going abnormal, neurotic. Everyone is asking from where to get, and no one is asking where to go and give, to whom to give.

The last question:

Daily in each of Your talks, You speak of awareness—total awareness, uninterrupted awareness, etcetera. You also said that it cannot be achieved by the mind, by repeating a thought—that it is to be felt. But how can one feel unless one achieves it? What is that feeling which is the precursor of achievement? How to imagine or project that which has not yet happened? Does that too happen by excluding mind? What is the whole process? How can it be made feasible?

When I say that awareness cannot be attained by mind, I mean that you cannot attain it by thinking about it. You can go on thinking about and about, but you will be moving in a circle. When I say that it cannot be attained by the mind, I mean that it cannot be attained by thinking. You have to practice it, you have to *do* it. It can be attained only by doing, not by thinking; that is the first thing. So don't go on thinking about what awareness is, how to achieve it or what will be the result. Don't go on thinking; start doing it.

When walking on the street, walk with awareness. It is difficult and you go on forgetting, but don't be afraid. Whenever you remember again, be alert. Take every step with full alertness, knowingly, remaining with the step, not allowing the mind to move somewhere else. While eating, eat; chew with awareness. Whatsoever you are doing, don't do it mechanically—and that is different. And when I say that it can be felt only, the meaning is this: for example, I can raise my hand mechanically, but then I can also raise my hand with full alertness. My mind is conscious that my hand is being raised. Do it, try it—once mechanically and then with alertness. You will feel the change. The quality changes immediately.

Walk with alertness, and you walk differently; a different grace comes to your walking. You move more slowly, more beautifully. If you walk mechanically—only because you know how to walk and there is no need to be alert, then the walking is

ugly, there is no grace in it. Do whatsoever you are doing with alertness, and feel the difference. When I say "feel," I mean observe. First do it mechanically and then with awareness, and feel the difference. And you will be able to feel the difference.

For example, if you eat with awareness, then you cannot eat more than is needed by the body. People go on coming to me and they say, "Put us on a diet. My weight is constantly increasing, the body is constantly hoarding. Put us on a diet."

I tell them, "Don't think of diet, think of consciousness. By dieting nothing will happen. You cannot do it. You will do it one day and the next day it will go. You cannot continue it. Rather, eat with awareness."

The quality changes. If you eat with awareness, you will chew more. With unconscious, mechanical habits, you simply go on pushing things into your stomach. You are not chewing at all, you are just stuffing. Then there is no pleasure, and because there is no pleasure you need more food in order to get the pleasure. There is no taste, so you need more food.

Just be alert and see what happens. If you are alert, you will chew more, you will feel the taste more, you will feel the pleasure of eating, and much more time will be taken. If you take half an hour to eat your meal, then by taking the same quantity of a meal with full awareness you will need one and a half hours—thrice the time. In half an hour you will have eaten only one-third of the quantity, and you will feel more fulfilled; you will have enjoyed the meal more. And when the body enjoys, it tells you when to stop. When the body has not enjoyed at all, it never says when to stop, so you go on. Then the body becomes dull. You never hear what the body is saying.

You are eating without being there; that creates the problem. Be there, and every process will be slowed down. The body will itself say, "No more!" And when the body says it, that is the right moment. If you are aware, you cannot trespass the body's order. You will stop. So allow your body to say something. The body is saying things every moment, but you are not there to hear it. Be alert and you will hear it.

And when I say, "Feel it," I know it is difficult. How can you feel awareness without being aware? I am not saying that you can feel Buddha's enlightenment right now, but one has to start somewhere. You may not get the whole ocean, but a drop— just a drop—will give you the taste, and the taste is the same. If even for a single moment you become aware, you have tasted buddhahood. It is momentary, a glimpse of it, but now you know more. And this will never happen to you through thinking; it will happen only through feeling.

The emphasis is on feeling because the emphasis is on a "lived" experience. Thinking is false; you can go on thinking about love and creating theories, you can even get a doctorate on the thesis of love, on what love is—without ever being in love. You may not know what love is; you may have never felt it. You can grow in knowledge without in any way growing in being. And these are two different dimensions. You can go on growing in knowledge. Your head will go on growing bigger and bigger, but you will remain the same tiny self.

Then nothing is growing really—only accumulation. When you start feeling things, you grow, your being grows. And one has to start somewhere, so start! There will be errors, there are bound to be. You will go on forgetting, it is natural. But don't get frustrated, don't throw the effort away saying, "I cannot do it." You *can* do it! The same possibility exists in you that existed in Jesus or Buddha. You are the seed; you are not lacking anything at all. You are just an arrangement, you are just a chaotic whole; everything is there. You can become a buddha, but a reorganization of your qualities is needed.

Right now you are chaotic because there is no arrangement. The arrangement comes in when you start being aware. Just by your being aware things start falling in line, and this chaos that you are becomes a symphony.

CHAPTER 49

Conscious doing

◆

T H E   S U T R A S

73 *In summer when you see the entire sky endlessly clear, enter such clarity.*

74 *Shakti, see all space as if already absorbed in your own head in the brilliance.*

75 *Waking, sleeping, dreaming, know you as light.*

**A**s I look in your eyes I never see you there—as if you are absent. You exist absently, and this is the core of all suffering. You can be alive without being at all present, and if you are not present your existence will become a boredom. And this is what has happened. So when I look in your eyes I don't find you there. You have yet to come, you have yet to be. The situation is there, and the possibility is there—you can be there any moment—but yet you are not.

To become aware of this absence is to begin the journey towards meditation, towards transcendence. If you are aware that somehow you are missing...you exist but you don't know why, you don't know how, you don't know even who exists within you. This unawareness creates all suffering, because, unknowingly, whatsoever you do will bring suffering. It is not what you do that is basic; it is whether you do it with your presence or with your absence that is significant.

Whatsoever you do, if you can do it with your total presence, your life will become ecstatic; it will be a bliss. If you do something without your presence there, absently, your life will be a suffering—bound to be. Hell means your absence.

So there are two types of seekers: one type of seeker is always in search of what to do. That seeker is on a wrong path, because the question is not of doing at all. The question is of being—what to be, how to be.

So never think in terms of action and doing, because whatsoever you do, if you are absent it will be meaningless.

Whether you move in the world or you live in a monastery, whether you function in the crowd or you move to an isolated spot in the Himalayas will make no difference. You will be absent here and you will be absent there, and whatsoever you do—in the crowd or in the isolation—will bring suffering. If you are not there, then whatsoever you do is wrong.

The second type, and the right type of seeker, is not in search of what to do, he is in search of how to be. The first thing is how to be.

One man came to Gautam Buddha. He was filled with much compassion, with much sympathy, and he asked Gautam Buddha, "What can I do to help the world?"

Buddha is reported to have laughed and said to the man, "You cannot do anything because you are not. How can you do anything when you are not? So don't think of the world. Don't think of how to serve the world, how to help others." Buddha said, "First be—and if you are, then whatsoever you do becomes a service, it becomes a prayer, it becomes compassion. Your presence is the turning point. Your being is the revolution."

So these are the two paths: the path of action and the path of meditation. They are diametrically opposite. The path of action is basically concerned with you as a doer. It will try to change your actions; it will try to change your character, your morals, your relationships, but never you. The path of meditation is diametrically opposite. It is not concerned with your actions; it is directly and immediately concerned with you. What you do is irrelevant. What you are is relevant. And that is basic and primary, because all action springs from you.

Remember, your actions can be changed and modified, can even be replaced by diametrically opposite actions, but they are not going to change you. Any outward change will not bring the inner revolution, because the outward is superficial and the innermost core remains untouched; by what you do it remains untouched. But the vice versa brings the revolution: if the innermost core is different, the surface automatically changes. So think a basic question; only then can we enter these techniques of meditation.

Don't be concerned with what you are doing. That may be a trick, that may be a device to escape from the real problem. For example, you are violent. You can make every effort to be nonviolent, thinking that by being nonviolent you will become religious; by becoming nonviolent you will come closer to the divine. You are cruel, and you may make every effort to be compassionate.

You can do it, and nothing will change and you will remain the same. Your cruelty will become a part of your compassion—and that is more dangerous. Your violence will become a part of your nonviolence—that is more subtle. You will be violently nonviolent. Your nonviolence will have all the madness of violence, and through your compassion you will be cruel.

You can even kill through your compassion; people have killed. There are so many religious wars—they are fought in the mood of compassion. You can kill very compassionately, very nonviolently; lovingly you can kill and murder, because you are killing for the sake of the person you are killing. You are killing him for himself, for his own sake, to help him.

You can change your actions, and this effort to change the actions may be just a device to escape the basic change. The basic change is this—first you must be. You must become more alert, more

conscious of your being, only then a presence comes to you. You never feel yourself, and even sometimes when you feel, you feel through others—through excitement, through stimulation, through reaction. Someone else is needed, and via someone else you can feel yourself. This is absurd.

Alone, without excitement, with no one there to become a mirror, you fall in sleep, you get bored. You never feel yourself. There is no presence. You live absently.

This absent existence is the nonreligious mind. To become filled with your own presence, with the light of your own being, is to become religious. So remember this as a basic point: that my concern is not with your actions. What you do is irrelevant. What you are—absent, present, aware, unaware—that's my concern. And these techniques we will enter are techniques to make you more present, to bring you here and now.

Either someone else is needed for you to feel yourself, or the past is needed—through the past, through past memories, you can feel your identity. Or the future is needed—you can project in your dreams. You can project your ideals, future lives, moksha. Either you need past memories to feel that you are, or you need a future projection, or someone else, but you alone are never enough. This is the disease, and unless you alone become enough, nothing will be enough for you. And once you alone have become enough unto yourself, you have become victorious, the struggle is over. Now there will be no suffering anymore. A point of no return has come.

Beyond this point there is beautitude, eternal bliss. Before this point you are bound to suffer, but the whole suffering, strangely, is your own doing. It is a miracle that you create your own suffering. No one else is creating it. If someone else is creating it then it is difficult to go beyond it. If the world is creating it then what can you do? But because you *can* do, it means no one else is creating your suffering—it is your own nightmare. And these are the basic elements of it.

The first thing: you go on thinking that you are, you believe that you are. This is simply a belief. You have never encountered yourself, you have never come face to face with yourself; you have never met yourself, there has been no meeting. You simply believe that you are. Throw this belief totally. Know well that you are yet to be, that you are not, because with this false belief you will never be able to transform. On this false belief your whole life will become false.

Gurdjieff used to say to his disciples, "Don't ask me what to do. You cannot do anything, because to do something first you will be needed. And you are not there, so who will do it? You can think about doing, but you cannot do anything."

These techniques are to help you, to bring you back; to help you to create a situation in which you can meet yourself. Much will have to be destroyed —all that is wrong, all that is false. Before the real arises the false will have to leave; it must cease. And these are the false notions—that you are. These are the false notions—that you are a soul, atma, you are Brahma. Not that you are not, but these notions are false.

Gurdjieff had to insist that there is no soul in you. Against all the traditions he insisted, "Man has no soul. Soul is simply a possibility—it can be, it may not be. It has to be achieved. You are simply a seed."

And this emphasis is good. The possibility is there, the potentiality is there, but it is not yet actual. And we go on reading the Gita and the Upanishads and the Bible, and we go on feeling that we are the soul—the seed thinking that it is the tree. The tree is hidden there, but it is yet to be uncovered. And it is good to remember that you may remain a seed, and you may die a seed—because the tree cannot come, the tree cannot sprout by itself. You have to do something consciously about it, because only through consciousness it grows.

There are two types of growth. One is unconscious, natural growth: if the situation is there, the thing will grow. But the soul, the atma, the innermost being, the divine within you, is a different type of growth altogether. It is only through consciousness that it grows. It is not natural, it is supernatural.

Left to nature itself it will not grow; just left to evolution it will never evolve. You have to do something consciously, you have to make a conscious effort about it, because only through consciousness it grows. Once the consciousness is focused there, the growth happens. These techniques are to make you more conscious.

Now we will enter the techniques.

73 Become the clarity of the cloudless sky.

The first technique: *In summer when you see the entire sky endlessly clear, enter such clarity.*

In summer when you see the entire sky endlessly clear, enter such clarity. Mind is confusion; there is no clarity. And mind is always crowded, always cloudy; never the open sky, cloudless, empty. Mind cannot be that. You cannot make your mind clear; it is not the nature of the mind to be so. Mind will remain unclear. If you can leave the mind behind, if you can suddenly transcend the mind and come out of it, clarity will happen to you. You can be clear, but not the mind. There is not such a thing as a clear mind; never has been and never will be. Mind means the unclarity, the confusion.

Try to understand the structure of the mind, and then this technique will be clear to you. What is mind? A continuous process of thought, a continuous procession of thoughts—associated, nonassociated, relevant, irrelevant—many multidimensional impressions gathered from everywhere. The whole life is a gathering, a gathering of the dust. And this goes on and on.

A child is born. A child is clear because the mind is not there. The moment mind appears, the unclarity, the confusion enters. A child is clear, a clarity, but he will have to gather knowledge, information, culture, religion, conditionings—necessary, useful. He will have to gather many things from everywhere, from many sources—opposite, contradictory sources. From thousands and thousands of sources he will gather. Then the mind will become a marketplace, a crowd, and because of so many sources, confusion is bound to be there. And whatsoever you gather, nothing is certain, because knowledge is always a growing affair.

I remember someone related an anecdote to me. He was a great searcher, and he told me this about his professor who taught him for five years in a medical college. The professor was a great scholar of his subject. The last thing he did was to gather his students and tell them, "One thing more I have to teach you. Whatsoever I have taught you is only fifty percent correct, and the remaining fifty percent is absolutely wrong. But the trouble is, I don't know which fifty percent is correct and which fifty percent is incorrect—I don't know."

The whole edifice of knowledge is such. Nothing is certain, no one knows, everyone is groping. Through groping we create systems, and there are thousands and thousands of systems. Hindus say something, Christians say something else, Mohammedans still something else—all contradictory, all contradicting each other; no agreement, no certainty—and all these sources are the sources for your mind. You collect: your mind becomes a junkyard; confusion is bound to be there. Only a person who doesn't know much can be certain. The more you know, the more uncertain you will become.

People, primitive people, were more certain and apparently appeared to be more clear. There was no clarity—simply unawareness of facts which could contradict them. If the modern mind is more confused, the reason is that the modern knows more. If you know more you will be more confused, because now you have more knowledge, and the more you know, the more uncertain you become. Only idiots can be certain, only idiots can be dogmatic, only idiots will never hesitate. The

more you know, the more the earth is taken away from your feet, the more hesitant you become. What I mean to say is, the more the mind grows, the more you will know the nature of the mind is confusion.

When I say only idiots can be certain, I don't mean that a Buddha is an idiot because he is not uncertain. Remember the difference. He is not certain, he is not uncertain—he is simply clear. With the mind, uncertainty; with the idiotic mind, certainty. With no mind both disappear—certainty and uncertainty.

Buddha is a clarity, a space, open space. He is not certain—there is nothing to be certain. He is not uncertain, because there is nothing to be uncertain. Only one who is seeking certainty can be uncertain. Mind is always uncertain and always seeking certainty; always confused and always seeking clarity. A buddha is one who has dropped the mind; and with the mind all confusion, all certainty, all uncertainty, everything is dropped.

Look at it in this way: your consciousness is just like the sky and your mind is just like the clouds. The sky remains untouched by the clouds. They come and go; no scar is left behind. The sky remains virgin: no record, no footprints, nothing of the clouds, no memory. They come and they go; the sky remains undisturbed. This is the case within you also: the consciousness remains undisturbed. Thoughts come and go, minds evolve and disappear. And don't think that you have one mind; you have many minds, it is a crowd. Your minds go on changing.

You are a communist, so you have a certain type of mind. You can leave it and you can become anticommunist. Then you have a different mind; not only different, quite the opposite. You can go on changing your minds just like your dress. And you go on changing. You may not be aware of it—these clouds come and go. Clarity can be achieved if you become aware of the sky, if your focus changes. You are focused on the clouds if you are unfocused on the sky. Unfocus on the clouds and focus on the sky. This technique says: *In summer when you see the entire sky endlessly clear, enter such clarity.*

Meditate on the sky—a summer sky with no clouds, endlessly empty and clear, nothing moving in it, in its total virginity. Contemplate on it, meditate on it, and enter this clarity. Become this clarity, this spacelike clarity.

If you meditate on open, unclouded sky, suddenly you will feel that the mind is disappearing, the mind is dropping away. There will be gaps. Suddenly you will become aware that it is as if the clear sky has entered in you also. There will be intervals. For a time being, thoughts will cease—as if the traffic has ceased and there is no one moving.

In the beginning it will be only for moments, but even those moments are transforming. By and by the mind will slow down, bigger gaps will appear. For minutes together there will be no thought, no cloud. And when there *is* no thought, no cloud, the outer sky and the inner become one, because only the thought is the barrier, only the thought creates the wall; only because of the thought the outer is outer and the inner is inner. When the thought is not there, the outer and the inner lose their boundaries, they become one. Really, boundaries never existed there. They appeared only because of the thought, the barrier.

To meditate on the sky is beautiful. Just lie down so you forget the earth; just lie down on your back on any lonely beach, on any ground, and just look at the sky. But a clear sky will be helpful—unclouded, endless. And just looking, staring at the sky, feel the clarity of it—the uncloudedness, the boundless expanse—and then enter that clarity, become one with it. Feel as if you have become the sky, the space.

In the beginning, if you only meditate on the open sky, not doing anything else, intervals will start appearing, because whatsoever you see enters you. Whatsoever you see stirs you within; whatsoever you see is pictured, reflected.

You see a building. You cannot simply see it; something immediately starts happening within you. You see a man, a woman; you see a car—you see anything. It is not just outside, something has started within, the reflection, and you have started reacting to it. So everything you see molds you, makes you, modifies you, creates you. The without is constantly related with the within.

To look into the open sky is good. Just the expanse is beautiful, with no boundaries there. Your own boundaries will disappear, because the no-boundary sky will reflect within you. And if you can stare without blinking your eyes it will be good. If you stare without blinking your eyes... because if you blink your eyes your thought-process will continue. Stare without blinking the eyes. Stare in the emptiness, move into that emptiness, feel that you have become one with it, and any moment the sky will enter within you.

First you enter into the sky and then the sky enters you. And there is a meeting: the inner sky meeting the outer sky. In that meeting is realization. In that meeting there is no mind, because the meeting can happen only when the mind is not there. In that meeting you are for the first time not your mind. There is no confusion. Confusion cannot exist without the mind. There is no misery, because misery also cannot exist without the mind.

Have you observed this fact anytime or not—that misery cannot exist without your mind? You cannot be miserable without your mind. The very source is not there. Who will supply you with this misery? Who will make you miserable? And the same is true from the opposite direction also: you cannot be miserable without your mind and you cannot be blissful with your mind. The mind can never be the source of bliss.

So if the inner and outer sky meet and mind disappears, even for a moment, you will be filled with a new life. The quality of that life is absolutely different. It is life eternal, uncontaminated by death, uncontaminated by any fear. In that meeting you will be here and now, in the present—because past belongs to thoughts, future belongs to thoughts.

Past and future are part of your mind. Present is existence—it is not part of your mind.

This moment doesn't belong to your mind. The moment that has gone belongs, the moment that is to come belongs to your mind. This moment never belongs to you. Rather, you belong to this moment. You exist here, right now here. Your mind exists somewhere else, always somewhere else.

Unload yourself.

I was reading one Sufi mystic. He was traveling on a lonely path, the way was deserted, and he saw a farmer with his bullock cart. The cart was stuck in mud. The road was rough. The farmer was carrying a big load of apples in his bullock cart, but somewhere on the rough road the tailboard of the wagon became unfastened and the apples were scattered. But he was not aware of it; the farmer was not aware of it.

When the cart got stuck in the mud, first he tried to bring it out somehow, but all efforts were in vain, so he thought, "Now I must unload my cart, then maybe I can pull it out." He looked back. Hardly a dozen apples were left—the load was already unloaded. You can feel his misery. The Sufi reports in his memoirs that that exasperated farmer made a remark. He said, "Stuck, by heck! Stuck!— and not a damn thing to unload!" The only possibility was that if he could unload the cart it could come out; but now—nothing to unload!

Fortunately you are not stuck in such a way. You can unload—your cart is too much loaded. You can unload the mind, and the moment the mind is not there, you fly; you become capable of flying.

This technique—to look into the clarity of the sky and to become one with it—is one of the most practiced. Many traditions have used this. And particularly for the modern mind it will be very useful, because on earth nothing is left. On earth nothing is left to meditate on—only the sky. If you look all around, everything is man-made, everything is limited, with a boundary, a limitation. Only the sky is still, fortunately, open to meditate on.

Try this technique, it will be helpful; but remember three things. One: don't blink—stare. Even if your eyes start to feel pain and tears come down, don't be worried. Even those tears will be a part of unloading; they will be helpful. Those tears will make your eyes more innocent and fresh—bathed. You just go on staring.

The second point: don't think about the sky, remember. You can start thinking about the sky. You can remember many poems, beautiful poems about the sky—then you will miss the point. You are not to think about it—you are to enter it, you are to be one with it—because if you start thinking about it, again a barrier is created. You are missing the sky again, and you are again enclosed in your own mind. Don't think about the sky. Be the sky. Just stare and move into the sky, and allow the sky to move into you. If you move into the sky, the sky will move into you immediately.

How can you do it? How will you do it—this moving into the sky? Just go on staring further away and further away. Go on staring—as if you are trying to find the boundary. Move deep. Move as much as you can. That very movement will break the barrier. And this method should be practiced for at least forty minutes; less than that will not do, will not be of much help.

When you really feel that you have become one, then you can close the eyes. When the sky has entered in you, you can close the eyes. You will be able to see it within also. Then there is no need. So only after forty minutes, when you feel that the oneness has happened and there is a communion and you have become part of it and the mind is no more, close the eyes and remain in the sky within.

The clarity will help the third point: *enter such clarity.* The clarity will help—the uncontaminated, unclouded sky. Just be aware of the clarity that is all around you. Don't think about it; just be aware of the clarity, the purity, the innocence. These words are not to be repeated. You have to feel them rather than think. And once you stare into the sky the feeling will come, because it is not on your part to imagine these things—they are there. If you stare they will start happening to you.

The sky is pure, the purest thing in existence. Nothing makes it impure. Worlds come and go, earths are there and then disappear, and the sky remains pure. The purity is there. You need not project it; you are simply to feel it—to be vulnerable to it so you can feel it—and the clarity is there. Allow the sky to happen to you. You cannot force it; you can only allow it to happen.

All meditations are really allowing something to happen. Never think in terms of aggression, never think in terms of forcing something. You cannot force anything. Really, because you have been trying to force, you have created all misery. Nothing can be forced, but you can allow things to happen. Be feminine. Allow things to happen. Be passive. The sky is absolutely passive: not doing anything at all, just remaining there. Just be passive and remain under the sky—vulnerable, open, feminine, with no aggression on your part—and then the sky will penetrate you.

*In summer when you see the entire sky
endlessly clear, enter such clarity.*

But if it is not summer what will you do? If the sky is clouded, not clear, then close your eyes and just enter the inner sky. Just close your eyes, and if you see some thoughts, just see them as if they are floating clouds in the sky. Be aware of the background, the sky, and be indifferent to thoughts.

We are too much concerned with thoughts and never aware of the gaps. One thought passes, and before another enters there is a gap—in that gap the sky is there. Then, whenever there is no thought, what is there? The emptiness is there. So if the sky is clouded—it is not summer-time and the sky is not clear—close your eyes, focus your mind on the background, the inner sky in which thoughts come and go. Don't pay much attention to thoughts; pay attention to the space in which they move.

For example, we are sitting in this room. I can look at this room in two ways. Either I can look at you, so that I am indifferent to the space you are in, the roominess, the room you are in—I look at you, I focus my mind on you who are here, and not on the room in which you are—or, I can change my focus: I can look into the room, and I become indifferent to you. You are there, but my emphasis, my focus, is on the room. Then the total perspective changes.

Just do this in the inner world. Look at the space. Thoughts are moving in it: be indifferent to them, don't pay any attention to them. They are there; note it down that they are there, moving. The traffic is moving in the street. Look at the street and be indifferent to the traffic. Don't look to see who is passing; just know that something is passing and be aware of the space in which it is passing. Then the summer sky happens within.

There is no need to wait for the summer, because our minds are such that they can find any excuse. They will say, "Summer is not here, and even if it is summer, the sky is not clear."

---

74 Feel the whole universe in your head.

The second technique: *Shakti, see all space as if already absorbed in your own head in the brilliance.*

See all space as if already absorbed in your own head in the brilliance. Close your eyes for this technique. When you do it, close your eyes and feel as if the whole space is absorbed in your own head. It will be difficult in the beginning. It is one of the advanced techniques, so it will be good to proceed towards it in steps. Do one thing: if you want to do this technique, start in steps.

First: while going to sleep, when just ready to sleep, lie down on your bed, close your eyes and feel where your feet are. If you are six feet tall, or five feet tall, just feel where your feet are, the demarcation. Then just imagine one thing: you have become six inches longer. Your height has lengthened, it has become six inches more. Just with closed eyes feel this. In imagination, feel that your height has become six inches more.

Then the second step: feel your head, where it is, just inside, and then feel that your head has also become six inches longer. When you can feel this, everything will be easy. Then you make it more. You feel that you have become twelve feet tall; or that you have filled the whole room. Now in your imagination you are touching the walls— you have filled the whole room. Then, by steps, feel that the whole house has come within you. And once you know the feel, it is very easy. If you can grow six inches taller, everything is easy then. If you can feel that you are not five foot, but you are five foot six, then nothing is difficult; this technique will be easy.

For three days go on feeling that; then for three days more, feel that you have filled the whole room. It is just a training of imagination. Then for three days the whole house is within you; then for three days you have become the sky. Then this technique will be very easy.

Shakti, see all space as if already absorbed in your own head in the brilliance.

Then you can close your eyes and feel that the whole sky, the whole space, is absorbed by your head. The moment you can feel this, the mind disappears, because the mind needs a very narrow space. With such vastness the mind cannot exist; it simply disappears. In such vastness mind is impossible. Mind can only be narrow, limited. In such infinite space there is no place for the mind to exist.

This technique is good. Suddenly the mind explodes and the space is there. Within a three-month period you can feel this. Your whole life will be different. But grow towards it in steps, because sometimes through this technique people become crazy, they lose balance. It is so tremendous, the impact is so tremendous—suddenly if you become aware that your head has absorbed the whole space, and then you see stars and moons moving

within you, the whole universe, you may become dizzy. In many traditions this technique is used very cautiously.

One of the Indian mystics of this century, Ramateertha, used this technique, and many suspect, many of those who know suspect that because of this technique he committed suicide. For him it was not a suicide, because for him—one who has known that the whole space has come within him—suicide is impossible, it cannot happen. No one is there to commit suicide. But for others, for those who were watching from outside, it was a suicide.

He started feeling that the whole universe was moving within him, within his head. His disciples thought that he was talking poetry. Then they started feeling that he had gone mad, because he started claiming that he was the universe and everything was within him. And then one day he just jumped from a mountain cliff into a river. Before jumping he wrote a beautiful poem saying, "I have become the universe. Now I feel this body as a burden, unnecessary, so I give it back. Now no boundary is needed. I have become the unbounded Brahma."

Someone with a psychiatric training will think that he has gone mad, it is just neurosis, but one who knows deeper dimensions of human consciousness will say he has become a *mukta,* an enlightened one. But to the ordinary mind it is a suicide.

With such techniques there is danger. That's why I say grow towards them gradually, because you don't know—anything is possible. Sometimes you are not aware of your own potentiality, sometimes you don't know how ready you are, and something can happen. So do it in steps.

First try your imagination with small things: just that the body has become bigger or has become smaller. You can go both the ways. You are five feet six: feel you have become four feet, three feet, two feet, one foot, you have become just a seed.

This is just a training; just a training so that you

can feel whatsoever you want to feel. Your inner mind is absolutely free to feel; nothing can hinder it from feeling anything. It is your feeling. You can grow and you can be small. Suddenly you become aware that it is you.

And if you can work well through this, you can come out of your body very easily. If you can grow and become small through imagination, you are capable of coming out of your body. You simply imagine that you are standing outside of your body and you will stand—but not immediately.

First work with small steps, and then when you feel that you are at ease and you don't become scared, then feel that you have filled the whole room—actually you will feel the touch of the walls. And then feel that the whole house has come within you—you will feel it within you. And then go on. Then, by and by, let the sky be felt in the head. And once you feel the sky in your head, absorbed there, the mind simply disappears. It has no business to do there.

For this technique it is good to be with some-one: to be with a teacher, or to be with a friend. Don't do it alone. Someone must be there to take care of you, to watch you. This is a school method. Where many people are working in a school, it is very easy, less harmful, less dangerous—because sometimes when the sky explodes within, for many days you may not become aware of your body. You may not come out, you may be so absorbed in the feeling, because time disappears; you cannot feel how much time has elapsed. The body disappears, you cannot feel the body. You become the sky. Someone must take care of your body; very loving care will be needed.

So with a master, or with a group, this technique is less harmful and less dangerous. And with a group that knows what is possible—what can happen and what should be done...because if in such a state of mind you are suddenly awakened, you may go mad, because time will be needed for your mind to come back. If suddenly brought back to the body, your nervous system cannot bear it. It is not made for

that. It has to be trained. So don't do it alone. You can do it in a group, with a few friends, in a lonely place. And do it in steps, not suddenly.

75 Remember yourself as light.

The third technique: *Waking, sleeping, dreaming, know you as light.*

Waking, sleeping, dreaming, know you as light. First start with waking. Yoga and tantra divide the life of man's mind into three divisions—the life of the mind, remember. They divide mind into three divi-sions: waking, sleeping, dreaming. These are not the divisions of your consciousness, these are the divi-sions of your mind, and the consciousness is the fourth.

They have not given any name to it in the East; they call it simply the fourth, *turiya*. These three have names. These are the clouds, they can be named—a waking cloud, a sleeping cloud, a dreaming cloud. They are all clouds, and the space in which they move—the sky—is unnamed, left simply as the fourth.

Western psychology has only recently become aware of the dreaming dimension. Really, only with Freud dreaming became important. But with Hindus, this is one of the most ancient concepts: that you cannot really know a man unless you know what he is doing in his dreams. Because whatsoever he is doing in his waking hours is more or less bound to be acting, false, because in the waking state of his mind he is forced to do many things.

He is not free. The society is there, rules are there, moralities are there. He is constantly strug-gling with his own desires: suppressing them, modi-fying them, moulding them in the mould the society allows. And the society never allows you to be your total being; it chooses. That is what a culture means—culture means a choice.

Every culture is a conditioning: a choice of cer-tain things and a denial of certain things. Your total being is not accepted anywhere; it is not—nowhere. Certain aspects are accepted here, certain aspects are accepted there, in this country or that, but nowhere is the total human being accepted. So the waking consciousness is bound to be false, pseudo, artificial, forced. You are not real there—just actors; not spontaneous—manipulated. Only in dreams are you free; only in dreams are you authentically yourself.

You can do whatsoever you like in your dreams. No one is concerned; you are alone. No one can penetrate, no one can look into your dreams. And no one is bothered: what you do in your dreams is your business, no one is concerned. They are absolutely private. Because they are absolutely private and related to no one, you can be free. So unless your dreams are known, your real face cannot be known. Hindus have been aware of it: dreams must be penetrated. But they are still clouds—private of course, freer, but still clouds, and one has to go beyond them also.

These are the three states: waking and sleeping and dreaming. Dreaming became very primary with Freud. Now sleeping has been touched. Now many sleep labs are working in the West to know what sleep is, because it seems to be very strange that we don't know what sleep is. What really happens to you in sleep is not yet known scientifically.

And if we cannot know what sleep is, it will be difficult to know what man is, because for one third of his life he will be sleeping. One third of your life! If you are going to live for sixty years, for twenty years you will be sleeping. It is such a major part. What are you doing while you are asleep? Something mysterious is going on, and it is so essential that life is not possible without it. Something deep is happening, but you are not aware.

Waking, you are a different person; dreaming, you are again a different person. In deep sleep, you are again a different person. You can't remember even your name while deep asleep. You don't know whether you are a Mohammedan or a Christian or a Hindu. Out of your deep sleep you can't answer who you are; rich or poor—no identity, no image.

In the waking layer you exist with the society. In the dreaming layer you exist with your own desires. In deep sleep you exist with nature, deep in the womb of nature. And yoga and tantra say that only beyond these three you exist in Brahma, in the cosmic whole. So these three must be crossed, passed, transcended.

There is one difference. The Western psychology is now interested in studying these states. Eastern seekers were interested in these states, but not in studying them. They were interested only in how to transcend them. This technique is a transcendental technique.

Waking, sleeping, dreaming, know you as light.

Very difficult. You have to start with waking. How can you remember in dreams? Can you create a dream consciously? Can you manipulate a dream? Can you have your own dreams of your own wishes? You cannot. How impotent man is! You cannot even create a dream of your own. They too happen to you; you are helpless. But there are certain techniques through which dreams can be created, and those techniques are very helpful in transcending, because if you can create, then you can transcend. But one has to start with waking.

While waking—moving, eating, working—remember yourself as light. As if in your heart a flame is burning, and your body is nothing but the aura around the flame. Imagine it. In your heart a flame is burning, and your body is nothing but a light aura around the flame; your body is just a light around the flame. Allow it to go deep within your mind and your consciousness. Imbibe it.

It will take time, but if you go on thinking about it, feeling it, imagining it, within a certain period you will be able to remember it the whole day. While awake, moving on the street, you are a flame moving. No one else will be aware of it in the beginning, but if you continue it, after three months others will also become aware. And only then, when others become aware, can you be at ease. Don't tell anyone. Simply imagine a flame, and your body as just the aura around it. Not a physical body, but an electric body. Go on doing it.

If you persist, within three months, or somewhere nearabout then, others will become aware that something has happened to you. They will feel a subtle light around you. When you come near them, they will feel a different warmth. If you touch them, they will feel a fiery touch. They will become aware that something strange is happening to you. Don't tell anyone. When others become aware, then you can feel at ease, and then you can enter the second step, not before it.

The second step is to take it into dreaming. Now you can take it into dreaming. It has become a reality. Now it is not an imagination. Through imagination you have uncovered a reality. It is real. Everything consists of light. You are light—unaware of the fact—because every particle of matter is light.

The scientists say it consists of electrons. It is the same thing. Light is the source of all. You are also condensed light; through imagination you are simply uncovering a reality. Imbibe it—and when you have become so filled with it, you can carry it into dreams, not before.

Then, while falling asleep, go on thinking of the flame, go on seeing it, feeling you are the light. Remembering it...remembering...remembering...you fall down asleep. And the remembrance continues. In the beginning you will start having some dreams in which you will feel you have a flame within, you are light. By and by, in the dreams also you will move with the same feeling. And once this feeling enters the dreams, dreams will start disappearing. Dreams will start disappearing: there will be less and less dreams and more and more deep sleep.

When in all your dreaming this reality is revealed —that you are light, a flame, a burning flame—all dreams will disappear. Only when dreams disappear can you carry this feeling into sleep, never before. Now you are at the door. When dreams have disappeared and you remember yourself as a flame, you are at the door of sleep. Now you can enter with the

feeling. And once you enter sleep with the feeling that you are a flame, you will be aware in it—the sleep will now happen only to your body, not to you.

This technique is to help you go beyond these three states. If you can be aware that you are a flame, a light, that sleep is not happening to you, you are conscious. You are carrying a conscious effort. Now you are crystallized around that flame. The body is asleep, you are not.

This is what Krishna says in the Gita: that yogis never sleep. While others are asleep, they are awake. Not that their bodies never sleep. Their bodies sleep —but only bodies. Bodies need rest, consciousness needs no rest; because bodies are mechanisms. Consciousness is not a mechanism. Bodies need fuel, they need rest. That's why they are born, they are young, then they become old, and then they die. Consciousness is never born, never becomes old, never dies. It needs no fuel, it needs no rest. It is pure energy, perpetual, eternal energy.

If you can carry this image of flame and light through the doors of sleep, you will never sleep again, only the body will rest. And while the body is sleeping, you will know it. Once this happens, you have become the fourth. Now the waking and the dreaming and the sleeping are parts of the mind. They are parts, and you have become the fourth—one who goes through all of them and is none of them.

Really, this is so simple. If you are in the waking state, and then you move into dreams, you cannot be either. If you are the waking state, then how can you dream? And if you are the dreaming state, how can you fall into sleep where there is no dream? You must be a traveler, and these states must be stations, so you can move from here and there and come back again. Again in the morning you will move into the waking state.

These are states, and the one who moves within these states is you. But that you is the fourth—and that fourth is what you call the soul. That fourth is what you call divine, that fourth is what you call the immortal element, the life eternal.

Waking, sleeping, dreaming, know you as light.

This is a very beautiful technique. But try it first in the waking state. And remember, when others become aware, then only have you succeeded in it. They will become aware. Then you can enter into dream, and then into sleep, and then you can awaken to that which you are—the fourth.

CHAPTER 50

Moving
to the roots

◆

Q U E S T I O N S

Isn't it a mistake to ignore the outer completely?

Are not all meditation techniques "doing"?

Does not the growth of the mind lead to clarity?

Why do we continue to create suffering?

The first question:

Last night You said that by changing the outer, the inner remains unchanged, untransformed. But is it not true that the right food, right labor, right sleep, right actions and behaviors are also important factors for inner transformation? Isn't it a mistake to ignore the outer completely?

he outer cannot change the inner, but the outer can help, or it can hinder. The outer can create a situation in which the inner can explode more easily. The thing to be remembered is this: that the outer transformation is not the inner. Even if you have done everything and the situation is there, the inner is not going to explode. The situation is necessary, it is helpful, but it is not the transformation. And those who get involved with the outer....

The outer is a vast phenomenon. You can go on changing for lives and you will never be satisfied, and something or other will remain to be changed, because unless the inner changes, the outer can never be perfect. You can go on changing it and polishing it and conditioning it. You will never feel satisfied. You will never come to a situation where you can feel, "Now the field is ready." So many have wasted their lives.

If your mind becomes obsessed with the outer —with food, with clothes, with behavior.... I am not saying to neglect them. No, what I am saying

is, don't get obsessed with them. They can be helpful, but they can become great hindrances if your mind becomes obsessed. Then it becomes an escape, then you are just postponing the inner change. And you can go on changing the outer. The inner is not even touched by it, the inner remains the same.

You might have heard one old Indian fable. In *Panchtantra* it is said that a mouse was very much afraid of a cat—constantly in fear, anxiety. He couldn't sleep, he would dream about the cat and he would tremble. A magician, just out of pity, transformed the mouse into a cat. The outer was changed, but immediately the mouse within the cat now became afraid of a dog. The anxiety was the same; only the object had changed. Previously it was the cat, now it was the dog. The trembling continued, the anguish remained, the dreams were still of fear.

So the magician changed the cat into a dog. Immediately the dog became afraid of the tiger, because the mouse within remained the same. The mouse was not changed; only bodies, the outer. The same anxiety, the same disease, the same fear remained. The magician changed the dog into a tiger. Immediately the mouse within the tiger became afraid of a hunter. So the magician said to the mouse, "Now be a mouse again, because I can change your bodies, but I cannot change you. You have the heart of a mouse, so what can I do?—the heart of a mouse!"

You can go on changing the outer, but the heart of the mouse remains the same. And that heart creates the problems. The shape will change, the form will change, but the substance will remain the same. And it makes no difference whether you are afraid of a cat, or of a dog, or of a tiger. The question is not of whom you are afraid; the question is that you are afraid.

The emphasis is—my emphasis is—that you must remain aware that your outer effort should not become a substitute for the inner transformation...one thing. Take every help that can be taken. It is good to have right food, but it is nonsense and madness to become obsessed with food. It is good to have right behavior, but it is neurotic to become obsessed with it. You should not become mad about anything.

In India there are many sects of sannyasins who are obsessed with food. The whole day they are thinking only of food: what to eat and what not to eat; who should prepare the food and who should not prepare the food. Once I was traveling with a sannyasin. He would take only milk, and only cow's milk, and only from those cows which were white; otherwise he would go without food. This man is mad.

Remember this: that the inner is important, significant. The outer is helpful, it is good, but you must not become focused on it. It must not become so important that the inner is forgotten. The inner must remain the inner and the central, and the outer, if possible, should be changed just as a help.

Don't ignore it completely. There is no need to ignore it, because really the outer is also part of the inner. It is not something opposite to it, it is not something contrary to it, it is not something imposed upon you—it is you. But the inner is the central, and the outer is the periphery. So give as much importance as a periphery needs, as a circumference needs, as a boundary needs—but the boundary is not the house. So take care of it, but don't become mad after it.

Our mind is always trying to find escapes. If you can become involved with food, with sex, with clothes, with the body, your mind will be at ease, because now you are not going towards the inner. Now there is no need to change the mind. Now there is no need to destroy the mind, to go beyond the mind. With the change of food, the same mind can exist. You may eat this or that—the same mind can exist. Only when you move inwards...the more inside you reach, the more this mind which you have has to cease. The inward path is the path towards no-mind.

The mind becomes afraid. It will try to find some escape—something to do with the outer. Then the mind can exist as it is. Whatsoever you do makes no difference. It is irrelevant what you do—this mind can exist, and this mind can find ways for how to remain the same. And sometimes, when you struggle with the natural outlet, your mind will find some perverted outlets which are more dangerous. Rather than being a help, they will become hindrances.

I have heard that Mulla Nasruddin fell down his stairs. His leg was fractured, so it was put in a plaster cast, and he was told that for three months he was not to go up and down the stairs. After three months he came to the doctor and the plaster was removed. Mulla asked, "Now can I go up and down the stairs?"

The doctor said, "Now you can go. You are absolutely okay."

Mulla said, "Now I am so happy, doctor. You cannot believe how happy I am. It was so awkward to go up and down the drainpipe the whole day. For three months, every day going up and down the drainpipe—it was so awkward, and the whole neighborhood was laughing at me. But you had told me not to go up and down the stairs, so I had to find a way."

This is what everyone is doing. If one outlet is blocked, then a perversion is bound to happen. And you don't know the ways of the mind—they are very cunning and very subtle. People come to me with their problems. The problem seems to be obvious—it is not. All problems seem to be obvious, clear—it is not so. Deep down something else is hidden, and unless that something else is known, discarded, gone beyond, the problem will remain. It will change its shape.

Someone is smoking too much and he wants to stop it. But smoking in itself is not a problem; the problem is something else. You can stop smoking, but the problem will remain, and it will have to come out in something else. When do you smoke? When you are anxious, nervous, you start smoking, and smoking helps you. You feel more confident, you feel more relaxed.

Just by stopping the smoking, your nervousness is not going to change. You will feel nervous, you will feel anxious; the anxiety will come. Then you will do something else. And you can find something which is a beautiful substitute; it looks so different. You can do anything. You can just use a mantra instead of smoking, and whenever you feel nervous you can say, "Ram, Ram, Ram"—anything continuously.

What are you doing with smoking? It is a mantra. You smoke in and out, you smoke in and out—it becomes a repetitive thing. Because of the repetition you feel relaxed. Repeat anything and the same will happen. But if you are using a mantra and saying, "Ram, Ram, Ram," no one is going to say that you are doing something wrong. And the problem is the same.

The problem has not changed; only you have changed the trick. Previously you were doing it with smoke; now you are doing it with a word. Repetition helps; any nonsense thing will help. You just have to repeat it continuously. When you repeat a thing it gives relaxation, because it creates a sort of boredom. Boredom is relaxing. You can do anything that creates a sort of boredom. Boredom is relaxing. You can do anything that creates boredom.

If you are smoking, everyone will say that it is wrong, and if you are chanting a mantra, no one is going to say that it is wrong. But if the problem is the same, I am saying that it is also wrong—rather, more dangerous than the previous one, because with smoking you were aware that it was wrong. Now, with this chanting of the mantra you are not aware, and this disease that you are unaware of is more dangerous and more harmful.

You can do anything on the surface, but unless deeper roots are changed, nothing happens. So with the outer remember this: be aware of it, and move from the surface towards the roots and find the root—why are you nervous? Someone is eating too much food. It can be stopped. You can force yourself to not eat too much. But why is one eating too much food? Why? Because this is not a bodily need, so somewhere the mind is interfering. Something has to be done with the mind; it is not a question of the body. Why do you go on stuffing yourself?

Too much obsession with food is a love need. If you are not loved well, you will eat more. If you are loved and you can love, you will eat less. Whenever someone loves you, you cannot eat more. Love fills you so much, you don't feel empty. When there is not love, you feel empty; something has to be stuffed in—you go on forcing food.

And there are reasons, root reasons, for it, because the first encounter of the child with love and food is simultaneous. From the same breast, from the same mother, he gets food and love—food and love become associated. If the mother is loving, the child will never take too much milk. There is no need. He is always secure in his love; he knows that whenever there is a need the food will come, the milk will be there, the mother will be there. He feels secure. But if the mother is nonloving, then he is insecure. Then he doesn't know whether, when he feels hungry, food will come, because there is no love. He will eat more. And this will continue. It will become an unconscious root.

So you can go on changing your food—eat this, eat that, don't eat this—but it makes no difference, because the basic root remains there. Then if you stop stuffing yourself with food, you will start stuffing with something else. And there are many ways. If you stop eating too much you may start accumulating money. Then again you have to be filled by something; then you go on accumulating money.

Observe deeply, and you will see that a person

who accumulates money is never in love, cannot be, because the money accumulation is really a substitute. With money he will feel secure now. When you are loved there is no insecurity; in love all fears disappear. In love there is no future, no past. This moment is enough, this very moment is eternity. You are accepted. There is no anxiety for the future, for what will happen tomorrow—there is no tomorrow in love.

But if love is not there, then the tomorrow is there. What will happen? Accumulate money, because you cannot rely on any person. So rely on things, rely on money and wealth. There are people who say, "Donate your money. Don't accumulate money. Be nonattached to money." But these are superficial things, because the inner need will remain the same—then he will start accumulating something else.

Stop one outlet and you will have to create another—unless the roots are destroyed. So don't be too much concerned with the outer. Be aware of whatsoever your outer personality is. Be aware of it, be alert, and from the periphery always move towards the roots to find what the cause is there. Howsoever disturbing, move to the roots. Once you come to know the roots, once the roots are exposed.... Remember this law: the roots can exist only in darkness—not only the roots of trees, but the roots of anything. They can exist only in darkness. Once they are brought to light, they die.

So move with your periphery; dig deep and go to the roots, and bring the roots to consciousness, to light. Once you have come to the root, it simply disappears. You have not to do anything about it. You have to do something only because you don't know what the problem is. A problem rightly understood disappears. Right understanding of a problem, a root understanding of the problem, becomes the disappearance of it. The first thing.

The second thing: whatsoever you do is superficial; it is not you in your totality. So don't judge a man by his actions, because action is very atomic. You see a person in anger, and you can judge that

this man is filled with hatred, violence, vengeance. But a moment later the anger disappears; the man becomes as loving as possible, and a different perfume, a different flowering, comes to his face. The anger was atomic. Don't judge the whole man. But this love is also atomic. Don't judge the whole man by this love.

Whatsoever you have done is not your total sum. Your actions remain just atomic—part of you of course, but your totality transcends them. You can be different immediately. And whatsoever is known about you by your behavior, by your actions, by your doings, you can contradict. You may have been a saint: you can become a sinner this very moment. No one could imagine that you, a saint, could do this. You can do it. It is not inconceivable. You may have been a sinner up to this moment, and the next moment you can jump out of it.

What I am saying is, your inner is so vast and so great that by your outer it cannot be judged. Your outer remains superficial, accidental. I will repeat it. Your outer remains accidental, your inner is the essence. So remember to uncover the inner, and don't get entangled with the outer.

One thing more: the outer is always of the past. It is always dead, because whatsoever you have done, you have done. It is always of the past, it is never alive. The inner is always alive, it is here and now, and the outer is always dead. If you know me —whatsoever I have done and said—you know my past, you don't know me. I am here, living. That is my inner point, and whatsoever you know about me is just the outer. It is dead, it is no more there.

Observe it in your own consciousness. Whatsoever you have done is not a bondage on you. It is no more, really; it is just a memory. And you are greater than that. Your infinite possibilities are there. It was only accidental that you are a sinner or you are a saint. It was only accidental that you are a Christian or a Hindu. But your innermost being is not accidental; it is essential.

The emphasis on the inner is the emphasis on

the essential. And that inner remains free, it is freedom. The outer is a slavery, because you can know the outer only when it has happened; then you cannot do anything about it. What can you do about your past? It cannot be undone, you cannot move backwards. You cannot do anything with the past; it is a slavery.

If you understand it rightly, then you can understand the theory of karma, the theory of actions. This theory—one of the most essential parts of Hindu realization—is that unless you go beyond karmas, you are not free; unless you have gone beyond all actions, you will remain in bondage. Don't pay much attention to the outer, don't get obsessed with it. Use it as a help, but continuously remember that the inner has to be discovered.

These techniques we are discussing here are for the inner, for how to discover it. I will tell you one thing. There have been traditions.... For example, one of the most important religious traditions has been Jainism. But Jainism pays too much attention to the outer; too much, so much so that they completely forget that there is anything like meditation, that there is anything like a science of yoga. They forget it completely.

They are obsessed with food, with clothes, with sleep, with everything—but with no effort towards meditation. Not that in their tradition originally there was no meditation, because no religion can be born without it, but they got obsessed somewhere with the outer. It became so important that they forgot completely that this whole situation is just a help; it is not the goal.

What you eat is not the goal. What you are is the goal. It is good if your eating habits help you to uncover the being. It is good. But if you become just obsessed with eating, continuously thinking about it, then you have missed the point. Then you are a food addict. You are mad, neurotic.

The second question:

Isn't it true that all meditation techniques are really doings which lead the seeker to his being?

In a way, yes; and in a deeper way, no. Meditation techniques are doings, because you are advised to do something. Even to meditate is to do something, even to sit silently is to do something, even to not do anything is a sort of doing. So in a superficial way, all meditation techniques are doings. But in a deeper way they are not, because if you succeed in them, the doing disappears.

Only in the beginning it appears like an effort. If you succeed in it, the effort disappears and the whole thing becomes spontaneous and effortless. If you succeed in it, it is not a doing. No effort on your part is needed then. It becomes just like breathing—it is there. But in the beginning the effort is bound to be, because the mind cannot do anything which is not an effort. If you tell it to be effortless, the whole thing seems absurd.

In Zen, where much emphasis is put on effortlessness, the masters say to the disciples, "Just sit. Don't do anything." And the disciple tries. Of course, what can you do other than trying? The disciple tries to just sit, and he tries to just sit, and he tries to not do anything, and then the master hits him on his head with his staff and he says, "Don't do this! I have not told you to try to sit, because that becomes an effort. And don't try not to do anything, because that is a sort of doing. Simply sit!"

If I tell you to simply sit, what will you do? You will do something, which will make it not a simple sitting; an effort will enter. You will be sitting with an effort, a strain will be there. You cannot simply sit. It looks strange, but the moment you try to simply sit, it has become complex. The very effort to simply sit makes it complex. So what to do?

Years pass, and the disciple goes on sitting and being blamed, condemned by the master that he is missing the point. But he simply goes on, goes on, goes on, and every day he is a failure, because the effort is there. And he cannot deceive the master.

But one day, just patiently sitting, even this consciousness to sit simply disappears. One day suddenly he is sitting—like a tree or like a rock—not doing anything. And then the master says, "This is the right posture. Now you have attained it. Now remember this: this is the way to sit." But it takes patience and long effort to achieve effortlessness.

In the beginning, effort will be there, doing will be there, but only in the beginning, as a necessary evil. But you have to remember constantly that you have to go beyond it. A moment must come when you are not doing anything about meditation—just being there and it happens; just sitting or standing and it happens; not doing anything, just being aware, it happens.

All these techniques are just to help you to come to an effortless moment. The inner transformation, the inner realization, cannot happen through effort, because effort is a sort of tension. With effort you cannot be relaxed totally; the effort will become a barrier. With this background in mind, if you make effort, by and by you will become capable of leaving it also.

It is just like swimming. If you know about swimming, you know that in the beginning you have to make effort—but only in the beginning. Once you know the feel of it, once you know what it is, the effort has gone; you can swim effortlessly. And even a good swimmer cannot say what swimming is, what exactly he is doing. He cannot explain to you what he is doing. Really, he is not doing anything. He is simply allowing himself to be in a deep responsive relationship with the water, with the river. He is not doing anything really. And if he is still doing, he is still not an expert swimmer —he is still amateur, still learning.

I will tell you one anecdote. In Burma, one Buddhist monk was ordered to make a design for the new temple, particularly for the gate. So he was making many designs. He had one very talented disciple, so he told that disciple to be near him. While he made the design the disciple was simply to watch, and if he liked it he had to say that it was okay, it was right. If he didn't like it then he had to say no. And the master said, "When you say yes, only then will I send the design. If you go on saying no, I will discard the design and will create a new one."

Hundreds of designs were discarded in this way. Three months passed. Even the master became afraid, but he had given his word so he had to keep it. The disciple was there, the master would make the design, and then the disciple would say no. The master would start another one.

One day the ink was just about to be finished, so the master said, "Go out and find more ink." The disciple went out. The master forgot him, his presence, and became effortless. His presence was the problem. The idea was constantly in his mind that the disciple was there, judging. He was constantly wondering whether he was going to like it or not, whether he would discard it again. This created an inner anxiety and the master could not be spontaneous.

The disciple went out. The design was completed. The disciple came in and he said "Wonderful! But why couldn't you do it before?"

The master said, "Now I understand why—because you were here. Because of you—I was making an effort to get your approval. The effort destroyed the whole thing. I couldn't be natural, I couldn't flow, I couldn't forget myself because of you."

Whenever you are doing meditation, the very effort that you are doing it, the very idea of succeeding in it, is the barrier. Be conscious of it. Go on doing, and be conscious of it. A day will come…just through patience a day comes when effort is not there. Really, you are not there, only meditation is. It may take a long time. It cannot be predicted, no one can say when it will happen. Because if something is to be achieved by effort, it can be predicted—that if you do this much effort you will succeed. But meditation is going to succeed only when you become effortless. That's why nothing can be predicted, nothing can be said about when you will succeed. You may succeed this very moment, and you may not succeed for lives.

The whole thing hinges on one thing: when your effort drops and you become spontaneous, when your meditation is not an act but becomes your being, when your meditation is just like love....

You cannot do anything about love, or can you? If you do anything, you falsify it. It will become artificial. It will not go deep. You will not be in it. It will become an acting. Love *is*—you cannot do anything about it.

You cannot do anything about meditation also. But I don't mean don't do anything, because then you will remain whatsoever you are. You have to do something, perfectly conscious that by only doing you will not achieve. Doing will be needed in the beginning. One cannot leave it; one has to go through it. But one has to go through it, one has to transcend it, and an effortless floating has to be achieved.

The path is arduous and very contradictory. You cannot find anything more contradictory than meditation—contradictory because it has to be started as an effort and it has to end as effortlessness. But it happens. You may not be able to conceive logically how it happens, but in experience it happens. A day comes when you just get fed up with your effort. It drops.

It happened to Buddha this way. For six years he was making every effort possible. No human being has been so obsessed with becoming enlightened. He did everything that he could do. He moved from one teacher to another, and whatsoever he was taught, he did it perfectly. That was the problem, because no teacher could say to him, "You are not doing well, that's why you are not achieving." That was impossible. He was doing better than any master, so the masters had to confess. They said, "This much we have to teach. Beyond this we don't know, so you go somewhere else."

He was a dangerous disciple—and only dangerous disciples achieve. He studied everything that was possible. Whatsoever he was told, he would do

it—absolutely as it was told. And then he would come to the master and say, "I have done it, but nothing has happened. So what next?"

The teachers would say, "You go somewhere else. There is one teacher in the Himalayas—go there." Or, "There is one teacher in some forest—go there. We don't know more than this."

He went around and around for six years. He did all that can be done, all that is humanly possible, and then he got fed up. The whole thing appeared futile, fruitless, meaningless. One night he relaxed all efforts. He was sitting under the bodhi tree, and he said, "Now everything is finished. In the world there is nothing, and in this spiritual search also there is nothing. Now there is nothing for me to do. Everything is finished—not only this world, but the other world also." Suddenly all efforts dropped. He was empty. Because when there is nothing to do, the mind cannot move. The mind moves only because there is something to do—some motivation, some goal. The mind moves because something is possible, something can be achieved, the future. If not today then tomorrow, but the possibility is there that one can achieve it—the mind moves.

That night Buddha came to a dead point. Really, he died that very moment, because there was no future. Nothing was to be achieved, and nothing could be achieved—"I have done everything. The whole world is futile and this whole existence is a nightmare." Not only the material world became futile, but the spiritual also. He relaxed. Not that he did something to relax—this is the point to understand: there was nothing to be tense about, therefore he relaxed. There was no effort on his part to relax.

Under the bodhi tree he was not trying for relaxation. There was nothing to do, nothing to be tense about, nothing to desire, no future, no hope. He was absolutely hopeless that night—relaxed. Relaxation happened. You cannot relax, because something or other is still there to be achieved. That goes on stirring your mind; you go on spinning and spinning around and around. Suddenly the spinning stopped, the wheel stopped—Buddha relaxed and fell asleep.

In the morning when he awoke, the last star was setting. He looked at the last star disappearing, and with that last star disappearing, he disappeared completely, he became an enlightened one. Then people started asking, "How did you achieve this? How? What was the method?"

Now you can understand Buddha's difficulty. If he said that he had achieved through some methods, then he was wrong, because he achieved only when there was no method. If he said that he had achieved through effort, then he was wrong, because he achieved only when there was no effort. But if he said, "Don't make any effort and you will achieve," then too he was wrong, because to his no-effort those six years of effort were the background. Without that effort, that six years' arduous effort, this state of no-effort could not have been achieved. Only because of that mad effort he came to a peak and there was nowhere further to go; he relaxed and fell down in the valley.

This has to be remembered for many reasons. Spiritual effort is the most contradictory phenomenon. Effort has to be made, with full consciousness that nothing can be achieved through effort. Effort has to be made only to achieve no-effort, only to achieve effortlessness. But don't relax your effort, because if you relax you will never achieve that relaxation which came to Buddha. You go on doing every effort, so automatically a moment comes when just by sheer effort you reach a point where relaxation happens to you.

For example, you may take it in a different way. As I see it, in the West, ego has been the central point: the fulfillment of the ego, the development of the ego, the achievement of a strong ego, has been the whole Western effort. In the East, it has been how to achieve egolessness, how to be a nonego, how to forget, surrender, dissolve yourself completely so that you are not. The East has been trying for egolessness, the West has been trying for

the perfect ego. But this is the contradictoriness of things: if you don't have a very developed ego, you cannot surrender. You can surrender only if you have a perfectly clear-cut ego. Otherwise you cannot surrender, because who will surrender?

So to me, both are half and both are in misery—East and West both. Because the East has taken egolessness, which is the end part, and the beginning part is missing.

Who will surrender the ego? The peak is not there, so who will create the valley? The valley is created only around a peak. The greater the peak, the deeper the valley. If you don't have an ego, or you have a very lukewarm one, surrender is not possible—or your surrender will be a lukewarm surrender, just so-so. Nothing will happen out of it; there will be no explosion.

In the West, the beginning part has been emphasized. So you can go on growing with your ego. It will create more and more anxiety. And when you have really created it, you don't know what to do with it, because the end part is not there.

To me, the spiritual search is both. Create a very great peak, create a perfect ego, just to dissolve it. That seems absurd—just to dissolve it, just to achieve a deep surrender, just to lose it somewhere. And you cannot lose something which you don't have. So in my view, humanity has to be trained for these two things together: help everyone to create a perfect ego, a fulfilled ego—but this is only half the journey—and then, help them to surrender it.

The greater the peak, the deeper will be the valley. The higher the ego, the deeper you will move in your surrender. And this is for everything. On the spiritual path, remember this continuous contradictoriness. Don't forget it even for a single moment. Become perfect egoists so that you can surrender, so that you can dissolve, melt. Do every effort that you can do, just to reach a point where effort leaves you and you are totally effortless.

The third question:

You said last night that the more the mind grows, the more we know that the nature of the mind is confusion. But isn't it true that this growth of the mind also leads to clarity?

Whatsoever I was just saying is related to this.

Yes, it leads to clarity, because only when you have a very mature mind do you become aware that you are confused. Even to become aware that mind is confusion, a very developed mind is needed. Those who are not aware that their mind is confusion are really not mature minds. They are childish, juvenile, still developing. Only a very mature mind can become aware of the quality of the mind, that it is confusion. And when you have developed the mind, only then is meditation possible, because meditation is the opposite goal.

Meditation means no-mind. But how can you achieve a no-mind if you have not achieved a mind? So achieve a mind just to lose it. And don't think that if ultimately one has to reach the state of no-mind, then what is the use of achieving a mind? —because if you don't achieve a mind, the ultimate is not going to happen to you. It can happen only if the mind is there. So I am not against mind, I am not against intellect. Really, I am not against anything. I am for everything, because everything can be used to reach the opposite pole.

There is a polarity, and the opposite pole cannot be reached if the polarity is not there. A madman cannot meditate. Why? Because he has no mind. But this no-mind is not the no-mind of Buddha. No-mind can have two dimensions: below mind and above mind. The above mind is no-mind, and the below mind is also no-mind. You can fall down from the mind: the mind is not there, but it is not meditation. You have to go beyond mind, only then is the Buddha's no-mind achieved. And always remember it, because they are so similar you can misunderstand the whole thing. They are so similar.

For example, a child is innocent. A saint is also innocent—a Jesus or a Krishna—but their innocence is not childish. It is childlike, not childish; because a child is innocent only because he is ignorant. He is innocent only as a negative thing, just the absence. Sooner or later everything will erupt; he is a volcano waiting to erupt. The innocence is just the silence before the volcano erupts.

A saint is one who has gone beyond. The eruption has happened; the volcano is silent again. But this silence is different. The first silence was very pregnant, something was present there. The silence was just on the surface; deep down that child was getting ready to be disturbed. The saint has passed the disturbance. The cyclone has gone. This silence, the innocence, appears similar, but there is a deep difference.

So sometimes an idiot can also appear to be saintlike. And idiots are saintlike, they are not cunning. To be cunning, intelligence is needed. They are not calculating; to be calculating, mind is needed. Idiots are simple, innocent, noncunning, noncalculating. They cannot deceive anyone. Not that they would not like to; they cannot. The very capacity is not there. They look like saints, and sometimes saints look like idiots, because the same thing has happened again, in a different, altogether different, dimension.

You can fall down below the mind, then too a no-mind happens. But it is not meditation; you have simply lost even that mind which was going to become a step towards meditation. So I am not against mind. Develop mind, develop intellect, but remember well—this is just a means, and a means which has to be forsaken, thrown away. It has to be used like a boat. You reach the other shore, you leave the boat. You forget about the boat completely.

The last question:

We very often feel that we create our own sufferings. In spite of this, why do we continue creating them? And when and how does one stop creating one's own suffering?

The first and very basic thing to be understood, is that whenever you say, *We very often feel that we create our own sufferings,* this is not the case. You never really feel that you are the creator of your own suffering. You may think so, because you have been taught so; because for centuries and centuries teachers have been teaching that you are the creator of your own suffering and no one else is responsible.

You have heard these things, you have read these things. They have become your blood and bone, they have become your unconscious conditionings, so sometimes you repeat like a parrot, *We create our own sufferings.* But this is not your feeling, this is not your realization, because if you realize it, then the other thing is impossible. Then you cannot say, *In spite of this, why do we continue creating them?*

If you really feel it, and if it is your own feeling that you are the creator of your own suffering, any moment you can stop—unless you want to create it, unless you enjoy it, unless you are a masochist. Then everything is okay, then there is no question. If you say, "I enjoy my suffering," then it is okay; you can go on creating it. But if you say, "I suffer and I want to go beyond it. I want to stop it completely—and I understand that I am the creator," then you are wrong. You don't understand it.

Socrates is reported to have said that knowledge is virtue. And there has been a long discussion for these two thousand years over whether Socrates was right or wrong—knowledge is virtue. Socrates says that once you know something, you cannot do contrary to it. If you know that anger is suffering, you cannot be angry. This is what Socrates means —knowledge is virtue. You cannot say, "I know anger is bad; still I move in it. What to do about it now?" Socrates says that the first thing is wrong. You don't know that anger is bad; that's why you go on moving in it. If you know, you cannot move in it. How can you move against your own knowledge?

I know that if I put my hand in the fire it is going to be painful. If I know, I cannot put my hand in. But if somebody else has told me, if I have heard through the tradition, if I have read in the scriptures that fire burns and I have not known fire, and I have not known any similar experience, only then can I put my hand into fire—and that too only once.

Can you conceive it—that you have put your hand into fire and you have been burned and you have suffered, and again you go and ask, "I know that fire burns, but in spite of it I go on putting my hand into the fire. What to do about it?" Who will believe that you know? And what type of knowledge is this? If your own experience of suffering and burning cannot stop you, nothing is going to stop you. Now there is no possibility, because the last possibility has been missed. But no one can miss it; that is impossible.

Socrates is right, and all those who have known, they will agree with Socrates—that agreement has a very deep point in it. Once you know.... But remember—the knowledge must be yours. A borrowed knowledge won't do; borrowed knowledge is useless. Unless it is your own experience, it is not going to change you. Others' experiences are of no help.

You have heard that you are the creator of your own suffering, but this is just in the mind. It has not entered your being, it is not your own knowledge. So when you are discussing, you can discuss about it cerebrally, but when the actual phenomenon happens, you will forget, and you will behave in the way you know, not in the way others know.

When you are at ease, cool, collected, silently discussing anger, you can say it is poison, it is a disease, evil. But when someone makes you angry then a complete change occurs. Now it is not an intellectual discussion, now you are involved. And the moment you are involved, you become angry. Later on again, retrospectively, when you again get cool, the memory will come back, your mind will again start functioning, and you will say, "That was wrong. It was not good of me to do that. I know anger is wrong."

Who is this "I"?—just intellect, just the superficial mind. You don't know—because when someone pushes you into anger, you throw this mind away. It is useful as far as discussion is concerned, but when a real situation arises, only the real knowledge will help. When there is no situation, you can go on. Even in a discussion the real situation can arise. The other can go on contradicting you so much that you become angry and then you will forget.

Real knowledge means that which has happened to you. You have not heard about it, not read about it, you have not collected information about it—it is your own experience. And then there is no question, because after that you cannot go against it. Not that you will have to make an effort not to go against it; simply you cannot go against it.

How can I? When I know this is a wall and I want to go out of this room, how can I try to pass through the wall? I know this is a wall, so I will search for the door. Only a blind man will try to go out through the wall. I have got eyes, I see what is a wall and what is a door. But if I try to enter the wall and tell you, "I know very well where the door is, and I know this to be a wall, but in spite of this, how can I stop myself from trying to enter the wall?" then that means that as far as I am concerned that door looks false. Others have told me that it is the door, but as far as I am concerned, I know that door is false. And others have told me that this is a wall, but as far as I see, I see the door here in this wall, and that is why I try.

In this situation you have to make a clear-cut distinction between what you know and what you have gathered as knowledge. Don't rely on information. From the greatest source—even if you collect from the greatest source—information is information. Even if a buddha says it to you, it is not your own, and it is not going to help you in any way. But you can remain thinking that it is your knowledge, and this misunderstanding will waste your energy, time and life.

The basic thing is not to ask what to do so that suffering is not created. The basic thing is to know that you are the creator of your suffering. Next time, whenever a real situation arises and you are in suffering, remember to find out whether you are the cause of it. And if you can find out that you are the cause of it, the suffering will disappear, and the same suffering will not appear again—impossible.

But don't deceive yourself. You can—that's why I say it. When you are suffering you can say, "Yes, I know I have created this suffering," but deep down you know that someone else has created it. Your wife has created it, your husband has created it, someone else has created it, and this is simply a consolation because you cannot do anything. You console yourself: "No one has created it, I have created it myself, and by and by I will stop it."

But knowledge is instant transformation; there is no by-and-by. If you understand that you have created it, it will drop immediately. And it is not going to come up again. If it comes again, it means the understanding has not gone deep. So there is no need to find out what to do, and how to stop. The only need is to go deep and to find out who is really the cause of it.

If others are the cause then it cannot be stopped, because you cannot change the whole world. If you are the cause, only then can it be stopped. That's why I insist that only religion can lead humanity towards nonsuffering. Nothing else can lead, because everyone else believes that the suffering is caused by others; only religion says that suffering is caused by you. So religion makes you the master of your destiny. You are the cause of your suffering, hence you can be the cause of your bliss.

CHAPTER 51

Coming back to existence

◆

76 *In rain during a black night, enter that blackness as the form of forms.*

77 *When a moonless rainy night is not present, close eyes and find blackness before you. Opening eyes, see blackness. So faults disappear forever.*

78 *Wherever your attention alights, at this very point, experience.*

nce a doctor, a very well-known historian and an eminent scholar, was staying in a village. The postmaster, the old postmaster of the village, became curious about this old man, this doctor. He was curious to know what kind of doctor he was, so one day he asked, "What kind of doctor are you, sir?"

The man said, "A doctor of philosophy." The old man had never heard about it. He was puzzled and he said, "I have never heard of any case of this disease here."

Don't laugh about it, because that old postmaster was right in a way—philosophy is a kind of disease. Of course, doctors of philosophy are not doctors; rather, they are the perfect victims of a disease.

Philosophy is not a specific disease, so you cannot think of it in terms of cases. It is born with the human being. It is as old as humanity or the human mind. And every human being is a victim, more or less—because thinking leads nowhere; or, it leads you in circles, vicious circles. You move much, and if you are expert you can move fast, but you reach nowhere.

This has to be understood very deeply, because if you cannot understand and feel this, you cannot take a jump into meditation. Meditation means the very anti approach—anti to philosophy. Philosophy means thinking and meditation means a state of nonthinking. They are polar opposites.

This is just human—to think about questions and to try to find out answers. But philosophy comes to no answers. Science comes to certain answers, religion comes to certain answers, but philosophy comes to no answers. And all the answers that philosophy appears to come to are just façades: if you dig deep in them you will find more questions and nothing else. So every answer leads to more questions—and this goes on and on.

Science comes to certain answers, because science depends not on thinking but on experimentation. Thinking is used as a help only, but the base is experimentation. That's why science has given some answers. Philosophers, known and unknown, have been working and working for centuries, but not a single answer, not a single conclusion has been achieved. It cannot be achieved. The very nature of thinking is such that if you use thinking as a help towards experimentation, something can be achieved; that's why science comes to certain answers.

But religion also comes to certain answers, because religion is also experimentation. Science experiments with the object, religion experiments with the subject, but both are experimentations and both depend on experiment. Between these two is philosophy—just pure thinking, abstract thinking, with no experiment. You can go on, you can go on, but you reach nowhere. Abstract thinking, speculative thinking, is thinking ad infinitum. You can enjoy, you can enjoy the journey, but there is no goal.

Religion and science are similar in a way—both believe in experiment. Religious experiment is of course deeper than scientific, because in science the experimenter himself is not involved. He is working with tools, working with things, working with objects; he remains aloof, he remains out of the experiment. Religion is a deeper science, because the experimenter himself becomes the experiment. There are no tools which are apart from him, no objects which are outside him. He is both—his tools, his objects, his method; he is everything. And he has to work upon himself.

It is arduous. Because you are involved, it is arduous. And because you are involved, the experiment will become experience. In science, the experiment will remain an experiment. The scientist will not be touched by it, will not be transformed by it. The scientist will remain the same. But in religion, passing through the experiment, you will be a different man altogether. You cannot come out the same; you are bound to change. That's why religious experiment becomes experience.

Remember this: you can go on thinking about God, about soul, about the other world, and you may make believe that you know something about God just by thinking about him. That will be false. You cannot know anything about God—the word "about" is absurd. You can know God, but you cannot know "about"—that "about" creates philosophy.

How can you know about God? Or, for example, how can you know about love? You can know love, you cannot know about love, because "about" means someone else knows and you believe in his knowledge. You collect and gather opinions. You say, "I know something about God." All knowledge which is "about" is false, dangerous, because you can be deluded by it.

You can know God, you can know love, you can know yourself, but forget that "about." That "about" is philosophy. The Upanishads say something, the Vedas say something, the Bible says something, the Koran says something, but for you, all that will become "about." Unless it becomes your experience it is futile, wasted.

This point must go deep within you, because you can go on thinking, and the mind is such that you can start thinking about meditation. You can make anything an object for thinking. Even about meditation you can think, and you can go on thinking about it—nothing will happen.

I am talking about so many methods. There is a danger: you may start thinking about these methods, you may become knowledgeable. That won't do, that is of no use. Not only is it of no use, it is dangerous—because meditation is experience, knowing "about" is worthless.

Remember this word 'experience.' Life's problems, all the problems of life, are existential, they are not speculative. You cannot solve them by thinking; you can solve them only by living them. Through living the future opens. Through thinking the future never opens. On the contrary, even the present closes.

You may not have observed: whenever you think, what happens? Whenever you think, you are closed. All that is present drops. You move on a dream path in your mind. One word creates another, one thought creates another, and you go on moving. The more you move in thinking, the further away you go from existence. Thinking is a way to go away. It is a dream-way; it is dreaming in concepts. Come back to the earth. Religion is very earthly in this sense; not worldly but very earthly, substantial. Come back to existence.

Life's problems can be solved only when you become deeply rooted in existence. Flying in thoughts you move away from the roots, and the further away you are, the less is the possibility of solving anything. Rather, you will confuse everything, and everything will become more entangled. And the more entangled, the more you will think, and the further away you will move. Beware of thinking!

Now we will enter the techniques.

76 Dissolve into darkness.

The first darkness technique: *In rain during a black night, enter that blackness as the form of forms.*

There has been one very old esoteric school about which you may not have heard. The school was known as the school of the Essenes. Jesus was taught in that school; he belonged to the Essenes' group. That Essene group is the only group all over the world that thinks of God as absolute darkness. The Koran says God is light, the Upanishads say God is light, the Bible says God is light. The Essenes' is the only tradition in the world which says that God is absolute blackness, absolute darkness, just an infinite black night.

This is very beautiful; strange, but very beautiful —and very meaningful. You must understand the meaning, then this technique will be very helpful, because this is the technique used by the Essenes to enter darkness, to become one with it.

Reflect. Why has God been symbolized everywhere as light? Not because God is light, but because man is afraid of darkness. This is human fear—we like light and we are afraid of darkness, so we cannot conceive of God as darkness, as blackness. This is human conception. We conceive of God as light because we are afraid of darkness.

Our gods are created out of our fear. We give them shape and form. That shape and form is given by us—it shows something about us, not about our gods. They are our creations. We are afraid in darkness, so God is light. But these techniques belong to the other school.

Essenes say that God is darkness, and there is something in it. One thing: darkness is eternal. Light comes and goes and darkness remains. In the morning the sun will rise and there will be light; in the evening the sun will set and there will be darkness. For darkness nothing will rise—it is always there. It never rises and never sets. Light comes and goes; darkness remains. Light always has some

source; darkness is without source. That which has some source cannot be infinite; only that which is sourceless can be infinite and eternal. Light has a certain disturbance; that's why you cannot sleep in light. It creates a tension. Darkness is relaxation, total relaxation.

But why are we afraid of darkness? Because light appears to us as life—it is; and darkness appears to be death—it is. Life comes through light, and when you die it appears you have fallen into eternal darkness. That's why we paint death as black, and black has become a color for mourning. God is light, and death is black. But these are our fears projected. Actually, darkness has infinity; light is limited. Darkness seems to be the womb out of which everything arises and into which everything falls.

The Essenes took this standpoint. It is very beautiful and very helpful also, because if you can love darkness you will become unafraid of death. If you can enter into darkness—and you can enter only when there is no fear—you will achieve total relaxation. If you can become one with darkness, you are dissolved, it is a surrender. Now there is no fear, because if you have become one with darkness, you have become one with death. You cannot die now, you have become deathless. Darkness is deathless. Light is born and dies; darkness simply is. It is deathless.

For these techniques, first you will have to remember that there should be no fear in your mind about darkness, about blackness, otherwise how can you do this experiment? First the fear must be dropped. So do one thing as a preliminary step: sit in darkness, put off the lights, feel darkness. Have a loving attitude towards it; allow the darkness to touch you. Look at it. Open your eyes in a dark room or in a dark night; have a communion, be together, imbibe a relationship. You will become afraid—then these techniques cannot be of any help, you cannot do them.

First a deep friendship with darkness is needed. Sometimes in the night when everyone has gone to sleep, remain with the darkness. Don't do anything, just remain with it. And just remaining with it will give you a deep feeling towards it, because it is so relaxing. You have not known it simply because of the fear. If you are not feeling sleepy, you will put on the light immediately, you will start reading or doing something, but you will not remain with the darkness. Remain with it. If you can remain with it, you will have new openings, new contacts with it.

Man has closed himself completely against darkness. There were reasons, historical reasons—because the night was very dangerous, and man was in the caves or in the jungles. In the day he was more secure: he could see all around, and no wild animals could attack him; or he could make some arrangements, some defense—at least he could escape. But in the night everywhere was darkness and he was helpless, so he became afraid—and that fear has gone into the unconscious; still we are afraid.

We are not living in caves now and we are not at the mercy of wild animals, no one is going to attack us—but the fear is there. It has gone deep, because for millions of years the human mind was afraid. Your unconscious is not your own; it is collective, it is hereditary, it has come down to you. The fear is there, and because of that fear you can have no communion with darkness.

One thing more: because of this fear, man started to worship fire. When fire was discovered, fire became a god. Not that fire is a god, but because of the fear of darkness. In the day there was light and no fear—man was more protected. In the night there was darkness, so when fire was discovered, of course, fire became a god—the greatest. The Parsis still go on worshipping fire. The worship of fire came into being because of the fear of darkness. In the night the fire became the friend, the protector, the divine security.

That fear is still there. You may not be aware of it, because no situations are there in which you can become aware of it, but one day put off the light in the night and sit—and the primitive fear will come

to you. In your own house you will start feeling that some wild animals are around. Some noise will come, and you will become afraid of wild animals—some danger is around. That danger is not around; that is in your unconscious.

So first you have to overcome your unconscious fear, and then you can enter these techniques, because these techniques are concerned with darkness. And Shiva is giving all the techniques that are possible.

My own experience with these techniques is very beautiful. If you can do them they are wonderful. You will enter a deep relaxation that you have never known. But first uncover your unconscious fears and try to live and love darkness. It is very blissful. Once you know, and once you are in contact with it, you are in contact with a very deep cosmic phenomenon.

So whenever you have the opportunity to be in the dark, and awake.... Because you can do two things: either you can put on the light or you can go to sleep. Both are tricks to escape the darkness. If you are asleep then you are not afraid, because you are not conscious. Or, if you are conscious, then you will put on the light. Don't put on the light and don't go to sleep. Remain with the darkness.

Many fears will be felt. Feel them. Be aware of them. Bring them to your conscious. They will come by themselves, and as they come, you remain just a witness. They will disappear, and very soon a day will come when you can be in darkness with total surrender, with no fear. With a total let-go you can be in darkness. Then a very beautiful phenomenon happens. Then you can appreciate the saying of the Essenes that God is darkness, absolute darkness.

In rain during a black night, enter that blackness as the form of forms.

All forms arise out of darkness and dissolve into darkness. Worlds come, are created out of darkness, and they fall back into darkness. Darkness is the womb, the cosmic womb. The undisturbed, the absolute stillness is there.

Shiva says that it will be good to do this technique in a rainy night when everything is black, when clouds are there and no stars can be seen and the sky is completely dark. In a black night when there is no moon...*enter that blackness as the form of forms.* Be a witness to that blackness, and then dissolve yourself into it. It is the form of all forms. You are a form—you can dissolve into it.

When there is light, you are defined. I can see you, the light is there. Your body has a definition. You are defined, you have boundaries. Boundaries exist because of the light. When the light is not there, boundaries are dissolved. In blackness nothing is defined, everything merges into every other thing. Forms disappear.

That may be one of the causes of our fear—because then you are not defined, then you don't know who you are. The face cannot be seen, the body cannot be known. Everything merges into a formless existence. That may be one of the causes of the fear—because you cannot feel your defined existence. Existence becomes vague and fear enters, because you don't know now who you are. The ego cannot exist: undefined, it is difficult to exist as an ego. One feels afraid. One wants light to be there.

Contemplating, meditating, merging, it will be easier to merge into darkness than to merge into light, because light gives distinctions. Darkness takes away all distinctions. In the light you are beautiful or ugly, rich or poor. The light gives you a personality, a distinctness—educated, uneducated, saint or sinner. The light reveals you as a distinct person. Darkness envelops you, accepts you—not as a distinct person; it simply accepts you without any definitions. You are enveloped and you become one.

The darkness is doing it always, but because you are afraid you cannot understand it. Put aside your fear and become one.

Enter that blackness as the form of all forms.

Enter that blackness.... How can you enter blackness? Three things: one, stare into blackness. Difficult. It is easy to stare at a flame, at any source of light, because it is there as an object, pointed; you can direct your attention to it. Darkness is not an object; it is everywhere, it is all around. You cannot see it as an object. Stare into the vacuum. All around it is there; you just look into it. Feel at ease and look into it. It will start entering your eyes. And when the darkness enters your eyes you are entering into it.

Remain with open eyes when doing this technique in the dark night. Don't close your eyes, because with closed eyes you have a different darkness. That is your own, mental; it is not real. It is *not* real. Really, it is a negative part; it is not positive darkness. Here is light: you close your eyes and you can have a darkness, but that darkness is simply the negative of the light. Just as when you look at the window and then you close your eyes you have a negative figure of the window. All our experience is of light, so when we close our eyes we have a negative experience of light which we call darkness. It is not real, it won't do.

Open your eyes, remain with open eyes in darkness, and you will have a different darkness—the positive darkness that is there. Stare into it. Go on staring into darkness. Your tears will start, your eyes will get sore, they will hurt. Don't get worried, just go on. And the moment the darkness, the real darkness which is there, enters in your eyes, it will give you a very deep soothing feeling. When real darkness enters in you, you will be filled by it.

And this entering of darkness will empty you of all negative darkness. This is a very deep phenomenon. The darkness that you have within is a negative thing; it is against the light. It is not the absence of light; it is against the light. It is not the darkness that Shiva is speaking of as the form of all forms—the real darkness that's there. We are so afraid of it that we have created many sources of light just as protection, and we live in a lighted world. Then we close our eyes and the lighted world reflects negatively inside. We have lost contact with the real darkness that is there—the darkness of the Essenes, or the darkness of Shiva. We have no contact with it. We have become so much afraid of it that we have turned ourselves completely away. We are standing with our backs to it.

So this will be difficult, but if you can do it, it is miraculous, it is magical. You will have a different being altogether. When darkness enters you, you enter into it. It is always reciprocal, mutual. You cannot enter into any cosmic phenomenon without the cosmic phenomenon entering in you. You cannot rape it, you cannot force any entry. If you are available, open, vulnerable, and if you give way for any cosmic realm to enter in you, then only will you enter into it. It is always mutual. You cannot force; you can only allow it.

It is difficult to find real darkness in cities now; difficult in our houses to find real darkness. With the unreal light we have made everything unreal. Even our darkness is polluted, it is not pure. So it is good to move to some remote place only to feel darkness. Just go to a very remote village where there is no electricity, or move to a mountain peak. Just be there for one week to experience pure darkness.

You will come back a different man, because in those seven days of absolute darkness, all the fears, all the primitive fears, will come up. You will have to face monsters, you will have to face your own unconscious. The whole humanity will...it will be as if you are passing through the whole of time, and deep from your unconscious many things will arise. They will look real. You may get afraid, scared, because they will be so real—and they are just your mental creations.

Many madmen in our mad asylums are suffering not from anything else but just from the primitive fears inside them which have erupted. The fears are there; the madmen are afraid, scared every moment of their lives. And we don't yet know how to allow those primitive fears to evaporate. If madmen can be helped to meditate on darkness, madness will disappear.

But only in Japan do they work a little towards this. With their madmen they behave absolutely differently. If someone goes mad, psychotic or neurotic, the Japanese method is to allow him to live in isolation for three weeks or for six weeks, as the case may need. They just allow him to live in isolation. No doctor, no psychoanalyst goes to him. Food is supplied, his needs are taken care of, and he is left alone.

In the night there is no light; in darkness he is alone—suffering of course, passing through many phases. Every care is taken, but no companionship is given to him. He has to face his own madness immediately and directly, and within three to six weeks the madness starts disappearing. Nothing has been done really; he has simply been left alone. This is the only measure that has been taken.

Western psychiatrists have become amazed. They can't understand really how it can happen, because they work for years—they psychoanalyze, they treat, they do everything, but they never leave the man alone. They never leave him to face his inner unconscious totally on his own. Because the more help you give, the more you make him helpless, because the more he depends on you. And the question is of an inner encounter; no one can help, really. So those who know, they will leave you to face yourself.

You have to come to terms with your unconscious. And this meditation on darkness will absorb all your madness completely. Try it. Even in your home you can try it. Every night, for one hour remain with darkness. Don't do anything, just stare into darkness. You will have a melting feeling, and you will feel that something is entering you and you are entering into something.

Staying, living with darkness for three months, for one hour a day, you will lose all feeling of individuality, of separation. Then you will not be an island, you will become the ocean. You will be one with darkness. And darkness is so oceanic: nothing is so vast, nothing is so eternal, and nothing is so near you, and of nothing are you so scared and afraid. It is just by the corner, always waiting.

In rain during a black night, enter that blackness as the form of forms.

Stare so that it enters into your eyes.

Secondly: lie down and feel as if you are near your mother. The darkness is the mother, the mother of all. Think: when there was nothing, what was there? You cannot think of anything else than darkness. If everything disappears, what will be there still? Darkness will be there.

Darkness is the mother, the womb, so lie down and feel that you are lying in the womb of your mother. And it will become real, it will become warm, and sooner or later you will start feeling that the darkness, the womb, is enveloping you from everywhere. You are in it.

And thirdly: moving, going to work, talking, eating, doing whatsoever, carry a patch of darkness within you. The darkness that has entered in you, just carry it. As we were discussing about the method of carrying a flame, carry darkness. And as I said to you that if you carry a flame and feel you are light, your body will start radiating a certain strange light and those who are sensitive will start feeling it, the same will happen with darkness.

If you carry darkness within you, your whole body will become so relaxed and calm, so cool, that it will be felt. And as when you carry light within you some people will become attracted to you, when you carry darkness within you some people will simply escape from you. They will become afraid and scared. They will not be able to bear so silent a being; it will become unbearable to them.

If you carry darkness within you, those who are afraid of darkness will try to escape from you; they will not come near you. And everyone is afraid of darkness. You will start feeling that friends are leaving you. Your family will get disturbed when you enter, because you enter like a pool of coolness, and everyone is agitated and excited. It will be difficult for them to look into your eyes, because your eyes will become deep like valleys, an abyss. If someone looks into your eyes he will become dizzy,

such a deep abyss will be felt there.

But you will feel many things. It will be impossible for you to get angry. Carrying darkness within, you cannot be angry. Carrying a flame you can be angry very easily, more easily than ever, because the flame can excite you. Carrying a flame you will feel more sexual than ever, because the flame will excite you, it will create passion. But carrying darkness within you, you will feel a deep asexuality happening to you. You will not feel sexual; you will not be able to easily get into anger. Passion will disappear. You will not feel that you are a man or a woman. You will feel that those words have become irrelevant, meaningless. You simply are.

Carrying darkness within for the whole day will help you very much, because then when you contemplate and meditate on darkness in the night, the inner darkness that you have carried the whole day will help you to meet—the inner will come to meet the outer.

And just by remembering that you are carrying darkness—you are filled with darkness, every pore of the body, every cell of the body is filled with darkness—you will feel so relaxed. Try it. You will feel so relaxed. Everything in you will be slowed down. You will not be able to run, you will walk, and that walk also will be slowed down. You will walk slowly, just as a pregnant woman walks. You will walk slowly, very carefully. You are carrying something.

And quite the opposite will happen when you are carrying a flame: your walk will become faster; rather, you would like to run. There will be more movement, you will become more active. Carrying darkness you will be relaxed. Others will start feeling that you are lazy.

In the days when I was at university, I was doing this experiment for two years. I became so lazy that even to get out of bed in the morning was difficult. My professors became very much disturbed about it, and they thought something had gone wrong with me—either I was ill, or I had become absolutely indifferent. One professor who loved me very much, the head of my department, became so worried that on my examination days he would come to fetch me from the hostel in the morning just to lead me to the examination hall so that I could be there on time. Every day he would see that I had entered the hall, and only then would he feel okay and go home.

Try it. It is one of the most beautiful experiences in life to carry darkness in your womb, to become dark. Walking, eating, sitting, doing whatsoever, remember, the darkness has filled you, you are filled with it. And then see how things change. You cannot get excited, you cannot be very active, you cannot be tense. Your sleep will become so deep that dreams will disappear and the whole day you will move as if intoxicated.

Sufis have used this method, a particular sect of Sufis, and those Sufis are known as drunken Sufis. They are drunk with this darkness. They make holes in the ground, and they lie down in the holes every night, and they meditate lying down in their holes—meditating on darkness, becoming one with it. And their eyes will show you that they are intoxicated. You can feel from their eyes such deep relaxation, such a relaxed vibration, that it can happen only if you are deeply intoxicated or feeling very sleepy. Only then can your eyes show that expression. They are known as drunken Sufis— and they are drunk with darkness.

---

77 Bringing out the inner darkness.

The second darkness technique: *When a moonless rainy night is not present, close eyes and find blackness before you. Opening eyes, see blackness. So faults disappear forever.*

I said that if you close your eyes the blackness will be false, so what to do if there is no moonless night, no dark night? if there is a moon and the moonlight is there? This sutra gives a key.

When a moonless rainy night is not present, close eyes and find blackness before you.

This blackness will be false in the beginning. You can make it real, and the method to make it real is—*opening eyes, see blackness.* First close your eyes, see blackness. Then open the eyes, and the blackness that you have seen within, see it without. If it disappears without, that means that your blackness that you have seen within was false.

This is a little bit more difficult. In the first you carry the real darkness within. In the second you carry the false out—go on carrying it. Close your eyes, feel darkness; open your eyes, and with open eyes see the darkness out. This is how you throw the inner false darkness out.

Go on throwing it. It will take at least three to six weeks, and then one day suddenly you will be able to carry the inner darkness out. The day you can carry the inner darkness out, you have come upon the real inner darkness. The real can be carried; the false cannot be carried.

And it is a very magical experience. If you can carry the inner darkness out, even in a lighted room you can carry it out, and a patch of darkness spreads before you. The experience is very weird, because the room is lighted. Or even in sunlight…if you have come to the inner darkness you can bring it out. Then a patch of darkness comes before your eyes. You can go on spreading it.

Once you know that it can happen, you can have darkness, dark as the darkest night, in the full sunny day. The sun is there, but you can spread the darkness. The darkness is always there; even while the sun is there the darkness is there. You cannot see it; it is covered by the sunlight. Once you know how to uncover it, you can uncover it.

In Tibet they have many methods just like this. They can bring things from the inner world to the outer world. You may have heard of one very famous technique; they call it "heat yoga." The night is cold, ice-cold, snow is falling, and a Tibetan monk, a Tibetan lama, can sit under the open sky with snow falling all around, the temperature below zero, and he can start perspiring. This is a medical miracle. How is he perspiring? He is bringing the inner heat out.

And the inner coolness or inner cold can also be brought out. In Mahavira's life it is related.... No one has tried to explain it up to now. Jainas think that he was just doing an austerity; it is not so. It is related that whenever it was summer, the hot season, and the sun was burning hot, he would always stand somewhere where there was no shade, no trees, none at all. He would stand in the burning sun in the days of summer, and in winter he would find a cool place, the coolest—under a tree, a shady tree, or near a river, or just where the temperature had gone below zero.

In the cold season he would find a cool place to meditate, and in the hot season he would find the hottest place to meditate. People thought that he was mad, and his followers think he was just doing austerities. It is not so. He was really trying some inner techniques like this.

When it was hot he was trying to bring his inner cold—and it can be felt only in a contrast. When it was cold outside he was bringing his inner heat—and it can be felt only when there is a contrast. He was not an enemy of the body, he was not against his body, as Jainas think. They think that he was killing his body, because if you can kill your body, you can kill your desire. This is sheer nonsense. He was doing nothing of the sort. He was bringing the inner out, and he was protected by the inner. Just as Tibetan lamas can create heat and they can perspire while snow is falling, Mahavira would stand under a hot burning sun and he would not perspire. He was bringing his inner cold, and that inner cold would come out and protect his body.

Similarly you can bring your inner darkness, and that feeling is very cool. If you can bring it, you are protected by it: no excitement, no passion will disturb you. Try it. These three things: stare in darkness with open eyes and allow the darkness to enter within. Secondly: feel darkness as a mother's womb all around; live with it; forget yourself more and more in it. And thirdly: carry a patch of darkness in your heart wherever you go.

If you can do this, the darkness will become the light. You will be enlightened through darkness.

When a moonless rainy night is not present,
close eyes and find blackness before you.
Opening eyes, see blackness.

That's the method. First feel it inside, feel it deeply so you can perceive it out. Then open the eyes suddenly and feel it out. It will take time.

So faults disappear forever.

And if you can bring the inner darkness outside, faults disappear forever, because if the inner darkness is felt, you have become so cool, so silent, so unexcitable, that faults cannot remain with you.

Remember this: faults can exist only if you are prone to be excited, if you tend to be excited. They don't exist in themselves; they exist in your capacity to get excited. Someone insults you, and you have no darkness within to absorb the insult; you become inflamed, you get angry, you get fiery, and then everything is possible. You can be violent, you can kill, you can do what only a madman can do. Anything is possible—you are now mad. Someone praises you: you again go mad to the other extreme.

All around you there are situations, and you are not capable of absorbing. Insult a buddha: he can absorb it, he can simply swallow it, digest it. Who digests that insult? An inner pool of darkness, silence. You throw anything poisoned; it is absorbed. No reaction comes out of it.

Try this, and when someone insults you, just remember that you are filled with darkness, and suddenly you will feel there is no reaction. You pass through a street, you see a beautiful woman or a man—you get excited.

Feel that you are filled with darkness; suddenly the passion will disappear. You try it. This is absolutely experimental, there is no need to believe it.

When you feel that you are filled with passion or desire or sex, simply remember the inner darkness. For a single moment close your eyes and feel darkness and see—the passion has disappeared, the desire is no more there. The inner darkness has absorbed it. You have become an infinite vacuum into which anything can fall and it will not return. You are now like an abyss.

That's why Shiva says: *So faults disappear forever.* These techniques appear so simple—they are. But don't leave them without trying them because they appear so simple. They may not challenge your ego, but still try them. It always happens that we never try simple things, because we think they are so simple they cannot be true. And truth is always simple, it is never complex. There is no need for it to be complex. Only lies are complex. They cannot be simple, because if they are simple they will be caught immediately.

And because something appears simple we think nothing is possible out of it. Not that nothing is possible out of it, but because our ego gets challenged only when something is very difficult. Many schools and many systems have simply complicated their methods because of you. There is no need, but they have to create complexities, unnecessary hurdles, to make them difficult so that you feel good because your ego is challenged. If something is very difficult and only few can do it, then you feel, "Now, this is something to do, because only a few can do it; rarely can someone do it."

These methods are absolutely simple. Shiva is not taking you into account. He is simply describing the exact method as it is—as simply as possible, as telegraphically as possible, only the bare essentials. So don't seek any ego challenge. These techniques are not to send you on an ego trip. They may not challenge you, but if you can try them, they will transform you. And challenge is not good, because with challenge you get feverish, you get mad.

78 Develop pure attentiveness.

A third technique: *Wherever your attention alights, at this very point, experience.*

What? What experience? In this technique, firstly you have to develop attention. You have to develop a sort of attentive attitude, only then will this technique become possible, so then wherever your attention alights you can experience—you can experience yourself. Just by looking at a flower you can experience yourself. Then looking at a flower is not looking at the flower only, but at the looker also—but only if you know the secret of attention.

You also look at a flower, and you may think you are looking at the flower, but you have started thinking about the flower and the flower is missed. You are no more there, you have gone somewhere else, you have moved away. By attention is meant that when you are looking at a flower, you are looking at a flower and not doing anything else—as if the mind has stopped, as if now there is no thinking and only a simple experience of the flower there. You are here, the flower is there, and between you two there is no thought.

Suddenly—if this is possible—suddenly, from the flower your attention will come back, bounce back to yourself. It will become a circle. You will look at the flower and the look will come back; the flower will reflect it, rebounce it. If there are no thoughts, this happens. Then you are not looking at the flower only, you are looking at the looker also. Then the looker and the flower have become two objects and you have become a witness of both.

But first attention has to be trained, because you have no attention at all. Your attention is just flickering, moving from this to that, from that to something further. Not for a single moment are you attentive. Even if I am talking here, you never hear all my words. You hear one word, then your attention goes somewhere else; then you come back, you hear another, then your attention goes somewhere else. You hear a few words, and you fill the gaps, and then you think you have heard me.

And whatsoever you carry with yourself, it is your own business, it is your own creation. Just a few words you have heard from me, and then you have filled the gaps, and whatsoever you fill in the gaps changes everything. I say a word, and you have started thinking about it. You cannot remain silent. If you can remain silent while hearing, you will become attentive.

Attention means a silent alertness with no thoughts interfering. Develop it. You can develop it only by doing it; there is no other way. Do it more and you will develop it. Doing anything, being anywhere, try to develop it.

You are traveling in a car, or in a train—what are you doing there? Try to develop attention; don't waste time. For half an hour you will be in a train: develop attention. Just be there. Don't think. Look at someone, look at the train or look outside, but be the look. Don't think anything. Stop thinking. Be there and look. Your look will become direct, penetrating, and from everywhere your look will be reflected back and you will become aware of the looker.

You are not aware of yourself because there is a wall. When you look at a flower, first your thoughts change your look; they give their own color. Then that look goes to the flower. It comes back, but then again your thoughts give it a different color. And when it comes back it never finds you there. You have moved somewhere else, you are not there.

Every look comes back; everything is reflected, "responsed," but you are not there to receive it. So be there to receive it. The whole day you can try it on many things, and by and by you will develop attentiveness. With that attentiveness do this:

Wherever your attention alights,
at this very point, experience.

Then look anywhere, but simply look. The attention has alighted—and you will experience yourself. But the first requirement is to have the capacity to be attentive. And you can practice it. There is no need for it to take some extra time.

Whatsoever you are doing—eating, taking a bath, standing under a shower—just be attentive. But what is the problem? The problem is that we do everything with the mind, and we are planning continuously for the future. You may be traveling in a train, but your mind may be arranging other journeys, programming, planning. Stop this.

One Zen monk, Bokuju, has said, "This is the only meditation I know. While I eat, I eat. While I walk, I walk. And while I feel sleepy, I sleep. Whatsoever happens, happens. I never interfere."

That's all there is—don't interfere. And whatsoever happens, allow it to happen; you be simply there. That will give you attentiveness. And when you have attention, this technique is just in your hand.

Wherever your attention alights,
at this very point, experience.

You will experience the experiencer; you will fall back to yourself. From everywhere you will be rebounded; from everywhere you will be reflected. The whole existence will become a mirror, you will be reflected everywhere. The whole existence will mirror you, and only then can you know yourself, never before.

Unless the whole existence becomes a mirror for you, unless every part of existence reveals you, unless every relationship opens you.... You are such an infinite phenomenon—ordinary mirrors won't do. You are such a vast existence within, that unless the whole existence becomes a mirror you will not be able to get a glimpse. When the whole universe becomes a mirror, only then will you be mirrored. In you exists the divine.

And the technique to make existence a mirror is this: create attention, become more alert, and then wherever your attention alights—wherever, on any object you alight—suddenly experience yourself.

This is possible, but right now impossible, because you don't fulfill the basic requirement. You can look at a flower, but that is not attention. You are just running near the flower, around and around. You have seen the flower while running; you have not been there for a single moment.

Then the whole life becomes meditative: *Wherever your attention alights, at this very point, experience.* Just remember yourself.

There is a deep reason why this technique can be helpful. You can throw a ball and hit the wall—the ball will come back. When you look at a flower or at a face, a certain energy is being thrown—your look is energy. And you are not aware that when you look, you are investing some energy, you are throwing some energy. A certain quantity of your energy, of your life energy, is being thrown. That's why you feel exhausted after looking in the street the whole day: people passing, advertisements, the crowd, the shops. Looking at everything you feel exhausted and then you want to close your eyes to relax. What has happened? Why are you feeling so exhausted? You have been throwing energy.

Buddha and Mahavira both insisted that their monks should not look too much; they must concentrate on the ground. Buddha says that you can only look up to four feet ahead. Don't look anywhere, just look on the path where you are moving. To look four feet ahead is enough, because when you have moved four feet, again you will be looking four feet ahead. Don't look more than that, because you are not to waste energy unnecessarily.

When you look, you are throwing a certain amount of energy. Wait, be silent, allow that energy to come back. And you will be surprised. If you can allow the energy to come back, you will never feel exhausted. Do it. Tomorrow morning, try it. Be silent, look at a thing. Be silent, don't think about it, and wait patiently for a single moment—the energy will come back; in fact, you may be revitalized.

People continuously ask me.... I go on reading continuously so they ask me, "Why are your eyes still okay? You must have needed specs long ago."

You can read, but if you are reading silently with no thought, the energy comes back. It is never wasted. You never feel tired. My whole life I have been reading twelve hours a day, sometimes even eighteen hours a day, but I have never felt any tiredness. In my eyes I have never felt anything, never any tiredness. Without thought the energy comes back; there is no barrier.

And if you are there you reabsorb it, and this reabsorption is rejuvenating. Rather than your eyes being tired they feel more relaxed, more vital, filled with more energy.

CHAPTER 52

Entering this moment

♦

Are not philosophical structures antimeditation?

Can problems be solved through thinking?

In gazing, does the object make a difference?

Can science and religion meet?

How to overcome impatience?

Kindly shed some more light on darkness.

The first question:

The other night You said that philosophies are anti-meditation. But on the other hand You agree that the Eastern philosophies such as tantra, yoga and Vedanta, are the writings of enlightened sages. Why do the enlightened sages leave behind them a strong structure of philosophical contemplation, if philosophies are antimeditation?

Philosophy is not darshan. Darshan is the Eastern term. Darshan means perception, philosophy means thinking. Hermann Hesse has coined a new word to translate darshan into Western languages. He calls it 'philosia'—'sia' comes from 'to see.'

Philosophy means to think, and darshan means to see. The two are basically different—not only different, but diametrically opposite, because when you are thinking you cannot see. You are so filled with thoughts that perception is blurred, perception is clouded. When thinking ceases, you become capable of seeing. Then your eyes are opened, they become unclouded. Perception happens only when thinking ceases.

For Socrates, Plato and Aristotle, and the whole Western tradition, thinking is the base. For Kanad, Kapil, Patanjali, Buddha, and the whole Eastern tradition, seeing is the base. So Buddha is not a philosopher, not at all; neither is Patanjali, nor Kapil or Kanad. They are not philosophers, they have seen the truth; they have not thought about it.

Remember well that you only think when you cannot see. If you can see, there is no reason to think. Thinking is always in ignorance. Thinking is not knowledge, because when you know, there is no need to think. When you don't know, you fill the gap by thinking. Thinking is groping in the dark. So Eastern philosophies are not philosophies. To use the word philosophy for Eastern darshan is absolutely wrong. Darshan means to see, to attain the eye, to realize, to know—immediately, directly, without the mediation of thinking and thought.

Thinking can never lead to the unknown. How can it lead? It is impossible. The very process of thinking has to be understood. When you think, what do you really do? You go on repeating old thoughts, memories. If I ask you a question—does God exist?—you can think about it. What will you do? All that you have heard, all that you have read, all that you have accumulated about God, you will repeat. Even if you come to a new conclusion, the newness of it will only be apparent, not real. It will be simply a combination of old thoughts. You can combine many old thoughts and create a new structure, but that structure will be apparently new, not new at all.

Thinking can never come to any original truth. Thinking is never original; it cannot be. It is always of the past, of the old, of the known. Thinking cannot touch the unknown; it is repetitively moving in the circle of the known.

You don't know truth, you don't know God. What can you do? You can think about it. You will move in circles, around and around. You can never come to any experience of it.

So the Eastern emphasis is not on thinking, but on seeing. You cannot think about God, but you can see. You cannot come to any conclusion about God, but you can realize. It can become an experience. You cannot get to it through information, through knowledge, through scriptures, through theories and philosophies; no, you cannot get to it. You can get to it only if you throw all knowledge. All that you have heard and read and collected, all the dust that your mind has collected, the whole past, must be put aside. Then your eyes are fresh, then your consciousness is unclouded, and then you can see it.

It is here and now—you are clouded. You have not to go somewhere else to find the divine or the truth—it is here. It is right there where you are. And it has always been so—only you are clouded, your eyes are closed. So the question is not to think more; the question is how to come to a nonthinking consciousness. That's why I say that meditation and philosophy are anti each other. Philosophy thinks, meditation comes to a no-thinking consciousness. And Eastern philosophies are not really philosophies. In the West, philosophies exist; in the East, only religious realizations.

Of course, when a Buddha happens, or a Kanad or a Patanjali happens, when someone comes to realize the absolute, he makes statements about it. Those statements are different from the Aristotelian statements, from Western philosophical conclusions. The difference is this: a Kanad, a Buddha, first comes to realize—the realization is the first thing—and then he makes statements about it. Experience is primary, and then he expresses it. Aristotle, Hegel and Kant, they think, and then through thinking and logical argument and dialectics, they reach particular conclusions. These conclusions are reached through thinking, through mind, not through any practice of meditation. Then they make assertions, then they make statements. The source is different.

For a Buddha, his statements are only as a vehicle to communicate. He never says that through his communication you will achieve the truth. If you can understand Buddha, that doesn't mean you have achieved the truth; that simply means you have gathered knowledge. You will have to pass through meditations, deep ecstasies, deep pools of the mind, only then will you come to the truth.

So truth is reached through a certain existential experience. It is existential, it is not mental. You must change to know it and to be it. If you remain the same and go on collecting information, you will become a great scholar, a philosopher, but you will not be enlightened. You will remain the same man; there will have been no mutation.

That's why I said that philosophy is one dimension, meditation is quite the contrary—the very opposite, the polar-opposite dimension. So don't think about life; rather, live it in depth. And don't think about ultimate problems; rather, enter this very moment into the ultimate. And the ultimate is not in the future—it is always there, timelessly there.

Someone else has also asked a similar question. He has asked:

Can problems be solved through thinking?

Yes, certain problems can be solved through thinking—only those problems which are created by thinking can be solved by it. But no real problem can be solved by it, no lived problem can be solved by it. It is not created by it, it is there in life itself. Thinking will not be of much help. Only in one way can thinking help you, and that is that through thinking and thinking and thinking you will stumble upon the truth that thinking is futile. And the moment you realize that thinking is futile for existential problems, it has helped you in a way. It is through thinking that you have come to this realization.

But problems which are created by thinking can be solved by thinking itself. For example, a mathematical problem: it can be solved by thinking, because the whole mathematics is created by thinking. For example, if there is no man on earth, will there be mathematics? There will be no mathematics. With the disappearance of human mind, mathematics will disappear. There is no mathematics in life and existence. In the garden, trees are there, but when you count, "One, two, three," three trees are not there, because the "three" is a mental thing. The trees are there, but the figures are not there. The figure three is in your mind. If you are not there, the trees will be there, but not three trees, only trees. The three is a quality given by the mind, it is a projected quality.

Mind creates mathematics, so any problem of mathematics will be solved by mind, it will be solved by thinking. Remember, you cannot solve a mathematical problem through nonthinking. No meditation will be of help, because meditation will dissolve the mind, and with the mind the whole mathematics will dissolve. So there are problems which are created by the mind; they can be solved. But there are problems which are not created by the mind, but are existential. Those problems cannot be solved by the mind. You will have to move deep in existence itself.

For example, love. It is an existential problem. You cannot solve it by thinking; rather, you will get more puzzled. The more you think, the less you will be in touch with the source of the problem. Meditation will be of help. It will give you insight, it will lead you to the unconscious roots of the problem. If you think about it, you will remain on the surface.

So remember, life problems cannot be solved by thinking. On the contrary, really, because of too much thinking you are missing all solutions, and more problems are created. For example, death. Death is not a problem created by thinking; you cannot solve it by thinking. Whatsoever you think, how can you solve it? You can console, and you can think that consolation is a solution—it is not. You can deceive yourself; that's possible through thinking. You can create explanations, and through explanations you can think that you have solved it. You can escape the problem through thinking, but you cannot solve it. And see the distinction clearly.

For example, death is there. Your beloved dies, or your friend, or your daughter—the death is there. Now what can you do? You can think about it. You can think and you can say that the soul is immortal—because you have read it. In the Upanishads it is said that the soul is immortal, only the body dies. You don't know it at all. If you really know, there is no problem—or is there a problem? If you really know that the soul is immortal, then death has not occurred; there is no problem at all. But the problem is there: death has occurred, and you are disturbed and deep in sorrow. Now you want to escape this sorrow, now somehow you want to forget this sorrow.

You can take the explanation that the soul is immortal—now, this is a trick. Not that the soul is not immortal—I am not saying that—but for you this is a trick. You are trying to deceive yourself. You are in sorrow, and now you want to escape this sorrow, so this explanation will be helpful. Now you can console yourself that the soul is immortal, no one dies, only the body—just as if one changes the clothes, or one changes the abode, so from one house to another the soul has gone. You can go on thinking, but you don't know anything about it. You have heard, you have collected information; but through these explanations you will be at ease. You can forget death.

Really this is no solution to the problem. Nothing has been solved. The next day someone else will die and the same problem will be there. Again someone will die and the same problem will be there. And deep down you know that you will have to die. You cannot escape death—and the fear is there. But you can go on postponing, and you can go on escaping through explanations. This won't do.

Death is an existential problem. You cannot solve it through thinking. You can create only fake solutions. What to do then? Then there is another dimension—the dimension of meditation, not of thinking, not of mentation. You just encounter the situation. Death has occurred. Your beloved is dead. Don't move into thinking, don't bring in the Upanishads and the Gita and the Bible. Don't ask the Christs and Buddhas. Leave them alone.

Death is there: face it, encounter it. Be with this situation totally. Don't think about it—what can you think? You can only repeat old rubbish. Death is such a new phenomenon, it is so unknown, that your knowledge is not going to help in any way. So put aside your mind, be in a deep meditation with death.

Don't do anything, because what can you do which can be of any help? You don't know. So be in ignorance. Don't bring false knowledge, borrowed knowledge. Death is there; you be with it. Face death with total presence. Don't move in thinking, because then you are escaping from the situation, you are becoming absent from here. Don't think. Be present with death.

Sadness will be there, sorrow will be there, a heavy burden will be on you—let it be there. It is part—part of life, and part of maturity, and part of the ultimate realization. Remain with it, totally present. This will be meditation, and you will come to a deep understanding of death. Then death itself becomes eternal life.

But don't bring the mind and knowledge. Remain with death; then death will reveal itself to you, then you will know what death is. You will move into the inner mansions of it. Then death will take you to the very center of life—because death *is* the very center of life. It is not against life; it is the very process of life. But mind brings the contradiction that life and death are opposites. Then you go on thinking, and because the root is false, the opposition is false, you can never come to any conclusion which can be true and real.

Whenever there is a lived problem, be with the problem without your mind—that's what I mean by meditation—and just being there with the problem will solve it. And if you have really been there,

death will not occur to you again, because then you know what death is.

We never do this—never with love, never with death, never with anything that is authentically real. We always move in thoughts, and thoughts are the falsifiers. They are borrowed, not your own. They cannot liberate you. Only the truth which is your own can become your liberation. And you can only come to your own truth through a very silent presence. With any problem, that fails. Thinking will not solve the real problems, but thinking can solve unreal problems created by thinking itself—because those problems follow the rules of logic. Life doesn't follow the rules of logic. Life has its own hidden laws, and you cannot force logic on them.

One point more about this: wherever you bring the mind, the mind dissects, analyzes. Reality is one, and mind always divides. And when you have divided a reality, you have falsified it. Now you can struggle for your whole life—nothing will be achieved, because basically the reality was one and the mind divided it into two, and now you are working with the division.

For example, as I was saying, life and death are one, but for the mind they are two and death is the enemy of life. It is not, because life cannot exist without death. If life cannot exist without death, how can death be the enemy? It is the basic situation. It makes life possible. Life grows in it; it is the soul. Without it life is impossible. But mind, thinking, divides it and puts it as a polar opposite. Then you can go on thinking about it. Whatsoever you think will be false, because in the beginning you have committed a sin—the sin of division.

When you meditate, divisions disappear. When you meditate, there cannot be divisions, because how can you divide in silence?

We are here. Everyone is thinking in his own mind something or other; then we are different, everyone is different, because your thought is yours, and my thought is mine. In my mind I have my own dreams and you have your own. There are many individuals here, but if we all are meditating —neither you are thinking nor I am thinking, the thinking has ceased—then there will not be so many individuals. Really, there will not be individuals at all. If we are all meditating then limitations have disappeared.

When I am meditating and you are meditating, there are not two persons, there cannot be, because two silences become one. They cannot be two, because how can you demark one silence from another silence? You cannot demark. You can demark one thought from another, one mind from another, but two silences are simply one—just like two zeros. Two zeros are not two; two zeros are one. You can put a thousand zeros, but they are one.

Meditation is creating a zero within—all limitations, all divisions disappear. And that gives you the real eye, the third eye, darshan. Now you have the real eyes to see. For these real eyes reality is clear, open, revealed. And with the reality revealed, there are no problems.

The third question:

What is the difference between gazing at an open clear sky, gazing at an enlightened master's photo, and gazing at the darkness?

The technique of gazing is not concerned really with the object; it is concerned with gazing itself. Because when you stare without blinking your eyes, you become focused, and the nature of the mind is to be constantly moving. If you are really gazing, not moving at all, the mind is bound to be in a difficulty.

The nature of the mind is to move from one object to another, to move constantly. If you are gazing at darkness or at light or at something else, if you are really gazing, the movement of the mind stops. Because if the mind goes on moving, your gaze will not be there; you will go on missing the object. When the mind has moved somewhere else, you will forget, you will not be able to remember what you were looking at. The object will be there physically, but for you it will have disappeared because your are not there; you have moved in thought.

Gazing, *tratak,* means not allowing your consciousness to move. And when you are not allowing the mind to move, in the beginning it struggles, struggles hard, but if you go on practicing gazing, by and by the mind loses struggling. For moments it stops. And when mind stops there is no mind, because mind can exist only in movement, thinking can exist only in movement. When there is no movement, thinking disappears, you cannot think, because thinking means movement—moving from one thought to another. It is a process.

If you gaze continuously at one thing, fully aware and alert…. Because you can gaze through dead eyes: then you can go on thinking. Only eyes, dead eyes, not looking at…just looking with dead men's eyes, but your mind will be moving. That will not be of any help. Gazing means not only your eyes, but your total mind focused through the eyes.

So whatsoever the object…. It depends: if you like light, it is okay. If you can like darkness, good. Whatsoever the object, if you look deeply it is irrelevant. The question is to stop the mind completely in your gaze, to focus it, so the inner movement, the fidgeting, stops; the inner wavering stops. You are simply looking at, not doing anything. That deep looking will change you completely. It will become a meditation.

And it is good; you can try it. But remember that your eyes and your consciousness should meet in the focusing. You must be really looking through the eyes; you must not be absent there. Your presence is needed—totally present. Then you cannot think, then thinking is impossible. There is only one danger: you may become unconscious, you may fall asleep. Even with open eyes it is possible that you may fall asleep. Then your gaze will become stony.

In the beginning the first trouble will be that you will be looking at, but you will not be present.

This is the first barrier. Your mind will move. Your eyes will be fixed, your mind will be moving—there will be no meeting of the eyes and the mind. This will be the first difficulty. If you win over it, the second difficulty will be that gazing with no movement, you will fall asleep. You will move into autohypnosis, you will be hypnotized by yourself. That's natural, because our mind knows only two states: either the constant movement or sleep. The mind knows only two states naturally: constant movement, thinking, or falling into sleep. And meditation is a third state.

The third state, meditation, means your mind is as silent as a deep sleep, and as alert and aware as in thinking—both these must be present. You must be alert, completely alert, and as silent as if deep in sleep. So Patanjali's *Yoga Sutras* say that meditation is a sort of deep sleep, with only one difference—that you are alert. Patanjali equates *sushupti* and samadhi: deep sleep and ultimate meditation. The difference is only that in deep sleep you are not aware, and in meditation you are aware, but the quality of both is deep silence—unrippled, unwavering silence, unmoving silence.

In the beginning it may happen that through staring you may fall asleep. So if you have become capable of bringing your mind to your focus and the mind is not moving, then remain alert, don't fall asleep. Because if sleep comes, you have fallen in the abyss, the ditch. Just between these two ditches —constant thinking and sleep—is the narrow bridge of being in meditation.

The fourth question:

You have said that science experiments with the objective, and religion with the subjective. But now there is a new growing science, psychology, or more accurately, depth psychology, which is both subjective and objective. So science and religion meet in depth psychology.

They cannot meet. Depth psychology, or the study of psychic phenomena, is again objective. And the method of depth psychology is the method of objective science.

Try to see the distinction. For example, you can study meditation in a scientific way. You can observe someone who is meditating, but then this has become objective for you. You meditate and I observe. I can bring all the scientific instruments to observe what is happening to you, what is happening there in you, but the study remains objective. I am outside. I am not meditating. You are meditating; you are an object to me.

Then I can try to understand what is happening to you. Even through instruments much can be known about you, but that will remain objective and scientific. So really, whatsoever I am studying is not the real thing that is happening to you, but the effects that your body is recording.

You cannot penetrate a buddha, what is happening to him, because really nothing is happening there. The deepest center of an enlightened man is nothingness. Nothing is happening there. And if nothing is happening, how can you study it? You can study something. You can study the alpha waves; what is happening to the mind, to the body, to the chemistry, you can understand. But really deep down, when someone becomes enlightened, there is not anything happening. All happening has ceased.

This is what is meant—the world has ceased. Now there is no *sansara*, no happening. He is as if he is not. That's why Buddha says, "Now I have become a no-atma, no-self. There is no one inside me. I am just an emptiness. The flame has disappeared, and the house is vacant." Nothing is happening. What can you record about it? At the most you can record that nothing is happening. If something happens it can be recorded objectively.

The method of science remains objective, and science is very much afraid of the subjective, for many reasons. Science and the scientific mind cannot believe in the subjective, because firstly it is private and individual and no one can enter in it. It cannot become public and collective, and unless something is public and collective nothing can be said about it. The person who is saying may be deceived, or may be deceiving others. He may be a liar, or he may be just in an illusion, not a liar. He may be thinking and believing that this has happened to him, and this may be just a delusion, a self-deception.

So for science the truth must be objective. Others must be able to participate in it, so we can judge whether it is happening or not. Secondly, it must be that it can be repeated; it must be repeatable. If we heat water it evaporates at a certain degree—it must be repeatable. So we repeat and repeat and again and again it evaporates at a certain degree. If it evaporates only once at a hundred degrees and never again, or sometimes at ninety and sometimes at eighty, it cannot become a scientific fact. It must be repeatable, and the same conclusion should be achieved through many repeated experiments.

But the subjective realization is not repeatable —it is not even predictable. And you cannot invite it; it happens. You cannot force it. You may achieve a deep meditation, you may have a very elated peak experience, but if someone says, "Repeat it here," you may not be able to repeat it. On the contrary, because someone says this and you make an effort to repeat it, this very effort may become the barrier. Even the presence of observers may be distracting. You may not be able to repeat it.

Science needs objective, repeatable experiments. And psychology, if it wants to be a science, must follow scientific rules. Religion is subjective. It is not concerned with proving any fact; rather, it is concerned with coming to an individual experiencing of it. And the deepest must remain individual, and the ultimate must remain private; it cannot become collective. Because unless everyone has come to the status of an enlightened one, it cannot become collective. You have to grow to achieve it.

So science and religion really cannot meet, because their approaches are different. Religion is absolutely private—the concern of the individual

with himself. Because of this, those countries which in the past have been more religious than others have remained individualistic. For example, India. India is individualistic. Sometimes it appears even selfish. Everyone is concerned with himself, his own growth, his own enlightenment; not concerned with others, indifferent to others, indifferent to society, social conditions, poverty, slavery. Everyone is concerned with himself, with growing to the ultimate peak. It also looks selfish.

Western countries are more socialistic, less individualistic. That's why the very concept of communism was impossible with the Indian mind. We have given a Buddha and a Patanjali, but we couldn't give a Marx. It had to come from the West where the society, the collective whole, is more important than the individual; where science is more important than religion; where that which happens objectively is more important than that which happens in your absolute privacy. That which happens in the privacy is dreamlike for the West.

Look at this: that which happens publicly we have called *maya,* illusion. Shankara says the whole world is illusion; only that which happens deep down within you, the ultimate, the Brahma that happens there is real, and everything else is unreal. Quite the opposite is the Western scientific attitude: that which happens within you is illusory; that which happens outside is the real. The reality is there outside, and the dream-world is there inside.

These are the two attitudes—so different, the approach so diametrically opposite, that there can be no meeting. There is no need also. Their dimensions are different, their spheres are different. They never trespass on each other; there is no conflict at all. And there need be no conflict. Science works with the objective world, and religion works with the individual, subjective world. They never cross each other. There cannot be any conflict.

And to me, when you are working with the outside world, work with a scientific attitude. When you are working with yourself, work with a religious attitude. And don't create any conflict; there is no need. Don't bring science for the inner world, and don't bring religion for the outer world.

If you bring religion to the outer world, you will create chaos. In India we have created it—it is a mess. If you bring a scientific attitude for the inner, you will create madness—the West has created it. Now the West is completely neurotic. And both have made the same mistake. Don't confuse the two, and don't try to bring the outer to the inner, or the inner to the outer. Let the subjective be subjective and let the objective be the objective. While you move outwards be scientific and objective, and while you move inwards be religious and subjective.

There is no need to create any conflict. There is none. The conflict arises only because we want to impose one attitude on both realms. We want either to be scientific totally, or to be religious totally—that's wrong. With the objective, the subjective approach will be false, dangerous, harmful; and vice versa.

The fifth question:

You have spoken about so many methods and techniques. The yearning to succeed in them is very great. How can we overcome our great impatience?

Two things to be remembered. One: spirituality cannot be an outcome of desire, because desire is the root cause of all our anxiety and anguish. And you cannot direct your desires to the spiritual realm. But it happens, it is natural, because we know only one movement—that is desire. We desire the things of the world. Someone desires riches, someone desires fame, someone desires prestige and power, or something else. We desire things of the world, and through this desiring we are frustrated.

And we are bound to be frustrated—it is irrelevant whether a desire is fulfilled or not. If it is not fulfilled, obviously we will be frustrated. If it is fulfilled, then too we will be frustrated, because whenever a desire is fulfilled, the desire is fulfilled, but the hope, the promise, is not fulfilled. You can get as much wealth as you desire, but the wealth was not desired really; something else was desired through it—that is never fulfilled.

You can achieve wealth, but the hope that was lingering around—the dream of happiness, of bliss, of some ecstatic life—that is not fulfilled. If wealth is not achieved you will feel frustrated. If wealth is achieved then too you will feel frustrated, because the promise is not fulfilled, the dream is not fulfilled. Everything is there. The means are there, and the end has escaped. The end is always elusive.

Through desire one comes to deep frustration. When this frustration happens you start looking for something absolutely other than this world—religious yearning is born, a religious longing...but again you start desiring. You become impatient; you want to achieve this and that. The mind has not changed. The object of desire is different: it was wealth, now it is meditation. It was power and prestige, now it is silence and peace. Before it was something, now it is something else. But the mind, the mechanism, the very working of your being, is the same. You were desiring A, now you are desiring B—but the desiring is there.

And desiring is the problem, not what you desire; that is not the problem. What you desire is not the problem—*that you desire* is the problem. Now you are again desiring and you will be frustrated again. If you achieve, you will be frustrated. If you don't achieve, you will be frustrated. The same will happen to you, because you have not been able to see the point, you have missed the point.

You cannot desire meditation, because meditation happens only when there is no desire. You cannot desire liberation, nirvana, because it happens only in a desireless state. It cannot be made an object of desire. So to me, and to all those who know, desiring is the world. Not that you desire worldly things—desiring, the very phenomenon of desiring, is the world.

And when you desire, impatience is bound to be

there, because the mind doesn't want to wait, the mind doesn't want to postpone. It is impatient. Impatience is the shadow of desire. The more intense the desire, the more impatience will be there. And impatience will create disturbance. So how will you achieve meditation? Desire will create movement of the mind, and then desiring will create impatience, and impatience will bring you to more disturbances.

So it happens, and I observe it daily, that a person who was living a very worldly life was not ordinarily so disturbed. When he starts to meditate, or to seek the religious dimension, he becomes more disturbed, more than ever. The reason is that now he has an even keener desire, more impatience. And with the worldly things, things were so real and objective that he could wait for them. They were always in his reach. Now in the spiritual realm things are so elusive, so far away, they never seem to be in reach. Life seems to be very short, and now the object of desire seems to be infinite—there is more impatience and then more disturbance. And with a disturbed mind, how can you meditate?

So this is the puzzle. Try to understand it. If you are really frustrated and you have come to feel that all that is outside is futile—money or sex or power or prestige, just futile—if you have come to this realization, then a deeper realization is also needed. If these things are futile, then desiring is even more futile: you desire and desire and nothing happens—and your desiring creates the misery.

Look at the fact that desiring creates misery. If you don't desire, there is no misery. So drop desiring! And don't create a new desire; simply drop desiring. Don't create a spiritual desire. Don't say, "Now I am going to seek God. Now I am going to find this and that. Now I am going to realize the truth." Don't create a new desire. If you create, it shows you have not understood your misery.

Look at the misery that desire creates. Feel that desire is misery and drop it. No effort is needed to drop it. Remember, if you make an effort you will create another desire. That's why you need some other desire, because then you can leave it. If some other desire is there, you can hang onto it. You can cling to the new desire and you can leave the old one. To leave the old is easy if some new is to be gained, but then you are missing the whole point. Simply leave desire because it is misery, and don't create a new desire.

Then there will be no impatience. Then meditation is not to be practiced really; it will start happening to you, because a nondesiring mind is in meditation. Then you can play with these techniques. And I say play.... Then you can play with these techniques; there is no practice. Practice is not a good word; the very word is wrong. Then you can play with these techniques, and you can enjoy playing, because there is no desire to achieve something and there is no impatience to reach somewhere.

You can play, and through play, when meditation is a play, everything is possible. And everything is possible immediately, because you are not disturbed, you are not impatient, you are not in any hurry, you are not going somewhere, not reaching somewhere. You are here and now. If meditation happens, okay. If it doesn't happen, it is still okay. Nothing is wrong with you because there is no desire, no expectation, no future. And remember, when meditation or no-meditation are similar to you, meditation has happened to you. You have reached. Now the goal has come, the ultimate has descended in you. This will look strange—that I say don't make meditation a practice, rather make it a play, a fun. Enjoy it while doing it, not for any result.

But our minds are very serious, deadly serious. Even if we play, we make it a serious thing. We make it a work, a duty. Play just like small children. Play with meditation techniques, and then much more is possible through them. Don't be serious about them; take them as fun. But we make everything serious. Even if we are playing, we make it serious. And with religion we have always been very serious. Religion has never been fun, that's why the earth has remained irreligious. Religion must become a fun and a festivity, a celebration—a celebration of the moment, enjoying whatsoever you are doing; enjoying so much and so deeply that mind ceases.

If you really understand me, these one hundred and twelve techniques will show you that everything can become a technique—if you really understand. That's why there are one hundred and twelve. Everything can become a technique if you understand the quality of the mind which brings meditation. Then whatsoever you do can become a technique. Be playful, celebrate it, enjoy it. Move so deeply in it that time ceases.

But time cannot cease if desire is there. Really, desire is time. When you desire, future is needed, because desire cannot be fulfilled here and now. Desire can be fulfilled only in the future somewhere, so you will need future to move. And then time destroys you. You miss eternity. Eternity is here.

So take meditation as a fun, a festivity, a celebration of anything. You are just digging outside in the garden—it can become a technique. Simply dig and enjoy and celebrate the very act. Become the act and forget the actor. The "I" is not there, only the action remains, and you are present to the action, blissfully present. Then ecstasy is there—no impatience, no desire, and no motivation.

If you bring motivation, desire and impatience to meditation, you will destroy the whole thing. And then the more you do, the more frustrated you will feel. You will say, "I am doing so much and nothing is happening." People come to me, they say, "I am doing this and I am doing that, and for so many months and for so many years, and nothing has happened."

One seeker from Holland was here, and he was doing a particular technique three hundred times every day. So he told me, "For two years I have been doing this technique three hundred times every day. Not a single day has been missed. I have left everything, because I have to do this three hundred times every day—and nothing has happened." And he was just on the verge of a nervous breakdown, because of the technique.

So I said, "The first thing is to leave this. Do anything whatsoever, but don't do this. You will go mad." He was deadly serious about it. It was a life-and-death problem for him. It had to be achieved.

And he said, "Who knows how many days are left? Time is short, and I must achieve it in this life. I don't want to be born again. Life is such a misery."

He will be born again and again. The way he is doing it, he will go more and more mad. But it is wrong—the whole attitude is wrong. Take meditation as a play, a fun, enjoy it, and then the very quality changes. Then it is not something you are doing as a cause to gain some effect. No, you are enjoying it here and now. It is the cause and it is the effect, both. It is the beginning and it is the end.

And then you cannot miss meditation. You cannot miss it, it will happen to you, because now you are ready to take it in. You are open. No one has said that meditation should be taken as a fun, but I say it. Make it a play. Just like small children, play with it.

The last question:

The other day You said that darkness is more fundamental to existence, while most religions hold the contrary view. Will You kindly shed some more light on this question, particularly in view of what modern science has to say about it? Does it not say that the last divisible components of matter are just electric energy?

Again the same division—light and darkness. They are two if you look at them through the mind. They are one if you meditate upon them. Whether you meditate on light or on darkness, it makes no difference. If you meditate, the other is dissolved into it. Then light is nothing but less darkness and darkness is nothing but less light; the difference is of degree. They are not two things opposed to each other; rather, two degrees of one phenomenon. And that one phenomenon is neither light nor darkness. That one of which these two are degrees is neither light nor darkness—or it is both. You can enter into it from light, you can enter into it from darkness.

Many religions have used light because it is more comfortable, easier. Darkness is difficult, more uncomfortable, and if you try to enter through darkness, you have chosen a more arduous path. That's why many religions have chosen light. But you can choose either; it depends on you. If you are adventurous, courageous, choose darkness. If you are afraid and don't want to go on an arduous path, choose light. Because both belong to one phenomenon which appears at one point as light, at another point as darkness.

For example, this room is filled with light. But it is not filled with the same light for everyone, or is it? If my eyes are weak then the light is not as light as it is for you. I see it as a little darker. Imagine if someone from Mars or from some other planet comes, who has very penetrating eyes. Then where you see light, he will see much light, more light than you see. And where you see darkness, he will see light. There are animals and birds who see in the night where you cannot see. For them it is light, for you it is darkness.

So what is light? and what is darkness?—one phenomenon. And how much you can penetrate into it, and how much it can penetrate into you...it depends on that penetration whether you call it light or darkness. These polar opposites just appear to be opposites. They are not, they are relative degrees of one phenomenon. So scientists say that the last divisible components of matter are just electric energy. But they don't say they are light; they say electric energy. Darkness is also electric energy, and light is also electric energy. Electric energy is not synonymous with light. If you give it the name electric energy, then light is one expression and darkness is another.

But there is no need to move into scientific discussion about it. It is useless. Rather, think about your own mind, what you like. If you feel at ease with light, enter through light. That is your door. If you feel at ease with darkness, enter through darkness. And both will lead to the same.

Many methods in these one hundred and twelve are concerned with light; a few are concerned with darkness. And Shiva is trying to explain all the methods possible. He is not talking to particular types; he is talking to all types. But there are a few persons who will like to enter through darkness. For example, a feminine mind, more passive, more receptive, will like to enter through darkness; it will be more acceptable. A male mind will like the light more.

You may not have observed the fact that many poets of the past and the present, many philosophers, and many others who have a deep insight into the human mind, have always compared the female with darkness, and the male with light. Light is aggressive, a male element; darkness is receptive, a female element. Darkness is like a womb.

So it depends: if you like darkness, good, enter through it. If you like light, enter through it. Sometimes even the opposite becomes appealing. You can try that also. There is no danger in trying anything, because every path leads to the same goal.

But don't go on thinking about what to choose. Don't waste time; rather, try. Because you can go on thinking forever about what will be suitable, what to do and what not to do, and why so many religions have insisted on light, and so few on darkness. Don't get worried about these things; they don't help. Rather, think about your own type, about what will be suitable for you, in what you will feel more comfortable, and then start it.

And then forget all others, because all of these one hundred and twelve methods are not for you. Even if you choose one method, for you it is enough. You need not go through one hundred and twelve methods; one method will do. So just be receptive and aware so that you can catch the method that is for you. You need not get worried about every other method; that is unnecessary. Choose one, play with it, and if you feel good and something is happening, then move into it and forget all the other one hundred and eleven. If you feel you have chosen wrongly, then throw it, choose another, and play with it. If you try this with four or five or six methods, you will fall upon the right one. But don't be serious—just play.

CHAPTER 53

From death to deathlessness

◆

79 *Focus on fire rising through your form from the toes
up until the body burns to ashes but not you.*

80 *Meditate on the make-believe world as burning to
ashes, and become being above human.*

81 *As, subjectively, letters flow into words and words
into sentences, and as, objectively, circles flow into
worlds and worlds into principles, find at last these
converging in our being.*

**A**ll the enlightened ones, all the religions, agree on one thing only. Their disagreements are many, but there is one agreement amongst all, and that is that man, because of his ego, is closed to the reality. The ego is the only barrier; the feeling that "I am." On this point Buddhas and Christs and Krishnas all agree. And because they all agree it seems to me that this is the basic thing in all religious endeavor. All else is accidental; this is essential—that you are debarred because of your own ego.

What is this ego? Of what does it consist? How does it arise? And why does it become so important?

Look at your mind—because you cannot understand the phenomenon of ego theoretically; you can only understand it existentially. Look at your mind, observe it, and you will come to a deep understanding. And if you can understand what the ego is, there is no problem; it can be dropped easily. Rather, there is no need to drop it. If you can understand it, the very understanding becomes the dropping, because the ego is created through your nonunderstanding, it is created through your sleepiness.

If you become alert about it, if you focus your consciousness towards it, it disappears. It disappears—just as when you bring light in a room and the darkness disappears. Even if you bring light to look at darkness, to see what darkness is...if you bring light it disappears. The ego exists because you have never been alert to your existence; it is a shadow of your nonalertness. So really, there is no need to drop it. If you can look at it, it drops by itself.

What is it? Have you ever felt any moment when there is no ego? Whenever you are silent, the ego is not. Whenever your mind is in turmoil, chattering, restless, the ego is there. Whenever you are relaxed, silent and calm, the ego is not. Just now, if you are silent, where is the ego? You will be there, but no feeling of "I." So try to understand it existentially.

Right now as I am speaking, you can observe the fact that if you are silent, totally alert, you are there, but with no feeling of "I." And just the contrary happens: if you are troubled, in conflict, in anxiety, you feel a centered ego within you. When you are in anger, in passion, violent, aggressive, you feel a crystallized ego within you. Whenever you are in love, in compassion, it is not there.

That's why we cannot love, because with the ego, love is impossible. That's why we go on talking so much about love, but we never are in love. And whatsoever we call love is more or less sex, it is not love; because you cannot lose your ego, and love cannot exist unless the ego has disappeared. Love, meditation, God, they all require one thing—the ego must not be there. That's why Jesus is right in saying that God is love, because both phenomena happen only when the ego is not.

If you know love, there is no need to know God—you have known him already. Love is just another name for it. If you know love, there is no need to go into meditation—you have gone already. Love is just another name for it. So many techniques of meditation are needed, and so many teachers, and so many schools of meditation are needed, because there is no love. If love exists, there is no need to practice anything, because the thing has happened already. And the thing is the disappearance of the ego.

So the first thing to be understood: whenever you are silent, the ego is not. And don't believe in me. I am not talking about a theory; this is a fact. You need not take my opinion, you can observe it in yourself. And there is no need to postpone it for the future; right now you can observe the fact that if you are silent, you are—but with no limitation, with no center. You exist without the center, there is no crystallized I. The presence is there, the consciousness is there, but there is no one who can say "I am."

When you are silent, the ego is not. And when you are not silent, the ego is. So ego is the disease, all diseases combined together, hence the emphasis on surrendering the ego. The emphasis is on surrendering the disease.

Secondly: if in silence for even a single moment you have the glimpse of your existence as egoless, then you can analyze it, and then you can enter the phenomenon of ego, of what it is. The mind is accumulated past. The mind is never here, it is never now. It is always from the past. It is accumulation. Mind is memory: all the experiences that you have gone through, all the information that you have come across, all the knowledge that you have gathered, heard, listened to, read—that is accumulated. The mind is constantly accumulating.

The mind is the greatest accumulator; it goes on accumulating. Even while you are not conscious it goes on accumulating; even while you are asleep the mind is accumulating. You may not be aware of it. While you are asleep, and there is noise in the road, the mind is accumulating. You can be hypnotized in the morning and you can be asked about it, and you will say everything, you will relate everything—whatsoever the mind has accumulated in

the night. Even if you have fallen in a coma, or you are unconscious, or you have fallen in a fit, the mind is accumulating.

The mind doesn't need your consciousness to accumulate; it goes on accumulating. Even while you were in the womb of your mother the mind was accumulating. And through hypnosis the memories of your days in the womb of your mother can be awakened. You don't remember anything about taking birth, but the mind was accumulating. Whatsoever was happening, the mind was accumulating. And now it can be awakened again. Through hypnosis the memory can be brought again to your focus. And millions of memories are being accumulated—this accumulation is the mind. Memory is the mind.

How is the I, the ego, created? The consciousness is within you, and around the consciousness all these memories are accumulated on the periphery. They are useful, and you cannot survive without them, they are needed, but then a new thing happens between these two, an epiphenomenon.

Consciousness is within, you are within, without the I. There is no I within. You are, without a center. On the periphery, every moment knowledge, experience, memories, accumulate. This is the mind. And whenever you look at the world, you look through the mind. Whenever you pass through a new experience, you look through the memories, you interpret it through the memories. You look at everything through the past. The past becomes a mediator.

Constantly looking through the past, you get identified with it—that identification is the ego. Let me put it in this way: the identification of the consciousness with the memories is the ego. You say, "I am a Hindu" or "I am a Christian" or "I am a Jaina." What are you doing? No one is born as a Christian, or a Hindu, or a Jaina, you are simply born as a human being. Then you are taught, then you are conditioned to think that you are a Christian, a Hindu, or a Jaina. This is a memory. You have been taught that you are a Christian. This is a memory, and now whenever you look through this memory you feel, "I am a Christian."

Your consciousness is not Christian; it cannot be. It is simply consciousness. You have been taught that you are a Christian. This teaching is accumulated on the periphery. Now you look through the glasses and the whole world is colored. Those glasses stick too much and too deeply with you, and you are never away from them, you never put them aside. You have become so accustomed to them that you have forgotten that there are spectacles on your eyes. Then you say, "I am a Christian."

Whenever you get identified with any memory, any knowledge, any experience, any name and form, that "I" is born. Then you are young, you are old; you are rich, you are poor; you are beautiful or you are not beautiful; you are educated or you are not educated; you are respected or you are not respected—then you go on getting identified with things which accumulate around you and the ego is born. Ego is identification with the mind.

That's why when you are silent the ego is not, because when you are silent the mind is not functioning. That's what silence means. Whenever the mind is functioning you are not silent. You cannot be—the functioning of the mind is the inner noise, the chattering, the constant chattering within you. When the chattering stops, or it is not there, or you have gone beyond it, or you have gone within, moved within, there is silence, and in that silence there is no ego.

But it happens only sometimes, and only for a moment, that you are silent. That's why you feel that those situations in which this happens are lovely. You start desiring those situations. You go to a hill, and while the sun is rising in the morning you look at it. Suddenly you have an upsurge of joy. You feel blissful, a beautitude descends upon you.

What has happened really? Because of the silent morning, and the silent rising of the sun, and the greenery, and the hill, suddenly your inner chatter-

ing has stopped. The phenomenon is so great—all around you such beauty, such peace and tranquility—that you have stopped for a moment. In that stopping you have realized a nonego state—for a single moment of course.

This can happen through many situations. In sex it happens, in music it can happen; in anything which is so great that you are overwhelmed, over-powered, and your constant chattering is put aside, forced aside for a moment, it will come again. Whenever you are egoless, accidentally or through some practice, you feel a subtle bliss which you have not felt before.

The bliss is not coming from outside. It is not coming from the hills or from the rising sun or from beautiful flowers; it is not coming from the sex act. It is not coming from outside. The outside is only creating an opportunity—it is coming from inside. So if you repeat the outer situation again and again it will not come, because you will get immune to it, you will get accustomed to it.

The same hill and the same morning...again you go there and you don't feel it. You feel something is missing. Because for the first time it was so new that it stopped your mind completely. The wonder was so great and the miracle was so new, you couldn't continue with the past chattering. It stopped—just in awe it stopped. But next time you go there you know everything. There is no awe, no mystery—the mind continues. This happens with every experience. In any experience, if you feel a joy, it will be destroyed if you repeat it, because then, in a repeated experience, you cannot put aside the mind.

So the second thing to remember is that mind is accumulation. Your consciousness is just hidden behind this accumulated past, and you are identified with it. Whenever you say, "I am this, I am that," you are creating the ego.

Thirdly: if you can understand this, then the third point is not difficult, and that third point is that mind has to be used. There is no need to get identified; you can use it as an instrument—and it *is* an instrument. There is no need to get identified with it. Remain always above it.

And really you are always above it, because you are here, now, always present, and mind is always past. You are always ahead of it. It is just lagging behind you, it is a shadow. This very moment is a new thing; your mind cannot have it. A moment later it will be absorbed in the memory, then the mind can have it. Every single moment you are free.

That's why Buddha has emphasized the moment so much. He says, "Remain in the moment and there will be no mind." But the moment is very atomic, it is very subtle; you can miss it easily. The mind is always the past—whatsoever you have known—and the reality that is passing just now is not part of the mind. It will become part of the mind a moment later.

If you can be aware of the reality here and now, you will remain always transcendental to the mind. And if you can remain transcendental to the mind —always above, never entangled in it, using it, but never getting involved in it, using it as an instrument, never getting identified with it—the ego will disappear. You will be egoless, and when you are egoless, nothing else is to be done. Then all else happens to you. You have become vulnerable, you have become open. Then the whole existence happens to you, then all the ecstasies are yours, then suffering is impossible.

Suffering comes through the ego. Bliss comes through the egoless gate.

Now we will enter the techniques—because these techniques are concerned with being egoless. Very simple techniques, but if you understand this background then you can do them, and much becomes possible through them.

---

79 Focus on fire.

The first fire technique: *Focus on fire rising through your form from the toes up until the body burns to ashes but not you.*

A very simple technique and very wonderful, very easy to do, but some basic requirements are to be fulfilled beforehand. Buddha liked this technique very much; he initiated his disciples into this technique.

Whenever someone was initiated by Buddha, the first thing was this: he would tell him just to go to the burning place and observe a body being burned, a dead body being burned. For three months he was not to do anything, but just sit there and watch. So the seeker would go to the burning place of the village. He would stay there for three months, day and night, and whenever a dead body would come there he would just sit and meditate. He would just look at the dead body; then the fire would be created and then the body would start burning. And for three months continuously he would not do anything else—just look at dead bodies being burned.

Buddha said, "Don't think about it. Just look at it." And it is difficult not to come upon the thought that sooner or later your body is going to be burned. Three months is a long time, and continuously, day and night, whenever there was a body to be burned, the seeker was to meditate. Sooner or later he would start seeing his own body on the burning pyre. He would start seeing himself being burned.

It will be helpful; if you want to do this technique, go to the burning place. Watch—not for three months, but at least watch one body being burned; observe it. Then you can do this technique easily with yourself. Don't think: simply watch the phenomenon, watch what is happening.

People go to burn their relatives' bodies, but they never watch. They start talking of other things, or about death; they argue and discuss. They do many things. They talk many things and gossip, but they never watch. It should be made a meditation. No talking should be allowed there, because it is a rare experience to see someone you loved being burned. You are bound to feel that you are also burning there. If you are seeing your mother being burned, or your father, or your wife, or your husband, you are bound to see yourself also there in the flames. That experience will help for this technique—the first thing.

The second thing: if you are very much afraid of death you cannot do this technique, because the very fear will protect you. You cannot enter into it, or you can just imagine on the surface, but your deep being will not be in it. Then nothing will happen to you. So remember the second thing: whether you are afraid or not, death is the only certainty. It makes no difference whether you are afraid or not, it is irrelevant. In life, nothing is certain except death. Everything is uncertain; only death is not accidental. And look at the human mind. We always talk about death as if it is an accident. Whenever someone dies we say his death was untimely. Whenever someone dies we start talking as if it has been an accident. Only death is not an accident—*only* death. Everything else is accidental. Death is absolutely certain. You have to die.

And when I say you have to die, it seems in the future, very far away. It is not so—you have already died. The moment you were born, you died. With birth, death has become a fixed phenomenon. One part of it has already happened—the birth; now only the second, later part has to happen. So you are already dead, half-dead, because once one is born, one has come into the realm of death, entered into it. Now nothing can change it, now there is no way to change it. You have entered into it. You are half-dead with birth.

Secondly: death is not going to happen in the end; it is already happening. It is a process. Just as life is a process, death is a process. We create the now—but life and death are just like your two feet, your two legs. Life and death are both one process. You are dying every moment.

Let me put it in this way: whenever you inhale, it is life, and whenever you exhale, it is death. The first thing a child does is to inhale. A child cannot exhale. The first thing is inhalation. He cannot exhale, because there is no air within his chest; he

has to inhale. The first act is inhalation. And the old man, while dying, will do the last act, which will be exhalation. Dying, you cannot inhale—or can you? When you are dying, you cannot inhale. The last act cannot be inhalation; the last act will be exhalation. The first act is inhalation and the last is exhalation. Inhalation is birth and exhalation is death. But every moment you are doing both—inhaling, exhaling. Inhalation is life, exhalation is death.

You may not have observed, but try to observe it. Whenever you exhale, you are more at peace. Exhale deeply and you will feel a certain peace within. Whenever you inhale, you become intense, you become tense. The very intensity of inhalation creates a tension. And the normal, ordinary emphasis is always on inhalation. If I tell you to take deep breaths, you will always start with inhalation.

Really, we are afraid of exhaling. That's why breathing has become shallow. You never exhale, you go on inhaling. Only the body goes on exhaling, because the body cannot exist with inhalation alone. It needs both: life and death.

Try one experiment. The whole day, whenever you remember, exhale deeply and don't inhale. Allow the body to inhale; you simply exhale deeply. And you will feel a deep peace, because death is peace, death is silence. And if you can pay attention, more attention, to exhalation, you will feel egoless. With inhalation you will feel more egoistic; with exhalation you will feel more egoless. Pay more attention to exhalation. The whole day, whenever you remember, exhale deeply and don't inhale. Allow the body to inhale; you don't do anything.

This emphasis on exhalation will help you very much to do this experiment, because you will be ready to die. A readiness is needed, otherwise the technique will not be of much help. And you can be ready only if you have tasted death in a certain way. Exhale deeply and you will have a taste of it. It is beautiful.

Death is just beautiful, because nothing is like death—so silent, so relaxing, so calm, so unperturbed. But we are afraid of death. And why are we afraid of death? Why is there so much fear of death? We are afraid of death not because of death, but because we don't know it. How can you be afraid of something you have never encountered? How can you be afraid of something that you don't know? At least you must know it to be afraid of it. So really you are not afraid of death; the fear is something else. You have never really lived—that creates the fear of death.

The fear comes because you are not living, so you are afraid—"I have not lived yet, and if death happens then what? Unfulfilled, unlived, I will die." The fear of death comes only to those who are not really alive. If you are alive, you will welcome death. Then there is no fear. You have known life; now you would like to know death also. But we are so afraid of life itself that we have not known it, we have not entered deep into it. That creates the fear of death.

If you want to enter this technique you must be aware of this deep fear. And this deep fear must be thrown away, purged, only then can you enter the technique. This will help: pay more attention to exhalation. And really, if you can pay all attention to exhalation and forget inhaling.... Don't be afraid that you will die; you will not die—the body will inhale by itself. The body has its own wisdom: if you deeply exhale, the body will take a deep inhalation by itself. You need not interfere. Then a very deep relaxation will spread all over your consciousness. The whole day you will feel relaxed, and an inner silence will be created.

You can deepen this feeling more if you do another experiment. Just for fifteen minutes in the day exhale deeply. Sit in a chair or on the ground, exhale deeply, and while exhaling close the eyes. When the air goes out, you go in. And then allow the body to inhale, and when the air goes in, open the eyes and you go out. It is just the opposite: when the air goes out, you go in; when the air goes in, you go out.

When you exhale, space is created within, be- cause breath is life. When you exhale deeply, you are vacant, life has gone out. In a way you are dead, for a moment you are dead. In that silence of death, enter within. Air is moving out: you close your eyes and move within. The space is there and you can move easily.

Remember, when you are inhaling to move inwards is very difficult, because there is no space to move. While exhaling you can move within. And when the air goes in, you go out; open the eyes and move out. Create a rhythm between these two. Within fifteen minutes you will feel so deeply relaxed, and you will be ready to do this technique.

Before doing this technique, do this for fifteen minutes so that you are ready—not only ready, but welcoming, receptive. The fear of death is not there, because now death appears like relaxation, death appears like a deep rest. Death appears not antagonistic to life, but the very source of it, the very energy of it. Life is just like ripples on the face of a lake, and death is the lake itself. When ripples are not there the lake is there. And the lake can exist without the ripples, but the ripples cannot exist without the lake. Life cannot exist without death. Death can exist without life, because it is the source. Then you can do this technique.

*Focus on fire rising through your form
from the toes up....*

Just lie down. First conceive of yourself as dead; the body is just like a corpse. Lie down, and then bring your attention to the toes. With closed eyes move inwards. Bring your attention to the toes and feel that the fire is rising from there upwards, every- thing is being burned. As the fire rises, your body is disappearing. Start from the toes and move upwards.

Why start from the toes? It will be easier, because the toes are very far away from your "I," from your ego. Your ego exists in the head. You cannot start from the head, it will be very difficult, so start from the farthest-away point. The toes are the most faraway point from the ego. Start the fire from there. Feel that the toes are burned, only ashes remain, and then move slowly, burning everything that the fire comes across. Every part—the legs, the thighs—will disappear.

And just go on seeing that they have become ashes. The fire is rising upwards, and the parts it has passed are no more there; they have become ashes. Go on upwards, and lastly the head disappears. Everything has become ashes...the dust has fallen unto dust...*until the body burns to ashes but not you.*

You will remain just a watcher on the hill. The body will be there—dead, burned, ashes—and you will be the watcher, you will be the witness. This witness has no ego.

This technique is very good to reach the egoless state. Why?—because so many things are implied in it. It appears simple; it is not so simple. The inner mechanism is very complex. First thing: your memories are part of the body. Memory is matter; that's why it can be recorded. It is recorded in the brain cells. They are material, part of the body. Your brain cells can be operated on, and if certain brain cells are removed, certain memories will disappear from you. Memories are recorded in the brain cells. Memory is matter; it can be destroyed. And now scientists say it can be replanted, it can be transplanted again.

Sooner or later we will find ways so that when a person like Albert Einstein dies we will be able to save his brain cells. And those brain cells will be able to be transplanted into a child, and that child will have all the memories of Albert Einstein without going through all those experiences. It is part of the body, memory is part of the body, and if the whole body is burned and has become ashes, you will not have any memory.

Remember, this is the point to understand: if the memory is still there, then the body remains and you have been playing tricks. If really you go deep in the feeling that the body is dead, burning, and the fire has completely destroyed it, you will not have any memory in that moment. In that moment of watching, there will be no mind. Everything will

have stopped—no movement of thought, just watching, just seeing what has happened.

And once you know this, you can remain in this state continuously. Once you have known that you can separate yourself from the body.... This technique is just a method to separate yourself from the body, just to create a gap between you and the body, just for a few moments to be out of the body. If you can do this, then you can remain in the body and you will not be in the body. You can go on living as you were living before, but you will not be the same again.

This technique will take at least three months. Go on doing it. It is not going to happen in one day, but if you go on doing it every day for one hour, within three months, someday suddenly your imagination will have helped and the gap will be created, and you will actually see the body gone to ashes. Then you can watch.

In that watching you will realize a deep phenomenon—that the ego is a false entity. It was there because you were identified with the body, with the thoughts, with the mind. You are neither —neither the mind nor the body. You are different from all that surrounds you; you are different from your periphery.

Apparently the technique seems simple, but it can bring you a deep mutation. But first go and meditate on the burning ghat, on the burning ground, so you can see how the body burns, how the body turns to dust again—so you can imagine easily. Then start from the toes and move very slowly. And before doing this technique, pay more attention to exhalation. Right before entering the technique, for fifteen minutes exhale and close the eyes; allow the body to inhale and open the eyes. For fifteen minutes feel a deep relaxation and then enter into it.

80 Imagine the whole world burning.

The second fire technique: *Meditate on the make-believe world as burning to ashes, and become being above human.*

If you can do the first, the second will be very easy. If you can come to imagine that your body is burning, it is not difficult to imagine that the whole world is burning—because your body is the world, and through your body you are related to the world. Really, only for your body are you related to the world—the world is extended body. If you can think and imagine that your body is burning, there is no difficulty in imagining it with the whole world. And the sutra says it is a make-believe world —just because you believe, it is there. The whole world is burning, disappearing.

But if you feel the first is very difficult, you can even start with the second. The second is very easy if you can do the first, and there is no need really to do the second if you have done the first. With your body, everything disappears automatically. But you can do the second directly also, if the first is very difficult.

I said start with the toes because they are very far away from the head, from the ego, but you may not even feel like starting from the toes. Then move still further away: start with the world, and then move nearer and nearer towards yourself. Start with the world and then come nearer. And when the whole world is just burning, it will be easy for you to burn in that whole burning world.

The second is: *Meditate on the make-believe world as burning to ashes, and become being above human.*

If you can see the whole world burning, you have gone above human, you have become superhuman. You have come to know a superhuman consciousness. You can imagine it, but a training of imagination is needed. Our imaginations are not very trained. They are very untrained, because there is no schooling for imagination. Intellect is trained, schools and colleges exist and a major part of life is spent in training the intellect. Imagination is not trained. And imagination has a very wonderful dimension of its own. If you can train your imagination, you can do wonders through it.

Start with small things, because it is difficult to jump to bigger things and you may be a failure. For example: this imagination that the whole world is burning—it cannot go very deep. First, you know it is imagination, and even if in imagination you think that the flames are everywhere, you will feel that the world is not burned, it is there still, because it is only your imagination. You don't know how imagination can become real. You have to feel it first.

Try a simple experiment before you enter this technique. Just close both your hands together, close your eyes, and just imagine that now your hands cannot be opened, they have gone dead, locked, and you cannot do anything to open them. In the beginning you will feel that you are just imagining and you can open them. But for ten minutes go on thinking that you cannot open them, you cannot do anything, your hands cannot be opened. And then after ten minutes try to open them.

Out of ten, four persons will immediately succeed, forty percent of people will immediately succeed: after ten minutes they cannot open their hands—the imagination has become real. Howsoever they struggle…and the more they struggle to open them, the more difficult it will be. You will start perspiring. You are seeing your own hands and you cannot open them. They are locked!

But don't be afraid. Just close your eyes again, and again imagine that now you can open them; only then will you be able to open them. Forty percent will succeed immediately. Those forty percent can move in this technique easily; there is no problem for them.

For the other remaining sixty percent it will be difficult, it will take time. Those who are very sensitive can imagine anything and it will happen. And once they feel that imagination can become real, then they have a feeling and they can move. Then you can do many things with your imagination. Already you are doing it without knowing it. Already you are doing it, but you are not aware.

A certain disease comes to the city—a French flu comes—and you become a victim of it. You can never think that out of one hundred cases, seventy percent are just because of imagination. Because the flu is there you start imagining that now you are going to fall prey to it—and you will fall. Many diseases are just caught through your imagination, many problems you create because of your imagination. You can also solve them once you know that it is you who are creating them. Train your imagination a little, and then this technique will be very helpful.

---

81 Everything converges in your being.

A third technique: *As, subjectively, letters flow into words and words into sentences, and as, objectively, circles flow into worlds and worlds into principles, find at last these converging in our being.*

That too is an imaginative technique. The ego is always afraid—afraid of being vulnerable, open, afraid something may enter and destroy it. So the ego creates a citadel around it; you start living in a walled prison. Nothing should be allowed to enter in you. You are afraid—if something comes in and disturbs, then what to do?—so it is better not to allow anything to come in. All communication stops. Even with those you love or you think that you love, there is no communication.

Look at a wife and husband talking. They are not talking to each other; there is no communication. Rather, they are avoiding each other through words. They are talking so that the communication can be avoided. In silence they will become vulnerable, in silence they will come closer, because in

silence the ego, the wall, will not be there. So the husband and wife, they will never be silent. They will be talking about something or other just to fill in time, and just so as not to be open to each other. We are so afraid of the other.

I have heard about Mulla Nasruddin, that one day as he was just walking out of his house his wife said, "Nasruddin, have you forgotten what day today is?"

Nasruddin knew about it—it was their twenty-fifth wedding anniversary—so he said, "I know it, I know it well."

The wife persisted, "Then how are we going to celebrate it?"

So Nasruddin said, "Darling, I don't know." And then he scratched his head, puzzled, and said, "How would it be if we keep two minutes' silence to celebrate it?"

You cannot remain silent with someone; you begin to feel restlessness. In silence, the other enters you. You are open, your doors are open, your windows are open. You are afraid. You go on talking, you go on creating devices to remain closed.

The ego is an enclosure, it is a prison, and the prison is accepted because we feel so insecure. The prison gives a certain feeling of security: you are protected, guarded. To do this technique, this third technique, the first and most basic thing is: know well that life is insecurity. There is no way to make it secure. Whatsoever you do is not going to help. You can create only a fiction of security—life remains insecure. It is the very nature of it, because death is involved in it, so how can life be secure?

And think for a moment: if life is really secure, it will be already dead. An absolutely totally secure life cannot be alive, because the very adventure is lost. If you are protected from all dangers you will be dead. In the very being of life there is adventure, danger, insecurity. Death is involved.

I love you...I have entered a dangerous path. Now nothing can be secure, but now I will try to make everything secure. For the sake of tomorrow, I will kill everything that is alive, because only then can I feel secure tomorrow also.

Love is transformed into marriage—marriage is a security. Love is insecure—the next moment everything can change. And you have invested so much, and in the next moment the beloved leaves you, or the friend leaves you, and you are left in a vacuum. Love is insecure. You cannot fix the future, you cannot predict. So love is killed and a secure substitute is found—that is marriage.

With marriage you can be secure; it is predictable. The wife will be your wife the next day; the husband will be your husband in the future also—but just because you have secured it. And now there is no danger. It is dead. The relationship is dead now, because only dead things can be permanent; alive things are bound to be changing. Change is the very quality of life, and in change is insecurity.

Those who want to enter deeper realms of life must be ready to be insecure, must be ready to be in danger, must be ready to move into the unknown, and must not try in any way to fix the future. The very effort will kill everything. And remember this also: that insecurity is not only alive, it is beautiful. Security is dull, ugly. Insecurity is alive and beautiful. You can be secure if you close your doors and windows and everything. Neither light enters nor air enters; no one enters. You are secure in a way, but you are not living, you have already entered your tomb.

This technique is possible if you are vulnerable, open, not afraid, because this technique is allowing the whole universe to enter in you.

As, subjectively, letters flow into words
and words into sentences, and as, objectively,
circles flow into worlds and worlds into principles,
find at last these converging in our being.

Everything converging in my being...I am standing under the open sky, and the whole existence, from everywhere, from every nook and corner, is converging in me—your ego cannot exist. In that openness where the whole existence is converging in

you, you cannot exist as an I. You will exist as an open space, but not as a crystallized I.

To do this technique start with a small step. Just sit under a tree. The breeze is blowing and the leaves of the tree are rustling. The wind touches you, it moves around you, it passes. But don't allow it just to pass you; allow it to move within you and pass through you. Just close your eyes, and as it is passing through the tree and there is a rustling of the leaves, feel that you are also like a tree, open, and the wind is blowing through you—not by your side but right through you.

The rustling of the tree will enter in you, and you will feel that from every pore of your body the air is passing. It is really passing through you. It is not only imagination, it is a fact—you have forgotten. You are not only breathing through the nose, you are breathing through the whole body—from every pore of it, from millions of pores. If you are allowed to breathe through your nose, but all the pores of your body are closed, painted, you will die within three hours. You cannot be alive just by breathing through the nose. Every cell of your body is a living organism, and every cell is breathing. The air is really passing through you, but you have lost the contact. So sit under a tree and feel.

In the beginning it will look like imagination, but soon it will turn into a reality. It is a reality—that the air is passing through you. Then sit under a rising sun, and not only feel that the rays of the sun are touching you, but that they are entering you and passing through you, so you become vulnerable, you begin to feel open.

And this can be done with everything. For example, I am speaking here and you are hearing me. You can hear just through the ears, or you can hear through the whole of the body. You can just try it right here, just with a change of the emphasis: you are not hearing my words through the ears only, you are hearing me through the whole of your body. And when you really hear, and when you really listen, it is the whole body that listens. It is not only a part, it is not a fragmented energy that listens, it is the whole of you. The whole of your body is involved in listening. Then my words are passing through you—from every cell, from every pore, you are drinking them. They are being absorbed from everywhere.

You can do this. Just go and sit in a temple. Many worshippers will be coming and going, and the bell of the temple will be hit again and again. Just listen with the whole of your body. The bell is ringing and the whole temple is agog; every wall of it is reflecting. To reflect this, in order to feel that the sound is converging on you, we created a round shape, so from everywhere the sound is thrown back. It converges upon you from everywhere, and you can listen to it through your whole body—every pore, every cell, listening, drinking, absorbing it, and it is passing through you. You have become porous; everywhere the door is open. You are not a barrier now to anything—the air, or the words, or the sound, or the rays, or anything. You are not a barrier, you don't resist anything.

When you come to feel that now you don't resist, you are not in a struggle, suddenly you will become aware that the ego is not there, because the ego exists only when you struggle. It is a resistance. Whenever you say no, the ego comes into existence; whenever you say yes, the ego is not there. So I call a man an *astik,* a real theist, who has said yes to the whole existence; there is no "no" in him, no resistance. He accepts everything, he allows everything to happen. Even if death comes, he will not close his door. The doors will remain open.

This openness has to be brought, only then can you do this technique, because this technique is saying that the whole existence is falling, converging on you—no resistance, welcoming, allowing it to converge. You will simply disappear, you will become a space, infinite space, because this infinite universe cannot converge on such a narrow atomic thing as the ego. It can converge only when you have become infinite like it, when you have yourself become an infinite space. But this happens. Slowly you have to become more and more sensitive and

you have to become aware of your resistances.

We are very resistant. If I touch you, you can feel that you are resisting the touch, you are creating a barrier, so my warmth cannot enter you, my touch cannot enter you. We don't allow each other to touch. If someone touches you, you become alert and the other says, "Excuse me." There is resistance everywhere. If I look at you, you resist, because the look can enter in you, it can penetrate deep, it can stir you, and then what will you do?

And this is not only with strangers. There is no need even with strangers, because no one is a stranger or everyone is a stranger. Just by living under one roof, how can the strangeness be destroyed? Do you know your father who has given you birth? He is a stranger. Do you know your mother? She remains a stranger. So either everyone is a stranger, or no one is a stranger. But we are afraid and create barriers everywhere. These barriers make us insensitive; then nothing can enter into us.

People come to me and they say, "No one loves. No one loves me." And I touch that man and I feel he is afraid even of touch. There is a subtle withdrawal. I take his hand in my hand and he has withdrawn. He is not there in the hand; only a dead thing is in my hand—he has withdrawn. And he says, "No one loves me." How can anyone love you? And even if the whole world loves, you will not feel it, because you are closed. Love cannot enter you; there is no gate, no door. And you are suffering in your own prison.

If the ego is there, you are closed—for love, for meditation, for God. So first try to be more sensitive, more vulnerable, open, allowing things to happen to you. Only then can the divine happen, because that is the last happening. If you cannot allow ordinary things to happen to you, how can you allow the ultimate? Because when the ultimate happens to you, you will be no more. You will simply be no more.

Kabir has said, "When I was seeking you, you were not there. And now, when you are there, where is that seeker Kabir? He is no more. So what type of meeting is this?" Kabir wonders, "What type of meeting is this? When I was there, the divine was not. Now the divine is there, but I am not. So what type of meeting is this?"

But really this is the only meeting, because two cannot meet. Ordinarily we think two are needed to meet—how will the meeting be there if there is only one? So the ordinary logic says that for a meeting at least two are needed, the other is needed. But for a real meeting, for a meeting which we call love, for a meeting which we call prayer, for a meeting which we call samadhi, ecstasy, one is needed. When the seeker is there, the sought is not; and when the sought has come, the seeker has disappeared.

Why is this so?—because the ego is the barrier. When you feel you are, you are so much that nothing can enter in you. You are filled with your own self. When you are not, then everything can pass through you. You have become so vast that even the divine can pass through you. The whole existence is now ready to pass through you, because you are ready.

So the whole art of religion is how not to be, how to dissolve, how to surrender, how to become an open space.

CHAPTER 54

The fire of awareness

◆

Q U E S T I O N S

How to preserve the vulnerable psyche from harmful vibes?

How can "I am" be dissolved in awareness?

Can we ever accept and develop in totality?

The first question:

A meditator who is vulnerable, passive, open and receptive, feels that with these characteristics he suffers due to the influence of the nonmeditative, negative and tense vibrations around him. Please explain how he can preserve his vulnerable psyche from the harmful vibrations.

f you are really vulnerable, nothing is negative for you—because the negative is your interpretation. Nothing is harmful to you—because the harmful is your interpretation. If you are really open, then nothing can harm you, nothing can be felt as harmful. You feel something is negative and something is harmful because you resist, because you are against it, because there is no acceptance of it. This has to be deeply understood.

The enemy exists there because you are protecting yourself against him. The enemy is there because you are not open. If you are open, then the whole existence is friendly; it cannot be otherwise. Really, you will not even feel it as friendly—it is simply friendly. There is no feeling even that it is friendly, because that feeling can exist only with the contrary feeling of enmity.

Let me put it in this way: if you are vulnerable, it means you are ready to live in insecurity. Deep down it means you are ready even to die. You will not resist, you will not oppose, you will not stand in the way. If death comes, there will be no resistance. You will simply allow it to happen. You accept existence in its totality. Then how can you feel it as death?

If you deny, then you can feel it as the enemy. If you don't deny, how can you feel it as the enemy? The enemy is created by your denial. Death cannot harm you, because the harm is your interpretation. Now no one can harm you; it has become impossible.

This is the secret of Taoist teaching. Lao Tzu's basic teaching is this: if you accept, the whole existence is with you, it cannot be otherwise. If you deny, you create the enemy. The more you deny, the more you defend, the more you protect, the more enemies are created. The enemies are your creation. They are not there outside; they exist in your interpretation.

Once you can understand this, then this question can never arise. You cannot say, "I am meditative, I am vulnerable, open, so now how am I to defend myself against negative vibrations around me?" Nothing can be negative now. What does the negative mean? The negative means that which you want to deny, that which you don't want to accept, that which you think is harmful. Then you are not open, then you are not in a meditative state.

This question arises only intellectually, this is not a felt question. You have not tasted meditation, you have not known it. You are simply thinking, and that thinking is just a supposition. You suppose, "If I meditate and become open, then I will be in insecurity. The negative vibrations will enter in me and they will be harmful. Then how am I to defend myself?" This is a supposed question. Don't bring supposed questions to me. They are futile, irrelevant.

Meditate, become open, and then you will never bring this question to me, because in the very opening the negative will have disappeared. Then nothing is negative. And if you think that something is negative, you cannot become open. The very fear of the negative will create the closure. You will be closed; you cannot open. The very fear that something can harm you…how can you become vulnerable? That's why I emphasize the fact that unless the fear of death disappears from you, you cannot become vulnerable, you cannot be open. You will remain closed in your own mind, in your own imprisonment.

But you can go on supposing things, and whatsoever you suppose will be wrong, because the mind cannot know anything about meditation, it cannot penetrate that realm. When it ceases completely, meditation happens. So you cannot suppose anything, you cannot think about it. Either you know it or you don't know it—you cannot think about it.

Be open—and in the very opening of yourself, all that is negative in existence disappears. Even death is not negative then. Nothing is negative. Your fear creates the negativity. Deep down you are afraid; because of that fear you create safety measures. Against those safety measures the enemy exists.

Look at this fact—that you create the enemy. Existence is not inimical to you. How can it be? You belong to it, you are just a part of it, an organic part. How can existence be inimical to you? You are existence. You are not separate; there is no gap between you and the existence.

Whenever you feel that the negative, the death, the enemy, the hate, is there, and if you are open, unguarded, existence will destroy you, you feel that you have to defend yourself. And not only defend —because the best way to defend is to be aggressive, to offend. You cannot be simply defensive.

When you feel that you have to defend yourself, you become offensive, because to offend, to be aggressive, is the best way to defend yourself.

The fear creates the enemy, and then the enemy creates defense, and then defense creates offense. You become violent. You are constantly on guard. You are against everybody. This point has to be understood: that if you are in fear, you are against everybody. Degrees may differ, but then your enemy and your friend are both your enemy. The friend is a little less, that's all. Then your husband or your wife is also your enemy. You have made an arrangement, that's all. You have become adjusted. Or it may be that you both have a common and a greater enemy, and against that common and greater enemy you both have become joined, you both have become one party—but the enmity is there.

If you are closed, the whole existence is inimical to you. Not that it is so—it appears to you that it is inimical. When you are open, the whole existence has become your friend. Now, when you are closed, even the friend is the enemy. It cannot be otherwise. Deep down you are afraid of your friend also.

Somewhere, Henry Thoreau or someone else has written that he prayed to God, "I will take care of my enemies, but you take care of my friends. I will fight with my enemies, but protect me from my friends."

Just on the surface is friendship; deep down is enmity. Your friendship may be just a façade to hide the enemy. If you are closed you can create only the enemy, because when you are open only then is the friend revealed. When you are open totally to someone, the friendship has happened. It cannot happen in any other way.

How can you love when you are closed? You live in your prison, I live in my prison, and whenever we meet, only the prison walls touch each other and we are hiding behind them. We move in our capsules: the capsules touch each other, the bodies touch each other, but deep down we remain isolated.

Even while making love, when your bodies have entered into each other, you have not entered. Only bodies are meeting; you remain still in your capsule, in your cell. You are just deceiving yourselves that there is communion. Even in sex, which is the deepest relationship, communion is not. It cannot happen because you are closed. Love has become an impossibility. And this is the reason—you are afraid.

So don't ask such questions; don't bring false questions. If you have known openness, you cannot feel that something can be harmful to you. Now nothing is harmful. That's why I say even death is a blessing. Your approach has become different. Now wherever you look, you look with an open heart. That open-heartedness changes the quality of everything, and you cannot feel that something is going to be harmful, you cannot ask how to defend —there is no need. The need arises because you are closed.

But you can go on supposing questions. People come to me and they say, "Okay, if we have realized God, then what?" They start with the question, "If?" There are no "ifs." In existence you cannot raise such questions. They are absurd, stupid, because you don't know what you are saying. "If I have realized God, then what?"

That "then what?" never arises, because with the realization you are no more, only God is. And with the realization there is no future, only the present is. And with the realization there is no worry, because you have become one with existence. So the question "then what?" never arises. This question arises because of the mind which is in constant worry, constant struggle, constantly thinking for the future.

The second question:

When I become more and more aware, my attention develops and there remains a feeling that I exist, I am present, I am aware. Please explain how this feeling can be dissolved into an egoless state of just awareness.

This is again a supposed question. *When I become more and more aware, my attention develops and there remains a feeling that I exist, I am present, I am aware.* This never happens, because as awareness grows, "I" decreases. In full awareness, you are, but there is no sense that "I am." In words, at the most, this can be said—that you feel a subtle am-ness, but there is no I.

You feel existence, and you feel it in abundance, a fulfilled moment, but the I is not there. You cannot feel "I exist"; you cannot feel "I am present"; you cannot feel "I am aware." That I is part of unawareness, inattention; part of your sleeping state. It cannot exist. It cannot exist when you are really alert and aware and conscious.

This is how supposed questions can arise. You can go on thinking about them, and nothing will be solved. If this happens—that you feel "I am; I am aware"—then you only have to note one thing, and that is that you are not alert, you are not aware. These feelings—"I am aware, I am conscious, I exist"—these are thoughts, then you are thinking them; they are not realized moments. You can think "I am aware"; you can go on repeating "I am aware"—that will not do. Awareness is not this repetition. And when you are aware, there is no need to repeat "I am aware." You are simply aware; the I is no more.

Try awareness. Right now be alert. Where is the I? You are—rather, you are more intensely—but where is the I, the ego? In the very intensity of consciousness, the ego is no more. Later on, when you lose awareness and thinking starts, you can feel "I am," but in the moment of awareness there is no I. Right now experience it. Silently you are here, you can feel your presence, but where is the I? The

I never arises. It arises only when retrospectively you think. When you lose awareness the I arises immediately.

Even if for a single moment you can experience simple awareness, you are, and the I is not there. When you lose awareness, when the moment has slipped, gone, and you are thinking, the I comes back immediately. It is part of the thought process. The very concept of I is a thought, it belongs to thinking. "I am" is a thought.

When you are alert and there is no thought, how can you feel that "I am"? The "am-ness" is there—but that too is not a thought, it is not thinking. It is there existentially, it is a fact. But you can turn the fact into thinking immediately, and you can think about this gap that existed where there was no I. And the moment you think, the I has come back. With thinking, the ego enters—thinking is the ego. With no-thinking, the ego is not.

So whenever you want to ask a question, first make it existential. Before giving me the question, test whether whatsoever you are asking is relevant or not. Such questions look relevant, just verbally, but they are like this: I say that the light has been put on, and then I ask, "The light has been put on and still the darkness remains, so what is to be done with the darkness?" The only thing is that the light is still off, it has not been put on, otherwise how can the darkness remain? And if the darkness is there, then the light is not there. And if the light is there, then the darkness is not there. They cannot be both together.

Awareness and the ego cannot be together. If awareness has come on, if it is there, the ego has disappeared. This is simultaneous; there is not even a single second's gap. The light is on and the darkness has disappeared. It is not that it disappears by and by, in steps, gradually. You cannot see it going outside; you cannot say that now the darkness is going out.

The light is there, and the darkness is immediately not there. There is not a single moment's gap, because if there is a gap then you can see darkness moving out. And if there is a single moment's gap, then there is no reason why there can't be a gap of one hour. There is no gap. The act is simultaneous. Really, the coming of the light and the going out of the darkness are two aspects of one phenomenon.

The same happens with awareness: when you are aware, the ego is not. But the ego can go on playing tricks, and the ego can say, "I am aware." The ego can say, "I am aware," and can befool you. Then the question will arise. And the ego wants to accumulate everything, even awareness. The ego not only wants wealth, power, and prestige; it wants meditation also, it wants samadhi also, it wants enlightenment also.

The ego wants everything. That which is possible must be possessed. The ego wants to possess everything—even meditation, samadhi, nirvana. So the ego can say, "Now I have achieved meditation," and then the question will arise. The meditation has been achieved, the awareness has come, but the ego remains, the misery remains. The whole burden of the past remains. Nothing changes.

The ego is a very subtle braggart. Be aware of it. It can deceive you. And it can use words, it can verbalize things. It can verbalize anything, even nirvana.

I have heard that once it happened that two butterflies were winging their way through the canyons of New York.

Just passing near the Empire State Building, the male butterfly said to the female, "You know, if I wanted to, just with one blow I could cause this Empire State Building to collapse."

One wise man happened to be there who heard this remark, so he called that male butterfly and asked, "What were you saying? You know very well that you cannot cause that Empire State Building to collapse with a single blow. You know it well, there is no need to tell you, so why did you say such a thing?"

The male butterfly said, "Excuse me, sir. I am very sorry. I was just trying to influence my girlfriend."

The wise man said, "Don't do it," and dismissed the butterfly.

The male butterfly went back to his girlfriend. Of course, the girlfriend asked, "What was the wise guy saying to you?"

So the male braggart said, "He begged me and said, 'Don't do it!' He was so afraid, trembling, nervous. He had heard that I was going to cause this Empire State Building to collapse, so he said, 'Don't do it!'"

The same is happening continuously. Those words were uttered by the wise man with a very different meaning. He meant, "Don't say such things," but the ego exploited him. Your ego can exploit anything, it is deeply cunning. And it is so experienced in cunning—experiences of millennia—that you cannot even detect where the cunning enters.

People come to me and they say, "Meditation has happened. Now what to do about my worries?" This is how the ego goes on playing tricks—and they are not even aware of what they are saying. "Meditation has happened, the kundalini has arisen—so what to do? The worries still continue."

Your mind wants to believe things, so without doing anything you go on believing, deceiving—wish-fulfillments. But the reality doesn't change by your wish-fulfillments: the worries continue. You can deceive yourself, you cannot deceive the worries. They will not just disappear because you say, "Meditation has happened and the kundalini has arisen, and now I have entered the fifth body." Those worries will not even hear what you are saying. But if meditation really happens, where are the worries? How can they exist in a meditative mind?

So remember this: that when you are aware, you are—but you are not the ego. Then you are unlimited, then you are infinite expanse, but with no center. There is no focused feeling of "I"; just unfocused existence, beginning nowhere, ending nowhere—just infinite sky. And when this I disappears, automatically the "you" disappears, because the "you" can exist only in reference to the I. I am

here; that's why you are there. If this I disappears from me, you are no more there. You cannot be. How can you exist?

I don't mean that you will not be there bodily, that you will not be there physically. You will be there as you are, but for me, you cannot be you. The "you" is meaningful in reference to my I; my I creates "you." One part disappears; the other disappears for me. Then simple existence is there; all the barriers have dissolved. With the ego disappearing, the whole existence becomes one. The ego is the divider—and the ego exists because you are inattentive. The fire of awareness will destroy it.

Try it more and more. Suddenly become alert. Walking on the street, immediately stop, take a deep breath, become alert for a moment. And when I say alert, I mean simply alert of whatsoever is happening—the traffic noise, people passing and talking, everything that is all around. Simply become alert. You are not there in that moment: existence is and the beauty of it.

Then the traffic noise doesn't appear to be noise, it doesn't look like a disturbance, because there is no one to resist it and fight it. It simply comes to you and passes; it is heard and heard no more. It comes and passes. There is no barrier against which it can strike. It cannot make a wound in you, because all wounds are made in the ego. It will pass. There will be no barrier to it on which it can strike; there will be no fight, no disturbance.

Remember this: the noise on the street is not the disturbance. When the noise of the street struggles against you, when you have a fixed notion that it is a disturbance, it becomes a disturbance. When you accept it, it comes and passes, and you are simply bathed by it; you come out of it more fresh. And nothing tires you then. The only tiring thing, that which goes on dissipating your energy, is this resistance which we call the ego.

But we never look at it in this way. The ego has become our life, the very gist of it. Really, there is no ego. If I say to someone—many times it happens—if I say to someone to dissolve this ego, immediately he stares at me as if with the question, the naked question, "If ego is dissolved, then where is life? Then I am no more."

I have heard that one very great politician, a big leader of a country, was asked, "You must be getting tired. The whole day, wherever you move, there is a crowd of autograph seekers."

That politician, that leader said, "It almost kills me—but this is only half of the truth." He must have been a very rare, honest man. He said, "It almost kills me—but almost. If there was no one seeking my autograph, it would kill me completely. This continuous crowd almost kills me, but the other thing would be more dangerous. It would kill me completely if there was no one to ask for my autograph."

So howsoever tiring the ego, howsoever wearing, you still feel it is life, and if the ego is not there, you feel life will disappear from your mind. You cannot conceive how life can exist without you, without there always being a reference point of I. It is logical in a way, because we have never lived without it. We have lived through it, we have lived around it; we know only one type of life, which is based on ego. We don't know any other life.

And because we have lived through it, we have not been really able to live. We are simply struggling to live, and the life never happens to us, it just bypasses us. It is always just in reach, in the hope—just tomorrow, the next moment, and we will be living. But it never comes, it is never achieved. It always remains a hope and a dream. But we go on moving, and because it is not coming, we move fast. That too is logical: if life is not happening to us, the mind can think only one thing—that we are not moving fast enough, so hurry, be speedy.

Once it happened that one of the great scientists, T.H. Huxley, was going to deliver a talk somewhere in London. He came to the station, to the suburban station, but the train was late, so he jumped into a cab and told the driver, "Hurry! Go at top speed!"

They were racing fast, when suddenly he realized that he had not given the address. But then he also remembered that he had himself forgotten the address. So he asked the driver, "Cabby, do you know where I am supposed to be going?"

He said, "No, sir. But I am going as fast as possible."

This is happening. You are going as fast as possible. Where are you moving, what is the destination? Why are you moving?—the hope that someday life will happen to you. And why is it not happening right now? You are alive—why is it not happening right now? Why is nirvana always in the future, always in the tomorrow? Why is it not today? And the tomorrow never comes—or whenever it comes it will always be the today and you will miss again. But we have lived only in this way. We know only one dimension of living—this so-called living we are already living—just dead, not alive at all, just pulling together anyhow, just waiting.

With the ego it will always remain a waiting—and a hopeless waiting. You can do it fast, you can make haste, but you will never reach anywhere: just by hurrying you will dissipate energy and you will die. And you have done that so many times. You have always been in a hurry, and in that hurry dissipating energy, and then only death comes and nothing else. You are hurrying for life, and only death comes and nothing else. But the mind, because it is accustomed to only one dimension, because it has known only one way—which is not even a way, but just appears to be a way—will say that if there is no ego, where is life?

But I say to you, if there is ego, there is no possibility of life, only promises. The ego is a perfect promise maker, it goes on promising you. And you are so unaware—no promise is ever fulfilled, but again you believe. When new promises are given, you again believe.

Look back! The ego promised many things, and nothing has been achieved through it. All the promises have fallen down. But you never look back, you never compare. When you were a child there were promises for youth: life will be there when you are older. Everyone was saying it, and you also were hoping that when you became older, all that was to happen would happen. Now those days have passed, the promise remains unfulfilled, but you have forgotten. You have forgotten the promise, you have forgotten that is has not been fulfilled. It is so painful to look at it that you never do.

Now you hope for the old age—that in old age sannyas will flower, meditation will happen to you. Then the worries will be over: your children will have gone to college, and everything will have become established. Then there will be no responsibility on you. Then you will be able to seek the divine. Then, in old age, the miracle is going to happen—and you will die unfulfilled.

It is not going to happen, because it never happens in hope, it never happens with hope. It never happens with the promise of the ego. It can happen right now—it can *only* happen right now. But then a very intense awareness is needed, so that you can throw all the promises, and all the hopes, and all the future programs, and all the dreams, and look directly here and now at what you are.

In that returning to yourself—your consciousness not moving somewhere ahead but returning to yourself—you become a circle of consciousness. This moment becomes eternal. You are alert and aware. In that alertness, in that awareness, there is no I, but simple existence, simple being. And simplicity comes out of that awareness.

Simplicity is not a loincloth, simplicity is not living in poverty, simplicity is not becoming a beggar. Those are very complex and very cunning things, very calculated. Simplicity is born when you have achieved a simple existence where no I exists. Out of that, simplicity arises, you become humble. Not that you practice it, because a practiced simplicity can never be simplicity. A practiced humbleness is just a hidden ego.

It happens: if you can be aware, it starts flowing

through you. You become humble; not against the ego, because a humbleness against the ego is again a different sort of ego—a more subtle ego and more dangerous, more poisonous. It is humbleness as the absence of ego; not as the opposite of the ego, just the absence. The ego has disappeared. You have come to yourself and known that there is no ego: simplicity arises, humbleness arises—they simply flow. You have not done anything for them; they are by-products, by-products of intense awareness.

So this type of question is foolish. If you feel that you are aware and still the I remains, know well that you are not aware. Make effort to be aware. And this is the criterion: when you are aware, the I is not; when you are aware, the I is not found there. This is the only criterion.

The third question:

One day You explained about the imbalance of object-centered Western culture and subject-centered Eastern culture, and You also mentioned that nowhere in any culture is the total human being accepted. Do You visualize such a coming culture which will be able to accept and develop the human being in his totality—objective as well as subjective?

This one-sided development has occurred as a natural fallacy, as a very natural fallacy. Try to understand the natural fallacy, because many things depend on it.

Whenever something is said, the opposite of it is denied. Whenever something is said, something is simultaneously denied. If I say "God is within," "God is without" is denied. I have not mentioned it at all. But if I say "God is without," then "God is within" is denied. If I say, "To be silent you have to move inwards," it is implied that if you move outwards, you will never be silent. So whatsoever is said in language always negates something.

This means that language can never cover the whole of life. Or, if you try to cover the whole of life, language becomes illogical, irrational. If I say, "God is within and God is without," it becomes meaningless. If I say, "Everything is God," it becomes meaningless. If I say, "Whether you go out or whether you go in, silence can be achieved," no meaning is carried then because I am saying both—both the opposites simultaneously. I am putting them together; they negate each other—and then nothing is said.

It has been tried. It has been tried many times that the whole of life be covered by linguistic expression. It has never been successful, and it cannot be. You can do it, but then your assertions become mystical; they don't carry any meaning. Logic has some requirements to be fulfilled—and language is logic.

If you ask me, "Are you here?" and I say, "Yes, in a sense I am here, and in a sense I am not here," or I say, "Both yes and no," then if you love me you will call me a mystic; if you don't love me, you will call me a madman—because how can both be? Either I am here—then I must say yes; or I am not here—then I must say no. But if I say yes and no both together, I am taking a jump out of the logical structure of the language.

Language is always a choice. Because of this, all the cultures, all the societies, all the civilizations become one-sided. And no culture can exist without language. Really, language creates the culture. Man is the only language animal; no other animal creates any culture or society or civilization. Only man creates culture and civilization and society. And with language, choice enters; and with choice, imbalance. No animal is imbalanced, remember. Only man is imbalanced. All animals exist in deep balance: trees and rocks and everything. Everything is balanced; only man is imbalanced. What is the problem?—that man lives through language. Language creates choice.

If I say to someone that he is both beautiful and ugly, the sentence carries no meaning. Ugly and beautiful both?—what do you mean? If I say, "You are beautiful," it is meaningful. If I say, "You are

ugly," it is meaningful. But if I say, "You are both. You are wise and foolish both," it cannot carry any meaning.

But reality is so. Really, no one is simply ugly and no one is simply beautiful. Wherever beauty exists, ugliness exists; wherever ugliness exists, beauty exists. They are part of one whole. And wherever wisdom exists, foolishness exists. You cannot find a wise man who is not also a fool, and you cannot find a fool who is not also a wise man.

It may be difficult for you to conceive, because whenever you say, "This man is a fool," you stop searching, you are closed, you have closed the door. You say, "This man is a fool." Now you are not going to search for his wisdom. And even if his wisdom is revealed to you, you will not listen to it. You will say, "This man is a fool. How can he be a wise man? It is impossible; something wrong has happened. He must have done it in a foolish way. This is something accidental. He cannot be wise." If you decide that this man is wise and then something foolish comes out of him, you cannot believe it, or you will have some explanations and you will rationalize it—that this must be wise.

Life is both together, but language divides. Language is a choice. Because of this, every culture creates its own choice-pattern. In the East they developed technology, they developed scientific research; they developed all that is now developed in the West. Five thousand years ago they developed everything, and then they felt the meaninglessness of it—as it is now felt in the West. They felt that it was useless.

When they felt that it was useless, they turned to the opposite extreme. They said, "Now turn within. Whatsoever is without is illusory, it leads nowhere. Turn within." Then science stopped growing, then technology stopped—and not only stopped: when they turned within, they started condemning all that was without. "Just live the life which is in! Leave all that is without!" They became against the world, life-negative, denying all that is material...only the spiritual, the pure spiritual.

Life is both. Really, to say life is both is not right. Life is one. That which we call material is just one expression of the spiritual, and that which we call spiritual is nothing but one expression of the material. Life is one. The within and without are not two opposite things, just two poles of one existence.

But whenever a society reaches to the extreme of one choice—because one choice is bound to be extremist—immediately you will miss the other, and that which you miss, you feel more. That which you have you can forget, but that which you miss you feel more. So the East, at the peak of scientific and technological development, felt the absurdity of it: it is useless, you cannot attain silence through it, you cannot attain bliss through it, so throw it away, renounce it, move inwards, move to the inner world. And then this inner movement automatically became a denial of the outer.

In the West that is happening now. Now the West has attained to a technological height; now the meaninglessness is felt. Now India has gone to the depths of poverty. It was bound to happen, because the Eastern mind started moving inwards. When you move inwards at the cost of all that is without, you are going to be poor, and you are going to be in bondage, and you are going to be in disease and suffering. That is bound to be so.

Now India is not interested in meditation, India is not interested in the inner world, India is not interested in nirvana. India is interested in modern technology. The Indian student is interested in engineering, in medical science. The Indian genius is going to the West to learn the know-how, atomic energy. And the Western genius is interested in coming to the East to know what meditation is, to know how to move in the inner space.

And they have achieved. For the first time in the history of man they have known how to move in outer space. They have reached the moon. Now that they have reached the moon the thing has become absurd. Now they are asking, "What will come out of it? Even if we have gone to the moon, what has happened?—man remains in the same

misery." The moon is not going to help, because you can transfer man to the moon, but he remains the same man. So movement in outer space seems to be of no use, a wastage of energy. How to move in inner space?

Now they turn to the East, and the East is turning to the West—again the choice. If the West turns to the East completely, within two or three centuries the West will become poor. Look at the hippies—they are already doing that. And if the new Western generation turns absolutely hippie, then who is going to work for the technology, and who is going to work for the industry, and who is going to work for the civilization that the West has achieved? It takes centuries and centuries to achieve something; you can lose it within a generation.

If the generation denies and says, "We are not going to the universities," what can you do? The old generation—how long can it prolong it? Twenty years and everything can disappear, just through the denial of the new generation—"I am not going to the university." And they are leaving, they are becoming dropouts. They say, "What is the use of big cars, of big houses, of a big technology, when there is no love? When there is no peace of mind, what is the use of all this wealth? What is the use of this high standard of living when there is no life? So leave this!"

Within two centuries the West can go to the very depths of poverty. It has happened in the East. In the days of the Mahabharata, almost the same technology was developed in the East. Then it was found to be of no use. And if the Indian mind turns to technology, within two generations religion will disappear—it has already disappeared—and just the word "meditation" will look out of date. If you talk about the inner, people will think you are not in your senses: "What do you mean by the inner? There is no inner."

This happens because of language—because language is a choice, and the mind moves to the extreme. And when it moves to one extreme, the other is lost. And with the other, many qualities disappear, and when they disappear you feel the hunger for them. Then you again move to the other extreme. Then something else is lost.

So no total culture has been born yet, and it cannot be born unless man learns to remain silent, unless silence becomes the very core of human mind. Not language but silence—because in silence you are whole, in language you are always part. Unless humanity starts living through silence—not through language, not through mind, but through the totality of the being—no total culture is possible. Only total human beings can constitute a total culture.

The human being is partial and fragmented. Every human being is just a fragment of that which he can be, that which he should be. He is just a fragment of his potentiality. These fragmentary human beings create fragmentary societies. Fragmentary societies have always been there. But now it seems possible that we may become aware of this whole nonsense of turning to extremes. And if this awareness becomes intense, and we don't move to the opposite, but rather we start to look at the whole....

For example, myself. I am not against the material, I am not against the spiritual. I am not for the spiritual, and I am not for the material. I am for both. There is no choice for me between the material and the spiritual, the inner and the outer. I am for both, because if you accept both, only then you become total and whole. But this is difficult to understand, to grasp, because of the heritage.

Whenever you see a spiritual man, you start looking to see whether he is poor or not. He must be poor, he must be living in a hut, he must be starving. Why? Why should he be poor and why should he be starving?—because the inner has to be chosen against the outer; that has become a part of the heritage. If you see a man living in luxury, you cannot believe that he is spiritual. How can he be spiritual?

What is wrong in luxury? And how is spirituality against luxury? Really, spirituality is the ultimate luxury. Really, only a spiritual man can be in luxury. He knows how to relax, and he knows how to enjoy, and he knows how to carry bliss wherever he moves. But the heritage has gone into the very cells of your brain. If you see a spiritual man walking in poverty, you feel that he must be authentic. How is poverty related to spirituality? and why? We have been choosing extremes. This is difficult to understand because of a long tradition—and you are not even aware of it.

Someone was just here, and he told me that in Wardha where Vinoba lives, it is very hot now the whole day—and he will not use a fan, he will not use a cooler, he will not use an air conditioner. Impossible! How can a spiritual man use an air conditioner? He cannot even use a fan. The man who had come from there was very much impressed. He said, "See, what a great spiritual man! He is not even using a fan."

Then I asked, "What is he doing?"

He said, "The whole day, from ten to five, for seven hours, he goes on putting cold cloths on his head and on his stomach."

Seven of Vinoba's hours wasted every day!—and what is the cost of a fan or a cooler or an air conditioner? And Vinoba's seven wasted hours every day...? But if there was a fan, this man would have felt that Vinoba is not spiritual. And somehow Vinoba is also agreeing with this type of attitude—that Vinoba's seven hours every day are not important.

Life is very short, and a genius like Vinoba is wasting seven hours unnecessarily. But he himself also feels that technology is somehow antispiritual. The outside and the inside—he has chosen the inside. But if you are choosing the inside, even putting on the wet cloth is outside. It is doing the same thing, only in a very primitive way. What are you doing? You are creating a sort of cooling. And you are wasting seven hours for it! This is at a very great cost. But we will say, "No, this is austerity, this is spirituality, and this man is great." This has gone to the very cells of our brains.

I accept life in its totality. The outer and the

inner both are there, and they both belong to me. And they must be balanced—you need not choose one at the cost of the other. And if you choose, you are falling a victim—victim of an extreme—and you will suffer for it.

Create a balance. The outer and the inner are not opposed, they are movements of the same energy, two banks of the same river, and the river cannot flow with only one bank. You can forget the other, but the other will be there. And the river can exist only if the other is there. You can forget it completely: then hypocrisy is born, because unnecessarily you have to go on hiding the other. There is no need.

The river cannot flow. Life flows between the inner and the outer, and both are essential. Life cannot exist with one. And the two are not really two. The two banks of the river only appear two; if you go deep in the river they are joined—the same

ground is appearing as two banks. The outer and the inner are the same ground, the same phenomenon.

If this insight goes deep, and human beings—and I am interested in human beings, not in cultures, not in societies, not in civilizations—if human beings become total and balanced, it is possible that someday humanity can become a balanced society. And only then will man be at ease. And only then will it be possible to grow without any unnecessary difficulty.

Now, rarely it happens that someone grows—rarely. Almost all the seeds are wasted. In millions, one seed grows and comes to flower. This seems sheer wastage. But if society is balanced—nothing is denied, nothing is chosen, but the whole is accepted in a deep harmony—then many will grow. Really, quite the reverse will be the case: it will happen rarely that someone will not grow.

CHAPTER 55

Only the unreal dissolves

◆

T H E   S U T R A S

82 *Feel: my thought, I-ness, internal organs—me.*

83 *Before desire and before knowing, how can I say I am? Consider. Dissolve in the beauty.*

Once a visitor asked many people in a small town about the mayor: "What type of man is your mayor?"
Said the priest, "He is no good."
Said the filling-station attendant, "He is a bum."

And said the barber, "I never in my life voted for that rascal."

Then the visitor met the mayor, a much maligned man, and the visitor asked, "What pay are you getting for your job?"

Said the mayor, "My goodness, I am not getting any pay for it. I have accepted this job just for the honor of it!"

This is the situation of the ego—only *you* think about your ego, no one else. Only you think that your ego is enthroned; for everyone else it is not so. No one agrees with your ego except you; everyone else is against it. But you go on living in a dream, in a delusion. You create your own image. You feel that image, you protect that image, and you think the whole world exists for it. This is a delirium, a madness. This is not reality.

The world is not existing for you. No one is concerned with your ego; no one at all. Whether you are or you are not, it makes no difference. You are just a wave. The wave comes and goes; the ocean is not worried about it. But you think yourself very important.

Those who want to dissolve the ego have first to recognize this fact. And unless you can put aside your egoistic structure, you will not be able to see the reality, because whatsoever you see, whatsoever you perceive, your ego distorts it. It tries to manipulate everything for itself. And nothing is for it, because reality cannot help anything which is false. Remember that.

Reality cannot support anything which is not, and your ego is the most impossible thing, the greatest falsity. It is not there; it is your creation, your imaginative creation. The reality cannot help it. The reality is always shattering it, always destroying it. Whenever your ego comes in contact with reality, the reality proves shocking. Just to defend yourself against these shocks which are always coming, continuously coming to destroy your ego, by and by you avoid seeing reality.

Rather than lose your ego, you try to avoid seeing the reality. And then around your ego you create a false world which you think is the reality. Then you live in your own world. You are not in contact with the real world, you cannot be, because you are afraid. You are living in a glasshouse of the ego. The fear is there: whenever the reality comes in contact, your ego may be destroyed, so it is better not to come in contact with the reality. We go on escaping from reality just to protect, to defend, this impossible ego.

Why do I call it impossible? Why do I say it is false? Try to understand this. The reality is one: the reality exists as a whole, as a totality. You cannot exist alone, or can you? If the trees are not existing you will not be able to exist, because they are producing oxygen for you. If the air disappears you will simply die, because that air is giving you vitality, life. If the sun goes out you will be no more here, because the warmth, the rays, they are your life.

Life exists as a cosmic totality. You are not alone, and you cannot exist alone. You exist in a world. You exist not as an atomic, separate, isolated existence; you exist in the cosmic whole as a wave. You are interrelated. And the ego gives you the feeling that you are individual, alone, separate, isolated. The ego gives you the feeling that you are an island—you are not. That's why the ego is false. It is unreal, and the reality cannot support it.

So there are only two ways. If you come in contact with reality, if you become open to it, your ego will dissolve—or you have to create your own dream-world, and then live in it. And you have created that world. Everyone is living in his own dream.

People come to me and I look at them, and I see that they are fast asleep, dreaming. Their problems are out of their dreams, and they want to solve them. They cannot be solved because they are not real. How can you solve an unreal problem? If it exists, it can be solved—but it is nowhere; it cannot be solved. An unreal problem—how can it be solved? It can be solved only by an unreal answer. But that unreal answer will create other problems which again will be unreal. And then you fall ad nauseam; there is no end to it.

If you want to come to meet reality…. And to meet reality is to meet God. God is not something hidden somewhere in the sky, it is the reality around you. God is not hidden; you are hidden in an unreality. God is the nearest immediate presence, but you are hidden in a capsule of your own unreal world and you go on protecting it—and the center of it is the ego.

The ego is unreal, because you are not isolated; you are one with reality. You exist as an organic part of it. You cannot be separated from it. If separated, not even for a single moment can you be alive. Every breath, and you are bridged with the cosmos; every moment you are moving in and out,

meeting the real and coming back.

You are a pulsation, not a dead entity, and that pulsation exists in a deep harmony with the real. But you have forgotten that pulsation. You have created a dead ego, a concept—"I am"—and this "I am" is always against the whole: defending itself, struggling, in conflict, in war. Hence the emphasis of all religions on dissolving the ego.

The first thing: it is unreal, that's why it can be dissolved. Nothing real can be dissolved. How can you dissolve it? If something is real, it cannot be destroyed; it will remain. And it will remain whatsoever you do. Only unreal things can be dissolved. They can disappear, they can simply evaporate into nowhere, into nothingness. Your ego can dissolve because it is unreal. It is just a thought, a notion; it has no substance to it.

Secondly: you cannot even carry this ego continuously for twenty-four hours. It is so unreal that you have to constantly fuel it, feed it. While you are asleep, the ego is not there. That's why in the morning you feel so fresh, because you have been in a deep contact with reality. The reality has rejuvenated you, revitalized you.

In deep sleep, your ego is not. Your name, your form, all have dissolved. You don't know who you are—educated or uneducated, poor or rich, a sinner or a saint—you don't know. In deep sleep you have fallen back to the cosmic whole; the ego is not there. In the morning you feel vitalized, fresh, young; energy has come to you from some deep source. You are again alive. But if in the night there are dreams and dreams and dreams, in the morning you feel tired because in the dreams the ego persists. In the dreams the ego persists, it is there, so it is not allowing you to fall into the original source. You will feel tired in the morning.

In deep sleep, the ego is not. When you are in deep love, the ego is not. When you are relaxed, silent, the ego is not. When you are absorbed in something so totally that you have forgotten, the ego is not. Listening to music, you have forgotten that you are—the ego is not. And really, the peace that comes to you is not coming through music; it is coming because you have forgotten the ego. The music is instrumental.

Looking at a beautiful sunrise or sunset, you forget yourself. Then suddenly you feel that something has happened to you. You are not there; something greater than you is there. This presence of the great...Jesus calls it God; that word is just symbolic. Mohammed calls it God; that word is just symbolic. "God" means greater than you—a moment when you feel that something greater than you is happening to you. And you can feel this only when you are not. While you are there, the greater cannot happen to you, because you are the barrier.

In any moment, if you are absent, God is present there. Your absence is the presence of the divine. Remember it always: your absence is the presence of the divine; your presence is the absence of the divine. So really the question is not how to reach God, the question is not how to attain God; the question is how to be absent.

You need not worry about the divine, you can forget it completely. There is no need to remember even the word "god." It is irrelevant, because the basic thing is not God, the basic thing is your ego. If it is not there, God happens to you. And if you try, if you make an effort to reach God, to attain God, or to be liberated, you may miss, because this whole effort may be ego-centered.

That's the problem for the spiritual seeker. It may be just the ego which is thinking to attain God. You cannot be satisfied by your worldly successes. You have achieved; in the outer world you have reached a certain status, position, prestige. You are powerful, you are rich, knowledgeable, respected, but your ego is not satisfied. The ego is never satisfied. And the reason?—the same. A real hunger can be satisfied. The hunger of the ego is false; it cannot be satisfied. Whatsoever you do will be futile. Because the hunger is false, no food can satisfy it. If the hunger is real, it can be satisfied.

All natural hungers can be satisfied—it is noth-

ing, not a problem at all—but unnatural hungers cannot be satisfied. In the first place they are not hungers—how can you satisfy them? And they are unreal; just emptiness exists there. You go on throwing food, and you are throwing food into an abyss, a bottomless abyss. You will not reach anywhere. The ego cannot be satisfied.

I have heard that when Alexander was coming to India someone said to him, "Have you ever meditated upon the fact that there is only one world, and if you win it then what will you do?"

And it is reported that upon hearing this Alexander became very sad and he said, "I have not thought about it, but it makes me very very sad. Really, there is only one world and I am going to win it. And when I have won it, what am I going to do then?"

Even this whole world will not quench your thirst, because the thirst is false, unreal. The hunger is not natural.

The ego can go in search of God. In almost ninety-nine cases out of a hundred this has been my feeling—that the ego is in search. And then the search is bound to be doomed from the very beginning, because the ego cannot meet the divine, and the ego is making every effort to reach it. Remember well, your meditation, your prayer, your worship, should not be an ego trip. If it is, you are unnecessarily wasting your energy. So be perfectly aware.

And this is only a question of awareness. If you are aware, you can find out how your ego moves and works. It is not difficult; no particular training is needed. You can close your eyes and you can see what the search is. You can ask the question whether you are really seeking the divine, or whether it is again just an ego trip—because it is respectable, because people think you are religious, because deep down you think, "How can I myself be satisfied unless I possess God?"

Is God going to be your possession? The Upanishads say that one who says that he has achieved God has not achieved, because the very assertion that "I have achieved God," is an ego assertion. The Upanishads say that one who claims that he has known has not known. The very claim shows that he has not known, because the claim that "I have known," comes from the ego—and the ego cannot know. The ego is the only barrier.

Now we will enter the techniques.

82 Feel, don't think.

First: *Feel: my thought, I-ness, internal organs—me.*

A very simple and a very beautiful technique. *Feel: my thought, I-ness, internal organs—me.* The first thing is not to think but to feel. These are two different dimensions. And we have become so intellect-oriented that even when we say that we are feeling, really we are not feeling, we are thinking. Feeling has completely stopped; it has become a dead organ in you. Even when you say, "I love," it is not a feeling, it is again a thought.

And what is the difference between feeling and thought? If you feel, you will feel yourself centered near the heart; if I say, "I love you," this very feeling of love will flow from my heart, the center will be near the heart. If it is just a thought, it will come from my head. When you love someone, try to feel whether it is coming from the head, or whether it is coming from the heart.

Whenever you feel deeply, you are headless. In that moment there is no head; there cannot be. The heart becomes your whole being—as if the head has disappeared. In feeling, the center of being is the heart. While you are thinking, the center of being is the head. But thinking proved very useful for survival, so we have stopped everything else. All other dimensions of our being have been stopped and closed. We are just heads, and the body is just a situation for the head to exist. We go on thinking; even about feelings we go on thinking. So try to feel. You will have to work on it, because that capacity, that quality, has remained retarded. You

must do something to reopen that possibility.

You look at a flower and immediately you say it is beautiful. Ponder over the fact, linger over the fact. Don't give a hurried judgment. Wait—and then see whether it is just from the head that you have said it is beautiful, or whether you have felt it. Is it just a routine thing, because you know a rose is beautiful, supposed to be beautiful? People say it is beautiful, and you have also said many times that it is beautiful.

The moment you see the rose, the mind supplies you, the mind says it is beautiful. Finished. Now there is no contact with the rose. There is no need; you have said it. Now you can move to something else. Without any communion with the rose...the mind didn't allow you even a glimpse of the rose. The mind came in between, and the heart couldn't come in touch with the rose. Only the heart can say whether it is beautiful or not, because beauty is a feeling, it is not a concept.

You cannot say from the head that it is beautiful. How can you say? Beauty is not mathematics, it is not measurable. And beauty is not really just in the rose, because to someone else it may not be beautiful at all; and someone else may just pass without looking at it; and to someone else it may even be ugly. The beauty doesn't exist simply in the rose, the beauty exists in a meeting of the heart with the rose. When the heart meets with the rose, beauty flowers. When the heart comes in deep contact with anything it is a great phenomenon.

If you come in deep contact with any person, the person becomes beautiful. The deeper the contact, the more beauty is revealed. But beauty is a phenomenon that happens to the heart, not to the mind. It is not a calculation, and there is no criterion by which to judge it. It is a feeling.

So if I say, "This rose is not beautiful," you cannot argue about it. There is no need to argue. You will say, "That is your feeling. And the rose is beautiful—this is my feeling." There is no question of argument. Heads can argue, hearts cannot argue. It is finished, it is a full stop. If I say, "This is my feeling," then there is no question of argument.

With the head, argument can continue and we can come to a conclusion. With the heart, the conclusion has already happened. With the heart, there is no procedure towards the conclusion; the conclusion is immediate, instantaneous. With the head it is a process—you argue, you discuss, you analyze, and then you come to a conclusion about whether this is so or not. With the heart it is an immediate phenomenon—the conclusion comes first. Look at it: with the head, conclusion comes in the end. With the heart, conclusion comes first, and then you can proceed to find the process—but that is the work of the head.

So when such techniques have to be practiced, the first difficulty will be that you don't know what feeling is. Try to develop it. When you touch something, close your eyes; don't think, feel. For example, if I take your hand in my hand and I say to you, "Close your eyes and feel what is happening," immediately you will say, "Your hand is in my hand." But this is not a feeling, this is a thinking.

Then I again say to you, "Feel, don't think." Then you say, "You are expressing your love." That too is again thinking. If I insist again, "Just feel, don't use your head. What are you feeling right now?" only then will you be able to feel and say, "The warmth." Because love is a conclusion. "Your hand is in my hand"—this is a head-oriented thought.

The actual feeling is that a certain warmth is flowing from my hand to your hand, or from your hand to my hand. Our life energies are meeting and the point of meeting has become hot, it has become warm. This is the feeling, the sensation, the real. But we go on with the head continuously. That has become a habit; we are trained for it. So you will have to reopen your heart.

Try to live with feelings. Sometimes in the day when you are not doing any particular business—because in business, in the beginning it will be difficult to live with feeling. There, head has proved very efficient, and you cannot depend on feeling.

While you are at home playing with your children the head is not needed, it is not a business—but there too you are with the head. Playing with your children or just sitting with your wife, or not doing anything, relaxing in a chair, feel. Feel the texture of the chair.

Your hand is touching the chair: how are you feeling it? The air is blowing, the breeze is coming in. It touches you. How do you feel? Smells are coming from the kitchen. How do you feel? Just feel, don't think about them. Don't start brooding that this smell shows that something is being prepared in the kitchen—then you will start dreaming about it. No, just feel whatsoever is the fact. Remain with the fact; don't move in thinking. You are surrounded from everywhere. Everywhere so much is converging on you. The whole existence is coming to meet you from everywhere, from all your senses it is entering you, but you are in the head, and your senses have become dead; they don't feel.

A certain growth will be needed before you can do this, because this is an inner experiment. If you cannot feel the outer, it will be very difficult for you to feel the inner, because the inner is the subtle. If you cannot feel the gross, you cannot feel the subtle. If you cannot hear the sounds, then it will be difficult for you to hear the inner soundlessness —it will be very difficult. It is so subtle.

You are just sitting in the garden, the traffic is passing by and there are many noises and many sounds. You just close your eyes and try to find the most subtle sound there around you. A crow is cawing: just concentrate yourself on that crow's noise. The whole traffic noise is going on. The sound is such, it is so subtle, that you cannot be aware of it unless you focus your awareness towards it. But if you focus your awareness, the whole traffic noise will go far away and the noise of the crow will become the center. And you will hear it, all the nuances of it—very subtle, but you will be able to hear it.

Grow in sensitivity. When you touch, when you

hear, when you eat, when you take a bath, allow your senses to be open. And don't think—feel.

You are standing under the shower: feel the coolness of the water falling on you. Don't think about it. Don't immediately say, "It is very cool. It is cold. It is good." Don't say anything. Don't verbalize, because the moment you verbalize, you miss feeling. The moment words come in, the mind has started to function. Don't verbalize. Feel the coolness and don't say that it is cool. There is no need to say anything. But our minds are just mad; we go on saying something or other.

I remember, I was working in a university, and there was a lady professor who would always be saying something or other. It was impossible for her to be silent in any situation. One day I was standing on the verandah of the college and the sun was setting. It was tremendously beautiful. And she was just standing by my side, so I told her, "Look!" She was saying something or other, so I said, "Look! Such a beautiful sunset."

So, very reluctantly she conceded. She said, "Yes, but don't you think there should be a little more purple just on the left?" It was not a painting; it was a real sunset!

We go on saying things, not even aware of what we are saying. Stop verbalizing; only then can you deepen your feelings. If feelings are deepened, then this technique can work miracles for you.

Feel: my thought….

Close your eyes and feel the thought. A continuous flow of thoughts is there, a continuum, a flux; a river of thoughts is flowing. Feel these thoughts, feel their presence. And the more you feel, the more will be revealed to you—layers upon layers. Not only thoughts that are just on the surface; behind them there are more thoughts, and behind them there are still more thoughts—layers upon layers.

And the technique says: *Feel: my thought.* And we go on saying, "These are my thoughts." But feel—are they really yours? Can you say "my"? The more you feel, the less will it be possible for you to

say that they are yours. They are all borrowed, they are all from the outside. They have come to you but they are not yours. No thought is yours—just dust gathered. Even if you cannot recognize the source from where this thought has come to you, no thought is yours. If you try hard, you can find from where this thought has come to you.

Only the inner silence is yours. No one has given it to you. You were born with it, and you will die with it. Thoughts have been given to you; you have been conditioned to them. If you are a Hindu, you have a different type, a different set of thoughts; if you are a Mohammedan, of course, a different set of thoughts; if you are a communist, again a different set of thoughts. They have been given to you, or you may have taken them voluntarily, but no thought is yours.

If you feel the presence of thoughts, the crowd, you can feel this also—that they are not yours. The crowd has come to you, it has gathered around you, but it doesn't belong to you. And if this can be felt—that no thought is mine—only then you can throw the mind. If they are yours, you will defend them. And the very feeling that "this thought is mine" is the attachment. Then I give it roots in myself. Then I become the soil and the thought can remain rooted in me. If anything that I can see is not mine is uprooted, then I am not attached to it. The feeling of "mine" creates attachment.

You can fight for your thoughts, you can even become a martyr for your thoughts, or you can become a killer, a murderer for your thoughts. And thoughts are not yours. Consciousness is yours, but thoughts are not yours. And why will this help?—because if you can see that thoughts are not yours, then nothing is yours because thought is the root of all. The house is mine and the property is mine and the family is mine—these are the outer things. Deep down the thoughts are mine. Only if thoughts are mine can all these things, the superstructure, be mine.

If thoughts are not mine then nothing matters, because this too is a thought—that you are my wife, or you are my husband. This too is a thought. And if basically thought itself is not mine, then how can the husband be mine? or how can the wife be mine? Thoughts uprooted, the whole world is uprooted. Then you can live in the world and not live in it.

You can move to the Himalayas, you can leave the world, but if you think that your thoughts are yours, you have not moved a single inch. Sitting there in the Himalayas, you will be as much in the world as here, because thoughts are the world. You carry your thoughts to the Himalayas. You leave the house—but the real house is inner, and the real house is built by the bricks of thought. It is not the outer house.

So this is strange, but this happens every day: I see a person who has left the world but still he remains a Hindu. He becomes a sannyasin and still he remains a Hindu or remains a Jaina. What does it mean? He renounces the world but he doesn't renounce the thoughts. He is still a Jaina, he is still a Hindu—the thought-world is carried still. And that thought-world is the real world.

If you can see that no thought is yours... And you will see, because you will be the seer and thoughts will become the objects. When you silently look at the thoughts, thoughts will be the objects and you will be the looker. You will be the seer, the witness, and thoughts will be flowing before you.

And if you look deeply and feel deeply, you will see that there are no roots. Thoughts are floating like clouds in the sky; they have no roots in you. They come and go. You are just a victim, and you unnecessarily become identified with them. About every cloud that passes by your house you say, "This is my cloud." Thoughts are like clouds: in the sky of your consciousness they go on passing and you go on clinging to each one. You say, "This is mine"—and this is only a vagrant cloud that is passing. And it will pass.

Go back in your childhood. You had certain thoughts, and you used to cling to them and you used to say that they were your thoughts. Then the

childhood disappeared, and with that childhood those clouds disappeared. Now you don't even remember. Then you were young: then other clouds which are attracted when you are young came to you and then you started clinging to them.

Now you are older, those thoughts are no more there, you don't even remember them. And they were so significant that you could have died for them, and now you don't even remember. Now you can laugh at the whole nonsense that you once thought that you could die for them, you could become a martyr for them. Now you are not ready to even give a single penny for them. They don't belong to you now. Now those clouds have gone but other clouds have come, and you are clinging to them.

Clouds go on changing but your clinging never changes. That's the problem. And it is not that only when you are no longer a child they will change; every moment they are changing. A minute ago you were filled with certain clouds; now you are filled with other clouds. When you came here, certain clouds were hovering over you; when you leave this room, other clouds will be hovering over you—and you go on clinging to every cloud. If in the end you find nothing in your hand, it is natural because nothing can come of clouds—and thoughts are just clouds.

This sutra says: *Feel*—be established in feeling first—then: *my thought*. Look at that thought which you have always been calling "my"—*my thought*. Established in feeling, looking at thought, the "my" disappears. And my is the trick because out of many my's, out of many me's, the "I" evolves—this is mine, this is my.... So many mine's; out of them the "I" evolves.

This technique starts from the very root. Thought is the root of all. If you can cut the feeling of "my" at the very root, it will not appear again, it will not be seen anywhere again. But if you don't cut it down there, you can go on cutting everywhere and it is useless; it will go on appearing again and again.

I can cut it. I can say, "My wife? No, we are

strangers, and marriage is just a social formality." I cut myself away. I say, "No one is my wife"—but this is very superficial. Then I say, "My religion." Then I say, "My sect." Then I say, "This is my religious book. This is the Bible, this is the Koran—this is *my* book." Then the "my" continues in some other field and you remain the same.

My thought, and then *I-ness.* First look at the traffic of thought, the process of thought, the river-like flow of thought, and find out whether any thought belongs to you or whether they are just passing clouds. And when you have come to feel that no thought is yours, to attach *my* to any thought is an illusion, then the second thing; then you can move deeper. Then be aware of *I-ness.* Where is this "I"?

Raman used to give a technique to his disciples: they were just to inquire, "Who am I?" In Tibet they use a similar technique, but still better than Raman's. They don't ask, "Who am I?" They ask, "Where am I?"—because the "who" can create a problem. When you inquire, "Who am I?" you take it for granted that you are; the only question is to know who you are. You have presupposed that you are. That is not contested, it is taken for granted that you are. Now the only question is *who* you are. Only the identity is to be known, the face is to be recognized, but it is there—unrecognized it is there.

The Tibetan method is still deeper. They say to be silent and then search within for where you are. Go on in the inner space, move to every point and ask, "Where am I?" You will not find it anywhere. And the more you seek, the more it will not be there. And asking "Who am I?" or "Where am I?" a moment comes when you come to a point where you are, but no "I"—a simple existence has happened to you. But it will happen only when thoughts are not yours. That is a deeper realm—*I-ness.*

We never feel it. We go on saying "I." The word "I" is used continuously—the most used word is "I"—but you have no feeling. What do you mean by "I"? When you say "I," what do you mean? What is connoted through this word? What is expressed? I can make a gesture, then I can say, "I mean this." I can show my body—"I mean this." But then it can be asked, "Do you mean your hand? Do you mean your leg? Do you mean your stomach?" Then I will have to deny, I will have to say no. Then the whole body will be denied. Then what do you mean when you say "I"? Do you mean your head? Deep down, whenever you say "I," it is a very vague feeling, and the vague feeling is of your thoughts.

Established in feeling, cut from thoughts, face I-ness, and as you face it, you find that it exists not. It was only a useful word, a linguistic symbol—necessary, but not real. Even a buddha has to use it, even after his enlightenment. It is just a linguistic device. But when a buddha says "I," he never means "I," because there is no one.

When you face this I-ness it will disappear. Fear can grip you at this moment, you can be scared. And it happens to many who move in such techniques deeply that they become so afraid that they run out of it.

So remember this: when you feel and face your I-ness you will be in the same situation as you will be when you die—the same, because "I" is disappearing, and you feel death is occurring to you. You will have a sinking sensation, you will feel you are sinking down and down. And if you get afraid, you will come out again and you will cling to thoughts because those thoughts will be helpful. Those clouds will be there: you can cling to them, and then the fear will leave you.

Remember, this fear is very good, a very hopeful sign. It shows that now you are going deep—and death is the deepest point. If you can go into death you will become deathless, because one who goes into death cannot die. Then death is also just around; never in the center, just on the periphery. When I-ness disappears you are just like death. The old is no more and the new has come into being.

This consciousness which will come out is absolutely new, uncontaminated, young, virgin. The old is no more—and the old has not even touched it.

That I-ness disappears, and you are in your pristine virginity, in your absolute freshness. The deepest layer of being has been touched.

So think of it in this way: thoughts, then below them I-ness, and thirdly:

Feel: my thought, I-ness, internal organs—me.

When thoughts have disappeared or you are not clinging to them—if they are passing it is none of your business, you are aloof and detached and unidentified, and the I-ness has disappeared—then you can look at the internal organs. These internal organs... This is one of the deepest things. We know the outer organs: with hands I touch you, with eyes I see you—these are the outer organs.

The internal organs are those through which I feel my own being. The outer are for others—I know about you through the outer. How do I know about me? Even that I am—how do I know about it? Who gives me the sensation of my own being? There are internal organs. When thoughts have stopped and when I-ness is no more, only then, in that purity, in that clarity, can you see the internal organs.

Consciousness, intelligence—they are internal organs. Through them I am aware of my own being, of my own existence. That's why if you close your eyes, you can forget your body completely, but your own feeling that you are remains. And it is conceivable that when a person dies... It is a fact—when a person dies, for us he is dead, but it takes a little time for him to recognize the fact that he is dead because the internal feeling of being remains the same.

In Tibet they have special exercises for dying and they say one must be ready to die. One of the exercises is this: whenever someone is dying, the master or the priest or someone who knows the *bardo* exercises will go on saying to him, "Remember, be alert, you are leaving the body." Because even when you have left the body it will take time to recognize that you are dead because the internal feeling remains the same; there is no change.

The body is only to touch and feel others. Through it you have never touched yourself, through it you have never known yourself. You know yourself through some other organs which are internal. But this is the misery—that we are not aware of those internal organs and our image in our own eyes is created by others. Whatsoever others say about me is my knowledge about myself. If they say I am beautiful or if they say I am ugly, I believe in it. Whatsoever my senses say to me through others, reflected through others, is my belief of myself.

If you can recognize the internal organs you are freed from society completely. That is what is meant when it is said in old scriptures that a sannyasin is not part of the society, because now he knows himself through his own internal organs. Now his knowledge about himself is not based upon others, it is not a reflected thing. Now he doesn't need any mirror to know himself. He has found the inner mirror, and he knows through the inner mirror. And the inner reality can be known only when you have come to the inner organs.

Internal organs... You can then look through those internal organs. And then—the me. It is difficult to express it in words. That's why the word "me" is used: any word will be wrong—"me" is also wrong—but the "I" has disappeared. So remember, this "me" doesn't have anything to do with "I." When thoughts are uprooted, when I-ness has disappeared, when internal organs are known, the "me" appears. Then for the first time my real being is revealed—that real being is called "me."

The outer world is no more, thoughts are no more, the feeling of ego is no more, and I have come to recognize my own internal organs of knowing, consciousness, intelligence—or whatsoever you call it—awareness, alertness. Then, in the light of this internal organ, "me" is revealed.

This "me" doesn't belong to you. This "me" is your innermost center, unknown to you. This "me" is not an ego. This "me" is not against any you. This "me" is cosmic, this "me" has no boundaries.

In this "me" everything is implied. This "me" is not the wave, this "me" is the ocean.

Feel: my thought, I-ness, internal organs. Then there is a gap, and suddenly the me is revealed. When this me is revealed, then one comes to know, *"Aham Brahmasmi.* I am God." This knowing is not any claim of the ego; the ego is no more there. You can mutate yourself through this technique, but first get established in feeling.

83 Change your focus to the gaps.

The second technique: *Before desire and before knowing, how can I say I am? Consider. Dissolve in the beauty.*

Before desire and before knowing, how can I say I am? A desire arises: with the desire, the feeling that "I am" arises. A thought arises: with the thought, the feeling that "I am" arises. Look for it in your own experience. Before desire and before knowing, there is no ego.

Sit silently, look within. A thought arises: you get identified with the thought. A desire arises: you get identified with the desire. In the identification you become the ego. Then think: there is no desire and there is no knowledge and no thought—you cannot get identified with anything. The ego cannot arise.

Buddha used this technique, and he said to his disciples not to do anything else but just one thing: when a thought arises, note it. Buddha used to say that when a thought arises, note that a thought is arising. Just inside, note it: now a thought is arising, now a thought has arisen, now a thought is disappearing. Just remember that now the thought is arising, now the thought has arisen, now the thought is disappearing, so that you don't get identified with it.

It is very beautiful and very simple. A desire arises. You are walking on the road; a beautiful car passes by. You look at it—and you have not even looked and the desire to possess it arises. Do it. In the beginning just verbalize; just say slowly, "I have seen a car. It is beautiful. Now a desire has arisen to possess it." Just verbalize.

In the beginning it is good, if you can say it out loud it is very good. Say out loud, "I am just noting that a car has passed, the mind has said it is beautiful, and now desire has arisen and I must possess this car." Verbalize everything, speak aloud to yourself and immediately you will feel that you are different from it. Note it.

When you have become efficient in noting, there is no need to say it aloud. Just inside, note that a desire has arisen. A beautiful woman passes; the desire has come in. Just note it—as if you are not concerned, you are just noting the fact that is happening—and then suddenly you will be out of it.

Buddha says: Note whatsoever happens. Just go on noting, and when it disappears, again note that now that desire has disappeared, and you will feel a distance from the desire, from the thought.

This technique says: *Before desire and before knowing, how can I say I am?*

And if there is no desire and if there is no thought, how can you say "I am"? *How can I say I am?* Then everything is silent, not a ripple is there. And without any ripple how can I create this illusion of "I"? If some ripple is there I can get attached to it and through it I can feel "I am." When there is no ripple in the consciousness, there is no "I."

So before desire, remember; when the desire comes in, remember; when the desire goes out, go on remembering. When a thought arises, remember. Look at it. Just note that a thought has arisen. Sooner or later it will go because everything is momentary, and there will be a gap. Between two thoughts there is a gap, between two desires there is a gap, and in the gap there is no "I."

Note a thought in the mind and then you will feel that there is an interval. Howsoever small, there is an interval. Then another thought comes; then again there is an interval. In those intervals there is no "I"—and those intervals you are your real being. Thoughts are moving in the sky. In those intervals you can look between two clouds, and the sky is revealed.

Consider. Dissolve in the beauty.

And if you can consider that a desire has arisen and a desire has gone and you have remained in the gap and the desire has not disturbed you... It came, it went. It was there, and it is now not there, and you have remained unperturbed, you have remained as you were before it. There has been no change in you. It came and it passed like a shadow. It has not touched you; you remain unscarred.

Consider this movement of desire and movement of thought but no movement in you. *Consider. Dissolve in the beauty.* And that interval is beautiful. Dissolve in that interval. Fall in the gap and be the gap. It is the deepest experience of beauty. And not only of beauty, but of good and of truth also. In the gap you are.

The whole emphasis has to go from the filled spaces to the unfilled spaces. You are reading a book: there are words, there are sentences, but between the words there are gaps, between the sentences there are gaps. In those gaps you are. The whiteness of the paper you are, and the black dots are just clouds of thought and desire moving on you. Change the emphasis, change the gestalt. Don't look at the black dots, look at the white.

In your inner being, look at the gaps. Be indifferent to the filled spaces, the occupied spaces. Be interested in the gaps, the intervals. Through those intervals you can dissolve into the ultimate beauty.

.

Discovering emptiness

◆

The first question:

In meditation, when the "I" drops temporarily and an emptiness is created within, after it a frustration is felt when that emptiness is not filled by the entry of the unknown. How can one learn to live with that emptiness?

mptiness is the unknown. Don't wait and don't hope that something is going to fill the emptiness. If you are waiting, hoping, desir-ing, you are not empty. If you are waiting that something, some un-known force, will descend upon you, you are not empty—this hope is there, this desire is there, this longing is there. So don't desire for something to fill you. Simply be empty. Don't even wait.

Emptiness is the unknown. When you are really empty the unknown has descended upon you. It is not that first you become empty and then the unknown enters. You are empty, and the unknown has entered. There is not a single moment's gap. The emptiness and the unknown are one.

In the beginning it appears to you as emptiness; that is only appearance, because you have always been filled by the ego. Really, you are feeling the absence of the ego; that's why you feel empty. First the ego disappears—but the feeling that the ego is no more creates the feeling of emptiness. Just the absence...something was there, and now it is not there. The ego has gone, but the absence of the ego

is felt. First the ego will disappear, and then the absence of the ego will disappear. Only then will you be really empty. And to be really empty is to be really filled.

That inner space which is created by the absence of the ego is the divine. The divine is not to come from somewhere else; you are already that. Because you are filled with the ego you cannot real-ize it, you cannot see it, you cannot touch it. A filmy barrier of the ego prevents you.

When the ego has dropped, the barrier has dropped. The curtain is no more there. Nothing is to come; whatsoever is to come is already there. Remember this: that nothing new is going to come to you. Whatsoever is possible is already there, actual. So the question is not of achieving; the question is only of discovering. The treasure is there, just covered—you uncover it.

When he became a realized man, Buddha was asked so many times, "What have you gained? What have you achieved?"

Buddha is reported to have said, "I have not achieved anything. Rather, on the contrary, I have lost myself. And that which I have achieved was already there, so I cannot say I have achieved it. I was unaware of it, now I have become aware. But I cannot say I have achieved it. Rather, on the con-trary, now I wonder how it was possible that I didn't know it before. And it was always there just by the corner—just a turning was needed."

Divinity is not a future, your divinity is the present. It is here and now. This very moment you are that—unaware, not looking in the right direction, or not tuned to it, that's all.

A radio is there: the waves are passing right now, but if the radio is not tuned to a particular wave, the wave is unmanifest. You tune the radio and the wave becomes manifest. A tuning is needed. Meditation is a tuning. When you are tuned, that which is unmanifest becomes manifest.

But remember: don't desire, because the desire will not allow you to be empty. And if you are not empty nothing is possible, because the space is not there, so your own unmanifest nature cannot be revealed. It needs space to be revealed. And don't ask how to live with emptiness. That is not the real question. Just be empty. You are not yet empty.

If once you know what emptiness is, you will love it. It is ecstatic. It is the most beautiful experience possible to mind, to man, to consciousness. You will not ask how to live with emptiness. You are asking that as if emptiness is something like a misery. It appears so to the ego. The ego is always afraid of emptiness, so you ask how to live with it as if it is some enemy.

Emptiness is your innermost center. All the activity is on the periphery; the innermost center is just a zero. All the manifest is on the periphery; the deepest core of your being is the unmanifest vacuum. Buddha has given it a name—*shunyata*. It means nothingness or emptiness. That's your nature, that's your being, and out of that nothingness everything comes, and everything goes back to it.

That emptiness is the source. Don't ask to fill it, because whenever you ask to fill it you will create more and more ego—ego is the effort to fill the emptiness. And even this desire that now something must descend upon you—a god, a divinity, a divine power, some unknown energy—this is again a thought. Whatsoever you can think about God is not going to be God; it is simply going to be a thought.

When you say the unknown, you have made it the known. What do you know about the unknown? Even to say that it is the unknown, you have known some quality about it—the quality of

its being unknown. The mind cannot conceive of the unknown. Even the unknown becomes known, and whatsoever the mind says is going to be just a verbalization, a thought process.

God is not the word 'god'. The thought of God is not God. And when there is no thought, only then will you come to feel and realize what it is. Nothing else can be said about it. It can only be indicated. And all indications are erroneous because they are all indirect.

This much can be said—that when you are not... And you are not only when there is no desire, because you exist with desire. Desire is the food through which you exist. Desire is the fuel. When there is no desire, no longing, no future, and when you are not, that emptiness is the fullness of existence. In that emptiness the whole existence is revealed to you. You become it.

So don't ask how to live with emptiness. First be empty. There is no need to ask how to live with it. It is so blissful—the deepest bliss it is. When you ask how to live with emptiness, you are really asking how to live with oneself. But you have not known yourself. Enter more and more into it.

In meditation sometimes you feel a sort of emptiness; that is not really emptiness. I call it just a sort of emptiness. When you are meditating, for certain moments, for a few seconds you will feel as if the thought process has stopped. In the beginning these gaps will come. But because you are feeling as if the thought process has stopped, this is again a thought process, a very subtle thought process. What are you doing? You are saying inside, "The thought process has stopped." But what is this? This is a secondary thought process which has started. And you say, "This is emptiness." You say, "Now something is going to happen." What is this? Again a new thought process has started.

Whenever this happens again, don't become a victim of it. When you feel a certain silence is descending, don't start verbalizing it, because you are destroying it. Wait—not for something— simply wait. Don't do anything. Don't say, "This is emptiness." The moment you have said it, you have destroyed it. Just look at it, penetrate into it, encounter it, but wait—don't verbalize it. What is the hurry? Through verbalization the mind has again entered from a different route, and you are deceived. Be alert about this trick of the mind.

In the beginning it is bound to happen, so whenever this happens again, just wait. Don't fall in the trap. Don't say anything—remain silent. Then you will enter, and then it will not be temporary, because once you have known the real emptiness you cannot lose it. The real cannot be lost; that is its quality.

Once you have known the inner treasure, once you have come in contact with your deepest core, then you can move in activity, then you can do whatsoever you like, then you can live an ordinary worldly life, but the emptiness will remain with you. You cannot forget it. It will go on inside. The music of it will be heard. Whatsoever you are doing, the doing will be only on the periphery; inside you will remain empty.

And if you can remain empty inside, doing only on the periphery, whatsoever you do becomes divine, whatsoever you do takes on the quality of the divine because now it is not coming from you. Now it is coming directly from the original emptiness, the original nothingness. If then you speak, those words are not yours. That's what Mohammed means when he says, "This Koran is not said by me. It has come to me as if someone else has spoken through me." It has come out of the inner emptiness. That's what Hindus mean when they say, "The Vedas are not written by man, they are not human documents, but the divine, God himself has spoken."

These are symbolic ways of saying something which is very mysterious. And this is the mystery: when you are deeply empty, whatsoever you do or speak is not from you—because you are no more. It comes from the emptiness. It comes from the deepest source of existence. It comes from the same source from which this whole existence has come.

Then you have entered the womb, the very womb of existence. Then your words are not yours, then your acts are not yours. It is as if you are just an instrument—an instrument of the whole.

If emptiness is felt only momentarily, and then it comes and goes like a flash, it is not real. And if you start thinking about it, even the unreal is lost. Not to think in that moment takes great courage. It is the greatest control I know. When the mind becomes silent and when you are falling empty, it takes the greatest courage not to think, because the whole past of the mind will assert. The whole mechanism will say, "Now think!"

In subtle ways, indirect ways, your past memories will force you to think—and if you think, you have come back. If you can remain silent in that moment, if you are not tempted by the mechanism of your memory and mind... This is really Satan—your own mind which tempts you. Whenever you are falling empty, the mind tempts you and creates something to think about—and if you start thinking, you are back.

It is said that when one of the great masters, Bodhidharma, went to China, many disciples gathered around him. He was the first Zen master. One disciple, who was to become his chief disciple, came to him and said, "Now I have become totally empty."

Bodhidharma slapped him immediately and said, "Now go and throw this emptiness also! Now you are filled with emptiness—throw this also. Only then will you be really empty."

You understand? You can be filled by the idea of emptiness. Then it will hover on you, it will become a cloud. He said, "Throw this emptiness also, and then come to me." If you say you are empty, you are not empty. Now this word 'empty' has become meaningful and you are filled with it. The same I say to you: throw this emptiness also.

The second question:

You have talked about transformation and mutation of man's mind, of man's unconscious into superconscious, and You have said that spirituality is an existential experimentation. But last night You said that the ego is a false entity and it has no substance and reality to it. Then does it mean that the whole spiritual experimentation is an existential transformation of the ego which is nonexistential?

No. The spiritual transformation is not the transformation of the ego; it is the dissolution of it. You are not going to transform the ego, because howsoever transformed, the ego will remain the ego. It may become superior, more refined, more cultured, but the ego will remain the ego. And the more cultured it becomes, the more poisonous. The more subtle, the more you will be in its grip, because you will not be able to be aware of it. You are not even aware of such a gross ego. When it becomes subtle you will not be aware of it; there will be no possibility.

There are ways to refine the ego, but those ways are not of spirituality. Morality exists on those methods. And that is the difference between morality and religion. Morality exists on methods of refining the ego; morality exists on respectability. So we say to a person, "Don't do this. If you do this, your respect is at stake. Don't do this—what will others think about you? Don't do this, you will not be honored. Do this and everyone will honor you."

The whole morality depends on your ego, a subtle ego. Religion is not a transformation of the ego, it is a transcendence. You simply leave the ego. And it is not that you leave it because it is wrong. Remember this distinction. Morality always says, "Leave that which is wrong, and do that which is right." Religion says, "Leave that which is false"—not wrong, but false. "Leave that which is unreal, and enter the real." With spirituality, truth is the value, not right. Because right may itself be false, and in a false world we need false rights to oppose wrongs.

Spirituality is not a transformation of the ego, it is a transcendence. You go beyond the ego. And this going beyond is really an awakening; it is a deep alertness to see whether the ego exists or not. If it exists, if it is a part, a real part of your being, you cannot go beyond it. If it is false, only then is transcendence possible. You can awaken out of a dream, you cannot awaken out of reality—or can you? You can transcend a dream, but you cannot transcend reality.

The ego is a false entity. And what do we mean when we say that the ego is a false entity? We mean that it exists only because you have not encountered it. If you encounter it, it will not exist. It exists in your ignorance; because you are not aware, it is there. If you become aware, it will not be there. If you become aware and some entity disappears just by your becoming aware, it means it was false. The real will be revealed in awareness and the false will disappear.

So really this too is not right to say—leave your ego—because whenever it is said, it gives a sense that the ego is something and you can leave it. You can even start struggling to throw this ego. The whole effort will be absurd. You cannot throw it, because only a reality can be thrown. You cannot fight with it. How can you fight with a shadow? And if you fight, remember, you will be defeated. Not because the shadow is very powerful, but because the shadow is not; you cannot defeat it. You will be defeated by your own stupidity.

Fight with a shadow and you cannot win—that is certain. You will be defeated. That too is certain, because you will dissipate your own energy in the fight. Not that the shadow is very powerful, but because the shadow is not. You are fighting with your own self, wasting your energy. Then you will be exhausted and you will fall down. And you will think that the shadow has won and you are defeated—and the shadow has not been there at all. If you fight with the ego you will be defeated. Rather, enter and try to find out where it is.

It is said that the emperor of China asked

Bodhidharma, "My mind is very restless. I am in constant inner turmoil. Give me some peace or give me some secret key to how I can enter into the inner silence."

So Bodhidharma said, "You come early in the morning, four o'clock, when there is no one here. When I am alone here in my hut you come—and remember, bring your restless mind with you. Don't leave it at home."

The emperor was very much disturbed, thinking that this man was mad. He said, "Bring your disturbed mind with you. Don't leave it at home, otherwise who am I going to silence? I will make it still, but bring it! Remember well."

The emperor left, but more disturbed than ever. He had been thinking that this man was a sage, a wise man, and he would give him some key, but whatsoever he said seemed to be foolish—how can one leave one's mind at home? He couldn't sleep. The eyes of Bodhidharma and the way he had looked at him...he was hypnotized, as if a magnet was pulling. He couldn't sleep the whole night, and at four he was ready. He didn't really want to go because this man was mad. And going so early, in darkness, when no one was there—this man could do anything.

But still, he was so attracted that in spite of himself he went. And the first thing that Bodhidharma asked... He was sitting before his hut with his staff in his hands, and he said, "Okay. So you have come. Where is your restless mind? Have you brought that? I am ready to silence it."

The emperor now said, "What are you talking about? How can one forget the mind? It is always there."

Bodhidharma said, "Where? Where is it? Show it to me so I can silence it, and you can go back."

The emperor said, "But it is not something objective. I cannot show it to you, I cannot put it in my hand. It is within me."

So Bodhidharma said, "Okay, close your eyes and try to find out where it is. And the moment you catch hold of it, open your eyes and tell me and I will still it." In that silence and with this madman, the emperor closed his eyes.

He tried and tried. And he was afraid also, because Bodhidharma was sitting with his staff— any moment he would hit. He tried and tried and tried. He looked everywhere, in every nook and corner of his being—where is that mind which is restless?

And the more he looked, the more he realized that the restlessness had disappeared. The more he tried to search...like a shadow it was not there.

Two hours passed, and he was not even aware of what had happened. His face became silent, he became like a buddha statue, and then with the rising sun Bodhidharma said, "Now open your eyes. It is enough. Two hours are more than enough. Now can you tell me where it is?"

The emperor opened his eyes. He was as silent as a human being can be. He bowed down his head at Bodhidharma's feet and said, "You have already silenced it."

Emperor Wu has written in his autobiography, "This man is miraculous, magical. Not doing anything he silenced my mind. And I also didn't do anything. I just entered myself and tried to find where it is. Of course he was right: first locate it, where it is. And just the effort to locate it, and it was not found there."

You will not find the ego. If you go in, if you search for it, you will not find it there. It has never existed. It is just a false substitute. It has some utility, that's why you have invented it. Because you don't know your real being, the real center, and without a center it is difficult to function, you have created a fiction, a fictitious center, and you function through it.

The real center is hidden. You have created a false center—the ego is a false center, a substitute center. Without a center it is difficult to exist, difficult to function. You need a center to function. And you don't know your real center, so the mind has created a false center. Mind is very skilled in creating substitutes. It always gives you a substitute if you cannot find the real, because otherwise you will go mad. Without a center you will go mad. You will get scattered, you will become fragmented; there will be no unity. So the mind creates a false center.

It is just like in dreaming. You dream you are feeling thirsty. Now, if this thirst becomes penetrating, the sleep will be disturbed, because then you will have to get up to drink water. Now your mind will give a substitute: the mind will create a dream. You need not get up, the sleep need not be disturbed—you dream that you are drinking water. From the fridge you are taking water and drinking. The mind has given you a substitute. Now you feel okay. The real thirst has not been quenched, simply deceived. But now you feel that you have drunk, you have taken water. Now you can sleep; the sleep can continue undisturbed.

In dreams the mind is constantly giving you substitutes just to protect sleep. And the same is happening while you are awake. The mind is giving you substitutes just to protect your sanity; otherwise you will be scattered in fragments.

Unless the real center is known, the ego has to function. Once the real center is known, there is no need to dream about water. When you have got the real water you can drink it. There is no need to dream about it. Meditation brings you to the real center. And with that very happening, the utility of the false disappears.

But this must be kept in consciousness—that the ego is not your real center. Only then can you start a search for the real. And spirituality is not a transformation of it. It cannot be transformed. It is unreal, it is simply not. You cannot do anything with it. If you are aware, alert, if you watch it within yourself, it disappears. Just the flame of your awareness and it is not there. Spirituality is a transcendence.

The third question:

If the ego is unreal, then does it not mean that the unconscious mind, the accumulation of memories in the brain cells, and the process of transformation that is the subject matter of spirituality, is also unreal, a dream process?

No. Ego is unreal; brain cells are not unreal. Ego is unreal; memories are not unreal. Ego is unreal; thought process is not unreal. Thought process is a reality. Memories are real, brain cells are real, your body is real. Your body is real, your soul is real. These are two realities. But when your soul gets identified with the body, the ego is formed—that is unreality.

It is just like this. I am standing before a mirror: I am real, the mirror is real, but the reflection in the mirror is not real. I am real, the mirror is also real, but the reflection in the mirror is a reflection, it is not a reality. Brain cells are real, consciousness is real, but when consciousness gets involved, attached, identified with the brain cells, the ego is formed. That ego is unreal.

So when you have awakened, when you have become enlightened, your memory is not going to disappear. The memory will be there. Really, it will be more crystal-clear. Then it will function more accurately because there will be no disturbance from the false ego. Your thought process will not disappear. Rather, for the first time you will be capable of thinking. Before that you were simply borrowing things. Then you will really be able to think. But then you, not the thought process, will be the master.

Before, the thought process was the master. You couldn't do anything about it. It continued on its own; you were just a victim. You wanted to sleep and the mind continued thinking. You wanted to stop it, but it would not stop. Really, the more you tried to stop it, the more stubborn it became. It was your master. When you become enlightened it will be there, but then it will be instrumental. Whenever you need it, you will be able to use it. Whenever you don't need it, it will not crowd your consciousness. Then it can be called and then it can also be stopped.

Brain cells will be there, the body will be there, memory will be there, thought process will be there. Only one thing will not be there—the feeling of "I" will not be there. This is difficult to understand.

Buddha walks, Buddha eats, Buddha sleeps, Buddha remembers. He has memory, his brain cells function beautifully. But Buddha has said, "I walk, but no one walks in me. I talk, but no one talks in me. I eat, but no one eats in me." The inner consciousness is no more the ego. So when Buddha feels hungry, he cannot feel like you. You feel, "I am hungry." When Buddha feels hungry, he feels, "The body is hungry. I am just the knower." And that knower is without any feeling of I.

The ego is the false entity, the only false entity —everything else is real. Two realities can meet, and in their meeting, a third epiphenomenon can be created. When two realities meet, something false can happen. But the false can happen only if there is consciousness. If there is no consciousness, the false cannot happen. Oxygen and hydrogen meet: a false water cannot happen. The false can happen only when you are conscious, because only consciousness can err. Matter cannot err, matter cannot be false. Matter is always true. Matter cannot deceive and cannot be deceived—only consciousness can. With consciousness is the possibility to err.

But remember another thing: matter is always real, never false, but also never true. Matter cannot know what truth is. If you cannot err, you cannot know what truth is. Both the possibilities open simultaneously. Human consciousness can err and can know that it has erred and can move away from it. That is the beauty of it. The danger is there, but danger is bound to be there. With every growth new dangers come in. For matter, there is no danger.

Look at it in this way. Whenever a new thing grows in existence, a new thing evolves, now dangers come with it into existence. For a stone there is no danger. Then there are small organisms.... In amoebas, sex doesn't exist in the way it exists in man or in animals. They simply divide their bodies. When one amoeba grows bigger and bigger, when it grows to a certain extent, its body automatically divides into two. The parent body divides into two. Now there are two amoebas.

Some bacteria can live eternally; because there is no birth, so there is no death. With sex entered birth; with birth entered death; with birth entered individuality; with individuality entered ego.

Every growth has its own potential dangers, but they are beautiful. If you can understand, there is no need to fall into them, and you can transcend them. And when you transcend, you mature and you achieve a greater synthesis. If you fall a victim, the greater synthesis is not achieved.

Spirituality is the peak, the last, the ultimate synthesis of all growth. The false is transcended and the real absorbed. And only the real remains; all the false drops away. But don't think that the body is unreal—it is real. Brain cells are real, the thought process is real. Only the relationship between the consciousness and the thought process is unreal. That is a tie. You can untie it. And the moment you untie it, you have opened the door.

The last question:

How can one know that the spiritual search in which one is involved is not an ego trip, but is an authentic religious search?

If you don't know, if you are confused, then know well that this is an ego trip. If you are not confused, if you know well that this is authentic, if there is no confusion at all, then it is authentic. And it is not a question of deceiving someone else. It is a question of deceiving or not deceiving oneself. If you are confused, in doubt, it is an ego trip, because the moment the authentic search is there, there is no doubt. Faith happens.

Let me put it in some other way. Whenever you

phrase such problems, the very confusion exactly shows that you are on the wrong path. Someone comes to me and he says, "Tell me. I don't know whether my meditation is going deep or not."

So I say, "If it is going deep, there is no need to come and ask me. The depth is such an experience, you will know it. And if you cannot know your depth, who is going to know about it? You have come to ask me only because you are not feeling the depth. Now you want someone else to certify you. If I say, 'Yes, your meditation is going very deep,' you will feel very good—this is an ego trip."

When you are ill, you know that you are ill. It may sometimes happen that illness may be very very hidden. You may not be aware of it. But the reverse never happens: when you are perfectly healthy, you know it. It is never hidden. When you are healthy, you know it. It may be that of your illness you may not be so aware, but of health—if health is there—you are aware of it, because the very phenomenon of health is a phenomenon of well-being. If you cannot feel your health, who is going to feel it? For your ill-health there may be experts to tell you what type of disease you have; there is no expert to tell you about your health. There is no need. But if you ask whether you are healthy or not, you are unhealthy; that much is certain. This very confusion shows it.

So when you are on a spiritual search, you can know whether it is an ego trip or an authentic search. And the very confusion shows that this is not an authentic search; this is a sort of ego trip. What is the ego trip? You are less concerned with the real phenomenon; you are more concerned with possessing it.

People come to me and they say, "You know, and you can know about us. Tell us whether our kundalini has arisen or not." They are not concerned with kundalini, not concerned really; they need a certificate. And sometimes I play and I say, "Yes, your kundalini has arisen," and immediately they are so happy. The person came very very gloomy and sad, and when I say, "Yes, your kun-

dalini is awakened," he is happy like a child.

He goes away happy, and when he is just going out of my room, I call him back and I say, "I was just playing. It is not real. Nothing has happened to you." He is again sad. He is not really concerned with any awakening; he is simply concerned with feeling good: now his kundalini has awakened, now he can feel superior to others.

And this is how many so-called gurus go on exploiting, because you are for your ego. They can give you certificates, they can tell you, "Yes, you are already awakened. You have become a buddha." And you are not going to deny it. If I say this to ten persons, out of ten, nine are not going to deny it. They will just feel happy. They were in search of such a guru who would say that they are awakened.

False gurus exist because of your need, because no authentic guru is going to say this to you, or give you any certificate—because any certificate is a demand from the ego. No certificate is needed. If you are experiencing it, you are experiencing it. If the whole world denies it, let them deny—it makes no difference. If the real experience is there, what does it matter who says that you have achieved and who says you have not achieved? It is irrelevant. But it is not irrelevant, because your basic search is the ego. You want to believe that you have achieved all.

And this happens many times: when you become a failure in the world, when you are in misery in the world, when you cannot succeed there and when you feel that your ambition remains unfulfilled and life is passing, you turn to spirituality. The same ambition now asks to be fulfilled here. And it is easy to be fulfilled here—easy, because in spirituality you can deceive yourself easily. In the real world, in the world of matter, you cannot deceive so easily.

If you are poor, how can you pretend that you are rich? And if you pretend, no one is deceived. And if you go on insisting that you are rich, then the whole society, the whole crowd around you, will think you have gone mad.

I once knew a man who started thinking that he was Pandit Jawaharlal Nehru. His family, his friends, everyone tried to persuade him: "Don't talk such nonsense, otherwise you will be thought to be mad."

But he said, "I am not talking nonsense. I am Pandit Jawaharlal Nehru."

He started signing "Jawaharlal Nehru." He would send telegrams to circuit houses, to officials, to collectors, to commissioners saying that "I am coming—Pandit Jawaharlal Nehru."

He had to be caught and chained in his house. I went to meet him—he lived in my village. He said, "You are a man of understanding, you can understand. These fools, no one understands me—I am Pandit Jawaharlal Nehru."

So I said, "Yes, that's why I have come to meet you. And don't be afraid of these fools, because great men like you have always suffered."

He said, "Right." He was so happy. He said, "You are the only man who can understand me. Great men have to suffer."

In the outer world, if you try to deceive yourself you will be thought mad, but in spirituality it is very easy. You can say that your kundalini has arisen. Just because you have a certain pain in your back, your kundalini has arisen. Because your brain is feeling a little unbalanced, you think centers are opening. Because you have a headache constantly, you think the third eye is opening. You can deceive and no one can say anything, and no one is interested. But there are false teachers who will say, "Yes, this is the case." And you will feel very happy.

An ego trip means that you are not interested in really transforming yourself; you are only interested in claiming. And the claim is easy, you can purchase it cheaply. And it is a mutual thing. When a guru, a so-called guru, says that you are an awakened man, of course he has made you awakened, so you have to pay respect to this guru. This is a mutual thing. You pay respect to him, and now you cannot leave that guru, because the moment you leave that guru what will happen to your awakening, your kundalini? You cannot leave. That guru depends on you because you give respect and honor to him, and then you will depend on him because no one else is going to believe that you are awakened. You cannot leave. This is a mutual bluff.

If you are really in search it is not so easy. And you don't need any witness. It is difficult and arduous; it may take even lives. And it is painful, it is a long suffering, because much has to be destroyed, much has to be transcended, long-established chains have to be broken. It is not easy. It is not a child's play. It is arduous, and suffering is bound to be there because whenever you start changing your pattern, all that is old has to be dropped. And all your investments are in the old. You will have to suffer.

When you start looking inwards for your ego and you don't find it, what will happen to your image that you have lived with? You have always thought you were a very good man, moral, this and that—what will happen to that? When you find that you are nowhere to be found, where is that good man? Your ego implies all that you have thought about yourself. Everything is implied in it. It is not something that you can throw easily. It is you, your whole past. When you drop it you become like a zero, as if you never existed before. For the first time you are born; no experience, no knowledge, no past—just like an innocent child. Daring is needed, courage is needed.

Authentic search is arduous. An ego trip is very easy. And it can be fulfilled very easily, because nothing is really fulfilled. You start believing; you start believing that something has happened to you. You are simply wasting time and energy and life. So if you are really with a master, he will constantly pull you back from your trip. He will have to watch that you don't become mad, that you don't start thinking in dreams. He will have to pull you back.

And it is a very very difficult thing, because

whenever you are pulled back you take revenge on the master. "I was going so high, and was just on the verge of exploding, and he says, 'Nothing is happening. You are just imagining.'" You are pulled back to the earth.

With a real master it is difficult to be a disciple. And disciples almost always go against their masters, because they are on their ego trips and the master is trying to bring them out of that. And these disciples create false masters. They have a need, such a great need, that anyone who fulfills their need will become their master. And it is easy to help your ego grow, because you are for it. It is very difficult to help your ego to disappear.

Remember well, and check every day and every moment that your search is not an ego trip. Go on checking it. It is subtle, and the ways of the ego are very very very cunning. They are not on the surface. The ego manipulates you from within; deep down, from the unconscious. But if you are alert, the ego cannot deceive you. If you are alert, you will come to know its language, you will come to know its feeling, because it is always going after experience. This is the key word.

The ego is always looking for the experience— sexual or spiritual, it makes no difference. The ego is greedy to experience this and to experience that: to experience kundalini and to experience the seventh body. The ego is always after experiences. The real search is not a greed for any experience, because any experience is going to frustrate you, is bound to frustrate you—because any experience is going to be repetitive. Then you will get fed up with it; then you will again demand some new experience.

The search for the new will remain with the ego. You will meditate, and if you are only meditating just to get a new thrill, because your life has become boring—you are fed up with your ordinary routine life, so you want to get some thrill.... You may get it, because man gets whatsoever he tries to find. That is the misery—whatsoever you desire, you will find. And then you will repent. You will get the thrill—then what? Then you get fed up

with it also. Then you want to take LSD or something else. Then you go on moving from this master to that, from this ashram to that, just in search of a new thrill.

The ego is a greed for new experiences. And every new experience will become old, because whatsoever is new will become old—then again.... Spirituality is not a search for experience really. Spirituality is a search for one's being. Not for any experience—not even for bliss, not even for ecstasy —because experience is an outer thing; howsoever inner, it is outer.

Spirituality is the search for the real being that is inside you: I must know what my reality is. And with that knowing, all greed for experiencing ceases. And with that knowing, there is no urge— no urge to move for any new experience. With the knowing of the inner true reality, the authentic being, all search ceases.

So don't move for an experience. All experiences are just tricks of the mind, all experiences are just escapes. Meditation is not an experience, it is a realization. Meditation is not an experience; rather, it is a stopping of all experience. Because of this, those who have really tried to express the inner happening—for example, Buddha—they say, "Don't ask what happens there." Or, if you insist, they will say, "Nothing happens there."

If I say to you that nothing will happen in meditation, what will you do? You will stop meditating. If nothing is going to happen there, what is the use? —that shows you are on an ego trip. If I say nothing happens there, and you still say, "Okay, I have known many happenings and I have known many experiences, and every experience proved to be frustrating".... You pass through it and then you know it was nothing; and then an urge to repeat, and then repetition also becomes a boredom. Then you move to something else.... This is how you have been moving for lives and lives; for thousands and thousands of lives you have been moving for experience.

If you say, "I have known experience. Now I

don't want any new experience, I want to know the experiencer," the whole emphasis changes. Experience is something outside you; the experiencer is your being.

And this is the distinction between true spirituality and false: if you are for experiences, the spirituality is false; if you are for the experiencer, then it is true. But then you are not concerned about kundalini, not concerned about *chakras,* not concerned about all these things. They will happen, but you are not concerned, you are not interested, and you will not move on these bypaths. You will go on moving towards the inner center where nothing remains except you in your total aloneness. Only the consciousness remains, without content.

Content is the experience. Whatsoever you experience is the content. I experience misery— then the misery is the content of my consciousness. Then I experience pleasure—then pleasure is the content. Then I experience boredom—then boredom is the content. And then you can experience silence—then silence is the content. And then you can experience bliss—then bliss is the content. So you go on changing the content. You can go on changing ad infinitum, but this is not the real thing.

The real is the one to whom these experiences happen—to whom boredom happens, to whom bliss happens. The spiritual search is not *what* happens, but to *whom* it happens. Then there is no possibility for the ego to arise.

CHAPTER 57

You are everywhere

♦

84 *Toss attachment for body aside, realizing I am everywhere. One who is everywhere is joyous.*

85 *Thinking no thing will limited-self unlimit.*

I have heard a story about an old doctor. One day his assistant phoned him because he was in very great difficulty—his patient was choking to death. A billiard ball was stuck in his throat, and the assistant was at a loss for what to do. So he asked the old doctor, "What am I supposed to do now?" The old doctor said, "Tickle the patient with a feather."

After a few minutes the assistant phoned again, very happy and jubilant, and said, "Your treatment proved wonderful—the patient started laughing and he spat the ball out. But tell me from where you learned this remarkable technique."

The old doctor said, "I just made it up. This has always been my motto: When you don't know what to do, do something."

But this will not do as far as meditation is concerned. If you don't know what to do, don't do anything, because mind is very intricate, complex, delicate. If you don't know what to do, it is better not to do anything, because whatsoever you do without knowing is going to create more complexities than it can solve. It may even prove fatal, it may even prove suicidal.

If you don't know anything about the mind... And really, you don't know anything about it. Mind is just a word. You don't know the complexity of it. Mind is the most complex thing in existence; there is nothing comparable to it. And it is the most delicate—you can destroy it, you can do something which cannot then be undone. These techniques are based on a very deep knowledge, on a very deep encounter with the human mind. Each technique is based on long experimentation.

So remember this: don't do anything on your own, and don't mix two techniques, because their functioning is different, their ways are different, their bases are different. They lead to the same end, but as means they are totally different. Sometimes they may even be diametrically opposite. So don't mix two techniques. Really, don't mix anything—use the technique as it is given.

Don't change it, don't improve it, because you cannot improve it, and any change you bring to it will be fatal. And before you start doing a technique, be fully alert that you have understood it. If you feel confused and you don't know really what the technique is, it is better not to do it, because each technique is to bring about a revolution in you.

These techniques are not evolutionary. By evolution I mean that if you don't do anything and just go on living, in millions of years meditation will happen automatically to you, in millions of lives you will evolve. In the natural course of time, you will come to the point to which a buddha comes through a revolution. These techniques are revolutionary. Really, they are shortcuts; they are not natural. Nature will lead you to buddhahood, to enlightenment—you will come to it one day—but then it is up to nature; you cannot do anything about it except just go on living in misery. It will take a very long time, really, millions of years and lives.

Religion is revolutionary. It gives you a technique which can shorten the lengthy process, and with which you can take a jump—a jump which will avoid millions of lives. In a single moment you can travel millions of years. So it is dangerous, and unless you understand it rightly, don't do it. Don't mix anything on your own. Don't change.

First try to understand the technique absolutely rightly. When you have understood it, then try it. And don't use this old doctor's motto that when you don't know what to do, do something. No, don't do anything. Nondoing will be more beneficial to you than any doing. This is so because the mind is so delicate that if you do something wrongly it is very difficult to undo it—very difficult to undo it. It is very easy to do something wrong, but very difficult to undo it. Remember this.

84 Detach yourself from your body.

The first detachment technique: *Toss attachment for body aside, realizing I am everywhere. One who is everywhere is joyous.*

Many points have to be understood. First: *Toss attachment for body aside.* There is a deep attachment to the body—bound to be, it is natural. You have been living in the body for many, many lives, from the very beginning. Bodies have changed, but you were always with a body, you were always embodied.

There have been certain moments and times when you were not embodied, but then you were not conscious. When you die from one body, you die in unconsciousness and then you remain unconscious. Then you are born again in a new body, but then too you are unconscious. The gap between one death and another birth is unconscious, so you don't know how you will feel when not embodied. You don't know who you are when you are not in a body. You know only one phenomenon, and that is of embodiment; you have always known yourself in the body.

This has been so long, so continuous, that you have forgotten that you are different from it. This is a forgetfulness—natural, bound to happen in the circumstances—hence the attachment. You feel you are the body—this is the attachment. You feel that you are not anything other than the body, not anything more than the body. You may not agree with me at this point, because many times you think that you are not the body, you are the soul, the self. But this is not your knowing; this is simply what you have heard, what you have read, and what you have believed without knowing.

So the first thing to be done is that you have to realize the fact that really this is your knowing—that you are the body. Don't deceive yourself, because deception will not help. If you think that you already know that you are not the body, then you cannot toss aside the attachment, because really for you there is no attachment, you already know. Then many difficulties arise which cannot be solved. A difficulty has to be solved at the beginning. Once you lose the beginning, you can never solve it; you have to come back again to the beginning. So remember well, and realize well that you don't know yourself as anything other than the body. This is the first basic realization.

This realization is not there. Your mind is befogged by whatsoever you have heard; your mind is conditioned by the knowledge of others—it is borrowed, it is not real. Not that it is false—those who have said it, they have known it—but for you it is false unless it becomes your own experience. So whenever I say something is false, I mean it is not your experience. It may be true for someone else, but it is not true for you. And truth is individual in this sense—that truth is truth only when experienced; not experienced, it is untrue. There are no universal truths. Every truth has to be individual before it becomes true.

You know, you have heard; this is part of your knowledge, part of an inheritance—that you are not the body—but it is not real for you. First toss aside this unreal knowledge. Face the fact that you know yourself only as the body. That will create a great tension in you—it was just to hide that tension that you gathered this knowledge. You go on believing that you are not the body and you go on living as the body, so you are divided, and your whole being becomes nonauthentic, pseudo.

Really this is a paranoid condition. You live as the body and you think and talk as the soul—then there is a struggle and a conflict and then you are constantly in an inner turmoil, a deep unease which cannot be bridged. So first encounter the fact you don't know anything about the soul, the self—all that you know is about the body.

This will release a very uneasy condition in you. All that is hidden will come up to the surface. In realizing this fact that you are the body, you will literally start perspiring. In realizing this fact that you are the body, you will feel very uneasy, strange, but that feeling has to be gone through; only then can you know what attachment to the body means.

Teachers go on saying that you should not be attached to your body, but the basic thing—what the attachment to the body is—is unknown to you. Attachment to the body is a deep identification with the body, but first you have to realize what this identification is. So put aside all your knowledge that has given you an illusory sense that you are the soul. Realize that you know only one thing, and that is the body. How does this create and how does this release hidden turmoil and a hidden hell within you?

The moment you realize you are the body, for the first time you realize the attachment. For the first time you grip the fact in your consciousness that this body which is born, and this body which is going to die, is you. For the first time you realize the fact that these bones, this blood—this is you. For the first time you realize the fact that this sex, this anger—this is you. So all the false images fall. You become real.

The reality is painful, very painful—that's why

we go on hiding it. It is a deep trick. You go on thinking about yourself as the self, and everything that you don't like, you throw on the body. So you say sex belongs to the body, love belongs to you. Then you say greed and anger, they belong to the body; compassion belongs to you. Compassion belongs to the self, and cruelty belongs to the body. Forgiveness belongs to the self, and anger belongs to the body. So whatsoever you feel is wrong, ugly, you throw to the body, and whatsoever you feel is beautiful, you go on being identified with. You create a division.

This division will not allow you to know what attachment is, and unless you know what attachment is and unless you suffer the misery of it and the hell of it, you cannot put it aside. How can you put it aside? You can put something aside only when it proves a disease, when it proves a heavy burden, when it proves a hell; only then can you put it aside.

Your attachment has not proved a hell yet. Whatsoever Buddha says and Mahavira says is irrelevant. They may go on saying that attachment is hell, but this is not your feeling. That's why you again and again ask how to be detached, how to be not attached, how to go beyond attachment. You go on asking this "how" only because you don't know what attachment is. If you know what attachment is, you will simply jump out of it, you will not ask "How?"

If your house is on fire you will not ask anyone, you will not go seeking a master to ask how to come out of it. If the house is on fire you will simply get out of it. You will not lose a single moment. You will not search for the teacher, you will not consult the scriptures. And you will not try to choose in what ways one has to come out, what means have to be adopted, and which door is the right door. These things are irrelevant when the house is on fire. When you know what attachment is, the house is on fire. You can put it aside.

To enter into this technique, first you have to throw the false knowledge of the self so that attachment with the body is revealed in its totality. It is going to be very difficult; it is going to be a deep anxiety and anguish to face it. It is not going to be easy, it is arduous, but once you face it, you can put it aside—and there is no need to ask how. It is absolutely a fire, a hell. You can jump out of it.

This sutra says: *Toss attachment for body aside, realizing I am everywhere.*

And the moment you toss aside the attachment, you will realize you are everywhere. Because of this attachment you feel you are limited by the body. It is not the body which is limiting you; it is your attachment to it. It is not the body which is making a barrier between you and the reality; it is your attachment to it. Once you know that the attachment is not there, there is no body to you. Rather, the whole existence becomes your body; your body becomes a part of the total existence. Then it is not separate.

Really, your body is nothing but existence come to you, existence reached to you. It is the nearest existence to you, that's all—and then it goes on spreading. Your body is just the nearest corner of it, and then the whole existence is there—it goes on spreading. Once your attachment is not there, there is no body to you; or, the whole existence has become your body. You are everywhere.

In the body you are somewhere; without the body you are everywhere. In the body you are confined to a particular space; without the body you have no confinement. That's why those who have known, they say the body is the imprisonment. Not that the body is the imprisonment; really, the attachment to it is the imprisonment. Once your eyes are not focused on the body, you are everywhere.

This looks absurd. To the mind who is in the body, this looks absurd, a madness—how can one be everywhere? To a buddha, whatsoever we say—that "I am here"—really looks like madness. How can you be somewhere? Consciousness is not a space concept. That's why if you close your eyes and try to find out where in your body you are,

you will be at a loss. You cannot find out where you are.

There have been many religions and many sects which have preached that you are in the navel. Some say that you are in the heart, some say that you are in the head, some say that you are in this center and that center, but Shiva says you are nowhere. That's why if you close your eyes and try to find out where you are, you cannot say. You are, but there is no "where" to you. You simply are.

In deep sleep you are not aware of the body. *You* are. In the morning you will say that the sleep was very deep, very blissful. You were aware of a deep bliss running throughout, but you were not aware of the body. In deep sleep where are you? When you die, where do you go? Continuously people ask, "When someone dies, where does he go?" But the question is absurd, foolish. It is related to our embodied consciousness—because we think that we are somewhere, so then when we die, where do we go? Nowhere.

When you die, you are not somewhere, that's all. You are not confined to a space, that's all. But if you have a desire to be confined, you will be confined again. Your desire leads you to new confinements. But when you are not in the body, you are nowhere, or everywhere—this depends on which word appeals to you.

If you ask Buddha, he will say you are nowhere. That's why he chooses the word 'nirvana'. Nirvana means you are nowhere. Just like a flame which has gone out—how can you say where the flame is then? He will say it is nowhere. The flame has simply ceased to be. Buddha uses a negative term—nowhere. That's what nirvana means. When you are not attached to the body you are in nirvana, you are nowhere.

Shiva chooses a positive term—he says everywhere—but both the terms mean the same. If you are everywhere, you cannot be somewhere. If you are everywhere, it is saying almost the same thing as saying that you are nowhere.

But in the body we are attached, and we feel

that we are confined. This confinement is a mental act; it is your own doing. And you can confine yourself to anything. You have a valuable diamond. Your being can be confined to it, and if the diamond is stolen you may commit suicide or you may go mad. What has happened? There are so many persons without a diamond: no one is committing suicide, no one is feeling any difficulty without a diamond, but what has happened to you?

Once you were also without a diamond; there was no problem. Now you are again without a diamond, but there is a problem. How is this problem created? It is your own doing. Now you are attached, confined. The diamond has become your body. Now you cannot live without it; it is impossible to live without it.

Wherever you get attached, it becomes a new imprisonment. And whatsoever we are doing in life is this: we go on creating more and more imprisonments, bigger and bigger jails to live in. Then we go on decorating those jails so that they look like home, and then we forget completely that they are jails.

This sutra says that if you toss aside the attachment with the body, realization happens that *I am everywhere*. You have an oceanic feeling, your consciousness exists without any location. Your consciousness exists without being tethered anywhere. You become just like a sky, enveloping all; everything is in you. Your consciousness has expanded to the infinite possibility. And then the sutra says: *One who is everywhere is joyous.*

Confined to a place you will be in misery, because you are always bigger than where you are confined. This is the misery—as if you are forcing yourself into a small bowl; the ocean is being forced into a small pot. The misery is bound to be there. This is the misery, and whenever this misery has been felt, the search for enlightenment arises, the search for the Brahma. Brahma means the infinite one. The search for moksha means the search for freedom. In a limited body you cannot be free; somewhere you will be a slave. Nowhere or everywhere you can be free.

Look at the human mind: whatsoever the direction, it is always for freedom, searching for freedom. It may be political, it may be economic, it may be psychological, it may be religious—whatsoever the direction, but the human mind is always groping for freedom. Freedom seems to be the deepest need. Wherever human mind finds any barrier, any slavery, any limitation, it fights against it. The whole human history is a fight for freedom.

Dimensions may be different: a Marx, a Lenin, they are fighting for economic freedom; a Gandhi, a Lincoln, they are fighting for political freedom. And there are thousands and thousands of slaveries, and the fight goes on. But one thing is certain—that somewhere, deep down, man is searching continuously for more and more freedom.

Shiva says, and all the religions say, that you can become politically free, but the struggle will not cease. Only one type of slavery will be no more, but there are other types of slaveries there, and when you are politically free then you will become aware of other slaveries. Economic slavery can cease, but then you will become aware of other slaveries—sexual, psychological. This struggle cannot cease unless you begin to feel and know that you are everywhere. The moment you feel you are everywhere, freedom is attained.

This freedom is not political, this freedom is not economical, not sociological. This freedom is existential. This freedom is total. That's why we have called it moksha, total freedom. And then only can you be joyous. Joy or bliss is possible only when you are totally free.

Really, to be totally free means joy. The joy is not a consequence, it is the very happening. When you are totally free you are joyous, you are blissful. This bliss is not happening as an effect. Freedom is bliss, slavery is misery. The moment you feel limited you are miserable; wherever you feel limited you feel miserable. When you feel unlimited, misery disappears. So misery exists in barriers, and bliss exists in a no-barrier land, in a no-barrier existence.

Whenever you feel this freedom, joy happens to

you. Even now, whenever you feel a certain freedom, even if it is not total, joy comes to you. You fall in love with somebody: a certain joy, a certain bliss happens to you. Why does it happen? Really, whenever you are in love with somebody, you have tossed aside your own attachment to the body. In a deep sense, now the other's body has also become your body. You are not confined to your own body now; somebody else's body has also become your body, it has also become your home, it has also become your abode. You feel a freedom. Now you can move into the other and the other can move into you. In a limited way a barrier has fallen. You are more than before.

When you love someone you are more than you ever were; your being has increased, expanded. Your consciousness is not limited like it was before; it has reached a new realm. You feel a certain freedom in love. It is not total, and sooner or later you will feel again confined. You feel extended, but still finite. So those who really love are sooner or later bound to fall into prayer.

Prayer means a greater love. Prayer means a love with the whole existence. You now know the secret. You know a key, a secret key—that you loved a person, and the moment you loved, the doors opened and the barriers dissolved, and at least for one person more your being was expanded, increased. Now you know the secret key. If you can fall in love with the whole existence, you will not be the body.

In deep love you become bodiless. When you are in love with someone you don't feel yourself as a body. When you are not loved, when you are not in love, you feel yourself more as a body, you become more aware of the body. The body becomes a burden; you have to carry it. When you are loved, the body has lost weight. When you are loved and you are in love, you don't feel gravitation has any effect on you. You can dance, you can fly really. In a deeper way the body is no more—but this is in a limited way. The same can happen when you are in love with the total existence.

In love, joy comes to you. It is not pleasure. Remember, joy is not pleasure. Pleasure comes to you through the senses; joy comes to you through being nonsensuous. Pleasures comes to you through the body; joy comes to you when you are not the body. When for a moment the body has disappeared and you are simply consciousness, then joy comes to you. When you are the body, pleasure can happen to you. It is always through the body. Pain is possible, pleasure is possible, through the body. Joy is possible only when you are not the body.

It happens ordinarily also, accidentally also. You are listening to music and suddenly gravitation is lost. You are so absorbed in it, you have forgotten your body. You are filled with music and you have become one with music. There is not a listener to it: the listener and the listened have become one. Only music exists; you are no more. You have expanded. Now you are flowing with musical notes, now there is no limit to you. The notes are dissolving into silence, and you are also dissolving into silence with them. The body is forgotten.

Whenever the body is forgotten, it is tossed aside unknowingly, unconsciously, and joy happens to you. Through tantra and yoga you can do it methodologically. Then it is not an accident; then you are the master of it. Then it is not happening to you; then you have the key in your hands and you can open the door whenever you want. Or you can open the door forever and throw away the key; no need to close the door again.

Joy happens in ordinary life also, but you don't know how it happens. The happening is always when you are not the body—remember this. So whenever you again feel any moment of joy, become aware of whether you are the body in that moment or not. You will not be. Whenever joy is, the body is not. Not that the body disappears—the body remains, but you are not attached to it. You are not attached to it, you are not tethered to it. You have jumped out.

You may have jumped out because of music, you may have jumped out because of a beautiful sunrise, you may have jumped out because a child was laughing, you may have jumped out because you were in love. Whatsoever the cause, but you have jumped out for a moment—out of the body. The body is there, but tossed aside; you are not attached to it. You have taken a flight.

Through this technique, you know that one who is everywhere cannot be miserable; he is joyous, he is joy. So the more you become confined, the more miserable. Expand, push your boundaries away, and whenever you can, leave the body aside. You look in the sky and clouds are floating: move with the clouds, leave the body here on the earth. And the moon is there: move with the moon. Whenever you can forget the body, don't miss the opportunity—go on a journey. And then you will become accustomed to what it means to be out of the body.

And this is only a question of attention. Attachment is a question of attention. If you pay attention to the body, you are attached. If the attention has moved away, you are not attached.

Look, for example: you are playing on the sports grounds; you are playing hockey or volleyball or something else. When you are deep in play, your attention is not on the body. Someone has hit your feet and the blood is flowing—you are not aware. The pain is there, but you are not there. The blood is flowing but you are out of the body. Your consciousness, your attention, may be flying with the ball, may be running with the ball. Your attention is somewhere else. The game finishes: suddenly you come back to the body, and the blood is there and the pain. And you wonder how it happened—when it happened and how it happened and how you were not aware of it.

To be in the body, your attention is needed to be there. So remember it—wherever your attention is, you are there. If your attention is in the clouds, you are there. If your attention is in the flower, you are there. If your attention is in money, you are there. Your attention is your being. And if your attention is nowhere, you are everywhere.

So the whole process of meditation is to be in a state of consciousness where your attention is nowhere, there is no object to it. When there is no object to it, there is no body to you. Your attention creates the body. Your attention is your body. And when attention is nowhere, you are everywhere— joy happens to you. It is not good to say that it happens to you: you *are* it. It cannot leave you now; it is your very being. Freedom is joy; that's why so much hankering after freedom.

---

85 Think of nothing.

The second detachment technique: *Thinking no thing will limited-self unlimit.*

That's what I was saying. If there is no object to your attention, you are nowhere; or, you are everywhere, you are free. You have become freedom. This second sutra says: *Thinking no thing*—or thinking nothing—*will limited-self unlimit.*

If you are not thinking, you are unlimited. Thinking gives you a limit, and there are many types of limits. You are a Hindu—it gives a limit. To be a Hindu is to be attached to a thought, to a system, to a pattern. You are a Christian—then again you are limited. A religious man cannot be a Hindu or a Christian. And if someone is a Hindu or a Christian, he is not religious—impossible— because these are thoughts. A religious man means not thinking thoughts; not limited by any thought, by any system, by any pattern; not limited by the mind—living in the unlimited.

When you have a certain thought, that thought becomes your barrier. It may be a beautiful thought —still it is a barrier. A beautiful prison is still a prison. It may be a golden thought but it makes no difference, it imprisons you all the same.

And whenever you have a thought and you are attached to it, you are always against someone, because barriers cannot exist if you are not against someone. A thought is always a prejudice; it is always for and against.

I have heard about a very religious Christian man who was a poor farmer. He belonged to the Society of Friends, he was a Quaker. Quakers are nonviolent; they believe in love, in friendship. He was coming from the city to his village on his mule-cart, and suddenly, apparently without any cause, the mule stopped and he would not budge. He tried, he persuaded the mule in Christian ways, he persuaded the mule in a very friendly way, a non-violent way. He was a Quaker: he couldn't beat the mule, he couldn't use strong words, he couldn't abuse, scold, but he was filled with anger. But how to beat the mule?

He wanted to beat him, so he said to the mule, "Behave rightly! Because I am a Quaker, I cannot beat you, I cannot scold you, I cannot be violent— but remember, mule, that I can sell you to someone who is not a Christian!"

The Christian has his own world, and the non-Christian is opposite. The Christian cannot conceive that the non-Christian can reach the kingdom of God. A Hindu cannot conceive, a Jaina cannot conceive, that others can enter into that realm of bliss—impossible. Thought creates a limitation, a barrier, a boundary, and all those who are not for are taken to be against. One who is not in agreement with me is against me.

How can you be everywhere? You can be with the Christian; you cannot be with the non-Christian. You can be with the Hindu, but you cannot be with the non-Hindu, with the Mohammedan. Thought is bound to be somewhere against —against someone or something. It cannot be total. Remember: thought cannot be total; only no-thought can be total.

Secondly: thought is always from the mind, it is always a by-product of the mind. It is your attitude, your speculation, your prejudice; it is your reaction, your formulation, your concept, your philosophy, but it is not existence itself. It is something about the existence; it is not existence itself.

A flower is there. You can say something about

it; that is a thought. You can say it is beautiful, you can say it is ugly, you can say it is sacred, but whatsoever you say about the flower is not the flower. The flower exists without your thoughts, and whenever you are thinking about the flower, you are creating a barrier between you and the flower.

The flower doesn't need your thoughts. It exists. Drop your thoughts, and then you can drop yourself into the flower. Whatsoever you say about a rose is meaningless; howsoever meaningful it appears, it is meaningless. What you say is not needed. It is not giving any existence to the flower. It is creating a film between you and the flower; it is creating a limitation. So whenever there is thought, you are debarred; the door is closed to existence.

This sutra says: *Thinking no thing will limited-self unlimit.*

If you don't think, if you simply are, fully alert, aware, but without any clouds of thought, you are unlimited. The body is not the only body—a deeper body is the mind. Body consists of matter; mind also consists of matter—subtle, more refined. Body is the outer layer, mind is the inner layer. And it is easy to be detached from the body. It is more difficult to be detached from the mind, because with the mind you feel you are more yourself.

If someone says that your body looks ill, you don't feel offended. You are not so attached; it is a little away from you. But if someone says your mind seems to be pathological, ill, you feel offended. He has insulted you. With the mind you are nearer. If someone says something about your body you can tolerate it. If someone says something about your mind, it is impossible to tolerate it, because he has hit deeper.

The mind is the inner layer of the body. Mind and body are not two: the outer layer of your body is the body and the inner layer is the mind. Just as if you have a house: you can see the house from the outside, and you can see the house from the inside. From the outside the outer layer of the walls will be seen; from the inside the inner layer.

The mind is your inner layer. It is nearer to you,

but it is still a body. In death your outer body drops, but you carry the inner, subtle layer with you. You are so attached to it that even death cannot separate you from your mind. Mind continues. That's why your past births can be known, because you are still carrying all the minds that you ever had. They are there. If you were a dog once, the dog mind is still with you. If you were a tree once, the tree mind is still with you. If you once were a woman or a man, you carry those minds. All the minds are carried by you. You are so attached to them that you never lose the grip.

In death the outer dissolves, but the inner is carried. It is a very subtle material thing. Really, just vibrations of energy, thought vibrations. You carry them, and according to your thought pattern that you carry, you enter a new body. According to the thought pattern, the desire pattern, the mind, you again create a new body for yourself. The blueprint is in the mind, and the outer layer is again accumulated.

The first sutra is to put aside the body. The second sutra is to put aside the mind, the inner body. Even death cannot separate you—only meditation can separate. That's why meditation is a greater death, it is a deeper surgery—deeper than death itself; that's why so much fear. People go on talking about meditation but they will never do it. They will talk, they can write about it, they can preach about it, but they will never do it. A deep fear exists about meditation, and the fear is of death.

Those who do meditation, they come one day or another to the point where they are scared, thrown back. They come to me and they say, "Now we cannot enter more. It is impossible." A point comes where one feels that one is dying. And that point is of a deeper death than any death, because now the innermost is being separated; the most inner identity is being shattered. One feels one is dying; one feels now one is moving into nonexistence. A deep abyss opens, infinite emptiness opens. One is scared, runs back to cling to the body so that one is not thrown,

because the earth beneath is moving, is being removed. A valley is opening, a nothingness.

So even if they try, people always try superficially; they play with meditation. They are unconsciously aware that if they move deep they will be no more. And that's right, the fear is true—you will not be yourself again. Once you have known that abyss, that *shunya,* the void, you will not be the same again.

You come back, but you are resurrected, a new man. The old has disappeared. You cannot find even a trace of it, of where it has gone. The old was the identity with the mind. Now you cannot be identified with the mind. Now you can use the mind, you can use the body, but they have become instruments; you are above them. Whatsoever you do, you can do, but you are not one with them. This gives freedom. But this can happen only when *thinking no thing,* hmm?

This is very paradoxical—*thinking no thing.* You can think about things, how can you think about no thing? What does this "no thing" mean? And how can you think about it? Whenever you think about something it becomes a thing, it becomes an object, it becomes a thought, and thoughts are things. How can you think no thing? You cannot, but in the very effort—the effort to think no thing—thinking will be lost, thinking will be dissolved.

You may have heard about Zen koans. Zen masters give an absurd puzzle to the seeker to think about—and it is something which cannot be thought. It is given knowingly just to stop thinking. For example, they say to the seeker: "Go and find out what your original face is—the face you had when you were not born. Don't think about this face which you have got; think of the face you had before birth."

How can you think about it? There was no face before birth; the face comes with the birth. The face is part of the body. You have no face; only the body has a face. Close your eyes and you have no face. You know about your face through the mirror. You have not seen it yourself, and you cannot see it, so how can one think about the original face? But one can try; the very effort will help.

The seeker will try and try—and it is impossible. He will come to the master again and again, asking, "Is this the original face?" And before he says it to the master, the master says, "It is wrong. Whatsoever you bring is going to be wrong."

For months together the seeker comes again and again. He finds something, imagines something, and he sees the face—"The original face is like this?" And the master says, "No." And every time this "No, no," and by and by he becomes more and more puzzled. He cannot think. He tries and tries and tries and fails. That failure is the basic thing. One day he comes to a total failure. All thinking stops in that total failure and he comes to realize that the original face cannot be thought. Thinking stops.

And whenever this last time happens to a seeker, when he comes to the master, the master says, "Now there is no need. I see the original face." The eyes have become vacant. The seeker has come not to say something, but just to be near the master. He has not found any answer. There was none. He has come for the first time without the answer. There is no answer to it. He comes silently.

Every time he had come he had some answer. The mind was there, the thought was there—he was limited by that thought. He had found or imagined some face—he was limited by that face. Now he has become original; now there is no limit. Now he has got no face, no idea, no thought. He has come without any mind. This is the state of no-mind.

In this state of no-mind, the limited-self un-limits. The limits are dissolved. Suddenly you are everywhere, suddenly you are everyone. Suddenly you are in the tree and in the stone and in the sky and in the friend and in the enemy—suddenly you are everywhere. The whole existence has become just a mirror—you are everywhere, mirrored. This state is the state of bliss. Now nothing can disturb

you, because nothing exists except you. Now nothing can destroy you; nothing exists except you. Now there is no death, because even in death you are. Now nothing is opposed to you. Alone, you exist.

This aloneness Mahavira has called *kaivalya,* total aloneness. Why alone?—because everything is involved, absorbed, has become you. You can express this state in two ways. You can say, "Only I am. *Aham Brahmasmi*—I am the God, the divine, the total. Everything has come unto me; all the rivers have dissolved into my ocean. Alone I exist. Nothing else exists." Sufi mystics say this, and Mohammedans could never understand why Sufis say such things. A Sufi says, "There is no God. Alone I exist." Or, "I am the God." This is a positive way of saying that now no separation is there. Buddha uses a negative way. He says, "I am no more. Nothing exists."

Both are true, because when everything is included in me, there is no sense in calling myself "I." The I is always opposed to the you; I is always opposed to thou. In relation to you it is meaningful. When there is no you, I becomes meaningless. So Buddha says there is no I, nothing exists. Either everything has become you, or you have become a nonbeing and you dissolve into everything.

Both the expressions are true. Of course, no expression can be totally true, that's why the opposite expression is always also true. Every expression is partial, part; that's why the opposite expression is also true—that too is part of it. Remember this. Whatsoever you express may be true and the opposite also may be true—the very opposite. Really, it is bound to be true, because every expression is only a part.

And there are two types of expression: you can choose the positive or you can choose the negative. If you choose the positive, the negative seems to be untrue. It is not; it is complementary. It is not really opposed to it. So whether you say Brahma, the total, or you say nirvana, nothingness, it is the same. Both connote the same experience, and the experience is this—thinking no thing, you come to know it.

Some basic things have to be understood about this technique. One: thinking, you are separated from existence. Thinking is not a relation, it is not a bridge, it is not a communication—it is a barrier. Nonthinking you are related, bridged; you are in communion. When you are talking to someone, you are not related. The very talk becomes a barrier. The more you talk, the further away you move. If you are with someone in silence, you are related. If the silence is really deep and there are no thoughts in your mind and both the minds are totally silent, you are one.

Two zeros cannot be two. Two zeros become one. If you add two zeros they don't become two, they become a bigger zero—one. And really a zero cannot be bigger—more big, or less big. A zero is simply a zero. You cannot add something to it, you cannot deduct something from it. A zero is whole. Whenever you are silent with someone, you are one. When you are silent with existence, you are one with it.

This technique says be silent with existence and then you will know what God is. There is only one dialogue with existence and that is in silence. If you talk with existence, you miss. Then you are enveloped in your own thoughts.

Try this as an experiment. Try it with anything as an experiment—even with a rock. Be silent with it—take it in your hand and be silent—and there will be a communion. You will move deep into the rock and the rock will move deep into you. Your secrets will be revealed to the rock and the rock will reveal its secrets to you. But you cannot use language with it. The rock doesn't know any language. Because you use language, you cannot be related to it.

And man has lost silence completely. When you are not doing anything, then too you are not silent; the mind goes on doing something or other. Because of this constant inner talk, this continuous inner chattering, you are not related to anything.

Not even to your beloved ones are you related, because this chattering goes on.

You may be sitting with your wife: you are chattering in your own mind; she is chattering in her own mind. Both are chattering. They are far away from each other, poles away. It is as if one is on one star, and the other on another star, and there is infinite space between them. Then they feel that the intimacy is not there, and then they blame each other—"You don't love me."

This is not the question really. Love is not possible. Love is a flower of silence. It flowers only in silence, because it flowers in communion. If you cannot be without thoughts, you cannot be in love—and then to be in prayer is impossible. But even if we do do prayer we chatter. To us, prayer is just chattering with God.

We have become so conditioned to chattering that even if we go to the church or to the temple we continue chattering there also. We chatter with God, we talk with God. This is absolute nonsense. God, existence, cannot understand your language. Existence understands only one language—that is of silence. And silence is neither Sanskrit nor Arabic nor English nor Hindi. Silence is universal; it doesn't belong to anyone.

There are at least four thousand languages on earth, and everyone is enclosed in his own language. If you don't know his language you cannot be related to him. You cannot be related. If I don't understand your language and you don't understand my language, we cannot be related. We are strangers. We cannot penetrate each other, we cannot understand, we cannot love. This is happening only because we don't know a basic universal language—that is silence.

Really only through silence is one related. And if you know the language of silence then you can be related to anything, because rocks are silent, trees are silent, the sky is silent—it is existential. It is not only human, it is existential. Everything knows what silence is; everything exists in silence.

If a rock is there in your hand, the rock is not

chattering within itself, and you are chattering— that's why you cannot be related to the rock. And the rock is open, vulnerable, inviting. The rock will welcome you, but you are chattering and the rock cannot understand the chattering—that becomes the barrier. So even with human beings you cannot be in a deep relationship; there can be no intimacy. Language, words, destroy everything.

Meditation means silence: not thinking about anything. Not thinking at all, just being—open, ready, eager to meet, welcoming, receptive, loving, but not thinking at all. Then infinite love will happen to you, and you will never say that no one loves you. You will never say it, you will never feel it. Now, whatsoever you do, you will say this and you will feel this. You may not even say it. You may pretend that someone loves you, but deep down you know.

Even lovers go on asking each other, "Do you love me?" In so many ways they go on inquiring continuously. Everyone is afraid, uncertain, inse-cure. In many ways they try to find out whether really the lover loves them. And they can never be certain, because the lover can say, "Yes, I love you," but it will not give any guarantee. How can you be at ease? How can you know whether he is deceiving you or not? He can argue, he can con-vince you. He can convince you intellectually, but the heart will not be convinced. So lovers are always in agony. They cannot be convinced of the fact that the other loves. How can you be con-vinced?

Really there is no way to convince through language. And you are asking through language, and while the lover is there you are chattering in the mind, questioning, arguing. You will never be convinced, and you will always feel that you have not been loved, and this becomes the deepest misery. And this is happening not because someone is not loving you; this is happening because you are closed within walls, you are closed within your thoughts. Nothing can penetrate. The thoughts cannot be penetrated unless you drop them. If you drop them the whole existence penetrates you.

This sutra says: *Thinking no thing will limited-self unlimit.*

You will become unlimited. You will become whole. You will become universal, you will be everywhere.

And then you are joy. Now you are nothing but misery. Those who are cunning, they go on deceiv-ing themselves that they are not miserable, or they go on hoping that something will change, some-thing will happen, and they will achieve at the end of life—but you are miserable. You can create faces, deceptions, false faces; you can go on smiling continuously, but deep down you know you are in misery. That is natural. Confined in thoughts you will be in misery. Unconfined, beyond thoughts— alert, conscious, aware, but unclouded by thoughts —you will be joy, you will be bliss.

CHAPTER 58

Go beyond karma

◆

Are not shortcuts against Tao?

Why are we not enlightened?

Are shortcuts a divine possibility?

Can You define "nondoing"?

The first question:

Techniques are shortcuts, revolutions, but are not these against Tao, *swabhav,* nature?

They are. They are against Tao, they are against swabhav. Any effort is against swabhav, Tao; effort as such is against Tao. If you can leave everything to swabhav, Tao, nature, then no technique is needed, because that is the ultimate technique. If you can leave everything to Tao, that is the deepest surrender possible. You are surrendering yourself, your future, your possibilities. You are surrendering time itself, all effort. This means infinite patience, awaiting.

If you can surrender everything to nature then there is no effort, then you don't do anything. You just float. You are in a deep let-go. Things happen to you, but you are not making any effort for them —you are not even seeking them. If they happen, it is okay; if they don't happen, it is okay—you have no choice. Whatsoever happens, happens; you have no expectations and of course, no frustrations.

Life flows by, you flow in it. You have no goal to reach, because with the goal effort enters. You have nowhere to go, because if you have somewhere to go, effort will come in; it is implied. You have nowhere to go, nowhere to reach, no goal, no ideal; nothing is to be achieved—you surrender all.

In this surrendering moment, in this very moment, all will happen to you. Effort will take time; surrender will not take time. Technique will take time; surrender will not take time. That's why I call it the ultimate technique. It is a no-technique. You cannot practice it—you cannot practice surrender. If you practice, it is not surrender. Then you are relying on yourself; then you are not totally helpless; then you are trying to do something— even if it is surrender, you are trying to do it. Then technique will come in, and with technique time enters, future enters.

Surrender is nontemporal; it is beyond time. If you surrender, this very moment you are out of time, and all that can happen will happen. But then you are not searching for it, not seeking it; you are not greedy for it. You have no mind for it at all: whether it happens or not, it is all the same to you.

Tao means surrender—surrender to swabhav, to nature. Then you are not. Tantra and yoga are techniques. Through them you will reach to swabhav, but it will be a long process. Ultimately after every technique you will have to surrender, but with techniques it will come in the end; with Tao, in Tao, it comes in the beginning. If you can surrender right now, no technique is needed, but if you cannot, and if you ask me how to surrender, then a technique is needed. So rarely in millions and millions of men one can surrender without asking how. If you ask "how," you are not the right type who can surrender, because the how means you are asking for a technique.

These techniques are for all those who cannot get rid of this how. These techniques are just to get rid of your basic anxiety about how—how to do it. If you can surrender without asking, then no technique is needed for you. But then you would not have come to me, you could have surrendered any time, because surrender needs no teacher. A teacher can teach only technique.

When you seek, you are seeking technique; every seeking is a seeking for technique. When you go to someone and ask, you are asking for a technique, for a method. Otherwise there is no need to go anywhere. The very search shows that you have a deep need for technique. These techniques are for you.

Not that without technique it cannot happen. It can happen, but it has happened to very few persons. And those few persons are also really not rare: in their past lives they have been struggling with techniques, and they have struggled so much with techniques that now they are fed up, they are bored. A saturation point comes when you have asked again and again, "How? How? How?"—and ultimately the "how" falls. Then you can surrender.

In every way technique is needed. A Krishnamurti can say that no technique is needed—but this is not his first life, and he couldn't have said this in his past life. Even in this very life many techniques were given to him, and he worked on them. You can come to a point through techniques where you can surrender—you can throw all techniques and simply be—but that too is through techniques.

It is against Tao, because you are against Tao. You have to be deconditioned. If you are in Tao then no technique is needed. If you are healthy then no medicine is needed. Every medicine is against health. But you are ill; medicine is needed. This medicine will kill your illness. It cannot give you health, but if the illness is removed, health will happen to you. No medicine can give you health. Basically every medicine is a poison—but you have gathered some poison; you need an antidote. It will balance, and health will be possible.

A technique is not going to give you your divinity, it is not going to give you your nature. It will destroy all that you have gathered around your nature. It will only decondition you. You are conditioned, and right now you cannot take a jump into surrender. If you can take it, it is good—but you cannot take it. Your conditioning will ask, "How?" Then techniques will be helpful.

When one lives in Tao, then no yoga, no tantra, no religion is needed. One is perfectly healthy; no medicine is needed. Every religion is medicinal. When the world lives in total Tao, religions will disappear. No teacher, no Buddha, no Jesus will be needed, because everyone will be a Buddha or a Jesus. But right now, as you are, you need techniques. Those techniques are antidotes.

You have gathered around yourself such a complex mind that whatsoever is said and given to you, you will complicate it. You will make it more complex, you will make it more difficult. If I say to you, "Surrender," you will ask, "How?" If I say, "Use techniques," you will ask, "Techniques? Are not techniques against Tao?" If I say, "No technique is needed; simply surrender and God will happen to you," you will immediately ask, "How?" Your mind!

If I say, "Tao is right here and now: you need not practice anything, you simply take a jump and surrender," you will say, "How? How can I surrender?" If I give you a technique to answer your "how," your mind will say, "But is not a method, a technique, a way, against swabhav, against Tao? If divinity is my nature, then how can it be achieved through a technique? If it is already there, then the technique is futile, useless. Why waste time with the technique?" Look at this mind!

I remember, once it happened that one man, a father of a young girl, asked composer Leopold Godowsky to come to his house and give an audition to his daughter. She was learning piano. Godowsky came to their house; patiently he heard the girl playing. When the girl finished, the father beamed, and he cried in happiness and asked Godowsky, "Isn't she wonderful?"

Godowsky is reported to have said, "She is wonderful. She has an amazing technique. I have never heard anyone play such simple pieces with such great difficulty. She has an amazing technique. Playing such simple pieces with such great difficulty, I have never seen anyone do before!"

This is what goes on happening in your mind. Even a simple thing you will make complicated, you will make difficult for yourself. And this is a way of defense, this is a defense measure, because when you create difficulty you need not do it—because first the problem must be solved and then you can do it.

If I say surrender, you ask how. Unless I answer your "how," how can you surrender? If I give you a technique, your mind immediately creates a new problem: "Why the technique? Swabhav is there, Tao is there, God is within you, so why this endeavor, this effort? Unless this is answered, there is no need to do anything."

Remember, you can go on in this vicious circle continuously for ever and ever. You will have to break it somewhere and come out of it. Be decisive, because only with decision is your humanity born. Only with decision do you become human. Be decisive. If you can surrender, surrender. If you cannot surrender, then don't create philosophical problems; then use some technique.

In both the ways the surrender will happen to you. If you can surrender right now, it is okay. If you cannot surrender, then pass through techniques —that training is needed. It is needed because of you, not because of swabhav, not because of Tao. Tao needs no training. It is needed because of you. And the techniques will destroy you. You will die through the techniques, and the innermost nature will evolve. You have to be shattered completely. If you can shatter it in a jump—surrender. If you cannot, then piecemeal—work on it through techniques.

But remember one thing: your mind can create problems which are tricks—tricks to postpone, to postpone decision. If the mind is not settled, you don't feel guilty. You feel, "What can I do? Unless something is absolute, clear-cut, transparent, what

can I do?" Your mind can create clouds around you, and your mind will not allow you to be transparent ever—unless you decide. With decision clouds disappear. Mind is very diplomatic, mind is political, and it goes on playing politics on you. It is very tricky, cunning.

I have heard, once Mulla Nasruddin came to visit his son and daughter-in-law. He had come for three days, but then he stayed for one week. Then the week passed, and he stayed for one month. Then the young couple started worrying—how to get rid of the old man? So they discussed how to get rid of him, and they hit upon a plan.

The husband said, "Tonight you prepare soup, and I will say that there is too much salt in it, it cannot be eaten, it is impossible to eat. And you have to say that there is not enough salt in it. We will argue and we will start quarreling, and then I will ask my father what his opinion is, what he says. If he agrees with me, then you get mad and tell him to go away. If he agrees with you, I will get sore and I will tell him to go away immediately."

The soup was prepared, and as it was planned, they started quarreling and arguing. And then the climax came. They were just on the verge of hitting each other and Nasruddin was sitting silently watching. And then the son turned towards him and said, "Pa, what do you say? Is there too much salt or not?"

So Nasruddin dipped his spoon in the soup, tasted it, meditated a moment upon the taste, and then said, "It suits me perfectly." He didn't take any side. The whole plan was futile.

Your mind goes on working in this way. It will never take any side, because the moment you take a side, action has to be there. It will not take any side; it will go on arguing. It will never decide anything; it will be always in the middle. Whatsoever is said will be argued, but it will never become a decision. And you can argue ad infinitum; there is no end to it. Only decision will give you action, and only action will become transformation.

If you are really interested in a deep revolution within you, then decide—and don't go on postponing. Don't be too philosophical; that is dangerous. For a seeker it is dangerous. For one who is not seeking really but just passing time, it is good, it is a good game. Philosophy is a good game if you can afford it. But I don't see that anyone can afford it because it is wasting time.

So be decisive. If you can surrender, then surrender. Then there is no "how" to it. If you cannot, then practice some technique, because only then through technique will you come to a point where surrender will happen.

The second question:

In the natural course, after millions of years and lives, one will be enlightened. But we might have already passed through millions of years and lives and yet are not enlightened. Why?

You cannot ask why. You can ask why only if you are doing something. If nature is doing something you cannot ask why; it is up to nature. And nature is not responsible; it is not going to answer you. It is completely silent. And for nature, millions of lives are nothing; for nature it may be just seconds. To you, millions of lives and years is a long history; for nature it is nothing. Nature is not worried, and nature is not interested in you particularly. Nature goes on working—someday it will happen, but you cannot ask why, because nature is silent.

If you are worried about why it has not happened yet, then you have to do something. If worry has entered you, then you have to do something. Only your doing will help you to come to a point where enlightenment can happen. Nature's ways are very patient, slow. There is no hurry, because for nature there is no limit to time. It is eternal. There is no beginning and no end. But man has come to a point: he has become conscious, he has started asking.

A tree never asks—even the bodhi tree under which Buddha became enlightened. The tree will never ask, "Why have I not become enlightened?—because I have also been existing for as many millions of years as you have existed, Gautam. Why?" The tree will never ask. The tree is absolutely natural. The questioning makes man unnatural. The unnatural has entered in you: you have started questioning why—why it has not happened yet.

This questioning is good, because it can lead you to a decisive moment where you can start working upon yourself. And man cannot leave it to nature, because man has become conscious. You cannot leave it to nature now. That's why man has created religions. No animal has any religion, there is no need: they are not asking, they are not in a hurry. In nature everything is unhurried—moving so slowly as if not moving at all; continuously repeating the same pattern, infinitely repeating the same circle.

Man has become conscious. Man has become conscious of time, and the moment you become conscious of time, you are thrown out of eternity. Then you are in a hurry. So as man's consciousness evolves more, he is more hurried, he becomes more and more time conscious. Go to a primitive society: they are not time conscious. The more civilized a society, the more time conscious. A primitive society is nearer nature: unhurried, it moves slowly. Just as nature moves, it moves. The more you become civilized, the more you become conscious of time. Really, time can be the criterion: how civilized a society is can be known by how time conscious it is. Then you are in a hurry, then you cannot wait, then you cannot leave it to nature. You have to take it in your own hands.

And man can take it in his own hands: he can do something and the process can be finished sooner. It can even be finished in a single moment. All that millions of years have not done, have not been able to do, you can do in a single moment. In that single moment you can become so intense that millions of years and millions of lives are traveled simultaneously.

That's possible—and because it is possible you

are worried. Your worry is a symptom you are not making actual that something which is possible—that is the worry, that is the human dilemma. You can do it and you are not doing it—that creates an inner worry, anguish. When you cannot do it the question never arises, there is no worry. The worry shows that it is possible now that you can jump—many lives which are unnecessary you can just bypass—and you are not bypassing.

You have become conscious, and you have come above nature. Consciousness is a new phenomenon. You have come above nature and now you can consciously evolve. Conscious evolution is revolution. You can do something about it. You are not just a victim, not just a puppet. You can take your destiny in your hands. That is possible, and because it is possible and you are not doing anything, it creates inner anxiety. And the more you become aware that this is possible, the more the anxiety will be felt.

A Buddha is very worried; you are not so worried. Buddha was very worried, in deep anguish, suffering. Unless he attained he would live in hell, because he was perfectly aware that something was absolutely possible, was just at hand, just by the corner, and he felt, "Still I am missing it. If I just stretch my hand it will happen—and my hand is paralyzed. Just a step and I will be out of it—and I cannot take that step. I am afraid of taking a jump."

When you are near the goal, and you can feel it and you can see it and still you go on missing, then you feel anguish. When you are very far away and you cannot feel it, you cannot see it, you are not even aware that there is a goal, you are perfectly unaware of any destiny, then there is no anxiety.

Animals are not in anguish. They appear happy—happier then man. What is the reason? Trees are even more happy than animals. They are perfectly unaware of what can happen, of what is possible, of what is just near at hand. They are blissfully unaware. There is no anxiety. They drift. Man becomes anxious, and the greater a man, the more anxiety will be there.

If you simply live, you are living an animal existence. Religious anguish arises the moment you become aware that something is possible—"The seed is there and I have to do something. I have to do something and the seed will sprout. The flowers are not very far away, and I can reap this crop"—but still nothing is happening. A very impotent state is felt.

That was Buddha's condition before he became a buddha. He was just on the verge of committing suicide. You will have to pass through that. And you cannot leave it to nature; you have to do something about it—and you can do. And the goal is not very far.

So don't be depressed if you feel anxiety. If you feel a very intense anguish within you, a suffering, agony, don't feel depressed about it—that's a good sign. That shows you are becoming more and more aware of that which is possible, and now you will never be at ease unless it becomes actual.

Man cannot leave it to nature because man has become conscious. Only a very minor part of his being is conscious, but that changes everything. And unless your total being becomes conscious, you cannot know again the simple happiness of the animal or of the trees. There is only one way to know it now: to become more and more alert, more and more aware, and more and more conscious. You cannot regress. There is no process for going back; no one can go back. You can either remain where you are and suffer, or you have to go forward and go beyond suffering. You cannot go back.

Total unconsciousness is blissful, total consciousness is blissful—and you are in between. A part of you has become conscious, and the major part of you is still unconscious. You are divided. You have become two, you are not one. The integration is lost. Animals are integrated and then saints are integrated. Man is disintegrated: a part remains animal and a part has become saintly. There is a struggle, conflict, and whatsoever you do you can never do with one heart.

So there are two ways. One is just to deceive yourself—that is to become totally unconscious again. You can take drugs, you can take alcohol, you can take intoxicants—you fall back to the animal world. You drug the part that has become conscious; you become totally unconscious. But this is a temporary deception; you will arise again. The effect of the chemical will be lost and your consciousness will become conscious again. The part which you have forcibly suppressed with alcohol or drugs or something else will arise again, and then you will feel more suffering, because then you can compare. You will feel more suffering.

You can go on drugging yourself. There are many methods—not only chemical. There are religious methods. You can use a *japa,* a mantra: you can chant it and create an intoxicating effect. You can do many things which can make you unconscious again, but that is going to be temporary, you will have to come out—and you will come out with a deeper suffering within you, because then you will be able to compare. If in unconsciousness this is possible, what will be possible in total consciousness? You will become more hungry for it, you will feel more starved.

Remember one thing: totality is bliss. If you are unconscious totally then too it is bliss, but you are not aware of it. Animals are happy but they are not aware of their happiness. So it is futile. It is just like when you are asleep you are happy, and whenever you are awake you are unhappy. Totality is bliss.

You can be total in consciousness also. Then there will be bliss and you will be perfectly aware of it. This is possible through *sadhana,* through methods, through practicing techniques which increase your consciousness. You are not enlightened because you have not done anything for it, but you have become aware that you are not enlightened. This has been done by nature; in millions of years nature has made you aware.

You may not be aware of the fact that man has stopped growing as far as body is concerned. We have skeletons that are millions of years old, but there is no visible change; they are similar to our skeletons. So for millions of years there has been no growth in the body, it has remained the same. Even the brain has not grown; it has remained the same. As far as body is concerned, evolution has done whatsoever could have been done. In a sense, man is now responsible for his own growth. And the growth is not going to be of the physical; the growth is going to be of the spiritual.

The skeleton of a buddha and your skeleton are not basically different, but you and Buddha are absolutely different. Evolution is working horizontally; methods, techniques, religions, they work vertically. Your body has stopped: it has come to a point, an omega point. Now there is no further growth for it. Horizontally, evolution has stopped; now a vertical evolution starts. Now, wherever you are, you have to take a jump vertically. That vertical evolution will be of consciousness, not of body. And you are responsible for it.

You cannot ask nature why, but nature can ask you why you are not enlightened yet, because everything is provided now. Your body has all that is needed: you have a buddha's body; exactly whatsoever is needed for the buddha to happen to you, you have got. Only a new arrangement, a new synthesis of all the elements that are given, and the buddha will happen to you. Nature can ask you why you are not enlightened yet, because nature has provided you with everything.

And nature asking you will not be irrelevant, but you asking nature is absurd. You cannot be allowed to ask. Now you are aware and you can do something. All the elements are given to you. The hydrogen is there, the oxygen is there, the electricity is there; you have to just make certain efforts and experiments and the water will happen.

All that is needed for you to be enlightened is with you, but it is scattered. You have to combine it, synthesize it, you have to make a harmony of it, and suddenly the flame will arise which becomes enlightenment. All these techniques are for that. You have got everything; just a know-how is needed, what to do, so that enlightenment happens to you.

The third question:

You say that millions of lives and millions of years of natural evolution can be avoided through reaching total awareness and total freedom. Can it not be argued that karma, with its natural forces of cause and effect, should not be interfered with by any shortcuts, or is it also the way of divinity to bring such a possibility within the reach of the evolving world, the evolving soul?

Everything can be argued, but argument leads nowhere. You can argue, but how is that argument going to help you? You can argue that the natural process of karma should not be interfered with—don't interfere then. But then be happy in your misery—and you are not. You want to interfere. If you can rely on the natural process, it is just wonderful—but then don't make any complaint. Don't ask, "Why is this so?" It is so because of the natural process of karma. You are suffering?—you are suffering because of the natural process of karma, and otherwise is not possible; don't interfere.

This is what the doctrine of fate, of *kismet* is—the doctrine of believing in fate. Then you are not to do anything: whatsoever is happening is happening, and you have to accept it. Then too it becomes a surrender, and you need not do anything. But the ability to accept totally is needed. Really there is no need to interfere—but can you be in such a state where you don't interfere? You are constantly interfering with everything. You cannot leave it to nature. If you can leave it, then nothing else is needed and everything will happen to you. But if you cannot leave it, then interfere. And you can interfere, but the process has to be understood.

Really, meditating is not interfering in the process of karma; rather, it is taking a jump out of it. Exactly it is not interfering; it is taking a jump out of the vicious wheel, out of the vicious circle. The circle will go on, and the process will come to

an end by itself. You cannot put an end to it, but you can be out of it, and once you are out of it, it becomes illusory.

For example, Raman died of cancer. His disciples tried to persuade him to go for treatment. He said, "Okay. If you like it and if it will make you happy, then treat me. But as far as I am concerned it is okay." The doctors were surprised, because his body was suffering, it was in deep pain, but his eyes were without any pain. His body was suffering deeply, but he was not suffering.

The body is part of the karma, it is part of the mechanical circle of cause and effect, but the consciousness can be beyond it, it can transcend it. He was just a witness. He was seeing that the body was suffering, that the body was going to die, but he was a witness. He was not interfering with it, not interfering at all. He was just watching whatsoever was happening, but he was not in the vicious circle, he was not identified, he was not within it then.

Meditation is not an interference. Really, without meditation you are interfering every moment. With meditation you go beyond; you become a watcher on the hill. Deep down in the valley things go on, they continue, but they don't belong to you. You are just an onlooker. It is as if they are happening to somebody else, or as if they are happening in a dream, or in a film on the screen. You are not interfering. You are just not within the drama itself —you have come out. Now you are not an actor, you have become a spectator. This is the only change.

And when you are just a witness, the body will complete immediately whatsoever has to be completed. If you have many karmas for suffering, and now that you have become a witness you are not going to be reborn again, the body will have to suffer in this life all the suffering that would have been in many lives. So it happens many times that an enlightened man has to suffer many bodily ills, because now there is no future birth, no future life. This is going to be the last body, so all the karmas and the whole process has to be completed, finished.

So it happens that if we look at Jesus' life through Eastern eyes, then the crucifixion is a different phenomenon. To the Western mind there is no succession of lives, no rebirth, no reincarnation, so they don't really have a very deep analysis of the crucifixion. They have a myth that Jesus suffered for us, his suffering was a salvation for us. But this is absurd; and this is not true to the facts also, because if Jesus' suffering has become a salvation for you, then why is humanity still suffering? It is suffering more than it ever suffered before.

After Jesus' crucifixion humanity has not entered into the kingdom of God. If he suffered for us, if his crucifixion was a repentance for our guilt and sin, then he is a failure, because the guilt continues, the sin continues, the suffering continues. Then his suffering was in vain, then the crucifixion didn't succeed.

Christianity has simply a myth. But the Eastern analysis of human life has a different attitude. Jesus' crucifixion was all his suffering accumulated through his own karmas. And this was his last life, he would not enter the body again, so the whole suffering had to be crystallized, concentrated, in a single point. That single point became the crucifixion.

He did not suffer for anyone else—no one can suffer for anyone else. He suffered for himself, for his past karmas. No one can make you free, because you are in the bondage because of your karmas, so how can Jesus make you free? He can make himself a slave, he can make himself a free man, he can liberate himself. Through the crucifixion the account of his own karmas closed. He was finished, the chain had come to an end. Cause and effect—they had come to an end. This body would not be born again; he would not enter into another womb. If he was not an enlightened person, then he would have had to suffer all this for many lives. It became concentrated in one point, in one life.

You cannot interfere, and if you interfere you will create more misery for yourself. Don't interfere with karmas, but go beyond, be a witness to them. Take them as a dream, not real; just look at them and be indifferent. Don't get involved. Your body suffers—look at the suffering. Your body is happy —look at the happiness. Don't get identified— that's all that meditation means.

And don't find alibis, don't find excuses. Don't say that this can be argued. You can argue anything, you are free to, but remember that your argument may be suicidal. You can argue against yourself, and you can create an argument which is not going to help you, which is not going to transform you; rather, it is going to become a hindrance. We go on arguing....

Just today one girl came to meet me. She asked me, "Tell me, is there really a God?" She was ready to argue that there is no God. I looked at her face, her eyes. She was tense, filled with argument; she wanted to fight about the point. Really deep down she wanted that there is no God, because if there is God you are in trouble. If there is God then you cannot remain whatsoever you are; then a challenge comes. God is a challenge. It means you cannot be satisfied with yourself; something higher than you is possible. A higher state, an absolute state of consciousness is possible. That's what God means.

So she was ready to argue, and she said, "I am an atheist and I don't believe in God."

I told her, "If there is no God, how can you not believe in him? And God is irrelevant. Your belief and your disbelief, your argument for and your argument against are related to you, not to God. Why are you concerned? If there is no God, why have you traveled so long, and why have you come to me to argue about something which is not? Forget and forgive him. Go to your home, don't waste your time. If he is not, then why are you worried? Why this effort to prove that he is not? This effort shows something about you. You are afraid. If God is, then it is a challenge. If God is not, then you can remain whatsoever you are; there is no challenge to life."

A person who is afraid of challenges, risks, dangers, of changing himself, of mutation, will always deny that there is God. The denial is his mind; the denial shows something about him, not about God.

I told her that God is not a thing which can be proved or disproved. God is not an object about which we can take some opinion for or against. God is a possibility within you. It is not something without; it is a possibility within you. If you travel to that possibility, he becomes real. If you don't travel up to that point, he is unreal. And if you argue against him then there is no point in traveling; you remain the same. And this becomes a vicious circle.

You argue that God is not, and because of it you never travel towards him—because it is an inner travel, an inner journey. You never travel, because how can you travel towards the point which is not? So you remain the same. And when you remain the same you never meet, you never encounter God. You never come to any feeling, to any vibration from him. Then it is proved more for you that he is not. And the more it is proved, the more you are far away, the more you are falling, the more the gap increases.

So it is not a question of whether God is or not, I told her. It is a question of whether you want to grow or not. If you grow, your total growth will be the meeting, your total growth will be the communion, your total growth will be the encounter. I told her one anecdote.

One windy morning, just as the spring was ending, a snail started traveling upwards on a cherry tree. Some sparrows which were just on a neighboring oak started laughing, because it was not the season and there were no cherries on the tree, and this poor snail was making so much effort to reach the top. They laughed at her expense.

Then one sparrow flew down, came near to the snail and said, "Darling, where are you going? There are no cherries yet on the tree."

But the snail never even paused; she continued her upward journey. Without pausing, the snail said, "But they will be there when I reach. They will be there when I reach there. It will take a long time for me to reach to the top, and by that time cherries will be there."

God is not, but he will be there by the time you reach. It is not something which is already there— it is never there. It is a growth. It is your own growth. When you reach to a point where you are totally conscious, God is. But don't argue. Rather than wasting your energy in arguing, use your energy in transforming yourself.

And energy is not much. If you divert your energy into argument you can become a genius in arguing. But then you are wasting it; it is at a great cost, because the same energy can become meditation. You can become a logician: you can make very logical arguments, you can find very convincing proofs or disproofs, but you will remain the same. Your arguments are not going to change you.

Remember one thing: whatsoever changes you is good. Whatsoever gives you growth, expansion, increase in consciousness, is good. Whatsoever makes you static and whatsoever protects your status quo is not good; it is fatal, suicidal.

The last question:

Sometimes I feel in a state of nondoing, very passive, but my awareness of what is happening around me seems less. In fact, I feel detached from things around me. This somehow means false passivity, as I imagine nondoing should be synonymous with increased awareness. Can You please define this state?

Ordinarily we are in a feverish state—active, but feverishly. If you become passive the fever will be lost. If you become passive, nondoing, if you relax within yourself, activity will be lost, fever will be lost, and the intensity that comes through fever will not be there. You will feel a little dull, you will feel as if your awareness is decreasing. It is not decreasing; only the feverish glow is decreasing.

And it is good, so don't be afraid of it, and

don't think that this passivity is not real. This is being said by your mind which needs and wants the feverish activity and the glow that comes through fever. Fever is not awareness, but in fever you can have a very unhealthy awareness, alertness. That is diseased; don't hanker for it. Allow it to go, fall into passivity.

In the beginning it will look like your awareness is decreasing rather than increasing. Allow it to decrease, because whatsoever decreases with passivity was feverish, that's why it decreases. Allow it to decrease. A moment will come when you will gain a balance. In that point of balance there will be no increase and no decrease. That is a healthy point; now the fever has gone.

On that point of balance, whatsoever awareness you have, that is real, that is not feverish. And if you can wait for that moment to come... It is difficult, because in the beginning you feel that you are losing grip, you are becoming really dead; your activity, your alertness, everything has gone—you are relaxing into death. It appears that way because whatsoever you know about life is feverish. It is not really life but just a fever, just a state of tension, just a state of hyperactivity. So in the beginning... And you know only one state—this state of fever. You don't know anything else so how can you compare?

When you become passive, relaxed, you will feel that something is lost. Allow it to be lost. Remain with passivity. A balancing point will come soon when you will be right at the point where there is no fever. You will be simply your own self —not pushed by someone else into activity, not pulled by someone else into activity. Now activity will start happening to you, but it will be spontaneous, it will be natural. You will do something, but you will not be pulled and pushed.

And what is the criterion by which to know whether this activity is not forced on you, is not feverish? This is the point: if the activity is spontaneous you will not feel any tension through it, you will not feel any burden. You will enjoy it. And the

activity will become an end unto itself; there will be no end. This will not be a means to reach somewhere else; it will be just an overflow of your own energy. And this overflow will be here and now; it will not be for something in the future. You will enjoy it.

Whatsoever it is—digging a hole in the garden, or pruning the trees, or just sitting, or walking, or eating—whatsoever you are doing will become absolute in itself, total action. And after it you will not be tired; rather, you will feel refreshed. A feverish activity tires you; it is ill. A natural activity nourishes you; you feel more energetic, more vital after it. You feel more alive after it. It gives you more life.

But in the beginning when you start becoming passive and you fall into nondoing, it is bound to be felt that you are losing awareness. No, you are not losing awareness. You are simply losing a feverish type of mentation, a feverish type of alertness. You will settle into passivity and a natural awareness will happen.

This is the difference between a feverish alertness and natural awareness. This is the difference: in feverish alertness there is a concentration; it excludes everything. You can concentrate on a thing. You are listening to me. If it is a feverish alertness then you listen to me and you are totally unaware of anything else. But if it is a passive awareness, not feverish, but balanced, natural, then if a car passes by, you hear that car also. You are simply aware. You are aware of everything, of whatsoever is happening around you. And this is the beauty of it—that the car passes by and you hear the noise but it is not a disturbance.

If you are feverishly attentive and you hear the car, you will miss listening to me; it will be a disturbance, because you don't know how to be totally, simply aware of everything that is happening. You know only one way: how to be alert of one thing at the cost of everything else. If you move to something else then you lose the contact with the first thing. If you are listening to me in a feverish mind, then anything can disturb you. Because your alertness goes there, then you are cut off from me. It is one-pointed; it is not total. A natural, passive awareness is just total; nothing disturbs it. It is not concentration, it is meditation.

Concentration is always feverish, because you are forcing your energy to one point. Energy by itself flows in all directions. If has no direction in which to move; it simply enjoys flowing all over. We create conflict because we say, "This is good to listen to; that is bad." If you are doing your prayer and a child starts laughing, it is a disturbance—because you cannot conceive of a simple awareness in which the prayer continues and the child goes on laughing and there is no conflict between the two; they both are part of a bigger whole.

Try this: be totally alert, totally aware. Don't concentrate. Every concentration is tiring, you feel tired, because you are forcing energy unnaturally. Simple awareness is inclusive of all. When you are passive and nondoing then everything happens around you. Nothing disturbs you and nothing by-passes you. Everything happens and you know it, you witness it.

A noise comes: it happens to you, it moves within you, then it passes, and you remain as you were. Just as in an empty room, if there was no one here the traffic would go on passing, the noise would come into this room, then it would pass—and the room would remain unaffected, as if nothing had happened. In passive awareness you remain unaffected. Everything goes on happening, just passes you, but never touches you. You remain unscarred. In feverish concentration everything touches you, impresses you.

One more point about this. In the Eastern psychology we have a word, *sanskar*—conditioning. If you are concentrating on something you will be conditioned, you will get a sanskar, you will get impressed by something. If you are simply aware—passively aware, not concentrating, not focusing yourself, just being there—nothing conditions you. Then you don't accumulate any sanskar, you don't accumulate any impressions. You go on remaining virgin, pure, unscarred; nothing touches you. If one can be passively aware, he passes through the world but the world never passes through him.

One Zen monk, Bokuju, used to say, "Go and cross the stream, but don't allow the water to touch you." And there was no bridge over the stream near his monastery.

Many would try, but when they crossed, of course the water would touch them. So one day one monk came and he said, "You give us puzzles. We try to cross that stream; there is no bridge. If there was a bridge, of course we could have crossed the stream and the water would not have touched us. But we have to pass through the stream—the water touches."

So Bokuju said, "I will come and I will cross and you watch." And Bokuju crossed. Of course, water touched his feet, and they said, "Look, the water has touched you!"

Bokuju said, "As far as I know, it has not touched me. I was just a witness. The water was touching my feet, but not me. I was just witnessing."

With passive alertness, with witnessing, you pass through the world. You are in the world, but the world is not in you.

CHAPTER 59

Watch from the hill

◆

T H E S U T R A S

86 *Suppose you contemplate something beyond percep-*
tion, beyond grasping, beyond not being—you.

87 *I am existing. This is mine. This is this. O beloved,*
even in such know illimitably.

Man is Janus-faced—animal and divine both. Animal belongs to his past, divine belongs to his future, and this creates the difficulty. The past has passed, it is no more; just a shadow of it lingers on. And the future is still the future, it has not yet come; it is just a dream, just a possibility. And between these two exists man —the shadow of the past and the dream of the future. He is neither and he is both.

He is both because the past is his—he was animal. He is both because the future is his—he can be divine. And he is not both, because the past is no more and the future is yet to be.

Man exists as a tension between these two: that which was and that which can be. This creates a conflict, a constant struggle to realize, to be something. In a sense, man is not. Man is just a step from the animal to the divine—and a step is nowhere. It was somewhere and it will be somewhere, but right now it is nowhere, just hanging in the air.

So whatsoever man is doing—whatsoever, I say —he is never satisfied in it, never content, because two diametrically opposite existences meet in him. If the animal is satisfied then the divine is in discontent. If the divine is satisfied then the animal is in discontent. A part is always in discontent.

If you move to the animal, in a way you satisfy part of your being, but immediately in that satisfaction dissatisfaction arises, because the opposite part, your future, is just contrary to it. The satisfaction of the animal is the dissatisfaction of the possibility of your future. If you satisfy your divine possibility the animal revolts; it feels hurt. A definite discontent arises within you. You cannot satisfy both, and satisfying one, the other is dissatisfied.

I remember one anecdote. One sports car enthusiast reached the Pearly Gates, and Saint Peter welcomed him. He had come with his Jaguar, and the first thing he asked Saint Peter was this: "Are there beautiful highways in heaven?"

Saint Peter said, "Yes, they have the most beautiful highways, but there is one difficulty—in heaven they don't allow automobiles."

The speed fiend said, "Then it is not for me. Then please arrange for me to be sent to the other place. I would like to go to hell. I cannot leave my Jaguar."

So it was arranged. He reached hell, he came to the gates, and Satan welcomed him and said that he was very happy to see him. He said, "You are just like me; I am also a lover of Jaguars."

The speed fiend said, "Fine, give me the map of your highways."

Satan became sad. He said, "Sir, we don't have any highways down here—that is the hell of it!"

This is the situation of man. Man is Janus-faced, a double being, split in two. If you satisfy one thing, then something becomes frustrating to your other part. If you do otherwise, then the other part is dissatisfied. Something is always lacking. And you cannot satisfy both, because they are diametrically opposite.

And everyone is doing this impossible thing, trying to do this—to have a compromise somewhere so both heaven and hell can meet; so body and soul, the lower and the higher, the past and the future, can somewhere meet and have a compromise. We have been doing that for many lives. It has not happened, and it is not going to happen. The whole effort is absurd, impossible.

These techniques are not concerned with creating a compromise within you. These techniques are to give you a transcendence. These techniques are not to satisfy the divine against the animal. That is impossible. That will create more turmoil within you, more violence, more struggle. These techniques are not to satisfy your animal against the divine. These techniques are just to transcend the duality. They are neither for the animal nor for the divine.

Remember, that is the basic difference between other religions and tantra. Tantra is not a religion, because religion basically means *for* the divine *against* the animal—so every religion is part of the conflict. Tantra is not a struggle technique, it is a transcendence technique. It is not to fight with the animal, it is not for the divine. It is against all duality. It is neither for nor against really—it is simply creating a third force within you, a third center of existence where you are neither animal nor divine. For tantra that third point is *advaita,* that third point is nonduality.

Tantra says you cannot reach the one by fighting through duality. You cannot come to a nondual point by choosing one thing. Choice will not lead you to the one; only a choiceless witnessing.

This is very foundational to tantra, and because of this tantra was never really understood rightly. It has suffered a long, a centuries-old misunderstanding, because the moment tantra says it is not against the animal, you start feeling as if tantra is for the animal. And the moment tantra says it is not for the divine, you then start thinking that tantra is against the divine.

Really, tantra is for a choiceless witnessing. Don't be with the animal, don't be with the divine, and don't create a conflict. Just go back, just go away, just create a gap between you and this duality and become a third force, a witnessing, from where you can see both the animal and the divine.

I told you that the animal is the past and the divine is the future, and past and future are opposed. Tantra is in the present. It is neither past nor future. Just this very moment, don't belong to the past and don't hanker for the future. Don't long for the future and don't be conditioned by the past. Don't allow the past to become a hangover and don't create any projections in the future. Remain true to this very moment, here and now, and you transcend. Then you are neither animal nor divine.

For tantra, to be such is to be God. To be such, in this suchness of the moment, where past is unrelated and future is not created, you are free, you are freedom.

These techniques are not religious in this sense, because religion is always opposed to the animal. Religion creates a conflict. So if you are really religious you will become schizophrenic, you will be split. All religious civilizations are split civilizations. They create neurosis, because they create inner conflict. They divide you into two, and one part of your being becomes the enemy. Then your whole energy is dissipated fighting with yourself.

Tantra is not religious in that sense, because tantra doesn't believe in any conflict, in any violence. And tantra says don't fight with yourself. Just be aware. Don't be aggressive and violent with yourself. Just be a witness, a watcher. In the moment of witnessing you are neither; both the faces disappear. In that moment of witnessing you are not human. You simply are. You exist without any label, you exist without any name. You exist without any category. You are, without being anyone in particular—a simple am-ness, a pure being. These techniques are for that pure being.

Now I will discuss the techniques.

86 Imagine the unimaginable.

The first technique: *Suppose you contemplate something beyond perception, beyond grasping, beyond not being—you.*

Suppose you contemplate something beyond perception—that which cannot be seen, which cannot be perceived. But can you imagine something which cannot be seen? Imagination is always of that which can be seen. How can you imagine something, how can you suppose something which cannot be perceived?

That which you can perceive you can imagine. You cannot even dream something which is not capable of being seen and perceived. That's why even your dreams are shadows of reality. Even your imagination is not pure imagination, because whatsoever you can imagine you have known somehow. You can create new combinations, but all the elements of the combination are known and perceived.

You can imagine a golden mountain flying in the sky like a cloud. You have not perceived such a thing ever, but you have perceived a cloud, you have perceived a mountain, you have perceived gold. These three elements can be combined. Imagination is not original; it is always a combination of something you have perceived.

This technique says: *Suppose you contemplate something beyond perception....*

It is impossible, but that's why it is worth doing, because in the very effort something will happen to you. Not that you will become capable of perceiving —if you try to perceive something which cannot be perceived, all perception will be lost. In the very effort, if you try to see something which you have never seen, all that you have ever seen will disappear.

If you persist in the effort, many images will come to you—you have to discard them, because you know that you have seen this; this can be perceived. You may not have seen it actually as it is,

but even if you can imagine it, it can be perceived. Discard it. Go on discarding. This technique says to persist for that which cannot be perceived.

What will happen? If you go on discarding, it is going to be an arduous effort, because many images will bubble up. Your mind will supply many images, many dreams; many conceptions will come, many symbols. Your mind will create new combinations, but go on discarding unless something happens which cannot be perceived. What is that?

If you go on discarding, nothing will happen to you as an object; only the screen of the mind will be there with no image, with no symbol, with no dream on it, no picture on it. In that moment a metamorphosis happens. When the screen is simply there without any image, you become aware of yourself. You become aware of the perceiver. When there is nothing to be perceived, the whole attention changes. The whole consciousness reflects back. When you have nothing to see, for the first time you become aware of your own self. You start seeing yourself.

This sutra says: *Suppose you contemplate something beyond perception, beyond grasping, beyond not being—you.*

Then you happen to yourself. For the first time you will become aware of the one who has been perceiving, who has been grasping, who has been knowing. But this subject is always hidden in objects. You know certain things but you never know the knower. The knower is lost in knowledge.

I see you, then I see someone else, and this procession goes on. From birth to death I will see this and that and that, and I will go on seeing and seeing. And the seer, the one who was seeing this procession, is forgotten; it is lost in the crowd. The crowd is of objects, and the subject is lost.

This sutra says if you try to *contemplate something beyond perception, beyond grasping*—which you cannot grasp with the mind—*beyond not being...*immediately the mind will say that if there is something which cannot be seen and cannot be grasped, it is not. The mind will immediately react that if something is not seeable, not perceivable, not graspable, then it is not. The mind will say that it doesn't exist. Don't become a victim of the mind.

This sutra says: ...*beyond perception, beyond grasping, beyond not being.* The mind will say that this is nothing, this cannot exist, this is a not-being. The sutra says, don't believe in it. There is something which is being beyond not-being, which exists and which cannot be perceived, which is not graspable: that is you.

You cannot perceive yourself, or can you? Can you imagine any situation in which you can encounter yourself, in which you can know yourself? You can go on using the word 'self-knowledge,' which is absolutely absurd, because you cannot know the self. The self is always the knower. It cannot be reduced to a known, it cannot be reduced to an object.

For example, if you think that you can know the self, then the self that you know will not be your self, but the one who is knowing the self will be the self. You will always remain the knower; you cannot become the known. You cannot put yourself in front of you; you will always recede back. Whatsoever you know cannot be yourself—this means that you cannot know it. You cannot know it the way you know other things.

I cannot see myself the way I see you. Who will see? Because every relationship of knowledge, seeing, perception, means that there are at least two things: the known and the knower. Self-knowledge is not possible in this sense, because there is only one. There the knower and the known are one; the observer and the observed are one. You cannot convert yourself into an object.

So the word 'self-knowledge' is just wrong, but it connotes something, it says something which is true. You can know yourself in a very different sense, in an altogether different sense from how you know other things. When there is nothing to be known, when all objects have disappeared, when all that can be perceived and grasped is no more, when you have discarded all, suddenly you become aware of yourself. And this awareness is not dual: there is no object and no subject. There is simply subjectivity.

This awareness is a different type of knowing. This awareness gives you a different dimension of existence. You are not divided in two. You are aware of yourself. You are not perceiving, you cannot grasp it, and yet it is existential—the most existential.

Try to think in this way. We have energy; that energy goes on moving to objects. Energy cannot be static. Remember it as one of the ultimate laws: energy cannot be static, it is dynamic. It cannot be otherwise. Dynamism is its very nature—energy moves. When I see you, my energy moves towards you. When I perceive you, a circle is made. My energy moves to you, then it comes back to me—a circle is made.

If my energy moves to you and doesn't come back, I will not know you. A circle is needed: the energy must go and then come back to me. With its coming back it brings you to me. I know you. Knowledge means that energy has made a circle. It has moved from the subject to the object, and then it has moved again and come back to the original source. If I go on living in this way—making circles with others—I will never know myself, because my energy is filled with energies of others. It brings those images, it delivers those images to me. This is how you gather knowledge.

This technique says to allow the object to disappear from there. Allow your energy to move in a vacuum, in emptiness. It goes from you, but there is no object to be grasped by it, no object to be perceived by it. It moves and comes back to you through emptiness; there is no object. It brings no knowledge to you. It comes vacant, empty, pure. It brings nothing. It brings only itself. It comes virgin—nothing has entered into it, it remains pure.

This is the whole process of meditation. You are sitting silently, your energy is moving. There is no object with which it can be contaminated, with which it can become entangled, with which it can become impressed, with which it can become one. Then you bring it back to yourself. There is no object, no thought, no image. Energy moves, the movement is pure, and then it comes back to you —virgin. As it left you it comes; it carries nothing. An empty vehicle, it comes to you, it hits you. There is no knowledge carried by it; it is coming only by itself. In that penetration of pure energy you become aware of yourself.

If your energy is bringing something else, then you will become aware of that something. You look at a flower. The energy is bringing the flower to you—the image of the flower, the smell of the flower, the color of the flower. The energy is bringing the flower to you. It is introducing you to the flower. Then you become acquainted with the flower. The energy is covered by the flower. You never become acquainted with the energy, the pure energy which is you. You are moving to the other and coming back to the source.

If there is nothing to impress it, if it comes unconditioned, if it comes as it had gone, if it brings itself, nothing else, you become aware of yourself. This is a pure circle of energy—energy moving not to something else, but within you, creating a circle within you. Then there is no one else, only you moving within yourself. This movement becomes self-knowledge, self-illumination. Basically, all meditation techniques, all of them, are different variations of this.

Suppose you contemplate something
beyond perception, beyond grasping, beyond
not being—you.

If this can happen, then for the first time you will become aware of yourself, of your being, of your existence—the subjectivity.

Knowledge is of two kinds: knowledge of objects, and knowledge of the subjectivity. Knowledge of the known, the knowable, and knowledge of the knower. And a man can know millions and millions of things, he can become acquainted with the whole world, but if he is not aware of the knower he is ignorant. He may be knowledgeable, but he is not wise. He may have collected much information, much knowledge, but the basic thing which makes one a knower is lacking—he is not aware of himself.

In the Upanishads there is a story. Svetketu, a young boy, came back from his master to his home. He had passed all his examinations, and he had passed well. All that the master could give him, he had collected. He had become very egoistic.

When he reached his father's house, the first thing the father asked Svetketu was this: "You seem to be too filled with knowledge, and your knowledge is making you very egoistic—the way you walk, the way you have entered the house. I have only one question to ask you: Have you known that which knows all, have you known that by knowing which everything is known—have you known yourself?"

Svetketu said, "But there was no course for it in the school, and the master never discussed it. I have known everything that can be known. You ask me anything and I will answer you. But what type of question are you raising? It was never discussed."

The father said, "Then you go back, and unless you know that by knowing which everything is known, and without knowing which nothing is known, don't come back. First know yourself."

Svetketu went back. He asked the master, "My father says I cannot be allowed to go back home, I cannot be welcomed there, because he says that in our family we have been brahmins not only by birth. We have been knowers, knowers of Brahma, brahmins, not only by birth but by real authentic knowledge. So he said, 'Unless you become a real brahmin, not by birth, but by knowing the Brahma, by knowing the ultimate, don't enter the house. You are not worthy of us.' So now teach me that."

The teacher said, "All that can be taught I have taught you. That is something which cannot be taught. So you do one thing: you simply be available for it. It cannot be directly taught. You simply be receptive; someday it will happen. You take all the cows of the ashram"—the ashram had many cows, they say four hundred—"you take all the cows to the forest. Remain with the cows; stop thinking, stop verbalizing, just become a cow. Remain with the cows, love them, and be silent as cows are silent. When the cows become one thousand, come back."

So Svetketu went with four hundred cows to the forest. There was no use in thinking, there was no one to talk to. By and by his mind became just like a cow's. He sat silently under the trees, and for many years he had to wait, because only when the cows became one thousand could he come back. By and by language disappeared from his mind. By and by society disappeared from his mind. By and by he became not a human being at all. His eyes became just like cows'.

And the story is very beautiful. The story says he forgot how to count—because if language disappears and verbalizations disappear... He forgot how to count, he forgot when he had to return. The story is beautiful. The cows said, "Svetketu, now we are one thousand. Now let us go back to the master's house. He must be waiting."

Svetketu came back, and the master said to the other disciples, "Count the cows."

The cows were counted and the disciples said, "Yes, there are one thousand cows."

And the master is reported to have said, "Not one thousand, one thousand and one—that's Svetketu."

He was standing amidst the cows, silent, just being there, with no thought, with no mind—just like a cow—pure, simple, innocent. And the master said, "You need not enter. Now go back to your father's house. You have known; it has happened to you. Why have you come again to me? It has happened to you."

It happens: when there is no object in the mind to know, the knower happens to you. When the mind is not filled by thoughts, when there is not a single ripple, when there is not a single wave, you are there alone. There is nothing other than you. Obviously you become aware of your self; for the first time you become filled by yourself. A self-illumination happens.

This sutra is one of the foundational ones. Try it. It is arduous, because the habit of thinking, the habit of clinging to objects, to that which can be perceived and that which can be grasped, is so deep-rooted, so ingrained, that it will take time and a very persistent effort not to be involved in objects, not to be involved in thoughts, but to just become a witness and discard them and say, "No, not this, not this."

The whole technique of the Upanishads is condensed in two words: *neti, neti*—not this, not this. Whatsoever comes to the mind, say, "Not this." Go on saying and discarding and throwing all the furniture out. The room has to be empty, totally empty. When emptiness is there, then that happens. If something else is there you go on being impressed by it, and you cannot know yourself. Your innocence is lost in objects. A thought-ridden mind is moving outwards. You cannot be related to yourself.

87 Feel "I am."

The second technique: *I am existing. This is mine. This is this. O beloved, even in such know illimitably.*

I am existing. You never enter deeply into this feeling: *I am existing.* You are existing, but you never dig deep into this phenomenon. Shiva says: *I am existing. This is mine. This is this. O beloved, even in such know illimitably.*

I will tell you one Zen anecdote. Three friends were walking along a road. Evening was just falling and the sun was setting when they became aware of a monk standing on a nearby hill. They started talking about the monk, wondering what he was doing there. One of them said, "He must be waiting for his friends. He must have gone for a walk from his hermitage and his friends are left behind, so he is waiting for them to come."

The other denied that and said, "This is not right, because if a person waits for someone, sometimes he will look backwards. But he is not looking backwards at all. So my assumption is this—that he is not waiting for anyone. Rather, he must have lost his cow. Evening is coming near, and the sun is setting, and soon it will be dark, so he is looking for his cow. He is standing there on the hilltop, and looking for where the cow is in the forest."

The third one said, "This cannot be right, because he is standing so silently, not moving at all, and it seems that he is not looking at all; his eyes are closed. He must be in prayer. He is not looking for any lost cow or waiting for some friends who have been left behind."

They couldn't decide. They argued and argued and then they said, "We must go to the top of the hill and ask the man himself what he is doing."

So they reached the monk. The first one said, "Are you waiting for your friends who are left behind to come?"

The monk opened his eyes and said, "I am not waiting for anyone. And I have neither friends nor enemies to wait for." He closed his eyes again.

The other one said, "Then I must be right. Are you looking for your cow which is lost in the forest?"

He said, "No, I am not looking for anyone— for any cow or anyone. I am not interested in anything except myself."

So the third one said, "Then certainly, definitely, you are doing some prayer or some meditation."

The monk opened his eyes and said, "I am not doing anything at all. I am just being here. I am just being here, not doing anything at all. I am just being here."

This is what Buddhists say meditation is. If you do something, it is not meditation—you have moved far away. If you pray, it is not meditation— you have started chattering. If you use some word, it is not prayer, it is not meditation—the mind has entered in. That man said the right thing. He said, "I am just being here, not doing anything."

This sutra says this: *I am existing*. Go deep into this feeling. Just sitting, go deep into this feeling— "I am existing, I am." Feel it, don't think it, because you can say it in the mind—"I am"—and it is futile. Your head is your undoing. Don't go on repeating in the head: "I am, I am existing." It is futile, it is useless. You miss the point.

Feel it deep down in your bones. Feel it all over your body. Feel it as a total unit, not in the head. Just feel it—"I am." Don't use the words 'I am'. Because I am relating to you, I am using the words 'I am'. And Shiva was relating to Parvati, so he had to use the words 'I am existing'. Don't. Don't go on repeating. This is not a mantra, you are not to repeat "I am existing, I am existing." If you repeat this you will fall asleep, you will become self-hypnotized.

If you go on repeating a certain thing, you become autohypnotized. First you get bored, then you feel sleepy, and then your awareness is lost. You will come back from it very much refreshed, just like after a deep sleep. It is good for health, but it is not meditation. If you are suffering from insomnia you can use chanting, a mantra. It is as good as any tranquilizer, or even better. You can go on repeating a certain word: repeating constantly in a monotonous tone you will fall asleep.

Anything that creates monotony will give you deep sleep. So psychoanalysts and psychologists go on telling people who suffer from insomnia to just listen to the tick-tock of the clock. Go on listening to it and you will fall asleep, because the tick-tock becomes a lullaby.

The child in the mother's womb sleeps continuously for nine months, and the heart of the mother goes on...tick-tock. That becomes a conditioning, a deep conditioning—the continuous repetition of the heart. That's why whenever someone takes you near his heart, you feel good. Tick-tock—you feel sleepy, relaxed. Anything that gives monotony gives relaxation; you can fall asleep.

In a village you can sleep more deeply than in a city, because a village is monotonous. The city is not monotonous. Every moment something new is happening; the traffic noises go on changing. In a village everything is monotonous, the same. Really, in a village there is no news, nothing happens; everything moves in a circle. So villagers sleep deeply, because life around them is monotonous. In a city, sleep is difficult, because life around you is very sensational; everything changes.

You can use any mantra: Rama, Rama, aum, aum—anything. You can use Jesus Christ; you can use Ave Maria. You can use any word and monotonously chant it, and it will give you deep sleep. You can even do this: Raman Maharshi used to give the technique "Who am I?" and people started using it as a mantra. They would sit with closed eyes and they would go on repeating: "Who am I? Who am I? Who am I?" It had become a mantra. That was not the purpose.

So don't make it a mantra, and sitting, don't say, "I am existing." There is no need. Everyone knows, and you know already that you are existing; there is no need, it is futile. Feel it—"I am existing." Feeling is a different thing, totally different. Thinking is a trick to escape from feeling. It is not only different, it is a deception.

What do I mean when I say to feel "I am existing"? I am sitting in this chair. If I start feeling "I am existing," I will become aware of many things: the pressure on the chair, the touch of the velvet, the air passing through the room, the noise touching my body, the blood circulating silently, the heart, the breathing that goes on continuously, and a subtle vibrating feeling of the body. Because the body is a dynamism, it is not a static thing, you are vibrating. Continuously there is a subtle trembling and while you are alive it will continue. The trembling is there.

You will become aware of all these multidimensional things. And the more you become aware of the many things that are happening.... If right now you become aware of whatsoever is happening within you and without, this is what is meant by "I am existing." If you become aware in this way, thinking will stop, because when you feel you are existing it is such a total phenomenon that thinking cannot continue.

In the beginning you will feel thoughts floating. By and by, the more you get rooted in existence, the more and more you settle down in the feeling of being; the thoughts will be far away, you will feel a distance—as if those thoughts are not now happening to you, but they are happening to someone else, very very far away. There is a distance. And then, when you are really rooted, grounded in the being, mind will disappear. You will be there with not a single word, not a single mental image.

Why does this happen?—because mind is a particular activity for relating with others. If I am to relate with you I will have to use my mind, language, words. It is a social phenomenon; it is a group activity. So even if you are talking while alone, you are not alone—you are talking to someone. Even when you are alone, when you are talking you are talking to someone; you are not alone. How can you talk alone? Someone is present in the mind and you are talking to him.

I was reading the autobiography of a professor of philosophy. He relates that one day he was going to take his daughter, who was five years old, to school, and after leaving her at the school he was going to go to the university to deliver his lecture. So he was preparing his lecture on the way, and he forgot all about his daughter who was sitting just by his side in the car, and he started lecturing out loud. The girl listened for a few moments and then she asked, "Daddy, are you talking with me or without me?"

Even when you are talking it is never without, it is always with—with someone. He may not be present, but to you he is present; for your mind he is there. All thinking is a dialogue. Thinking as such is a dialogue, it is a social activity. That's why if a child is brought up without any society, he will not know any language. He will not be able to verbalize. It is society which gives you language; without society there is no language. Language is a social phenomenon.

When you get grounded within yourself, there is no society, there is no one. You alone exist. Mind disappears. You are not relating to anyone, not even in imagination, so mind disappears. You are there without the mind, and this is what meditation is—being without the mind. Being perfectly alert and conscious, not unconscious, feeling existence in its totality, in its multidimensionality—but the mind has suddenly disappeared.

And with the mind many things disappear. With the mind, your name; with the mind, your form; with the mind, that you are a Hindu or a Mohammedan or a Parsi; with the mind, that you are good or bad; with the mind, that you are a saint or a sinner; with the mind, that you are ugly or beautiful—everything disappears. All that is labeled on you suddenly is not there. You are in your pristine purity. In your total innocence you are there; in your virginity—grounded, not floating, rooted in that which is.

With the mind you can move into the past. With the mind you can move into the future. Without mind you cannot move into the past or into the future. Without mind you are here and now—just this moment is all eternity. Nothing exists except this moment. Bliss happens. You need not go on any search. Rooted in the moment, rooted in the being, you are blissful. And this bliss is not something which is happening really to you —you are it.

I am existing. Try it. And you can do it anywhere. Just riding in a bus, or traveling in a train, or just sitting, or lying down on your bed, try to feel existence as it is; don't think about it. Suddenly you will become aware that you have not known many things which are continuously happening to you. You have not felt your body. You have your

hand, but you have not ever felt it—what it says, and what it continuously goes on informing you: how it feels.

Sometimes it is heavy and sad, sometimes it is happy and light. Sometimes everything flows in it, sometimes everything is dead. Sometimes you feel it alive, dancing, sometimes as if there is no life in it —frozen, dead, hanging on you, but not alive.

When you start feeling your being, you will come to know the moods of your hands, of your eyes, of your nose, of your body. It is a big phenomenon; there are subtle nuances. The body goes on telling you and you are not there to hear it. And existence all around you goes on penetrating you in subtle ways, in many ways, in different ways, but you are not aware. You are not there to receive it, to welcome it.

When you start feeling existence, the whole world becomes alive to you in a totally new way you have not known. Then you pass through the same street and the street is not the same, because now you are grounded in existence. You meet the same friends but they are not the same, because you are different. You come back to your house and the wife you have lived with for years is not the same.

Now you are aware of your own being, you become aware of the other's being. When the wife becomes angry, you can enjoy even her anger, because now you can feel what is happening. And if you can feel it, anger may not look like anger; it may become love. If you can feel it deep down, then anger shows that she still loves you; otherwise she would not be angry, she would not bother. She still waits for you the whole day. She is angry because she loves you. She is not indifferent.

Remember, anger or hate are not the real opposites of love—indifference is the real opposite. When someone is indifferent to you, love is lost. If someone is not even ready to be angry with you, then everything is lost. But ordinarily if your wife is angry you react more violently, you become aggressive. You cannot understand the symbolic meaning of it. You are not grounded in yourself. You have not really known your own anger; that's why you cannot understand others' anger.

If you know your own anger, if you can feel it in its total mood, then you know others' anger also. You are angry only when you love someone, otherwise there is no need. Through anger the wife is saying that she still loves you, she is not indifferent to you. She has been waiting, waiting, and now the whole waiting has become anger.

She may not say it directly, because the language of feeling is not direct. And that has become a big problem today—because you cannot understand the language of feeling, because you don't know your own feelings. You are not grounded in your own being. You can understand only words, you cannot understand feelings. Feelings have their own way of expression, and they are more basic, more real.

Once you get acquainted with your own existence, you will become aware of others' existence also. And everyone is so mysterious, and everyone is such a deep abyss to be known—an infinite possibility of being penetrated and known. And everyone is waiting that someone should penetrate, go deep, and feel his or her heart. But because you have not known your own heart, you cannot know anyone else's. The nearest heart remains unknown, so how can you know others' hearts?

You move as a zombie, and you move in a crowd of zombies. Everyone is fast asleep. You have only this much alertness: that you pass through fast-asleep people and without any accident you come to your home, that's all. This much alertness you have got. This is the minimum which is possible to man, that's why you are so bored, so dull. Life is just a long heaviness, and deep down everyone is waiting for death, in order to be delivered from life. Death seems to be the only hope.

Why is this happening? Life can be infinite bliss. Why is this so boring? You are not grounded in it. You are uprooted, uprooted and living at the minimum. And life really happens when you live at the maximum.

This sutra will give you a maximum of existence. Thought can give you only a minimum; feeling can give you the maximum. Through mind there is no way to existence; through heart is the only way.

I am existing. Feel it through the heart. And feel this existence is mine. *This is mine. This is this.* This is very beautiful. *I am existing.* Feel it, be grounded in it; then know *this is mine*—this existence, this overflowing being is mine.

You go on saying that this house is mine, this furniture is mine. You go on talking about your possessions, and you never know what you really possess. You possess total being. You possess the deepest possibility, the centermost core of existence in you. Shiva says: *I am existing.* Feel this. *This is mine.*

This too is not to be made a thought; remember that continuously. Feel it—this is mine, this existence—and then you will feel gratitude. How can you thank God? Your thankfulness is superficial, formal. And look what a misery...even with God we are formal. How can you be grateful? You have not known anything to be grateful for.

If you can feel yourself rooted in existence, merged in it, overflowing with it, and allow even dancing with it, then you will feel, "This is mine. This existence belongs to me. This whole mysterious universe belongs to me. This whole existence has been existing for me. It has created me. I am a flower of it."

This consciousness that has happened to you is the greatest flower that has happened to the universe. And for millions and millions of years this earth was preparing for you to exist.

This is mine. This is this. To feel, "This is what life is, *this is this*—this suchness. I was unnecessarily worried. I was unnecessarily a beggar, unnecessarily thinking in terms of begging. I am the master."

When you are rooted, you are one with the whole, and the existence exists for you. You are not a beggar; you become an emperor suddenly. *This is this.*

O beloved, even in such know illimitably.

And while feeling this, don't create a limit to it. Feel it illimitably. Don't create a boundary to it. There is none, it ends nowhere. The world begins nowhere; the world ends nowhere. Existence has no beginning and no end. You also don't have any beginning; you also don't have any end.

Beginning and end are because of the mind — mind has a beginning and mind has an end. Go backwards, travel backwards into your life: there comes a moment where everything stops — there is a beginning. You can remember back to when you were three years of age, or, at the most, two years of age — that is rare — but then memory stops. You can travel backwards to when you were two years of age. What does it mean? And you cannot remember anything previous to that, previous to that age of two years. Suddenly there is a blank, you don't know anything.

Do you remember anything about your birth? Do you know anything about the nine months in your mother's womb? You were, but the mind was not there. Mind started around the age of two; that's why you can remember back to that age. Then there is no mind, memory stops. Mind has a beginning, mind has an end, but you are beginningless.

If in deep meditation, in such meditation you can come to feel existence; then there is no-mind — a beginningless, endless flow of energy, of cosmic force, an infinite ocean around you, and you are just a wave in it. The wave has a beginning and an end — the ocean has none. And once you know that you are not the wave but the ocean, all misery has disappeared.

What is deep down in your misery? Deep down there is death. You are afraid of some end which is going to be there. It is absolutely certain; nothing is so certain as death — the fear, the trembling. Whatsoever you do, you are helpless. Nothing can be done — death is going to be there. And that goes on and on inside in the conscious and unconscious mind. Sometimes it erupts in the conscious — you become afraid of death. You push it down, and then it continues in the unconscious. Every moment you are afraid of death, of the end.

Mind is going to die, you are not going to die — but you don't know yourself. You know something which is just a created thing: it has a beginning, it is going to have an end. That which begins must end. If you can find within your being something which never begins, which simply is, which cannot end, then the fear of death disappears. And when the fear of death disappears, love flows through you, not before it.

How can you love when there is going to be death? You can cling to someone, but you cannot love. You can use someone, but you cannot love. You can exploit someone, but you cannot love.

Love is not possible if fear is there. Fear is the poison. Love cannot flower with fear deep inside. Everyone is going to die. Everyone is standing in a queue waiting for his time. How can you love? Everything seems nonsense. Love appears nonsense if death is there, because death will destroy everything. Even love is not eternal. Whatsoever you do for your beloved, for your lover, you cannot do anything because you cannot avoid death — it is just waiting behind everything.

You can forget it, you can create a façade, and you can go on believing that it is not going to be there, but your belief is just superficial — deep down you know it is going to be there. And if death is there, then life is meaningless. You can create artificial meanings, but they won't help much. Temporarily, for some moments, they can help, and again the reality erupts and the meaning is lost. You can just deceive yourself continuously, that's all — unless you come to know something which is beginningless and endless, which is beyond death.

Once you come to know it, then love is possible, because then there is no death. Love is possible. Buddha loves you, Jesus loves you, but that love is absolutely unknown to you. That love has come because fear has disappeared. Your love is just a mechanism to avoid fear. So whenever you love, you feel fearless. Someone gives you strength.

And this is a mutual phenomenon: you give strength to someone and someone gives strength to you. Both are weak, and both are seeking someone, and then two weak persons meet and they help each other to be strong—this is just wonderful! How does it happen? It is just a make-believe. You feel that someone is there behind you, with you, but you know no one can be with you in death. And if someone cannot be with you in death, how can he or she be with you in life? Then it is just postponing, just avoiding death. And because you are afraid, you need someone to make you fearless.

It is said, somewhere Emerson has written, that even the greatest warrior is a coward before his wife. Even a Napoleon is a coward, because the wife knows that he needs her strength, he needs her in order to be himself. He depends on her. When he comes back from the war, from the fighting, he is trembling, afraid. He rests in her, he relaxes in her. She consoles him; he becomes just like a child. Every husband is a child before the wife. And the wife?—

she depends on the husband. She lives through him. She cannot live without him; he is her life.

This is a mutual deception. Both are afraid—death is there. They both try to love each other and forget death. Lovers become, or appear to be, fearless. Lovers even sometimes can face death very fearlessly, but that is just appearance.

Our love is part of fear—just to escape from it. Real love happens when there is no fear—when death has disappeared, when you know you never begin and you are never going to end. Don't think it. You can think it, because of the fear. You can think, "Yes, I know I am not going to end, there is no death, the soul is immortal." You can think because of fear—that will not help.

If you move deep in meditation it will happen. Fear will disappear, because you know yourself endlessly. You go on spreading endlessly—back into the past, forward into the future, and this very moment, this present moment, in the depth of it you are there. You simply are—you never begin, you are never going to end.

Feel this illimitably—infinitely.

CHAPTER 60

Liberate yourself – from yourself

◆

Q U E S T I O N S

Are not freedom and surrender contradictory?

Is not this that, Brahma?

Does the desire for divinity have to be transcended?

How to get rid of fear?

What is this sound of water flowing?

The first question:

You say that religion is total freedom or *moksha*, and You also stress the importance of surrender in religion. But are not freedom and surrender contradictory terms?

hey appear contradictory but they are not. And they appear so because of the language; existentially they are not. Try to understand two things. First: you cannot be free remaining as you are, because as you are is your bondage. Your ego is the bondage. You can be free only when this ego point disappears—this ego point is the bondage.

When there is no ego, you become one with existence, and only that oneness can be freedom. While you exist separately, this separation is false. Really you are not separate, you cannot be; you are part of existence—and not a mechanical part, but an organic part. You cannot exist for a single moment separated from existence. You breathe it every moment; it breathes you every moment. You live in a cosmic whole.

Your ego gives you a false feeling of separate existence. Because of that false feeling, you start fighting existence. When you fight you are in bondage. When you fight you are bound to be defeated, because the part cannot win against the whole. And because of this fight with the whole, you feel in bondage, everywhere limited. Wherever you move, a wall comes. That wall is nowhere in existence—it moves with your ego, it is part of your separate feeling. Then you struggle against existence. In that struggle you will be defeated constantly; in that defeat you feel bondage, limitation.

By surrender it is meant that you surrender the ego, you surrender the separating wall, you become one. That is reality, so whatsoever you are surrendering is just a dream, a concept, a false notion. You are not surrendering reality; you are just surrendering a false attitude. The moment you surrender this false attitude you become one with existence. Then there is no conflict.

And if there is no conflict you have no limitation; nowhere there comes a bondage, a boundary. You are not separate. You cannot be defeated, because there is no one to be defeated. You cannot die, because there is no one to die. You cannot be in misery, because there is no one to be in misery. The moment you surrender the ego, the whole nonsense is surrendered—misery, bondage, *dukkha*, hell—everything is surrendered. You become one with existence. This oneness is freedom.

Separation is bondage. Oneness is freedom. Not that you become free, remember this—you are no more. So it is not that you become free—you are no more. Really, when you are not, freedom is. How to express it is a problem. When you are not, freedom is. Buddha is reported to have said, "You are not going to be in bliss. When you are not, the bliss is. You are not going to be liberated. You are going to be liberated from yourself."

So freedom is not freedom of the ego; freedom

is freedom *from* the ego. And if you can understand this—that freedom is freedom from the ego—then surrender and freedom become the same, then they mean the same. But if you take the ego as the standpoint from which to think, then the ego will say, "Why surrender?—because if you surrender, then you cannot be free. Then you become a slave. When you surrender, you become a slave."

But really, you are not surrendering to someone. This is the second point to be understood: you are not surrendering to someone; you are simply surrendering. There is no one who will take your surrender. If there is someone and you surrender to him, then it is a sort of slavery. Really, there is not even a God to whom you are surrendering. And when we talk about a God, that is just to find you something to help you to surrender.

In Patanjali's *Yoga Sutras,* God is talked about just to help you to surrender. There is no God. Patanjali says there is no God, but it will be difficult for you to surrender to no one; it will be difficult for you to simply surrender. To help surrender, God is talked about. So God is just a method. This is rare, very scientific—God is just a method to help you surrender. There is no one who is going to take your surrender. If there is someone and you surrender, then it is a slavery, a bondage. This is a very subtle and deep point: there is no God as a person; God is just a way, a method, a technique.

Patanjali relates many techniques. One of them is *ishwara pranidhan*—the idea of God. There are many methods to reach surrender; one method is the idea of God. That will help your mind to surrender, because if I say, "Surrender," you will ask, "To whom?" If I say, "Simply surrender," it will be difficult for you to conceive. Try to understand in a different way. If I say to you, "Simply love," you will ask, "Whom? What do you mean by 'simply love'? If there is no one to be loved, how to love?" If I say, "Pray," then you will ask, "To whom? Worship whom?" Your mind cannot conceive of nonduality. It will ask, it will raise a question, "To whom?"

Just to help your mind, so that the mind's question is satisfied, Patanjali says that God is just a way, a technique. Worship, love, surrender—to whom? Patanjali says, "To God." Because if you surrender, then you will come to know that there is no God—or you yourself are that to which you have surrendered. But this will happen when you have surrendered. God is just a trick.

It is said that even to surrender to a God who is nowhere seen, who is invisible, is difficult, so scriptures say, "Surrender to the guru, to the master." The master is visible and a person, so then the question becomes relevant—if you surrender to a master then it is a slavery, because a person is there and you are surrendering to him. But then too you will have to understand again a very subtle point—even more subtle than the notion of God. A master is a master only when he is not. If he is, then he is not a master. A master becomes a master only when he is not. He has achieved nonbeing; there is no one.

If someone is sitting here in this chair, then there is no master; then it is going to become a slavery. But if there is no one sitting in this chair, a nonbeing, one who is not centered anywhere, one who has surrendered—not to anyone, but simply surrendered and achieved nonbeing, has become a nonperson—who is simply there, not concentrated in an ego, diffused, not concentrated anywhere, then he can become a master. So when you are surrendering to a master, again you are surrendering to nobody.

This is a deep question for you. When you are surrendering, if you can understand that this is simply surrendering, not a surrender—surrendering, not a surrender… A surrender is to someone. A surrendering is something on your part. So the basic thing is surrendering—the act, not the object. The object should not be important, but the one who is surrendering is important. The object is just an excuse—just an excuse.

If you can understand, then there is no need to surrender to anyone—you can simply surrender.

Then there is no need to love someone—you can simply love. You are significant, not the object. If the object is significant, you will create a bondage out of it. So even a God who is not will become a bondage; even a master who is not will become a bondage. But that bondage is created by you; it is a misunderstanding. Otherwise surrendering is freedom. They are not contradictory.

The second question:

While "this is this" also includes "this is that," and "that is Brahma," how is it that the sutra emphasizes only "this is this"?

For a very particular reason—because tantra, deep down, is interested only in the here and now. "This is this" means that which is here and now. "That" goes a little further away.

Secondly, for tantra there is no division between this and that. Tantra is nondualistic—this is the world, and that is Brahma; this is the mundane, the material, and that is consciousness, the spiritual— for tantra there is no distinction like this. "This" is all, "that" is included in it. This very world is divine.

And tantra makes no distinction and no categorization of higher and lower: "this" means the lower, and "that" means the higher; "this" means that which you can see and touch and know, and "that" means the invisible that you cannot see and cannot touch, you can only infer. For tantra there is no distinction of higher and lower, of visible and invisible, of matter and mind, of life and death, of world and Brahma—no distinction.

Tantra says, "This is this" and "that" is included in it. But the emphasis on *this* is beautiful. It says here and now, whatsoever is, this is all. And everything is in it; nothing is excluded. The near, the intimate, the ordinary, is all.

It is a very well-known saying of Zen mysticism that if you can become just ordinary, you have become extraordinary. Only the person who is at ease with his ordinariness is extraordinary. Because everyone hankers to be extraordinary, so the desire to be extraordinary is very ordinary. Everyone— you cannot find a person who is not trying to be extraordinary in some way, so the desire, the lust to be extraordinary, is a part, a basic part of the ordinary mind. Zen masters say, "So to be ordinary is the most extraordinary thing in the world. To be just ordinary is rare. Very rarely it happens that someone is simply ordinary."

One Japanese emperor was in search of a master, so he went from one teacher to another, but no one could satisfy him. Because one old man had said that the real master would be most ordinary, he went on searching, but he couldn't find an ordinary man. He came back to the old man who was just on his dying bed, and he said, "You have put me to great trouble. The way you defined the master—that he will be simple, ordinary—has become a problem for me. I have been searching all over the country, and no one satisfies me. So give me some clue how to find the master."

The dying man said, "You have been searching in wrong places. You have been searching in wrong places! You have been going to persons who are in some way extraordinary, and then you try to find the ordinary. Move in the ordinary world. And really you are still trying to find the extraordinary. Now you define him as ordinary, but you are still searching for the extra-ordinary. Now the definition has changed. Now you define him as the most ordinary, but the rare, the exceptional. You are still on this search. Don't do that, and the moment you are ready and not searching in this way, the master will come to you."

The next morning while he was sitting, he tried to understand what the old man had said, and he felt that he was right. The desire left him. A beggar appeared—and he was the master. And he had known that beggar his whole life. He was always coming, that beggar was coming daily to the palace, so the emperor asked the beggar, "How did it happen that I couldn't recognize you before?"

The beggar said, "Because you were searching

for the extraordinary. I was here, but you were searching there. You missed me continuously."

Tantra says "this" not "that," particularly in this technique. There are techniques in which "that" is discussed, but "this" is most tantric—this, here and now, the most intimate. Your wife, your husband—this—your friend, the beggar, may be the master. But you are not looking at this; you are looking at that, there, somewhere in the clouds. You cannot even conceive that near you can be that quality of being—you cannot conceive. Because you think you already know the near, so you search for it far away. You already feel that you know "this," so now the only thing to be found is "that."

This is not true. You don't know "this," you don't know the near. The near is as unknown as the faraway. Have a look around you. You are not acquainted with anybody, you don't have any knowledge of anybody. Do you know the tree you pass every day? Do you know your friend with whom you have lived your whole life? Or do you know yourself, who is the nearest? Do you know your body, the breath that comes and goes continuously? Do you know it? Nothing is known. Even "this" is not known, so why hanker after "that"?

This technique says, if "this" is known, "that" will be known automatically, because that is implied in this. The faraway is hidden in the near, in the intimate. But the human mind hankers for the faraway. This is an escape. It is an escape to think of the faraway, because then you can go on thinking forever, and you can go on postponing living—because life is "this." If you think about it and if you contemplate about it, you will have to change yourself.

I am reminded of one anecdote. Once it happened, a Zen master was appointed as a preacher in a temple. No one knew that he was a Zen master. The congregation gathered and the first sermon was delivered. Everyone was thrilled; it was just beautiful. No one had heard such a thing before. The next day an even greater crowd came to the temple, but the master repeated the same sermon. So they got

bored—"What type of man is he?"

Then on the third day they came again, not in so great a number, but the master repeated the same sermon again. So many left just in the middle; only very few were left, and those few were there only to ask, "Have you got only one sermon? And are you going to deliver it every day?" One spokesman blurted out and asked the priest, "What type of preaching is this? Thrice we have heard you, and you go on repeating exactly the same thing, in exactly the same words. Don't you have any other lectures, any other sermons?"

The priest said, "I have quite a few, but you have not done anything about the first one. Unless you do something about the first one, I am not going to deliver the second. It is unnecessary."

The crowd stopped coming. No one would come near the temple, because the moment anyone would come, the Zen priest would start the first sermon. It is said that people stopped passing that way, that temple—"That priest is there, and if you happen to be there he will give you the same sermon again."

He must have been a very deep knower of the human mind. The human mind wants to think but never wants to do anything—action is dangerous. Thinking is good, because you go on being the same. If you think about the faraway, the distant, there is no need to change yourself. The Brahma, the absolute, cannot change you, but the neighbor, the friend, the wife, the husband—if you look at them, you will have to change yourself. And it is a trick not to look at them.

You look at the that to forget the this—and this is life, and that is simply a dream. You can think about God, because that thinking is impotent; it is not going to do anything. You will continue thinking about God and you will remain the same. This is a trick to remain the same. If you think about your wife, if you think about your child, if you penetrate deep in the intimate near, you cannot remain the same—action will come out of it.

Tantra says, "Don't go far away. He is here, this very moment, just near you. Be open, and look at the this, and the that will take care of itself."

The third question:

You have said that tantra teaches man to transcend both his craving for his animalistic past, and also his craving for the divine. Does it mean that divinity is part of the world, and that too has to be transcended? And what is it that goes beyond both?

You will have to understand many things. First: the nature of desire. Divinity is not what you call it. The God that you talk about is not the God of reality; it is the God of your desire. So it is not a question of whether the divine is part of the world, that is not the question. The real question is, can you desire the divine without making him part of the world?

Look at it in this way. It has been said again and again that unless you leave desiring, you cannot attain to him, the ultimate. You cannot attain to the divine if you don't leave desiring. Leave desiring and you can attain to him. You have heard it many times, but I wonder whether you understand it or not. More or less, you will be misunderstanding it. Hearing this, you start desiring the divine—and that is to miss the whole point.

If you leave desiring, the divine will happen to you. Then you start desiring the divine, so your divine will be part of the world. That which can be desired is the world. This is how I define it: that which can be desired is the world. So the divine cannot be desired, and if you desire it, it has become part of the world.

When desiring stops, the divine happens. When you are not desiring anything, the divine is there—then the whole world is divine. You will not find the divine somewhere in contradiction, in opposition to the world—contrary to the world. When you are not desiring, everything is divine; when you are desiring, everything is the world. Your desiring creates the world: whatsoever you desire becomes the world. This is not the world that you see—the trees and the sky and the sea and the rivers and the earth and the stars. This is not the world—that

which you desire is the world.

A flower is there in the garden. The moment you pass the tree, and you look at the flower, and the smell of the flower comes to you, look within. If you are not desiring that flower, if there is not even a slight urge to possess it, not even a slight ripple of desire to have it, that flower becomes divine. You will have the divine face through it. But if the desire is there to possess it, or a jealousy arises about the owner of the tree, you have created a world; the divine has disappeared. It is your desire that changes the quality of existence; your desire makes it the world. When you are nondesiring, the whole world becomes divine.

Now I will read this question again.

You have said that tantra teaches man to transcend both his craving for his animalistic past, and also his craving for the divine.

Tantra teaches only to transcend craving. It is irrelevant *what* you crave—*that* you crave is the point. You can go on changing the objects. You crave money, you crave power, you crave prestige—you crave for the world. Then you change. You get fed up with it, you are bored. Or you have attained whatsoever you craved, and now you are not fulfilled; you feel frustrated. You start a new craving.

Now you crave the divine. You crave moksha, nirvana, liberation—now you crave God. The object has changed; you have not changed—your craving remains the same. It was running after prestige and power and money. Now it is running after divine power. It is running after the ultimate, moksha, the absolute freedom, but the craving is there.

Ordinarily, religious people go on changing their objects of desire. Desire remains the same, unchanged. And it is not the objects which create the problem; it is the desire, the craving, which creates the problem. Tantra says it is futile to go on changing objects. It is wasting time and life and energy. Changing objects won't help—drop craving. Don't crave. Don't crave for freedom, because craving is bondage. Don't crave for the divine, because craving is the world. Don't crave for the inner, because craving is the outer. So it is not a question of transcending this craving or that— simply drop craving. Don't crave, don't desire. Just be yourself.

When you don't desire, what happens? When you don't crave, what happens? You are non-moving; all movement ceases. You are not in a hurry to reach anywhere. You are not serious. There is no hope and there is no frustration. You don't expect anything; nothing can frustrate you. There is no desire; you cannot be a failure. Of course, there is not going to be any success either.

When you are not craving, not desiring, what happens? You are simply left alone, moving nowhere. There is no goal, because craving creates the goal. There is no future, because craving creates the future. There is no time, because craving needs time to move. Time stops. Future drops. And when there is no craving, mind drops, because mind is nothing but craving, and because of that craving you have to plan and think and dream and project.

When there is no craving, everything drops. You are simply in your purity. You exist without moving anywhere; inside, all ripples disappear. The ocean remains, but the waves are not there. This is what divineness is for tantra.

So look at it in this way: craving is the barrier. Don't think of the object; otherwise you will be deceived by yourself. You will change one object for another, and then time will be wasted. Again you will get frustrated, and then you will again change the object. You can go on changing objects infinitely, unless you realize that it is not the object which creates the problem, it is your craving. But craving is subtle and the object is gross. The object can be seen, and craving can be seen only when you go deep down and meditate upon it; otherwise, craving is not seen.

You can marry a woman or a man with great dreams and hope, and the greater the dreams, the greater the hope, the greater will be the frustration. An ordinary arranged marriage cannot be such a failure as a love-marriage is bound to be, because with an ordinary arranged marriage there is not much hope, there is not much dreaming. It is businesslike; there is no romance, no poetry. There is no peak to it; you are traveling on plain ground. So arranged marriages never fail. They cannot fail, because there is no point. How can you fail in an arranged marriage? You were never on a height, so you cannot fall. Love-marriages fail. Only love-marriages can fail, because with a great poetry, with a great dreaming force, they come up. They touch heights, on the waves you rise high, and then you will have to fall down.

So old countries, those who have knowledge, experience, they have come to settle for arranged marriages. They don't talk about love-marriages. In India they never talk about love-marriages. They have also tried in the past, and then they felt that a love-marriage is going to be a failure. Because you expect too much, you will be frustrated, and the proportion of frustration will be the same. Whatsoever you desire and dream gives you expectations —they cannot be fulfilled.

You marry a woman; if it is a love-marriage, you expect much. Then you get frustrated. The moment you get frustrated, immediately you start thinking about another woman. So if you say to your wife, "I am not interested in any other woman," and she feels you have become indifferent to her, you cannot convince her—it is impossible, it is unnatural. The moment you become indifferent to your wife, the wife knows instinctively that you have become interested in someone else.

This is how mind functions. You become aware of the woman that you have married, and you feel the frustration is coming because of her—"This was not a right choice."

This is ordinary logic. "This was not a right choice. This woman is not for me. I have chosen a wrong partner, so the conflict has arisen." Now you will try to find another partner.

You can go on that way ad infinitum. You may marry all the women on the earth, and still you will be thinking in the same way—that "This woman is not right for me." And the subtle craving which is creating all trouble is not seen. It is subtle. The woman is seen; the craving is not seen. It is not the woman or the man who is frustrating you; it is your craving, your desire, which is frustrating you.

If you can come to understand this, you have become wise. If you go on changing objects, you are ignorant. If you can come to feel yourself and the craving which is creating the whole thing, you have become wise. Then you don't go on changing one object for another; you simply drop the very effort to possess, to desire, to crave.

The moment this craving is not there, the whole world becomes divine. It has always been so, only your eyes were not open to see. Your eyes were filled with craving. Eyes filled with craving, the divine appears as the world. Open eyes, unfilled, unclouded by craving, the world appears as the divine.

The world and the divine are not two things, not two existences, but two ways of looking at the same thing, two approaches to the same thing, two outlooks, two types of perception. One perception clouded with craving, another perception unclouded with craving. If you can look unclouded, and your eyes are not filled with tears of frustration and dreams of hope, there is nothing like the world; only the divine exists—existence is divine. This is what tantra means. And when tantra says transcend both, tantra is not concerned with either this or that—tantra is concerned only with transcendence, so there is no craving.

And what is it that goes beyond both? That cannot be said, because the moment anything is said about it, it comes within the two. Whatsoever can be said about God will be false, just because it is said.

Language is dualistic. There is no nondual language—there cannot be. Language is meaningful only because of dualism. I say light; immediately in your mind bubbles up the word "darkness" or "black." I say day, and immediately in your mind comes "night." I say love, and just behind it is hidden "hate." If I say light and there is no darkness, how will you define it?

We can only define words because of their opposite terms. I say light, and if you ask me what light is, I say that which is not darkness. If someone asks you what mind is, you say that which is not body. If someone asks what body is, you have to say that which is not mind. All terms are circular, so basically meaningless, because neither do you know anything about the mind, nor do you know anything about the body. When I ask about the mind, you define it with the body, and the body is undefined. When I ask you about the body, you define it with the mind, which is itself undefined.

This is good as a game. Language is good as a game—language *is* a game. But we never feel that the whole thing is absurd, circular; and nothing is defined, so how can you define anything? When I ask about the mind, you bring in the body—and the body is undefined. With an undefined term, you define mind. And then when I ask, "What do you mean by body?" you have to define it with the mind. This is absurd—but there is no other way.

Language exists through the opposite, so language is dualistic. It cannot be otherwise. So nothing can be said about the nondual experience. Whatsoever is said will be wrong. It can be indicated, symbols can be used for it, but silence is the best. That which can be said about it is silence. Everything else can be defined, talked about—not the ultimate. You can know it, taste it, you can be it, but nothing can be said about it. Only negatively we can say something, but only negatively. We cannot say what that is; we can only say what that is not.

The whole mystic tradition is simply using negative terms for it. If you ask what that ultimate is, they will say, "That ultimate is not this, not that. It is neither life nor death. It is neither light nor darkness. It is neither near nor far. It is neither I nor you." They will speak in this way—but this makes no sense.

Drop craving and you come to know it face to face. And the experience is so deep and individual, nonverbal, nonlinguistic, that even when you come to know it, you cannot say anything about it. You will become silent. Or at the most you can say this that I am saying; you can say, "Nothing can be said about it."

Then what is the point of talking so much? Then why do I go on saying something to you if nothing can be said? Just to bring you to that point where nothing can be said. Just to push you to that abyss where you can take a jump out of language. Up to that point, language can be helpful. Up to the point when you take the jump, language can be helpful, but the moment you have taken the jump, it is silence, it is beyond language.

So I can push you to the very end of the world through language—to the very end of the world—but not a single inch into the divine through language. But this pushing you up to the very end will be helpful, because then you can see with your own eyes that there is this blissful abyss beyond. And then that beyond will call you by itself; then the beyond will attract you; then the beyond will become a magnet, a pull. It is impossible then for you to come back, to retreat. The abyss is so enchanting—the abyss of silence—that before you know, you will have taken a jump.

That's why I go on talking, knowing well that all that I am saying will not help you to know it. But it will help you to take a jump. It is methodological. It will look contradictory, paradoxical, if I say that all language that I am using or that the mystics have ever used, is to bring you to the temple of silence—to force you into silence, to call you unto silence. It looks paradoxical. Then why use language? I can use silence also, but then you will not understand.

When I have to talk to madmen, I have to use a mad language. It is because of you I am using language. It is not that anything can be expressed by it; only your inner chattering can be destroyed by it. It is just as if you have a thorn in your foot—

another thorn can pull it out. The other one is also a thorn. Your mind is filled with words, with thorns. What I am trying to do is to pull those words out of you. What I am using are also words. You are filled with poison. What I am giving you is again a dose of poison, just an antidote—it is also a poison. But a thorn can pull out another thorn; then they can both be thrown.

When I have talked to you to the point where you are ready to be silent, throw all that I have said to you; it is useless, it is even dangerous to carry it. When you have come to realize that language is useless, dangerous, that inner verbalization is the only barrier, and when you are ready to be silent, then remember well—don't carry whatsoever I have said to you. Because the truth cannot be said, and all that can be said cannot be true. Be unburdened of it.

The last thing Zarathustra said to his disciples is very beautiful. He had taught them, he had given them glimpses, he had stirred their souls, he had challenged them to the ultimate adventure. The last thing he said to them was, "Now I am leaving you. Now beware of Zarathustra."

So they asked, "What are you saying? Beware of Zarathustra? You are our teacher, our master, our only hope."

And Zarathustra said, "All that I have said to you, now beware of it. Don't cling to me, otherwise I will become a bondage to you."

When one thorn has pulled out your thorn, throw the other one also with it. When I have prepared you to move into silence, then beware of me. Then whatsoever I have said has to be thrown; it is rubbish, of no use. It has utility only up to the point before you are ready to take a jump into silence. Nothing can be said about that which transcends both. Only this much can be said—and this is too much really. If you can understand, this is enough to indicate towards it.

I am saying this—that if your mind becomes totally vacant of words, you will know it. When you are not burdened with thoughts, you will realize it, because it is already there. It is not something which is going to happen; it has already happened within you. You are just an expression of it. But you are so much engrossed, involved, with thoughts, with clouds, that you miss the key. You are too concentrated on the clouds; you have forgotten the sky. Allow the clouds to disperse, and the sky has always been there just waiting for you. The beyond is waiting for you. Just drop the duality and it is there.

The fourth question:

You have said that one who is in fear cannot love, nor can he reach godhood. But how is one to get rid of his fear according to tantra?

Why do you want to get rid of fear? Or have you become afraid of fear? If you have become afraid of fear, this is a new fear. This is how mind goes on creating the same pattern again and again. I say, "Don't desire and then you will reach the divine." So you ask, "Really? If we don't desire, then will we reach the divine?" You have started desiring the divine.

I say to you, "If there is fear, love cannot be," so you become afraid of fear. You ask, "How can one get rid of fear?" This is again a fear, and more dangerous than the first one, because the first one was natural; the second one is unnatural. And it is so subtle that you are not aware of what you are asking—how to get rid of fear?

The question is not of getting rid of anything; the question is only of understanding. Understand fear, what it is, and don't try to get rid of it, because the moment you start trying to get rid of anything, you are not ready to understand it—because the mind which thinks to get rid of it is already closed. It is not open to understand, it is not sympathetic. It cannot contemplate quietly; it has already decided. Now the fear has become the evil, the sin, so get rid of it.

Don't try to get rid of anything. Try to understand what fear is. And if you have fear, then accept it. It is there. Don't try to hide it. Don't try to create the opposite. If you have fear, then you have fear. Accept it as part of your being. If you can accept it, it has disappeared already. Through acceptance, fear disappears; through denial, fear increases.

You come to a point where you know that you are afraid, and you come to understand, "Because of this fear, love cannot happen to me. So okay, what can I do? The fear is there, so only one thing will happen—I will not pretend love, or I will say to my beloved or my lover that it is because of fear that I am clinging to you. Deep down I am afraid. I will become frank about it; I will not deceive anyone, nor myself. I will not pretend that this is love. I will say this is simply fear. Because of fear, I cling to you. Because of fear, I go to the temple, or to the church, and pray. Because of fear, I remember God. But then I know that this is not prayer, this is not love, this is only fear. I am fear, so whatsoever I do, it is there. I will accept this truth."

A miracle happens when you accept a truth. The very acceptance changes you. When you know that there is fear in your being and you cannot do anything about it, what can you do? All that you can do is pretend, and pretensions can go to the very extreme, to the other extreme.

A very fearful man can become a very brave man. He can create an armor around him. He can become a daredevil, just to show that he is not afraid, just to show others that he is not afraid. And if he can go into danger, he can deceive himself that he is not afraid. But even the bravest man is afraid. His whole bravery is just around him; deep down he trembles. Not to be aware of it, he takes a jump into danger. He becomes engaged with the danger so that he is not aware of the fear—but the fear is there.

You can create the opposite, but this is not going to change anything. You can pretend that you are not afraid—that again makes no change. The only transformation that can happen is that you become simply aware that "I am fear. My whole being is trembling, and whatsoever I do is because of the fear." You have become true to yourself.

Then you are not afraid of fear. It is there, a part of you; nothing can be done about it. You have accepted it. Now you don't pretend, now you don't deceive anyone, nor yourself. The truth is there, and you are not afraid of it. The fear starts disappearing, because a person who is not afraid to accept his fear has become fearless—that is the deepest fearlessness that is possible. He has not created the opposite, so there is no duality in him. He has accepted the fact. He has become humble before it. He doesn't know what to do—no one knows—and nothing can be done, but he has stopped pretending; he has stopped using masks, faces. He has become authentic in his fear.

This authenticity, and this fearlessness to accept the truth, changes you. And when you don't pretend, don't create a false love, don't create a deception around you, don't become a pseudo person, you have become authentic. In this authenticity, love arises; fear disappears, love arises. This is the inner alchemy of how love arises.

Now you can love, now you can have compassion, sympathy. Now you don't depend on anyone, because there is no need. You have accepted the truth. There is no need to depend on anyone; there is no need to possess and be possessed. There is no hankering for the other. You accept yourself—through this acceptance, love arises. It fills your being. You are not afraid of fear, you are not trying to get rid of it. It simply disappears when accepted.

Accept your authentic being and you will be transformed. Remember: the ability to accept, a total acceptance, is the most secret key of tantra. Don't reject anything. Through rejection you will be crippled. Accept everything—whatsoever it is. Don't condemn it, and don't try to get rid of it.

There are many things implied in it. If you try to get rid of it, you will have to cut your being into departments, fragments, parts. You will be crippled. When you throw one thing, something else is also thrown with it—the other part of it—and you become crippled. Then you are not total. And you cannot be happy unless you are total and whole. To

be whole is to be holy. To be in fragments is to be ill and diseased.

So I will say, try to understand fear. Existence has given it to you. It must have some deep meaning, and it must have some hidden treasure, so don't throw it. Nothing is given without any meaning. Nothing exists within you which cannot be used in a higher symphony, in a higher synthesis.

All that exists in you, whether you understand it or not, can become a step. Don't think of it as a hindrance; allow it to become a step. You can take it that it is hindering the path—it is not hindering. If you can ride above it, if you can use it, stand on it, a new view of the path will be revealed to you on a higher level. You will be able to look deep into the possibility, into the future, into the potentiality.

Fear is there for certain purposes. Try to understand this. One: if there is no fear, you will become too egoistic, and there will be no going back. If there is no fear, as you are you will never try to merge into existence, into the cosmos. Really, if there is no fear you will not be able to survive at all. So it is doing something for you. Whatsoever you are, it is playing a role in it.

But if you try to hide it, destroy it, create the opposite of it, you will be divided and you will become fragmentary, disintegrated. Accept it and use it. And the moment you know that you have accepted it, it disappears. Just try to think: if you accept your fear, where is it?

One man came to me and he said, "I am very much afraid of death." He had cancer, and death was very near; any day it could happen. And he could not postpone it. He knew it was going to happen. Within months it would be there, or even within weeks.

He was really physically, literally, trembling, and he said, "Just give me one thing: how can I get rid of this fear of death? Give me some mantra, or something which can protect me and give me courage to face death. I don't want to die trembling in fear." The man said, "I have been to many saints. Many things they have given—they were very kind. Someone has given me a mantra, someone has given me some sacred ashes, someone has given me his picture, someone has given something else, but nothing helps. Everything is in vain. Now I have come to you as the last resort. Now I will not go to anyone anymore. Give me something."

So I told him, "Still you are not aware. Why are you asking for something?—just to get rid of fear? Nothing will help. I cannot give you anything; otherwise, as others have proved failures, I will also prove a failure. And they gave you something because they don't know what they are doing. I can say only one thing to you: Accept it. Tremble if trembling is there—what to do? Death is there, and you feel a trembling, so tremble. Don't reject it, don't suppress it. Don't try to be brave. There is no need. Death is there. It is natural. Be afraid totally."

He said, "What are you saying? You have not given me anything. Rather, on the contrary, you say to accept."

I said, "Yes, you accept. You just go and die peacefully with total acceptance."

After three or four days he came again, and said, "It works. I couldn't sleep for so many days, but for these four days I slept deeply, because it is right, you are right." He said to me, "You are right. Fear is there, death is there, nothing can be done. All the mantras are just hocus-pocus; nothing can be done."

No doctor can help, no saint can help. Death is there, a fact, and you are trembling. It is just natural. A storm comes and the whole tree trembles. It never goes to any saint to ask how not to tremble when a storm is passing by. It never goes for a mantra to change it, to protect it. It trembles. It is natural; it is so.

And the man said, "But a miracle has happened. Now I am not so afraid." If you accept, fear starts disappearing. If you reject, resist, fight, you give energy to fear. That man died peacefully, unafraid, fearless, because he could accept fear. Accept fear and it disappears.

The last question:

By the use of techniques similar to the second technique You discussed yesterday, I hear some sounds like the flowing of a river or a stream. May I know what that sound is? If I have understood rightly, there should be no thoughts or sound, and there should be complete silence. Then what is this sound?

In the beginning, before silence happens to you, sound will happen. So this is a good sign. Words, language, verbalization, disappear; the second layer is of sound. But don't fight with it; enjoy it. It will become musical, beautiful. You will be filled by its music, and you will become more alive through it.

When mind disappears, a natural inner sound appears. Allow it to happen. Meditate on it. Don't fight with it; just be a witness to it—it will deepen. And if you don't fight with it and don't create any struggle, it will disappear by itself, and when it disappears you will fall into silence. Words—sound—silence. Words are human, sounds are natural, silence is cosmic.

So this is a good sign. This is what is called *nada,* the inner sound. Hear it, enjoy it, be a witness to it. It will disappear. And don't be disturbed and feel that it should not be there. If you say it should not be there, or if you hurry to get rid of it in any way, you will come to the first layer again—to the words. Remember this. If you fight with this second layer of sound, you have started thinking about it and words have entered. If you say anything about this sound, you have lost the second, deeper layer, and you are thrown back again to the first. You have come to the mind.

Don't say anything, don't think about it. Don't even say that this is sound. Just listen to it. Don't create any word around it. Don't give it any name or form. Let it be as it is. Allow it to flow, and you be a witness. The stream flows, and you are sitting on the bank, just a witness—not even knowing the name of the stream, not knowing where it is going, not knowing from where it is coming.

Just sit nearby the sound, and sooner or later it will disappear, and when it disappears there will be silence. This is a good sign. You have touched a second layer. But if you try to think about it, you will lose it; you will be thrown back to the first. If you don't think about it and can enjoy in witnessing, you will go deeper to the third layer.

CHAPTER 61

Techniques to become one with the whole

◆

88 *Each thing is perceived through knowing. The self shines in space through knowing. Perceive one being as knower and known.*

89 *Beloved, at this moment let mind, knowing, breath, form, be included.*

I have heard one anecdote. In a Conservative Party rally, Lord Mancroft was invited to speak. He came right on time, reached the rostrum and said to the public—he was looking a little flustered—he said, "Forgive me for shortening my speech a little, but the fact is that my house is on fire." And that fact is everybody's fact. Your house is also on fire, but you don't even seem a little flustered. Everybody's house is on fire, but you are not aware—not aware of death, not aware that your life is just passing through your hands.

Every moment you are dying, every moment you are losing an opportunity which cannot be regained. The time that is lost is lost; nothing can be done to regain it, and your life becomes shorter and shorter every moment.

This is what I mean when I say that your house is also on fire. But you don't seem even a little flustered, you don't even seem to be worried about it. You are not aware of the fact that the house is on fire. The fact is there, but your attention is not there. And everybody thinks that there is enough time to do something. There is not enough time, because whatsoever has to be done is so much that the time is never enough.

Once it happened that the devil was waiting for years and years and nobody was coming to hell. He was waiting to welcome people, but the earth was running so well and people were so good that no one was coming to hell. Of course he became very worried. He called an emergency council. His greatest disciples gathered together to discuss the situation. Hell was passing through a great crisis and this could not be tolerated. Something had to be done. So he asked for advice: "What should we do?"

One disciple suggested, "I would go to the earth and I would talk to people and try to convince them that there is no God and religions are false, and whatsoever the Bible, the Koran and the Vedas say is nonsense."

The devil said, "This won't do, because we have been doing this since the very beginning and it has not influenced people very much. Through such teaching you can convince only those who are already convinced. So it is of no use; it is not of much use."

Then the second disciple, subtler than the first, said, "I will go and teach people and try to convince people that whatsoever the Bible, the Koran and the Vedas say is right. There is heaven, there is God, but there is no devil and no hell, so don't be afraid. And if we can make them less afraid, they will not bother about religion at all, because all religion is based on fear."

The devil said, "Your proposal is a little better. You may be able to, you may succeed in convincing a minority, but the majority will not listen to you. They are not as much afraid of hell as they are greedy for heaven. Even if you convince them that there is no hell, they will still want to enter into heaven, and they will try to be good for that. So this also won't do much."

Then the third disciple, the subtlest of them all,

said, "I have an idea. Give me a chance to try it. I will go and say that whatsoever religion says is absolutely true—there is God and there is devil and there is heaven and there is hell—but there is no hurry."

And the devil said, "Right! You have the right system. You go!"

And it is said that since then there has never been a crisis in hell. Rather, they are worried about overpopulation.

This is how our minds are functioning: we always think there is no hurry. These techniques we are talking about will be of no use if your mind thinks there is no hurry. Then you can go on postponing and death will come first. That day will not come when you think there is a hurry, when you think that now the moment has come. You can go on postponing. This is what we have been doing with our lives.

You have to be decisive to do something. You are in a crisis—the house is on fire. Life is always on fire because death is always there hidden behind it; any moment and you may not be anymore. And you cannot argue with death. You cannot do anything. When death happens, it happens. Time is very short. Even if you live for seventy years or for a hundred years, it is very short. What you have to do with yourself to transform, to mutate, to become a new being, is such a great work. Don't go on postponing.

Unless you feel it as an emergency, a deep crisis, you will not do anything. Unless religion becomes a very critical process for you, and you feel that unless something is done to transform you, your whole life is just wasted.... If you feel this very keenly and deeply and honestly, only then will these techniques be of any help. Because you can understand them—but understanding is of no use unless you do something about it. Really, unless you do something about it, you have not understood them, because understanding must become action. If it is not becoming action then it is only acquaintance, not understanding.

Try to understand this distinction. Acquaintance is not understanding. Acquaintance will not force you to actions. It will not force you to any change. It will not force you to do something about it. You will gather it in the mind; it will become information. You will become more knowledgeable. But at death everything stops. You go on collecting many things, never doing anything about them. They become just a burden on you.

Understanding means action. When you understand a thing, immediately you start working on it, because if it is right and you feel it is right, you have to do something about it. Otherwise everything remains borrowed, and borrowed knowledge cannot become understanding. You can forget that it is borrowed—you would like to forget that it is borrowed, because to feel that it is borrowed means that your ego is hurt. So you go on forgetting that it is borrowed. By and by you start feeling that it is your own. That is very dangerous.

I have heard an anecdote. The congregation of a church was very bored by the minister. A point came when the members of the church said directly to the minister, "Now you have to leave."

The minister said, "Give me one more chance, only one chance, and if then you say so, I will leave."

So next Sunday the whole town gathered in the church to see what that minister was going to do now that only one chance was left to him. They never suspected, they never imagined, that such a beautiful sermon was going to be delivered on that day. They had never heard such a thing.

Surprised, delighted, they enjoyed it, and when the sermon was finished they gathered around the minister and they said, "You need not leave. You remain here. We have never heard such a thing before—never in our lives. Be here and remain here, and of course, with an increase in your stipend."

But then one man, a very prominent member of the congregation, asked, "Tell me one thing only. When you started your lecture you raised your left hand with two fingers raised, and when you closed your lecture you raised your right hand, again with two fingers raised. So what is the meaning of this symbol?"

The minister said, "The meaning is easy. Those fingers are symbolic of quotation marks. That sermon was not mine — it was borrowed."

Always remember those quotation marks. It is very good to forget them, you feel good, but all that you know is within quotation marks; it is not your own. And you can drop those quotation marks only when something has become your own experience.

These techniques are to change knowledge into experience. These techniques are to change acquaintance into understanding. That which belongs to a Buddha or to a Krishna or to a Christ, through these techniques can belong to you — that can become your own. And unless it becomes your own, no truth is true. It may be a grand lie, a beautiful lie, but no truth is true unless it becomes your experience — individually, authentically your own.

Three things. First: always remember that your house is on fire. Second: don't listen to the devil. He will constantly say to you that there is no hurry. And thirdly: remember, acquaintance is not understanding.

Whatsoever I am saying here will make you acquainted. It is needed, but it is not enough. It starts you on a journey, but it is not the end. Do something so that knowledge doesn't remain knowledge, doesn't remain as memory, but becomes your experience and your life.

---

88 Know the knower and the known.

Now the first technique: *Each thing is perceived through knowing. The self shines in space through knowing. Perceive one being as knower and known.*

Whenever you know something, it is known through knowing. The object comes to your mind through the faculty of knowledge. You look at a flower: you know this is a roseflower. The roseflower is there and you are inside. Something from you comes to the roseflower, something from you is projected on the roseflower. Some energy moves from you, comes to the rose, takes its form, color and smell, and comes back and informs you that this is a roseflower.

All knowledge, whatsoever you know, is revealed through the faculty of knowing. Knowing is your faculty; knowledge is gathered through this faculty. But knowing reveals two things: the known and the knower. Whenever you are knowing a roseflower, your knowledge is half if you forget the knower who is knowing it. So while knowing a roseflower there are three things: the roseflower — the known; and the knower — you; and the relationship between the two — knowledge.

So knowledge can be divided into three points: knower, known and knowing. Knowing is just like a bridge between two points — the subject and the object. Ordinarily your knowledge reveals only the known; the knower remains unrevealed. Ordinarily your knowledge is one-arrowed: it points to the rose but it never points to you. Unless it starts pointing to you, that knowledge will allow you to know about the world, but it will not allow you to know about yourself.

All the techniques of meditation are to reveal the knower. George Gurdjieff used a particular technique just like this. He called it self-remembering. He said that whenever you are knowing something, always remember the knower. Don't forget it in the object. Remember the subject.

Just now you are listening to me. When you are listening to me, you can listen in two ways. One, your mind can be focused towards me — then you forget the listener. Then the speaker is known but the listener is forgotten. Gurdjieff said that while listening, know the speaker and also know the listener. Your knowledge must be double-arrowed, pointing to two points — the knower and the known. It must not only flow in one direction towards the object. It must flow simultaneously towards two directions—the known and the knower. This he called self-remembering.

Looking at a flower, also remember the one who is looking. Difficult, because if you do try it, if you try to be aware of the knower, you will forget the rose. You have become so fixed to one direction that it will take time. If you become aware of the knower, then the known will be forgotten. If you become aware of the known, then the knower will be forgotten.

But a little effort, and by and by you can be aware of both simultaneously. And when you become capable of being aware of both—this Gurdjieff calls self-remembering. This is one of the oldest techniques that Buddha used, and Gurdjieff again introduced it to the Western world.

Buddha called it *samyak smriti*—right mindfulness. He said that your mind is not in a right mindfulness if it knows only one point. It must know both. And then a miracle happens: if you are aware of both the known and the knower, suddenly you become the third—you are neither. Just by endeavoring to be aware of both the known and the knower, you become the third, you become a witness. A third possibility arises immediately, a witnessing self comes into being, because how can you know both? If you are the knower, then you remain fixed to one point. In self-remembering you shift from the fixed point of the knower. Then the knower is your mind and the known is the world, and you become a third point, a consciousness, a witnessing self.

This third point cannot be transcended, and that which cannot be transcended is the ultimate. That which can be transcended is not worthwhile, because then it is not your nature—you can transcend it.

I will try to explain it through an example. In the night you sleep and you dream. In the morning you wake and the dream is lost. While you are awake there is no dream; a different world comes into your view. You move in the streets, you work in a factory or in an office. Then you come back to your home, and again you fall asleep at night. Then this world that you knew while you were awake disappears. Then you don't remember who you are. Then you don't know whether you are black or white, poor or rich, wise or foolish. You don't know anything. You don't know if you are young or old. You don't know if you are man or woman. All that was related with the waking consciousness disappears; you enter the world of dreams. You forget the waking world, it is no more. In the morning, again the dreaming world disappears. You come back.

Which is real?—because while you are dreaming, the real world, the world that you knew when you were awake, is no more. You cannot compare. And while you are awake, the dreaming world is no more. You cannot compare. Which is real? Why do you call the dreaming world unreal? What is the criterion?

If you say, "Because it disappears when I am awake," this cannot be the criterion, because your waking world disappears when you are dreaming. And really, if you argue this way, then the dreaming world may be more real, because while you are awake you can remember the dream, but while you are dreaming you cannot remember the waking consciousness and the world around it. So which is more real and more deep? The dreaming world completely washes away the world that you call real. Your real world cannot wash away the dreaming world so totally; it seems more solid, more real. And what is the criterion? How to say? How to compare?

Tantra says that both are unreal. Then what is real? Tantra says that the one who knows the dreaming world and the one who knows the waking world, he is real—because he is never transcended. He is never canceled. Whether you dream or whether you are awake, he is there, uncanceled.

Tantra says that the one who knows the dream, and the one who knows that now the dream has stopped, the one who knows the waking world, and the one who knows that now the waking world has disappeared, is the real—because there is no point when it is not, it is always there. That which cannot be canceled by any experience is the real. That which cannot be transcended, beyond which you cannot go, is your self. If you can go beyond it, then it was not your self.

This method of Gurdjieff's, which he calls self-remembering, or Buddha's method, which he calls right-mindfulness, or this tantra sutra, lead to one thing. They lead within you to a point which is neither the known nor the knower, but a witnessing self which knows both.

This witnessing self is the ultimate, you cannot go beyond it, because now whatsoever you do will be witnessing. Beyond witnessing you cannot move. So witnessing is the ultimate substratum, the basic ground of consciousness. This sutra will reveal it to you.

Each thing is perceived through knowing.
The self shines in space through knowing.
Perceive one being as knower and known.

If you can perceive in yourself one point which is both knower and known, then you have transcended object and subject both. Then you have transcended matter and mind both; then you have transcended the outer and inner both. You have come to a point where the knower and the known are one. There is no division.

With the mind, division will remain. Only with the witnessing self division disappears. With the witnessing self you cannot say who is the known and who is the knower—it is both. But this has to be based on experience; otherwise it becomes a philosophical discussion. So try it, experiment.

You are sitting near a roseflower: look at it. The first thing to do is be totally attentive, give total attention to the rose, so that the whole world disappears and only the rose remains there—your consciousness is totally attentive to the being of the rose. If the attention is total then the world disappears, because the more the attention is concen-

trated on the rose, the more everything else falls away. The world disappears; only the rose remains. The rose becomes the world.

This is the first step—to concentrate on the rose. If you cannot concentrate on the rose, it will be difficult to move to the knower, because then your mind is always diverted. So concentration becomes the first step towards meditation. Only the rose remains; the whole world has disappeared. Now you can move inwards; now the rose becomes the point from where you can move. Now see the rose, and start becoming aware of yourself—the knower.

In the beginning you will miss. When you shift to the knower, the rose will drop out of consciousness. It will become faint, it will go away, it will become distant. Again you will come to the rose, and you will forget the self. This hide-and-seek play will go on, but if you persist, sooner or later a moment will come when suddenly you will be in-between. The knower, the mind, and the rose will be there, and you will be just in the middle, looking at both. That middle point, that balancing point, is the witness.

Once you know that, you have become both. Then the rose, the known, and the knower, the mind, are just two wings to you. Then the object and the subject are just two wings; you are the center of both. They are extensions of you. Then the world and the divine are both extensions of you. You have come to the very center of being. And this center is just a witness.

Perceive one being as knower and known.

Start by concentrating on something. When the concentration has come to be total, then try to move inwards, become mindful of yourself, and then try to balance. It will take time—months, even years. It depends on how intense is your effort, because it is the most subtle balancing to come between the two. But it happens, and when it happens you have reached the center of existence. In that center you are rooted, grounded, silent, blissful, in ecstasy, and duality is no more. This is what Hindus have called samadhi. This is what Jesus called the kingdom of God.

Just understanding it verbally will not be of much help, but if you try, from the very beginning you will start to feel that something is happening. When you concentrate on the rose, the world will disappear. This is a miracle—when the whole world disappears. Then you come to understand that it is your attention which is basic, and wherever you move your attention, a world is created, and from wherever you remove your attention, the world drops. So you can create worlds through your attention.

Look at it in this way. You are sitting here. If you are in love with someone, then suddenly only one person remains in this hall; everything else disappears, it is not there. What happens? Why does only one person remain when you are in love? The whole world drops really; it is phantomlike, shadows. Only one person is real, because now your mind is concentrated on one person, your mind is totally absorbed in one person. Everything else becomes shadowlike, a shadow existence—it is not real for you.

Whenever you can concentrate, the very concentration changes the whole pattern of your existence, the whole pattern of your mind. Try it—on anything. You can try it on a buddha statue or a flower or a tree or anything, or just on the face of your beloved or your friend—just look at the face.

It will be easy, because if you love some face it is very easy to concentrate. And really, those who tried to concentrate on Buddha, on Jesus, on Krishna, they were lovers. So it was very easy for Sariputta or for Maudgalyan or for the other disciples to concentrate on Buddha's face; they loved Buddha. The moment they looked at Buddha's face they were easily flowing towards it. The love was there; they were infatuated.

So try to find a face—any face you love will do—and just look in the eyes and concentrate on the face. Suddenly the whole world drops; a new dimension has opened. Your mind is concentrated on one thing; then that person or that thing becomes the whole world.

When I say this, I mean that if your attention is total towards anything, that thing becomes the whole world. You create the world through your attention. Your world you create through your own attention. And when you are totally absorbed, flowing like a river towards the object, then suddenly start becoming aware of the original source from where this attention is flowing. The river is flowing; now become aware of the origin.

In the beginning you will get lost again and again; you will shift. If you move to the origin, you will forget the river and the object, the sea towards which it is flowing. It will change: if you come to the object, you will forget the origin. It is natural, because the mind has become fixed to either the object or to the subject.

That's why so many people go into retreats, they just leave the world. Leaving the world basically means leaving the object so that they can concentrate on themselves. It is easy. If you leave the world and close your eyes and close all your senses, you can be aware of yourself easily, but again that awareness is false because you have chosen one point of duality. This is another extreme of the same disease.

First you were aware of the object—the known, and you were not aware of the subject—the knower. Now you are fixed with the knower and you have forgotten the known, but you remain divided in duality. And this is the old mind again in a new pattern. Nothing has changed.

That's why my emphasis is not to leave the world of the objects. Don't leave the world of the objects. Rather, try to become aware of both the subject and the object simultaneously, the outer and the inner simultaneously. If both are there, only then can you be balanced between them. If one is there you will get obsessed with it.

Those who go to the Himalayas and close themselves, they are just like you only standing in a reverse position. You are fixed with the objects, they are fixed with the subject. You are fixed with the outer, they are fixed with the inner. Neither you are free nor they, because you cannot be free with the one. With the one you become identified. You can be free only when you become aware of the two. Then you can become the third, and the third is the free point. With one you become identified. With two you can move, you can shift, you can balance, and you can come to a midpoint, an absolute midpoint.

Buddha used to say that his path is a middle path—*majjhim nikai*. It has not been really understood why he insisted so much on calling it the middle path. This is the reason: because his whole process was of mindfulness—it is the middle path. Buddha says, "Don't leave the world, and don't cling to the other world. Rather, be in-between. Don't leave one extreme and move to the other; just be in the middle, because in the middle both are not. Just in the middle you are free. Just in the middle there is no duality. You have come to one, and the duality has become just the extension of you—just two wings."

Buddha's middle path is based on this technique. It is beautiful. For so many reasons it is beautiful. One: it is very scientific, because only between two can you balance. If there is only one point, imbalance is bound to be there. So Buddha says that those who are worldly are imbalanced, and those who have renounced are again imbalanced in the other extreme. A balanced man is one who is neither in this extreme nor that; he lives just in the middle. You cannot call him worldly, you cannot call him otherworldly. He is free to move; he is not attached to any. He has come to the midpoint, the golden mean.

Secondly: it is very easy to move to the other extreme—very easy. If you eat too much you can fast easily, but you cannot diet easily. If you talk too much you can go into silence very easily, but you cannot talk less. If you eat too much, it is very easy not to eat at all—this is another extreme. But to

eat moderately, to come to a midpoint, is very difficult. To love a person is easy; to hate a person is easy. To be simply indifferent is very difficult. From one extreme you can move to the other.

To remain in the middle is very difficult. Why? Because in the middle you have to lose your mind. Your mind exists in extremes. Mind means the excess. Mind is always extremist: either you are for or you are against. You cannot be simply neutral. Mind cannot exist in neutrality: it can be here or there—because mind needs the opposite, it needs to be opposed to something. If it is not opposed to anything it disappears. Then there is no functioning for it; it cannot function.

Try this. In any way become neutral, indifferent—suddenly mind has no function. If you are for, you can think; if you are against, you can think. If you are neither for nor against, what is left to think?

Buddha says that indifference is the basis of the middle path. *Upeksha*, indifference—be indifferent to the extremes. Just try one thing: be indifferent to the extremes. A balancing happens.

This balancing will give you a new dimension of feeling where you are both the knower and the known, the world and the other world, this and that, the body and the mind. You are both, and simultaneously neither—above both. A triangle has come into existence.

You may have seen that many occult, secret societies have used the triangle as their symbol. The triangle is one of the oldest occult symbols just because of this—because the triangle has three angles. Ordinarily you have only two angles, the third is missing. It is not there yet, it has not evolved. The third angle is beyond both. Both belong to it, they are part of it, and still it is beyond and higher than both.

If you do this experiment you will help to create a triangle within yourself. The third angle will arise by and by, and when it comes then you cannot be in misery. Once you can witness, you cannot be in misery. Misery means getting identified with something.

But one subtle point has to be remembered—then you will not even get identified with bliss. That's why Buddha says, "I can say only this much—that there will be no misery. In samadhi, in ecstasy, there will be no misery. I cannot say that there will be bliss." Buddha says, "I cannot say that. I can simply say there will be no misery."

And he is right, because bliss means when there is no identification of any type—not even with bliss. This is very subtle. If you feel that you are blissful, sooner or later you will be in misery again. If you feel you are blissful, you are preparing to be miserable again. You are still getting identified with a mood.

You feel happy: now you get identified with happiness. The moment you get identified with happiness, unhappiness has started. Now you will cling to it, now you will become afraid of the opposite, now you will expect it to remain with you constantly. You have created all that is needed for misery to be there and then misery will enter, and when you get identified with happiness, you will get identified with misery. Identification is the disease.

At the third point you are not identified with anything: whatsoever comes and passes, comes and passes; you remain a witness, just a spectator—neutral, indifferent, unidentified.

The morning comes and the sun rises and you witness it. You don't say, "I am the morning." Then when the noon comes, you don't say, "I have become the noon." You witness it. And when the sun sets and darkness comes and the night, you don't say, "I am the darkness and the night." You witness it. You say, "There was morning, then there was noon, then there was evening and now there is night. And again there will be morning and the circle will go on and I am just an onlooker. I go on witnessing."

If the same becomes possible with your moods—moods of the morning and moods of the noon and moods of the evening and the night, and they have their own circle, they go on moving—you

become a witness. You say, "Now happiness has come—just like a morning. And now night will come—the misery. The moods will go on changing around me, and I will remain centered in myself. I will not get attached to any mood. I will not cling to any mood. I will not hope for anything and I will not feel frustrated. I will simply witness. Whatsoever happens, I will see it. When it comes, I will see; when it goes, I will see."

Buddha uses this many times. He says again and again that when a thought arises, look at it. A thought of misery, a thought of happiness arises—look at it. It comes to a climax—look at it. Then it starts falling down—look at it. Then it disappears—look at it. Arising, existing, dying, and you remain just a witness; go on looking at it. This third point makes you a witness, *sakshin*, and to be a witness is the highest possibility of consciousness.

89 Include everything in your being.

The second technique: *Beloved, at this moment let mind, knowing, breath, form, be included.*

This technique is a little difficult, but if you can do it, then very wonderful, beautiful. Sitting, don't divide. Sitting in meditation, be inclusive of all—your body, your mind, your breath, your thinking, your knowing, everything. Be inclusive of all. Don't divide, don't create any fragmentation. Ordinarily we are fragmenting; we go on fragmenting. We say, "The body is not me." There are techniques which can use that also, but this technique is totally different; rather, the opposite.

Don't divide. Don't say, "I am not the body." Don't say, "I am not the breath." Don't say, "I am not the mind." Just say, "I am all"—and be all. Don't create any fragmentation within you. This is a feeling. With closed eyes include everything that exists in you. Don't get yourself centered anywhere—be uncentered. The breath comes and goes, the thought comes and moves. The form of your body will go on changing. You have not observed this.

If you sit with closed eyes, you will feel that sometimes your body is big, sometimes your body is small; sometimes it is very heavy, sometimes just light, as if you can fly. You can feel this increasing and decreasing of the form. Just close your eyes and sit and you will feel that sometimes the body is very big—filling the whole room; sometimes it is so small—just atomic. Why does this form change? As your attention changes, the form of the body changes. If you are inclusive, it will become big; if you exclude—this is not I, this is not I—then it will become very minute, very small, atomic.

This sutra says: *Beloved, at this moment let mind, knowing, breath, form, be included.*

Include everything in your being and don't discard anything. Don't say, "This is not I," say, "I am," and include everything in it. If you can do this just sitting, wonderful, absolutely new happenings will happen to you. You will feel there is no center; in you there is no center. And with the center gone, there is no self, there is no ego; only consciousness remains—consciousness like a sky covering everything. And when it grows, not only your own breath will be included, not only your own form will be included; ultimately the whole universe becomes inclusive to you.

Swami Ramateertha used this technique for his own *sadhana*. A moment came when he started saying, "The whole world is in me, and the stars move in me."

Somebody was talking to him and said, "It is very beautiful here in the Himalayas." Ramateertha was staying in the Himalayas, and the man said to him, "It is very beautiful here in the Himalayas."

And Ramateertha is reported to have said, "Himalayas? The Himalayas are in me."

The man must have thought that he was mad. How could the Himalayas be in him? But if you practice this meditation, you can feel that the Himalayas are in you. Let me explain how it is possible.

Really, when you look at me you cannot look at the one who is here sitting in the chair. Really you are looking at a picture of me which is in you, in your mind. How can you know me here on this chair? Your eyes carry just a picture. Not even a picture—just rays of light enter in your eyes. And then the eyes don't go themselves to the mind; just rays passing through the eyes go inside. And your nervous system which carries those rays cannot carry them as rays; it transforms them into chemicals. So only chemicals travel, and these chemicals are decoded and you see me in your mind.

You have never been out of your mind. The whole world that you know, you decode it in your mind, you know it in your mind. All the Himalayas and all the suns and the stars and the moons, they are there in your mind in a very subtle existence. If you close your eyes and feel that everything is inclusive, you will know that the whole world is moving within you. And once you feel this—that the whole world is moving within you—all your individual misery is lost. You are no more an individual. You have become the absolute, the nonindividual. You have become the whole existence.

This technique expands your consciousness. Now in the West, many drugs are being used to expand consciousness—LSD, marijuana, and other drugs. In India also, in the old days, they were used, because they give a false feeling of expansion. All those who use drugs, for them this technique will be beautiful, very helpful, because their hankering is for expansion.

When you take LSD, you are no more confined in yourself, you have become inclusive of all. There have been cases… One girl jumped from a seven-story building because she felt that she could not die, death was impossible. She felt that she could fly, and she felt that there were no barriers, there was no fear. She jumped out of a seven-story building and died, shattered. But in her mind, under the influence of the drug, there was no limitation, no death.

Expansion of consciousness has become a fad, because when you expand you feel high. The whole world, by and by, becomes included in you. You become great, infinitely great, and with greatness, with expansion, all your individual miseries fall. But through LSD or marijuana or other drugs, this is only a false feeling.

Through this technique, this feeling becomes real—really the whole world comes within you. There are two reasons for this. One: our individual consciousness is not really individual; deep down it is collective. We look like islands, but all the islands deep down are connected to the earth. We look like islands, different—I am conscious, you are conscious—but your consciousness and my consciousness somewhere deep down are one. It is connected to the earth, the basic ground.

That's why many things happen which look inexplicable. If you meditate alone it will be more difficult to enter into it, but if you meditate with a group it is very easy, because the whole group works as a unit. In meditation camps I have felt and observed that after two or three days your individuality is no more; you become part of a greater consciousness. And very subtle waves are being felt, very subtle waves start moving, and the group consciousness evolves.

So when you dance, you are not really dancing, but the group consciousness is dancing; you are just a part of it. The rhythm is not only within you, the rhythm is also without you. The rhythm is all around you. In a group you are not. The superficial phenomenon of being islands is forgotten and the deeper phenomenon of being one is realized. In a group you are nearer to the divine; alone you are further away, because again you become concentrated on the ego, on the superficial difference, on the superficial separation. This technique helps, because really you are one with the universe. It is only a question of how to dig it or how to fall into it and realize it.

Being with a friendly group always gives you energy. Being with someone who is antagonistic, you always feel that your energy has been drained out. Why? If you are with a friendly group, in a

family, and you are sitting, relaxing, just being together, you feel energized, vitalized. Meeting a friend, you feel more alive than you were before. Just passing an enemy, you feel that you have lost some energy, you feel tired. What happens?

When you are meeting a friendly sympathetic group, you forget your individuality; you drop down to the basic level where you can meet. When someone is antagonistic, you become more individual, egoistic; you cling to your ego. Because of that clinging you feel tired. All energy comes from the roots; all energy comes with the feeling of a collective being.

In the beginning, doing this meditation you will feel a collective being arising, and then ultimately a cosmic consciousness arises. When all differences are lost, all boundaries disappear and existence remains as one piece, one unit, one whole; then everything is included. This effort to include everything starts from your own individual existence. Include.

Beloved, at this moment let mind, knowing, breath, form, be included.

The basic point is to remember inclusiveness. Don't exclude. This is the key for this sutra—inclusiveness, include. Include and grow. Include and expand. Try it with your body, and then try it with the outside world also.

Sitting under a tree, look at the tree, then close your eyes and feel that the tree is within you. Look at the sky, then close your eyes and feel that the sky is within you. Look at the rising sun, then close your eyes and feel that the sun is rising within you. Feel more inclusive.

A tremendous experience will happen to you. When you feel that the tree is within you, immediately you will feel more young, more fresh. And this is not imagination, because the tree and you both belong to the earth. You both are rooted in the same earth and ultimately rooted in the same existence. So when you feel that the tree is within you, the tree *is* within you—this is not an imagination—

and immediately you will feel the effect. The tree's aliveness, the greenery, the freshness, the breeze passing through it, will be felt within you in your heart. Include more and more existence and don't exclude.

In many ways, many world teachers have been teaching this. Jesus says, "Love your enemy as yourself." This is an experiment in inclusiveness. Freud used to say, "Why should I love my enemy as myself? He is my enemy, so why should I love him as myself? And how can I love?" His question seems relevant, but he is not aware of why Jesus says to love your enemy as yourself. It is not for any social politics, not for any change in society, not to create a better society, but to give you an expanded feeling of being and consciousness.

If you can include the enemy within yourself, he cannot harm you. That doesn't mean that he cannot kill you; he can kill you, but he cannot harm you. The harm comes when you exclude him. The moment you exclude him, you become the ego, separate, alone, cut off from existence. If you include the enemy within you, then everything is included. When the enemy can be included, then why not the tree and why not the sky?

The emphasis for the enemy is that if you can include the enemy in your being, you can include everything; then there is no need to exclude anything. If you feel that your enemy is included within you, then even your enemy will give you vitality, energy. He cannot be harmful to you. He can kill you, but even while he is murdering you, he cannot harm you. That harm comes from your own mind when you exclude.

But the case with us is totally, diametrically opposite—even friends are not included. Enemies are excluded, and even friends are not included. Even your lover, your beloveds, are not included. While being with your lover, you are not merging in him or her. You remain separate, you control yourself. You don't want to lose your identity. Because of this, love has become impossible.

Unless you lose identity how can you love? You want to remain yourself, and your lover wants to remain himself, and no one is ready to merge, no one is ready to include. Both exclude, both are bracketed in themselves; there is no meeting, no merging, no communion. If even lovers are not included, then it is bound to be that your existence is the poorest possible. You are alone, poor, a beggar. With the whole existence included, you are the emperor.

So remember this: make it a style of life to include. Not only a meditation, but a style of life, a way of living. Try to include more and more. The more you include, the more you expand, the more your boundaries recede to the very corners of existence. One day only you are; the whole existence is included. This is the ultimate of all religious experience.

Beloved, at this moment let mind, knowing, breath, form, be included.

CHAPTER 62

Right now is the goal

◆

Q U E S T I O N S

How do You reconcile "hurrying" with "playing?"

How to include my enemy into my being?

The first question:

Yesterday You said that one should hurry towards the goal because whatever time we have is very little. However, some time ago You also said that the whole process of attaining the goal should be an effortless play. How would You reconcile the two words "hurry" and "play"?—because the one who hurries never gets the joy of playing.

The first thing: don't try to reconcile different techniques. When I say don't be in a hurry, forget time completely, don't be serious, don't make any effort, surrender, be in a let-go, this is a different technique. This is suitable only for a part of humanity—all cannot do this technique—and the type of person who can do this cannot do the opposite one. This technique is for the feminine mind. All females are not necessarily feminine, and all males are not necessarily masculine, so when I say a feminine mind, I don't mean females.

A feminine mind means a mind who can surrender, who can be receptive like a womb, who can be open, passive. Half of humanity can be of this type, but the other half is totally opposite. As man and woman are the two halves of humanity, in just the same way the feminine mind and the masculine mind are the two halves of the human mind.

The feminine mind cannot make effort. If it makes effort it will never reach anywhere. The effort will be the undoing for it; it will only create anguish and tension and no achievement. The very working of the feminine mind is to wait and allow things to happen.

Just like a woman: even if she is in love, she will not take the initiative. And if a woman takes the initiative, you have every reason to be afraid and escape, because that attitude is the male attitude—in the feminine body there is a masculine mind, and you will be in difficulty. If you are really male, immediately the woman will lose attraction. If you are feminine—male in the body but feminine in the mind—only then can you allow the woman to take initiative and you will be happy. But then physically she is a woman and you are a man; mentally you are feminine and she is masculine, she is male.

A woman will wait. She will never utter the words "I love you" before you have uttered them and you have committed yourself. In the very waiting is the feminine power. The male mind is aggressive, it has to do something. It has to move and go and take initiative.

The same happens on the spiritual path. If you have an aggressive mind, a male mind, effort is necessary. Then make haste; then don't lose time and opportunity. Then create an urgency and crisis so that you can put all your being into your effort. When your effort has become total you will achieve. If your mind is feminine, then there is no hurry at all. There is no time.

You may or may not have observed that women have no sense of time—they cannot have. So the husband is standing outside the house and he is

873

honking the horn and saying, "Come down!" And the wife says, "I have told you a thousand times that I am coming in one minute. Continuously for two hours I have been telling you that I am coming in one minute. So don't get mad. Why are you honking the horn?"

The feminine mind cannot have a sense of time. It is the male, aggressive mind who is time-worried, time-conscious. They are totally different.

The feminine is not in any hurry—there is no hurry. Really, there is nowhere to reach. That's why women cannot become great leaders, great scientists, great warriors—they cannot become. And if sometimes there are freak women, they have a male mind. For example, Joan of Arc, or Laxmi Bai: they are only feminine in body; the mind is not feminine at all, it is masculine.

For the feminine mind there is no goal, and our world is man-oriented. So women cannot be really great in a man-oriented world, because greatness is related to the goal. Some goal has to be achieved; then you become great—and the feminine mind is not after any goal. Here and now she is happy. Here and now she is unhappy. There is nowhere to move.

The feminine mind exists in the moment. That's why the feminine curiosity is never for the faraway; it is always about the neighborhood. She is not interested in what is happening in Vietnam, she is interested in what is happening in the other house—the intimate, the here. The man looks absurd: "Why are you worried about what Nixon is doing or what Mao is doing?" The woman is interested in the love affairs that are going on in the neighborhood. She is curious about the near; the far is meaningless. Time doesn't exist.

Time exists for those who have a goal to reach. Remember, time can exist only when you have to reach somewhere. If you don't have to reach anywhere, what is the meaning of time? Then there is no hurry.

Look at this situation from a different angle. The East is feminine and the West is masculine. The East has never been concerned much about time;

the West is mad after time. The East has been very leisurely, moving slowly as if not moving at all; no change, no revolution—such a silent evolution that it creates no noise anywhere. The West is just mad: every day revolution is needed, and everything has to become a revolution. Unless everything is changing, it seems we are not going anywhere; we have become static. If everything is changing and everything remains in an upheaval, then the West feels that something is happening. And the East thinks that if there are upheavals, it means we are diseased. Something is wrong; that's why there is change. If everything is okay, there is no need for any revolution, for any change.

The Eastern mind is feminine. That's why in the East we have praised all the feminine qualities: compassion, love, sympathy, nonviolence, acceptance, contentment—all feminine qualities. In the West all the masculine qualities are praised: will, willpower, ego, self-esteem, independence, rebellion—these are the values praised there. In the East—obedience, surrender, acceptance. The basic attitude is feminine in the East and masculine in the West.

These techniques are not to be compromised, are not to be in any way synthesized. The technique of surrender is for the feminine mind. The technique of effort, will, endeavor, is for the masculine mind. And they are bound to be polar opposites, so if you make any synthesis between the two you will create a hodge-podge—meaningless, absurd, and even dangerous. It will not be of use for anyone.

So remember this. These techniques many times will look contradictory, because they are meant to be for different types of mind, and there is no effort to make any synthesis. So if you feel something is contradictory, don't get uneasy about it—it is. And only very small minds become afraid of contradiction—very small minds, petty minds. They become uneasy, they feel a discomfort. They think everything must be noncontradictory, everything must be consistent. This is nonsense, because life is inconsistent.

Life is contradictory itself, so truth cannot be

uncontradictory; only lies can be uncontradictory, only lies can be consistent. Truth is bound to be inconsistent, because it has to cover everything that is in life. It has to be total. And life is contradictory. There is man and there is woman: what can I do and what can Shiva do? And man is totally the polar opposite to woman—that's why they are attracted; otherwise there would be no attraction. Really, the opposite type of being, the difference, creates the attraction. The polar opposite becomes a magnetic force. That's why when man and woman meet there is happiness, because when two polar opposites meet they negate each other. They negate each other because they are opposites. They negate each other, and for a single moment when man and woman really meet—not just bodily, but totally; when their beings meet in love—for a single moment both disappear. Then there is neither man nor woman; pure existence exists—that's the bliss of it.

The same can happen within you also, because deep analysis shows that within you also there is a polarity. Now modern deep psychoanalytic approaches have revealed that the conscious mind and the unconscious mind are polar opposites within you also. If you are a man, your conscious mind is masculine, your unconscious mind is feminine. If you are a woman, your conscious mind is feminine, your unconscious mind is masculine. The unconscious is the opposite of the conscious. In deep meditation there comes a deep orgasm, an intercourse, a love, between your conscious and unconscious—they become one. When they become one you attain to the highest bliss possible.

So man and woman can meet in two ways. You can meet a woman outside you; then this meeting can be only momentary, very momentary. For a single second the peak comes, and then things start falling away. There is another meeting of man and woman that happens within you: your conscious and unconscious mind meet. When this happens, this meeting can be eternal. The sexual pleasure is also a glimpse of the spiritual—only momentary— but when the real meeting happens within, then it

becomes samadhi, then it becomes a spiritual phenomenon.

But you have to start from your conscious mind, so if your conscious mind is feminine, surrender will be helpful. And remember, being a woman is not necessarily synonymous with having a feminine mind. That creates the difficulty. Otherwise everything would be very easy: then women would follow the path of surrender and men would follow the path of will. But it is not so easy. There are women who have masculine minds—their very approach towards life is aggressive—and they are growing every day.

The women's liberation movement will create more and more masculine women. They will be more and more aggressive, and the path of surrender will not be for them then. And because women are becoming competitive with man, man is regressing from aggression; he is becoming more and more feminine. More and more the path of surrender will be useful for man in the future.

So you have to decide about yourself. And don't think in terms of valuation; don't think that you are a man, so how can you have a feminine mind? You can have, and nothing is wrong in it, it is beautiful. And don't think that you are a woman, so how can you have a masculine mind? Nothing is wrong in it, it is beautiful. Be authentic towards your own mind. Try to understand what type of mind you have, then follow the path that is for you, and don't try to create any synthesis.

Don't ask me how I am going to reconcile these two. I am not going to. I am never for reconciliation, and I am not for noncontradictory statements. They are stupid and childish. Life is contradictory, and that's why life is alive. Only death is consistent and noncontradictory.

Life lives through opposition, through encountering the opposite pole, and this opposition, challenge, creates energy. It releases energy, and life moves through it. This is what Hegelians say: a dialectical movement—thesis, antithesis, and then the synthesis again becomes a thesis and creates its own antithesis, and this goes on. Life is not monotonous. It is not logical. It is dialectical.

You must understand the difference between logical and dialectical. The question is because you think life is logical, so you ask how you will reconcile, because logic always reconciles; logic cannot tolerate the contradictory. Logic *cannot* tolerate the contradictory. Logic has to somehow explain that it is not contradictory, and if it is contradictory then both cannot be true; then one must be wrong. Both can be wrong, but both cannot be true. Logic tries to find noncontradiction everywhere.

Science is logical. That's why science is not totally true to life, cannot be. Life is contradictory, illogical. It works through the opposite. It is not afraid of the opposite, it uses the opposite. The opposites are only apparently opposite; deep down they work together. It is dialectical, not logical. It is a dialogue between the opposites—a continuous dialogue.

Think for a single moment: if there is no contradiction, life will be dead, because from where will come the challenge? From where will come the attraction? From where will the energy be released? It will be monotonous, dead. Life is possible only because of dialectics, because of the opposite. Man and woman is the basic opposition, and then the challenge creates the phenomenon of love. And the whole life moves around love. If your lover and you become so totally one that there is no gap at all, you both will be dead. You will not be able to exist then. You both will disappear from this dialectical process.

You can only exist in this life if oneness is never total, and you have to move away again and again to come near. That's why lovers fight. That fight creates dialectics. The whole day they will fight. They will go far away from each other, they will become enemies. This means that they have now come to be really polar opposites; they have moved as far away as possible. The lover starts thinking how to kill this woman, and the woman starts thinking how to get rid of this man. They have

moved to the very farthest corner possible. And then again in the evening they are making love.

When they are far away, so far away, again the attraction comes. Again they look from such a faraway point that they feel attracted. Then they have become simply man and woman again, not lovers. Then they are man and woman, strangers. They will fall in love again. They will come near. A point will come when they will become one for a single moment, and that will be their happiness, their joy.

But the moment they have become one, the process of going away starts again. In the very moment when the wife and husband are one, if they can be a witness to it, they will see they have started being separate again. The very moment the peak comes, the process starts to be different, to be separate, to be opposite. This moving goes on— again and again you come near and go away.

This is what I mean: life creates energy through polarities. Without polarities life cannot exist. If two lovers really become one, they disappear from life. They are liberated really. They will have no rebirth again; there will be no life in future. If two lovers can become so totally one, their love has become the deepest meditation possible. They have achieved what Buddha achieved under the bodhi tree. They have achieved what Jesus achieved on the cross. They have achieved nonduality. Now they cannot exist.

Existence as we know it is dual, dialectical, and these techniques are for you who exist in duality. So there will be many contradictions, because these techniques are not philosophy; these techniques are meant to be done and lived. They are not mathematical formulas; they are actual life processes. They are dialectical, they are contradictory. So don't ask me to reconcile them. They are not the same, they are opposite.

Try to find out what is your type. Can you relax? Can you let go? Can you be in a passive moment, not doing anything?—then all the techniques which require will are not for you. If you cannot relax, and if I say to you to relax and you immediately ask me how to relax, that "how" shows your mind. That "how" shows that you cannot relax without making an effort. Even for relaxation you need some effort, so you ask "how?" Relaxation is relaxation; there is no how to it. If you can relax, you know how to relax, you simply relax. There is no effort, no method.

Just as in the night you go to sleep—you never ask how to go to sleep. But there are persons who have insomnia. If you say to them, "I just put my head on the pillow, and it's okay, I am asleep," they cannot believe you. And their suspicion is meaningful. They cannot believe you; you are deceiving—because they also put their head on the pillow. They go on putting their head the whole night—nothing happens.

They are going to ask how—how to put the head on the pillow? There must be a secret which you are not telling them. You are deceiving; the whole world is deceiving them. Everybody says, "We just go to sleep. There is no how to it. There is no technology." They cannot believe you, and you cannot blame them. You say, "We simply put down our heads, close our eyes, put off the light, and we are asleep."

They also do the same procedure, they do the same ritual, and they do it more correctly than you have ever done, but nothing happens. The light is off, they have closed eyes, lying on their bed—nothing is happening. Once you lose the capacity to relax, then technique is needed. Then they need technique; then without technique they will not be able to sleep.

So if you have a mind which can relax, then surrender is for you. And don't create any problems—then simply surrender. At least half of you can do this. You may not be aware, but fifty percent is the possibility, because masculine and feminine minds exist in a proportion. They are always fifty-fifty, almost exactly fifty-fifty, in every realm, because a man cannot exist without a woman opposing him. There is a deep balance in nature.

Do you know?—one hundred and fifteen boys are born to one hundred girls, because boys are weaker than girls, so by the time they are sexually mature fifteen boys will have died. One hundred and fifteen boys are born for every one hundred girls. Girls are stronger: they have more stamina, more resistance. Boys are weak, they don't have so much resistance, so one hundred and fifteen boys are born for one hundred girls. Then fifteen boys die. The moment they become sexually mature, by the age of fourteen, the number will be the same. For each man a woman exists, for each woman a man exists, because there is an inner tension. They cannot exist without it; that polar opposite is needed.

And similar is the case with the inner mind also. The existence, nature, needs a balance, so half of you are feminine and can be deeply in surrender very easily. But you can create problems for yourself. You may feel that you can surrender, but you think, "How can I surrender?" You feel that your ego may be hurt. You become afraid of surrendering, because it has been taught to you: "Be independent. Remain independent, don't lose yourself. Don't give your control to someone else. Always be in control."

This has been taught; these are taught difficulties. So you can feel that you can surrender, but then other problems arise which have been given to you by society, culture and education. And they create problems. If you really feel that surrender is not for you, then forget it. It is not to be worried about. Then put all your energy into effort.

So these are the two extremes. One: if you are a really feminine mind, you have nowhere to go, there is no goal, no God to be achieved, no future heaven—nothing. Don't be in any hurry now, remain true to the moment, and all that can be achieved by the male mind through hurry, effort, you will achieve here and now without any effort. Right now you are at the goal, if you can relax.

The male mind will have to run round about and round about until it is tired completely, and then it falls down; only then it can relax. Aggression, effort, endeavor, are necessary for the male mind to be exhausted. When that exhaustion happens, then it is possible for it to relax and to surrender. That surrender will come only in the end; for the feminine mind it is always in the beginning. You reach the same happening but the ways of reaching are different.

So when I said yesterday, "Don't waste time," I said it to the male mind. If I said be in a hurry and create such an emergency that your total energy and being becomes pinpointed, concentrated, and only in that concentrated effort your life will become a flame, this is for the male mind, the masculine mind. For the feminine mind, relax and you are already a flame.

Because of this, you have Mahavira, you have Buddha, you have Jesus, Krishna, Rama, Zarathustra, Moses, but you don't have a similar list of women. Not because women have not achieved such a state of mind—they have achieved, but their ways are different. And this whole history has been recorded by man, and man can understand only the masculine mind. Man cannot understand the feminine mind, that's the problem. It is really very difficult.

A man cannot understand that a woman, just by being a simple housewife, can achieve something which a buddha achieves with so much difficulty, so arduously. A man cannot conceive, it is impossible for him to conceive, that a woman can achieve just by being a housewife: living moment to moment, enjoying moment to moment, just near and here and now, and not bothering about anything else—no goal, no spirituality; just loving the children, loving the husband, just being an ordinary woman, but blissful. No need to make such arduous effort as a Mahavira is making—twelve years of long, arduous effort. But man will appreciate Mahavira, because he can appreciate effort.

If you achieve a goal without the effort, for man it is not worth it. He cannot appreciate it. He can appreciate someone, a Tensing, a Hillary, reaching the Everest—not because Everest is worth it, but because so much effort is needed and it is so dangerous. And if you say that you are already on the Everest he will laugh, because Everest is not meaningful—the effort to reach it is meaningful. The moment Everest becomes easy to reach, for the masculine mind all attraction is lost. There is nothing to be achieved on the Everest. When Hillary and Tensing reached there, nothing was there to be achieved, but the masculine mind feels such a glory.

When Hillary reached there, I was in a university; all the professors were just thrilled. I asked one woman professor, "What do you say about Hillary and Tensing who have reached the top of Everest?"

She said, "I cannot understand why there is so much fuss about it. What is the point? What have they gained by reaching there? Even reaching to the market, to a shop, would have been better."

For the feminine mind it is useless. Going to the moon—why such danger? There is no necessity. But for the masculine mind, it is not the goal. Really, the effort is the thing, because then he proves that he is masculine. The very effort, the very aggression, and the very possibility of death, give him the thrill.

Danger is very appealing to the masculine mind. For the feminine mind it has no appeal at all. Because of this, human history is really half recorded. The other half has been totally unrecorded, left unrecorded. We don't know how many women became buddhas; it is impossible to know, because our measurement, our criterion, cannot be applied to the feminine mind.

So first decide about your own mind. First meditate about your own mind—what type of mind you have got—then forget all those methods which don't belong to you. And don't try to reconcile them.

The second question:

You have said, "Learn to include more and more of existence into your being. Draw energy from the root source of all existence. Be inclusive even of your enemy." How can I be inclusive of my enemy while at the same time going fully into the emotion of hatred? Does this not lead to suppression?

I have said to be inclusive even of your enemy, but I have not said to start from the enemy. Start from the friend. As you are right now, you are not even inclusive of the friend. Start from the friend. Even that is difficult—to include the friend into your being, to allow him to enter in you and penetrate you, to be open to him, vulnerable. Start from the friend. Start from the lover, the beloved. Don't jump to the enemy.

And why do you jump to the enemy?—because then you can say, "It is impossible, it cannot be done," so you can discard it. Start from the first step. You start from the last. How can the journey become possible? You always start from the last step. The first has not been taken yet, so the last is only in the imagination. And you feel it is impossible. Of course it is impossible. How can you start from the end? The enemy is the last point to be included.

If you can include your friend it becomes possible, because only friends become enemies. You cannot make someone an enemy without making him first your friend. Or can you? Friendship will be needed first if you want to make someone your enemy. Friendship will be the first step.

Buddha is reported to have said, "Don't make friends, because that is the first step towards making enemies." Buddha says, "Be friendly; don't make friends. If you make friends you have already taken the first step; now it is not very far from when you will make enemies."

Include the friend. Start from the near, begin from the beginning. Only then is it possible, you don't feel any difficulty. When you have to include the friend and be inclusive of the friend, it is diffi-

cult enough, because it is not a question of the friend or the enemy. It is a question of your opening. Even for the friend you are closed; even with the friend you remain guarded; even with the friend you have not revealed your being totally, so how can you include him?

You can include him only when there is no fear, when you are not afraid, when you can allow him to move within you, and you are not making any security arrangements. Even with the beloved you are closed; you have not opened your mind. Still there are a few things which are secret, private. If you have privacy you cannot be open, you cannot be inclusive, because then the privacy can be known, then your secrets can become public. It is not easy to include even a friend, so don't think it is difficult to include an enemy—it is impossible right now.

That's why Jesus' teaching became impossible, and Christians became pseudo. They had to, because Jesus says, "Love your enemies," and you are not even capable of loving your friends. He gives you an impossible goal. You are bound to become hypocrites, pseudo; you will not be authentic. You will talk about loving—loving your enemies—and you will hate your friends. I am not saying that.

So the first thing: don't think of the enemy right now. That's a trick of your mind. Think of the friend. The second thing: the question is not to include someone; the question is to be inclusive. That's a quality of your consciousness. Create the inclusiveness, create the quality.

How can you create the quality?—for that is the technique. You are sitting near a tree. Look at the tree. It is outside you, but if it is really outside you, you cannot know it. Something of it has already traveled within you; that's how you can know the tree is there. It is green—but do you know that the green exists in you, not in the tree? When you close your eyes, the tree is not green.

Now scientists say this—that the color is given by you. Everything in nature is colorless; there exists no color. Color comes into being when rays traveling from a particular object meet your eye. Then the color is created. So color is given by your eye. It is a meeting of the tree and you where greenness happens. The flowers are there in bloom: the scent comes to you, and you smell it. But that fragrance also is given by you; it is not in nature. Only waves are coming towards you which you translate as smell. It is your nose which smells it. If you are not there, there will be no smell.

There have been philosophers like Berkeley or Nagarjuna or Shankara who say the world is unreal, it exists in your mind, because whatsoever we know about the world is really given by us. Because of this, Immanuel Kant, a German thinker and philosopher, says that the thing in itself cannot be known; whatsoever we know is not the thing, it is our projection.

Your face looks beautiful to me. Your face is neither beautiful nor ugly; it is my attitude. It is I who make you beautiful or ugly. It depends on me; it is my feeling. If you are alone in the world and there is no one to say that you are ugly or beautiful, you will not be either—or will you be? If you are alone on the earth, will you be beautiful or ugly? Will you be intelligent or foolish? You will be nothing. Really you cannot exist alone on the earth. You cannot be.

If you are sitting near a tree, meditate. Open your eyes and look at the tree, and then close your eyes and look at the tree within. If you try it—again open the eyes, meditate on the tree and then close the eyes and look at the tree within—in the beginning the tree within will be a faint shadow of the tree without, but if you continue, by and by it will come to have the same reality and being as the tree without.

And if you continue and persist, which is difficult, a moment comes when the outer tree becomes just a shadow of the inner. The inner becomes more beautiful, more alive, because now your inner consciousness is the soil for it. Now it is rooted in the inner consciousness. Now it is feeding on the consciousness, really. It is something rare.

So when Jesus or people like Jesus talk about the kingdom of God, they talk in such colorful language that we think that either they are mad, or just in hallucination. They are neither. They have learned how to include existence. Their own inner consciousness has become now a life-giving phenomenon. Now whatsoever is planted within becomes alive. It is more colorful, more fragrant, more vital—as if it doesn't belong to this world, this mundane world; it belongs to some other world. Poets know this a little. Mystics know it very deeply, but poets also know it a little. They have a glimpse. They can feel the world included in them.

Try it—to be inclusive. This is what I mean when I say to be inclusive: let the tree go in and be rooted there. Let the flower go in and allow it to flower there. You cannot believe it, because there is no way unless you experience it. Concentrate on a bud, a bud of a roseflower. Concentrate on it, go on concentrating on it, and allow it to be transferred to the inner.

And when really your inner experience of the bud has become so real that the outer, the real bud, the so-called real bud, appears to be just a shadow of it—the real idea is now inside, the real essence is inside, and the outer is just a faint copy—when you have come to this point, close your eyes and concentrate on the inner bud. You will be amazed, because the inner bud will start opening. It will become a flower, and such a flower you have not known. And you cannot meet that flower outside. Now this is a rare phenomenon, when something starts growing within you, opening, blooming.

In this way be inclusive, and then by and by allow your boundaries to expand. Include your lovers, your friends, your family, include strangers, and then by and by you will be able to include the enemy. That will be the last point. And when you can include the enemy and you can allow him to enter in you and be rooted there and become part of your consciousness, then nothing is inimical to you. Then the whole world has become your home.

Then nothing is strange, no one is alien, and you are at ease in it.

But be aware of the cunning mind. The mind will always say to you something which you cannot do, and when you cannot do it, the mind will say, "These are absurd things. Leave them." The mind will set a target which cannot be reached. Always remember that, and don't be a victim of your own mind. Always start from somewhere which is possible; don't jump to the impossible. If you can grow in the possible, the impossible is only the other end of it. It is not opposite to it; it is only the other end. It is the same spectrum—the other end of the spectrum.

One question more is included in it: *How can I be inclusive of my enemy while at the same time going fully into the emotion of hatred? Does this not lead to suppression?*

This is a subtle point to be understood deeply. While you hate, I don't say suppress it, because whatsoever is suppressed is dangerous. And if you suppress something you cannot be open ever. Then you create a private world which will not allow you to include others. You will always be afraid of this which you have suppressed, because any moment this can come out. So first thing: don't suppress anger, hatred, or anything. But there is no need to express it on someone.

You express it on someone because you feel the other is responsible—that is wrong. The other is not responsible; only you are responsible. You feel hate because you are hateful, and the other only gives you an opportunity, nothing else. If you come and abuse me, you simply give me an opportunity to bring out whatsoever is in me. If there is hate, hate comes out. If there is love, then love will come out. If there is compassion, then compassion will come out. You are just an opportunity for me to be revealed.

If hate comes out, don't feel that the other is responsible. He is just instrumental. We have a beautiful word in Sanskrit for it—*nimitt*—instrumental. He is not the cause; the cause is always

within. He is just the instrument to bring the cause out. So just be thankful to him—be thankful that he makes you aware of your own hidden hate. He is a friend. You convert him into an enemy because you impose all responsibility on him. You think that he is creating the hatred. No one can create anything in you, remember that forever.

If you go to Buddha and abuse him, he is not going to hate you, he is not going to be angry with you. Whatsoever you do, you cannot make him angry. Not because your effort is less, but because the anger is not there; you cannot bring it out. The other is not the source of hate, so don't throw it on him. Just be thankful to him, be grateful to him, and the hate that is within you, throw it out into the sky—the first thing.

The second thing: be inclusive about hate also. That's a deeper realm, a deeper dimension. Be inclusive of hate also.

What do I mean when I say this? Whenever there is something bad, whenever something which you call bad, evil, happens, you never include it in yourself. Whenever something good happens, you include it. If you are loving, you say, "I am love." When you hate, you never say, "I am hate." When you have compassion, you say, "I am compassion." When you are angry, you never say, "I am anger." You always say, "I am angry"—as if anger has happened to you; as if you are not anger—it is just a happening from outside, something accidental. And when you say, "I am love," it seems something essential, not something accidental that has happened to you, not something that has come from without. It is coming from within.

Whatsoever is good, you include it. And whatsoever is bad, you don't include it. Be inclusive of the bad also. Because you *are* hate, you *are* anger, and unless you feel this deeply—that "I am hate" —you will never go beyond it.

If you can feel, "I am anger," a subtle process of transformation sets in immediately. What happens when you say, "I am anger"? Many things happen. First: when you say, "I am angry," you are different from the energy you call anger. This is not true, and from an untrue base nothing true can happen. This is not true—this anger is you; this is your energy. It is not something separate from you.

You separate it because you create a false image of yourself—that you are never angry, that you are never hateful, that you are always loving, that you are always kind and sympathetic. You have created a false image of yourself. This false image is your ego. This ego goes on saying to you, "Cut anger, cut hate, they are not good"—not because you know they are not good, but because they don't give you the image; they don't feed your ego and your image.

You are a good man, respectable, nice, cultured —you have an image. Sometimes you fall down from the image—those are accidents. You regain your image again. Those are not accidents; really, they are more true about you. When you are angry, your true self is revealed more truly than when you are smiling falsely. When you show your hate, you are more authentic than when you pretend love.

The first thing is to be authentic, true. Include hate, include anger, include everything that is in you. What will happen? If you include everything, your false image will fall forever, and that's very good. That's just beautiful that you are relieved of the false image, because it goes on creating complexities. With the image falling your ego will fall, which is a door to spirituality.

When you say, "I am anger," how can you have your ego? When you say, "I am hate, I am jealousy, I am cruelty, I am violence," how can you have the ego? The ego can be had easily when you say, "I am Brahma, I am the supreme God." Then it is easy. "I am *atma*, the supreme self"—then it is easy. But when you say, "I am jealousy, hate, anger, passion, sex," you cannot have the ego. With the false image the ego falls; you become true, natural. Then it is possible to understand your reality. Then you can approach your anger without any anti-attitude. It is you. You have to understand that it is your energy.

And if you can be understanding about your anger, the very understanding changes and transforms it. If you can understand the whole process of anger and hate, in the very process of understanding it disappears, because a basic ingredient to being angry and hateful is to be ignorant about it, to be unaware about it, to be unalert about it. So whenever you are not alert, you can be angry. When you are alert, you cannot be angry. The alertness absorbs all energy which becomes anger.

Buddha has said again and again to his monks, "I don't say not to be angry. I say while you are angry, be alert." This is really one of the fundamentals for mutation. I don't say not to be angry. I say: while angry, be alert. Try it. When anger comes, be alert. Look at it. Observe it. Be conscious of it, don't be sleepy. And the more alert you are, the less anger. In a moment when you are really alert, anger is not —the same energy becomes alertness.

Energy is neutral. The same energy becomes anger, the same energy becomes hate, the same energy becomes love, the same energy becomes compassion. The energy is one; these are all expressions. And there are basic situations in which energy can become a particular mood. If you are unalert, energy can become anger, energy can become sex, energy can become violence. If you are alert, it cannot become—the alertness, awareness, consciousness, doesn't allow it to move in those grooves. It moves on a different plane—the same energy.

Buddha says, "Walk, eat, sit. Whatsoever you do, do, but do it fully conscious, mindful, aware that you are doing it."

Once it happened that Buddha was walking and a fly came and sat on his head, on his forehead. He was talking to some monks, so without really paying any attention to the fly, he just waved his hand and the fly left his forehead. Then he became aware that he had done something not fully aware, because his awareness was towards the monks to whom he was talking, so he said to the monks, "Excuse me for a single minute." He closed his eyes and he raised his hand again. The monks were amazed at what he was doing, because now there was no fly. He raised his hand again and waved his hand near the spot where the fly was—although it was not there now. He brought his hand back and then he opened his eyes and said, "You can ask now."

But those monks said, "We have forgotten what we were asking. Now we want to ask you what you did. There was no fly—it was there previously—so what did you do?"

Buddha said, "I did as I should have done before—fully consciously raising the hand. It was not good of me. Something had been done unconsciously, automatically, robotlike."

Such alertness cannot become anger, such alertness cannot become hate—impossible. So first include hate, anger, all that is thought to be bad. Include it in yourself, include it in your image, so that your ego falls down. You come down on the ground from the sky. You become true.

Then don't throw it on someone else. Let it be there; express it to the sky. Be fully alert. If you are angry, go in a room, be alone, and be angry and express your anger—and be alert. Do whatsoever you would have done with the person who was instrumental. You can take his picture there, or just put a pillow there and say, "You are my father," and give a good beating. Be fully alert. Be fully alert about what you are doing, and do it.

It will be a deep realization. The anger will be expressed, and you will be alert. And you will be able to laugh; you will be able to know what stupid things you are doing. But you could have done this to your real father—you are only doing it to the pillow. And if you really do it authentically, you will feel very kindly, very loving towards your father. When you come out of the room and when you look at your father's face you will feel very sympathetic, very loving. You would even like to ask him to forgive you.

This is what I mean by being inclusive. No suppression is meant. Suppression is always dangerous, poisonous. With whatsoever you suppress, you are creating inner complexes which will continue and which will make you ultimately mad. Suppression is bound to become madness. Express, but don't express on anyone. There is no need. That is stupid, and creates a vicious circle. Express alone, meditatively, and be alert while expressing.

CHAPTER 63

Start creating yourself

◆

90 *Touching eyeballs as a feather, lightness between them opens into heart and there permeates the cosmos.*

91 *Kind Devi, enter etheric presence pervading far above and below your form.*

Once it happened in a church that after a very long, dry sermon, the minister announced that there would be a meeting, a brief meeting of the board, right after the benediction. After the services a stranger approached the minister; he was the first man. The minister thought, "There has been some misunderstanding," because the man was absolutely a stranger. He didn't even look like a Christian; his appearance was that of a Mohammedan, so the minister said, "It seems you have misunderstood the announcement. There is going to be a meeting of the board."

The stranger said, "So I have also heard—and if there was someone here more bored than me then I would like to meet him."

But this seems to be the situation of everyone. Look at people's faces, or at your own face in a mirror, and you will feel you are the most bored, and it seems impossible that there can be someone else who is more bored than you. The whole life seems to be a long boredom—dry, dreary, meaningless; somehow you are carrying it as a burden.

Why has this happened? Life is not meant to be a boredom. Life is not meant to be a suffering. Life is a festival, a celebration, a peak of joy—but that is only in poetry, in dreams, in philosophies. Sometimes a Buddha, a Krishna, appears to be in a deep celebration, but they look like exceptions, really unbelievable; not real, just ideal. It seems they never happen. They are our wish-fulfillments, myths, dreams and hopes, but not realities. The reality seems to be our face—bored, in anguish, and with suffering impressed on it—and the whole life is just a carrying on somehow.

Why has this happened? And this must not be the basic reality of life, this cannot be, because this happens only to man. The trees, the stars, the animals, the birds...nowhere else does it happen. Except for man, no one is bored. And even if sometimes pain happens, it is momentary; it never becomes an anguish. It never becomes a constant obsession; it is not always on the mind. It is a momentary thing, an accident; it is not carried over.

Animals can be in pain, but they are not in suffering. Pain looks like an accident; they get over it. They don't carry it, it doesn't become a wound. It is forgotten and forgiven. It goes into the past; it never becomes a part of the future. When pain becomes a constant thing, a wound, not an accident but a reality, essential, as if you cannot exist without it, then it becomes a problem—and that problem has arisen only for the human mind.

Trees are not in suffering. There seems to be no anguish. Not that death doesn't occur to them; death occurs, but it is not a problem. Not that painful experiences are not there; they are there, but they don't become life itself. Just on the periphery they happen and disappear. Deep down in the inner core, life remains celebrating. A tree goes on celebrating. Death will happen, but it happens only once, it is not carried over constantly. Except for man, everything is in a festive mood. Only man is bored—boredom is a human phenomenon. What has gone wrong? Something must have gone wrong.

In a way this can be a good sign also. Boredom is human. You can define the human being through boredom. Aristotle has defined the human being as rational. That may not be exactly true; it is not a hundred percent true, because the difference is only of degree. Animals are also rational—less rational, but not absolutely irrational. There are animals which are just below the human mind. They too are rational in their own way—not as much as man, but not completely devoid of reason. The difference is only of degrees, and man cannot be defined by reason alone. But through boredom you can define him: he's the only bored animal.

And this boredom can come to such a climax that man can commit suicide. Only man can commit suicide; no animal commits suicide. That is an absolutely human phenomenon. When boredom comes to such a point that even hope becomes impossible, then you drop dead by yourself, because then there is no sense in carrying all this. You can carry this boredom, this pain, because somewhere the tomorrow is yet hopeful. This is bad today, but tomorrow something will happen. Because of that hope you go on carrying.

I have heard, once it happened that one Chinese emperor sentenced his prime minister to death. The day the prime minister was to be hanged, the emperor came to see him to say goodbye. He had been his devoted servant for many many years, but he had done something which irritated the emperor so much that he had sentenced him to death. But remembering that this was going to be the last day, the emperor came to meet him.

When the emperor came, he saw the prime minister weeping, and tears were rolling down from his eyes. He couldn't imagine that death could be the cause, because he was a brave man, so he asked, "It is impossible to imagine that you are weeping because you are going to die this evening—it is impossible to conceive. You are a brave man, and I have known your bravery so many times, so it must be something else. What is it? If I can do something I will do it."

The prime minister said, "Now nothing can be done and it is of no use to say it to you, but if you insist, then I am still your servant—I will obey you and tell you."

The emperor insisted, so the prime minister said, "It is not my death, because that is not of much importance—man has to die one day; any day death will be—but I am weeping because I have seen your horse standing outside."

The emperor asked, "Because of the horse? Why?"

The prime minister said, "I was looking for my whole life for this type of horse, because I have learned one ancient secret—that I can teach horses to fly—but only of a particular type. This is the type, and this is my last day. I am not worried about my death, but just that one ancient art will be lost with me. That's why I am weeping."

The emperor was thrilled, excited—if the horse could fly, this would be something—so he said, "How many days will it take?"

The prime minister said, "At least one year—and then this horse will start flying."

So the emperor said, "Okay, for one year I will make you free, but remember, if in one year the horse is not flying you will be again sentenced and hanged. But if the horse is flying you will be forgiven, and not only forgiven, I will give you half of my kingdom, because I will be the first emperor in history who has a flying horse. So come out of the jail and don't weep."

The prime minister rode, happy and laughing, on the horse to his house. But the wife was still weeping and crying and she said, "I have heard, the news has reached before you—but one year only? And I know you know no art, and this horse cannot fly. This is just a trick, a deception, so if you could ask for one year why couldn't you ask for ten years?"

The prime minister said, "That would be too much. As it is, it is already too much—the horse flying is already too much. Then asking for ten years would have been obviously a trick. But don't weep."

But the wife said, "It makes me still more sad that now I will be living with you and after one year you will be hanged. This one year is going to be a suffering."

The prime minister said, "Now I will tell you one ancient secret you don't know. In this one year the king can die, the horse can die, I can die. Or, who knows?—the horse can learn to fly! One year!"

Just hope—and man lives through hope because he is so bored. When boredom comes to a point where you cannot hope, when hopelessness is absolute, you commit suicide. Boredom and suicide are both human. No animal can commit suicide, no tree can commit suicide.

Why has this happened? What is the reason behind it? Has man forgotten completely how to live, how to celebrate, how to be festive? While the whole existence is festive, how has man retreated out of it and created a sad milieu around him?

It has happened. Animals live through instinct; they don't live through awareness. They live through instinct, mechanically. Nothing has to be learned, they are born with whatsoever they need to know. Their life runs on a smooth instinctive plane; there is no learning. They have an inbuilt program, a blueprint in their cells, for all that they need to live and be happy, so they go on living mechanically.

Man has lost instinct; now there is no blueprint to live. You are born without any blueprint, without any inbuilt program. No mechanical lines are available for you to move on. You have to create your own path. You have to substitute instinct with something which is not instinct, because instinct has dropped. You have to substitute your instinct with intelligence, with awareness. You cannot live mechanically. You have gone beyond that stage where mechanical life is possible—it is not possible for you. You cannot live like animals and you don't know how to live in some other way—this is the problem.

You don't have a natural inbuilt program to follow. Without a program you have to face exis-

tence. And boredom, suffering, is bound to be your destiny if you cannot create such awareness that you can live through awareness rather than living through instinct. You have to learn everything, this is the problem. No animal needs to learn anything. You have to learn everything, and unless you learn it you cannot live it. You have to learn how to live. No animal needs it.

This learning is the problem. You learn many things: you learn how to earn money, you learn mathematics, you learn history, you learn science, but you never learn how to live. That is creating the boredom. The whole of humanity is bored because a basic thing remains untouched. And it cannot be left to instinct, because there are now no instincts to live. For man, instinct has dropped; that door is closed. You have to build your own program. You are born without a map.

This is good, because existence thinks you are so responsible you will create your own map. This is a glory. This is magnificent. This makes man the highest, the peak of existence, because existence leaves you free. No animal is free: he has to live and follow a particular program that existence gives to him. When he is born, he is born with a program—he has to follow it. He cannot go astray, he cannot choose. There are no alternatives given to him. For man, all alternatives are open, and with no map to move with.

If you don't learn how to live, your life will become a dreary affair. This has happened. Then you can go on doing many things and still you will feel you are not alive. Dead—deep down something is dead, not alive. You go on doing things because you have to. Just to live you go on doing things, but that "just to live" is not life. There is no dance in it, no song in it. It has become a business. There is no play in it, and obviously you cannot enjoy it. These techniques of tantra are to teach you how to live. They are to teach you not to depend on animal instinct, because it is no more there. It has become so faint it cannot work for you, it cannot function.

It has been noted, observed, that if a human child is brought up without the mother, he will never be able to learn love, he will never be able to love. For his whole life he will remain without love, because now there is no instinct; he has to learn it. Even love has to be learned. A human child who is brought up without love cannot learn it. He will not be able to love. If a mother is not there, and if a mother doesn't become a source of happiness, of ecstasy, then no woman can become a source of happiness and ecstasy for that child. When he becomes mature, grown-up, he will not be attracted to women, because now instinct is not functioning.

This will not happen to animals: in the right moment they will start functioning. They will become sexual, they will move towards the opposite sex—that is instinctive, mechanical. With man nothing is mechanical. If you don't teach a human child language, he will not learn it. If you don't teach it, he is not going to have it. It is not natural; there is no instinct for it. Whatsoever you are is because of your learning. Man is less nature and more culture. Animals are simply nature.

Man is less natural and more cultural, but one dimension, the basic and the most foundational, remains uncultured—that is the dimension of being alive. You take it as if you already have it; it is taken for granted. That is wrong. You don't know how to live, because just to breathe is not synonymous with living. Just to eat and sleep and just carry on the bodily affairs is not synonymous with living. You are existing, that's right, but you are not alive.

A buddha is alive, not simply existing. That aliveness can come only if you learn it, if you become aware of it, and if you search for it and if you create situations in which it can evolve. Remember this: for man, mechanical evolution is not. Conscious evolution has taken place, and now you cannot do anything about it—you have to move into conscious evolution. You cannot fall back. You can stick where you are—then you will get bored.

That's what is happening. You are not moving. You go on accumulating physical things, so things are moving, not you. Your riches go on accumulating, they are growing—your bank balance is growing, not you. You are not increasing at all. On the contrary, you may be shrinking, decreasing, but you are not increasing. Unless you do something consciously, you are lost. A conscious effort is needed. It is not asked from the animals because they are not responsible. So you have to understand one very basic thing: with freedom comes responsibility. And you can be free only if you are responsible.

Animals are not responsible, but they are also not free. They are not free; they have to follow a particular pattern. They are happy because nothing can go wrong. They are following a predetermined course, they are following a pattern which has been worked out in millennia, in centuries of evolution. It has been worked out and found correct. They are following that, there is no possibility of going wrong.

There is every possibility for you to go wrong, because there is no plan, there is no map, there is no pattern. Your life ahead is not charted. You are free. But then a great responsibility falls on you, and that responsibility is to choose rightly, to work rightly, and to create your future through your effort. Really, the human being has to create himself through his own effort.

What existentialists in the West say is true. They say man is born without an essence, or you can say without a soul. Sartre, Marcel, Heidegger, they say that man is born without an essence. He is born as an existence, and then through his own effort he creates the essence. He is born only as a possibility, and then through his own effort he creates the soul. He is born only as a form, and then through his own conscious effort he creates the substance.

Just the contrary is the case for all nature: every animal, every plant, is born with an essence, with a soul, with a program, with a fixed destiny. Man is born as an opening with no fixed destiny—this creates burden, this creates responsibility. This gives you fear, anguish, anxiety. And then wherever you are, if you don't do anything you get stuck. That getting stuck creates boredom.

You can be alive, happy, festive, joyful, only when you are moving, when you are growing, when you are increasing, when you are creating the soul; really when you are pregnant with the divine, and when the divine is growing in your womb, when you are going to give birth.

For tantra, God is not the beginning, God is in the end. God is not the creator, but the ultimate peak, the omega point, of evolution. It is the last, not the first; not the alpha but the omega. And unless you become pregnant and unless you carry a child within you, you will be bored, because then your life is futile—nothing is going to come out of it; no fruit is going to come out of it. That creates boredom.

You can make this opportunity a source of evolution, or you can miss the opportunity and can make it a point of suicide. It depends on you—because only man can commit suicide, only man can grow spiritually. No animal can grow spiritually. Because man can destroy himself, he can also create. Remember, both the possibilities move simultaneously. No animal can destroy himself—impossible. You cannot conceive of a lion thinking about suicide, to jump from a cliff and end the whole thing—no, impossible. No lion can think of it. Howsoever brave, no lion can think of ending himself, destroying himself. He's not free.

You can conceive of destroying yourself. It is impossible to find a human being who has not thought many times to destroy himself. And if you can find a human being who has not thought of committing suicide, then either he is animal or God. That is very basically human—the possibility to destroy. But that also opens another door; simultaneously both the doors open—you can create also. You can create yourself, because you can destroy yourself.

No animal can create himself. You can create

yourself, and unless you start creating, you will be destroying. Unless you create yourself, start creating…. And it is not a thing to create yourself, it is a process—you have to go on creating. Unless you reach to the ultimate, you have to go on creating. Unless the god is born within you, you have to go on creating. If you are not creating, you will be bored—uncreative life is boredom. All these techniques are to help you to create, to be reborn, to become pregnant.

Now I will take the techniques.

The first technique—this technique is very easy and really wonderful. You can do it, anyone can do it. There is no question of type; anyone can do this technique, and for everyone this will be helpful. Even if you cannot move very deeply in it, then too it will be helpful. It will refresh you.

Whenever you are bored, it will immediately refresh you. Whenever you are tired, it will immediately revitalize you. Whenever you are in a mood where you feel fed up with the whole thing, immediately a new surge of energy will flow within you. So for everyone, even if you are not meditating on it, it will be helpful, a medical help. It will give you health. And it is very easy to do, no prerequisites.

---

90 Touch your eyes lightly.

The sutra is: *Touching eyeballs as a feather, lightness between them opens into heart and there permeates the cosmos.*

Before entering the technique, some introductory remarks about it. First, something has to be understood about the eye, because the whole technique depends on it.

The first thing: whatsoever you are, whatsoever you appear from without, is false, but your eyes cannot deceive. You cannot create false eyes. You can create a false face; you cannot falsify your eyes. That is impossible—unless you become a perfect master like a Gurdjieff. Unless you become a perfect master of all your energies, you cannot falsify your eyes. No ordinary human being can do that. You cannot falsify your eyes.

That's why if someone looks in your eyes, stares in your eyes, you feel offended, because he is trying to find the real thing. And at that point you cannot do anything—your eyes will reveal the true self. So it is not good manners to stare in anybody's eyes. Even while talking you go on avoiding the eyes. Unless you are in love with someone, unless someone is ready to be true with you, you cannot stare. There is a limit.

Psychologists have observed that thirty seconds is the limit. With a stranger you can stare for thirty seconds, not more. If you stare more, you have started being aggressive, and the other will immediately start to feel uneasy. You can stare from a faraway point, because then no one is aware. If you are a hundred feet away I can go on staring at you, but if you are just two feet away it becomes impossible.

In a crowded train, or in a crowded elevator, sitting or standing just close together, you never look at each other's eyes. You can touch the body—that is not so offensive—but you never look into each other's eyes because that will be too much, too near, and you will penetrate the real man. The first thing to remember: eyes have no personality. They are pure nature, they have no personality.

The second thing to remember: you move into the world almost only through the eyes; they say eighty percent. Those who have been working with eyes, the psychologists, they say that eighty percent of contact with the world is through the eyes. Eighty percent of your life moves out through the eyes.

That's why whenever you see a blind man, you feel pity. You never feel so much pity and sympathy when you see a deaf man, but when you see a blind man, suddenly you feel sympathy and compassion. Why?—because he is eighty percent nonalive. A deaf man is not so nonalive. Even if your feet are cut and your hands are cut, you will not be so

unalive, but a blind man is eighty percent closed; he lives only twenty percent.

Through your eyes eighty percent of your energy moves out. You are moving into the world through the eyes. So when you get tired, the first thing is the eyes. Later on, other parts of the body will be affected; the eyes will be the first to be drained of energy. If you can refresh your eyes, you can refresh your whole body, because they are eighty percent of your energy. If you can revitalize your eyes, you have revitalized yourself.

In a natural surrounding you never feel as tired as you feel in an unnatural city, because in a natural surrounding your eyes are continuously fed. The greenery, the fresh atmosphere—everything relaxes your eyes and feeds them. In a modern city everything exploits your eyes and nothing feeds them. So move to a remote village, or to a hilltop where nothing artificial is in the milieu, where everything is natural, and you will see a different type of eyes. The twinkling, the quality, will be different—fresh, animal-like, penetrating, alive, dancing.

In a modern city eyes are dead, just living on the minimum. They don't know what festivity is. They don't know what freshness is. The eyes are unaware of any life flowing through them; they are just being exploited. Eighty percent of your energy moves from your eyes, so you have to be perfectly aware, and you have to learn an art about this movement, this energy, and the possibility of the eyes.

In India we have been calling blind men *prajna-chakshu*—wisdom-eye—for a particular reason, because every misfortune can be transformed into a great opportunity. Eighty percent of the energy moves through the eyes, and when a person is blind, he is eighty percent not alive; eighty percent of his contact with the world is lost.

He is very poor as far as the world without is concerned, but if he can use this opportunity—this opportunity of being blind—then he can use this eighty percent of his energy for his inner world, this eighty percent that you cannot use ordinarily unless you know the art. So eighty percent of his energy is with him, it is a reservoir, and the energy that normally moves out can move within. If he knows how to allow it to move within, he will become a wisdom-eye.

A blind man is not a prajna-chakshu, a wisdom-eye, just by being blind, but he can be. He doesn't have ordinary eyes, but he can get the eyes of wisdom. The possibility is there. We named him prajna-chakshu just to make him aware that he should not be sorry that he doesn't have eyes; he can create an inner eye. And eighty percent more energy is with him which is not with those who have eyes. He can move it, he can use it.

Even if the blind man is not aware, he becomes more silent than you are. He becomes more relaxed. Look at a blind man: he is more silent, his face is more relaxed, he seems to be at ease with himself, no discontent. This will not be the case with a deaf man. He will be more restless than you, and he will become cunning. But a blind man is never cunning, never restless, never calculative, but basically trusting, in a deep faith with existence.

Why does this happen?—because the eighty percent of energy, even if he doesn't know anything about it, is moving within. It becomes a constant fall, just like a waterfall. Even unaware, it goes on falling on his heart. The same energy that moves out goes on falling on his heart—that changes the quality of his being. In ancient India the blind man was very much respected—very much respected. In deep respect we called him prajna-chakshu, wisdom-eye.

The same you can do with your eyes, and this technique is for that: to help your energy which moves out to fall back upon yourself, upon your own heart center. If it falls on the heart, you become as light as possible. You feel as if the whole body has become a feather, as if gravitation has absolutely no effect on it. And immediately you are connected with the deepest source of your being, which revitalizes you.

For tantra, deep sleep revitalizes you not because of sleep, but just because the energy which was moving out moves in. If you know the secret, then what an ordinary man is doing in six hours or eight hours of sleep, you can do within minutes. What an ordinary man is doing in eight hours, really he is not doing. He is allowing nature to do something, and he is not aware of what it is. A mysterious process is happening in your sleep. One of the basic things is that your energy is not moving out; it goes on falling on your heart, and that revitalizes you. You are in a deep bath with your own energy.

Something more about this moving energy. You might have observed that whenever there is a dominant man, he always stares in your eyes. Whenever there is a dominated man, he looks down. Slaves, servants, or anyone who is inferior to someone, will never stare in the eyes of the superior. But the superior can stare. Kings can stare, but standing before a king, standing in the audience of the king, you are not supposed to stare. That would be an offense. You have to look down.

Really, with your eyes your energy moves. It can become a subtle violence. And not only in man, even in animals. When two strangers meet, two animals meet, they stare each other in the eye just to judge who is going to be the superior and who is going to take the role of the inferior. And once one animal looks down, the thing is decided. Then they will not fight; the thing is over. It is now taken for granted who is superior.

Even children play the game of staring into each other's eyes, and whoever looks away is defeated. And they are right. When two children stare into each other's eyes, whosoever becomes first uncomfortable and starts fidgeting and starts looking away and avoiding the look of the other is defeated. The one who goes on staring is stronger. If your eyes can defeat the other's eyes, it is a subtle indication that you are stronger than the other.

On the stage when someone comes to speak or to act, he becomes very afraid, a great trembling happens. Even with those who are long in the profession, old actors...when they come on the stage a fear grips them, because so many eyes are staring; there is so much aggressive energy. There is so much energy from the thousands of people staring at them that they suddenly start trembling deep down. A fear grips them. A subtle energy is flowing through the eyes, a very subtle energy. The subtlest, the most refined of physical forces, is flowing through the eyes. And the quality of the energy changes with you.

From the eyes of a Buddha a different type of energy is flowing, from the eyes of a Hitler a totally different type. If you look at Buddha's eyes, they accept you, they welcome you, they become a door. If you look at Hitler's eyes, they reject you, they condemn you, they push you away, they throw you away. For Hitler, his eyes are like weapons; for Buddha, his eyes are compassion. The quality of the eyes changes. Sooner or later we must come to measure the eye energy, and then there will be no need to know much about the man; just the eye energy and its quality will show what type of man is hidden behind. Sooner or later that will be possible.

This sutra, this technique: *Touching eyeballs as a feather, lightness between them opens into heart and there permeates the cosmos.*

Touching eyeballs as a feather…. Use both your palms, put them on your eyes, and allow the palms to touch the eyeballs—but just like a feather, with no pressure. If you press you miss the point, you miss the whole technique. Don't press; just touch like a feather. You will have to adjust, because in the beginning you will be pressing. Put less and less pressure until you are just touching with no pressure at all—just your palms touch the eyeballs. Just a touch, just a meeting with no pressure, because if the pressure is there, then the technique will not function. So—like *a feather*.

Why? Because a needle can do something which a sword cannot do. If you press, the quality has changed—you are aggressive. And the energy that is flowing through the eyes is very subtle: a small pressure and it starts fighting and a resistance is created. If you press, then the energy that is flowing through the eyes will start a resistance; a fight, a struggle will ensue. So don't press; even a slight pressure is enough for the eye energy to judge.

It is very subtle, it is very delicate. Don't press—like a feather, just your palm is touching as if not touching. Touching as if not touching, no pressure —just a touch, a slight feeling that the palm is touching the eyeball, that's all.

What will happen? When you simply touch without any pressure, the energy starts moving within. If you press, it starts fighting with the hand, with the palm, and moves out. Just a touch and the energy starts moving within. The door is closed; simply the door is closed and the energy falls back. The moment energy falls back, you will feel a lightness coming all over your face, your head. This energy moving back makes you light.

And just between these two eyes is the third eye, the wisdom-eye, the prajna-chakshu. Just between these two eyes is the third eye. The energy falling back from the eyes hits the third eye. That's why one feels light, levitating, as if there is no gravitation. And from the third eye the energy falls on the heart. It is a physical process: just drip, drip, it drops, and you will feel a very light feeling entering in your heart. The heartbeats will slow down, the breathing will slow down. Your whole body will feel relaxed.

Even if you are not entering deep meditation, this will help you physically. Any time in the day, relax on a chair—or if you don't have any chair, when just sitting in a train—close your eyes, feel a relaxed being in the whole of your body, and then put both your palms on your eyes. But don't press—that's the very significant thing. Just touch like a feather.

When you touch and don't press, your thoughts will stop immediately. In a relaxed mind thoughts cannot move; they get frozen. They need frenzy and fever, they need tension to move. They live through tension. When the eyes are silent, relaxed, and the energy is moving backwards, thoughts will stop. You will feel a certain quality of euphoria, and that will deepen daily. So do it many times in the day. Even for a single moment, touching will be good. Whenever your eyes feel exhausted, dry of energy, exploited—after reading, seeing a film, or watching TV—whenever you feel it, just close the eyes and touch. Immediately there will be the effect. But if you want to make it a meditation, then do it for at least forty minutes. And the whole thing is not to press. Because it is easy for a single moment to have a featherlike touch; it is difficult for forty minutes. Many times you will forget and you will start pressing.

Don't press. For forty minutes, just remain aware that your hands have no weight; they are just touching. Go on being aware that you are not pressing, only touching. This will become a deep awareness, just like breathing. As Buddha says to breathe with full awareness, the same will happen with touching, because you have to be constantly mindful that you are not pressing. Your hand should just be a feather, a weightless thing, simply touching.

Your mind will be totally there, alert, near the eyes, and the energy will be flowing constantly. In the beginning it will be just dropping in drops. Within months you will feel it has become a river-like thing, and within a year you will feel it has become a flood. And when it happens—*touching eyeballs as a feather, lightness between them*—when you touch you will feel lightness. You can feel it right now. Immediately, the moment you touch, a lightness comes. And that *lightness between them opens into the heart;* that lightness penetrates, opens into the heart. In the heart, only lightness can enter; nothing heavy can enter. Only very light things can happen to the heart.

This lightness between the two eyes will start dropping into the heart, and the heart will open to receive it—*and there permeates the cosmos.* And as the falling energy becomes a stream and then a river and then a flood, you will be washed completely, washed away. You will not feel that you are. You will feel simply the cosmos is. Breathing in, breathing out, you will feel you have become the cosmos. The cosmos comes in and the cosmos goes out. The entity that you have always been, the ego, will not be there.

This technique is very simple, without any danger, so you can experiment with it as you like. But because it is so easy, you may not be able to do it. The whole thing depends on touch without pressure, so you will have to learn it. Try it. Within a week it will happen. Suddenly someday when you are just touching with no pressure, immediately you will feel what I am saying—a lightness and an opening in the heart, and something dropping from the head into the heart.

91 Experience your etheric body.

The second technique: *Kind Devi, enter etheric presence pervading far above and below your form.*

The second can be done only if you have done the first. It can be done separately also, but then it will be very difficult. But if you do the first, then it is good to do the second—and very easy.

Whenever this happens—that you feel light, levitating, as if you can fly—suddenly you will become aware that around your body form there is a bluish light. But that you can see only when you feel that you can levitate, that your body can fly, that it has become light, completely free of any burden, completely free of any gravitation towards the earth.

Not that you can fly—that is not the point. Sometimes it happens. Sometimes it happens that it comes to such a balancing point that your body goes up. But that is not the goal, and don't think about it at all. This much will do: if you feel with closed eyes that your body has gone up. When you open your eyes you will see you are just sitting on the ground, so don't become worried about it.

If with closed eyes you feel as if your body has gone up and you feel there is no weight to it, this is enough. For meditation this is enough. But if you are trying to learn levitation, then it is not enough. But I am not interested in that, and I will not tell you anything about it. This much is enough—that you feel that your body has no weight, it has become weightless.

Whenever you feel this weightlessness, just with closed eyes become aware of the form of your body. Just with closed eyes, feel your toes and their form, and the legs and their form, and then the form of the whole body. If you are sitting in *siddhasana,* just like a buddha, then feel the form while sitting like a buddha. Just inside try to feel the form of your body. It will become apparent, it will appear before you, and you will simultaneously become aware that just around the form there is a bluish light.

Do it with closed eyes in the beginning. And when this light goes on spreading and you feel an aura, a bluish aura, all around the form, then sometimes while doing it in the night with no light in a dark room, open your eyes and you will see it exactly around your body—a bluish form, just light, blue light, all around your body. If you want to see it actually, not with closed eyes but with open eyes, do it in a dark room with no light at all.

This bluish form, this bluish light, is the presence of the etheric body. You have many bodies. This technique is concerned with the etheric body, and through the etheric body you can enter into the highest ecstasy. There are seven bodies, and every body can be used to enter into the divine; every body is just a door.

This technique uses the etheric body, and the etheric body is the easiest to realize. The deeper the body, the more difficult; but the etheric body is just near you, just near the physical. It is just near. The second form is of the etheric—just around you, just around your body. It penetrates your body and it is also around your body just like a hazy light, a blue light, hanging all around like a loose robe.

Kind Devi, enter etheric presence pervading
far above and below your form.

Far above, below—everywhere around your form. If you can see that blue light around you, thinking will stop immediately, because for the etheric body, no thinking is needed. And the blue light is so calming, so soothing, so relaxing. Even ordinarily blue light is so soothing. Why?—because it is the light of your etheric body. The blue sky is so soothing. Why?—because it is the color of your etheric body, and the etheric body is very soothing.

Whenever someone loves you, whenever someone touches you with deep love, he touches your etheric body. That's why you feel it as such a soothing thing. It has even been photographed. Two lovers in deep love, making love: if their intercourse can continue beyond a certain limit, beyond forty minutes, and there is no ejaculation, around both the bodies, deep in love, a blue light appears. It has even been photographed.

And sometimes there have been very strange phenomena, because this light is a very subtle electric force. All around the world, many times it has happened that a new couple, staying in a new room on their honeymoon, or on their first night when they don't know each other's body and they don't know what is possible... If both the bodies are in a certain vibration of love, of attraction, of deep involvement and commitment—open, vulnerable to each other, ready to become one space—then sometimes it has happened accidentally that their bodies have become so electrified, their etheric body becomes so alive, that things in the room start falling.

Very strange phenomena: a statue is there on the table—suddenly it falls down. The glass on the table suddenly breaks. There is no one else, only the couple making love, and they have not even touched the glass. Or suddenly something catches fire... These cases have been reported to many police stations all around the world, and much investigation has been done, and then it was found that two persons in deep love can create such an electric force that it may affect things around them.

That force also comes through the etheric body. Your etheric body is your electric body. Whenever you are overflowing with energy, you have a bigger range to your etheric body. Whenever you are sad, depressed, you don't have any etheric body near your body. It recedes back into the body. So with a sad person, a depressed person, you will also feel sad. If a really sad person enters in this room, you will feel that something has gone wrong, because his etheric body affects you immediately. He becomes an exploiter, because his own etheric forces are so depressed they start feeding on others'.

A sad person will make you sad, a depressed person will make you depressed, an ill person will make you ill, because it is not only that which you see that he is; something hidden is constantly working. Even if he has not said anything, even if he is smiling outwardly, if he is depressed he will exploit you. Your etheric body will lose its energy—he will exploit, he will feed on you. When someone is happy and he enters, immediately you feel a happiness around you, because he is throwing so much etheric force. He is really giving you a feast; he is feeding you. He has so much he is overflowing.

When a Buddha moves around, or a Christ, or a Krishna, they are constantly giving you a feast, constantly you are guests. And when you come after seeing a Buddha, you feel so refreshed, so alive, so vitalized, so rejuvenated. What has happened? Buddha may not have said anything. Even a darshan, just a look, and you feel something has changed within you, something has entered within you.

What is entering? He is so overflowing with his energy…. And whosoever is at peace with himself is always overflooded, because his energy is not wasted in unnecessary nonsense in which you are wasting your energy. He is always overflooded, and whosoever comes can take. Jesus says, "Come unto me. If you are heavily burdened, come unto me. I will unburden you." Really he is not doing anything; it is just his presence.

It is said that whenever a godman, a tirth-ankara, an avatara, a Christ, moves on the earth, around him a particular milieu is created. Jaina yogis have even measured it. They say it is twenty-four miles. Twenty-four miles is the radius around a tirthankara, and for twenty-four miles in the whole radius everyone is flooded with his energy: knowing, not knowing, friend or enemy, following him or opposing him, it makes no difference.

If following, you are flooded more, because you are more open; if opposing, you are flooded, but not so much because you are closed—but the energy is flooding. A single man is such a reservoir; a single man, if undisturbed, silent, at ease, at home, is such a reservoir that for twenty-four miles around him in all directions a milieu is created. And in that milieu you are on a constant feast.

This happens through the etheric body. The etheric body is your electric body. The body that we see is the physical, the material. This is not really life. Life comes to this body because of the electric, the etheric body. That is your *prana*, that is your vitality.

So Shiva says: *Kind Devi, enter etheric presence….*

First you will have to become aware of the form that surrounds your physical form, and when you have become aware, then help it to grow, help it to increase and expand. What can you do?

Just sitting silently, looking at it, not doing anything, just looking at the bluish form around you, not doing anything, just looking at it, you will feel it is increasing, spreading, becoming bigger and bigger. Because when you are not doing anything, the whole energy goes to the etheric. Remember this. When you are doing anything, the energy is taken out of the etheric.

Lao Tzu says, "Nondoing, no one is stronger than me. Not doing anything at all, and no one is stronger than me. Those who are strong by doing can be defeated." Says Lao Tzu, "I cannot be defeated, because my energy comes from nondoing." So the secret is not doing anything.

What was Buddha doing under the bodhi tree? —not doing anything. He was not doing in that moment. He was not. Just sitting he achieved the ultimate. It looks puzzling. We are doing so much effort and nothing is achieved, and Buddha was not doing anything under the bodhi tree and he achieved the ultimate.

When you are not doing anything, your energy is not moving out. It goes to the etheric. It is accumulated there. Your etheric body becomes an electric reservoir. And the more it grows, the more you become silent. The more you become silent, the more it grows. And once you know how to give energy to the etheric body and how not to waste it unnecessarily, you have come to realize, you have come to know about a secret key.

Then you can be festive. Really, only then can you be festive. As you are now, drained of energy, how can you be festive? How can you celebrate? How can you blossom? Flowers are part of the luxury. When the tree is overflowing with energy, then flowers come. Flowers are always luxury.

If the tree is starved, flowers won't come, because even for the leaves there is not enough food, even for the roots there is not enough food. There is a hierarchy: first the roots will be fed, because they are the most basic. If they disappear, then there is no possibility for the flowers. Then the trunk will be fed, then the branches will be fed. If everything goes okay and energy is still there, then the leaves will be fed, and if still the food is there and the tree is totally satisfied and no food is needed, no energy is needed to exist and survive, suddenly it blooms. The overflowing energy becomes flowers. Flowers are a feast for others. It is a presentation. It is a gift from the tree to you.

And the thing happens in man also. A buddha is a tree which has flowered. Now the energy is so overflowing that he has invited all and sundry to come and share.

First try the first technique and then try the second. You can do it separately also, but it will be more difficult to realize the bluish form of the etheric body.

CHAPTER 64

Choicelessness is bliss

◆

Q U E S T I O N S

How is it that most choose suffering?

How can we hope for an enlightened society?

The first question:

Is it that there are only two alternatives before man —a life of abiding sorrow and suffering or one of divinity and bliss—and this choice lies with him? How is it that most have chosen the path of sorrow and suffering?

t is a very significant question, but very delicate also. The first thing to be understood is that life is very paradoxical, and because of that many things happen. These are the two alternatives: either man can be in heaven or in hell—and there is no third possibility. Either you can be in deep suffering, or you can be without suffering and in deep bliss. These are the only two possibilities, two openings, two doors, two modes of being.

Then the question necessarily arises why man chooses to be in suffering. Man never chooses to be in suffering, man always chooses to be in bliss— and there comes the paradox. If you choose to be in bliss, you will be in suffering, because to be in bliss means to be choiceless. This is the problem. If you choose to be in bliss you will be in suffering. If you don't choose, if you simply remain a witness, nonchoosing, you will be in bliss. So it is not a question of choosing between bliss and suffering; deep down it is a question of choosing between choosing and nonchoosing.

Why does it happen that whenever you choose you are in suffering?—because choice divides life: something has to be cut and thrown away. You don't accept the total. You accept something in it and you deny something, that's what choice means. And life is a totality. If you choose something and deny something, that which you deny will come to you, because life cannot be divided. And that which you deny, just because you deny it, becomes a powerful thing over you. You really become afraid of it.

Nothing can be denied. You can only close your eyes to it. You can only escape. You can become inattentive towards it, but it is always there hidden, waiting for the moment to assert. So if you deny suffering—if you say you are not going to choose suffering—then in a subtle way you have chosen it. Now it will always be around you—one thing.

Life is totality—the first thing; and life is change—the second thing. These are basic truths. You cannot divide life. Secondly: nothing is stagnant, and nothing can be. So when you say, "I am not going to suffer. I am going to choose a blissful mode of living," you will cling to happiness. And whenever you cling to something, you want it, you hope it will be permanent. And nothing can be permanent in life. Life is a flux.

So when you cling to happiness, you are again creating suffering, because this happiness will pass away; nothing can remain. It is a river, and the moment you cling to a river, you are creating a situation in which you will be frustrated, because the river will move. Sooner or later you will find that the river has gone far away. It is not now with you:

your hands are empty and your heart is frustrated.

If you cling to bliss, there will be moments of bliss, but they are going to pass away. Life is a flux. Nothing can be permanent here except you. Except you, nothing is eternal here, and if you cling to a changing thing, when it is gone you will suffer. And it is not only that when it is gone you will suffer; if you have the mind of clinging, while it is there you will not be able to enjoy it, because you will be constantly afraid that it is going to be lost.

If you cling you will miss the opportunity also. Later on you will suffer and right now you will not enjoy, because the fear is just around the corner— sooner or later it has to go. The guest has come to your house, and you know he is a guest and tomorrow morning he will leave. You start suffering for the future—tomorrow morning he will leave— and that pain, that suffering, that anguish, comes upon you right now. You cannot be happy while the guest is in your home. While the guest is with you, you cannot be happy because you are already in anxiety and anguish that tomorrow morning he will leave. So while he is there you will not be happy, and when he is gone you will be unhappy. This is what is happening.

The first thing: life cannot be divided. If you divide, only then can you choose. And that which you choose is fluxlike—sooner or later it will be gone—and that which you have denied will fall over you; you cannot escape it. You cannot say, "I will live only in the days and I will escape the nights." You cannot say, "I will live only with the ingoing breath and I will not allow the outgoing breaths."

Life is a rhythm of opposites. The breath comes in and goes out: between these two opposites— ingoing and outgoing—you exist. Suffering is there, happiness is there. Happiness is just like the ingoing breath, suffering is just like the outgoing breath; or day and night—the rhythm of opposites. You cannot say, "I will live only if I am happy. When I am not happy, I will not live."

You can take this attitude, but this attitude will make you suffer more. No one chooses suffering, remember. You ask why man has chosen to suffer. No one has chosen to suffer. You have chosen not to suffer, you have chosen to be happy, and you have chosen strongly. You are doing everything to be happy and that's why you are in suffering, why you are not happy.

So what is to be done? Remember that life is total. You cannot choose—the whole life has to be lived. There will be moments of happiness and there will be moments of suffering, and both have to be lived; you cannot choose. Because life is both —otherwise the rhythm will be lost, and without rhythm there will be no life.

It is just like music. You hear some music: there are notes, sounds, and after each sound there is silence, a gap. Because of that gap, that interval of silence, and the sound—because of both the opposites—music is created. If you say, "I will choose only sounds and I am not going to take the gaps," there will be no music. It will be a monotonous thing, it will be dead. Those gaps give life to sound. This is the beauty of life—that through opposites it exists. Sound and silence, sound and silence—that creates music, the rhythm. The same is with life. Suffering and happiness are two opposites. You cannot choose.

If you choose you have become a victim; you will suffer. If you become aware of this totality of the opposites and the way that life functions, you don't choose—the first thing. And when you don't choose there is no need to cling, there is no meaning in clinging. When suffering comes you enjoy the suffering, and when happiness comes you enjoy the happiness. When the guest is at home you enjoy him, when he has gone you enjoy the suffering, the absence, the pain. I say enjoy both. This is the path of wisdom: enjoy both, don't choose. Whatsoever falls upon you, accept it. It is your fate, it is how life is, and nothing can be done about it.

If you take this attitude, there is no choosing. You have become choiceless. And when you are choiceless, you will become aware of yourself, because now you are not worried about what happens, so you are not outgoing. You are not worried about what is happening around you. Whatsoever happens you will enjoy it, you will live it, you will go through it, you will experience it, and you will gain something out of it, because every experience is an expansion of consciousness.

If there is really no suffering you will be poor for it, because suffering gives you depth. A man who has not suffered will always remain on the surface. Suffering gives you depth. Really, if there is no suffering you will be saltless. You will be nothing, just a boring phenomenon. Suffering gives you tone, a keenness. A quality comes to you which only suffering can give, which no happiness can give. A man who has remained always in happiness, in comfort, who has not suffered, will not have any tone. He will be just a lump of being. There cannot be any depth. Really, there cannot be any heart. The heart is created through suffering; through pain you evolve.

If a man has only suffered and he has not known any happiness, then too he will not be rich, because richness comes through opposites. The more you move in opposites, the higher, the deeper you evolve. A man who has simply suffered will become a slave. He who has not known any moments of happiness will not be really alive. He will become an animal; he will just exist anyhow. There will be no poetry, no song in the heart, no hope in the eyes. He will settle down to his pessimistic existence. There will be no struggle, no adventure. He will not move. He will be simply a stagnant pool of consciousness, and a stagnant pool of consciousness is not conscious—by and by he will become unconscious. That's why if there is too much pain you fall unconscious.

So just happiness will not be of much help, because there will be no challenge. Just pain will not be of much growth, because there will be no reason to struggle, to hope, to dream; there will be no fantasy. Both are needed, and life exists between both as a very delicate tension, a subtle tension.

If you understand this, then you don't choose. Then you know how life functions, how life is. This is the way, this is the way of life—it moves through happiness, it moves through suffering and gives you tone, and gives you meaning, and gives you depth. So both are good.

I say both are good. I don't say choose between the two—I say both are good, don't choose. Rather, enjoy both; rather, allow both to happen. Be open, without any resistance. Don't cling to one and don't resist the other.

Let no-resistance be your motto: I will not resist life. Whatsoever life gives to me, I will be ready to take it, available, and I will enjoy it. The nights are also good and beautiful, and suffering has a beauty of its own. No happiness can have that beauty. Darkness has its own beauty; day has its own beauty. There is no comparison and there is no choice. Both have their own dimensions to work in.

The moment this consciousness arises in you, you will not choose. You will be just a witness, and you will enjoy—this choicelessness will become bliss. This choicelessness will become bliss. Bliss is not contrary to suffering; bliss is a quality which you can bring to anything whatsoever—even to suffering.

Buddha cannot suffer, but that doesn't mean that suffering doesn't happen to him. Remember, suffering happens as much to Buddha as it happens to you, but he cannot suffer because he knows the art of enjoying it. He cannot suffer because he remains blissful. Even in suffering he remains festive, meditative, alive, enjoying, open, nonresistant. Suffering happens to him, but he is not touched. Suffering comes and goes, just like a breath coming in and going out. He remains himself. The suffering cannot push him aside. The suffering cannot push him off his feet. Nothing can push him—neither suffering nor happiness. You exist like a pendulum: everything pushes you—everything. You cannot even be really happy, because happiness will also kill you. You get so involved in it.

I remember, once it happened that a poor school-master—very old, poor, retired—won a lottery. The wife was afraid and she thought, "This is going to be too much for the old man. Five thousand dollars is too much for him. Even a five-dollar note gives him so much happiness, so five thousand dollars may kill him."

She ran to the church, to the nearby church, and went to the priest and told him what had happened. She said, "The old man is out, but he is just coming back, this is his time to return, so do something. Five thousand dollars—just the news will kill him!"

The priest said, "Don't be afraid. I know the human mind and the way it functions. I know the psychology. I will come."

So the priest came to the house. The moment they arrived the old man also arrived, so the priest started. He said, "Suppose you won a lottery of five thousand dollars—what would you do?"

The old man thought about it, pondered over it, and he said, "I would give half of the money to the church."

The priest fell down dead. It was too much.

Even happiness will kill you, because you get so involved. You cannot remain out of anything. Suffering or happiness, whatsoever comes to your door, you get so involved in it you are just pushed off your feet. You are no more there. Just a breeze comes in the house and you are no more there.

What I am saying is that if you don't choose, if you remain alert and aware that this is how life is —days and nights come and go, suffering and happiness—you just witness. There is no clinging to happiness, no hankering for happiness, and no escape from suffering. You remain in yourself—centered, rooted. This is what bliss is.

So remember, bliss is not something opposite to suffering. Don't think that when you become blissful there will be no suffering—nonsense. Suffering is part of life. It ceases only when you are not. When you completely disappear from the body, suffering ceases. When there is no birth, suffering

ceases. But then you are lost in the totality, then you are no more—a drop has just fallen into the ocean and is no more.

While you are, suffering will continue. It is part of life. But you can become aware: then suffering happens somewhere around you, but it never happens to you. But then happiness also never happens to you. Don't think that happiness will go on happening to you and suffering will not happen —both will not happen to you. They will just happen around, just on the periphery, and you will be centered in yourself. You will see them happening, you will enjoy them happening, but they will happen around you; they will not happen to you.

This becomes possible if you don't choose. That's why I said this is delicate, subtle. Because of the paradoxical life, you choose happiness and you fall in suffering. You try to escape from suffering, and more and more suffering is invited. So you can take it as an ultimate law: whatsoever you choose, the opposite will be your fate. I say it as an ultimate law: whatsoever you choose, the opposite will be your fate.

So whatsoever is your fate, remember, you have chosen it by choosing the opposite. If you are suffering, you have chosen your suffering by choosing happiness. Don't choose happiness and suffering disappears. Don't choose at all. Then nothing can happen to you, and everything is a flux except you. That has to be understood very deeply.

Only you are the constant factor in existence, nothing else. Only you are the eternity, nothing else. Your awareness is never a flux. Suffering comes, you witness it. Then happiness comes, you witness it. Then nothing comes, you witness it. Only one thing remains constant—witnessing— and witnessing is you.

You were a child.... Or, if you move even further backwards, once you were just an atomic cell. You cannot even imagine it—just an atomic cell in your mother's womb, not even visible to the naked eyes. If that cell comes before you and you encounter it, you will not be able to recognize that once you were that. Then you were a child, then you became young, and now you are old, or lying on your deathbed. Many things happened. Your whole life has been a flux; nothing remained the same for even two moments.

Heraclitus says you cannot step twice in the same river—and this he says for the river of life. You cannot have two similar moments. The moment that has gone cannot be repeated. It is gone forever; you cannot have it again. The same cannot exist. In such a great flux, only one thing within you remains the same—the witnessing.

If you could have witnessed in your mother's womb, the quality of consciousness would have been the same. If you could have witnessed when you were a child, the quality of witnessing would have been the same. Young or dying, while just dying on your bed, if you can witness, the quality of consciousness will be the same.

The only one thing deep down within you is your witnessing self, your consciousness—that remains the same; everything else changes. And if you cling to any object of the world of change, you will suffer. Nothing can be done about it. You are trying to do the impossible, that's why you suffer. I know you never choose, but that is not the point— if you suffer, you have chosen it indirectly.

Once you become aware of this indirectness of life, this paradoxical quality of life, you will stop choosing. When choice falls, the world has disappeared. When choosing falls, you have entered the absolute.

But that is possible only when the choosing mind disappears completely. A choiceless awareness is needed and then you will be in bliss. Rather, you will be the bliss. And I will repeat again: suffering will continue to happen, but now nothing can make you suffer. Even if you are suddenly thrown into hell, just by your presence there, for you it will be a hell no more.

Someone asked Socrates where he would like to go, so Socrates said, "I don't know whether there is a hell and a heaven. I don't know whether they are there or not, but I will not choose between them. My only prayer will be this: allow me to be alert wherever I am. Let me be fully aware wherever I am. Whether it is hell or heaven, that is irrelevant." Because if you are fully alert, hell disappears—hell is your being not aware. If you are fully aware, heaven appears—heaven is your being fully aware.

Really there are no such geographical places as hell or heaven. And don't go on thinking in childish terms that someday you will die and God will send you to heaven or hell according to your doings, according to whatsoever you have done on earth. No, you carry your hell and heaven within you. Wherever you move, you carry your hell or heaven with you.

Even God cannot do anything. If suddenly you meet him, he will look like a hell. You carry your hell within you; you project it wherever you are. You will suffer. The encounter will be just death-like, intolerable. You may become unconscious. Whatsoever happens to you, you carry within you. The seed of consciousness is the seed of the whole existence.

So remember, if you suffer you have chosen it: consciously, unconsciously, directly, indirectly, you have chosen it. It is your choice and you are responsible. No one else is responsible.

But in our mind, in our confused mind, everything is upside-down. If you suffer, you think you suffer because of others. You suffer because of you. No one can make you suffer. That is impossible. And even if someone makes you suffer, it is your choice to be in suffering through him. You have chosen him and you have chosen a particular type of suffering through him. No one can make you suffer—it is your choice. But you always go on thinking that if the other changes, or if the other is doing something else, you will not suffer.

I have heard, Mulla Nasruddin was filling out a report because he had crashed his car into a parked car. He was filling out a report, and many things were asked. When he came to the part where it was asked what the driver of the other vehicle could have done to avoid the accident, he filled it, "He should have parked the car somewhere else. The car was parked there; he should have parked it somewhere else—because of him the accident has happened."

And this is what you are doing. Always the other is responsible: he should have done something or other and there would have been no suffering. No, the other is not responsible at all. You are responsible, and unless you take this responsibility consciously upon you, you will not change. The change will become possible, easily possible, the moment you realize that you are responsible for it.

If you have suffered, it was your choice. This is what the law of karma is, nothing else: you are wholly responsible. Whatsoever happens—suffering or happiness, hell or heaven—whatsoever happens, ultimately you are totally responsible. This is what the law of karma is: total responsibility is with you.

But don't be afraid, don't be scared by it, because if the total responsibility is with you, then suddenly a door of freedom opens—because if you are the cause of your suffering, you can change. If others are the cause, then you cannot change. Then how can you change? Unless the whole world changes, you will suffer. And there seems to be no way to change others—then suffering cannot end.

But we are so pessimistic that even such beautiful doctrines as the law of karma we interpret in such a way that they don't free and liberate us, but rather, on the contrary, they make us more burdened. In India the law of karma has been known for at least five thousand years or even more, but what have we done? It is not that we have taken responsibility upon ourselves; we have thrown all the responsibility on the law of karma—that it is happening because of the law of karma and we cannot do anything, nothing can be done; because of the past lives this life is such.

The law of karma was to free you. It was giving you total freedom towards yourself. No one else

can make any suffering for you—this was the message. If you are suffering you have created it. You are the master of your fate, and if you want to change it, immediately you can change it and the life will be different. But the attitude....

I have heard, once two friends were talking. One was a bonafide optimist, the other a bonafide pessimist. Even the optimist was not too happy about the situation. The optimist said, "If this economic crisis continues and these political catastrophes continue and the world remains the same as it is, immoral, then we are going to be reduced to begging soon."

Even he was not too hopeful about it—the optimist. When he said, "We are going to be reduced to begging," the pessimist said, "From whom? From whom are you going to beg if this condition continues?"

You have a mind, and you go on bringing your mind to everything. Really, you transform the quality of every teaching and doctrine. You defeat Buddhas and Krishnas so easily because you convert the whole thing; you color it in your own way.

You are totally responsible for whatsoever you are and for whatsoever world you are living in. It is your creation. If this goes deep in you, you can change everything. You need not suffer. Don't choose, be a witness, and bliss will happen to you. Bliss is not a dead state. Suffering will go on continuing around you. So it is not a question of what happens to you; it is a question of how you are. The total ultimate meaning comes from you, not from the happening.

The second question:

Last night You talked about boredom. How can we hope for an enlightened society when in order to maintain society most people must perform boring, monotonous and repetitive tasks?

Again: nothing is boring, nothing is repetitive and monotonous—you are, and you bring your quality to everything that you do. No act is boring in itself, and no act can be nonboring in itself—it is you who make it boring or nonboring. And the same act can be a boredom to you this moment and the next moment it may become a blissful thing. Not that the act has changed; your mood, the quality you bring to the act, has changed. So remember, you are not bored because repetitive acts have to be done. Rather, on the contrary, you are bored—that's why they appear repetitive.

For instance, children want to repeat things. They go on playing the same game again and again. You get bored. What are they doing? The same game again and again? They go on asking for the same story. They enjoy it again and again, and they say, "Tell me that story again."

What is the matter? You cannot conceive of it, it looks stupid. It is not. They are so alive that nothing is repetitive for them. You are dead and everything is repetitive for you. They go on repeating the same game. The whole day they can go on, and if you stop them they will scream and cry and they will resist you, saying, "Don't destroy our game." And you cannot understand what they are doing the whole day.

They have a different quality of consciousness. Nothing is repetitive for them. They enjoy it so much that the very enjoyment changes the quality, and then they enjoy it again—and they enjoy it more, because now they know the know-how. The third time they enjoy it even more, because now they are acquainted with everything. They go on enjoying; their enjoyment goes on increasing. Your enjoyment goes on decreasing.

What is the matter? Is the act itself boring, or is something wrong with your mode of being, your mode of consciousness?

Look at it from another angle. Two lovers will go on repeating the same acts every day. They will kiss and they will hug—they are the same acts. And they would like to go on doing that ad infinitum. If you give them time, they will go on repeating to the very end of existence. Looking at two lovers, you will get bored. What are they doing?—

the same thing every day? And if you give them the whole day, they will go on hugging, loving, embracing, kissing. What are they doing?

Lovers have again become children. That's why love is so innocent—it makes you a child again. Now they are enjoying the game. They are again children. They have thrown the whole nonsense of maturity. They are playing with each other's body, and to them nothing is repetitive. Each kiss is something absolutely new, unique. It was never so before, it will never be the same again. Each moment of love has its own individual existence, nonrepetitive; that's why they go on enjoying.

The economic law of diminishing returns doesn't apply to it. For love, there is no law of diminishing returns; rather, increasing returns. That's why economists cannot understand love, mathematicians cannot understand love. All those who are efficient in calculation cannot understand love, because this is absurd: it defies all laws, all mathematics—it goes on increasing.

When I was a student, when my teacher of economics explained to us about the law of diminishing returns, I asked him about love, "What do you say about love?"

He became disturbed, and when I said that just the contrary—the law of increasing returns—applies to love, he said to me, "You go out of the class. You cannot understand economics." He said, "This law is universal."

I said, "Don't say it is universal, because what about love?"

Two lovers appear to us as if they are repeating. To them, they are not repeating. But to a prostitute the law of economics will apply, because for her, love is not love, it is a commodity—something to be sold, something which can be purchased. So if you go and kiss a prostitute, for her it is boredom, repetition, and someday she will say. "This is nonsense. I am bored of being kissed and kissing the whole day. It is intolerable." She will say that it is a repetitive act.

That's what I want to show you—the distinction. For a lover it is not repetitive; for a prostitute it is repetitive. So, really, the act itself is not repetitive; it is your quality that you bring to it. Whatsoever you do, if you love it, it will never be repetitive. If you love your doings, your acts, there will be no boredom. But you don't love.

I go on talking to you every day. I can go on ad infinitum. I love it. It is not repetitive for me. From eternity to eternity I can go on talking with you. Communication, to communicate with your heart, is love to me. It is not a repetitive act, otherwise I would get bored.

I have heard, one small child went with his father and mother to the church one Sunday, and then the next and the next. On the third Sunday this little child asked his father, "God must be getting bored, because there are the same faces every day in the church. For three Sundays we have been coming here—the same faces! God must be bored, seeing them turning up again and again every Sunday."

But God is not bored. The whole existence has been repeating continuously. It looks like repetition to us, but if there is a being, a total being, something like a God, he is not bored. If he is bored there is no need to continue. He can stop. He can say, "No more!" He can say, "Finished!" But he is not bored. Why?

He loves—whatsoever is happening is his love. He is a creator, not a worker, not a laborer. He is a creator.

A Picasso is not bored, he is a creator. If your act becomes creation, you will not be bored. And your act becomes creation if you love it. But the basic difficulty is that you cannot love whatsoever you do because you hate yourself—that's the problem. So whatsoever you do, you hate it, because basically you hate yourself.

You have not yet accepted yourself, you have not yet thanked existence for your existence. From your heart there is no thank-you towards God. Really, you have a grudge—"Why have you created me?" Deep down you go on asking, "Why

have I been thrown into existence? What is the purpose?" Think, if suddenly God meets you, what will be the first question you will ask? You will ask, "Why have you created me? to suffer? to be in agony? to be unnecessarily wandering through lives and lives? Why did you create me? Answer!"

You have not accepted yourself so how can you accept your acts? Love yourself. Accept yourself as you are. Because action is secondary, it flows from your being; if I love myself then whatsoever I do I love it—and if I don't love it I stop it. What is the need to continue?

But you don't love, and the source is unloved so the products of that source cannot be loved. Whatsoever you do—you may be an engineer or you may be a doctor or a chemist or a scientist—whatsoever you do, you will bring hate to it. Your hate makes it repetitive. You hate it, and you go on finding excuses for why you are doing it. You say, "I am doing it for my wife, for my children." And your father was doing it for you, and his father was doing it for him, and your children will do it for their children, and no one will enjoy life.

These are tricks. You are simply a coward. You cannot escape from it, because it gives you security, safety, income, bank balance. Because you are a coward, you cannot stop doing it and you cannot start doing that which you love. Then you go on putting everything on your children, on your wife, and they are also doing the same.

Ask the child. He is going to the school, he is bored. He says, "I am going for my father. He feels happy. If I don't go he feels very miserable." And your wife?—she is doing everything just for you and the children. No one is really existing for himself. No one loves himself enough to exist for himself. Then everything goes wrong. The source is poisoned, and then all that comes out of that source is poisoned.

And don't think that if you change your job, you will love it. No, you will bring your quality to the new job also. In the beginning it may be a sensation, something new, but sooner or later you will settle down and it will be the same. Change yourself, love yourself, and love whatsoever you do —howsoever small, it makes no difference.

I am reminded of an anecdote. It happened that when Abraham Lincoln became president, on the first day when he was inaugurating the Senate, someone who was very jealous of his power, his prestige, his success, stood and said to Abraham Lincoln, "Lincoln, don't forget that your father was a shoemaker."

It was absolutely irrelevant, absurd, and the man who said this added, "Your father was a shoemaker, and he used to make shoes for my family. Don't forget him."

It was just to insult him, and the whole Senate laughed because everyone was jealous. Deep down everyone was feeling, "This chair belongs to me, and this man has usurped it." Of course, whenever someone succeeds, he succeeds in some cunning way; only you succeed rightly. This is how we adjust to others' successes—it was by cunning, by some wrong techniques somehow that he reached. This is how we can tolerate it and console ourselves. So the whole Senate laughed.

But Abraham Lincoln said something which is beautiful. He said, "It is so good of you to remind me of my father. I know he was a shoemaker—but I have never seen such a shoemaker. He was unique, he was a creator, because he loved shoemaking. And I cannot think myself as successful as he was, because I don't love this presidency as much as he loved shoemaking. He enjoyed it, he was blissful. I will never be as blissful in this presidency as he was just as a shoemaker.

"But why have you remembered him this moment? I know," said Abraham Lincoln, "that my father was making shoes for your family, but they never complained, so I hope the shoes were all right. But you remember him in this moment, without any relevance—I feel some shoe is still pinching. I am his son, I can repair it."

If you love yourself, if you love your work, you live in a different milieu. In that milieu nothing is repeated. Repetition appears only to a bored mind. Don't say that you are bored because of repetitive acts. Acts appear repetitive because you are bored —then whatsoever you do will appear repetitive.

But look at life—life enjoys repetition. The seasons move in a circle. The sun moves in a circle —every day, every morning, it arises. And the summer comes and the winter comes and the rains come and they go on moving. In a deep way the whole existence is repetitively moving. It seems creation is just like a child's play. The trees are not bored, and the sky is not bored. The sky never says, "Now again the clouds?" For so many many millennia the sky has been seeing the clouds— every rainy season the clouds come and they start moving. Look at life! It is repetitive.

The word is not good; the word "repetitive" is not good. Rather, it will be better to say it goes on playing the same game. It enjoys it so much that it wants to repeat it again. And it goes on increasing; it goes on moving towards a climax. Why does man get bored with repetition? Not because repetition is boring, but because you are so bored that everything will be boring.

Once it happened that Sigmund Freud was asking a patient questions; just the preliminary basic questions that he asked before the psychoanalysis could start. He asked, "Look at the bookcase, and what does it immediately remind you of?"

The man looked at the books, not really looking at all, and he said, "It reminds me of a woman, a beautiful woman."

This was good for Freud, because it was falling in with his theory that everything is sexual, so he said, "Okay." Then he took his handkerchief and said, "Look at this. What does this remind you of immediately?—whatsoever comes to your mind."

The man laughed and said, "A beautiful woman."

Freud was overjoyed. Really that was his theory —that every man is basically concerned with sex and nothing else. Man thinks of woman, woman thinks of man—and that is all thinking. So he said, "Look at the door." There was no one at the door, there was no one even moving in the street. He said, "Look, there is no one. This absence—what do you feel? What do you immediately remember?"

The man said, "A beautiful woman."

Now even Freud was a little disturbed whether this man was just deceiving him or not, so he said, "It seems too much. Everything makes you remember a woman!"

The man said, "That is not the point. Whether it is a bookcase or a handkerchief or an empty door is not the point. Really, I never think of anything except of women. I never think of anything else, so whatsoever you say is irrelevant. I think only of women. It is not that everything reminds me of them; I am thinking only of women—it is not a question of any reminding."

So really it is not a question that this act makes you bored or that act makes you bored, or repetition or monotony or tedious jobs make you bored. The real thing is that you are bored whether you do something or not. If you are simply relaxing in a chair you will be bored. Not doing anything you will be bored. You will say, "There is nothing to do and I am bored. Nothing to do—I am bored." The whole week you are bored because of the tedious job, and on the weekend you are bored because there is nothing to do. The whole life you are bored because of doing a repetitive job in a factory, in an office, in a shop. Then when you retire you are bored, because now there is nothing to do.

It is not a question of anything else. Something is not creating boredom in you; you are bored, and you go on bringing your boredom to everything that you touch. You have heard of King Midas—whatsoever he touched became gold. You are also a King Midas—whatsoever you touch becomes boredom. You have an alchemical touch: you can change everything into a boredom; everything, I say.

Don't think of changing jobs, actions; think of changing the quality of your consciousness. Be more loving to yourself. The first thing to remember is to be more loving to yourself. The moralists have poisoned the whole world. They say, "Don't love yourself, this is selfishness." They say, "Love others, don't love yourself. The love of the self is sin."

And I say to you that this is absolute nonsense—and not only nonsense; it is dangerous nonsense. Unless you love yourself you cannot love anybody, it is impossible, because a man who is not in love with himself cannot be in love with anybody. If you are in love with yourself, only then can your overflowing love reach somebody.

A man who has not loved himself will hate himself, and if you yourself hate yourself, how can you love anybody else? You will hate others also. You can only pretend. And when you cannot love yourself, how do you expect others to love you? Everyone is condemned in his own eyes. The whole moralistic teaching gives you only one thing: techniques of self-condemnation—how to condemn yourself, how you are bad, a criminal, guilty, a sinner.

Christianity says that your being a sinner is not a question of what you do; you are born a sinner. It is not a question of whether you do some sin or not; no, you are a born sinner. Man is born in sin. Adam, the first man, committed the sin, and you are descendants. The sin has been committed, nothing can be done. Now it cannot be undone, and you are born into sin—Adam's sin.

If you are born in sin, how can you love yourself? If your very being is guilt, how can you love yourself? And if you cannot love yourself, you cannot love anybody. The love must happen at home first—you are the home—and only when it overflows can it reach to others. And when it overflows, it overflows into your acts, into whatsoever you do. Whether you paint or make a shoe or anything—just cleaning the street—whatsoever you do, if you are in deep love, if you are in deep love with yourself, it flows into everything you do. It flows even when you are not doing anything. It goes on flowing, it becomes your very existence, and then nothing is boring.

People come to me; sometimes very sympathetically some friends ask me, "The whole day you are sitting in one room, not even looking out of the window. Don't you get bored?" I am with myself, why should I get bored? They say, "Just sitting alone, don't you get bored?"

If I hate myself I will get bored, because you cannot live with a person you hate. You get bored with yourself; you cannot be alone. Even if you are alone for a few moments you get fidgety, you get uncomfortable, an uneasiness comes into your being. You long to meet someone, because you cannot remain with yourself. The company is so boring—your own company. You cannot look at your own face. You cannot touch your hand lovingly; no—impossible.

They ask me—and their asking is relevant to their own reference, because they will get bored if they are alone—they ask me, "Don't you go out sometimes?" There is no need. Sometimes they ask me, "People come to you with the same problem again and again. Don't you get bored?"

Because everyone has the same problem… You are so unoriginal you cannot even create an original problem. Everyone has the same problem. Some are related with your love, with your sex, with your peace of mind, with your confusion, or something else—some psychology, some pathology, something—but man can be easily divided into seven categories, and there are the same questions, the seven basic questions, and people go on asking them. So friends ask me, "Don't you get bored?"

I never get bored, because each individual is unique to me, and because of the individual, the problem he brings is not a repetition because the context is different, the individual is different. You come with your love problem, another comes with his love problem: both look similar but they are not, because two individuals are so different—their difference changes the quality of the problem.

So if you categorize, you can categorize into seven categories—but I never categorize. Each individual is so unique that he cannot be put with anyone else. No category can be made. But then you have to have a very keen awareness to penetrate to the very root where the individual is unique. Otherwise, on the surface everyone is alike.

Just on the surface everyone is alike, with the same problems, but if you penetrate deep, if you are alert and ready to move with the person to the deeper core of his being, the deeper you go, the more original, individual and unique a phenomenon comes into being. If you can see to the very center, this person before you is unrepeatable. He has never been before, he will never be again. He is just unique. And the mystery then overfills you—the mystery of the unique person.

Nothing is a repetition if you know how to penetrate, how to be loving and alert. Otherwise everything is repetitive. You are bored because you have a consciousness which creates boredom. Change the consciousness, and there will be no boredom. But you go on changing objects—that will not make any difference.

CHAPTER 65

Destroy the limits

◆

92 *Put mindstuff in such inexpressible fineness above, below and in your heart.*

93 *Consider any area of your present form as limitlessly spacious.*

L ife is not a problem but a mystery. For science life is a problem, but for religion it is a mystery. A problem can be solved, a mystery cannot be solved—it can be lived but it cannot be solved. Religion offers no solutions, no answers. Science offers answers; religion has none. This is the basic difference, and before you make any effort to understand what religion is, this basic difference in the very approach of a religious mind and a scientific mind is to be deeply understood.

When I say that science looks at life as a problem, as something which can be solved, the whole approach becomes intellectual. Then the mind is involved, not you. You are out of it. The mind manipulates, the mind tackles, the mind penetrates and analyzes. The mind argues, doubts, experiments, but you as a totality are out of it. Hence this very puzzling phenomenon: a scientist may be a very keen intellectual as far as his own department of research is concerned, but in ordinary life he will be just as ordinary a human being as anyone else— nothing special, just ordinary. In his own branch of knowledge he may be a genius, but in life he is just ordinary.

Science includes only your intellect, not your totality. An intellect has a violence, it is aggressive. That is why very few women can be scientists— aggression is not natural to them. Intellect is male, aggressive, violent: that is why men are more scientific and women are more religious. Intellect tries to dissect, divide, analyze, and whenever you dissect an alive thing, the life disappears. Only dead parts are left in your hands.

That is why science never touches life. Really, whatsoever it touches becomes dead. When science says there is no soul or there is no God it is meaningful, not because there is no soul or no God, but because this shows that the very approach of the scientific mind is such that you cannot touch life anywhere. Wherever science touches, death happens. In the very method, in the very way, in the very approach of division, analysis, dissection, life is bracketed out.

One thing: intellect is violent and aggressive, so the ultimate outcome through intellect can only be death, not life. It is partial, not total, and parts are dead. Life is an organic unity. You can know life through synthesis, not through analysis. The greater the synthesis the higher the forms of life that evolve. God is the ultimate synthesis, the total unity, the wholeness of existence. God is not a puzzle but the ultimate synthesis of all that is; matter is the ultimate analysis of all that is.

So science comes to atomic materiality and religion comes to cosmic consciousness. Science moves downwards to the last, lowest denominator and religion moves upwards to the highest denominator. They move in opposite dimensions. So science transforms everything into a problem, because if you have to tackle it scientifically, you first have to decide whether it is a problem or not. Religion takes mystery as the base. There is no problem, life is not a problem. The emphasis is that it cannot be solved.

A problem means something solvable, something which can be known, something knowable. It may not be known right now, but it is not unknowable. At the most it may be unknown, but that unknownness will disappear and it will be transformed into a known thing.

So really, religion cannot ask a question like, "What is life?" This is absurd. Religion cannot ask such a question as, "What is God?" This is nonsense. The very approach of religion is not to create problems. Religion can ask how to be more alive, how to be in the very current of life, how to live abundantly; religion can ask how to be a god—but it cannot ask what God is.

We can live mysteries, we can become one with them, we can lose ourselves in them; we can have a totally difference existence, the very quality changes—but nothing is solved, because nothing can be solved. And all that appears to be solvable, all that appears to be knowable, is only because we are taking it in fragments. If we look at the whole then nothing is knowable, we just go on pushing the mystery backwards.

All our answers are temporary, they appear to be answers only to lazy minds. If you have a penetrating mind you will come again upon the same mystery, only it has been pushed back, a step back. Just behind the answers the question is hidden. You have simply created a façade of an answer, just a curtain over the mystery.

If you can feel the distinction, then from the very beginning religion takes on a different shape, a different color and a different view. The whole perspective changes. These techniques that we are discussing here are not to solve anything—they don't take life as a problem. Life is there. It has been a mystery and will remain a mystery. Whatsoever we do we cannot demystify it, because to be mysterious is the very quality of it. That life is mysterious is not something accidental, it is not something which can be separated, it is the very life itself. So to me, the more you enter into the mysterium, into the mysterious, the more religious you become.

A really religious man will not say that he believes in God; he will not say that God exists. These things seem to be very superficial, they seem to be like answers given to certain questions. A religious man cannot utter such profanities—that God is. It is such a profound phenomenon, such a mysterious thing, that to say anything will be profane. So whenever someone asked Buddha whether God existed or not, he remained silent. You are asking a thing which cannot be answered. Not that there is no God, but to answer such a thing will make it answerable. Then life will become a problem which can be answered. Then the mystery disappears. So Buddha said, "Don't ask me any metaphysical questions."

Questions can only be physical. Physics can answer them. Metaphysical questions are not there, they cannot be, because metaphysics means the mystery.

These techniques are to help you to move more deeply into mystery, not into knowledge.

Or you can look at it in a different way: these techniques are to help you to be unburdened of your knowledge. They are not to help you to increase your knowledgeability, because knowledgeability is the barrier. The door is then closed for the mystery. The more you know, the less you are capable of penetrating deep into life. The original wonder must be recaptured, because in a childlike sense of wonder nothing is known and everything becomes a mystery. And if you move into the mystery, the deeper you move, the deeper the mystery becomes. Then a moment comes when you can say that you don't know anything. That is the right moment.

Now you have become meditative. When you can feel a deep ignorance, when you become aware that you don't know anything, you have come to the right balancing point from where the door of the mystery can open. If you know, then the door is closed; if you are ignorant, fully alert that you don't know anything, the door suddenly opens. The very feeling that you don't know opens the door.

So take these techniques not as knowledge, but as a help to make you more innocent. Ignorance is innocent, knowledge is always a sort of cunningness, cleverness. If you can use your knowledge to be ignorant again, then you have used it rightly. This is the only use of all the scriptures, of all the knowledge, of all the Vedas—to make you childlike again.

92 Be aware of moments of no-thought.

Now the first technique: *Put mindstuff in such inexpressible fineness above, below and in your heart.*

Three things. First, if knowledge is important then the head is the center; if childlike innocence is important then the heart is the center. The child lives in the heart; we live in the head. The child feels; we think. Even when we say that we feel, we think that we feel. Thinking becomes primary for us, feeling becomes secondary. Thinking is the tool for science, feeling is the tool for religion.

You must start to be a feeling organism again. And both the dimensions are different. When you think, you remain separate; when you feel, you melt.

Think about a flower, a roseflower. When you think, you are separate, there is a gap, a distance, a space. For thinking, space is needed; for thoughts to move, distance is needed. Feel the flower and the gap disappears, the distance drops, because for feeling, distance is the barrier. The closer you come, the more you feel. A moment comes when even closeness appears to be a sort of distance—and then melting happens. Then you cannot feel the boundaries of where you are and where the flower is, of where you end and where the flower begins. Then boundaries melt into each other: the flower enters you in a way, you enter the flower in a way. Feeling is losing the boundaries; thinking is creating the boundaries. That is why thinking always insists on definitions, because without definitions you cannot create boundaries.

Thinking says define first, and feeling says don't define. If you define, feeling stops.

The child feels; we think. The child comes close to existence, he melts and allows the existence to melt into him. We are isolated, imprisoned in the head. We are like islands.

This sutra says to come back to the heart center. Start feeling things. It will be a great experiment if you start feeling things. Whatsoever you do, give a certain amount of your time and energy to feeling. You are sitting here, you can listen to me—but that will be part of thinking. You can also feel me here but that will not be a part of thinking. If you can feel my presence, then definitions are lost. Then really, if you come to a moment of feeling, you don't know who is speaking and who is listening. This can happen right this very moment. Then the speaker becomes the listener and the listener becomes the speaker, then really they are not two. Rather, they are two poles of one phenomenon: on one pole is the speaker, on another pole is the listener. But these are just poles, isolated. They are not real. The real thing is just in-between these two —the life, the flow. Whenever you feel, something other than your ego becomes important. Object and subject lose their definitions. A flow, a wave, exists—on one pole the speaker, on another pole the listener, but life is the wave.

Head gives you clarity, and because of this clarity much confusion has come into being because the head defines clearly, marks boundaries, makes maps. With reason, everything is clear-cut; no vagueness, no mystery is allowed. All that is vague is rejected, only the clear is real. Reason gives you a clarity, and because of clarity, a great misunderstanding arises. Clarity is not reality. Reality is always unclear, vague. Concepts are clear, reality is mysterious; concepts are rational, reality is irrational.

Words are clear, logic is clear, life is not clear. The heart gives you a melting vagueness. It reaches reality more intimately, but it is not clear. And because we have chosen clarity as the goal, we have been missing reality. You must have unclear eyes to enter reality again. You must be vague, you must be ready to enter into something which cannot be conceptualized, into something which is not logic, into something which is staggering and real, staggering and alive.

Clarity is dead. It remains fixed. Life is a flux, nothing is fixed, nothing remains the same the next moment. How can you be clear about it? If you insist too much on clarity you will lose contact with it. That is what has happened.

This sutra says that the basic thing is to come back to the heart center—but how to come to it? *Put mindstuff in such inexpressible fineness above, below and in your heart.*

The word "mindstuff" is not a good translation of the original Sanskrit word *chit*. But English has no other equivalent. So it is good in a way, it carries the meaning, not of "mind" but of "mindstuff."

Mind means mentation, thinking, thought, and mindstuff means the background upon which these thoughts float—just as in the sky the clouds move. Clouds are the thoughts and the sky is the background upon which they move. That sky, consciousness, has been called mindstuff. Your mind can be without thoughts; then it is chit, then it is pure mind. When it has thoughts it is impure mind.

If your mind can be without thought, then it is very subtle, the subtlest thing possible in existence. You cannot conceive of a more subtle possibility. Consciousness is the most subtle thing. So when there are no thoughts in the mind, you have pure mind. The pure mind can move towards the heart, the impure mind cannot. By impurity I don't mean any immoral thoughts in the mind; by impurity I mean all thoughts—thought as such is impure.

Even if you are thinking of God it is an impurity, because the cloud is moving. The cloud is very white, but the cloud is there and the purity of the space is not there. A cloudless sky is not there. A cloud may be a black cloud, a sexual thought moving in the mind, or the cloud may be a white cloud, beautiful, a prayer moving in the mind, but in both cases the pure mind is not there. It is impure, clouded. And if the mind is clouded you cannot move to the heart.

This has to be understood because with thoughts you cling to the head. Thoughts are the roots, and unless those roots are cut you cannot fall back to the heart.

The child remains in the heart only up to the moment that thoughts crystallize, that thoughts start floating in his mind. Then they take root; then through education, culture, cultivation, they become rooted; then by and by the consciousness moves from the heart to the head. The consciousness can remain in the head only if there are thoughts. This is basic. If there are no thoughts, consciousness immediately drops back to its original innocence in the heart.

Hence so much emphasis on meditation, so much emphasis on nonthinking, on thoughtless awareness, on choiceless awareness, or on Buddha's "right mindfulness," which is just mindfulness without any thought, just being aware. What happens then? A very great phenomenon happens because when the roots are cut, immediately consciousness drops back to the heart, to the original place where it had been. You become a child again.

Jesus said, "Only those who are like children will enter into the kingdom of my God." He refers to those persons whose consciousness has come back to the heart. They have become innocent, childlike.

But the first basic requirement is to *Put mindstuff in such inexpressible fineness....*

Thoughts can be expressed. There is not a single thought which is inexpressible, nor can there be. If it is inexpressible you cannot think it; if you can think it, it is expressible. There is not a single thought which you can say is inexpressible. The moment you can think it, it has become expressible —you have already expressed it to yourself.

Consciousness, pure consciousness, is inexpressible. That is why mystics go on saying that they cannot express what they know. Logicians always raise the question that if you know, then why can't you say it? And their argument has meaning and significance. If you really say that you know then why can't you express it?

For a logician, knowledge must be expressible —that which can be known can be made known to others, there is no problem. If you have known it, then where is the problem? You can make it known to others. But the mystic's knowledge is not of thoughts. He has not known it as a thought, he has known it as a feeling. So really, it is not good to say, "I know God." It is better to say, "I feel." It is not good to say, "I have known God." It is better to say, "I have felt him." That is a more accurate description of the phenomenon because the "knowledge" is through the heart; it is like feeling, it is not like knowledge.

Put mindstuff in such inexpressible fineness.... Mindstuff, consciousness, chit, is inexpressible. If a single thought is moving, it is expressible. So, to *Put mindstuff in such inexpressible fineness* means to come to a point where you are conscious, but not conscious of any thought; where you are alert, but there is no thought moving in the mind. This is a delicate point and very difficult—you can miss it easily.

We know two states of mind. One is when thoughts are there. When thoughts are there, you cannot move to the heart. Then we know another state of mind—when thoughts are not there. When thoughts are not there, you fall asleep. Then too, you cannot move to the heart. Every night, for a few moments, for a few hours, you fall out of thinking. Thoughts cease, but you don't reach to the heart because you are unconscious. So a very delicate balance is needed. Thoughts must cease as they cease in deep sleep, when there is no dream— and you must be as alert as you are while awake. These two points must meet. Mind must be as thoughtless as it is in deep sleep, but you must not be asleep, you must be perfectly alert, aware.

When awareness and this thoughtlessness meet, it is meditation. That is why Patanjali says that *samadhi* is like *sushupti.* The highest ecstasy, samadhi, is like the deepest sleep, with only one difference: in it you are not asleep. But the quality is the same—thoughtless, dreamless, undisturbed, without a single ripple, totally calm and quiet, but alert. When you are aware and there is no thought, you will feel a sudden transformation in your consciousness. The center changes. You are thrown back. You are thrown to the heart. And from the heart, when you look at the world, there is no world, there is only God. From the head, when you look towards existence, there is no God, there is only material existence.

Matter, material existence, the world, and God are not two things, two outlooks, two perspectives. They are the same phenomenon looked at from two centers of being.

Put mindstuff in such inexpressible fineness above, below and in your heart. Be totally in it, merged, immersed. Be simply consciousness, above, below, in the heart; the whole heart surrounded by simple consciousness; not thinking anything in particular, just being aware, with no word, with no verbalization, not thinking at all, just being.

Put mindstuff above, below, and in your heart, and everything will become possible to you. All the doors of perception will be cleansed and all the doors of mysteries will be opened. Suddenly there will be no problem, and suddenly there will be no misery—it is as if the darkness has disappeared completely. Once you know this you can move back to the head but you will not be the same. Now you can use the head as an instrument. You can work with it, but now you are not identified with it, and even while working with it and looking at the world through it, you will know that whatsoever you are seeing is because of the intellect. Now you are acquainted with a higher standpoint, a deeper view—and any moment you want to you can drop back.

Once you know the passage and how consciousness drops back, how your age, your past, your memory and your knowledge disappear and you become a newborn child again—once you know this secret, this passage, you can travel to that point as many times as you like, and you can be refreshed again and again. If you have to move to the head, you can use it; you can move in the ordinary world, working but not getting involved in it, because deep down you know that that which is known by the intellect is partial. It is not the whole truth. And a partial truth is more dangerous than a lie, because it appears to be true and you can be deceived by it.

Some more points. When you move to the heart, you look at existence as a total being. The heart is not departmental, the heart is not a fragment of you, the heart means you in your totality. Mind is a fragment, hand is a fragment, leg is a fragment, stomach is a fragment, the whole body taken in parts is fragmented. The heart is not a fragment. That is why my hand can be cut off and I will be alive. Even my brain can be removed and I will be alive, but if the heart is gone, I am gone.

Really, my whole body can be removed but if my heart is beating I am alive. The heart means your wholeness, so when the heart fails, you are no longer there. All other things are just parts, disposable. If the heart is beating you will remain intact. The center of the heart is the very core of your existence.

I can touch you with my hand, that touch will give me a certain knowledge about you, about your skin, whether it is smooth or not. The hand will give a certain knowledge to me, but that knowledge will be partial because the hand is not my wholeness.

I can see you. My eyes will give a certain knowledge from a different standpoint but that will not be the whole. I can think about you—again the same thing. But I cannot feel you in part. If I feel you at all I feel you in your wholeness. That is why, unless you know through love, you never know the wholeness of any person.

Only love can reveal the whole personality to you, the whole being, the essential, the total, because love means knowing through the heart, feeling through the heart. So to me, feeling and knowing are not two fragments of your being. Feeling is your whole being and knowing is just a fragment of it.

To religion love is the highest knowledge. That is why religion is expressed more in poetic terms than in scientific ones. Scientific terms cannot be used, they belong to the realm of knowing. Poetry can be used. And those who have come to know reality through love, whatsoever they say becomes poetry. The Upanishads, the Vedas, the sayings of Jesus or Buddha or Krishna, they are all poetic statements.

It is not just a coincidence that all the old religious scriptures are written in poetry. It has a significance. It shows that there is some affinity between the world of a poet and the world of a mystic. The mystic is also using the language of the heart.

The poet is only a mystic in certain moments of flight, just as when you jump you can go away from the gravitation of the earth, but you again come back to it. A poet means a person who has been for some seconds on a flight into the world of the mystics. He has had some glimpses. A mystic is one who has gone beyond gravitation completely, who lives in the world of love, who lives through the heart. This has become his very abode. For the poetic person it is just a glimpse; sometimes he falls down from the head to the heart. But this is just for the time being—again he goes back to the head. So if you see a beautiful poem, don't try to see the poet who has written it because you will not meet the same person. You will be disappointed because you will meet a very ordinary man. He had a glimpse. For certain moments reality was revealed to him and he came down to the heart. But he doesn't know the passage; he is not the master of it. It has been a happening and he cannot move to it by his own will.

When Coleridge died he left about forty thousand incomplete poems. He really completed only seven poems in his whole life. He became a great poet, one of the greatest in the world, but he was asked many times, "Why do you go on piling up incomplete poems, and when are you going to complete them?"

He said, "I cannot do anything. Sometimes a few lines come to me and then they stop. So how can I complete them? I will wait. I will have to wait. If it happens again and the glimpse comes to me, and I again have the world revealed to me, the reality, then I will complete it. But on my own I can do nothing." He must have been a very sincere poet. To find such sincere poets is difficult, because the tendency of the mind is to supply. If three lines have come then you will supply the fourth, and the fourth will kill all the three because it will come from a much lower state of mind—when you are back on the earth.

When you jumped, and you were freed for some moments from gravitation, you had a different dimension of being.

A poet moves on the earth but sometimes he jumps. In those jumps he has glimpses. A mystic lives in the heart. He doesn't move on the earth, the heart has become his abode. So he doesn't really create poetry but whatsoever he does becomes poetic, whatsoever he says becomes poetry. Really, a mystic cannot use prose because his prose is also poetry—it is coming through the heart, it is coming through love.

Put mindstuff in such inexpressible fineness above, below and in your heart. The heart is your total being, and when you are total you can know the total—remember this. Only the similar can know the similar. When you are fragmentary you cannot know the total. As within, so without. When you are total within, the total reality without is revealed to you; you have become capable of knowing it, you have earned the right to know it. When you are fragmented within, the reality is fragmented without. So whatsoever you are within will be the without for you.

Deep in the heart the whole world is different, the gestalt is different. I am looking at you. If I am looking at you through the head, through intellect, through one of my parts of knowing, then a few friends are here, individuals, egos—separate. But if I am looking at you through the heart, then individuals are not here. Then just an oceanic consciousness is here and individuals are just waves. If I look at you through the heart, then you and your neighbor are not two; then the reality is between you and your neighbor. You are just two poles, and the real is just in-between. Then here there is an ocean of consciousness in which you exist as waves. But waves are not separate, they are linked together. And you are melting every moment into the other, whether you know it or not.

The breath that was within you just a moment ago has left you—now it is moving into your neighbor. Just a moment before it was your life and you would have died without it, and now it is moving into your neighbor. It is his life now. Your body is continuously radiating vibrations, you are a radiator, so your life energy is constantly moving into the neighbor and his life energy is moving into you.

If I look at you from my heart, if I look at you with loving eyes, if I look at you totally, then you are just radiating points, and life is moving continuously from you to others and from others to you....

And not only just in this room, this whole universe is a constant flux of life energy. It goes on moving. There are no individual units, it is a cosmic whole. But through intellect the cosmic never appears, only fragments, atomic fragments, appear. And this is not a question which can be comprehended through intellect. If you try to comprehend through intellect it will be impossible to comprehend it. It is a totally different outlook, from a different point of existence.

If you are total within, the totality without is revealed to you. Some have called that revelation God-realization; some have called it *moksha,* liberation; some have called it *nirvana,* cessation. Different words, altogether different words, but they signify the same core, the same essence.

One thing is basic to all these expressions—the individual disappears. You may call it God-realization, then you are no longer an individual; you can call it liberation, then you are no longer a self; you can call it cessation—as Buddha has called it—then just as a lamp, a flame, ceases to be, disappears, disperses, you cannot find it anywhere again, you cannot locate it, it has gone into nonbeing, so the individual disappears. But this point has to be pondered over. Why do all religions say that the individual, the self, the ego, disappears when you realize the truth? If all religions emphasize this, this means that the self must be illusory—otherwise how can it disappear? The self must not be there really, only then can it disappear. This may seem paradoxical, but this is so; only that which is not can disappear. That which is will persist in being, it cannot disappear.

Just because of the head a false entity has come into being—the individual. If you come down to the heart, the false entity disappears. It was a creation of the head. From the heart the cosmic is, the individual is not; the whole is, the parts are not. And remember, when you are not, you cannot create a hell; when you are not, you cannot be in misery; when you are not, there can be no anxiety, no suffering. All anxiety, all suffering, exists because of you—the shadow of the shadow. The self is unreal, the ego is unreal, and because of that unreal self many unreal shadows are created. They follow you, you go on fighting with them, but you will never be victorious because the base goes on being hidden within you.

Swami Ramateertha has said somewhere that he was staying in a house, in a poor villager's house. The small child of the villager was playing just in front of the hut, and the sun was rising and the child saw his shadow. He tried to catch it, but the more he moved, the more the shadow would move ahead. The child started crying. He was a failure. He tried in every way to catch it, but it was impossible. To catch a shadow is impossible—not because a shadow is such a difficult thing to catch,

it is impossible because the child was moving to catch it. When he was moving, the shadow moved ahead. You cannot catch a shadow because a shadow has no substance, and only a substance can be caught.

Ramateertha was sitting there. He was laughing and the child was crying, and the mother was at a loss about what to do. How to console the child? So she said to Ramateertha, "Swamiji, can you help me?" Ramateertha went to the child, caught the child's hand and put it on his head—the shadow was caught. Now that the child had put his hand on his head, the shadow was caught. The child started laughing. Now he could see that his hand had caught the shadow.

You cannot catch a shadow, but you can catch yourself. And the moment you catch yourself, the shadow is caught.

Suffering is just a shadow of the ego. We are all like that child, fighting with suffering, anxiety, anguish, and trying to disperse them. We can never be victorious. It is not a question of strength—the whole effort is absurd, impossible. You must catch the self, the ego, and once you catch it, suffering suddenly disappears. It was just a shadow.

There are persons who start fighting with the self. It has been taught, "Disperse the self, be egoless, and you will be in bliss," so they start fighting the self, the ego. But if you fight you are still believing that the self exists. Your fight will give food to it, it will become an energy-giving thing to it, you will be feeding it. This technique says don't think of the ego, just move from the head to the heart and the ego will disappear. The ego is a projection of the head. Don't fight with it. You can go on fighting for lives together, but if you remain in the head you cannot win.

Just change the standpoint, just move from the head to a different standpoint, to a deeper standpoint of the being, and the whole thing changes because now you can look from a different perspective. From the heart there is no ego. Because of this we have become afraid of the heart. We never allow it to have its own way, we always interfere with it, we always bring mind into it. We try to control the heart through the mind because we have become afraid—if you move to the heart, you lose yourself. And this losing is just like death. Hence the incapacity to love, hence the fear of falling in love—because you lose yourself, you are not in control. Something greater than you grips you and takes possession. Then you are not on sure ground and you don't know where you are moving. So the head says, "Don't be a fool, move with reason. Don't be mad."

Whenever someone is in love everyone thinks that he is mad. He himself thinks that something has gone crazy: "I am not in my senses!" Why does it happen? Because now there is no control. Something is happening that he cannot control, he cannot manage and manipulate. Rather, something is manipulating him, a greater force has taken him over. He is possessed....

But unless you are ready to be possessed there can be no God for you. Unless you are ready to be possessed there is no mystery for you, and no bliss, no benediction. One who is ready to be possessed by love, by prayer, by the cosmos, means one who is ready to die as an ego. Only that one can know what life really is, what life has to give. What is possible becomes immediately actual, but you must put yourself at stake.

This technique is beautiful. It doesn't say anything about your ego. It doesn't say anything about it. It simply gives you a technique, and if you follow the technique, the ego will have disappeared.

93 Consider the body limitless.

The second sutra: *Consider any area of your present form as limitlessly spacious.*

This is the same, through a different door. The basic essential is the same, that is, to destroy limits. Mind creates limits. If you don't think, you move

into the unlimited. Or, from a different door, you can try with the unlimited and you will fall from the mind. The mind cannot coexist with the unlimited, with the undefined, unbordered, infinite. The mind cannot exist with the unbordered, so if you can try something limitless, the mind will disappear.

This technique says, *Consider any area of your present form as limitlessly spacious.* Any area. You can just close your eyes and imagine that your head has become infinite. Now there are no boundaries to it. It goes on and on and on and there is no boundary to it. Your head has become the whole cosmos, without any boundaries. If you can imagine this, suddenly thoughts will stop. If you can imagine your head as infinite, thinking will not be there. Thinking can exist only in a very narrow mind. The narrower it is, the better for thinking. The greater the mind, the less the thinking, and when the mind becomes total space, there is no thinking at all.

Buddha is sitting under his bodhi tree. Can you imagine what he is thinking? He is not thinking at all. His head is the whole cosmos. He has become spacious, infinitely spacious. This technique is good for those who can imagine, it will not be good for all. For those who can imagine, and for whom the imagination becomes so real that you cannot really say whether it is imagination or real, it will work. Otherwise it will not be of much use. But don't be afraid, because at least thirty percent of people are capable of such imagination. These people are very powerful.

If your mind is not very educated it will be easy for you to imagine. If it is educated then the creativity is lost, then your mind is just a storage space, a bank. And the whole education system is a banking system. They go on banking and dumping stuff onto you. Whatsoever they feel has to be dumped onto you, they do. They use your mind for storage—then you cannot imagine. Then whatsoever you do is just repeating that which has been taught to you.

So those who are uneducated, they can use this technique very easily. And those who have come out of university without being distorted by it, they can also use it. Those who are really still alive, even after so much education, they can do it. Women can do it more easily than men. All those who are imaginative, dreamers, they can do it very easily.

But how to know whether you can do it or not?

You can do a small experiment before entering it. Just lock both your hands together and close your eyes. For five minutes, anytime, relax in a chair, lock both your hands together, and just imagine that the hands are so locked that even if you try, you cannot open them. It will look absurd to you because they are not locked, but you just go on imagining that they are.

For five minutes go on thinking, and then say three times in your mind, "Now I will try to open my hands but I know it is impossible. They are locked and they cannot be opened."

Then try to open them. Thirty percent of you will not be able to open your hands. They will be really locked, and the more you try, the more you will feel that it is impossible. You will start perspiring—you cannot open your own hands. Then this method is for you. Then you can try this method.

If you can easily open your hands and nothing has happened, this method is not for you. You will not be able to do it. But don't get scared if your hands do not open, and don't try too much, because the more you try, the more difficult it will be. Just close your eyes again and imagine that now your hands are unlocked. You will need five minutes again to go on imagining that when you try to open them, they will open immediately.

Unlock the same way as you locked them, just through imagination. And if this is possible, that your hands become locked just by imagination and you yourself cannot open them, then this technique will work miracles for you. And in these one hundred and twelve techniques there are many which work with imagination. For all those techniques this hand-locking experiment will be good. Just remember, experiment whether or not the technique is for you.

Consider any area of your present form as limitlessly spacious. Any area... You can consider the whole body. Just close your eyes and consider that the whole body is spreading, spreading, spreading, and then the boundaries are lost. It has become infinite. What will happen? You cannot even conceive of what will happen. If you can conceive that you have become the cosmos—that is the meaning, the infinite—all that is bound up with your ego will not be found there. Your name, your identity, all will be lost. Your poorness or richness, your health or your disease, your miseries—all will be lost, because they are part of the finite body. With an infinite body they cannot exist. And once you know this, come back to your finite body. But now you can laugh. And even in the finite you can have the sense, the feel of the infinite. Then you can carry it.

Try. And it will be good if you try from the head, because that is the base of all illness. Close your eyes, lie down on the ground or sit on a chair and relax. Just look within the head. Feel the walls of the head spreading, expanding. If you feel that it will be very staggering, then try it slowly. First think that your head has come to occupy the whole room. You will actually feel your skin touching the walls. If you can lock your hands, this will happen. You will feel the coolness of the walls which your skin is touching. You will feel the pressure.

Go on moving. Your head has gone beyond—now the house has come within your head, then the whole town has come within your head. Go on spreading. Within three months, slowly, you can come to the point where the sun rises in your head, it starts moving in your head. Your head has become infinite. This will give you a deep freedom such as you have never known, and all the misery that belongs to this narrow mind will disappear. In such a state, Upanishadic seers could say, "*Aham Brahmasmi*—I am the divine, I am the absolute." In such ecstasy "*Ana'l haq*" was uttered.

Mansoor cried in ecstasy, "*Ana'l haq, ana'l haq*—I am God." Mohammedans couldn't understand him. Really, no sectarian will be able to understand such things. They thought he had gone mad, but he was not mad, he was the sanest person possible. They thought he had become an egoist. He said, "I am God." So they killed him. While he was being killed, with his hands cut off, he was laughing and he was saying, *"Ana'l haq, aham Brahmasmi*—I am God."

Someone asked, "Mansoor, why are you laughing? You are being murdered."

He said, "You cannot murder me. I am the whole. You can murder only a part. How can you murder the whole? Whatsoever you do to it cannot make any difference."

Mansoor is reported to have said, "If you really wanted to kill me, you should have come at least ten years before. Then I was. Then you could have killed me, but now you cannot kill me, because I am no more. I myself have killed the ego which you could have killed and murdered."

Mansoor was practicing certain Sufi methods of this type, the type in which one goes on expanding until the expanse becomes so infinite that one is no more. Then the whole is and the individual is not. In these past few decades, these past two or three decades, in the West psychedelic drugs have become very significant. And the attraction is really one of expansion, because under the influence of the drug your narrowness, your limitations, are lost. But it is a chemical change, nothing spiritual happens out of it. It is just a forced violence on the system—you force the system to break.

You can have a glimpse that you are no longer confined to anything, that you have become infinite, liberated. But this is because of the chemical enforcement. Once back, you will be again in the narrow body, and now this body will feel more narrow than before. Again you will be confined to the same imprisonment, but now the imprisonment will be more intolerable because you have had a glimpse. And because that glimpse was through a chemical you are not master of it, you will become a slave, you will become addicted. Now you will need it more and more.

This technique is a spiritual psychedelic. If you practice it, a spiritual change will take place which will not be chemical and of which you will be the master.

Take it as a criterion: if you are the master, then the thing is spiritual. If you are the slave, then beware—the thing may appear to be spiritual, but it cannot be. Anything that becomes addictive, powerful, enslaving, imprisoning, is leading you towards more slavery, more "unfreedom"—whatsoever the appearance.

So take it as a criterion that whatsoever you do, your mastery must grow through it. You must become more and more the master of it. It is said, and I repeat it again and again, that when meditation has really happened to you, you will not need to do it. If you still need to do it, it has not yet really happened, because that too has become a slavery.

Even meditation must disappear. A moment must come when you need not do anything. Then just as you are, you are divine; just as you are, you are the bliss, the ecstasy.

But this technique is good for expansion, for expanding the consciousness. Before trying it, try the hand-locking experiment, so that you can feel. If your hands become locked, you have a very creative imagination, it is not impotent. Then you can work miracles through it.

CHAPTER 66

A buddha is a nobody

♦

Q U E S T I O N S

What do You mean by mystery?

I feel myself ordinary but untransformed.

Is there such a thing as good and bad?

Can we reverse imagination?

The first question:

Last night You said that when there are no thoughts in the mind, the mind becomes an empty space and the doors to all the mysteries are opened. I feel this inner space deeply and clearly but there is nothing special that I feel as mystery.

Will You explain what You mean by the mystery and how it is felt?

he inner emptiness itself is the mystery. You cannot feel it and you cannot know it. You become it. You *are* it. When the inner space is there, then you are not. You cannot observe it. If you observe it, then the inner space has not yet appeared. Who will observe it? If you can observe it you are separate from it, so it is not inner, it is outer. It is "out" to you. The inner has not yet become empty, it is filled. The ego is there—in a very subtle form; as an observer or onlooker, it is there. The inner is not empty yet, because when the inner is empty, you are not.

So the first thing to remember is that you will not be a witness to the mystery, you will be the mystery. You will not be able to observe it because you cannot be separate, there cannot be any duality.

One thing...when the inner is really empty, you are not, because you are the thing by which the inner is filled. Because of you it is not empty; because of you the space is covered, occupied. When you dissolve, when you simply disappear, only then the inner emptiness is there. So you will not be a witness to the mystery. Until you are not, the mystery will not be revealed; when you are not, the mystery will be revealed. So if you say that you feel inner emptiness it means you are not the emptiness; emptiness is something that is happening to you, around you, but you are not empty. So really this emptiness is just a thought of emptiness—that is why you can say that now your inner space has become empty. This is a thought; this emptiness is not real, this emptiness is just part of the mind. The observer is there so the object must be there. You can make emptiness an object, a thought.

It is reported that Bokuju became empty like this. He must have come across this type of emptiness. He came to his master and he said, "Now there is nothing, I have become empty."

The master said, "Go out and throw this nothingness also. This nothingness is still something, why are you carrying it? If you have really become nothing you will not be able to report it. Who will carry it? Who will feel in it a certain achievement?" The master said to Bokuju, "You have done well, you have become empty; now go and throw out this emptiness also."

You can be filled with emptiness—that is the problem. And if you are filled with emptiness you are not empty.

The second thing...what do I mean by mystery? Whatsoever you understand, I don't mean, because you think that a mystery will be something very amazing, staggering, shocking, that you will be thrown off the ground. That is not the point. Mystery is the simple pure existence with nothing amazing about it, nothing staggering. You will not be pushed aside, not thrown, not shocked, not puzzled. Mystery is nothing mysterious really. This very ordinary existence—accept it as it is without creating any problem. When you don't create a problem this existence is the mystery; when you create the problem you are destroying the mystery. Now you are in search of a solution, some answer. The same mind goes on. If you hear me talking about the mystery then you think about something very special. There is nothing special in existence. Only for the ego does the word 'special' exist.

It is reported that when Lin Chi achieved enlightenment he laughed. His disciples asked, "Why are you laughing?"

He said, "I am laughing for this. I was endeavoring for thousands and thousands of lives for this —it is so ordinary."

This is the mystery: nothing special.

It is said of Dogen, another Zen master, that when he achieved enlightenment disciples asked him, "What was the first thing that you wanted to do after it?"

Dogen is reported to have said, "I wanted a cup of tea."

It was so ordinary. But for the ego these things are not appealing. If I say that enlightenment is so ordinary that you would like to have a cup of tea after it, then you will feel that the whole thing is nonsense—why endeavor? Then the ego comes in. The ego wants something special, something rare, something that does not usually happen, that has happened only to you, which has not happened to just anyone. The ego wants something special, extraordinary.

Reality is not extraordinary; it is happening everywhere. And if it has not happened to you then that is special!—because it is there, always present. Not for a single moment is it absent. Enlightenment is happening every moment, it is the very core of existence—but you are deaf and blind. It is nothing special.

To be a buddha, to be enlightened, is the most ordinary phenomenon. When I say "ordinary" I mean: it must be so. If it looks very extraordinary it is because of you, because you create so many hurdles—and you love them. First you create the obstacle, and then you try to cross it. And then you feel very elated. In the first place, there is no obstacle. But your ego will not feel good—you must create a long route to come to the point that was the nearest, the most intimate one. And you had never missed it!

So don't seek something mysterious. Just be simple and innocent, and then the whole existence opens to you. You will not go mad, you can simply smile at the absurdity of the whole thing that was so near but you could not attain it. And there was no barrier. It was, in a sense, always within you. It was a miracle how you went on missing it.

If the emptiness is real, all that is there, the whole of it, the reality, will be opened to you. Not that it is closed right now—it is open, *you* are closed. Your mind is occupied. When your mind is empty, unoccupied, you will be open to it, and there will be a meeting. And then everything is beautiful in its total ordinariness. Hence it is said that one who has known becomes absolutely ordinary. He is one with the reality. To be hankering for the special is the way of the ego, and all the ways of the ego create gaps and distances between you and the real. Be empty and everything will have happened to you.

Not that you will have much to report: there is nothing to be reported. It is thought that Buddhas and Krishnas, or those who have attained the ultimate, cannot describe it because it is so complex. No, they cannot describe it because it is so simple. Complex things can be described, remember. Simple things cannot be described. The more complex a thing is, the easier the description is, because in a complexity you can divide, contrast, compare. With a simple thing you cannot do anything.

For example, if I ask you, "What is yellow?" what will you say? Yellow is so simple, there is nothing complex about it. If I ask, "What is water?" you can say, "H_2O." It is complex: there is hydrogen, there is oxygen, so you can define it. But if I ask you, "What is yellow?" at the most you can say that yellow is yellow. But that is a tautology, it makes no sense. What will you do if I say, "What is yellow?" You may indicate a yellow flower, you may indicate a yellow sun rising, but you are not saying anything, you are indicating.

A simple thing can only be indicated; a complex thing can be defined, divided, analyzed. Buddhas are silent, not because they have encountered a very complex reality, they are silent because of a phenomenon so simple that it can only be indicated, not defined. So they can lead you towards it but they cannot say anything about it.

That mystery is not a complex thing, it is very simple, the simplest possible. But you can only meet with it when you have also become simple. If you are complex, you cannot meet it. There is no meeting ground. Only when you have become simple, totally simple, innocent, empty, the reality and you meet. Then there is a reflection of it in you. It echoes in you. It enters into you.

But don't wait for anything special. Nirvana is nothing special. When I say this, what is happening to your mind? When I say this nirvana is nothing special, what do you feel? How do you feel? You feel a little disappointed. In the mind the question must be arising, "Then why struggle? Then why make any effort? Then why meditate? Then why these techniques?"

Look at that mind; that mind is the problem. The mind wants something special. And because of that desire the mind goes on creating special things. In reality there is nothing special: either the whole of reality is special or nothing is special.

Because of this desire, the mind has created heavens, paradises. And it is not satisfied with one, it goes on creating many. Christians have one heaven, Hindus have seven—because there are so many good people, there must be a hierarchy. The supreme good, where should they go? There is no

end to it. In Buddha's days there was a sect who believed in seven hundred heavens. You have to place the egos: the highest ego must go to the highest heaven.

I was looking at a book of the Radhaswamis. They say there are many divisions—fourteen divisions. Only their guru has reached to the last. Buddha is somewhere in the seventh, Krishna somewhere in the fifth, Mohammed somewhere in the third. Only their guru has reached to the fourteenth. And everyone else is given a place, categorized. Only their guru is special. This is the desire to be special. And everyone is according to his desire.

I have heard an anecdote. In a Sunday school the priest was giving a religious lesson to the very small boys of the neighborhood. He talked much about what good people would achieve—the crowns of glory and a heavenly reward. Those who are good would be crowned in heaven. Then at the end of his talk he said, "Who will get the biggest crown?"

There was silence for a while; then a little boy, the hatmaker's son, stood up confidently and said, "The one who has the biggest head."

This is what we are all doing. Our definition of the biggest head may differ but we have a conception of something special in the end, and because of that "special" we go on moving. But remember, because of that "special" you are not moving anywhere at all, you are moving in desires. And a movement in desire is not a progress, it is circular.

If you can still meditate—knowing well that nothing special is going to happen, that you will just come to a reconciliation with the ordinary reality, that you will be in harmony with this ordinary reality—if with this mind you can meditate, then enlightenment is possible this very moment. But with this mind you won't feel like meditating—you will say, "Leave everything if nothing special is going to happen."

People come to me and they say, "I have been meditating for three months and nothing has happened yet."

A desire...and that desire is the barrier. It can

happen in a single moment if desire is not there.

So don't desire the mysterious. Really, don't desire anything. Just be at ease, at home with reality as it is. Be ordinary—to be ordinary is wonderful. Because then there is no tension, no anguish. To be ordinary is very mysterious because it is so simple. To me, meditation is a play, a game; it is not a work. But to you it goes on being work; you think in terms of work.

It will be good to understand the distinction between work and play. Work is end-oriented, not enough in itself. It must lead somewhere, to some happiness, to some goal, to some end. It is a bridge, a means. In itself it is meaningless. The meaning is hidden in the goal.

Play is totally different. There is no goal to it, or, it itself is the goal. Happiness is not beyond it, outside it; to be in it is to be happy. It will not give you any happiness outside of it, there is no meaning beyond it—all that is there is intrinsic, internal. You play, not because of any reason, but because you enjoy it right now. It is purposeless.

That's why only children can play really; the older you grow, the less capable you become of playing. Because of more and more purpose, more and more you ask why, why should I play? More and more you become end-oriented: something must be achieved through it, in itself it has no meaning. Intrinsic value loses meaning for you. Only children can play because they don't think of the future. They can be here timelessly.

Work is time; play is timeless. Meditation must be like play, not end-oriented. You must not meditate to achieve something because then the whole point is lost. You cannot meditate at all if you are meditating *for* something. You can meditate only if you are playing with it, enjoying it, if nothing is to be achieved out of it, if it is beautiful in itself. Meditation for meditation's sake…then it becomes timeless. And then the ego cannot arise.

Without desire, you cannot project yourself into the future, without desire you cannot start expectations, and without desire you will never be disappointed. Without desire, time really disappears: you move from one moment of eternity to another moment of eternity. There is no sequence…and then you will never ask why nothing special is happening.

For myself, I have not come to know the mystery yet. The very play is the mystery; being timeless, desireless, is the mystery. And to be ordinary is the "goal", if you allow me to use the word. To be ordinary is the goal. If you can be ordinary you are liberated, then there is no *sansara* for you, no world for you.

This whole world is a struggle to be extraordinary. Some try it in politics, some try it in economics, some try it in religion. But the lust remains the same.

The second question:

Not only in meditation but in routine life also, I constantly feel a oneness with the existence, egolessness, timelessness. Yet I feel myself ordinary. And I do not find in me the total transformation about which You talk very often.

This is good. This is the goal. You should not create a problem out of it. You should relax and be ordinary.

But why do you feel it? Why do you feel that you remain ordinary? Somewhere there must be the desire to be extraordinary, to be not ordinary. Only in contrast to that can you feel ordinary, and then a certain sadness will follow. But why not be ordinary? What do I mean when I say, "Be ordinary"? I mean that whatsoever the case is—be.

One young man came to me just a few days ago, and he said, "I am an egoist and whenever I listen to you, I feel that I am wrong. So how to be egoless?"

I told him, "You be simply egoistic, and accept the fact that you are so and don't struggle. Don't try to be egoless. You are an egoist, so feel it and be it."

He felt very disappointed because really he was searching for a new way for the ego. He was searching for egolessness. And I said, "Be whatsoever you are," so that that desire would be cut and the ego couldn't move. And I told him, "For three months don't come to me and don't fight the ego—accept it, it is there. It is part of you, it is how you are. Don't fight with it, and don't think in terms of the contrary, how to be egoless, because that is the way of the ego. Accept it. Acceptance is the death."

But the young man said, "But every religion says be egoless, and I want to be egoless."

Who is this "I" that wants to be egoless? The ways of the ego are very subtle. When I was talking to him I felt he was not listening to me. If I gave him some technique to do to be egoless, he would be ready and accepting, receptive, because then the ego could start work. But I was saying, "Don't talk about egolessness, just be whatsoever you are. And for three months don't struggle; then come to me."

He tried. After three months he came again and he said to me, "It has been very hard to accept, but because you told me, I tried. Now give me some technique, give me some key to go beyond this ego." The whole effort was false, because if you accept then there is no desire to go beyond.

Whenever you feel yourself to be ordinary you try to be extraordinary in some way. But everyone is ordinary: to be ordinary is to be real. It may be that to you someone looks extraordinary because you compare him with yourself, but a genius in himself is as ordinary as anybody, and he feels himself ordinary. A roseflower is ordinary, a lotus flower is ordinary, but if the rose starts comparing and starts thinking about how to be a lotus flower then problems arise. And if the lotus starts thinking about the beautiful perfume that comes from the roseflower, then the roseflower becomes extraordinary.

When you compare, in comparison extraordinariness happens—otherwise everything is ordinary. In itself everything is as it is. Don't compare and don't hanker after it. If you hanker then meditation will disappoint you, because meditation will bring you to a point where you feel your total ordinariness. Be receptive to it, welcome it. It is good. It

shows that meditation is progressing, deepening. But somewhere the desire for the extraordinary is still there and that is creating the barrier.

If that desire disappears, you will not feel yourself as ordinary. You will simply be. How can you feel that you are ordinary? You will simply be, and to be, to be so simply that you don't feel whether you are ordinary or extraordinary, is to attain.

It is good, don't be disappointed by it. If you are disappointed then remember that you are carrying a desire, and that desire is creating poison. Why is there this madness? Why does it come and happen to everyone? This whole world is mad because of this: everyone is trying to be something special, somebody.

Life happens to you only when you are nobody. When you are so empty that there is no one, then the whole of life flows through you without any barrier, without any obstacle, without any hindrance. Then the flow is total and complete.

When you are somebody, you become a rock, you disturb the flow—life cannot move through you. There is a struggle, a resistance, and of course you create much noise. And you may think that because you are creating so much noise you are something extraordinary.

Be an empty vessel, a passage with no resistance, so that life can flow through it, flow through it easily. Then no noise will be created. You may not be able to feel that you are, because you only feel that you are when you fight. The more you fight, the more you feel.

Life flows so smoothly through you that you may even completely forget that you exist. There is no barrier, no resistance, no rejection, no negation. And you are so welcoming that you even forget that you are.

It was heard about one Zen master that he would call his own name many times during the day. In the morning he would call, "Bokuju?" and then he would say, "Yes sir, I am here." Bokuju was his name. And his disciples would ask why he did this. He would say, "I go on forgetting. I have

become so smooth that I have to remind myself—
'Bokuju?' And then I say, 'Yes sir, I am here.'"

Life can become such a smooth flow, such a
silent river, that no noise is created. But if you are
bent upon being something, somebody, extraordinary, special, then life cannot flow through you.
Then there is a constant struggle between life and
you, between your small ego and the cosmos.

This is creating madness. The whole earth has
become a mad planet. And this madness cannot be
helped by treatments, therapies, because it is so
basic a style of life that it is not a pathology. This is
how we are living. Our whole style of life is mad.
So you cannot be helped through therapies unless
the whole lifestyle changes.

There are only two lifestyles: ego-oriented and
egoless-oriented. You must be somebody...this is
one way of life. Then madness is the outcome.
Really, the madman is the most extraordinary man.
He has achieved extraordinariness because now he
is completely uprooted from reality, he is not
concerned with the reality at all. Now he lives
isolated in himself, he has created his own world.
Now the dream is the real and the real has become
just a dream. Everything is upside-down.

You cannot convince a madman that he is
wrong, because he is very logical. Madmen are very
rational and logical.

One madman used to come out of his house
every day in the morning and chant some mantras
and make some gestures. So whosoever was passing would ask, naturally, what he was doing. And
the madman would say, "I am protecting this
neighborhood from ghosts."

So the person who was asking would say, "But
there are no ghosts in this neighborhood."

And the man would say, "See, because of my
chanting mantras, there are no ghosts."

He is rational, you cannot convince him—
ghosts are not there because of his chanting. But he
lives now in his own subjective dream-world and
you cannot pull him out.

If you think yourself somebody—nobody can

be somebody, that is not in the nature of things—
but if you think yourself somebody, then a part of
you has gone mad. That somebodiness is your
madness. And the more this cancer of somebodiness grows, the more you will be cut off from reality.

A buddha is a nobody. All his doors are open.
The wind comes and blows, the rains come and
blow, the sunrays enter and pass, the life flows, but
he is not there. This is what I mean when I say
meditation has happened to you. And this is very
ordinary, natural, real.

The third question:

**You are often saying that this is good or bad, or
this is right or wrong. Is this a language just for us
as we are not able to realize the oneness of everything, or is there such a thing as good and bad?**

No, it is simply a language. For me there is nothing
good and nothing bad. But this will be too dangerous for you. Truth can be dangerous. Really, only
truth can be dangerous—lies are never so dangerous because they are not potential. They have no
force in them.

Truth can be very shattering. It is the truth that
there is no good, no bad, that nothing is right,
nothing is wrong. Everything is as it is; all condemnation, division, is futile—but this will be dangerous for you. This will be too much for you, you
will misunderstand it. You cannot understand it;
when there is nothing good, nothing bad, you
cannot understand it, and you will have your own
interpretation of it.

If I say there is nothing good, nothing bad, you
will think that now whatsoever you have been
thinking of up to now as bad, there is no need to
think of it as such. So it will become a license for
you and you will start double thinking. You will
think that for yourself there is nothing good, nothing bad, but for others you will not allow the same.
If you can allow the same for others also, then you
have understood; then it is not a license, it is a free-

dom. But the mind must be one; there should not be double standards.

Why do I say that there is nothing good and nothing bad? Because goodness and badness are interpretations, they are not reality.

If there is a flower outside in the garden, you can call it beautiful and somebody else can call it ugly. The flower is neither. The flower exists there as it is in its authenticity, and it is not bothered about your interpretations. But to you it is either beautiful or not. That beauty and ugliness is interpretation, not reality. It is your mind which says that it is beautiful or ugly. The flower will not be affected by it, but you will be. If you say that it is beautiful, your behavior will be of one kind; if you say that it is ugly, your behavior will be different. You will be affected by your interpretation.

And I am talking to you, so I have to constantly remember that whatsoever I say, your behavior will be affected. Unless you come to a point where the whole emphasis has changed from doing to being, when you are not interested in doing and you are only interested in being, you cannot understand what I mean when I say that there is nothing good or bad. Things are as they are.

But it is only possible to understand this when you are deeply centered in the being. And if you are centered in the being, then whatsoever you do will be good. Then there is no danger. But right now you are not centered in the being, you are centered on the periphery. You are continuously choosing what to do and what not to do.

Really, you have not asked the question, "What to be?" You have always been asking what to do and what not to do and whether it will be good or not. You never ask the question, "What to be?" And unless being becomes more important than doing, there is good and there is bad—for you. Then something has to be done and something has not to be done.

How do I make this difference and why? If there is really no good and no bad then how and why is this difference made?

To me, this is again a difference I make for you: I call something good if it leads to your being, where everything will become good, and I call something bad if it leads you away from the being. If you go on being away from yourself, everything will become bad.

To help you to come to yourself, to your home, I call something good or bad, or, something right or wrong. It is better to use the words 'right' and 'wrong' than the words 'good' and 'bad' because I am more concerned with techniques of how to bring yourself to your being. So a technique can be right if it brings you to your being; a technique can be wrong if it doesn't bring you to your being or if it becomes a hindrance, or moves you into by-paths, or moves you on ways which will become cul-de-sacs and will not lead you anywhere.

But if you ask me, ultimately there is nothing good, nothing bad, nothing right, nothing wrong. And if you can understand this right now, then start living in a way where nothing is wrong and nothing is right—and this is for you as far as you are concerned with others, and for others as far as they are concerned with you.

Jesus says, "Do unto others as you would like them to do unto you." This is the basic principle of "one standard," and this is the whole of the teaching of all those who want to help you to come to yourself—there is one standard where nothing is good and nothing is bad, not only for you but for everyone.

It is easy to say that to steal is not bad if you are stealing, but if someone else is stealing something from you then it becomes difficult to say that stealing is not bad.

I have heard about a thief. For the fourth time he was caught and the judge asked him, "You get caught again and again, what is the matter? If you are not so efficient, why go on doing it?"

The man said, "It is not a question of efficiency. I am alone and the work is too much."

So the judge said, "Then why don't you have a companion, a partner?"

The thief said, "Morals have become so low that you cannot depend on any partner."

Even a thief thinks in terms of morality, for others—"Morals have gone so low that you cannot depend on a partner. So I have to do all the work myself and the work is too much."

This is the deepest teaching of all the knowers: there is nothing to choose. Everything is accepted. If you can accept it in its totality, you are transformed. But if you are cunning and want to deceive yourself, then this total acceptability will be dangerous.

So I say many things to you just because of you, and just in between I also go on communicating that which I would really like to say to you. But it can be given only very indirectly. You are so dangerous, so suicidal, that you can commit something which will be harmful to you.

I am talking about a higher truth—not only a higher truth, but an ultimate truth. Naropa, in his song, says that only an inch difference sets heaven and hell apart. An inch difference between what is good and what is bad sets heaven and hell apart.

And you will have to live in anguish because you have created the division. Bring all the dualities nearer, closer, and let them merge. Let the good and bad merge into each other, the darkness and the light merge into each other, life and death merge into each other. Then there is *advaita,* then there is oneness. That oneness brings freedom, transformation.

The fourth question:

It is our imagination, through autosuggestions, that has established us in the world of the finite, in the world of names and forms, in the world of pains and pleasures. Can the same instrument be used to reach the infinite, the absolute, the blissful? The same instrument in the reverse order?

You have come to this house, soon you will be going back, and the same path will be used again—but in the reverse order. While you were coming here your face was towards me and when you go back, your back will be towards me. But the path will be the same. No other path is needed to go back home. Only the direction changes.

The way which you have traveled to come into darkness will be the way, is the way, the only way—you will have to travel back that way. The way that has brought you into misery and anguish will be the way which will lead you towards bliss and ecstasy. There is no other way, there is no need. And remember, don't follow any other way; otherwise you will never reach home.

You have to be alert to follow the same path again. The only change is in the direction—it is a total about-turn. Hypnosis, autosuggestion, they create this world; de-hypnosis, de-autosuggestion will lead you back to the real. There is no finite world, the world is infinite. It is your superimposition, your hypnosis, that makes it look finite. Withdraw your hypnosis and the world is infinite—it has always been so.

All techniques of meditation are similar to hypnosis. This creates a problem. It creates a problem when people go on asking about the difference between hypnosis and meditation. There is no difference. The path is the same but the direction is different.

In hypnosis you are falling more and more asleep, losing awareness; in meditation you are coming out of sleep, gaining awareness. It is the same path. In hypnosis you are conditioning yourself, in meditation you are unconditioning yourself—but the process is the same. Meditation is hypnosis in reverse. So whatsoever you have done with yourself you have to undo it, that's all.

Try to do a very simple experiment which will be revealing: you can hypnotize yourself. Close your room and make it completely dark, then put a small candle just in front of your eyes. Then without blinking your eyes, stare at the flame, and just go on thinking that you are falling asleep, you are falling asleep. A deep sleep is descending upon you—just let this thought be floating there, within. Go on staring at the candle and let this thought be there as a cloud hovering over you. You are falling asleep, you are falling asleep. When you do it, you have to say, "I am falling asleep. Sleep is descending. My limbs are relaxing."

You will immediately feel a subtle change, and within three minutes you will feel that the body has become heavy. Any moment you can fall. The lids of the eyes are heavy and now it is very difficult to go on staring at the flame. The eyes want to close. Everything has become numb.

Now you can feel that this is what hypnosis is: being more sleepy, falling into unawareness, becoming more unconscious. Feel the feel of it, what is happening, how your mind has become cloudy. The clarity has gone, aliveness has gone, you are becoming dead. Your body feels more weighty. This will give you the sensation of how your consciousness can become unconsciousness.

Try this for seven days so that you can feel completely what it is, and how you descend into the well. With more and more darkness, more sleep, more unconsciousness, at the last moment suddenly you will not be there and the flame will have disappeared. You are fast asleep. You can feel the grave.

Then after one week try the other experiment. Have the same room, the same flame, the same way of staring, but a different thought in the mind, "I will become more alert, I am becoming more and more alert, more alive, more alert. The body is becoming more and more weightless." Let this thought be there and go on staring at the flame— you will feel a sudden surge of life awareness and consciousness.

Within seven days you can come to a point where you will feel so alert that you will feel as if the body is not. On one pole of the whole spectrum is deep sleep where you forget yourself completely; on the other pole there is deep awareness where everything is forgotten, you remember only yourself.

Then there are many mid-stages. The stage we are in is just in the middle—half asleep, half awake. So whatsoever you do, you are doing it half

asleep, half awake. Both the processes are the same, they are the same process.

Thought in an intense state becomes reality; thought condensed becomes a thing. One thought kept continuously in the consciousness transforms you, becomes a seed. So if you are struggling to be more and more alert, you are deconditioning yourself, moving in the other direction. Gurdjieff calls it self-remembering—he says, "Continuously remember yourself." Buddha says, "Don't forget yourself whatsoever you are doing; continuously go on hammering that you are doing it." And he is so particular that he says to his monks, "While you are walking and your left foot comes up, remember that your left foot is coming up. Now the foot is going down, now the right one is coming up, now the right is going down. Remember that the breath is coming in, that the breath is going out. Remember continuously, whatsoever is happening and use every happening as a situation to remember. Don't do anything in an unconscious state, a sleepy state." And Buddha says that this is enough. If you can work like this for twenty-four hours, sooner or later you will have de-hypnotized yourself. You will have become aware, alert.

Hypnosis and meditation are the same process in diametrically opposite directions. You can use hypnosis to awaken you; you can use hypnosis to fall deep into sleep. And if you become master of the art of hypnosis, you have got the key to open all the doors of life.

If you are not the master of the key of hypnosis, then you are a victim of many, many forces. This is worth understanding: if you don't know what hypnosis is then you are a victim. Everybody is trying hypnosis on you—I say everybody! They may not be doing it knowingly, but everybody is trying. There are different ways, methods. The whole world is filled with hypnotic tricks: the same advertisement in the newspaper, on the television and on the radio. It goes on hammering, it becomes a hypnotic thing.

In the mind you go on repeating, "Lux is the

best soap." You go on repeating it. Wherever you move it is written on the walls; in films you see it, on the TV screen it is there, on the radio it is there, in magazines, in newspapers, in anything: "Lux Toilet Soap." It goes on and on. You become hypnotized by it. Then you go to the shop and the man behind the counter asks you, "What soap do you need?" You say, "Lux Toilet Soap." You are asleep. You are not saying it consciously, it has been hammered in and now it is built in.

Crores of rupees are spent on advertising just to hypnotize you. Those advertisements have to be repeated continuously. Repetition is the way. Then there is imprint, and you become unconscious about it; then suddenly it comes out of your mouth, "Lux Toilet Soap." And you think that you are choosing. You are not the chooser.

The whole education system is hypnotic. That's why for the teacher a higher place is needed. It must be measured scientifically because there is a particular point—the way I am sitting here is at a wrong point, this is not right. Your eyes should be in a tension looking at me, in much tension, not relaxed—then you are easily hypnotized.

Hitler used every proportion. He had an expert committee to measure how much distance from the audience and how much height was needed so that the eyes are correctly at a tension where they become easily hypnotized and sleepy. And then all the lights would be put off—in Hitler's lecture hall the only lights would be on Hitler. Nobody could see anywhere else, and so you were forced to look only at him. In a particular situation a particular tension was created. In this tension he would go on saying something for a while. The things that he wanted to put into you would be said later on,

when the whole audience had become sleepy. Then the words would simply move into the unconscious and start functioning.

Now they have invented subliminal advertisements in films. As you watch a film, between two scenes, just for a fraction of a second, the advertisement will be flashed. You will not be able to read it, you will not even know what has happened. Simply watching the film, suddenly for a few seconds the advertisement will be there—but you will not be continuously aware of it.

Only two persons in a hundred can feel that something has happened. Only those who have very keen eyes can feel that something was in between. Ninety-eight percent will not feel it, but the unconscious has read it. It has entered you.

There was one experiment about it in an American film. They flashed a particular brand of cold drink on the screen, something new. Only two percent of the people became aware that there was an advertisement, ninety-eight percent were fully unaware, but in the interval many people went out and asked for the drink. They were not aware that there had been an advertisement because it had been so fast.

Hypnosis is all around. Education uses it, politics uses it, the market uses it—everyone is using it. And if you are not aware then you are a victim. Become aware. If you become aware, you can use it—not to hypnotize others, but to de-hypnotize yourself. And if you can become completely de-hypnotized, you are free, you are liberated.

And there is no conflict between meditation and hypnosis. The conflict is in the directions—the process is the same.

CHAPTER 67

Go beyond
mind and matter

♦

94 *Feel your substance, bones, flesh, blood, saturated with the cosmic essence.*

95 *Feel the fine qualities of creativity permeating your breasts and assuming delicate configurations.*

P hilosophers all over the world have been arguing for centuries about what basic stuff the universe is made of, what the substance is. There have been propositions, systems, that say that matter is the basic reality and mind is just an outgrowth, that matter is basic and mind is just a by-product, that mind is also material, only subtle. Charwaka proposed this in India, Epicurus in Greece, and even today, Marxists and other materialists go on talking in terms of matter. Just opposite to this, there has been a second system of thinking which says that mind rather than matter is the basic stuff, and that matter is nothing but a form of mind. Vedanta and other idealist philosophies of the world have reduced everything to mind.

Just at the beginning of this century, it was thought that the materialists had become victorious because physics and other scientific investigations were proving, or appeared to be proving, that matter was the basic substance. But just two or three decades ago the whole thing changed completely. One of the greatest scientists of this age, Eddington, said, "Now we can say that the universe appears to be more like a thought than like a thing." And as the physicists Max Planck and Einstein worked deeper, they came to realize that the deeper one penetrates matter, the more matter disappears—something more than matter, more beyond than matter, appears to be there. You can call it mind more easily than matter because it is a form of energy. One thing is certain: it is not material in the old sense at all.

For tantra, for yoga, there has been no choice. Tantra doesn't say that either matter or the mind is the basic reality. Tantra has a third standpoint, and I think that that standpoint is ultimately going to win. Tantra says mind and matter are both forms of something which we can call "X." Neither matter nor mind is substantial but a third entity, which exists in both but which is not confined to either, is the real—these two are the manifestations. Matter and mind are not realities, but forms of a third reality, a basic reality, which remains hidden. Whenever it manifests itself, it manifests itself either as matter or as mind.

So the whole conflict between mind and matter, and their followers, is baseless, because the ultimate substratum that physics has now come to know is really neither like matter nor like mind. The division has disappeared, the duality has disappeared. The behavior of the basic substance is very vague; sometimes it behaves like matter, and sometimes it behaves like mind.

You may be surprised to know that physics cannot say anything about individual atoms—they are unpredictable, just like any human being. Nothing can be said about the individual atom and how it is going to behave. It appears that it has a certain independence; no causality can predict how it is going to behave. We can predict mass behavior, but we cannot predict the behavior of an individual atom. Sometimes it behaves in cause–effect terms, like matter, and sometimes it behaves like mind, as if it has a will of its own, as if it has a choice.

With tantra, this idea of physics fits very well. But why does tantra say that the basic reality is the third, the unknown, the "X"? Not because tantra is interested in propounding any theory about reality, no. It is proposed just as a help for *sadhana*, just as a help for spiritual growth. If it is so—that the reality is the third, and mind and matter are just two manifestations—then you can enter the reality through two doors: either from matter or from mind. If you try to enter from matter, then there are certain techniques to use. Hatha yoga is a technique to enter the reality through matter, through the body. You have to do something with the body, you have to transform the body, you have to crystallize certain chemical phenomena in the body, and then you will enter into the reality.

Or you can enter directly through the mind. Raja yoga and other methods are used to enter through the mind. And for tantra, both are right.

You cannot say to tantra, "How can a body posture, a particular body posture, be helpful to enter reality?" Tantra says it can be helpful. A certain body posture is not a mere body posture, because body is the manifestation of the reality. So when you give your body a certain posture, you are giving the reality a certain form. And there are postures with which you can easily enter into yourself. A certain food can be helpful. A certain practice of breathing can be helpful. These are material things—food, breathing, body—but you can enter through them.

And similar is the case with mind: just working with mind also you can enter. Many times the question may have arisen in your mind about Shiva telling Parvati certain techniques which look just imaginary. The question is bound to arise: how can imagination be helpful?

Even imagination is a mode of reality because the mind is a manifestation of reality. And when you change the imagination in the mind, you are changing the mode of reality. For tantra nothing is unreal. Even a dream has its own reality—and it affects you. So a dream is not a mere dream. A dream is as real as anything else because it affects you, it changes you. You are different because you dreamed it; you will never be the same because a certain dream has happened. So if you dream that you are a thief, in the morning you will say that it makes no difference, it was just a dream. But for tantra it is not so. A dream of stealing, of theft, has changed you. Your reality is different in the morning; you cannot be the same. Whether you recognize it or not, it has affected you. It will affect your behavior, your future—it has become a seed.

Even a dream is not irrelevant. And you think that dreams are just dreams. That is not so, because you cannot create a dream consciously, you cannot choose a dream. It happens to you as anything else happens to you. Can you choose a dream? Can you think about a dream that you will dream tonight? Can you choose it? Can you will it? You cannot will it, because to will a dream will need many changes in your reality. Only then will a dream come. A dream is just like a flower. A roseflower comes on a rosebush, and you cannot change the flower unless you change the whole process, from the seed onwards. You cannot just change the flower. A dream is a flowering. If you can change the dream, you can change reality.

So many times, many techniques will appear imaginary—but they are also real. And tantra is trying to change your imagination. If the imagination can be changed, then the hidden reality behind it will automatically be different.

The techniques that we will discuss today start from your imagination, from your dreaming, from your mind. Three things have to be remembered. One: whatsoever happens to your mind is not superficial—it is happening because of you, it is happening because you happen to be in a certain situation. So two things can be done: either change the situation, then you will have to start from the body because body is the situation; or if you are not starting with the situation, then change the happening. It will persist, it will not be easy to change it, but if you make an effort and you go on making the effort, if you are stubborn and are not defeated, then the very effort will change it.

One thing is certain: you may not achieve the goal that you were thinking of, but the fact that you make this effort will bring a change. You will be different: whether you succeed or fail, you will be different. The very effort will be counted.

Thirdly, don't think that mind is just mind, and don't think that dreaming is just dreaming. If you can direct your dreaming—and now there is a therapy in the West called Directed Daydreaming—if you can direct your dreaming, you are directing yourself. And many things will become different.

There is an old Tibetan technique called The Lion's Roar. If you are angry, sexual, filled with hatred, jealousy, then the Tibetan master will give you this technique, The Lion's Roar. You have to sit before a mirror, and you are to imagine that you are a lion, not a man. You have to make your face like a lion, you have to put your tongue out, and you have to roar. And you have to practice it so that the imagination becomes so true that you forget that you are a man daydreaming that he is a lion. And when the point comes when you have really fallen prey to your own imagination, and you have become the lion, and a real roar comes out of you, suddenly you are transformed. In that roar, all hatred, anger, sex, disappears, and you will fall into a deep silence such as you have not known before.

In old Tibetan monasteries they have a special room with many mirrors. Whenever someone is suffering from something like anger, hatred, or jealousy, he is to be sent to that mirrored room and he has to remain there until he comes to a climax. And when he comes to the climax, the whole monastery will know, because a real lion will be roaring there. To us, he has gone mad. The whole monastery will gather and welcome the man, and he will come out a totally different man. It may take three days, it may take seven days. Food will be supplied to him, but he is not allowed to come out. He has to persist in imagining that he is a lion, until from the very

roots of the unconscious the roar comes. The whole body is involved, every cell of it; every cell in it roars, and in that roar everything is thrown out. It is the deepest catharsis possible. And you will never see that man angry again because now the poison is not there. For the first time the face will become human.

Your face cannot be human because so much is suppressed there. The jealousy, the hatred, the anger that you have suppressed, is there—layers upon layers are just hidden under the skin. They are making your face. But they can be released—just by this daydream, a directed daydream.

In the West they now have another technique they call psychodrama. That too is one of the oldest Buddhist methods—to become a part of a drama, to act it so totally that you forget that you are simply acting. The acting becomes action, and you are not the actor, you become a real doer in it. It changes you.

Tantra says that if you can change dreaming, imagination, if you can change your mind and the pattern of it, the reality behind will be different. Because it is deeply rooted in reality, you can move through the mind. These techniques are just to change the way and the style in which your mind has been behaving up to now.

94 Feel yourself saturated.

The first technique: *Feel your substance, bones, flesh, blood, saturated with the cosmic essence.*

Try with simple experiments. For seven days try one simple experiment: feel your blood, your bones, your flesh, your body, filled with sadness—every cell of the body sad; dark night around you; very heavy, depressed; not a single ray of light; no hope, gloomy, just as if you are going to die. Life is not throbbing in you; you are just waiting for death. It is as if death has already settled, or is settling. For seven days contemplate on the feeling that death has entered throughout the body; it has penetrated deep to the bone, to the very marrow. Go on thinking in this way, don't disturb this mood. And then, after seven days, see how you feel.

You will be just a dead weight. All feeling will have disappeared, the body will not be felt as alive. And what have you done? You have been eating, you have been doing everything the same as you have always been doing; the only change has been in the imagination—there is a new pattern of imagination around you.

If you succeed in it... You will succeed. Really, you have already succeeded in it; you are doing it, you are expert in doing this, unknowingly. That's why I say start with sadness. If I say be filled with bliss, it will be very difficult. You cannot conceive of it. But if you can do it with sadness, then you will become aware that if sadness can happen to you, why not happiness? If you can create a sad milieu around you and become a dead thing in it, then why can't you create an alive milieu around you and be alive, dancing? The other becomes conceivable.

Secondly, you will become aware that whatever sadness you have been suffering was not real. You were the creator of it, you were the author; unknowingly you have been doing this. It seems difficult to believe that your sadness is your imagination, because then the whole responsibility falls on you. Then no one else is responsible, then you cannot throw it on God, on fate, on others, on society, on wife, on husband—you cannot throw it anywhere. You are the creator, and whatsoever is happening to you, you are creating it.

Try it for seven days, consciously. And then, I say, you will never be sad again—because you will have known the key.

Then for seven days try just being in a stream of bliss—floating in it, every breath giving you ecstasy. Just feel it. Start with sadness for seven days and then for seven days move to the contrary. And when you move to the direct opposite, you will feel it better because the contrast will be there.

Then only can you try this experiment—because it is deeper than happiness. Sadness is the surface, happiness is the middle, and this is the last core, the innermost core, the cosmic essence. *Feel your substance, bones, flesh, blood, saturated with the cosmic essence*—with eternal life, with divine energy, with cosmic essence. But don't start it directly because then you will not be able to touch it. Start from sadness, then move to happiness, and then try the origin, the very origin of life—the cosmic essence. And feel yourself filled with it.

In the beginning you will become aware again and again that you are simply imagining it, but don't stop. Even imagination is good. Even that you can imagine something worthwhile is good. You are imagining, and in the very imagination you are changing. It is you who are imagining. Go on imagining, and by and by you will forget completely that you are imagining it—it will have become a reality.

One of the greatest books ever written is the Buddhist scripture, *Lankavatara Sutra*. Buddha says again and again to his disciple Mahamati, he goes on saying again and again, "Mahamati, this is only mind. Hell is mind. Heaven is mind. The world is mind. Enlightenment is mind."

Mahamati asks again and again, "Just mind? Just mind? Even *nirvana*, enlightenment, just mind?"

And Buddha says, "Just mind, Mahamati."

When you understand that everything is just mind, you are freed. Then there is no bondage, then there is no desire. In *Lankavatara Sutra*, Buddha says that the whole world is just like a magical world, a city of Gandharva, as if a magician has created a world. Everything appears to be there, but it is there only because of the thought form.

But don't start with outer reality, that is too far. That too is mind, but it is very far away from you. Start from the very near, you own moods, and you will be the master if you can feel and know that they are your own creation.

Whenever you start thinking in terms of sadness, you become sad, and you become receptive to all the sadness around you. Then everybody helps you to be sad. Everybody helps, the whole world is always ready to help you, whatsoever you do. When you want to be sad, the whole world is helpful, cooperative. You have become receptive. Really, you fall to a certain wavelength where only sadness can be received. So even if someone comes to cheer you up, he will make you more sad. He will not look friendly, he will not look understanding; you will feel that he is insulting you because you are so sad and he is trying to cheer you up. He thinks your sadness is superficial. He is not taking you seriously.

And when you are ready to be happy, you are on a different wavelength. Now you are attuned to all the happiness that this world can give, now everywhere flowers start flowering, now every sound and noise becomes musical—and nothing has happened. The whole world remains the same, but you are different. You have a different pattern of looking, a different attitude, a different perspective; through that perspective a different world comes to you.

But start with sadness because you are expert in that. I was reading a sentence of some old Hassid mystic—I liked it very much. He says there are certain people who, if their whole life becomes a bed of roses, will not be happy until they develop some allergy towards the roses. Roses cannot make them happy unless they develop some allergy. Roses cannot make them happy; only when they become allergic will they start feeling alive. They can be attuned only to sadness, to illness, to disease, they cannot be aware of anything else. They go on finding sadness. They are searchers after wrong—something wrong, something sad, depressed, dark. They are death-oriented.

I have been meeting hundreds and hundreds of persons deeply, intimately, closely. When they start talking about their sadness I have to be serious—otherwise they will not feel that I am sympathetic, they will not feel good about it. Then they will

never turn to me again. I have to be sad with their sadness and serious with their seriousness to help bring them out of it…and this is their own creation, and they are making every effort to create it. And if I try to bring them out, they create every type of barrier—not knowingly of course, because no one will do it knowingly.

This is what the Upanishads call ignorance. Unknowingly you go on disturbing your own life, you go on creating more problems and anxieties, and whatsoever happens will not make any difference because you have a pattern—whatsoever happens. There are persons who come to me and say, "We are lonely." So they are unhappy. And the next moment someone comes and says he cannot find a place where he can be lonely, so he is unhappy. Then there are persons who have too much work on their minds, so they are unhappy, and there are persons who have no work, so they are unhappy. A person who is married is unhappy, a person who is not married, he is unhappy. It seems it is impossible for man to be happy. That's what I mean when I say you are experts—you are very efficient in finding ways and means to be unhappy. And you always succeed.

Start from sadness, and for seven days be completely unhappy for the first time. That will transform you totally, because once you know that consciously you can be unhappy, you will become conscious whenever you become unhappy. Then you will know what you are doing: it is your own doing. And if you can be unhappy by your own mind, then why can't you be happy? There is no difference, the pattern is the same. And then you can try this.

Feel your substance, flesh, blood, bones, saturated with the cosmic essence. Feel as if the divine is flowing through you: you are not, but the cosmic exists in you, God exists in you. When you feel hungry, he feels hungry—then to give food to the body becomes worship. When you feel thirsty, he feels thirsty—the cosmic in you. When you feel sleepy, he feels sleepy, he wants rest, relaxation.

When you are young, he is young in you. When you fall in love, he falls in love. Be saturated with him, and be *totally* saturated with him. Don't make any distinction. Good or bad, whatsoever happens is happening to him. You just withdraw, you are no longer there, only he is there. So good or bad, hell or heaven, whatsoever happens, happens to him. All the responsibility is thrown onto him and you are no more. The "no-moreness" that this technique can bring you is the ultimate in religion.

But you have to be saturated with it. And you don't know any saturation, you don't feel your body as porous, you don't feel that in your body a life energy is flowing. You think of yourself as something solid, dead, closed. Life can happen only when you are vulnerable, open, not closed. Life moves through you, and whatsoever happens is happening to the life energy, not to you—you are just a fragment. And all the boundaries that you have created around you are false, they are not real.

You cannot exist alone. If you are alone on the earth, can you exist? You cannot exist alone. You cannot exist without the stars. Somewhere Eddington says that the whole existence is like a spider's web—the whole existence is a spider's net. If you touch the net anywhere, the whole vibrates; if you touch existence anywhere, the whole vibrates. It is one. If you touch a flower you have touched the whole cosmos; if you look into your neighbor's eyes you have looked into the cosmos. Because the whole net is one, you cannot touch any part without touching the whole, and no part can exist without the whole.

When you start feeling this, the ego will disappear. The ego exists only when you take a certain part as the whole. When you make a part the whole, the ego exists. When you come to know the right proportion, that the part is part, and the whole is whole, the ego disappears. Ego is just a misunderstanding.

And this technique, to feel oneself saturated with the cosmic, is just wonderful!

From the very early morning, when you feel life awakening, when you feel that the sleep has gone, the first thought must be of this saturation—now the divine is opening, coming back out of sleep, not you. So Hindus, who have been one of the most penetrating races in the world, will start their first breath with the name of God. Now it has become a formality and the essential has been lost, but this was the root of it—that at the moment you become alert in the morning you must not remember yourself, you must remember the divine. The divine must become the first remembrance—and the last, at night, when you are falling asleep. The divine must be remembered; he must be the first and the last. And if he is really the first in the morning and the last at night, he will be with you the whole day, in the middle also.

You must drop into sleep saturated with him. You will be surprised, because the quality of your sleep will be different. While falling into sleep tonight, please don't *you* fall into sleep, let the divine fall into sleep. While you are preparing the bed, prepare it for the divine—the guest is coming. And while you are lying on the bed, let the divine be there, not you—treat yourself as the guest. And while dropping into sleep go on feeling that the divine exists, he saturates every breath, he pulsates in the blood, he beats in the heart. Now he is tired after a whole day of work, now he wants to sleep.

And in the morning you will feel that you have been sleeping in a different way. The quality of the sleep will be cosmic, because the meeting will be deep at the source.

When you feel yourself as divine, you fall into the abyss because then there is no fear. Otherwise, even in the night while you are sleeping you are afraid to fall deeply into it. Many people are suffering from sleeplessness—not because of any other tension, but because they are afraid to fall asleep, because sleep appears like an abyss, a bottomless thing. I have known a few persons who are afraid.

One old man came to me and said that he could not sleep because he was afraid. I asked, "Why are you afraid?"

He said, "I am afraid because if I really sleep, and I die, I will not be conscious, alert. And I can die because now I am old—and I don't like the idea of dying in sleep. At least let me be aware and alert of what is happening."

You go on clinging to something so that you cannot fall into sleep, but when you feel that the divine is there, you have accepted. Then the abyss is also divine. Then you fall very deeply into the very original sources of your being—and the quality will be different.

And when you arise in the morning and you feel that sleep has gone, remember that the divine is arising. The whole day will be different.

And be saturated—whatsoever you do, or you don't do, let the divine do it—simply allow it to be done. Eat, sleep, work, but let the divine do it. Only then can you be saturated, can you become one with it. And once you feel, even for a single moment—even for a single moment, I say—that the peak has come, that you are not, that the divine has saturated you completely, you are enlightened. In that single moment, that timeless moment, you will become aware of the whole mystery of life. Then there is no fear and then there is no death. Now you have become life itself. It goes on and on; it never ends, it never begins. Then life is ecstasy.

And the concepts of *moksha*, of heaven and paradise, are just childish, because they are not really something geographical. They are symbols of this ultimate state of being: when the individual has dissolved into the cosmos or when the individual has allowed the cosmos to dissolve into him; when the two have become one, when mind and matter, both the manifestations, have come back to the original source, the third. The whole search is for that. That is the only search, and you will not be satisfied until this is achieved. Nothing can be a substitute for it. You can go on moving for lives and lives, but unless this is achieved, your search will be constantly haunting you. You cannot rest.

This technique can be very helpful and there is no danger in it; you can practice it without a master. Remember this: all the techniques that start with the body are dangerous without a master—because the body is a very complex phenomenon, very complex. It is a mechanism, and without someone who knows exactly what is going on, it is dangerous to start—you may disturb the mechanism, and then it will be difficult to repair it. All the techniques that start directly from mind are based on imagination, and are not dangerous because the body is not touched at all. They can be done even without a master—although it will be difficult because you don't have any self-confidence. A master is not really going to do anything, but he becomes a catalytic agent. He is not going to do anything—really nothing can be done—but with just his presence, your confidence and trust are touched, and it helps. With just the feeling that the master is there, you move confidently. Because he is present, you are not afraid; because he is with you, you can move into the unknown, the uncharted. But with body techniques he is very necessary, because the body is a mechanism and you can do something which cannot be easily undone. You can harm yourself.

One man came to me, he was doing *shirshasana* —standing on his head for hours together. In the beginning it was very good and he felt very relaxed and cool the whole day. But then problems followed, and he became very disturbed when the coolness disappeared and he became hot all over. He became almost mad. And because he thought that shirshasana helped in the beginning, and he became very cool, and felt very collected, silent, relaxed, he did it more because now he felt so disturbed. He thought more shirshasana would help him—and shirshasana was really the cause.

The mind mechanism, the brain, needs only a certain amount of blood to circulate through it; if less blood is circulating, you will be in difficulty. And with everyone it is different. It depends. That's why you cannot sleep without pillows. If you try to sleep without pillows, you cannot sleep, or you will sleep less because more blood flows into the head.

Those pillows help you. Your head is high so less blood flows, and for sleep, less blood is needed. If more blood flows, then the brain is alert, it cannot relax. If you do too much of shirshasana, your sleep may be completely lost. You may not be able to sleep at all.

And there are dangers. It has been recorded that seven days is the longest you can go without sleep —only seven days. After that you will go mad, because very subtle tissues of the brain will break, and they cannot be replaced easily. While you are standing on your head in shirshasana, all the blood is flowing downwards towards the head. So I have not seen anyone doing shirshasana who is in any way intelligent. If a person is doing much shirshasana, he is bound to become stupid, because the very subtle tissues of the brain will be destroyed. With so much blood passing through, delicate tissues cannot exist.

So it has to be decided by a master who knows how much will be helpful to you—a few seconds, or a few minutes. And this is just an example. All the bodily postures, asanas, techniques, have to be done with a master. They are never to be done alone because you don't know your body. Your body is such a big thing, you cannot even conceive of it. The small head, your head, has millions of cells in it. And those millions of cells are interrelated. Scientists say that the interrelationship is as complex as the whole universe.

Old Hindu seers have said that the whole cosmos exists in the head in miniature. The whole complexity of the universe is there in miniature. If the whole relationship of all the cells can be understood, you have understood the whole complexity of the universe. You are not aware of any cells, and about any relationship you are not aware. And it is good that you are not aware, otherwise you will go mad with such a big war going on. It can go on only unconsciously.

The blood circulates, but you are not aware of it. Only just three centuries ago it was discovered that blood circulates in the body. Before that it was thought that the blood was static, not circulating. Circulation is a very recent concept. And man has been in existence for millions of years but no one could feel that the blood was circulating. You cannot feel it. Much speed, much work is going on there. It is a big factory, your body, and one of the most delicate ones. It is constantly repairing itself, constantly renewing itself. For seventy years, if you don't make any trouble for it, it will run smoothly. We have not created any mechanism up to now that can take care of itself for seventy years. So when you start any work on your body remember to be near a master who knows about what he is telling you to do. Otherwise don't do it.

But with imagination there is no problem. It is a simple phenomenon. You can start it.

---

95 Concentrate on the breasts, or on the root of the penis.

The second technique: *Feel the fine qualities of creativity permeating your breasts and assuming delicate configurations.*

A few important points before I enter this....

Shiva is talking to Parvati, to Devi, his consort, so this technique is specifically for women. There are a few points to be understood. One: the male body and the female body are similar, but still, different in many, many ways. And the difference is always complementary. Whatsoever is positive in the male body will be negative in the female body; and whatsoever is positive in the female body will be negative in the male body. That is why when they meet in deep orgasm, they become one organism. The positive meets the negative, the negative meets the positive, and both become one—one circle of electricity. Hence, so much attraction for sex, so much appeal. This appeal is not because man is a sinner or immoral, it is not because the modern world has become too licentious, it is not because of obscene films and literature—it is very deep rooted, very cosmic.

The attraction is because both male and female are half circuits, and there is an inherent tendency in existence to transcend whatsoever is incomplete and to become complete. This is one of the ultimate laws—the tendency towards completion. Wherever you feel something is lacking, you feel that you would like to fill it, to make it complete. Nature abhors incompleteness, any type of incompleteness. The male is incomplete, the female is incomplete, and they can have only one moment of completion —when their electric circuits become one, when the two are dissolved. That's why the two most important words in all languages are love and prayer. In love you become one with a single individual; in prayer you become one with the whole cosmos. And love and prayer are similar as far as their inner workings are concerned.

Male and female bodies are similar, but their positive and negative poles are different. When a child is born in the mother's womb, for a few weeks, at least for six weeks I think, he is neutral— he is neither male nor female. He has the tendency, but the body is still just in the middle. Then after six weeks the body will become either male or female. If it becomes female, then the polarity of sex energy will be near the breasts, the positive pole —because the female vagina is the negative pole. If the child is male, the sex center, the penis, will be the positive pole, and the breasts are also there —the whole mechanism is there—but they are negative. In the female body a counterpart to the penis exists, the clitoris, but it is nonfunctional. Just like male breasts, the feminine clitoris is nonfunctional—it has no function.

Physiologists have been raising questions about why there are breasts in the male body when there appears to be no need because a child is not going to be fed. What is the need? They are negative poles. Hence so much attraction of the male mind towards female breasts—they are positive electricity. So much poetry, literature, painting, sculpture, everything, is concerned with female breasts.

Really, it seems man is less concerned with the whole of the feminine body, and more concerned with the breasts. And this is not something new. The oldest primitive paintings in the caves are of breasts, so emphatically of breasts that the whole body is just around them. Breasts are basic.

This technique is for women because their positive electricity pole is in the breasts. Really, as far as the vagina is concerned, it is more or less insensitive. The breasts are the most sensitive parts, and the whole creativity of the feminine body is around the breasts.

That is why Hindus have been saying that unless a woman becomes a mother she is not fulfilled. The same is not true for men—no one will say that unless a man becomes a father he is not fulfilled. To be a father is accidental. It may be, it may not be. It is not very basic, and a man can remain without being a father without losing anything. But a woman will lose something because her whole creativity, her whole functioning, comes only when she becomes a mother. When her breasts become the center of her being she becomes total. And she cannot come to the breasts unless a child is there to call. So men marry women to get wives, and women marry men to become mothers—not to get husbands. Their basic sole interest is to have a child who will call their womanhood. So really, husbands are always afraid, because the moment a child is born they move to the periphery of the woman's interest—the child becomes the center. So fathers always feel jealous because the children come in between, and now the woman is more interested in the children than in the father of the children. He has become a peripheral existence— necessary for survival but nonessential. Now the basic need has been fulfilled.

In the West now there is a trend, a fashion, not to feed children directly from the breasts. This is very dangerous because it means that the woman will not come to the creative center of her being. When a man loves a woman he can love her breasts, he will love them, but he cannot call them mother. Only a small child can call them mother. Or if the love is very deep—so deep that the husband becomes just like a child—then it is possible. Then the woman forgets completely that she is just a consort and she becomes a mother to her lover. Then there will be no need for a child; she can become a mother and the center of being can happen near the breasts.

This technique says: *Feel the fine qualities of creativity permeating your breasts and assuming delicate configurations.* The whole creativity of feminine existence is rooted in motherhood. That is why women are not interested in any other type of creativity. Man is a creator; woman is not a creator. She has not painted, she has not created great poetry, she has not written big books, she has not created great religions—she has not done anything really. But man goes on creating, he is mad. He goes on inventing, creating, making, constructing. Tantra says that this is because man is not a creator by nature—he remains unfulfilled, tense. He wants to become a mother, he wants to become a creator, so he creates poetry, he creates books, he creates many things, he will "mother" many things. But a woman is at ease. If she can really become a mother she is fulfilled, she is not interested. It is only when a woman cannot become a mother, cannot love, cannot really come to the peak of her creativity, that she will start thinking about doing something else. So basically, uncreative women will become creators—poets and painters—but they will always be second-rate, they cannot be first-rate. It is just as impossible for them to be creators of paintings and poetry and other things, as it is impossible for man to create a child. He cannot become a mother; that is biologically impossible, and he feels the gap. To fill the gap he goes on doing many things—but still even a great creator is not as fulfilled, or only very rarely, as a woman is if she really becomes a mother.

A buddha is fulfilled because he has created himself. He is reborn, he has given rebirth to himself, he is a new man, he is both father and mother to himself now. He can feel fulfilled.

A woman can feel fulfilled more easily. Her creativity is just around the breasts. That's why all over the world, women are concerned so much with their breasts—it is as if their whole existence is concentrated there. They are always alert about their breasts—hiding or exhibiting, but always concerned. The breasts are their most secret part, their treasure, their center of being—of being mother, of being a creator.

Shiva says: *Feel the fine qualities of creativity permeating your breasts and assuming delicate configurations.* Just concentrate on the breasts, become one with them, forget the whole body. Move your total consciousness to the breasts and many phenomena will happen to you. If you can do this, if you can concentrate totally near the breasts, the whole body will lose weight, and a very sweet, deep sweetness will envelop you. It will pulsate around you, within you, above, below, everywhere—a deep feeling of sweetness.

Really, all the techniques that have been developed have been developed more or less by man, so they always give centers which are easier for men to follow. As far as I know, only Shiva has given some techniques which are basically for women. A man cannot do this. Really, if a man tries to concentrate near the breasts he will become very uneasy. Try it. Even within five minutes you will start perspiring and you will become very uneasy, because male breasts are negative, they will give you negativity. You will feel uneasy, uncomfortable, that something is going wrong in the body, ill.

But female breasts are positive. If women concentrate near the breasts, they will feel very happy, very blissful, a sweetness will pervade all over their being and their body will lose gravity. They will feel light, as if they can fly. And with this concentration many things will change; you will become more motherly. You may not become a mother but you will become more motherly. To everyone your relationship will become motherly—more compassion, more love will happen. But this concentration near the breasts should be done very relaxedly, not tensely. If you are tense about it there will be a division between you and the breasts. Relax and melt into them, and feel that you are no more, that only the breasts are there.

If man has to do the same he will have to do it with the sex center, not with the breasts. Hence the importance of the first *chakra* in all kundalini yogas. He has to concentrate just at the root of the penis—there he has the creativity, there he is positive. And remember this always: never concentrate on anything negative because with the negative everything negative will follow. With the positive, everything positive will follow.

When the two poles of man and woman meet, negative is in the upper part of man, positive is in the lower; and negative is in the lower part of woman and positive in the upper. These two poles of positive and negative meet and a circle is created. That circle is blissful, but it is not ordinary. In ordinary sexual acts, the circle does not happen—that is why you feel so attracted towards sex, and so repelled also. You feel so much for it, you need it so much, you ask for it so much, but when it is given, when it is there, you feel frustration—nothing happens. It is possible only when both the bodies are very relaxed and very open to each other without any fear, without any resistance. Then the let-go is so complete that the electricities can merge and meet and become a circle.

Then there is a very strange phenomenon.... Tantra has recorded it but you may not have heard of it. This phenomenon is a very strange one. When two lovers really meet and become a circle then a flickering happens. For a moment the lover becomes the beloved and the beloved becomes the lover, and the next moment, again the lover is the lover and the beloved is the beloved. The male becomes the female for a moment, then the female becomes the male for the moment—because the energy is moving, and it has become one circle. So it will happen that the male will be active for a few minutes and then he will relax and the female will

become active. That means that now the male energy has passed to the female body and she will act while the male will remain passive. And this will go on. Ordinarily you are man and woman; in deep love, in deep orgasm, it will happen that for moments man will become woman, and the woman will become man. It will be felt, absolutely felt and recognized, that the passivity changes.

In life there is rhythm; in everything there is rhythm. When you take a breath, the breath goes in—then for a few seconds it stops, there is no movement. Then again it moves, out it goes—and again there is a stop, a gap, no movement. Movement, no movement, movement. When your heart beats, there is one beat, gap, another beat, gap. The beat means male, the nonbeat gap means female.

Life is rhythm. When two persons meet, male and female, it becomes a circle: there will be gaps for both. You will be a woman and suddenly there will be a gap and you are no longer a woman, you have become a man. You will be man and woman and man. When these gaps are felt you can feel that you have achieved a circle. This circle is represented in Shiva's symbol—the *shivalinga*. This circle is represented by the *yoni* of Devi and *linga* of Shiva. It is a circle. It is one of the peak phenomena of two high energies meeting.

This technique will be good. *Feel the fine qualities of creativity permeating your breasts and assuming delicate configurations.* Simply relax, move into the breasts, let your breasts become your whole being. Let the whole body be just a situation for the breasts to exist, your body has become secondary, just a background, and the breasts are emphasized, and you are totally relaxing in them, moving in them. Then your creativity will arise. The feminine creativity arises only when the breasts become active. Merge into them and you will feel creativity arising.

What does it mean when creativity arises? You will have many visions around you. Buddha and Mahavira have said in their past lives that when they are born their mothers will see certain visions, certain dreams. Because of those dreams, it could be predicted that a buddha was going to be born. Sixteen visions would follow each other.

I have been experimenting with this. If a woman really melts into her breasts, certain visions will follow in a certain sequence. She will start seeing certain things. To different women there will be different sequences, but I will tell you a few. One, there will be figures, human figures, and if the woman is going to give birth to a child, then the figure of the child will appear. If total melting has happened in the breasts then the woman can see what type of child is going to be born to her. The figure will appear, and then it will be more clear. If she is not going to be a mother soon or she is not pregnant, then very unknown scents, perfumes will happen around her. The breasts can become sources of very delicate perfumes which are not of this world, which cannot be created chemically; sounds, harmonious sounds will be heard; all the realms of creativity can appear in new and many configurations. All that has happened to great painters and poets will happen to the woman if she can melt into her breasts.

And this will be so real that it will change her total personality—she will become different. And if she goes on with these visions, by and by they will drop, and a moment will come when nothingness, void, emptiness will happen—*shunyata* will happen. This shunyata is the highest of meditations.

So remember this: if you are a woman, don't concentrate on the third eye. It will be better for you to concentrate near the breasts—on the breasts, right on the two nipples of the breasts. Concentrate there. And the second thing: don't concentrate on one breast—concentrate on both simultaneously. If you concentrate on one, your body will immediately be disturbed. Even paralysis is possible if you concentrate on only one. So just concentrate on both simultaneously, melt into them and allow whatsoever happens to happen.

Just go on watching and don't get attached to any rhythm because the rhythms will be very beautiful, just heavenly. Don't get attached. Go on watching them and be a witness. A moment will come when they will start disappearing—and when shunyata, nothingness, happens, when just space, just space remains and the breasts have disappeared, then you are under the bodhi tree.

CHAPTER 68

Energy enjoys itself playing

◆

Q U E S T I O N S

Is not imagination also desire?

Yesterday You said that mind is reality....

Why do You emphasize changing the center?

Why different techniques for men and women?

The first question:

It has been said that no desire, neither worldly nor religious, can lead towards freedom. But a positive imagination of happiness and bliss is also a sort of desire. Then isn't it true that imagination is also desire and hence creates tensions?

magination is not desire. Imagination is just a play. Desire is a totally different thing. You can base your imagination on desire, you can project your imagination through desire—then it will be a bondage. If you simply play with imagination without any desire—not to reach anywhere, not to get anything out of it, but just as a game, then it is not desire and not binding. These techniques of imagination can be helpful only if you are playing with them. If you get serious, you lose the point.

But the question is relevant because, really, you cannot conceive of anything which you can do without desire. Even if you are playing, you can play only to reach somewhere, to get something, to win. If there is nothing in the future, you will lose interest. You will say, "Then why? Then why play at all?"

We are so end-oriented that we turn everything into a means. This must be remembered: meditation is the ultimate play, it is not a means to something, it is not a means to enlightenment. Enlightenment happens in it, but it is not a means to it. It is not a means to ultimate freedom. Ultimate freedom happens in it, but it is not a means to it. You cannot use it as a cause to effect something. This has been one of the most puzzling things: all through the centuries, those who have known go on insisting on meditation for meditation's sake. Don't desire anything out of it, enjoy it in itself, don't move out of it—and the consequence will be enlightenment. Remember, consequence—not effect. Meditation is not a cause, but if you are deep in meditation, enlightenment happens. Really, being deep in the play is enlightenment.

But the mind always turns everything into work. It says, "Do something because this will be the profit from it." Imaginary or real, the mind needs something to hang onto, to project onto. Only then can it devote itself. That is how mind functions—it functions in the present for the future. The future may be illusory, it may not ever happen, but if the mind can hope for the future then it can work. This is what is called desire: working in the present for the future. The end is always somewhere else; the means are here but the end is somewhere else. This division of end and means, this gap, is desire. If you are playing, there is no desire because the end is here and the means are also here. While playing there is no future; you are simply merged so much in it that the future disappears.

Look at children playing. Look at their faces, at their eyes. Now they are in eternity. They are happy because they are playing. Happiness will not result in an end, it is here right now. Moment to moment they are happy—not that something great is going to happen later on, it is happening already. They are in eternity. But their minds are still not developed. We will force them to develop because this play will not be of much help in the world. They will have to learn work. They will have to divide means and end. They will have to create a gap between this moment and the future, and we will teach them to sacrifice the present for the future. This is the way of the world, the way of the market, the way of desire. Desire makes everything utilitarian.

In meditation you will become a child again, playing, with no idea of the future, enjoying this very moment, enjoying the very act in itself, intrinsically. Then imagination is not desire. Then you can play with it, and it is one of the most beautiful things possible. And this playing, this being in the moment, totally absorbed, is enlightenment. The moment it happens you are transformed.

So enlightenment is never in the future, it is always in the present; and it is not a work to be done, it is a game to be played.

That is the meaning of the Indian concept of *leela*. God is playing, he is not engaged in work. This world is not utilitarian, it is just a play of energy. Energy enjoys itself playing; it divides itself and then plays the game of hide and seek. So, really, Indian seers have never said that God is the creator, they say that God is the player—because the very word "creation" carries much seriousness about it, as if there is some end and something has to be achieved. God creating the world? This is absurd, because it means that something is lacking, so God is creating the world to achieve something. Or it means that there is a future, so God also lives in desire.

Jainas and Buddhists could not understand the Hindu concept of leela, so they completely denied God—because if God creates the world, then he desires. So Jainas and Buddhists say that if God desires, then God is part of the world; he himself is not free, he himself is not liberated. So they com-

pletely denied the concept of God because they say that God means one who is beyond desire. And they say that Mahavira is a god, he is beyond desire, but Brahma is not a god because he creates the world, he desires the world. They couldn't follow the concept of leela.

The concept of leela is totally different from the concept of creation. God is just playing and you cannot ask "Why?" because a play has no "Why?" to answer. If children are playing can you ask, "Why are you playing?" They will say, "We are playing, so we are playing." Playing is good in itself—the energy is moving, abundant energy is overflowing.

The older you grow the less you play. Why? Because now your energy is not so overflowing. Now you have become economical. Now you know that you have a certain amount of energy and you have to channel that energy for work, to achieve something. Children are just overflowing. Their energy is so much that they have to play. The play is just overflowing energy, too much energy moving. Then they enjoy the very moment. A child is jumping, running, but not to reach some goal. Running itself is a beautiful experience of vital energy, an experience of vitality, an experience of being alive, of overflowing so abundantly that you can throw out the energy without any economical mind behind it.

God means absolute energy, infinite energy. God cannot be economical. He has so much, so infinitely much, that he can only play. And this play goes on and on, there is no end to it. There cannot be because the energy is infinite. And you cannot ask "Why?" Energy moves, there is no "why" to it. If God created the world you can ask, "Why? Why have you created the world?" But if he is simply playing you cannot ask "Why?"

When you also become a player, you become divine. If you are a worker you are human; if you are a player you have become divine. Then you share in the game. That's why we have called Krishna the absolute *avatara*. We have not called

Rama the absolute avatara, we call him a partial avatara—a partial coming of the divine to the world. But Krishna we call an absolute coming. The difference is that Rama is serious. He is still utilitarian, end-oriented: this is right and that is wrong. Only in work do right and wrong exist: this should be done and that should not be done, this is good and that is bad. For Krishna everything has become a play so everything is arbitrary—just rules of the game.

If you follow the rules, and if you follow them knowing that this is a game and that the rules have to be followed, it is good. If you don't follow, nothing is wrong; really, you are playing the reverse game of not following. If you obey, you follow the game of obedience; if you don't obey, you follow the game of disobedience, the game of rebelliousness. But nothing is wrong. What you want to play is your choice. And if you are not serious and are happy whatsoever you do, you are enlightened.

There are rules because a game has to be played with others. If you are playing alone there is no question of rules; then you can change your rules any moment you like. But because you are playing with others, rules have to be followed so that you can play with them. There isn't any other reason behind it. Morality is a rule, love is a rule, society is just a rule—agreed-upon rules that we are going to play a game so we will agree. If you don't want to play the game then you can be rebellious, but don't be serious about it. Then play the game of being rebellious. And if someone kills you, murders you, or crucifies you, you know that you were playing the game of a rebellious leader, so you have been killed. There is no condemnation. You were not with the established rules, so the established rules were against you—it is okay. Then nothing is wrong, and you don't have to complain.

Once you become aware that the concept of work, utility, reaching somewhere, the goal, is the bondage, it doesn't mean that you stop playing the game in the market. You go on playing, but you know that this is a game. It doesn't mean that you

divorce your wife—you go on playing the game of marriage. But know well that this is a game. Don't get serious about it. And if you want to play the game of divorce, you can play it, but remember, don't get serious about it. Divorce or marriage—these are alternative games; being a worldly man or becoming a sannyasin—these are alternative games. But don't be serious about it. Be light-hearted, festive. And whatsoever you choose, you can play; and whatsoever consequences follow, you will welcome them because there is nothing serious about them.

Once this deepens in your consciousness—and it will deepen if you start playing with meditation—it will be a good beginning. Because in meditation you alone are the player, that's why it can be a good beginning, the right beginning. You are alone playing the game so you can forget society and society will not come to interfere. This is a solo game, meditation, a solo game. You play alone.

So whatsoever you want to play you can play, but forget the ends. If there are ends you have also turned meditation into a work. Just play it, enjoy it, love it. It is beautiful in itself. There is no need for any other end to beautify it.

People come to me and they say, "We are enjoying meditation, but tell us what is going to happen. What will be the end result?"

I tell them, "This *is* the end result—that you are enjoying. Enjoy it more!"

But they go on insisting, "Tell us something about it. What will be the end result? Where will we reach to?" They are not concerned at all where they are; they are always concerned with where they will reach to. The mind cannot exist in the present so it goes on giving you excuses to move into the future. Those excuses are the desires. So if you desire to be a god, to be a buddha, your meditation will be a sort of desire, and then it is not meditation. If you don't desire anything, you just enjoy being here, you just celebrate being alive, you enjoy the inner energy playing in imagination, in visions, in emptiness, whatsoever you choose, and you are totally one with this moment of enjoyment, then it is meditation. Then there is no desire, and, with no desire, the world drops. With a nondesiring, playful mind you have entered. You are already in it.

But this has to be hammered into your mind again and again because your mind is a transformer. It transforms anything into a desire—anything; it can transform even nondesire into a desire. People come to me and they say, "How does one achieve the state of nondesire? How to achieve the state of nondesire?" Now this has become the desire. Your mind has a transforming mechanism: whatsoever you put in will come out as a desire.

Be alert of this and enjoy moments so much that no energy is left to move into the future. Then, any day, any moment, it will happen to you that suddenly all the darkness falls; suddenly all that is a burden disappears; suddenly you are freed. But the emphasis should be more and more on play, the present, here and now—and less and less on the future.

The second question:

Yesterday You said that mind is reality, dream is reality. Then why do gurus like You take the trouble to teach us that mind is the only barrier, mind is the only obstacle?

Gurus and disciples are mind phenomena. Because your mind needs gurus, there are gurus. You create them. Because you want to be taught, there are teachers. You need them.

This is a game. When I say marriage is a game, don't think that I would not say that guru and disciples is a game. It is a game. Some people enjoy it, so they play it. If you enjoy it, play it deeply; if you don't enjoy it, forget it. But this is one of the most beautiful of games. It goes even deeper than marriage.

It is one of the most beautiful, most refined of games—and only when a culture reaches the peak does this game develop, never before. So, really, only in India has the game developed. The game of the guru and the disciple came into being here. Now the West is discovering it for the first time because now the West is reaching to a peak. This game is the most luxurious. It is not ordinary, so only people who can afford it can play it. And if you know that this is a beautiful game and you enjoy it, you can play it. But don't get serious about it. And disciples can be forgiven if they are serious, but when teachers are serious it is absurd. It cannot be forgiven if they are not even aware that this is a game.

In reality all games disappear, but for the mind, games exist. By this I am not saying that you should stop playing, I am only saying that you should become aware that this is a play and then if you enjoy it go on playing it. If you don't enjoy it, then stop. Once you become aware that everything in life, every relationship, is a sort of game, you are already free, because you are in bondage only because of the seriousness. You are in bondage because you think everything is so serious. Nothing is so serious. But it is difficult to conceive of this whole life as a game.

Why is it so difficult? Because then the ego falls flat. If everything is a game, the ego cannot stand. The ego needs food. Seriousness is the food. It feeds on it. So when you become a disciple, if you are just playing, your ego cannot get strong through it because you know that this is a play.

What is there to be so egoistic about? People start thinking that they are disciples of a very great guru. The guru may not be great or he may be great, that is not the point—but the disciple thinks, "I am the disciple of the greatest guru." That becomes a vitamin and the ego grows on it, becomes stronger.

That's why disciples go on fighting about gurus. No one can believe that his guru is number two, he is always number one. And it is not about whether he is number one or not—that is not the point; it is because you can be number one only if your guru is number one. The ego of the disciple depends on the height of the guru. If someone says something against your guru, why do you feel so hurt? Your ego is hurt. *Your* guru means *your* ego, embodied, and if someone says something against your guru, you cannot tolerate it. It is impossible because it is a direct hit at your ego.

But for disciples it can be tolerated. They are ignorant and whatsoever they do, they will do wrongly. That is agreed upon. But so-called gurus are also playing the game very seriously. They cannot laugh; it is impossible for them to laugh about the whole game. A guru is really a guru when he knows that the whole thing is a game and that in the game he is helping to make you more aware. And a moment will come when you will also laugh, a moment will come when you will be able to look back—and then you will feel very grateful because for you it was so serious and for the guru it was never anything. But he was playing the game so seriously with you and making every effort—as if he was leading you somewhere.

Remember, it is "as if" because there is nowhere to lead you to. You have to be here. So all the efforts which appear to be leading you somewhere are just devices. You cannot be led anywhere. You are already at home, you have never left it. You are rooted in the reality, in the truth. So all these games of leading, guidance, gurudom, are to bring you to situations where you will find everything that you wanted to find already there.

But you cannot understand nonseriousness. The ego doesn't know that language. Every religion is born as a play, and every religion becomes a church, very serious, deadly serious. Every religion is born as a dance, as a song, as a festivity, and then everything goes dead and serious. Religion cannot be serious really. It must be ecstatic, it must be the highest peak of bliss. How can it be serious?

Christians go on thinking and believing that Jesus never laughed. Look at Krishna—you cannot find any common ground between them. Not that Jesus was like that, but Christians have made him serious because only around a serious Jesus is a serious church possible. And then the whole game of popes—so serious, so burdened. Jesus must

have been a very lighthearted man, laughing, enjoying, eating, drinking, dancing. He must have loved life very deeply.

That was the sin. That was the reason why he was crucified. Those who crucified him were very serious. They were the old established church. Really, they did not crucify Jesus, they crucified the festivity of him—and there would have been no Christianity if he had not been crucified, because he was a very joyous man. The moment Jews crucified him the whole thing became very serious; death became the point. And the figure on the cross is of course very serious: dead. Christianity arose around the dead body and the cross. The cross became the symbol—not Jesus laughing in a village, drinking at a party, eating with friends, or staying in a prostitute's home. No, they were not to become the symbols. The cross became the symbol, and with the cross, seriousness—dead seriousness. And because of that cross and the crucified Jesus, Christianity went against life. All that is alive became sin.

And every religion goes on doing this in its own way.

Those who are very sophisticated will not do it in this way, they will do it in another way. We have not transformed Krishna—India is a very sophisticated land, it will not do such a thing—but we have never taken him to our heart. He is just a myth, beautiful.

The Gita became more important than Bhagavad; Krishna's life is not so important for Hindus, but his message delivered on the war field is very important. Why? Because it is a serious thing. A war field is nearer to death than to life. Krishna's life is very much alive, but that has become a myth and nobody bothers about it. His few words uttered on the war field have become more important than his whole life. And then there are pundits who go on explaining that his life is just symbolic, it is not real. His playing with the *gopis* is not real—gopis are just symbols of senses, not real. They are not real women of bone and flesh, no. Gopis are not women, they are symbolic. And pundits are very efficient in doing such tricks. They say that Krishna is the soul and the gopis are the senses of the body—the senses are dancing around the soul.

This is a sophisticated country. They kill Krishna, they crucify Krishna, but in a very sophisticated way. His festivity is killed; it becomes symbolic, meaningless, and his whole real life is pushed aside. He was dancing with real women, but that is shocking because we cannot conceive of Krishna dancing with real women. We can allow him to dance with symbolic women but not with real women. We will be shocked. Life shocks us. We have become so dead that anything alive shocks us.

Every religion is born in festivity—and when the festivity dies know well that the religion is dead. Whenever a new religion is born, all the old religions will be against it because again the festivity will be there. Just as when a child is born—every child is born as a player, festive, alive, celebrating, irresponsibly celebrating, not believing in the future, believing in the here and now—the whole society will be against him; the whole society will try to put him right before he goes astray. He must be put on the right track.

The same happens with every new religion.

So when I talk of meditation as a dance, or when I talk about sannyas as an inner celebration and happiness, an affirmation of life, of course all those who belong to old traditions will say, "You call this sannyas?" And in a way they are right because whatsoever they have been believing that sannyas is, is not this. They have been believing in dead men—the more dead, the more they say, "Now this is real renunciation." When life has been renounced, they call it sannyas—but I call it sannyas when life is being lived in its totality.

But this is how it will be always. When I am no more, you will turn it into a serious thing. You will give explanations of what the real meaning is. But the real meaning is always obvious, there is no need to give any explanation. All explanations are to explain away—to bring in something which was not there.

Gurus, disciples, awakened ones and ignorant ones...this is a great play, a cosmic play. Ignorant ones need awakened ones; awakened ones cannot play solo, alone—they need ignorant ones. But the master knows that this is a play and is not serious about it.

The third question:

You said last night that a change in the outer or inner and physical or mental aspects can bring a change in consciousness. That means that changes on the periphery also affect the consciousness, the center. But then why do You emphasize changing the center, instead of changing the outer, the periphery?

This is the trouble: you go on catching the words and missing the meaning.

The periphery also belongs to you; it is part of the center. The periphery is part of the center, it is the outer part of the center, but it is not different from the center. Can you create a periphery without the center? Or can you create a center without the periphery? They are not separate, they are one. The periphery is the center looked at from without. If you change your periphery, the center will also be affected for two reasons: firstly, the periphery is part of the center, and secondly, what will change the periphery but the center? What will change the periphery? The center will change the periphery.

But my emphasis on starting the work from the center is still there because if you start changing the periphery it will take a longer time to reach to the center. That which can be done in a single moment may take many lives, because you have to travel from the periphery to the center—backwards from the superficial to the depth.

If you start work from the center, the periphery automatically changes. When the center is different, the periphery will follow it because the periphery cannot go away from you. For example, I will not tell you to try to be nonviolent at the periphery—it is an unnecessary wastage of time and effort. Be nonviolent at the heart, be compassionate, loving, at the heart—and the periphery will follow. You can forget it completely because whatsoever happens at the periphery comes from the center, so if at the center you are compassionate, the periphery will follow. And this compassion will be totally different because the periphery will not know that this is compassion; the periphery will not feel elated that this is compassion; the periphery will be blissfully unaware—the compassion will follow you like a shadow. This is the easiest course.

What I mean is this: if you want to change a tree, change the roots. Of course, the leaves of the tree are also the tree, and you can also try to change the leaves. If you change the leaves the roots will be affected but it is going to be a very long process because the flow is from the roots to the leaves, the flow is not from the leaves to the roots. You are following a reverse direction from that of nature. If you go on changing the leaves, after many, many lives you may affect the pattern of the roots, but this is going to be unnecessarily long. You can do it immediately if you change the pattern at the roots. The leaves will change and will become different.

So when I emphasize the center, I don't mean that the periphery is separate from the center. And when I emphasize the center, I don't mean that you cannot affect the center from the periphery—you can, but this is the longest route possible. If you choose to travel the long route it is up to you. Nothing is wrong in it. If you enjoy the journey, then the long route is good; if you just want to see the side views then the long route is good. Otherwise start from the center.

It is like this: we are sitting here and you are listening to me, so a center is created in this room—you become the periphery, I become the center. A group soul exists. You are centered towards me. If someone wants to affect this room and this group soul, it is better to start from me than from you. Because if I change my mind, effects will come soon, but if someone starts from you, it is going to

be a very long effort. Because for one thing, you are many and first he has to change you one by one, and then he must try to change me through you. This is going to be very long, and it may not succeed ever. The other is easier. If he changes me and if you are attached to me as the center, immediately there will be effects.

In your body, in your being, the same phenomenon is happening. There is the center and there is the periphery of your life. With a direct hit at the center the periphery will follow—it has to follow, there is no other way to go. Changing the periphery is a piecemeal affair: you change one fragment and ninety-nine other fragments remain as the old; then when you move to another fragment, those ninety-nine others will change the one you tried to change—they will make it again the old. The whole pattern will be against it. I can change one habit—much effort will be needed—but not your whole pattern because your center goes on giving you all the old habits. I have changed only one habit and there are thousands of habits. This changed habit is just from the surface, forced. The moment you become unaware, all the other habits and the pattern will change it again into the old. So much effort is wasted working on the periphery.

I have seen people who have been working their whole life for ordinary things. For example, someone has been trying for his whole life to stop smoking—this has been the whole aim, the only aim, and he has not achieved it. I tell such a person that even if you achieve it, what is achieved? The whole life is lost just in trying to stop smoking. It is not worth it. When you reach to the divine source, to God, you will only be able to say that you have stopped smoking. This won't be worth telling. And the whole life has been spent trying to stop smoking and even that has not been achieved. This is piecemeal work. And the problem is not smoking; you are fighting against a current by changing a small wave—and the whole river goes on flowing. If you change a wave, the whole river will change the wave back again into itself, because the pattern, the built-in pattern, goes on being flashed from the center to the periphery. It is a built-in program: whatsoever is happening on the periphery has happened already in the center. That's why it is happening there. The periphery comes to know about things which have been happening very deeply.

Move to the cause and don't be too much concerned with the effect.

This is scientific. Change the center. Don't try to stop smoking, don't try to stop this and that—follow the deepest pattern. Why is smoking there? Why is this obsession with sex there? Why is this obsession with money there? Why are you a miser? Why do you go on clinging to dead money? You can donate it—it will not make any difference. Donating will not help, you will again gather. And donating in itself will be an investment for the future, it will be part of your bank balance. You cannot donate just in play, can you? You can donate very seriously when it is said that the donation will lead you to heaven. Then you can donate. To me a donor who is giving his money for some future end in paradise is more clinging to his money than a person who can throw away all his fortune in a game of cards. This person is less greedy. He can play with it, and his achievement is deeper. He may look immoral because morality is created by the donators. They will say, "You are wasting money." They never waste money; they always invest it. And this man is mad, immoral, wasting money. But this man is less greedy, and this man can move deeper more easily than the greedy man who is donating for some paradise or something.

You can change outer things, but even the change will deep down have the same pattern. The pattern has to be uprooted and transformed. That's why I emphasize starting from the center. But don't think that I mean that if you cannot start from the center, don't start from the periphery. That is not what I mean. If you can't start from the center, please start from the periphery. Something is better than nothing. It will take much time, or you may

not ever be able to do it, but still the very effort will be good.

I am reminded of an incident. In a waiting room of an airport, a young woman was crying steadily. Everyone around was aware of it, but no one knew what to do. Then one fellow took courage. He came near the woman, tried to console her, said some soothing things, put his arm around her, and asked, "What can I do? Is there anything I can do to help you to stop crying?"

But she was not listening. She continued crying, so he squeezed her a little more tightly and then again asked, "Is there anything I can do to stop you from crying?"

The woman said at last, "I am afraid not. This is hayfever, but still, please, keep on trying."

That's what I say to you. From the periphery it is difficult because it is like hayfever. It is almost impossible, but please, keep on trying. Something may happen. Who knows?

But if you are really interested, start from the center.

The fourth question:

Why should there be a difference in techniques for men and women?

Because they are different. They are as different as possible. They are polar opposites. Really, the more relevant question would be this: Why should there be similar techniques?

There are techniques which are being used by both men and women, not because they are suited to women, but really because special techniques were never developed for them. They have been a neglected part of humanity. All the techniques were developed by men. Basically man was experimenting with himself: he knew about his energy pattern, his routes of energy, his passages of energy. He worked on these. And then he was talking to other men—so techniques were developed by men for men. Women were never considered.

Women cannot enter a Mohammedan mosque.

They are not to be a part of Islam really; the mosque exists only for men. For many years Buddha insistently denied women initiation. Mahavira initiated many women, he never denied them initiation, but no techniques were developed for them. All the techniques were for men. Women worked through them. That's why the results were never so miraculous, never; they were always so-so, bound to be.

Really, there is no need for three hundred religions in the world, there is only need for two religions: one for men and one for women. And those two religions need not be in conflict, they can be married together. They will become one. There is no need of any conflict. If a man and a woman can fall in love and live together as a single unit, those two religions can fall in love—they should.

The whole physiology, the whole psychology, every layer of the feminine consciousness is different from man's—not only different, just the opposite. For example, kundalini yoga...it is not for women at all. But many will be shocked if I say that—and women particularly will be shocked. They will think that something has been taken out of their hands. It is not for them at all because kundalini is based on the positive sex center for man. The positive sex center is at the root of the penis—for men, not for women. For women that center is negative, and energy cannot be raised from a negative center. So almost always it is the case—this is my observation—that whenever women say they are feeling kundalini arising in them, they are imagining. It cannot happen but they are very imaginative, more imaginative than men. So if I work with ten women and ten men, nine women will feel the energy arising and only one man will feel the energy arising. This is miraculous because it cannot happen! They go on coming to me and I say, "Okay, it is happening." What to do? It is impossible, scientifically impossible, because energy can come only from a positive pole.

Totally different techniques should be developed, totally different techniques—but because man and woman live so near, so close together, they go on forgetting that they are different.

Nothing is similar, and it is good that nothing is similar, because that's why they can become one circle of energy. They are complementary, they fit into each other. But because they fit that doesn't mean that they are similar—they fit because they are not similar.

And whenever two similar types of bodies and minds try to fit into each other, this is perversion. So I say that homosexuality is a perversion. In the West, now, it has become more and more prevalent. Now homosexuals think they are progressive: they have their clubs, parties, institutions, magazines, propaganda, everything. And their number is rising. In certain countries it has come to nearabout forty percent. Sooner or later homosexuality will become a pattern all over, a normal pattern. If people insist, you have to allow it because the government has to serve the people. If two men want to live together in marriage, it is no one's business to create obstacles. It's okay. If two women want to live together, married, it's no one's business. It's their own affair. But this is basically unscientific. It is their affair, but unscientific. It is their affair and no one needs to interfere.

But their minds are unenlightened about the very basic pattern of human energy and its movement. Homosexuals cannot develop spirituality, it is very difficult. Their whole pattern of energy movement is disturbed. The whole mechanism is shocked, perverted. And now if homosexuality grows too much in the world, very different techniques will have to be developed, unknown before, to help them to move towards meditation.

When I say a man and woman are two counterparts of one whole, I mean they are complementary. And the complementariness is possible only when their opposite poles meet. Look at it in this way: the vagina is the negative pole in the feminine body and the breasts are the positive pole. This is the rod of magnetism: the positive pole near the breasts, the negative pole near the vagina. For man the negative pole is at the breasts, and the positive pole is at the penis. So when breasts meet—male and female—negative and positive are meeting; and when sex centers meet in coitus, negative and positive are meeting. Now both magnetic rods are meeting at their opposite poles, now there is a circle—the energy can flow, the energy can move.

But this circle will happen only when a man and woman are in love. If they are not in love, then only their sex centers will meet—one positive pole will meet with one negative pole. There will be an exchange of energy, but linear. A circle cannot be made. That's why without love you never feel satisfied.

Sex without love becomes just a trifle, it is not moving deep. Energy moves, but in a line—a circle is not made. And when a circle is there you become one, not before. When you are deep in love, then breasts also meet, never before. So the sex act is very easy, the love act is more complex. The sex act is just physical—two energies meeting and dissipating. Hence, if there is only sex, sooner or later you will feel frustrated: you waste energy and nothing is gained. The gain happens only when there is a circle. If the circle is totally there, then both the partners will come out of the sex act more energetic, more alive, more charged, with more energy flowing. If there is only the sex act, both partners will come out of it discharged, faint. They have lost energy. Sleep will follow because all they are feeling is weak.

In this "one pole meeting," men are at more of a loss than women. That's why women can become prostitutes—because the positive pole is man and the negative pole is woman. Energy flows from man to woman but not vice versa. So a woman can be in twenty or thirty sex acts in one night, a man cannot. A man cannot be in two. It depends on age, how his energy is moving—because nothing is gained. So to me, if prostitution is bad it is not because of prostitution, it is because a circle is impossible. You are not charged, you simply waste your energy. If there is love, then man and woman meet on two poles. Man gives to the woman and the woman returns it back. This is reciprocal, mutual.

For females, meditation will be good if it starts from the breasts. That is their positive pole. Because of this, many strange things become possible, happen. Man always likes to enter the woman immediately. He is not interested in foreplay because his positive pole is always ready. And women are always reluctant to enter into the sex act immediately, without any foreplay, because their negative pole is not ready. And it cannot be ready—unless the man starts loving the woman from the breasts, the negative pole will not be ready. They can yield but they will not participate. And man thinks the sex act is simple. Why waste time? Enter the woman immediately—and he is finished within minutes. But the woman was not a part, she was not aroused. That's why women have a hankering that their lovers should touch their breasts, love their breasts—a deep hankering. Only when their breasts have become filled with energy does their second pole of the magnetic rod, which is negative, respond. Then they are alive to it, then they can participate, then communication is possible—and then they will melt. Foreplay is a must.

Marriages become dry because in the beginning when you meet a new woman you play with her body before. You are not certain whether she will allow you a direct approach, so you play. You just feel the ground to see whether she is ready. But when she is your wife, you take her for granted—there is no need. Wives are so dissatisfied with their husbands, not because their husbands are not loving but because they are wrongly loving. They don't think that a woman exists in a different way, that her body responds in a different way just opposite to them.

This concentration at the breasts, melting into them, will give a new feeling to the female meditator—a new feeling about her own body, because now from the center she can feel the whole body vibrating. Just by loving the breasts of a woman she can be brought to a deep orgasm because the negative pole will automatically go on responding.

There are many other things. If you start from the breasts, meditating on the nipples... Don't follow the route that you have read in books because that is meant for men. Simply don't follow any chart, just allow the energy itself to move. It will happen in this way: with just a vague suggestion your breasts will become filled with energy, they will radiate energy, they will become hot, and then immediately your vagina will respond. And only after your vagina responds and vibrates will your kundalini start working. The route will be different and the way the kundalini will arise will be different.

In man it arises very actively, forcibly. That's why they have called it a serpent rising. Very forcibly, suddenly, with a jerk, the serpent unfolds. And it is felt on many points. Those points are called *chakras*. Wherever there is resistance, the snake forces itself. Just as the penis enters the vagina, so the passage is similar for man. When the energy arises it is as if the penis inside is moving.

And the snake is a phallic symbol. Really, not to use direct language, not to call it penis, they have called it a snake. You must have heard the story of the Garden of Eden where the serpent persuaded Eve to eat the fruit of the tree of knowledge. Now scholars are working and they say that this serpent is also just a phallic symbol, used so as not to say it directly. So it is not a question, really, of eating the fruit of knowledge; it is a question of sexuality.

The same symbol has been used similarly in India: the serpent rises just like a penis erecting, in jerks, and moving inwards.

This will not be the feeling for woman. The feeling will be quite the opposite. As a woman feels when the penis has entered the vagina—the melting sensation, the welcoming, the vagina giving way, vibrating very, very delicately, in a very receptive mood, loving, welcoming—the same will be the phenomenon inside. When the energy rises, it will be a receptive, passive rise, as if a passage is opening—not a serpent rising, but a door opening, and a passage opening, and something giving way. It will be passive and negative. With men something is entering; with women something is opening, not entering.

But no one has worked on it, never before, because no one has taken any cognizance of women. But for the future, I think that now it is a must—the feminine body should not be neglected. Much research and work is needed, but it is very difficult to work because of so much puritanical, moralistic nonsense. It is very difficult to work and to create a map of how the feminine body will respond to the phenomena.

But this is how I feel it will be: everything will be just the opposite. It must be so. It cannot be similar. But the ultimate thing will be the same.

CHAPTER 69

You are unknown to yourself

◆

96 *Abide in some place endlessly spacious, clear of trees, hills, habitations. Thence comes the end of mind pressures.*

97 *Consider the plenum to be your own body of bliss.*

 an is born alone and dies alone, but between these two points he lives in society, he lives with others. Aloneness is his basic reality; society is just accidental. And unless man can live alone, can know his aloneness in its total depth, he cannot be acquainted with himself. All that happens in society is just outer; it is not you, it is just your relations with others. You remain unknown. From the outside you cannot be revealed.

But we live with others. Because of this, self-knowledge is completely forgotten. You know something about yourself, but indirectly—it is said to you by others. It is strange, absurd, that others should tell you about yourself. Whatsoever identity you carry is given to you by others; it is not real, it is just a labeling. A name is given to you. That name is given as a label because it will be difficult for society to be related to a nameless person. Not only is the name given, the very image that you think yourself to be is given by society: that you are good, that you are bad, that you are beautiful, that you are intelligent, that you are moral, a saint, or whatsoever. The image, the form, is also given by society, and you don't know what you are. Neither your name reveals anything, nor the form that society has given to you. You remain unknown to yourself.

This is the basic anxiety. You are there, but you are unknown to yourself. This lack of knowledge about oneself is the ignorance, and this ignorance cannot be destroyed by any knowledge which others can give to you. They can say to you that you are not this name, you are not this form, you are "soul eternal," but that too is given by others, that too is not immediate. Unless you come to yourself directly, you will remain in ignorance— and ignorance creates anxiety. You are not only afraid of others, you are afraid of yourself— because you don't know who you are and what is hidden in you. What is possible, what will erupt out of you the next moment, you don't know. You go on trembling and life becomes a deep anxiety. There are many problems which create anxiety, but those problems are secondary. If you penetrate deeply, then every problem will ultimately reveal that the basic anxiety, the basic anguish, is that you are ignorant of yourself—of the source from where you come, of the end to where you are moving, of the being who you are right now.

Hence every religion says to move into solitude, into aloneness, so that you can for a time leave society and all that society has given to you, and face yourself directly.

Mahavira lived for twelve years alone in the forest. He would not speak during those days, because the moment you speak you have moved into society. Language is society. He remained completely silent, he would not speak. The basic bridge had been cut so that he would be alone. When you don't speak you are alone, deeply alone; there is no way to move to the other. For twelve long years he lived alone without speaking. What was he doing? He was trying to find out who he was. It is better to put away all labels, it is better to move away from others so that there is no need for the social image. He was destroying the social image. He was throwing away all the garbage that society had given; he was trying to be totally naked, without any name, without any form. That's what Mahavira's nakedness means. It was not just throwing away the clothes, it was deeper. It was the nudity of being totally alone. You also use clothes for society: they are to hide your body, or they are to cover you in the eyes of others, because society doesn't approve of your whole body. So whatsoever society doesn't approve of, you have to hide. Only particular parts of the body are allowed to be in the open. The society chooses you in parts. Your totality is not approved of, not accepted.

The same is happening with the mind, not only with the body. Your face is approved of, your hands are approved of, but your whole body is not approved of, particularly the parts of the body that can give any hint of sex. They are disapproved of, not accepted. Hence the importance of clothes. And this is happening with the mind also: your total mind is not accepted, only parts of it. So you have to hide the mind and suppress it. You cannot open your mind. You cannot open your mind to your deepest friend because he will judge. He will say, "This is what you think? This is what goes on in your mind?" So you have to give him only that which can be accepted—a very minute part—and all else that is in you has to be hidden completely. That hidden part creates many diseases. The whole psychoanalysis of Freud consists only of bringing the hidden part out. It takes years before the person is healed. But the psychoanalyst is not doing anything, he is simply bringing the suppressed part out. Just to bring it out becomes a healing force.

What does it mean? It means the suppression is the illness. It is a burden, a heavy burden. You wanted to confess to someone; you wanted to tell, to express; you wanted someone to accept you in totality. That is what love means—you will not be rejected. Whatsoever you are—good, bad, saint, sinner—someone will accept you in your totalness,

he will not reject any part of you. That's why love is the greatest healing force, it is the oldest psychoanalysis. Whenever you love a person you are open to him, and just by being open, your cut, divided parts are brought together. You become one.

But even love has become impossible. Even with your wife you cannot tell the truth. Even with your lover you cannot be totally authentic, because even his or her eyes are judging. He or she also wants an image to be followed, an ideal—your reality is not important, the ideal is important. You know that if you express your totality you will be rejected, you will not be loved. You are afraid, and because of this fear love becomes impossible.

Psychoanalysis brings the hidden part out, but the psychoanalyst is not doing anything, he is simply sitting there listening to you. No one has listened to you, it seems. That is why you now need professional help. No one is ready to listen to you, no one has the time, no one has much interest in you. So professional help has come into being— you are paying someone to listen. And then year in, year out, he will listen to you every day, or twice a week, or thrice a week, and you will be healed. This is miraculous! Why should you be healed just by listening? It is because someone pays attention to you without any judgment and you can tell anything that is in you. And just by telling, it comes up and becomes a part of the conscious. When you cut off something, deny something, prohibit something, suppress something, you are creating a division between the conscious and the unconscious, the accepted and the rejected. This division has to be thrown.

Mahavira moved into aloneness so that he could be as he was with no fear of anybody. Because he didn't have to show a face to anybody he could throw away all the masks, all the faces. Then he could be alone, totally naked, as he is, under the stars, by the river and in the forest. No one would judge him and no one would say, "You are not allowed to be like this. You should behave. You should be like this."

Leaving society means leaving the situation where suppression has become inevitable. So nudity means to be as one is, with no barriers, no withholding. Mahavira moved into silence, into loneliness, and he said, "Unless I find myself—not the self that others have given to me, that is false, but the self that I am born with—I will not return to society. Unless I know who I am I will not return to society. Unless I have come directly face to face with my reality, unless I have encountered the essential in me, not the accidental, I will not speak, because it is useless to speak."

You are the accidental. Whatsoever you think you are is the accidental part. For example, you are born in India; you could have been born in England or in France or in Japan. That is the accidental part. But just by being born in India, you have a different identity. You are a Hindu, you think yourself a Hindu—but you would have thought yourself a Buddhist in Japan, or a Christian in England,or a communist in Russia. You have not done anything to be a Hindu, it is just an accident. Wherever you were you would have joined yourself with the situation. You think yourself religious but your religion is just accidental. If you had been born in a communist country, you would not have been religious, you would have been as irreligious there as you are religious here. You are born into a Jaina family so you don't believe in God—without your having discovered that there is no God. But just by the side of your house another child is born on the same day, and he is a Hindu. He believes in God and you don't. This is accidental, it is not essential. It depends on circumstances. You speak Hindi, someone speaks Gujarati, someone speaks French—these are accidents. Language is accidental. Silence is essential; language is accidental. Your soul is essential; your self is accidental. And to find the essential is the search, the only search.

How to find the essential? Buddha moved in silence for six years. Jesus also moved into a deep forest. His followers, the apostles, wanted to go with him. They followed him and at a certain moment, at a certain point, he said, "Stop. You should not come with me. Now I must be alone with my God." He moved into the wilderness. When he came back he was a totally different man; he had faced himself.

Loneliness becomes the mirror. Society is the deception. That's why you are always afraid of being alone—because you will have to know yourself, and you will have to know yourself in your nudity, in your nakedness. You are afraid. To be alone is difficult. Whenever you are alone, you immediately start doing something so you are not alone. You may start reading the newspaper, or you may put on the TV, or you may go to some club to meet some friends, or you may go to visit some family—but you must do something. Why? Because the moment you are alone your identity melts, and all that you know about yourself becomes false and all that is real starts bubbling up.

All religions say that man must move into solitariness to know himself. One need not be there forever, that is futile, but one has to be in solitude for a time, for a period. And the length of the period will depend on each individual. Mohammed was in solitude for a few months; Jesus for only a few days; Mahavira for twelve years and Buddha for six years. It depends. But unless you come to the point where you can say, "Now I have known the essential," it is a must to be alone.

---

96 Look into unlimited space.

This technique is concerned with loneliness. *Abide in some place endlessly spacious, clear of trees, hills, habitations. Thence comes the end of mind pressures.*

Before we enter this technique three other points about loneliness must be understood. One: to be alone is basic, foundational—that is how your being is. In the mother's womb you are alone, totally alone, and psychologists say that the hankering for nirvana, for enlightenment, for salvation, for paradise, is really a deep imprinted memory of the experience of the mother's womb. You have known it, the total aloneness, and the bliss of it. You were alone, you were God. No one else was there. No one disturbed you, no one interfered. Alone, you were the master. With no conflict the peace was intrinsic. Silence was there, no language. You were deep in yourself. You are not consciously aware of the fact but it is deeply imprinted, it is there hidden in the unconscious.

Because of this, psychologists say that everyone thinks that life in childhood was beautiful. And every country and every race thinks that somewhere in the past was the golden age—somewhere in the past, life was blissful. Hindus call it *satyuga*, age of truth. In the past, somewhere, the very, very past, before history began, everything was beautiful and blissful. There was no conflict, no strife, no violence. Only love prevailed. That was the golden age. Christians say that Adam and Eve lived in Eden, in the garden, in absolute innocence and blissfulness. Then came the fall. So the golden age is before the fall. Every country, every race, every religion, believes that the golden age was somewhere in the past, and the strangeness is that howsoever deeply into the past you move, this was always believed to be so—always.

In Mesopotamia a stone has been found which is six thousand years old. There is an inscription on it. If you read it you will feel that it is the editorial of today's morning newspaper. The inscription says that this age is the age of sin, everything has gone wrong, the son doesn't believe in the father, the wife doesn't believe in the husband. Darkness has set. Where are those days, the days of the past, those golden days? This is a six-thousand-year-old inscription!

Lao Tzu says that in the days of the past, in the days of the ancients, everything was beautiful. Then Tao prevailed, then there was nothing wrong, and because there was nothing wrong, no one preached. There was nothing wrong to be changed, trans-formed, and there was no priest, no preacher, no moral leaders, because everything was so right. Lao Tzu says that in those days, those old days, there was no religion. There was no need because Tao prevailed. Everyone was so religious that there was no need for religion. There were no sages then, because there were no sinners. Everyone was such a sage that, naturally, no one was aware of who was a sage and who was a sinner.

Psychologists say that this past never existed. This past is just the deep memory within every individual of the womb. It existed, really. Tao was in the womb, and everything was beautiful, everything was as it should be. Completely unaware of the world, the child is moving in bliss. The situation of the child in the womb is just as it is for Vishnu on his *sheshnaga*. Hindus believe that Vishnu is lying on his couch, a serpent couch, floating on the ocean of bliss. Really, that is the child's position in the womb. The child floats. The mother's womb is just like the ocean.

You may be surprised to know that the water in which the child floats in the mother's womb has the same constituents as the ocean water—very similar, the same salts, everything. It is ocean water, soothing. And the womb always keeps the right temperature for the child. The mother may be shivering with cold, that makes no difference. For the child it is always the same temperature in the womb. He is warm, blissfully floating, with no worries, no anxieties, no responsibilities, alone. He is not aware of the mother; mother doesn't exist for him. This *sanskar*, this imprint, is carried on by you. This is the basic reality, how you were before you entered society, and this will be the reality again when you go out of society and die. You will again be alone.

And between these two points of loneliness your life is filled with many events. But those events are accidental. Deep down you remain alone because that is your basic reality. Around that aloneness many things happen: you get married, you become two, then you have children and you become many. Everything goes on happening—but just on the periphery. The deep stratum remains totally alone. That is your reality. You may call this your *atma*, your essence.

In deep solitude this essence has to be recaptured. So when Buddha says that he has achieved nirvana, really he has achieved this loneliness, this basic reality. Mahavira says he has achieved *kaivalya*. The very word "kaivalya" means loneliness, the alone. Just below the turmoil of events that aloneness is there. It runs through you like a thread running in a mala. The beads are apparent, but the thread is not. But the beads are hanging on the thread, and the beads are many and the thread is one. Really, the mala is a symbol of this reality. The thread is the reality and the beads are just the events which go on hanging on it. And unless you penetrate and come to the basic thread, you will be in anguish, you will be in suffering.

You have a history—that history is accidental. And you have a nature—that nature is nonhistorical. You are born on a certain date, to certain parents, in a certain society, in a certain age; you are educated in a certain way. Then you enter a particular profession, you fall in love with a woman, you have children. These dramas are beads, events, history, but deep down you are always alone. And if you forget yourself completely because of these events you have missed the very purpose of being here. Then you have lost yourself in the drama and you have forgotten the actor who was not part of it, who was just playing the role. All these things are roles.

Because of this India does not have written histories. Really, it is very difficult to be certain about when Krishna was born, when he died; when Rama was born, when he died—or whether he was ever born or not or is just a myth. We have not written his history, and this is the reason: we in India are concerned with the thread and not with the beads. Really, in the religious world, Christ is the first historical person, but had he been born in India he would not have been historical. We in India are always looking for the thread, the beads are irrelevant. But the West is more oriented towards events, facts—temporal things—than to the essential and the eternal. History is the drama.

In India, we say that Ramas and Krishnas go on being born in every age. They have been repeated many times before and they will be repeated many times afterwards, so there is no need to carry on the records. When they are born is irrelevant. What their being is—the thread—that is the meaningful. So we are not concerned if they were really historical persons or not, we are not concerned with outer things that happen to a being, we are concerned with the being itself and whether anything happens to it or not.

When you move into solitude you are moving to the thread; when you move into solitude, you are moving into nature. If you are really alone, not even thinking of others, you will feel the world of nature around you for the first time. You will become attuned to it. Right now you are attuned to society. If you fall from this attunement to society, you will be attuned to nature. When the rains come —they are always coming but you cannot understand the language of the rains—they don't say anything to you, they don't mean anything to you; at the most some utilitarian thing about water being needed is realized. So there is some use, but you don't have any dialogue, you cannot understand the language of the rains, the rain has no personality for you.

But if you leave society for a time and remain in aloneness, you will start feeling a new phenomenon: the rains will come and they will talk to you. Then you will feel their moods—some day the rain is very angry and some day it is very soothing and loving. Some day the whole sky is depressed, and some day it is dancing. Some day the sun rises as if without any will of its own, forced, doing the work; and some day on its own—now it is not a work but a play.

You will feel all the moods around you. Nature has its own language but it is silent, and unless you are silent you cannot understand it.

The first layer of attunement is with society, the second layer of attunement is with nature, and the third layer, the deepest, is with Tao or Dharma. That is the pure existence. Then the trees, then the rains, then the clouds, they are also left behind. Then, just existence…. Existence has no moods. Existence is always the same. Existence is always the same: always festive, exploding with energy. But one has first to move from society to nature—then from nature to existence. When you are attuned with existence you are totally alone, but this aloneness is different from that of the child in the womb. The child is alone, but it is not that he is really alone, he is unaware of anything else. He is enclosed in darkness, that's why he feels alone. The whole world exists around him but he is not aware of it. His aloneness is that of ignorance. When you become consciously silent, one with existence, your aloneness will not be surrounded by darkness, it will be surrounded by light.

For the child in the womb the world is not, because he is unaware. For you the world will not be, because the world and you have become one.

When you reach the deepest being you are alone again because the ego is lost. The ego is given by society. It can persist a little even when you are in nature although it will not be as much as it is in society. When you move alone, your ego starts disappearing—because it is always in relationship. Look at this phenomenon: with every individual your ego changes. If you are talking to your servant, look inside, look at the ego, see how it is. If you are talking to your friend, look within, see how the ego is. You are talking to your beloved, look within, see whether the ego is or is not.

If you are talking to an innocent child, look within—the ego will not be there because it will be stupid to be an egoist with an innocent child. You will feel that this would be stupid, so while playing with children you become a child. The child doesn't know the language of ego. And being egoistic with a child you will look awkward. So when you play with children they pull you down, they bring you

back to your own childhood. When you are talking with a dog, or playing with a dog, the ego that the society has given to you cannot exist because with a dog there is no question of ego. If you are walking with your dog—a very beautiful and costly dog—and someone crosses the street, even the dog seems to give you ego. But the dog is not giving you ego, it is the man who is passing. You become straight, you feel elated because you have a very beautiful dog and the man looks jealous.

The ego is there. If you move into a forest the ego disappears. Hence the insistence of all religions to move, at least for a time, into the world of nature.

This sutra is simple: *Abide in some place endlessly spacious*—on some hilltop from where you can see endlessly, from where the vision never comes to any end. If you can see endlessly and there is no end to your vision, the ego will dissolve. Ego needs limits, boundaries. The more defined the boundaries, the easier it is for the ego to exist.

Abide in some place endlessly spacious,
clear of trees, hills, habitations. Thence comes
the end of mind pressures.

Mind is very subtle. You can live on a hilltop where there is no one, but if you can see a cottage deep down in the valley you will start talking with that cottage, you will be in relationship with it—the society has come. You don't know who lives there, but someone lives there, and that becomes the boundary—you will start dreaming about who lives there and your eyes will search each day to see who lives there. The cottage will become a symbol of humanity.

So the sutra says *without habitations*—even without trees, because it has been known that people who live alone start talking with trees. They make friendships, they create a dialogue. You cannot understand the difficulty of a man who has gone to be lonely. He wants someone so he will say "Hello" to the tree and "How are you?" And trees are beings. If you are really honest, they will start replying, there will be a response.

So you can create a society. The meaning of the sutra is this: be in some place and be alert that you don't create a society again. You may start tending a tree, loving a tree. You may feel that the tree is feeling thirsty so you should bring some water— you have started a relationship and with a relationship you are not alone.

So this is the emphasis: move to such a place but have it in your mind that you are not going to create any relationship. Leave all relationship and the world of relationship behind, and be alone there. In the beginning it is going to be very difficult because your mind is created by society. You can leave society but where will you leave the mind? The mind will follow you like a shadow. The mind will haunt you. The mind will start torturing you. Faces will come in your dreams—they will try to pull you. You will try to meditate but thoughts will not cease. You will start thinking of your house, you will start thinking of your wife, of your children. It is human.

And it does not happen to you only—it has happened to Buddha and to Mahavira. It has happened to everyone. Even a Buddha is bound to think of Yashodhara during six long years of loneliness. In the beginning, when the mind was following him, he must have been sitting under a tree pretending to meditate, and Yashodhara must have followed him. He loved that woman, and he must have felt guilty because he had left her—and without saying anything to her. Nowhere is it mentioned that he thought about Yashodhara, but I say he must have thought of her. It is so human, it is so natural; to think that he never thought again of Yashodhara would be very inhuman and would not be fair to Buddha. Only by and by, after a long struggle, would he have been able to throw off the mind.

But mind will persist because it is nothing but society—society internalized. Society has entered into you—that is your mind. You can escape from society, the outer reality, but the inner will follow you.

Many times Buddha must have been talking with Yashodhara, with his father, with the small child he left behind. The face of his child must have followed him. It was there in his mind when he left. The night he left he went into Yashodhara's room, just to see the child for the last time. The child was only one day old; Yashodhara was sleeping and the child was clinging to her breast. He looked at the child. He wanted to take the child into his hands because this was his last opportunity. He had not touched him yet and now he might never return so there would be no meeting. He was leaving the world. He wanted to touch and kiss the child but then he became afraid, because if he took the child up in his hands, Yashodhara might be awakened. Then it would be very difficult for him to leave— she would start weeping and crying. He had a human heart. It was beautiful that he thought of it, that if she started crying it would be very difficult for him to leave. Then all that he had created in his mind—that this world was useless and futile— would disappear. He would not be able to see Yashodhara crying. He loved that woman. So he left, he moved out of the room without making any noise.

This man could not leave Yashodhara and the child easily. No one could. When he was begging it was bound to come to his mind—his palace and everything. He was a beggar of his own accord. The past would persist, it would hammer the mind again and again: "Come back." Many times he would think, "I have made a mistake." It is bound to be so. Nowhere is this recorded and sometimes I think about making a diary about what happened to Buddha's mind during those six years—a diary about what happened to his mind, what was going on.

Mind will follow like a shadow wherever you go. So it is not going to be easy, it has never been easy for anyone. It will be a long struggle to make yourself again and again alert; again and again to be a witness; again and again not to fall a victim. And to the very last the mind follows. Unless you are desperate, unless you feel that you are incurable, that nothing can be done, the mind will go on haunting you. It will try in every way. It will create fantasies, reveries, dreams; it will create all types of allurements, seductions. It is written in the lives of all the seers that Satan comes, the Devil comes, to seduce. No one comes—only your mind. Your mind is the only Devil and no one else. It will try in every way. It will say to you, "I will give you the whole world, come back." It will make you depressed: "You are a fool—the whole world is enjoying and you have come to this hilltop. You are mad. All this religious stuff is humbug, come back. Look, the whole world is not insane and they are enjoying." And the mind will give such beautiful pictures of everyone who is enjoying and the whole world will be more attractive to you than ever. All that you have left behind will pull you backwards.

This is the basic struggle. And this is just because the mind is a mechanism of habits, of mechanical persistence. On the hilltop the mind will feel like hell—nothing is good there, everything is wrong. The mind will create negativity all around you: "What are you doing here? Have you gone mad?" The world that you have left behind will become more and more beautiful to your eyes and the place that you are in will become more and more ugly. But if you persist and you remain aware that this is what the mind is doing, this is what the mind is bound to do, and if you don't get identified with the mind, a moment comes when the mind leaves you, and with it all the pressures. When the mind leaves you, you are unburdened, because it is the only burden. Then there is no worry, no thought, no anxiety, you have entered the womb of existence. Unworried, you float. A deep silence explodes within you.

The sutra says, *Thence comes the end of mind pressures*. In such solitude, in such loneliness, one thing more has to be remembered: the crowd exerts a deep pressure on you, whether you know it or not.

Now, after working on animals, scientists have come to a very basic law. They say that every animal has a certain space as his territory. If you enter that space then the animal becomes tense and he will attack you. Every animal has a certain space around him. He will not allow anybody to enter, because the moment someone enters, he feels the pressure. You hear many birds singing in the trees. You don't know what they are doing. Scientists say now, after years of study, that whenever a bird is singing in the trees he is doing many things. One, he is calling for his girlfriend. Another, he is alerting all the male competitors that this is his territory—don't enter it. And if someone enters the territory a fight will ensue. And the girlfriend will just wait and see who wins, because whoever gets the territory will get her. She will just wait, and the one who wins will stay there and the one who is defeated will have to leave. By many means every animal creates territory: by sound, by singing, by body odor. No competitor should enter that territory.

You may have seen dogs pissing all around. Scientists say that they create their territory by pissing. The dog will go and piss on this pole and on that pole. He will not piss on one place—why? You can do it on one place, why move so much? He is creating territory. His urine has a particular odor and with it he creates a territory. No one should enter, it is dangerous. He lives secluded in his own territory, master of it.

There are many studies going on. They have tried putting many animals in one cage with all their needs fulfilled—better than they can fulfill them themselves in a forest. But they go mad because they don't have space. When someone is always around they are tense, afraid, ready to fight. This constant readiness to fight gives such tensions that there are heart failures or they go mad. Animals even commit suicide because the pressure becomes so much. And many abnormalities develop which are never found in the wild state. Monkeys in the wild are totally different. When caged in a zoo they start behaving abnormally. In the beginning it was thought that it was the bondage that was creating the problem. Now it is known that it is not the bondage. If you give them the proper space that they need in a cage they are happy. Then there is no problem. But they have an intrinsic feeling of space. When someone enters that space, pressure comes to their minds. Their minds start to be tense, strained; they cannot sleep right, they cannot feed right, they cannot love right.

Because of these studies, scientists now say that the whole of humanity is going crazy and mad because of overpopulation. The pressure is so great, you are never left alone: in the train, in the bus, in the office, everywhere, crowds and crowds. Man also has a need of space, to be left alone. But there is no place, you are never alone. When you come to your home, your wife is there, the children are there, and the relatives keep on coming. And they still think that the guest is God! You are already crazy because the pressure is too much all around you. You cannot say to anyone, "Leave me alone." If you say to your wife, "Leave me alone," she will get angry: "What do you mean?" She has been waiting for you the whole day. Mind needs space to be relaxed.

This sutra is really beautiful and very scientific. *Thence comes the end of mind pressures.*

When you move alone on a solitary hilltop you have space all around you, endless space. The pressure of the crowd, the pressure of others around you, leaves you. You will sleep more deeply. You will have a different quality of awakening in the morning. You will feel free. An inner pressure circle is not there. You will feel unimprisoned, unfettered.

This is good. But we have become so addicted to crowds that only for a few days—three or four days—will you feel good, then the desire will arise to go again to the crowd. Every holiday you go on, you want to come back after three days. Because of the pattern, the habit, you feel useless. Alone you feel useless, alone you cannot do anything, and even if you do something, no one will know about it, no one will see you doing it, no one will appreciate it. You cannot do anything alone because all

your life you have been doing something for others. You feel useless.

So remember, if you ever try this solitary madness, drop the idea of utility. Be useless. Only then can you be alone. Because really, utility has been forced on your mind by society. Society says, "Be of some utility, don't be useless." Society wants you to be an economic unit, a thing, efficient, utilitarian. Society doesn't want you to be just a flower. No, even if you are a flower then you must be worth being sold. Society needs you to be in the market, you must have some utility. Only then are you of use, otherwise not. Society goes on preaching that use is the goal of life, the purpose of life. This is nonsense.

I am not saying be useless. I am saying that this use is not the goal. You have to live in society, to be useful to it, but to remain capable of being useless at any moment. That capacity must be retained; otherwise you become a thing and not a person. When you move into solitariness, aloneness, this will become a problem. You will feel yourself useless.

I have been working with many people. Sometimes I suggest that they go for three weeks or three months into total loneliness, silence. And I tell them that after seven days they will want to come back and their mind will find all the reasons for not being there so that they can come back. I tell them not to listen to those arguments and to make it a point that for the time they have decided upon they will not leave. They say to me that they are going of their own will, so why should they leave? I tell them that they don't know themselves. This will not be there for more than three to seven days; afterwards they will long to return, because society has become alcoholic, it is an intoxicant. In sober moments you can think about being alone, but when you are alone, within three days you will think, "What am I doing? This is useless." So I tell them to be useless and not to think in terms of utility.

Sometimes it has happened that they have remained there for three weeks or three months, and then they come and they say, "It was beautiful, I was very happy, but this idea continued to hammer: 'What is the use?'" They say, "I was happy, very silent, I enjoyed it. But this idea was constantly in the background: 'What is the use? What am I doing?'" Remember, use is for society. Society uses you and you use society. This is a reciprocal relationship.

But life is not for use. It is nonutilitarian, purposeless; it is a play, a celebration. So when you move into solitariness to do this technique, be prepared from the very beginning that you are going to be useless, and enjoy it, don't feel sad about it. You cannot conceive of what arguments the mind will bring. You will say, "The world is in such trouble and you are sitting in silence here. Look what is happening in Vietnam and what is happening in Pakistan and what is happening in China; and your country is dying, there is no food, there is no water. What are you doing here meditating? What is the use? Will it bring socialism to the country?"

Mind will bring beautiful arguments; mind is the great arguer. It is the Devil—it will try to persuade you, it will convince you that you are wasting time. But don't listen to it. From the very beginning be prepared: "I am going to waste time. I will not be of any use. I will simply enjoy being here."

And don't be concerned with the world. The world goes on. It is always in trouble, it has been always in trouble and it will remain always in trouble. That is the way of the world. You cannot do anything so don't try to be a great world reformer, a revolutionary, a messiah. Don't try.

You simply be yourself and enjoy your solitariness, just like a rock or a tree or a river—useless! What is the use of a rock just lying there under the rains, under the sun, under the stars? What is the use of this rock? No use—the rock enjoys itself being that way. Just be a rock. There are rock gardens in Japan, in Zen monasteries; they make rock gardens particularly for this. There are no trees in the garden, just sand and rock. A solitary rock just sits there, and the master says to the disciple, "Go, and be just a rock, just like that rock. Don't be bothered about the world. That rock remains there whatsoever happens to the world. It is not worried. It is always in meditation."

Unless you are really prepared to be useless, you cannot be solitary, you cannot be in solitude. And once you know the depth of it you can come back to society. You must come back because solitariness is not a style of life—it is just a training. It is not a way of life, it is just a deep relaxation to change the perspective. It is just falling out of step with society to have a look at yourself, who you are, alone. So don't think that this is a style of life. Many have made it a style of life. They are in error, they are absolutely in error. They have made a medicine food. It is not a style of life, it is just medicinal. You fall out for a time being just to have a perspective, a distance, to see what you are and what society is doing to you. When you are out of it, you can have a better look. You can observe. Without being concerned, without being in it, you can become an observer from the hilltop, you can become a witness. You are so far away…unprejudiced, undisturbed, you can look.

So note it, this is not a way of life. I am not saying leave the world and become hermits somewhere in the Himalayas—no. But sometimes leave, relax, be useless, be alone, exist like a rock, be independent, free from the world, be a part of nature—and you will be rejuvenated, reborn. Then come back and move in society and in the crowd again, and try to carry that beauty, that silence that happened to you when you were alone. Now carry it, don't lose contact with it. Move deep into the crowd but don't become a part of it. Let the crowd be there outside you—you remain alone.

And when you become capable of being alone in the crowd, you have achieved real aloneness. It is easy to be alone on a hilltop; the whole of nature helps you, and nothing is a barrier. To be back in the marketplace, in the shop, in the office, in the family, and to remain alone—that is an achievement. Then it is something you have achieved and it is not just accidental, something that happened because of the hills. Now the quality of consciousness has changed. So remain alone in the crowd. The crowd will be there outside but don't allow it to enter in. Protect whatsoever you have gained. Defend it, don't allow it to be disturbed. And whenever you feel that the feeling has become dull, that you are missing it, that society has disturbed it, that the dust has gathered around, that the fresh spring is no longer fresh, that it is polluted—move again. Fall out of society to renew it, to make it alive again. Then come back and move in the crowd. And then a moment will come when that original spring will remain fresh and no one will be able to pollute it or contaminate it. Then there is no need to move anywhere.

So this is just a technique, not a style of life. Don't become a monk, don't become a nun, don't move to a monastery to live there forever. That is nonsense. If you live forever in a monastery you will never be able to know whether you have attained what you have attained, or whether the monastery has just given it to you. It may be accidental, not essential. The essential has to be tested. The essential has to be set against society; it has to be brought to the touchstone. And when it never breaks, when you can depend on it, when nothing can change it, then it has become a crystallization.

---

97 Fill endless space with your bliss body.

The second technique: *Consider the plenum to be your own body of bliss.*

This second technique is concerned with the first. Consider space to be your own body of bliss. Meditating on a hilltop with endless space before you, you can do it. Consider it to be filled with your own body of bliss.

There are seven bodies. The bliss body is the last body, so the more you enter within, the more you feel yourself to be blissful. You are nearing the bliss body, the layer of bliss. It is just around your essential soul, which is the first body from within outwards, or the last body from without inwards. Just around your being, the essential soul, is the layer of bliss. It is called the bliss body. Sitting on a hilltop, looking at the endless sky, feel that the whole space, the whole plenum, is filled with your bliss body. Feel that your bliss body has increased and the whole space is filled with it.

How will you feel it? You don't know what bliss is so how to imagine it? It will be better to try first to feel that the whole space is filled with silence, not with bliss. Feel it filled with silence. Nature will be helpful about it because in nature even noises are silent. In cities even silence is noisy. Natural sounds are silent because they don't disturb, they are harmonious. So don't think that silence is necessarily soundlessness. No, a musical sound can be silent because it is so harmonious—it doesn't disturb you. Rather, it deepens your silence. So when you move into nature, the breeze blowing, the stream, the river, the wind or whatsoever sounds there are, are harmonious, they make a whole. They are not disturbing. You can listen to them and the very listening will deepen your silence. So first feel that the whole space is filled with silence; feel deeply that it is growing more and more silent, that the sky has become silence around you.

And when you feel that the sky has become silence, only then should you try to be filled with bliss. As silence deepens you will have the first glimpse of bliss. As tension increases, you have the first glimpse of misery, strain; as silence deepens you will feel at ease, at home, relaxed, and the first glimpse of bliss will come to you. And when that glimpse comes, then you can imagine that the whole space is now filled with that bliss. *Consider the plenum to be your own body of bliss*—the whole sky becomes your body of bliss.

You can do it separately, there is no need to join it to the first, but the same requirements are needed

—endless space, silence, no human beings around you. Why this insistence on no human beings around you? Because the moment you see a human being you will start reacting in the old ways. You cannot see a human being without reacting. Something or other will happen to you immediately. He brings you back to your old patterns. If you don't see human beings you forget that you are human, and to forget that you are human, part of society, is good. It is good to remember simply that you are, even if you don't know what. You don't belong to anybody, to any society, to any group, to any religion. This nonbelonging will be helpful.

So it will be good if you move alone somewhere and do this, practice this. Alone this technique will be helpful, but remember to start with something that you can feel. I have seen people doing techniques which they cannot feel. If you cannot feel, if you don't have any experience, even a glimpse, then the whole thing becomes false.

A man came to me and he said, "I am practicing that God is everywhere."

So I asked him, "How can you practice? What do you imagine? Have you any taste, any feeling of God? Only then will it be easy to imagine; otherwise you will be simply thinking that you are imagining and nothing will happen."

Remember this for any technique you do. At the start you must do something you are acquainted with; you may not be totally acquainted with it, but a little glimpse will be necessary. Only then can you progress, step by step. But don't jump into something which is absolutely unknown to you because then you cannot feel it and you cannot imagine it.

Because of this, many masters, particularly Buddha, completely dropped the word "god". Buddha said, "You cannot work with it. It is the very end, and you cannot bring the end into the beginning. So begin from the very beginning." He said, "Forget the end, the end will follow automatically." And he said to his disciples, "Don't think of God. Think of compassion, think of love." So he doesn't say that one should feel that God is everywhere; one should simply feel compassion for everyone who is there—for the tree, for human beings, for animals. Simply feel compassion. Feel sympathetic, create a love...because love you know, howsoever little. There has been something like love in everybody's life. You may not have loved, but someone may have loved you, your mother at least. You must have looked into her eyes: she loved you.

"Just be motherly to existence," Buddha says, "and feel deep compassion. Feel that the whole world is filled with your compassion. Then everything else will follow."

Remember this as a basic law: always start with something you can feel because only then can the unknown enter through it.

CHAPTER 70

Suffer the pain of aloneness

◆

Q U E S T I O N S

Aloneness is so painful. What to do?

How to reconcile aloneness with wholeness?

To minimize or maximize?

Is sex the longing to return to the womb?

Whom do You mean by "we"?

The first question:

Confrontation of oneself in aloneness is very fearful, very painful. What to do?

t is fearful and it is painful, and one has to suffer it. Nothing should be done to avoid it, nothing should be done to divert the mind, nothing should be done to escape from it. One has to suffer it and go through it. This suffering, this pain, is just a good sign that you are near a new birth, because every birth is preceded by pain. It cannot be avoided, and it should not be avoided because it is part of your growth. This pain and this suffering is known traditionally as *tapascharya*, austerity. This is the meaning of *tapas*—arduous austerity, effort.

But why is this pain there? This should be understood because understanding will help you to go through it, and if you go through it knowingly, you will come out of it more easily, and sooner.

Why is there pain when you are alone? The first thing is that your ego gets ill. Your ego can exist only with others. It has grown in relationship, it cannot exist alone. So if the situation is one in which it can exist no more, it feels suffocated, it feels just on the verge of death. This is the deepest suffering. You feel just as if you are dying, but it is not you who is dying but only the ego which you have taken to be yourself, with which you have become identified. It cannot exist because it has been given to you by others. It is a contribution.

When you leave others you cannot carry it with you. Think of it in this way: when you are in society, people think you are a very good person. This goodness cannot exist when you are lonely and alone because this is what people thought about you. Now those people are there no more. Your image cannot be helped. It has become foundationless. By and by it will disappear and you will feel very bad because you were such a good person and now you are no more. And not only good people will suffer—if you are a bad person that too was given by others to you. That too is a way of getting attention. When many people consider you bad they give you attention. They cannot be indifferent to you, they have to be aware of you. You are somebody, a bad man, dangerous. When you move into loneliness, you become nobody. That bad image will disappear and you were feeding on it, your ego was feeding on it. So bad men and good men are not basically different—both are gaining their egos. Their mediums differ, but their goals are the same.

The bad depends on others, the good also. They exist in society. The saint and the sinner, they exist in society. Alone you are neither a saint nor a sinner. So in aloneness all that you know about yourself will fall; by and by it will disappear. You can prolong your ego for a certain period—and that too you will have to do through imagination—but you cannot prolong it for long. Without society you are uprooted; the soil is not there from where to get food. This is the basic pain. You are no longer sure who you are: you are just a dispersing personality, a dissolving personality. But this is good, because unless this false you disappears, the real cannot emerge. Unless you are completely washed and become again clean, the real cannot emerge.

This false you is occupying the throne. It must be dethroned. By living in solitariness all that is false can go. And all that is given by society is false — really, all that is given is false, all that is born with you is real. All that is you by yourself, not contributed by someone else, is real, authentic. But the false must go. And the false is a great investment; you have invested so much in it, you have been looking after it so much. All your hopes hang on it, so when it starts dissolving you will feel fearful, afraid, trembling. What are you doing to yourself? You are destroying your whole life, the whole structure.

There will be fear. But you have to go through this fear, only then will you become fearless. I don't say you will become brave, no; I say you will become fearless. Bravery is just part of fear. Howsoever brave you are, the fear is hidden behind. I say fearless. You will not be brave, there is no need to be brave when there is no fear. Bravery and fear both become irrelevant. They are both aspects of the same coin. So your brave men are nothing but you standing on your head — just in *shirshasana*. Your bravery is hidden within you and your fear is on the surface; their fear is hidden within and their bravery is on the surface. So when you are alone you are very brave, when you think about something you are very brave, but when a real situation comes you are fearful.

It is said about soldiers, the greatest of them, that before going to the front they are as afraid as anyone. The inside is trembling, but they will go. They will push this trembling aside into the unconscious; and the more the inner trembling is there, the more they will create a façade that they are brave around them. They will create an armor. You look at that armor — it looks brave, but deep down they are filled with fear. One becomes fearless only when one has gone through the deepest fear of all — that is the dissolving of the ego, the dissolving of the image, the dissolving of the personality.

This is death because you don't know if a new life is going to emerge out of it; during the process you will know only death. Only when you are dead as you are, as the false entity, only then will you know that the death was just a door to immortality. But that will be the end. During the process you are simply dying. Everything that you cherished so much is being taken away from you — your personality, your ideas, all that you thought was beautiful. All is leaving you. You are being denuded. All the roles and robes are being taken away. In the process fear will be there, but this fear is basic, necessary, inevitable — one has to pass through it. You should understand it, but don't try to avoid it, don't try to escape from it because every escape will bring you back again, you will move back into the personality.

Those who go into deep silence and solitude, they always ask me, "There will be fear, so what to do?" I tell them not to do anything, just to live the fear. If trembling comes, tremble. Why prevent it? If an inner fear is there, and you are shaking with it, so shake with it. Don't do anything. Allow it to happen. It will go by itself. If you avoid it — and you can avoid it, you can start chanting Rama, Rama, Rama; you can cling to a mantra so that your mind is diverted. You will be pacified and the fear will not be there. You have pushed it into the unconscious. It was coming out — which was good, you were going to be free from it — it was leaving you and when it leaves you, you will tremble. That is natural because from every cell of the body, of the mind, some energy which has always been there pushed down, is leaving. There will be a shaking, a trembling; it will be just like an earthquake. The whole soul will be disturbed by it, but let it be. Don't do anything. That is my advice. Don't even chant the name of Rama. Don't try to do anything with it because all that you can do will again be suppression. Just by allowing it to be, by letting it be, it will leave you — and when it has left, you will be altogether a different man.

The cyclone has gone and you will now be centered, centered as you never were before. And once you know the art of letting things be, you will know one of the master keys which opens all the inner doors. Then whatsoever the case is, let it be, don't avoid it.

If just for three months you can be in total solitude, in total silence, not fighting with anything, allowing everything to be, whatsoever it is, within three months the old will be gone and the new will be there. But the secret is allowing it to be, howsoever fearful, painful, howsoever apparently dangerous, deathlike. Many moments will come when you will feel as if you will go mad if you don't do something and involuntarily you will start to do something. You may know that nothing can be done, but you will not be in control and you will start to do something.

It is just as if you are moving through a dark street in the night, midnight, and you feel fear because there is no one around and the night is dark and the street is unknown—so you start whistling. What can whistling do? You know it can do nothing. Then you start singing a song. You know nothing can be done by singing a song, the darkness cannot be dispelled, you will remain alone, but still, it diverts the mind. If you start whistling, just by whistling you gain confidence and you forget the darkness. Your mind moves into whistling and you start feeling good.

Nothing has happened. The street is the same, the darkness is the same, the danger, if there is any, is there, but now you feel more protected. All is the same, but now you are doing something. You can start chanting a name, a mantra, Rama, Rama, that will be a sort of whistling. It will give you strength. But that strength is dangerous, that strength will again become a problem, because that strength is going to be your old ego. You are reviving it again.

Remain a witness, and allow whatsoever happens to happen. Fear has to be faced to go beyond it. Anguish has to be faced to transcend it. And the

more authentic the encounter, the more face to face, the more looking at things as they are, the sooner the happening will be there.

It takes time only because your authenticity is not intense. So you may take three days, three months, or three lives—it depends on the intensity. Really, three minutes can also do—three seconds can also do. But then you will have to pass through a tremendous hell, with such an intensity that you may not be able to bear it, to tolerate it. If one can face whatsoever is hidden in oneself, it passes, and when it has gone, you are different. Because all that has left you was part of you before, and now it is no longer a part.

So don't ask what to do. There is no need to do anything. Nondoing, witnessing, effortlessly facing whatsoever is, not even making a slight effort, just allowing it to be…remain passive and let it pass. It always passes. When you do something, that is the undoing because then you interfere.

And who will interfere? Who is afraid? The same which is the disease will interfere. The same ego which has to be left behind will interfere.

I told you that the ego is part of the society. You left the society but you don't want to leave the part that society has given to you. It is rooted in society; it cannot live without society. So either you have to leave it or you have to create a new society in which it can live.

So you can create an alternative society, that is one of the greatest tricks of the mind. It has always been so. You can create a different society, you can create an ashram. Twenty people who think they want to live in solitude can create a monastery—then the monastery has become an alternative society. So they move from society but they create another society, so basically nothing changes. They remain the same. Rather on the contrary, they may become more egoistic because now they are the chosen few, the elect. They have left the world but they have created another world, and the same pattern of relationship moves again. Then there is the chief, then there are the disciples, then there is a master, and all hierarchy and everything comes in, in miniature form. And then there are good disciples, there are bad disciples, there are successful ones and the unsuccessful ones...so it is the same. In a small group the whole society is there.

That will not do. Now this is happening in the West. A great number of young people are leaving society because they feel that society is rotten, decadent, dying, and they feel it is so decadent that it cannot be changed. This is a very new thing. Young people always think that the society is rotten, but they think it can be changed, transformed, so a revolution is needed. Only in the last stage of a society or civilization does this happen—people start thinking that nothing can be done, that revolution is nonsense, that society is so dead that no one can revive it, that you cannot change it. So you just drop out of it. You cannot do anything, the house is on fire—so you simply escape from it.

This is what is happening in the West: hippies, beatniks, yippies, others, all dropping out of society. But they are creating another society, an alternative society. Hippies themselves have become an alternative society. In ordinary society if you have long hair, others will look at you as if you have gone astray. Something is wrong. In the hippie society if you have short hair, you are wrong! Something is wrong with you. What is the difference?

In ordinary society if you live in a dirty way you are wrong—you are unmannerly, uncultivated, uneducated, unacceptable. But in a hippie society if you live very cleanly then something is wrong with you. Then you are still clinging to the old mind which said that cleanliness is next to God. God has died a long time ago, now the second thing, cleanliness, has also died. It cannot exist without God.

The same condemnation and the same appreciation is there. You can create an alternative society with just the opposite rules but it makes no difference—your ego can be fed again. It has been transplanted, a new soil has been formed.

To be solitary means not to create an alternative society. Just move out of society, and then whatso-ever society has given you will leave you. It can exist only in a milieu, in the social milieu, it cannot exist out of it. You will have to drop it. It will be painful because you are so adjusted to it, everything is so arranged. It has become such a comfort to be adjusted, where everything is convenient. When you change and move alone, you are leaving all comforts, all conveniences, all that society can give —and when society gives something to you, it also takes something from you: your liberty, your soul.

So it is an exchange—and when you are trying to get to your soul in its purity you have to stop the bargaining. It will be painful, but if you can pass through it, the highest bliss is just near. Society is not as painful as loneliness, society is tranquilizing, society is convenient, comfortable. But it gives you a sort of sleep. If you move out of it inconvenience is bound to be there. All types of inconveniences will be there. Those inconveniences have to be suffered with the understanding that they are part of solitude, part of regaining yourself.

This is tapas, this is austerity, and you will come out of it new, with a new glory and dignity, a new purity and innocence.

The second question:

Last night You said that total aloneness is the essential nature, is the ultimate reality of man. Another day You explained that individuality is false and man is a wave in the organic whole of existence. How is a reconciliation possible between aloneness and wholeness?

There is no need of reconciliation. Aloneness *is* wholeness. But aloneness doesn't mean individuality. You are an individual because of society. When you are totally alone you will not be an individual.

An individual means a part of a society, a unit of a society. When you are in the crowd you are an individual; when you move out of the crowd, not only is the crowd dropping behind, the individual also is dropping behind. That individuality was given to you. Individuality and society are two poles of one phenomenon. Alone you are not an individual; the individual has to exist in a pattern of society. It is just as when I said that alone you are neither good nor bad, alone you are neither saint nor sinner, alone you are neither beautiful nor ugly, alone you are neither wise nor foolish. Both the dualities drop. The dichotomy drops.

The individual exists in society; the individual is the unit of society. Alone you are not an individual, so don't think that you will become an individual when alone. No, you will not be an individual. If there is no society, how can you be an individual? You will be there, and that aloneness will be wholeness. The ego will drop, and it is the ego that gives you the feeling of individuality.

Alone doesn't mean that you are an individual, alone means that now the dichotomy of society and individual is no longer there. This will give you wholeness. You are not part of anything now, you have become the whole.

This is difficult to express because in language it appears absurd. You cannot imagine how you will not be an individual if you are alone, because if you think and imagine yourself on a hilltop, sitting alone somewhere in a Himalayan cave, you will think of yourself as an individual—because you don't know what aloneness is. Aloneness means that all thought, all mind, all individuality that was given by society has been left behind. You will become just a space, an emptiness, nobody. Sitting in a Himalayan cave there will be no one who is sitting, just a space.

Buddha was meditating under a tree. It was a full-moon night and some young people had come to the forest. They had brought much alcohol with them and a young prostitute. But they took so much alcohol and they became so intoxicated that the prostitute escaped. When they became aware that the girl had left them, they started to search for her. Where did she go?

In their search they reached Buddha who was sitting under a tree meditating. So they said to him, "You must have seen a young, beautiful, nude girl passing by here because this is the only way and it is a full-moon night. So you must have seen a beautiful young girl, nude, passing by. Did you see her?"

Buddha opened his eyes and said, "Someone passed by, but I cannot say whether the one who passed was a woman or a man. I cannot say whether the person who passed was beautiful or ugly. And I cannot say whether the person who passed was clothed or naked. Someone did pass—I heard the footsteps."

They were amazed and they said, "This is impossible!"

Buddha said, "I would not have believed this myself before. When I was a part of society it would have been impossible, but now that I have left society I have left all the conceptions of society as well. Now only nature happens around me. So I heard the sound of someone passing; there was just a sound which reached into my inner space, that is all. Someone passed."

You become a silent inner space. You are not an individual because you are not a mind. To drop the mind solitude is suggested. And with the mind everything drops. A moment comes when you don't know who you are—and that is the moment from where real knowledge will start.

A moment comes when you forget completely who you are, and all that you knew before is no longer there, all the old leaves have fallen. Now this is the moment, and now there will be an interval for a time being. This interval will be of much anguish because the old has left and the new has not yet come. When the old leaves drop from the tree, the tree will be naked for a few days, just waiting for the new to emerge. The new leaves are coming, they are on the way, the old have left a place. Now that the place is vacant the new are flowing towards the space and sooner or later they will emerge. But you will have to wait.

While meditating in aloneness, society will drop, the mind will drop, the ego will drop and there will be a gap. You will have to pass through that gap also. Now the tree is waiting for the new leaves to come…but one cannot do anything. What can the tree do? Nothing can be done to bring them sooner, they will take their own course.

It is good that the old have dropped—because now the place is there, space is there for the new to emerge. Now there will be no barrier.

So there is an autumn of the inner mind. Leaves will drop. It will be painful. You have lived with those old leaves for so long that you will feel that you are losing something. And then there will be a winter of waiting, an inner winter, when you will be nude—with no leaves, a naked tree against the sky—and you don't know what is going to happen. Now everything has stopped. Now no bird comes to sing on your branches; now no one comes to sit under you, under your shadow, to wait, to relax. Now you are not in any way aware of whether you are dead or whether a new life is going to happen to you. This is the gap, the interval.

Christian mystics have called it the dark night of the soul—before the sunrise. All artificial lights have been put off. The night has become very dark. And the moment nearest to the sunrise will be the darkest.

So there is a winter of the inner soul when there are no leaves, and no birds sing, and no one comes to wait under you and relax. You feel dead. Everything has stopped. All movement is gone. This has to be passed—because then there will be spring, new leaves will come, new life, new flowers. A totally new dimension will appear within you.

But remember the autumn, remember the winter; only then is spring possible. The autumn is also part of the spring—if you can understand—it is making the way for the spring to happen. So autumn is not against spring, it is just the beginning of it. And the gap is also necessary, because in the gap you become ready. The old has left. You are not tormented by it now, not burdened by it. You are pregnant—but pregnancy is waiting, the new child is growing. Before it emerges, manifests itself in the world, it will have to hide deep in the unconscious, because every seed has to go deep into darkness, underneath, hidden. Only then does life happen to it. If you put the seed in the sunlight nothing will happen to it. It needs deep darkness, a womb. So there will be winter while you are pregnant: all movement ceases, you just have to carry the burden—consciously, understandingly, lovingly, hoping, praying, waiting. And then there will be spring. It has been always so. Man is also a tree.

And remember, aloneness is wholeness, they are not contradictory. Ego is part, ego is fragmented, ego cannot be whole, ego is against the whole. In aloneness ego disappears. You become one with the whole and the boundary disappears. When you are really alone you are the cosmos, you are Brahma.

The third question:

In the first technique taken last night it is said that to abide in loneliness is to minimize relationship. But on previous occasions You said that one should maximize the relationship with limitless expansion.

Do either. Either expand yourself so much that nothing remains unrelated to you, then you will disappear; or be so totally alone that nothing remains related to you, then too you will disappear.

You are in the middle, where something is related and something is not related, where someone is a friend and someone is an enemy, where someone belongs to you and someone doesn't belong to you, where there is a choice. You are in the middle. Move to either extreme. Become related to everyone, to everything that exists, and you will disappear. It is so tremendous a phenomenon to be related to everything that you cannot exist, you will be flooded. Your ego is so narrow, it can exist with only a few relationships—and in those too it is against something, otherwise it could not exist. If you are friendly to everything that is in the world, you disappear. If you want to exist as an ego you can be friendly; but you must also be inimical to someone; you must love someone and you must hate. Then you can exist between these two contradictions—the ego can exist. Either love everything that is and you will disappear, or hate it and you will disappear. They look contradictory. They are not. The technique is the same. The technique is the same whether you love all or whether you hate all. The hatred of everything is known in the East as *vairagya,* as renunciation. This is hatred of everything, withdrawing your love completely, feeling that everything is useless, not worth anything.

If you can hate so totally you will become total —then you cannot exist. You can exist only when two contradictions are there: love and hate. Between these two you balance. It is just like a man walking on a rope: he has to balance between right and left. If he moves to the left completely he will fall; if he moves completely to the right he will fall. So whether you move to the right or to the left makes no difference. Choose one, and you will fall down from the rope.

If you want to be a man on a rope, you have to balance, sometimes to the left, sometimes to the right. And really the balance is a science. Whenever you lean to the left you will immediately have to lean to the right because the left will create the possibility of falling. To counterbalance it you will have to lean to the right, and when you lean to the right the possibility comes that you can fall. So you will have to lean to the left. That is why you go on moving between love and hate, between friend and enemy, between this and that, like and dislike, attraction and repulsion. You are moving on a rope, continuously. If you don't understand this your life will be a total misunderstanding.

I have been studying many, many people and this is one of the basic problems of all. They love, then they hate, and they cannot understand why they hate when they love also. This is how they balance—and this balancing gives you the ego, your personality. If you really want to be without the ego, choose either extreme. Move to the left, love, and don't balance it by the right—you will fall from the rope. Or move to the right, hate, and hate totally, and don't move to the left. You will fall from the rope.

Mahavira says be detached from everything— that is hate—and Krishna says love. That is why Jainas can never understand the message of Krishna —impossible. And Hindus have not taken any note of Mahavira. They have not even mentioned his name in their scriptures, not a single mention, they have not even taken note, because he says to be so unattached from everything that it becomes hatred. Krishna says love, and love so deeply that hate falls completely from the mind. Both are the same. They look contradictory to you, they are not.

Either you lean to the left or to the right—it makes no difference, you will fall to the ground, you will not be on the rope, that is certain. That rope is the ego or the world, the *sansara,* and you are balancing yourself. Many people love me but I know that sooner or later they will balance and they will hate. And when they hate they get disturbed. They should not get disturbed because that is how they can be on the rope. But they cannot hate long. Again they will have to balance.

In the morning you love, in the evening you hate, in the morning you love again. Unless you are ready to leave the ego the balancing will continue. It can continue infinitely—infinitely it can continue, the rope is endless. But once you get fed up with the whole game, once you feel that this is nonsense—balancing each time with hate and love and each time moving to the opposite direction again and again; this is nonsense—then you can move to one, either love or hate, and drop from the rope. And once you drop from the rope, you are enlightened. The balance is sansara, the world.

The fourth question:

Man has an inherent longing to enter into the womb. Kindly explain whether or not man's lust for the sexual act, penetration, symbolizes his inherent longing for this return.

Yes. It is part of it. Everything in nature wants to return to the source. This is one of the laws. Whatsoever happens in between is irrelevant, every circle comes to the end or to the very beginning—to the original source.

Man is born out of the womb. Whenever he is in distress or depression, whenever there is too much responsibility in the world, too much burden, things become heavy, he wants to return to the womb. Hence this attraction, lust, to enter the woman. You cannot enter, you cannot become a child again, so the sexual act becomes a symbolic act, the penetration becomes symbolic. You are again in the womb. That is why sex is so relaxing, so soothing. All the tensions are gone, your mind is unburdened. In this moment at least you are ecstatic. It is a catharsis, you are purged of much dirt.

So sex becomes a release, a relaxation, and the woman becomes a womb. This is part of the attraction, part of the lust. You may not be aware of it, but all that we have created for comfort is womb-like. In a room, closed, at body temperature, silent, you can relax easily. It is womblike. And if all the qualities of the womb are there in your sleeping room, you will sleep deeply. Even a clock on the wall helps you. It goes on tick-tock, tick-tock; it is the same as the heart of the mother going tick-tock, tick-tock, for the child in the womb. He goes on listening to it. The tick-tock rhythm is helpful; the mattress, the pillows, all the things we use are really womblike. Now scientists are of the mind that sooner or later we will make exactly womblike sleeping chambers, exactly the same, because they will give you the deepest sleep possible.

The ultimate conception of nirvana is also womblike. In the womb the child is so free, free of all responsibilities. He never comes to know any desire. Before the desire is there it is fulfilled. That is what Hindus call *kalpavriksha*. In heaven there are trees under which you sit and when a desire comes to your mind, immediately it is fulfilled. There is no gap, no time gap, between desire, demand, and supply. There is no time gap. When the desire is there it is fulfilled.

This is happening in the womb, it is kalpavrik-sha, the wish-fulfilling tree. A child never becomes aware that he is hungry—before there is hunger, it is fulfilled. The child never becomes aware that he is thirsty—before there is thirst, the thirst is fulfilled. He never becomes aware of any strife, any strain; he is silently served by the cosmos around him. Psychologists say that that is why the child in the womb cannot be conscious, because for consciousness, strife is needed, struggle is needed. Consciousness grows only when there is demand, then a time gap, and then supply. That time gap makes you conscious. If there is no time gap, if whatsoever you need is fulfilled immediately, you will fall asleep. So the child is asleep for nine months together—not for a single moment does he become alert. There is no need to be alert. All needs are fulfilled. There is no pain, no suffering, no tension, so alertness is not possible.

The child sleeps, and when he is born it is such a shock that Freud says that no one ever recovers from it. It is traumatic. It remains like a wound in you. And I think he is right. When the child is born it *is* a shock! He is thrown out of the Garden of Eden, out of paradise. Everything was so beautiful—it was so beautiful that he was asleep. It was so comfortable that there was no need to be awake for even a single moment. It was a dreamland, and now he has been thrown out forcibly. There is every possibility that the unconscious of the child struggles to remain in the womb. It is difficult to say whether it is so or not, but there is every possibility that the unconscious of the child struggles to remain in the womb. He creates every difficulty in coming out. Hence the pain and the struggle; he is being thrown out, expelled.

And the first moment out of the womb is bound to be the greatest suffering that the child will ever suffer—even death will not be such a suffering—because in the first moment on his own he will have to breathe, and the world has started with all its worries. Now he will be the center and he will be responsible and he will have to carry his own burden. He is thrown out of the mother. He will have to breathe and to cry when he is hungry, and now nothing is certain; whether when he is hungry he will be fulfilled or not, is not certain. It will depend, he has become dependent. Now for every need he has to struggle.

But then we provide every comfort for our children, in every way, so the shock is not so much, not too much. The mother goes on fulfilling his needs immediately. Because of this the child comes to feel that he is the center of the world and the whole world has to follow him. Just a cry and the whole world has to fall at his feet. This gives a very egoistic beginning. So every child is very egoistic. And then other shocks are bound to follow because this is only the first birth, just the beginning of births. Those who know human phenomena deeply say that the whole life is a continuous birth. There are many births. A day will come when the mother will refuse to breast-feed the child. Now he has to depend on food, he has to chew it. Responsibility grows. Now the food has to be chewed, digested. The milk was something else. The child was not doing anything, simply sucking. He was a sucker.

Every day responsibilities will grow and he will be thrown away, away from the mother. And the further away he is thrown, the more the world surrounds him. The world is hostile—the womb was never hostile, it was so friendly. The world is not friendly; there is competition, and everyone is interested in himself and no one is interested in you. The world is not your mother.

When a child moves to the school he is moving into a hostile world, with traumas and traumas and many shocks. And it goes on. The ultimate break happens when the child falls in love with a woman. He is becoming grown up. This is the last break with the mother; now the last link is broken. But still this man-child will go on behaving as if his wife is his mother. She is not. She is interested in herself, and he is interested in himself. Both are interested in themselves. They are egos. And every husband goes on trying to get the wife to behave like his mother. That is the struggle. She cannot behave like

that—she has her own interests. The mother was totally devoted.

So every man is frustrated with his wife because no wife can be a mother. It is not a question of good and bad wives—no wife can be a mother. Every man is frustrated. I have not yet seen a man who is not frustrated with his wife. It seems impossible not to be frustrated because the desire is so impossible.

But the husband feels good when he enters the woman, the wife. Again he is in the womb. This is a symbolic penetration. In those few moments he forgets all the worries, the world, everything. He is again a child. Look at a man deep in love with his wife, or beloved—his face will look like a child's. All the tensions have gone. So it is not just coincidence that when in love the wife will call the husband "baby."

I was just reading an anecdote. It was midnight and a house was on fire. At the last moment a woman was pulled out of it. She was mad and crying, "My baby has remained inside." And then suddenly the baby appeared. On the balcony stood a three-hundred-and-sixty-pound man, and he said, "Don't get worried, I am alive and I am coming." And the whole crowd was wondering what the matter was!

But they were deep in love, just lying together, and the man was a baby at that moment. In all ways mind is seeking a womblike state again, but you cannot enter the womb, even in a sexual act. You just seem to be.

The only possibility of entering the womb again is not physical, it is psychological, or, on deeper layers, spiritual. If you can be one with the cosmos you will be in the womb again, and this is something which cannot be taken away from you. Then the whole existence becomes a mother. So to me, those religions that have said that God is not a father but a mother are more scientific. Those who have called their God "father" are not so scientific, because a father is not a very essential thing, it is just accidental. Father has not always existed. The word 'mother' is very very much older than 'father.' Even the word 'uncle' is older than 'father,' because five thousand years back there was no marriage. Groups lived together, the child knew his mother but he didn't know who the father was, so all the male members of the group were uncles. 'Uncle' is an older word than 'father.' All the males were uncles because there was no certainty who the father was.

Father is a later arrival. When one male dominated a woman and pushed away all the other males, father came into being. And it is not certain whether it is going to remain, because the family is dispersing. It is not something eternal, just institutional. The father seems to be going; in the future he cannot stay. For father there is no hope! He will drop. Uncles will again become important. Mother is basic; father is social and can be discarded. It depends on the institution, on the way society thinks. But mother cannot be discarded. So those religions that think of God as the mother are really deeper. When you enter God the mother and become one with it, you have entered the eternal womb. Now there will be no pain, there will be no suffering. Now you will never be thrown out.

The last question:

You said we are concerned with threads, not the essence. But whom do You mean by "we"? Because as we are we are concerned with beads, with events. We live in events.

When I say that we are concerned with the thread, with the essence, the foundational, the real, by "we" I don't mean you—you as you are, no, but you as you can be, yes. You are double, and that which you are right now is not the real. It is just a false thing, just an image which can be discarded easily. The real you is that which can be known only when all the masks are thrown away. So when I say "we" are concerned with the thread, I include you in your reality—not as egos, but as souls. You are two: one as you appear to be and one as you are. The appear-

ance is concerned with events, concerned with beads, the superficial. The inner, the one that you are, is not concerned with events; it is not concerned with time at all. It is concerned with the eternal.

I will tell you a story of one of Buddha's past lives, when he was not yet a buddha; in that life Buddha was as ignorant as anyone. He heard about a man who had become enlightened, so he went to touch his feet and to have a *darshan*. He touched the feet of the enlightened one, and when he was rising, he was amazed to see the enlightened man touching his feet. He said, "What are you doing? I am ignorant, unenlightened, a sinner, and you are enlightened, the purest light I have ever seen. Why should you touch my feet? I have come to touch your feet, why should you touch my feet?"

The enlightened one laughed and said, "I am not touching your feet. I am touching the feet of the essential, of the soul that is hidden within you. That is already enlightened. You may know it later on, and when you know, remember. One day you will come to know the reality before which I have bowed down. You don't know it right now, your own treasure you don't know, but I know my treasure and the moment I have known my treasure, I have known everybody else's treasure."

The enlightened one said to Buddha, "The moment I became enlightened I knew the essential reality of all. You can go on deluding yourself, that is up to you, but I can penetrate and I can see the purest light within you. Remember me when you realize it."

And when Buddha became enlightened in his next life, he said to his disciples, "I didn't understand what that awakened one was saying. It was a mystery. But now I can see what he meant. Now the appearance has come, and whatsoever I am now I was at that moment also. He must have bowed to this."

So when I say "we," I include you in your possibility, not in your appearance. Your appearance is just a dream, but you are not aware of it because if you become aware that you are dreaming, the dream has ceased. You are not aware of the real you. If you become aware, the appearance will disappear. I am aware—so you can understand my difficulty. I see you as enlightened ones. You are already that. You are just playing the game of being ignorant, just trying to deceive yourself, but whatsoever you do makes no difference to the innermost reality. It remains innocent, pure, absolutely pure.

You are here. If I look at your surface, you have to be taught many things. But if I look to your inner, there is no need to teach you anything, there is no need to do anything. That is what I mean when I say, "We are concerned with the thread, the essence, not with the beads, the events, the outer."

Remember this. Someday when you become enlightened you will know what my meaning was when I said "we," and who was included. It is certain that you are not included as you are here, just before me, the appearance, no—but as you have always been and as you will always be when this curtain is thrown away, when these clouds disappear and the sun rises. I can see the sun behind the clouds.

You are so identified with the clouds that you cannot even believe me. If I say you are already enlightened, how can you believe it? You will say I must be deceiving you or playing a trick. This is the truth, but truth is difficult to understand. And you have to travel long before you come to yourselves, you have to travel long before you come to realize that your home is the goal, that you have been always in the place that you wanted to reach.

CHAPTER 71

Forget the periphery

◆

98 *In any easy position gradually pervade an area between the armpits into great peace.*

99 *Feel yourself as pervading all directions, far, near.*

◆

Life without is a cyclone—a constant conflict, turmoil, struggle. But it is only so on the surface—just as on the surface of the ocean are waves, maddening noise, constant struggle. But this is not all of life. Deep down there is also a center—soundless, silent, no conflict, no struggle. In the center, life is a noiseless flow, relaxed, a river moving with no struggle, with no fight, no violence. Towards that inner center is the search. You can get identified with the surface, with the outer. Then anxiety and anguish follow. This is what has happened to everyone: we are identified with the surface and with the struggle that goes on there.

The surface is bound to be disturbed, nothing is wrong in it. And if you can be rooted in the center, the disturbance on the surface will become beautiful, it will have a beauty of its own. If you can be silent within, then all the sounds without become musical. Then nothing is wrong; it becomes a play. But if you don't know the inner core, the silent center, if you are totally identified with the surface, you will go mad. And everyone is almost mad.

All religious techniques, techniques of yoga, meditation, Zen, are basically to help you to be again in contact with the center, to move within, to forget the periphery, to leave the periphery for the time being and to relax into your own being so deeply that the outer disappears completely and only the inner remains. Once you know how to move backwards, how to step down into yourself, it is not difficult. It becomes as easy as anything. But if you don't know, if you know only the mind clinging to the surface, it is very difficult. Relaxing into one's self is not difficult; nonclinging to the surface is.

I have heard a Sufi story…. Once it happened that a Sufi fakir was traveling. It was a dark night and he lost his way. It was so dark he couldn't even see where he was moving. Then suddenly he fell into an abyss. He was terrified. He didn't know what was down there in the darkness or how deep the abyss was, so he caught hold of a branch and started praying. The night was cold. He cried but there was no one to listen, only his own voice echoed back. And the night was so cold that his hands were becoming frozen and he knew that sooner or later he would have to leave the branch —it was going to be difficult to keep on holding it. His hands were getting so frozen that they were already slipping from the branch. Death was absolutely near. Any moment he would fall and die. And then the last moment came. You can understand how terrified he was, dying moment by moment. Then the last moment came and he saw the branch slipping out of his hands. And his hands were so frozen that there was no way to hold on, so he had to fall.

But the moment he fell he started dancing—there was no abyss, he was on clear ground. And he had suffered all night….

This is the situation. You go on clinging to the surface, afraid that if you leave the surface you will be lost. Really, clinging to the surface you are lost.

But deep down there is darkness and you cannot see any ground; you cannot see anything else than the surface. All these techniques are to make you courageous, strong, adventurous, so that you can stop the holding on and fall within yourself. That which looks like an abyss, dark, bottomless, is the very ground of your being. Once you leave the surface, the periphery, you will be centered.

This centering is the aim. Once you are centered you can move to the periphery but you will be totally different. The quality of your consciousness will have changed altogether. Then you can move to the periphery but you will never *be* the periphery again—you will remain at the center. And remaining centered at the periphery is beautiful. Then you can enjoy it; it will become a beautiful play. Then there is no conflict, it is a game. Then it will not create tensions within you and there will be no anguish and no anxiety around you. And any moment that it becomes too much, too heavy on you, you can go back to the original source—you can have a dip. Then you will be refreshed, rejuvenated, and you can move to the periphery again. Once you know the way…and the way is not long. You are not going anywhere else than into your own self, so it is not long. It is just near. The only barrier is your holding on, holding to the periphery, afraid that if you leave it you will be lost. The fear feels just as if you are going to die. Moving to the inner center is a death—death in the sense that your identity with the periphery will die, and a new image, a new feeling of your being will arise.

So if we want to say in a few words what tantra techniques are, we can say that they are a deep relaxation into oneself, a total relaxation into oneself.

You are always tense, that is the holding, the clinging. You are never relaxed, never in a state of let-go. You are always doing something; that doing is the problem. You are never in a state of non-doing, when things are happening and you are just there not doing anything. Breath comes in and goes out, the blood circulates, the body is alive and throbbing, the breeze blows, the world goes on

spinning around—and you are not doing anything. You are not a doer, you are simply relaxed and things are happening. When things are happening and you are not a doer, you are totally relaxed. When you are a doer and things are not happening but are being manipulated by you, you are tense.

You relax partially while you are asleep, but it is not total. Even in your sleep you go on manipulating, even in your sleep you don't allow everything to happen. Watch a man sleeping: you will see that he is very tense, his whole body will be tense. Watch a small child sleeping: he is very relaxed. Or watch an animal, a cat—a cat is always relaxed. You are not relaxed even while asleep; you are tense, struggling, moving, fighting with something. On your face there are tensions. In dreams you may be fighting, protecting—doing the same things as when you were awake, repeating them in an inner drama. You are not relaxed; you are not in a deep let-go. That's why sleep is becoming more and more difficult. And psychologists say that if the same trend goes on, soon the day will come when no one will be able to sleep naturally. Sleep will have to be chemically produced, because no one will be able to fall naturally into sleep. The day is not very far off, you are already on the way towards it, because even while asleep you are only partially asleep, partially relaxed.

Meditation is the deepest sleep. It is total relaxation plus something more; you are totally relaxed and yet alert. Awareness is there. Total sleep with awareness is meditation. Fully alert, things are happening but you are not resisting, not fighting, not doing. The doer is not there, the doer has gone into sleep. Only a witness is there, a nondoer alertness is there. Then nothing can disturb you.

If you know how to relax then nothing can disturb you. If you don't know how to relax then everything will disturb you. I say *everything*. It is not really something else that disturbs you, everything else is just an excuse. You are almost always ready to be disturbed. If one thing doesn't disturb you, then something else will; you will get disturbed. You are ready, you have a tendency to get disturbed. If all the causes are withdrawn from you even then you will get disturbed. You will find some cause, you will create some cause. If nothing comes from without, you will create something from within—some thought, some idea—and you will get disturbed. You need excuses.

Once you know how to relax nothing can disturb you. Not that the world will change, not that things will be different—the world will be the same, but you don't have the tendency, you don't have the madness; you are not constantly ready to be disturbed. Then all that happens around you is soothing—even the traffic noise becomes soothing if you are relaxed. Even the marketplace becomes soothing. It depends on you. It is an inner quality. The more you go towards the center the more the quality arises, and the more you move towards the periphery the more you will be disturbed. If you are too disturbed, or if you are prone to be disturbed, that shows only one thing: that you are existing near the periphery—nothing else. It is an indication that you have made your abode near the surface. And this is a false abode because your real home is at the center, the very center of your being.

98 Feel the peace in your heart.

Now we will enter the techniques. *In any easy position gradually pervade an area between the armpits into great peace.*

This is a very simple method but it works miraculously. Try it. And anyone can try it, there is no danger. The first thing is to be in an easy relaxed position—relaxed in a position that is easy for you. Don't try a particular position or *asana*. Buddha sits in a particular posture; it is easy for him. It also can become easy for you if you practice it for a time, but in the very beginning it will not be easy for you. And there is no need to practice it. Start from any posture that comes easy to you right now.

Don't struggle with the posture. You can sit in an easy chair and relax. The only thing is your body must be in a relaxed state.

So just close your eyes and feel, all over the body. Start from the legs—feel whether there is some tension or not. If you feel there is some tension, do one thing: make it more tense. If you feel there is some tension in the right leg, then make that tension as intense as possible. Bring it to a peak—then suddenly relax so that you can feel how the relaxation settles there. Then go all over the body just looking everywhere for some tension. Wherever you feel the tension make it more so, because it is easy to relax when it is intense. In just a mid-state it is very difficult because you cannot feel it. It is easy to move from one extreme to another, very easy, because the very extreme creates the situation to move to the other. So if you feel some tensions in the face, then strain all the face muscles as much as possible, create tension and bring it to a peak. Bring it to a point where you feel that no more is possible—then suddenly relax. In this way see that all parts of the body, all the limbs are relaxed.

And be particular about the face muscles, because they carry ninety percent of the tensions; the rest of the body carries only ten percent. All your tensions are in the mind, so the face becomes the storage. So strain your face as much as possible, don't be shy about it. Make it intensely anguished, anxious—and then suddenly relax. Do it for five minutes so that you can feel that every limb in the whole body is relaxed. This is an easy posture for you—you can do it sitting, or lying in bed, or howsoever you feel is easy for you. *In any easy position gradually pervade an area between the armpits into great peace.*

The second thing: when you feel that the body has got to an easy posture, don't make much fuss about it. Just feel that the body is relaxed, then forget the body. Because really, remembering the body is a sort of tension—that's why I say don't make much fuss about it. Relax it and forget it.

Forgetting is relaxation.

Whenever you remember too much, that very remembering brings a tension to the body. You may not have observed this, but there is a very easy experiment to try. Put your hand on your pulse and count it. Then close your eyes, bring your attention to your pulse for five minutes, and then count. The pulse will now be beating faster, because giving the attention for five minutes gives tension to it. So really, whenever a doctor counts your pulse it is never the real count—it is always more than it was before the doctor started counting it. Whenever the doctor has taken your hand in his hand you have become alert. And if the doctor is a lady doctor you will be more alert, and it will go faster. So whenever a lady doctor counts your pulse, reduce it by ten; then that will be exactly your pulse count. Otherwise there will be ten more counts per minute.

Whenever you bring your consciousness to any part of the body, that part becomes tense. You become tense when someone observes you; the whole body becomes tense. When you are alone you are different. When someone enters the room you are not the same. The whole body is going at a faster rate, you have become tense. So don't make much fuss about relaxation or you will be obsessed with it. For five minutes simply relax easily and forget. Your forgetting will be helpful and it will bring a deeper relaxation to the body.

…Gradually pervade an area between the armpits into great peace. Close your eyes and just feel the area between the two armpits, the heart area, your chest. First feel it just between the two armpits with your total attention, total awareness. Forget the whole body, remember just the heart area between the two armpits, the chest, and feel it filled with great peace. The moment the body is relaxed, peace automatically happens in your heart. The heart becomes silent, relaxed, harmonious. And when you forget the whole body and bring your attention just to the chest and consciously feel it filled with peace, much peace will happen immediately.

There are areas in the body, particular centers, where particular feelings can be created consciously. Between the two armpits is the heart center, and the heart center is the source of all the peace that happens to you, whenever it happens. Whenever you are peaceful, the peace is coming from the heart. The heart radiates peace. That is why people all over the world, every race, without any distinction of caste, religion, country, cultured or uncultured, have felt this, that love arises from somewhere near the heart. No scientific explanation exists. Whenever you think of love you think of the heart. Really, whenever you are in love you are relaxed, and because you are relaxed you are filled with a certain peace. That peace arises from the heart. So peace and love have become joined, associated. Whenever you are in love you are peaceful; whenever you are not in love you are disturbed. Because of peace the heart has become associated with love.

So you can do two things. You can search for love, then sometimes you will feel peace. But this path is dangerous, because the other person whom you love has become more important than you; the other is the other, and you are becoming in a way dependent. So love will give you peace sometimes but not always. There will be many disturbances, many moments of anguish and anxiety, because the other has entered. Whenever another enters there is bound to be some disturbance, because you can meet with the other only on your surface. The surface will be disturbed. Only sometimes when the two of you will be so deeply in love with no conflict, only then will you sometimes be relaxed and the heart will glow with peace.

So love can only give you glimpses of peace, but nothing really established, rooted. No eternal peace is possible through it, only glimpses. And between two glimpses there will be deep valleys of conflict, violence, hatred and anger.

The other way is to find peace not through love, but directly. If you can find peace directly—and this is the method for it—your life will become filled with love. But now the quality of love will be different. It will not be possessive; it will not be centered around one. It will not be dependent and it will not make anyone dependent on you. Your love will become just a lovingness, a compassion, a deep empathy. And now no one, not even a lover, can disturb you, because your peace is already rooted and your love comes as a shadow of your inner peace. The whole thing has become reversed.

So Buddha is also loving but his love is not an anguish. If you love you will suffer, if you don't love you will suffer. If you don't love you will suffer the absence of love; if you love you will suffer the presence of love, because you are on the surface and whatsoever you do can only give you momentary satisfaction—then again the dark valley.

First be established in peace on your own, then you are independent, then love is not your need. Then you will never feel imprisoned when you are in love; you will never feel that love has become a sort of dependence, a slavery, a bondage. Then love will be just a giving: you have too much peace so you want to share it. Then it will be just a giving with no idea of return; it will be unconditional. And it is one of the secrets that the more you give, the more it happens to you. The more you give and share, the more it becomes your own. The deeper you enter into the treasury, which is infinite, the more you can go on giving to everybody. It is inexhaustible.

But love must happen to you as a shadow of inner peace. Ordinarily the reverse is the phenomenon: peace happens to you just as a shadow of love. Love must happen to you as a shadow of peace, then love is beautiful. Otherwise love also creates ugliness, it becomes a disease, a fever.

...Pervade an area between the armpits into great peace. Become aware of the area between the armpits and feel that it is filled with great peace. Just feel peace there and you will feel it is filled. It is always filled but you have never been alert about it. This is only to increase your alertness, to bring you nearer home.

When you feel this peace you are farther away from the surface. Not that things will not be happening there—but when you try this experiment and when you are filled with peace you will feel a distance; the noise is coming from the street but there is a great distance now, a great space. It happens, but it brings no disturbance; rather, it brings you a deeper silence. This is the miracle. The children will be playing, someone will be listening to the radio, someone will be quarreling, and the whole world will be going around, but you will feel that a great distance has come between you and everything. That distance comes because you have retreated from the periphery. Things are happening on the periphery and they will appear to you as if they are happening to someone else. You are not involved. Nothing disturbs you so you are not involved—you have transcended. This is the transcendence.

And the heart is naturally the source of peace. You are not creating anything, you are simply coming to a source which is always there. This imagining will help you become aware that the heart is filled with peace—it is not that the imagining will create the peace. This is the difference between the tantra attitude and Western hypnosis. Hypnotists think that you are creating it by imagination, but tantra thinks that you are not creating it by imagination, you are simply becoming attuned to something that is already there. Whatsoever you can create by imagination cannot be permanent: if it is not a reality then it is false, unreal, and you are creating a hallucination.

So it is better to be disturbed and real than to be in a hallucination of peace, because that is not a growth, you are simply intoxicated by it. Sooner or later you will have to come out, because sooner or later the reality will shatter the illusion. Reality has to shatter all illusions; only a greater reality cannot be shattered.

A greater reality will shatter the reality which is on the periphery; hence Shankara and others say that the world is illusion. Not that the world is illusion, but they have come to know a higher reality and from that altitude this world looks dreamy. It is so far away, the distance is so infinite that it cannot be felt as real. The noise on the street will be as if you are dreaming about it—it is not real. It cannot do anything. It just happens and passes and you remain untouched. And when you are untouched by reality how can you feel that it is real? The reality is felt only when it penetrates you deeply. The deeper the penetration, the more you feel it as real.

Shankara says the whole world is unreal. He must have come to a point from where the distance is so vast, so tremendously vast, that all that happens there becomes just like a dream. It comes but no reality comes with it because it cannot penetrate. Penetration is the proportion of reality. If I throw a stone at you it hits you. The hit penetrates you and that penetration makes the stone real. If I throw a stone and it touches you but doesn't penetrate you, deep down you will hear the thud of the falling stone on you, but there will be no disturbance. You will feel it as false, unreal, maya, illusory. But you are so near the periphery that if I throw a stone at you, you will be hurt. Not the body—the body will be hurt in either case. If I throw a stone at a buddha the body will be hurt as your body will be hurt, but a buddha is not on the periphery, he is rooted in the center. And the distance is so great that he will hear the thud of the stone without being hurt. The being will remain untouched, unscarred. This unscarred being will feel the stone as if it is something thrown in a dream. It is illusory. So Buddha says that nothing has substance to it, everything is substanceless, without any substance. The world is empty of substance—which is the same thing as Shankara saying that the world is illusory.

Try this. Whenever you are able to feel the peace between your two armpits filling you, pervading your heart center, the world will look illusory. This is a sign that you have entered meditation—when the world feels and appears to be illusory. Don't think that the world is illusory, there is no need to think it—you will feel it. It will

suddenly occur to your mind, "What has happened to the world?" The world has suddenly gone dreamy. It is there, a dreamlike existence, without any substance. It looks so real, just like a film on the screen. It can even be three-dimensional. It looks like something, but it is a projected thing. Not that the world is a projected thing, not that it is really unreal—no. The world is real but you create the distance, and the distance gets more and more. And you can understand whether the distance is getting more and more or not by knowing how you are feeling about the world. That's the criterion. That is a meditative criterion. It is not a truth that the world is unreal—if the world has become unreal, you have become centered in the being. Now the surface and you are so far away that you can look at the surface as being something objective, something other than you. You are not identified.

This technique is very easy and will not take much time if you try it. With this technique it sometimes even happens that with the very first effort you will feel the beauty and the miracle of it. So try it—but if you don't feel anything with the first effort, don't be disappointed. Wait, and go on doing it. And it is so easy that you can go on doing it anytime. Just lying on your bed at night you can do it; just in the morning when you feel that you are now awake you can do it. Do it first and then get up. Even ten minutes will be enough. Ten minutes at night just before falling asleep, do it. Make the world unreal, and your sleep will be so deep that you may not have slept like that before. If the world becomes unreal just before falling asleep, dreaming will be less, because if the world has become a dream then dreams cannot continue. And if the world is unreal, you are totally relaxed because the reality of the world will not impinge itself upon you, hammer on you.

I have suggested this technique to people who suffer from insomnia. It helps deeply. If the world is unreal, tensions dissolve. And if you can move from the periphery, you have already moved to a deep state of sleep—before the sleep comes you are already deep into it. And then in the morning it is beautiful because you are so fresh, so young; your whole energy is vibrating. It is because you are coming back to the periphery from the center.

And the moment you become alert that now sleep is no more, don't open your eyes. First do this experiment for ten minutes, then open the eyes. The body is relaxed after the whole night and is feeling fresh and alive. You are already relaxed, so it will not take much time. Just relax. Bring your consciousness to the heart just between the two armpits; feel it filled with deep peace. For ten minutes remain in that peace, then open the eyes. The world will look totally different because that peace will also be radiated from your eyes. And the whole day you will feel different—not only will you feel different but you will feel that people are behaving differently with you. To every relationship you contribute something. If your contribution is not there, people behave differently because they feel you are a different person. They may not be aware of it, but when you are filled with peace everyone will behave differently towards you. They will be more loving and more kind, less resistant, more open, closer. A magnet is there. Peace is the magnet. When you are peaceful people come nearer to you; when you are disturbed everyone is repelled. And this is so physical a phenomenon that you can observe it easily. Whenever you are peaceful you will feel everyone wants to be closer to you, because that peace radiates, it becomes a vibration around you. Circles of peace move around you and whosoever comes near wants to be nearer to you—like you want to move under the shadow of a tree and to relax there.

A person who is peaceful within has a shadow around him. Wherever he goes everyone would like to be closer to him, open, trusting. A person who has inner turmoil, conflict, anguish, anxiety, tensions, repels people. Whosoever comes near becomes afraid. You are dangerous. To be near you is dangerous, because you will give whatsoever you have. You

are constantly giving it. So you may want to love someone but if you are very disturbed within, even your lover will be repelled and he will want to escape from you because you will drain his energy and he will not feel happy with you. And whenever you leave him, you will leave him tired, exhausted, because you don't have a life-giving source, you have a destructive energy within you.

So not only will you feel you are different, others will also feel that you are different.

Your whole lifestyle can change if you move a little closer to the center—and the whole outlook and the whole outcome. If you are peaceful the whole world becomes peaceful to you. It is just a reflection. Whatsoever you are is reflected all over. Everyone becomes a mirror.

99 Expand in all directions.

The second technique: *Feel yourself as pervading all directions, far, near.*

Tantra and yoga both think that your narrowness is the problem. Because you have made yourself so narrow, so tightly narrow, you feel always in bondage. The bondage is not coming from anywhere else; the bondage is coming from your narrow mind. And it goes on being narrower and narrower and you are very confined. That confinement gives you the feeling of bondage. You have an infinite soul and an infinite being but that infinite being feels imprisoned. So whatsoever you do, you feel limitations everywhere. Wherever you move, a point of cul-de-sac comes. You cannot move beyond it. Everywhere there is a boundary. There is no open sky to fly.

But that boundary is created by you—that boundary is your own creation. You have created it for certain reasons, for security, safety. You have created a boundary, and the narrower the boundary, the more you feel secure. If you have a very large boundary you cannot watch over all of it, you cannot be alert and watchful everywhere. It becomes vulnerable. Narrow the boundary and you can watch it: you can remain closed, you are not vulnerable, you feel safe. The safety, the security has created the boundary. But then you feel a bondage.

This is how the mind is paradoxical. You go on asking for more safety and you go on asking for more freedom. Both cannot be together. If you want freedom you will have to lose safety, security. In any case the safety is just illusory, it is not really there. Because death is going to happen—whatsoever you do, you are going to die—all your safety, security, is just a façade, nothing will help. But afraid of insecurity you create boundaries, you create big walls around you and then the open sky is closed. And then you suffer! And then you say, "Where is the open sky?" and "I want freedom and I want to move!" But you have created these boundaries.

So this is the first thing to remember before you do this technique; otherwise it will not be possible to do it. With your boundaries intact you cannot do it. Unless you stop creating boundaries you will not be able to feel or do it.

...*Pervading all directions, far, near.* No boundaries, becoming infinite, becoming one with infinite space.... This will be impossible with your mind. How can you feel it? How can you do it? First you will have to stop doing certain things.

The first thing is that if you are too concerned about security and safety then remain in bondage. Really, prison is the most secure place. No one can harm you there. No one out of prison is as secure, as guarded, as the prisoners. You cannot kill, you cannot murder a prisoner. It is difficult. He is more guarded than a king. You can murder a president or a king, it is not so difficult. Every day they go on killing them. But you cannot kill a prisoner. He is so safe that those who want to be safe, really, must be in prisons, they must not live outside. To live out of a prison is dangerous, it is full of hazards. Anything can happen. So we have created mental prisons around us, psychological prisons around

us, and we carry those prisons with us, they are portable. You need not remain with them, they move with you. Wherever you go, your prison goes with you.

You are always behind a wall. Only sometimes, rarely, do you stretch your hand out of it to touch someone. But only a hand—you never come out of your prison. So whenever we meet, it is simply meeting hands out of prisons. Out of windows we stretch a hand, afraid, scared, and ready any moment to withdraw the hand. Both the parties are doing the same—only hands touch. And now psychologists say that even that is just an appearance, because hands have their own armor around them. No hand is ungloved. Not only Queen Elizabeth uses gloves, you also have gloves so that no one can touch you. Or even if someone touches, there is only a hand, dead. You are already withdrawn, afraid—because the other creates fear. As Sartre says, "The other is the enemy."

The other will look like an enemy if you are so armored. With an armored person there can be no friendship. Friendship is impossible, love is impossible, communion is impossible. You are afraid. Someone may make you a possession, someone may overpower you, someone may make you a slave. Afraid of this, you have created a prison, a safety wall around you. Cautiously you move, cautiously you take every step. Life becomes a drudgery, life becomes a boredom. If you are too cautious, life cannot be an adventure. If you are protecting yourself too much, hankering after security too much, you are already dead.

So remember one basic law: life is insecurity. And if you are ready to live in insecurity, only then will you be alive. Insecurity is freedom. If you are ready to be insecure, constantly insecure, you will be free. And freedom is the door to the divine.

Afraid, you create a prison—you become dead, more and more dead. And then you call, "Where is God?" And then you question, "Where is life? What does life mean? Where is bliss?" Life is there waiting for you, but you have to meet it on its own terms. You cannot have your own terms, life has its own terms. And the basic term is: remain insecure. Nothing can be done about it. You can only create an illusion, and in that illusion you can waste your life. Nothing can be done about it. Whatsoever you do is just a deception.

If you fall in love you become afraid that this woman can leave you or this man can leave you. Fear enters immediately. You were never afraid when you were not in love. Now you are in love: life has entered and insecurity has entered with it. One who never loves anybody is never afraid that anyone will leave him. The whole world can leave him, he is not afraid. You cannot harm him. He is secure. The moment you love someone, insecurity has entered because life has entered. And with life, death has entered. The moment you love you have become afraid: this person can die, this person can leave, this person can love somebody else! Now to make things secure, you must do something—you must get married. So a legal bondage is made so that it is now difficult for this person to leave you. Now society will protect you, the law will protect you, the policeman, the judge, will all protect you. Now if this person wants to leave, you can drag him to the court, and if he wants a divorce he will have to prove something against you. Even then it will take three or five years. Now you have created safety around you.

But the moment you are married you are dead. The relationship is not alive. Now it has become a law, not a relationship. Now it is a legal phenomenon, not an alive thing. The court cannot protect life; the court can only protect bargains. The law cannot protect life; the law can only protect laws. Now marriage is something which is dead. It can be defined, love cannot be defined. Marriage is definable, love is indefinable. Now you have come under the world of definitions.

But the phenomenon is already dead. The moment you wanted it to be secure, the moment you wanted to enclose it so that no new thing happens to it, you are imprisoned in it. Then you will suffer. Then you will say that this wife has become a bondage to you. The husband will say this wife has become a bondage to him. And then you fight because you have each become an imprisonment for the other. Now you fight. Now love has disappeared, there is only conflict. That is what happens because of the hankering for security.

And this has happened in everything. Remember it as something basic: life is insecure. This is the very nature of it. So when there is love, suffer the fear that the beloved can leave you, but don't create security. Then love will grow. The beloved can die and you cannot do anything, but that will not kill love. Love will grow more.

Security can kill. Really, if man were immortal, I say love would be impossible. If man were immortal it would be difficult to love anybody. It would be so dangerous to fall in love. Death is there and life is just like a dewdrop on a trembling leaf. Any moment the breeze will come and the dewdrop will fall and disappear. Life is just a wavering. Because of that wavering, because of that movement, death is always there. It gives intensity to love. Love is possible only because there is death. Love becomes intense because there is death. Think…if you know your beloved is going to die the next moment, all meanness will go, all conflict will go. And this one moment will become eternity. And there will be so much love that your whole being will be poured into it. But if you know the beloved is going to live, there is no hurry. You can fight and you can postpone the loving for later on. If life is eternal, if the body is immortal, you cannot love.

Hindus have a beautiful myth. They say in heaven where Indra rules—Indra is the king of heaven—there is no love. There are beautiful girls, more beautiful than on the earth, and deities. They have sex, but there is no love because they are immortal.

So it is recorded in one of the Indian stories that Uruvasi, the chief of the heavenly girls, asked permission of Indra to move to earth for a few days to love a man. "What nonsense!" Indra said. "You can love here! And you will not find such beautiful persons on the earth."

Uruvasi said, "They are beautiful but they are immortal, so there is no charm. They are really dead."

They are really dead because there is no death to make them alive. They will always be there. They cannot die, so how can they be alive? That aliveness exists against death. A man is alive because death is there constantly, fighting. Against the background of death life exists.

So Uruvasi said, "Give me permission to move to the earth. I want to love someone." Permission was given so she came down to earth and fell in love with Pururva, a young man.

But there was a condition from Indra. Indra made the condition that she could go to the earth, she could love someone, but she must tell the man who loved her not to ask anything about who she was. This is difficult for love because love is curious. Love wants to know everything about the beloved, everything. The whole unknown has to be made known. The whole mystery has to be entered and penetrated. So Indra cunningly made a condition which Uruvasi didn't understand the craftiness of. So she said, "Okay. I will tell my lover not to be curious about me, not to ask who I am. And if he asks, immediately I will leave him, I will come back." And she said to Pururva, "Don't ever ask anything about me, who I am. The moment you ask I will have to leave earth."

But love is curious. Because of this Pururva must have become more curious about who she was. He could not sleep. He would go on looking at Uruvasi. Who is she? Such a beautiful woman, made of dream stuff, doesn't look earthly, doesn't look substantial. Perhaps she comes from somewhere else, some unknown dimension. He became more and more curious. But he also became more and more afraid, because she might leave. He became so afraid that in the night when he went to sleep he would take a fragment of her sari in his hand because he was not confident about himself. Any moment he could ask, the question was always

there. Even in his sleep he could ask. And Uruvasi said that even in sleep he could not ask about her. So he slept with a part of her sari in his hand.

But one night he couldn't contain himself—and he thought that now she loved him so much that she would not leave. So he asked. And Uruvasi had to disappear—only a fragment of her sari remained in Pururva's hand. And it is said that he is still searching for her.

In heaven there cannot be love because there is no life really. Life exists here on earth, where death exists. Whenever you make anything secure, life disappears. Remain insecure, that is the very quality of life itself. Nothing can be done about it. And it is beautiful!

Just think—if your body was immortal, it would be ugly. You will start finding ways and means of committing suicide. And if it is impossible, against the law, you will suffer so much you cannot even imagine. Immortality is a very long thing. Now in the West they go on thinking about euthanasia, because people are now living longer. So a person who reaches the age of a hundred wants the right to kill himself. And really, the right will have to be given. We made it a law not to commit suicide when life was very short. Really, in Buddha's time to be forty or fifty was much; the average life was just about twenty. In India, just two decades ago, the average life was twenty-three. Now in Sweden the average life is eighty-three. So people can very easily live to be a hundred and fifty.

In Soviet Russia there are fifteen hundred people who have reached the mark of a hundred and fifty. Now, if they say they have the right to kill themselves, because now it is too much, we will have to give them the right. It cannot be denied them. Sooner or later suicide will be one of the birthrights. You cannot deny it if a person wants to die—not for any reason, just because now life has no meaning. It has been too long already. A person living at a hundred doesn't feel like living. Not that he is frustrated, not that there is no food—everything is there, but life has no meaning.

So think of immortality. Life will be totally meaningless. The meaning comes with death. Love has meaning because love can be lost. Then it throbs, vibrates, pulsates. It can be lost, you cannot be certain about it! You cannot think anything about it for tomorrow because it may not be there. You have to love the lover and the beloved with the view that tomorrow may never be there at all. Then love becomes intense.

So first, withdraw your efforts to create a secure life. Just by withdrawing, your walls around you will fall. For the first time you will feel rains coming to you directly, the wind blowing at you directly, the sun rising to you directly. You will be under the open sky. It is beautiful. And if it looks horrible to you, it is only because you have become accustomed to living in a prison. You will have to get accustomed to this new freedom.

This freedom will make you more alive, more flowing, more open, more rich, more radiant. But the more radiant you are, the higher the peak of your aliveness, the deeper will be the death near you—just near. You can rise only against death, the valley of death. The peak of life and the valley of death are always near and in proportion.

That's why I always say that Nietzsche's dictum is to be followed. It is a very religious dictum. Nietzsche says, "Live dangerously." Not that you have to seek danger positively, there is no need to seek danger positively. Don't create protections. Don't create walls around you. Live naturally, and that will be dangerous, dangerous enough. There is no need to seek any danger.

Then you can do this technique. *Feel yourself as pervading all directions, far, near.* Then it is very easy. If walls are not there, you will already be feeling yourself pervading everywhere. Then there is no point at which you end. You simply begin in the heart and end nowhere. You have a center and no periphery. The periphery goes on expanding—on and on. The whole space is surrounded by it. Stars move in it, earths are born and dissolve, planets arise and set. The whole cosmos becomes your periphery. In this vastness where will your ego be? In this vastness where will your suffering be? In this vastness where will your mean mind be? The mediocre mind, where will it be? It cannot be there in such vastness, it simply disappears. It can exist only in a narrow field. It can exist only when it is walled, enclosed, encapsulated. The encapsulation is the problem. Live dangerously and be ready to live in insecurity.

And the beauty is that even if you decide not to live in insecurity, you will! You cannot do anything!

I have heard about a king. He was very afraid of death....

Kings are more afraid. They are more afraid because they have exploited so many people; they have pushed, crushed; they have played many political games on so many people, they have made many enemies. A real king has no friend, he cannot have, because the closest friend is also an enemy, just waiting for an opportunity to kill him, to be in his place. A man in power cannot have any friends. A Hitler, a Stalin, a Nixon, they cannot have friends. They just have enemies who are parading around them as friends, and just waiting for the right chance to push them aside from the throne. Whenever they get the chance they do everything. Just a moment ago they were friendly, but their friendliness is a strategy, their friendliness is a tactic. A man who is in power cannot have friends. So Lao Tzu says, "If you want friends, don't be in power." Then the whole world will be friendly to you. If you are in power, then you are your only friend, everyone is your enemy.

...So the king was very afraid. He was very scared of death, it was all around. He was haunted by the idea that everyone around him was going to kill him.

He couldn't sleep, so he asked his wise men, his counselors, what to do. They told him to make a palace with only one door. At the door he should put seven rings of military men: the first watching the palace, the second watching the first, the third ring watching the second. With only one door no one could enter and the king would be safe.

The king built the palace with only one door, and with seven rings of soldiers watching each other. The news spread all over and another king from a nearby state came to see it. He was also afraid. News had reached him that his neighbor had built such a secure palace that it was impossible to kill him. He came to visit his neighbor and together they appreciated very much the idea of only one door and every safety—no danger.

While they were looking at the door a beggar just sitting at the corner of the street started laughing. So the king, the owner of the palace, asked the beggar, "Why are you laughing?"

The beggar replied, "I am laughing because you have made one error. You should go inside and close, seal this door also. This door is dangerous, someone can enter it. A door means that somebody can enter. And even if nobody else enters, at least death will enter. So you do one thing: go inside and let this door be also closed. Then you will be really safe because death cannot enter."

But the king said, "That means I would be already dead, if I closed this door also."

The beggar said, "You are already ninety-nine percent dead—you are only as much alive as this door. That is the danger, to be this much alive. Leave this aliveness also."

Everyone in his own way is creating a palace around him where nothing can enter and he can remain in peace. But then you are already dead. And peace happens only to those who are alive; peace is not a dead thing.

Remain alive, live dangerously, live a vulnerable life, open, so that everything can happen to you. And let everything happen to you. The more that happens to you the richer you will be. Then you can practice this technique. This technique is then very easy, you will not even need to practice it. Just think, and you will be pervading the whole space.

CHAPTER 72

Start living in insecurity

♦

Please explain Buddha's love.

Doesn't spiritual love become marriage?

Can one live in insecurity and not be anxious?

What is the need of transcendence?

The first question:

You said that love is possible only with death. Then will You please explain Buddha's love.

or an ignorant person love is always part of hate, it always goes with hate. For the ignorant mind hate and love are just two aspects of the same coin. For the ignorant mind love is never pure. And that is the misery of love—because the hate becomes a poison. You love a person and you hate the same person also. But you may not be doing both simultaneously, so you are not aware of it. When you love a person you forget about the hatred part, it goes below, it goes into the unconscious and it waits there.

Then when your love is tired, it falls into the unconscious and the hate part comes up. Then you hate the same person. And when you hate you are not aware that you also love—now the love has gone deep down into the unconscious. This goes on, just like night and day. It goes on moving in a circle. It becomes a misery.

But for a buddha, for one who is enlightened, the dichotomy, the dualism, disappears. Everywhere—not only as far as love is concerned—the whole life becomes a oneness. Then there is no dichotomy, the opposite doesn't exist.

So really, to call Buddha's love "love" is not good, but we have no other term. Buddha himself never used the word 'love'; he used the word 'compassion'. But that too is not very good, because your compassion is always mixed with your cruelty, your nonviolence is always mixed with your violence—whatsoever you do will have its opposite just nearby. You exist between contradictions; hence the tension, the anguish, the anxiety. You are not one; you are always two. You are a crowd, divided into many fragments, and those fragments are opposing each other. Your being is a tension; Buddha's being is a deep relaxation. Remember, tension exists between two opposite poles, and relaxation is just in the middle, where two opposing poles are no longer opposing. They negate each other—and there is a transcendence.

So Buddha's love is basically different from what you know as love. Your love is a dis-ease; Buddha's love is total relaxation. There is no head part to it, so the quality of it changes completely. Many things will be in Buddha's love which cannot be in ordinary love.

First, it cannot be hot. The hotness comes from hate. It is not passion, rather it is compassion. It is not hot, it is cool. To us, a cool love means something which has gone wrong. Buddha's love is cool, there is no heat to it. It is not like the sun, it is like the moon. It will not create passion in you, it will create a deep coolness.

Secondly, Buddha's love is not really a relationship—your love is a relationship. Buddha's love is his state of being. Really, he does not love you, he *is* love. This distinction must be understood clearly. If you love a person, your love is an act, you do something, you behave in a certain way, you create a relationship, a bridge. Buddha's love is just his being, it is just how he is. He is not loving towards you, he is just love. He is just like a flower there in the garden—you pass by and the perfume comes to you. It is not that the flower is sending its perfume to you especially—when there was no one passing by, the perfume was there. And if no one ever passes by, the perfume will still be there.

When your lover is not with you, when your beloved is not with you, the love disappears, the perfume is not there. It is an effort on your part, it is not simply your being. You have to do something to bring it out. When no one is there and Buddha is sitting alone under his bodhi tree, then too he is a lover. It looks absurd that then too he is a lover—there is no one to be loved but still he is a lover. This being a lover is his state. And because it is his state, it is never a tension. Buddha cannot get tired of his love. You will get tired, because it is something you are doing. So lovers get tired of each other if there is too much love; they get tired, they need gaps, intervals, to recuperate. If you are with your lover for twenty-four hours, he will get fed up because it is too much attention. Twenty-four hours of doing something is too much.

Buddha is not doing something, he is not tired of his love. It is his very being, it is just as if he is breathing. As you are never tired of breathing, you are never tired of being, so he is not tired of his love.

And then the third thing follows: you will be aware that you love, Buddha will not be at all aware—because awareness needs the contrary. Buddha is so filled with love that he will not be aware. If you ask him he will say, "I love you." But he is not aware of it. It is flowing so silently from him, it has become so intrinsic a part, that he cannot be aware of it. You will become aware that he loves, and if you are open and receptive you will become more aware that he loves you more. It depends on your capacity, on how much you can receive. But to him it is not a gift. He is not giving anything to you—he is this way, he happens to be

this way. Whenever you become aware of your total being, enlightened, liberated, the dichotomy drops from your life. Then there is no duality. Then life becomes a harmony—nothing is against anything.

Because of this harmony, much peace happens. There is no disturbance. Disturbance is not created from without, it is within you. The contradiction goes on creating the disturbance, although you may find excuses without. For example, watch what happens with your lover, or a friend, a deep friend, very intimate, close. Live with him, and just watch what is happening to you. When you meet you are very elated, ecstatic, dancing. But how much can you dance? And how ecstatic can you feel? Minutes later you are down, the elation has gone, and after a few hours you are bored, you are thinking of escaping to somewhere else. And after a few days you will be fighting.

Just watch what is happening.

This is all coming from within, but you will find excuses outside. You will say that now this man is not as loving as he was when he came; now this man is disturbing me, he is making me angry. And you will always find that he is doing something to you, you will never be aware that your dichotomy, your duality of mind, the opposites within, are doing something. We are never aware of our own workings of the mind.

I have heard that a very famous, glamorous Hollywood actress went to a studio for her photograph. The photograph had been taken the day before. The photographer presented the photograph to her, but she was annoyed, furious. She said, "What have you done? You have taken my photographs before and they were heavenly!"

The photographer said to the actress, "Yes, but you have forgotten that I was twelve years younger when I took your photographs. I was twelve years younger, you forget that."

We never look within at what is happening. If the photograph is not okay to you, something is wrong with the photographer—it is not that twelve years have passed and you are older. It is an inner process, the photographer is not concerned at all, but the photographer must have been a very wise man! He said, "You forget that I was twelve years younger then."

Buddha's love is totally different, but we don't have any other word for it. The best that we have is "love." But if you can remember this, then the quality changes completely.

And note one thing, think about it deeply. If Buddha is your lover, will you be satisfied? You will not be, because you will feel that it is cold, that there is no passion in it. You will feel that he loves you as he loves everyone—you are nothing special. You will feel that his love is not a gift—he is this way, that is why he is loving.

You will feel his love to be so natural that you will not be satisfied with it. Think inside. You cannot be satisfied with a love which is without hate, and you cannot be satisfied with a love which is with hate. This is the problem. Either way you will be unsatisfied. If love is with hate, you will be unsatisfied, always ill, because the hate part will disturb you. If love is without hate, you will feel that it is cold. And it is happening to Buddha so naturally that even if you were not there it would be happening—so it is nothing special for you. So your ego will feel unsatisfied. And it is my feeling that if you have a buddha or a nonbuddha to choose as your lover, you will choose the non-buddha...because you can understand his language. The nonbuddha is at least just like you. You will be fighting, you will be quarreling, the whole thing will be just a mess, a mad mess, but still you will choose a nonbuddha—because a buddha will be so high that you cannot understand the way he loves unless you rise.

With a nonbuddha, with an ignorant person, you need not transform yourself, you can remain the same. He is not a challenge. Really, just the contrary happens to lovers. When two lovers meet and fall in love, they both try to convince each other that they are very high. They bring out the best that

is within them. They appear to be on the peak. But it takes much arduous effort! You cannot remain on this peak. So when you start settling down you come back down to the earth.

So lovers are always frustrated with each other, because they thought the other was just divine, and when they settle, when everything becomes just mundane, just ordinary, they think the other was deceiving. No, he was not deceiving, he was just presenting himself in his best colors, that is all. He was not deceiving anybody, he was not consciously doing anything. He was just presenting himself in his best colors—and the same was done by the other. But you cannot go on presenting yourself like that for long because it becomes arduous, difficult, heavy. So you come down.

When two lovers settle, when they start to take each other for granted, then they appear very mean, very mediocre, very ordinary—just the opposite to what they appeared to be before. Then they were angels; now they appear to be just disciples of the devil. You fall down, you come to your ordinary level.

Ordinary love is not a challenge, but it is rare to fall in love with someone who is enlightened. Only very fortunate ones fall in such a love—it is rare. It happens only when you have been searching for an enlightened person for lives together. Only if this has happened do you fall in love with an enlightened person. Falling in love with an enlightened person is in itself a great achievement—but then there is a problem. The problem is that the enlightened person is a challenge. He cannot come down to your level, that is not possible, that is impossible. You have to go to his peak; you have to travel, you have to be transformed.

So love becomes a *sadhana* if you fall in love with a buddha. It becomes a sadhana, the greatest sadhana that is possible. Because of this, whenever there is a Buddha or a Jesus, or a Lao Tzu, many around them are able to reach to peaks in one life that they could not have reached in many lives. But the secret is if they can fall in love. It is not unimaginable, it is imaginable. You may have been there in the time of Buddha, you must have been somewhere around. Buddha might have passed through your village or town and you may not have even heard him, you may not have seen him. Because even to hear a buddha or to see a buddha or to come near to him, a certain love is needed, a certain search is needed on your part.

When someone falls in love with an enlightened person it is meaningful, very meaningful, but arduous will be the path. It is easy to fall in love with an ordinary person, there is no challenge, but with an enlightened person the challenge will be much, and the path will be difficult, because you will have to travel all the way upwards. And those things will be disturbing. His love will be cold, his love will look as if it is for everyone, his love will not have the hatred part.

This has been my experience. Many people fall in love with me, and then they start to play the game—the ordinary game. Knowingly or unknowingly, they start to play it. In a way it is natural. They start expecting things from me, ordinary expectations, and their mind works in the duality. For example, if you love me you will feel happy if you can make me happy. This is how love feels, it wants to make the other happy. If you can make me happy, you will feel happy—but you cannot make me happy, I am already!

If you fall in love with me, you will feel dejected, you will feel very disappointed because you cannot make me happy, you cannot make me more happy. There is nothing more. If you cannot make me happy you will feel unhappy, and so you will try to make me unhappy! Because at least if you can do that, that too will be a satisfaction. You will try to make me unhappy—unknowingly, you are not alert, you are not aware of it. If you are aware you will not do it. But you will try—your unconscious mind will try to make me unhappy. If you can make me unhappy, then you can be certain that you can make me happy also. But if you cannot make me unhappy you are totally disappointed. Then you

will feel that you are not related to me at all, because this is what relationship means to you.

Ordinary love is a disease, because the duality goes on persisting. And to understand the love of an enlightened person is difficult. Intellectually there is no way to understand it. You have to fall in love, and then you have to be alert about your own mind because that mind will go on disturbing.

Buddha became enlightened, then he came back to his home—he came back after twelve years. His wife, whom he had loved very much, was very angry, furious. All these twelve years she had been waiting and waiting—someday this man will come back. And she had much revenge in her mind, because this man had done an injustice to her, he was unfair. Suddenly one night he had disappeared. At least he could have said something, then it would have been fair, but without saying anything he simply disappeared, leaving her and their small child.

For twelve years she waited, and then Buddha came. She was furious, she was mad.

Buddha's nearest, closest disciple was Ananda. Ananda had always followed him like a shadow. When Buddha was entering the palace he said to Ananda, "Please don't come with me."

Ananda asked why—because he had an ordinary mind, he was not enlightened. He became enlightened only when Buddha died. He said, "Why? Are you still thinking in terms of wife and husband? That you are going to meet your wife? Are you still thinking in terms of wife and husband?" He was shocked. How can a buddha, an enlightened person, say, "Don't come with me. I am going to meet my wife"?

Buddha said, "That is not the point. She will get more furious seeing that I have come with someone. She has been waiting for twelve years. Let her be mad alone. She belongs to a very ancient family, very cultured, so she will not be angry before you, she will not express anything—and she has been waiting for twelve years. So let her explode, don't come with me. I am not a husband to her now, but she is still a wife. I have changed, but she has not changed."

Buddha went alone. Of course she was furious, she started crying and weeping and screaming and saying things. And Buddha listened. She asked again and again, "If you loved me at all, why did you leave? Why did you go away?—and without telling me! If you loved me at all, tell me this."

And Buddha said, "If I didn't love you, why should I have come back?"

But these are two different things, totally different. She was not ready to hear what he would say. She went on insisting, "Why did you leave me alone? You tell me that you never loved me, then everything is settled."

And Buddha said, "I did love you. I still love you, that is why I have come back after twelve years."

But this love is different: she was angry and Buddha was not angry. If he had also been angry because she was screaming and weeping and crying, she could have understood. If he had also been angry and had beaten her, she could have understood. Then everything would have been okay—he was still the old man. The twelve years would have disappeared completely and they would have loved again. There was no problem. But he was standing silently and she was mad. Only she was mad, he was smiling. This was too much! What type of love is this? It must have been very hard for her to understand.

Just to taunt Buddha she told her son, who was now twelve years old, "This is your father, look at him, an escapist. You were just one day old when he escaped. This is your father. He is a beggar, and he gave birth to you. Now ask about the heritage. Spread your hands before him, he is your father. Ask him what he has to give to you." She was taunting Buddha, she was angry, naturally.

And Buddha called Ananda, who was standing outside, and said, "Ananda, come and bring my begging bowl." When the begging bowl was given to Buddha, he gave it to his son, Rahul, and said,

"This is my heritage. I initiate you into sannyas." This was his love.

But Yashodhara got more mad. She said, "What are you doing? If you love your son, you will not make him a beggar, a sannyasin."

Buddha said, "I make him a beggar because I love him. I know what real heritage is, and that I am giving to him. My father was not so wise, but I know what is worth giving and I am giving it."

These are two different dimensions, two different languages, never meeting anywhere. He is loving. He must have loved his wife; that is why he came back. He must have loved his son; that is why he initiated him. But no father can understand this....

When Buddha's father heard about this—he was an old man, ill—he came running out and he said, "What have you done? Are you bent on destroying my whole family? You escaped from the house, you were my only son. Now my hopes are on Rahul, he is your only son. And you have initiated him into sannyas. So my family is cut. Now there is no possibility for the future. What are you doing? Are you an enemy?"

And Buddha said, "Because I love my son, I give him what is worth giving. Neither your kingdom nor your family and its tree is significant. It will make no difference to the world whether this tree goes on growing further or not. But the phenomenon of sannyas that Rahul is initiated into is something significant. I also love my son."

Two fathers talking... Buddha's father was again pleading with him, "You come back. I am your father. I am old, I am angry. You have disappointed me. But still I have a father's heart and I will forgive you. Come, my doors are open. Come back. Throw this sannyas, come back, my doors are open. This kingdom is yours, I am waiting. I am very old but I have a deep love for you and I can forgive." This is love.

Then there is the other father, Gautam Buddha himself, giving initiation to his son to leave the world. That too is love.

But both loves are so different that it is not good to call them by one name, one word—but we don't have any other.

The second question:

Last night You said that love is alive because it is insecure, and marriage is dead because it is secure. But isn't it true that love in the spiritual depth becomes marriage?

No! It never becomes marriage. The deeper it goes the *more* love it becomes, but never a marriage. By marriage I mean an outer bond, a legal sanction, social approval. And I say that love never becomes a marriage because it is never secure. It remains love. It becomes more love, more and more, but the more it is, the more insecure it is. There is no security.

But if you love, you don't care about security at all. When you don't love, only then do you care about security. When you love, the very moment is so much that you don't care about the next moment, you don't care about the future. What happens tomorrow is not your concern—because what is happening right now is so much. It is too much, it is unbearably much. You don't care.

Why does security come to the mind? It comes because of the future. The present is not enough so you are afraid about the future. Really, you are not rooted in the present. You are not living in the present. You are not enjoying it. It is not a bliss. The present is not a bliss—then you hope for the future, then you plan for the future, then you want to make every security for the future.

Love never wants to make any security, it is secure in itself. That is the point. It is so secure in itself that it never thinks about any security; what will happen in the future is not a concern at all—because the future is going to grow out of the present, and if the present is so alive, so blissful, the future will grow out of it. Why worry about it?

When the present is not a bliss, when it is a misery, then you are worried about the future. Then you want to make it secure, safe. But remem-ber, no one can make anything secure. That is not in the nature of things. The future will remain inse-cure. You can do only one thing: live the present more deeply. That is all you can do. If any security happens through that, that is the only security. And if it is not happening, it is not happening—nothing can be done.

But our mind works in a completely suicidal way. The more miserable the present is, the more you think about the future and want to make it secure. And the more you move into the future, the more the present will be miserable. Then you are moving in a vicious circle.

This circle can be broken, but the only way to break it is to live the present moment so deeply that this moment becomes the eternity in its depth. The future is going to be born out of it—it will take its own course, you need not worry about it.

So I say that love never thinks of security be-cause love is so secure in itself. Love is never afraid of insecurity. If it is there at all, if love is there at all, it is not afraid of insecurity. Life is insecure, but love is not afraid of insecurity. Rather, love enjoys insecurity because it gives color to life, changing seasons and moods, it gives tone. It is beautiful. The changing life is beautiful because there is always something to discover, there is always some-thing to encounter which is new.

Really, two lovers move in a constant discovery of each other. And the landscape is infinite. A loving heart is an infinite landscape. You can never finish it. There is no end to it, it goes on and on, spreading on and on. It is as spacious as space itself.

Love is not worried about insecurity, love can enjoy it. It gives a thrill. Only those who cannot love are afraid of insecurity, because they are not rooted in life. Those who cannot love are always secure in life. They waste their life just making it secure—and it is never secure. It cannot be.

Security is the quality of death; safety is the quality of death. Life is insecure, and love is not afraid of it. Love is not afraid of life, insecurity, because it is so grounded. If you are not grounded and you feel a cyclone coming, you will be afraid. But if you are grounded you will welcome the cyclone, it will become an adventure. If you are rooted, the passing cyclone will become a challenge. You will be shaken to the very roots by it; every fiber will become alive. Then, when the cyclone has gone, you will not think that it was bad, a misfortune. You will say it was fortunate, a blessing, because all the deadness has been taken away by the cyclone. All that was dead has moved with it and all that was alive has become more alive.

Look at the trees after the cyclone has gone. They are vibrating with life, pulsating with life, radiant, vital; energy is filling them. Because the cyclone gave them an opportunity to feel their roots, to feel their "groundedness." It was an opportunity to feel themselves.

So one who is rooted in love is never afraid of anything. Whatsoever comes is beautiful, a change —insecurity. Whatsoever happens is beautiful. But it never becomes a marriage. When I say it never becomes a marriage I don't mean that lovers should not marry, but that marriage should not become a substitute for love. It should only be the outer garb, it should not be the substitute. And it will never become a marriage because lovers never take each other for granted.

What I mean is that it is deeply psychological— lovers never take each other for granted. Once you start taking the other for granted, the other has become a thing. Now he is not a person. So marriage reduces the partners into things. A husband is a thing, a wife is a thing—predictable, very predictable.

I have been staying in many families all over this country and I have come to know many wives and many husbands. They are not persons at all. They are predictable. If the husband asserts a sentence it can even be said what the wife will say; how the wife will react is predictable. And if the wife says something mechanically the husband will

reply to it mechanically, it is certain. They are playing the same role again and again. Their life is just like a gramophone record when something goes wrong, when the needle sticks at a point and it goes on repeating. It is as predictable as that. You can tell what is going to happen again and again—the husband and wife are stuck somewhere, they have become phonograph records. Then they go on repeating. That repetition creates boredom.

I was staying with a family.... The husband said to me, "I have become afraid to be alone with my wife. Only when someone else is there are we both happy. We cannot even go for a holiday without taking someone with us because that someone gives something new. Otherwise we know what is going to happen. It is so predictable that it is not worth anything. We know it already." It is just as if you are reading the same book, again and again and again.

Lovers are not predictable—that is the insecurity. You don't know what is going to happen— and that is the beauty. You can be fresh and young and alive. But we want to make things of each other because a thing can be manipulated easily. And you need not be afraid of a thing. You know its whereabouts, its behavior. You can plan beforehand what to do and what not to do. By marriage I mean an arrangement in which two persons fall to the level of things.

Love is not an arrangement, it is a moment-to-moment encounter, alive. Full of danger of course, but life is so. Marriage is safe, there is no danger; love is unsafe. You never know what is going to happen, the next moment is unknown, remains unknown.

So love is entering every moment into the unknown—that is what Jesus means when he says, "God is love." God is as unknown as love. And if you are not ready to be alive and in love and insecure, you cannot move into God, because that is a greater insecurity, a greater unknownness. So love prepares you for prayer. If you can love, and remain with an unknown person without reducing him to a thing, without becoming predictable, encountering moment to moment, you are getting ready for prayer.

Prayer is nothing but love—love for the whole existence. You are living with existence as you are living with your lover: you don't know the mood, you don't know the season, you don't know what is coming. Nothing is known. You go on uncovering it—it is an endless journey.

The third question:

Can one who is not enlightened live in total insecurity and not be anxious, depressed and miserable?

Total insecurity and the capacity to live in it are synonymous with enlightenment. So one who is not enlightened cannot live in total insecurity, and one who cannot live in total insecurity cannot become enlightened. These are not two things, they are just two ways of saying the same thing. So don't wait until you have become enlightened to live in insecurity, no! Because then you will never become enlightened.

Start living in insecurity—that is the way towards enlightenment. And don't think about total insecurity. Start from where you are. As you are you cannot be total in anything, but one has to make a start. In the beginning it will create anxiety, in the beginning you will feel miserable—but only in the beginning. If you can pass the beginning, if you can tolerate the beginning, the misery will disappear, the anxiety will disappear.

The mechanism has to be understood. Why do you feel anxiety when you feel insecure? It is not because of insecurity, but because of the demand for security. When you feel insecure you feel anxious, anxiety arises. It is not arising because of insecurity, it is arising because of the demand to make life a security. If you start living insecurely and don't demand security, the anxiety will disappear when the demand goes. The demand is creating the anxiety.

Insecurity is the very nature of life. It is an insecure world for a Buddha; for a Jesus it is also

insecure. But they are not anxious because they have accepted the fact. They have become mature enough to accept a reality.

This is my definition of maturity and immaturity. A person I call immature is one who goes on fighting against reality for fictions and dreams. This man is immature. Maturity means coming to terms with reality, throwing away dreams, and accepting the reality as it is. Buddha is mature. He accepts: it is so. For example, although there is death, an immature person goes on thinking that everyone may die but he is not going to die. An immature person goes on thinking that by the time he dies something will be discovered, some medical elixir, which means he will not die. An immature person goes on thinking that it is not the rule to die. Of course, many have died, but in everything there are exceptions, and he goes on thinking that he is an exception.

Whenever someone dies you feel sympathetic, you feel, "Poor man, he has died." But it never comes to your mind that his death is your death also. No, you bypass it. You just don't touch such delicate matters. You go on thinking that something or other will save you—some mantra, some miracle-maker guru. Something will happen and you will be saved.

You are living in stories, children's stories. A mature person is one who looks at the fact and accepts that life and death are together. Death is not the end, it is the very peak of life. It is not something like an accident which happens to life; it is something which grows in the very heart of life. It grows and comes to a peak. So he accepts and then there is no fear of death. He accepts that security is not possible. You can create a façade: you can have a bank balance, you can donate much money to have some security in heaven, you can do everything. But deep down you know nothing is really secure. The bank can cheat you, and no one knows that the priest is not a cheat, the greatest cheat. No one knows. They write letters....

In India there is a Mohammedan sect, the head priest of which writes letters to God. You donate a particular amount of money and he will write a letter. The letter will be put with you in your tomb, in your grave. It will be put with you so you can produce the letter. The money goes to the priest, the letter goes with you. But nothing is secure.

A mature person comes to terms with reality, he accepts it as it is. He doesn't demand. He is not a demander. He doesn't say, "It should be so." He looks at the fact and says, "Yes, it is so." This coming to terms with reality will make it impossible for you to be miserable—because misery comes when you demand. Really, misery is nothing else than an indication that you are moving against reality. And reality cannot be changed by you, you will have to be changed by reality. You will have to come to terms, you will have to yield.

This is what the meaning of surrender is: you will have to yield. The reality cannot yield, the reality is as it is. Unless you yield, you will suffer. The misery is created by you because you go on fighting. It is just as if the current of a river is flowing towards the sea and you are trying to swim upcurrent. You feel the river is against you. The river is not against you. It has not even heard about you, it doesn't know you at all. The river is simply flowing to the sea. It is a river's nature to flow to the sea, to move to the sea and to fall into it.

You are trying to move upstream. And there may be some foolish fellows sitting or standing on the bank who go on inspiring you: "You are doing well. You shouldn't be worried because sooner or later the river will have to yield. You are simply great, go on doing it! Those who are great, they have won over the river." There are always foolish people who go on giving you inspiration, giving you more enthusiasm.

But no Alexander, no Napoleon, no great man, no one has ever been able to go upstream. Sooner or later the stream takes over. But when you are dead, you cannot enjoy the bliss that was possible while you were alive: the bliss of surrendering, of accepting, of becoming so one with the stream that there is no conflict.

But those foolish people on the bank will say, "You have yielded, you are defeated, you are a failure." Don't listen to them, just enjoy the inner freedom that comes with yielding. Don't listen to them.

When Buddha stopped trying to flow upstream, all those that knew him said, "You are an escapist. You are a failure, you have accepted defeat."

Don't listen to what others say. Feel the inner feeling. Feel what is happening to you. If you feel good flowing with the stream, this is the way. This is Tao for you. Don't listen to anybody, just listen to your own heart. Maturity accepts, whatsoever there is.

I have heard an anecdote…. A Mohammedan, a Christian and a Jew were asked a question. The question was the same. Someone asked all three, "What would you do if a tidal wave forces the ocean onto the land and you are drowned in it?"

The Christian said, "I will make the sign of the cross on my heart, and pray to God to allow me into heaven, to open the doors."

The Mohammedan said, "I will take the name of Allah, and will say that this is *kismet*, this is fate—and drown."

The Jew said, "I will thank God and accept his will and learn to live under water."

This has to be done. One has to accept the will of existence, the will of the universe, and learn how to live in it. This is the whole art. A mature person accepts whatsoever is here, doesn't demand, doesn't talk about any heaven.

The Christian was doing—he was asking, he was saying, "Open the doors of heaven." But he was also not a pessimist who simply accepts and is drowned. The Mohammedan was doing that. The Jew accepted, welcomed rather, and said, "This is the will, now I must learn how to live under water. This is God's will."

Accept the reality as it is and learn how to live in it with a yielding heart, with a surrendered ego.

The last question:

You said yesterday that life exists with death. Then please explain what is the need of transcendence.

This is the need. There is the need. Life exists with death...if you can understand this, you have transcended. You accept life, you don't accept death. Or do you? You accept life but you reject death, and because of that you are always in trouble. You are in trouble because death is part of life. When you accept life, death is going to be there, but you reject death. When you reject death you have rejected life also because they are not two. So you will be in trouble.

Either accept the whole, or reject the whole.

That is transcendence.

And there are two ways of transcending. Either accept both, life and death together, or reject both, life and death together—then you have transcended. These are the two ways, the negative and the positive. The negative says, "Reject both." The positive says, "Accept both," but the emphasis is that *both* should be there, whether accepted or rejected. When both are there they negate each other, just like minus and plus. They negate each other, and when they are not, you have transcended.

You are attached either to life or attached—sometimes—to death, but you never accept both. I have come across many people who are so dejected about life that they have started to think about committing suicide. First they are attached to life, then life frustrates—not that life frustrates, attachment frustrates, but they think life is frustrating—so they become attached to death. Now they start thinking about how to destroy themselves, how to commit suicide, how to die. But the attachment is there. Previously it was to life, now it is to death. So a person who is attached to life and a person who is attached to death are not different. Attachment is there and that attachment is the problem. Accept both.

Just think. What will happen if you accept both life and death? Immediately a silence will come to the mind, because they negate each other. Life and death both disappear when you accept them—then you have transcended, you have gone beyond. Or reject both—it is the same thing.

Transcendence means going beyond duality. Attachment means remaining within duality, attached to one against the other. When you accept both or reject both, attachment falls, your tie is undone. Suddenly you float into a third dimension of being, where neither life is nor death.

That is nirvana, that is moksha—where both the dualities are not, but oneness, isness, is. And unless you transcend, you will always be in misery. You can change your attachment from this to that, but you will be in misery.

Attachment creates misery. Rejection also creates misery. Whatsoever you choose, it is up to you. You can choose a positive path, like Krishna. He says, "Accept. Accept both." Or you can choose a path like Buddha, who says, "Reject both." But do something with both together, then transcendence follows immediately. Even if you *think* of both, there will be transcendence. And if you can do it in real life, a new being is born. That being doesn't belong to the earth of duality, that being belongs to an unknown realm—the realm of nirvana.

CHAPTER 73

Fear
of transformation
goes deep

◆

100 *The appreciation of objects and subjects is the same for an enlightened as for an unenlightened person. The former has one greatness: he remains in the subjective mood, not lost in things.*

101 *Believe omniscient, omnipotent, pervading.*

Many people seem to be interested in meditation, but that interest cannot be very deep because so very few are transformed through it. If the interest is really deep, it becomes a fire by itself. It transforms you. Just through intense interest you start becoming different. A new center of being arises. So many people seem to be interested but nothing new arises in them, no new center is born, no new crystallization is achieved. They remain the same.

That means they are deceiving themselves. The deception is very subtle but it is bound to be there. If you go on taking medicine, having treatments, and the illness remains the same—rather, on the contrary, it goes on increasing—then your medicine, your treatment, is bound to be false. Maybe deep down you don't want to be transformed. That fear is very real—the fear of transformation. So on the surface you go on thinking that you are deeply interested, but deep down you go on deceiving.

The fear of transformation is just like the fear of death. It is a death, because the old will have to go and the new will come into being. You will be there no more, something totally unknown to you will be born out of you. Unless you are ready to die, your interest in meditation is false, because only those who are ready to die will be reborn. The new cannot become a continuity with the old. The old must be discontinued. The old must go. Only then can the new come into being. The new is not an outgrowth of the old, the new is not continuous with it—the new is totally new, and it comes only when the old dies. There is a gap between the old and the new; that gap gives you the fear. You are afraid. You want to be transformed but simultaneously you want to remain the old. This is the deception. You want to grow, but you want to remain you. Then growth is impossible; then you can only deceive, then you can go on thinking and dreaming that something is happening, but nothing will happen because the basic point has been missed.

So there are many people all over the world who are very interested in meditation, *moksha, nirvana,* and nothing is happening. There is so much noise about it but nothing real is happening. What is the matter?

Sometimes the mind is so cunning that because you don't want to be transformed, the mind will create a superficial interest so that you can say to yourself, "You are interested, you are doing whatsoever can be done." And you remain the same. And if nothing happens, you think that the technique you are using is wrong, the guru you are following is wrong, the scripture, the principle, the method, is wrong. You never think that even with a wrong method transformation is possible if the real interest is there; even with a wrong method you will be transformed. If you are really interested in transformation, you will become different even if following a wrong guru. If your soul and your heart is in your effort, no one can mislead you except yourself. And nothing is a barrier to your progress except your own deceptions.

When I say that even a wrong master, a wrong

method, a wrong principle, can lead you to the real, I mean that the real transformation happens when you are intensely involved in it, not through any method. The method is just a device, the method is just a help, the method is secondary—your being involved in it is the fundamental thing. But you go on doing something—not even doing, you go on talking about doing. And words create an illusion: you think so much about it, you read so much about it, you listen so much about it that you start feeling you are doing something. So-called religious persons have developed many deception devices.

I have heard that a motorist, driving along a road, saw the school building on fire. The teacher of the small school of that small village was Mulla Nasruddin. He was sitting under a tree. The motorist called to him, "What are you doing there? The school building is on fire!"

Mulla Nasruddin said, "I know about it."

The motorist was much excited. He said, "Then why are you not doing something?"

Mulla Nasruddin said, "Ever since it started I have been praying for rain. I *am* doing something."

Prayer is a trick to avoid meditation, and the so-called religious mind has developed many types of prayer. Prayer can also become a meditation—when it is not only a prayer, it is a deep effort, a deep involvement. Prayer can also become meditation, but ordinarily prayer is just an escape. To avoid meditation, people go on praying. To avoid doing anything they pray. Prayer means that God must do something, someone else must do. Prayer means that we are passive—something must be done to us.

Meditation is not prayer in that sense; meditation is something you do to yourself. And when you are transformed, the whole universe behaves differently to you, because the universe is nothing but a response to you, whatsoever you are. If you are silent, the whole universe responds to your silence in thousands and thousands of ways. It reflects you. Your silence is multiplied infinitely. If you are blissful, the whole universe reflects your

bliss. If you are in misery, the same happens. The mathematics remains the same, the law remains the same: the universe goes on multiplying your misery. Prayer won't do. Only meditation can help because meditation is something to be done authentically by you, it is a doing on your part.

So the first thing I would like to say to you is be constantly alert that you are not deceiving yourself. You may be doing something and still deceiving yourself.

I have heard that Mulla Nasruddin once came running into a post office, grasped the postmaster by the lapel, shook him, and said, "I have gone crazy. My wife has disappeared!"

The postmaster felt sorry and he said, "Really, she has disappeared? Unfortunately this is a postal department—you have to go to the police department to report this disappearance."

Mulla Nasruddin shook his head negatively and said, "I am not going to be caught again. In the past my wife also disappeared and when I reported it to the police department, they found her. I am not going to be caught again. If you can take the report, take it, otherwise I am going."

He wants to report to feel good, to feel that he has done whatsoever can be done. But he doesn't want to report to the police department because he is afraid.

You go on doing things just to feel good, just to feel that you are doing something. But really you are not ready to be transformed. So all that you do just passes as useless activity—not only useless, harmful also, because it is a wastage of time, energy, and opportunity. These techniques of Shiva are only for those who are ready to do. You can ponder over them philosophically—that means nothing. But if you are actually ready to do, then something will start happening to you. They are alive methods, not dead doctrines. Your intellect is not needed; your totality of being is required. And any method will do. If you are ready to give it a chance, any method will do. You will become a new man.

I will repeat again: methods are devices. If you

are ready, then any method can do. They are just tricks to help you to take the jump, they are just like jumping boards. From any jumping board you can jump into the ocean. The jumping boards are insignificant; what color they are, what wood they are made of is irrelevant. They are simply jumping boards and you can take a jump from them. All these methods are jumping boards. Whatsoever method takes your fancy, don't go on thinking about it, do it!

Difficulties will arise when you start doing something—if you don't do anything there will be no difficulty. Thinking is very easy to do because you are not really traveling, but when you start doing something, difficulties arise. So if you see that difficulties have arisen, you can feel that you are on the right track—something is happening to you. Then old barriers will break, old habits will go, there will be change, there will be disturbance and chaos. All creativity comes out of chaos. You will be created anew only if all that you are becomes chaotic. So these methods will destroy you first, then only will a new being be created. If there are difficulties, feel fortunate—that shows growth. No growth is smooth...and spiritual growth cannot be smooth, that is not its nature. Because spiritual growth means growing upwards, spiritual growth means reaching into the unknown, reaching into the uncharted, difficulties will be there. But remember that with each difficulty that is passed you are crystallized. You become more solid. You become more real. For the first time you will feel something centering within you, something becoming solid.

As you are now you are just a liquid phenomenon, changing every moment, nothing stable. Really you cannot claim any "I"—you don't have one. You are many "I"s just in a flow, a riverlike flow. You are a crowd, not an individual yet. But meditation can make you an individual.

This word 'individual' is beautiful; it means indivisible. Right now as you are, you are divided. You are only many fragments clinging together anyhow without any center being there, without

any master in the house, with only servants. And for a moment any servant can become the master.

Every moment you are different because you are not—and unless you are, the divine cannot happen to you. To whom can it happen? You are not there. People come to me and they say, "We would like to see God." I ask them, "Who will see? You are not there. God is always there, but you are not there to see. It is just a passing thought that you want to see God." The next moment they are not interested; the next moment they have forgotten all about it. A persistent, intense effort and longing is needed. Then any method will do.

Now we should enter the methods.

---

100 Remain detached.

The first method: *The appreciation of objects and subjects is the same for an enlightened as for an unenlightened person. The former has one greatness: he remains in the subjective mood, not lost in things.*

This is a very beautiful method. You can start it as you are; no other prerequisite is needed. The method is simple: you are surrounded by persons, things, phenomena—every moment something is around you. Things are there, events are there, persons are there—but because you are not alert, you are not there. Everything is there but you are fast asleep. Things move around you, persons move around you, events move around you, but you are not there. Or, you are asleep.

So whatsoever happens in your surroundings becomes a master, becomes a force over you; you are dragged by it. You are not only impressed, conditioned by it, you are dragged by it.

Anything can catch you, and you will follow it. Somebody passes—you look, the face is beautiful, and you are carried away. The dress is beautiful, the color, the material is beautiful—you are carried away. The car passes by—and you are carried away. Whatsoever happens around you catches you. You are not powerful. Everything else is more powerful than you. Anything changes you; your mood, your being, your mind, depend on other things. Objects influence you.

This sutra says that enlightened persons and unenlightened persons live in the same world. A buddha and you both live and move in the same world—the world remains the same. The difference is not in the world, the difference happens in the buddha: he moves in a different way. He moves among the same objects but he moves in a different way. He is his own master. His subjectivity remains aloof and untouched. That is the secret. Nothing can impress him; nothing from the outside can condition him, nothing can overpower him. He remains detached; he remains himself. If he wants to go somewhere, he will go, but he will remain the master. If he wants to pursue a shadow, he will pursue it, but it is his own decision.

This distinction must be understood. By "detachment" I don't mean a person who has renounced the world—then there is no sense and no meaning in detachment. A detached person is a person who is living in the same world as you—the difference is not in the world. A person who renounces the world is changing the situation, not himself. And you will insist on changing the situation if you cannot change yourself. That is the indication of a weak personality. A strong person, alert and aware, will start to change himself, not the situation in which he is, because really the situation cannot be changed. Even if you can change the situation, there will be other situations. Every moment situations go on changing so every moment the problem will be there.

This is the difference between the religious and the nonreligious attitude. The nonreligious attitude is to change the situation, the surrounding. It doesn't believe in you, it believes in situations: when the situation is okay, you will be okay. You are dependent on the situation: if the situation is not okay, you will not be okay. So you are not

an independent entity. For communists, Marxists, socialists, and all those who believe in changing the situation, you are not important; really, you don't exist. Only the situation exists and you are just a mirror which reflects the situation. The religious attitude says that as you are you may be a mirror, but this is not your destiny. You can become something more, someone who is not dependent.

There are three steps of growth. Firstly, the situation is the master, you are just dragged by it. You believe that you are, but you are not. Secondly, you are, and the situation cannot drag you, the situation cannot influence you because you have become a will, you are integrated and crystallized. Thirdly, you start influencing the situation: just by your being there, the situation changes.

The first state is that of the unenlightened; the second state is of the person who is constantly aware but as yet unenlightened—he has to be alert, he has to do something to be alert. The alertness has not become natural yet so he has to fight. If he loses consciousness or alertness for a single moment, he will be under the influence of the thing. So he has to stand on his toes continuously. He is the seeker, the *sadhak,* the one who is practicing something.

The third state is that of the *siddha,* the enlightened one. He is not trying to be alert, he simply is alert—there is no effort to it. Alertness is just like breathing: it goes on, he does not have to maintain it. When alertness becomes a phenomenon like breathing, natural, *sahaj,* spontaneous, then this type of person, this type of centered being, automatically influences situations. Situations change around him—not that he wishes them to change, but he is powerful.

Power is the thing to be remembered. You are powerless so anything can overpower you. And power comes through alertness, awareness: the more alert, the more powerful; the less alert, the less powerful. Look…while you are asleep even a dream becomes powerful because you are fast asleep, you have lost all consciousness. Even a dream is powerful, and you are so weak that you cannot even doubt it. Even in an absurd dream you cannot be skeptical, you will have to believe it. And while it lasts, it looks real. You may see just absurd things in the dream, but while you are dreaming, you cannot doubt. You cannot say this is not real, you cannot say this is a dream, you cannot say this is impossible. You simply cannot say it because you are so fast asleep. When consciousness is not there even a dream affects you. While awake, you will laugh and you will say, "It was absurd, impossible, this cannot happen. This dream was just illusory." But you have not noticed that while it was there you were influenced by it, you were totally taken over by it. Why was a dream so powerful? The dream was not powerful—you were powerless. Remember this: when you are powerless even a dream becomes powerful.

While you are awake, a dream cannot influence you, but reality, the so-called reality around, does. An awakened person, an enlightened person, has become so alert that your reality also cannot influence him. If a woman passes, a beautiful woman, you are suddenly carried away. Desire has arisen, the desire to possess. If you are alert, the woman will pass by, but the desire will not arise—you have not been influenced, you have not been taken over. When this happens for the first time, when things move around you and you are not influenced, you will feel a subtle joy of being. For the first time really you feel that you are; nothing can drag you out of you. If you want to follow, that is another thing. That is your decision. But don't deceive yourself. You can deceive, you can say, "Yes. The woman is not powerful, but I want to follow her, I want to possess her." You can deceive, many people go on deceiving, but you are deceiving nobody except yourself. Then it is futile. Just take a close look: you will know the desire is there. The desire comes first, and then you start rationalizing it.

For an enlightened person, things are there and he is there but there is no bridge between him and the thing. The bridge has broken. He moves alone. He lives alone. He follows himself. Nothing else

can possess him. Because of this feeling we have called this attainment moksha—total freedom, *mukti*. He is totally free.

All over the world, man has searched for freedom; you cannot find a man who is not hankering after freedom in his own way. Through many paths man tries to find a state of being where he can be free, and he resents anything that gives him a feeling of bondage. He hates it. Anything that hinders, that makes him imprisoned, he fights. He struggles against it. Hence so many political fights, so many wars, revolutions; hence so many continuous family fights—wife and husband, father and son, all fighting each other. The fight is basic. The fight is for freedom. The husband feels confined, the wife has imprisoned him—now his freedom is cut. And the wife feels the same. They both resent each other, they both fight, they both try to destroy the bondage. The father fights the son because every stage of growth in the son means more freedom for him, and the father feels he is losing something: power, authority. In families, in nations, in civilizations, man is hankering after only one thing—freedom.

But nothing is achieved through political fights, revolutions, wars. Nothing is achieved, because even if you get freedom, it is superficial—deep down you remain in bondage. So every freedom proves a disillusionment. Man longs so much for wealth, but as far as I understand it, it is not a longing for wealth, it is a longing for freedom. Wealth gives you a feeling of freedom. If you are poor, you are confined, your means are limited—you cannot do this, you cannot do that. You don't have the money to do it. The more money you have, the more you feel you have freedom, you can do anything you like. But when you have all the money and you can do all that you wish, imagine, dream about, suddenly you feel this freedom is superficial, because inside your being knows well that you are powerless and that anything can attract you. You are impressed, influenced, possessed by things and persons.

This sutra says that you have to come to a state of consciousness where nothing impresses you, you can remain detached. How to do it? Throughout the whole day the opportunity is there to do it. That is why I say this method is good for you to do. Any moment you can become aware that something is possessing you. Then take a deep breath, inhale deeply, exhale deeply, and look at the thing again. While you are exhaling look at the thing again, but look just as a witness, as a spectator. If you can achieve the witnessing state of mind for even a single moment, suddenly you will feel you are alone, nothing can impress you; at least in that moment nothing can create desire in you. Take a deep breath and exhale it whenever you feel that something is impressing you, influencing you, dragging you away from you, becoming more important than yourself. And in that small gap created by the exhalation look at the thing—a beautiful face, a beautiful body, a beautiful building, or anything.

If you feel it is difficult, if just by exhaling you cannot create a gap, then do one thing more: exhale, and stop inhalation for a single moment so the exhalation has thrown all the air out. Stop, don't inhale. Then look at the thing. When the air is out, or in, when you have stopped breathing, nothing can influence you. In that moment you are unbridged—the bridge is broken.

Breathing is the bridge. Try it. It will be only for a single moment that you will have the feeling of witnessing, but that will give you the taste, that will give you the feeling of what witnessing is. Then you can pursue it. Throughout the whole day, whenever something impresses you and a desire arises, exhale, stop in the interval, and look at the thing. The thing will be there, you will be there, but there will be no bridge. Breathing is the bridge. Suddenly you will feel you are powerful, you are potent. And the more powerful you feel, the more *you* will become. The more things drop, the more their power over you drops, the more crystallized you will feel. Individuality has begun. Now you have a center to refer to, and any moment you can move to the center and the world disappears. Any moment you can take shelter in your own center,

and the world is powerless.

This sutra says, *The appreciation of objects and subjects is the same for an enlightened as for an unenlightened person. The former has one greatness: he remains in the subjective mood, not lost in things.* He remains in the subjective mood, he remains within himself, he remains centered in consciousness. Remaining in the subjective mood has to be practiced. As many opportunities as you can get, try it. And every moment there is an opportunity, every single moment there is an opportunity. Something or other is impressing you, dragging you out, pulling you out, pushing you in.

I am reminded of an old story. A great king, Bharathari, renounced the world. He renounced the world because he had lived in it totally and he had come to realize that it was futile. It was not a doctrine to him, it was a lived reality. He had come to the conclusion through his own life. He was a man of strong desire, he had indulged in life as much as possible, then suddenly he realized it was useless, futile. So he left the world, he renounced it, and he went to a forest.

One day he was meditating under a tree. The sun was rising. Suddenly he became aware that just on the road, the small road which passed nearby the tree, lay a very big diamond. As the sun was rising, it was reflecting the rays. Even Bharathari had not seen such a big diamond before. Suddenly, in a moment of unawareness, a desire arose to possess it. The body remained unmoved, but the mind moved. The body was in the posture of meditation, *siddhasana,* but the meditation was no longer there. Only the dead body was there, the mind had moved—it had gone to the diamond.

Before the king could move, two men came from different directions on their horses and simultaneously they became aware of the diamond lying on the road. They pulled out their swords, each one claiming that he had seen the diamond first. There was no other way to decide so they had to fight. They fought and killed each other. Within moments two dead bodies were lying there next to the diamond. Bharathari laughed, closed his eyes, and went into meditation again.

What happened? He again realized the futility. And what happened to these two men? The diamond became more meaningful than their whole life. This is what possession means: they threw away their life just for a stone. When desire is there, you are no more—desire can lead you to suicide. Really, every desire is leading you to suicide. When you are in the power of a desire, you are not in your senses, you are just mad.

The desire to possess arose in Bharathari's mind also; in a fragment of a moment the desire arose. And he might have moved to get it but before he could, the other two persons came and fought, and there were two dead bodies lying on the road with the stone there in its own place. Bharathari laughed, closed his eyes, and went into his meditation again. For a single moment his subjectivity was lost. A stone, a diamond, the object, became more powerful. But again the subjectivity was regained. Without the diamond the whole world disappeared, and he closed his eyes.

For centuries meditators have been closing their eyes. Why? It is only symbolic that the world has disappeared, that there is nothing to look at, that nothing is worth anything, even to look at. You will have to remember continuously that whenever desire arises, you have moved out of your subjectivity. This is the world, this movement. Regain, move back, get centered again! You will be able to do it: the capacity is there with everyone. No one ever loses the inner potential, it is always there. You can move. If you can move out, you can move in. If I can go out of my house, why can I not come back within it? The same route is to be traveled; the same legs are to be used. If I can go out, I can come in. Every moment you are moving out, but whenever you move out, remember—and suddenly come back. Be centered. If you feel it difficult in the beginning then take a deep breath, exhale, and stop. In that moment look at the thing which was attracting you. Really, nothing was attracting you,

you were attracted. That diamond lying there on the road in the lonely forest was not attracting anybody, it was simply lying there being itself. The diamond was not aware that Bharathari had been attracted, that someone had moved from his meditation, from his subjectivity, had come back into the world. The diamond was not aware that two persons had fought for it and lost their lives.

So nothing is attracting you—*you* get attracted. Be alert and the bridge will be broken and you will regain balance inside. Go on doing it more and more. The more you do it, the better. And a moment will come when you will not need to do it because the inner power will give you such a strength that the attraction of things will be lost. It is your weakness which is attracted. Be more powerful and nothing will attract you. Only then for the first time are you master of your own being.

That will give you real freedom. No political freedom, no economic freedom, no social freedom can be of much help. Not that they are not desirable, they are good, good in themselves, but they will not give you the things which the innermost core of your being is longing for—the freedom from things, from objects, the freedom to be oneself without any possibility of being possessed by anything or anybody.

---

101 Believe that you are all-powerful.

The second technique is similar in a way, but it is from a different dimension. *Believe omniscient, omnipotent, pervading.*

This too is based on inner power, inner strength. It is very seedlike. Believe that you are omniscient, all-knowing; believe that you are omnipotent, all-powerful; believe that you are pervading, all-pervading.... How can you believe it? It is impossible. You know you are not all-knowing, you are ignorant. You know you are not all-potent, you are absolutely powerless, helpless. You know you are not all-pervading, you are confined in a small body. So how can you believe it? And if you believe it, knowing well that this is not the case, the belief will be useless. You cannot believe against yourself. You can force a belief, but it will be useless, meaningless. You know it is not so. A belief becomes useful only when you know that it is so.

This has to be understood. A belief becomes powerful if you know that this is the case. True or untrue is not the point. If you know that this is the case, a belief becomes truth. If you know that this is not the case, then even a truth cannot become a belief. Why? Many things have to be understood.

Firstly, whatsoever you are is your belief: you believe in that way, you have been brought up in that way; you have been conditioned in that way, so you believe in that way. And your belief influences you. It becomes a vicious circle. For example, there are races where man is less powerful than woman, because those races believe that a woman is stronger, more powerful, than man. Their belief has become a fact. In those races, man is weaker and woman is stronger. The women do all the work that ordinarily, in other countries, men would do, and men do the work that in other countries women would do. Not only that, their bodies are weak, their structure is weak. They have come to believe that this is so. The belief creates the phenomenon. Belief is creative.

Why does this happen? Because mind is more powerful than matter. If mind really believes something, matter has to follow. Matter cannot do anything against the mind because matter is dead. Even impossibilities happen.

Jesus says, "Faith can move mountains." Faith *can* move mountains. If it cannot, it only means that you don't have faith—not that faith cannot move mountains. Your faith cannot move them because you don't have the faith.

Now much research is going on on this phenomenon of belief, and science is coming to many unbelievable conclusions. Religion always believed in them but science is finally coming to the same

conclusions. It has to because many phenomena are being investigated for the first time. For example, you may have heard about placebo medicines. There are hundreds and hundreds of "pathies" in the world—allopathy, ayurvedic, yunani, homeopathy, naturopathy—hundreds, and they all claim that they can cure. And they do cure, their claims are not false. This is the rare thing—their diagnosis is different, their treatment is different. There is one illness and there are a hundred and one diagnoses, and a hundred and one treatments, and every treatment helps. So the question is bound to be raised whether it is really the treatment that helps or the belief of the patient. This is possible.

In many ways, in many countries, in many universities, in many hospitals, they are working. Just water or something nonmedicinal is given but the patient believes that a medicine has been given. And not only the patient, the doctor also believes it, because he also is not aware. If the doctor is aware whether it is medicine or not, it will have an effect, because the doctor gives a belief to the patient more than a medicine. So when you pay more and you have a greater doctor, you get well better and sooner. It is a question of belief. If the doctor gives you a four-penny medicine, just four pennies, you know well that nothing is going to happen. How can such a big patient with such a disease, such a great phenomenon, be cured by four pennies? Impossible! The belief cannot be created.

Every doctor has to create around him an aura of belief. It helps. So if the doctor knows that it is just water that he is giving, he will not give his belief with faith. His face will show, his hands will show, his whole attitude and behavior will show that he is giving just water, and the unconscious of the patient will be affected. The doctor must believe. The more he believes the better, because his belief is infectious. The patient looks at the doctor. If the doctor feels confident—"Don't worry, this is a new treatment, a new medicine and this is going to help you. It is a hundred percent certain, there is no doubt about it" —if the whole personality of the doctor gives the impression of a hundred percent hope, then already, even before taking the medicine, the patient is being cured. The cure has already started. Now they say that whatsoever you use, thirty percent of the patients will be cured almost immediately; whatsoever you use—allopathy, naturopathy, homeopathy, or any "pathy"—whatsoever you do, thirty percent of the patients will be cured immediately.

Those thirty percent are believers. That's the ratio. If I look at you, into you, thirty percent are potential, are ones who can immediately be transformed. Once they get the belief, it will immediately start working. One third of humanity can be immediately transformed, changed, to new orders of being without any difficulty. The question is only how to create the belief in them. Once the belief is there, nothing can debar them. You may be one of those fortunate ones, one of the thirty percent. But a great misfortune has happened to humanity, and that is that those thirty percent are condemned. Society, education, civilization, all condemn them. They are thought to be stupid people.

No, they are more potential people. They have a great power but they are condemned, and impotent intellectual people are praised—because they are potent with language, words, reason, they are praised. Really, they are simply impotent. They cannot do anything in the real world of inner being, they can just go on with their mind. But they possess the universities, they possess the news media, they are the masters in a way. And they are artists in condemnation. They can condemn anything. And this thirty percent of potential humanity, those who can believe and can get transformed, they are not so articulate—they cannot be. They cannot reason, they cannot argue, that's why they can believe. But because they cannot argue their case they have themselves become self-condemning. They think something is wrong. If you can believe, you start feeling that something is wrong with you; if you can doubt, you think something is great with you. But doubt is not a force. Through doubt no one ever got to the innermost being, to the ultimate ecstasy, no one, ever.

If you can believe, then this sutra will be helpful. *Believe omniscient, omnipotent, pervading.* You are that already, so just by believing it, all that is hiding you, all that is covering you, will fall down immediately. But even for those thirty percent it will be difficult because they are also conditioned to believe in something which is not the case. They are also conditioned to doubt, they are also trained to be skeptical; and they know their limitations, so how can they believe? Or if they believe, people will think they are mad. If you say that you believe that inside you is the all-pervading, the omnipotent, the divine, the all-powerful, then people will look at you and think you have gone crazy. How can you believe such things unless you are mad?

But try something. Start from the very beginning. Get a little feeling of this phenomenon, then belief will follow. If you want to use this technique, do this. Close your eyes and just feel that you have no body, feel as if the body has disappeared, melted away. Then you can feel your all-pervadingness. With the body it is difficult. That's why many traditions go on teaching that you are not the body because with the body, limitation comes in. It is not difficult to feel that you are not the body, because you are *not* the body. It is just a conditioning, it is just a thought that has been forced upon your mind. Your mind has been impregnated with the thought that you are the body.

There are phenomena which demonstrate this. In Sri Lanka, Buddhist monks walk on fire. They do in India also, but the Sri Lankan phenomenon is very rare—they walk for hours and they are not burned.

It happened once, just a few years ago, that a Christian missionary went to see the fire-walk. They do it on the night when Buddha became enlightened, a full-moon night, because they say that on that day it was revealed to the world that the body is nothing, matter is nothing; that the inner being is all-pervading and the fire cannot burn it. But to do this for one year the monks who walk on the fire purify their bodies, through *pranayama,* breathing processes, and fasting. They meditate to purify their minds, empty their minds. For one year continuously they prepare. They live in isolated cells just feeling that they are not in their bodies. For one year continuously a group of fifty or sixty monks goes on thinking that they are not their bodies. A year is a long time. Thinking every moment only one thing, that they are not their bodies, continuously hammering that the body is illusory, they come to believe it. Then too they are not forced to walk on the fire. They are brought to the fire and then whosoever thinks that he will not be burned, jumps into it. A few remain doubting, hesitating—they are not allowed to jump because this is not a question of fire burning or not, this is a question of their doubt. If they hesitate a little they are stopped. So sixty are prepared and sometimes twenty, sometimes thirty people jump into the fire and they dance in it for hours together without getting burned.

A missionary came to see it in 1950. He was very surprised but he thought that if belief in Buddha could do this miracle, then why not belief in Jesus? So he thought for a while, hesitated a little, but then, with the idea that if Buddha could help, Jesus would also help, he jumped. He got burned, badly burned; he had to be hospitalized for six months. And he couldn't understand the phenomenon. It was not a question of Jesus or Buddha, it was not a question of belief in someone, it was a question of belief. And that belief has to be hammered into the mind. Unless it reaches to the very core of your being, it will not start working.

That Christian missionary went back to England to study about hypnosis, mesmerism, and allied phenomena, and what happens during firewalking. Then they invited two monks to Oxford University to give a demonstration. The monks went. They walked on fire. The experiment was tried many times. Then the two monks saw that one professor was looking at them, and he was looking so deeply and he was so involved that his eyes, his face, were ecstatic. The two monks went to the professor and said to him, "You can also come with us." Immediately he ran with them, jumped into the fire, and nothing happened. He was not burned.

The Christian missionary was also present, and he knew well that this professor was a professor of logic, a man who is professionally doubtful, whose profession is based on doubt. So he said to the man, "What! You have done a miracle. I couldn't do it, and I am a believer."

The professor said, "In that moment I was a believer. The phenomenon was so real, so fantastically real, it gripped me. It was so clear that body is nothing and mind is everything and I felt so ecstatically in tune with the two monks that when they invited me, there was not a single hesitation. It was simple to walk, it was just as if there was no fire."

There was no hesitation, no doubt—that is the key.

So first try this experiment. Sit with closed eyes for a few days just thinking that you are not your body—not only thinking but feeling that you are not your body. And if you sit with closed eyes a distance is created. Your body goes on moving away and away. You go on moving inwards. A great distance is created. Soon you can feel that you are not the body. If you feel you are not the body, then you can believe you are all-pervading, omnipotent, omniscient, all-knowing, all-powerful. This all-powerfulness or this all-knowingness is not concerned with so-called knowledge; it is a feeling, an explosion of feeling—that you *know*. This has to be understood, particularly in the West, because whenever you say that you know, they will say, "What? What do you know?" Knowledge must be objective. You must know something. And if it is a question of knowing something you cannot be all-pervading, no one can be, because there are infinite facts to be known. No one can be all-knowing in that sense.

That's why in the West they laugh when Jains claim that Mahavira was *sarvagya*, all-knowing. They laugh, because if Mahavira was all-knowing, then he must have known all that science is discovering now and even that which science will discover in future. But that doesn't seem to be the case. He says many things which are obviously contradictory to science, which cannot be true, which are not factual. His knowledge, if it is all-pervading, should never be erroneous, but there are errors.

Christians believe that Jesus was all-knowing. But the modern mind will laugh because he was not all-knowing—all-knowing in the sense of knowing all about the facts of the world. He didn't know that the earth was circular, that the earth was a globe—he didn't know. He knew that the earth was flat ground. He didn't know that the earth had been in existence for millions and millions of years, he believed that God created it just four thousand years before him. As far as facts, objective facts are concerned, he was not all-knowing.

But this word "all-knowing" is totally different. When the Eastern sages say all-knowing, they don't mean knowing all about the facts—they mean all-conscious, all-aware, fully inside, fully conscious, enlightened. They are not concerned with knowing something, they are concerned only with the pure phenomenon of knowing—not knowledge, but the very quality of knowing. When we say that Buddha knows we don't mean that he knows what Einstein knows. He doesn't know that. He is a knower. He knows his own being and that being is all-pervading. That feeling of isness is all-pervading. And in that knowing nothing remains to be known, that is the point. Now there is no curiosity to know anything. All questions have dropped. Not that all answers have been achieved: all questions have dropped. Now there is no question to be asked. All curiosity has gone. There is no problem to be solved. This inner quietness, this inner silence, filled with inner light, is infinite knowing. This is what is meant by omniscient. It is subjective awakening.

This you can do. But it will not happen if you go on adding more knowledge to your mind. You can go on adding knowledge for lives together—you will know something but you will never know all. The all is infinite; it cannot be known in that way. Science will always remain incomplete, it can

never be complete—that's impossible. It is inconceivable that it can be complete. Really, the more science knows, the more it comes to know that more has to be known.

This all-knowingness is an inner quality of awakening. Meditate, and drop your thoughts. When you don't have any thoughts you will feel what this omniscience is, what this all-knowledge is. When there is no thought, consciousness becomes pure, purified; in that purified consciousness you don't have any problem. All questions have dropped. You know yourself, your being, and when you know your being, you have known all, because your being is the center of everybody's being. Really your being is everybody's being. Your center is the center of the universe. In this sense, the Upanishads have declared, *Aham Brahmasmi*—I am the Brahma, I am the absolute." Once you know this little phenomenon of your being you have known the infinite. You are just like a drop of the ocean: if even one drop is known, all the secrets of the ocean become revealed.

Believe omniscient, omnipotent, pervading. But this will come through faith, this you cannot argue with yourself. You cannot convince yourself with some argument, you will have to dig deep within you for such feelings, for sources of such feelings.

This word "believe'" is very significant. It doesn't mean that you have a conviction, because conviction means a rational thing. You are convinced, you have argued it over, you have proofs for it. Belief means you don't have any doubts about it, not that you have proofs. Conviction means you have proofs. You can prove, you can argue. You can say, "This is so." You can reason it out. Belief means you don't have any doubts. You cannot argue it, you cannot rationalize, you will be defeated if you are asked. But you have an inner grounding—you feel it is so. It is a feeling, not a reasoning.

But remember that such techniques can work only if you work with your feeling, not with your reasoning. So it has happened many times that very ignorant people, uneducated, uncultured, reach heights of human consciousness and those who are very cultured—educated, reasonable, rational—miss.

Jesus was just a carpenter. Friedrich Nietzsche writes somewhere that in the whole New Testament there was only one person really worth something, who was cultured, educated, philosophically knowledgeable, wise—that man was Pilate, the Roman governor who ordered Jesus to be crucified. Really he was the most cultured man, the governor-general, the viceroy, and he knew what philosophy was. At the last moment, when Jesus was going to be crucified, he asked, "What is truth?" It was a very philosophical question.

Jesus remained silent—not because this puzzle was not worth answering, Pilate was the only person who could have understood deep philosophy—Jesus remained silent because he could speak only to those who could feel. Thinking was not of any use. He was asking a philosophical question. It would have been good if he had asked in a university, in an academy, but asking Jesus a philosophical question was meaningless. He remained silent because it was futile to answer. No communication was possible. But Nietzsche, himself a man of reason, condemns Jesus. He said he was uneducated, uncultured, unphilosophical—and he couldn't answer, that's why he remained silent. Pilate asked a beautiful question. If he had asked it of Nietzsche, Nietzsche would have talked about it for years together. "What is truth?" This one question is enough to talk about and discuss for years. All of philosophy is just this business: "What is truth?" One question and all the philosophers are involved in it.

Nietzsche's criticism is really a criticism by reason, a condemnation by reason. Reason has always condemned the dimension of feeling because feeling is so vague, so mysterious. It is there, and you cannot say anything about it. Either you have got it or you haven't got it; either it is there or it is not there. You cannot do anything about it and you cannot discuss it. You also have many beliefs but those

beliefs are just convictions; they are not beliefs because you have doubts about them. You have crushed those doubts by your arguments, but they are there. You are sitting on top of them, but they are there. You go on fighting with them, but they are not dead. They cannot be. That's why your life may be that of a Hindu, or a Mohammedan, or a Christian, or a Jaina, but it is only because of conviction. Faith is not there.

I will tell you an anecdote. Jesus told his disciples to go by boat to the other bank of a lake where they were staying, and he said, "I will be coming later." They went. When they were just in the middle of the lake a great wind came and there was much turmoil and they were afraid. The boat was rocking and they started crying and screaming. They started crying, "Jesus, save us!"

The bank where Jesus was was very far away, but Jesus came. It is said that he came running on the water. And the first thing he said to his disciples was, "Men of little faith, why are you crying? Don't you believe?" They were scared. Jesus said, "If you believe, then come out of the boat and walk towards me." He was standing on the water.

They saw with their own eyes that he was standing on the water, but still it was difficult to believe. They must have thought in their minds that it was a trick, or it was maybe just an illusion, or this was not Jesus. Maybe it was just the devil, luring them or something. So they started looking at each other, "Who will walk?"

Then one disciple got out of the boat and walked. Really, he could walk. He couldn't believe his own eyes. He was walking on the water. When he came close to Jesus he said, "How? How is it happening?"

Immediately the whole miracle disappeared. The "How?"—and he was under water. Jesus pulled him out and said, "Man of little faith, why do you ask how?"

But reason asks "Why?" and "How?" Reason asks, reason questions. Faith is the dropping of all questions. If you can drop all questions and believe, then this technique can work miracles for you.

CHAPTER 74

Sensitivity is awareness

◆

Q U E S T I O N S

How to be sensitive and yet detached?

Why can You not heal Your own body?

To make earnest efforts or "Leave it to me"?

Did Jesus really believe the earth is round?

The first question:

With deepening meditation, one becomes more and more sensitive to objects, events and persons. But due to this heightened sensitivity one feels a sort of deep intimacy with everything, and this usually becomes a cause of subtle attachments. How to be sensitive and yet detached?

ow to be sensitive and yet detached? These two things are not contraries, they are not opposites. If you are more sensitive, you will be detached; or if you are detached, you will become more and more sensitive. Sensitivity is not attachment, sensitivity is awareness. Only an aware person can be sensitive. If you are not aware you will be insensitive. When you are unconscious you are totally insensitive—the more consciousness, the more sensitivity. A buddha is totally sensitive, he has optimum sensitivity, because he will feel and he will be aware to his total capacity. But when you are sensitive and aware you will not be attached. You will be detached, because the very phenomenon of awareness breaks the bridge, destroys the bridge, between you and things, between you and persons, between you and the world. Unconsciousness, unawareness, is the cause of attachment.

If you are alert, the bridge suddenly disappears. When you are alert there is nothing to relate you to the world. The world is there, you are there, but between the two the bridge has disappeared. The bridge is made of your unconsciousness. So don't think and feel that you become attached because you are more sensitive. No. If you are more sensitive you will not be attached. Attachment is a very gross quality, it is not subtle.

For attachment you need not be aware and alert. There is no need. Even animals can be attached very easily, rather, more easily. A dog is more attached to his master than any man can be. The dog is completely unconscious so attachment happens. That is why in the countries where human relationship has become poor, such as in the West, man goes on seeking relationship with animals, with dogs, with other animals, because the human relationship is no longer there. Human society is disappearing and every man feels isolated, alienated, alone. The crowd is there but you are not related to it. You are alone in the crowd and this aloneness scares. One becomes afraid and fearful.

When you are related, attached to someone, and someone is attached to you, you feel you are not alone in this world, in this strange world. Someone is with you. That feeling of belonging gives you a sort of security. When human relationship becomes impossible then men and women try to make relationships with animals. In the West they are very deeply related to dogs and other animals, but here in the East, although you may be worshipping cows you are not related to them. You may go on saying that you worship the cow as a divine animal, but your cruelty has no end.

In the East you are so cruel with your animals

that the West cannot even conceive of how you can go on thinking that you are nonviolent. All over the world, particularly in the West, there are many societies to protect animals from the cruelty of men. You cannot beat a dog in the West. If you beat it, it will be a criminal act and you will be punished for it. What is happening really is that human relationship is dissolving—but man cannot live alone. He must have a relationship, a belonging, a feeling that someone is with him. Animals can be very good friends because they get so attached; no one, no man, can get that attached.

For attachment, awareness is not necessary; rather, awareness is the barrier. The more aware you become the less you will be attached, because the need for attachment disappears. Why do you want to be attached to someone? Because alone you feel you are not enough. You lack something. Something is incomplete in you. You are not a whole. You need someone to complete you. Hence, attachment. If you are aware, you are complete, you are a whole; the circle is now complete, nothing is lacking in you—you don't need anyone. You, alone, feel a total independence, a feeling of wholeness.

That doesn't mean that you will not love persons; rather, on the contrary, only you *can* love. A person who is dependent on you cannot love you; he will hate you. A person who needs you cannot love you. He will hate you because you become the bondage. He feels that without you he cannot live, without you he cannot be happy, so you are the cause of both his happiness and unhappiness. He cannot afford to lose you. This will give a feeling of imprisonment: he is imprisoned by you and he will resent it, he will fight against it. Persons hate and love together, but this love cannot be very deep. Only a person who is aware can love, because he doesn't need you. But then love has a totally different dimension: it is not attachment, it is not dependence. He is not dependent on you and he will not make you dependent on him; he will remain a freedom and he will allow you to remain

a freedom. You will be two free agents, two total, whole beings, meeting. That meeting will be a festivity, a celebration—not a dependence. That meeting will be a fun, a play.

That is why we have called Krishna's life *Krishna-leela,* the play of Krishna. He loves so many persons but there is no attachment. The same is not true on the part of the *gopis* and the *gopals,* the friends and the girlfriends of Krishna. The same is not true. They have become attached, so when Krishna moves from Vrindavan to Dwaraka, they weep and cry and suffer. Their anguish is great because they think that Krishna has forgotten them. He has not forgotten, but there is no pain because there was no dependence; he is as whole and happy in Dwaraka as he was in Vrindavan and his love is flowing as much in Dwaraka as it was in Vrindavan. The objects of love have changed but the source of love remains the same. So whosoever comes near him receives the gift. And this gift is unconditional; nothing is required as a return, nothing is asked as a return.

When love comes through an aware consciousness it is just a pure gift with no condition, and the person who is giving it is happy because he is giving it. The very act of giving is his bliss, his ecstasy.

So remember that if you feel that through meditation you have become more sensitive, then automatically you will become less attached, more detached. Because you will be more grounded in yourself, you will be more centered in yourself, you will not use somebody else as your center. What does attachment mean? Attachment means that you are using someone else as your center of being, Majnu is attached to Laila: he says he cannot live without Laila. That means the center of being has been transferred. If you say that you cannot live without this or that, then your soul is not within you. Then you are not existing as an independent unit, your center has moved somewhere else.

This movement of the center from yourself to something else, to the other, is attachment. If you are sensitive, you will feel the other, but the other will not become the center of your life. You will remain the center and out of this centering the other will receive many gifts from you. But they will be gifts, they will not be bargains. You will simply give because you have too much, you are an overflowing. And you will be thankful that the other has received it. That will be enough and that will be the end.

That is why I go on saying that the mind is a great deceiver. You think that you are meditating and that that is why you have become sensitive. Then the question of why you get attached arises. If you get attached, that is a clear symptom that the sensitivity is not because of awareness. Really, it is not sensitivity at all. It may be sentimentalism, that is a totally different thing. You can be sentimental: you can cry and weep over small things, you can be touched, and a storm can be created very easily within you—but that is sentimentalism, not sensitivity.

Let me tell you a story. Buddha was staying in a village; a woman came to him, weeping and crying and screaming. Her child, her only child, had suddenly died. Because Buddha was in the village, people said, "Don't weep. Go to this man. People say he is infinite compassion. If he wills it, the child can revive. So don't weep, go to this Buddha."

The woman came with the dead child, crying, weeping, and the whole village followed her—the whole village was affected. Buddha's disciples were also affected; they started praying in their minds that Buddha would have compassion. He must bless the child so that he will be revived, resurrected.

Many disciples of Buddha started weeping. The scene was so touching, deeply moving. Everybody was still. Buddha remained silent. He looked at the dead child, then he looked at the weeping, crying mother and he said to the mother, "Don't weep, just do one thing and your child will be alive again. Leave this dead child here, go back to the town, go to every house and ask every family if someone has ever died in their family, in their house. And if you

can find a house where no one has ever died, then from them beg something to be eaten, some bread, some rice, or anything—but from the house where no one has ever died. And that bread or that rice will revive the child immediately. You go. Don't waste time."

The woman became happy. She felt that now the miracle was going to happen. She touched Buddha's feet and ran to the village, which was not a very big one—very few cottages, a few families. She moved from one family to another, asking. But every family said, "This is impossible. There is not a single house—not only in this village but all over the earth—there is not a single house where no one has ever died, where people have not suffered death and the misery and the pain and the anguish that comes out of it."

By and by the woman realized that Buddha had been playing a trick. This was impossible. But still the hope was there. She went on asking until she had gone around the whole village. Her tears dried, her hope died, but suddenly she felt a new tranquility, a serenity, coming to her. Now she realized that whosoever is born will have to die. It is only a question of years. Someone will die sooner, someone later, but death is inevitable.

She came back and touched Buddha's feet again and said to him, "As people say, you really do have a deep compassion for people." No one could understand what had happened. Buddha initiated her into sannyas, she became a *bhikkhuni*, a sannyasin. She was initiated.

Ananda asked Buddha, "You could have revived the boy. He was such a beautiful child and the mother was in such anguish."

But Buddha said, "Even if the child was resurrected, he would have had to die. Death is inevitable."

Ananda said, "But you don't seem to be very sensitive to people, to their misery and anguish."

Buddha replied, "I am sensitive; you are sentimental. Just because you start weeping, do you think you are sensitive? You are childish. You don't understand life. You are not aware of the phenomenon."

This is the difference between Christianity and Buddhism. Christ was reported to have done many miracles of reviving people. When Lazarus was dead, Jesus touched him and he came back to life. We in the East cannot conceive of Buddha touching a dead man and bringing him back to life. To ordinary persons, to the ordinary mind, Jesus would look more loving and compassionate than Buddha. But I say to you that Buddha is more sensitive, more compassionate, because even if Lazarus was revived, it made no difference. He still had to die. Finally Lazarus had to die. So this miracle was of no use, of no ultimate value. One cannot conceive of Buddha doing such a thing.

Jesus had to because he was bringing something new, a new message to Israel. And the message was so deep that people would not understand it, so he had to create miracles around it—because people can understand miracles but they cannot understand the deep message, the esoteric message. They can understand miracles, so through miracles they might become open and able to be receptive to the message. Jesus was carrying a Buddhist message to a land which was not Buddhist; an Eastern message to a country which had no tradition of enlightenment, of many buddhas.

We can conceive that Buddha was more sensitive than his disciples who were weeping and crying. They were sentimental.

Don't misunderstand your sentimentality for sensitivity. Sentimentality is ordinary; sensitivity is extraordinary. It happens through effort. It is an achievement. You have to earn it. Sentimentality is not to be earned; you are born with it. It is an animal inheritance which you already have in the cells of your body and your mind. Sensitivity is a possibility. You don't have it already. You can create it, you can work for it—then it will happen to you. And whenever it happens, you will be detached.

Buddha was totally detached. The dead child was there but he didn't seem to be affected at all. The woman, the mother, was miserable and he was

playing a trick on her. This man seems to be cruel and this playing of a trick seems to be too much for a mother whose child has died. He gave her a riddle, and he knew well that she would come back empty-handed. But I say again that he has real compassion because he was helping this woman to grow, to be mature. Unless you can understand death you are not mature; and unless you can accept death, you don't have a center within your being. When you accept death as a reality, you have transcended it.

Buddha used the situation. He was less concerned with the dead child and more concerned with the alive mother because he knew that the dead child would come back to life again—there was no need for the miracle. But if the child was revived the mother might have lost an opportunity. For lives together she might not again have a meeting with a buddha. So in the East only third-rate *sadhus* have been doing miracles; the first-rate have never done any—they work on a higher level. Buddha is also doing a miracle but the miracle is being done on a very high level. The mother is being transformed.

But it is difficult to understand because our minds are gross and we only understand sentimentality, we cannot understand sensitivity. Sensitivity means an alertness which feels everything that happens around. And you can feel only when you are not attached. Remember this: if you are attached you are no longer there to feel, you have moved out of you. So if you want to know the truth about someone don't ask his friends, they are attached. And don't ask his enemies, they are also attached, in the reverse order. Ask someone who is neutral, neither a friend nor an enemy. Only he can say the truth.

Friends cannot be believed, enemies cannot be believed; but we believe either the friends or the enemies. Both are bound to be wrong because they don't have a neutral witnessing, they don't have a detached view. They cannot stand aloof and look because they have an investment in the person.

Friends have an investment and enemies have an investment. They see according to particular viewpoints, and with those viewpoints they are attached. You cannot feel life in its totality if you are attached. The moment you feel you are attached, you have taken a viewpoint. The totality is lost; only a fragmentary thing is in your hands. And fragments are always lies because only the whole is true.

Meditate, become more sensitive, and take it as a criterion that you will go on becoming more and more detached. If you feel that attachment is growing, then you are erring somewhere in your meditation. These are the criteria. And to me, attachment cannot be destroyed and detachment cannot be practiced. You can only practice meditation—and detachment will follow as a consequence, as a by-product. If meditation really flowers within you, you will have a feeling of detachment. Then you can move anywhere and you will remain untouched, unafraid. Then when you leave your body, you will leave it unscratched. Your consciousness will be absolutely pure, nothing foreign has entered into it. When you are attached, impurities enter into you. This is the basic impurity: that you are losing your center and somebody else or something else is becoming your center of being.

The second question:

If faith can move mountains, why can You not heal Your own body?

I don't have any body.

This feeling that you have a body is absolutely wrong. The body belongs to the universe; you don't have it, it is not yours. So if the body is ill or if the body is healthy the universe will take care of it. And a person who is in meditation should remain a witness, whether the body is healthy or ill.

The desire to be healthy is part of ignorance. The desire not to be ill is also part of ignorance. And this is not a new question—this is one of the oldest questions. It has been asked of Buddha; it

has been asked of Mahavira. Ever since there have been enlightened persons, the unenlightened have always asked this question.

Look…Jesus said faith can move mountains, but he died on the cross. He couldn't move the cross. You or someone like you must have been present there waiting. The disciples were waiting because they knew Jesus, and he had been saying again and again that faith could move mountains. So they were waiting for some miracle to happen—and Jesus simply died on the cross. But this was the miracle: he could be a witness to his own death. And the moment of witnessing one's own death is the greatest moment of being alive.

Buddha died of food poisoning. He suffered for six months continuously, and there were many disciples who were waiting for him to do a miracle. But he suffered silently and died silently. He accepted death.

There were disciples there who were trying to cure him, many medicines were given to him. A great physician of those days, Jivaka, was Buddha's personal physician. He used to move with him wherever he went. Many times people must have asked, "Why does this Jivaka go with you?" But it was Jivaka's own attachment. Jivaka was moving with Buddha because of his own attachment, and the disciples who were trying to help Buddha's body remain alive longer in this world, even if only for a few days more, were also attached.

For Buddha himself, illness and health were the same. That doesn't mean that illness will not give pain. It will! Pain is a physical phenomenon, it will happen. But it will not disturb the inner consciousness. The inner consciousness will remain undisturbed, it will remain as balanced as ever. The body will suffer, but the inner being will remain just a witness of the whole suffering.

There will be no identification—and this I call the miracle. This is possible through faith.

And no mountain is bigger than identification—remember. The Himalayas are nothing; your identification with your body is a greater mountain.

The Himalayas may be moved or not moved through faith, that is irrelevant, but your identification *can* be destroyed.

But we cannot conceive of anything which we do not know, we can think only according to our minds. We think according to where we are; the pattern remains the same.

Sometimes my body is ill, and people come to me and they say, "Why are you ill? You should not be ill; an enlightened person should not be ill." But who told you that it is so? I have never heard about any enlightened person who was not ill. Illness belongs to the body. It has no concern with your consciousness or whether you are enlightened or not.

And sometimes it happens that enlightened persons are more ill than unenlightened ones. There are reasons…. Now that they don't belong to the body, they don't cooperate with the body; deep down they have broken themselves from the body. So the body remains but the attachment and the bridge is broken.

Many illnesses happen because of the separation that has happened. They are in the body but their cooperation is no longer there. That is why we say an enlightened person will never be born again —because now he cannot make any bridge with any body again. The bridge is broken. While he is in the body, then too, really, he is dead.

Buddha attained enlightenment when he was nearabout forty. He died when he was eighty so he lived forty years more. On the day he was dying, Ananda started crying and said, "What will happen to us? Without you we will fall into darkness. You are dying and we have not yet become enlightened. Our own light is not yet lit and you are dying. Do not leave us!"

Buddha is reported to have said, "What? What are you saying, Ananda? I died forty years before. This existence was just a phantom existence, a shadow existence. It was running along somehow, but the force was not there. It was just a momentum from the past."

If you are pedaling a bicycle, and then you stop and there is no pedaling, you are not giving any cooperation to the cycle, it will go on moving for a little while just because of the momentum, the energy that you gave it in the past.

The moment someone becomes enlightened, the cooperation is broken. Now the body will take its own course. It has a momentum. From many lives in the past, momentum has been given to it. It has a life span of its own which will be completed, but now, because the inner force is no longer with it, the body is prone to be more ill than ordinarily. Ramakrishna died of cancer; Raman died of cancer. To the disciples it was a great shock, but because of their ignorance they could not understand.

One thing more has to be understood. When a person becomes enlightened, this is going to be his last life. So all the past karmas and the whole continuum has to be fulfilled in this life. The suffering—if he has anything to suffer—will become intense. For you there is no hurry, your suffering will be spread out over many lives. But for a Raman this is the last. All that is there from the past has to be completed. There will be an intensity of everything, of all karmas. This life will become a condensed life.

Sometimes it is possible—this is difficult to understand—to suffer in a single moment the sufferings of many lives. In a single moment, the intensity becomes much because time can be condensed or spread out.

You know already that sometimes when you sleep you see a dream, and when you are awake again you know that you have been asleep for only a few seconds. But you have seen such a long dream. It is possible that even a whole life can be seen in a single dream.

What has happened? In such a small period of time how could you see such a long dream? There is not a single layer of time as we ordinarily understand, there are many layers of time. Dream time has its own existence. Even while awake time goes on changing. It may not change according to the clock because a clock is a mechanical thing, but psychological time goes on changing.

When you are happy, the time flows fast. When you are unhappy, the time slows down. A single night can be eternity if you are in suffering, and a whole life can become a single moment if you are happy and blissful.

When a person becomes enlightened, everything has to be closed; this is a closing time. Many millions of lives have to be closed and all the accounts have to be cleared, because there will be no chance anymore. After his enlightenment an enlightened person lives in a different time altogether and whatsoever happens to him is qualitatively different. But he remains a witness.

Mahavira died of stomach pain, something like an ulcer—for many years he suffered. His disciples must have been in difficulty because they have created a story around it. They could not understand why Mahavira should suffer, so they have created a story which shows something about the disciples, not about Mahavira.

They say that a person who had a very evil spirit, Goshalak, was the cause of Mahavira's suffering. He threw his evil force on Mahavira and Mahavira absorbed it only because of his compassion—and that is why he suffered. This shows nothing about Mahavira but something about the difficulty of the disciples. They cannot conceive of Mahavira suffering so they had to find a cause somewhere else.

One day I was suffering from a cold—it is my constant companion. So somebody came and he said, "You must have taken somebody else's cold." That doesn't show anything about me, it shows something about him. It is difficult for him to conceive of me suffering. So he said, "You must have somebody else's cold." I tried to convince him, but it is impossible to convince disciples. The more you try to convince them, the more they believe that they are right. In the end he said to me, "Whatsoever you say I am not going to listen. I know! You have taken somebody else's illness."

What to do? The body's health and illness is its own affair. If you want to do something about it, you are still attached to it. It will take its own course; you need not be much worried about it.

I am only a witness. The body is born, the body will die; only the witnessing will be there. It will remain forever. Only witnessing is something absolutely eternal—everything else goes on changing, everything else is a flux.

The third question:

Last night You explained in detail about how seekers deceive themselves by not making earnest and sincere efforts toward meditation. But with many of the seekers who earnestly ask You for meditation techniques, You simply say to them to leave everything to You and that You will look after their spiritual progress. But many seekers feel dissatisfaction about their spiritual transformation that way. In this case, please explain how these seekers are deceiving themselves.

Firstly, when they ask for a technique, I give them a technique. This is a technique: Leave everything to me. This is one of the most powerful techniques possible. And don't think that it is easy; it is very difficult, sometimes impossible. It is difficult to leave everything to somebody, but if you can, in that very surrender your ego has disappeared; in that very surrender, your past has disappeared; in that very surrender a new point is born—you are different. Up to now you were living with your own ego; from now onwards you will be living without the ego, you will be following a path of surrender.

So don't think that this is not a technique! It is a technique—one of the very basic techniques. And I don't give it to any and everybody. I give it only to particular persons who are very egoistic, because for them any technique will create trouble. Their ego will exploit it. They will become more egoistic through it. They can practice anything except this, but by that practice their ego is not going to be destroyed; rather, it will be more fulfilled. They will become great meditators. They can renounce the world, but their ego will be strengthened whatsoever they do. Whenever I feel that this seeker has such a subtle ego that any method will be poisonous to him, then only do I say, "Leave everything to me." Not that this is going to be the end, but this is going to be the beginning. And this is going to be the right beginning for all those who are ego-centered. If they can leave everything to me, then I will start giving them other techniques—but only then. Then other techniques will not prove poisonous. Once the ego is not there those techniques will transform them. And if their surrender is so total that nothing is left to be transformed, then there will be no need for any other technique. This too is possible, and this is possible only for those who are very egoistic; only they can surrender totally.

This will look confusing, paradoxical—but remember, you can leave something only if you have it. If you don't have a very strong ego, what can you leave? What can you surrender? It is just like asking a beggar to surrender all his riches. He will be ready, he will say, "Okay," but his okay means nothing. It is absolutely futile because he has nothing to lose. And if you have a very strong ego, that means a very concentrated ego, crystallized, you can leave it totally because it will be difficult to leave it in parts. It is so concentrated and crystallized that it will be difficult to leave it in fragments. Either you can leave it or not. It is one of the paradoxes of life that for surrender a very authentic ego is needed to be there in the first place. So to me, a right education will consist in creating strong egos, to the very extreme, where a great suffering is born out of them, and then—surrender. Only then is surrender possible.

This has been my experience. People coming from the West have stronger egos than the Eastern people because in the West there is no concept of surrender, no concept of obedience, no concept of guru and disciple. Really, the Western mind cannot conceive of what a guru is. And they cannot conceive of someone surrendering to anybody. The whole Western education, culture and civilization is based on ego, ego-fulfillment. And Western psychologists say that to be mentally healthy, you must have a strong ego. So all the Western psychologies help the ego to be strong: a child's ego must be strengthened in every way otherwise he will become mentally ill.

But Eastern religions say that unless you leave the ego you cannot know the ultimate truth, you cannot know what life's mystery is. Both seem to be contradictory, but they are not. To me, the Western training must be there in the beginning with every person all over the world. Every person should be given a strong ego. By the age of thirty-five you should reach to the peak of your ego; at the age of thirty-five it should be at its peak, strong, as strong as possible. Only then will surrendering happen. So whenever Western seekers come to me and I tell them to leave things to me, they are very hesitant, resistant. And it seems impossible, but sometimes, when surrender happens, they achieve a much deeper realization.

With Eastern people surrender is not very difficult. They are ready. You say, "Surrender," they say, "Yes." There is not a single hesitation on their part. They don't have very strong, developed egos. They can surrender it—but that surrender is impotent. It will not help. So it almost always happens that with the Eastern person I immediately give him a technique to work on, so that it helps his ego. With Western people I immediately say, "Surrender." They have already reached that point within them so they can surrender; their very hesitancy shows that they can surrender. But their surrender is going to be a struggle, and when it is a struggle it is a *sadhana*. When it is a struggle it means something; it is going to transform them.

So firstly, when I say, "Leave everything to me," this is a technique; and I say it only to people who have very developed egos. Secondly...*but many seekers feel dissatisfaction about their spiritual transformation that way.* Right, these are the people to whom I say, "Surrender." They feel very dissatisfied. They want something to do, they don't want to surrender. I know they will feel dissatisfied because their ego will resist; it will try in every way not to surrender. But that cannot be helped. They will have to pass through this dissatisfaction, and they will have to understand that leaving everything to me is just the beginning. If they cannot do that, I am not going to give them any technique right now. They can leave me, or leave everything to me. There is no other alternative. Once I say to someone, "Leave everything to me," I am not going to give any technique to him. I know that it will be difficult and arduous—but it has to be so. The more difficult, the more arduous, the better, because that means he has a more evolved ego, and it is struggling. He will have to come someday—to me or to someone else, it is irrelevant—and he will have to surrender it.

The master is not so relevant; the surrendering is relevant. Where you surrender is of no significance. You can surrender to a stone buddha, that will do. Surrendering transforms you. It is putting your ego aside, unburdening yourself; living for the first time not out of the past but moving into the present, fresh and young, unburdened.

And the third thing: *In this case, please explain how these seekers are deceiving themselves.* They can deceive themselves. They can say to me, "Yes, we leave everything to you," and go on withholding everything. They can deceive themselves that they have surrendered and they can go on insisting on their own ways. Surrender cannot be partial, it can be only total—and then you cannot set your conditions, your likes and dislikes.

It happened just a few days ago. A man came to me and he said, "I will leave everything to you. Whatsoever you say, I will do."

I told him, "Repeat it again slowly, 'Whatsoever you say, I will do.'" He repeated it. I told him to repeat it again and go more slowly.

He became a little disturbed and said, "Why?" And he also became aware of why I was saying go slowly. He said, "You may be right. I should not say this, because it is very difficult to leave everything to you and it will be difficult to follow whatsoever you say." So I told him to make it conditional, to be exact so that he could not change. He said, "Right. Whatsoever I like—give me the freedom to choose."

This is how you can deceive. Inside *you* remain the master; you go on choosing what to do and what not to do. And as it happens, whatsoever you choose is going to be wrong because the mind that is choosing is wrong; otherwise there would have been no need to come to me. When I say surrender it means that now you will not choose, now I will choose and you will follow. And if you can follow totally, the day is not far away when I will say, "Now there is no need. Now you can choose."

You must disappear; the surface, the superficial ego must disappear. Then your own being comes into being. I am not going to keep you following me for ever and ever. That is not a very happy business. When your ego is no longer there, your own guru, the inside master, has come into being. The outer guru is nothing but a representative of the inner one. Once the inner is there, the outer is not needed. And your own guru will say to you, "Now follow yourself. Move alone. Now you don't need anybody to guide you, the inner guide has come into being. Now you have your own inner light, you can see through it. It will show you the path."

But right now, as you are, it is not possible. You don't have any light. You cannot see. And wherever your mind leads you it will be wrong. This mind has been leading you for lives and it always leads you into particular patterns. It has old habits and it leads you accordingly. It is a mechanical thing. Just to create a break, surrender is needed. If you surrender to something, even for a few days, there will be a gap between now and your past. A new force has entered within you. Now you cannot continue with the past; your way, as it has always been, cannot be any more. A turning will happen. This gap is what is meant by surrender.

But you can deceive. You can say, "Yes, I surrender," and you may not have surrendered. Or you may think that you have surrendered but unconsciously you are fighting. Not only in surrender, but in everything where a let-go is needed, we fight.

In the West much research is going on about the phenomenon of sex, because people are becoming less and less capable of deep orgasms. They have sex but no ecstasy comes out of it. It has become a boring affair. They feel only frustrated, only weakened through it. And then it becomes a routine. They don't know what to do. A deep ecstasy through the orgasm is its significance. If it doesn't happen it is futile and useless and even harmful.

Many schools of psychology go on working on the questions: "What has happened to man? Why is he not achieving orgasm through sex? Why is there so much dissatisfaction?" All the researches indicate that the reason is that man cannot surrender—that is why he cannot achieve orgasm. Even while making love, while deep in sex, your mind remains in control. You go on controlling. You are not in a let-go. You are afraid to let go because if you allow the sex energy to move uncontrolled you don't know where it will lead. You may go mad, you may even die. That is the fear. So you remain in control.

You go on manipulating your body. This manipulation from the mind doesn't allow the whole body to become a flow of energy. Then sex becomes a local affair, the whole body is not involved, the whole body is not in an inner dance; the ecstasy is missed. You lose energy and you don't gain anything—there is bound to be frustration. So psychologists say that you will not achieve a deep ecstasy unless you are in a deep let-go, unless the mind is not there and the ego is not there; unless the body has taken over with its own force, its own momentum, and is moving by its own unconscious sources; unless *you* are not there. That ecstasy can give you a first glimpse of the ultimate ecstasy that happens in a total let-go of your ego with the divine, with the universe.

Samadhi, the ultimate goal of all yoga and tantra, is a deep orgasm with the universe itself, with the existence itself. The guru is just trying to help you, to bring you to a point where you can at least surrender the ego. Then a deep ecstasy will happen between you and your master. Wherever there is a let-go, ecstasy happens—that is the law.

So if you can surrender to a guru, don't listen to anybody. Even if the whole world says that this guru is wrong, don't listen to it. If you can surrender, this guru is right. You will achieve an ecstatic moment through him. And if the whole world says that this guru is right, and you cannot surrender, he is useless for you. So wherever you have the feeling of surrendering, there is your guru, your master.

Search for the place, search for the person in whose presence you can allow a let-go, in whose presence you can drop your mind even for a time. Once this force from the outside enters into you, your path will be different, your life will have taken a new turning.

You can deceive yourself: you can go on thinking that you have surrendered but you know well inside that you have not surrendered. And remember: you cannot deceive a master—he knows. And he will go on insisting unless the let-go really happens. You can maneuver, you can play a game, but you cannot deceive a master. You can put your head to his feet but that gesture means nothing. It may be just a superficial gesture, you are not bowing down at all. But if bowing down really happens, the master can work.

So whenever I say, "Surrender," or "Leave it to me and I will take care," I mean it. Exactly whatsoever I say I mean it. I want to create a gap within you, a discontinuity with the past. Once the gap is there, you will sooner or later become capable of going on your own. But before that, if you go on your own, you will continue the past story. Nothing new is possible. For the new, something from the outside must enter you, must push you onto a new path.

The last question:

You said that Jesus didn't know that the earth is round. So for Christians who believe that Jesus was God, this seems very strange. Isn't it implied that an enlightened one like Jesus, who knew deep occult sciences, must also know many astronomical and astrological facts about planets, the universe, and the interrelationship of celestial bodies? Please explain.

No, Jesus was not concerned. When Jesus said that the world was flat, he was using the knowledge that was prevalent in those days. He was not concerned about whether the world was round or flat; it was meaningless to him. He was more concerned about those persons who were living on this flat or round earth.

The concern has to be understood. It is absolutely futile for Jesus to discuss these things. What difference does it make? For example, you know from the geography books that the world is round. If your geography books were teaching that the world is flat, as they were teaching in the past, what difference will it make to you? Will you be a better man? Will you be more meditative on a flat world or on a round earth? What difference will it make to your being and the quality of your consciousness? It is irrelevant.

Jesus was concerned with your consciousness, and he would not unnecessarily argue about things which are useless. Only unenlightened persons are dragged into unnecessary things. If you had told Jesus that the world was round, he would have said yes. It makes no difference to him because that was not his concern. The prevalent idea was that the world was flat. And really, to the ordinary mind, the world is still flat. It looks flat. The roundness is a scientific fact, but Jesus was not a scientist.

For example, I know that it is a scientific fact that the sun never rises and never sets. The earth is moving around, the sun is not moving. But still I use the words 'sunset' and 'sunrise'. Sunrise is basically wrong. The very word is wrong, because the sun never rises. Sunset is wrong, the sun never sets. So after two thousand years, someone can say that this man was unenlightened because he said the sun rises: sunrise, sunset. Didn't he know these small things?

But if I am to change every word then I will be fighting unnecessarily and that is not going to help anybody. Jesus simply used the prevalent knowledge —and the prevalent idea was that the earth was flat. He was not concerned about it. If he were here today, he would say that the earth is round. But even that is not exactly scientific, because the earth is not exactly round. Now they say it is like an egg, not exactly round. The shape is like an egg. But who knows?—the next day they may change and say that this is not so. Science goes on changing, because as it becomes more accurate, as it attains to more knowledge, as more facts are known, as more experiments are done, things change. But a person like Jesus or Buddha is not concerned about these facts.

Remember one thing: science is concerned with facts, religion is concerned with truth. Facts are not its concern, truth is its concern. Facts are about objects, truth is about you, your consciousness. So every enlightened person has to use the prevalent knowledge about facts. But you should not judge Jesus or Buddha by that—you are judging wrongly. They can be judged only by what they have said about the truth, about the intrinsic truth of human consciousness. About that they are always absolutely right although their language differs.

Buddha speaks in one language, Jesus in a different one, Krishna in another. They use different factual knowledge, they use different techniques, devices, but the central core of their teaching is the same. And that, if you allow me to say it, is how to attain to total awareness.

Awareness is the basic teaching of all the enlightened ones. They use many parables, techniques, devices, symbols, myths, but those are irrelevant. You can cut them away, you can put them aside and just bring out the basic core. The basic core of all the awakened persons is awareness. So Jesus goes on telling his disciples how to be more awake—not to be sleeping, not to move in dreams, but to be alert, awake.

He used to tell a parable. He said that it happened once that a great lord, a great master, a very rich man, went on a faraway journey. He told his servants that they had to be always alert because he would be back any moment, *any* moment, and whenever he came back, the house should be ready to receive him. He could come back any moment. The servants had to be alert, they couldn't even sleep. Even at night they had to be ready because the master could come any moment.

Jesus used to say that you have to be alert every moment because any moment the divine can descend into you. You may miss. If the divine knocks at your door and you are fast asleep, you will miss.

You have to be alert. The guest can come at any moment, and the guest is not going to inform you beforehand that he is coming.

Jesus said just like the servants of that master, remain alert continuously, remain aware, waiting, watchful because any moment the divine can penetrate you. And if you are not alert, he will come, knock, and go back. And that moment may not be repeated soon; no one knows how many lives it may take before the divine will again knock at your door. And if you have become habitually asleep, you may have missed that knock many times already and you may miss it again and again.

Be alert. That is the basic core. All else is only to be used to reach it. So just because Jesus says the earth is flat, he doesn't become unenlightened. And just because you know the earth is round, you don't become enlightened. It is not so easy!

CHAPTER 75

Seek the rhythm of opposites

◆

102 *Imagine spirit simultaneously within and around you until the entire universe spiritualizes.*

103 *With your entire consciousness in the very start of desire, of knowing, know.*

104 *O Shakti, each particular perception is limited, disappearing in omnipotence.*

105 *In truth forms are inseparate. Inseparate are omnipresent being and your own form. Realize each as made of this consciousness.*

One of the greatest poets, Walt Whitman, is reported to have said, "I contradict myself because I am big. I contradict myself because I contain all the opposites, because I am all." The same thing can be said about Shiva, about tantra.

Tantra is the search for the rhythm of opposites, of contradictions. Contradictory, opposite standpoints become one in tantra. This has to be deeply understood; only then will you be able to understand why there are so many contradictory, different techniques. Life is a rhythm between opposites: male and female, positive and negative, day and night, birth and death. Between these opposites moves the river of life. The opposites are the banks —they appear to be contradictory, but they are cooperative. The appearance is false. Life cannot exist without this rhythm between the opposites. And life contains all. Tantra is neither for this nor for that—tantra is for all. Tantra has no standpoint of its own, really; all standpoints that are possible are contained in it. It is big. It can contradict itself because it contains all. It is not partial, it is the whole. Hence it is holy.

All partial standpoints are bound to be profane; they cannot be holy if they don't contain the opposite. They may be logical and rational, but they cannot be alive. Wherever life exists, it exists through its opposite. It cannot exist alone, the opposite is a must.

In Greek mythology, two gods are at polar opposites: Apollo and Dionysius. Apollo is the god of order, discipline, virtue, morality, culture, and Dionysius is the god of disorder, chaos, freedom, nature. Both are polar opposites. Almost all religions are more or less based on the Apollonian standpoint. They believe in reason, they believe in order, they believe in virtue, they believe in discipline, control…really they believe in the ego.

But tantra is basically different: it contains both. It contains the Dionysian standpoint also. It believes in nature, it believes in chaos, it believes in laughing and dancing and singing; it is not just serious, it is both. It is *both* serious and nonserious. Nietzsche writes in one of his letters, "I can believe only in a dancing god." He couldn't find any dancing god. Had he known something about Shiva then the story of his life would have been totally different. Shiva is the dancing god. Nietzsche knew only about the Christian god. That is the only standpoint—very serious. Sometimes the seriousness of the Christian god looks absurd, childish, because the opposite is denied completely. You cannot conceive of a Christian god dancing. Impossible! Dancing looks too earthly. And you cannot conceive of a Christian god laughing—or can you? It is impossible. The Christian god cannot laugh. Laughter will look too worldly. The Christian god is the very spirit of seriousness and Nietzsche couldn't believe in it.

And I think that no one can believe in such a god because it is half, it is not the whole. Only persons like Billy Graham can believe in it. Somewhere Billy Graham says very seriously that when you are reading sexy magazines you must remember that God is looking at you. This looks foolish. You are reading a sexy magazine and God is seeing you reading the sexy magazines!

This very attitude is stupid. It is stupid because it doesn't contain the opposite. You will become stupid and dead if the opposite is denied. But if you can move to the opposite easily with no contradiction, if you can be serious and you can be laughing, if you can sit like a Buddha and you can dance like a Krishna—and there is no inherent opposition between these two, you can move from being a Buddha towards being a Krishna easily and smoothly—if you can do this, you will be alive. And if you can do this you will be a tantric, because tantra is the basic search for the rhythm which exists between the opposites, for the river which flows between the opposites.

So tantra goes on working on all and every technique possible. Tantra is not for someone, it is for all. Every type of mind can move through tantra. Every type of mind cannot be Christian, every type of mind cannot be Hindu, every type of mind cannot be Buddhist. A particular type of mind will be attracted by Buddha, a particular type by Jesus, a particular type by Mohammed. Shiva contains all. Shiva can have an appeal for every type possible. The total, the whole has been included, it is not a partial standpoint. That is why tantra has no sect. You cannot create a sect around the whole, you can create a sect only around a fragment. You can live the whole, but you cannot create a sect. A sect can be created only when you are for something and against something else. If both the opposites are contained, how can you create a sectarian mind? Tantra is the essential religion, it is not a sect. Hence so many techniques.

People keep on coming to me and asking, "There are so many techniques and one technique contradicts the other?" Yes, it contradicts the other because it is not meant for a particular mind. In these hundred and twelve techniques, all the types, all the possible types of humanity have been included. Please don't be concerned with all the techniques, otherwise you will get confused. You simply find that which suits you, that which appeals to you. Towards it you will feel a deep affinity, an attraction; you will fall in love with it. Then forget all the remaining one hundred and eleven techniques. Forget them. You just stick to the one that works for you. In these one hundred and twelve techniques, only one technique is for you. If you try many techniques you will get confused, because to try so many techniques you will need a very big mind which can absorb contradiction. That is not possible right now. One day it may become possible. You can become so complete, so total, that you can move easily with many techniques. Then there will be no problem. But then there will also be no need! Right now is the need. Find your technique.

I can be helpful to you in finding which technique will be suitable for you. And if you feel that other techniques are contradictory to the technique that suits you, don't think about them. They are contradictory, but they are not for you. At least they are not for you now. One day it may become possible that when you don't have the ego within, you can move to the opposite without any problem. The ego creates the problem. It is stuck somewhere, it clings to something, it is not liquid, it cannot flow. And Shiva is flowing in all directions.

So remember, don't start thinking about these techniques: that this technique is against that. Shiva is not trying to create a system, he is not a system maker. Shiva is giving all the techniques without any systematizing. They cannot be systematized, because a system means that the contradictory, the opposite, must be denied. And here the opposite is included. It is both Apollo and Dionysius, it is both serious and laughing; it is both immanent and transcendent, it is both earthly and unearthly—because it is all.

Now we should enter the techniques.

102 Imagine spirit within and without.

The first technique: *Imagine spirit simultaneously within and around you until the entire universe spiritualizes.*

First you must understand what imagination is. It is condemned very much nowadays. The moment you hear the word "imagine" you will say this is useless, we want something real, not imaginary. But imagination is a reality, it is a capacity, it is a potentiality within you. You can imagine. That shows that your being is capable of imagination. This capacity is a reality. Through this imagination you can destroy or you can create yourself. That depends on you. Imagination is very powerful. It is potential power.

What is imagination? It is getting into an attitude so deeply that the very attitude becomes reality. For example, you may have heard about a technique which is used in Tibet. They call it heat yoga. The night is cold, snow is falling, and the Tibetan lama will be standing naked under the open sky. The temperature is below zero—you would simply start dying, you would freeze. But the lama is practicing a particular technique. That technique is that he is imagining that his body is a burning fire and he is imagining that he is perspiring—the heat is so much that he is perspiring. And he actually starts perspiring although the temperature is below zero and even the blood should freeze. He starts perspiring. What is happening? This perspiration is real, his body is really hot—but this reality is created through imagination.

You just try some simple technique so that you can feel how reality can be created through imagination. Unless you feel it, you cannot work with this technique. Just count your pulse. Sit in a closed room and count your pulse. And then for five minutes just imagine that you are running. Imagine that you are running, it is hot, you are taking deep breaths, you are perspiring, and your pulse rate is

going high. After imagining this for five minutes again count your pulse. You will see the difference: your pulse rate will be high. You have worked it just by imagination, you were not really running.

In old Tibet, Buddhist monks used to do exercise only through imagination. And those techniques can be of much use for modern man, because it is difficult to run in the street, difficult to have a long walk, difficult to find a lonely street. You can just lie down on the floor in your room and imagine that for one hour continuously you are taking a long fast walk. Just in imagination go on walking. And now even medical experts say that the effect would be the same as if it were a real walk. Once you get in tune with your imagination, the body starts functioning.

You are already doing many things without knowing that it is your imagination working. Many times you create illnesses just through imagination; you imagine that now this disease is there, infectious, it is all over the place. You have become receptive, now there is every possibility that you will fall ill—and that illness is real. But it has been created through imagination. Imagination is a force, an energy, and the mind moves through it. And when the mind moves through it, the body follows.

It happened once in a university hostel in the United States that four students were trying an experiment in hypnosis. Hypnosis is nothing but imagination power. When you hypnotize a person, he is really falling into deep imagination, and whatsoever you suggest will start happening. So they suggested many things to a boy that they had hypnotized. Four boys tried hypnosis on one. They tried many things and whatsoever they said, the boy immediately followed. When they said, "Jump," the boy started jumping. When they said, "Weep," the boy started weeping. When they said, "Tears are flowing from your eyes," tears started flowing. Then just as a joke they said, "Now lie down. You are dead!" And the boy lay down and he was dead.

This happened in 1952. After that they made a

law against hypnosis in the United States. No one should try hypnosis unless some research work is involved; unless some medical institute, or some psychological department of some university authorizes you. Only then can you experiment. Otherwise it is dangerous—the boy simply believed, imagined, that he was dead, and he was dead.

If death can occur through imagination, why not life, why not more life?

This technique is based on the power of imagination. *Imagine spirit simultaneously within and around you until the entire universe spiritualizes.*

Just sit in a lonely place where no one will disturb you—a lonely secluded room will do. Or if you can get somewhere outside it will be better, because when you are near nature you are more imaginative. When there are only man-made things around you, you are less imaginative. Nature is dreaming, and it gives you a dreaming force. Alone you become more imaginative; that's why you are afraid when you are alone. It is not that ghosts are going to trouble you, but alone your imagination can work, and your imagination can create ghosts or anything you want it to. When you move alone, your imagination is more potential; when someone else is there, your reason is in control, because without reason you cannot be related to the others. When there is no one there, the mind relaxes and you regress to a deeper imaginative layer of the being. When you are alone, imagination starts functioning.

Many experiments have been done with sensory deprivation. If a person can be deprived of all sensory stimuli—if you are closed in a soundproof room with no light entering it, no possibility of being related to any other human being, no pictures on the walls, nothing in the room to which you can relate—after one, two or three hours you will start relating to yourself. You will become imaginative. You will start talking to yourself. You will question and you will answer. A monologue will start in which you will be divided. Then suddenly you will start feeling many things which you cannot understand. You will start hearing sounds, but the room is soundproof, no sound can come in. Now you are imagining. You may start smelling perfumes, but no perfume is there. Now you are imagining. After thirty-six hours of sensory deprivation, you cannot make any difference between what is real and what is imaginary—impossible. After thirty-six hours of sensory deprivation, imagination becomes reality and reality becomes illusory.

That is why seekers in the old days would move to the mountains, to the lonely places, where they could lose the distinction between the real and the unreal. Once the distinction is lost, your imagination is in full force. Now you can use it and you can be creative through it.

For this technique sit in a lonely place: if the surrounding is natural, it is good; if not, then a room can also do. Then close your eyes and imagine a spiritual force is felt within and without. Within you a river of consciousness is flowing and it is going all over the room, overflowing. Within and without, around you, everywhere, spirit is present, energy is present. And don't imagine it only in the mind, start feeling within the body—your body will start vibrating. When you feel that the body has started vibrating, it shows that the imagination has started functioning. Feel that the whole universe by and by is spiritualized—everything, the walls of the room, the trees around you, everything has become nonmaterial, it has become spiritual. Matter is no more.

That is the reality also. Physicists say that matter is illusory and energy is real, and wherever you see solid things, that solidity is just an appearance, it is not there. As physics enters deeper into the world of matter, matter disappears. Only energy, immaterial energy, remains indefinable.

Through imagination you are reaching to a point where, by your conscious effort, you are destroying the structures of the intellect, the patterns of the intellect. You feel that there is no matter, only energy, only spirit, within and without. Soon you will feel that within and without have disappeared. When your body becomes spiritual and you feel it is energy, then there is no distinction between the within and the without. The boundaries are lost. Now there is only a flow, an ocean, vibrating. This is the real also—you are reaching to the real through imagination.

What is imagination doing? Imagination is only destroying the old concepts, matter, old patterns of the mind which go on looking at things in a certain way. Imagination is destroying them. And then the reality will be revealed.

Imagine spirit simultaneously within and around you until the entire universe spiritualizes—until you feel that all distinctions have disappeared, all boundaries have dissolved and the universe has become just an ocean of energy. That is the fact, also. But the deeper you proceed in the technique, the more scared you will become. You will feel as if you are going mad, because your sanity consists of distinctions, your sanity consists of this so-called reality and when the reality starts disappearing, you will feel that simultaneously your sanity is disappearing. Saints and insane persons move in a world which is beyond our so-called reality. They both move, but the insane persons fall and saints go beyond. The difference is very small but it is very great also. If without any effort on your part you lose your mind and the distinctions, the real and the unreal, you will become insane. But if you destroy the concepts with conscious effort, you will become "un-sane," not insane. That "un-sanity" is the dimension of religion. It is beyond sanity. But conscious effort is needed. You should not be a victim, you should remain a master. When it is your effort which is destroying the patterns of the mind, you look into the unpatterned reality.

The unpatterned reality is the only reality; the patterned reality is just imposed. That's why now anthropologists say that every society, every culture, looks at the same reality but finds a different reality there, because their patterns, their concepts are different. There are many cultures in the world, primitive cultures. They look at the same

world in a very different way; their interpretation is totally different. The reality is the same for us and for them, but the pattern looked through is different. For example, Buddhists say that there is no substance in the world, the world is a process. There is nothing substantial. Everything is in movement—or even that may not be the right thing to say. Movement is the only thing. When we say that everything is in movement, again there is the old fallacy—it is as if there is something which is moving. Buddha says there is nothing which is moving—only movement is there. That is all that there is.

So in a Buddhist country like Thailand or Burma, they don't have any corresponding word for "is" in their languages. When the Bible was translated into Thai for the first time, it became a problem to translate it because in the Bible it is said that "God is." You cannot say that "God is" in Burmese or in Thai; you cannot say it. Whatsoever they say will mean, "God is becoming." Everything is moving, nothing is. When a Burmese looks at the world, he looks at movement. When we look, when particularly the Greek-oriented Western mind looks, there is no process, only substance. There are dead things, not movements. Even when you look at a river, you see the river as "is." The river is not there—the river just means a movement, something which is constantly becoming. And a point never comes where you say it has become, it is a process without end. When we look at a tree, we say the tree "is." The Burmese language has nothing to say. They can only say that the tree is becoming, the tree is flowing, the tree is growing, the tree is in process. If the child is brought up with this pattern in the mind, then everything is a process; the world, the reality, will be totally different. For you it is different—and the reality is one and the same. But what mind do you bring to it to interpret it? Then it changes.

Remember one basic thing: unless the pattern of your mind is thrown away, unless you are "de-patterned," unless your conditioning is thrown away and you are deconditioned, you will not know what reality is—you will know only interpretations. Those interpretations are the workings of your own mind.

Unpatterned reality is the only reality. And this technique is to help you to unpattern, to decondition, to dissolve from the mind the words which have gathered there. You cannot look because of them. Whatsoever looks real to you, let it be dissolved.

Imagine energy, not substance—nothing static, but process, movement, rhythm, dance—and go on imagining until the entire universe spiritualizes. If you persist, within three months of intensively working for just one hour every day, you can move to this feeling. Within three months you can have a different feeling of the whole existence around you. Matter is no longer there, only immaterial, oceanic existence, just waves, vibrations. When this happens then you know what God is. That ocean of energy is God. God is not a person, God is not somewhere sitting on a throne in heaven; there is no one sitting there. God is the totality of all that is. The whole creative energy of existence is God. But we have a pattern of thinking. We say God is the creator. God is not the creator; rather, God is the creative force, the very creation itself.

It has been forced again and again on our minds that somewhere in the past, God created the world—and then and there creation finished. Christians have a story that within six days God created the world and on the seventh day he rested. That's why the seventh day, Sunday, is a holiday. God took a holiday on that day. In six days he created the world, for ever and ever, and since then there has been no creation. Since the sixth day there has been no creation. This is a very dead concept.

Tantra says God is the very creativity. Creation is not an historical event that happened somewhere in the past—it is happening every moment, God is creating every moment. But again language creates a problem and we say, "God is creating." It feels that God is someone who goes on creating. No, the very creativity that goes on moving and moving every moment, that very creativity is God. So you are in creation every moment. This is a very alive concept. It is not that God has created something somewhere and since then there has been no dialogue between man and God, there has been really no connection, no relationship—he created and the thing was finished. Tantra says that every moment you are being created, every moment you are in deep relationship with the divine, with the source of creativity. This is a very alive concept.

Through this technique you will have a glimpse of the creative force, within and without. And once you can feel the creative force and the touch, the impact of it, you will become totally different, you will never be the same again. God has entered you. You have become an abode.

103 Do not fight with desire.

The second technique: *With your entire consciousness in the very start of desire, of knowing, know.*

The basic thing about this technique is *entire consciousness*. If you can bring your entire consciousness to anything, it will become a transforming force. The transformation happens whenever you are entire in it—in anything. But that is difficult, because wherever we are, we are only there in part, never in entirety.

You are here listening to me. This very listening can become a transformation. If you are entirely here, this very moment here and now, if listening is your entirety, that listening will become a meditation. You will enter a different realm of ecstasy, a separate reality. But you are not entire. That is the problem with the human mind, it is always partial. A part is listening; other parts may be somewhere else, or may be asleep, or may be thinking about what is being said, or arguing inside. That creates a division and division is a dissipation of energy. So when doing anything bring your entire being to it. When you are not holding anything back, not even a minor part is separate, when you have taken a jump, total, whole, your whole being has come into it, then any act becomes meditative.

It is reported that one day Rinzai was working in his garden—Rinzai was a Zen master—and somebody approached. The man had come to ask some philosophical questions. He was a philosophical seeker. He didn't know that the man who was working in the garden was Rinzai himself. He thought he must be a gardener, a servant, so he asked, "Where is Rinzai?"

Rinzai said, "Rinzai is always here." Of course, the man thought that this gardener seemed to be mad because he said that Rinzai was always here. So he thought it would not be good to ask anything of this man again and he started moving off to ask someone else. Rinzai said, "Don't go anywhere, because you will not find him anywhere. He is always here." But he escaped from this madman.

Then he inquired from others and they said, "The first man you met is Rinzai."

So he came back and said, "Forgive me, I am sorry, I thought you were mad. I have come to inquire about something. I want to know what truth is. What should I do to know it?"

Rinzai said, "Do whatsoever you want to do, but do it entirely."

The point is not what you do, that is irrelevant. The point is that you do it entirely.

"For example," Rinzai said, "when I am digging this hole in the earth, my entirety is there in the act of digging. There is no Rinzai left behind. The whole has gone into the digging. Really there is no digger left, only the digging. If the digger is left, then you are divided."

You are listening to me. If the listener is left, then you are not entire. If there is only listening and there is no listener left behind you are entire, here and now. Then this very moment becomes a meditation.

In this sutra Shiva says, *With your entire consciousness in the very start of desire, of knowing, know.* If a desire arises within you, tantra doesn't say to fight it. That is futile. No one can

fight a desire. It is foolish also, because whenever you start fighting with something within you, you are fighting with yourself, you will become schizophrenic, your personality will be split. And all these so-called religions have helped humanity to by and by become schizophrenic. Everybody is split, everybody is divided and fighting with himself because so-called religions have told you, "This is bad. Don't do this." If the desire comes, what to do? You go on fighting with the desire. Tantra says don't fight the desire. But that doesn't mean that you become a victim of it. That doesn't mean that you indulge in it. Tantra gives you a very subtle technique. When desire arises, be alert just at the beginning with your entirety. Look at it with your entirety. Become the look, don't leave the looker behind. Bring your total consciousness to this arising desire. This is a very subtle method, but wonderful. Miraculous are its effects.

Three things have to be understood. Firstly, when desire has already arisen you cannot do anything. Then it will take its full course, it will complete its circle, and you cannot do anything. Just in the beginning something can be done—the seed should be burned then and there. Once the seed has sprouted and the tree has started growing, it is difficult, almost impossible, to do something. Whatsoever you do will create more anguish, dissipation of energy, frustration, weakness. When the desire arises, just at the beginning, just at the first glimpse, the first flicker that a desire is arising, bring your total consciousness, the entirety of your being to look at it. Don't do anything. Nothing else is needed. With the entire being the look is so fiery that the seed is burned, with no struggle, with no conflict, with no antagonism. Just a deep look with the entire being and the arriving desire disappears completely.

And when a desire disappears without a fight, it leaves you so powerful, with such immense energy, with such tremendous awareness, you cannot imagine it. If you fight, you will be defeated. Even if you are not defeated and you defeat the desire, that too will amount to the same thing. No energy will be left. You will feel frustrated whether you win or get defeated. In both cases you will be weak in the end, because the desire was fighting with your energy and you were fighting with the same energy. The energy was coming from the same source, you were taking from the same source, so the source will be weakened whatsoever the result. But if the desire disappears just in the beginning, without any conflict—remember, this is basic: without any fight, with just a look, not even an antagonistic look, not even with a mind to destroy, with no enmity, just a total look—in the intensity of that total look the seed is burned. And when the desire, arising desire, disappears, just like smoke in the sky, you are left with tremendous energy. That very energy is bliss. That will give you a beauty of its own, a grace.

The so-called saints who are fighting their desires are always ugly. When I say ugly, I mean they are always mean, fighting. Their whole personality becomes graceless, and they are always weak, always lacking energy, because all their energy is used up in the inner fight. Buddha is totally different, and the grace that has come to Buddha's personality is the grace of desires disappearing without any struggle or fight, without any inner violence.

With your entire consciousness in the very start of desire, of knowing, know. In that very moment simply know, look, see. Don't do anything. Nothing else is needed. All that is needed is that your total being should be there, present. Your total presence is needed. This is one of the secrets of achieving the ultimate enlightenment without any violence. And remember, you cannot enter into the kingdom of God with violence. No, those doors shall never open for you, howsoever much you knock. Knock and go on knocking; you may break your head but those doors will never open. But for those who deep inside are nonviolent and not fighting with anything, those doors are always open, they were never closed.

Jesus said, "Knock and the doors shall be opened unto you." I say to you that there is no need even to knock. Look, the doors are open. They have always been open. They were never closed. Just take a deep look, entire, total, whole.

104 The limits of perception.

The third technique: *O Shakti, each particular perception is limited, disappearing in omnipotence.* Whatsoever we see is limited, whatsoever we feel is limited, all perceptions are limited. But if you can become aware, then every limited thing is disappearing into the unlimited. Look at the sky. You will see a limited part of it, not because the sky is limited but because your eyes are limited, your focus is limited. But if you can become aware that this limitation is because of the focus, because of the eye, it is not the sky that is limited, then you will see the boundaries melting into the unlimited. Whatsoever we see becomes limited because of our seeing. Otherwise existence is unlimited, otherwise everything is melting into something else. Everything is losing its boundary, every moment waves are disappearing into the ocean—and there is no end to anything and there is no beginning. Everything is everything else also.

Limitation is forced by us. It is because of us, because we cannot see the infinite, that we divide it. We have done it in everything. You make a fence around your house and you say, "This land belongs to me and beyond the fence is somebody else's land." But deep down your land and your neighbors' land are one. The fence is just because of you. The land is not divided, the neighbors and you are divided—because of your mind.

Nations are divided because of your mind. Somewhere India ends and Pakistan starts, but just a few years back India was where Pakistan now is. At that time India used to continue up to the limits of Pakistan, the present-day limits. But now Pakistan is divided, there is a barrier. But the land remains the same.

I have heard a story that happened when India

and Pakistan were divided. There was a madhouse, a mad asylum, just on the boundary of India and Pakistan. The politicians were not very worried about where the madhouse went, to Pakistan or to India, but the superintendent was very worried. So he asked where the madhouse was going to be, whether it was going to be in India or in Pakistan.

Somebody from Delhi informed him that he should ask the inmates, the madmen, and take a vote as to where they wanted to go.

The superintendent was the only man who was not insane and he tried to explain. He gathered all the madmen together and told them, "Now it is up to you, wherever you want you can go. If you want to go to India, you can go to India. If you want to go to Pakistan, you can go to Pakistan."

But the madmen said, "We want to remain here. We don't want to go anywhere."

He tried and tried to explain. He said, "You will remain here, don't worry about it. You will remain here, but where do you want to go?"

Those madmen said, "People say we are mad, but you look more mad. You say you will remain here, and we will remain here, so why worry about going anywhere?"

The superintendent was at a loss as to how to explain the whole thing. There was only one way. He erected a wall, and divided the madhouse into two equal parts. One part became India, another part became Pakistan. And it is reported that sometimes madmen from the Pakistan madhouse came over the wall, and the madmen from India they also jumped over the wall, and they're still much confused about what is happening. "We are in the same place, and you have gone to Pakistan, and we have gone to India, and no one has gone anywhere!"

Those madmen are bound to be at a loss, they will never be able to understand, because in Delhi and Karachi there are bigger madmen.

We go on dividing. Life, existence, is not divided. All demarcations are man-made. They are useful if you don't go mad about them and if you

know that they are just artificial, man-made, utilitarian, not real, not true; that they are just myths, that they help but they don't go any deeper.

O Shakti, each particular perception is limited, disappearing in omnipotence. So, whenever you see anything limited, always remember that beyond the limit it is disappearing, the limitation is disappearing. Always look beyond and beyond.

This you can make a meditation. Just sit under a tree and look, and whatsoever comes into your view, just go beyond, look beyond, and don't stop anywhere. Just find where this tree is melting. This tree, this small tree just in your garden, has the whole of existence in it. It is melting every moment. If the sun does not rise tomorrow this tree will die, because this tree's life is bound together with the life of the sun. The distance between them is very long; for the sunrays to reach earth takes time, ten minutes' time. Ten minutes' time is very long, because light travels at a very fast speed, tremendous. Light travels one hundred and eighty-six thousand miles in one second and it takes ten minutes for light to reach this tree from the sun. The distance is tremendous, vast. But if the sun is no longer there, the tree will immediately disappear. They exist together. The tree is melting every moment into the sun and the sun is melting into the tree. Every moment the sun is entering into the tree, making it alive…. The other thing is as yet unknown to science, but religion says another thing is also happening—because in life nothing can exist without response. If the sun is giving life to the tree, the tree must be giving life back to the sun, because in life there is always a response, and energy equalizes. The tree must be giving life to the sun. They are one. Then the tree has disappeared, the limitation has disappeared.

Wherever you look, look for the beyond and don't stop anywhere. Go on and on and on, until you lose your mind, until you lose all your limited patterns. Suddenly you will be illumined. The whole existence is one. That oneness is the goal. And suddenly mind is tired of pattern, limitation, boundary—and as you insist on going beyond, as you go on pulling it beyond and beyond, the mind slips, suddenly it drops, and you look at existence as a vast oneness, everything melting into each other, everything changing into the other.

O Shakti, each particular perception is limited, disappearing in omnipotence. You can make a meditation out of it. Sit for one hour and work it out. Don't create any limitation anywhere. Whatsoever the limitation, just try to find the beyond, and move and go on moving. Soon the mind becomes tired because mind cannot cope with the unlimited. Only with the limited can it be related. With the unlimited, it cannot be related: it gets bored, it gets tired, it says, "Enough, now stop!" But don't stop, go on moving. A moment will come when mind is left behind and only consciousness is moving. In that moment you will have the illumination of oneness, of nonduality. That is the goal. That is the highest peak of consciousness. And that is the greatest ecstasy possible to human mind, and the deepest bliss.

---

105 Realize the oneness of existence.

The fourth technique: *In truth forms are inseparate. Inseparate are omnipresent being and your own form. Realize each as made of this consciousness.*

In truth forms are inseparate. They appear separate, but every form is joined together with other forms. It exists—rather it is more correct to say that it coexists with other forms. Our reality is a coexistence. It is really an inter-reality, an inter-subjectivity. For example, think of yourself alone on this earth. What will you be? The whole of humanity has disappeared, you are left alone after a third world war, alone in the world, alone on this big earth. Who will you be?

The first thing is that it is impossible to conceive of yourself alone. It is impossible, I say, to conceive of yourself alone. You will try and try and you will

see that someone is just standing there—your wife, your children, your friends—because you cannot exist alone, even in imagination. You exist with others. They give you existence. They contribute. You contribute to them and they contribute to you.

Who will you be? Will you be a good man or a bad man? Nothing can be said, because goodness and badness exist in relation. Will you be beautiful or ugly? Nothing can be said. Will you be man or woman? Nothing can be said, because whatsoever you are, you are related to someone else. Will you be wise or foolish? By and by you will see that every form has disappeared. And with these other forms, all forms within you have also disappeared. You are neither foolish nor wise, neither good nor bad, neither ugly nor beautiful, neither man nor woman. Then what will you be? If you go on eliminating all forms, soon you will realize that only nothing remains. We see forms as separate, but they are not. Every form is linked with others. Forms exist in a pattern.

This sutra says, *In truth forms are inseparate. Inseparate are omnipresent being and your own form.* Even your form and the form of the whole existence are inseparate. You are one with it. You cannot be without it. And the other thing is also true but difficult to conceive: the universe cannot be without you. The universe cannot be without you just as you cannot be without the universe. You have been existing in many, many forms always and you will exist always in many, many forms. But you will be there. You are an intrinsic part of this universe. You are not alien, you are not a stranger to it, you are not an outsider. You are an insider, an intrinsic part. And the universe cannot afford to lose you because if it loses you, it will lose itself. Forms are not separate, they are inseparate. They are one. Only the appearance gives demarcations and boundaries. This can become a realization if you ponder over it, penetrate into it; it becomes a realization, not a doctrine, not a thought, but a realization that, "Yes, I am one with the universe and the universe is one with me."

This is what Jesus was saying to the Jews. But they felt offended because Jesus said, "I and my father in heaven are one." Jews felt offended. What was he claiming? Was he claiming that he and God are one? This was blasphemy. He must be punished. But he was simply teaching a technique, nothing else. He was simply teaching a technique that forms are not separate, that you and the whole are one—"I and my father in heaven are one." But this was not a claim, this was just a suggested technique. And when Jesus said, "I and my father are one," he didn't mean that you and the father and the divine are separate. When he said "I," every "I" is represented. Whenever "I" exists, that "I" and the divine are one. But it can be misunderstood, and both Jews and Christians misunderstood. Even Christians misunderstood, because they say he was the only begotten son of God, the only begotten son, so that no one else can claim that he also is a son of God.

I was reading a very funny book. The title is *Three Christs*. In a madhouse, there were three men, and all the three claimed that they were Christ —this is an actual fact not a story—so one psycho-analyst studied all three. Then the thought came to his mind that it would be very funny to introduce them to each other to see what would happen—how they would introduce themselves and what their reaction would be. So he brought all three together and left them in a room to introduce themselves.

The first one said, "I am the only begotten son, Jesus Christ."

The other laughed and in his mind he thought he must be mad! He said, "How can you be? I am Jesus Christ. You are also part of that whole. A fragment of that consciousness is in you also. But Jesus Christ, the only son of God—that I am."

The third thought that both were foolish, that both had gone insane. He said, "What are you talk-ing about? Look at me. The son of God is here."

Then the psychoanalyst asked them separately, "What is your reaction?"

They all said, "Both the others are mad. The other two have gone crazy."

And this is not only the case with madmen. If you ask Christians what they think about Krishna —because he claims that he is God—they will say that there is only one, one penetration of the beyond, and that is Jesus Christ. At only one time in history did God penetrate into the world, and that was with Jesus Christ. Krishna is good, a great man but not divine, not God himself.

If you ask Hindus, they will laugh at Jesus. The same madness goes on, and the reality is that every-one is the only begotten son of God—everyone. The otherwise is not possible. You come from the same source, whether you are Jesus or Krishna or A, B, C, anybody or nobody, you come from the same source. And every "I," every consciousness, is immediately related to the divine. Jesus was giving only a technique. He was misunderstood.

This technique is the same. *In truth forms are inseparate. Inseparate are omnipresent being and your own form. Realize each as made of this consciousness.* Not only realize that you are made of this consciousness, realize that everything around you is made of this consciousness. Because it is very easy to realize that you are made of this conscious-ness, it can give you a very egoistic feeling, it can be a deep fulfillment to the ego. But realize that the other is also, then it become a humbleness.

When everything is divine you cannot have any egoistic mind. When everything is divine, you are humbled. Then there is no question of your being somebody, or something above; then the whole of existence is divine, and wherever you look, you look at the divine. The looker and the looked-at are both divine because forms are not separate. Under-neath all forms is hidden one formlessness.

Life is sex energy

◆

The first question:

We have always heard that tantra is basically concerned with sex energy and sex center techniques, but You say that tantra is all-inclusive. If there is any truth in the former standpoint, the majority of techniques in *Vigyan Bhairav Tantra* seem to be nontantric. Is this true?

The first thing is to understand sex energy. As you understand it, it is just a part, one part, one fragment of the life force, but as tantra understands it, it is just synonymous with life. It is not a part, not a fragment—it is life itself. So when tantra says "sex" energy it means "life" energy. The same is true about Freudian concepts of sex energy. Freud was also very much misunderstood in the West. It appeared to people that he was reducing life to sex, but he was doing the same thing that tantra has been doing for so long.

Life is sex. The word 'sex' is not confined to reproduction, the whole play of life energy is sex. Reproduction is just a part of that play. Wherever two energies are meeting—negative and positive—sex has entered.

It is difficult to understand. For example, you are listening to me; if you ask Freud, or if you ask tantra masters, they would say that listening is passive, feminine, and speaking is male. Speaking is a penetration of you and you are receptive to it. Between a speaker and a listener a sex act is hap-

pening because the speaker is trying to penetrate you and the listener is receiving. The energy in the listener has become feminine, and if the listener has not become feminine there will be no phenomenon of listening. That is why the listener has to be totally passive. He should not think while listening because thinking will make him active. He should not go on arguing within because argument will make him active. While listening, he should be simply listening, not doing anything else. Only then can the message penetrate and become illumined. But then the listener has become feminine.

Communication happens only when one party has become male and the other party has become female, otherwise there can be no communication. Wherever negative and positive meet, sex has happened. It may be on the physical plane—positive and negative electricity meet and sex has happened. Wherever polarities meet, opposites meet, it is sex. So sex is a very wide, a very spacious term, it is not concerned only with reproduction. Reproduction is only one type of phenomenon which is included in sex. Tantra says that when the ultimate bliss and ecstasy comes inside you, it means your own positive and negative pole have come to a meeting—because every man is both man and woman, and every woman is both man and woman. You are born not only from woman or from man, you are born out of a meeting of the opposites. Your father has contributed, your mother has contributed. You are half your mother and half your father and they both coexist within you. When they meet within, ecstasy happens.

Buddha sitting under his bodhi tree is in a deep inner orgasm. The inner forces have met, they have melted into each other. Now there will be no need to seek a woman outside because the meeting has happened with the inner woman. And Buddha is nonattached to, or detached from, woman outside, not because he is against woman, but because the ultimate phenomenon has happened within. Now there is no need. An inner circle has become whole, now it is complete. That is why such grace comes to Buddha's face. It is the grace of being complete. Now nothing is lacking, a deep fulfillment has happened, now there is no further journey. He has achieved the ultimate destiny. The inner forces have come to a meeting and now there is no conflict. But it is a sexual phenomenon. Meditation is a sexual phenomenon, that is why tantra is said to be sex-based, sex-oriented—and all these hundred and twelve techniques are sexual.

Really, no meditative technique can be non-sexual. But you have to understand the wideness of the term 'sex'. If you don't understand you will be confused, and misunderstanding will follow.

So whenever tantra says sex energy it means the élan vital, the life energy itself. They are synonymous. Whatsoever we call sex is just one dimension of life energy. There are other dimensions. And really it should be so. You see a seed sprouting, somewhere flowers are coming on a tree, the birds are singing—the whole phenomenon is sexual. It is life manifesting itself in many ways. When the bird is singing it is a sexual call, an invitation. When the flower is attracting butterflies and bees it is an invitation, because the bees and butterflies will carry the seeds of reproduction. Stars are moving in space…. No one has yet worked on it but it is one of the oldest tantra concepts that there are male planets and female planets—otherwise there would be no movement. It must be so because the polarity is needed, the opposite is needed to create magnetism, to create attraction. Planets must be male and female. Everything must be divided into these two polarities. And life is a rhythm between these

two opposites. Repulsion and attraction, coming nearer and going far…these are the rhythms.

Tantra uses the word "sex" wherever the opposites meet. It is a sexual phenomenon. And how to make your inner opposites meet is the whole purpose of meditation. So all these hundred and twelve methods are sexual. They cannot be anything else, there is no possibility. But try to understand the wideness of the term "sex."

The second question:

You said that existence is a wholeness, that everything is related, that things are melting into each other, that the tree cannot be without the sun and the sun also cannot exist without the tree. In reference to the above, please explain how ignorance and enlightenment are related to each other.

They are related. Enlightenment and ignorance are two polar opposites. Enlightenment can exist only because there is ignorance. If ignorance disappeared from the world, enlightenment would disappear simultaneously. But because of our dualistic thinking we always think that opposites are opposites. They are complementary, they are not really opposite. They are complementary because one cannot exist without the other. So they are not enemies; birth and death are not enemies, because death cannot exist if there is no birth. Birth creates the base for death to exist.

But if there were no death, birth could not exist. Death creates the base—so whenever someone is dying, someone else is being born. At one point there is death, at the next point immediately there is birth. They look opposite, they work in opposition as far as the surface is concerned, but deep down they are friends helping each other.

It is easy to misunderstand about ignorance and enlightenment because we think that when a man becomes enlightened, ignorance has disappeared completely. This is the ordinary standpoint about enlightenment, that ignorance has disappeared completely. No, that is not right. Rather, on the contrary, when a person becomes enlightened, enlightenment and ignorance have both disappeared, because if one is there the other is bound to be there; one cannot exist without the other. They exist together or they disappear together. They are aspects of one thing, two faces of one coin. You cannot make one face of the coin disappear and retain the other.

So when a person becomes a buddha, really, at that moment both have disappeared—ignorance and enlightenment both. Just consciousness is left, pure being is left, and the conflicting, opposing, helping opposites have disappeared. That is why when Buddha is asked what happens to an enlightened man, he remains silent many times. He says, "Don't ask this because whatsoever I say will be untrue. Whatsoever I say will be untrue. If I say that he has become silent it means the opposite of silence must exist there, otherwise how can you feel silence? If I say he has become blissful, then anguish must exist side by side. How can you feel bliss without anguish?"

Buddha says, "Whatsoever I say will be untrue." So he remains consistently silent about the state of an enlightened person, because all our terms are dual. If you say light, and if someone insists, "Define it," how are you going to define it? You will have to bring darkness in, only then can you define it. You will say that light is where darkness is not—or something like that.

One of the greatest thinkers of the world, Voltaire, used to say that you can communicate only if you define your terms first. But that is impossible. If you have to define light, you will have to bring darkness in. And then if it is asked what darkness is, you will have to define it by light, which is undefined. All definitions are circular. They used to say, "What is mind?" and the definition was, "Not matter." And, "What is matter?" and the definition was, "Not mind."

Both terms are undefined and you are playing a trick with yourself. You define one term by another term which itself needs definition. The whole language is circular and the opposite is necessary.

So Buddha says, "I will not even say that the enlightened person exists," because existence is possible only if nonexistence is also present. So he will not even say that you exist after enlightenment, because existence has to be defined by nonexistence. Nothing can be said then because all language consists of the polar opposite. That is why in the Upanishads it is said that if someone says that he is enlightened, know well that he is not, because how can he feel that he is enlightened? Some ignorance must have remained because a contrast is needed.

If you write on a blackboard with white chalk, the blacker the board the whiter will be the writing. You cannot write on a white board with white chalk. If you do, there will be no writing; the contrast is needed. If you feel that you are enlightened that shows that the blackboard is right there—only then could you feel it. If the blackboard has really disappeared, the writing would have also disappeared. It happens simultaneously. So a buddha is neither ignorant nor wise, he simply is. You cannot put him on any pole of any duality. Both the poles have disappeared.

When they disappear how does it happen? When both poles meet they negate each other and disappear. In another way you can say Buddha is both the most ignorant person and the most enlightened. The polarity has come to its extreme point, there has been a meeting, and the meeting has canceled both. The minus and plus have come together. Now there is neither minus nor plus, because they cancel each other. The minus has canceled the plus and the plus has canceled the minus; they have both disappeared and a pure being, an innocent being is left. You cannot say it is wise, you cannot say it is ignorant—or you can say it is both.

Enlightenment means the point from where you take a jump into the nondual. Before that point is duality. Everything is divided.

Someone asked Buddha, "Who are you?"

He laughed and said, "It is difficult to say."

But the man insisted. He said, "Something can be said because you are. Something meaningful can be asserted because you are."

But Buddha said, "Nothing can be said. I am, but even to say this leads me into untruth."

Then the man took another route. He asked, "Are you a man or a woman?"

Buddha said, "It is difficult to say. Once I was a man, but then my whole being was attracted towards women. When I was a man, my mind was filled with women, and when women disappeared from my mind, my man also disappeared with them. Now I cannot say. I don't know who I am and it is difficult to define."

When duality is no more, nothing can be defined. So if you are aware that you have become wise it means that foolishness persists. If you think that you have become blissful, it means that you are still in the world, in the realm of anguish. If you say that you feel a very deep well-being, a health, that means that disease is still possible. The opposite will follow you; if you carry one the other will follow. You have to drop both. And the dropping happens when both meet.

So the basic science of all religion is how to allow your inner opposites to meet so that they disappear and not a trace is left. You will disappear with the disappearance of the opposite. You as you are will no longer be there and something totally new and unknown, something unimaginable, will come into being. That something is called Brahma, you can call it God. Buddha prefers the term *nirvana*. The word 'nirvana' simply means cessation of all that was, total cessation of the past. And you cannot use your past experience and knowledge to define this new. This new is indefinable.

Ignorance and enlightenment are also part of duality. For us Buddha looks enlightened because we are in ignorance. For Buddha himself he is neither. It is impossible for him to think in terms of duality.

The third question:

Will You please tell us why Krishnamurti is against techniques, whereas Shiva is for so many techniques?

Being against techniques is simply a technique. Not only Krishnamurti is using that technique, it has been used many times before. It is one of the oldest techniques, nothing is new about it.

Two thousand years ago Bodhidharma used it. He introduced into China what is now known as *Ch'an* or Zen Buddhism. He was a Hindu monk, a monk from India. He believed in no-technique. Zen is based on no-technique. Zen masters say that if you do something you will miss, because who will do? You? You are the disease, and out of you nothing else can be born. Who will make the effort? Your mind, and your mind has to be destroyed— and you cannot destroy the mind itself with help from the mind. Whatsoever you do, your mind will be more strengthened.

So Zen says there is no technique, no method, there is no scripture and there can be no guru. But the beauty is that Zen has created the greatest of gurus and Zen masters have written the best scriptures in the world. And through Zen thousands and thousands of people attained nirvana—but they say there is no technique.

So it has to be understood that no-technique is really one of the foundational techniques. The emphasis is on "no" so that your mind is negated. Mind can have two attitudes—yes or no. These are the two possibilities, the two alternatives, just as they are in everything. No is the feminine and yes is the male. So you can use the method of no, or you can use the method of yes. If you follow the method of yes, then there are many methods—but you have to say yes and there can be many yes's. If you follow no, then there are not many methods, only one, because there cannot be many no's.

Look at this point: there are so many religions in the world, so many types of theists. There are at least three hundred religions in existence right now.

So theism has three hundred temples, churches, scriptures. But there is only one type of atheism, there cannot be two. Atheists have no sects. When you say there is no God, the thing is finished. You cannot differentiate between two no's, you cannot make any difference. But when you say, "Yes, there is God," then there is a possibility of difference, because my yes will create my own God and your yes will create your own God. Your yes may be said to Jesus, my yes may be said to Krishna—but when you say no, then all no's are similar. That is why on the earth there are no sects in atheism.

Atheists are all alike. They don't have any scripture, they don't have any church. When they don't have any positive attitude there is nothing to differ about, a simple no is enough. The same has happened about techniques: no has only one technique, yes has one hundred and twelve, or many more even are possible. You can create new combinations.

Someone has said that the method I teach, the dynamic method of meditation, is not included in these one hundred and twelve methods. It is not included because it is a new combination, but all that is in it is there in the hundred and twelve methods. Some parts are in one technique, some other part is in some other technique. These hundred and twelve are the basic methods. You can create thousands out of them, there is no end to it. Any number of combinations is possible.

But those who say there is no method can have only one method. You cannot create much out of no. So Bodhidharma, Lin Chi, Bokuju, Krishnamurti, have only one method. Really Krishnamurti comes just after a succession of Zen masters. He is talking Zen. Nothing is new about it. But Zen always looks new, and the reason is that Zen doesn't believe in scriptures, doesn't believe in tradition, doesn't believe in techniques.

So whenever no arises again it is fresh and new. Yes believes in tradition, in scriptures, in masters. Whenever yes is there, it will have a long beginningless tradition. Those who have said yes,

Krishna or Mahavira, they go on saying that they are not saying anything new. Mahavira says, "Before me twenty-three *tirthankaras* have taught the same." And Krishna says, "Before me, this seer gave this message to that seer, that seer gave the message to that, and it has been coming down. I am not saying anything new."

Yes will always be old, eternal. No will always look new, as if it has suddenly come into being. No cannot have traditional roots. It is unrooted. That is why Krishnamurti looks new. He is not.

What is this technique of denying technique? It can be used. It is one of the subtlest ways to kill and destroy the mind. Mind tries to cling to something that is a support; mind needs support to be there, it cannot exist in a vacuum. So it creates many types of supports—churches, scriptures, Bible, Koran, Gita; then it is happy, there is something to cling to. But then with this clinging the mind remains.

This technique of no-technique insists on destroying all supports, so it will insist that there is no scripture. No Bible can be of help because the Bible is nothing but words; no Gita can be of any help because whatsoever you come to know through the Gita will be borrowed, and truth cannot be borrowed. No tradition is of any help because truth has to be achieved authentically, individually. You have to come to it, it cannot be transferred to you. No master can give it to you because it is not something like property. It is not transferable, it cannot be taught because it is not information. If a master teaches you, you can learn only words, concepts, doctrines. No master can make you a realized one. That realization has to happen to you and it has to happen without any help. If it happens through some help then it is dependent and then it cannot lead you to ultimate freedom, to *moksha*.

These are the parts of this no-technique. Through these criticisms, negations and arguments, supports are destroyed. Then you are left alone with no guru, no scripture, no tradition, no church, nowhere to move, nowhere to go, nowhere to be dependent. You are left in a vacuum. And really, if you can conceive of this vacuum and are ready to be in it, you will be transformed. But mind is very cunning. If Krishnamurti says to you that these are things—no support, no clinging, no master, no scripture, no technique—you will cling to Krishnamurti. There are many clinging to him. The mind has again created a support and then the whole point is lost.

Many people come to me and they say, "Our minds are in anguish. How to come to the inner peace, how to attain the inner silence?" And if I give them some technique they say, "But techniques cannot help because we have been listening to Krishnamurti."

Then I ask them, "Then why have you come to me? And what do you mean when you ask, 'How to attain silence?' You are asking for a technique and you are still going to listen to Krishnamurti. Why? If there is no master and if the real cannot be taught, then why are you going on listening to him? He cannot teach you anything. But you go on listening to him and you are being taught. And you have now started to cling to this no-technique. So whenever someone gives you technique, you will say, 'No, we don't believe in techniques.' And you are still not silent. So what has happened? Where have you missed the train? If you really need no technique, if you don't have any technique, you must have attained. But you have not attained."

The basic point has been missed. The basic point is that for this no-technique technique to work you must destroy all support, you must not cling to anything. And it is very arduous. It is almost impossible. That is why so many people for these last forty years have been listening to Krishnamurti but nothing has happened to them. It is so arduous and difficult, almost impossible to remain unsupported, to remain totally alone and to be alert that the mind is not allowed to create any support. Because mind is very cunning, it can create subtle supports again and again. You may throw away the Gita, but then you fill the space with Krishnamurti's books. You may laugh at Mohammed, you may laugh at

Mahavira, but if someone laughs at Krishnamurti you get angry. Again in a roundabout way you have created a support, you are clinging.

Nonclinging is the secret of this method. If you can do it, it is good; if you cannot do it, then don't deceive. Then there are methods. Use them! Then be clear that you cannot be alone so you will take someone's help. Help is possible. Through help also, transformation is possible.

These are the opposites—no and yes, these are opposites. You can move from either but you must decide about your own mind and its working. If you feel that you can be alone…

Once it happened that when I was staying in a village a man came and he said to me, "I am confused. My family is trying to arrange a marriage for me." He was a young man, just fresh from university. He said, "I don't want to be involved in all that. I want to become a sannyasin, I want to renounce all. So what is your advice?"

I told him, "I never went to ask anybody, but you have come to take my advice. When you have come to take advice it shows that you need support, that you need help. It will be difficult for you to live without a wife. That too is a support."

You cannot live without a wife, you cannot live without your husband, but you think you can live without a guru? Impossible! Your mind needs support in every way. Why do you go to Krishnamurti? You go to learn, you go to be taught, you go to borrow knowledge; otherwise there is no need.

Many times it has happened that friends will say, "It would be good if you and Krishnamurti meet."

So I tell them, "You go and ask Krishnamurti and if he wants to meet, I will come. But what is going to be there? What will we do? What will we talk about? We can remain silent. What is the need?"

But they say, "It would be good if you both meet. It would be good for us. We will be happy to listen to what you say."

So I tell them a story. Once it happened that a Mohammedan mystic, Farid, was traveling. When they came near the village of Kabir, another mystic, the followers of Farid said that it would be very good if they both meet. And when it became known to Kabir's disciples, they also insisted that, as Farid was passing, they should invite him in. So Kabir said, "It is okay." Farid also said, "It is okay. We will go, but don't say anything when I enter Kabir's hut, remain quite silent."

For two days Farid stayed in Kabir's hut. There was total silence. They sat silently for two days and then Kabir came to the edge of his village to give a send-off to Farid—and in silence they departed. The moment they departed the followers of both started asking. The followers of Kabir asked him, "What was this? It became a boredom. You were sitting silently for two days, not even a single word was spoken, and we were so eager to hear."

Farid's followers also said, "What was this? It seems weird. For two days continuously we were watching and watching and waiting and waiting for something to come out of this meeting. But nothing came out."

Farid is reported to have said, "What do you mean? Two persons who know, cannot talk; two persons who don't know, can talk much, but it is useless, even harmful. The only possibility is one person who knows, talking to one who doesn't know."

And Kabir said, "Whoever uttered a single word would have proved that he didn't know."

You go on asking for advice, you go on searching for supports. Realize it well that if you cannot remain without support, then it is good to find a support, a guide, knowingly. If you think that there is no need, that you are enough unto yourself, then stop seeking Krishnamurti or anybody. Stop going and remain alone.

It has happened also to persons who were alone but the phenomenon is very rare. Sometimes to one person in millions it happens—and that too is not without any cause. That person may have been seeking for many lives; he may have been finding many supports, many masters, many guides, and now a point has come where he can be alone. Only

then it happens. But whenever it happens to a person that he achieves the ultimate alone, he starts saying that it can happen to you also. It is natural.

Because it happened to Krishnamurti alone, he goes on saying that it can happen to you. It cannot happen to you! You are in search of support and that shows that alone you cannot do it. So don't be deceived by yourself! Your ego may feel good that "I don't need any support!" Ego always thinks in terms of "I alone am enough," but that ego will not help. That will become the greatest barrier possible.

No-technique is a technique, but only for very specific people; for those who have struggled in many lives and have now come to a point where they can be alone, that technique is a help. And if you are that type of person, I know well you will not be here. So I am not worried about that person, he will not be here. He cannot be here. Not only here, he cannot be anywhere with any master, listening, seeking, searching, practicing. He will not be found anywhere. So we can leave him, we need not discuss him.

These techniques are for you. So this is how I will conclude. Krishnamurti is talking for the person who cannot be there and I am talking for persons who are here. Whatsoever Krishnamurti is saying is absolutely right but the persons to whom he is saying it are absolutely wrong. The person who can be alone, who without any method, any support, any scripture, any guru, can reach, is not going to listen to Krishnamurti because there is no need, there is no meaning. And those who are going to listen, they are not of that type, they will be in deep difficulty—and they are. They need support and their mind goes on thinking that there is no need for support. They need a guru and their mind goes on saying that the guru is a barrier. They need techniques and logically they have concluded that techniques cannot help. They are in deep trouble, but the trouble is created by themselves.

Before you start doing something you must try to understand what type of mind you have got, because ultimately the guru is not meaningful, ultimately your mind is meaningful. The ultimate decision is going to come through your mind, the destiny is to be fulfilled through your mind—so understand it, without any ego confusing you. Just understand if you need support, guidance, techniques, methods to work with. If you need them, find them. If you don't need them, there is no question: be alone, unclinging, move alone, unclinging. The same will happen through both ways. Yes and no are two opposites and you have to find out what your path is.

The last question:

You said that Shiva is not a system maker and sects cannot form around his teachings. But persons like Buddha, Mahavira, Jesus, Gurdjieff, seem to be great system makers. Why do they have to be system makers? Please explain the pros and cons of system making. Are You a multisystem maker?

There are two possibilities: you can create a system to help people, create multisystems to help people, or the other, you can try to destroy systems to help people. Again the yes and no. Again the polar opposites. And in both ways you can help people.

Bodhidharma is a system destroyer, Krishnamurti is a system destroyer, the whole tradition of Zen is system destroying. Mahavira, Mohammed, Jesus, Gurdjieff, are great system makers. The problem is always that we cannot understand these two contradictory things simultaneously together; we think that either one can be right but both cannot be. If system makers are right, then our mind says that system destroyers must be wrong. Or if system destroyers are right, then system makers must be wrong. No, both are right.

A system means a pattern to follow, a clear-cut map to follow so that no doubt arises, no indecisiveness arises and you can follow with absolute faith. Remember this: a system is created to create faith, to create trust. If everything is clear, then there will be trust more easily. If all your questions are answered mathematically, then you will be in a state of no doubt and you can proceed. So sometimes Mahavira answers your absurd questions also. They are futile questions, meaningless, but he will answer. And he will answer in such a way that it helps you to have trust, because that quality of trust is needed.

When someone tries to penetrate into the unknown a deep trust is needed; otherwise it will be impossible to move. It will be so dangerous you will get scared. It is dark, the path is not clear, everything is chaos and every step leads you into more and more insecurity. Hence system making is needed so that everything is planned: you know everything about heaven and hell and the ultimate moksha, and from where you will move, from where you will pass. Every inch has been mapped. That gives you a security, a feeling that everything is okay. People have been there before and you are not moving into a no-man's land, you are not moving into the unknown. A system makes it appear as if it is known. That is to help you, just to give you support. And if you have faith then you will have energy to move. If you are doubtful, you will dissipate energy and movement will be difficult.

System makers have tried to answer all types of questions and they have created a neat and clean map. With that map in your hand you feel everything is okay, you can proceed. But I tell you, every system is just artificial. Every system is just to help you. It is not true. No system can be true. It is a device. But it helps because your whole personality is so untrue that even untrue devices help. You live in lies and you cannot understand truth. A system means less lies and then even less lies and then by and by, by and by, you will come nearer and nearer to the truth. When the truth is revealed to you the system will become meaningless, it will simply drop.

When Sariputta became enlightened, came to the ultimate goal, he looked back from that point and saw that the whole system had disappeared. Whatsoever he had been taught was not there. So he said to Buddha, "The whole system that was taught to me has disappeared."

Buddha said to him, "Keep silent, don't tell the others! It has disappeared, it has to disappear because it was never there, it was a make-believe, but it helped you to come to this point. Don't tell those who have not come yet, because if they know that there is no knowledge where they are going to they will stop. They cannot go into the unknown unguarded, alone they cannot go."

It happens many times. It has been my own experience that people come to me and they say, "Now meditation is going deep but we are scared." An ultimate feeling is bound to come when you feel a "dying" fear, as if death is approaching near. When meditation comes to its peak it is deathlike. I tell them, "Don't worry, I am with you." Then they feel okay. I cannot be there—impossible! No one can be there. This is untrue. No one can be there, you will be alone. That point is one of total aloneness. But when I say, "I will be there, you don't worry, you go ahead," they feel okay and they move. If I say, "You will be alone and no one is going to be there," they will step back. The point has come where fear is bound to be there. The abyss is there and they are going to fall—I must help them to fall. So I say that I am there, you just take the jump. And they take the jump! After the jump they will come to know that no one was there, but now, now the whole thing is finished. They cannot come back. This is a device.

All systems are devices to help: to help people who are full of doubts, to help people who have no trust, to help people who have no confidence. To help people to move into the unknown without fear, systems are created. In those systems everything is just like a myth, that is why there are so many systems. Mahavira creates his own—that system is created according to the needs of his followers. So he creates a system. It is a myth, but very helpful, because many moved through it and reached to the truth. And when they reached they knew that the system was false—but it worked.

Buddha defines truth as that which works. His definition of truth is that which works—if a lie can

work, it is true, and if a truth cannot work, it is false.

There are so many systems, and every system helps. But every system cannot help everybody. That is why the old religions insisted that a person should not be converted into a new religion, because although the mind can after a time be conditioned in a system and can be changed, deep down you will never change, and a new system will never become useful for you. A Hindu can become a Christian, a Christian can become a Hindu, but after the age of seven the mind is almost fixed, conditioned. So if a Hindu becomes a Christian he will remain a Hindu deep down and the Christian system will not help him. And he has lost contact with his own system which might have worked.

Hindus and Jews have always been against conversion. Not only against conversion—if someone wants to enter their religion voluntarily, they will resist. They will say, "No, follow your own path." Because a system is a great unconscious phenomenon, it has to be deep in the unconscious, only then can it help. Otherwise it cannot help and it is an artificial thing. It is just like language. You can never speak any language as you speak your mother-tongue, it is impossible. Nothing can be done about it. Howsoever efficient you become in somebody else's language it will remain superficial. Deep down your mother-tongue will continue to influence it. Your dreams will be in your mother-tongue; the unconscious will function with the original language. Anything can be imposed on and above it, but it cannot be replaced.

Religious systems are like language, they are language. But if they penetrate deep, they help because you feel confident. The system is irrelevant but the confidence is relevant. You feel trusting so you move with a sure step—you know where you are moving. And this knowing helps.

But there are system destroyers also and they also help. There is a rhythmic circle, just like day and night—again day comes, again night comes. They help because sometimes it happens that when there are so many systems people get confused, and rather than moving with the maps, the maps become so heavy that they cannot carry them. It happens always.

For example, a tradition, a very long tradition, is helpful because it will give confidence because it is so long. But because it is so long it is heavy also, it has become a dead weight. So rather than helping you to move, you cannot move because of it. You have to be unburdened. So there are system destroyers who destroy the system from your mind and unburden you and help you to move. They both help, but it depends. It depends on the age, it depends on the person who is to be helped.

In this age systems have become very heavy and confused. For many reasons the whole point has been lost. Before, each system lived in its own world: a Jaina was born Jaina, lived Jaina, died Jaina. He did not study Hindu scriptures, it was prohibited. He did not go to the mosque or the church, that was a sin. He lived within the walls of his system. Nothing alien ever penetrated his mind, so no confusion was there.

But all that has been destroyed, and everyone is acquainted with everything else. Hindus are reading the Koran and Mohammedans are reading the Gita. Christians are moving to the East and the East is moving to the West. Everything is confused. The confidence that used to come from a system is no longer there. Everything has penetrated your mind and things are jumbled up. Jesus is not alone there, Krishna has penetrated and Mohammed has also penetrated. And they have contradicted each other within you. Now nothing is certain.

The Bible says this, the Gita says exactly the contrary. Mohammed says this, Mahavira is just the opposite. They have contradicted. You are no longer anywhere. You don't belong, you are simply standing there confused. No path is yours. In such a state of mind, system destroying can be helpful. Hence the great appeal of Krishnamurti in the West. He does not have so much appeal in the East because the East is still not as confused as the West,

because the East is still not as educated about others. The West is obsessed about knowing about others. They know too much. Now no system is real, they know that everything is a make-believe, and once you know it, it will not work.

Krishnamurti appeals to them because he says leave all systems. If you can leave all systems you will become unconfused—but it depends on you. It may happen, as it happens almost always, that all the systems will remain there and this new system of destroying all systems will also enter. So one more disease is added.

Jesus goes on speaking, Krishna goes on speaking, Mahavira goes on speaking—and then Krishnamurti also enters. Your mind becomes the Tower of Babel—so many tongues and you cannot understand what is happening. You just feel crazy.

If you can believe in a system, so far so good; if you cannot believe in any system, then drop all. Then be completely clean, unburdened. But don't be just in the middle of these two alternatives. And it appears that everyone is just in the middle. Sometimes you move to the right, sometimes to the left, then again to the right and then to the left—just like the pendulum of a clock. You go from this side to that, this side to that. This movement may appear to you as if you are proceeding. You are not proceeding anywhere. Every step cancels some other step, because when you move to the right and then to the left you go on contradicting yourself. In the end you are just confused, puzzled, a chaos.

Either be unburdened completely—that will be helpful. You will be clean, innocent, childlike, and you can fly—or if that understanding seems too dangerous to you, if you are afraid of unburdening because that will lead you into a vacuum, into an emptiness, if that unburdening looks dangerous and you are scared, then choose a system. But there are many who go on saying to you that everything is the same—the Koran says the same, the Bible says the same, the Gita says the same, their message is the same. These people are the great confusers. The Koran, the Bible, the Gita, they don't say the same, they are systems, clear-cut systems, different. Not only different, but sometimes contradictory and opposite.

For example, Mahavira says that nonviolence has to be the key. If you are violent, even slightly violent, the door of ultimate reality is closed for you. This is a technique. To become totally nonviolent needs a complete cleansing of your mind and body—both. You have to be purified completely, only then will you become nonviolent. This process of becoming nonviolent will purify you so totally that the very process will become the end.

Just the opposite is Krishna's message. He says to Arjuna, "Don't be afraid of killing because the soul cannot be killed. You can kill the body but you cannot kill the soul. So why be afraid? And the body is already dead, so that which is dead will be dead and that which is alive will remain alive. You need not be concerned. It is just a play."

He is also right, because if you can come to realize this point—that the soul cannot be destroyed—then the whole life becomes a play, a fiction, a drama. And if the whole life becomes a drama, even murder and suicide become a drama to you, not just in thinking, but you realize the fact that everything is just a dream. Death too will make you a witness, and that witnessing will become transcendence… you will transcend the world. The whole world becomes a drama—there is nothing good, nothing bad, just a dream. You need not worry about it.

But these two things are totally different. They lead to the same point ultimately but you should not mix them. If you mix them, you will suffer. System makers have been there to help you, system destroyers have been there to help you. But it seems that no one has been able to help. You are such, so adamant and so cunning, you always find some loopholes to escape through.

Buddha and Krishna and Jesus—every century they go on teaching certain things. You go on listening but you are very clever. You listen and yet you don't listen. And you always find something, some hole, from where you can escape. Now the trick of the modern mind is that if there is a system, if Gurdjieff is teaching, then people will go to him and say, "Krishnamurti says no system." These same people will go to Krishnamurti—Krishnamurti teaches no-system—and they will say, "But Gurdjieff says that without a system nothing can be done." So while near Gurdjieff they use Krishnamurti as a loophole to escape, while near Krishnamurti they use Gurdjieff as a trick to escape. But they are not deceiving anybody, they are simply destroying themselves.

Gurdjieff can help, Krishnamurti can help, but they cannot help against you. You must be certain about certain things. One, either you need help or you don't need it. Second, either you can move into the unknown without any fear or you cannot. And third, without any method, without any technique, without any system, can you proceed a single inch or can't you? These three things you have to decide within you. Analyze your mind, open it, look into it and decide what type of mind you have got. If you decide that you cannot do it alone then you need a system, a master, a scripture, a technique. If you think that you can do it alone then there is no need for anything else. You are the master, you are the scripture, you are the technique. But be honest, and if you feel that it is impossible to decide—it is not so easy to decide—if you feel confused, then first try a master, a technique, a system. And try it hard, to the very extreme, so that if something is going to happen, it happens. If nothing is going to happen then you come to a point where you can decide that now you will leave all, you will be alone. That too will be good.

But my suggestion is that you should always start with a master, a system, a technique, because in both ways it will be good. If you can achieve through it, it is good; if you cannot achieve through it, then the whole thing becomes futile and you can drop it and then you can proceed alone.

Then you will not need Krishnamurti to tell you that no master is needed, you will know it. Then you will not need any Zen teaching to tell you to throw away your scriptures and burn them, you will have already burned them.

So it is good to proceed with a master, with a system, with a technique—but be sincere. When I say be sincere I mean that you should do whatsoever you can do with a master, so that if something can happen, it happens. If nothing can happen, then you can conclude that this is not the path for you and you can move alone.

CHAPTER 77

Become each being

◆

106 *Feel the consciousness of each person as your own consciousness. So, leaving aside concern for self, become each being.*

107 *This consciousness exists as each being, and nothing else exists.*

108 *This consciousness is the spirit of guidance of each one. Be this one.*

♦

Existence as such is one. The human problem arises because of human self-consciousness. Consciousness gives everyone a feeling that they are separate, and the feeling that you are separate from existence creates all the problems. Basically this feeling is false, and whatsoever is based on a falsity will create anguish, will create problems, will create confusion. And whatsoever you do, if it is based on this false separateness, it will go wrong.

So from the very beginning the problem of human anguish has to be tackled. How does it arise? Consciousness gives you a feeling that you are the center of your being, and consciousness makes you aware that others are "other," that you are different from them. This difference is just because you are conscious. While you are asleep there is no difference—you are again merged with the universe. Hence so much bliss comes out of sleep. In the morning you feel refreshed, rejuvenated, again alive, fresh.

What is happening in deep sleep? You are losing your ego, you are losing yourself, you are falling into a unity with the universe. That falling back into the unity makes you fresh and alive, and in the morning you feel blissful. All the anguish disappears; all conflict, all disturbance disappears; all fear, all death disappears—because death is possible only if you are separate. If you are not separate, then death is impossible. Who is going to die if you are not separate? Who can suffer if you are not

separate? So all tantra, yoga and other methods of meditation are just to make you aware that separateness is false and inseparateness is real. And if you can become aware of that you will be totally different, because the center will have disappeared from you and it will take its right place in the universe. You will be just a wave on this vast ocean. You will not be separate so you will not be afraid. You will not feel insecure. You will not feel the anguish of approaching death and annihilation. All that disappears with the ego.

Hindus have always believed that *samadhi* is conscious sleep. In sleep it happens automatically that you are no more. The existence is, and you are no more; but you are deeply unconscious so you don't know what is happening. If this same phenomenon can happen consciously, you become enlightened. Buddha moves to the same source, to the same source that you move every night in deep sleep, in dreamless sleep. But Buddha moves to that source consciously, alert, aware. He knows where he is moving to, he knows what is happening, and when he comes back from that deep source, he comes totally different. The old has disappeared and a new being, a new energy has arisen out of it.

Of this being, the center is the universe; and with this transfer of the center, all your worry, all your anguish, all your hell disappears, simply disappears. It is not solved, it is simply not there. It cannot exist there without the ego. So how to be consciously deep asleep? How to move into sleep consciously? How to remain alert while you are losing the ego?

The ego is a by-product, a by-product of your

whole upbringing, a by-product of the natural course of life. It has to be there. There is no other way. No being can evolve without being involved with the ego. But a point comes when the ego can be dropped and should be dropped, and the being should transcend it.

The ego is just like the shell of the egg. It is needed, it protects. Just like the shell of a seed, it is needed, it protects. But the protection can become dangerous also, if it protects too much. If it goes on protecting and doesn't allow the seed to sprout, then it becomes a hindrance. It must dissolve into the earth so that the inner life evolves out of it. It must die.

The seed must die. Every man is born as a seed. The ego is the outer covering; it protects the child. If a child is born without the ego, without the feeling that "I exist," he cannot survive. He will not be able to protect himself, he will not be able to struggle, he will not be able in any way to exist. He needs a strong center. Even if it is false, it is needed. But a moment comes when this help becomes a hindrance. It protects you from outside, but it becomes so strong that it will not allow you, the inner being, to spread, to go beyond it, to sprout. So ego is needed—and then ego-transcendence is needed.

If someone dies with the ego, he has died as a seed. He has died without really attaining the destiny that was possible, without attaining existence consciously. These techniques are for how to destroy this seed.

106 Become each being.

The first technique: *Feel the consciousness of each person as your own consciousness. So, leaving aside concern for self, become each being.*

Feel the consciousness of each person as your own consciousness. In reality it is so, but it is not felt so. You feel your consciousness as yours, and others'

consciousnesses you never feel. At the most you infer that others are also conscious. You infer because you think that because you are conscious, other beings like you must be conscious. This is a logical inference; you don't feel them as conscious.

It is just like when you have a headache you feel your headache, you have a consciousness of it. But if someone else has a headache, you infer—you cannot feel the other's headache. You simply infer that whatsoever he is saying must be true and he must have something like you. But you cannot feel it.

The feeling can come only if you become conscious about others' consciousnesses—otherwise it is a logical inference. You believe, you trust, that others are saying something honestly, and whatsoever they are saying is worth believing because you also have similar types of experiences.

There is a logical school which says that nothing can be known about the other, it is impossible. At the most there can be an inference but nothing certain can be known about others. How can you know that others have pain like you, that others have anxieties like you? Others are there but we cannot penetrate them, we can only just touch their surface. Their inner being remains unknown. We remain closed in ourselves.

The world around us is not a felt world, it is just inferred—logically, rationally. The mind says it is there but the heart is not touched by it. That is why we behave with others as if they are things not persons. Our relationship with persons is also as it is with things. A husband behaves towards his wife as if she is a thing; he possesses her. The wife possesses the husband just like a thing. If we behaved with the other as if they were persons then we would not try to possess them, because only things can be possessed.

A person means freedom. A person cannot be possessed. If you try to possess them, you will kill them, they will become things. Our relationship with others is really not an I-thou relationship, deep down it is just an I-it relationship. The other is just a thing to be manipulated, to be used, exploited. That is why love becomes more and more impossible, because love means taking the other as a person, as a conscious being, as a freedom, as something as valuable as you are.

If you behave as if everything is a thing, then you are the center and things are just to be used. The relationship becomes utilitarian. Things have no value in themselves—the value is that you can use them, they exist for you. You can be related to your house—the house exists for you. It is a utility. The car exists for you, but the wife doesn't exist for you and the husband doesn't exist for you. The husband exists for himself and the wife exists for herself. A person exists for himself; that is what being a person means. And if you allow the person to be a person and don't reduce him to being a thing, you will by and by start feeling him. Otherwise you cannot feel. Your relationship will remain conceptual, intellectual, mind to mind, head to head—but not heart to heart.

This technique says, *Feel the consciousness of each person as your own consciousness.* This will be difficult because first you have to feel the person as a person, as a conscious being. Even that is difficult.

Jesus says, "Love your neighbor as you love yourself." This is the same thing—but the other must first become a person for you. He must exist in his own right, not to be exploited, manipulated, utilized, not as a means but an end in himself. First, the other must become a person; the other must become a thou, as valuable as you are. Only then can this technique be applied. *Feel the consciousness of each person as your own consciousness.* First feel that the other is conscious, and then this can happen—you can feel that the other has the same consciousness that you have. Really, the other disappears, only a consciousness flows between you and him. You become two poles of one consciousness flowing, of one current.

In deep love it happens that the two persons are not two. Something between the two has come into being and they have just become two poles.

Something is flowing between the two. When this flow is there you will feel blissful. If love gives bliss, it gives bliss only because of this: that two persons, just for a single moment, lose their egos—the "other" is lost and oneness comes into being just for a single moment. If it happens, it is ecstatic, it is blissful, you have entered paradise. Just a single moment, and it can be transforming.

This technique says that you can do this with every person. In love you can do it with one person, but in meditation you have to do it with every person. Whosoever comes near you, simply dissolve into him and feel that you are not two lives, but one life, flowing. This is just changing the gestalt. Once you know how, once you have done it, it is very easy. In the beginning it seems impossible because we are so stuck in our own egos. It is difficult to lose it, difficult to become a flow. So it will be good if in the beginning you try with something that you are not very scared or afraid of.

You will be less afraid of a tree so it will be easier. Sitting near a tree, just feel the tree and feel that you have become one with it, that there is a flow within you, a communication, a dialogue, a melting. Sitting near a flowing river just feel the flow, feel that you and the river have become one. Lying under the sky, just feel that you and the sky have become one. In the beginning it will be just imagination but by and by you will feel that you are touching reality through imagination.

And then try it with persons. This is difficult in the beginning because there is a fear. Because you have been reducing persons to things, you are afraid that if you allow someone to be so intimate he will also reduce you to a thing. That is the fear. So no one allows much intimacy; a gap is always to be kept and guarded. Too much closeness is dangerous because the other can convert you into a thing, he can try to possess you. That is the fear. You are trying to convert others into things, and others are trying to convert you—and no one wants to be a thing, no one wants to become a means, no one wants to be used. It is the most degrading phenomenon to be reduced to just a means to something, not valuable in yourself. But everyone is trying. Because of this there is a deep fear and it will be difficult to start this technique with persons.

So start with a river, with a hill, with the stars, with the sky, with trees. Once you come to know the feeling of what happens when you become one with the tree; once you come to know how blissful you become when you become one with the river, how without losing anything you gain the whole existence—then you can try it with persons. And if it is so blissful with a tree, with a river, you cannot imagine how much more blissful it will be with a person, because a person is a higher phenomenon, a more highly evolved being. Through a person you can reach higher peaks of experience. If you can become ecstatic with even a rock, with a person you can feel a divine ecstasy happening to you.

But start with something that you are not much afraid of, or, if there is a person you love, a friend, a beloved, a lover, of whom you are not afraid, with whom you can be really intimate and close without any fear, with whom you can lose yourself without getting scared deep down that he may turn you into a thing—if you have someone like that, then try this technique. Lose yourself consciously into him. When you lose yourself consciously into someone, that someone will lose himself into you; when you are open and you flow into the other, the other starts flowing into you and there is a deep meeting, a communion. Two energies melt into each other. In that state there is no ego, no individual—simply consciousness. And if this is possible with one individual, it is possible with the whole universe. What saints have called ecstasy, samadhi, is just a deep love phenomenon between a person and the whole universe.

Feel the consciousness of each person as your own consciousness. So, leaving aside concern for self, become each being. We are always concerned with our own self. Even while we are in love, we are concerned with our own self, that is why love

becomes a misery. It can become heaven but it becomes a hell, because even lovers are concerned with their own selves. The other is loved because he gives you happiness, the other is loved because you feel good with him, but the other is still not loved as if he is something valuable in himself or herself. The value comes through your enjoyment. You are gratified, you are satisfied in some way, that is why the other has become significant. This is also using the other.

Concern for the self means exploitation of the other. And religious consciousness can come into existence only when the concern for the self is lost, because then you become nonexploitive. With existence your relationship becomes one not of exploitation, but of sheer sharing, sheer bliss. You are not using, you are not being used—it becomes a sheer celebration of being.

But concern for the self has to be thrown away ...and it is very deep-rooted. It is so deep-rooted that you are not even aware of it. In one of the Upanishads it is said that the husband loves his wife, not for the wife, but for himself; and the mother loves the child, not for the child, but for herself. The concern for the self is so deep-rooted that whatsoever you do, you do for yourself. This means that you are always gratifying the ego, feeding the ego, feeding a false center which has become a barrier between you and the universe.

Lose the concern for the self. If even sometimes, even for a few moments, you can lose concern for the self and can become concerned with the other, with the other's self, you will be entering a different reality, a different dimension. Hence so much emphasis on service, love, compassion, because compassion, love, service, mean concern for the other's self, not your own.

But look...human mind is so cunning that it has converted service, compassion and love into concerns for the self. A Christian missionary serves, and his service is sincere. Really, no one else can serve so deeply and intensely as a Christian missionary. No Hindu can do that, no Mohammedan can do that, because Jesus has emphasized service so much. A Christian missionary is serving poor people, ill people, diseased people, but deep down he is concerned with himself, not with them. This service is just a method to reach heaven. He is not concerned with them, he is not really concerned with them at all, he is concerned with his own self. Through service he can achieve a greater self, so he is doing service. But he has missed the basic point, because service means the concern for the other — the other is the center and you have become the periphery.

Try it sometimes. Make someone the center — then his happiness becomes your happiness, his misery becomes your misery. Whatsoever happens, happens to him and flows to you. But he is the center. If once, even once, you can feel that the other is the center and you have become just a periphery to him, you have entered a different type of existence, a different dimension of experience, because in that moment you will feel a deep bliss, unknown before, unexperienced before. Just by making the other the concern, you will lose all misery. In that moment there will be no hell for you; you have entered paradise.

Why does it happen? It happens because the ego is the root of all misery. If you can forget it, if you can dissolve it, all misery dissolves with it.

Feel the consciousness of each person as your own consciousness. So, leaving aside concern for self, become each being. Become the tree, become the river, become the wife, become the husband, become the child, become the mother, become the friend — it can be practiced every moment of life. But in the beginning it will be difficult. So do it for a least one hour every day. In that hour, whatsoever passes around you, become that. You will wonder how it can happen. There is no other way to know how it can happen — you have to practice it.

Sit with the tree and feel that you have become the tree. And when the wind comes and the whole tree starts shaking and trembling, feel that shaking and trembling in you; when the sun rises and the whole tree becomes alive, feel that aliveness in you; when a shower of rain comes and the whole tree is satisfied and content, a long thirst, a long awaiting has disappeared and the tree is completely satisfied and content, feel satisfied and content with the tree. And then you will become aware of the subtle moods, of the nuances of a tree.

You have seen that tree for many years, but you don't know its moods. Sometimes it is happy, sometimes it is unhappy. Sometimes it is sad, dead, worried, frustrated; sometimes it is very blissful, ecstatic. There are moods. The tree is alive and it feels. And if you become one with it, then you will feel it. Then you will feel whether the tree is young or old; whether the tree is dissatisfied with its life or satisfied; whether the tree is in love with existence or not — is anti, against, furious, angry; whether the tree is violent or there is a deep compassion in it. As you are changing every moment, the tree is also changing. If you can feel a deep affinity with it, what they call empathy...

Empathy means you have become so sympathetic that really you become one. The moods of the tree become your moods. And then, if this goes deeper and deeper and deeper, you can talk, you can have a communication with the tree. Once you know its moods you start understanding its language, and the tree will share its mind with you. It will share its agonies and ecstasies.

And this can happen with the whole universe.

For at least one hour every day try to be in empathy with something. In the beginning you will look foolish to yourself. You will think, "What kind of stupidity am I doing?" You will look around and you will feel that if someone looks or someone sees or someone comes to know, they will think you have gone crazy. But only in the beginning. Once you enter this world of empathy the whole world will look crazy to you. They are missing so much unnecessarily. Life gives in such abundance and they are missing it. They are missing because they are closed; they don't allow life to enter into them. And life can enter you only if you enter life through many, many ways, through many paths, through multidimensions. Be in empathy for at least one hour every day.

This was the meaning of prayer in the beginning of every religion. The meaning of prayer was to be in an affinity with the universe, to be in a deep communication with the universe. In prayer you are talking to God—God means the totality. Sometimes you may be angry with God, sometimes thankful, but one thing is certain—you are in communication. God is not just a mental concept, it has become a deep, intimate relationship. That is what prayer means.

But our prayers have gone rotten because we don't know how to communicate with beings. And if you cannot communicate with beings, you cannot communicate with the Being—Being with a capital B; it is impossible. If you cannot communicate with a tree, how can you communicate with the total existence? And if you feel foolish talking to a tree, you will feel more foolish talking to God.

Leave one hour aside every day for a prayerful state of mind. And don't make your prayer a verbal affair, make it a feeling thing. Rather than talking with the head, feel it. Go and touch the tree, hug the tree, kiss the tree; close your eyes and be with the tree as if you are with your beloved. Feel it. And soon you will come to a deep understanding of what it means to put the self aside, of what it means to become the other.

Feel the consciousness of each person as your own consciousness. So, leaving aside concern for self, become each being.

---

107 Know only consciousness exists.

The second technique: *This consciousness exists as each being, and nothing else exists.*

Scientists used to say in the past that only matter existed, nothing else. Great systems of philosophy arose based on the concept that only matter existed. But even those who believed that matter existed had to concede that there was something like consciousness. Then what was it? They said that consciousness was just an epiphenomenon, just a by-product of matter. It was nothing but matter in disguise, something very subtle but still material. But this half century has seen a very great miracle happen.

Scientists tried and tried to find out what matter was, but the more they tried, the more they came to realize that there was nothing like matter. Matter was analyzed and it was found that it had disappeared. Nietzsche had said just a hundred years before, "God is dead." With God dead there can be no consciousness because God means the totality of consciousness. But within a hundred years matter is dead—and it is dead not because religious people believe it so but because scientists have come to a definite conclusion that matter is just appearance. It appears to be as it is because we cannot see very deeply. If we can see deeply it disappears, and then energy is left.

This phenomenon of energy, this nonmaterial energy force, has been known by mystics since long ago. In the Vedas, in the Bible, in the Koran, in the Upanishads—all over the world mystics have penetrated into existence and have always concluded that matter is just an appearance; deep down there is no matter, only energy. With this science now agrees. And the mystics have said one thing more which science has yet to agree with—but with which it will have to agree one day! The mystics have come to another conclusion also. They say that when you penetrate deep into energy, energy also disappears and only consciousness remains.

So these are the three layers. Matter is the first layer, the surface. If you penetrate the surface then the second layer becomes apparent; you can perceive the second layer which is energy. Then if you penetrate energy, the third layer becomes illumined. That third layer is consciousness. In the beginning, science said that mystics were just dreaming, because science saw only matter and nothing else. Then science tried to penetrate, and the mystics' second layer was uncovered: matter is just apparent, deep down it is nothing but energy. And the mystics' other claim is: penetrate more into energy and energy also disappears, then there remains only consciousness. That consciousness is God. That is the *deepest* core.

If you penetrate into your body, these three layers are there. Just on the surface is your body. The body looks material, but deep down there are currents of life, *prana,* vital energy. Without that vital energy your body would be just a corpse. It is alive, with something flowing in it. That flowing something is energy. But deeper, still deeper, you are aware, you can witness. You can witness both your body and your vital energy. That witnessing is your consciousness.

Every existence has three layers. The deepest is the witnessing consciousness. In the middle is vital energy and just on the surface is matter, a material body.

This technique says, *This consciousness exists as each being, and nothing else exists.* What are you? Who are you? If you close your eyes and try to find out who you are, ultimately you are bound to come to a conclusion that you are consciousness. Everything else may belong to you, but you are not that. The body belongs to you, but you can be aware of the body—and that which is aware of the body becomes separate. The body becomes an object of knowledge and you become the subject. You can know your body. Not only can you know, you can manipulate your body, you can activate it or make it inactive. You are separate. You can do something with your body.

And not only are you not your body, you are not your mind either. You can become aware of your mind also. If thoughts move, you can see them, and you can do something with them: you can make them disappear completely, you can become thoughtless, or you can concentrate your consciousness on one thought and not allow it to move from there. You can focus yourself on it and make it remain there, or you can allow a riverlike flow of thoughts. You can do something with your thoughts. You can even dissolve them completely until there is no thought—but still you are. You will know that there are no thoughts, that a vacuum has come into being; but you will be there, witnessing that vacuum.

The only thing you cannot separate yourself from is your witnessing energy. That means you are that. You cannot separate yourself from it. You can separate yourself from everything else: you can know that you are not your body, not your mind, but you cannot know that you are not your witnessing because whatsoever you do you will be the witness. You cannot separate yourself from witnessing. That witnessing is consciousness. And unless you come to a point from where separation becomes impossible, you have not come to yourself.

So there are methods by which the seeker goes on eliminating. He goes on eliminating—first the body, then the mind, and then he comes to the point where nothing can be eliminated. In the Upanishads they say, *Neti, neti*—this is a deep method—"this is not, that is not." So the seeker goes on knowing, "This is not, this is not me, this is not I." He goes on and on until ultimately he comes to a point where he cannot say, "This is not I." Just a witnessing self remains. Pure consciousness remains. This pure consciousness exists as each being.

Whatsoever is in existence is just a phenomenon of this consciousness, just a wave, just a crystallization of this consciousness—and nothing else exists. But this has to be felt. Analysis can be helpful, intellectual understanding can be helpful, but it has to be *felt* that nothing else exists, only consciousness. Then behave as if only consciousness exists.

I have heard about Lin Chi, a Zen master. As he was sitting one day in his hut someone came to see him. The man who came was angry. He may have been fighting with his wife or with his boss or something, but he was angry. He pushed open the door in anger, he threw down his shoes in anger and then he came, very respectfully, and bowed down to Lin Chi. Lin Chi said, "First go and ask forgiveness from the door and from the shoes."

The man must have looked at Lin Chi very strangely. There were other people also sitting there and they started laughing. Lin Chi said, "Stop!" and then said to the man, "If you don't do it then leave. I will have nothing to do with you."

The man said, "It will look crazy to ask forgiveness from the shoes and from the door."

Lin Chi said, "It was not crazy when you expressed anger. Will it now be crazy? Everything has a consciousness. So you go, and unless the door forgives you, I am not going to allow you in."

The man felt awkward but he had to go. Later on he became a monk himself and became enlightened. When he became enlightened he related the whole anecdote and he said, "When I stood before the door, asking forgiveness, I felt awkward, foolish. But then I thought that if Lin Chi says so, there must be something in it. I trusted Lin Chi, so I thought that even if it is foolish, do it. In the beginning whatsoever I was saying to the door was just superficial, artificial; but by and by I started to get warm. And Lin Chi was waiting and he said that he would watch. If the door forgave me, only then could I come in; otherwise I had to stay there until I had persuaded the door and the shoes to forgive me. By and by I became warm. I forgot that many people were looking. I forgot about Lin Chi—and then the concern became sincere and real. I started to feel that the door and the shoes were changing their mood. And the moment I realized that the door and the shoes had changed and that they were feeling happy, Lin Chi immediately said that I could come. I had been forgiven."

This incident became a transforming phenomenon in his life because for the first time he became aware that everything is really a crystallization of consciousness. If you cannot see it, it is because you are blind. If you cannot hear it, it is because you are deaf. There is nothing the matter with the things around you; everything is condensed consciousness. The problem is with you—you are not open and sensitive.

This technique says, *This consciousness exists as each being, and nothing else exists.* Live with this notion. Be sensitive to this and wherever you move, move with this mind and this heart—that everything is consciousness and nothing else exists. Sooner or later, the world will change its face. Sooner or later, objects disappear and persons start appearing everywhere. Sooner or later, the whole world will be suddenly illumined and you will know that you were living in a world of dead things just because of your insensitivity. Otherwise everything is alive—not only alive, everything is conscious.

Everything deep down is nothing but consciousness. But if you leave it as a theory, if you believe in it as a theory, then nothing will happen. You will have to make it a way of life, a style of life—behaving as if everything is conscious. In the beginning it will be an "as if" and you will feel foolish, but if you can persist in your foolishness, and if you can dare to be foolish, soon the world will start revealing its mysteries.

Science is not the only methodology to use to enter the mysteries of existence. Really, it is the crudest methodology, the slowest. A mystic can enter existence in a single moment. Science will take millions of years to penetrate that much. The Upanishads say that the world is illusory, that matter is illusory, but only after five thousand years can science say that matter is illusory. The Upanishads say that deep down energy is conscious—science will take another five thousand years. Mysticism is a jump; science is a very slow movement. The intellect cannot jump; it has to argue—argue every fact, prove, disprove, experiment. But the heart can jump immediately.

Remember, for the intellect a process is necessary, then comes the conclusion—process first, then the conclusion—logical. For the heart, conclusion comes first, then the process. It is just the reverse. That is why mystics cannot prove anything. They have the conclusion, but they don't have the process.

You may not be aware, you may not have noticed, that mystics simply talk about conclusions. If you read the Upanishads you will find only conclusions. When for the first time they were translated into Western languages, Western philosophers couldn't see the point—because there was no argument. The Upanishads say, "There is Brahma" —without any argument. How do you reach this conclusion? What is the proof? On what premises do you declare, "There is Brahma"? The Upanishads don't say anything, they simply come to a conclusion. The heart reaches a conclusion immediately. And when the conclusion is reached, you can create the process. That is the meaning of theology.

Mystics reach the conclusion and theologians create the process. Jesus reached the conclusion and then the theologians—Saint Augustine, Thomas Aquinas—they created the process. That is secondary. The conclusion has been reached, now you have to find the proofs. The proof is in the life of the mystic. He cannot argue about it. He himself is the proof—if you can see it. If you cannot see, then there is no proof. Then religion is absurd.

Don't make these techniques theories. They are not. They are jumps into experience, jumps into conclusion.

---

108 Become your own inner guide.

The third technique: *This consciousness is the spirit of guidance of each one. Be this one.*

The first thing is that you have the guide within you but you don't use it. And you have not used it for so long, for so many lives, that you may not even be aware that a guide exists within you.

I was reading Castaneda's book. His master, Don Juan, gives him a beautiful experiment to do.

It is one of the oldest experiments.

On a dark night, on a very hilly track, dangerous, without any light, Castaneda's master said, "You simply believe in the inner guide and start running." It was dangerous. It was a hilly track, unknown, with trees, bushes, abysses. He could fall anywhere. Even in the daylight he had to be alert walking there, and at night everything was dark. He could not see anything and his master said, "Don't walk, run!" He couldn't believe it! It was simply suicidal. He became scared—but the master ran. He ran off just like a wild animal, and came running back. And Castaneda could not understand how he was doing it. Not only was he running in this darkness, but each time he came running directly to him, as if he could see. Then by and by Castaneda gathered courage. If this old man could do this, why not he? He tried, and by and by he felt an inner light coming in. Then he started running.

You only *are* whenever you stop thinking. The moment you stop thinking, the inner happens. If you don't think, everything is okay—it is as if some inner guide is working. Your reason has misguided you. And the greatest misguidance has been this: you cannot believe in the inner guide.

First, you have to convince your reason. Even if your inner guide says, "Go ahead," you have to convince your reason and then you miss opportunities. Because there are moments…you can use them or you can miss them. Intellect takes time, and while you are pondering, contemplating, thinking, you miss the moment. Life is not waiting for you. One has to live immediately. One has to be really a warrior, as they say in Zen, because when you are fighting in the field with your sword, you cannot think. You have to move without thinking.

Zen masters have used the sword as a technique for meditation, and they say in Japan that if two Zen masters, two meditative persons, are fighting with those swords, there can be no conclusion. No one can be defeated and no one is going to win, because both are not thinking. The swords are just not in their hands, they are in the hands of their inner guide, the nonthinking inner guide, and before the other attacks, the guide knows and defends. You cannot think about it because there is no time. The other is aiming at your heart. In a flash of a moment the sword will penetrate the heart. There is no time to think about it, about what to do. When the thought, "penetrate the heart" occurs to him, simultaneously the thought, "defend" must occur to you—simultaneously, with no gap—only then can you defend. Otherwise you will be no more.

So they teach swordsmanship as a meditation and they say, "Be moment to moment with the inner guide, don't think. Allow the inner being to do whatsoever happens to it. Don't let the mind interfere." This is very difficult because we are so trained with our minds. Our schools, our colleges, our universities, the whole culture, the whole pattern of civilization, teach our heads. We have lost contact with the inner guide. Everyone is born with that inner guide but it is not allowed to work, to function. It is almost paralyzed, but it can be revived.

This sutra is for that inner guide. *This consciousness is the spirit of guidance of each one. Be this one.* Don't think with the head. Really, don't think at all. Just move. Try it in some situations. It will be difficult, because the old habit will be to start thinking. You will have to be alert: not to think, but to feel inwardly what is coming to the mind. You may be confused many times because you will not be able to know whether it is coming from the inner guide or from the surface of the mind. But soon you will know the feeling, the difference.

When something comes from the inner, it comes from your navel upwards. You can feel the flow, the warmth, coming from the navel upwards. Whenever your mind thinks, it is just on the surface, in the head, and then it goes down. If your mind decided something, then you have to force it down. If your inner guide decides, then something

bubbles up in you. It comes from the deep core of your being towards the mind. The mind receives it, but it is not of the mind. It comes from beyond—and that is why the mind is scared about it. For reason it is not reliable because it comes from behind—without any reason with it, without any proofs. It simply bubbles up.

Try it in certain situations. For example, you have lost your path in a forest. Try it. Don't think—just close your eyes, sit down, be meditative, and don't think because it is futile—how can you think? You don't know. But thinking has become such a habit that you go on thinking even in moments when nothing can come out of it. Thinking can think only about something which is already known. You are lost in a forest, you don't have any map, there is nobody you can ask. What are you thinking about? But still you think. That thinking will be just a worry, not a thinking. And the more you get worried, the less the inner guide can be competent.

Be unworried. Sit down under a tree, and just allow thoughts to drop and subside. Just wait, don't think. Don't create the problem, just wait. And when you feel a moment of nonthinking has come, then stand up and start moving. Wheresoever your body moves, allow it to move. You just be a witness. Don't interfere. The lost path can be found very easily. But the only condition is: don't let the mind interfere.

This has happened many times unknowingly. Great scientists say that whenever a great discovery has been made, it was never made by the mind; it was always made by the inner guide.

Madame Curie was trying and trying to solve a mathematical problem. She did her best, all that was possible; then she got fed up. For days together, weeks together, she had been working and nothing had come out. She was feeling just mad. No path was leading to the solution. Then one night, just exhausted, she fell down and slept. And in the night, in a dream, the conclusion bubbled up. She was so concerned with the conclusion that the dream was broken, she awoke. Immediately she wrote down the conclusion—because there was no process in the dream, just a conclusion. She wrote it down on a pad and then slept again. In the morning she was puzzled; the conclusion was right, but she didn't know how it had been achieved. There was no process, no method. Then she tried to find the process; now it was an easier affair because the conclusion was in hand, and it is easy to go back from the conclusion. She won the Nobel Prize because of this dream—but she always wondered how it happened.

When your mind gets exhausted and cannot do any more, it simply retires. In that moment of retirement the inner guide can give hints, clues, keys. The man who won the Nobel Prize for the inner structure of a human cell, saw it in a dream. He saw the whole structure of the human cell, the inner cell, in a dream, and then in the morning he just made a picture of it. He himself couldn't believe that it could be so, so he had to work for years. After years of work he could conclude that the dream was true.

With Madame Curie it happened that when she came to know this inner process of the inner guide, she decided to try it. Once there was a problem which she wanted to solve, so she thought, "Why worry about it, and why try? Just go to sleep." She slept well, but there was no solution. So she was puzzled. Many times she tried: when there was a problem immediately she would go to sleep. But there was no solution. First, the intellect has to be tried completely; only then can the solution bubble up. The head has to be completely exhausted, otherwise it goes on functioning even in a dream.

So now scientists say that all the great discoveries are intuitive, not intellectual. This is what is meant by the inner guide.

This consciousness is the spirit of guidance of each one. Be this one. Lose the head and drop into this inner guide. It is there. Old scriptures say that the master or the guru—the outer guru—can be helpful only in finding the inner guru. That is all.

Once the outer guru has helped you to find the inner guru, the function of the outer guru is no more.

You cannot reach to the truth through a master; you can reach only to the inner master through a master—and then this inner master will lead you to the truth. The outer master is just a representative, a substitute. He has his inner guide and he can feel your inner guide also, because they both exist on the same wavelength—they both exist in the same tuning and the same dimension. If I have found my inner guide, I can look into you and feel your inner guide. And if I am really a guide to you, all my guidance will be to lead you to your inner guide.

Once you are in contact with the inner guide, I am no longer needed. Now you can move alone. So all that a guru can do is to push you down from your head to your navel, from your reasoning to your intuitive force, from your argumentative mind to your trusting guide. And it is not like this only with human beings, it is so with animals, with birds, with trees, with everything. The inner guide exists, and many new phenomena have been discovered which are mysteries.

There are a number of cases. For example, the mother fish dies immediately after she lays the eggs. Then the father helps the eggs to be fertilized, and then he dies. The eggs remain alone without a mother and without a father. They mature. Then new fish are born. These fish don't know anything about father, mother, parents; they don't know from where they came. But although these particular fish live in a particular part of the sea, they will move to the part from where the father and mother had come to lay the eggs. They will move to the source. This has been happening again and again, and when they want to lay eggs they will come to this bank, lay the eggs, and die. So there is no communication between parents and their children but the children somehow know where they have to go, where they have to move—and they never miss. And you cannot misguide them. It has been tried, but you cannot misguide them. They will reach to the source. Some inner guide is working.

In Soviet Russia they have been experimenting with cats, with rats, and with many small animals. A cat, a mother cat, was separated from her children and the children were taken deep down into the sea; she could not know what was happening to her children. Every type of scientific instrument was attached to the cat to measure what was going on within her mind and her heart, and then one child was killed, deep in the sea. Immediately the mother became aware. Her pulse rate changed. She became puzzled and worried, her heartbeat increased…as soon as the child was killed. And the scientific instrument said that she was feeling severe pain. Then after a while everything became normal. Then another child was killed—again the change. And the same with the third child. It happened every time, exactly at the same time, without any time-gap. What was happening?

Now Soviet scientists say the mother has an inner guide, an inner feeling-center and it is joined to her children, wherever they are. And she immediately feels a telepathic relationship. The human mother will not feel so much. This is puzzling. It should be quite the otherwise: the human mother should feel more because she is more evolved. But she will not because the head has taken everything into its hands and the inner centers are all lying paralyzed.

This consciousness is the spirit of guidance of each one. Be this one. Whenever you are puzzled in a situation and you cannot see how to get out of it, don't think; just be in a deep nonthinking and allow the inner guide to guide you. In the beginning you will feel afraid, insecure, but soon, when you come every time to the right conclusion, when you come every time to the right door, you will gather courage and you will become trusting.

If this trust happens, I call it faith. This really is religious faith—the trust in the inner guide. Reasoning is part of the ego. It is you believing in yourself. The moment you go deep within you, you have come to the very soul of the universe. Your inner guide is part of the divine guidance. When you follow it, you follow the divine; when you follow yourself, you are complicating things, and you don't know what you are doing. You may think yourself very wise. You are not.

Wisdom comes from the heart, it is not of the intellect. Wisdom comes from the innermost depth of your being, it is not of the head. Cut your head off, be headless—and follow the being, whatsoever, wheresoever it leads. Even if it leads into danger, go into danger, because that will be the path for you and your growth. Through that danger you will grow and become mature.

Even if the inner guide leads you to death, go into it, because that is going to be the path for you. Follow it, trust it, and move with it.

CHAPTER 78

The inner guide

◆

Some of these techniques seem too advanced.

How to recognize the inner guide?

Will the intuitive person not become weak intellectually?

.

The first question:

Some of the techniques in the one hundred and twelve methods seem to be end results and not techniques, such as those that say to "become universal consciousness" or "be this one," et cetera. It seems that we need techniques to achieve these techniques. Were techniques like these meant for very advanced persons who could just become cosmic at a mere suggestion?

uch techniques were meant not for very advanced persons, but for very innocent persons— simple, innocent, trusting. Then just a suggestion is enough. You have to have something to do because you cannot trust. You don't have faith. Unless you do something, nothing can happen to you because you believe in action. If something happens to you suddenly without any doing on your part, you will be scared and you will not believe it. You may even bypass it; you may not even record in the mind that it happened. Unless you *do,* you cannot feel something happening to you—this is the way of the ego.

But for an innocent person, for an innocent, open mind, just a suggestion is enough. Why? Because really, the innermost being is not something to be achieved in the future—it is here and now, it is already the case. Whatsoever is to be attained is here, present in you right this very moment. If you can trust without any effort, it can become revealed. It is not a question of time, of you having to work it out. It is not somewhere far away that you have to travel to. It is *you.* You may call it God, you may call it nirvana or whatsoever you like—it is *you* already. So even a suggestion, if believed totally, can reveal it to you. That's why so much significance is given to *shraddha,* trust, faith. If a person can believe in the master, just a hint, a suggestion, an indication—and in a flash everything will be revealed.

The basic point to be understood is this: there are things which you cannot attain right now because time will be needed to produce them. They are not with you. If I give you a seed, it cannot immediately become a tree. Time will be needed, and you will have to wait and work. Then the seed cannot become the tree immediately. But you are really the tree already. It is not a seed which has to be worked on, it is a tree hidden in darkness, it is a tree which is covered, it is a tree which you are inattentive to—that's all. Your inattention is the cover. You are not looking at it, that's all. You are looking somewhere else and that's why you are missing it. In a trusting moment the master can tell you, just by a suggestion, that it is here. And if you can believe, if you can look in that dimension in trust, it will be revealed to you.

These techniques are not for advanced people; they are for simple, innocent people. Advanced people are, in a way, difficult. They are not innocent, they have been working, they have attained something, and they have a subtle ego behind it. They know something so they are not innocent, they cannot believe. You will have to argue and convince them—and then too they will have to make some efforts. By an innocent mind, I mean a mind which is not arguing. It is just like a small child. The child goes with his father hand in hand, he is not afraid. Wheresoever the father is leading, he must be leading in the right direction. The father knows—so the child need not worry about it. He is not thinking of the future, what is going to happen is not his concern. He is enjoying the very journey; the end is not the problem at all. For the father it may be a problem. He may be afraid. He may be wondering whether they have lost the path or not, whether they are on the right path or not. But for the child it is not a problem. He knows that the father knows. That's all. And wherever the father leads, he will follow—and he is happy at this very moment.

A trusting disciple, an innocent mind is just like a child—and the master is more than a father. Once the disciple surrenders, he trusts. Then at any moment, when the master feels that the disciple is tuned, that the disciple is in harmony, he will just give a hint.

I have heard about a Zen master, Bokuju.... He struggled hard to attain enlightenment, but nothing happened. Really, with a hard struggle sometimes nothing will happen, because the hard struggle is through the ego. And through hard struggle the ego becomes more hard. He did whatsoever could be done but the goal was no nearer. Rather, on the contrary, it was further away; further away than when he had started the journey. He was puzzled, confused, so he came to his master. The master said, "For a few years just completely stop any effort, any goal, any destination. Just forget, and live moment to moment near me. Don't do anything. Simply eat, sleep, walk, and just be near me. And don't raise any question...just see me, my presence. And don't make any effort because nothing is to be achieved. Forget the achieving mind because the achieving mind is always in the future —that's why it goes on missing the present. Just

forget that you have to achieve anything."

Bokuju believed in his master. He started living with him. For a few days, a few months, ideas floated in, thoughts came, and sometimes he would become uneasy and would think, "I am wasting time. I am not doing anything. How can it happen without doing anything? If it couldn't happen through such hard effort, how is it going to be easily attained by not doing anything?" But, still, he believed in the master. By and by the mind slowed down, and in the presence of his master he started to feel a subtle calm flowing—a silence would fall from the master onto him. He started feeling a merging. Years passed. He completely forgot that he was. The master became the center and he started to live like a shadow.

Then the miracle is possible—this happening itself is the miracle. One day, suddenly, the master called his name, "Bokuju, are you here?" Just this, "Bokuju, are you here?" And he said, "Yes, master." And, it is said, he became enlightened.

There was nothing like a technique, not even a suggestion—just, "Bokuju, are you here?" The total presence had been called: Are you here, not moving anywhere, not gone somewhere else? With total intensity, are you present here? And Bokuju said, "Yes, master." In that "yes" he became totally present there.

It is said that the master started laughing and Bokuju started laughing, and the master said, "Now you can go. Now you can move out there and help people by your presence."

Bokuju never taught any method. He would simply ask this much, "Just be near. Remain present." And whenever a disciple was in tune, he would call the name of the disciple and ask, "Are you here?" This was the whole technique.

But this technique will need a grounding of your mind, a deep innocence. There are many techniques which are simple, the simplest possible: just a saying, "Be this one"—just a hint. But it must have been said by the master in a certain moment. "Be this one" cannot always be said. It must have been said in a certain tuning, when the disciple was totally one with the master, or totally with the universe, merged. Then the master says, "Be this one"—and suddenly the focus will change and the last part of the ego will dissolve.

These methods worked in the past but now it is difficult, very difficult, because you are so calculating, you are so clever. And being clever is just against being innocent. You are so calculating, you know too much arithmetic. This calculation goes on and on in the mind; whatsoever you do, it is always calculated, planned. You are never innocent, never open, receptive; you believe too much in yourself. Hence you go on missing. These methods won't be helpful for you unless you prepare. That preparation can be very long, and you are very impatient.

This age is basically the most impatient age that has ever happened on this earth. Everyone is impatient, everyone is too time-conscious, and everyone wants to do everything immediately. Not that it cannot be done—it can be done immediately. But with such time-consciousness it is impossible. People come to me and they say that they have come only for one day. The next day they are going to Sai Baba, and after meeting him they will go to Rishikesh, and then they will go somewhere else. Then they return frustrated and they think there is nothing that India can give. It is not a question of whether India can give something or not, the question is always whether you can receive it or not. You are in such a hurry and you want something immediately. Just like instant coffee, you think of instant meditation, instant nirvana. It is not possible. Nirvana cannot be packaged, cannot be made instant. Not that it is impossible to make it instant, it can become instant—but it can become instant only with the mind which is not after the instant. That's the problem. It can become instant. Immediately, this moment, it can happen. Not even a single moment is needed. But only to one who is relaxed about time completely, to one who can wait for infinity—for him it will happen instantly.

This looks paradoxical but this is the case. If you can wait for eternity, you will not need to wait at all. But if you cannot wait for even a single moment, you will have to wait for eternity. You will have to wait because the mind which says, "Let it happen immediately," is a mind which has already moved from the moment. It is running, it is standing nowhere, it is just on the move. A mind which is on the move, on the way, cannot be innocent.

You may not be aware of it but innocent people are always without time-consciousness. Time lingers slowly. There is no hurry to go anywhere, they are not running. They are enjoying moment to moment. They are chewing each moment. And each moment has its own ecstasy to deliver. But you are in such a hurry that it cannot be delivered. While you are here, your hands are in the future, your mind is in the future—you will miss this moment. And this will be always the case; you will always miss the now. And *now* is the only time! The future is false, the past is just memory. The past is no more, the future is yet to be—and all that ever happens is the now. Now is the only time.

So if you can be prepared to slow down a little, to become noncalculating, playing like children, here and now, then these simple techniques can work miracles. But this century is too time-conscious. That's why you ask, *It seems that we need techniques to achieve these techniques.* No. These are techniques, not end results. They look like end results because you cannot conceive of how they can work. They can work in a particular mind; they cannot work in other types of mind. And really, those who know, they say that all the techniques will ultimately bring you to the innocence where the phenomenon happens. When the phenomenon happens, it will be because the techniques will have brought you to that innocence—if the innocence is there.

But it is difficult now because nowhere is innocence taught; everywhere we are teaching cleverness. Universities are not to make you innocent, they are to make you clever, cunning, calculating.

The more clever you are, the better you will be in the struggle of life. You can gain much wealth, prestige, power, if you are calculating. If you are innocent, you will prove to be stupid; if you are innocent, then you will be nowhere in this competitive world. This is the problem: in this competitive world you may not be anywhere, but in that noncompetitive world of nirvana, if you are innocent, you will be somewhere. If you are calculating you will not be anywhere in the world of nirvana, but in this world you will be somewhere. And we have chosen this world to be our goal.

Old universities differed completely, their orientation was totally different. Nalanda or Takshsila did not teach calculation, they did not teach cleverness. They were teaching innocence. Their orientation was different from Oxford or Kashi or Cambridge; their orientation was totally different. They were creating a different type of mind. So it almost always happened that a person who studied in Takshsila or Nalanda would become a *bhikkhu*, a sannyasin, in the end. By the time he graduated from university he would renounce this world. Those universities were antiworld; they were preparing for some other dimension. They were preparing you for something else which cannot be measured in terms of this world. These techniques were for those type of people. Either they were innocent by their nature or they were training themselves to be innocent.

When Jesus said to his followers, "If someone hits you on one cheek, you give him the other," what is he intending to do? He is trying to make you innocent. Only a foolish person would do this. When someone hits you on one cheek, a calculating mind will say, "Hit him hard, immediately." And a really calculating mind will say, "Before someone hits you, hit him. Because attack is the best defense." Ask Machiavelli, he is the cleverest mind. He says, "Before someone attacks you, you attack him, because attack is the best defense. Once someone has attacked you, you are already weak; he has already gained over you. Now the race is not equal. He is ahead of you. So don't allow the enemy to go ahead. Attack before anybody attacks you."

This is a calculating mind, this is a clever mind. Machiavelli was read by every prince and every king in medieval Europe, but he was such a clever person that no king would employ him. He was read—his book was the bible for power politics, every prince would read his book *The Prince* and they would follow it—but no king was ready to employ him because he was such a clever man. It was better to keep him away; he was dangerous, he knew too much. He said, "Virtue is not good, but pretending to be virtuous is. Don't be virtuous, but pretend always that you are virtuous. That is the real good because then you gain from both the ends: from vice you gain, and from virtue also." This is the calculating mind. Go on pretending that you are virtuous, and always praise virtue. But never be really virtuous. Always praise virtue so others know that you are a virtuous person. Always condemn vice—but don't be afraid to use it.

Jesus says, "When someone hits you on one cheek, give him the other. And if someone takes your coat, snatches it, give him your shirt also. And if someone forces you to carry his load for one mile, tell him that you are ready to carry it for two miles." This is patent foolishness, but very meaningful. If you can do this, these techniques will be for you. Jesus is preparing his disciples for sudden enlightenment. Just think about it. If you can be so innocent, so trusting that if the other is hitting you, he must be hitting you for your good—so give him the other cheek also, and let him hit it. The other's goodness is believed in, trusted in; no one is your enemy. When Jesus says, "Love your enemies," this is the meaning. No one is your enemy; don't see the enemy anywhere. That doesn't mean that there will not be enemies and there will not be people who will exploit you. There will be. They will exploit you. But be exploited—and don't be cunning. Just look at that dimension: be exploited but don't be cunning. Be exploited but don't be mistrusting, don't disbelieve, don't lose faith. That is more valuable than anything others can cheat you of. Nothing else is so valuable.

But how do our minds function? If one man deceives you, the whole of humanity is evil. If one man is dishonest or you think that he is dishonest, then you don't believe in man at all. Then the whole of humanity has become dishonest. If one Jew is a miser, then the whole race of Jews is miserly. If one Mohammedan is bigoted, then all Mohammedans are. Just one is enough for us to lose our faith in all. Jesus says, "Even if all are dishonest, you should not lose faith, because faith is more valuable than what these dishonest people can take from you by their dishonesty." So really, if you lose faith you are losing something; otherwise nothing is lost.

For such innocent people these techniques are enough, they will not ask for anything more. You say, and it happens to them. Just on hearing the master many have become illumined—but in the past, not in this age.

I have heard a story about Rinzai. He was a very poor bhikkhu, a poor sannyasin, a beggar. As he was sleeping in his hut a thief entered. There was nothing in the hut except a blanket that he himself was using. He was sleeping on the floor, covered with his blanket. Then he became very uncomfortable and started to think, "What an unfortunate fellow! He has come so far from the village to find something, and there is nothing in my hut. What misery! How to help him? The only thing is this blanket." And he was under it and the thief would not have the courage to snatch the blanket, so he slipped out from under it, left it there and slipped into a dark corner. The thief took the blanket and went away. The night was very cold, but Rinzai was happy that the thief had not gone back empty-handed.

Then he sat at the window of his hut. The night was cool, and the full moon was in the sky. He wrote a small haiku, a small poem. In the haiku he said, "If I could have given this moon to that thief, I would have." This mind! What has he lost? Just a blanket. What has he gained? The whole world, all

that can be gained. He has gained innocence, trust, love.

For this man no technique is needed. His master would say, "Just look. Be aware. Be alert." And that would do.

The second question:

How to differentiate between the dictates of the unconscious mind and that of the inner guide? How can one recognize that the inner guide has come into function?

The first thing: because of Freud, much misunderstanding has arisen around the word 'unconscious'. Freud completely misunderstood it, misinterpreted it. And he has become the very basis of modern knowledge about mind. To Freud, unconscious meant simply the repressed conscious, the suppressed part of the conscious. So all that is evil and bad, immoral, has been suppressed. Because the society cannot allow it, it has to be suppressed within. For Freud, that repressed part is the unconscious—but not for mystics.

Freud is not a mystic; he has not entered his own unconscious. He has been simply observing cases of patients: ill people, abnormal people, mad, insane, pathological. He has been studying the pathological mind, and through the study of the pathological mind—and that, too, from without—he concluded that just underneath the conscious there is an unconscious mind. That unconscious mind carries all that has been suppressed from the childhood, all that society has condemned. The mind has suppressed it, just to forget that it is there.

But it is there—and it goes on functioning. And it is very powerful: it goes on changing the conscious, it goes on playing tricks with the conscious. The conscious is really impotent before it, because whatsoever is repressed is repressed only because it is so powerful that society cannot cope with it. So society has been repressing it and society doesn't know what else to do with it. For example, sex. It is so powerful that if you don't repress it you won't know what to do with it. It will lead you into dangerous paths. And it is such a forceful energy that the whole society will become chaotic if it is allowed completely. No marriage could exist, no love could exist, everything would be just a chaos if it was allowed total freedom—because then man would behave like an animal. If there were no marriage, no family, the whole society would be destroyed. Society depends on the unity of the family; the family depends on marriage; marriage depends on sex suppression. Everything that is natural, forceful, has been inhibited, tabooed—so forcibly that you feel guilty about it and you go on fighting with it. Society has not only created policemen outside, it has created inner policemen, your conscience—a double arrangement so that you don't go astray, so that you cannot be natural, you have to be unnatural.

Now modern psychologists say that insanity is part of civilization—no civilization can be without madness. But mad people are suffering because you have forced such an order over them that their natural instincts are crushed. They have been crippled. It may be that your madmen are more powerful than you, that's why their inner instincts have revolted and they have thrown their conscience, their mind, everything, overboard. That's why they are mad. A better concept of humanity, a better organization, a better discipline with more knowledge and wisdom, may use them. They may prove geniuses; they may prove very talented people. They are. But they have such a force in them that they cannot repress themselves. And society will not allow them to move because they are wild. Freud came to the conclusion that civilization needs the unconscious, the repressed part.

But really, for tantra and yoga this unconscious is not the unconscious, it is just between the conscious and the unconscious, a small boundary. It is subconscious. The conscious has forced something down, but the conscious knows about it. It is not really unconscious, you know about it. You may not want to recognize it, you may not want to be attentive to it, because you are afraid that if you give it attention it will come up. You have forced it into darkness but you are conscious about it. The Freudian unconscious is not really unconscious, it is only subconscious. It is not dark night, it is in the light, you can see it.

Tantra talks about the real unconscious which is not suppressed by you but which is your deepest being. And your conscious is just one part of it which has come into light, the one-tenth part which has seen the light, which has become conscious. Nine parts, nine-tenths, are just hidden underneath. That unconscious is really your source of life-energy, of being. Your conscious mind is one-tenth of the whole mind and this conscious mind has created its own center. That center is the ego. This center is false because it doesn't belong to the whole mind, it is not the center of the whole mind. It is just a center of the conscious part, a fragment. The fragment has created its own center and that center goes on pretending it is the center of the whole being. No, your total mind has a center: that center is called the guide. That center is in the unconscious and it will be revealed only when five fragments, or half of the mind, come into light. Then the center which is the guide will be revealed. It is hidden in the unconscious.

So you need not be afraid of the unconscious; it is the Freudian unconscious you are afraid of. It is something to be afraid of. But this Freudian unconscious can be thrown out in catharsis. Hence my great insistence on catharsis. This Freudian unconscious can be thrown out in catharsis: whatsoever you wanted to do and you have not done, do it, meditatively. Don't do it *to* anyone because that will create a chain of events—and you will not be in control. Just do it in a vacuum. If you are angry, do it in a vacuum. If you feel sexuality, throw it into the sky. If you feel anything, just allow it to move from your inwards outwards. Express it. A meditative catharsis will relieve you of the Freudian unconscious. With the technique that I am teaching —if it is followed—the Freudian unconscious will simply disappear. And only when this Freudian unconscious disappears can you penetrate the real unconscious. It is just in between, between the conscious and the unconscious. You just go on throwing your rubbish things into a room and you close it; you go on accumulating a junkyard—Freudian unconscious is just a junkyard. Don't throw it in, I say, throw it out. When it moves in, you will become pathological, you can go insane. When it moves out you will become fresh, young, unburdened.

For this age, catharsis is a must. No one can reach the inner guide without catharsis. And once you are in deep catharsis you need not be afraid. Then the real unconscious will start revealing itself, then it will penetrate into your conscious, and then for the first time you will become aware of your vast territory. You are not such a small fragment, you have a very vast being, and this vast being has a center. That center is the inner guide.

How to differentiate between the unconscious and the inner guide? How to differentiate between the Freudian unconscious and the inner guide? It will be difficult if you don't go through catharsis. But you can feel a difference by and by because the Freudian unconscious is just a repressed thing. If something appears in you with a violent force, know well that this violent force is coming because you have repressed it in the first place. If something simply appears in you without any violence, just bubbles up silently, easily, without any sounds, even soundlessly, then know that this is the real unconscious. From the guide something is coming to you. But you will become proficient only when you go through catharsis. Then you will know what is happening.

Whenever anything comes from the Freudian unconscious you will feel disturbed, it will make you uneasy, uncomfortable; and whenever something comes from the guide you will feel such serenity, you will feel so happy, so at ease, so at home, that you cannot imagine it. You will simply feel that this is the thing. Your total being is in harmony

with it, there is no resistance. You know this is the right, this is the good, this is the truth—and nobody can convince you otherwise. With the Freudian unconscious you can never be serene, you can never be still and calm; you will be disturbed. It is a sort of disease that has come up—and there will be a fight with it. So it is better if you pass through deep catharsis, then the Freudian unconscious will become silent, by and by.

And just as bubbles come up from a riverbed, come up to the very surface of the water, you will feel bubbles coming up from the very bed of your being. They will come to your conscious mind. But their very coming will give you a deep tranquility—a feeling that nothing can be more right than this. But before it happens you have to unburden yourself of the Freudian unconscious. And that can happen only if you are in a let-go, because the innermost being is so nonviolent that it will not assert itself.

The Freudian unconscious will want to assert itself; every moment it is trying to assert itself and you are pushing it back. This is the difference. It wants to assert itself, it wants to become active, it wants to lead you somewhere, it wants to manipulate you—and you are resisting it, fighting it.

The real unconscious, the guide, is not assertive. If you allow it, if you invite it, prayerfully, it will come to you just like an invited guest. You have to be in a let-go. Only then will it come. When it feels you are ready, when it feels it will not be denied, rejected, when it feels it will be welcomed, then it will come to you.

So you have to do two things: catharsis for the Freudian unconscious, and training in let-go and surrender for the real guide, the real unconscious. These two things done, you will know the difference.

The difference really cannot be taught to you—you will know it. When it happens, you will know it. How do you know the difference between when there is pain in your body and when the whole body feels a well-being? When the whole body is filled with well-being and when your head has a headache, how do you feel what the difference is? You simply know it. You cannot define it, you simply know it: you know what a headache is and you know what well-being is.

The real guide will always give you a feeling of well-being, and the Freudian unconscious will always give you a feeling of headache. It is a turmoil, it is an inner conflict, it is anguish, it is pain suppressed. So whenever it comes you will feel painful all over.

Because of this Freudian unconscious, many things have become painful which are not naturally painful—for example, sex. Because society has repressed sex, it has become painful. One of the most blissful things in natural life is sex. But it has become painful. If you move into sex you will feel frustrated, you will feel guilty, at the end you will feel weakened, and you will decide never to have sex again. This is not because of natural sex, this is because of the unconscious. Sex has become painful. It has been so repressed that it has become ugly and painful. Otherwise it is one of the most natural ecstasies. If a child is never taught that sex is bad and a sin he will enjoy it, and every time he will feel a deep well-being flowing all over the body.

Men feel more well-being than women—because women are repressed more. No one requires that a boy should be a virgin but everyone requires, even the boy himself, that the girl he is going to marry should be a virgin. Even playboys require that the girl should be a virgin. Women's unconscious has been repressed more than men's, that's why only a few women achieve orgasm. And that, too, in the West—in the East not more than five percent of women, at the most, achieve any enjoyment in sex. Ninety-five percent are simply fed up with it. That's why when sadhus and monks teach that sex is sin, women always agree. They gather in multitudes around monks because the thing appeals to them, it is right. Because they are so suppressed they have never known any bliss out of it.

In India, while making love, women are not supposed to move, be active. They have to lie still like a corpse. If they are active their man will become suspicious: they are enjoying sex and this is not the sign of a good woman. A good woman is one who doesn't enjoy. In the East they will say that if you want to marry, marry a good woman, and if you want to enjoy, then have a friendship with a bad woman—because only bad women can enjoy. This is unfortunate. The woman is not supposed to move, to be active, she should be just dead. How can she achieve orgasm when the energy is not moving?

And if she cannot enjoy it she is bound to be against the husband and she is bound to think that the husband is evil. Every day Indian women come to me and they say that they are fed up with sex and their husbands are forcing them again and again to have sex. They don't like it, they are disgusted. And why are the husbands not so disgusted? Why are the women disgusted? The reason is that they have a greater repressed unconscious about sex than men.

Sex will become painful. If you have suppressed it, it is a headache. Anything can become a headache—just suppress it, that is the trick. It will become a suffering. And anything can become blissful—just express it, don't suppress it.

This Freudian unconscious is all that you know right now. You don't know about the real unconscious, the tantra unconscious—that's why you are afraid. And afraid, you cannot let go. Afraid, you cannot lose control. You know that if you lose control, immediately the suppressed instincts will take over. Immediately, whatsoever you have repressed will come to the mind and it will insist on being acted out. That's why you are afraid. Catharsis is needed first so the fear goes. And then you can let go. And if you let go, a very silent force will start flowing to your conscious mind and you will feel a well-being, you will feel that you are at home, you will feel that everything is good, you will feel that you are blessed.

How can one recognize that the inner guide has

come into function? This will be the first sign: you will start feeling good, good about yourself. Remember, you always feel bad about yourself. I almost never come across a person who feels good about himself. Everyone is condemning himself, everyone thinks he is bad. And when you think you are bad how do you suppose that someone else is going to love you? And when no one loves you, you feel frustrated. But you yourself don't love you. You have never touched your hand lovingly, you have never felt your body lovingly, you have never thanked God that he has given you such a beautiful body, such a beautiful organism. No, you just feel disgusted. And the religions, the so-called religions have taught you to feel condemned—this body is a bag of sins. You are carrying a burden.

When the unconscious is released you will feel suddenly that you are accepted, you are not bad. Nothing is bad. The whole of life becomes deep down a blessing. You feel blessed. And the moment you feel blessed, all others around you become blessed; you can bless them, you can feel happy. Because you feel condemned, you feel bad about yourself and you think the same about others. How can you love another's body if you condemn your own body? If you are against your own body, how can you love another body? You will condemn— deep down you will condemn. Really, religions have prepared you to become just ghosts. They don't want you to be with the body, they want you to be just unembodied spirits. Everything has been so condemned…and you have taken it for granted.

I have seen in scriptures, in many scriptures, that it is written that your body has nothing but blood, fat, phlegm—just to condemn it. I don't know what these persons who were writing these scriptures wanted. Did they want gold to be there? silver? diamonds? or what? Why is blood condemned? Why is blood bad? Blood is life! But they have condemned it and we have accepted the condemnation. They must be mad, insane.

Jainas always say that their *tirthankaras* never urinated, they don't defecate. Such bad things. But why is urine bad? What do you want to urinate instead of urine? And what is bad in it? But it is such a bad thing. And psychologists say that because the sex center and the urinating organ are the same in man, sex has become condemned. And in woman the sex center is just in the middle, on one side defecation and on the other side urination; sex cannot be good if it is between two such bad things. The condemnation of sex has come because we have condemned defecation. But why? Why condemn it? What is bad? But we accept condemnation and when we accept, then there are problems.

Your whole body is condemned by neurotic people. They may have written scriptures but that doesn't make any difference. They may have been great leaders—neurotics almost always are. They are great leaders because they are so fanatic that they can immediately get a following. And there are always people who worship fanaticism. Anyone who says something strongly will have people falling at his feet saying he is the right leader. And he may be just neurotic, just mad. These neurotic people have condemned you and you have accepted them, you have been conditioned by them.

When the unconscious flows in you, a subtle well-being will come. You will feel good: everything is good, and everything is divine. Your body comes from the divine, your blood also, your urine also. Everything is divine. When the unconscious flows in you, everything is divine, everything becomes spiritual. Nothing is bad, nothing is condemned. This will be the feeling, and then you will fly. You will become so light you cannot walk. Then nothing is a burden on your head. Then you can enjoy small things in a very great way. Then every trivial thing becomes a beauty. But that beauty is given by you—whatsoever you touch becomes golden because deep down you are so filled with bliss.

This will be the first thing that will happen to you—a goodness about yourself. And, when the unconscious starts flowing into your conscious, the second thing will be that you will become less world-oriented, less intellectual, more total. Then if you are happy you will not just simply say that you are happy—you will dance. Just saying, "I am happy," is pale, meaningless. I see people who say, "I am happy"—but just look at their faces! I know people who say, "I love you," but their body is not expressing anything. Words are dead but we have substituted them for life. When the unconscious flows in you, this will be the difference: you will live with your total being. When you feel happy, you will dance. Then you will not simply say, "I am happy"—you will *be* happy. That's the difference. You will not say, "I am happy"—there is no need to say it because you will be happy. Then there will be no need to say to someone, "I love you"—you will *be* love. Your whole being will show the feeling, you will vibrate with love. Anybody passing nearby will feel that you love; anyone just touched by your hand will feel a subtle energy has entered into him. There is a warmth in your presence, a happiness.

This will be the second thing. First, you will feel a goodness about yourself and about everything; and second, you will become total. When the guide takes you, you will be total.

The third question:

When that intuition starts functioning, is surrender the only technique for that intuition, or the inner guide? Does a person living through intuition always succeed? How do You value success and failure? Is it not true that the person living intuitively will become weak intellectually?

Surrender is the only technique for the inner being to become active.

Does a person living through intuition always succeed? No, but he is always happy—whether he succeeds or not. And a person not living intuitively is always unhappy, whether he succeeds or not. Success is not the criterion because success depends on many things. Happiness is the criterion because happiness depends only on you. You may not suc-

ceed because others are competitors there. Even if you are working intuitively, others may be working more cunningly, more cleverly, more calculatingly, more violently, more immorally. So success depends on many other things; success is a social phenomenon. You may not succeed.

Who can say that Jesus succeeded? Crucifixion is not a success, it is the greatest failure. A man crucified when he was just thirty-three—what type of success is this? No one knew about him. Just a few villagers, uneducated people, were his disciples. He had no position, no prestige, no power. What type of success is this? Crucifixion cannot be said to be success. But he was happy, he was totally blissful—even when being crucified. And those who were crucifying him would remain alive for many years but they would remain in misery. So really, who was undergoing crucifixion? That is the point. Those who crucified Jesus, were they undergoing crucifixion? Or was Jesus, who was crucified? He was happy. How can you crucify happiness? He was ecstatic. How can you crucify ecstasy? You can kill the body but you cannot kill the soul. Those who crucified him, they lived, but their life was nothing but a long, slow crucifixion—misery and misery and misery.

So the first thing is that I don't say that if you follow the inner guide you will always succeed—in the sense that the world recognizes success; but in the sense that a Buddha or a Jesus recognizes success, you will succeed. But that success is measured by your happiness, your bliss—whatsoever happens is irrelevant, you will be happy. Whether the world says that you have been a failure, or the world makes you a star, a success, it doesn't make any difference. You will be happy whatsoever the case; you will be blissful. Bliss is success to me. If you can understand that bliss is success, then I say you will succeed always.

But to you bliss is not success; success is something else. It may even be misery. Even if you know that it is going to be a misery, you long for success. Ask political leaders—they are in misery. I have not seen any political leader who is happy. They are just miserable, but still they are trying for higher posts, trying to get still higher on the ladder. And those who are already above them are in misery, and they know it. But we are ready to be miserable if success comes to us. So what is success to us? Success is egoistic fulfillment, not bliss. It is just so that people will say that you have succeeded. You may have lost everything—you may have lost your soul; you may have lost all that innocence that gives bliss; you may have lost all that peace, silence, that brings you nearer to the divine; you may have lost all, and become just a madman—but the world will say you are a success.

For the world, ego gratification is the success; for me it is not. For me, to be blissful is success—whether anyone knows about you or not. It is irrelevant whether anyone knows about you or not, whether you live totally unknown, unheard of, unnoticed. But if you are blissful, you have succeeded.

So remember this distinction because there are many people who would like to be intuitive, who would like to find the inner guide, just to succeed in the world. For them the inner guide will be a frustration. In the first place, they cannot find it. In the second place, even if they can find it, they will be miserable, because what they are aiming at is recognition by the world, ego fulfillment—not bliss.

Be clear in the mind: don't be success-oriented. Success is the greatest failure in the world. So don't try to succeed; otherwise you will be a failure. Think of being blissful. Every moment think of being more and more blissful. Then the whole world

may say you are a failure but you will not be a failure. You have attained.

Buddha was a failure in the eyes of his friends, family, wife, father, teachers, society—he was a failure. He had become just a beggar. What type of success is this? He could have been a great emperor: he had the qualities, he had the personality, he had the mind. He could have been a great emperor but he became a beggar. He was a failure, obviously. But I say to you he was not a failure. If he had become an emperor then he would have been a failure because he would have missed the real life. What he attained under the bodhi tree was the real and what he lost was unreal.

With the real you will succeed in the inner life; with the unreal...I don't know. If you want to succeed in the unreal then follow the path of those who are working in cunningness, cleverness, competition, jealousy, violence. Follow their path, the inner guide is not for you. If you want to gain something of the world, then don't listen to the inner guide.

But ultimately you will feel that although you have won the whole world, you have lost yourself. Jesus says, "And what does a man get if he loses his soul and gains the whole world?" Who will you call a success: Alexander the Great or Jesus the Crucified? So if—and that "if" has to be understood well—if you are interested in the world, then the inner guide is not a guide for you. If you are interested in the inner dimension of being then the inner guide, and only the inner guide, can help.

1103

CHAPTER 79

The philosophy of emptiness

◆

109 *Suppose your passive form to be an empty room with walls of skin — empty.*

110 *Gracious one, play. The universe is an empty shell wherein your mind frolics infinitely.*

111 *Sweet-hearted one, meditate on knowing and not-knowing, existing and not-existing. Then leave both aside that you may be.*

112 *Enter space, supportless, eternal, still.*

These techniques are concerned with emptiness—they are the most delicate, the most subtle. Even to conceive of emptiness seems impossible. Buddha used all these four techniques for his disciples and *bhikkhus,* and because of these four techniques he was totally misunderstood. Buddhism got completely uprooted from Indian soil just because of these four techniques.

Buddha said that there is no God. If there is God, you cannot be totally empty. You may not be there but the God will be there, the divine will be there. And your mind can deceive you, because your divine may be just your mind playing tricks. Buddha said that there is no soul, because if there is any soul, atma, you can hide your ego behind it. Your ego will be difficult to leave if you feel that there is some self within you. Then you cannot be totally empty because you will be there.

Just to prepare the ground for these techniques of emptiness, Buddha denied everything. He was not an atheist but he appeared to be an atheist because he said that there is no God, he said there is no soul, he said there is nothing substantial in existence—existence is empty. But this was just to prepare the ground for these techniques. Once you enter emptiness you have entered all—you may call it the divine, you may call it God, or atma, soul, whatsoever you like—but you can enter the truth only when you are totally empty. Nothing should be left of you.

Hindus thought that Buddha was destroying religion, that he was teaching irreligion. And people who heard him, even they couldn't follow, because whenever you go somewhere, you go to seek something—you never go to seek emptiness. So those who went to hear him were seeking something—nirvana, moksha, the other world, heaven, truth—but they were seeking something. They had come to gratify their ultimate desire: to find the truth. That is the last desire. And unless you are completely desireless, you cannot know the truth; the very condition of knowing is to be totally desireless.

So one thing is certain: you cannot desire truth. If you desire it, the very desire will become the barrier. There were masters before Buddha who were teaching, "Don't desire, be desireless." But they were talking about God, about the kingdom of God, heaven, paradise, moksha, the ultimate freedom and liberation—and they were saying, "Be desireless." Buddha felt that you cannot be desireless if there is something to be attained. You may pretend that you are desireless, but this pretension, desirelessness, is also from some desire to be fulfilled. It is false. The masters say that you cannot attain to ultimate bliss with desire, and you want to attain ultimate bliss—so you start being desireless, you try to be desireless, so that you can attain the ultimate bliss. But the desire is there. You are trying to be desireless just because of the desire. So Buddha said that there is no God to be attained. Even if you desire, there is no one to be attained... so be desireless. There is no moksha somewhere,

1107

there is no goal. Life is meaningless and goal-less.

His emphasis is beautiful and wonderful—no one has tried that way. He destroyed all the goals just to help you to be desireless. If the goals are there, how can you be desireless? And if you are not desireless, you will not attain to the goal—this is the paradox. He destroyed all the goals—not that those goals are not there, they are there and they can be attained—but if you want to attain them, if you desire to attain them, it becomes impossible. The very basic condition is that you must be desireless, then the ultimate happens to you. So Buddha says there is nothing to be desired, desires are futile. Drop all desires and when there is no desire you will be empty.

Just imagine, if there is no desire within you, what will you be? You are nothing but a bundle of desires. If all desires go, you simply disappear. Not that you will not exist—you will exist, but as an emptiness. You will be there just like a vacant room: no one is there, just a *shunya*, a nothingness. Buddha has called this nothingness *anatma, anatta*, no-soulness. You will not feel any center, that "I am"; there will be just am-ness, no "I" to it, because "I" is nothing but accumulated desires, condensed desires, crystallized desires—many, many desires have become your "I."

It is just as in physics. Physicists say that if you analyze matter, then matter is nothing but atoms; there is nothing to join the atoms, each atom is surrounded by vacant space. If you have a rock in your hand, there is no rock, just atoms of energy, and between two atoms, infinite space. Even a rock is spacious, porous. They say that soon we will be able to pull that space out from anything.

H. G. Wells has written a story…. In the twenty-first century, a passenger starts calling for coolies in a big station. Other passengers who are traveling in the same compartment with this passenger cannot understand, because he has no luggage, just a packet of cigarettes and a small matchbox. That is all his luggage, and he goes on calling for coolies. A big group gathers and a passenger asked, "Why?

Why are you calling? You don't have anything. You can carry this matchbox and this packet of cigarettes yourself. What are you going to do with these two dozen coolies?"

The passenger laughs and he says, "Try; try that matchbox. That matchbox is not ordinary. One railway engine is condensed into it."

It will be possible soon. Space can be pulled out and then it can be again forced in, and the engine will take its shape again. Then big things can be carried without much problem. The weight will remain the same but the shape, the form, will become smaller and smaller. A matchbox can contain a railway engine, but the weight will remain the same, because space has no weight. You can pull out the space but you cannot pull out the weight. The weight will remain the same because weight is contained by the atoms, not by the space. They say that the whole earth can be condensed into the form, the shape, of one apple, but the weight will remain the same. And if you pull apart all these atoms, if you take one atom out, and then another, and then another, if you take all the atoms out, nothing will be left behind—so matter is just an appearance.

Buddha has analyzed the human mind in a simpler way; he is one of the greatest scientists possible. He says your ego is nothing but desires, atomic desires. There are millions of desires; they make you. If you go on pulling out desires one by one, a moment will come when there is no desire left, you have disappeared…just space, just vacant space remains. And this, Buddha says, is nirvana. This is the cessation of your being completely; you are no more. And Buddha says this is silence: unless you are completely gone, silence cannot descend on you.

Buddha says you cannot be silent because you are the problem; you cannot be peaceful because you are the disease; and you can never be blissful because you are the only barrier. The bliss can come at any moment, but you are the barrier. When you are not, bliss will be there; when you are not, peace will be there; when you are not, silence will be there; when you are not, ecstasy will be there. When your inner being is totally empty, this emptiness itself is bliss. That's why Buddha's teachings are called *shunyavad,* the philosophy of emptiness, or the philosophy of zero.

These four techniques are to attain this state of being, or you can call it this state of no-being—there is no difference. You can give it a positive term, as Hindus and Jainas have called it, soul, or you can give it a more appropriate but negative term, as Buddha has called it, anatta, no-selfness or no-soulness. It depends on you. But whatsoever you call it, there is no one to be named and called, there is just infinite space. That's why I say that these are the ultimate techniques, the most delicate, the most difficult—but the most wonderful. And if you can work with any of these four techniques, you will gain the unattainable.

109 Feel your body as empty.

The first technique: *Suppose your passive form to be an empty room with walls of skin—empty.*

*Suppose your passive form to be an empty room with walls of skin...*but inside, everything empty. This is one of the most beautiful techniques. Just sit in a meditative posture, relaxed, alone, your backbone straight and the whole body relaxed—as if the whole body is hanging on the backbone. Then close your eyes. For a few moments go on feeling relaxed, more relaxed, becoming calmer and calmer and calmer. Do this for a few moments, just to be in tune. And then suddenly start feeling your body is just walls of skin and there is nothing inside, there is no one inside, the house is vacant. Sometimes you will feel thoughts passing, clouds of thoughts moving, but don't think that they belong to you. You are not. Just think that they are roaming in a vacant sky—they don't belong to anyone, they don't have any roots.

Really this is the case: thoughts are just like clouds moving in the sky. They don't have any roots and they don't belong to the sky, they simply roam in the sky. They come and they go and the sky remains untouched, uninfluenced. Feel that your body is just walls of skin and there is no one inside. Thoughts will still continue—because of old habit, old momentum, old cooperation, thoughts will go on coming. But just think that they are rootless clouds moving in space—they don't belong to you, they don't belong to anybody else. There is no one to whom they can belong—you are empty. It will be difficult, but because of the old habits, nothing else. Your mind would like to catch some thought, be identified with it, move with it, enjoy it, indulge in it. Resist! Just say there is no one to indulge, there is no one to fight, there is no one to do anything with this thought.

Within a few days, a few weeks, thoughts will slow down, they will become less and less. The clouds will start disappearing, or, even if they come, there will be great gaps of cloudless sky when there will be no thought. One thought will pass, then another will not come for a period. Then another will come and then there will again be an interval. In those intervals you will know for the first time what emptiness is. And the very glimpse of it will fill you with such deep bliss you cannot imagine.

Really it is difficult to say anything about it, because whatsoever is said in language will refer to you, and you will not be there. If I say that you will be filled with happiness it will be nonsense. You will not be there, so how can I say you will be filled with happiness? Happiness will be there. Just within the four walls of your skin, happiness will be there, vibrating—but you will not be there. A deep silence will descend on you, because if you are not, no one can create a disturbance. You always go on thinking that somebody else is disturbing you: the traffic noise on the road, children playing around you, the wife working in the kitchen... somebody is disturbing you. Nobody is disturbing you; you are the cause of the disturbance. Because you are there, anything can disturb you. If you are not there, then disturbances will come and pass through the emptiness without touching it. You are there—very touchy, a wound; anything immediately hurts you.

I have heard about a scientific story…. It happened after the third world war that all were dead; now there was no one on the earth, only trees and hills were there. One big tree thought to create a great noise, as it used to create in the past. It fell down from a big rock, it did everything that was possible, but there was no noise—because for noise your ears are needed, for sound your ears are needed. If you are not there, sound cannot be created. It is impossible. I am speaking here; I am making sound because you are here. If no one is here, I may go on speaking, but sound cannot be created. But I can create it myself because I myself can hear it. If no one is there to hear, sound cannot be created, because sound is a reaction of your ears.

If no one is there on the earth, the sun will rise but it cannot create light. It seems absurd. We cannot conceive of it because we always think that the sun will rise and there will be light. Your eyes are needed. Without your eyes, the sun cannot create light. It may go on rising but it will be futile because the rays will pass in emptiness. There will be no one who can react and who can say that this is light. Light is a phenomenon of your eyes; you react. Sound is a phenomenon of your ears; you react. What do you think…a rose is there in the garden, but if no one passes, will there be perfume? A rose alone cannot create perfume—impossible. You and your nose are needed—someone to react and interpret that this is perfume, this is rose perfume. However hard a rose tries, without a nose it will not be a rose at all.

The disturbance on the street is not there really, it is within your ego. Your ego reacts and says that this is a disturbance. It is your interpretation. Sometimes in a different mood you may enjoy it, then it will not be a disturbance. You may enjoy it in a

different mood, and then you will say, "This is beautiful. What music!" But in a sad moment even music will become a disturbance. But if you are not there, just space, emptiness, there can be neither disturbance nor music. Things will just pass through you unnoticed, because unstruck, there is no wound to react, there is no one to respond; not even an ego will be created. This is what Buddha calls nirvana.

And this technique can help you.

Suppose your passive form to be an empty room with walls of skin—empty. Sit in a passive state, inactive, not doing anything…because whenever you do something the doer comes in. Really there is no doer. Only because of the doing you imagine that there is one. Buddha is difficult only because of this. Only because of linguistic forms have problems arisen.

We say a man is walking. If you analyze this sentence, it means that there is someone who is walking. But Buddha says there is only a process of walking, there is no one who is walking. You are laughing. Because of language it appears that there is someone who is laughing. Buddha says there is laughter but no one inside who is laughing. When you laugh, remember this, and find out who laughs. You will never find anyone—there is simply laughter. There is no one behind it doing it. When you are sad, there is no one who is sad, there is simply sadness…. Look at this. Simply sadness. It is a process: simply laughter, simply happiness, simply unhappiness. There is no one behind it.

Only because of language do we go on thinking in terms of two. If there is movement, we say there must be someone who has moved—the mover. We cannot conceive of movement alone. But have you ever seen the mover? Have you ever seen the one who laughs? Buddha says there is life, the process of life, but no one inside who is alive. And then there is death, but no one dying. For Buddha you are not a duality—the language creates a duality. I am speaking. It seems that I am someone who is speaking—but Buddha says there is only speaking, there is no one who is speaking. It is a process, it belongs to no one.

But for us this is difficult because our mind is deeply rooted in dualism. Whenever we think of some activity we conceive of some actor inside, some doer. That's why a passive, inactive form is good in meditation because then you can fall into emptiness more easily. Buddha says, "Don't meditate, be in meditation." The difference is vast. I will repeat. Buddha says, "Don't meditate, be in meditation"—because if you meditate, the doer has come in; you will go on thinking that you are meditating. Then meditation has become an act.

Buddha says, "Be in meditation." That means be totally passive, don't do anything, and don't think that there is any doer. That's why sometimes, when the doer is lost in the doing, you feel a sudden upsurge of happiness. It comes because you have become one. With a dancer a moment comes when dance takes over and the dancer disappears. Then happens a sudden blessing, a sudden beautitude, a sudden ecstasy. He is filled with unknown bliss. What has happened? Only the doing remained and the doer was no more.

At the war front, soldiers sometimes attain to very deep bliss. It is difficult to conceive of because they are so near death—at any moment they can die. In the beginning it makes them afraid, they tremble in fear. But you cannot continue trembling and fearing every day, continuously. One becomes accustomed, one accepts death—then the fear disappears. And when death is so near and with any wrong movement you may be dead immediately, the doer is forgotten, and only duty remains, only doing remains. And one has to be so deeply in the doing that one cannot go on remembering that "I am." That "I am" will create trouble, you will miss. You will not be totally in the activity. And life is at stake so you cannot afford duality. Action becomes total. When action is total, you suddenly feel you are happy as you have never been before.

Warriors have known very deep springs of joy that ordinary life cannot give to you. That may be the reason why war is so appealing. And that may be the reason why *kshatriyas,* warriors, have attained to moksha more than brahmins, because brahmins are always thinking and thinking—much mental activity. Twenty-four Jaina *tirthankaras,* Rama, Krishna, Buddha, were all kshatriyas, warriors. They have attained to the highest peak.

No businessman has ever been heard to attain to that peak. He lives in such security that he can afford to be dual. Whatsoever he is doing, it is never total. Profit cannot be a total activity. You can enjoy it, but it is never a life-and-death problem. You can play with it, but nothing is at stake. It is a game. A business is playing a game, the game of money. The game is not very dangerous, so businessmen almost always remain mediocre. Even a gambler may attain to higher peaks of bliss than a businessman, because a gambler moves into danger. He stakes everything that he has got—and in that moment of total stake the doer is lost.

That may be the reason why gambling is so appealing, war is so appealing. As far as I understand, behind whatsoever is appealing, there must be some ecstasy lurking somewhere, some hint of the unknown somewhere, some glimpse of the deep mystery of life hidden somewhere there. Otherwise nothing can be appealing.

Passivity.... Any posture that you take in meditation should be passive. In India we have evolved the most passive *asana,* the most passive posture; that is *siddhasana.* And the beauty of it is that in this siddhasana posture, as Buddha sits, the body is in the deepest of passive states. Even while lying down you are not so passive; even while sleeping, your posture is not so passive, it is active. Why is a siddhasana so passive? For many reasons. In this posture the body is locked, closed. The body has an electric circle: when the circle is closed and locked, the electricity moves round and round inside the body, it does not leak out. Now it is a proved scientific phenomenon that in certain postures your body leaks energy. When the body is leaking energy, it has to create energy continuously. It is active. The body dynamo has to work continuously because you are leaking. When energy is leaking from the outside body, the inside body has to be active to replace it. So the most passive state will be when no energy is leaking.

Now in Western countries, particularly in England, they treat patients just by making a circle of their body electricity. In many hospitals these techniques are being used and they are very helpful. A person lies on the floor on a net of wires. The net of wires is just to make a circle of his body electricity. Just half an hour is enough, and he will feel so relaxed, so filled with energy, so strong, that he cannot believe that when he came he was so weak.

In all the old cultures, people used to sleep in a particular direction in the night just so that energy didn't leak out—because the earth has a magnetic force. To use that magnetic force you have to lie in a particular direction—then the force in the earth will magnetize you the whole night. If you are lying opposite to it the force is fighting with you and your energy will be destroyed. Many people in the morning feel very depressed, very weakened. This should not be so, because sleep is meant to rejuvenate you, to give you more energy. But there are many people who are energetic when they go to bed but in the morning they are just dead. There can be many reasons for it but this may be one: they are lying in the wrong direction. If they are lying against the earth magnet they will feel dissipated.

So now scientists say that the body has an electric circuit which can be locked, and they have studied many yogis sitting in siddhasana. In that state the body is leaking the minimum energy; energy is preserved. When energy is preserved the inner batteries need not work, there is no need for any activity. So the body is passive. In this passivity, you can become more empty than if you are active.

In this siddhasana posture your backbone is straight and the whole body is also straight. Now many studies have been done. When your body is straight, totally straight, you are least influenced by the gravitation of the earth. That's why if you sit in a posture which is inconvenient, which you call inconvenient, the inconvenience is caused because your body is affected by more gravitation. If you are sitting straight then gravitation is least effective, because it can pull only your backbone, nothing else. That's why it is difficult to sleep while standing. It is almost impossible to sleep while standing in a *shirshasana,* on your head.

For sleep you have to lie down. Why? Because then the earth has the maximum pull on you—and the maximum pull makes you unconscious. For sleep you have to lie down on the ground, so the earth's gravitation touches the whole of your body and pulls every cell of it. Then you become unconscious. Animals are more unconscious than man because they cannot stand erect. Evolutionists say that man could evolve because he could stand erect, on two feet; the gravitational pull is less. Because of that he could become a little more aware.

In siddhasana, the gravitational pull is at its minimum. The body is inactive and passive, closed inside, it has become a world unto itself. Nothing is moving out, nothing is coming in. Eyes are closed, hands are locked, feet are locked—energy moves in a circle. And whenever energy moves in a circle, it creates an inner rhythm, an inner music. The more you hear that music, the more you feel relaxed.

Suppose your passive form to be an empty room, just like an empty room, *with walls of skin —empty.* Go on dropping into that emptiness. A moment will come sometime when you feel everything has disappeared; that there is no one, nobody, the house is vacant, the lord of the house has disappeared, evaporated. In that gap, in that interval, when you are not present inside, the divine will be present. When you are not, God is. When you are not, bliss is. So try to disappear. Try to disappear from within.

110 Be playful in activity.

The second technique: *Gracious one, play. The universe is an empty shell wherein your mind frolics infinitely.*

This second technique is based on the dimension of play. That has to be understood. If you are inactive, it is good to fall into deep emptiness, into the inner abyss. But you cannot be empty the whole day and you cannot be passive the whole day. You will have to do something. Activity is a basic requirement, otherwise you cannot be alive. Life means activity. So you can be inactive for a few hours, but for the rest of the twenty-four hours you will have to be active. And meditation should be something which becomes your style of life, it should not be a fragment. Otherwise you will gain it and lose it. If you are inactive one hour then for twenty-three hours you will be active. The active forces will be more, and they will destroy whatsoever you attain in your inactivity. The active forces will destroy it. And the next day you will again do the same: for twenty-three hours you will accumulate the doer and in one hour you will have to drop it. It will be difficult. So your mind must change its attitude about work and activity. Hence the second technique.

Work should be considered as play, not as work. Work should be considered as play, just a game. You should not be serious about it; you should be just like children playing. It is meaningless, nothing is to be achieved; just the very activity is enjoyed. You can feel the distinction if you play sometimes. When you work it is different: you are serious, burdened, responsible, worried, anxious, because the result, the end result, is the motive. The work itself is not worth enjoying. The real thing is just in the future, in the result. In play there is no result, really. The very process is blissful. And you are not worried, it is not a serious thing. Even if you look serious, it is just pretending. In play you enjoy the very process; in work the process is not being enjoyed—the goal, the end, is important. The process has to be tolerated anyhow. It has to be done because the end has to be achieved. If you could achieve the end without this, you would drop activity and jump to the end.

But in play you would not do that. If you could achieve the end without playing, then the end would be futile. It has meaning only through the process. For example, two football teams are on the playing ground. Just by throwing a coin they can decide who will win and who will be defeated. Why go through so much effort, unnecessarily exerting yourself? The thing can be decided very easily just by tossing a coin. The end will be there. One team can win, another can be defeated. Why work for it? But then there will be no meaning, no significance. The end is not meaningful, the very process is the meaning. Even if no one wins and no one is defeated the game was worth it. The activity in itself is enjoyed.

This dimension of play has to be applied to your whole life: whatsoever you are doing, be there in that activity so totally that the end is irrelevant. It may come, it has to come, but it is not on your mind. You are playing, you are enjoying.

That's what Krishna means when he tells Arjuna to leave the future in the hands of the divine. The result of your activity is in the hands of the divine, you simply do. This simple doing becomes a play. That's what Arjuna finds difficult to understand, because he says that if it is just play, then why kill, why fight? He understands what work is but he cannot understand what play is. And Krishna's whole life is just a play. You cannot find such a nonserious man anywhere. His whole life is just a play, a game, a drama. He is enjoying everything but he is not serious about it. He is enjoying it intensely but he is not worried about the result. What happens is irrelevant.

It is difficult for Arjuna to understand Krishna, because he calculates, he thinks in terms of the end result. He says in the beginning of the Gita, "This whole thing seems to be absurd. On both sides my friends and my relatives are lining up to fight. Whosoever wins, it will be a loss, because my family, my relatives, my friends, will be destroyed. Even if I win, it will not be worth anything because to whom am I going to show my victory? Victories are meaningful because friends, relatives, family will enjoy them. But there will be no one, the victory will be just over dead bodies. Who will appreciate it? Who will say, 'Arjuna, you have done a great deed'? So whether I am victorious or I am defeated, it seems absurd. The whole thing is nonsense." He wants to renounce. He is deadly serious. And anyone who calculates will be that deadly serious.

The setting of the Gita is unique. War is the most serious affair. You cannot be playful about it, because lives are involved, millions of lives are involved—you cannot be playful. And Krishna insists that even there you have to be playful. You don't think about what will happen in the end, you just be here and now. You just be a warrior playing. Don't get worried about the result, because the result is in the hands of the divine. And it is not even the point if the result is in the hands of the divine or not. The point is that it should not be in your hands. You should not carry it. If you carry it then your life cannot become meditative.

This second technique says, *Gracious one, play.* Let your whole life be just a play. *The universe is an empty shell wherein your mind frolics infinitely.* Your mind goes on playing infinitely. The whole thing is just like a dream in an empty room. While meditating, one has to look at the mind just frolicking, just like children playing, jumping out of overflowing energy, that's all. Thoughts jumping, frolicking, just a play—don't be serious about them. Even if a bad thought is there, don't feel guilty. Or if there is a very great thought, a very good thought—that you want to serve humanity and transform the whole world, and you want to bring heaven onto earth—don't get too much ego through it, don't feel that you have become great. This is just a frolicking mind. Sometimes it goes down, sometimes it comes up—it is just overflowing energy, taking many shapes and forms. Mind is just an overflowing spring, nothing else.

Be playful, Shiva says: *Gracious one, play.* The attitude of the player means he is enjoying the activity, it is good in itself. No profit motive is involved; he is not calculative. Just look at a businessman: whatsoever he is doing, he is calculating about the profit, what he is going to attain out of it. A customer comes. The customer is not a person, he is just a means. What can be profited out of him? How can he be exploited? Deep down he is calculating what is to be said, what is to be done. Everything is calculated just to manipulate, just to exploit. He is not concerned with this person, he is not concerned with the deal, he is not concerned with anything—he is concerned only with the future, the profit.

Look at the East: in the villages still, a businessman is not just a profit maker, and the customer has not come just to purchase something. They enjoy it. I remember my old grandfather. He was a cloth merchant, and I and my whole family were puzzled because he enjoyed it so much. For hours together it was a game with the customers. If something was worth ten rupees, he would ask fifty rupees for it—and he knew this was absurd, and his customers knew it too. They knew that it must be worth nearabout ten rupees, and they would start from two rupees. Then a long haggling would follow—hours together. My father and my uncles would get angry. "What is going on? Why don't you simply say what the price is?" But he had his own customers. When they came, they would ask, "Where is Dada, where is grandfather? because with him it is a game, a play. Whether we lose one rupee or two, whether it is more or less, that is not the point!"

They enjoyed it. The very activity in itself was something worth pursuing. Two persons were communicating through it. Two persons were playing a game and both knew it was a game—because of course a fixed price was possible.

In the West now they have fixed prices, because

people are more calculating and more profit-motivated. They cannot conceive of wasting time. Why waste time? The thing can be settled within minutes. There is no need. You can just write the exact price. Why fight for hours together? But then the game is lost and the whole thing becomes a routine. Even machines can do it. The businessman is not needed; the customer is not needed.

I have heard about a psychoanalyst who was such a busy man and who had so many patients that it was difficult to have personal contact with everyone. So he would feed his tape-recorder for a particular patient and the tape-recorder would say whatsoever that psychoanalyst wanted to say to the patient.

Once it happened that it was the appointed time of a patient who was a very rich man. The psychoanalyst was entering a hotel. Suddenly he saw the patient sitting there, so he asked, "What are you doing here? It was your time with me."

The patient said, "I am so busy that I have fed my words to my own tape-recorder. Both the tape-recorders are talking to each other. Whatsoever you have to say to me, my tape-recorder has recorded, and whatsoever I have to say to you, your tape-recorder has recorded it from my tape-recorder. This saves time, and we are both free." If you are too calculating then persons disappear, and more and more mechanization comes in.

Even now in villages in India the haggling goes on. It is a game and worth enjoying. You are playing. It is a match between two intelligences, and two persons come in deep contact. But it is not time-saving. Games can never be time-saving. And in games you don't worry about the time. You are carefree, and whatsoever is going on, you enjoy it right in that moment.

Being playful is one of the deepest bases of all meditative processes. But we are businesslike; we are trained for it. So even when we meditate, we are looking for the end, for the result. And whatsoever happens, you will be unsatisfied.

People come to me and they say, "Yes, meditation is growing, progressing. I'm feeling more happy, a little more silent, at ease, but nothing else is happening." What nothing else? I know that people like this are bound to come someday and say, "Yes, I am feeling nirvana, but nothing else is happening. I am blissful, but nothing else is happening." What nothing else? He is looking for some profit, and unless some very visible profit comes into his hands, something which he can deposit in a bank, he cannot be satisfied. Silence and happiness are so vague, you cannot possess them, you cannot show them to anyone.

Every day it happens that people come to me and they say that they are sad. They are expecting something which should not be expected even in business—and they are expecting it in their meditations. The business mind comes into meditation with the whole training of business—what profit can be made out of it?

The businessman is not playful, and if you are not playful, you cannot be meditative. Be more and more playful. Waste time in play. Just playing with children will do. Even if there is no one, you can jump and dance alone in the room and be playful. Enjoy. But your mind will go on insisting, "What are you doing, wasting time? You can earn something out of this time. You can do something, and you are just jumping, singing and dancing. What are you doing? Have you gone mad?"

Try it. Snatch whatsoever time you can get out of your business, and be playful. Whatsoever—you can paint, you can play on a sitar, anything you like—but be playful. Look for no profit out of it, see no future in it, just the present. And then—then you can be playful inside also. Then you can jump on your thoughts, play with them, throw them here and there, dance with them, but not be serious about them.

Many people are just unconscious as far as their mind is concerned. Whatsoever happens in their mind, they are unconscious about it; they are drifting in it without knowing where the mind leads them. If you can be aware of any track of the mind you will be puzzled at what is happening. Mind moves through associations. A dog barks on the street. The bark comes to your head—and now you have started. You may move to the very end of the world through this barking of the dog. You may remember some friend who had a dog. Then this dog is dropped and that friend has come into the mind and he had a beautiful wife, and the wife was beautiful…and now you are moving. You can go to the very end of this world and you will never remember that a dog just played a trick on you; it just barked and put you on the track, and you started to move.

You will feel very awkward at what scientists say about this. They say that this track is fixed in your mind. If the same dog in the same situation barks again, you will follow this track again: the friend, the dog, the wife, the beautiful wife—you will go the same way again.

Now they have tried many experiments with electrodes in the human brain. They touch a particular spot in the brain and then a particular memory is released. Suddenly you see that you are five years old, playing in a garden, running after a butterfly. Then the whole sequence is there: you feel pleasant, everything is nice, the air, the garden, the smell, everything comes alive. It is not simply memory, you relive it. Then the electrode is pulled out and the memory stops. If the electrode again touches the same spot, again the same memory starts: you are again five years old, in the same garden, with the same butterfly, the same smell, the same sequence of events. When the electrode is pulled out, the memory disappears, but put the electrode back in the same spot and the memory comes again.

It is just as if you are remembering something mechanically. And it always starts from a certain beginning and ends at a particular end, and then starts from the beginning…. Just as you record something on a tape-recorder, your brain has millions of memories, millions of cells recording, and it is all mechanical.

These experiments on the human brain are very strange and very revealing. Memories can be revived again and again, again and again. One experimenter tried three hundred times and the memory was the same—it was recorded. The person on whom the experiment was done became aware and he felt that it was very, very weird because he was not the master, he could not do anything. When the electrode touched the place, the memory started and he had to see it. During three hundred times he by and by became a witness. He started seeing the memory but then he became aware that he was different and this memory was different. This experiment can be helpful, very helpful for meditators, because when you know your mind is nothing but a mechanical recording around you, you are separate.

This mind can be touched. Now scientists say that sooner or later we will cut all the centers which give you anguish, anxiety, because again and again the same thing is touched and the whole thing has to be relived.

I have been trying many experiments with many disciples. Do the same thing and they move in the same vicious circle, again and again, again and again—unless they become a witness that this is a mechanical thing.

You are aware that if you say the same thing to your wife—each week, the same thing—she will react. After seven days, when she has forgotten, say the same thing: she will react. Then record…the reaction is going to be the same. You know, your wife knows, a pattern becomes fixed—and it goes on. Even a dog can start your pattern just by barking. Something is touched, an electrode has entered. You have started on a journey.

If you are playful in life then you can be playful inside with the mind also. Then be as if you are watching something on a TV screen: you are not involved, you are just a spectator, an onlooker. Look, and enjoy it. Don't say good, don't say bad, don't condemn, don't appreciate, because those are serious things. If a naked woman comes onto your screen, don't say that this is bad, that some devil is playing a trick on you. No devil is there to play a trick upon you. Look at it as if it is just on the screen, a film screen. And be playful about it: say to the lady, "Wait!" Don't try to push her out because the more you push her out, the more she will come in—ladies are difficult. And don't follow her. If you follow then you will be in trouble. Don't follow, don't fight—this is the rule. Just look and be playful. Just say a "hello" or "good morning." Just look and don't be disturbed at all. Let the lady wait. She will go by herself, as she came: she moves on her own. She is not related to you, she is just something in the memory. Struck by some situation she came there, just a picture. Be playful with it. If you can be playful with your mind it will drop very soon, because mind can be there only if you are serious. Seriousness is the link, the bridge.

Gracious one, play. The universe is an empty shell wherein your mind frolics infinitely.

---

111   Beyond knowing and not-knowing.

The third technique: *Sweet-hearted one, meditate on knowing and not-knowing, existing and not-existing. Then leave both aside that you may be.*

…Meditate on knowing and not-knowing, existing and not-existing. Meditate on the positive aspect of life and then on the negative—then put both aside because you are neither. *Then leave both aside that you may be.*

Look at it in this way. Meditate on a birth: a child is born, you are born. Then you grow, you become young—meditate on this whole growth. Then you become old, then you die. From the very beginning…imagine the very moment when your father and mother conceived you, and into the womb of the mother you came, just the first cell. From there look to the very end, where your body is burning on a funeral pyre and all your relatives are standing around you. Then put both aside—the one who was born and the one who has died. Just put both aside and then look within. There you are—that which is never born and which is never going to die.

…Knowing and not-knowing, existing and not-existing. Then leave both aside that you may be. You can do it with any positive–negative polarity. You are sitting here. I look at you, I know you. When I close my eyes, you are no longer there, I don't know you. Then put aside both the knowledge that I have known and the knowledge that I don't know—you will be empty, because when you put both knowledge and no-knowledge aside you will be empty.

There are two types of people: some are filled with knowledge and some are filled with ignorance. There are people who say, "We know." Their ego is bound up with their knowledge. And there are people who say, "We are ignorant." They are filled with their ignorance. They say, "We are ignorant. We don't know." One is identified with knowledge, the other is identified with ignorance—but both possess something, both cherish something. Push both aside, knowing and not-knowing, so that you are neither—neither ignorant, nor knowing. Put aside both positive and negative. Then who are you? Suddenly the "who" will be revealed to you. You will become aware of the beyond, that which transcends. Putting aside both positive and negative, you will be empty. You will be no one, neither wise nor ignorant. Put both hate and love aside, put both friendship and enmity aside. When both the polarities are put aside you are empty.

But this is a trick of the mind: it can put one aside but never the two together. It can put one aside—you can put ignorance aside, then you cling to knowledge. You can put pain aside, but then you cling to pleasure. You can put enemies aside, but then you cling to friends. And there are a few people who do just the reverse: they will put friends aside and cling to the enemies, they will put love aside and cling to hate, they will put wealth aside and cling to poverty, and they put knowledge, scriptures, aside and cling to ignorance. These people are great renouncers. Whatsoever you cling to they put it aside and cling to the opposite—but they cling all the same.

Clinging is the problem, because if you cling you cannot be empty. Don't cling; this is the message of this technique. Just don't cling to anything, positive or negative, because with nonclinging you will find yourself. You are there, but because of the clinging, you are hidden. With nonclinging you will be exposed, you will be uncovered. You will explode.

---

112 Enter the space within.

The fourth technique: *Enter space, supportless, eternal, still.*

Three qualities of space have been given in this technique. Supportless: there can be no support in space. Eternal: it can never end. Still: it will be soundless, it will be silent. Enter this space, it is within you.

But the mind always asks for support. People come to me and if I say to them, "Just sit silently, with closed eyes, and don't do anything," they say, "Give me some *avalamban,* some support. Give me some mantra as a support, because I cannot sit." Just sitting is difficult. If I give them a mantra, it is okay. They can go on repeating the mantra. Then it is easy. With support you are never empty, that's why it is easy. Something must go on, you must be doing something. Doing, the doer remains; doing, you are filled. You may be filled with *omkar,* aum, Rama, Jesus, Ave Maria, anything—you may be filled with anything, but you are filled; then you are okay. Mind resists emptiness. It wants always to be filled by something else, because if it is filled it can be. If it is not filled it will disappear. In emptiness you will attain to no-mind. That's why mind asks for support.

If you want to enter inner space, don't ask for support. Drop all supports, mantras, gods, scriptures, whatsoever gives you a support. If you feel you are supported, drop it, and just move inside—supportless. It will be fearful, you will feel scared. You are moving to where you can be lost completely. You may not be able to come back, because all supports will be lost. Your contact with the bank is lost and where this river will lead you, no one knows. Your support is lost. You may fall into an infinite abyss. Hence, fear grips you, and you ask for some support. Even if it is a false support, you enjoy it. Even a false support is helpful, because for the mind it makes no difference whether a support is real or false—it must be a support, that's the point. You are not alone, something is there and supporting you.

It happened once that a man came to me…. He was living in a house where he felt there were spirits and ghosts, and he was very worried. Through worries, he started seeing more illusions. Through worries, he became ill, weak. His wife said, "If you live any longer in this house, I am leaving." His children were sent to some relative's house.

The man came to me and he said, "It has become very difficult now. I see them clearly. They walk in the night. The whole house is filled with spirits. You help me."

So I gave him one of my pictures and said, "Take it. Now I will tackle those spirits. You simply sleep silently, you need not worry. Really, I will tackle them, I will see to them. Now it is my business. And don't interfere. Now you need not be concerned."

The man came the next day. He said, "I slept, it was so beautiful! You have done a miracle!" And I had not done anything but give a support. Through support the mind was filled. It was no longer vacant, someone was there.

In ordinary life you are leaning on many false supports, but they help. And unless you become strong enough, you will need them. That's why I say that this is the ultimate technique—no support.

Buddha was dying, and Ananda asked him, "Now you are leaving us, what shall we do? How shall we attain? How shall we proceed now? When the master is gone, we will be wandering in darkness for many, many lives. No one is there to lead us, to guide us; the light is going out."

So Buddha said, "It will be good for you. When I am no more, you become your own light. Move alone, don't ask for any support, because support is the last barrier."

And it happened. Ananda had not become enlightened. For forty years he was with Buddha, he was the closest disciple, he was just like a shadow to Buddha, moving with him, living with him; he had had the longest contact with him. For forty years Buddha's compassion was falling over him, raining over him—for forty years. But nothing happened, Ananda remained as ignorant as ever. And the day after Buddha died, Ananda became enlightened—the next day, the very next day. The very support had been the barrier. When there was no more Buddha, Ananda could not find any support. It is difficult. If you live with a buddha, and the buddha goes, then no one can be a support to you. Now no one will be worth clinging to. One who has been clinging to a buddha cannot cling to anybody else in this world. This whole world will be vacant. Once you have known a buddha and his love and compassion, then no love, no compassion can compare. Once you have tasted that, nothing else is worth tasting. So Ananda was alone for the first time in forty years, totally alone. There was no way to find a support. He had known the highest support; now lower supports would not do. The next day he became enlightened. He must have

moved into the inner space...*supportless, eternal, still.*

So remember, don't try to find any support. Be supportless. If you are trying to do this technique, then be supportless. That is what Krishnamurti is teaching: "Be supportless. Don't cling to a master. Don't cling to a scripture. Don't cling to anything."

This is what every master has been doing. A master's whole effort is first to attract you towards him, so that you start clinging to him. When you start clinging to him, when you become close and intimate with him, then he knows that the clinging must be cut. And you cannot cling to anyone else now, that is finished. You cannot move to anyone else, that is impossible. Then he cuts the clinging, and suddenly you are left supportless. It will be miserable in the beginning. You will cry and you will weep and you will scream and the whole being will feel that you are lost. Into the very deepest depth of misery you will fall. But from there one arises alone, supportless.

Enter space, supportless, eternal, still. That space has no beginning, no end. And that space is absolutely soundless. There is nothing—not even a sound vibrating, not even a ripple. Everything is still.

That point is just within you. Any moment you can enter it. If you have the courage to be supportless, this very moment you can enter it. The door is open. The invitation is for all, all and everyone. But courage is needed; courage to be alone, courage to be empty, courage to dissolve and melt, courage to die. And if you can die within to your inner space, you will attain to the life which never dies, you will attain to *amrit,* to immortality.

CHAPTER 80

All and nothing mean the same

◆

Q U E S T I O N S

If there is no one inside us, why call it the being?

How can an enlightened one make decisions?

Why do mystics live in quiet places?

How do You know consciousness is eternal?

What will my enlightenment do for the rest of the world?

The first question:

You said that really there is no one inside us, there is only a void, an emptiness, but then why do You often call it the being, the center?

Being or nonbeing, nothing or all —they look contradictory but they both mean the same. All and nothing mean the same. In dictionaries they are opposites but in life they are not. Nobody understands. Look at it in this way: if I say that I love all, or if I say that I love no one, it means the same. If I love someone, then only is there a difference. If I love all, it means the same as loving no one. There is no difference then. The difference is always in degrees, relative.

And these are both two extremes, they have no degrees; the total and the zero have no degrees. So you can call the total a zero, or you can call a zero the total. That's why some enlightened persons have called the inner space emptiness, *shunya*, the void, nothingness, nonbeing, *anatma*—and some have called it the inner being, the absolute being, *Brahma, atma*, the supreme self. These are the two ways to describe it. One is positive, the other is negative. Either you have to include all or to exclude all—you cannot describe it with any term which is relative. An absolute term is needed. Both the contradictory poles are absolute terms.

But there have been some enlightened persons who have remained totally silent. They have not called it anything, because whatsoever you call it— whether you call it being or nonbeing—the moment you give it a name, a term, a word, you have erred, because it includes both.

For example, if you say, "God is alive," or "God is life," it is meaningless, because then who will be death? He includes all. He must have death in him as completely as life, otherwise to whom will death belong? And if death belongs to someone else and life belongs to God—then there are two Gods, and then there will be many problems which cannot be solved. God must be both life and death. God must be both the creator and the destroyer. If you say God is the creator, then who is the destroyer? If you say God is good, then who will be evil?

Because of this difficulty, Christians, Zoroastrians, and many other religions have created a Devil side by side with God—because to whom will the evil belong? They have created a Devil. But nothing is solved, the problem is only pushed one step back because then it can be relevantly asked, "Who has created the Devil?" If God himself creates the Devil, then he is responsible. And if the Devil is something independent, not related to God, then he himself becomes a God, a supreme power. And if God has not created the Devil, how can God destroy him? It is impossible. Theologians go on giving some answer to a question but that answer again creates more questions.

God created Adam, then Adam became evil. He was expelled. He disobeyed God and he was expelled from the heavenly world. It has been asked again and again, and relevantly, why did

Adam become evil? The possibility must have been created in him by God—the possibility to be evil, to go wrong, to disobey. If there was no possibility, no inherent tendency, then how could Adam go wrong? God must have created the tendency.

And if the tendency for evil was there, another thing is also certain: the tendency to overcome it was not so strong, the tendency to fight it was not so strong. The evil tendency was stronger. Who created this strength? No one except God can be responsible. Then the whole thing seems to be a hoax. God creates Adam; he creates an evil tendency in him, a strong evil tendency which he cannot control; then he goes wrong; then he is punished. God should be punished, not Adam! or you have to accept that some other force exists side by side with God. And that other force must be stronger than God, because the Devil can tempt Adam and God cannot protect him. The Devil can provoke and seduce and God cannot protect. The Devil seems to be a stronger God.

There is a church, recently born in America, called the Church of Satan, the Church of the Devil. They have a high priest, just like the pope of the Vatican, and they say that history proves that the real God is the Devil. And they look logical. They say, "Your God, the God of good, has always been defeated, and the Devil has always been victorious. The whole of history proves it. So why worship a weak God who cannot protect you? It is better to follow a strong God who can seduce you but who can protect you also, because he is stronger." The Church of the Devil is now a growing church. And they seem logical, this is what history proves.

This duality—to save God from the negative pole—creates problems. In India we have not created the other pole. We say God is both the creator and the destroyer, the good and the bad. This is difficult to conceive of because the moment we say "God" we cannot conceive of him being bad. But in India we have tried to penetrate the deepest mystery of existence—that is, oneness.

Somehow, good and bad, life and death, negative and positive, meet somewhere, and that meeting point is existence, oneness. What will you call that meeting point? Either you will have to use a positive term, or a negative one, because we don't have any other terms.

If you use positive terms, then you call it Being with a capital B—God, Absolute, Brahma—or if you want to use a negative term, then you call it nirvana, nothingness, shunya, nonbeing, anatma. Both indicate the same. It is both and your inner being is also both. That is why sometimes I call it being, and sometimes I call it nonbeing. It is both. It depends on you. If the positive appeals to you, then call it being. If the negative appeals to you, then call it nonbeing. It depends on you. Whatsoever feels good, whatsoever you feel will give you maturity, growth, evolution, call it that.

There are two types of persons: one who cannot feel any affinity with negativity and the other who cannot feel any affinity with the positive. Buddha is the negative type. He cannot feel affinity with the positive, he feels affinity with the negative; he uses all negative terms. Shankara doesn't feel affinity with the negative; he talks about the ultimate reality in positive terms. Both say the same thing. Buddha calls it "shunya," and Shankara calls it "Brahma." Buddha calls it the void, nothing, and Shankara calls it the absolute, the all. But they are saying exactly the same thing.

Ramanuja, one of Shankara's greatest critics, says that Shankara is just a hidden Buddhist. He is not a Hindu, he only appears to be because he uses positive terms. That is all the difference there is. Wherever Buddha says nothing, he says Brahma; all else is the same. Ramanuja says that Shankara is the great destroyer of Hinduism because he has brought Buddhism in from the back door by just using a trick—wherever a negative term is used, he uses a positive term, that's all. He calls him a *prachchhanna-buddha,* a crypto-Buddhist. And he is right in a way because there is no difference. The message is the same.

So it depends on you. If you feel an affinity with silence, nothingness, then call that great being Emptiness. If you don't feel an affinity, if you feel afraid, then call that emptiness The Great Being. But then your techniques will be different. If you feel scared with emptiness, aloneness, nothingness, then the four techniques I talked about last night will not be of much use to you. Forget them. There are other methods about which I have been talking. Use positive techniques.

But if you are ready and have the courage to be supportless, to move into emptiness, alone, ready to cease completely, then these four techniques will help you tremendously. It depends on you.

The second question:

If there is absolute emptiness inside an enlightened one, then how is it that he seems to be making decisions, discriminating, liking this or disliking that, saying yes or no?

This will really look like a paradox. If an enlightened one is simply emptiness, then for us it becomes a paradox. Then why does he say yes or no? Why does he choose? Why does he like some things and dislike other things? Why does he talk? Why does he walk? Why does he live at all?

For us this is a problem; but for the enlightened one it is not a problem. Everything is done out of emptiness. The enlightened one is not choosing. It looks like choice to us but the enlightened one simply moves in one direction. That direction comes from the emptiness itself.

It is just like this. You are walking. Suddenly a car comes in front of you and you feel that an accident will happen. You don't decide what to do. Do you decide? How can you decide? There is no time. A decision will take time. You will have to ponder and think, weigh up the pros and cons, decide whether to jump this way or that. You don't decide, you simply jump. From where does that jump come? Between the jump and you there is no thinking process. Suddenly you become aware that

the car is in front of you and you jump. The jump happens first. Then later on you can think. In that moment you jump through hastiness; your whole being jumps without any decision.

Remember, decision is always of the part, it can never be of the whole. Decision means that there was a conflict. One part of your being was saying, "Do this," another part was saying, "Don't do this." That's why the decision was needed. You had to decide, argue, and one part had to be pushed aside. That's what decision means. When your totality is there, there is no need to decide, there is no alternative. An enlightened one is total within himself, total emptiness. So whatsoever comes out, it comes out of his totality, not out of any decision. If he says "yes" it is not a choice: there was no "no" to be chosen, there was no alternative. Yes is the response of his total being. If he says no, then no is the response of his total being. That's why an enlightened man can never repent. You will repent always. Whatsoever you do, it makes no difference —whatsoever you do, you will repent. If you want to marry a woman, if you decide yes, you will repent, if you decide no, you will repent. Because whatsoever you decide is a partial decision, the other part is always against. If you decide, "Yes, I will marry this woman," one part of your being is saying, "Don't do this, you will repent." You are not total.

When difficulties arise... They are bound to arise because when two different persons start living together, difficulties are bound to arise. There will be conflicts, there will be a struggle to dominate, there will be power politics. Then the other part will say, "Look! What did I say? I was insisting that you shouldn't do this, and you have done it." But that doesn't mean that if you had followed the other part, there would have been no repentance. No! The repentance would have been there, because then you would have married some other woman, and the conflict and the struggle would have happened. Then the other part would go on saying, "I was saying marry the first woman. You have missed an opportunity. A heaven is lost, and you are married to a hell."

You will repent, whatsoever the case, because your decision cannot be total. It is always against a part, and that part will take revenge. So whatsoever you decide, if you do good you will repent, if you do bad you will repent. If you do good, then your mind, the other part, will go on saying that you have missed an opportunity. If you do bad, then you will feel guilty. An enlightened being never repents. Really he never looks backwards. There is nothing to look backwards at. Whatsoever is done is done with his totality.

So the first thing to be understood is that he never chooses. The choice happens to his emptiness; he never decides. That doesn't mean that he is indecisive. He is absolutely decisive, but he never decides. Try to understand me. The decision happens in his emptiness. This is how his whole being acts: there is nothing more to it. If you are walking and a snake crosses your path, you jump suddenly, that's all. You don't decide. You don't consult a master and a guide. You don't go to look into books in the library about what to do when a snake crosses the path—how to do it, what the technique is. You simply jump. And remember, that jump is coming from your total being, it has not been a decision. Your total being has acted that way, that is all. There is nothing more to it.

To you it seems as if an enlightened one is choosing, deciding, discriminating, because you are doing that every moment, and you cannot understand something which you have not known at all. An enlightened one happens to be doing things without any decision, without any effort, without any choice—he is choiceless. But that doesn't mean that if you give him food and stones, he will start eating stones. He will eat the food. To you it will look as if he has decided not to eat the stones, but he has not decided. That is simply foolish, it doesn't occur to him; he eats the food. This is not a decision—only an idiot person would decide whether to eat stones or food. Stupid minds decide; enlight-

ened minds simply act. And the more mediocre the mind, the more effort has to be made for a decision.

That's what worry means. What is worry? There are two alternatives and no way to decide between them—and the mind goes on, one moment this side, another moment that side. This is what worry is. Worry means you have to decide and you are trying to decide, but you cannot decide. So you are worrying, puzzled, moving in vicious circles. An enlightened one is never worried. He is total. Try to understand this. He is not divided, he is not split, there are not two beings in him. But in you there is a crowd: not only two, there are many, many persons living in you, many voices, just a crowd. An enlightened one is a deep unity, he is a universe. You are a multiverse. This word 'universe' is beautiful. It means one—uni. You are a "multiverse," there are many worlds in you.

The second thing to be understood is that whatsoever you do, before doing it, there is thinking, thought. Whatsoever an enlightened person is doing, there is no thinking, no thought. He is doing it.

Remember, thinking is needed because you have no eyes to see. Thinking is a substitute. It is just like a blind man groping his way on a path with a stick. A blind man can ask people who have eyes how they grope, what type of sticks they use to grope their way on the path. And they will simply laugh; they will say that they don't need sticks, they have eyes. They simply see where the door is, they need not grope for it. And they never think about where the door is. They see and they pass through it. But a blind man cannot believe that you can simply pass through a door. First you will have to think about where the door is. First you will have to inquire; if someone is there you will have to ask where the door is. And even if the direction is given, you will have to grope for it with your stick—and then too there may be many pitfalls. But when you have eyes, if you want to go out, you simply look...you don't think about where the door is, you don't decide. You simply look, the door is there, you pass through it. You never think that this is a door, you simply use it and you act.

The same is the situation with unenlightened minds and enlightened minds. An enlightened mind simply looks. Everything is clear. He has a clarity, his whole being is light. He looks around and he simply moves, acts—he never thinks. You have to think because you don't have eyes. Only blind men think; they have to think because they don't have eyes. They need substitute eyes, and thinking provides that.

I never say that Buddha or Mahavira or Jesus are great thinkers. That would be just nonsense. They are not thinkers at all; they are knowers, not thinkers. They have eyes, they can see, and through their seeing they act. Whatsoever comes out of a buddha comes out of emptiness, not out of a mind filled with thoughts. It has come out of an empty sky. It is the response of emptiness.

But for us it is difficult, because nothing comes to us in that way. We have to think about it. If someone asks a question, you have to think about it. And even then you can never be certain that whatsoever you are saying is the answer. A buddha answers; he doesn't think. You question him, and the emptiness simply responds. That response is not a thought-over thing, it is a total response. His being behaves that way. That's why you cannot ask for consistency from a buddha. You cannot. Thought can be consistent, a thinker is bound to be consistent—but an enlightened person cannot be consistent, because each moment the situation changes, and each moment things come out of his emptiness. He cannot force. He cannot think. He does not really remember what he said yesterday. Every question creates a new answer, and every question creates a new response. It depends on the questioner.

Buddha enters a village. One man asks, "Is there God?" Buddha says, "No."

In the afternoon, another man asks, "Is there God?" Buddha says, "Yes."

Then in the evening, a third one asks, "Is there God?" Buddha remains silent. In just one day: in the morning, no; in the afternoon, yes; in the evening, silence—neither yes nor no.

Buddha's disciple, Ananda, became puzzled. He had heard all three answers. In the night when everyone had retired, he asked Buddha, "Can I ask you a question? Just in one day you have answered one question in three ways—and not only differently, contradictorily. My mind is puzzled. I cannot sleep if you don't answer. What do you mean? In the morning you say yes, in the afternoon no, in the evening you remain silent. And the question was the same."

Buddha said, "But the questioners were different. And how can different questioners ask the same question?" This is really beautiful, very deep. He said, "How can different questioners ask the same question? A question comes out of a being, it is a growth. If the being is different, how can the question be the same? In the morning when I said yes, the man who was asking was an atheist. He had come to get my confirmation that there is no God. And I could not confirm his atheism, because he was suffering because of it. And because I could not be a part in his suffering and I wanted to help him, I said, 'Yes, God exists.' That's how I tried to destroy his so-called atheism. In the afternoon, when the other person was there, he was a theist and he was suffering through his theism. I couldn't say yes to him because that would have been a confirmation—which he had come for. Then he would go and say, 'Yes, whatsoever I was saying is right. Even Buddha says so.' And the man was wrong. I could not help a wrong man in his wrongness, so I had to say no to destroy whatsoever he is, to shatter his mind.

"And the man who came in the evening was neither. He was a simple, innocent man and he was not asking for any confirmation. He had no ideology; he was really a religious person. So I had to be silent. I said to him, 'Be silent about this question. Don't think about it.' If I had said yes, it would have been wrong because he was not there to find a theology. If I had said no, it would have been wrong, because he was not to be confirmed in any atheism. He was not interested in thoughts, in ideas, in theories, doctrines, no; he was a real religious man. How could I utter any word before him? I had to be silent. He understood my silence. When he went away, his religiousness had deepened."

Buddha said, "Three persons cannot ask the same question. They can formulate it in a similar way—that is another thing. The questions were all 'Does God exist?' Their formulation was the same, but the being from where the question was coming was totally different. They meant different things by it: their values were different, their associations with words were different."

I remember, once it happened that Mulla Nasruddin came back to his house one evening. The whole day he had been involved in a football match. He was a fan. In the evening when he entered the house, his wife was reading a newspaper, and she said, "Look, Nasruddin, there is something for you. It is reported here that a man has given his wife in return for a season ticket for the football matches. You are also a fan, a mad fan, but I cannot conceive that you would do the same —or would you? Would you exchange me just to get a season ticket for the football matches?"

Nasruddin thought hard, and then he said, "Of course I would not—because it is ridiculous and criminal. The season is half over."

Every mind has its own orientation. You may use the same words but because you are different, those same words cannot be the same.

Then Buddha said another thing, and that is even more significant. He said, "Ananda, why are you disturbed? You were not a party; you should not listen, because not a single answer was given to you. You should remain indifferent; otherwise you will go mad. Don't move with me because I will be involved with many, many types of persons. And if you listen to everything that is not said to you, you

will get confused and crazy. You just leave me; otherwise remember to listen only when I speak to you. At other times don't listen. Whatsoever I say is not your business. It was not said to you and it was not your question at all, so why should you be worried? You were not related. Someone asked, someone else replied. Why are you unnecessarily worried about it? If you have the same question, ask, and then I will answer. But remember, my answers are not to the questions, but to the questioners. I respond. I look at the man, I see through the man, the man becomes transparent—and this is my response. The question is irrelevant; the questioner is relevant."

You cannot ask for consistency from an enlightened person. Only unenlightened, ignorant persons can be consistent, because they don't have to look. They just follow some ideas. They carry dead ideas, consistently. For their whole life they will carry something and they will remain consistent to it. They are stupid, that's why they can remain consistent. They are not alive, they are dead.

Aliveness cannot be consistent. That doesn't mean that it is wrong—aliveness is consistent, but very deeply, not on the surface. Buddha is consistent in all the three answers, but his consistency is not in the answers—his consistency is in his effort to help. He wanted to help the first man, he wanted to help the second man, he wanted to help the third man. For all three, compassion was there, love was there. He wanted to help them—that is his consistency. But it is a deep current. His words are different, his answers are different, but his compassion is the same.

So when an enlightened person speaks, answers, that answer is a total response of his emptiness, of his being. He echoes you, he reflects you, he is a mirror. He has no face of his own. Your face is mirrored in his heart. So if an idiot comes to meet Buddha, he will meet an idiot—Buddha is just a mirror. And that man will go and spread the rumor that Buddha is an idiot. He has seen himself in Buddha. If someone sensitive, understanding, mature, grown-up comes, he will see something else in Buddha; he will see his own face. There is no other way—you go on seeing mirrors in persons who are totally empty. Then whatsoever you carry is your interpretation.

It is said in old scriptures that when you reach an enlightened person, remain totally silent. Don't think, otherwise you will miss the opportunity of meeting him. Just remain silent, don't think; absorb him, but don't try to understand him through your head. Absorb him, drink him, allow your total being to be open to him. Let him move within you, but don't think about him—because if you think, then your mind will be echoed. Let your total being be bathed in his presence. Only then will you have a glimpse of what type of being, of what type of phenomenon you have come in contact with.

Many came to Buddha. They came and went. They carried their own opinions, and they went out and they spread them. Very few, really very few, understood—and that is how it should be, because you can understand only according to you. If you are ready to melt and change and be transformed, only then can you understand what an enlightened person, what an enlightened being is.

The third question:

You said that noise and disturbances are not outside in the world, but are because of our own minds and ego. But why do the saints and mystics always live in unnoisy, uncrowded places?

Because they are still not saints and mystics. They are still endeavoring, still working. They are seekers, not *siddhas;* they have not reached. Noise will disturb them, the crowd will disturb them. The crowd will pull them back to its own level. They are still weak, they need protection. They are still not confident. They cannot move into temptation; they have to protect themselves in the lonely solitude where they can grow and become strong. When they are strong there will be no problem. Mahavira moved into the wilderness. For twelve years he was alone, silent, not talking, not moving in villages or cities; then he became enlightened. Then he came back to the world. Buddha was in total silence for six years. Then he came back to the world. Jesus or Mohammed, or anyone—when they are growing they need protected conditions. When they have grown, then there is no problem.

So if you find a mystic afraid of moving in a crowd, then know well that he is still a child, growing. Otherwise why should a mystic be afraid of moving in crowds? Nothing can be done to him by the crowd, by the noise, by the world, by the objects of the world. With all this madness around him, nothing can be done to him. He cannot be touched. He can move and he can live—anywhere it happens for his emptiness to live, he can live.

But in the beginning it is good to be alone, to be in a harmonious, natural surrounding. So remember, don't think that because you live in a noisy Bombay you are a mystic, or you have grown up and have become a siddha. If you want to grow you will also have to move sometimes, for some definite periods, into loneliness—out of the crowd, out of the concerns of the world, relations of the world, objects of the world—into such a place where you can be alone and not disturbed by others. As you are now you can be disturbed, but once you have the strength, once you have the inner power, once you are crystallized and you know that now no one can shatter your inner center, you can move anywhere. Then the whole world is lonely. Then wherever you are is wilderness. Then the space of silence moves with you because you are the creator of it. Then around you, you create your own inner silence, and wherever you move, you are in silence. No one can penetrate that silence. No noise can disturb it.

But unless the crystallization has happened, don't believe that you will not be disturbed. You are disturbed, whether you know it or don't know it. Really, you are so disturbed that you cannot know it. You have become accustomed to disturbance. Every nerve is on edge; you are continuously disturbed. Right now you don't feel the disturbance —to feel the disturbance sometimes you need to be not disturbed. Only then can you feel it in contrast. You are continuously disturbed but you have become accustomed to it, habituated to it. You think this is how life is. It would be good if you move into the Himalayas for some time. It would be good to go into some remote village, a remote forest, and be alone for a few days' silence—as if the whole of humanity has disappeared. Then come back to Bombay. Then you will know what disturbance you have been living in. You will be suddenly disturbed. Now you have a contrast. You had an inner music, now it is shattered. For seekers solitariness is good; for siddhas it is irrelevant.

And there are two types of wrong people. With the first type, if you say to them that it is they who are disturbed, the situation is irrelevant, then they will never go into solitariness to have a glimpse of what silence is. Then they will remain here and they will say, "Nothing disturbs us. It is us really, not the surrounding. So we remain here." And they are disturbed but their theory will become a rationalization. Then there are other people, the other type of wrong people, who, if you tell them to move into silence, to solitude, because it will help, they will move—but then they will never come back. Then it becomes an addiction and they will remain weak forever, they will always feel afraid of coming back to the world. Then their solitariness has not been a help; rather, it has become a hindrance. They are not stronger through it, they have become weaker. Now they cannot move in the world. Both these types are wrong.

Be the third type, which is the right type. In the beginning, know well that you are disturbed by circumstances; so sometimes try, manage, to move out of them. Then when you are out of them, whatsoever silence you attain, bring it back to your circumstances and try to preserve it. If you can preserve it in the circumstances, then only will the theory have become an experience. Then you know that nothing disturbs. Then you know it is you ulti-

mately who are disturbed or not disturbed. But make it an experience—just as a theory it is useless.

The fourth question:

It is one thing to realize cosmic consciousness on earth, and transcend body. But how do realized ones know for sure that this consciousness is eternal and will remain after the death of the body?

The first thing is, they don't bother about it. They are not worried about whether it will remain or not. It is you who are worried. They don't think of the next moment. The next life is just irrelevant; even the next day, the next moment, is not a point of concern. It is you who always ask about something in the future, something of the future. Why? Because your present is just empty, your present is just nothing, your present is just rotten, your present is such a suffering that you can tolerate it only if you go on thinking of the future and the paradise and the life ahead. Just here now there is no life so you pitch your mind into the future just to escape from the present, the ugly present.

One who is realized is here and now, totally alive. All that can happen has happened. There is no future to it. Whether death is going to kill him or not is not a concern at all. It is the same. Whether he disappears or remains, it makes no difference. This moment is so rich, so absolutely rich, this moment is so intense, that his whole being is here and now.

Ananda asked Buddha again and again, "What will happen to you when your body dies?"

And Buddha insisted again and again, "Ananda, why are you so concerned about the future? Why don't you look at me, at what is happening now?"

But again, after a few days, he would ask, "What happens to an enlightened one when his body dies?" He is afraid about himself. He is afraid. He knows that when the body dies there is no possibility of reviving it, there is no possibility of remaining, there is no possibility of being. And he has not attained anything. The light will just go out —it has been a futile thing. If that happens without his attaining anything, he will simply disappear. So the whole thing was meaningless, the whole suffering was meaningless, leading nowhere. He was concerned; he wanted to know if something survives after the body.

But Buddha says, "I am here and now. What will happen in the future is not a concern at all."

So the first thing is that a realized one is not bothered. That is one of the signs of a realized one —he is not bothered by the future.

And the second thing: you asked, How does he know for sure? Knowledge is always sure. Certainty is inherent, intrinsic, to knowledge. You have a headache. Can I ask you, "How can you say for sure that you have a headache?" You will say, "I know." I can ask, "But how are you sure that your knowledge is right and not wrong?" But no one asks such nonsensical questions. When the headache is there, it is there—you know it. Knowledge is intrinsically certain. When one is enlightened, he knows he is enlightened; he knows that he is not this body; he knows that inside he is just a vast space—and space cannot die. Things can die, space cannot die.

Just think about this room. We can destroy this building, this Woodlands, but we cannot destroy the roominess in this room. Can you destroy it? The walls can be destroyed, but we are sitting here in this roominess, space. The walls can be destroyed, but how can you destroy this room— not the walls, the space here? The whole of Woodlands may disappear—it will disappear one day—but this space will remain. Your body will disappear and because you don't know the inner space, you are afraid. You want to know it for sure. But an enlightened man knows that he is the space —not the body, not the walls, but the inner space. The walls will drop, they have dropped many times, but the inner space will remain. It is not something he has to find proofs for, it is his immediate knowledge. He knows it, that's all. Knowledge is intrinsically certain.

If your knowledge is uncertain, then remember it is not knowledge. People come to me and they say, "Our meditation is going very well. We are feeling very happy." And then suddenly they ask me, "What do you say about it? Is our happiness really there? Are we really happy?" They ask me! They are not certain about their happiness. What type of knowledge is this? They are simply pretending, but they cannot deceive themselves. They are thinking, they are hoping, they are wishing—but they are not happy. Otherwise what is the need to ask me? I will never go to ask anybody whether I am happy or not. Why should I? If I am happy, I am happy. If I am not, I am not. Who else can give proof of it? If I cannot be a witness, who will be a witness for me, and how can the other be a witness?

So sometimes I play games. Sometimes I say, "Yes, you are happy. You are absolutely happy." And they become more happy just by hearing me. And sometimes I say, "No, you don't show anything, there is no indication. You are not happy, you must have been dreaming." And they drop, their happiness disappears, they become sad. What type of happiness is this? Just by saying that you are happy it increases; and just by saying that you are not, it disappears! They are just trying to be happy but they are not. This is not knowledge, this is just wish-fulfillment. They hope, and they think they can deceive themselves. By thinking that they are happy, believing that they are happy, finding some proof, finding some certificate from somewhere that they are happy, they think that they will create happiness. It is not so easy. When something happens in the inner world, you know it has happened, you don't need any certificate. You don't need one! The very search for someone to approve is childish. It shows that you long for happiness, but you have not attained it. You don't know it, it has not happened to you.

One who has realized is always certain, and when I say certain, sure, absolutely sure, I don't mean that he feels some uncertainty somewhere, and against that uncertainty he feels certain—no. He is simply certain. There is no question of uncertainty. I am alive. Am I certain about it, sure about it? There is no question. There is no question of certainty. It is absolutely certain, it does not have to be decided. I am alive.

Socrates was dying and someone asked him, "Socrates, you are dying so easily, so happily. What is the matter? Are you not afraid? Are you not scared?"

Socrates said a very beautiful thing. He said, "Only two things are possible after I am dead: either I will be or I will not be. If I am not, then there is no question: no one is there to know it, to know that I am not. The whole thing simply disappears. And if I am there, then there is no question —I am. Only two are the possibilities: either I will be, or I will not be, and both are okay. If I am, then the whole thing continues. If I am not, then there is no one to know, so why be worried?"

He was not an enlightened one, but he was a very wise man. Remember, this is the difference between a wise one and an enlightened one. A wise one thinks deeply, penetrates intellectually into everything, and comes to a conclusion. He is a very wise man. He says that there are two alternatives. Logically he penetrates into the phenomenon of death: "Only two are the possibilities: either I simply disappear, I am no more; or I will remain." Is there any third alternative? There is no third alternative. So Socrates says, "I have thought about both. If I remain, then there is no question to be worried about. If I am no more, there is no one to worry. So why be worried now? I will see what happens." He is not in the know, he doesn't know what is going to happen, but he has thought about it wisely. He is not a buddha, he is the keenest intellectual possible. But if you can become wise—not enlightened, because enlightenment is neither wisdom nor ignorance, the duality has been transcended—even if you can become wise, you will feel relaxed; even if you can become wise, you can feel very contented.

But wisdom is not the goal of tantra or yoga.

Tantra and yoga aim for the superhuman, the point where wisdom and ignorance are both transcended: where one simply knows and does not think, where one simply looks and is aware.

The last question:

I certainly want to become enlightened. But if I do, what difference does it make for the rest of the world?

But why are you worried about the rest of the world? Let the world worry about itself. And you are not worried about what will happen to the rest of the world if you remain ignorant....

If you are ignorant, what happens to the rest of the world? You create misery. Not that you knowingly do it—you *are* misery, so whatsoever you do, you sow seeds of misery all around. Your hopes are meaningless; your being is significant. You may think you are helping others—you hinder them. You may think you love others—you may be simply killing them and murdering them. You may think you are teaching others, but you may be simply helping them to remain ignorant forever— because what you hope, what you think, what you wish, is not significant. What you are is significant.

Every day I see people around who are loving to each other—but they are killing each other. They think they are loving, and they think they are living for the other, and without them the life of their family, their beloveds, their children, their wives, their husbands, will be miserable—but it is miserable with them. And they try in every way but whatsoever they do, it goes wrong. It is bound to be so, because they are wrong. Doing is not of much importance; the being from where it comes, originates, is. If you are ignorant, you are helping the world to become a hell. It is already—this is what has happened through you. Wherever you touch, you will create hell.

If you become enlightened, whatsoever you do —or you need not do anything—just your being, your presence will help others to flower, to be happy, to be blissful. But that should not be your concern. The first thing is how to be enlightened.

You ask me, "I want to be enlightened." But that wanting seems to be very impotent, because immediately you say "but." Whenever "but" comes in, it shows the desire is impotent. "But what will happen to the world?" Who are you? What do you think about yourself? Does the world depend on you? Are you running it? managing it? Are you responsible? Why give so much importance to yourself? Why feel so important?

This feeling is part of the ego, and this worrying about others will never allow you to move to a peak of realization, because that peak is achieved only when you drop all worries. And you are so efficient in accumulating worries that you are simply wonderful. Not only your own, you go on accumulating others' worries—as if yours are not enough. You go on thinking about others, and what can you do? You can only get more and more worried and mad.

I was reading a viceroy's journal, Lord Wavell's journal. The man seems to be very sincere, deeply honest, because some remarks he makes are just superb. One remark he makes in the journal is: "Unless these three old men, Gandhi, Jinnah and Churchill, die, India will be in trouble." These three men, Gandhi, Jinnah, Churchill—and these three were helping in every way! Churchill's own viceroy writes in a journal that these three men should die soon—and he hopefully even gives their ages: Gandhi, seventy-five, Jinnah, sixty-five, Churchill, sixty-eight—because these three are the problem. Can you think of Gandhi imagining that he is the problem—or Jinnah, or Churchill? All are doing their best to solve the problem of this country! And Wavell said that these three are the problem, because all three are adamant, stubborn; every one of these three has the absolute truth and the other two are absolutely wrong. These three absolutes cannot meet anywhere—the other two are simply wrong. There is no question about it.

Everyone thinks as if he is the center and he has

to worry about the whole world, and change the whole world, transform the whole world, create a utopia. All that you can do is just change yourself. You cannot change the world. You can create more mischief trying to change it, you can create more chaos, you can harm, and you can puzzle. Already the world is too puzzled. You can puzzle it more and confuse it more.

Please leave the world to itself. You can do only one thing, and that is, you can achieve inner silence, inner bliss, inner light. If you achieve this, you have helped the world very much. Just by changing one ignorant spot into an enlightened flame, just by changing one person from darkness into light, you have changed a part of the world. And this changed part will have its own chain reactions. Buddha is not dead. Jesus is not dead. They cannot be dead because there is a chain reaction—from one lamp, from one flame, another flame takes over. And a successor is created, and they go on living.

But if your light is not there, if your lamp is without a flame, you cannot help anyone. The first basic thing is that you must attain your inner flame. Then others can share, then you can kindle others' light also; then it becomes a succession. Then you may disappear from the body but your flame goes on passing from hand to hand. Up to eternity it goes on and on. Buddhas never die, enlightened persons never die, because their light becomes a chain reaction. And unenlightened persons never live, because they cannot create any chain, they don't have any light to share, no flame to kindle someone else's flame.

Please be concerned with yourself only. Be selfish, I say, because that is the only way you will become selfless, that is the only way you can become a help and a blessing to the world. Don't be worried about it; that is not your concern. The greater your worries are, the greater you think your responsibilities are. And the greater your responsibilities, the more you feel yourself as being great. You are not. You are simply mad.

Get out of this madness of helping others. Just help yourself, that's all that can be done.

And then many things happen...but they happen as a consequence. Once you become a source of light, things start happening. Many will share it, many will be enlightened through it, many will attain life, more life, abundant life through it. But don't think about it. You cannot do anything about it consciously. Only one thing can be done, and that is, you can become conscious. Then everything follows.

Jesus says somewhere, "Enter into the kingdom of God first. Seek ye first the kingdom of God, then all else shall be added unto you."

I repeat the same.

List of Meditations

*Illustrated cards have been created for each of the meditations
in The Book of Secrets, as a playful and intuitive aid to exploring
the techniques. These cards are presented on an interactive CD-ROM,
which can be previewed at www.osho.org/secrets.*

About Osho

Never Born, Never Died—Only visited this planet Earth between December 11, 1931 and January 19, 1990.

With these literally immortal words, Osho both dictates his epitaph and dispenses with his biography. In the year before his departure, he even does away with his own name. "Osho" is derived from the "oceanic" experience described by William James, he says. "It is not my name, it is just a healing sound." And, taking his leave, he promises to continue to be available and asks that he always be referred to in the present tense.

So what to say about Osho? The ultimate deconstructionist? He gathers thousands of disciples, but insists they are not his followers but his friends. In his daily talks he repeatedly emphasizes that he is not conveying a belief system but rather dismantling all beliefs, and in the meantime giving his audience an opportunity to sit silently, alert, listening without the interference of the mind—in other words, to have a taste of meditation. He makes use of contemporary therapies not to "fix" people's problems but to show them how to stop creating problems in the first place. His revolutionary contribution to the science of inner transformation is to invent a number of active meditations designed to release the accumulated stresses of contemporary life and thereby clear the space for a silence that is not enforced but natural and effortless. He tells scandalous jokes, he contradicts himself almost daily, he seems to take special delight in being controversial and outrageous.

What to say about Osho? Really, he is such that each individual must discover him in his own time, in his own way. The less said the better and ultimately, better to let Osho speak for himself:

"I am not teaching philosophy to you, I am sharing my truth with you. Don't ask for definitions. If you have the courage, then take a plunge into the experience that is made available here: take a jump into meditation, and you will know."

A complementary audiobook is available for The Book of the Secrets, *published by Audio Renaissance.*

OTHER TITLES BY OSHO INCLUDE:

The Osho Zen Tarot
Meditation: The First and Last Freedom

and a series of audiobooks on major spiritul traditions including
Zen, Sufism, Buddhism and Taoism.

Osho Commune International

Osho Commune International has been established by Osho as a place where people can visit for a few days, weeks, or months, and have a firsthand experience of his vision. Located in Poona, India, about 120 miles southeast of Bombay, the Commune offers a variety of programs in which visitors can take part, including a full daily meditation program, many different types of therapies and self-discovery workshops, plus world-renowned programs and trainings in the healing arts, esoteric sciences, creative arts, and even a meditative sports program.

Osho Commune does not provide residential accommodation, but the surrounding neighborhood offers a wide choice of hotels, guest houses and private apartments for visitors. Commune facilities include several vegetarian restaurants serving organic food, a health and recreation spa, and modern, air-conditioned facilities for most workshops and meditation programs. The highlight of each day is the evening meeting—a two-hour celebration of music, dance, and a silent meditation watching one of Osho's videotaped discourses.

Up-to-date travel information and program details are available on line at the Osho International web site, http://www.osho.org

For further information:

http://www.osho.org

A comprehensive web site in different languages, featuring Osho's meditations, selections from his talks, books and tapes, an on-line tour of Osho Commune International, and listings of Osho information centers worldwide.

Osho Commune International
17 Koregaon Park
Pune 411 001 (MS)
India
Tel: +91 (212) 628 562
Fax: +91 (212) 624 181
Email: osho-commune@osho.org

Osho International
570 Lexington Avenue
New York, N.Y. 10022
USA
Toll-free information: +1 (800) CALL OSHO
Tel: +1 (212) 588-9888
Fax: +1 (212) 588-1977
Email: osho–int@osho.org